The Cambridge Encyclopedia of Africa

The Cambridge Encyclopedia of
AFRICA

General Editors

Roland Oliver
Professor of the History of Africa
School of Oriental and African Studies
University of London

Michael Crowder
Editor, History Today
Research Professor
Lagos University Centre for Cultural Studies
1975–8

CAMBRIDGE UNIVERSITY PRESS
Cambridge London New York New Rochelle
Melbourne Sydney

Editorial Director: James R. Clark
Managing Editor: Barbara Horn
Executive Editor: Roger G. Thomas
Designer: Terry Smith
Maps: Swanston and Associates
Drawings: Rod Sutterby
Diagrams: Martin Causer
Index: Marion Johnson

Published by the Press Syndicate of the University of Cambridge,
The Pitt Building, Trumpington Street, Cambridge, CB2 1RP
32 East 57th Street, New York, NY 10022
296 Beaconsfield Parade, Middle Park,
Melbourne 3206, Australia

Created, designed and produced by
Trewin Copplestone Books Limited, London

© Trewin Copplestone Books Limited, 1981

First published by Cambridge University Press 1981

Library of Congress catalogue card number: 79–42627

British Library Cataloguing in Publication Data
The Cambridge encyclopedia of Africa
    1. Africa–Dictionaries and encyclopedias
    I. Oliver, Roland   II. Crowder, Michael
    960'.03   DT3

ISBN 0 521 23096 9

Set in Linotron Plantin and Univers by Tradespools Ltd, Frome
Separation by Scanplus Ltd, London
Made and printed in Italy by New Interlitho S.P.A., Milan

Contributors

A. A.   **Anthony Atmore**
Centre of International and Area Studies, University of London

A. D. B.   **Anthony D. Buckley**
Ulster Folk and Transport Museum

A. D. R.   **Dr A. D. Roberts**
School of Oriental and African Studies, University of London

A. O'C.   **Dr Anthony O'Connor**
University College, University of London

A. P. H.   **Adrian P. Hewitt**
Overseas Development Institute, London

A. R.   **Alan Rake**
Editor, *African Business*

A. W.   **Dr Andrew Warren**
University College, University of London

B. L.   **Bernard Lanne**
Centre d'Études et de Documentation sur l'Afrique et l'Outre-Mer, Paris

B. W.   **Dr Brian Wood**
University College, University of London

B. W. H.   **Professor B. W. Hodder**
School of Oriental and African Studies, University of London

C. F.   **Christopher Fyfe**
Centre of African Studies, University of Edinburgh

C. S.   **Dr Christopher Stevens**
Overseas Development Institute, London

C. S. C.   **Dr Christopher Clapham**
University of Lancaster

D. B. B.   **Professor David Birmingham**
University of Kent

D. B. C.   **David B. Coplan**

D. C. O'B.   **Dr Donal B. Cruise O'Brien**
School of Oriental and African Studies, University of London

D. D.   **Desmond Davies**

D. G.   **Derek Gjertsen**

D. G. A.   **Professor Dennis Austin**
University of Manchester

D. H.   **Dr David Hilling**
Bedford College, University of London

D. K.   **Mr David Killingray**
Goldsmiths' College, University of London

D. O. A.   **Dr David Oluwayumi Atteh**
College of Technology, Ilorin

D. W.   **David Williams**

D. W. P.   **Dr David W. Phillipson**
Glasgow Museums and Art Galleries

E. D.   **Dr Elizabeth Dunstan**

F. W. K.   **Professor Franklin W. Knight**
Johns Hopkins University

G. A.   **Guy Arnold**

G. B. L.   **Dr G. B. Lamb**
Institute of Development Studies, University of Sussex

G. M.   **Dr George Murdoch**

G. R. A.   **Dr George Reid Andrews**
Social Science-Research Council, New York

G. W. K.   **Dr Gary W. Knamiller**
University of Leeds

H.-H.K. **Hans-Heino Kopietz**
School of Oriental and African Studies, University of London

I.L. **Professor Ian Linden**
University of Bath

J.A.K. **J. Arouna Karimu**
Fourah Bay College, University of Sierra Leone

J.B. **Professor John Blacking**
The Queen's University of Belfast

J.B.L.M. **James Mayall**
London School of Economics and Political Science

J.D.F. **Professor J.D. Fage**
Centre of West African Studies, University of Birmingham

J.D.H. **Professor John D. Hargreaves**
University of Aberdeen

J.E.C. **James Cunningham**

J.F.C. **Dr Jeff Crisp**

J.F.M. **Dr J. Forbes Munro**
University of Glasgow

J.G. **Professor Josef Gugler**
University of Connecticut

J.H. **Julius Holt**
International Disaster Institute, London

J.L.C.-T. **Professor J.L. Cloudsley-Thompson**
Birkbeck College, University of London

J.-L.V. **Dr Jean-Luc Vellut**
Université Catholique de Louvain

J.M. **Professor John Middleton**
School of Oriental and African Studies, University of London

J.O.C.O. **Dr J.O.C. Onyemelukwe**
University of Ibadan

J.O.H. **Professor John O. Hunwick**
Center for Arabic Studies, American University in Cairo

J.P. **John Picton**
School of Oriental and African Studies, University of London

J.P.O. **Dr John Peter Olinger**

J.S. **Dr John Seaman**
The Save the Children Fund, London

J.S.O. **Professor J.S. Oguntoyinbo**
University of Ibadan

J.S.R. **Professor James S. Read**
School of Oriental and African Studies, University of London

J.W. **Dr J. Woodburn**
London School of Economics and Political Science

K.M.B. **Professor Michael Barbour**
New University of Ulster

L.E.L. **Dr. L.E. Larson**

L.P. **Dr Laurel Phillipson**

M.B. **Dr Michael Brett**
School of Oriental and African Studies, University of London

M.B.T. **Martin B. Thorp**
University College, Dublin

M.C. **Michael Crowder**
Editor, *History Today*

M.E. **Michael Etherton**
Ahmadu Bello University, Zaria

M.E.S. **Dr Monica Schuler**
Wayne State University

M.J. **Marion Johnson**
Centre of West African Studies, University of Birmingham

M.S. **Marcel Soret**
Académie des Sciences d'Outre-Mer, Paris

M.W.D. **Dr M.W. Daly**

P.A.S. **Pamela Ann Smith**

P.C.L. **Professor Peter C. Lloyd**
University of Sussex

P.D.C. **Dr Paul Collins**
University of Ghana

P.H. **Peggy Harper**

P.H.T. **Professor P.H. Temple**
University of Birmingham

P.M. **Philip Modiano**
Cooperative Development Agency, London

P.M.M. **Professor Phyllis M. Martin**
Indiana University

P.N.B. **Dr P.N. Bradley**
University of Newcastle upon Tyne

P.R. **Dr Paul Richards**
University College, University of London

P.R.B. **Dr Randall Baker**
University of East Anglia

P.S. **Mr Paul Sherlock**
Oxfam, Oxford

P.W. **Dr Peter Warwick**

R.A.C. **Professor R.A. Caulk**
Camden College, Rutgers University

R.A.P. **Robert Plumptree**
Commonwealth Forestry Institute, Oxford

R.C. **Dr Robert Cornevin**
Académie des Sciences d'Outre-Mer, Paris

R.G.T. **Roger G. Thomas**

R.K.P.P. **Dr Richard K.P. Pankhurst**

R.L.B. **Dr Robin Bidwell**
Middle East Centre, University of Cambridge

R.M.D. **Dr Robin Derricourt**

R.M.P. **Professor R. Mansell Prothero**
University of Liverpool

R.M.S. **Richard Synge**

R.P. **Dr René Pélissier**

R.R. **Dr Richard Rathbone**
School of Oriental and African Studies, University of London

R.S. **Dr Ralph Schram**
Bureau of Hygiene and Tropical Diseases, London

R.W.S. **Robert William Shenton**
University of Toronto

S.D. **Susan Denyer**

S.G. **Dr Sandy Gow**
Northern Lights College, British Columbia

S.J.M. **Simon McBride**

S.K.P.-B. **Keith Panter-Brick**
London School of Economics and Political Science

T.A. **Tony Avirgan**

T.H. **Tony Hodges**

W.G.F. **Professor William G. Flanagan**
Coe College, Iowa

W.H.A. **Professor William H. Alexander**
Howard University

W.M.F. **W.M. Freund**
Centre for the Study of Social History, University of Warwick

5

Contents

8   List of maps
9   Index

THE AFRICAN CONTINENT

The Physical Environment
33   Geology and geomorphology
40   Climate
45   Hydrology
46   Soils
48   Vegetation
52   Fauna

The Peoples
57   The development of mankind
74   Languages
78   Ethnic groups

THE AFRICAN PAST

Before European Colonization
89   The Ancient Nile Valley
95   The Copper and Iron Ages
100   Classical North Africa
105   North-East Africa before the rise of
        Islam
112   The spread of Islam in North Africa
117   Islam and Christianity in North-East
        and East Africa
125   Bantu Africa
130   The Western and Central Sudan
136   Europe, North Africa and the Sahara
        1250–1835
141   The Portuguese in Africa c.1450–1650
145   The slave trade era
151   The prelude to European occupation
        c.1820–85

The European Occupation
156   The Scramble for Africa
158   African resistance
160   French expansion: North Africa
161   French expansion: Tropical Africa
163   British expansion
164   Belgian expansion
165   Portuguese expansion
166   German expansion
167   Italian expansion
168   Spanish expansion
169   Southern Africa
171   Ethiopia
172   Liberia
173   Egypt
175   The First World War

European Rule 1919–39
177   Colonial doctrines and practices
178   French North Africa
179   French Black Africa
181   British West Africa
183   British East Africa
184   British Central Africa
186   Egypt and the Sudan
187   Italy and the Horn
188   Belgian Africa
190   Portuguese Africa
190   Spanish Africa
191   Southern Africa

The Struggle for Independence
193   Pan-Africanism and African
        nationalism to 1939
195   The Second World War
196   The Maghrib
199   Libya, Egypt and the Sudan
200   French West Africa
202   French Equatorial Africa and
        Cameroon
203   Madagascar

204   The Horn of Africa
205   Belgian Africa
207   British West Africa
210   British East Africa
213   British Central Africa
215   South Africa
217   Portuguese Africa
219   The colonial legacy

CONTEMPORARY AFRICA

Africa since Independence
223   Algeria
224   Angola
224   Benin
225   Botswana
226   Burundi
226   Cameroon
227   Cape Verde Islands
227   Central African Republic
228   Chad
228   Comoro Islands
229   Congo
229   Djibouti
230   Egypt
231   Equatorial Guinea
232   Ethiopia
233   Gabon
233   The Gambia
234   Ghana
235   Guinea
236   Guinea-Bissau
236   Ivory Coast
237   Kenya
238   Lesotho
239   Liberia
239   Libya
240   Madagascar
241   Malawi

241 Mali
242 Mauritania
242 Mauritius
243 Morocco
244 Mozambique
245 Namibia
245 Niger
246 Nigeria
248 Réunion
248 Rwanda
248 São Tomé and Príncipe
249 Senegal
249 Seychelles
249 Sierra Leone
250 Somalia
251 South Africa since 1961
253 Sudan
254 Swaziland
255 Tanzania
256 Togo
257 Tunisia
257 Uganda
258 Upper Volta
259 Western Sahara
260 Zaire
261 Zambia
262 Zimbabwe

Government
264 Ideologies
265 Forms of government
267 Legal systems

Utilization of Natural Resources
270 Energy
274 Water resources
277 Forestry and timber
280 Minerals
283 People as a resource
287 Hunting and gathering
290 Pastoralism

294 Agriculture and fishing
305 Environmental hazards
311 Conservation

Political Economy
315 Development
326 Agriculture and peasantry
330 Craft production
334 Mineral exploitation
337 Industrialization
346 Industrial location
348 Wage labour
351 State ownership and indigenous
    entrepreneurship
354 Appropriate technology
357 Regional groupings
360 Transport
365 Markets
369 Finance and banking
371 Trade patterns
376 White settlerdom in South Africa
378 Tourism

Society
381 The changing family
382 Social stratification
384 Urbanization
388 Ethnicity and communalism
391 Traditional medicine
392 Modern medicine
397 Education
403 Communications media

Religion
406 Traditional religions
408 Christianity
410 Islam

Arts and Recreation
413 Traditional arts and crafts
425 Traditional architecture

431 Contemporary painting and
    sculpture
434 Dance
436 Drama and cinema
440 Literature
442 Traditional music
446 Popular music
451 Sport
454 Entertainment and leisure

AFRICA AND THE WORLD

Inter-African Relations
459 Pan-Africanism since 1958
460 The Organization of African Unity
461 The Economic Commission for
    Africa
462 Regional groupings: a listing

International Relations
463 Neo-colonialism
464 Africa and the USA
465 Africa and the USSR
466 Africa and China
467 Africa and the Third World

The Black Diaspora
469 The Muslim world
472 Europe
475 The Caribbean and Guyanas
478 Latin America
481 North America

485 Further reading
492 Acknowledgements

List of maps

32   Tectonics
34   Geology
37   Relief and landforms
40   Mean annual sunshine hours
40   Average global temperature (°C): January
41   Average global temperature (°C): July
41   Surface pressure and air masses: January
42   Surface pressure and air masses: July
42   Annual rainfall (millimetres)
43   Rainfall peaks
43   Annual rainfall variability
44   Days (mean) with thunderstorms per year
45   Physiological climate: January
45   Physiological climate: July
47   Soils
51   Major vegetation zones
66   Major pre-iron age archaeological sites
71   Probable areas of domestication of selected African crops
76   Major languages
89   The ancient Nile Valley
100   Classical North Africa
107   North-East Africa before the rise of Islam
112   The spread of Islam in North Africa
117   Islam and Christianity in North-East Africa
126   Bantu Africa
131   West African peoples and states 12th-17th centuries
135   West African peoples and states 18th and 19th centuries
136   Europe, North Africa and the Sahara
174   Africa in 1914
222   The States of Africa
290   Distribution of cattle and tsetse fly
294   Desertification risk
295   Staple crops: cassava and wheat
295   Staple crops: millets, sorghum and yams
296   Staple and cash crops: maize
296   Staple and cash crops: oil palm and dates
297   Staple and cash crops: groundnuts and citrus
297   Staple and cash crops: bananas and ensete
298   Cash crops: rubber and tobacco
298   Cash crops: coffee, sugar and grapes
299   Cash crops: cocoa and tea
299   Cash crops: cotton and cloves
313   National parks approved by the IUCN (1978)
340   Manufacturing in Africa: factory workers as a proportion of total population
363   Transport
368   Market periodicity in West Africa

Index

An asterisk against a name or word in the text indicates that there is an entry on this subject, or substantial further reference to it, which can be found elsewhere in the book by looking it up in the Index

ABAKO, see *Alliance des Bakongo*
Abbas, Ferhat 197, 223
Abbasids 113, 114, 115, 471
Abbas II Hilmi, khedive 173
Abd al-Kader, Amir 160
Abd al-Mumin 116 137
Abd al-Rahman al-Mahdi, Sayyid 199
Abd al-Wadids 137
Abd el-Krim, Mohammed 190, 196
Abeokuta 393
Abidjan 367, 394–5
Abomey 161
Aborigines Rights Protection Society 193
Abrahams, Peter 441
Abua language 77
Abu Bakr 116
Abu Inan, sultan 138
Abu Simbel 92
Abu Yazid 114
Acacia 49–50, 279
Accra 81, 142, 181, 206, 209, 347, 361, 369, 395, 407, 451
Acheampong, Col Ignatius 234–5
Achebe, Chinua 431, 440
Acheulian 60–4, 67
Achimota College 207
Acholi people 82, 258
Achour, Habib 257
Action Group (Nigeria) (AG) 209, 246
Adal 122–4
Adamawa-Eastern language 77
Adangme 77, 81
Addis Ababa 105, 120, 124, 167, 188, 229, 394, 433
   Conference (1972) 254, 397
   Treaty (1896) 172
Aden Abdullah Osman 204
Aden 111, 163, 167
Ade, Sunny 449, 450
administration 92, 112, 160, 162, 164, 172, 181, 384, 388, 473
administrators 116, 143, 231
Adowa battle 167, 172
Adrar Bous (Niger) 69, 72
Adulis port 106–9, 111
Advisory Council of the N. Sudan 199
Afar (Djibouti) 33, 36, 61, 78, 105, 229, 426
al Afdal 115–16

Affade language 75
Afonso I 143
AFRC, see Armed Forces Revolutionary Council (Ghana)
African Agricultural Credit Commission 370
African Amateur Boxing Association 451
African Boxing Union (ABU) 451
African Churches 409–10
African Development Bank 370
African diaspora 469–84
African Football Confederation 451
African Morning Post 181, 209
African National Congress (South Africa) (ANC) 192–3, 215–17
   (Northern Rhodesia) (ANC) 213
African National Council (Zimbabwe) (ANC) 263
African Orthodox Church 484
Africans, formally educated 164, 193
African socialism 207, 265, 269
Africa Proconsularis 101–3
African-Portuguese interaction 141–5, 151
Afrifa, Brigadier Akwasi 234
Afrikaans 77–8, 216, 252, 376
Afrikaners 78, 171, 191–2, 213, 216, 376–7
Afrikaner National Party, see National Party
Afrikanische Gesellschaft in Deutschland 152
Afrique noire française (French Black Africa) 179
Afro-Americans, see Americans, black
Afro-Asian partnership, bloc 118, 230, 467, 468
Afro-Asian People's Solidarity Organization 466
Afro-Asiatic languages 75, 81, 105
Afro-Brazilians 478–80
Afro-Latin Americans 479–80
Afro-Portuguese 143
Afro-Shirazi Party (Zanzibar) (ASP) 212
AG, see Action Group (Nigeria)
Agadir 141
age-sets 83, 86, 105, 128, 434
Agew 105–6, 108, 109, 111, 121, 123
Aghlabids 114, 470

agricultural peoples 49, 71, 79, 81–2, 85, 96, 102, 131, 242, 284, 392
   production 148, 151, 183, 225, 229, 326, 372, 383
   work-force 258, 276, 284–5, 305, 348–50
agriculture 131, 127, 275, 295–304, 326–30, 342–4
   African 189, 205, 210–11, 240, 249–50, 295–304, 326, 349, 389
   compulsory under colonial rule 166, 181, 183, 196, 217, 326
   early 64, 72–3, 96, 131
   modernization, investment 324, 346, 350, 370–1, 383
Ahidjo, Ahmadou 202, 226
Ahmadu (Tokolor) 161
Ahmadu Bello University 355
Ahmadu Lobbo, Seku 134
Ahmed Abdallah 228–9
Ahmed Badly 123
Ahmed ibn Ibrahim al-Ghazi 120, 124
Al Ahram 403
Ahomadegbe, Justin 225
aid 286, 321, 467–8
Aidoo, Ama Ata 437
Aïr 50, 52
Air Afrique 358, 463
air transport 179, 358, 359, 362, 373, 378, 379, 462, 463
Ait Benhaddan 425
Aja 133
Ajaokuta 361
Aja states 148
Ajuran 110
Akan area, 97, 132, 142, 182
   kingdoms, states 132–3, 409
   language (=Twi-Fante) 77–8
   people 78, 80, 132, 148, 235, 382, 435, 436
Akhnaton, king 92
Akintola, S. L. 246
Akinyele 367–8
Akolo, Jimoh 433
Aksum, Ethiopia 73, 94, 105, 108–9, 111, 120, 122
   period, dynasty 106–7, 111, 121
Akuapem people 235
Akuffo, Lt Gen Fred 234

Akwamu 148
Akwete 334
Akyem 148
Aladura (Church of the Lord), 392, 409
el-Alamein, battle 199
Alawites (Morocco) 139–40, 198, 259, 470
Alcazarquivir (al-Qasr al-Kabir) battle 139
alcoholics 394
Alexander the Great 93, 101, 106
Alexandria 108, 112, 136–8, 140, 156, 200, 347, 365, 369, 384, 408
Alexis, Jacques Stéphen 478
Algeria 223–4, 265–8, 284, 383, 390, 404–5, 451
   agriculture, pastoralism 240, 293, 303–5, 330
   Arab, Turkish 113–16, 137–8
   archaeology 62, 69, 72
   economy 281–3, 349, 369–72
   external relations 357, 462, 466–7, 474
   French 153, 158, 160, 177–9, 197, 220
   independence struggle 197–8, 202, 217, 257, 464
   physical 36, 38, 43
   resources 270, 272, 279, 281–3, 324, 334, 336, 365
   Roman 101–2, 104
Algerians 160, 162, 176, 198, 284, 390
Algiers 139–40, 152, 160, 365, 394, 468
Ali al-Mirghani, Sayyid 199
Ali Shermarke, Abdar-Rashid 204, 250
Ali Soilhi 228–9
Ali Yusuf, Shaykh 173
All-Africa Games 451, 455
Allal el Fassi, see el-Fassi, Allal
Alliance des Bakongo (ABAKO) 206
Allied Powers (First World War) 158, 168, 175
Allies, Allied forces (Second World War) 195, 199, 202–3, 216
All Peoples Congress (Sierra Leone) (APC) 250
Almohads 116, 137, 470

Almoravids 79, 116, 132, 137, 411, 470

ALN, see *Armeé de la Liberation Nationale* (Algeria)

Aluko, T. M. 440

aluminium 226, 234, 281, 336, 273, 374

Alwa 110, 119

Amax 335

Ambo (= Ovambo) people 78, 245

Ambriz 224

Amda Siyon, Emperor 122–3

Amda Siyon II 124

Amenhotep III 94

American and Foreign Anti-Slavery Society 482

American Colonization Society 172, 464

Americans 145–6, 157, 194

Americans, black 153, 172, 193–4, 205, 447–8, 450, 459, 464, 472–3, 477–84

American War of Independence 473, 482, 484

Americo-Liberian people 80, 153, 239

Amhara 78, 85–6, 111, 120–22, 188

Amharic language 75, 78, 106, 120

Amin, Idi 240, 248, 256, 258, 266, 354, 358, 362, 379

Anang people 81

ANC, see African National Congress (South Africa)

ANC, see African National Council, (Zimbabwe)

ancestors 83, 392, 406, 407, 414, 443

Ancient Egypt, see Egypt, ancient

Anderson, Benjamin 172

Anderson, Marian 483

Andriananjato, Richard 203

Angas language 75

Anglo-American Corporation 185, 261

Anglo Egyptian Sudan 173, 199, 253

Anglo-Egyptian treaty, alliance 187, 199

Anglo-Ethiopian boundary commission 188

Anglophone Africa 264, 357, 360, 370, 440, 451, 456

Angola 33, 65, 268–9, 272, 281, 283, 303

labour 165, 190, 349

liberation struggle 217, 219, 243, 252, 256, 262, 265, 460, 464, 465–7

literature 441

modern 328, 372, 378, 381

peoples 78, 82, 125, 285, 287, 478–9

Portuguese trade 128, 143, 148–9, 155, 169

Portuguese colonization 125, 130, 158, 165–6, 190, 219, 408

sculpture 413, 420–1

Anikulapo-Kuti, Fela 449, 450

animal husbandry 278, 290–4, 356, 360, 462

animal numbers 54, 293–4, 312

Anjouan, see Nzawani

Ankrah, Lt. General Joseph 234

Annaba, (Bone) = Hippo 104

annexation 154, 162, 165, 168, 171

Annobón 169

Ansar 199, 254

Antananarivo 394–5

Antara 471

antelope 54, 311–12

anti-colonialism 195, 200, 205, 207, 265, 403, 410, 459, 464–5, 467, 477

Antigua 476

anti-slavery activities 152–3, 163

Anyi people 78

Aosta, Duke of 188

apartheid 192, 215–16, 245, 251–2, 268, 376–8, 437, 452, 460, 465, 468

APC, see All People's Congress (Sierra Leone)

Apithy, Sourou Migan 225

apprenticeship systems 402, 413

appropriate technology 354–6

Arab Africa 459

Arabia, 52, 78, 105–6, 109–110, 113, 117–18, 119, 410–11, 469–71

Arabia, South 78, 105–6, 109–110, 119

language, script 101, 106, 108

Arabic language 78–9, 84, 111, 113, 117–18, 160, 179, 242, 390, 403, 405, 438, 441

Arabic, modern 438

Arabic-speaking peoples 404, 456

Arabi Pasha 173

Arab League 197–8, 229, 231, 240, 254

Arab traders 118–20, 125, 128, 154, 383, 469, 478

Arabs 78–9, 85, 119, 130, 284, 382, 393, 408

East Africa, Zanzibar 85, 99, 163, 184, 211–12

North Africa 104, 110–15, 196, 242

Arab Socialist Union 230, 240

Arab-Swahili people, see also Swahili 129, 154

Aragon 116, 138

architecture 118, 425–30

Arden-Clarke, Sir Charles 208

Areogun 413

Argentina 478–80

Arguin 141

Argungu fishing festival 455–6

arid zone 46, 48, 74, 79, 307, 360

aristocrats 83, 184, 411, 446

Argobba 120, 122

Arma 111, 139

Armah, Ayi Kwei 440

Armed Forces Revolutionary Council (Ghana) (AFRC) 234

armed revolts 476

Armée de la Libération Nationale Algeria (ALN) 223

Armstrong, Louis 483

armies, precolonial 100, 112–13, 116, 124, 130, 135–6, 140, 142, 158–9, 470–1

colonial 158–9, 162, 166, 175–6, 195–6, 473–4

modern 223, 234–5, 266

Aro 149, 198

arrows 67–8, 287, 332

art 80–1, 85–6, 91–2, 94, 97–8, 413–14, 418, 455, 472, 478

art, tourist 432–3

artisans 97, 197, 383, 447, 479

arts 80, 116, 380, 401, 413–50, 455

Arusha Declaration 255, 353

Arusi people 81

Asante 78, 148–9, 154, 158, 163, 208, 235, 334, 388, 406, 414, 423

Ashanti, see Asante

Ashanti Goldfields 335

Asia 57, 89, 93, 95, 106, 117, 164, 459, 467

iron 95

trade, shipping 90–1, 93, 118, 154, 363, 374

al-Ashraf Khalil 136

Asia Minor 52, 469

Asians 353, 376, 383, 475

Askia Muhammad 132-3

Asmara 167, 172

ASP, see Afro-Shirazi Party (Zanzibar) 211

Assab 167

assassination 199, 216, 218, 223, 227, 229, 234, 237, 246–7, 250, 260

Aswan 93, 273–4, 277, 285, 396, 467

athletics 451, 455

Atiman, Dr Adrien 393

Atlantic Charter 195

Atlantic Islands 143

Atlantic ocean 33, 36, 41–2, 141

Atlas Mts, High 51, 116

Atlas ranges 33, 36, 38, 45, 48, 50, 100, 102, 160

atomic energy 274, 335

Augustine, St (of Hippo) 104, 108

Aures Mts 102

australopithecines 57–61

'authenticity' 228, 256, 260

Autochthonous Negro Party (Uruguay) 481

Autorité de Développement Integré de la Région du Liptako-Gourma 462

Avungara people 79

Awash river, plain 120, 122, 124

Awdaghast 115–16

Awolowo, Obafemi 209, 246

Awoonor, Kofi 440

Axim 142

Axis powers 186, 195, 197, 199

Aybeg 116

Ayn Jalut, battle 136

Ayyubids 116, 136

Azande people 78

Azbi dist 106, 108, 111

al Azhar Mosque 116

Azikiwe, Nnamdi 181–2, 403

Azores 143, 217, 465, 478

Azzamur 141

'Babu' (A. R. Mohamed) 212

Bachama language 75

Badagri 148

Bagamoyo 128

Bagaza, Jean-Baptiste 226

Baggara (= Baqqara) people 79, 84

Baghdad 113, 136, 470

Baghirmi 470

Bagirmi people 79

Bahadur, Sultan 470

Bailundu rebellion 165

Bakari, Djibo 245

Baker, Ginger 449

Bakwe language 77

Balewa, Sir Abubakar Tafawa 246

Balogun, Ola 439

Bamako 195, 395, 447

Bamangwato people 86

Bambara 75, 79, 83, 134, 148, 419, 432

Bambuk 132

Bamileke 79, 226, 428, 429

Bamoun 428–9

bananas 117, 128, 295, 372, 428

Banda, Dr Hastings Kamuzu 214, 241

Bandiagara escarpment 413, 429–30

Bandung Conference 230, 467–8

Bangui 451

Bani River 132

Banjul 234, 347

banks 304, 369–71, 463

European 70, 164–5, 168, 188, 220, 324

nationalization 244, 258, 353

Bantu Africa 97, 99, 125–30

Bantu Education Act 215–16

Bantu languages 74, 77, 118

speakers, 73, 77–9, 81–4, 116, 125, 199, 252, 376, 478

Bantu National Congress (Southern Rhodesia) 214

Bantustans 215–16, 251–2, 286, 376, 460

Banu Hilal 115

Baoule, see Baule

Baqqara, see Baggara

Baraba 434

Barbados 475, 478

Barbarossa, 138–9

Bardo, Treaty of 160

Barghawata 116

Baring, Sir Evelyn (Lord Cromer) 173

Barotse, see Lozi

Barrera, Angel (Gov.) 169

Barth, Heinrich 151

Barwe kingdom 128

rebellion 166

Barya-Kunaina people 106

Basarwa 437

Basotho National Party (Lesotho) 238

Basotho Congress Party (Lesotho) (BCP) 238

Basra 470
al Basri, Mohammed 243
Bassa language 77
Bassey, Hogan 'Kid' 451–2
Bassiri, Mohammed 259
Basutoland 171, 192, see also Lesotho
Bata 169
Bathurst 393, see also Banjul
Bauchi 361
Baule (= Baoule) 77, 79, 161, 420
bauxite 150, 235, 281, 335–6, 342, 351, 372
Baybars 136
Bayi, Filbert 452
BCP, see Basotho Congress Party (Lesotho)
beads 72, 95–7, 107, 118, 128, 132, 141, 143–4, 414, 422
Bechuanaland 171, 192
Bechuana people, see Tswana
Bedauye language 75
Beduin people 78–9
Begho 97
Behanzin, king 161
Beide Maryam 124
Beier, Georgina 433
Ulli 433
Beira 190, 262
railway 185, 261
Beja 79, 105, 106, 108, 111
Bekwarra language 77
Belgian colonial rule 85, 164, 177, 184, 188–9, 205–6, 333
Congo (later Zaire) 188–9, 194, 204, 206, 260, 265, 268, 311, 433
investments 164–5, 261
Ruanda, Urundi, 175, 183, 248
Belgians 261, 395, 464
Belgium 152, 164–5, 188, 195, 206, 463, 465
Belgrade 468
Bemba 77, 79, 130
Benader Coast 118
Ben Barka, Mehdi 243
Ben Bella, Ahmed 198, 223
Bendjedid, Chadli 223
Benghazi 239, 451
Benguela 128, 143, 149, 155
railway 190, 262
Beni Hasan tombs 91
Benin art 97, 142, 413, 416–17
city, kingdom 80, 97, 133, 142–3, 408, 413–14, 431–2, 436
people (= Bini), see Edo
Benin, Republic of 75, 77, 80, 86, 179, 224–5, 375, 395–6, 426, 432, 462–3
Ben Khedda, Ben Jousef 223
Ben Saleh, Ahmed 257
Benue-Congo languages 77, 79, 81, 86
Benue valley 36, 132, 361
Béranger, Paul 242
Berber language 75, 84, 100, 104, 116
chieftains, princes 95, 104, 115
people 79, 86, 112, 113, 115–16,
130, 131, 133, 179, 181, 190, 382, 390, 411
Berlin Conference 157–8, 164, 172
Berta language 75
Beti, Mongo 431, 440
Betsileo 83, 111, 120
Betsimaraka people 83
Beys (Algeria) 139
Egypt 140
Tunis(ia) 139–40, 160, 179, 198, 257
Biafada language 75
Biafra 81, 209, 246, 391
Bida 334
Bie province (Angola) 224
Bight of Benin 141, 147, 151
Bigo 125
Bijaya (= Bougie) 115, 138
Bikila, Abebe 451
Biko, Steve 252
Bilal 469
Bilma 38, 132
Bilsen, Prof. von 260
Bini (Benin), see Edo
birds 52–3, 55, 56, 314
Bisa language 77
people 128
Bismarck, O. von 157, 166
Bissandugu 135
Bizerta 257
Blaawbank valley 58–9
Black Africa 159, 175, 179, 217, 237, 242, 390, 431, 449, 459
Black Africans 469, 474
Black Americans 153, 172, 193–4, 205, 447–8, 450, 459, 464, 472–3, 477–84
Black People's Convention (South Africa) 252
blacksmiths 332, 337, 447
Black Star Line 365, 484
Blair, Henry 482
Blake, Eubie 483
blindness 310, 311, 394, 396
Bloc Démocratique Sénégalais 200–1
Blue Nile 306, 469
Blyden, Edward Wilmot 193
Bobo people 79
Boers 78, 130, 154, 155, 376, 383
Boganda, Barthélémy 202, 227
Bokassa Jean-Bedel (Emperor) 227–8, 266
Boki language 77
Bondu 133
Bonelli, Capt, Emilio 168
Bongo language 75
Bonny 81
Bontemps, Arna 483
Bophuthatswana 'homeland' 252, 376, 379
Borana people 81
Bore, see Annaba
Borgawa 133
Borgu 132–3, 158
Bornu 81, 131–4, 140
Botswana 33, 225, 268, 355–6, 372–3, 378, 395, 402, 437, 462
language, people 77, 85–6, 287
minerals 268, 281–2
Botswana Democratic Party 225
Botswana Independence Party 225
Botswana National Front 225
Botswana People's Party 225
Bouabid, Abderrahim 243
Bouaké 395
Boucetta, Mohammed 243
Bougie (= Bijaya) 115
Boumedienne, Houari 321
Bourguiba, Habib 197–8, 257, 266
boxing 451, 453
BP (British Petroleum) 335–6
Brass (city-state) 81, 413, 416
brass 142, 147, 416, 432
brass bands 437, 446, 455
Brathwaite, Edward K. 478
Brava 119
Brazil 143, 145–6, 149, 151, 155, 190, 468, 478–80
Brazilian slave traders 155
Brazilian Negro Front 480
Brazza, Savorgnan de 162
Brazzaville 179, 196, 202, 394–5, 451
Conference 195, 202, 463
bricks, brickwork 90, 347, 428
Brink, André 441
Britain 374, 377, 463, 465, 474
armies, expeditions 140, 155, 172–3, 195
colonies 84–5, 157, 177
nineteenth century 151, 153–4, 156, 182
twentieth century 162, 163, 171, 177, 211, 213, 214, 262
British Cameroons 202, 447
Central Africa 184, 213, 358
citizenship 250
Commonwealth Empire 171, 216–17, 242, 269, 368, 484
East Africa 183, 210, 311
expansion 134, 140, 155, 163, 172–3, 195; Egypt 177, 230; Ethiopia 188, 204; Liberia 172; Togo-Cameroon 175
High Commission Territories 171, 192
West Africa 181, 207, 264, 358
West Indies 475
British influence, Madagascar 162
North Africa 160, 239
Somalia 250
Southern Rhodesia 169
Zanzibar 129
British South Africa Company (BSAC) 163, 170, 184, 185, 192, 213, 261
British trade, traders 146, 149, 151, 155, 165
Broederbond 216
Broken Hill, see Kabwe
Brong people 235
bronze 91, 95–6, 416
Bronze Age 91, 95, 413
Brooke, Edward 483
Broom, Robert 58
Bruce, Blanche K. 483
Brutus, Dennis 440–1
BSAC, see British South Africa Company
Bubangi people 130
Budongo forest 54
Buduma language 75
Bugeaud, Marshal 160
Buganda kingdom 128–9, 163, 184, 210–11, 257–8, 388, 409
Buhen 93
building materials 93, 148, 277, 278–9, 425–30
Bukoba 410
Bulawayo 130, 361
Bunche, Ralph 484
Bunyoro kingdom, Bunyoro-Kitara state 84, 125, 128
Bure 132, 135
bureaucracy 78, 383, 388
Burma 195–6, 396
Burundi (Republic) 85, 125, 226, 248, 287, 372, 462–3
kingdom 175
Bururi province 226
Busa language 77
Bushman language, people 81, 287, 413, 415, 422, 437, see also Khoisan
Bushong people 82
Busia, Dr Kofi 234–5
Buthelezi, Gatsha 252
Butiama 211
'Butua' kingdom, see also Rozvi 128
Byzantine Africa 104, 112, 115
Egypt 112
Byzantium, see Constantinople

Cabinda oil wells 219, 224
Cabo Juby 169
Cabora Bassa 24, 273, 300
Cabo San Juan 169
Cabral, Amilcar 218, 227
Luiz 236
Caesarea (= Cherchel) 101
Caillié, René 384
Cairo, Arab 115, 123, 137, 140
modern 87, 197–8, 200, 316, 338, 362, 403, 469–70
Calabar 393
caliphs, caliphate 113–14, 116, 148, 158
camels 71, 73, 78–9, 95, 104–5, 130–1, 291, 360, 415
Cameron W. L. 164
Cameroon 34, 35, 48, 54, 97–8, 175
French 179, 181
German 157, 166–7, 175, 179
northern 133, 202, 413
peoples, languages 75, 77, 79, 81, 287
Republic 202, 226, 269, 349, 361, 358, 372, 380, 440, 461, 467
resources 270, 272, 280, 281, 374
southern 202
western 48, 422, 428

Canary Islands 52, 168
cane sugar 328
Cape (South Africa) 141, 149, 152, 155, 169, 170, 177, 203, 279, 296, 369, 376
Cape Bojador 141
Cape Coast 80, 145
Cape Coloureds 79, 82, 215, 252–3, 376, 411
Cape Delgado 144
Cape Province (South Africa) 40, 50, 53, 68, 79
  archaeology, palaeontology 57–8, 65, 67, 68, 74, 97
  modern 130, 192, 252, 393
Cape Town 149, 155, 365, 377
Cape Verde 141–3, 165, 218–19, 227, 236, 462
capital, capitalism 152, 162, 164, 169, 177, 179, 189, 206, 217, 219–20, 238, 265, 285, 304, 320–22, 325–6, 336, 339, 353, 369–70, 376–7, 383, 459–60
capital goods 346, 371, 374
capital-intensive technology 189, 325, 335
capital investment 273, 460
caravans 108–10, 121, 129, 141, 143, 149–50, 165, 469
Caribbean 146, 168, 194, 459, 467–8, 474–5, 477, 479–81, 484
Carter, Jimmy 465
Carthage 95, 100–4, 112, 130, 384
Carver, George Washington 482
Casablanca 160, 179, 196, 357, 359, 365, 394
cash-crops 185, 293, 297–8, 304, 307, 319, 326, 348, 368, 375, 477
cassava 72, 84, 128, 294–6, 308, 310, 319, 328, 341, see also manioc
caste 85, 479–80
Castro, Fidel 468
cattle 94–5, 129, 134, 140, 166, 291–2, 302, 396
cattle disease 172, 276, 291–2, 302
cattle keeping 71–4, 78–82, 85, 98, 105, 117–18, 125, 128–30, 290–4, 302
CEAO, see Communauté Economique de l'Afrique de l'Ouest
cement 337, 345, 347, 354, 428
Central Africa 33, 40, 42–3, 64, 69, 82, 429, 447, 449
Central Africa, nineteenth/twentieth century 152, 154, 162, 165, 214, 308, 311, 316, 348, 477
  nationalism 193–4, 211
Central African Empire 266
Central African Republic 75, 78–9, 227, 281, 361–2, 376, 462–3
  colony 179, 202
Central Sudan 130–2
Centre Maghrebien d'Etudes Industrielles 462
centres of learning, religious 113, 119, 122, 124, 384

cereals, cereal agriculture 72, 73, 328
Césaire, Aimé 194, 440, 478
Ceuta 138, 141, 168
CFA, see Communauté Financière Africaine
Chad 228, 240, 262–4, 294, 304, 395–6
  colony 179, 202
  economic 270, 274, 281, 349, 361–2, 370, 372
  language, people 75, 79
Chad basin 33, 36
Chad-Frolinat-Libya dispute 246
Chad National Liberation Front, see Frolinat
Chadic language 75, 81
Chagga people 79, 427, 428
Chama Cha Mapinduzi Revolutionary Party (Tanzania) 256
Chamba language 77
Chamber of Deputies (Ethiopia) 204, 232
Changamire state 144
Chaouen 190
Chaouia 160
Chari-Nile languages 75, 79, 84
chartered companies 163, 164, 166, 170
Charter of National Action (Egypt) 230
Cheops, see Khufu
Chephren, see Khafre
Cherchel (= Caesarea) 101
Chewa 83, 128–9, see also Marawi
chiefs 181–4, 207, 235, 263, 267, 368, 382, 409, 414, 428
Chifunyise, Stephen 437
China, Chinese 57, 141, 212, 224, 231, 242, 262, 348, 393, 466–7, 495
Chipata 241
Chipembere H. B. M. 241
Chisiza, Yatuta 241
Chokwe people 82, 130, 413, 420–21
cholera 309, 311, 319, 395
Chopi people 445
Christian empires, kingdoms 78, 84, 106, 111, 115, 118–23, 137, 141, 144, 408, 411, 470
Christianity 78, 108, 110, 144, 162, 219, 390, 406, 408–10, 432
Christian mercenaries, North Africa 138, 139
  captives 140
  janissaries 138
Christian missions 152, 189, 193, 408–9, 446, 477
Christian-Muslim wars 472
Christians 79, 81–3, 86, 121, 209, 408–10, 469
chrome, chromium 185, 213, 281, 283, 372, 465
Church, Aksum 108
  Congo-Zaire 106, 205
  Egypt 108, 112–13
  Ethiopia 121, 123, 144–5
  North Africa 103, 119
  Rwanda 248

Church Health Association 394
Church Missionary Society (CMS) 152–3
Churches Christian 392
  Catholic 144–5, 231, 410
  Coptic 408
  'Ethiopic' 193
  Greek 108
  Syriac 109
  United Methodist, Zimbabwe 263
  Zionist 193
CILSS, see Comité permanent inter-Etats du Lutte contre la Sechèresse du Sahel
Cirta (= Constantine) 101, 139
Ciskei 'homeland' 252
cities 100, 102, 104, 284, 302, 381, 384–8, 447
citimukulu 79
citizenship 50, 100, 172, 179, 181, 203
city states 115, 118, 125, 128, 144, 148–9, 154
civil service 90, 153, 225, 237, 266, 383, 388, 435
civil war 256, 390
  America 481–2, 484
  Angola, Mozambique 128, 219, 224, 465–6
  Ethiopia/South Arabia 110, 145
  Nigeria 148, 246, 266, 285, 299, 384
  Sudan 253–4
clan 80, 419, 428
Clark, J. P. 436
class 83, 86, 205, 237, 326, 377, 382–4, 411, 447, 449, 460, 480
Cleopatra, queen 93
clerks 113, 194, 205, 383, 388, 411, 474
'click' languages 82
clients 112, 120, 125
climate 40–6, 48–9, 52, 74, 177, 278–9, 294, 312, 328
  droughts 165, 251, 258
  and tourism 378, 380
cloth 95, 102, 107, 118, 132, 136, 137, 141, 143, 147, 226, 337
clothing 330, 332, 337, 373
cloves 129, 149–50, 184, 229
CMS, see Church Missionary Society
coal 165, 179, 225, 245, 261, 270, 274, 282–3, 336, 342
coastal areas, peoples 237, 408
coastal trade, markets 118, 143, 146–7, 149, 150
cobalt 179, 260–1, 281, 283, 334, 372
cocoa 294, 297–8, 304–5, 316, 360, 368, 372, 388
  Ghana 78, 163, 234, 300, 328, 375
  other West Africa 163, 165, 190, 226, 257, 307, 328
cocoa farms plantations 169, 182, 208, 234, 248
coffee 146, 297, 316, 328, 368, 372, 388
  Central Africa 164, 190, 217, 219, 224, 227, 328, 342

East Africa 29, 81, 183, 220, 303, 326, 328, 342, 373
  Ethiopia 122, 342
  West Africa 165, 226, 237, 257, 307, 328
Cohen, Sir Andrew 211
Coloe 106–7
colonial administration 163, 177–8, 189, 193, 219–20, 403, 408, 477
  army 455
  economy 177–8, 219–20, 320, 369
  experience 436, 446
  legacy 219–20, 347
  medical services 394
  period 361, 378, 386, 397, 400, 410, 456, 464, 466
  policy, practice 163, 177–8, 187, 189, 320, 440
  powers 159, 172, 195, 319, 388, 395
  press 403
  rule 269, 357, 383–4, 389, 409, 432
  rulers 78, 163, 369
  self-government 192
  society 449
  structure 264
Colonial Development and Welfare programme 195
colonialism 293, 378, 404, 410, 465, 467–8
colonies, colonial states 159, 161, 163, 326, 383, 389
colonization 304, 411, 473
colons 'settlers' 178–9, 197–8
Colony, Sierra Leone 250
colour bar 185, 191–2, 206, 213, 376, 409, 469, 476
Coloureds, see Cape Coloureds
Comité de la Liaison Trans-Saharienne 463
Comité de l'Unité Togolaise 256
Comité inter-Etats des Riverains due Fleuve Sénégal 462
Comité permanent Consultatif du Maghreb 462
Comité permanent inter-Etats du Lutte contre la Sècheresse du Sahel (CILSS) 462
Comités Culturels et de Plein Air 402
commerce 92, 135, 240, 349, 384
commercial advertising 404
  agriculture 220, 344, 348, 389
  capital 163, 324
  centres 446
  felling, forestry 279
  networks 135, 149, 164
  penetration 153, 161
  rivalry 100
  ties 368
  treaties 154
Common Man's Charter (Uganda) 257, 353
communalism 196, 235, 266, 388–90
Communauté Economique de l'Afrique de l'Ouest 257, 358, 375, 462
Communauté Financière Africaine 358

communications 130, 220, 240, 328, 349, 374–5, 380–1, 389, 412
communications media 403–5
communism, communists 195, 200, 230, 254, 264, 459–60
communist bloc 230, 240, 374, 467
Comoro Islands 53, 228–9
Conakry 201, 218, 236, 394
concessionary companies 162, 166
Condominium 173, 187
Conference of East and Central African States 462
Conference of Ministers 461
Congo areas, rivers 65, 82, 152, 157, 162, 478–9
   Basin 197
   crisis 465
   forests 97, 154, 445
   Free State 155, 157, 164–6
   lower 189, 205–6
Congo, French 164, 202
Congo Republic 48, 82, 179, 227, 229, 272, 280–3, 287, 334–5, 353, 358, 361, 372, 395, 405, 440,
Congo-Kinshasa, see Zaire
Conombo, Joseph 258
conquest 107, 135, 158, 161, 163, 193
Conseil Suprême de la République (Burundi) 226
conservation 311–14
Constantine (city), see Cirta
Constantine, Emperor 103, 108, 111
Constituent Assembly (Nigeria) 247
Constitutional Reform Party (Egypt) 173
construction 90, 220, 349, 472
Conseil-Général (Senegal) 180–1
consuls 140, 151, 152, 154, 163, 166
consumer goods 220, 373–5, 388, 475
contract labour 238, 248
Conventional Basin of the Congo, see Congo Basin
Convention People's Party (Ghana) (CPP) 207–8, 234
conversion 119, 120, 123, 133, 143, 409, 412
Cook, Dr Albert 393
cooking 330, 337, 368, 394
cooperatives 223–4, 236, 257, 305, 317, 320, 330, 348
copper 96–7, 141, 190, 373, 384, 413, 416, 462
   East Africa 99, 118, 280, 361
   Egypt/Sudan 89, 91, 95, 342
   North-West Africa 132, 280
   southern Africa 128–9, 275, 280, 336
   Zaire/Zambia 125, 135, 213–4, 220, 260–1, 274, 281, 334–6, 351, 372, 386
Copper Age 95
Copperbelt 79, 185, 205, 214, 281, 285, 348
Coptic language 108, 111
   Church 108, 112, 115, 119, 408
Copts 110, 112–13, 123

Corisco Islets 169, 231
corporations 336, 338, 347
corruption 266, 328, 354, 383
   in particular countries 226–7, 229, 234, 237, 239–40, 245, 247, 258, 260–1
corsairs 138, 140, 160
Cosmas Indicopleustes 109, 111
Cotonou 225, 395
cotton 146, 294, 297, 302, 308, 326, 388, 481–2
   Egypt/Sudan 173, 254, 294, 297, 328, 342–3
   Uganda 81, 85, 164, 184, 220, 303
   other Africa 143, 185, 224, 226–7, 234, 372
cotton cloth, yarn 99, 334, 343–4, 413
cotton growing 184, 189, 217, 337, 413, 471
Council of Government (French Africa) 180
Council of Guinea 201
coups 266–7, 269
   in particular African countries 199, 204, 207, 212, 223–36, 239–46, 248, 250, 253–4, 260
   Lisbon 219, 465
courts 133, 236, 368, 445
cowries 99, 145
CPP, see Convention People's Party (Ghana)
crafts 70, 83, 90, 93, 96, 98, 316, 331–4, 337, 367, 401, 472
craftsmen 81, 84, 89–90, 97, 330, 402
credit 330, 369–70
Creole people, Sierra Leone 77, 80, 153, 209, 250, 438, 459
   Fernando Po 169
   Guinea Bissau 165
   Mauritius 242
Cromer, Lord (Sir Evelyn Baring) 173
crops 248, 275–7, 302, 342–3, 383, 400
Cross River 413
Cross River languages 77, 148
Crowther, Samuel Ajayi 153
Crusades 16, 115, 116, 136
Cuba 475, 477–8
   slave trade 149, 151, 155, 475, 480
   relations with Africa 167, 219, 224, 229, 231, 241, 245, 265–6
Cuima 361
Cullen, Countee 483
cultivation 69, 72–4, 105, 118, 122, 130, 136, 312
cultural activities 380, 455
   change 446, 455
   exchange 447
   nationalism 193, 210, 448
   cultures 283, 401, 445
currencies – cloth, shell 127, 333
currency 99, 147, 188, 212, 225, 234, 261, 315, 358, 369, 375, 462–3
Currency Boards 369–70
Cushitic languages, speakers 73, 75, 78–9, 81, 85–6, 105, 120–21, 124

customary law 267, 269, 411
customs duties 129, 147, 154, 212, 375
   unions 227, 238, 318, 357–8, 375, 462
cyclones 305–6
Cyrenaica, classical 67, 69, 100–1, 103–4, 112
   modern 167–8, 187, 199, 239, 469

Dabban 69
Dabola 347
Dacko, David 227–8
da Costa, Manuel Pinta 248
Dadié, Bernard 436
Dagaari language 77
Dagbani language 77
Dagomba (Dagbon) 80, 133, 138, 148
Dahlak Islands 111, 123
Dahomey 80, 148–9, 161, 372
   colony 179–80
   Republic, see also Republic of Benin 224
Daima 46
Dakar, French 154, 161, 179, 181, 193, 196, 200–1, 249
   post-colonial 380, 393–5, 431, 433, 451
Damascus 470
Damas, Léon 478
Damot state 105, 120–22
dams 275, 285, 301, 307
Danakil 78, 426
Dan language 75
Danes, 148, 151, 153
Dan language 75
Danquah, J. B. 181, 207–8
Dar es Salaam 196, 218, 262, 361–2, 365, 396, 404, 459
Dar Fertit 469
Darfur 75, 140, 469–70
Dar Runga 469
Dar Tichit 73
Dart, Raymond 58–9
da Souza family, Togo 257
Davies, William Broughton 393
Davis, Jefferson 482
Dawit II 122–3
Daza language 75
de Assis, Machado 480
De Beers 140, 190, 335
De Bono, General 187
Debre Damo 109, 121, 123
Debre Libanos 121, 123
debt 146, 160, 184–5, 322, 381
decolonization 202, 210–1, 217–18, 250, 336, 349, 358, 451, 459–60, 468, 474
de Gaulle, General 195, 198, 200, 202
Deir el Bahari 91–2
DELCO 336
Del Wambera 124
Democratic Party (Uganda) 211

Democratic Republic of the Congo, see Congo Republic
Democratic Turnhalle Alliance (Namibia) (DTA)
Dendi language 75
Denkyira 148
dependency (economic) 220, 320, 322, 337, 383, 463, 477
Derg 232
desert 42–3, 46, 50, 52–5, 69, 100, 102, 115–16, 242, 278, 284, 360, 380
desert edge 49, 98
desertification 293–4, 307, 328
Destour (Constitution) Party (Tunisia) 197–8
Deutsch, André 405
Deutsche Gesellschaft zu Erforschung Äquatorialafrikas 152
Deutsche Kolonialgesellschaft für Südwestafrika 166
Deutsch-Ostafrikanische Gesellschaft 166
development 195, 204, 208, 213, 219–20, 228, 304, 315–26, 369–70, 438, 462
   banks 370, 462–3
   economics 320
Dey (Algiers) 139, 160
Dhlo-Dhlo (Zimbabwe) 99
Dhu Raydan 109
Diagne, Blaise 181, 193
diamond cutting 242
   mining 170, 281, 335
diamonds 280–1, 334–5, 351, 372
   South Africa 130, 155, 169, 280, 334, 377
   other African countries 190, 211, 225, 227, 238, 250
Dias de Novais, Paulo 143
Dibango, Manu 449
Diégo Suarez 162
diet 310, 394–5, 481
Die Transvaler 216
Dikko 134
Dinguiray 134
Dinka 75, 80, 93, 429
Diocletian, Emperor 103
Diop, Mahjmout 249
Diori, Hamani 245
Dire Dawa 122
Dir Somali 122
disease 177, 276–7, 284, 308–11, 319, 358, 395–6, 400
   beliefs 391–2, 406
   plant, animal 292, 304, 312
Diula (= Dyula) people 80, 83, 132–3, 135, 148
divination 79, 392, 407–8, 417
'divine' king 81, 85, 125
Djemaa, assembly of notables, Western Sahara 260
Djerma language 75
Djibouti (Afar) 33, 75, 77, 167, 204, 229, 250
doctors 179, 319, 383, 391, 395, 417

Doe, Master Sergeant Samuel 239
Dogali battle 172
Dogon 77, 80, 429–30
domba 444
Dombo, king 128
domestic servants 90, 149, 388, 473, 479
Dominican Republic 477
do Nascimento, Abdias 480
Donatus, Donatists 103–4
Dongola battle 111
donkeys 71, 130, 360
Dorobo 287
Douala 227, 382
Douglass, Frederick 482
drama 436–9, 455–6
Dra valley 471
Drew, Charles 482
drinking water 275, 277
drought 147, 219, 225, 277, 284, 287, 292–4, 302, 305, 307–8, 358, 462
see also Sahelian drought
drugs 396
drum music 437, 442–5
dry season 301–2, 425, 456
DTA, see Democratic Turnhalle Alliance (Namibia)
Du Bois, W. E. B. 194, 477, 483
Durban 252, 365, 377, 447
Dutch Antilles 474
East Indies 149, 177
West Indies Company 146
Dutch language 77, 146
people 128, 130, 376
settlers, South Africa 155
shipping 145
traders 129, 145, 149, 153, 164
Duval, Gaetan 242
dyeing 133, 333, 422
Dyola language 75
Dyula people, see Diula

Early Iron Age 73–4, 98–9, 430
Early Stone Age 59, 64, 67
earthquakes 305, 307
East Africa 264, 267, 302, 308, 328, 384–5, 390–2, 404, 411, 452
arts 413–14, 423, 425, 427–8, 437–9, 440–1, 449
British 163–4, 183–4, 210–12
coast 78, 85, 109, 117, 119, 125, 127, 141, 146, 149, 154, 267, 408, 469
expatriates 284, 383, 467
First World War 175
German, see German East Africa
highlands 81, 177
independence 194, 203
industry, trade 348, 356, 369, 374
lakes, interlacustrine area 48, 54, 70, 98, 128, 150, 361
missionary activity 152
Portuguese 44, 145, 165
tourism, game 312, 314, 378–80
trade 119, 150, 152

East Africa Protectorate (= Kenya) 163, 183
East African Common Services Organization 212, 462
East African Community 318, 358, 375, 379, 462
East African Currency Board 369
East African High Commission 212, 462
East Central Africa 154
eastern Africa 33, 41, 45, 48, 117, 312, 334, 409
Eastern Province, Tanganyika 211
Eastern Region, Nigeria 209, 246, 301
ECA, see Economic Commission for Africa
Economic Commission for Africa (ECA) 328, 341, 359, 372, 461, 463
economic communities 357, 359, 462
Economic Community of the Great Lakes Countries 462
Economic Community of West African States (ECOWAS) 257, 318, 358, 375–6, 462
economic benefit 378–80
cooperation 462–3, 314–26
development 171, 180, 205, 314–26, 382, 388, 461
independence 241, 325, 351, 354
policy 177, 462
surplus 362
system 383
ECOWAS, see Economic Community of West African States
Edea 226
Edo language, people 77, 79–80, 413
education 220, 264, 286, 305, 315, 319–20, 322, 328, 371, 382–3, 388, 390, 397–402
Egypt, North Africa 168, 173, 179
in Europe 472–4
mission 408–9, 446
South Africa, Central Africa 189, 213, 240, 248, 252, 263
West Africa 153, 163, 181–2, 207, 218, 227, 247, 250
educational broadcasting, 404, 405
publications 405
EEC, see European Economic Community
Efik people 81, 148
Efik-Ibibio language 77
Egypt, ancient 71–2, 89, 91, 93–5, 103–5, 112, 120, 384
agriculture 140, 297, 303, 328, 330, 342, 372
Christian 108, 110–11, 121
industry 137, 318, 336, 338, 347, 373
Islamic 110–16, 136
miscellaneous 33, 153, 168, 267, 284–5, 395–6, 404–5, 487
nineteenth century 156, 162–3, 167, 403
Ottoman 139, 152–3, 156, 162, 171, 173

Roman 106–7
resource 270, 275, 281–3, 339
twentieth century 175, 186, 199, 200, 230–1, 362, 369, 378–80, 459, 462, 466–71
Egypt/Sudan relations 84, 93, 105, 155, 171, 199, 23, 240
Egziabeher, god 109
EIC, see *Etat Independent du Congo*
E.K.'s Band 449
Ekwensi, Cyprian 440, 441, 456
elders 267, 408, 434
elections 197, 246, 250, 256, 388, 390, 483
electricity 155, 244, 270, 272–4, 388, 456
electronics 242, 318, 354
Eleni, Empress 124
elephants 52, 54, 103, 150, 150, 311, 312, 314
elites 150, 158, 193, 220, 264, 333–4, 380–4, 432, 473, 480
North Africa, Egypt 179, 187
East and Central Africa 127, 265, 285
West Africa 182–3, 200, 209, 235, 286
southern Africa 213, 447
colonial 154, 176, 446, 448
ruling 351, 403
urban 377, 390, 403–4
Elizabethville, see Lumbumbashi
Ellington, Duke 483
Elmina 80, 142, 145, 408
Elobey Island 169
emancipation 473, 477, 480, 482
emigration 151, 159, 227
emirates 81, 134, 411
empires 79, 100–1, 113–16, 140, 148, 227, 266
Ethopia 78, 105, 107, 120–4
medieval Sudanic 83, 85, 96, 130–2
employment 267, 303, 322, 325, 338, 343, 348–9, 381–2, 386, 388, 400, 402
Enarya kingdom 105
'enclave' economies 335, 347
energy 270–4, 283, 304, 320, 356
Engel's Law 341
England 334, 453, 472, 475
English 276, 403, 481
companies 145, 148, 168
language, law 77, 226, 234, 267
entertainment 404–5, 414, 443, 455
entrepôt 138, 144, 154
entrepreneurs 149, 353, 354, 383
environment 294, 306, 426
Enwonwu, Ben 433
Equatorial Africa, French, see French Equatorial Africa
Equatorial Guinea 231, 462
Equatorial zone 40, 42–3, 45, 48–9
Eritrea 86, 105–6, 120–21, 123–4, 167, 172, 187, 199, 204, 232–3
Eritrean Liberation Front 232
erosion, see soil erosion

Esie 413
Eskender, Emperor 124
Etat Independent du Congo (EIC), see Congo Free State
Ethiopia 69–70, 121–4, 137, 144–5, 150, 152, 155, 204, 210
agriculture etc 71–3, 287, 292, 294, 297, 303
culture 330, 413, 426–7, 433
drought 311, 388
Islam 111, 469–71
Italy 162, 184, 194, 204
North, North-East 61, 119, 172
other states 459–60, 462, 468
peoples 78, 81, 85–6
physical 33, 36, 38, 41, 306–9
post-1945 232, 265, 269–70, 272, 349, 362, 395–6, 408–9, 451–2
resources 52, 274, 279–80, 372
Somalia, Eritrea 204, 228, 264, 266
South, South-West 60, 108
Ethiopian government 307
Ethiopic language, script 75, 106, 108, 158
ethnicity, ethnic groups 78–86, 193, 219, 382, 384, 388–90, 406, 475–6
Etienne, Eugène 162
Europe 36, 45, 57, 61, 65, 69, 71, 378–80, 395, 477
economic 81, 128–9, 138–40, 145–6, 151, 163, 184, 318, 333–7, 374
political 140, 143, 187
cultural 445, 482
North African 140, 160
Ethiopia 124
South Africa 128
European Economic Community (EEC) 202, 227, 232, 242, 335, 357–9, 374, 464, 468
Europeans 79, 113, 138, 141, 159, 229, 362, 384, 403
merchants 138, 140–1, 163, 220, 369
settlers, farmers 130, 151, 160, 164, 171, 183, 210, 215, 220, 325, 475
labour force 205
Eusebio 453
Ewe, Ewe-Fon languages, people 77, 80, 133, 235, 256, 423
Eweland, Ewe unification 157, 256
Ewondo-Fang language 77
Ewostatewos, Abba 123
exchange 292, 307, 326, 367, 369
Executive Councils 182, 207–9
exile 198, 204, 227, 229, 231, 241, 249, 254–5, 258, 260, 404
exploitation 220, 285, 463
exploration 129, 141, 151–2, 161, 164, 168–9, 172, 190, 336, 351
export credits 324
crops 184, 275, 320, 326, 328, 330, 369, 372
economy 164, 245, 321

industry 167, 339, 371
 processing 242, 337
exporters 358
exports 163, 280, 294, 320, 339, 342,
 346, 361, 371–2
extended family 301, 381, 387, 482
Exxon 335
Eyadema, General Gnassingbe 256
Ezana, king 109

Faal, Louis 451
factories, factory workers 338–9, 349,
 386, 455, 465, 482
faith-healing 392–3
Falasha 'outsiders' 123
Faleme 132
Fali language 77
family 267, 269, 284, 300–1, 381–2,
 386, 409, 411, 481
famine 115, 166, 172, 217–19, 307–8,
 388, 394, 396
Fang (= Pangwe, Pahouin) people 80,
 190, 431
Fanon, Frantz 265
Fante (= Fanti) 80, 148, 235
Faras 110
Far East 136, 141, 144–5, 195
farmers 79–86, 106, 120, 125, 128,
 163–4, 184, 194, 211, 307–8,
 434
farms, farming, see also agriculture
 48, 160, 168, 179, 214, 301, 317,
 337, 356
Farouk, king 200
Fashoda expedition 158, 162
el-Fassi, Allal 196, 243
FASU, see Federation of African
 University Sports
Fatimids 114–16, 470
Faidherbe, Louis 154
fauna 52–6, 314
Fauset, Jessie 483
Faranah 201
Fayum 57, 72
Fazughli 119
Federal Islamic Republic of the
 Comoros 229
Federation (Central African) 214
Federation of African University
 Sports 451
female labour 190
fencing 302
Fernando Po (Macias Nguema Byogo)
 169, 231
fertilizer 304, 317, 322, 328, 329
Fes 113, 137–40, 160, 179, 196, 333
 Treaty 161
Festac 380, 431, 455–6
Fetu 142
feudalism 84, 254, 292
Fezzan 95, 100, 102, 114, 132, 140,
 199, 239
FIDES, see Fonds d'Investissement
 et de Développement
 Economique et Sociale

film 437, 439, 456
finance 153, 173, 349, 369–70
fire 49, 63, 96, 278, 312
firearms 129, 134, 143–4, 149
First World War, see World War, First
fish 56, 148, 259, 413, 462
fishermen 81–2, 84, 95, 132, 303, 434
fishing 69, 72–3, 81, 89, 118, 165,
 249, 287, 292, 295, 303
FLN, see Front de Libération
 Nationale (Algeria)
'flood retreat agriculture' 275, 306
floods 305–6
FNLA, see Frente Nacional de
 Libertaçâo de Angola
Fonds d'Investissement et de
 Développement Economique et
 Sociale 195, 202
Fon people 80, 161, see also Ewe
food 130, 220, 240, 278–9, 287, 302,
 304, 326, 358, 367, 372, 375
 crops 128, 270, 304–5, 330, 342,
 476
 imports 227, 233–4, 249, 261, 286,
 305, 328, 330, 373
 processing 236, 238, 356, 373
 production 69–73, 106, 236, 238,
 254, 262, 308, 317, 320–22,
 326, 328;
 for Europe 151, 171
 for war 175, 186, 196
 subsidies, aid 231, 245, 258, 289
football 451, 453, 456
Force, Charles L. 403
forced labour 162, 175, 180–1, 195,
 203, 348, 386
Force Publique (police, Congo) 205–6
foreign aid 277, 323
foreign exchange 322, 328, 370–1,
 379, 388
 particular countries 227, 230, 233–
 4, 238, 250, 261–2, 343
foreign firms 354, 383
foreign indebtedness 153, 172, 220,
 260
foreign investment 230, 236, 241,
 322, 324–5, 338, 351, 371, 377
forest products 127, 277, 342
forestry 49, 279, 361, 342
forests 48–9, 69, 70, 73, 96, 98, 132,
 148, 164, 226, 270, 275, 277–80,
 314, 379, 407, 479
Fort Jesus, Mombasa 144
Fort Lamy 196
Fort Ternan, Kenya 57
Fourah Bay College 153
France 100, 151, 195, 197, 265, 335,
 394, 463–4, 465, 472, 475
 and Africa 162, 177, 202, 228, 378–
 9
 and North Africa 138, 140, 153–4,
 160–1, 178–9, 196–8, 223–4
 and Tropical Africa 161–2, 172, 175,
 180–1, 188, 200–2, 230, 235,
 241
 Africans 193, 230, 304, 451, 472,
 474

trade with Africa 145–6, 148–9,
 155, 334, 374
 Indian Ocean sugar islands 129,
 149, 247, 475
Franco, General 190, 243, 260
 Francoist Spain 259–60
Franco-Mauritian people 242
Francophone Africa, Africans 193,
 194, 201, 264, 360, 440, 451, 456
 countries, zone 201, 249, 351, 357,
 370, 460, 463, 464
Franco-Spanish expedition, West
 Sahara 259
Franco-Spanish treaties 168
Franc Zone 257, 358, 370
Freedom Charter of South Africa 215,
 217
freed slaves 152, 162, 239, 464, 477
Free French 195, 202–3
Free Officers Movement (Egypt)
 (Society of Free Officers) 200,
 230
Freetown 80, 153, 181, 193, 205, 209,
 250, 393, 408, 447, 454
free trade 157, 177, 462
Frelimo, see Frente de Libertaçâo de
 Moçambique
French Africa 157, 161–3, 166, 169,
 172, 180–1, 449
 aid, development funds 202, 203,
 257
 bases 203, 247, 249
 capital 245
 citizenship 160
 colonial troops 159, 162
 Equatorial Africa (FEA) 162, 179,
 195, 202, 207, 264, 338
 expansion 134–5, 153, 157–8,
 160–1, 190, 333, 464
 Federations 179–80, 202, 249, 258
 language 77, 181, 226, 403, 439
 North Africa 167–8, 178–9, 195
 settlers, Madagascar 203; North
 Africa, see colons; Réunion
 247; South Africa 376
 Somaliland 167
 Soudan (later Mali) 179, 241
 West Africa 161–2, 179, 195, 200–
 1, 207, 236, 242, 264, 311, 358
French Union 202
'French Community' 202
Frente de Libertaçâo de Moçambique
 (Frelimo) (Mozambique
 Liberation Front) 218–19, 244,
 256
Frente Nacional de Libertaçâo de
 Angola (FNLA) 219, 224, 465
Frente Popular para la Liberación de
 Sakiet el Hamra y Rio de Oro, see
 Polisario
Frolinat (Chad National Liberation
 Front) 228
Front de Libération Nationale (FLN)
 198, 223, 266, 466–7
Front pour la Défense des Institutions
 Constitutionelles (Morocco)
 (FDIC) 243

fruit 279, 280, 328, 362, 372
Frumentius 108–9
Fugard, Athol 437, 439
Fula language 75, 133
Fulani (= Fulbe, Peul) people 81, 86,
 133–4, 148, 291–3, 382, 391,
 422
Fulbe, Fulfulde, Peul, see Fulani
funduq 'hotel-warehouse' 138
Funj 119
Fur language 75
Fustat 112, 114–5
Futa Jalon 69, 133–4, 148, 161, 292
Futa Toro 133–4

Gabon 149, 155, 162, 179, 202, 233,
 287, 380, 393
 foreign relations 227, 231, 249,
 462–3, 467
 resources 272–3, 280–3, 324, 334–
 5
 trade, industry 347, 361–2, 368,
 371–2
Gadabursi clans 122
Ga, Ga-Adangme people, language
 (Gã) 71, 81, 133, 235, 407, 447
Galabat 172
Galla (= Oromo) people 81, 105, 232,
 309
Gambia River 46, 132, 141, 143, 147,
 360, 396
 Colony 75, 154, 163
The Gambia 85–6, 207, 209, 233–4,
 307, 347, 379–80, 462
 agriculture 297, 302, 328, 372
 health 310, 393, 395
game parks, reserves 287, 311, 314,
 379–80
Ganda 77, 81, 84–5, 210, 385
Gande, Oumarou 439
Ganga, Jean Claude 452
Gao 85, 96, 114, 131–3, 384
Garamantes 95, 100–2, 130
Garoua 361
garrisons 122, 124, 164, 237, 446
Garvey, Marcus 194, 477, 480, 483
Gaza kingdom 130
Gazankulu 'homeland' 252
Gbaga language 77
Gebre Mesqel 110–1
Gedi tombs 118
Geez (= Ethiopic) language, script
 106, 108, 111, 121
General People's Congress (Libya) 240
generàl strike 198, 213, 245, 249
Geneva Conference (Rhodesia) 263
geology 33–8
German Colonial Company for South
 West Africa (Deutsche
 Kolonialgesellschaft für
 Sudwestafrika) 166
German colonies156, 166–7, 175, 183
 expansion 152, 154, 163, 166
German East Africa 159, 163, 166–7,
 175, 184

German East Africa Company (*Deutsche-Ostafrikanische Gesellschaft*) 166
Germany 151–2, 156, 161, 166, 173, 195, 199, 384, 413, 474
Gezira irrigation 48, 187, 306, 342
Ghana, mediaeval, ancient 83, 85, 97, 114–16 131–3, 470
Ghana, modern republic 75–8, 80–1, 164, 207–8, 234–5, 266, 394–6, 405–7, 451
  agriculture 73, 297, 300, 302, 326, 328, 330
  cultural 334, 343–4, 437, 440, 447–9
  external relations 357, 459, 462–3, 466–8
  Nkrumah 230, 265, 321, 354
  resources 270, 272–3, 280, 303, 335
  social 159, 381, 409, 414
  trade and industry 96–7, 338, 347–51, 353–4, 361–2, 365, 372, 375
Gildo 104
giraffe 55, 312
Gisaka 128
Giscard d'Estaing, President 236
Gisenyi 248
Gishen monastery 122–4
Gitarama 248
Giza near Cairo 90
Gladstone, W. E. 157
glass 99, 102, 107, 144, 334, 347
Glass and Grant 447
gmelina 278
goats 71–2, 165, 238, 292, 302, 427
goat-skins 302, 333
Gobedra near Aksum 73
Gobir 132, 134
Gofa language 75
Gola language 75
gold 280, 372, 475, 479
  East Africa 99, 118–9, 144, 384
  Egypt 89, 94, 140
  Ethiopia 109
  South Africa 155, 169, 190, 280, 377
  West Africa 95, 103, 114–16, 132–3, 139, 141, 143, 148, 280, 334–5, 351, 411
  Zimbabwe 127, 185, 213, 280
Gold Coast 141–3, 147–8, 153–5, 163, 182, 193, 207, 219, 264, 403–4, 468
Golden Stool (Asante) 78
goldfields 97, 121, 128, 132, 148, 169, 191
gold-mines, mining 98, 128, 146, 148, 169, 190, 252, 386, 471, 477
gold trade 97, 111, 116, 119, 125, 128, 132–3, 138, 141, 144, 149, 384
Gondar 188
Gonja people, state, 80–1, 133, 148
Gordianus, Emperor 103
Gordimer, Nadine 441

Gordon, General C. 164
Gorée 161, 181, 393
Gorst, Sir Eldon 173
Gouled, Hassan 220
government 265–7, 324, 370, 403
Gowon, Lt.-Colonel Yakubu 246
Graduates General Congress (Sudan) 187, 199
grain 100–2, 112, 118, 140, 160, 292–3, 295, 307, 319
Granada 116, 138, 141
Grande Comoro see Ngazidja 228
grass, grasslands 49, 52, 54, 68, 73, 125, 296, 302, 312
Graziani General (Viceroy) 188
grazing 72, 130, 204, 291–2, 294
Great Depression 156, 183–4
Great Lakes/Swahili coast 84
Great Zimbabwe 18, 99, 116, 127, 170, 384, 413
Greece, Greeks 93, 95, 100–2, 104, 107–9, 111, 115, 140, 376, 408, 472
Greenberg, J. H. 74–5
Green Revolution 305
Gregory, exarch 112
Griqualand 155
  West 169
Grillo, Yusuf 433
Gross Domestic Product (GDP) 280, 303–4, 315, 328, 376
Gross National Product (GNP) 315, 335, 338, 358, 399
groundnut oil 154, 338, 373
groundnuts 153–4, 219, 249, 295, 297–8, 308, 328, 338, 342, 360, 388
  Gambia 154, 204, 328, 360, 372
  Guinea-Bissau 154, 236
  Nigeria 333, 338, 342
  Senegal 154, 300, 303, 328, 338
'groundnuts', Bambara, Hausa 72
ground nut scheme 275
Group Areas Act 215
Grunitsky, Nicolas 256
grupes dinamizadores (dynamizing groups) 244
Guedira, Ahmed Reda 243
guerrillas 159, 197, 202, 210, 218–19, 224, 226, 232, 243–5, 251, 262, 263
Guèye, Lamine 200
Guggisberg, Sir Gordon 181
Guillén, Nicolás 477–8
Guinea 45, 48–9, 75, 82–3, 133, 235–6, 265–6, 269, 321, 379
  agriculture 297, 317
  industry 325, 338, 347, 351, 353–4
  resources 274, 281, 335
  external relations 357–8, 374, 460, 462–4, 466–7
  colonial 155, 161, 201–2
Guinea-Bissau 75, 154, 165, 217–19, 227, 236, 265, 321, 462, 464
Guinea Coast 100, 141, 149
Guinea, Portuguese, see Guinea-Bissau

guitar, guitar bands 446–7, 449
Gulf of Aden 120, 163
Gulf of Guinea 141, 168
gum 148
gunpowder 165
guns 138, 147, 150, 158
Guraghé language 106
Gur language, see also Voltaic 79, 80, 84, 85
Gurma language 77
Guyana, Guyanese 195, 475–8
Gwandu 134
Gwari 435
Gwede, Focus 241

Habshi 469
Habte-Weld, Aklilu 232
Habyarimana, General Juvenal 248
Hadar 61
Hadith (Sayings of the Prophet) 113, 116
Hadya 122
Hadza 77, 287–8
Hafsid 116, 137–8
Haile-Maryam, Maj. Mengistu 232
Haile Selassie, Emperor 187–8, 195, 204, 232, 265
Haiti 475, 477–8, 482
Al-Hajj Umar 134, 161
Al Hakim, Tewfik 438
Hallilu, Adamu 439
Hamdallahi 134
Hamilcar Barca 101
'Hamitic' languages 75
Hammadids 115
Hanafi 267
Hannibal 101
Hanno 100
Haoulti 106
Haquedin II 122
Harakat Tahrir Saguiet El-Hamra wa Oued Ed-Dahab 259
Harar 73, 120, 122, 204
  Harari language 106, 120
Harper, Peggy 436
Hassanien, Mohammed 451
Hassan I, Sultan (Morocco) 160
  Hassan II, king 243, 260
Hathor, goddess 91
Hatshepsut, queen 92
Haua Fteah 67–9, 72, 125
Hausa language, people 75, 81, 132, 246, 411, 471
  arts 333, 413, 429–30, 439
  states 132, 134, 140, 148, 446
Hawiya Somali people 119
al-Hayqutan 471
Head, Bessie 441
health, health care 181, 218, 220, 276, 309–11, 315, 390–6, 402, 408–9, 474
Hearne, John 478
heavy industry 223, 342–3, 345–6, 371
Hehe people 81

Hejaz 110
Hellenistic culture 384
Henderson, Fletcher 483
herbalists 391, 393
herdsmen 73–4, 81, 83, 85–6, 98, 125, 128, 130, 211, 312, 395
Herero people 81, 159, 166, 175
Hertzog, J. B. M. 192
hides 133–4, 141, 302, 342–3
High Commissioner (Egypt) 173
  French (Dakar) 180
higher education 397, 399, 463
High God 392, 406
highlife 435, 447–9
hijra 134, 159
Hinton, William A. 482
Hippo = Annaba, (Bone) 104
hippopotamus 52, 54, 312
Hittites 92
Hoare, Sir Samuel 188
hoes 96, 99, 330, 332, 337, 366
Hofrat en Nahas 342
Hoggar 33, 36, 50, 62, 102
Holland, see also Dutch 151, 216, 472–5
Holt, John (Company) 182
Holy Apostles of Aiyetoro 303
Holy Ghost Fathers (= *La Congrégation du St Esprit*) 152
Holy Land 136
  Holy places, Islam 137
holy men 114, 116, 119, 139
holy war 116, 120, 138, 148, 411
'Homelands' (= Bantustans) 215, 245, 251–2, 253, 376–7, 379
Home, Lord 263
Homo, hominids 33, 57–62, 64–5, 67, 69–70
Hong Kong 439, 454, 456
Hope Waddell Institute 393
Horn of Africa, see also Somalia, Ethiopia, Eritrea 46, 70, 75, 94, 105, 124, 204, 254, 307–8, 466, 469
horses, horsemen 95, 116, 119, 124, 130–2, 136, 141, 415
Horton, J. Africanus 153, 393
hospitals 319, 391, 393–4
hotels 353, 378–9
Hottentot language, people, see also Khoisan 77, 81
Houphouët-Boigny, Félix 200–1, 237, 265
House of Representatives 483
House of Tekle Haymanot 123
  House of Ewostatowos 123
houses, housing 286, 330, 349, 353, 388, 390, 425–30, 474
Hova people, see Merina
Huambo 224
Huggins. Godfrey (Lord Malvern) 185, 213–14
Hughes, Langston 483
Huguenots 149
human development 57–74
hunter-gatherers 68–71, 74, 81, 84, 98, 275, 284, 287–9, 445

hunters, hunting 67, 69, 85, 95, 105–6, 118, 155, 287, 314, 415, 434
Husaynids (Tunis) 139
Hussayn Kamil, Sultan 173
Hussein, Ebrahim 437, 438
Hutu people 85, 226, 248, 382
hydro-electricity 219, 226, 261, 270, 272–4, 277, 281, 285, 307
hydrology 45
'Hyksos' kings 91–2

Ibadan 49, 86, 305, 391, 394–5, 422
Ibadites 114–15
Iberian peninsula, see also Spain, Portugal 95, 138, 141, 472
Ibero-Maurusian 69–70
Ibiam, Dr. Akanu 393
Ibibio people 81, 413
Ibn Battuta 118–19
Ibn Misjah 471
Ibn Shikla 470–1
Ibn Tumart 116
Ibn Yasin 116
Ibo people see Igbo
Ibrahim ibn al-Aghlab 113
Ibrahim ibn Shikla 470
ICU, see Industrial and Commercial Workers' Union of Africa
ideologies 264–5
Idoma language 77
Idris, Idrisids 113
Idris Aloma 132
Idris, king (Sayyid Idris al-Mahdi al-Sanusi) 199, 239
Ifat 122
Ife 86, 97, 413, 415–16
Ifni 168, 190
Ifriqiya 112–16, 137–8
Igala 334
Igbo (= Ibo) language, culture 77, 414, 439
    people 81, 143, 148–9, 154, 209, 246, 381
Igbo-Ukwu 96–7, 130, 413, 416
Ijaw, see Ijo
Ijebu 382
Ijo language, people (= Ijaw) 77, 81, 148, 434, 436
Ikere-Ekiti 424
Ikhshidid dynasty 114–15, 471
Ilaje 303
Ilesha 394
Ilorin 134–5
imam, imamate 115, 134, 135
Imbangala 149
Imerina monarchy 162
IMF, see International Monetary Fund
Imhotep 90
immigration 169, 171, 185, 213, 217, 233, 473, 480
Immorality Act (South Africa) 215
imperialism 155, 199, 459, 463–5, 477
import-export companies 182

imports 280, 294, 333, 334, 336, 346, 358, 367, 373
import substitution 318, 338, 342, 346, 351, 373
income 302, 315, 321, 335, 354, 369, 376, 384, 387
income tax 212, 263, 304, 462
independence 193–4, 202–3, 206–9, 211, 213, 224, 465, 477
    struggle 193–4, 197–200, 211, 213, 218, 256, 403, 438, 461, 463
Independent Churches 194, 408–9
independent schools 194
India 115, 117, 141, 144, 177, 467–9, 475, 482
Indian Ocean 26, 163, 203, 247, 306, 380, 465
Indian Ocean trade 114, 117, 128, 138, 140–1, 149, 384, see also slave trade
Indian people 79, 154, 183–4, 190, 211, 215, 253, 376, 411, 467, 479
India, trade 107, 116, 136–7, 143, 149, 154, 184, 334, 337, 469
indigenization 269, 336, 352–4, 370
indigénat 179, 181, 195
indigo 141, 143, 146, 414, 422
indirect rule 135, 164, 167, 177, 183, 193, 267, 447
Indo-Mauritian 242
Indonesia 77, 475
industrial activity 315, 318, 338
    areas 179, 447
    investment 324
    location 339, 346–8
    products 280
Industrial and Commercial Workers' Union of Africa (South Africa) (ICU) 192, 194
Industrial Conciliation Act (Rhodesia) 184
Industrial Development Corporations 353
industrialization 234, 286, 318, 336–46, 348, 370, 375, 384–6, 461
    limited 233, 238, 240, 286, 316
    South Africa 191, 377, 383
Industrial Revolution 151, 384
industrial workers 189, 341
industry 151, 318, 383–4, 474
infant and child mortality 277, 284, 309, 388
infectious disease 309–10
infertility 310
inflation 196, 231, 234, 241, 247, 262, 328, 346, 370–1, 373, 379
information 368, 404
infrastructure 224, 238, 286, 307, 320–22, 325, 336, 346–8, 351, 354, 405
Inga hydro-electric scheme 261, 274
Ingombe Ilede 99, 127
inheritance 267, 269, 411
initiation 413, 419, 444
insurance 244, 292, 353
Intermediate Technology (IT) 354–5
Intermediate Technology

Development Group (ITDG) 354–6
International African Association 152
international agencies 358, 388, 396
International Commission on Education 402
International Court of Justice 260
International Development Association 370
International Finance Corporation 370
International Institute of Tropical Agriculture 305
International Livestock Centre 294
International Monetary Fund (IMF) 234, 261, 371
International Olympic Committee 452
International Standard Industrial Classification 341
International Telecommunication Union 405
International Union for the Conservation of Nature (IUCN) 311
intolerance 409, 412
invasion 115, 155, 160, 162, 168, 194, 203, 225, 229–30, 235, 256, 258
investment 320–21, 342, 351, 370, 377, 388, 462–3, 465
    agriculture 302, 304–6, 383
    mining 336,
    see also foreign investment
Investment Policy Decrees 353–4
iqta ('fief') 136
Iraq 112–15, 469
Iraqw 75, 422
iron 92, 106–7, 118, 233
    mines 242, 250–1
    ore 239, 282, 332, 335–6, 342, 361–2, 365, 372
iron and steel industry 213, 339, 345, 361, 373
Iron Age 70, 94–7, 125
    bars 109, 141, 147, 330, 332
    bells 125, 128
    objects 98
    tools 95, 99
iron working 83, 94–6, 98–99, 117, 125, 130, 132, 332, 413, 415
Ironsi, Major-General J. I. Aguyi 246
irrigation 274–5, 277, 285, 294, 297, 302, 306, 311, 317
    East Africa, Ethiopia 79, 117, 317
    Nile Valley 48, 90, 173, 187, 275, 297
    North Africa 102, 240
Isaac, Glynn 60
Isandhlwana battle 158
Islam 80, 97, 133–5, 141, 406, 410–12, 432, 445–6, 469–71
    spread 78, 112–16, 119–20, 132–3, 150, 154, 384, 432
    North Africa 79, 196, 380,
    see also Muslims
Islamic brotherhoods 389–90
Islamic expansion 411
Islamic influence 80, 97, 150, 154, 446

Islamic law, learning 133, 267, 411, 469
Islamic socialism 269
Ismail al-Azhair 199
Ismail, Khedive 153
Isoma 392
Israel 240, 460, 468
    Israel/Egypt wars 200, 230–1
Israeli-occupied territories 404
Israel–Uganda relations 258
Issas people 229
Istanbul 139–40, 471
Istiqlal (Independence) party, Morocco 197, 243
IT, see Intermediate Technology
Italian colonies 167, 175, 187
Italian Somaliland 268
Italians 136, 171–2, 395
Italo-German invasions, Egypt 195
Italy 100, 138, 175, 187, 195, 250, 303, 472
    and the Horn 187–8, 194–5, 204, 265
    and Tunisia 160
ITDG, see Intermediate Technology Development Group
Iteso people, see Teso
Ituri 165, 287
IUCN, see International Union for the Conservation of Nature
ivory carving, objects 89, 125, 154, 413, 416
    poaching 314
    trade Congo 162, 164
    East and Central Africa 107, 118, 128–30, 144, 149–50, 154, 227, 384
    Egypt 93–4
    Sahara 95, 102–3, 133
    West Africa 141, 148
Ivory Coast 48, 77–9, 88, 135, 161, 236, 351, 378–80, 383, 396, 405
    arts 414, 432–3, 436
    colony 179, 181
    economic 272, 279, 281, 283, 297, 328, 337–8, 348, 362, 372–3, 375
    external relations 358, 461–3
    independent 200, 202, 228, 236, 237
Iwo Eleru 69–70, 73
Iyasu 204
Iyesus Moa 122–3

al-Jahiz 471
Jalonke 134
Jamaica 146, 153, 281, 450, 476–8
James, C. L. R. 478
Jameson, L. S. 171
    Jameson Raid 171
Jamestown 407
Jan Hofmeyer School of Social Studies 218
Janjero kingdom 105
Janjira 470

Japan 141, 195, 203, 245, 303, 335, 337, 339, 374, 379
Javouhey, Ann Marie 393
Jawara, Dauda 209, 233–4
Jawhar 115
jazz 447, 483
Jebel Irhoud, Morocco 67
Jebel Uweinat 70
Jellud, Major Abd al-Salam 240
Jemaa 415
Jema river 105
Jenne 132–4, 148
Jerusalem 111, 115–16, 121, 231, 471
Jesuits, Ethiopia 145
Jeunesse Révolutionnaire Rwagasore (Burundi) 226
Jeux Inter-Africains 451
Jews 103, 108–11, 123, 143, 160, 408, 469, 472
jihads 81, 133–4, 148, 411, 469
Jinja 347
Jipcho, Ben 452
Johannesburg 58, 169, 171, 191, 379, 447, 465
Johnson, Lyndon B. 465
Jolof 86, 147
Jonathan, Chief Leabua 238–9
Jones, Alfred 369
Jones, Eldred 441
Jones, Eugene K. 483
Jos Plateau 63, 75, 96, 332, 415
Juba river, basin 118, 204
Jugurtha 101
Jukun language 73, 77
Jukunoid language 77
Juno, goddess 102
Justinian, Emperor 104, 108, 110

Kaarta kingdom 79, 134, 148
kabaka 81, 210–1
Kabaka Yekka party 258
Kabao 427
Kabwe (Broken Hill) 67, 437
Kabyle people 79
Kabylia Mountains 102, 104
Kadake-Ngwenya railway 361
Kadalie, Clements 192, 194
Kadero 72
KADU, see Kenya African Democratic Union
Kaduna 49, 362, 437
Kaduna State Housing Authority 353
Kafue copper 185
Kafur 471
Kainji 285, 303, 396
Kairouan 112–13, 115
Kakongo state 149
Kalahari desert 77, 437, 444–5
  plateau 40–1, 43, 45, 67–8
  sands 33
'Kalahari' field 282
Kalambo Falls 62–3, 67–8
Kaleb, king 109–11
Kalemba 68

Kalenjin people 81
Kalonga 129
Kamau, Johnstone (= Kenyatta, Jomo) 210, 403
Kamba language, people 77, 81, 150
Kambari language 77
Kambona, Oscar 255
Kampala 393
Kampala, OAU Conference 247
Kandoa 46
Kanem 131–2, 134
Kanem–Bornu 133
Kanembu 75, 134
al-Kanemi, Sheikh Muhammad 134
Kani, John 437, 439
Kankan 347
Kano 132–3, 301–2, 342, 470
KANU, see Kenya African National Union
Kanuri language, people 75, 77, 81
Kaposwa 68
Kapwepwe, Simon 262
Karakum 52
Karamanlis 139–40
Karanga language, people 75, 85
Karari industry 60, 62
Kariba 273, 285, 306, 396
Karimi merchants 137
Karimojong 292
Kariuku, J. M. 237
Karume, Abeid 211
Kasai 165, 188, 205–6, 260
Kasanje kingdom 128, 130, 149
Kasavubu 260
Kasese 361
Kasoma 437–8
Katanga, see also Shaba 33, 130, 150, 165, 185, 205, 206, 260, 334, 386
Katla language 75
Katoto 128
Katsina 49, 132–3
Kaunda, Kenneth 213, 214, 261–2
Karari stone industry 62
'Kavirondo' people 82
Kayes 154
Kayibanda, Grégoire 248
Kazembe 82, 128, 129, 130
KBS industry 60, 62
Kebre Neghest 'Glory of the Kings' 106, 111, 122
Keino, Kip 452
Kei river 128
Keita, Modibo 241
Kemant language 75
Kennedy, John F. 217, 465
Kenya 33, 54, 237–8, 265, 311–12, 265, 356, 375, 378–80, 400, 403–5, 451–2
  agriculture 220, 284, 293–4, 302, 304, 326, 328, 330
  arts 425, 439, 449
  colony 163, 183–5, 188, 210, 212
  industry 338, 342, 347–9, 351, 353–4
  people 82, 154, 287, 332
  resources 275, 279–81
  trade 304, 328, 362, 372–5

Kenya African Democratic Union (KADU) 210, 237
Kenya African National Union (KANU) 37, 210, 237
Kenya African Union 210
Kenya Central Association 403
Kenya highlands 36, 82, 129–30, 163–4, 210
  North 60, 85, 307
  South 68, 73, 75, 81
  West 128
Kenya People's Union (KPU) 237
Kenyatta, Jomo 194, 210, 237, 265, 403
Kerekou, Colonel Mathieu 225
Keren battle 199
Kgatla people 86
Khafre king (= Chephren) 90
Khama, Sir Seretse 225
Khani 99
Khartoum 69, 72, 187, 196, 395, 433, 451
Kharijites 113–14
Khatmiyya Sufi Order 199
Khider, Mohamed 223
Khoi people 149
Khoisan language, people 12, 74, 77, 79, 97–9
Khoisanoid type 70
Khufu king (= Cheops) 90
Kikuyu Central Association 183, 193, 210
Kikuyu language, people (= Gikuyu) 77, 81, 82, 130, 164, 183, 210, 237, 311, 425
Kilembe 361
Kilimanjaro 38, 79, 393, 427
Kilo Moto 188
Kilwa 118, 120, 125, 129, 144, 149, 154, 384
Kilwa hinterland 129
Kimberley 130, 170
Kimbanguist movement, churches 189, 194
Kimbundu language, people 77, 82, 217
kingdoms 78–86, 99, 119, 125, 149, 161, 163, 184, 210
  ancient Egypt 94, 96–7
  Ethiopia 105
  Kongo 127, 141, 165
kings, kingship 106, 164, 199, 226, 239, 243, 254, 257, 266, 382, 384, 408, 413, 414, 416, 424, 445
King, Martin Luther 484
'King of the Bush' 417
King of the Water 416
King's African Rifles 446
kingship, sacred 105
Kinshasa 454, 456
kinship 381, 382, 387, 425, 482
Kintampo 73
Kinyarwanda language, see Rwanda
Kipsigis people 81
Kirundi language, see Rundi
Kisama salt mines 143
Kisangani (Stanleyville) 206

Kisenyi 461
Kissi language 75
Kissinger, Henry 263, 465
Kisumu 237, 347
Kitawala (Watchtower) movement 194, 205
Kitchener, Lord 173
Kizlar Agha 471
Koalib language 75
Kofi, Vincent 433
kola nuts 132, 133, 147–8
Kololo people 82, 130
Komenda 142
Kongo 77, 82, 127–8, 141, 145, 165, 408, 413, 420
Konso 420
Koobi Fora 58, 60–1
Kordofan 75, 312
Kordofanian languages 75
Korean War 213, 234
Kotey, David 'Poison' 453
Kotoka, Brigadier Emmanuel 234
kouloughlis 139
Koumbi-Saleh 384
Kountche, Lt.-Colonel Seyni 245
Kpelle language, people 75, 78
KPU see Kenya People's Union
Krim, Belkacem 223
Krio language 77, 80, 454
Kromdraai 58–9
Kruger Park 312
Kruger, President 169, 171
Kru language, people 77, 82
Kuba 82, 413–14, 420–22
Ku Klux Klan 483
Kumasi 78, 148, 347, 355–6, 433
Kumba 394–5
Kunama language 75
Kunene, Masisi 441
!Kung Bushman 287–8, 288–9, 444–5
Kurama language 77
Kuri language 75
Kush 94, 109, 111
Kutep language 77
Kuwait 230
Kwa languages 77, 78–81, 84, 86
Kwango river, valley 149
Kwanyama people 165
Kwanza river 128, 143
Kwararafa 81, 132
kwashiorkor 310, 319, 394
Kwazulu 'homeland' 252
Kwena people 86
Kwilu revolt 189

labour 90, 220, 286, 301–2, 319, 348, 372
  conscription, recruitment 166, 189, 231
  force, stable 335, 386
  migration 190, 284, 285, 295, 335, 348, 377, 383, 447, 474;
    Central Africa 185, 213, 224;
    East Africa 82; France 197,

304; South Africa 86, 169, 185, 190, 244, 304; West Africa 304
mine, plantation 167, 178, 181, 188, 190, 335
unrest 246–7, 325, 477
Americas 146, 475, 478–80
Central Africa 188–90
East Africa 166
southern Africa 86, 130, 184–5, 190–1, 215, 304, 376–7
West Africa 143, 169
labourers 149, 175, 188, 231, 383, 388, 471
labour-intensive technology 296, 325
labour market 192, 348
Labour Party, South Africa 192
Mauritius 242
Ladipo, Duro 456
Laetolil 60–1
La Giiera 168
Lagos 361–2, 365, 380, 405, 451, 454, 456
colony 154, 161, 163, 181, 209, 369
people 196, 285, 316, 382
Lagos Conference 402
La Guma, Alex 441
laibon 83
Lake Abaya 105
Lake Besaka 73
Lake Chad 69, 131–2, 162, 303, 358, 427
basin, area 33, 45–6, 75, 96, 462
Lake Chad Basin Commission 462
Lake Haiq 122
Lake Kainji 303
lake kingdoms 128
Lake Kisale 125
lake levels 69, 72–3
Lake Malawi (= Nyasa) 150, 163, 393
Lake Rudolph, see Lake Turkana
lakes 43–4, 46, 56, 69, 303, 360, 379
Lake Tanganyika and Kivu Basin Commission 462
Lake Tana 109, 123
area 121
Lake Tanganyika 45
area 125, 150
Lake Turkana (= Rudolph) 46, 60–1, 69
Lake Victoria 44, 46, 57, 64, 68–9, 75, 85, 128–9, 163, 361, 414
Lake Volta 303, 361
Lalibela, emperor 121
Lalibela churches 121
Lambaesis 102
Lambaréné 393
Lambo, Dr T. A. 393
Lamizana, Lt.-Colonel Sangoule 258
Lamming, George 478
Lamtuna people 116
Lamu Islands 119
Lancaster House Conference 263
lançados 143, 145
land 284, 302, 342, 353, 382, 387–9
alienation 166, 170, 178–9, 183–4, 191, 193, 217, 245, 304, 383

policy 155, 192, 214, 252, 263, 348
reform 210, 223, 230, 232, 238, 269, 284, 317, 330
rights, tenure 164, 263, 267, 269, 301, 326, 383, 390
shortage 183, 210, 223, 294, 301, 306, 477, 484
use 211, 267, 312
Land Apportionment Act (Southern Rhodesia) 184
landforms 37–8
land-locked countries 262, 361, 362
landlord-chiefs 210
landowners 102, 104, 112, 128, 152, 287
Land Tenure Act (Rhodesia) 263
Landuma language 75
Lane, Lunsford 482
Lango 82, 258
languages 74–7, 252, 283, 300, 389, 404, 406, 438, 443, 445
Lapido, Duro 437
Larabanga 426
Larashe 141
La Rochelle 161
Larsen, Nella 483
Lasta 109, 111, 121–2
Later Iron Age 98–9, 125
Late Stone Age 64, 67–9, 73
Latin America 374, 446–9, 467, 478–81, 484
Latin language, culture 101–2, 104, 113
Lattier, Christian 433
Laurenço Marques 190
Lausanne, Treaty 168
Laval, Pierre 188
Lavigerie, Cardinal 152
law and order 91, 163, 246
Lawata people 104
Laws, Dr Robert 393
Lawson family, Togo 257
lawyers 383
Laye, Camara 440
League of Nations 187–8, 204
Mandate 158, 175, 179, 180, 183, 192, 202, 211, 244
Leakey, Mary 59–60
Leakey, Richard 60
leather, leatherwork 133, 138, 330, 332, 333, 343
Lebanese 176, 383, 467
Lebanon 91, 100
Lebne Dengel 124
Lebowa 'homeland' 252
Lega 414
legal systems 113, 267–9, 381, 469, 473
Legislative Councils 182, 208–9
legitimate trade 130, 153
leishmaniasis 396
Leopold II, king 152, 157, 164–5
Leopoldville (= Kinshasa) 205–6
Lepcis 101
leprosy 309, 311, 394, 396
Lesotho 36, 70, 85, 238, 238, 268, 281, 303, 349, 378, 460, 462

Lessing, Doris 441
Letseng-la-Terai 281
Lettow-Vorbeck General von 175
Levantine enterprises 353
Lewis, W. A. 320
Liberation Committee 460
Liberation Rally (Egypt) 230
liberation struggle 255, 262, 466, 468
Liberia 42, 45, 153, 172, 239, 265, 269, 380, 403, 408, 451
agriculture 293, 297
external relations 459, 462, 464, 488
industry, trade 347, 365, 372
labour 169, 349
minerals 280–2, 329, 335–6, 361
peoples, languages 75, 77, 80, 82, 153, 193, 393, 447, 477
Libreville 162, 347, 395
Libya 33, 41, 239–40, 266, 269, 279, 337, 370, 405, 451
ancient 95, 100–1, 112
external relations 228, 254, 404, 459, 462, 469
Italian 167, 175
oil 272, 283, 303, 324–5, 334–5, 365, 371–2
Libyan Campaign 195, 199
desert 115
light industry 321, 343, 371, 389
Lilongwe 241
Limann, Hilla 234
Limba language 75
Limpopo river, area 128–30, 170, 336
Lingala language 77
lingua franca 75, 77, 85, 154
linguistic institutes 401
lions 54, 311, 312
Liptako-Gourma region 358
Lisbon 141, 218–19, 465, 472
Lisbon coup 24, 219
Lisette, Gabriel 228
literacy 41, 78, 143, 251, 390, 400, 441
literature 91, 440–1,
Liverpool School of Tropical Medicine 394
livestock 170, 183, 278, 307, 311, 347, 411
Livestock and Meat Economic Community 462
Livingstone, David 151, 361, 393
Livingstonia Hospital 393
loans 273, 322, 353, 460
Loango 143, 147, 149
Lobengula 84
Lobito 262, 365
Locke, Alain 483
Lods, Pierre 433
Logone 427
Loi Cadre 'framework law' 200, 202–3
Lomé Convention 227, 242, 374, 464, 468
Lomé Treaty of Association 358
London Anti-Slavery Conference 482
London Missionary Society 152
London School of Hygiene and

Tropical Medicine 394
long-distance trade 96, 105–6, 119–20, 122, 130, 132, 147, 367, 411
Longuda language 77
Lonrho 335
loom 330, 333–4
Lothagam 61, 69
Lovedale Missionary Institution 393
Lowasera 69
Lower Tugela 216
Lozi (= Barotse) people 79, 82, 130
kingdom 128
Lualaba river 125
Luanda 143, 145, 149, 155, 165, 217, 224
Luapula river 128
Luba language, people 79, 82, 125, 130, 445
Lubumbashi (= Elisabethville) 205–6, 433
Lubwa 213
Luchazi people 82
Lugard, Frederick (Lord) 164, 177, 182
Lugbara 392
Luhya people 82
Luluabourg mutiny 205
lumber 190, 278, 280, 338, 477
Lumpa Church 410
Lumumba, Patrice 206, 260, 265
Lunda people, empire 82, 120, 127, 128, 143, 149, 165, 421
Luo language, people 75, 82, 237
Lusaka 263, 404, 461
Luso-African 165
Luthuli, Albert 216
Luvale people 82, 128
Luxor (ancient Thebes) 91, 93
Luyia language 77
Luzira 413–14
Lyautey, General 161, 179
Lydenburg 98, 413
Lyon, G. F. 469
Lyttelton, Oliver 211

McCoy, Elijah 482
McEwan, Frank 433
McKay, Claude 483
Maasai (Masai) language 75
Maban language 75
Machel, Samora 244
machine-gun 152, 158
machinery 304, 335, 337–8, 371, 373
Macias Nguema Byogo, see Fernando Po
Macina 133–4
macumba 480
Macupa Bridge, Mombasa 163
Madagascar 40, 42–3, 45, 48, 52–4, 77, 82–3, 287
pre-colonial, colonial 117, 149, 162
modern 203, 240, 247, 280–1, 297, 380, 384, 395, 463
Maddy, Yulisa 438
Madeira 143, 197–8, 478
Madrid agreement 242

Maffey, Sir John 187
Maga, Hubert 225
al-Maghili, Muhammad, 133
Maghrib 48, 50, 69, 79, 95, 284, 362, 382
  history, see also North Africa 113, 114, 116, 137, 138, 140, 179
Magill, S. F. 393
Mago 100
Maguzawa people 81
Mahdia 114–15
al-Mahdi, 470
Mahdi 114, 116, 411
Mahé Islands 249
Mahfouz, Naguib 441
Mahfuz 124
Mahram deity (= Ares) 108–9
Maiduguri 361
maize 72, 128–9, 145, 287
  imports 261–2
  marketing 190, 304
maize-growing 86, 249, 295–7, 301. 328
Maji Maji rebellion 159, 166
Makapansgat 59, 61
Makeda, queen 106, 111
Makeni 454
Makerere College 211, 393, 395
Makonde people 83, 129
Makonnen, Ras 204
Makua language, people 77, 83, 129
Makurdi 361
Makuria 110
Malagasy language 77, 117
  French relations 280
  people 82, 162, 203
Malagasy Republic 440
Malan, D. F. 192, 215
malaria 158, 277, 284, 309–10, 319, 396
Malawi 83–4, 86, 130, 150, 214, 241, 269
  agriculture 297, 304, 328, 372
  modern 279, 349, 354, 361, 379, 394–5, 460, 462
Malawi Congress Party (MPC) 241
Malayo-Polynesian language 77, 82, 117
'Malays' 79, 411
Mali, Republic 241, 269–70, 310, 314, 395–6, 402
  culture 413, 429–30, 480, 447
  economy 270, 274, 349, 353, 360, 370, 372
  external relations 357–8, 375, 460, 462–3, 466–7
  people, language 75, 78, 79–80, 83, 85–6, 390
Mali empire 83, 93, 97, 131–3, 135, 138, 141
Malik Anbar 470–1
Maliki 267, 411
Malikite school 113
Malik Sarwar 470
Malik Si 133
Malindi 144, 384
Malinke language, people, see also

Maninka, Mandingo 75, 83, 131–2, 135
Malloum, General Félix 228
malnutrition 284, 310–1, 319, 394, 396
Malvern, Lord, see Godfrey Huggins
Mamluks 116, 136, 138–9
Mamprusi (Mamprugu) 133
al-Mamun, 470
mancala 455–6
Mancham, James 249
Manchester Pan-African Congress, see Pan-African Congress
Mandate, Mandates Commission, see League of Nations
Mande language 75, 77, 79–80, 83, 85–6, 132–3
  traders 132, 142–3, 148
Mandela, Nelson 217
Manding language, people, see Mande
Mandinka people 209, 234
Mane people 147
Manekweni 127
manganese 233, 282, 335, 351, 361, 372
Mang'anja people 129
Mangbetu 75, 83
Mangoche Hills 241
manikongo (ruler, Kongo) 143
Maninka language 75
manioc 145, see also cassava
manpower 283, 285
Mansa Musa 133
al-Mansur al Dhahabi, Ahmed 132, 135, 139
manufactured goods 179, 317, 337, 354, 358, 386, 463, 468
manufacturing industry, sector 220, 303, 318, 320, 337–8, 346, 349
  state 353–4
  Central and East Africa 213, 241, 375
  Mauritius 242
  North Africa 321
manufacturing licences 353
manumission 469, 472, 476
Manyema 130
Manyika people, kingdom 85, 128
Mapungubwe 128
Maravi people, kingdom 83, 129, 418
Marc Aurel 403
Margai, Sir Albert 250
Margai, Sir Milton 150, 209
Margi language 75
Marinids 137–8
market economy 102, 390
  garden 160
  week 367
marketing boards 320, 326, 351
marketing systems 86, 328, 476–7
markets (demand) 328, 349, 460–1
  mass 378–9
markets, market places 131, 365–8
  Central Africa 143–4, 149
  East Africa 118, 150
  Ethiopia 106, 109, 122, 124

North Africa 115, 366
  West Africa 97, 149
Maroon communities 476
Marrakesh 116, 138–9, 160, 384
marriage 267, 269, 288, 381, 413, 425, 434, 435, 479
marronage 476
Martinique 440, 475, 478
Marxism, Marxism-Leninism 179, 225, 229, 232, 244, 249, 377, 459
Maryland 481–2
Masaesylii 101
Masai (Maasai) 83, 130, 164, 293, 311, 391, 422, 425, 434
Masalit language 75
Mascarene Islands 53
Maseru 349, 378
Masingir Dam 306
Masinissa 101–2
Masisi 205
Maskara 139, 160
masks 406, 414, 416, 418, 431, 478
massacre 218, 227, 258
mass audience 436, 456
Massawa Islands, port 122, 144, 167, 171, 187
mass education 397
mass media 448, 456
mass-produced goods 151
mass support 480
Massylies 101
Matabele, see Ndebele people
Matadi 205, 361
Matamba 128, 149
Matanzima, Chief Kaiser 252
Matara 106, 109
material culture 426, 434
Matos, Luis Palés 478
matrilineal 79, 81, 83
Matzeliger, Jan 482
Mau-Mau 82, 210, 410
Mauretania 101–4
Mauretania Caesariensis 101–3
Mauritania 73, 75, 84, 242–6, 260, 274, 290, 303, 307
  economy 349, 370
  external relations 357, 375, 462
  history 95, 131, 141, 162, 179, 408
  minerals 281, 335–6, 351, 361–2, 365, 372
Mauritius 129, 149, 242, 349, 357, 372–3, 379, 395, 463, 467
Mawlay Abd al-Rahman 140
Mawlay al-Rashid 139
Mawlay Ismail 139
Mawlay Youssef, Sultan 198
Mayotte (Comoro Islands) 162, 228–9
mazimbabwe 127
Mazrui 154
Mbasogo, Lt.-Colonel Teodoro Oblang Nguema 232
Mbembe language 77
Mbida, André-Marie 202
mbira 421, 444
Mboya, Tom 237
Mbugu language 75
Mbum language 77

Mbundu people 82, 127–8, 143, 149
Mbuti Pygmies 85, 287
MDRM, see Mouvement Démocratique de la Rénovation Malgache (Madagascar)
meat 109, 279, 287, 292–4, 302, 328, 342, 372, 375, 388
Mecca, Medina 110, 114–15, 120, 134, 140, 412, 469, 471
mechanics 356
mechanization 300, 317, 377
Medea 139
media 404, 450, 456
medical care 286, 319, 388, 393, 395, 396, 408
medical practitioner 201
medical training 393
medicinal plants 391
medicine, modern 201, 392–6, 473
  traditional 390–1
Mediterranean economy, trade 93, 95, 100, 138, 384, 408
  culture 89, 108, 137
Mediterranean sea 36, 53, 410, 472
  Eastern 72, 104–6
  Western 100, 104
  coasts 40, 43, 50, 101, 167, 378, 380
Mediterranean slave trade 472
Medjerda valley 102
Meqelé 111
Mehalla el Kubra 347
Melilla 139, 168, 190
Mende language, people 75, 209, 392
Menelik I, Emperor 111, 155, 167, 171, 172, 204
Mengo hospital 393
Mensah, E. T. 448
Menuhotep I 91
Merca 119
mercantile state 109
mercenaries 138, 236
merchants 16, 97, 110, 114, 116, 120, 124, 141, 146, 153, 157, 184, 369
Mereb river 106, 120
Merina (= Hova) people 83, 203
Meroe 94, 96
Mers el-Kebir 139
Messali al-Haji 197
Mestiri, Ahmed 257
metal goods 118, 342, 343
  tools 96
metal working 80, 413
metallurgy 74, 89, 95
metals 127, 334, 335, 373, 414
Mexico 475, 478–80
Micombero, Michel 226
microliths 65, 66, 68–70
Middle Congo, see Moyen Congo
Middle East 52, 114, 136, 138, 141, 152, 210, 284
middlemen 148, 305, 328, 354, 369
Middle Stone Age 64–5, 68–9
migrants 258, 322, 348
migration 240, 253, 258, 292–4, 316, 322, 326, 381, 383, 386–8, 412, 455, 483

Mijikenda people, see Nyika
military 135, 161, 203, 470
  bases 203, 239–40, 449, 465
  force 151, 153, 161, 199, 203
  presence 166, 230
  rule 178–9, 199, 266, 351
  technology 465
Military Revolutionary Council 199
milk, milking 125, 193, 205
millenarian movements 189, 193, 205
millet 72, 295–6, 304, 307, 328
Mills, Florence 483
Milner, Sir Alfred 171
Mimoun, Alain 451
mineral exploitation 177, 283, 303,
    334–5, 338, 351
  oils 154
  prospecting 157, 165, 185, 246,
    283, 336
  resources 191, 233, 244, 252, 275,
    321, 337, 342, 358, 462
minerals 220, 261, 342, 369, 371–2
miners 185, 215, 243, 395
mines 167, 185, 238, 285, 348, 386,
    447, 455, 478
minimum wage 388
mining 151, 163, 220, 280, 336, 348,
    351, 361–2, 384
  Central Africa 99, 188–9, 248
  North Africa 179, 190
  Latin America 479, see also gold
    mining, copper mining etc.
mining industries 165, 185, 213, 244,
    295, 334–5, 349
  centres 169, 388
mining camps 189
mining capital 324, 335
ministries of education 401, 402
Mirambo 150
Al Misr 403
missionaries, Christian 129, 138, 143–
    4, 152–3, 157, 162–3, 165, 189,
    383, 403
  Islamic 115
mission churches 383, 408, 410
  education, schools 193, 383, 446,
    455
  hospitals 393
missions 152, 161, 190, 193, 393,
    403, 408
Mittleholzer, Edgar 478
Mkomazi Game Reserve 314
MLSTP, see *Movimente de
    Libertação de São Tomé e
    Principe*
MMM, see *Mouvement Militant
    Mauricienne* (Mauritius)
MNC, see *Mouvement National
    Congolais*
MNR, see *Mouvement National
    Révolutionnaire* (Congo)
Mobutu, Joseph-Désiré = Mobutu
    Sese Seko 206, 228, 256, 260–1
Mobutu Sese Seko 261, 265, 449
Moçamedes 361
modernization 177, 183, 332, 348,
    389–90, 436

agriculture 330, 346
arts 448, 450, 454
nineteenth century 140, 153, 160,
    162, 193, 204, 232, 264
Modisane, Bloke 441
Moeshoeshoe II, king 239
Mogadishu 118–19, 144, 187
Moghul imperialism 470
Mohamed, A. R. ('Babu') 212
Mohamed Haji Ibrahim Egal 204
Mohammed, Brigadier Murtala 247
Mohammed V (Morocco) 196–8, 243
Moheli, see Mwali
Moi, Daniel arap 237–8
Mombasa 119, 128, 144–5, 149–50,
    154, 347, 362, 365, 369, 384,
    408
Monastir 198
Mondlane Eduardo 218–19, 244
money 334, 370, 377, 387
money economy 293, 387
moneylenders 305
Mongo people 84
Monomotapa, see Mwenemutapa
Monophysites 108, 110, 112
monopoly 145, 149, 152, 162, 164,
    220, 240, 416
Monrovia 172, 239, 347, 357, 359,
    408, 447
Montague Cave 67
Montevideo 479
Montgomery, Benjamin 482
Montreux Convention 187
Moors (people) 84, 472
Mopti 360
*Mouvement Révolutionnaire National
    pour le Développement*
    (Rwanda) 248
Moraba, Kori 450
moran 83
Morel, E. D. 165
Moré language (= Mossi) 77
Morho Naba 84
Morocco 36, 41, 43, 103, 279
  history 67, 95, 112, 115–6, 132,
    137–41, 388
  French 174, 198
  modern 243, 267, 290, 303, 373,
    378, 380, 404, 425
  external relations 223, 224, 241,
    259–60, 266, 459, 462, 464,
    469–71
  minerals 272, 281–2, 335, 365
  coast 65, 168;
    Atlantic 103, 116, 138
    North 101, 113–14, 168
    South, South East 114–15
  'Morocco leather' 302, 333
Morocco, modern 179, 198, 243,
    259–60
Morocco, Spanish 116, 190, 196
  French 153, 159–60, 179, 196
  revolts, independence struggle 17,
    159, 168, 198
Moshi 393
Moshoeshoe II 239
Moshweshwe, king 85, 130

mosque 113, 115, 118, 133, 368, 384,
    426
Mosque of the Kaba 471
Mossi 84, 133
  languages, see Moré
mountains 45, 50, 379–80
Mount Kenya 52, 396
Mouri 145
Mouride Muslim brotherhood 389
*Mouvement Démocratique de la
    Rénovation Malgache*
    (Madagascar) (MDRM) 203
Mouvement Militant Mauricienne
    (Mauritius) (MMM) 242
Mouvement National Congolais
    (MNC) 206, 265
*Mouvement National pour la
    révolution culturelle et sociale*
    (Chad) 228
Mouvement National Revolutionaire
    (Congo) (MNR) 229
*Mouvement Populaire de la
    Révolution* (Zaire) 260, 449
Mouvement Populaire (Morocco) 243
*Mouvement pour l'Evolution
    Sociale de l'Afrique Noire*
    (Oubangui-Chari) 202
*Movimento de Libertação de São
    Tomé e Principe* (MLSTP) 248–9
*Movimento Popular de Libertação de
    Angola* (MPLA) 219, 224, 245,
    460, 465–6, 467
Moyen Congo colony 179, 181, 202
Mozambique 33, 36, 48, 83, 86, 306
  history 127, 130, 144, 158, 165,
    185, 190
  liberation struggle 219, 226, 252,
    256, 262–3, 269
  modern 217, 244, 265, 272–3, 281–
    2, 321, 328, 330, 361, 372
  arts 437, 441, 445
  foreign relations 464–5, 469, 478
Mozambique Company 166
MPC, see Malawi Congress Party
Mphahlele, Ezekiel 441
MPLA, see *Movimento Popular de
    Libertação de Angola*
Msiri 130
Mubarak Shah 470
mud building 429, 430
Mufo 65
Mugabe, Robert 263, 456
Muhammad Ali 140, 152
Muhammad ibn Yusuf (= Mohammed
    ben Yusef, Mohammed V of
    Morocco) 198
Muhammad Idris, Amir 168
  descent from 113–14, 139
Muhammad, the Prophet 110–1
Muizz, monarch 115
Mulago 393
Mulai Hafid, Sultan 161
mulattoes 143, 172, 472
Mulay Ismail 470–1
multilateral finance aid 370
multi-national corporations 351, 354
Multinational Programming and

Operational Centres 461
'multi-racial' society 211
Mulungushi Declaration 353
Mumias 82
Murabitun = Almoravids 116
  murabits (marabouts) 139
Murray, Kenneth 433
Murzuq 140
Musa ibn Nusayr 112
music 71, 85, 380, 404, 442–5, 447–
    50, 454, 478, 480
musicians 90, 435, 442–5, 447–50,
    470–1
Muslim brotherhoods 230, 389–90
Muslim peoples, areas, 78–81, 83–6,
    111, 166, 179, 208, 267, 308, 412
  forces 124, 141, 429
  kingdoms, states 79, 111, 120–22,
    124, 132–5, 144, 154, 411
  traders 111, 118–9, 469
  world 469–71
Muslims 132, 133, 134, 411, 429
Mustafa, Ibrahim 451
Mustafa Kamil 173
al-Mustansir 470
Mustapha El-Ouali Sayed 259
al-Mutanabbi 471
Mutesa II, King Frederick 210, 258,
    297
Mutwa, Credo 437
Muwahhidun (= Almohads) 116
Muwale, 214
Muzorewa, Bp. Abel 263
Mwali (Moheli) (Comoro Islands) 228
Mwambutsa IV, Mwami 226
Mwangi, Meji 441
Mwata Yamvo 128, 130
Mwenemutapa kingdom
    (= Monomotapa) 128, 144, 170
Myalism 476
myth 435, 437
Mzilikazi 84, 130

Nacala 241
Nairobi 130, 210, 294, 316, 369, 387,
    396, 403, 451, 456
Nama people 159, 166, 175
Namibia 245, 262, 281–3, 303, 334–5,
    372, 404, 465
  archaeology 68, 70
  German 157, 175
  language, people 77–8, 81–2, 287
  physical 33, 40, 43, 46, 48
Namibian border 165, 224–5
Nandi people 81, 159
Naod 124
Napata 94
Napoleon, Emperor 140, 160, 475
  Napoleonic wars, armies 140, 154,
    156, 160
Napoleonic Codes 268
Narosura, 73
Nasera, 68
Nasser, Gamal Abdel 200, 230, 404,
    459, 467

Nasser, Said 451
Natal 48, 70, 84, 155, 169, 193, 216, 376
National Association for the Advancement of Coloured People (USA) 483
National Charter (Algeria) 223, 266
National Christian Council of Kenya 356
National Congress of British West Africa 193–4
National Council of Nigeria and the Cameroons (NCNC) 209, 246
National Council of Nigerian Citizens (NCNC) 246
National Development Corporation of Tanzania 353
nationalism 176, 193–7, 264, 390, 448, 460
  North Africa 223, 259
  north-eastern Africa 153, 173, 186–7, 199, 204
  Madagascar 203
  Mozambique 218
  West Africa 181, 207
nationalization 336, 338, 349, 351, 353, 370
  Central Africa 224, 244, 260
  Egypt, North Africa 223, 230
  Ethiopia, East Africa 232, 237, 258
  Madagascar 280
  West Africa 248, 257
National Negro Business League (USA) 483
national parks 311–4
National Party (South Africa) (NP) 192, 215–16, 252, 376, 452
National Party (Egypt) 173
National Supply Company of Nigeria 353
National Union (Egypt) 230
National Urban League (USA) 483
Native Authorities 182–3
Native Labour Corps (South Africa) 176
Native Lands Acts 376
Native National Congress (South Africa) 176
natural gas 272, 283
naval base 141, 169, 249
navy 120, 151, 203
NCNC, see National Council of Nigeria and the Cameroons; National Council of Nigerian Citizens
Ndau people 85
Ndebele (= Matabele) people, country 84, 130, 159, 170, 214
Ndembu people 82, 392
  chiefdom 165
Ndiseye, Prince Charles → Nfare V, Mwami 226
Ndjamena 395
Ndola 361
Ndongo 143, 148
Near East, see also Middle East 67, 69, 71, 72, 173, 199, 254
Nefertiti, queen 92

negroid peoples 60, 70, 97, 98
'Negroid' population of Egypt 93
Neguib, General 200, 230
negus (military title) 107
Negus Neghast 'King of Kings' 107
neo-colonialism 265, 357, 459, 460, 464
neo-mercantilism 177
négritude 194, 201, 440, 478
Néo-Destour Party 197–8, 257
Neto, Agostinho 218–19, 441, 468
New Orleans 483
newspapers 209, 403, 456
New York 341, 483
Ngaoundéré 227, 361
Ngazidja (Grande Comoro) 228
Ngizim language 75
ngola a kiluanje (Ndongo ruler) 143
Ngoni people, kingdoms 84, 130
Ngouabi, Marien 229
Ngoyuo state 149
Nguema, Francisco Macias 231
Nguesso, Colonel Denis Sasson 229
Ngugi wa Thiong'o 431, 438, 440–1
Nguni language, people 77, 82, 84, 86, 128–30
Ngwenyama, king 254
Niamey 395, 461
Niassa Company 166
Niger-Congo languages 75, 77
Nigeria 33, 48–9, 96–7, 312, 393–5, 400, 403–5, 411–12, 453
  arts 334, 380, 413, 425, 432, 436, 440, 446–7, 449–50, 454
  agriculture etc. 297–8, 300–1, 303, 305, 326, 328
  eastern 60, 150, 163, 381, 390, 393
  economic 274, 298, 324–5, 342, 349, 362, 365, 369–70, 384, 456
  Jos Plateau 63
  manufacture 318, 338, 343, 348, 351, 353–5
  minerals 270, 280, 282–3, 334–6
  modern 154, 159, 175, 182, 193, 202, 207–8, 434
  Northern 131, 134, 158, 164, 182, 209, 301–2, 333, 380, 411, 433
  oil 272, 324, 336, 365, 371, 374
  people 75, 77, 81, 84, 86, 301, 316
  political 246, 269, 266–7, 285, 384, 462–3, 465–6
  southern 163, 209
  western 181, 382, 391, 394
Nigerian Enterprises Promotion Decree 354
Nigerian Federation 353
Nigerian National Democratic Party 246
Nigerian National Petroleum Corporation 351
Nigerian National Shipping Line 365
Nigerian Youth Movement 194
Niger-Kordofanian languages 75, 77
Niger mission (CMS) 153
Niger, upper 131–2

Niger Republic 245, 279, 281, 290, 307, 339, 361–2, 396
  arts 333, 429, 439, 446
  external relations 358, 375, 461–3
  French colony 162, 175, 179, 181, 202
  language, people 75, 77, 81, 85, 340
Niger river 130, 285, 303, 361
  Bend 96, 114, 131–3, 142
  Delta 42, 45, 77, 81, 148–9
  delta 303, 362, 434
  Guinea 36, 45
  interior delta 69
  Middle Niger Bend 75, 96, 114, 161, 192
  Middle 75, 161
  Saharan 36, 46
  trade 38, 151, 157–8, 193
  Upper 45, 79, 143, 147, 154, 161
Nile 36, 38, 46, 89–92, 108, 119, 152, 187, 273, 285, 360–1, 396
  Blue 45, 94, 105, 109, 119–20, 123, 167
  Delta 284
  upper 45, 72, 75, 80, 82, 85, 89, 411
  Valley, basin 40–1, 45–6, 48, 65, 69, 301; ancient 89, 93, 95; people 84, 284, 316; routes 136, 411, 469
  White 46, 119, 158, 163
Nile Waters Agreement 187
Nilo-Saharan languages 75, 81, 85
Nilotes 82, 292
Nilotic languages 73
  East (= Paranilotic) 75
  West (= Nilotic) 75
al-Nimeiri, Pres Jaafar 231, 253
Nimeiri, Major General Jaafar 254
Nippon Steel 335
Nixon, President 465
Nkomo, Joshua 214, 263
Nkroful 207
Nkrumah, Kwame 182, 207, 265, 321, 403
  Ghana 207–8, 234–5, 351, 354, 448
  abroad 206, 230, 357, 459, 463, 468
Nkumbala, Harry 213
Nobatia 110
Nobel Peace Prize 484
nobles 83, 86, 90, 112
Nogal (Italian Somaliland) 187
Nok 96, 413, 415–6
nomads 100, 104, 114–16, 132, 140, 168, 251, 287, 294, 302
non-alignment 230, 244, 249, 255–6, 464–5, 467, 468
non-Arab African States 399
North Africa 45, 50, 75, 137–140, 279
  agriculture 140, 275, 300, 305, 307, 328, 375
  Arab, Ottoman 79, 113, 132, 139–41, 472
  archaeology 63, 65, 67, 69–72, 95
  Atlantic 100, 140
  Christian 408
  classical 78, 84, 100–3

coast 95, 100
  colonial 167, 193, 195–6
  independent 269, 318, 348–9, 367, 371, 378, 380, 383, 403–5, 413, 445
  Islam 384, 390, 410–2, 469–71, 492
  stock-rearing 138, 140, 475
North America 281, 378, 380, 403, 477, 481
North Atlantic Treaty Organization 217, 465
north-eastern Africa 71, 105, 111, 118–19, 145, 156, 187, 302
northern Africa 33, 41, 45, 52, 75, 79, 365
northern Ghana 133, 297, 304
Northern Nigeria, Protectorate 163, 164
Northern Peoples Congress (Nigeria) (NPC) 209, 246
Northern Rhodesia 14, 185, 220, 261, 273, 404
Northern Rhodesian Congress 214
North Kavirondo Central Association (Kenya) 183
north-western Africa see also Maghrib, North Africa 41, 72, 141, 168, 177, 380
Nortje, Arthur 441
Nouira, Hedi 257
NP, see National Party (South Africa)
NPC, see Northern Peoples Congress (Nigeria)
Ntshona, Winston 437, 439
Nuba Hills 75, 84
Nuba people 84, 109, 419
Nubia 46, 65, 69, 71, 75, 91–4, 110–12, 115, 137, 408, 470–1
Nubi people 84
nuclear power 274, 281
Nuer (Sudan) 291
Numidia (modern Algeria) 100–1
Numidia, Roman province 101–3
Nupe language, people, 77, 84, 133–5, 334, 425
Nusayb 471
nutrition 315, 318, 328, 394
Nwoka, Demas 433
Nyabusora, 63
Nyakyusa people 84, 429
Nyamwezi people 84, 129–30, 150
Nyanja people, see also Maravi 83
Nyasaland 163, 185, 193, 213, 241
Nyasaland Congress 214
Nyerere, Julius 211, 253, 255, 265–6, 321, 356–7, 402–3
Nyika (= Mijikenda) people 84
Nyoro people 84
Nzawani (Anjouan) 228
Nzinga, queen 128

oases 101–2, 140, 278
OAU, see Organization of African Unity
oba (Benin ruler) 143

Obama, Jean-Baptiste 436
Obasanjo, General Olusegun 247
Oberlin College 218
Obey, Ebenezer 449
Obiechina, Emmanuel 441
Obote, Milton 211, 257–8
OCAM, see *Organisation Commune Africaine et Mauricienne*
OCAMM, see *Organisation Commune Africaine, Malgache et Mauricienne*
OCCEAC, see *Organisation Commune pour la Coopération de l'Afrique Centrale*
ocean fishing 295, 303
    shipping 360, 365
Odinga, Oginga 237–8
OERS, see *Organisation des Etats Riverains du Fleuve Sénégal*
Office de la Recherche Scientifique et Technique Outre-Mer 395
officials 133, 379, 383, 411, 479
offshore oilfields 229, 233, 237
Ogaden 105, 120, 229, 233, 250, 460, 466
Ogoni language 77
Ogoué valley 162
Ogunde, Hubert 437, 439, 456
Ogungbesan, Kolawole 441
Ogunmola, Kola 456
oil 231, 254, 272, 283, 290, 305, 365
    Algeria 179, 198, 223–4, 272
    Libya 240, 272, 303, 335
    Nigeria 272, 286, 336, 351, 465
    others 226, 229, 231, 233
oil companies 262, 272
oil fields, oil wells 198, 219, 230–1, 272, 283, 362
oil imports 234, 248, 261, 270, 274, 304
oil palms 294, 301, 337
oil prices 234, 245, 273, 283, 336–7, 346, 371–2, 460, 468
oil producers 324, 371–3, 374
oil refining 227, 238, 244, 272, 342, 353
Oil Rivers Protectorate 163
Ojukwu, Colonel Chukwuemeka Odumegwu 246
Okeke, Simon 433
Okeke, Uche 433
Okello, John 212
Okiek 287, 289
Okigbo, Christopher 440
Okosun, Sonny 450
Okot p'Bitek 440
Old Dongola 110–11, 119
Old Oyo 97
Olduvai 46, 59–63
olives 101–2, 104, 153, 294, 297
Olokun 416
Olorgesailie 62
Olowe 413, 424
Olympic Games 451
Olympio, Sylvanus 256, 257
Oman 128, 154
Omani, Arabs 128, 145, 149–50

clove plantations 149
Omo river, valley 60–1, 67, 105, 306
Omotic (= western Cushitic) language 75, 105
onchocerciasis 311, 396
one-party state 203, 226, 229, 230–1, 235, 237, 244, 250, 254, 262
Onitsha Market literature 441, 456
Onobrakpeya, Bruce 433
Opango, Colonel Joachim Yhombi 229
OPEC, see Organization of Petroleum Exporting Countries
Operation Feed the Nation 305
Opobo 153
oracles 149, 267, 408
Oran 139
Orange basin 45
Orange Free State 43, 48, 86, 155, 376–7
    Orange Rivery Colony 171
Organic Law (Egypt) 173
Organisation Commune Africaine et Malgache 357, 463
Organisation Commune Africaine, Malgache et Mauricienne 463
Organisation Commune Africaine et Mauricienne 463
Organisation Commune pour la Coopération Economique de l'Afrique Centrale 463
Organisation des Etats Riverains du Fleuve Sénégal 462
Organisation pour la Collaboration et Coopération contre les Grandes Endemies 395
Organisation pour la Mise en Valeur du Fleuve Sénégal 462
Organization of African Unity (OAU) 242, 254, 339, 357, 405, 451, 459–61, 464, 466–8
    Conferences 232, 247, 250, 258
Organization of Petroleum Exporting Countries (OPEC) 224, 234, 274, 336, 371, 468
Oromo, see Galla people
Oron, Oron-Ibibio 413, 420
Osei Tutu 78
Oshogbo 433
Osi-Ilorin 413
Osiris, god 91
ostriches 52, 55, 133
Ottoman Empire 116, 132, 138–40, 145, 152–3, 160, 162, 168, 173, 469, 471
Ouagadougou 84, 395
Oubangui-Chari 179, 202, 227, 358
Oudjda 160
Oued Isly 160
Oujda group 223
Oulata 427
Ould Daddah, Moktar 242
Ould Salek, Lt.-Colonel Mustapha 242
Ouologuem, Yambo 440
Ousmane, Sembène 439–40, 456
Ovambo 78, 245
overgrazing 73, 278–9, 292, 316
overpopulation 219, 292, 315–16

overseas trade 118, 129, 148–9
Ovimbundu kingdom 128, 130
    workers 224
Owen Falls 277, 396
ox-ploughing 302–3, 355
Oyo 134, 148–9
Ozidi Saga 435

p'Bitek, Okot 440
PAC, see Pan Africanist Congress (South Africa)
Padmore, George 477
Pahouin, see Fang people
PAIGC, see *Partido Africano da Independência da Guiné e Capo Verde*
painting 413, 422, 431, 444, 478
PAI, see *Parti Africain de l'Independence* (Senegal)
PAL, see Progressive Alliance of Liberia
palaces 90, 113–5, 138, 241, 417, 425, 432
Palestine 91–2, 110–11, 115, 136, 140, 200, 460
Palestine Liberation Organization 224, 231, 460
palm fibres 333
    kernels 163, 297
    products 196, 297, 304, 307, 360
    wine 447
palm-oil 129, 153–5, 163, 297, 300, 328, 373, 388
    Central Africa 164, 188
palm-oil mills 300, 337
palm-oil trade 80, 156
    West Africa 78, 81, 143, 298, 326, 372
Pan-Africanism 193, 207, 234, 265, 357, 460–1, 467, 474, 476–7
Pan-Africanist Congress (South Africa) (PAC) 216–17
Pan-African Congress 194, 207, 210, 459–60
Panama 480
pan-Arabism 459–60
Pangwe, see Fang people
paper 280, 337–8, 347
Paranilotic, see Nilotic, language
Paris 370, 440, 474
Park, Mungo 151
Parks, Rosa 484
Parmehutu, see *Parti de l'Emancipation du Peuple Hutu* (Rwanda)
Parti Africain de l'Independence (Senegal) (PAI) 249
Parti Congolais du Travail (PCT) 229
Parti de l'Emancipation du Peuple Hutu (Rwanda) (*Parmehutu*) 248
Parti de l'Unité Togolaise 256
Parti Démocratique de Guineé (PDG) 201–2, 235
Parti Démocratique de la Cote d'Ivoire 200–1, 237

Parti Démocratique Sénégalais 249
Parti des Déshérités Malgache (Madagascar) 203
Partido Africano da Independência da Guiné e Capo Verde (PAIGC) 218–19, 227, 237
Parti du Congrès de l'Indépendance de Madagascar 203
Parti du Peuple Algérien (PPA) 197
Parti du Peuple Mauritanien (PPM) 241
Parti Progressiste Nigerien 245
Parti Progressiste Tchadien (PPT) 228
Parti Social Démocrate (Madagascar) 203, 240
Parti Socialiste (Senegal) (PS) 249
passes, pass-laws 184, 215, 217
Pasteur Institute 394
pastoralism 73, 149, 275, 287, 290–4
pastoral peoples, societies 49, 78, 95, 284, 289, 307, 316, 391
    East Africa 111, 164, 237, 328
    Horn of Africa 51, 120, 122, 124, 307
    South Africa 81, 155
    Western Sudan 79, 131, 308, 328
pasture 49, 129, 277
Pate 119
Paterson, Reverend Edward 433
Paton, Alan 441
Patriotic Front (Zimbabwe) (PF) 263
patronage 239, 384, 446
PCT, see *Parti Congolais du Travail*
PDG, see *Parti Démocratique de Guinée*
peasant agriculture 264, 287, 301, 304
peasants 159, 196, 275, 300, 316, 326–8, 330, 383, 388
    Central Africa 85, 217, 228, 335
    eastern Africa 84, 184, 190, 210
    Egypt 108, 112–13, 173, 186
    Ethiopia 123, 232
    Europe 472
    North Africa 102, 104, 197, 223
    West Africa 159, 201, 249
Pedi people 85
Pemba 129, 150, 211–12
Pentecostalism 410
Peoples' National Assembly (Guinea Bissau) 236
People's National Party (Ghana) (PNP) 234
People's Progressive Party (Gambia) (PPP) 233–4
People's Redemption Council (Liberia) (PRC) 239
People's Republic of Angola 224
People's Republic of Benin 225
People's Republic of China 466
pepper 141, 143
Pétain (Vichy) 195, 202
perfume 133, 229, 248
Periplus of the Erythraen Sea 107, 109, 111, 118
permanent settlement 69, 71, 73, 89
Persian Gulf 117–18, 144, 154, 336, 469, 471

Persia, Persians 93, 104, 110, 114, 116, 118, 144, 471
pests 277, 304, 358
petro-chemicals 336, 339
petroleum 324, 325, 334–6, 342, 345–6, 351, 353, 372–3, 477
petroleum-refining 337, 345
petrol rationing 227
Peul, see Fulani people
PF, see Patriotic Front (Zimbabwe)
Phoenicians 95, 100
phosphates 179, 243, 245, 251, 257, 259–60, 282, 335–6, 365, 372
pidgin languages 77, 302
pigs 302
pilgrimage 110, 111, 133, 137, 412, 469
pirates 111, 138, 140
Pires, Aristides Pereira Pedro 227
pit props 279
plantation production 190, 279, 348, 475, 477, 480
plantations 165, 167, 181, 237, 258, 275, 300, 316, 353, 473, 478–9
plantation slavery 469
plantation workers 165, 217, 388, 395
planters 177, 185
Plateau languages 77
Pliya, Jean 436
plough 73, 105–6, 302, 330
plural society 149, 377
PNP, see People's National Party (Ghana)
poetry 201, 441, 443, 471, 478
Polisario (Western Sahara) (Frente Popular para la Liberacion de Sakiet el Hamra y Rio de Oro) 224, 242–3, 259–60
political authority 326, 351, 367
  centralization 132
  institutions 131, 283, 413
  parties 193, 230, 410
  prisoners 230, 237
  system 132, 406
  unification 358
politicians 383, 404, 446, 469
polygyny 382, 409, 425
pombeiros 143, 145
Pomongwe 67
Pondo people 84
'poor white' 191, 248
Popular Democratic Republic of Angola 224
popular music 435, 446, 450, 455–6
population 70, 78–86, 97, 239, 283–6, 348, 358, 376, 383, 403
  decline 184, 302
  density 48, 315–6, 328; high 48, 73, 150, 248, 258, 307, 367; low 225, 284, 287, 315, 328, 403
  distribution 275
  growth 49, 98, 128, 227, 283, 326, 334, 372, 386, 412; East and Central 99, 183, 328, 312; Madagascar 240; Southern Africa 191

movement 74, 99, 105, 125, 284
  pressure 99, 296, 300, 328
  rural 286, 301, 305, 308
  urban 206, 212, 252, 317, 381, 384, 366, 386
Pore society 82, 85
porters 150, 388, 472, 482
Porto Novo 148, 161
ports 262, 321, 336, 339, 347, 361–2, 365, 472
  East and South Africa 190, 196, 244, 361, 377
  North Africa 101, 104, 138, Red Sea 106, 167, 171, 229
  West and Central Africa 148, 188, 196, 361
Portugal 116, 120, 124, 139, 157, 169, 195, 235, 376, 472–3
  policy 151, 177, 273, 395, 408
  slave trade 82, 146, 148–9, 151, 155, 472, 478
Portuguese in Africa 141–5, 165–6, 190, 217–9, 268, 326, 393, 465
  Angola 128, 149, 158, 224, 245
  East Africa 99, 128, 154
  Guinea Bissau 154, 218–9, 236
  Kongo 124, 127–8, 143
  Mozambique 124, 130, 158, 244, 273, 453
  North Africa 138
  West Africa 411
Portuguese India 124
  Latin America 478
Portuguese language 77, 118–19, 145, 464
possession 407–8, 443, 471
potter's wheel 330
pottery 330–2, 413–14, 432
  early 69, 72–4, 89, 94, 97–9, 102, 125
  sculpture 413–5
  trade 118, 128
poultry farms 302
poverty 308–9, 316, 326, 330, 349, 380, 383–4, 387–8, 400, 402, 468, 480
power 346, 348
power development 275
power-generating stations 321
PPA, see Parti du Peuple Algérien
PPM, see Parti du Peuple Mauritanien
PPP, see Progressive People's Party (Liberia)
PPT, see Parti Progressiste Tchadien
prazeros 144, 148–9, 165
PRC, see People's Redemption Council (Liberia)
presidentialism 266
press 230, 390, 403–4
Prester John 124, 141, 408
prestige 311, 334, 402, 411, 423
prestige projects 277
price agreements 182, 208, 326
price controls 196
prices, exports 176, 220
  agricultural 196, 317, 326, 328, 330, 371–2

mineral 213, 245, 257, 261, 342
prices, food 238, 243, 493
prices, imports 304, 346, 460 see also oil prices
prices, slaves 472
priest-chiefs 80
priests 202, 267, 407, 408, 434
primary products 317, 318, 320, 322, 371–2
Principe, see São Tomé and Principe
printing 337, 343, 401, 403
processing 189, 328, 336, 371, 373
produce-grading 304
produce marketing boards 320
production 383, 397, 400, 402, 461
productivity 342
profits 338, 368, 378, 383
Progess Party (Ghana) 234
Progressive Alliance of Liberia (PAL) 239
Progressive People's Party (Liberia) (PPP) 239
Promotion of Bantu Self Government Act 252
protectorate 157, 166, 161, 163, 168, 172–3, 179, 186, 190, 197–8, 209, 238
proto-Ethiopic language 78, 106
'proto-Mediterranean' 70
PS, see Parti Socialiste (Senegal)
Ptolemy 93, 101
  Ptolemaic kings 93, 106
public health 179, 284
  investment, debt 353, 371
  sector 250
  services, utilities, works 347–9, 351, 353, 374, 388
Puerto Rico 475, 477–8
Punic Wars (Phoenician) 101
  language 101–2, 104
PUNS, see Sahara National Union (West Sahara)
Purified National Party (South Africa) 192
Purvis, Robert 482
pygmies 54, 84–5, 287
pyramids 90, 91, 94

Qaddafi, Muammar 231, 240, 266
Qadiriyya 134
al Qahira (= Cairo) 115
el-Quafi, Mohammed 451
Qala 115
Qalawan 136
Queen of Sheba, Saba 106, 111, 122
Quran 113, 116, 267, 469
  Quranic School 201
Qus 136
Qwaqwa 'homeland' 252

Rabat 197
Rabemananjara, Jaques 203
Rabérivelo, Jean-Joseph 440

racial discrimination 386, 479, 480
racism 131, 467, 480, 484
'radical' states 467
radio 175, 343, 345, 403–4, 435, 441, 446, 456
raiding 81, 86, 122, 146, 292
rail transport 145, 229, 241, 261–2, 361, 389, 482
railway construction 151, 154, 161–4, 169, 179, 384
  recent 227, 233, 235–6, 361
  routes 229, 261–3, 346
railways 162, 188, 190, 219, 229, 333, 342, 358, 362
rainfall 40–5, 48–9, 69, 98, 248, 275, 278, 290, 292, 305–7, 360, 456
rain forest 49, 52–4, 98
rais, corsair captain 139
Ramantsoa, General Gabriel 240
Ramesses I, II, III, 92
Ramgoolam, Sir Seewoasagar 242
Rand, see Witwatersrand
Ras Alula 171
Rassemblement Démocratique Africain (RDA) 195, 201
Rassemblement du People Togolais (RPT) 256–7
Ratsirika, Lt.-Commander Didier 240
Rawlings, Lieutenant Jerry 234
raw material exports 321, 362, 371, 383–4, 463
  to Asia 118, 353
  to Egypt 93
  to Europe and America 151, 175, 195, 239, 260, 346
raw materials imports 338, 346, 347, 373
raw materials local 238, 330, 336, 342, 347, 425
RDA, see Rassemblement Démocratique Africaine
Real Sociedad Geográfica Española 168
rebellions 190, 193, 197, 203, 261, 388
'recaptives' 153, 172
recession 189, 318, 328
recording, music 446, 448, 456
recruitment 175, 190, 285, 349, 386
Red Sea 36, 44, 73, 469
  routes, invasions, voyages 114–15, 120, 136–7, 144–5, 155, 195
  North 110
  South 73, 111
  trade 469
referendum 200, 202, 204, 235, 243, 259–60
refining – metals 336, 373, see also oil refining
refugees 119, 146, 149, 152, 229, 251, 285, 289, 307
reggae 450
Regional Development Corporations 353
regional groupings 357–9, 462–3
regionalism 248
religion 389, 401, 408–10, 446, 469
  syncretic 480

traditional 406–8
Remond, Charles 482
René, Albert 249
Régimen de castas 479
republic 100, 155, 172, 200, 210, 216–17, 226, 230, 234, 237, 464, 479
Republic of Benin, see Benin Republic
Republic of Congo, see Congo Republic
Republic of South Africa, see South Africa
research 212, 358, 462
'reserve' 184–5, 215, 376, 377
resettlement 285, 306
Reshe language 77
'residencies' 167, 183
Resident, French 162
    British 184
    Resident Minister (British) 207
resistance 134, 158–61, 163, 165–6, 170, 252, 259
Reth, king 188
Réunion 129, 149, 162, 248, 372
Revels, Hiram R. 483
revenue 116, 126, 153, 162–4, 238–9, 338, 358
    from taxes 155, 214, 229, 304, 343
revolt 163, 175, 189, 194, 198, 232, 259
Revolutionary Command Council
    (Egypt) 230
    (Libya) 240
RF, see Rhodesian Front
rhinoceros horn 107, 118, 314
Rhodes, Cecil 136, 163, 170–1
Rhodesia (now Zimbabwe) 163, 169, 262, 269, 304, 404, 460, 465
    war 225, 244
Rhodesian amalgamation 185, 213–4
Rhodesian Bantu Voters Association 193
Rhodesian Front (RF) 214, 262–3
Rhodesia Selection Trust 185
rhythm 435–6, 442–4, 480
rice 294–5, 297, 301, 328, 342, 358
    Madagascar 82, 117
    Mozambique 190
    West Africa 72, 225, 234, 239, 307, 310
rice imports 236
rice-growing, America 146, 481
Rif 168, 190, 196
Rift valley, East Africa 33, 36, 38, 45, 50, 52, 58–60, 274
    Ethiopia 105, 120, 122
    Kenya 62, 73, 81, 83
    Tanzania 83
rigged elections 197, 246, 250, 256
Rillieux, Norbert 482
rinderpest 166, 293, 302
Rio Muni 169, 190, 231
riots 206, 208, 232, 246
risk 292, 336, 371
ritual 292, 382, 392, 406, 408, 413, 414, 434, 436, 443–4
Rivera, Primo de 190
'river blindness' 311, 396

River Niger Basin Commission 462–3
river-rail transport system 154
rivers 45–6, 130, 164, 303, 358, 360, 426
river transport 132, 154, 360–1
RNC, see Royal Niger Company
road construction 188, 190, 227, 348
roads 78, 179, 220, 305, 307, 312, 321, 346, 389
road transport 353, 362, 378
Roan Selection Trust 261, 335
Roberto, Holden 219
Roberts, President J. J. 172
Robeson, Paul 483
Rochereau 449
rock art 70, 72, 95–6, 413, 415
Rolong people 86
Romain-Defossés. Pierre 433
Roman Africa 93, 95, 102, 104, 115, 130
    influence 95, 109–10
Romano-Berber kingdoms, princes 104, 112
Rome 95, 101, 102, 104, 107, 384, 472
Ron language 75
Roosevelt, Franklin 195, 198, 465
Rossing mine 281
Rostow, W. W. 320
Rotimi, Ola 436
Rouch, Jean 439
Roumain, Jacques 478
Rovuma river 154
Royal Dutch Tropical Institute 396
Royal Niger Company 135, 157, 163
royalties 185, 213, 224, 261
Roye, Edward James 172
Rozvi people 128, 130
RPT, see *Rassemblement du Peuple Togolais*
Ruanda 175, 183, see also Rwanda
Ruanda-Urundi 268
rubber 129, 162, 164–6, 196, 239, 297, 300, 305, 349, 372, 388
Rufisque 161, 181
Rugambwa, Cardinal Laurian 410
Ruhengeri 248
ruling party 228, 235, 237, 248, 255, 351
Runga language 75
rural development 211, 322, 326, 328, 356
rural-urban migration 285, 328, 386–8
Rusinga Islands 57
Russia, see also USSR 151, 162, 303
Ruvu-Mnyusi 361
Rwanda 248, 287, 301, 357, 374, 382, 384, 461–3
    archaeology, history 63, 125
Rwanda/Burundi 292
Rwanda language, people 77, 85, 128

Saadians 139
Saba ('= the South') 106, 109–10
Sabratha 101

Sabredin 122
Sadat, President Anwar 230–1
Sadian dynasty 470
Sadiq al-Mahdi, Sayyid 254
Sahara 36, 38, 89, 130
    archaeology 65, 413
    central 40–1
    climate, vegetation 42–3, 45, 50, 65, 72–3
    eastern 75
    margin 38, 46, 71, 95–6, 103
    oases 342
    oilfields 198
    people, language 75, 79, 84, 86, 102, 104, 113, 131, 140, 295, 411
    southern 42, 69, 72, 132
    trade, see trans-Saharan trade
    western 95, 116
Saharan Arab Democratic Republic 260
Saharan National Union Party (Spanish Sahara) (PUNS) 260
Sahel 46–9, 130, 133, 275, 278, 312, 328, 348–9, 384, 390
    people 78, 81, 86
Sahelian drought 43, 249, 258, 284, 307, 309, 326, 388, 462
    states 316, 411
Sahraoui Republic, proposed 242
    nationalism 259–60, see also Western Sahara
Saint-Domingue 146, 473, 475–6
Saint Louis 154, 161, 181
Saint Lucia 478
Saint Mark 108
Saint Stephen monastery 122
Sakalava people 83, 162
Sakiet Sidi Youssef 257
Sakkara 90
Saladin 116
Salah ben Youssef 198
es-Salahi, Ibrahim 433
Salazar, António 190, 217, 219
Salé (= Salee) 140
Salisbury 361, 403
Salisbury Workshop 433
salt 95, 109, 128, 132–3, 143, 147–8, 165, 270, 292, 426, 471
Samori 135, 159, 161
Sandawe language 77
sande society 82
Sanga copper and iron 125
Sango (god) 434
Sango language 77
Sanhaja nomads 132
San Pedro 365
San people 70, 287, 444
Santa Cruz, Nicomedes 480
Santeria 476
Santiago 142
Sanusi, Sanusiyya 168, 175, 199, 239
Sao 413
Saõ Tiago Island 218
São Salvador 224
São Tomé 141, 143, 145, 165, 219
    and Principe 248–9

Sarakole people 85
Sara language 75
Saudi Arabia 230
savanna 49–50, 52–5, 290, 295, 301, 396, 411
    man 58, 85, 96, 99
    East, South and Central Africa 125, 287, 310
    West Africa 130–1, 148, 154, 161, 382
savanna fringes 130, 293
Savimbi, Jonas 219
Sawaba party (Niger) 245
sawing 279–80, 337–8, 347, 356
Sayyid Ali ibn Hamoud 184
Sayyid Muhammad Abdille Hassan 158
Sayyid Said ibn Sultan 149, 154
schistosomiasis 311, 319, 396
school-leavers 250, 319, 356
schools 393, 399, 402, see also education
Schumacher, E.F. 354
Schweitzer, Dr Albert 393
Scramble for Africa 75, 153, 156, 164–5, 167, 173, 193
SCSA, see Supreme Council for Sports in Africa
sculpture 91, 93, 96–7, 413–4, 420, 424, 431, 444
sea communications 106, 117, 138, 140, 203
Seadedin 122–3
seamen 472
'Sea Peoples' 92
Sebitwane 130
secession 206, 209, 211, 246, 260, 390
Second World Festival of Black and African Arts and Culture 455–6, see also *Festac*
Second World War 320, 336, 338, 384, 428, 447–9, 474, 477
'secret societies' 82–3, 85
sects 408–9, 410
sedentarization 259, 289
Sefawa 134
Segou 79, 134, 148, 292, 412
segregation 213, 263, 483–4
Sekondi 347, 350
Seku Ahmadu, see Ahmadu (Tokolor)
Seku Akmadu Lobbo, see Ahmadu Lobbo, Seku
self-employment 349 388, 402
semi-arid region 46, 81, 290, 360
Semitic language, speakers 73, 78, 86, 105, 120, 122, 124
    Ethiopia 105–6
Semliki 54
Sena 144
Senegal (republic) 33, 131, 249, 266, 390, 393, 395, 405
    agriculture, etc 220, 297–8, 300, 303, 328, 338
    arts 414, 433, 439–40
    colony 154, 158, 160–1, 163, 179, 181, 193, 200–1

economy 272, 274, 307, 334, 378–80

foreign relations 234, 236, 375, 411, 462–3

language, people 75, 83, 85–6, 292, 383, 390

phosphates 282, 335, 351, 365

Senegal river, valley 132–4, 137, 141, 306, 360

Senegambia 142, 147, 150, 209

Senghor, Léopold 194, 200–1, 249, 266, 389, 403, 431, 440

Sennar 119

Senufo language, people 77, 85, 431

separate development 245, 252, 268, 377

separatist Churches 409

Sékou Touré 165, 266, 321

Septimus Severus, Emperor 102

Serengeti National Park 311, 312, 314

Serer people 85–6

Seretse Khama 225

servants 376, 472, 482

Seti I, king 92

Setif 197

settled cultivators 302

settlements 73, 74, 97

settlement schemes 284, 330

settlers 166–7, 177–8, 264, 403, 437

  Central Africa 143, 206, 217

  East Africa 143, 164, 183, 193, 210–11, 238

  Indian Ocean 162, 203

  North Africa 160, 178–9, 383

  southern Africa 130, 155, 177, 184, 191, 213–14, 219, 244, 295, 369, 376–7

Seville 472

Seychelles 53, 249, 357, 378–9

Shaba Province (formerly Katanga) 99, 125, 128, 256, 261, 281, 334, 386, 460, 464

Shafii 113, 267, 411

Shagari, Shehu 247

Esh Shaheinab 72

Shaka 86, 130

Shama 142

shanty towns 196, 286, 383, 387, 447

shares 354, 370, 378

Sharia 267, 469

Sharifs 139

Sharpeville shooting 216–17, 251, 377

Shata, Alhaji Muhamman 455

Shaykh al-Balad ('Head of the City') 140

Shaykh Umar, see Al-Hajj Umar

sheep 71, 74, 98, 138, 302, 427

Sherbro 413

Shewa 105, 120–3

Shibraim, Ahmed Mohamed 433

shifting cultivation 278, 284, 300

Shiites 113, 115

Shilluk people 85

Shimbra-Kure battle 124

Shimenzana 121

shipping 118–19, 138, 141, 151, 358, 364–5

Shirazi dynasty 118

Shire Highlands 185

Shluh people 79

Shoa 155

Shona language 77, 214
  people 84, 85, 159, 170

shrines 406, 413, 428–9

Siad Barre, Major General Mohammed 250

Sicily 100–1, 113, 115, 138, 472

Sidama kingdom, people 85, 105, 111, 120–1

Sidi Muhammad 140

Sierra Leone 33, 42, 45, 75, 249–50, 307, 392–3, 395, 397, 403, 408
  agriculture 154, 295, 297, 300
  arts 413, 447, 454, 456
  foreign relations 462, 473, 484
  history 141, 147, 153, 163, 193
  minerals 281, 334–6, 351, 372
  oil imports 272, 274
  political 209, 264, 269

Sierra Leone People's Party (SLPP) 249–50

Sierra Leone Railway 361

Sierra Leone Youth Movement 181

Sijilmasa 115–16

silk 106, 118, 414, 422–3, 423

silver 89, 100, 141, 479

silver mines 143, 472

Silvestre, General 190

Sinai oilfields 230–1

single-party system 256, 265, 269

sisal 183, 224, 238, 300, 328

Sisala language 77

Sithole, Reverend Ndabaningi 214, 263

skilled workers 217, 479, 482

skins 95, 133, 314

slave armies 113, 130, 138, 469–70

slave labour 165, 348, 471–2, 478, 480

slave-raiding 117, 302

slavery 469, 472, 479, 481–2

slaves, Africa 86, 100, 129, 136, 138, 149, 376
  America, Europe 472, 474, 480–2
  Muslim world 140, 469–71
  sources 117, 129, 148–50, 302, 411

slave trade 141, 145–50, 153, 165, 184, 408, 437
  abolition 151–5, 163, 475, 480, 481–2
  Atlantic 81, 128, 130, 133–4, 143, 165, 472
  Europe 141, 472, 478
  Indian Ocean 144–5, 469
  Mediterranean 136, 469, 472
  Nile 111–2, 114
  overseas 150
  Red Sea 111, 118, 123, 469
  slave traders 80, 82, 411
  trans-Saharan 95, 114, 132–3, 145, 411, 469, 481

slavery, abolition 155, 484

sleeping sickness 395–6

SLPP, see Sierra Leone People's Party

smallpox 146, 293, 394–6

small stock 292, 302, 305

smelting 89, 282, 332, 334, 336, 342

Smith, Ian 214, 262–3

smuggling 234, 241, 250, 375

Smuts, J. C. 191, 215

Soames, Lord 263

soaps 153, 354, 356

Soba 119

Sobhuza II (Swaziland) 254

Sobukwe, Robert 217

socialism 194, 201, 229, 249, 269, 322, 325, 353, 370, 405
  North Africa 223, 240
  Tanzania 212, 255, 322, 379

Socialiste Destourien Party (Tunisia) 257

social revolution 91, 182

social security 384, 387

social services 185, 214, 320, 330

social stratification 125, 237, 383–4, 446

social welfare 318, 320, 348, 382

Sociedad de Africanistas y Colonistas 168

Société Générale de Belgique 188

Society of Free Officers, see Free Officers Movement

Sofala 118, 144, 384

soil erosion 238, 263, 277–9, 284, 304

soils 36, 46–9, 275, 279
  fertility 105, 183, 284, 296, 301, 308, 316

Sokoto Caliphate 134–5, 148, 158–9, 163

solar energy 40, 274, 336

soldiers 114, 143, 157, 159, 162, 175, 195–6, 447, 473–4, 477

Solomonic dynasty myth 111, 122

Somalia 250, 269, 274, 287, 330, 353, 372, 395
  British forces 210
  foreign relations 204, 210, 229, 460, 465
  Islam 119–20, 412
  pastoralism 290, 294, 307
  Trust Territory 204

Somaliland, British 163, 167, 188, 204
  French Somali Coast 204
  Italian 167, 187

Somaliland National League 204

Somali language, script 75, 85, 118, 250
  coast 119, 154, 163, 411
  pastoralists 120, 122, 124, 293
  people 70, 85, 105, 118, 124, 204, 232–3, 250

Somali Republic (Somalia) 204, 250
  revolt 167

Somali Youth League 204

Sonatrach national oil co, Algeria 223

Songhai, Songhay 75, 85, 97, 131, 132–3, 139, 384, 474

songs 404, 443–4, 449

Sonhrai people see Songhai

Soninke language, people (= Sarakole) 75, 80, 83, 85, 131–3

Sonni Ali 132

sorghum 72, 98, 106, 295, 304, 307, 328, 342, 356

Sorko 132

Soshangane 130

Sotho people, language 85–6, 130
  Sotho/Tswana people 128

South Africa 57–8, 215, 252, 279, 391, 395, 397, 403–5, 410
  arts 413, 428, 437, 447, 449–51
  agriculture, fishing 297, 300, 303
  energy 270, 272–4
  foreign relations 157, 175, 217, 224, 254, 259–62, 265, 267
  inter-war 184, 191–2
  labour 185, 190–2, 285–6, 348, 386
  language, people 84, 86
  law 208, 267–8
  mines, minerals 169, 280–3, 285, 334–6, 345–9, 386
  political organizations 193, 215
  post-1945 213, 216–18, 237–8, 241, 244–5, 251, 256, 261–2
  Second World War 186
  tourism, national parks 312, 378, 380
  trade, industry 338, 341, 346, 361, 365, 372, 386
  whites 130, 149, 155, 199, 376–7, 380, 383

South African Broadcasting Services 404

South African National Olympic Committee 452

South African Party 191–2

South African Republic 169

South African Students' Organization 252

South African War 171, 446

South America 52, 146, 459, 478–80

South Arabia 78, 105–6, 109–10, 119
  language, script 101, 106, 108

South East Asia 314

south-eastern Europe 469

southern Africa 155, 169–70, 369, 384, 413, 456, 466, 468
  agriculture etc. 275, 284, 296, 302, 304
  language, people 77, 82, 84–5, 316
  national parks, tourism 312, 378, 380
  physical 33, 36, 38, 45, 47–9, 306
  religion 390, 408–9, 411

Southern Cameroons, see Cameroons, South

Southern Confederacy 482

southern Europe 378

Southern Rhodesia 14, 159, 171, 183–5, 192, 216, 220, 262, 273, 433

southern Sudan see Sudan, South

South India 289

South Korea 339

South Ndebele 'homeland' 252

South West Africa 159, 166–7, 175, 192, 245

South West Africa People's Organization (SWAPO) 245, 262, 404
south-western Africa 41, 79
South Yemen 73
sovereignty 460, 464
Soviet, see USSR
Soviet-Egyptian treaty of friendship 231
Soweto 252, 377
Soyinka, Wole 405, 431, 436–7, 440
Spain 145, 151, 168, 195, 472–3, 475, 478
  ancient 95, 100–1
  Arab, reconquest 112–4, 116, 137–9, 141, 410, 469–70
Spanish Civil War 190
Spanish language 77
Spanish expansion 168
Spanish Africa 138, 168–9, 175, 190, 231, 260, 268, 478
  Guinea 190
  Sahara 167–8, 190, 224, 242–3, 259
spices 136, 138, 140, 362
spirits 147, 338, 392, 406–7, 414, 425, 443
sport 451–3, 455–6
squash 456
Stack, Sir Lee 186–7
Standard Bank 369–70
Standard Bank of British South Africa 369
Stanley, Henry Morton 151, 164
Stanleyville 206
starvation 258, 307, 311
state 93, 96, 148, 159, 167, 350–4, 388–90
state enterprise 138, 223, 261, 336, 349, 351, 353, 405
  ownership 351–3
state-run farms 317
states, eastern and southern Africa 84, 99, 144, 150, 155
  Central Africa 82, 149, 164
  North Africa 104, 160, 171, 223
  West Africa 78–80, 86, 147–8, 202, 411
State Trading Corporation of Tanzania 353
status 286, 292, 419, 422
  of women 409
steam power 152
steel 282, 336–7, 346, 374, 482
Stellenbosch 216
Sterkfontein 58–9, 61
Stevens, Siaka 209, 250
Stewart, Dr James 393
stock rearing 276, 290, 295, 476
stone artifacts 73, 74, 90, 413
  tools 58–63, 64, 67, 89, 95, 98
  walls 99, 127
Straits of Gibraltar 104, 168
strikes 194, 335
  pre-1960 185, 191, 205, 208, 215
  post-1960 232, 239, 242, 249, 252, 257
Student Non-Violent Coordinating Committee (USA) 484

subsistence agriculture 220, 249, 275, 304, 306, 316, 322, 326, 335, 348
subsistence economy 103–4, 270, 284, 294, 307, 315, 328, 383
Sudan, Central and Western 95, 114–6, 130–5, 137–40
'Sudanic' belt 89, 469
Sudanic, central, language 75, 83
Sudanic, eastern, language 75, 80–2, 85, 99
Sudan, Nilotic 33, 275, 280–1
  Anglo-Egyptian 186–7, 188, 199, 230
  history 94–5, 105, 109, 111, 117, 119, 155, 171–3
  people, language 75, 77–9, 84–5
Sudan Republic 80, 199, 253–4, 267, 269, 312, 380, 396, 404, 427, 433
  agriculture and pastoralism 290–3, 297–8, 306–7, 342, 372
  external relations 199, 459, 462, 469
  North 253
  religion 109, 408, 411–2
  South 253–4, 285, 312
Sudan Socialist Union 254
Suez Canal 152, 154, 174–5, 187–8, 199–200, 272
  company, shares 153, 230
Suez route 195
  war 200, 467
Sufism (Islamic mysticism) 134, 139, 199, 411
sugar 294, 297, 302, 342–4
  Americas 143, 145–6, 475, 477, 479, 481
  Egypt and Sudan 337, 342
  Europe and Atlantic islands 138, 143, 472
  Indian Ocean islands 242, 248, 372
  Mozambique 166, 190
  Persia 471
  West Africa 143, 230
sugar mills 337, 347
sugar refining 338, 482
Suhaym 471
Sukuma language, people 77, 85
  Sukuma Federation 85
Sulaiman Bal 134
Sulayman, Sultan, Morocco 140
Sundiata 132
Sunna (Custom of the Prophet) 113
  Sunnites 113, 115, 119
supply companies 320
Supreme Council for Sports in Africa (SCSA) 451
Surinam 474–5
Susu 132–3
Susu language 75
Sutherland, Efua 436
Suto people 85
Swahili, Arab-Swahili traders, caravans 144, 150, 165, 438, 441
  city states, settlements 99, 129, 144, 149, 411
  language 77, 118, 125, 129, 154, 211

swamp rice 297
Swazi 'homeland' 252
Swaziland 84–5, 171, 192, 254, 268, 279, 378–9, 462
  minerals 270, 282, 335, 361
Swazi people 84, 85, 382
Sya language 77
Syphax, king 101–2
Syria 92, 103–4, 112, 114–16, 126, 140, 152, 224, 230–1

Taban lo Liyong 440
Tabora 129, 150
Tafari Makonnen (= Haile Selassie) 204
Tahert 114
Taita Hills 183
Takedda 95
Takoradi 347, 365
Takrur 131–3
Tal al-Kabir battle 173
Tallensi people 159
Talodi language 75
Tamasheq language 75
Tanala people 83
Tananarive 162
Tanga 128
Tanganyika, see also German East Africa 183, 185, 211, 212, 275, 357, 467
Tanganyika African Association 193, 211
Tanganyika Africa National Union (TANU) 211–12
Tangier (= Tingi) 103, 141, 197
tanneries 152, 333, 337
TANU, see Tanganyika Africa National Union, Tanzania African National Union
TanZam, see Tazara
Tanzania 211, 285–6, 393, 395, 402, 411, 427–9, 452
  agriculture 297, 301–2, 328, 372
  archaeology, history 58–9, 70, 128–9
  coast, islands 118
  early man 59, 70
  economy 231–2, 274–5, 280–2, 338, 351, 353, 355–6
  government 266–7, 269, 321–2
  North 73
  people, languages 75, 77, 79, 81, 83–6, 287, 467
  physical 33, 48, 54
  population movement 285–6, 306, 381
  south-eastern 130
  wild-life, tourism 311–2, 379–80
Tanzania Africa National Union (TANU) 255
Tanzania Tourist Corporation 379
Tarfaya 169
tariff 304, 338, 354, 374
Tassili 415
Taung 57–8

Taushi, Sarkin 455
Tawana people 86
taxation 214, 224, 263, 283, 293, 304, 325–6, 335–6, see also revenue
  pre-colonial 103, 108, 112, 115, 137, 152
  colonial 163, 166, 175, 177, 181–2, 185, 348
taxes 112, 115, 137, 163, 181–2, 293, 304, 348
tax farms 113, 115, 139–40
tax concessions 249, 338, 351, 354
taxis 362, 456
Tazara (TanZam) railway 261–2, 264, 361, 402, 467
tea 185, 213, 238, 241–2, 297, 299–300, 303–4, 316, 328, 342, 372
teachers 205, 207, 400–1, 402, 467
Tebessa (= Thebeste) 102
technical assistance 236, 405, 460
  skills 318, 393
technicians 383
technology, agricultural 328
  handicraft 304, 330, 334, 425–6
  imported 143, 217, 325, 337, 370, 432, 436
Technology Consultancy Centre, Kumasi, Ghana 355
Teghaza 471
Tekeze, valley 107, 109, 111, 121, 123
Tekle Haymanot, Saint 173
Tekrur kingdom 86
television 401, 404, 405, 441, 456
Tema 347, 365
Temne language, people 75, 85, 209
temples 91, 93, 94, 106, 109
Tenere desert 72
terms of trade 304, 317, 321, 328, 372
Ternefine 62
Teso language, people (= Iteso) 75, 85, 396
Tete 128, 144
Tetela 206
Tewodros I 123, 195
textiles Asian 118, 144
  demand 337
  handicraft 333, 356, 401, 413
  local manufacture 152, 213, 242, 318, 342, 354, 373
  mills, American 482
theatre 380, 436–7, 439, 441, 455–6
Thebes, tombs, kings 91–2
Theodora 110
Theveste = Tebessa 102
Thiong'o, Ngugi wa, see Ngugi wa Thiong'o
Third World 459–60, 464, 467–8
Thlaping people 86
Thonga 391
Thurman, Wallace 483
Thysville riots 206
Tibesti 33, 36, 50, 52, 413
Tiemassas 69
Tiger, Dick 451–2
Tigre province 106, 108–9, 120–4, 172, 430
Tigrinya language 75, 86, 106–7

Tijaniyya 134
timber 118, 162, 190, 226–7, 229, 233, 277–80, 314, 342, 353, 372, 388
Timbuktu 96, 132–3, 139, 292, 384
tin 96, 100, 196, 282, 334, 335, 336, 343, 415
Tin Can Island, Lagos 365
Tingi (= Tangier) 103
tinkhundla tribal communities (Swaziland) 254
Tippu Tib 150
Tiris El-Gharbia 260
Tiv language, people 77, 86, 159, 382, 434–5
Tlemcen 116, 137–8
tobacco growing, Africa 185, 213, 220, 241, 297–8, 328, 388; America 146–7, 181
    processing 146–7, 481
    trade 133
Togo 77, 80, 256, 370, 375, 380, 395–6, 437, 462–3
    German, French 152, 166–7, 179–80
    phospates 282, 335–6, 351, 365
Tokolor (= Toucouleur) empire, people 86, 161
Tolbert, William 239
Tombalbaye, François 228
tombs 90–2, 95, 103, 108, 118
Tonga-Korekore people 85
Tonga people 86
Tongogara, Josiah 263
tools 91, 95, 99, 330
Toomer, Jean 483
torodbe 133–4
Tororo 347
Touan, Jules 452
Touba 389
Toucouleur, see Tokolor
Touré, Sékou 201–2, 235–6, 321
tourism 234, 238, 242, 249, 257, 311–12, 378–80, 432, 456, 463
towns 97, 102, 122, 128, 284, 389–90
townships 100
tractors 300, 328, 355
trade, international 317, 320
    intra-African 374
    maritime 111, 384
    pre-colonial – eastern, southern, central Africa 99, 118, 127–30, 144, 155, 411; Nile Valley 72, 89–91, 93, 115, 411; North Africa, Western Sudan 95–6, 114, 132–4, 411, 472; Red Sea, Ethiopia 106, 109, 119–20, 122–4, 136, 145; West, West-Central Africa 97, 141, 143, 148–9, 302
    'Scramble' period 153–4, 161–3, 165
    colonial 194, 206, 351, 369, 464
    post-colonial 240, 248, 317, 324, 353, 369–75, 464; internal 287, 302, 333, 360, 367
trade unions 335, 350, 383, 477

Central Africa 205, 335
    North Africa 197, 240, 257
    southern Africa 185, 191, 213
    West Africa 201, 209, 237, 249, 335
Trade Winds 41–2
traders, African 382, 388, 408
    non-African 153, 379, 383, 467
trading centres 100, 106, 120, 132
    peoples, African 78–84, 86, 93, 132–4, 142, 143, 148, 472; European 129, 141–3, 145, 411
    networks 138, 142–3, 148, 150, 333–4
    states 81–2, 109, 122
traditional arts 401, 413, 425, 434–5, 456
    festivals 380
    medicine 391–2
    religion 133, 390, 406, 409, 412, 432
    rulers 133, 164, 193, 269, 326
Trans-African Highway 362, 463
trans-Atlantic slave trade 128, 143, 146, 198, 383, 472, 481
Transkei 84, 86, 239, 376, 460
    'homeland' 252
transport 286, 346, 349, 353, 361–5, 371, 373, 390
    difficulties 227, 233, 262, 379–80
    new, improved 262, 336, 347–8, 358, 368, 381, 461
    pre-industrial 90, 130, 148, 426
trans-Saharan highway 463
trans-Saharan trade 130–3, 137, 140–1, 145, 333, 348, 469, see also slave trade
    traders 79, 85, 95, 114, 130, 132, 148, 291
Transvaal 33, 43, 49, 85–6, 128–30, 169, 190
    archaeology 58, 61, 99
    railway 166
    Republic, see South African Republic
Traoré, Colonel Moussa 241
Treaty of Rome 358
Trek, Great, see Great Trek
Tribal Trust Lands, Rhodesia 263
tribute 91, 112, 122, 138, 146, 148–9
Trinidad 475
Tripoli 101–2, 116, 139–40
Tripolitania 101–2, 104, 114, 137, 199, 239
    Italian penetration 167–8
Tripolitanian National Congress Party (Libya) 239
tropical crops 242, 305, 371
tropical disease 146, 284, 394
tropical fruits 236, 249
tropical rain forest 48–9, 53, 84, 96, 277, 279, 287, 290
Trotter, William Monroe 483
Trouvoada, Miguel 248
trucks 362, 432, 456
True Whig Party (Liberia) (TWP) 172, 239, 265

trusteeship 177, 204
trypanosomiasis 290, 302, 311, 396
Tsavo National Park 312
tsetse fly 127, 130, 290, 302, 311, 360, 396
tshikona 444
Tshombe, Moise 260
Tsimety people 83
Tsiranana, Philibert 203, 240
Tsonga 129
Tswana (= Bechuana) people 81, 85, 86, 129–30
Tswana-Sotho language 77
Tuareg people 79, 86, 116, 175, 292, 332–3
tuberculosis 310, 388, 394–5
Tubman, William 239
Tulunid dynasty 114
Tumbuka language 241
Tumtum language 75
Tunis 137–40, 179, 384, 394
Tunisia 220, 240, 257, 266–7, 330, 373, 378–80, 459, 462–3
    French 160–1, 176, 178–9, 197–9
    history 69, 95, 100–2, 104, 114, 137–9, 153, 470
    minerals 179, 272, 282, 334–5
Turkey 92, 115–6, 124, 138–9, 175, 186
Tuskegee Institute 482
Tutankhamen 92
Tutmosis I 92, 94
Tutsi, Tutsi-Hima 85, 128, 226, 248, 292–3, 382
Twa people 85
Twi language 78
    Twi-Fante language, see Akan
typhoid 309, 395

UAM, see Union Africaine et Malgache
UAMCE, see Union Africaine et Malgache de Coopération Économique
UANC, see United African National Congress (Rhodesia)
UDEAC, see Union Douanière et Economique de l'Afrique Centrale
UDEAO, see Union Douanière de l'Afrique de l'Ouest
UDI, see Unilateral Declaration of Independence
UDV, see Union Démocratique Voltaique (Upper Volta)
Ufipa 334
Uganda 210–12, 256–8, 383, 390, 393–6, 403, 409, 451
    agriculture 292, 297, 302, 304, 328, 342
    archaeology, history 65, 72, 125, 128
    arts 333, 413–14, 433, 440, 445
    British 163–4, 184
    economy 270, 281, 347, 353, 361–2, 370, 372, 375

external relations 240, 146, 256, 258, 354, 357–8, 466–7
    people, languages 75, 81–2, 84–5, 287
    wildlife, tourism 54, 311, 379
Uganda Asians 258, 354, 467
Ugandan Development Corporation 353
Uganda People's Congress (UPC) 211, 257
UGCC, see United Gold Coast Convention
UGTT, see Union Générale Tunisienne du Travail
Uitlanders 169, 171
ujamaa 285, 317
Ujiji 156
Ukamba Members Association 183
ulama (sing. alim) 'the wise' 113
Ulcinj 471
Umar Walasma 122
Umayyad dynasty 113–14
Umbundu language 77
Umma Party 254
Um Nyobe, Ruben 202
UMOA, see Union Monétaire Ouest-Africaine
Umuahia 433
UN, see United Nations
UNCTAD, see United Nations Commission for Trade and Development
underdevelopment 219–20, 269, 463, 468
underemployment 250, 368
UNDP, see United Nations Development Programme
unemployment 286, 316, 319, 330, 349, 381, 387–8, 394, 400
    Caribbean 477
    Central Africa 205, 217, 229, 233
    East Africa 238
    Indian Ocean Islands 240, 248
    North Africa 223, 243
    southern Africa 252, 356, 377
    West Africa 227, 234
UNESCO 402
UNFP, see Union Nationale des Forces Populaires (Morocco)
União Nacional de Índependência Total de Angola (UNITA) 219, 224, 465, 466–7
UNICEF 356
Unilateral Declaration of Independence (UDI) 214, 62–3, 362, 460
Union Africaine et Malgache 357, 463
Union Africaine et Malgache de Coopération Économique 463
Union Camerounaise 202
Union Démocratique du Peuple Malien 241
Union Démocratique pour la Défense des Intérêts Africains (Congo) 229
Union Démocratique Voltaique (UDV) 258

Union des Etats de l'Afrique Centrale 228
Union des Populations du Cameroun (UPC) 202, 226, 466
Union Douanière et Economique de l'Afrique Centrale 227–8, 339, 358, 463
Union Douanière et Economique de l'Afrique de l'Ouest 462
Union Générale Tunisienne du Travail (UGTT) 257
Union Minière du Haut Katanga 205, 260, 335, 386
Union Monétaire Ouest-Africaine 463
Union Nationale Camerounaise 226
Union Nationale des Forces Populaires (Morocco) (UNFP) 243
Union Nationale Rwandaise 240
Union Progreŝsiste Sénégalaise 249
Union of South Africa 171, 175
Union Socialiste des Forces Populaires (Morocco) 243
Union Soudanaise (Mali) 241
UNIP see National Independence Party
UNITA, see *União Nacional de Independência Total de Angola*
United African National Congress (Rhodesia) (UANC) 263
United Arab Republic 230
United Federal Party (Rhodesia) 214
United Gold Coast Convention (UGCC) 207–8
United National Independence Party (Zambia) (UNIP) 213–14, 261
United Nations (UN) 199, 204, 230, 245, 259, 320, 322, 395, 461, 465, 468
　Commissioner 239, 245
　Commission for Trade and Development (UNCTAD) 468
　Development Programme (UNDP) 359, 461
　mission 260
　Security Council 245
　Trusteeship, Trust Territory 202, 204, 211, 218, 226, 256
　troops 230, 260
　UN-supervised election, Namibia 245
United Negro Improvement Association 194
United Party (South Africa) 192, 215, 234
United Progressive Party (Zambia) (UPP) 262
United Republic of Cameroon 226
Unité pour le Progrès National, (Burundi) 226
Universal Negro Improvement Association 477, 483
universities 393, 400–1, 479
University of Dar es Salaam 393, 437
UN Sahelian Office 462
UNSO, see UN Sahelian Office
UP, see United Party (The Gambia)

UPC, see *Union des Populations du Cameroon*
UPC, see Uganda People's Congress
UPP, see United Progressive Party (Zambia)
Upper Guinea 143, 147, 150
Upper-Katanga 188
Upper Niger see Niger, Upper
Upper Volta 258, 266, 274, 307, 349, 372, 375, 396
　external relations 358, 462–3
　French 179, 181
　languages, people 75, 77, 79, 84
Uprona, see *Unité pour le Progrès National* (Burundi)
uranium 227, 233, 245, 274, 281, 335
urban areas 133, 322, 347, 348, 376
　growth 205, 285–6, 387–8
　life 362, 365, 367, 381, 388
　populations, see under population
urbanization 93, 362, 368, 381, 384–8, 412, 446, 456
Uruguay 478, 480
Urundi 183, see also Burundi
USA 146, 151, 195, 292, 304, 312, 336
　black Americans 473, 477, 479, 481–4
　universities 207, 209, 227
USA and Africa 187, 217–9, 230–2, 235–6, 243, 250, 257, 263, 399, 464–5
　economic 154, 165, 320–22, 335–7, 374, 377–9, 467
　Liberia 153, 172, 175, 239, 269, 464
US Navy 153
　Air Force 217
Usambara 128
USSR 172, 195, 230–1, 235, 237, 241, 249–50, 259–60, 464–8, 477
　army, navy 224, 245, 249, 465
Usuman dan Fodio 134
Uteve 128
Uwaifo, Victor 449
U Tam'si, Tchicaya 440

Vaal 65
Vai language, people 75, 86
Valencia 472
Vandal invasions 104
Vasco da Gama 141, 144
vegetable oils 154, 347, 373
vegetation 48–9, 52, 67, 130, 270, 314
Venda 443–4
Venda 'homeland' 252
Venezuela 478, 479–80
Verdier (firm) 161
vernacular 404–5
Versailles Conference 176
Verwoerd, Hendrik 216
veterinary medicine 293
Vichy Government, 195, 202–3
Victoria (Cameroon) 227
Vieira, José Luandino 440–1

Vili kingdoms 128, 130, 149
Villa Cisternos 168
villages 89, 97, 98–9, 104, 128, 236
'villagization' 285, 356
viral diseases 291–3
Vodun 476
Volta-Congo languages 77
Voltaic (= Gur) language 77
Volta Region 235, 396
Volta river 38, 45, 77, 161, 273, 285, 396
　Volta River Project 234
Volubilis (= Walila near Fes) 101
voluntary associations 194, 390, 447
Vorster, Balthazar 237, 241, 263

Wadai 140
Wade, Abdoulaye 249
Wadi Halfa 173
Wafd Party, government (Egypt) 186–7
wage labour 167, 184–5, 190, 215, 285, 316, 348–9, 383, 473, 481
　female 349
wages 169, 183, 196, 250, 305, 335, 348–9, 376, 386–7, 477
Wag-Lasta 109
Walasma family 122
　empire 122
　sultan, Adal 123–4
Walcott, Derek 478
Walila = Volubilis 101
Walker, David 482
Wallace-Johnson, I. T. A. 181–2
Wal-Wal 188
war 124, 129, 135, 146, 155, 320, 394, 396, 474, 475
warriors 79, 85, 83, 86, 116, 119, 120, 136
Al Watan 403
Watchtower movement, see Kitawala
water 187, 227, 246, 274–6, 292, 348, 358, 379
waterholes 312
water resources 274–7
Waters, Ethel 483
water supply 275, 277, 284, 285, 286, 319, 322, 346, 356, 395
water transport 360
Wattisids 138–9
wax 133, 138, 141, 164, 414
weapons 91, 95, 97, 99, 107, 330
weaving 80, 333, 334, 356, 414, 422–3
Webb, Ellsworth 452
Webi Shebele river 119
Welensky Sir Roy 214
Wello province, Ethiopia 78, 120
wells 275, 278, 293
Wesleyan Methodists 152
West Africa 153–4, 193, 380, 384, 403, 477
　arts 384, 413, 414, 430
　agriculture, pastoralism 292, 295–7, 326

British 154, 163, 181, 207
　coast 77, 79, 141, 143, 290, 294, 390–1, 408, 472
　forest 54, 64, 71, 96, 177, 302
　French 162–3, 175, 200
　French-speaking 193–4
　gold 95, 103, 141
　health 177, 310–1, 391–2
　Muslims 264, 411–2, 469
　people 62, 69–70, 73, 80–81, 86, 383, 467, 472, 478
　physical 33, 36, 41–2, 44–5, 49, 306
　Portuguese 141, 145
　sahel, savanna 293, 328, 411, 469
　slave trade 147, 153
　trade, industry 153, 155, 338, 375
West African Clearing House 371
West African Currency Board 369
West African Economic Community 462
West African Pilot 181, 209
West African Regional Group 462
West African Students Union 194
West Atlantic language 75, 81, 85–6
West Central Africa 141, 143, 147, 149, 154–5, 164, 177
　Portuguese 41, 145, 154
western Africa 40–2, 44, 365, 408
Western capital 336, 383
　culture 140, 197, 381, 405, 433, 446
　technology 244
　world 149, 177, 220, 222
Western Europe 136, 141, 151, 164
western Nigeria 246, 367
Western Sahara 242, 259, 365
Western Sudan 96, 130–1, 141, 143, 148, 161
West Germany 217, 236, 256, 374, 377–9
West Indians 193, 459, 474, 477
West Indies 52, 146, 369, 403, 473, 475, 477, 484
West Somali Liberation Front 466
wheat 71–3, 149, 261, 294–5, 297, 328, 342
　emmer 72, 89
White Fathers (*La Société de Notre-Dame d'Afrique*) 152, 393
white immigration 185
White Nile 469
white population 183–5, 211, 213, 217, 224, 261, 376
　miners 191
　minority 386
　planters, farmers 213, 262, 304
　trade unions 191, 213
　working class 191–2
'white' Highlands 210
'white' South Africa 377, 451
white nationalism 214, 216
　power 184, 376, 382, 481
white settlerdom 155, 376
white settlers, see settlers
WHO, see World Health Organization
Whydah 148

wilaya, see *département*
wildlife conservation 311, 312, 380, 415
Williams, Daniel Hale 482
Williams, Eric 478
Williams, Sylvester H. 477
Wilson, Harold 262
Wilson, Woodrow, President 176
Windward Coast 148
wine 102, 149, 165, 220, 297, 375
Wingate, Sir Reginald 186
witchcraft 79
'witchdoctors' 393, 408
'witches' 392, 408–9, 412, 417
Witwatersrand 170, 191, 338
Witwatersrand recruiting 166, 180, 280
  gold 169
wives 382, 386, 387, 427, 470
Wolde, Mamo 452
Wollo Province 232
Wolof languages, people (= Jolof) 75, 86
women 197, 218, 230, 236, 355, 382, 387, 408–9, 411, 425, 429, 434, 437
wood 89, 93, 277–9, 342, 414
woodcarving, sculpture 79, 81, 82–3, 413, 431
Woods, Granville 482
Woodson, Carter G. 483
wool 138, 155, 302, 342, 414
workers 213, 223, 236, 303, 319
working class 447, 449
World Bank 305, 320, 322, 324, 335, 359, 370
World Council of Churches 394
World Health Organization (WHO) 393, 395–6
world trade 140, 151, 320, 326, 371
World War, Second 175, 185, 188, 195, 197, 199, 202–5, 210, 213, 215–16;
  after 96, 181, 194, 198
  First 159, 165, 173, 175, 179, 188, 193, 195, 197, 199, 361, 393, 446–7, 473;
    after 167, 181, 186–7, 192, 194, 248

writing 85–6, 90–1, 93–4, 101, 106, 108, 111, 251
Wuchale treaty 172

Xhosa 77, 84, 86, 129–30, 270

Yacé, Phillipe 237
yam 72, 294, 296, 319, 341
Yaméogo, Maurice 258
yams 73, 78, 295, 304, 328
Yao people, traders 86, 129–30, 150
Yaoundé 227, 395, 461
Yeha 106
Yeke 150
Yekuno Amlak, Emperor 122
Yemen 107, 110, 115, 122–4, 200, 230, 470
Yeskwa language 77
Yhombi-Opango, Colonel Joachim, see Opango
Yishaq 123
Yohannes IV, Emperor 155, 167, 171–2
Yoruba 77, 80, 86, 143, 153, 246, 382, 391
  arts 334, 413–14, 431, 434–7, 449, 454
  states 130, 133–4, 148, 416
Youlou, Abbé Fulbert 202, 229
Young Kavirondo Association 193
Young Tunisians 197
Yugoslavia 471
Yusuf ibn Tasfin 116
Yusuf Pasha 140

Zafar 109–10
Zaghawa language 75
Zaghlul, Saad 186–7
Zagwe (= ze Agew) 'of the Agew' dynasty 120–22
Zaire 33, 48–9, 260–1, 285, 311, 384, 390, 395, 411
  agriculture, forestry 279, 295, 298

archaeology, history 99, 125, 165, 205
  arts 414, 428, 445, 449, 454
  economy 274, 336, 353–4, 360–2, 371–2, 386
  external relations 219, 229, 243, 262, 357, 462–4, 467
  minerals 280–3, 324, 334, 336, 349, 351
  Mobutu 228, 256, 265, 269
  peoples, language 75, 77–9, 82–5, 287
Zaire basin 36, 45, 47–9, 125
  river 36, 45, 127, 130, 141, 143, 149, 164
Zaire-Oubangui 361
Zama battle 101
Zamana Mesafent 'era of princes' 155
Zambezi 273, 285, 306, 396
Zambezi basin, valley 45, 65, 70, 82, 128, 144, 149, 165
  lower 128
  middle 129, 136
  upper 68, 128, 130
Zambezi, area south of 70, 127, 144, 219
  area north of 171
Zambia 95, 392
Zambia 213–4, 261–2, 269, 285, 395, 405, 410, 435, 453
  archaeology, history 62, 67–8, 99, 128, 130, 165
  economy 270, 272–4, 279, 343, 349, 351, 353, 355, 361–2
  external relations 241, 244, 263, 461–2, 467–8
  minerals 220, 280–2, 324, 334–6, 349, 351, 372
  peoples 82–4, 86, 287
Zambia African National Congress (ZANC) 213
ZANC see Zambia African National Congress
Zande language 77
Zanj 118, 469, 471
ZANU see Zimbabwe African National Union
Zanzibar 78, 85, 152, 184, 211–2, 267
  Arab state 85, 128, 150, 154

cloves 129, 150, 184
  Germans 157, 163
  union with Tanganyika 256, 467
Zanzibar Nationalist Party (ZNP) 211–12
ZAPU, see Zimbabwe African People's Union
zar 471
Zaria 132, 355, 430, 433
Zarid, Sinaika 451
Zarma, see Djerma language
Zawditu (daughter of Menelik) 204
Zawila 114
zawiya 139
Zeila 119–20, 122
Zenati language 75
Zezuru people 85
Zimbabwe 33, 84–5, 216–7, 220, 262–3, 269, 441, 456
  agriculture 220, 297, 303
  archaeology, history 67, 70, 99, 127–8
  economy 261, 270, 273, 303, 341, 343, 361–2, 372
  minerals 99, 118, 280–2, 335–6
Zimbabwe, kingdom, see Great Zimbabwe
Zimbabwe African National Union (ZANU) 214, 244, 263
Zimbabwe African People's Union (ZAPU) 214, 263
Zimbabwe–Rhodesia 263
zinc 185, 282
Zionism 460
Zirids 115
Ziyanids (= Abd al-Wadids) 116, 137–8
ZNP, see Zanzibar Nationalist Party
Zombepata 67
Zoser, king, see Djoser
Zouerate 362
Zugwalla Mountain 124
Zulu 77, 84, 86, 158, 216, 382, 434, 442
  kingdom 86, 99, 130, 155
Zumbo 128
Zungeru 209
Zwangendaba 130

THE AFRICAN CONTINENT

Tsavo National Park, Kenya: a water-hole in the dry season

TECTONICS

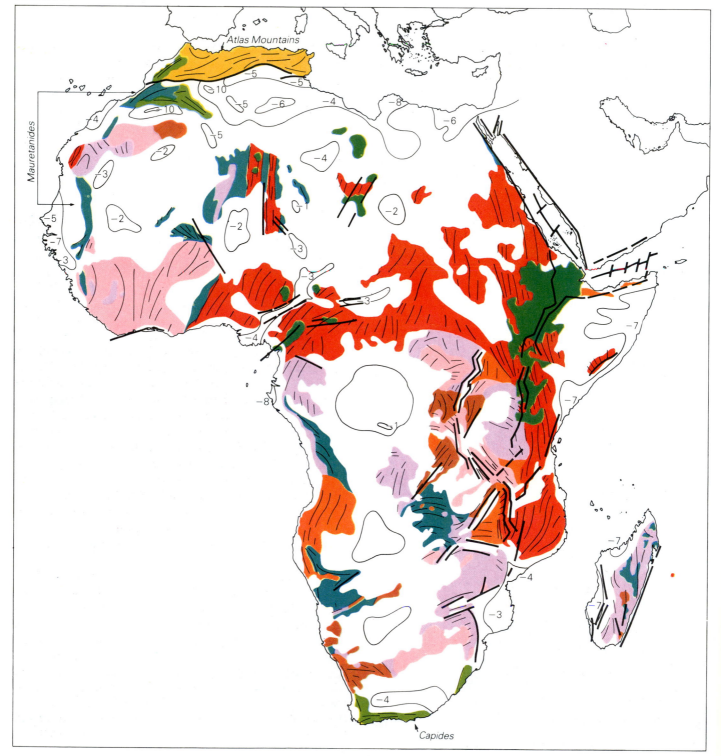

Geology and geomorphology

Within its 30 million sq km Africa contains widely diverse environments. Vast plains, resplendent volcanoes, arid wastes, soaring mountains and palm-fringed beaches are but a fraction of this diversity. In its rocks is a record of Earth history from 3500 million years ago (MYA) and an immeasurable storehouse of wealth.

Geology

Africa is an immense platform, or 'shield', of crystalline rocks partly covered by sedimentary rock and by lava flows. Varying in age from 3500 MYA to 500 MYA and exposed over 56 per cent of the continent, the crystalline rocks are complex and varied. They consist mainly of schists, quartzites, migmatites, gneisses and granites, the products of several rock-forming cycles, each lasting 300–1000 million years, which commenced with the accumulation of thick layers of sediments, and sometimes lavas, on and around an existing shield. Changes due to pressure and heat (metamorphism and granite formation) ensued, and finally the old shield and new additions were welded together and stabilized to form a new, larger shield.

Four such cycles built the present African shield. Rocks resulting from the 'Archean' cycle, 3500–2500 MYA, can be seen in Tanzania,

KEY

Sedimentary cover rocks

Form lines of sedimentary base (figures indicate thousands of metres below surface of maximum thickness: where none are given depths are not known)

Cainozoic lavas

MAJOR ROCK-FORMING CYCLES

Alpine — 25±25 million years ago (MYA)

Hercynian — 290±50 MYA

Damaran — 550±100 MYA

Pan-African

Kibaran — 1100±200 MYA

Eburnian — 1850±250 MYA

Archean — pre-2500 MYA

Undifferentiated

Components of the African shields

Generalized fold-trend lines

Major rift-type faults and flexures operative in the Cainozoic

Zimbabwe, Transvaal (South Africa) and Sierra Leone. There the shield consists largely of irregular linear belts of greenstone schists (metamorphosed sediments and volcanics) and granulites (re-metamorphosed older shield rocks) lying vertically between large granite intrusions. The 'Eburnian' cycle 2500–1700 MYA, created bodies of strongly folded gneisses (coarse-grained, banded, meta-morphosed rocks) schists and granites in western and central Africa. The 'Kibaran' cycle, ending at 1100 MYA, fringed and intersected the Eburnian rocks. The final 'Pan-African'-Damaran cycle of 560–350 MYA involved 50 per cent of the continent. Its mobile belts form a network around the West African, Congo and Kalahari blocks. Sedimentary troughs, partly metamorphosed, folded and granite-intruded, occur in Katanga (Zaire), Namibia, Angola, Egypt and the Hoggar region of the Sahara. In Sudan, Mozambique, Nigeria and central Africa pre-existing shield rocks were thermally and chemi-cally reactivated. The Capides were folded in a dying phase of this cycle, while in the Mauretanides mountain-building continued spasmodically through to 275 MYA. On the Tectonic map opposite these are referred to as the 'Hercynian' rock-forming cycle. Since then, excluding the Atlas region, Africa has experienced vertical movements, vulcanicity, rift faulting and continental separation.

The sedimentary rocks that rest upon the shield are mainly sandstones, mudstones and limestones. Derived from the erosion of adjacent uplifted areas, the sediments were deposited either in shallow seas which extended across the continental margins at various times or in large interior basins. They display homogeneous properties over great distances. Thick glacial tills occur in the older rocks. Fossils range from the earliest life forms to *Homo sapiens*. Most of the cover rocks are flat-lying or only gently warped, but some were involved in shield cycles and consequently are deformed.

Although the formation of sedimentary rocks has characterized the entire history of the continent, there are five distinct cover series of wide extent today. Each was initiated and terminated by major vertical movements of the shield, the consequent domes and basins of which produced the relief patterns necessary for renewed erosion and sedimentation.

The late Pre-Cambrian cover, 1000–650 MYA, is preserved in West and Central Africa. It contains thick glacial deposits and was terminated by the Pan-African cycle. The Paleozoic cover, 600–250 MYA, is extensive in northern Africa, where its thick sandstones build massive escarpments and plateaux. The Karroo cover accumulated between 320 and 180 MYA in southern and eastern Africa and on the other southern continents that were then joined in the Gondwana super-continent. It also includes glacial tills and coal measures. It is capped by the Stormberg lavas, which heralded the breakup of Gondwanaland. The Mesozoic cover of northern Africa, 275–60 MYA, records a long initial period of continental deposition followed by widespread marine transgressions from the Tethyan and Atlantic

GEOLOGY

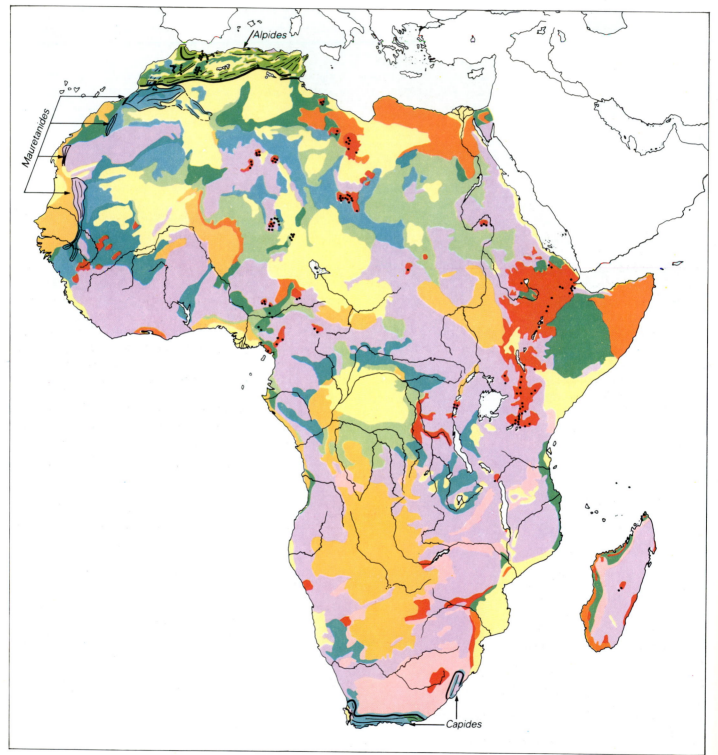

Evidence of past volcanic activity: a crater lake in western Uganda with the Ruwenzori Mountains in the background

oceans during the Cretaceous and Eocene periods at the end of the Mesozoic and beginning of the Cainozoic eras. These rocks are found, for example, in the folded Atlas ranges and the oil-bearing basins around Africa's coastlines. The final cover, of Cainozoic age, commenced around 50 MYA and is still forming, especially in Botswana and the Sahara. In central and southern Africa it is called Kalahari sand, and in northern Africa it includes marine deposits in Libya, Egypt and Senegal and continental deposits elsewhere, e.g. the Lake Chad basin.

The volcanic rocks comprise lavas and igneous intrusions in three age groups: the Mesozoic lavas, sills and granites of West Africa, the Karroo and the Sahara; the Eocene flood basalts of Tibesti and East Africa; and the recent vulcanicity for which Africa is particularly noteworthy. In Ethiopia, Afar (Djibouti), Kenya, Tibesti and Cameroon are numerous volcanoes, and great expanses and thick layers of lava flows. This vulcanicity is associated with impressive uplift and faulting of the shield and in East Africa with the Rift Valley system. The fundamental mechanism seems to be an invasion and partial melting of the crust by volatiles from below it. The process is working more slowly in northern Africa than beneath the East African Rift system.

The fragmentation of Gondwanaland and the emergence of Africa as a separate continent commenced about 180 MYA with massive outpourings of lavas and igneous intrusions. Fractures, flexures

---

KEY

SEDIMENTARY COVER ROCKS

Quaternary: aeolian, lacustrine, alluvial and marine deposits

Cainozoic: marine deposits

Cainozoic: continental deposits

Mesozoic: marine deposits of mainly Jurassic and Cretaceous age

Mesozoic: marine, folded (Atlas Alpide mountains) deposits of mainly Jurassic, Cretaceous and early Cainozoic age

Mesozoic: continental deposits of mainly Jurassic and Cretaceous age

'Karroo': continental cover rocks, including lavas

Paleozoic: continental cover rocks of Cambrian-Carboniferous age

Upper Pre-Cambrian: continental cover rocks, 1000–c. 570MYA

Pre-Cambrian: shield of Archean and Proterozoic age

VOLCANIC ROCKS

Lavas: mostly of Cainozoic-Quaternary age, also of Mesozoic 'Karroo' age

Volcanoes: active or recently extinct

Fold axes in rock-building belts

NON-SHIELD, FOLDED ROCK-BUILDING SYSTEMS
Alpides   (Atlas) of Cainozoic age
Mauretanides of Paleozoic age
Capides   of Paleozoic age

Rock-building fronts of the Alpides and Capides

(regional warping caused by adjacent uplift and subsidence) and rift faults, e.g. the Benue valley (Nigeria) and Lebombo monocline (a one-direction fold) in Mozambique, gradually defined the new coastlines. The first marine sediments, of Jurassic age (before the Cretaceous period of the Mesozoic era), were deposited in narrow troughs, the embryonic Indian and Atlantic oceans. Today, these initial phases can be seen in the Red Sea region. There the process started about 25 MYA, when the Afro-Arabian shield and East Africa were strongly uplifted and enveloped with lavas. Rift faulting, vulcanicity and crustal thinning – still active in the Afar – split the dome, and the sea invaded, thus completing the first phase of continental separation and sea floor spreading. The Red Sea, once a terrestrial rift valley, is now an arm of the Indian Ocean, widening by about 6 cm per year. Africa contains 16 uplifted shield areas and 29 rift valleys which have developed since the disruption of Gondwanaland.

These rearrangements of the Earth's crust by continental separation and sea floor spreading (collectively embraced in the theory of plate tectonics) which separated Africa from the other southern continents also brought it closer to the Eurasian landmass. The Atlas Mountains – together with all the mountains of southern Europe – were created by this slow, inexorable conjunction during the last 65 million years. (The Mediterranean Sea is but a remnant of the earlier Tethys Ocean that separated the two landmasses.) In the Atlas thick Mesozoic sediments, undeformed on the African shield to the south, were folded, faulted and overthrust in several mountain-building paroxysms. In the southern Atlas the folds are more simple and the mountain chains are separated by wide plateaux. In Morocco, northern Algeria and Tunisia lie the high limestone mountains and deep fault troughs of the more intensely deformed Alpine domain.

Geomorphology

The Relief map opposite shows that Africa is high in the south-east and low in the north-west. It also shows the large topographic basins and elevated rims, e.g. Chad, Zaire, characteristic of African relief. Both patterns stem from slow vertical tectonic movements of the last 25 million years. Rivers flow from the uplifted rims and focus in the basins, and the often curious courses of the largest rivers have developed from the slow interlinking of these basins. The Saharan and Guinea Nigers connected within the last 50 000 years, the Nile is an amalgam of several earlier drainage systems, and the Zaire headwaters have been truncated by uplift along the western Rift Valley.

Plains are the dominating feature of Africa's landscape. In the drier regions and in areas of deposition they are astonishingly horizontal and smooth. In the humid zone permanent valleys provide slightly more diversified local relief. The surprising inselbergs (isolated bare-rock hills) and the wall-like escarpments which punctuate and often terminate the plains only strengthen the impression of Africa's vast

flatness. Most of the plains are erosional in origin and are called planation surfaces. They are produced during long periods of denudation when the land surface is reduced to gentle slopes at altitudes determined by regional base levels of erosion. Thus when uplift is slight, new plains are eroded rapidly within the thick layers of decomposed rock underlying the old plains. Where uplift is rapid and considerable, the old plains are elevated but not destroyed, and erosion is concentrated around the flanks of the uplift in escarpments and rugged dissection zones. Slowly these encroach upon the high plains and in their wake new low level plains are created. The erosional debris accumulates in interior basins or offshore and, if fossiliferous, can be used to date the planation surface.

Some geomorphologists recognize between three and five major planation surfaces formed during the last 130 million years. Especially in southern Africa and perhaps also in West Africa they form a staircase raising Africa's topography from the coastal lowlands to the interior in a series of escarpment defined steps. Those surfaces initiated approximately 65 MYA are called the 'African' surfaces. They are underlain by a distinctive deep weathering layer. The most extensive planation surfaces are those which developed from about 25 MYA after widespread uplift. Other geomorphologists believe that local patterns of planation surfaces are far more complex than this simple model. They stress the important effects of local tectonic histories and rock types upon the extent, number and properties of these plains.

Mountain country, in both low and high Africa alike, e.g. Ruwenzori (Uganda/Zaire), Tibesti and Hoggar in the Sahara, and in Ethiopia, Kenya, and Lesotho, rises to maxima of 3000–6000m.

KEY

LANDFORMS

▚▚▚▚	Prominent escarpments
🌫️	Areas of shifting sand dunes (ergs)
●	Active volcanoes

GEOMORPHIC ZONES

═══	Humid geomorphic zone
━━━	Arid geomorphic zone

COASTAL FORMS

∿	Indented beach coasts
⋮⋮⋮	Beaches and lagoons
⋯⋯	Straight beaches, spits
‒ ‒	Depositional coasts, most with beaches
⋯⌣	Deltas
⋰⋰⋰	One or more of estuaries, rias, inlets, bays, often with headlands, beaches and spits
ʌʌʌ	Straight cliffy coasts
ʌʌʌ	Indented cliffy coasts, often with beaches
⟂	Mangroves
⌒⌒	Coral reefs

RELIEF AND LANDFORMS

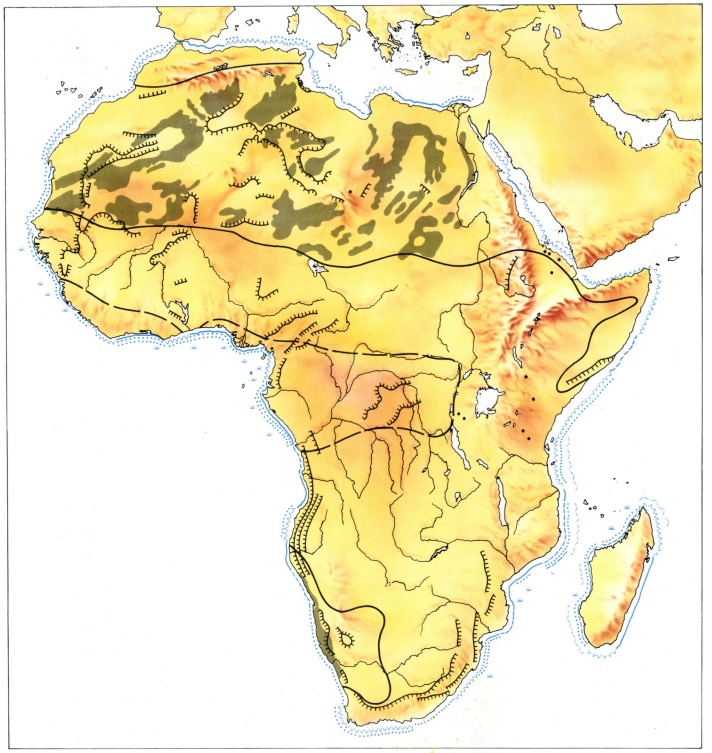

Deeply eroded into gorges and plateaux, the mountain ranges have been produced by locally enhanced uplift and vulcanicity. Hills 500–1000m higher than their surrounding plains are usually caused by locally more resistant rocks which have withstood erosion.

Different rock types expectedly generate their own distinctive landforms. Africa is particularly renowned for its bare granite inselbergs. Rising abruptly from plains or as buttresses in hill country, they vary from blocky bouldery tors to smooth domes, and from a few metres to over 1000m in height. They occur best in unjointed granites. Some develop as escarpments, and dissection zones retreat, the harder granites remaining as residual hills; others are born as resistant domes beneath thick layers of decomposed rock and are later exposed when the weathered layers are eroded. The tough schists and quartzites commonly generate long ridges while gneisses and well-fractured granites frequently underlie subdued, rolling topography. Plateaux, mesas, gorges and steep escarpments are associated with the hard or porous sandstones of the sedimentary covers. Volcanoes and calderas (an enlarged volcanic crater formed by the explosion or collapse of the cone), large and small, pristine and eroded, and tabular lava flows are typical in the volcanic areas.

Landforms and surface materials also vary with climate.* In the humid zone rock outcrops are rare and a 5–50m thick layer of soil and weathered rock blankets even the steepest hills. This layer is composed of gritty clay, pale at depth but coloured bright red by iron oxides nearer the surface with dense concentrations of iron oxide nodules just below the soil layer. Landslides are a frequent occurrence. Landforms are characteristically convex, with hemispherical hills, and flat swampy valleys.

In the seasonally dry savanna lands, weathering layers are usually thinner, rocks outcrop more frequently and the iron oxides tend to concentrate into distinctive gravel or hardpan layers. These can be commonly observed as ledges around valley sides or on top of weathered rock mesas. Streamless small valleys are another characteristic landform.

More than half of Africa is arid and semi-arid. In the desert mountains water-based processes have produced sombre-coloured bare rock hillsides, screes and sandy floored seasonal watercourses (wadis). Bare, rocky sandstone plateaux are intricately dissected into gorges, plains are veneered by gravel and sand sheets, calcium carbonate crusts ('calcretes') or saline evaporitic basins. Fine sands, eroded from sandstone plateaux and transported by occasional floods, have accumulated in lower lying areas. There they have been moulded by the desert winds into the red-gold sand 'seas' for which the Sahara is justly famous. These 'seas' are enormous–the Bilma dune field stretches 1300km and the Great Eastern Erg of Algeria covers 196000sq km. The dunes are built into a variety of patterns: closely spaced linear ridges parallel to the wind, crescentic ridges transverse to the wind, conical dunes with radiating sharp crested ridges, and huge sand ridges, 250m high, 2km wide, 2–5km apart and scores of kilometres long with smaller dunes on their backs. Each pattern reflects a particular interplay between sand quantity, grain size, wind velocity and direction. Bewilderingly complex in detail, the dune systems when seen on satellite photographs or from a high-flying aircraft display a remarkably geometric overall pattern closely reflecting prevailing wind directions.

The African coastline is distinctive for its beautiful beaches, often stretching many kilometres between rare rocky headlands. Amply supplied with sands from the weathered rocks inland, they are moulded by surf and waves and by the powerful longshore drifts they generate. Intricate lagoons, swamps and old beach ridges often lie behind the beaches and indicate a history of coastal outgrowth during the past 4000 years. Mangrove swamps and their maze-like creeks characterize flat coasts with fine sediments. Coral reefs along the eastern coasts protect palm-fronded beaches. Cliff coasts and bays are common along north-western coasts, in southern Africa and in Somalia.

Many of Africa's landforms demonstrate profound environmental changes, especially those of the past 50000 years. During glacial epochs climates became cooler and drier. Glaciers grew on Ruwenzori and Kilimanjaro (Tanzania) and formed anew in the Atlas Mountains and Ethiopia. The deserts expanded and today extensive fossil dune systems can be seen in the drier savannas. During the non-glacial periods deeper penetrations of moist air brought enhanced rainfall to the deserts, wadis flowed further and more frequently, lakes and marshes expanded along the Saharan fringe, in the Rift Valley basins and in Okavango (Namibia). The last major dry period lasted from 20000 to 12000 years before the present (BP), the last pluvial period from 12000 to 5000 BP.

Man is also a creator of landforms, his are the gullies, the eroded soils,* the alluviated valleys, the overgrazed, windswept pastures and the new lakes on the Nile, the Niger and the Volta as well as the much older soil-protective terracing in the ancient densely peopled areas. African landforms are thus a mosaic of features large and small, young and old, etched from a complex of rocks by contrasting climates and processes during a long period of time.   *M.B.T.*

African landforms: (1) plains underlain by deeply-weathered crystalline rocks, near Zaria, northern Nigeria; (2) dome-shaped granite inselbergs sharply distinguished from the deeply-weathered surrounding plains, near Kwatarkwashi, northern Nigeria; (3) mountain country: the High Atlas Mountains south of Marrakesh, Morocco; (4) humid tropical landscape: a view across the Sewa River, Sierra Leone; (5) coastal landscape: sand dunes and mangrove swamps between Lamu and Malindi, Kenya; (6) arid landscape: part of the 220km-long Great Fish River Canyon, Namibia

(1)

(2)

(3)

(4)

(5)

(6)

Climate

Sunshine

Atmospheric processes depend mainly on solar radiation. Local variations in heat balance determine patterns of air pressure, which, in turn, control wind-flows. Temperature is directly influenced by solar radiation and, in conjunction with wind-flow, leads to a control of rainfall, humidity and evaporation. Prior consideration, then, must be given to the distribution of solar radiation, for it is the most significant factor for understanding the distribution of other atmospheric phenomena.

The latitudinal location of Africa astride the Equator ensures that most of the continent receives a high level of insolation (solar radiation actually reaching the Earth's surface) all year round. At the Equator the lengths of day and night are approximately equal throughout the year while at the northern and southern extremities of the continent daylight duration ranges between 14 hours and 29 minutes in summer and 9 hours and 51 minutes in winter.

In January when the sun is overhead in the southern hemisphere, the region of the longest total sunshine duration lies in the south-west corner of the continent, where the Cape Province of South Africa receives over 350 hours of sunshine. This value decreases northwards into central Africa where, because of dense cloud cover, the average January figure is only 150 hours of sunshine. North of the Equator there is an increase in the total duration of sunshine up to a maximum of 300 hours in parts of the Nile basin and central Sahara because of cloudless skies. The Mediterranean coast receives only 150 hours.

In July the pattern is reversed. The heart of the Sahara receives the longest sunshine duration, with an average of over 400 hours. This value drops to only about 100 hours along the coast of western Africa, again because of cloud cover. In the southern hemisphere monthly totals increase to over 300 hours on the Kalahari Plateau.

On an annual basis two zones of maximum sunshine duration can be identified: central Sahara (over 4000 hours) and the Kalahari Plateau (over 3600 hours). In the northern hemisphere annual totals decrease southwards from the Sahara to the coast of West Africa where the annual total is about 1600 hours. In the southern hemisphere there occurs an east–west increase with values ranging from 2000 hours in Madagascar to over 3600 hours in Namibia.

Temperature

Two main factors influence temperature pattern in Africa: solar radiation and elevation. Since the annual variation of radiation is very small, the range of monthly average temperature variations is also small, i.e. between 3°C and 6°C. The daily range of temperature is

MEAN ANNUAL SUNSHINE HOURS

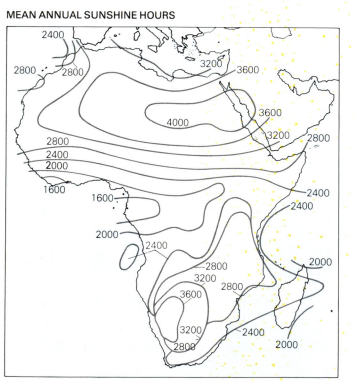

AVERAGE GLOBAL TEMPERATURE (°C): JANUARY

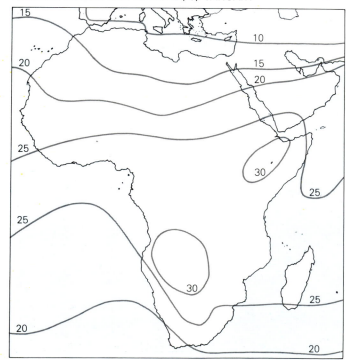

somewhat greater, however, ranging from less than 10°C in many coastal areas to over 15°C in south-west Libya. Even so, temperature variations are generally less pronounced in Africa than in temperate latitudes.

In January the 25°C isotherm encompasses most of eastern, western and central Africa with two isolated peaks (about 30°C) on the Ethiopian highlands and Kalahari Plateau; beyond this broad band the isotherms show a zonal pattern declining to 10°C along the northern African coast and 20°C around the coasts of South Africa.

In July zonal patterning is much in evidence from the southern-most tip to about latitude 8°N; values range from 15°C to 30°C. The interior of the Sahara in Libya, Morocco and the Nile Valley records the highest values (over 35°C). The cooling effects of cool ocean currents are seen in the indentation of the isotherms along the coasts of south-western Africa (Cold Benguela Current) and north-western Africa (Cold Canary Current).

General circulation and air masses

The general atmospheric circulation pattern of air mass movements in Africa between the tropics is dominated by three features: the large Subtropical High Pressure (STHP) air masses over the Sahara and south Atlantic Ocean, the air-flows termed 'Trades' (Trade Winds), which move towards the Equator from these air mass cells, and the

Inter-Tropical Discontinuity (ITD), which is sometimes coincident with the equatorial trough (the low pressure zone upon which the NE and SE Trades converge). Superimposed upon this basically simple pattern are irregularities due to elevation, moisture sources, multiple airstream structure, and other weather conditions.

In January the NE Trades blow southwards from the central Sahara. They are usually very dry and often dust-laden. On occasions, turbulent dust storms occur; these are called *haboob* in north-east Africa. Areas affected are subject to wide daily ranges of temperature of about 17°C and low relative humidity (often less than 10 per cent). Over parts of eastern Africa, the Trades blow across the Indian Ocean where the lowest layers become moist, yielding only meagre rainfall even when forced up the plateau. Over West Africa the dry dust-laden winds originating from the desert are known as the *harmattan*. Weather conditions are similar to those of the *haboob*. In the coastal areas the NE Trades override the moister but shallow SW Monsoon winds.

KEY

Subtropical High Pressure air masses		Inter-Tropical Discontinuity
Air-flows		Other zones of convergence

AVERAGE GLOBAL TEMPERATURE (°C): JULY

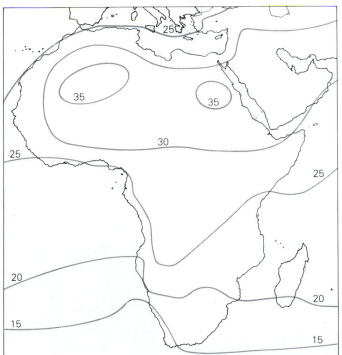

SURFACE PRESSURE AND AIR MASSES: JANUARY

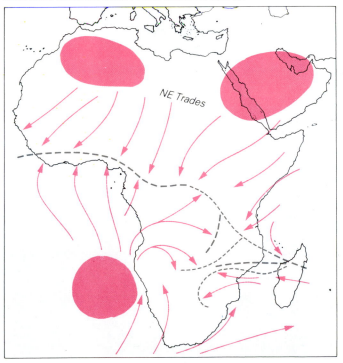

Initially western African monsoon winds blow north-westwards, being steered by the St Helena STHP cell in the South Atlantic, but swing round across the Equator to become the SW Monsoon winds of the West African coast and the Westerlies of the Zaire basin. Along the coast of West Africa the SW Monsoon directly confronts the oncoming NE Trades but little happens because, as mentioned earlier, the drier air overrides the more humid equatorial air.

In East Africa, the SE Trades, a warm moisture-laden airstream, produces variable amounts of rainfall along the coast and inland. One of the main features of this air mass is that although it is moist, it is not very deep because it is overlain by drier air at 2km aloft.

In July a thermal low pressure zone over the Sahara is fully developed and the ITD has moved northwards to about latitude 20°N. In West Africa the moisture-laden SW Monsoon begins to advance inland from February in the wake of the ITD and by July this air mass envelopes extensive areas of West and central Africa including the southern Sahara. The airstream lies deep over the coast but is very shallow over the desert, where it is overlain by the much weakened

Trade flow. Rainfall is usually moderate to heavy, though it is sporadic and unreliable along the desert margins. Nearer the coast, light but prolonged rains are experienced over wide areas when the ITD has reached its northernmost position.

On the east coast the SE Trades airstream is deeper than in January and flows northwards across the Equator, then eastwards to become part of the Indian Summer Monsoon. Despite its depth there is not much increase in rainfall. This is because the air appears to be divergent over much of eastern Africa; over central and southern Africa the air recurves southwards. Such spreading of the airstream does not permit much shower activity.

Rainfall

The heaviest rainfall occurs in the region astride the Equator, especially from the Niger delta to the Zaire River basin and central Zaire. Along the coast of Sierra Leone and Liberia and along the east coast of Madagascar annual totals exceed 2000mm. North of the Equator rainfall decreases generally northwards until about latitude

KEY

- Subtropical High Pressure air masses
- Air-flows
- Inter-Tropical Discontinuity
- Other zones of convergence

KEY

- 0–250mm
- 250–500mm
- 500–1000mm
- 1000–1500mm
- 1500–2000mm
- over 2000mm

SURFACE PRESSURE AND AIR MASSES: JULY

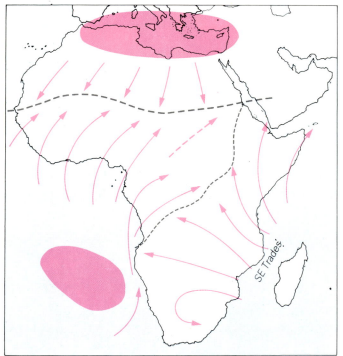

ANNUAL RAINFALL (MILLIMETRES)

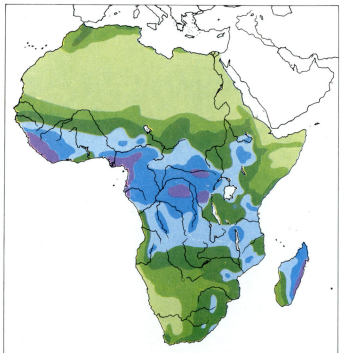

18°N, where the mean annual total is less than 250mm, except along the Mediterranean coast (Morocco, Algeria, Tunisia), where the annual total ranges between 250 and 1000mm. The situation in the southern hemisphere is more complex. Broadly speaking, there is a zonal north–south decrease in rainfall from the Equator to the Tropic of Capricorn; beyond this latitude an east–west pattern becomes more apparent, with the east coast of Madagascar receiving over 2000mm of rainfall and the coast of Namibia in the same latitude recording less than 250mm per year. Superimposed upon this are the effects of topography and large lakes, which increase precipitation in isolated instances.

Africa is an area of well-defined wet and dry seasons. The two periods of maximum rainfall occur roughly between June and August in the northern hemisphere, and December to February in the southern hemisphere. These correspond to the times of maximum rainfall activity associated with the ITD. The areas roughly between latitudes 9°N and 18°S receive heavy rainfall lasting 8–12 months with some regions having marked double maximum (two peaks of particularly heavy rainfall during the rainy season) and 'little dry season' characteristics (a short dry but cloudy period in the middle of the rainy season). Beyond this zone, the single maximum characteristic predominates in the rest of northern Africa and most of southern Africa except the south-eastern coast, parts of the Transvaal and the Orange Free State. In this zone of single maximum type the length of the rainy season decreases from about 8 months to about 3–4 months on the edge of the desert.

Rainfall in Africa varies in reliability both over space and time. This variability is most marked in the semi-arid and arid areas where droughts such as the Sahelian drought* of the early 1970s caused great havoc to human beings, livestock and crops. The highest rainfall variability of over 40 per cent occurs in the Sahara and Kalahari while the lowest year to year variability occurs in the heart of the continent astride the Equator in Uganda. On a geological time scale even more marked fluctuations are known to have occurred and there is evidence for periods when the Sahara was definitely moister than it is now.

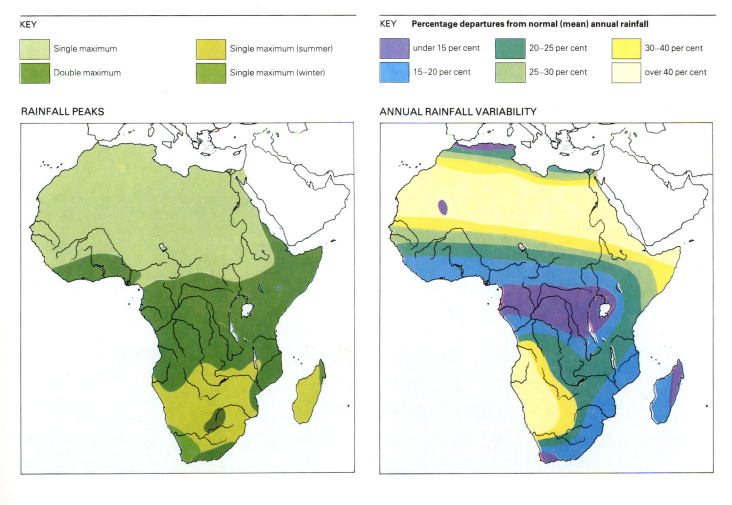

KEY

	Single maximum		Single maximum (summer)
	Double maximum		Single maximum (winter)

RAINFALL PEAKS

KEY   Percentage departures from normal (mean) annual rainfall

	under 15 per cent		20–25 per cent		30–40 per cent
	15–20 per cent		25–30 per cent		over 40 per cent

ANNUAL RAINFALL VARIABILITY

An interesting feature of tropical rainfall is the occurrence of 'tropical disturbances'. The main condition for the formation of any tropical disturbance is the presence of warm and humid air masses in which no inversion exists. This type of air mass encourages instability and vertical uplift during which period a large amount of latent heat of condensation is released to reinforce the vertical ascent. Heating of the Earth's surface is one of the main causes of convection currents. Such convection cells frequently form into thunderstorms, which are the smallest and most common tropical disturbances. Other phenomena associated with this convective activity include linear systems, easterly waves and tropical cyclones.

Thunderstorms are purely local affairs, rarely reaching up to 10km in diameter. Their duration is limited to 1–2 hours. It is generally estimated that thunderstorms will develop when instability reaches a height of about 8000m. This explains the high frequency of occurrence in the equatorial region, which is characterized by continuous cloud cover for most of the year. The time of occurrence of thunderstorms depends mainly on the factor which initiates the

process. Convectional (or thermal) thunderstorms and those caused by sea breezes, such as along the coast of West Africa, occur mainly during the afternoon. Those over lakes (such as on the coast of Lake Victoria) and seas, or those caused by land breezes, occur mainly during the night or early hours of the morning. Seasonally, thunderstorms show frequencies of occurrence which are closely related to the properties of the prevailing air masses: they are therefore generally rare during seasons when stable or dry air masses prevail over an area and most frequent at the beginning and end of the rainy season when convective activity is most virile.

Linear systems consist mainly of numerous thunderstorms, organized in lines or bands which, because of common origin, develop and move more or less as an organized system. These 'squall lines', as they are known, can be hundreds of kilometres long, while their width is usually about 10–30km. They normally consist of uninterrupted cumulonimbus clouds, but exhibit zones of stronger and weaker thunderstorm activity. Their origin is generally due to a combination of factors, of which convergence and convection are the most important. Such disturbance lines occur at the beginning and end of the rainy seasons in West Africa mainly due to confluence.

Physiological climate indices

One method of determining the impact of temperature and humidity on human beings is through the Effective Temperature (ET) index; the distribution of the ET index in Africa in January and July is shown on the accompanying maps. The most notable characteristics are the broad areas covered by *Extremely Hot*, *Sultry* and *Mild* in July and by *Sultry*, *Hot* and *Warm* in January. Physiological indices show high variability from humid to cold and dry. Only a few areas, such as along the west coast and the Red Sea, possess anything approaching truly uncomfortable conditions, but unfortunately it is these areas that were prominent in early writings on Africa and so formed the stereotype of Africa as a steaming, sultry continent. Actually, over most parts of the continent, the climatic stress factors are not appreciably different from elsewhere in the world and, in fact, are less than those in the mid-latitudes with their hot summers and freezing winters.

J.S.O.

KEY

under 5	20–60	over 80
5–20	60–80	

DAYS (MEAN) WITH THUNDERSTORMS PER YEAR

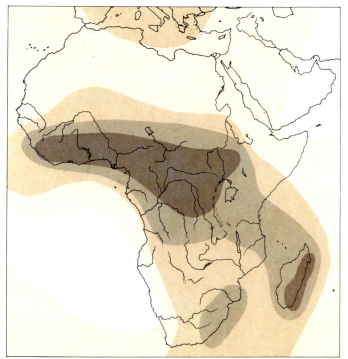

KEY Physiological climate: January/July

Extremely hot		Keen	
Sultry		Cool	
Hot		Mild	
Warm			

PHYSIOLOGICAL CLIMATE: JANUARY

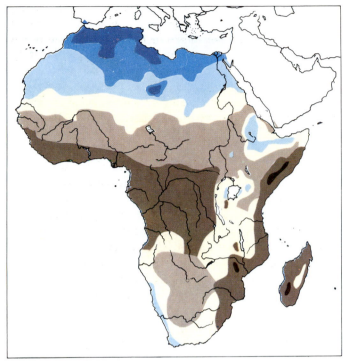

PHYSIOLOGICAL CLIMATE: JULY

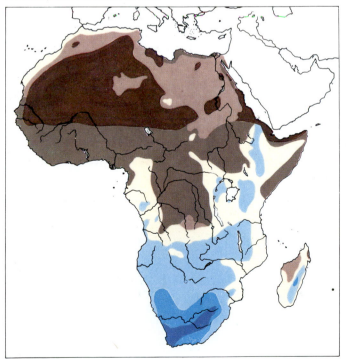

Hydrology

Africa contains five of the world's largest drainage basins – all draining to the sea – the Zaire, the Niger, the Nile, the Orange and the Zambezi. Extensive parts of the continent are areas of internal drainage, e.g. Lake Chad and sections of the East African Rift Valley. While the drainage basin pattern is largely controlled by the geological history of the continent, it is the regional climatic variations that are responsible for the variations of annual and seasonal water discharge. Over large areas of semi-arid Africa perennial flow is restricted to major watercourses and most small rivers and streams are intermittent, drying up during varying periods of the year. Over large areas of arid Africa, e.g. the Sahara and Kalahari, permanent watercourses do not exist and drainage is ephemeral.

Thus annual runoff or discharge is low to very low in most parts of northern, southern, and eastern Africa. It only becomes considerable in inter-tropical West (e.g. the lower Niger) and Central Africa (the Zaire headwaters) and high (greater than 100cm) in Guinea, Sierra Leone, Liberia, the Niger delta, Cameroon and in north-eastern Madagascar. Overall the African continent contributes 17 per cent of global runoff compared to 18 per cent from North and Central America, an area two-thirds its size. This anomaly reflects the high evaporation rates general over Africa, where an overall mean of 67cm of precipitation is counterbalanced by 51cm evaporational loss to yield 16cm runoff (cf. Europe, which has a 24cm runoff from an area one-third the size). These gross values are, of course, approximate and fail to give proper emphasis to the large geographical variations in total runoff and to the seasonality of most African river regimes.

River regimes (seasonal and longer term discharge variations) vary widely because of the markedly fluctuating relationships of precipitation amounts and evaporative demands over their basins. Discharge variations can also be exaggerated through tributaries flooding at different times from the main stream, e.g. the Blue Nile, or damped down through excessive losses to ground water storage in alluvial areas, e.g. the Upper Nile and Upper Niger during the flood season. Only in the main Zaire basin, where there is a double rainy season, considerable cloudiness, and moderate evaporation, is a high discharge maintained throughout the year. By contrast most of the rainier parts of West Africa display a strongly-marked seasonal maximum discharge and a low-flow period of three to four months. In some cases the low-flow period may be much longer, e.g. five to seven months for the Volta, and longer still for many of the major rivers of eastern Africa. Seasonality of discharge is also strongly marked in North and South Africa, both experiencing 'Mediterranean' rainfall regimes. Nowhere in Africa is snow melt of hydrological significance – though snow falls on the Atlas Mountains and on the high peaks of East Africa where there are small glaciers on the Equator.

In savanna areas many major rivers are highly seasonal: a riverbed near Kondoa, Tanzania in the dry season

Surface drainage is affected by the large lake basins, some fossil, most geologically recent. A good example is the lake zone of East Africa. Lake Victoria is the largest, and Lake Tanganyika the deepest of East African lakes. These lake basins contain vital evidence for interpreting the history of climate* (e.g. Lake Chad) and the evolution of mankind (e.g. Olduvai* and Lake Turkana*). Present-day lakes are often important natural river flow regulators (e.g. Lake Victoria's effect on the White Nile). While the African rivers with their numerous sections of rapids and erratic flow have frequently impeded penetration of the interior (the Gambia and Nile are exceptions), the lakes have often been the goal of explorers searching for the sources of the great rivers.   *P.H.T.*

Soils

Soil zones in Africa correlate broadly with climate,* the most important soil-forming factor at the continental level.

The arid zone

Shifting sands and bare rock occupy only about a fifth of the 1100 million hectares of African deserts and their margins. More than half the area comprises Saharan soils known as *yermosols*, with shallow soil profiles over gravel or pebble beds. Other soils of the Sahara's rims, and of the Horn of Africa and the Namib, include those termed *xerosols* (which contain slightly more humus than *yermosols*), *regosols* (with a better developed surface soil layer than in either *yermosols* or *xerosols*, and without hard subsoil pans of lime or gypsum) and

arenosols (deep quartz-sandy profiles with limited clay formation in the subsoil). The aridity encourages accumulation in depressions of lime, gypsum and sodium salts, but alluvial deposits of the Nile in Nubia, and also of the Niger's desert reaches in Mali, are kept largely salt-free by regular flooding. The *fluvisols* (soils forming on recent alluvium) along these major rivers and the small but important areas, at oases, of *vertisols* (dark-coloured cracking clays) and *gleysols* (periodically waterlogged soils) support, with irrigated food cropping, 100 or more inhabitants per sq km whereas the rest of the arid zone has a population density of less than 4 per sq km overall, and in large tracts is uninhabitable.

The Sahel and other semi-arid to subhumid terrain

As the rains progressively increase in amount away from desert areas, and begin to show marked seasonality, permitting fast-growing annual crops to mature during the wetter months, the soils in general improve also. A decrease in gravel and stone content and an increase in depth are accompanied by the build-up of plant nutrient levels

KEY

World Soil Map units – only the most prominent soils are identified in each tract mapped – (Small islands around Africa – not shown on this map – are nearly all volcanic, with fertile andosols and thin lithosols)

EASIER SOILS FOR FARMING (provided moisture is not lacking)

Vertisols	Luvisols and acrisols
Nitosols	Luvisols and cambisols
Luvisols	Irrigated fluvisols in Egypt

DIFFICULT SOILS (with major fertility and/or management problems)

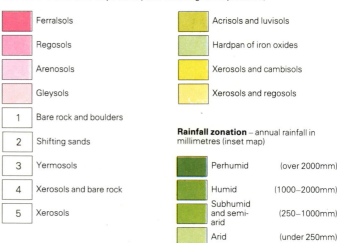

Ferralsols	Acrisols and luvisols
Regosols	Hardpan of iron oxides
Arenosols	Xerosols and cambisols
Gleysols	Xerosols and regosols
1 Bare rock and boulders	
2 Shifting sands	
3 Yermosols	
4 Xerosols and bare rock	
5 Xerosols	

Rainfall zonation – annual rainfall in millimetres (inset map)

Perhumid	(over 2000mm)
Humid	(1000–2000mm)
Subhumid and semi-arid	(250–1000mm)
Arid	(under 250mm)

SOILS

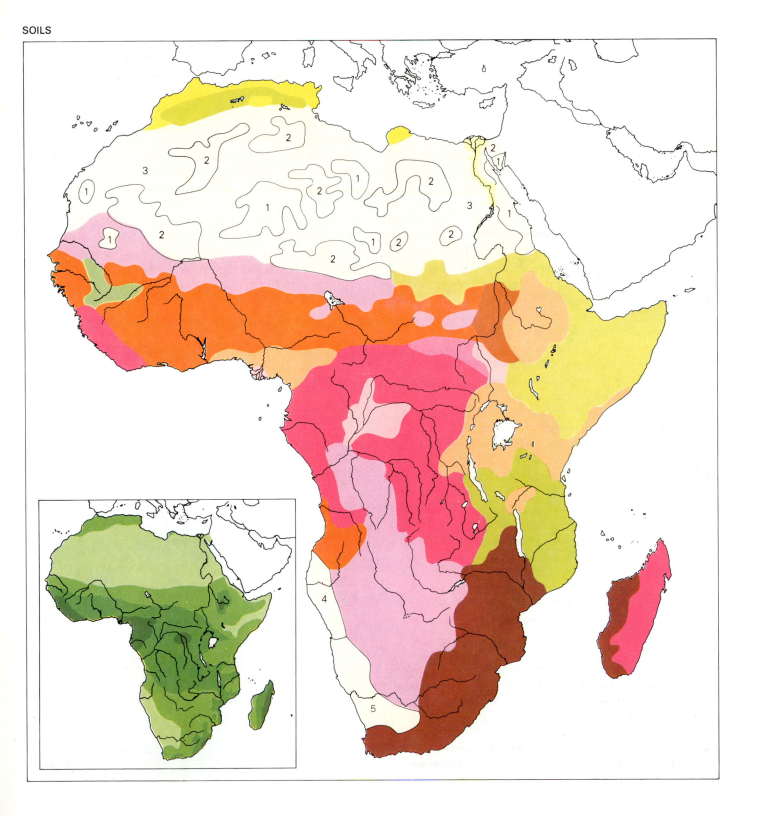

(such as the bases potassium, calcium and magnesium, and several trace elements). There is often, however, a lack of phosphorus and almost always low organic matter and nitrogen. But the overriding uncertainty to farmers in this belt–known where it borders the southern edge of the Sahara as the Sahel★ (from the Arabic *sahil*, 'coast')–is soil moisture supply.

The *xerosols*, *regosols* and *arenosols* bordering the arid zone are generally succeeded by *luvisols* (soils with marked clay accumulation in lower horizons and relatively high base status, but with productivity often reduced by the presence of ironstone gravel or hardpan). As an exception, throughout Namibia and the western Cape Province of South Africa, Kalahari deposits give rise to *arenosols* not only in the subhumid but also in the humid zone, along a wide sandy corridor reaching through Angola as far north as Zaire and Congo. South-eastern Africa and western Madagascar, however, are characterized by *luvisols* and associated soils, e.g., *vertisols* in the Transvaal and *planosols* (sandy top abruptly overlying claypan) in the Orange Free State. In eastern Africa *luvisols* are replaced as dominant soils by *nitosols* (soils characterized by weathered but well-structured profiles of medium to heavy texture) and there are also in both the east and the west sizeable areas of *acrisols* (as *luvisols*, but with low base status), particularly common in Tanzania. The Nile basin of central Sudan, including the Gezira irrigation scheme, is floored by *vertisols*. The Maghrib (western North Africa) has its own distinctive soils: *xerosols* and *cambisols* (soils with rather immature profiles, often unleached and fairly fertile) in valleys of the Atlas grade to *luvisols* and *cambisols* on lower ground. Out of 900 million hectares in the entire zone, about half has 'easier' soil agriculturally and a population density of 24 per sq km. The other half, more difficult farmland, currently has a population density of 8 per sq km.

The humid and perhumid tropics and subtropics

There are 1000 million hectares of Africa with average yearly rainfall greater than 1000mm. Despite quite long dry seasons, which are the norm even in some of the wetter localities, the soils other than those in constant-renewal sites (*fluvisols* and *gleysols*) have been leached of bases, impoverished in all plant nutrients and virtually reduced to low-activity clay particles and rubbly quartz sand in a fabric of iron and aluminium oxides (soils called *ferralsols*–also known as *oxisols* or *latosols*). Most of the tropical regions of Africa, receiving over 2000mm mean annual rainfall (the perhumid zones), have these end-product soil profiles, except for the *nitosols* and other better land (not, however, without problems of erosion and poor productivity) in southern Nigeria and western Cameroon. In the humid zone, receiving annual rainfall of about 1000 to 2000mm, there is a threefold division on the continent, with *ferralsols* (plus *gleysols* and, in the south-west, *arenosols*) of the Zaire basin and surrounding areas giving way north-westwards to a rather more productive region of

luvisols and *acrisols* (reaching into Ivory Coast and Guinea) and south-eastwards to disconnected moister tracts through Mozambique and Natal with *luvisols* predominating. The perhumid east coast and humid central strip of Madagascar has *ferralsols*. Humid areas in the upper Nile lakes catchment and the Ethiopian highlands are endowed with *nitosols* among complexes of other soil types.

Africa's humid areas, as defined, have average population densities of 39 per sq km on their 'easier soils' and 11 per sq km on difficult soils. The perhumid areas average 64 per sq km on easier soil and 17 per sq km elsewhere. Clearly the challenge to human occupation of Africa's wet climatic belt is being met, but living standards are still low there on the whole. Blends of traditional farming methods★ (seedbed shaping, mulching, manuring, intercropping) with agronomic research findings in the fields of plant breeding and plant nutrition promise greater understanding soon of the capabilities of some among the 'difficult' soils, notably *ferralsols* and *acrisols*.   G.M.

Vegetation

Africa spans the tropics and extends both north and south into temperate latitudes. From Algeria to the Cape, a range of differing climatic regimes★ are fundamental in shaping Africa's vegetation.

Forest

Near the Equator high rainfall and constantly high temperatures throughout the year, except in mountainous areas, enable tropical rain forest to flourish. No other type of vegetation in the world is so

Tropical forest in Nigeria

luxuriant, for in sheer bulk of living material it can exceed temperate forests by 60–80 per cent and its annual productivity is second to none. Throughout most of the Zaire River basin, and the southern fringe of West Africa, the tropical rain forest dominates, but only occupies some 9 per cent of the continent's land mass. However, increased agricultural pressure through population growth,★ and the inroads carved out by modern forestry,★ threaten the long term conservation of these extensive tracts. Contrary to popular belief, the interior of the rain forest is not an impenetrable jungle. The deep shade cast by three strata of trees, the highest of which may exceed 40m, all but prevents plant growth on the forest floor. The range of plant adaptations to this constantly warm and humid environment is remarkable. Buttress roots, lianes (climbers), epiphytes (plants growing non-parasitically on others, such as mosses and ferns), 'drip-tip' evergreen leaves, and a uniquely prolific variety of trees make the tropical rain forest the richest vegetation type on the globe.

Savanna

Away from the equatorial region, where annual rainfall drops below 1500mm, the climate becomes increasingly seasonal. An initially short dry period gradually increases in length and severity. In Nigeria, for example, at Ibadan in the south it lasts for five months; at Kaduna in the centre, it extends for a further two months, and in the far north at Katsina, it has further increased to eight and a half months. A climatic gradient such as this has profound effects on vegetation. At first the closed, evergreen canopy of the rain forest gives way to a more open, deciduous one, and gradually the stature and variety of the trees change. Savannas, consisting of scattered trees and grasses, clothe the land, and as aridity becomes dominant in the annual climatic cycle, so grasses gain ascendancy over trees. Within this gradient, changes in the form and function of individual plants clearly demonstrate the increasing severity of the dry season. Trees are more open and spreading, their bark becomes thick and fire-resistant, and thorns and hooks appear on the thinner branches. Above all, leaf morphology undergoes radical change. The small, glistening, oval-shaped leaves of the rain forest are replaced by large and coarse ones such as are found on many of the *Ficus* (fig family) species. They may become lobed, as in *Bauhinia* (a family of leguminous climbers, trees and shrubs), and eventually deeply divided, pinnate or bipinnate, as in the *Acacias*. Size of leaves varies dramatically, but generally decreases with reduced rainfall, as does the height of trees. In the Sahel★ zone in the far north, small thorn shrubs are dominant, such as *Acacia senegal*, from which gum arabic is derived. Beneath and between the savanna trees, a variety of grasses offer valuable forage to both domestic cattle and wild game alike. In the more humid savanna areas dense elephant grass (*Pennisetum*) grows to 5m. With increasing aridity, individual tussocks of grasses such as *Hyparrhenia*, *Imperata* and *Andropogon* are more widely

spaced and rarely grow as tall. Eventually a zone of short annual grasses is found, e.g. in the central Sahel, while on the desert fringes, even these disappear and all that remains are drought-resistant *Panicum* and *Aristida* tussocks.

The savannas therefore occupy a long climatic gradient covering vast areas of the continent. The relationship between savanna and aridity is not always obvious, however, for both soil type★ and topography complicate the climatic pattern. Moreover, these regions have for long supported both agricultural★ and pastoral★ peoples, and the impact of man on the vegetation has compounded that of the physical environment. Only in rare instances are pristine savannas to be found. The clearance of woodland for agriculture and fuel, the continuous grazing of domestic animals, and the frequent use of fire to control pasture has led to the gradual impoverishment of the savanna. Fire-resistant trees, as well as those possessing thorns which dissuade grazing animals, are abundant. Indeed, the impact of fire has been such that in many areas, e.g. southern West Africa, 'derived' savannas now occupy climatic zones which may have been capable of supporting rain forest.

Savannas are not confined to West Africa. Throughout the majority of the eastern and southern parts of the continent similar vegetation can be found. In fact, 55 per cent of Africa's land mass supports savanna vegetation of one form or another. Thus the 'derived' and southern Guinea savannas of West Africa find their equivalent in southern Zaire, while the 'high grass-low tree' savanna is found as the northern Guinea savanna of West Africa and the more luxuriant form of 'Miombo' in East and South Central Africa. Though the individual species may vary, the form of these different grades of savanna is essentially the same.

Savanna vegetation: baobab trees in Madagascar

Desert vegetation

The majority of the rest of the continent is occupied by deserts (comprising 27 per cent of Africa's land surface). The Sahara dominates the north of the continent and its vast expanses are virtually empty of plant life, save for the small areas fed by subterranean water, or by the rare flash-floods which debouch from mountains. The few oases that exist are usually intensively cultivated, though where natural vegetation still survives, the ubiquitous *Acacias* form open 'savanna' vegetation. From the air, thin lines of these, and other trees such as date-palms, jujube and tamarisks mark the edges of wadis (seasonal watercourses).

Below: desert vegetation, an oasis in the Sahara at Insalah, Algeria. Bottom: temperate vegetation, a valley in the Atlas Mountains, Morocco

Temperate vegetation

There remain two broad categories of African vegetation. Firstly, at the northern and southern extremes of the continent, temperate climates give rise to vegetation types quite unlike the inter-tropical savannas. The northern littoral fringes the Mediterranean, and supports typical Mediterranean plants. Thus the High Atlas Mountains are covered with pine and cedar forests, or oak woods, while the lower slopes support *maquis*, a dense shrub community found throughout the Mediterranean lands. On the southern slopes of the Atlas a thin band of steppe grassland marks the northern edge of the desert. Remnants of this temperate vegetation also survive on the high mountains of the Sahara (Hoggar, Aïr, Tibesti and Jebel Marra). These relics indicate that in former (Pleistocene) times, climates in the north and central Sahara were sufficiently cool and moist to support much more extensive Mediterranean vegetation.

The southern tip of the continent also experiences a Mediterranean type of climate, and although the specific plants are once again different, their ecological role, and their overall form, bear strong resemblance to the vegetation of the Maghrib. Thus the *fynbos* of the Cape, dominated by members of the *Proteaceae* (a large family of flowering shrubs and small trees), is a parallel of the *maquis*, while the northern steppes are matched by the more extensive, though degraded grassland of the veldt.

Montane vegetation

A final environment of Africa is that provided by the mountain chains of the Rift Valley in East Africa and Ethiopia, as well as those of Cameroon and Madagascar. Although many of these mountains are located in the tropics, their high altitude modifies the climate to such

KEY

Tropical rain forest

'Derived' savanna/high grass-low tree savanna – humid (southern Guinea savanna)

High grass-low tree savanna (northern Guinea savanna; humid Miombo)

Acacia-tall grass savanna (Sudan savanna; Miombo)

Acacia-short grass savanna (Sahel; thorn veldt)

Sub-desert steppe

Desert

Mediterranean-type vegetation

Temperate grassland (veldt)

Montane vegetation

MAJOR VEGETATION ZONES

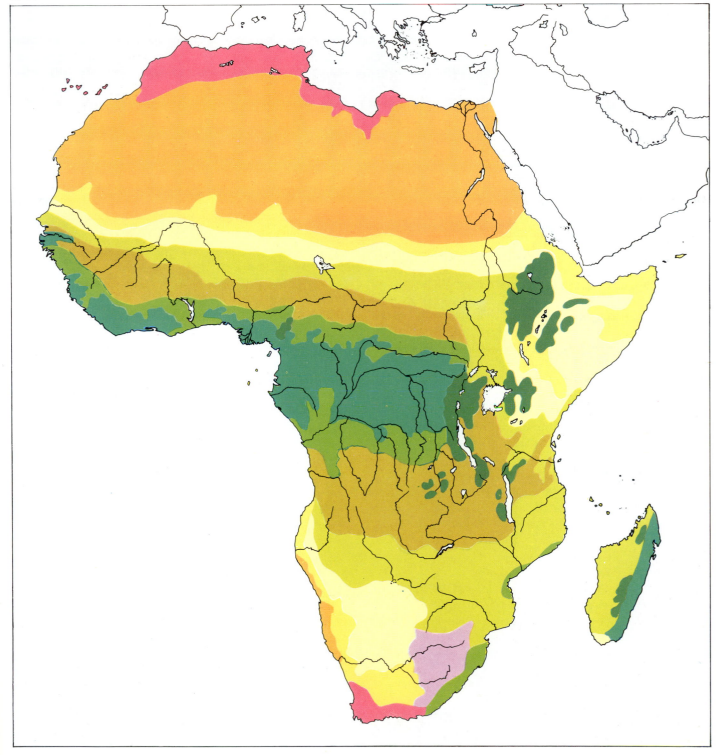

Montane vegetation: Mount Kenya, Kenya

Fauna

The fauna of the African continent includes elements of the Palaearctic zoogeograpical region (North Africa including the Canary Islands), as well as the Ethiopian (Africa south of the Sahara) and Madagascan regions – all of which are distinguished by their own characteristic plants and animals.

Zoogeographical regions

The Mediterranean coastal strip of northern Africa enjoys a warm temperate climate,* with hot, dry summers and comparatively warm, wet winters. Its fauna is similar to that of much of the Middle East: the Sahara to the south forms an integral part of the Great Palaearctic desert, which stretches almost continuously from Senegal across northern Africa and Asia Minor to northern India, Karakum and Mongolia. The Sahara is not uniformly desert. In its driest central regions, there are isolated mountains, such as Tibesti, Hoggar and Aïr, in which Palaearctic species spread far to the south while Ethiopian species reach northwards.

The Ethiopian zoogeographical region, which covers the continent of Africa south of the Sahara, also includes the southern corner of the Arabian peninsula. Its mammalian fauna is most varied, consisting of 38 families, excluding bats, while in number of endemic (confined to a particular region) families it ranks second only to the Neo-tropical (South America, most of Mexico and the West Indies). There are 12 endemic families: giraffes, hippopotamuses, aardvarks, otter shrews, golden moles, elephant shrews, and six families of rodents. The Ethiopian region shares with the Palaearctic the families of jerboas, dormice, coneys and wild horses, and with the Oriental region, apes, monkeys, lorises, elephants, rhinoceroses, pangolins, chevrotains and bamboo-rats. Hedgehogs, porcupines, civets, hyenas and pigs have affinities with both the Palaearctic and Oriental regions, while shrews, squirrels, rabbits, weasels, dogs, cats, bovids, and cricetid and murid mice have a world-wide distribution.

Birds are numerous in Africa south of the Sahara and, like the mammals, have strong affinities with the Orient. Exclusive to the Ethiopian region are ostriches, secretary birds, hammerheads, crested touracos, helmet shrikes and mousebirds. The many kinds of snakes include pythons, vipers, cobras, and mambas, which are endemic. Girdle-tailed lizards are also unique, and chameleons nearly so – only four of the 50 known species of chameleon are found outside the African continent and none of them occurs further away than India. Amphibians are less distinctive, but clawed toads of the genus *Xenopus* and the frog family *Phrynomeridae* are endemic.

In contrast, the Ethiopian fish fauna is extremely diverse, including characens, lung-fishes and several endemic families, including the mormyrids or elephant-snout fishes. Although

an extent that the cold summits of some of the tallest peaks are permanently snow-capped. A range of bizarre vegetation types survives in these extreme environments. Though each mountain system is individual, broad zones of vegetation can be distinguished, particularly in the Rift Valley. Depending on location, rain forests or savannas clothe the lower slopes, although they rarely extend to high altitudes. Quite often a semi-permanent cloud layer causes perpetual mists and dripping water, within which dense forests are found. The dwarfed trees of this 'cloud' forest are covered with epiphytic mosses and ferns, while at slightly higher altitudes a zone of bamboo thickets is normally encountered. Above the cloud layer, drier and cooler conditions exist, and the vegetation once again changes; firstly to a community of tree heaths dominated by *Erica arborea* and later to alpine vegetation characterized by giant *Hypericum* and *Senecio* plants, whose nearest relatives can be found in temperate Europe. Finally on the coolest and driest peaks, open tussock grasslands may be found.

Determinants of vegetation distribution

The vegetation of Africa is primarily controlled by climate, in particular by the amount and duration of available water. Within any one moisture regime local soil and topographic conditions can modify the general characteristics of the vegetation. This is nowhere more evident than in the savanna, where abrupt changes in the form of the vegetation reflect variation in these latter variables. However, the constraints imposed by the physical environment are overshadowed by human activity. Through the clearance of woodland, and the use of fire over many centuries, it has contributed to the opening up and desertification of savannas, and the general regression of the vegetation away from its climatic optimum.   *P.N.B.*

mormyrids possess electric organs–which are used both to detect prey and for purposes of orientation in muddy water–they are not related to the electric eels of the Amazon. On the other hand, the African lung-fish *Protopterus* is related to the South American lung-fish *Lepidosiren*. Characins or tiger fishes are likewise found also in the Neotropical region.

Africa was in the centre of Gondwanaland, the more southerly of the two land masses into which the world was divided until the Triassic period, some 200 million years ago; so it is not surprising that the older, and less mobile components of its fauna should be related more closely to those of the other southern continents, while the birds and mammals show closer affinities with the Oriental and Palaearctic realms. These were created by the break-up of the northern land mass, Laurasia, and are now actually closer in distance since Africa was originally separated from Europe and Asia by the huge Tethys Ocean, of which the Mediterranean represents only a vestige.

The vertebrate fauna of Madagascar and its offshore islands, including the Seychelles, Comoro and Mascarene islands, lacks the variety of the Ethiopian fauna. There are no large mammals or strictly freshwater fishes, while many families of Old World birds, reptiles and amphibians are also lacking. In the main, the fauna of Madagascar show African affinities but, undoubtedly, some of the birds and amphibians are more closely related to Oriental forms. The many endemic families and genera indicate a long period of isolation – indeed Madagascar has probably been an island since the early part of the Mesozoic era, some 220 million years ago.

Madagascar lacks true monkeys, antelopes, horses, elephants, aardvarks, lizards, vipers, cobras, worm-snakes, agamid and monitor lizards, soft-shelled turtles, and toads. At the same time, it possesses three families of lemurs, tenrecs, a subfamily of rodents, a family of bats, and 11 species of *Viverridae* (civets and genets) which are endemic to Madagascar. One of these, the fossa (*Cryptoprocta ferox*), a rapacious carnivore, about twice the size of a cat but with very short legs, is specially noteworthy as possible representing a group ancestral to both *Felidae* (the cats) and *Viverridae*.

A species of hippopotamus lived in Madagascar during the Pleistocene but became extinct about a million years ago, while huge flightless elephant-birds (*Aepyornis*) survived there until early historical times. Other endemic birds, still living, include the thrush-sized mesites, the couas–relatives of the cuckoos–ground-rollers, the curol or cuckoo-roller, the asity or false sunbird, and the vangas. The Seychelles have 14 endemic species of birds, a giant tortoise (*Geochelone gigantea*), a genus of legless burrowing amphibians, and some archaic frogs.

African biomes and their faunas

The Earth can be subdivided into a number of 'biomes', or major plant associations, depending on temperature, precipitation and evapotranspiration (the sum of evaporation and transpiration). From the Equator, a traveller in Africa moving north or south would pass through the following major biomes–equatorial and tropical rain forest, savanna, and desert. The Mediterranean coastline and the Cape region of southern Africa enjoy a western margin type of climate with hot, dry summers and comparatively warm, but wet, winters. In addition, Africa possesses various montane and freshwater biomes.

Rain forest

The fauna of the equatorial and tropical rain forest biome can be subdivided into a number of ecological groups, according to their ways of life. For instance, some animals have acquired arboreal habits and are adapted for tree climbing. Others are terrestrial, but have to be able to push through dense undergrowth. Subterranean forms are relatively scarce compared with the numerous burrowers of the savanna and desert biomes. The forest floor is inhabited by 'cryptozoic' animals which lead hidden lives in their concealed, micro-environments.

Chimpanzees in the Gombe Stream Game Reserve, Tanzania

Arboreal animals are numerous in rain forest, because vegetation is scanty at ground level, where there is little light, and the tree-tops provide an abundant supply of such staple foods as fruit and termites. It is because the seasons are almost absent and fruit is obtainable throughout the year that the rain forest can support fruit-eating animals such as parrots, hornbills, fruit-bats and chimpanzees, which would be quite unable to find a regular supply of their favourite diets in any other biome of the world. At the same time, the diversity of species present in rain forest may be one of the factors limiting the size and abundance of larger animals because few single, constant sources of food are available. All the larger mammals, even those that are arboreal, tend to range rather widely. For instance, chimpanzees in the Budongo forest move from one part of the forest to another as the fruits of different trees ripen. In contrast, gorillas can find almost anywhere the pithy stems and roots on which they live, and so travel in compact slow-moving groups, feeding as they go.

Many forest animals are adapted for arboreal life, and even primarily ground-living species, such as leopards, pangolins, rodents and insectivores are usually adept climbers. Most tree-dwellers are branch runners which live and move about on the upper surface of large branches. These include lemurs in the Madagascan forests, pangolins and squirrels. Guereza monkeys, gorillas and chimpanzees swing from branch to branch, tree to tree, suspended by their long arms. Chameleons and tree-snakes have prehensile tails, while the ventral scales of the latter are usually stiffened by transverse keels which give added traction on surfaces of rough bark. The vine or twig snake (*Thelotornis kirtlandii*) has a long, whip-like body which can be stiffened into a rod by muscular contraction so that the snake is able to reach across gaps between one branch and another.

The feet of arboreal animals may be prehensile or non-prehensile. In the latter, the claws are usually well developed, as in squirrels and leopards. Prehensile hands and feet are modified for grasping by one or more of the digits being inserted so that it can be opposed by the other digits. Primates have an opposable thumb and, except in man, an opposable big toe as well. In anthropoid apes, and most monkeys, the digit is flattened, a modification which gives more gripping power, and the claws are replaced by nails. Opposable digits are also found in parrots, woodpeckers and chameleons, while adhesive pads are sometimes found, either on the tips of the digits or on the soles of the feet of tree-hyraxes, geckoes and tree-frogs.

Those who come fresh to the rain forest are usually disappointed by the apparent scarcity of animal life. This is partly because the fauna is dwarfed by the luxuriance of the vegetation, and partly because the most active, abundant, and brightly-coloured species live in the upper storeys of the trees. At ground level most animals – those which can be classified as terrestrial – are hidden behind a tangle of tree-trunks, vines and lianas, branches and roots. Mammals tend to be smaller than their relatives outside the rain forest which helps them to push between the trees. For instance, forest elephants are smaller than bush elephants: they have small tusks and rounded ears. Forest buffaloes are smaller than the plains sub-species, and the same is true of leopards. The pygmy hippopotamus, like the human pygmy, is a forest dweller, as is the royal antelope (*Neotragus pygmaeus*) of the coastal forests of West Africa. This is the smallest ruminant in the world, but many other dwarf antelopes, such as *Hylamus batesi* of Cameroon and *H. harrisoni* of the Semliki forest (Uganda), are not much larger. The forest-hog (*Hylochoerus meinertzhageni*) and the bongo (*Boocerus euryceros*) appear to be somewhat exceptional in their large size.

Cryptozoic animals include members of most, if not all, terrestrial phyla. They are usually small in size, with thin exoskeletons, and are completely dependent upon a moist environment. Many of them are blind, and the sense of vision is largely replaced by tactile and chemical senses. Powers of locomotion are not well developed among the cryptozoa, for these animals seldom need to move far from one part to another of their uniform environment. Wingless insects are common, while those that do possess wings are not strong fliers. Other distinctive characters of the cryptozoa, as compared with other groups of animals of the African forests, include the lack of effective respiratory mechanisms; reduction of secondary sexual characters, which distinguish males from females; development from eggs that do not possess an impervious shell, and are therefore laid in clusters coated with mucus; the continuation of moulting throughout life and even after maturity has been reached; inactivity; and a lack of diversity in form and colour.

Savanna

Park-like savanna woodlands are found where the dry season is longer, and the rainfall less heavy than in rain forest. Wooded savanna grades into tropical grassland steppe and from this to desert. In East Africa, and elsewhere, savanna is maintained by regular burning of the grass, and there is a delicately balanced interaction between climate, soil, vegetation, animals and fire.

While the fauna of the rain forest is remarkable chiefly for the extraordinary wealth and variety of species present, animal life in the savanna is characterized by the immense number of individuals of certain species. The mammals tend either to be large cursorial (adapted for running) forms, such as elephants, giraffes, buffaloes, antelopes and zebras, or else are small burrowing rodents and insectivores. More than 40 species of large vegetarian mammals along with their attendant carnivores – lions, leopards, cheetahs, hyenas, jackals and hunting dogs – inhabit the African savannas, not counting the smaller antelopes. In any one habitat, such as the bushy grasslands of Kenya or the wooded savanna of Tanzania, as many as 15 or 16 species of large game animals may be found together, and population densities are often greater than in any other terrestrial

Kudu, giraffe and zebra drinking, Etosha Pan, Namibia

Addax in the Sahara

biome. Such concentration does not, however, lead to severe competition, because each animal has its own food preferences and feeds from different levels of the vegetation – elephant and giraffe from the tops of trees, antelope on bushes at different heights above the ground, zebras and impala on grass, while wart-hogs grub up underground roots. Species with overlapping food preferences, such as wildebeeste and buffalo, occupy different habitats, while different species may occupy the same place at different seasons of the year.

A few savanna herbivores, such as the elephant and rhinoceros, are large enough to be immune from the attacks of predators. Others, such as rodents, obtain protection by burrowing. Many, however, rely on camouflage to evade detection, and good vision and speed to escape from their enemies.

Desert

In the African deserts where plant life is scanty, the fauna is correspondingly reduced in comparison with that of the savanna. Even completely barren deserts, however, are inhabited by a few beetles and other insects which feed on dry vegetation and grass seeds, blown often from a considerable distance.

The mammals most independent of water are desert rodents, such as jerboas and gerbils. By hiding throughout the day in comparatively cool and moist burrows, they can subsist solely on the metabolic water obtained from the breakdown of dry food. They excrete extremely concentrated urine, and have dry faeces. Desert rodents do not sweat, but can cool themselves in emergencies by salivating

copiously and wetting the chin and throat. The desert tortoise (*Geochelone sulcata*) can, likewise, cool itself by salivation. Large mammals, such as antelope, asses and camels, cannot escape the daytime heat, but endure a rise of body temperature so that they store excess heat during the day and lose it at night when the air cools. They use some water in sweating, but this is reduced to a minimum. The oryx and addax can even survive without drinking at all.

Birds tend to inhabit the fringe of the desert, and never go very far from water. Small species utilize shade as far as possible to protect themselves from the sun while larger forms, such as vultures and hawks, soar in the upper air. The large ostrich must also drink from time to time, or eat very succulent food, but it possesses salt-excretory nasal glands that enable it to live off brackish water.

Reptiles are conspicuous members of the desert fauna and, like darkling beetles, scorpions, and camel spiders, are able to maintain stable, yet not excessive body temperatures, by behavioural and, to a lesser extent, physiological means. Water loss through transpiration is reduced to a minimum, nitrogenous waste is excreted in the form of insoluble uric acid – with very little loss of water – and diurnal (active during the day) forms avoid the sun's heat by seeking shade, or else by adopting suitable postures after optimum body temperature has been reached.

Mountains

From rain forest at the foot of a tropical mountain one passes, with increasing altitude, through belts of deciduous and coniferous forest to alpine meadows and finally to a region of snow and ice. The forest is rich in wild animals, big game extending as far as the ericaceous or moorland belt. At higher altitudes hyraxes, duikers and rats are the most important herbivores. They tend to be larger and more hairy than their relatives of the plains. Reptiles tend to be scarce. The cryptozoic habit of the fauna is most striking nearest the summit, where spring-tails and insects predominate. Many of the latter are flightless, as on remote islands.

Lakes and rivers

Africa is rich in the possession of many great lakes, large rivers, papyrus swamps and salt-marshes, each with its own distinctive fauna. The Ethiopian region has one of the most diversified fish faunas of the world. The great lakes are also inhabited by an assortment of unusual animals, including jellyfish (*Limnocnida* spp.), and some highly specialized worms, molluscs and crustaceans. African waters are the home of crocodiles and are justly famous for the richness of their bird life, which includes flamingoes, spoonbills, storks, and the shoebill of the papyrus swamps. Temporary rainpools support a rich fauna which includes tadpole shrimps (*Triops* spp.). Mangrove swamps and coral reefs, found along the coast, occur only in tropical climates.   *J. L. C.-T.*

Right: rock hyraxes. Below: lesser flamingo on Lake Nakuru, Kenya

The development of mankind

The span of human prehistory in Africa is much longer than it is in any other part of the world. As a result of the archaeological discoveries of the last several decades, there can now be little reasonable doubt that it was on this continent that man-like creatures, or hominids first evolved. The hominid evolutionary process leading to modern man (*Homo sapiens*) has been traced back in greater or lesser detail to over 3 million years ago. For at least half of this time man may have been an exclusively African creature. At the other end of the time-scale, history as studied through written records and oral traditions covers only a relatively brief and recent period in much of Africa. Archaeology and the associated disciplines used to reconstruct prehistoric events and processes are thus of paramount importance in elucidating even the recent African past. The importance of archaeology to the study of man in Africa needs no further stress. However, despite or because of archaeology's recognized value to African studies, it is necessary to emphasize the sparseness of the evidence on which any synthesis must at present be based. Although the tempo of research is increasing, there remain large regions where virtually no scientific excavations or intensive archaeological surveys have been conducted. Fully studied sites are few in relation to the vastness of the continent, and the geographical and chronological distribution of these sites is extremely uneven.

The emergence of man

The idea that humans first evolved in Africa is as old as the idea that they have evolved at all. In 1871 Charles Darwin wrote, in *The Descent of Man*, 'It is therefore probable that Africa was formerly inhabited by extinct apes closely allied to the gorilla and chimpanzee; and as these two species are now man's nearest allies it is somewhat more . . . probable that our early progenitors lived on the African continent than elsewhere.' It was more than half a century later that material evidence began to be found in support of this hypothesis. The first firm evidence for human evolution was provided by hominid fossils discovered in Europe and Asia. Investigations in China and Java produced what were reasonably interpreted as the earliest known remains of man. It was not until 1925, with the discovery of what was subsequently identified as the skull of a juvenile australopithecine at Taung in the Cape Province of South Africa, that it was accepted that African fossil evidence might be found to substantiate Darwin's hypothesis. Since then hominid remains have been recovered with increasing frequency in East and South Africa, sometimes from datable archaeological contexts. In the decades since 1959 there has been a very greatly increased accumulation of the material evidence on which a reconstruction of human evolution may be based.

Pre-human evolution requires a brief consideration here, as it is the essential background to African prehistory. Remains of *Aegyptopithecus* from the Fayum Depression in lower Egypt date from the Oligocene of almost 30 million years ago. This creature (the earliest known ape) was quadrupedal, with well-developed forelimbs suited to life in forest trees. The evolutionary sequence is continued by *Dryopithecus* from 20 million year-old deposits on Rusinga Island, near the eastern shore of Lake Victoria. These fossils may be not far removed from the point of separation of the evolutionary lines that led respectively to modern man and to the modern great apes. The former line seems to be next represented in the fossil record by *Ramapithecus*, which is known from Europe, India and Africa and is dated to about 12 million years ago. Despite the fragmentary nature of the remains (no limb bones yet having been discovered), it has been suggested that *Ramapithecus* may have had a partly bipedal gait and have inhabited a more open environment than was favoured by the earlier primates. A single battered stone found associated with *Ramapithecus* remains at Fort Ternan in western Kenya is not widely accepted as being a deliberately produced artefact.

There is then a major gap in the fossil record of the early African hominid ancestors, with only uninformative fragments represented, until about 3.5 million years ago. The fossil record then resumes at this later period with a confusing diversity of early hominids. The significance of this material, much of which has been discovered only within the last decade, is still a matter of intense debate. There is as yet no consensus as to the number of species represented, for we still lack any very clear understanding of the amount of variation that might have existed between the individuals of a single population, or of the regional variation present in a single species. The problem is exacerbated by the fragmentary nature of much of the evidence and the scarcity of fossil material other than teeth and skull fragments. Many questions remain to be answered concerning the relationships of the early hominid species to one another and their cultural – e.g. tool making and tool using – capacities and absolute chronologies.

Laymen, and even some professionals, are apt to think of research into human origins as primarily a glorious fossil hunt. This is, however, only a small part of the story, just as the hominid fossils are a small, albeit important, portion of the total body of evidence concerning human evolution. Man's separation from the rest of the animal kingdom is more a result of the intellectual and behavioural activities that comprise human culture than it is a result of his purely physical attributes. It is impossible to study behaviour patterns in prehistoric or present day populations without reference to the environmental context in which the behaviour took place. A major facet of research into human origins must therefore be directed towards reconstructing the natural environments in which the various populations lived. Archaeological investigations that attempt to elucidate the behaviour patterns and activities of the early hominids are equally important. Our interest is not just in man's physical evolution, but also in his cultural and social evolution. Unfortunately for the prehistorian, the simpler the life style, the fewer are the traces that it will leave in the archaeological record, making efforts at reconstruction and interpretation correspondingly tenuous. For this reason use must be made of all possibly relevant sources of information, including studies of the conduct and social organization of the modern non-human primates.

Owing to the fragmentary nature and varied quality of the evidence (to which it is expected that much will be added in the next few years) and to the controversial status of some important fossils, it is not yet practicable to give a complete synthesis of the earliest stages of human prehistory. Instead, it is best to present the data by means of a review of the major sites that have yielded evidence of the early hominids.

The earliest sites

The oldest archaeological sites fall into two groups: former caves on the dry inland plateau of South Africa, and open sites preserved in sediments of the great Rift Valley in eastern Africa. To a certain extent, this distribution reflects the accidents of preservation and subsequent exposure, but it also strongly suggests that the early man-like creatures preferred an open savanna tropical environment.

At Taung in the Cape Province of South Africa is a limestone quarry that was the first site in Africa to yield fossil remains of an immediately pre-human hominid. Blocks of fossil-bearing rock removed in 1924 were examined by Raymond Dart, who recognized a virtually complete juvenile skull as representing a hitherto unknown

hominid genus, with an upright posture and bipedal gait, which he named *Australopithecus*. This infant specimen had a cranial capacity akin to that of a modern adult chimpanzee. Dart's initial publication of *Australopithecus africanus* in 1925 attracted little serious attention until the discovery of further apparently related specimens in the Transvaal more than a decade later.

Three sites–Sterkfontein, Swartkrans and Kromdraai–are located in close proximity in the Blaawbank Valley not far west of Johannesburg. The initial fossil discovery, announced by Robert Broom in 1936, came from the site of Sterkfontein. Similar deposits at the other two sites yielded hominid fossils in the following decade. Like Taung, the Blaawbank Valley localities were originally caves in which the bones of a variety of animals had been concentrated by some natural agency–perhaps the activity of hyenas. Among them were bones of *Australopithecus africanus* and of a more heavily built and muscular species, *Australopithecus robustus*. A few other specimens have been attributed to an early form of the genus *Homo*, which is better known from sites in East Africa. Stone tools, a few of them flaked on both sides, have been recovered from the upper levels of the Sterkfontein deposits. There is no certain means of attributing the manufacture of these tools to any particular one of the three hominid species represented at the site. Also, these Transvaal sites do not enable us to reconstruct much about the life-style of the hominids, to consider the non-hominid fossils as representatives of the prey of the hominids, or to date the deposits very accurately. Faunal studies have enabled provisional relative ages to be assigned to

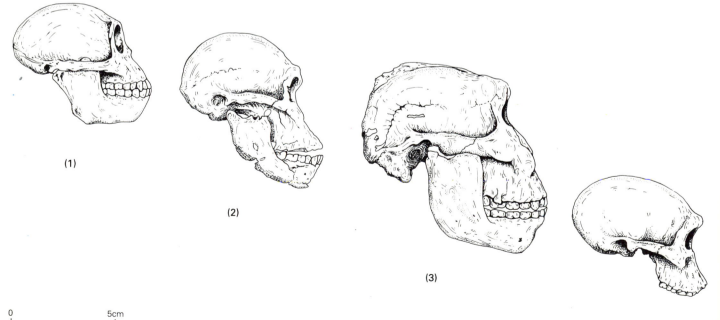

(1)

(2)

(3)

0   5cm

(4)

them, with Kromdraai being the most recent site and the lower levels at Sterkfontein the oldest. Comparisons with dated East African sites suggest that the Blaawbank sequence covers the period from about 3 million to 1.5 million years ago.

Makapansgat, probably the oldest of all the South African australopithecine sites, is also in a former cave, located 200km north of Pretoria. In many respects the material recovered from this site resembles that from Sterkfontein. Claims by Dart that many of the broken animal bones represent an 'osteodontokeratic' (bone, tooth and horn) tool-making tradition of *Australopithecus* are not now generally accepted. Similar bone fracture patterns and the selective accumulation of particular types of bones may be encountered outside hyenas' dens.

In 1959 the main centre of interest for early African hominid research shifted northwards to Olduvai Gorge, on the western edge of the great Rift Valley in northern Tanzania. Early Stone Age artefacts had been known for many years from the long sequence of deposits exposed by the downcutting of the gorge. Four principal superimposed beds contain a succession of stone tool industries, that from bed I, known as Oldowan, representing what was arguably then the oldest known prehistoric industry. Despite the abundance of faunal remains, no early hominid fossils were recovered from Olduvai until 1959, when the well preserved skull of a robust australopithecine was discovered by Mary Leakey on a living floor in bed I, associated with Oldowan artefacts. Dating of the surrounding rock indicated an age for this level in the order of 1.75 million years. At first sight it appeared reasonable to regard the hominid represented, *Australopithecus boisei* (a very near relative of *Australopithecus robustus*), as the inhabitant of this small temporary campsite and the maker of the tools. Such a conclusion was rendered less than convincing by the subsequent discovery of a somewhat earlier living floor on which similar stone tools were associated with remains of a more advanced hominid, generally attributed to the genus *Homo*, described as *Homo habilis*. Since only one type of stone industry is represented in bed I at Olduvai, it is logical to suppose that this was the handiwork of the most developed hominid present. Subsequent research at Olduvai suggests that the gracile australopithecine, *Australopithecus africanus* was also present about 1.7 million years ago, and that both *Australopithecus boisei* and *Homo* coexisted there until 1 million years ago, by which time *Homo habilis* was replaced by, or evolved into, *Homo erectus*, and *Australopithecus* had finally become extinct. From about 1.5 million years ago the Olduvai industrial succession also became more complicated, with apparently contemporaneous sites yielding assemblages that are attributed respectively to early Acheulian and developed Oldowan industries; the nature of these, and their possible significance, is discussed below.

Reconstructions of skulls: (1) *Ramapithecus*; (2) *Australopithecus africanus*; (3) *Australopithecus boisei*; (4) *Homo habilis* (Olduvai); (5) *'1470'* (Koobi Fora); (6) *Homo erectus* (Koobi Fora); (7) *Homo sapiens rhodesiensis*; (8) modern West African negroid

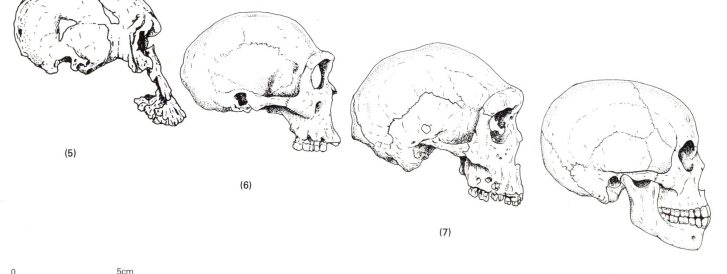

(5)

(6)

(7)

0   5cm

(8)

Laetolil, not far from Olduvai, has been known for many years as a site that yielded faunal remains considerably older than those from the bottom of the Olduvai sequence. No hominid fossils were recovered until 1974, but since then several mandibles have been found in a context dated to as long ago as 3.5 million years. The initial publication attributed these specimens to *Homo*, which would make them by far the earliest representatives of this genus, but subsequent research has cast doubt on this identification. The most spectacular, and in some ways the most informative, of Mary Leakey's discoveries at Laetolil is a trail of footprints made by a fully bipedal hominid.

Below: one of the hominid footprints preserved by volcanic ash at Laetolil, Tanzania, discovered by Mary Leakey. Bottom: a view of the Plio/Pleistocene fossil-bearing deposits at Koobi Fora, Kenya

Formed in mud that subsequently dried, the trail was preserved by a fall of volcanic ash. The footprints and stride-length are both very small. There can be no doubt that they date from the same period as the hominid fossils.

Further north in the East African Rift Valley is Lake Turkana (formerly Lake Rudolf) in northern Kenya. Along its north-eastern shore is Koobi Fora an extensive area of eroded sediments in which, since 1970, Richard Leakey, Glynn Isaac and their collaborators have discovered a mass of data relating to Plio/Pleistocene hominids, their activities, technology, environment and faunal contemporaries. Unfortunately there has been considerable uncertainty about the chronology of these deposits, and early claims for ages in the 2.5 to 3 million year range are now treated with reserve. It now appears likely that few, if any, of the signs of early hominid activity at Koobi Fora are more than 2 million years old, which makes them broadly contemporary with the beginning of the Olduvai sequence. The relative abundance of hominid fossils at Koobi Fora permits major amplification of the picture presented at Olduvai. Both gracile and robust australopithecines are represented as well as early *Homo*, but here again two strains have been recognized, differentiated mainly by their relative brain-size. By 1.5 million years ago, it is clear that the large-brained form had evolved into a creature recognizable as *Homo erectus*, and by this time the gracile australopithecine was probably already extinct.

The earliest stone tool assemblage at Koobi Fora is that from the KBS site, best dated to about 1.8 or 1.7 million years ago. It consists of simple flakes, a few of them minimally modified, and shows less reliance on chopper forms than do the broadly contemporary Oldowan industries. The site appears to have been located in the sandy bed of a seasonal stream, its area probably limited by the availability of shade, and has suffered virtually no disturbance since it was abandoned. No fossil hominid remains were preserved on this particular site, but it nevertheless provides a more detailed picture of the behavioural patterns and micro-environments favoured by the early hominids, since most of the latter's physical remains have not been found in primary contexts. By 1.5 million years ago a distinctive and much more complex stone industry was being produced in the Koobi Fora area. Named the Karari industry, it is typified by heavy pick-like tools, roughly circular cores and flakes with rough marginal trimming. Again, no hominid fossils have been found in direct association with occurrences of the Karari industry, but the date of its appearance is broadly the same as that of *Homo erectus*. Acheulian industries are markedly absent from the Koobi Fora area.

The Omo River is the northern affluent of Lake Turkana, draining a large area of southern Ethiopia. In its lower reaches it cuts through a deep series of Plio/Pleistocene deposits which are centred only some 250km to the north-northwest of those at Koobi Fora. Several lines of evidence combine to suggest that the earlier part of the Omo Valley sequence falls within the period between 3 and 2 million years ago. Hominid fossils occur through the greater part of this time-span: most are very fragmentary but they appear to indicate the presence of both gracile australopithecines and *Homo*. From about 2.5 million years ago, stone artefacts make their appearance. They are mostly tiny flakes and chips of quartz, differing markedly from those from KBS at Koobi Fora probably because of the nature and flaking properties of the available raw material. The gracile australopithecine (*Australopithecus africanus*) is not represented in the Omo sequence after about 2 million years ago, but the robust form *Australopithecus boisei* evidently inhabited the region alongside *Homo* for much of the following million years.

Hadar is located in the hot, arid Afar Rift of north-eastern Ethiopia, over 1000km north of Lake Turkana. Sediments there are demonstrably earlier than those at Olduvai, Koobi Fora or Omo. There is fossil evidence for the presence between 3.5 and 3 million years ago of a gracile australopithecine and, less convincingly, for a more advanced hominid, which has been tentatively identified as a representative of *Homo*. At Hadar particular interest attaches to the discovery of the large part of a gracile hominid skeleton (concerning the taxonomic attribution of which there is considerable controversy) and the report that remains of several, possibly related, individuals have been found in close proximity.

Australopithecus and early *Homo*

Broadly speaking, and based on the evidence from eastern and southern Africa for the evolution and activities of the earliest hominids up to about 1 million years ago, there can be no reasonable doubt that several distinct types of hominid existed in close proximity to one another and that they exploited broadly similar environments. The precise number of parallel hominid lineages, and their taxonomic relationships, remains a matter for controversy both because of the very fragmentary nature of most of the fossils and since there is much uncertainty about the variation that can exist between individuals of a single species or genus within a limited period of time. (We are now considering a time-depth for the genus *Homo*, for example, which is five or six times as long as that which was generally considered likely less than a quarter of a century ago.) Sexual size difference also may have been considerable, yet this remains poorly understood because the sex of so few of the early hominid fossils can be ascertained.

The general picture, however, is one which emphasizes the long florescence of *Australopithecus africanus*, the gracile form of *Australopithecus*, which probably survived until less than 1.5 million years ago. When this creature first appeared is uncertain, but it may have been present as long ago as 5 million years at Lothagam, west of Lake Turkana. The robust australopithecine is in evidence by 2 million years ago and was probably extinct by 1 million years ago.

Two kinds are recognized: *Australopithecus robustus* in South Africa and *Australopithecus boisei* in eastern Africa. *Homo* has been claimed as long ago as 3.5 million years at Laetolil and Hadar, but both these identifications are open to dispute. There are indications of *Homo* in the Omo Valley rather before 2 million years ago and well preserved specimens from Olduvai and Koobi Fora from 1.7 million years ago. From at least the latter period the small-brained *Homo habilis* existed alongside a larger-brained form, and by 1.5 million years ago at Koobi Fora the latter type is recognizable as *Homo erectus*.

Stone tool industries

The evidence for the earliest stone tool industries is even more fragmentary: the only sequence of any length and completeness is from Olduvai. It must, of course, be anticipated that the earliest objects used as tools would not have been deliberately modified and may not therefore be recognizable in the archaeological record even if they have survived. Materials other than stone would most probably have been employed initially, and for these the chances of preservation are very slight. No artefacts have been reported from Laetolil. Some have been recovered in the later part of the Hadar sequence but their precise position and typology have not yet been made known. The small simple quartz flakes from about 2.5 million years ago onwards in the Omo Valley have already been noted: they at present rank as the oldest undisputed human artefacts. Somewhat more advanced are the KBS industry from Koobi Fora and the early Oldowan from Olduvai: both date from around 1.8 to 1.7 million years ago. By 1.5 million years ago the process of development and diversification had evidently accelerated. At Olduvai both Developed Oldowan and early Acheulian industries are attested side by side for the next half million years, when the Oldowan finally disappears from the record. It is to these last-mentioned industries that the few stone artefacts from the Transvaal sites of Sterkfontein and Makapansgat probably belong. The Karari industry at Koobi Fora belongs to the same general period.

The query inevitably arises: to what extent can particular industries be correlated with one or other of the early hominid species? No confident answer may be given. It is logical to suppose that the earliest artefacts will have been the work of one of the more advanced hominids present at the same place and time. We cannot answer the basic question of whether *Australopithecus* ever made stone tools, or whether this was the prerogative of *Homo*. It is debatable whether the two parallel industries attested at Olduvai between 1.5 and 1 million years ago were made by two distinct types of hominid. While this remains a possible explanation, it has also been suggested that the Developed Oldowan and early Acheulian occur in different micro-environments and that they may thus represent different activities or patterns of resource exploitation. There is reasonably good evidence, as will be noted below, from

Ternifine in Algeria about 900 000 years ago, and slightly later in Bed II at Olduvai, for the association of *Homo erectus* with an Acheulian industry: it is plausible to suggest that this correlation may hold good for the earlier Acheulian phases also.

Before about 1.5 million years ago, the artefact densities on all sites are low and the areas of scatter are small, suggesting that they represent encampments occupied by a few individuals for a short period of time. In some cases they appear to represent the butchery site of a single carcase – whether killed by the hominids themselves or by some other agency it is not possible to ascertain. Be that as it may, it is reasonably clear that by this time hominids had already developed such social fundamentals as the ability to cooperate, to share food resources, and to establish a home base. Meat was evidently an important part of the diet, and it must be remembered that stone tool manufacture will greatly have facilitated meat-eating by a creature that did not retain the physical attributes, such as elongated canine teeth, possessed by other primate meat-eaters. The known sites of this period show a clear preference for dry, open situations in savanna country, but in close proximity to open water.

The Acheulian industrial complex

As noted above, the Acheulian first appeared in the archaeological record at Olduvai Gorge about 1.5 million years ago. Initially, other industries such as Karari and Developed Oldowan coexisted with it. By 1 million years ago these other industries are no longer represented; the Acheulian alone survived and it had spread to most parts of Africa except the densely forested regions. It was at about this time that many areas of West and North Africa were first settled by man. Throughout Africa and, indeed, many parts of the Old World, the Acheulian industries display considerable typological standardization. They also show remarkably little change through time, for the Acheulian remained the dominant tool-making tradition until about 100 000 years ago.

The early Acheulian assemblages and sites exhibit several new, even radically new, departures attesting to changes in the behaviour and abilities of their makers as compared with those of the preceding industries. The stone tools are generally larger and more finely made than are Developed Oldowan artefacts – bifacially flaked tools more than 18cm long are common – and the quality of their workmanship suggests a high degree of skill and even a sense of artistry on the part of the craftsmen who produced them. The most characteristic tool type of the Acheulian is the almond-shaped, bifacially flaked handaxe; other large bifacial tools, including straight-edged cleaver forms, are also common, as are a variety of scrapers and other smaller tools made on flakes with one or more trimmed edges.

Two other differences from the Oldowan are of very great importance. Living floors and occupation sites of the Acheulian period, such as those at Kalambo Falls in the extreme north of

Zambia, and at Olorgesailie in the Kenya Rift Valley, are very much larger than any of the few undisturbed Oldowan campsites that have been discovered. Oldowan sites are often only a few metres in diameter and yield relatively few artefacts; Acheulian sites may be a hundred metres across. Besides being larger, with correspondingly greater numbers of artefacts, Acheulian sites are more widely

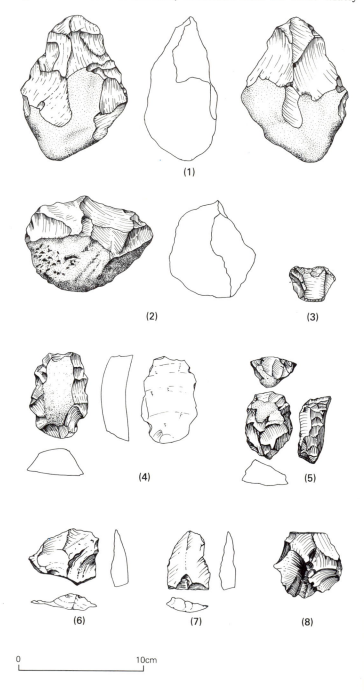

(1)

(2)   (3)

(4)   (5)

(6)   (7)   (8)

0   10cm

dispersed, being found in all parts of Africa except the most densely forested. Also, if we exclude a few possible early sites in southern Europe, the Acheulian is the first stone tool-making tradition to be found outside of Africa. Dates for European and Near Eastern Acheulian sites, the oldest being less than a million years, make it apparent that the tradition was carried by the tool makers moving out of Africa.

Despite their remarkable standardization through space and time, the Acheulian stone tools remain enigmatic objects. No wholly convincing suggestions have been put forward as to the use to which the ubiquitous handaxes were put: it seems probable indeed that they served many different functions, including that of meat chopper. Cleavers have been shown by experiment to be very serviceable tools for skinning game.

From all of this we can begin to construct a picture of hominid populations who were able to procure food and to organize themselves socially – presumably through the use of well developed language – on a sufficient scale to allow them to live in large groups on at least some occasions. At both Olorgesailie and Olduvai Gorge evidence has been uncovered that whole herds of animals were sometimes killed and butchered by Acheulian hunters: a large antelope, springbok and giant baboon. Such activities could only have been carried out successfully as a result of close group cooperation and probably some advance planning. Evidence for the controlled use of fire has been claimed from the site of Kalambo Falls (where it may have been used to assist in the shaping and hardening of wood), from Nyabusora in Rwanda and from the Jos Plateau of Nigeria. As we have noted, some makers of the Acheulian industries moved into new territories where they were able to adapt themselves to, and flourish in, the new environments they encountered. The many different details of the assemblages recovered from different sites probably reflect both necessary local adaptations to the immediate environments and the cultural traditions and preferences of their makers. A general, overriding trend towards the production of more refined and smaller tools in the later Acheulian took place only very slowly.

It may be inferred from their stone artefacts alone that the makers of the Acheulian were probably different from the earlier hominid populations; and, indeed, fossil material recovered from Acheulian sites in East and North Africa belongs apparently exclusively to *Homo erectus*, a large brained, beetle-browed hominid whose general appearance and basic physical abilities may not have been very different from those of modern man.

Left: the earliest East African stone industries: (1, 2, 3) Oldowan; (4, 5) Karari; (6, 7, 8) KBS industry. Right: Late Acheulian artefacts from Kalambo Falls, Zambia: (1, 2) flake tools; (3) cleaver; (4) handaxe

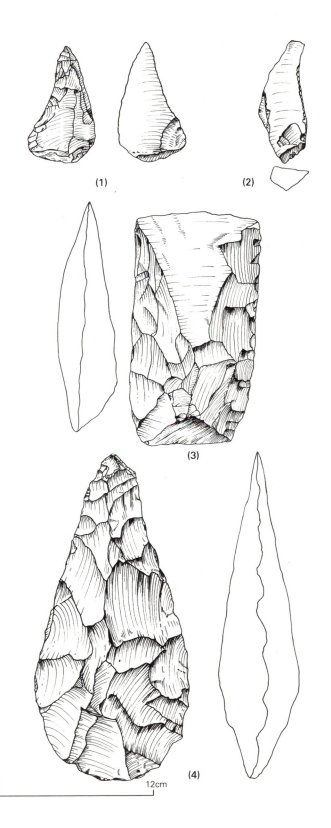

(1) (2)

(3)

(4)

0   12cm

Regional diversification

Following the relatively uncomplicated Acheulian comes a period, commonly referred to as the Middle Stone Age, in which there was a proliferation of local stone tool-making traditions whose relationships to one another are not as yet well understood. It should be stressed at this point that terms such as 'Early Stone Age', 'Middle Stone Age' or 'Late Stone Age' are used by prehistorians of Africa in a purely informal and provisional sense: they do not indicate finite periods of time but general technological stages. Our ignorance of the detailed prehistory of this period reflects in part the limited amount of research that has been done on Middle Stone Age sites: it is generally the earliest periods and the first beginnings, whether of tool-making or of agriculture, that tend to attract the most research interest; and few undisturbed Middle Stone Age sites with good faunal associations or other economic evidence have been discovered. This was a period that saw the invention of several new techniques of stone tool production and their adoption at different times and to different degrees by populations who were presumably also making the gradual transition from *Homo erectus* to *Homo sapiens*. The pattern of prehistory is one of alternating periods of diversification and consolidation; and the period between about 100 000 and 40 000 years ago seems to have been one of much diversification.

While bifacial handaxes and cleavers continued to be produced throughout the Acheulian period, they gradually became smaller and eventually tended to be less numerous in the total assemblages, their place being taken by new forms of bifacial core tools and by smaller implements made on retouched flakes. An emphasis on flake tools is characteristic of most Middle Stone Age traditions. Frequently the cores from which the flakes were struck were first carefully trimmed to a round or triangular shape so that the flakes struck from them required little additional retouching before they could be used as spear points or as cutting or scraping tools. So common are prepared cores and the flakes struck from them on post-Acheulian sites that, until recently, the presence of such artefacts was taken as an automatic indication of a Middle Stone Age date even in the absence of any corroborating evidence, while the presence of large bifaces was thought to be indicative of the Early Stone Age. These too facile assumptions have further obscured our knowledge of the period in question. Until more evidence is available, the Middle Stone Age must be considered on a regional basis.

In the forested regions of West and Central Africa and extending to the eastern shores of Lake Victoria and to some of the major river valleys of southern Africa heavy bifacially worked core tools continued to be produced. These included very large, roughly shaped triangular picks, forms similar to the older handaxes but often more crudely shaped except along their cutting edge, some large flat cleavers made on pre-shaped flakes 15–20cm long, and, in Central Africa, long narrow lanceolate and leaf-shaped points, some of which

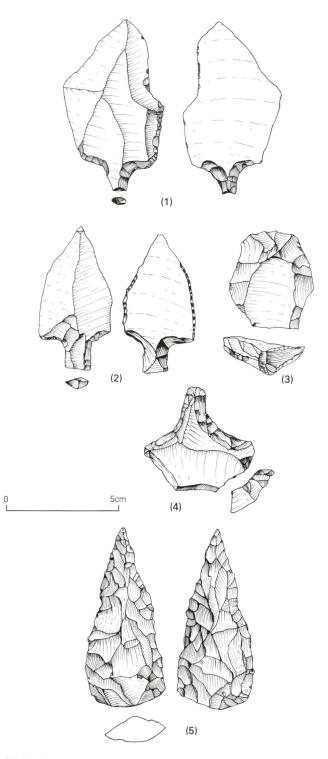

Middle Stone Age artefacts: (1, 2, 3, 4) North African Aterian; (5) Bambata industry from Zambia

are among the most beautiful stone tools produced at any period in African prehistory. These assemblages, which are generally undated, are named Sangoan after a type-site in south-western Uganda. Some extraordinarily large pre-formed flake tools have been found mainly in the Vaal and middle Zambezi valley basins in association with the more characteristic Sangoan picks and axes as well as with smaller flake tools. That they have no obvious successor in the archaeological record may indicate a merging or consolidation with the dominant Middle Stone Age tendency to produce much smaller pre-formed flake tools.

In the Congo and Angola areas a succession of industries has been recognized as developing on from the Sangoan. Here, fine bifacial axes and points continued to be produced with a steady diminution in size of the artefacts. The Lupemban successor to the Sangoan has been dated to more than 40000 years old, as at Mufo in Angola. It has been suggested, not unreasonably, that the retention of the larger bifacial tool forms in the Sangoan and its successor traditions represents a special adaptation to living in heavily wooded areas, but the nature of such an adaptation has yet to be demonstrated.

In most other parts of the African continent, the period from about 100000 years ago saw the general abandonment of large bifacially worked implements and a heavy emphasis on flake tools made to more or less standardized patterns. In parts of North Africa the local industries were not dissimilar to their contemporary European counterparts of the Middle Palaeolithic period. They include tools made on neat parallel-sided blades and many fine triangular points, often with their butt ends tanged to facilitate hafting. Such points are usually about 5–8 or 10cm long, too long to have served as arrow heads, and so must have served as spear points or knives. The very earliest of these North African industries have been dated to about 80000 years ago or somewhat less on the Moroccan coast; and the complex was widespread from Nubia to Senegal before 40000 years ago, including parts of the Sahara, which was then more habitable than it is now. There were many regional and temporal differences in the Middle Stone Age industries of North Africa. While tanged points are characteristic of the Aterian found in western North Africa, those forms are absent in the Nile Valley and Nubia. Levalloiso-Mousterian industries in the latter areas are, in fact, very similar to their European counterparts.

The site of Klasies River Mouth, a cave complex in the southern Cape of South Africa, is of particular interest because of the faunal remains preserved with a long sequence of Middle Stone Age industries that ended more than 38000 years ago. These include mainly specimens of antelope, especially eland, and the young of giant buffalo, also abundant shellfish remains and the bones of seals and penguins. A fairly specialized adaptation to a rich environment seems to be indicated with, not surprisingly, an emphasis on those species that were the easiest to hunt.

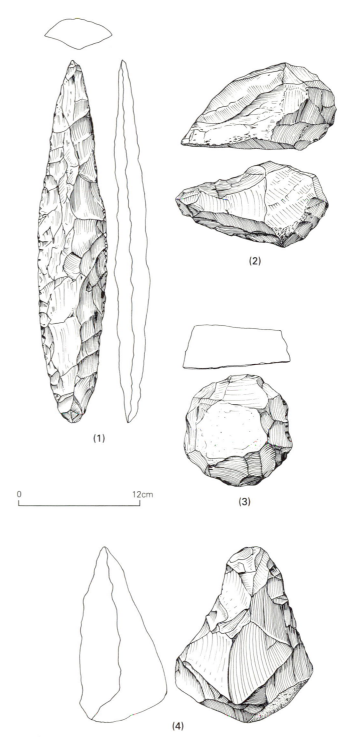

0 _____ 12cm

Sangoan and Lupemban artefacts: (1) lanceolate point; (2, 3) scrapers; (4) pick

MAJOR PRE-IRON AGE ARCHAEOLOGICAL SITES

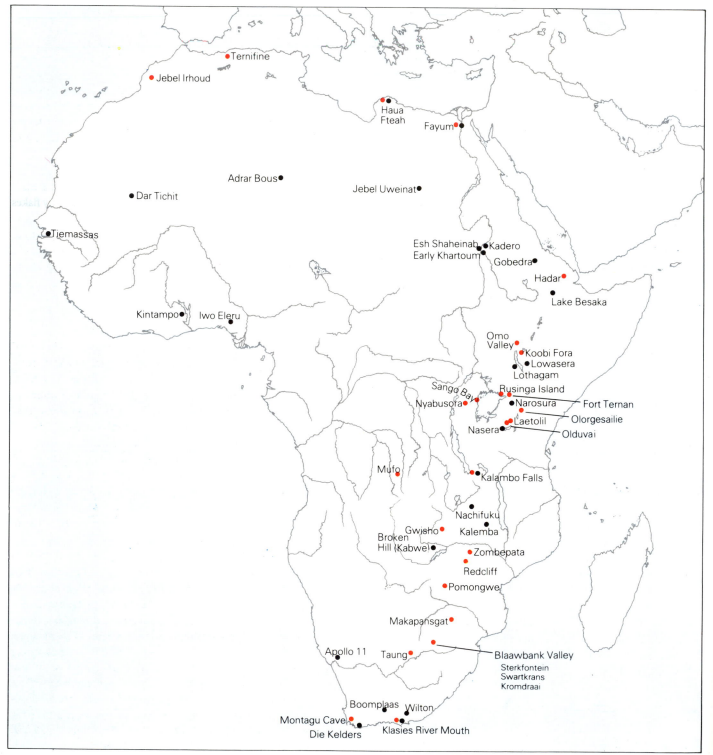

Ternifine

Jebel Irhoud

Haua Fteah

Fayum

Adrar Bous

Dar Tichit

Jebel Uweinat

Tiemassas

Esh Shaheinab
Early Khartoum
Kadero

Gobedra

Hadar

Lake Besaka

Kintampo
Iwo Eleru

Omo Valley

Koobi Fora
Lowasera
Lothagam

Sango Bay
Nyabusora
Rusinga Island
Narosura
Fort Ternan
Olorgesailie
Laetolil
Olduvai
Nasera

Mufo

Kalambo Falls

Nachifuku

Gwisho
Kalemba

Broken Hill (Kabwe)

Zombepata

Redcliff

Pomongwe

Makapansgat

Apollo 11
Taung
Blaawbank Valley
Sterkfontein
Swartkrans
Kromdraai

Boomplaas
Wilton

Montagu Cave
Die Kelders
Klasies River Mouth

Another site in the Cape, Montagu Cave, is also of interest in demonstrating the range of stone industries manufactured during the Middle Stone Age. From levels in a stratified sequence radiocarbon-dated to more than 50 000 years ago comes an assemblage in which the expected retouched flake tools are accompanied by other smaller specimens made on steeply retouched, or 'backed', blades and blade fragments in forms more characteristic of Late Stone Age industries. However, this new element does not persist in the prehistoric record, nor does it reappear for about another 15 000 years. Attempts have been made to associate the first occurrences of this new technique, scattered in time from about 50 000 to 10 000 years ago and in space from the Cape to the Horn, under the industrial terms Magosian (now discarded), Howieson's Poort or Evolved MSA, but this association seems unlikely.

In Zimbabwe and Zambia, Middle Stone Age assemblages have been described from both rock-shelter and open sites, although many of the latter are from unstratified and undatable contexts. Mention has already been made of the Lupemban industry dated to about 46 000 years ago at Kalambo Falls. Contemporary industries with a strong emphasis on retouched flake tools, termed Bambata, have been dated to between 37 000 and 42 000 years ago at the Zimbabwean shelter sites of Zombepata, Redcliff and Pomongwe. Similar material comes from an undated context, an ancient cave uncovered during copper mining operations at Broken Hill near Kabwe in Zambia. Also from the same site, and arguably associated with (or earlier than) the artefacts, comes a beautifully preserved fossil skull of a rather heavily muscled subspecies of modern man, *Homo sapiens rhodesiensis*.

Possibly the earliest *Homo sapiens* remains yet recovered in Africa come from the Omo River valley in southern Ethiopia and could be as old as 100 000 years. Examples of *Homo sapiens neanderthalensis* come from a number of sites in North Africa—Jebel Irhoud in Morocco, Haua Fteah in Cyrenaica, and others—in contexts about 40 000 to 80 000 years old. After this date the more heavily muscled and beetle-browed human types evolved into, or were replaced by, fully modern man, *Homo sapiens sapiens*.

Our knowledge of early *Homo sapiens* is based on such scanty evidence that we can do little more than conclude that the period was one of much diversity in human type as well as in stone-working traditions. The Broken Hill skull apparently belonged to an individual with somewhat neanderthaloid characteristics, but different enough to be separately designated; while the neanderthals of North Africa differ both from the Zambian specimen and, to some extent, from the neanderthals of Europe and the Near East. The differences are not great, but they are larger than are generally recognized between any present-day human populations.

Looking backwards, we see that during the first part of the Early Stone Age a certain amount of apparently aimless divergence took place in both human and cultural evolution. Several early hominids flourished in the same or similar environments and several indistinctly defined tool-making traditions have been recognized. Eventually the evolutionary momentum was seen to lie with *Homo erectus* and with the Acheulian cultural variants, other lines having apparently led to dead ends. A similar score, played at a much faster tempo, can be recognized in the Middle Stone Age. With the fading out of the Acheulian a new period of experimentation began with the appearance of large crude bifaces, very fine medium and small bifaces, extremely large and very small flake tools, and many flakes made to predetermined shapes. With time, two general trends exercised a dominant influence: the replacement of core by flake tools and a steady diminution in size of all stone artefacts. Industries in which these two trends are well expressed first appeared at very approximately the same time as, or somewhat after, *Homo sapiens sapiens* replaced his predecessors.

Microlithic industries

As has been shown above, Middle Stone Age developments in several regions included the first establishment of stone-working technologies based upon the production of steeply backed microliths. Industries with microlithic tools made their first appearance at markedly different times in different parts of Africa, from far back in the Upper Pleistocene on the southern coast to only about 3000 years ago in parts of the Karroo and the Kalahari fringelands. At one time these microlithic industries were thought to define a distinct cultural phase whenever they occurred in Africa and to be attributable to a distinct period of time within the last few thousand years. Both the cultural phase and the time period were called the Late Stone Age. More recent research has now discredited this facile equation of industrial technique, culture and temporal period.

In several areas of Africa where there is sufficient environmental evidence, the initial appearance of microlithic techniques has been shown to have taken place at times when there was a local shift from more open to more densely wooded vegetation patterns. Accompanying this was a shift from the hunting of the larger animals of the open plains to the smaller woodland species. The changing environmental circumstances required new hunting techniques; and gradually the use of the bow with a microlith-tipped arrow and various small tools came to replace the larger stone implements of the Middle Stone Age. In parts of South Africa microlithic technologies appear to have developed on at least two separate occasions: firstly during the well watered high sea-level phase of the last interglacial, and again during the final millennia of the Pleistocene.

KEY

●	Early Stone Age sites	●	Later Stone Age sites

There is now little doubt that the development of local microlithic industries was largely the result of parallel indigenous developments, not the result of diffusion from a single centre. This conclusion is substantiated by several long, dated sequences of stratified archaeological deposits which span the periods that saw the inception of microlithic technologies in their respective areas. These sites include the Haua Fteah in Libya, Nasera in northern Tanzania, Kalemba in eastern Zambia, Apollo 11 in Namibia, and Klasies River Mouth on the Cape coast of South Africa.

Excluding those of the last interglacial in South Africa, the earliest fully microlithic industries of sub-Saharan Africa are those which occur in the highlands of the eastern half of the subcontinent, stretching from Lake Victoria and southern Kenya to northern and eastern Zambia. Tiny, pointed, backed bladelets and varied stone scrapers are the characteristic tool types of these industries. Stones with holes bored in them are found in Zambian deposits, but not at sites further to the north. The larger bored-stones resemble objects which, in later periods, are known to have been used as weights for digging-sticks, while other examples are much smaller and probably served other functions. This early microlithic industry, known in Zambia as 'Nachikufan I', made its appearance about 17 000 BC and continued with little significant change for about 7000 or 8000 years.

Subsequently, microlithic industries became virtually ubiquitous in eastern and southern Africa. Exceptional areas included the Kalahari, which was apparently uninhabited until only a few thousand years ago, and the upper Zambezi valley, where the open grassy plains allowed a late persistence of Middle Stone Age industrial techniques. Elsewhere, most of the microlithic industries were characterized by geometrical backed forms, chiefly lunates, which replaced the single-pointed types of Nachikufan I and its counterparts. These industries show considerable regional variation,

the significance of which is not yet apparent. In some local industries, such as those of the southern Cape coast, small convex scrapers far outnumber the backed microliths; and when a number of these Late Stone Age assemblages are compared, a great range in the frequencies of specific tool types can be seen. Despite this variability, there has been a tendency among archaeologists to subsume most of these industries under the generic name 'Wilton', after a site near Alicedale in the eastern Cape. This has helped to obscure the very real differences between most of the assemblages so designated, while exaggerating the idiosyncrasy of those, such as the later Nachikufan phases of northern Zambia and the Kaposwa from the site of Kalambo Falls, which have been given different names. It now appears that temporal, economic, cultural and regional factors all influenced the composition of individual tool kits. At sites with a stratified sequence of microlithic industries, there has been noted a steady decrease in artefact size with the passage of time, the later assemblages having smaller tools than the earlier.

A large proportion of the dated archaeological occurrences of this period in eastern and southern Africa are from cave or rock-shelter sites where little has been preserved apart from the stone artefacts and, on occasions, associated faunal remains. Only rarely has vegetable matter survived, leading to an unbalanced representation of the tool kits and diet of the Late Stone Age people. Particular importance therefore attaches to the dry cave deposits of southernmost Africa and to the few waterlogged sites, such as those at Gwisho hot springs in southern Zambia, where there has been an excellent preservation of organic materials. From these sites, it may be demonstrated that, at least in some areas, wood was used for bows, arrows and link-shafts, digging-sticks, pegs and wedges, and bark for trays. Bags and clothing were made of sewn leather. Leaves were used as a wrapping material for valuables, while grass and soft undergrowth were collected for use as bedding. Vegetable foods were varied and often assumed considerable importance in the total diet, as they do among most modern hunter/gatherer groups. Remains of plant foods have also provided important information concerning the seasonality of settlements, confirming the often less detailed evidence of the faunal remains. In the south-western Cape, for example, it now seems that some hunter/gatherer groups moved regularly between their coastal winter settlements and summer haunts further inland.

On the fringes of the equatorial forest a local, largely microlithic, industry, known as the Tshitolian, gradually developed from the preceding Lupemban tradition. The microlithic component of its variants appears to have been more strongly attested in the forested river valleys than it was in apparently contemporaneous assemblages recovered from the more open savanna. The chronology of these processes remains poorly understood, but the Tshitolian industries were apparently well developed by about 8000 BC. During the preceding millennia the forest had gradually expanded from its

Microlithic tool types

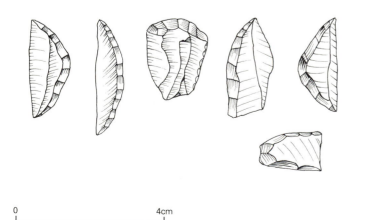

0   4cm

shrunken late Pleistocene confines until it covered an area considerably greater than it does today.

Comparable developments almost certainly took place in West Africa. Here, however, full understanding is hampered by the very incomplete coverage of archaeological research. Most Late Stone Age occurrences are isolated and undated: virtually none has well preserved and described organic materials in association with the stone industries. One of the very few long dated sequences is that at Iwo Eleru in the forest of south-western Nigeria. Here, a fully microlithic industry was established at least as early as 10 000 BC. Unlike the contemporary industries from south-central Africa, ground stone axes do not appear in the Iwo Eleru succession until a much later date, as will be shown below. In the far west, as at Tiemassas in southern Senegal, a local development of a microlithic industry from a Middle Stone Age predecessor may also be discerned. In several other regions of West Africa – in parts of eastern Nigeria, for example, and on the Futa Jalon plateau of Guinea – the advent of microlithic technology appears to have taken place considerably later, in some cases not until after the beginnings of West African pottery manufacture about the 4th millennium BC. Especially in some of these non-microlithic industries, crudely flaked hoe-like implements are a prominent feature. These may indicate a strong reliance upon tuberous plant foods and, possibly, the early beginnings of yam cultivation.

In parts of North Africa a markedly contrasting situation prevailed. At Haua Fteah, for example, the local Middle Stone Age Levalloiso-Mousterian industry was abruptly replaced in about 38 000 BC by a blade industry, the Dabban, of a type known in Europe and the Near East as Upper Palaeolithic. Related industries are known in parts of the Nile Valley, where, however, they did not become common until about 15 000 BC. By this time, as in Nubia, the Nile Valley industries were predominantly microlithic. They show much local variation even over short distances; and this feature appears to reflect a range of micro-environments, exploitation patterns, seasonal settlement and territoriality. In Cyrenaica, the Dabban at Haua Fteah was replaced about 14 000 BC by a fully microlithic industry, the Ibero-Maurusian, which is also found in the Maghrib further to the west. About the 7th millennium BC the Ibero-Maurusian in turn was replaced by industries of the Capsian complex. Any direct connection between the North African Capsian and the much earlier blade industries of Ethiopia and the Horn must be regarded as unlikely. In the coastal areas of Algeria and Tunisia, Capsian industries are found on large shell middens: elsewhere intensive hunting and gathering practices are attested which continued until the development of food production.

The beginning of permanent settlement

During the period between the 9th and the 3rd millennia BC the upper Nile Valley and the southern Sahara saw a major rise in the water levels in rivers and lakes. The exact reasons for this remain imperfectly understood: greater rainfall and increased cloud cover, lower evaporation rate and denser vegetation may have been linked with the retreat of the ice sheets of the last glaciation and with the associated rise in sea level. Whatever their cause, these high lake levels had a major effect on the physical environment of an area which is now largely desert or semi-desert. The water of Lake Turkana then stood 80m above its present level and maintained an outflow channel to the Nile. Lake Chad covered an area much greater than that of the present Lake Victoria, while rivers that now flow for only a few days in a year were probably then perennial.

The Late Stone Age people who lived in the vicinity of these rivers and lakes were able to exploit enormously rich sources of food, mainly fish, obtainable with very little expenditure of effort. This enabled them to establish permanent or semi-permanent settlements, often on a larger scale than had been possible for their hunter/gatherer predecessors. Despite the wide dispersal of these lakeside fishing settlements, from Lake Turkana in the east to the inland Niger delta in the west, some items of the fisherfolk's material culture were remarkably uniform. Fish were caught by means of harpoons with characteristic barbed bone heads. Pottery made its first local appearance at this time, and may well have been an independent invention. It was decorated with designs of parallel wavy lines, often apparently executed by dragging a catfish spine across the damp clay. On the other hand, the chipped stone industries display considerable variations, which appear to be rooted in distinct local traditions traceable to the period before the development of the fishing adaptation. It is thus most satisfactory to regard these sites as representing a common adaptation, with many shared features, to a common economic opportunity, rather than to consider them as belonging to a single uniform culture. One of the most intensively investigated sites is that known as Early Khartoum, within the modern Khartoum conurbation. Other noteworthy occurrences are at Adrar Bous in Niger and at Lothagam and Lowasera beside Lake Turkana. As will be shown below, the settled life-style that such sites afforded eventually proved to be of major importance for the beginnings of African food production.

The emergence of recent African populations

It is in the context of these regional Late Stone Age industries that we can make our first tentative correlations between communities represented in the African archaeological record and the ancestors of the present day populations. In North Africa no human skeletal remains have yet been found in association with a Dabban industry. Comparable technology in Europe, however, seems almost always to have been the work of *Homo sapiens sapiens*. Ibero-Maurusian skeletons are, by contrast, plentiful and belong to a heavily built population known as Mechta-Afalou. Though there can be no doubt about its attribution to *Homo sapiens sapiens*, it has been plausibly suggested that it represents a local North African derivative from a neanderthaloid ancestor. By contrast, many of the skeletal remains recovered from Capsian sites are more slender and lightly built. They are generally designated 'proto-Mediterranean'.

In the West African forest zone, the evidence from Iwo Eleru suggests that by the time of the earliest microlithic industries a recognizably negroid population had already emerged. Generalized negroid characteristics have also been recognized with varying degrees of confidence in skeletal remains from the northern savanna and as far to the east as Early Khartoum. In East Africa the picture is less clear. Published references to the presence of caucasoids have been widely misinterpreted, but should be understood as referring to peoples akin to the modern Somali. Recent research emphasizes the negroid affinities of the skeletal characteristics of several early populations in this region as far back as the 16th millennium BC. Skeletons displaying negroid affinities also occur associated with microlithic industries at least as far south as the Zambezi, but others have been described as being predominantly khoisanoid* types. These become more frequent with increasing distance to the south. Interpretation of this admittedly very fragmentary evidence is rendered even more difficult by the fact that the modern reference populations on which these attributions are based are the result of thousands of years of interaction between precisely those groups that we are attempting to distinguish. All that may safely be said of the physical affinities of the peoples of eastern and southern Africa during the last ten millennia BC is that with the passage of time populations that more closely resemble those of the modern inhabitants of Africa may be discerned: khoisanoid, negroid and north-east African caucasoid.

Rock art

Most of the surviving rock art of Africa is attributable to the early food producing communities, discussed below. In most regions, however, the earliest extant examples seem to have been the work of the makers of the microlithic industries. There are no good reasons for assuming that these represent the first examples produced: it is more likely that the earliest manifestations of rock art have not survived on the exposed rock faces and in the shallow shelters where they had been painted or engraved. The one firm indication of the great antiquity of African rock art comes from the Apollo 11 cave in southern Namibia, where paintings occur in contexts dated to as far back as 40 000 years ago.

In North Africa and the Sahara several long stylistic sequences of rock paintings and engravings have been identified, those of Tassili and Jebel Uweinat being particularly well known. The earliest series depicts exclusively wild animals and may be held to predate the

Rock painting at Silozwane Cave, Matopo Hills, Zimbabwe

arrival of the domestic species which are shown in the later series. In West Africa, Ethiopia and the Horn it is unlikely that any of the now extant art predates the local beginning of food production.

Further south, however, in the regions where stone-tool-using hunter/gatherers continued in occupation until the advent of the Iron Age* communities, the rock-shelters of central Tanzania contain an extensive range of paintings which are almost certainly attributable to the former group. In Zambia pre-Iron Age rock art is rare, but south of the Zambezi there are major concentrations of such paintings and engravings. In Zimbabwe the sequence evidently spans the beginning of the Iron Age and confirms the stratigraphic indications that hunter/gatherer groups survived long after the arrival of the Iron Age immigrants. Much of the surviving rock art in southern Africa, especially the paintings of the Cape, highland Natal and Lesotho, lies outside the areas that were settled by Iron Age peoples, and here it has proved possible to evaluate this art in the light of recorded beliefs of the San and related indigenous peoples, providing an invaluable insight into its purpose and meanings. These paintings may be seen as the final flowering of an artistic tradition that formerly extended as far north as modern Tanzania.

Food production

None of the African prehistoric societies described in the preceding sections practised any form of food production. Among these peoples a diet of wild vegetables was supplemented by meat and fish derived from species over whose breeding and movement men exercised almost no deliberate control. For many years prehistorians have emphasized the importance of the so-called food producing, or 'neolithic', revolution. This has been seen as one of the greatest single steps in the course of human social and economic evolution.

Specialization in crafts and in less materially productive activities has been seen as a result of food production and the storage of food surpluses. So too, population growth, permanent settlements, and the development of elaborate sanctions to support increasingly complex norms of social behaviour have been considered as dependent upon the attainment of a food producing economy.

While this traditional view holds good in broad outline in the African context, it represents a considerable over-simplification. Recent studies of the few remaining non-food producing peoples of Africa – the hunters and gatherers* – has amply shown that life for them is not an unremitting search for food; and that, except in particularly bad years, they have more time to devote to the non-productive arts – music, dance and social intercourse – than do their agricultural neighbours.

Also, the development or adoption of techniques of food production can no longer be considered as a revolutionary event. Rather, it was a gradual process whose polar extremes are defined by the terms 'wild' and 'domestic'. Nowhere are the intermediate possibilities of semi-domestication more clearly apparent today than in Africa. In the forest fringes of West Africa, for example, the oil palm tree (Elaeis guineensis) is owned and protected, but is rarely planted. Along the southern margin of the Sahara certain species of wild cereals are preserved for intensive exploitation as a food resource in times of famine; and a similar situation may have prevailed in the Nubian Nile Valley between 15 000 and 10 000 BC. In Ancient Egypt* it seems that herds of wild antelope were enclosed and some of the males perhaps castrated.

Examples such as these make it apparent that various stages in the processes of plant and animal domestication may have taken place at many times and in many places. Initially, far more species were involved than retained prominence in the major farming societies of the recent past. The eventual prevalence of a restricted range of domesticated species has imparted a misleadingly simple appearance to the processes that were involved. These points are directly relevant to the current debate concerning the extent to which food production in Africa may have been the result of indigenous innovation rather than a response to external stimuli.

The classic view is that both plant and animal domestication throughout Africa, Europe and Western Asia are derived from the original development of these techniques in the Near East about 10 000 years ago. Certainly such important crops as wheat and barley were first cultivated in the Near East, and sheep and goats, and perhaps cattle, were first domesticated there. However, the total picture is complex.

The contribution of the domesticated animals of Near Eastern origin to the food producing economies of Africa has been very great. Local wild North African bovids and sheep and goats may not themselves have been domesticated, but they must have interbred and contributed genetically to the domestic herds. The donkey, however, was probably first domesticated in north-eastern Africa, as was the cat, although the latter's direct economic importance has been negligible. The camel is a much more recent introduction from Asia. South of the Sahara possible wild prototypes for any of the domesticated animals are completely unknown, so the ancestors of all the economically significant domesticated animals must have been introduced to the subcontinent from some external source or sources.

PROBABLE AREAS OF DOMESTICATION OF SELECTED AFRICAN CROPS

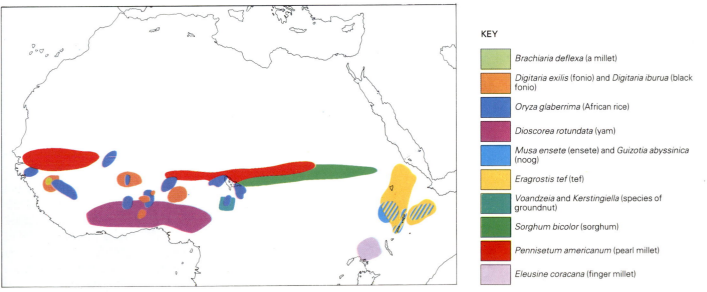

KEY

Brachiaria deflexa (a millet)

Digitaria exilis (fonio) and Digitaria iburua (black fonio)

Oryza glaberrima (African rice)

Dioscorea rotundata (yam)

Musa ensete (ensete) and Guizotia abyssinica (noog)

Eragrostis tef (tef)

Voandzeia and Kerstingiella (species of groundnut)

Sorghum bicolor (sorghum)

Pennisetum americanum (pearl millet)

Eleusine coracana (finger millet)

Cultivated plants in Africa present a markedly different picture. Wheat and barley must have been introduced directly or indirectly from the Near East, as there is no evidence for any African prototypes for these grains. These two cereals have been of major economic importance only in parts of North Africa, the Nile Valley, and the Ethiopian highlands. South of the Sahara, if we discount crops such as maize and cassava which were introduced from the New World within the past five centuries, most of the significant cultivated plants are of indigenous species. While it may perhaps be argued that the people who were responsible for these developments might have been acquainted with the idea of plant cultivation as practised in more northerly regions, there can be little reasonable doubt that sub-Saharan agriculture was an essentially indigenous development or series of developments.

In Egypt the earliest positive archaeological evidence for food production comes from the Fayum, where it is dated to the 5th millennium BC. In the context of the known prehistory of the eastern Mediterranean as a whole this is a surprisingly late date, but it must be pointed out that the immediate precursors of the Fayum people have not yet been recognized in the archaeological record. There is thus little justification for regarding the Fayum date as referring to the inception of farming in Egypt. The Egyptian farmers cultivated barley and emmer wheat, the grains of which were stored in basket silos. Their pottery and flaked stone industry show no very strong affinity to contemporary material from the Near East.

Further to the west, at Haua Fteah in Cyrenaica, the commencement of animal domestication may be placed at about the beginning of the 5th millennium BC. It appears possible that cereal agriculture was not adopted in this region or further west in North Africa until significantly later times. In Algeria and adjacent parts of north-western Africa, on the other hand, bones of domestic cattle are attested by the late 7th millennium – appreciably earlier than any comparable evidence yet reported from Egypt. It may be that there were earlier herdsmen in the lower Nile Valley whose archaeological remains have not been discovered. However, the possibility remains that the first Algerian domestic cattle were descended not from their Near Eastern counterparts, but from the indigenous short-horned wild cattle of north-western Africa. Detailed archaeological and osteological studies may be expected to throw further light on this problem.

There is abundant evidence that much of the territory that now comprises the Sahara Desert was formerly rich grazing country. Rock paintings, probably dating from between the 7th and the 3rd millennia BC, depict wild animals that now are found only in more southerly, better-watered areas, as well as domestic cattle and occasional small livestock. In the southern Sahara and the Sudanese Nile Valley were located the lake-shore and riverside settlements of the harpoon-fisherfolk, described above. By late in the 5th millennium BC some of these people had acquired domestic cattle. This was at about the same time as a major fall in lake levels, as is attested particularly clearly at Adrar Bous, on the edge of the Tenere desert in north-eastern Niger. The available radiocarbon dates seem to indicate a southward spread of cattle from their early centre in Algeria, and it is reasonable to link this with the desiccation of the Sahara which set in at this time.

The 4th millennium BC also saw the beginnings of food production in the valley of the middle Nile. At the site of Esh Shaheinab, about 50km north of Khartoum, artefacts indicate a tradition which was a continuation of that found at Early Khartoum. However, the fish-based economy here was supplemented by the herding of goats and possibly also sheep. From about the same period of time and general area, but further from the Nile, is the recently investigated site at Kadero. Here, about 90 per cent of the recovered animal bones are of domesticated species, including cattle, and there is also evidence of cereal agriculture. Some form of mobile settlement pattern, perhaps seasonal transhumance, may have been practised. Both the style of pottery found at these sites and the evidence of a trade in the fine stones used for the manufacture of beads indicate connections with the southern Sahara. Further to the east, related archaeological sites have been reported from the valley of the Atbara near the foot of the Ethiopian highlands.

Studies of the development of African agriculture are limited by the scarcity of incontestable evidence of domesticated plant foods. Many of the artefacts used in agricultural production and in vegetable food preparation may be used as well for wild as for domesticated crops. This fact, combined with the superior preservation of bone as compared with vegetable matter, has tended to cause archaeologists to overemphasize the importance of animal foods in prehistoric societies both before and after the advent of food production.

Current views on the initial cultivation of the indigenous African crops must, in the absence of much hard evidence, be based largely on botanical arguments such as the distribution of wild prototypes of the early crops, and on environmental fluctuations of the last several thousand years. The map on page 71 shows the probable homelands of many of the most important African food crops. Sorghum and most millets were probably first cultivated in the savanna country between the Senegal and the confluence of the Blue and White Niles. Finger millet seems to have been first cultivated in the Ethiopian highlands, or possibly in what is now northern Uganda. Teff, a cereal crop now only grown on a significant scale in Ethiopia, is undoubtedly indigenous to that region, as is the banana-like ensete of southern Ethiopia. The other main centre of early African plant domestication was West Africa, where fonio millet, legumes (such as Bambara and Hausa 'groundnuts'), guinea rice and the African species of yam must first have been domesticated.

South of the Sahara the beginnings of plant cultivation are

associated with the gradual desiccation of the 5th, 4th and 3rd millennia BC, and with the accompanying changes in human settlement patterns. The territory where many of the African crops were first cultivated is the southern part of the area occupied by the Late Stone Age fisherfolk, some of whom had already become herders of domestic animals. Their settled or semi-settled life-style would have facilitated the eventual adoption of agriculture, which environmental changes may have necessitated. As the high water levels receded and fish populations decreased desertification would have set in, perhaps exacerbated by overgrazing and the removal of bush in the areas of densest settlement. Southward movement of peoples and herds from the less hospitable parts of the Sahara may have greatly increased population densities in some areas and served as a stimulus for the more extensive exploitation and eventual cultivation of some vegetable foods. Whether such developments were completely independent of any knowledge of cereal cultivation on the Near Eastern pattern is a question which cannot yet be answered.

By about the 4th millennium BC pottery and ground stone artefacts began to appear as components of Late Stone Age industries in several areas of West Africa. The basic features of the industries are essentially continuous with those of earlier times in the same region, while the innovations are best regarded as introductions from the north. The sites of Iwo Eleru in the forest of south-western Nigeria, and Kintampo in Ghana are illustrative of these cultures. Around Kintampo dwarf cattle and small livestock were introduced during the 2nd millennium BC. Stone grater-like objects recovered from the deposits may have been used in the preparation of yams, but this has not been convincingly demonstrated. Yam cultivation, which is of great economic importance in parts of West Africa, and which may be a practice of considerable antiquity, is effectively invisible in the archaeological record.

Viewing West Africa as a whole, it is clear that the adoption of food production techniques was a gradual process, which took place at different times in different areas. The beginning of cereal cultivation is best illustrated at Dar Tichit in southern Mauritania, where, from the mid-2nd millennium BC onwards, plant exploitation passed rapidly through stages characterized by the intensive collection of a wide range of grasses to the near-exclusive cultivation of bulrush millet.

On the opposite side of the continent, the highlands of Ethiopia were another early centre of food production, although direct archaeological evidence for this is still scarce. The many varieties of wheat and barley that grow here indicate that their cultivation has a considerable local antiquity in this the most southerly region of Africa where they were grown in pre-colonial times. Archaeological remains of teff have not yet been recognized in Ethiopia, but traces of it occur in South Yemen dated to early in the last millennium BC.

Considerably earlier, possibly as old as 3000 BC, are seeds of cultivated finger millet from Gobedra rock-shelter near Aksum. They occur at the stage in a Late Stone Age sequence at which pottery also occurs for the first time. Evidence for the presence of camels at this time, if correctly associated, is more problematic but may indicate that contacts across the southern Red Sea had already begun at this early period. Linguistic evidence suggests that the use of the plough in cereal cultivation may predate the arrival of Semitic-speakers in the mid-1st millennium BC. The ensete-based planting economy of the southern Ethiopian highlands may be of comparable antiquity. The date at which cattle were first herded in Ethiopia also remains unknown, but it was certainly earlier than the mid-2nd millennium BC, when cattle are attested archaeologically at Lake Besaka, west of Harar, and at Gobedra. Ancient Egyptian records also indicate the presence of cattle and of cultivated cereals around the southern end of the Red Sea at this period.

To the south, in Kenya, there is much more archaeological evidence from which to reconstruct a picture of the inception of plant and animal domestication. On the northern plains cattle were herded as early as the mid-3rd millennium BC by people who used pottery and stone bowls. The descendants of the earlier harpoon fisherfolk continued their traditional ways of life along the margins of the shrinking lakes for some centuries after the advent of pastoralism. It may not have been until a thousand or more years later that domestic stock were first herded in the Rift Valley highlands of southern Kenya and northern Tanzania. In this limited area a complex of Late Stone Age pastoral traditions is now recognized. Wild species dominate the faunal assemblages recovered from some sites, while cattle or small stock are more frequent at others. Substantial open air settlements, such as Narosura in southern Kenya, have been located; and rock-shelters were also occupied. Both mass cremation burials and individual interments under piled stone cairns have been located. It is not yet known whether any of these early East African pastoral communities practised any form of plant cultivation. Arguments have been advanced to link these groups with early speakers of Cushitic and Nilotic languages. Some of these pastoralists appear to have remained in control of the central Rift Valley highlands at least until the middle of the 1st millennium AD, long after the regions to the east and west had been settled by Bantu-speaking Early Iron Age populations.

So far, this account of early African food production has been restricted to the regions north of the Equator. The general pattern of development has been the gradual adoption and spread of the techniques of pastoralism and agriculture; not always concurrently. In most cases, the first farmers in any particular region were native inhabitants of that area. In the more southerly latitudes, on the other hand, a markedly contrasting situation prevailed. The advent of food production in the south seems to have been brought about by means of a major population movement, which was responsible for introducing Early Iron Age culture through the enormous region of Africa that has been occupied by speakers of Bantu★ languages within the last thousand years. Here it is sufficient to point out that techniques of metallurgy, pottery manufacture, crop cultivation and the herding of domestic animals seem to have been introduced throughout this area (where they were previously unknown) during the millennium which followed 500 BC.

In southernmost and south-western Africa the stone-tool-using folk were not displaced or absorbed, as were their counterparts elsewhere, by the Early Iron Age newcomers. It may have been that the Bantu-speakers could not adapt their agriculture to the more arid climate or that it was not worth their while to do so. However, despite the failure of the Bantu-speakers to spread into the extreme south-west of the continent, pottery and domestic sheep are attested on the south and south-western Cape coasts and in some inland regions from around the beginning of the Christian era. Cattle may be almost as early as sheep in these areas, but this has yet to be confirmed. Key sites of this period are Boomplaas in the Cape Folded Mountains, and Die Kelders on the coast. While it is possible that the Cape coastal pottery, which shows no clear affinity to any known Iron Age wares, could have been a local invention, the same cannot be true of the domestic stock, in the absence of any local wild prototypes. Most probably the animals were descended from herds kept by Early Iron Age folk in what is now Angola. The adoption of livestock in the Cape further complicated a settlement pattern which was based upon seasonal movement between inland regions where hunting and collecting were practised, and the coast where shellfish provided the basis for subsistence. Thus were begun the life-styles which were continued by the Khoisan inhabitants of the Cape until the time of European settlement.

Throughout the vast span of human prehistory in Africa many forces have been at work, some few leaving clear traces in the archaeological record, some guessed at, and others forever unknown. Food resources, climate, topography and all other features of the natural environment have had a part to play. Cultural factors have been even more important. Once our ancestors began to walk upright and to fashion tools new opportunities became open to them. So too, the sharing of knowledge made possible by language, new technical skills and inventions, and new social patterns have all shaped and faciliatated man's evolutionary progress. To a very large extent, man's destiny has been shaped in Africa; and it has been shaped by himself.

D. W. P. & L. P.

Late Stone Age artefacts: (1, 2, 3) potsherd and bone harpoon heads from Early Khartoum, Sudan; (4, 5, 6, 7) stone artefacts, stone bowl and pottery vessel from Narosura, a site of Late Stone Age pastoralists in southern Kenya

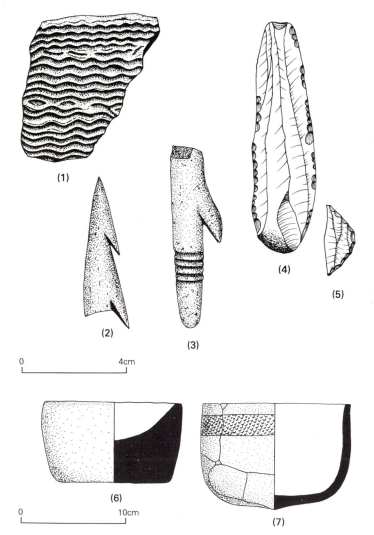

(1)

(2)

(3)

(4)

(5)

0   4cm

(6)

(7)

0   10cm

Languages

Although no one is certain of the precise number of languages spoken today in Africa, scholars are in general agreement that they exceed 1000 and that Professor J.H. Greenberg's classification of the languages of Africa into four *phyla* (sing. *phylum*, major language families) is probably the most convenient framework within which any brief description can be written. That is not to say that Greenberg's classification is accepted totally by all scholars – there is, for example, considerable controversy about some of his sub-classifications within the four *phyla* – but it is widely used by Africanists and there is little controversy about the four *phyla* themselves or, at the lowest level, about the groupings of closely related languages. In the following paragraphs an outline of Greenberg's classification is given, taking each *phylum* in turn, and the more significant areas of controversy are indicated.

Afro-Asiatic

Afro-Asiatic covers North Africa, much of the Sahara, and the Horn of Africa. Though so wide in geographical spread it is an area in parts only thinly populated. It derives its name from its inclusion of languages both from Africa and the Middle East. This *phylum* includes languages such as *Ancient Egyptian* and *Berber* which used to be referred to as Hamitic. This latter term is no longer accepted as having any linguistic validity, though some scholars still use the term Hamito-Semitic as synonymous with Afro-Asiatic. The *phylum* is divided into five language families.

SEMITIC includes all the Semitic languages, e.g. *Hebrew* spoken outside Africa; *Arabic* spoken outside Africa and throughout northern Africa and as far south as Mauritania and Kenya; *Amharic*, *Tigré* and *Tigrinya* of Ethiopia.

BERBER consists of the *Berber* languages spoken in Mauritania, Morocco, Algeria, Mali, Niger, and in small pockets across northern Africa, e.g. *Tamasheq* and *Zenati*.

CUSHITIC, whose languages are spoken mostly in the Horn of Africa and parts of the western edge of the Red Sea, is subdivided into five: Northern Cushitic, e.g. *Bedauye* of Sudan; Central Cushitic, e.g. *Kemant* of Ethiopia; Eastern Cushitic, e.g. *Somali* of Somalia, Djibouti, Ethiopia and Kenya; Western Cushitic (some scholars prefer to group Western Cushitic under the term Omotic), e.g. *Gofa* of Ethiopia; and Southern Cushitic, e.g. *Iraqw* and *Mbugu* of Tanzania.

ANCIENT EGYPTIAN (extinct but has been studied from written records).

CHADIC, which takes its name from Lake Chad, includes *Hausa*, indigenous to Nigeria and Niger, but spoken widely as a trading *lingua franca* from Ghana to Sudan, *Margi* of Nigeria, the lakeside languages of *Buduma*, *Affade*, *Ngizim* and *Kuri*, and languages spoken on the Jos Plateau of Nigeria such as *Ron*, *Angas* and *Bachama*.

Nilo-Saharan

Nilo-Saharan is possibly the most controversial of the *phyla*, partly because so little work has been done on most of its languages. It is also the most scattered geographically. It covers much of eastern Sahara, the upper Nile valley and stretches down south-east of Lake Victoria and has scattered pockets within the main Afro-Asiatic area. It is divided into six language families.

SONGHAI described by some as a single language with several dialects, e.g. *Dendi* of Niger, Benin and Nigeria and *Djerma* (or *Zarma*) of

Niger and Nigeria. It is found in two areas along the valley of the middle Niger and in small pockets further north.

SAHARAN covers the main part of the eastern Saharan area and includes such languages as *Kanuri* of Niger, Nigeria, Chad and Cameroon, *Kanembu* of Niger, *Daza* of Niger and Chad, and *Zaghawa* of Chad and Sudan.

MABAN lies south-east of Saharan and includes *Runga* of Chad and the Central African Republic, *Karanga* of Chad, and *Masalit* of Chad and Sudan.

FUR is a single language spoken in the Darfur province of Sudan.

CHARI-NILE is subdivided into four: Eastern Sudanic, subdivided again, includes the Western Nilotic languages e.g. *Dinka* and *Luo*, and Eastern Nilotic, e.g. *Maasai* of Kenya and Tanzania and *Teso* of Uganda, as well as the *Nubian* languages of Sudan and Upper Egypt. Western and Eastern Nilotic are sometimes labelled Nilotic and Paranilotic respectively. Central Sudanic, subdivided again, includes *Bongo* of Sudan, the *Sara* languages of Chad and the Central African Republic, and *Lugbara* and *Mangbetu* of Zaire and Uganda. *Kunama* is a single language spoken in Ethiopia. *Berta* is a single language spoken on either side of the Sudan-Ethiopia border.

Niger-Kordofanian

Greenberg's third *phylum* is Niger-Kordofanian, which covers two distinct but related families: Kordofanian and Niger-Congo.

Kordofanian

Kordofanian covers only a small area in the Nuba Hills of the Kordofan region of Sudan and is subdivided into five language families, including such languages as *Koalib*, *Tegali*, *Talodi*, *Tumtum* and *Katla*.

Niger-Congo

By contrast with Kordofanian, Niger-Congo covers most of the central, largely equatorial belt across Africa and much of southern Africa, and its languages are spoken by more than half the population of the continent. It consists of six language families.

WEST ATLANTIC, the most westerly, is subdivided into: Northern West Atlantic, e.g. *Wolof* and *Dyola* of Senegal, Gambia and Guinea, *Biafada* of Guinea-Bissau, and *Fula*, which has spread from Senegal north to Mauritania and east to Sudan; and Southern West Atlantic, e.g. *Landuma* of Guinea, *Temne* of Sierra Leone, *Limba* of Sierra Leone and Guinea, *Kissi* of Guinea, Sierra Leone and Liberia, and *Gola* of Liberia.

MANDE (the name originally referred to the homeland of the people speaking a language known as *Malinke* or *Maninka*) moving eastward from West Atlantic, is subdivided into: Western Mande, e.g. the Manding languages spoken from Senegal to Ghana, e.g. *Bambara*, *Maninka* and *Vai*, *Susu* of Guinea, *Soninke* of Senegal and Mali,

MAJOR LANGUAGES

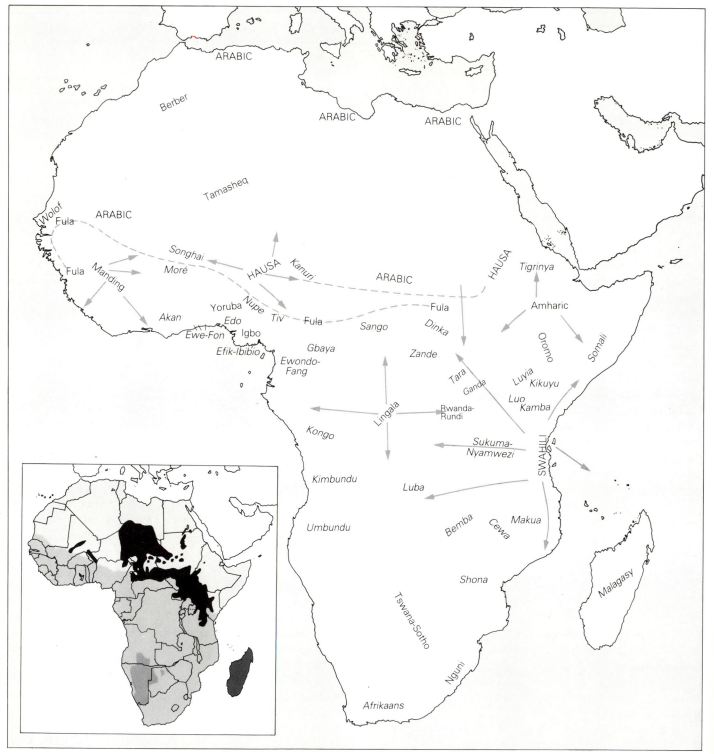

Mende of Sierra Leone, *Kpelle* of Liberia and *Sya* of Mali and Upper Volta; and Eastern Mande, e.g. *Dan* of Liberia and Ivory Coast, *Bisa* of Upper Volta and Ghana, and *Busa* of Benin and Nigeria.

VOLTAIC (or GUR) takes its name from the Volta River within whose basin a considerable number of this family's languages are spoken. It stretches from Mali and Upper Volta south into northern Ivory Coast, Ghana, Togo, Benin, Niger and Nigeria, e.g. *Dogon*, *Dagaari*, *Dagbani*, *Gurma*, *Moré* (*Mossi*), *Sisala* and the *Senufo* languages.

KWA (whose name derives from the word for 'people' in many of its languages) extends in a band along the coast of West Africa from Liberia to eastern Nigeria. It includes the *Bassa* and *Kru* languages of Liberia, *Bakwe* and *Baule* of Ivory Coast, *Akan* (*Twi-Fante*) and *Gā-Adangme* of Ghana, *Ewe-Fon*, *Yoruba*, *Nupe*, the *Edo* languages, *Idoma*, *Igbo* and *Ijo*.

BENUE-CONGO is subdivided into four: Plateau, contains languages spoken around the Plateau region of Nigeria, e.g. *Kurama*, *Reshe*, *Kambari*, *Yeskwa* and *Birom*. Jukunoid covers an area south and south-east of Plateau and extending across the border into Cameroon, e.g. *Jukun*, *Mbembe* and *Kutep*. Cross-River which stretches from the Niger delta across the border into Cameroon includes *Bekwarra*, *Boki*, *Efik-Ibibio* and the *Ogoni* and *Abua* languages. Bantoid includes *Tiv*, most of the southern half of Cameroon and on south and south-east through the rest of southern Africa. This means that this subdivision of Benue-Congo, itself a subdivision of Niger-Congo, a branch of Niger-Kordofanian, contains all the Bantu languages, e.g. *Swahili*, *Kongo*, *Rwanda*, *Rundi*, *Kimbundu*, *Umbundu*, *Lingala*, *Luba*, *Sukuma*, *Luyia*, *Kamba*, *Ewondo-Fang*, *Shona*, *Bemba*, *Cewa-Nyanja*, *Kikuyu*, *Ganda*, *Makua*, *Tswana-Sotho*, the *Nguni* languages, e.g. *Xhosa* and *Zulu*, and many other Bantu languages.

ADAMAWA-EASTERN stretches from the Adamawa region of Nigeria across to south-western Sudan and northern Zaire. It is subdivided into two: Adamawa, e.g. *Longuda* of Nigeria, *Chamba* of Nigeria and Cameroon, and *Mbum* and *Fali* of Cameroon; and Eastern, e.g. *Gbaya*, *Sango* and *Zande*.

There is controversy about several of the above six language families, for example, many would prefer to treat Mande as a group outside Niger-Congo. Some linguists do not regard Kwa as a viable group, choosing to put Kwa and Benue-Congo together as one group; others have put Voltaic, Kwa and Benue-Congo into one Volta-Congo family. Perhaps the best known debate concerns the placing of the Bantu languages in the Bantoid subdivision of Benue-Congo.

Khoisan

Khoisan covers the smallest geographical area of all the *phyla* and is concentrated mostly in and around the Kalahari Desert in Namibia, Botswana, Zimbabwe and South Africa. It includes, principally, the click languages of the Bushman and Hottentot peoples but, in addition, small pockets in Tanzania where *Sandawe* and *Hadza* are spoken. Some scholars have objected to the grouping of both Bushman and Hottentot languages together, claiming they do not belong in the same family. Others have objected to *Sandawe* and *Hadza* being included.

Malayo-Polynesian

In addition to much older African languages included within Greenberg's four *phyla*, mention must be made of *Malagasy*. *Malagasy* is a language of non-African origin, of the Malay family, belonging to the Malayo-Polynesian *phylum*. It was introduced into the island of Madagascar during the 1st millennium AD by settlers coming from Indonesia.

Other languages

English, French, Portuguese and Spanish are languages of non-African origin, not shown on the map, used as *linguae francae* in various parts of Africa. Most ex-colonial states in Africa are multilingual and such languages are used as national languages in the majority of them. In addition, pidgins and creoles based on European languages are in use in many parts of Africa. By definition a pidgin is used as a trade language and is not a mother tongue. A creole has developed and become the mother tongue of the group using it. One example of a creole language is *Krio* of Sierra Leone, based on English; another is *Afrikaans* of South Africa, based on Dutch.

Ultimately, it must be stressed how comparatively little is still known about the rich and complex languages of Africa and what an enormous amount of research remains to be done if all the existing problems and controversies regarding the relationships of African languages to each other are to be resolved. *E.D.*

KEY

Major languages (languages spoken by more than 1 million people)

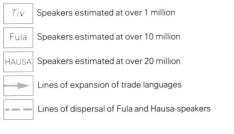

Tiv	Speakers estimated at over 1 million
Fula	Speakers estimated at over 10 million
HAUSA	Speakers estimated at over 20 million
→	Lines of expansion of trade languages
---►	Lines of dispersal of Fula and Hausa-speakers

Language phyla (major language families – inset map)

▢	Afro-Asiatic	▢	Khoisan
▢	Nilo-Saharan	▢	Malayo-Polynesian
▢	Niger-Kordofanian		

Ethnic groups

There are some thousand societies or ethnic groups in Africa: the number is approximate mainly because of the difficulty in defining what is a society or ethnic group, and also because of the many gaps in our ethnographic knowledge of African peoples. The very short, selective list of peoples given here includes the numerically largest groups and some that, although small in numbers, are either well known in the Africanist literature or have had attention drawn to them for some other reasons.

Many names of African ethnic groups are complicated. For example, the Bantu-speaking peoples use prefixes to denote number, so that a single 'Swahili' is MSwahili, the plural of which is WaSwahili; the language is known as KiSwahili. In this list such names are given only in the root form: 'Swahili'.

The figures given for population size are approximate only. In many cases the information needed to give detailed figures is not available. The figures given here are the most accurate that can be found. Cross-references indicated by 'qv' are to other entries *within* this article.

AFAR (also known as DANAKIL): a Cushitic-speaking people living in Djibouti and Ethiopia. They are nomadic camel herders of desert areas. Collectively and individually highly independent, they are much feared by surrounding groups. Population *c*.150 000.

AFRIKANERS: those inhabitants of South Africa who are of Dutch ancestry and who speak Afrikaans. They are often called Boers, the Afrikaans word for 'farmers'. Population *c*.2 million.

AKAN: a cluster of Twi (Kwa)-speaking peoples of the forest belt of Ghana and Ivory Coast, growing yams as staple crops and producing palm-oil and cocoa for export. They comprise several kingdoms, all recognizing matrilineal descent and with a long urban and trading tradition. The best-known and largest state is that of Asante (qv). Total population *c*.5 million.

AMBO (OVAMBO): a Bantu-speaking people of Namibia and Angola. They are mixed farmers, with many cattle, and are divided into several small kingdoms and chiefdoms. Population *c*.250 000.

AMHARA: one of the Semitic-speaking peoples of Ethiopia. Since *c*. AD 1300 the politically dominant groups have spoken Amharic, which is derived from a proto-Ethiopic tongue introduced from southern Arabia as much as 5000 years ago. The Amhara homeland (present day Wello province) did not accept Christianity until *c*.800–1000 after which the Amhara moved southwards. From 1260 to 1974 the Christian empire of Ethiopia was ruled by Amhara dynasties which,

by intermarriage and cultural assimilation, incorporated people from almost every ethnic group of the empire. Population *c*. 6 million.

ANYI (AGNI): a Kwa-speaking people of the Ivory Coast, one of the Akan peoples (qv). They comprise several small chiefdoms. Population *c*.200 000.

ARAB: a Semitic-speaking people originating in Arabia, now dispersed widely throughout northern Africa, with elements in the Sahel* zone of West Africa, Sudan, and on the East African coast. They are virtually all Muslims. Among pastoralist groups such as the Beduin the basic cultural and political unit is the tribe, under the authority of its sheikh. In the towns of North Africa this traditional organization has been lost but the culture of the nomadic groups is still regarded as the ideal. The spread of Islam* through the continent has been largely part of the expansion of Arab groups as traders and, in East Africa, as colonial rulers based on Zanzibar.*

ASANTE (ASHANTI): a Kwa-speaking Akan (qv) people of southern Ghana. The Asante form a confederacy of chiefdoms, founded by the ruler Osei Tutu in the late 17th century with the establishment of the Golden Stool at Kumasi. The confederacy reached its fullest extent in the early 19th century, equipped with a powerful military organization, an elaborate network of roads, and an efficient bureaucracy some of whose members were literate in Arabic. Asante traditional culture and religion are still strong today, with rich ceremonial and art of international fame. Population *c*.1 million.

AZANDE: a Central Sudanic-speaking people of the south-west Sudan Republic, Zaire and the Central African Republic. The Azande are an ethnically mixed cluster of agricultural peoples who were formed into

Asante notables and horn-blowers at a ceremonial gathering

a series of kingdoms by the Avungara in the 18th century. They are known for their elaborate system of beliefs in witchcraft and divination. Population *c*.800 000

BAGGARA (BAQQARA): a nomadic Beduin Arabic-speaking people of the Sudan Republic, keeping cattle in the arid region between the Nile and Lake Chad. They are descended from Arabs who migrated during the Middle Ages from Egypt to Chad and then eastwards. They are renowned as warriors, and lack any single or centralized political authority. Population *c*.5 million.

BAGIRMI: a Chari-Nile-speaking and ethnically mixed people of Chad. They are agriculturalists and traders. In the 16th century they formed a Muslim kingdom that was important in trans-Saharan trade. Traces of the state survive, but without its former power. Population *c*.1 million.

BAMBARA: a Mande-speaking people of Mali. Today sedentary farmers, they are divided into many small chiefdoms, and known for their elaborate cosmology and religion. Earlier they had founded two important states at Segou, on the Niger, *c*.1650 and at Kaarta *c*.1753–4. Population *c*.1.2 million.

BAMILEKE: a cluster of Benue-Congo-speaking peoples of the highlands of southern Cameroon. They comprise some 90 small kingdoms, are sedentary farmers and are famed as woodcarvers. Population *c*.600 000.

BAROTSE: see LOZI.

BAULE (BAOULE): a Kwa-speaking people of the Ivory Coast. Formerly an important state, they are today divided into small chiefdoms. They are renowned for their art. Population *c*.800 000.

BEDUIN: Arabic-speaking nomads of parts of the Sahara and neighbouring arid regions. Most African Beduin are camel herders, although the Baggara (qv) keep cattle. They are divided into largely independent tribal groups, each controlled by its sheikh and council of lineage heads.

BEJA: a cluster of Cushitic-speaking peoples of the north-eastern Sudan Republic. Most are Muslim and are cattle and camel herders. Population *c*.400 000.

BEMBA: a Bantu-speaking people of northern Zambia. An offshoot of the former Luba empire to the west, they are matrilineal and recognize the authority of a ruler, the *citimukulu*. They are slash-and-burn shifting agriculturalists; today many work on the Copperbelt. Population *c*.150 000.

BENIN (BINI): see EDO.

BERBER: the indigenous population of northern Africa and the Sahara, speaking an Afro-Asiatic language. They retained their independence until conquered or seriously affected by Arabs who invaded North Africa between the 7th and 12th centuries; most of the Berber tribes ultimately accepting Islam. Although in the more fertile parts of the Maghrib Berbers are sedentary farmers, others are nomadic or transhumant pastoralists of the Sahara, often with elaborate caste-like forms of social stratification. Historically, among other things, they are significant as leaders of the Almoravid* movement. The best-known Berber groups include the Kabyle, Shluh, and Tuareg (qv). Total population over 10 million.

BOBO: a Gur-speaking people of Upper Volta. They are farmers living in the savanna whose political and social organization is 'segmentary': i.e. they are organized in relatively small units on the basis of kinship structures rather than through centralized chiefships or kingdoms. Population *c*.300 000.

BUSHMEN: see KHOISAN.

CAPE COLOURED PEOPLE: a people of South Africa, of mixed ancestry (European, Khoisan, and Asian) who speak Afrikaans. Most are Christian, with a Muslim minority (the 'Malays'). Most live in the cities and towns of Cape Province. Population *c*.2 million.

CEWA: see MARAVI.

CHAGGA: a Bantu-speaking people living on the lower slopes of Mount Kilimanjaro, Tanzania. They practise an efficient means of irrigation, using wooden aqueducts to take water from the snows over long distances. They are of ethnically mixed origins, and comprised many chiefdoms until a paramountcy was established in the 19th century. They are wealthy coffee farmers. Population *c*.300 000.

Cape Coloured family

Fulani woman

Dinka man and boy

Galla woman

CREOLES: the inhabitants of Freetown, Sierra Leone, the descendants of freed slaves from the New World who were resettled in the 19th century. They speak Krio, and until recently retained a dominant position in the social and political life of the nation. Population *c*.45 000. The Americo-Liberians of Liberia have a similar history.

DAGOMBA: a Gur-speaking people of northern Ghana. Today peasant farmers, they form a state which was founded in the 14th century but reduced by the 18th century by invasions of Gonja (qv). Population *c*.150 000.

DINKA: an Eastern Sudanic-speaking people of the Upper Nile in the Sudan Republic. They are transhumant cattle herders occupying a vast area of low-lying and often swampy country. Lacking centralized political authority, they comprise many sub-groups recognizing only the authority of religious chiefs ('masters of the fishing spear'). Population *c*.1 million.

DIULA (DYULA): a congeries of Mande-speaking groups, probably of Soninke (qv) origin, widely dispersed throughout West Africa as traders. They have long been Muslim. Population *c*.200 000.

DOGON: a Gur-speaking people of central Mali. Living in isolated mountainous country under the authority of priest-chiefs, they have retained their traditional customs and elaborate religious beliefs despite strong Islamic influence in the surrounding plains. Population *c*.200 000.

EDO: a Kwa-speaking people of southern Nigeria, the population of the kingdom of Benin; whose political and religious ruler, the *oba*, lives in Benin City. The ruling dynasty is historically closely linked with the Yoruba (qv). They are famed for their carving, metal-casting and other arts. Population *c*.1.3 million.

EWE: a cluster of Kwa-speaking peoples of Togo and south-eastern Ghana, tracing their ultimate origins to south-western Nigeria. Most Ewe groups have centralized political authority, sometimes partly based on Akan (qv) patterns, but this usually has very limited authority and much power remains with clan heads. They are farmers and, on the coast and rivers, fishermen. They are renowned for their weaving. Population *c*.1 million.

FANG (also known as PANGWE and PAHOUIN): a cluster of Bantu-speaking peoples of Gabon and Cameroon. They migrated from savanna country into their present coastal forest habitat in the 19th century. They are today wealthy farmers, lacking any traditional state organization. Population *c*.1 million.

FANTE (FANTI): one of the Kwa-speaking Akan (qv) peoples of southern Ghana. They comprise several traditional states, each under the authority of a royal chief and of military companies (*asafo*). They were formerly the trading partners of early European enterprises, living in coastal towns such as Elmina and Cape Coast. Population *c*.400 000.

FON: a Kwa-speaking people of the Republic of Benin. They are intensive farmers, and were palm-oil and slave traders during the height of the kingdom of Dahomey in the 18th and 19th centuries. They are famed as weavers and artists. Population *c*.1 million.

FULANI (FULBE, PEUL): a people speaking a West Atlantic language, dispersed across the Sahel* zone of West Africa from Senegal to Cameroon. They are predominantly Muslim, and comprise both transhumant cattle keepers and also sedentary agricultural groups. Both are typically minority elements living among other peoples. The pastoralist groups are egalitarian, the sedentary ones having chiefs and systems of ranking. They initiated several jihads (holy wars), and in some areas, such as northern Nigeria, where they overthrew the Hausa (qv) rulers of existing states in the early 19th century, established kingdoms by the conquest of indigenous peoples. Population c.7 million.

GĀ: a Kwa-speaking people of Ghana, the original inhabitants of the city of Accra. Traditionally fishermen, they have for long been involved in the trade of the coastal towns. Population (with the related Adangbe) c.700 000.

GALLA (also known as OROMO): a cluster of Cushitic-speaking peoples of Ethiopia and northern Kenya. Traditionally pastoralists, those groups in northern Ethiopia today are farmers, the southern Galla remaining cattle herders. These latter (including the Borana and Arusi) have retained much of their traditional organizations and religion, the northern Galla having become mostly Muslims or Christians. Population c.10 million.

GANDA: a Bantu-speaking people of southern Uganda, the population of the largest traditional kingdom of the area, founded about the 12th century. The king, the *kabaka*, ruled with the help of bureaucratic chiefs. In the 19th century most Ganda became Christian but there is a significant Muslim minority. Until the troubles of the 1970s in Uganda they were wealthy farmers growing cotton and coffee. The kingship was abolished by the Uganda government in 1967. Population c.1 million.

GONJA: a Kwa-speaking people of northern Ghana. Farmers in a semi-arid region, they are of diverse origins and were formed into a formerly important but highly decentralized trading state in the 17th century. Population c.100 000.

HAUSA: a Chadic (Afro-Asiatic)-speaking people of Nigeria and Niger. They are intensive farmers, and famed craftsmen. Hausa traders are found throughout West Africa. Most Hausa were conquered by the Fulani (qv) in the early 19th century and today form the populations of the Muslim emirates of Nigeria. A minority, the Maguzawa, have retained their traditional religion. Population c.12 million.

HEHE: a Bantu-speaking people of south-central Tanzania. Formerly a cluster of independent chiefdoms, they were amalgamated into a single polity in the 19th century, but greatly weakened by German colonial government. Population c.200 000.

HERERO: a cluster of Bantu-speaking peoples of Namibia and neighbouring areas. They were once pastoralists but today are mainly settled farmers. They recognize both patrilineal and matrilineal descent. Under severe treatment during German colonial rule, their numbers greatly declined. Population c.700 000.

HOTTENTOT: see KHOISAN.

IBIBIO: a cluster of Benue-Congo-speaking peoples of south-eastern Nigeria including the Efik and the Anang. They are agriculturalists and fishermen, and are renowned for their art. Population c.2 million.

IGBO (IBO): a Kwa-speaking people of eastern Nigeria. They are a congeries of many small and traditionally autonomous communities, some ruled by kings ad others lacking centralized political authority. Local government is controlled by a complex system of rankholders ('title holders') based on age, wealth and achievement. They are renowned as traders throughout Nigeria, and their art is famous. The Igbo established the short-lived state of Biafra* in the 1960s. Population c.7 million.

IJO (IJAW): a Kwa-speaking people of southern Nigeria. Traditionally fishermen in the swamps of the Niger delta, the western Ijo live in scattered villages; the eastern Ijo took part in the early European trade in palm-oil and slaves and after the 16th century developed several city-states (Bonny, Brass, etc). Population c.500 000.

JUKUN: a Benue-Congo-speaking people of north-eastern Nigeria, believed to be the descendants of the medieval state of Kwararafa. The ruler is famed as a 'divine' king. Population c.30 000.

KALENJIN: a cluster of Eastern Sudanic-speaking peoples of the Rift Valley region of Kenya. Traditionally cattle pastoralists and renowned as aggressive raiders, most are today sedentary intensive farmers. The best-known are the Nandi and Kipsigis. Population c.500 000.

KAMBA: a Bantu-speaking people of central Kenya, closely related to the Kikuyu (qv). They are mixed farmers and known as woodcarvers. During the 19th century they controlled much of the trade between the East African highlands and the coast. Population c.1 million.

KANURI: a Nilo-Saharan-speaking people of north-eastern Nigeria. They formed the empire of Bornu, which reached its greatest extent in the 16th century. Its rulers became Muslim in the 11th century and today the Kanuri are all Muslim. Population c.1.4 million.

KHOISAN: the term now used for the Bushmen and Hottentot peoples of southern Africa. The Bushmen (San) were hunters and gatherers and today are mostly cattle herdsmen for other African groups such as the Tswana (qv); the Hottentots (Khoi) were pastoralists, and today are represented only by groups of mixed ancestry in Namibia, most

Herero women returning from market

other Hottentots having become extinct or merged into the Cape Coloured people (qv). Khoisan speak 'click' languages. Total population c.100 000.

KIKUYU (GIKUYU): a Bantu-speaking people of the central highlands of Kenya, and the largest ethnic group in that country. They are intensive farmers, with a very high population density. They lack traditional chiefship, government being by elders and councils selected by age, and by prophetic leaders. During the 1950s they were involved in the Mau Mau rising, and have since provided many of the political leaders of the Kenya nation. Population c.2 million.

KIMBUNDU: a Bantu-speaking people of western and central Angola. They are farmers and comprise many small chiefdoms. They should not be confused with the Mbundu (qv). Population c.1.2 million.

KONGO: a Bantu-speaking people of Zaire, Angola, and Congo, living near the mouth of the River Congo. The Kongo kingdom, founded in the 14th century, was partially converted to Christianity by the Portuguese, with its capital at San Salvador. By the 18th century, after much Portuguese slaving, it declined, but its memory provides a focus for ethnic loyalty today. Population c.1 million.

KPELLE: a Mande-speaking people of Liberia and Guinea. They are rice farmers, organized into several chiefdoms. The men's *poro* and the women's *sande* 'secret societies' are politically important. Population c.400 000.

KRU: a Kwa-speaking people of Liberia. They are known as fishermen and boatmen throughout West Africa from Senegal to Cameroon. Population c.1 million.

KUBA: a cluster of Bantu-speaking peoples of central Zaire. They are matrilineal in descent, practising agriculture. They were formed into a kingdom about 1600 under a king of the Bushong sub-group. They are famed for their art. Population c.80 000.

LANGO: an Eastern Sudanic-speaking people of northern Uganda. They are agriculturalists, lacking traditional chiefs. They are closely related to the Acholi and other groups of the upper Nile valley. Population c.400 000.

LOZI (BAROTSE): a Bantu-speaking people of western Zambia, living in the flood-plain of the upper Zambezi. The kingdom was conquered in the mid-19th century by Kololo invaders, a Nguni (qv) people from southern Africa. Population c.400 000.

LUBA: a cluster of Bantu-speaking peoples of south-eastern Zaire. They are agriculturalists and fishermen, and were formerly united under a single ruler. Today they comprise several autonomous chiefdoms. They are known for their woodcarving and other arts. Population c.1.5 million.

LUHYA: a cluster of Bantu-speaking people of western Kenya. Each group is traditionally autonomous, only the Wanga, under chief Mumias, having formed a small trading state in the 19th century. Despite lack of political cohesion, the sense of Luhya cultural identity is very high. Population c.1 million.

LUNDA: a cluster of Bantu-speaking peoples astride the borders of Zaire, Angola and Zambia. They are agriculturalists. During the 17th and 18th centuries they formed some of the largest conquest states of Central Africa (Lunda, Kazembe); others lack centralized political authority. The Lunda were formerly renowned as rulers and traders throughout Central Africa. The best-known groups include the Chokwe, Luchazi, Luvale, and Ndembu. Population c.1.5 million.

LUO: an Eastern Sudanic-speaking people of western Kenya, often known as 'Kavirondo'. Unlike most other Nilotes, who are traditionally pastoralists, the Luo are agriculturalists and fishermen. They generally lack traditional chiefs, and provide migrant labourers throughout East Africa. Population c.2 million.

MAKONDE: a Bantu-speaking people of northern Mozambique and south-eastern Tanzania. They are sedentary farmers, recognizing matrilineal descent and lacking any centralized political authority. They are famous as woodcarvers, producing sculptures that often draw on Makonde folklore for themes. Population c.1 million.

MAKUA: a Bantu-speaking people of northern Mozambique and southern Tanzania. They are settled farmers, and many have accepted Islam. Population c.3 million.

Malagasy woman and children

MALAGASY: the peoples of the island of Madagascar. Comprising some 50 ethnic groups, they are of diverse origins. The strongest element is that from Indonesia, and the Malagasy languages are Malayo-Polynesian. The north-western coasts are inhabited by many Swahili (qv) and other Bantu groups from the African mainland. The traditional economy is based on agriculture, rice being the usual staple, although cattle are kept in many areas. Before colonial rule the various groups were politically autonomous, most lacking centralized political authority. The main exception were the Merina of the central highlands, where a powerful kingdom was established in the 16th century. The most numerous peoples include the Merina (often known as Hova, the term for the commoners of the state), Betsimaraka, Betsileo, Tsimety, Sakalava, and Tanala. The traditional religions are mostly based on ancestor worship. Today most Malagasy are Protestant Christians, with a strong Muslim minority in the north-west. Total population *c.*8 million.

MALINKE (MANDINGO): a cluster of Mande-speaking peoples of Mali, Guinea, Senegal and neighbouring areas. They are sedentary farmers, their various communities being under the authority of an hereditary noble class. Malinke groups founded the medieval empire of Mali. Population *c.*1.5 million.

MANDE (MANDING): a group of Mande-speaking people of West Africa. They developed agriculture early. Mande groups founded the medieval empires of Ghana and Mali. They include the Bambara, Dyula, Malinke, Mende, and Soninke (qqv).

MANGBETU: a cluster of Central Sudanic-speaking peoples in north-eastern Zaire. In the 19th century they comprised a powerful kingdom ruled by an aristocracy to which alone the name Mangbetu is properly given. They are renowned for their craftsmanship, especially in wood and iron. Population *c.*1 million.

MARAVI: a cluster of Bantu-speaking peoples of Malawi and Zambia. They are matrilineal, and have rulers who arrived during the 15th and 16th centuries. The best-known Maravi groups are the Cewa and the Nyanja. Population *c.*2 million.

MASAI: an Eastern Sudanic-speaking people of the Rift Valley area of Kenya and Tanzania. They are nomadic cattle herders, organized in a complex age-set system which provides the warriors (*moran*), under control of ritual leaders (*laibons*). Population *c.*230 000.

MBUNDU (OVIMBUNDU): a Bantu-speaking people of southern Angola, comprising some 20 indigenous chiefdoms. Today mixed farmers, they were formerly long-distance traders over much of Central Africa, from the Great Lakes to the Atlantic. They should not be confused with the Kimbundu (qv). Population *c.*1.7 million.

MENDE: a Mande-speaking people of Sierra Leone. Mainly rice-farmers, they comprise several chiefdoms. Community life is largely in the hands of the men's *poro* and women's *sande* 'secret societies'. Population *c.*1 million.

Masai man

MONGO: a cluster of Bantu-speaking peoples of central Zaire. They are sedentary cassava farmers, organized into many small chiefdoms. Population *c*.5 million.

MOORS: a popular term for the Muslim inhabitants of North Africa, Mauritania and the Sahara, both Arabic- and Berber-speaking.

MOSSI: a Gur-speaking people of Upper Volta. They are sedentary farmers, comprising several chiefdoms under a powerful paramount, the Morho Naba of Ouagadougou, who rules a feudally organized kingdom. Population *c*.1.8 million.

NDEBELE (MATABELE): a Bantu-speaking people of Zimbabwe and northern South Africa. They originated in the 19th century as an offshoot of the Nguni (qv) and moved northward conquering some of the indigenous Shona peoples, and establishing a state under Mzilikazi and his successor Lobengula. Population *c*.1.5 million.

NGUNI: a cluster of Bantu-speaking peoples of southern Africa. Originally occupying Natal and Transkei, they expanded rapidly in the early 19th century in a series of migrations. The main groups today include the Zulu, Swazi and Xhosa (qqv) of South Africa and Swaziland; the Ndebele (qv) of Zimbabwe; and the Ngoni of Zambia, Malawi and Tanzania. All are organized into patrilineal clans under the political control of powerful chiefs aided by councils. Total population *c*.7 million.

NUBA: a Chari-Nile-speaking cluster of people of the Nuba Hills in the western Sudan Republic. They are farmers, isolated from the Baggara (qv) of the surrounding plains. Population *c*.500 000.

NUBI: a term used for the Arabic-speaking descendants of Sudanese troops used in the Egyptian occupation of the Sudan; today most inhabit Uganda and Zaire.

NUBIANS: the Chari-Nile-speaking occupants of the Nile valley between Aswan and Khartoum, Sudan Republic, the descendants of the people of the medieval Christian kingdoms of Nubia. *c*.300 000.

NUPE: a Kwa-speaking people of central Nigeria. Farmers and fishermen, organized in a kingdom, they are mostly Muslims, and are known as craftsmen and traders. Population *c*.1 million.

NYAKYUSA: a Bantu-speaking people of southern Tanzania. They are intensive farmers and famed for their unique pattern of villages, each occupied only by men of the same age and their families. Population *c*.400 000.

NYAMWEZI: a Bantu-speaking people of central Tanzania. They are mixed farmers, comprising several chiefdoms. They were formerly important as long-distance traders between the Great Lakes and the Swahili coast. Population *c*.500 000.

NYANJA: see MARAVI.

NYIKA (also called MIJIKENDA): a cluster of Bantu-speaking peoples of the coast of Kenya. Farmers and fishermen, they are mostly Muslim. Population *c*.700 000.

NYORO: a Bantu-speaking people of western Uganda. The original state of Bunyoro-Kitara, founded in the 14th or 15th century with a pastoralist ruling class and farming peasants, was predominant in the interlacustrine area until weakened by the Ganda and British. The kingship was abolished by the Uganda government in 1967. Population *c*.400 000.

OVAMBO: see AMBO.

PEUL: see FULANI.

PONDO: a Bantu-speaking people of Transkei, South Africa, closely related to the Xhosa (qv). They are organized into strongly patrilineal clans and powerful chiefdoms. Population *c*.200 000.

PYGMIES: small-statured inhabitants of central Africa, the descendants of the presumed autochthonous occupants of the tropical forests. Traditionally hunters and gatherers, Pygmy bands are typically in a

Pygmy woman

symbiotic relationship with non-Pygmy groups, and many have become farmers and herders in the surrounding savanna areas. The basic unit of organization is a small band, lacking any powerful forms of political or other authority. The best-known groups are the forest-dwelling Mbuti of Zaire and the Twa of the Great Lakes savannas. All speak the languages of their non-Pygmy neighbours. Total population c.200 000.

RUNDI, RWANDA: Bantu-speaking peoples of the republics of Burundi and Rwanda. Although separated by historical enmity, their cultures and organizations are similar. Both are caste-ridden societies, comprising three elements: the Tutsi; a largely endogamous cattle-owning class which provided the despotic kingship and the warrior aristocracy; the Hutu, peasantry who form the great majority of the population; and the Pygmy hunters called Twa. All speak the Bantu languages called Rwanda and Rundi. Large centralized kingdoms emerged during the 17th and 18th centuries. Although this system was maintained under Belgian colonial rule, it has been changed drastically since independence. Population: Rundi, c.3.5 million; Rwanda, c.3.7 million.

SENUFO: a cluster of Gur-speaking peoples of the Ivory Coast and southern Mali. They lack elaborate forms of political authority, and are intensive agriculturalists. They are famed for their plastic art and music. Population c.800 000.

SERER: a West Atlantic-speaking people of Senegal and The Gambia. They are sedentary farmers. The traditional political organizations of Serer communities varied considerably, some having powerful chiefs and others merely local headmen. Population c.500 000.

SHILLUK: an Eastern Sudanic-speaking people living along the Nile south of Khartoum in the Sudan Republic. They are farmers, with many cattle, and form a kingdom under the *reth* or king, the proto-type of the 'divine kingship' in ethnographic studies. Population c.120 000.

SHONA: a cluster of Bantu-speaking peoples of eastern Zimbabwe. They are mixed farmers, organized traditionally into many small chiefdoms. The main groups include the Zezuru, Karanga, Manyika, Tonga-Korekore, and Ndau. Population c.1 million.

SIDAMA: a cluster of Cushitic-speaking peoples of southern Ethiopia, of mixed origins. They are farmers, with the *ensete* ('false banana') as staple, and lack centralized political authority. They have for long been subjected to Amhara domination, but have mostly retained their traditional religion. Population c.1.5 million.

SOMALI: the Cushitic-speaking people of Somalia and parts of Kenya, Ethiopia, and Djibouti. They are mainly transhumant herders, divided into many traditionally autonomous and warlike groups, but with a powerful sense of cultural unity, based largely on Islam and the written Somali language. Population c.4 million.

SONGHAY (SONHRAI): a cluster of Nilo-Saharan-speaking peoples of Niger and eastern Mali. They were the dominant group in the medieval empire of Songhay, with its capital at Gao, which reached its height in the 16th century, controlling much of the Saharan caravan trade. Population c.1 million.

SONINKE (also called SARAKOLE): a Mande-speaking people of eastern Senegal and Mali. Today settled farmers, they are the descendants of the founders of the medieval empire of Ghana. Population c.400 000.

SOTHO: a cluster of Bantu-speaking peoples widely dispersed over southern Africa, their unity being linguistic and cultural, and not political. They comprise the Suto (qv) of Lesotho, the Tswana (qv) of Botswana, and the Pedi and others of the Transvaal. Population c.3 million.

SUKUMA: a Bantu-speaking people of Tanzania, living south of Lake Victoria. Mixed farmers, they are divided into many small autonomous chiefdoms, which today form the Sukuma Federation. Population c.1.5 million.

SUTO: a Bantu-speaking people comprising the population of Lesotho. They were formed into a state in the 19th century by King Moshweshwe. Population c.1 million.

SWAHILI: a cluster of Bantu-speaking peoples of the coast and islands of East Africa. They are ethnically and culturally an amalgam of African groups and Arab immigrants who have entered the area continually since ancient times. The greatest expansion of Swahili culture came after the establishment of the Arab colonial state of Zanzibar. Swahili is widely spoken as a *lingua franca* in East and Central Africa. Population c.500 000.

SWAZI: a Bantu-speaking people living in Swaziland; one of the Nguni cluster (qv). They were formed into a kingdom in the early 19th century, and remain independent today. Population c.500 000.

TEMNE: a West Atlantic-speaking people of Sierra Leone. They are farmers and organized into many small chiefdoms. The chief's office is largely religious, his authority being linked with the *poro* and *ragbenle* 'secret societies'. Population c.750 000.

TESO (ITESO): an Eastern Sudanic-speaking people of central Uganda. Lacking traditional chiefs, they were partially conquered by the Ganda in the late 19th century, but later regained their independence under the British. Unlike most other Eastern Sudanic-speakers, who are cattle herders, the Teso are wealthy and progressive cotton farmers. Population c.400 000.

Left: Tuareg man

Right:
Yoruba men

TIGRE: a cluster of peoples of Ethiopia and Eritrea. The northern Tigre were originally Cushitic-speakers, but now speak Tigrinya, a Semitic language. They are of diverse ethnic origins and mostly nomadic herders and Muslim. The southern Tigre are closely related to the Amhara (qv) and are agriculturalists. Population c.4 million.

TIV: a Benue-Congo-speaking people of the Middle Belt of Nigeria. They are agriculturalists, with complex systems of marketing. They lack traditional chiefship and have largely retained their traditional customs and religion. Population c.1 million.

TOKOLOR (TOUCOULEUR): a West-Atlantic-speaking people of Senegal, related to the Wolof, Serer, and Fulani (qqv). They have been Muslim since the 11th century, and formed the kingdom of Tekrur from the 10th to the 18th centuries. Population c.500 000.

TONGA: a cluster of Bantu-speaking peoples of Zambia and Malawi. They are intensive maize farmers, and lack any form of centralized traditional chiefship. Population c.300 000.

TSWANA (BECHUANA): a cluster of Bantu-speaking peoples of Botswana who formerly occupied much of the Transvaal and Orange Free State. Linguistically one of the Sotho group (qv). They are mixed farmers and herders in a semi-arid environment, supplying many migrant labourers to South Africa. The most important chiefly groupings include the Bamangwanto, Kgatla, Kwena, Tawana, Rolong, and Thlaping. Population c.800 000.

TUAREG: a Berber people of the central Sahara and the northern Sahel* zone of West Africa. They have a system of ranks, comprising nobles, commoners and slaves, and have always been feared as raiders throughout the region. They have their own form of writing. Population c.300 000.

VAI: a Mande-speaking people of Liberia, famed for their indigenous system of writing. Population c.200 000.

WOLOF (JOLOF): a West Atlantic-speaking people of Senegal and The Gambia. They are farmers and many are traders in the coastal cities. Traditionally they were grouped into a state with elaborate distinctions of hierarchy, from paramount chief to slaves. Population c.1.5 million.

XHOSA: a Bantu-speaking people of the Transkei, South Africa, one of the Nguni cluster (qv). They are mixed farmers, today supplying much labour to the Republic of South Africa. Population c.300 000.

YAO a cluster of Bantu-speaking peoples of Tanzania, Malawi, and Mozambique. They are organized into many small chiefdoms, and were famous as traders in the 19th century, when most of them accepted Islam. Population c.1 million.

YORUBA: a cluster of Kwa-speaking peoples of south-western Nigeria and the Republic of Benin. Although some north-eastern Yoruba are organized according to kinship groups and lack centralized chiefships, most groups are organized in culturally similar but politically autonomous kingdoms, all tracing their origins to the kingdom of Ife. Each is ruled by a king who is both the political and religious head. The Yoruba are traditionally highly urbanized, Ibadan being the largest pre-colonial city in Black Africa. Their traditional religion flourishes today, although many Yoruba are Muslims and Christians. They are famed for their art. Population c.12 million.

ZULU: a Bantu-speaking people of South Africa, one of the Nguni group (qv). Traditionally mixed farmers, they were formed into a kingdom by Shaka in the early 19th century, but were conquered and broken by the British in the Zulu Wars. They were a formidable fighting force, their regiments being based on age-sets of warriors. Population c.3 million.

THE AFRICAN PAST

Seated copper figure, in the style of Ife, from the Nupe village of Tada, Nigeria

The ancient Nile Valley

Ancient Egypt was the first urban civilization of the continent; it linked the changing world of western Asia and the Mediterranean to the African interior. The Sahara Desert, which separated these two worlds, was broken by the fertile strip of the Nile Valley for over 2000km. The Nile allowed communication and encouraged permanent and dense settlement on the fertile land created by the annual deposits of river silts. The Nile supported the first African states, the first African metallurgy, and the first African civilization. From the mid-4th millennium BC Ancient Egypt was a focus for trade and for societies far beyond the valley boundaries, while deliberate imperial policy expanded the Egyptian state south, east and occasionally west.

Aquatic resources had encouraged a more settled life of fishing and food-collecting societies in the sub-Saharan 'Sudanic' belt, on the Sudanese Nile and in the still fertile parts of the Sahara until the 4th millennium BC. In the Nile Valley itself exploitation of wild plant and animal resources developed about 5000 BC with the adoption of domestic animals and cereal crops (emmer wheat and barley) from South-West Asia: the winter rainfall regime of Egypt precluded the successful domestication of African food plants. The technique of making and firing pottery, probably discovered independently in Africa, was a feature of these Nile Valley neolithic communities, which used stone tools in the agricultural economy.

Significant changes came with the prehistoric communities termed 'Predynastic' because they antedate the historically known sequence of Egyptian royal families. The Predynastic economy was sufficiently productive to support skilled (if still part-time) craftsmen. Slate, wood and ivory were carved, flint and gold were mined, and there was trade to and from the valley. Copper is found early in the Predynastic period of Upper Egypt (the valley proper) although it was not yet cast, and was used mainly for decoration. Smelting of ore and casting molten copper for use as tools and weapons were established in the later Predynastic, after c.4000 BC. Gold and silver were used for objects of personal adornment.

The later Predynastic groups of the 4th millennium had already developed some of the features of subsequent Egyptian civilization: for example, larger villages built in mud brick, and the formal burial of the dead with everyday objects for use in the afterlife. Religious rituals involving cow horns or dancing figures, emblems of later deities, and boat shrines are shown on decorated pottery. Closer

Detail from a Book of the Dead, 21st Dynasty, c. 1000BC

KEY

| | Fertile flood plain of the Nile | Bigo | Towns | MALI | States and regions |

THE ANCIENT NILE VALLEY

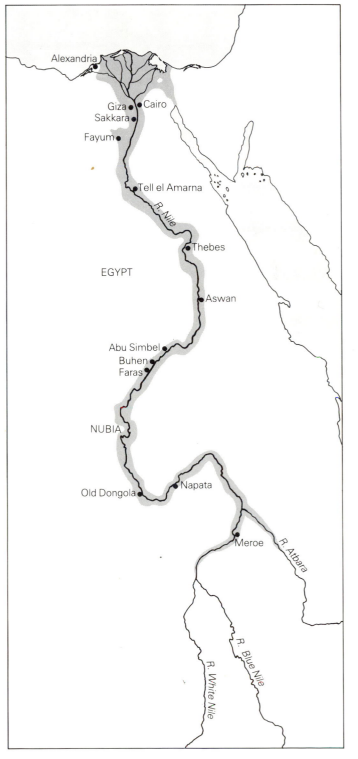

settlement, communal ritual, and some craft specialization and trade probably reflected cooperation in agriculture, particularly in the irrigation needed to cultivate the fertile silt-lands after the annual Nile floods. Differential wealth is shown in grave form and contents.

A revolutionary development, the Unification Period of a century or less, led to the founding of the Egyptian state and the 1st Dynasty. Local rulers, perhaps important in agricultural and religious roles, came to dominate the two areas of Upper Egypt and Lower Egypt (the Nile delta). We see scenes of this period carved in relief on stone maces in a style that anticipates the classic canons of Egyptian art. By 3100 BC, earlier according to some calculations, the Archaic period was established with an Egyptian state unified under a single king. The gods, their ritual and worship, were established; monumental brickwork was used for tombs of kings and nobles and for fortification of towns; specialist craftsmen were supported by the surplus from the land, and there was a state, personified in the monarch, with a unified social system. Most important, writing – the tool for commerce, religion and politics – had begun.

The Pyramid Age and Egyptian society

After four centuries of Archaic Egypt, the 'Pyramid Age' of the Old Kingdom was established from about 2700 BC. Old Kingdom Egypt gained its wealth not from conquest, although there were raids south and east; only partly from trade (more with Asia than with other parts of Africa), but mainly from agriculture. Local administrative 'nomes' (territorial divisions) accumulated some of the wealth of farming; but it is unclear to what extent local irrigation, apportionment of land after the annual floods, and agricultural marketing were centrally administered rather than cooperative in the Old Kingdom. Centralized seasonally produced wealth, though,

Painted limestone relief of musicians at a feast, in a nobleman's tomb at Sakkara, 5th Dynasty, *c.* 2400 BC

could be redistributed in the agriculturally inactive season in exchange for labour. Hence the construction of the pyramids, permanent royal tombs for the pharaoh (king), could both re-emphasize the centralized state and guarantee economic security by providing work through the lean season.

The royal palaces of the pharaohs, and the buildings of nobles, civil servants, domestic servants and craftsmen which made up a royal capital, were of mud brick, destined to dissolve back into the soil. Egyptian official religion propagated the notion of an afterlife which reproduced the patterns of terrestrial life and society: the use of stone for a permanent tomb dates from the first Old Kingdom king, Djoser (Zoser), whose architect Imhotep was credited with the design of the Step Pyramid. This construction, overlying an underground tomb, forms only one part of a large funeral complex at Sakkara. This architectural style developed under subsequent Old Kingdom pharaohs. The Great Pyramid of Khufu (Cheops), at Giza near Cairo, is the pinnacle of Old Kingdom architecture: 147m high, 230sq m at the base, linking achievements of sophisticated mathematics and technology with the organization of massive resources of labour which was engaged in quarrying stone, transport and construction.

The Sphinx at Giza belongs with the pyramid of Khafre (Chephren), part of the cult complex that sought to protect the pharaoh's interests after his death, a cult with its staff of priests like those of the divine cults in the towns. Beyond the pyramids of the pharaoh and his queens were the tombs of his entourage, from rich nobles to the more humble. All were buried with domestic goods to give them comfort in the next life, but all were buried beyond the edge of cultivable land, which was conserved for the present life.

Egyptian writing, in its hieroglyphic form, had evolved for trade

The Step Pyramid complex of Djoser at Sakkara, attributed to the architect Imhotep, 3rd Dynasty, *c.* 2650 BC

and commerce, and to mark ownership. It used pictures of real objects (in standardized form) as letters for consonants, syllables or for explanatory glosses to a word. A cursive script, hieratic, was used for everyday writing. In the Old Kingdom a true literature evolved, best known in the Pyramid Texts, religious inscriptions on the chamber walls of the later pyramids. These integrated the doctrine of the sun-god, Atum, with the resurrection of soul and body to the god Osiris. Magical spells in the texts allowed the king to take his place among the gods. By the 5th Dynasty, private tombs also reflect the Osiris cult and its concept of the afterlife.

The classic style of Egyptian art was closely linked to its religious functions. Standing and seated figures of the king had a votive role, while sculptures of members of his household stood by to accompany him into the afterlife. While the skills of stone carving developed and gained in sophistication, the basic canons of representation established by the Old Kingdom remained constant.

In bas-relief carving and in painting direct on plaster, art itself took on the role of hieroglyphic writing: direct representational statement in which detail was all important, requiring the human body to be shown frontally, the face in profile but the eye in full. A horizontal panel design for scenes overcame a lack of depth perspective but did not inhibit a freedom of expression of scenes from daily life, which, preserved in the aridity of tombs, bring to life the society of Ancient Egypt, in agriculture and craft, domestic life and recreation.

Development and change

Following the 6th Dynasty from about 2200 BC, there occurred a period of social change and breakdown of the formal social order. In the 'First Intermediate Period' trade with Asia was reduced, the state system of law and order was substantially weakened and the tightly structured hierarchy of wealth and rank was shaken, if not shattered. Underlying the social revolution may have been the inability of the state to respond to a series of successive failures of the annual Nile flood, which was essential to prosperous agriculture. When the Middle Kingdom emerged with the reunification of Egypt by the Theban, Mentuhotep I of the 11th Dynasty (c.2050 BC), the state was not so clearly all-powerful, and the unity of the land was maintained partly by a greater administrative complexity. The prosperity of the Middle Kingdom lay partly in expanded trade in other parts of Africa and in Asia, although probably not the actual expansion of formal rule. Tombs at Beni Hasan have paintings showing symbolic scenes of men bringing foreign tribute. Evidence of close links with Palestine is demonstrated by many Asiatic names found in the Egyptian delta, while the Lebanese port of Byblos, closely linked by sea trade to Egypt, had a temple to the Egyptian goddess Hathor.

Thebes (modern Luxor) was the city of the founders of the Middle Kingdom, and in the nearby desert they began the tradition of Theban royal burial. The Mentuhotep Temple of Deir el Bahari consists of a small pyramid set over two raised forms within the natural framework of rock cliffs. Stonemasons prepared massive royal coffins; the Coffin Texts developed the religious themes of the afterlife and different theological systems.

Daily life is seen not only in wall scenes but in wooden models of domestic activities, which contrast with the stern and grandiose royal statuary. Excavations have revealed the complexity of the towns of the Middle Kingdom, and have uncovered the fortresses which guarded the southern reaches of the Nile. This was also the Age of Bronze, when cast alloyed metal replaced copper in the manufacture of tools and weapons.

In a second collapse of the social order, from about 1780 to 1570 BC, administration devolved on numerous local rulers who probably ruled contemporaneously. Among these, the 'Hyksos' kings, of Asiatic descent, became most prominent. Changes in the relative prominence of religious cults reflected these political developments, until the followers of the sun-god, Amen-Re, again from Thebes, challenged the Hyksos, and united the land from the south. With this establishment of what is now called the New Kingdom, Egypt's great imperial era was born. The firm restoration of state administration at home was symbolized by mighty temples dedicated to the gods at Thebes and beyond.

The wealth of Africa: tribute of gold, papyrus, panther skins and apes from Nubia; a wall painting in a nobleman's tomb at Thebes, 18th Dynasty, c. 1400 BC

The Egyptian army, having driven out the Hyksos, was to penetrate south to establish a wider African empire along the Nile, under Tutmosis I. A ruling queen, Hatshepsut, extended commerce further south to Punt, and built a great funerary temple at Deir el Bahari to mark her royal strength. Her nephew, and successor, Tutmosis III, marched into Asia to defeat an alliance of Levantine princes, and continued to campaign successfully in the region, establishing vassaldoms under resident commissioners. Booty was brought back to Egypt and for the cult of Amen-Re. Successive pharaohs maintained the imperial strength, the administrative structure and the theological establishment.

The exception came with the revolution of Akhnaton, the king from about 1378 to 1362 BC. He rejected the Amen-Re cult and replaced its secular base with a new city at Tell el-Amarna. He also organized a new administration, instituted the worship of a single new deity (the sun disc Aton) and encouraged a new, more expressive, art style. Following the death of Akhnaton and his queen, Nefertiti, the earlier order was quickly re-established. This return is symbolized by the magnificence of the grave goods of the young king Tutankhamen, from one of the few Theban royal tombs that was not later despoiled by robbers.

From 1320 to 1085 BC achievements of great magnificence are attached to kings named Seti and Ramesses. These 19th and 20th Dynasty kings maintained administrative strength, strict laws, widespread monument-building and visible wealth. Some continued foreign campaigning. Seti I fought in Palestine and Syria; his son Ramesses II extended further to the land of the Hittites—iron-using warriors with a Turkish base—and, after battle, treaties were drawn. Ramesses III held back the attack on Egypt of the 'Sea Peoples', but thereafter Egypt's territorial power was restricted to Africa.

The temple building of this later New Kingdom in Egypt included both the dramatic and imposing cult temples of many sites, and the funerary temples of Thebes. In Nubia, to the south, the great rock-cut temple of Abu Simbel dates to the reign of Ramesses II.

The two rock-cut temples of Ramesses II (1304–1237 BC) of the 19th Dynasty at Abu Simbel in Nubia; shown during work to raise them above the flood level of the Aswan High Dam

Entrance to the Temple at Luxor, with pylon and obelisk of Ramesses II, 19th Dynasty

Architecture, religious cults and formal art may be seen at their pinnacle in the New Kingdom.

The Late Period, which followed this climax of Egypt's political power, maintained a creative expressiveness in craft and sculpture, and in literature and theology despite changing political structures and rule by royal dynasties of diverse origin. These changes led to a brief Assyrian occupation in 671 BC which, among other things, brought iron into Egypt. The Saïte period of the 26th Dynasty (663–525 BC) was a time of contact with the Mediterranean world and its developing trade: but the new vitality of this period was set in the mould of the ancient tradition of Egypt rather than that of the changing wider world. This tradition persisted for a further five centuries, although a greater mystical element in popular religion can be traced, and traded goods are found in burial and town sites alike. A new form of handwriting, demotic, was used for daily purposes during the Saïte period.

Persian kings ruled Egypt from 525 to 404 BC, when they lost the land, but the Nile again became part of the Persian Empire in 343 BC. It was thus inevitable that Alexander the Great, the Macedonian conqueror of the Persians, should conquer Egypt in 332 BC. Alexander's general, Ptolemy, and his Ptolemaic successors, ruled Egypt with the titles and formality of the ancient pharaohs. Greek began to be used in inscriptions: the use of Greek alongside hieroglyphs and demotic on the Rosetta Stone has enabled modern scholars to begin to decipher the ancient Egyptian language. Real cultural change did not come until the defeat and death in 30 BC of the last Ptolemaic ruler, Cleopatra. Egypt became part of a Roman empire, whose rulers were more determined than previous foreign invaders to impose a new culture on the Nile Valley.

Egypt and the south

Influences from other parts of Africa as well as from Asia were intertwined with local Nile Valley developments in the origins of Egyptian civilization, as in its subsequent history. The religious and economic patterns of ancient Egypt developed along the banks of the Nile, but elements of civilization–the state, craft specialization, monumental architecture, urbanization and writing–evolved contemporaneously with developments in South-West Asia, doubtless with some shared and exchanged knowledge, and long before they did in the rest of Africa. Egypt drew raw materials from Africa, but also gained from trade and expeditions into Asia. Dynastic change often reflected the activities of migrant communities, who entered Egypt from other parts of Africa and from Asia. Despite claims and counter-claims the population of ancient Egypt cannot be characterized either as 'Asiatic' nor as 'Negroid', but reflected a balance and mix of origins and groups; while Egypt's language was a member of a family widespread in north-eastern Africa: Afro-Asiatic.*

Egypt was a focus for trading and nomadic groups from the more arid areas west, east and south of the Nile Valley; and the valley's products spread through localized trade. Wood, precious stones and building materials were brought down the Nile. Gold was mined in Nubia, the valley beyond the first cataract of Aswan, and brought to Egypt. Ivory and ebony were traded along the Nile corridor.

The systematic exploitation of Nubia was expanded during the Middle Kingdom under the guard of solid fortresses: first at Buhen, then elsewhere. By the time of the New Kingdom, the 'Royal Son of Kush' was one of the highest positions in the land, with specific responsibilities for Africa to the south. The Egyptian rule and administration of Nubia probably extended south of the fourth

Slaves bringing geese for counting: a scene from a private tomb of the New Kingdom at Thebes

cataract. New forts were built by Tutmosis I in the late 16th century BC, and by his successors. Amenhotep III, about 1405 BC, extended conquests to their limit with a punitive expedition which killed or captured 1052 'negroes', their families and servants. Also known to ancient Egypt was Punt, possibly the lowland and coastal part of the Horn of Africa. Expeditions took place in the Middle and New Kingdoms to trade for ivory and gold, cattle and apes, scents and other items.

With the end of the New Kingdom, Egyptian control of Nubia and beyond weakened. Communities now entirely influenced by Egyptian culture continued in the area. That which developed as Napata came to rule Egypt itself as the 25th or Kushitic Dynasty from c.750 BC until its power was broken c.655 BC. By the 7th century BC the Napatans had probably established far to the south, in what is now the Sudan Republic, a new town which was to be of great importance in African history: Meroe. From the early 6th century BC it became the capital of a kingdom. Iron working came south to Kush by the 6th century BC, and a major strength of Meroe was its iron manufacture. Meroe was a major industrial centre for iron working by the 3rd–4th centuries AD. The largest of the Meroitic towns, Meroe was the site of over 40 royal burials in chambers below distinctive pyramids, often faced with sandstone blocks.

Meroitic painted pottery from Faras in Nubia

Statue of a Kushitic administrator at Thebes, 25th (Kushitic) Dynasty, c. 700 BC

Meroitic temples are generally influenced by Egyptian patterns, and Amen was worshipped at Meroe, although his large temple was mainly of mud brick. The Meroitic lion god, Apedemek, was also worshipped at a temple at Meroe and lion statues are found at several sites. Reliefs on the stone of temples have an art style clearly developed from that of Egypt. In small objects design was also influenced by Egypt, but Meroitic civilization developed its own distinctive and high quality pottery styles, often with fine painted design decoration. A cursive form of writing developed from Egyptian hieroglyphs, but the language it presents is still undeciphered.

The spread of Meroitic civilization extended from northern Nubia to the Blue Nile, but sites away from the Nile Valley are rare, and very few Meroitic objects seem to have reached into other parts of Africa. Meroe was attacked by a Roman expedition in AD 61 and the land remained known to the Roman world after this. The final fall of Meroe came later, however, perhaps at the hands of the people of Aksum* in about AD 350. Meroitic power was, however, already weakened before this date, and a millennium of Iron Age civilization in the Sudan drew to a close.

R.M.D.

The Copper and Iron Ages

Settled societies equipped with stone tools* reached a stable pattern in much of Africa as fishermen, pastoralists, or 'neolithic' agriculturalists in the north and west of the continent. Changes in settlement and in social formation were brought about with the introduction of metallurgy. In the southern half of Africa, by contrast, crop agriculture was first introduced by communities already equipped with an iron-working technology.

Copper was smelted in pre-dynastic Egypt* early in the 4th millennium BC, and was used for cast objects. The full technology of alloying copper to make bronze took 2000 years more to be widespread in Egypt. The origins of these new technologies lay in South-West Asia, which supported true Bronze Age civilizations.

The Metal Ages elsewhere in Africa were significantly later. A copper industry is known from Mauritania in the western Sahara, dating back to at least the 5th century BC, and copper was mined early in the 1st century BC at Takedda in what is now northern Niger. Copper was widely available in the area and was mined and hammered into tools and weapons within small-scale agricultural societies. Influences on the development of this industry may have come from the Iberian peninsula through the Maghrib, and some of the tool forms suggest European parallels. The Maghrib itself had little copper or bronze, although there is evidence of cultural contact between the late Neolithic Age of Morocco and the Copper Age of Spain.

The Metal Age of Africa beyond the Nile was essentially an Iron Age, and later African prehistory and early history is of Iron Age communities and Iron Age civilization. Iron technology was an Asiatic development and was introduced to North Africa from western Asia. Egypt had iron tools and weapons only from the 7th century BC, over four centuries later than the origins of iron working in Asia. Iron was never significant to the cultural development of Egypt, but underlay the strenth of Meroe and subsequent cultures of the Sudan.

North-West and West Africa

As far as the spread of iron technology is concerned, developments elsewhere in North Africa were more important. The pastoralists of dry rocky ranges and the Sahara edge were in contact with the Nile Valley to the east, and to the north-west with settled farmers of the coastal Maghrib. Some Greek colonies and the Phoenician settlements from Iron Age Asia on the Mediterranean coast, and especially at the Tunisian site of Carthage,* influenced these indigenous societies. The potential for trade—an exchange of foodstuffs for Mediterranean goods—stimulated more productive agriculture under Berber chieftains. But outsiders—Phoenician, then Roman—

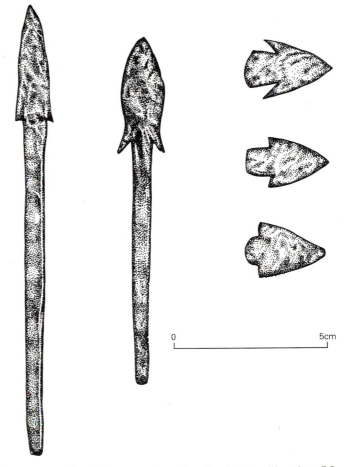

Copper arrowheads from western Mauritania, 1st millennium BC

played an increasing part in agriculture until coastal North Africa was thoroughly absorbed in the wider Mediterranean economy as 'the granary of Rome'.

The mobile Libyan communities trading across the Sahara remained much more independent. They were able to trade Saharan salt for West African gold, Mauritanian copper, slaves, ivory, skins and other African products and, in turn, exchanged these for imported goods, notably cloth and beads. In the last centuries BC these Saharan traders used horse-drawn chariots: these are depicted on the rocky hills of the desert region, part of the sequence of cultural self-portraits which range in subject from hunting and cattle pastoralism to camels (introduced in Roman times). One such group, combining Saharan trade with mixed agriculture was the Garamantes* of the Libyan Fezzan. Politically independent, the Garamantes were influenced by Carthage and Rome, had militarily strong settlements, and tombs with inscriptions. They met Roman expeditions in battle and were well known in the Classical world.

Most of the African trade took place within the savanna of the Western Sudanic belt: the area of West Africa between the southern edge of the Sahara and the northern borders of the tropical forest. It was probably here that iron objects, and the knowledge of iron smelting and iron working, first passed to members of West African societies. It has often been assumed that Meroe was the source of West African iron technology, but it seems no less probable that the technology followed the trade routes from the North African coast. The Saharan rock drawings of chariots suggest two routes from North Africa to the Sudanic area: to the bend of the Niger at Gao (in what is now the Republic of Mali) and to the west of Timbuktu. These trade routes laid the commercial basis of the medieval Western Sudanic kingdoms.

The Iron Age in West Africa, particularly in Nigeria and Ghana, has been investigated by archaeologists since the Second World War. So far, evidence of the earliest Iron Age in West Africa comes from Nok on the Jos Plateau of the Middle Belt of Nigeria, and from related sites. Nok figurines* of terracotta mark the beginning of our knowledge of Nigerian sculpture. The tradition is thought to have begun after the middle of the 1st millenium BC. Evidence of iron smelting is accompanied by examples of Nok art, which indicates the elements of broader social change that accompanied the technical innovation of iron working into stone-tool using agricultural communities. Beads made from locally mined tin are among the finds, possibly dating to the Nok period. Wattle and daub huts housed the people of the Nok culture.

The gradual nature of much of the Iron Age transition is seen at Daima, south-west of Lake Chad. One level of a mound of continuous settlement shows that neolithic herders acquired iron in the first centuries AD. Certain traditions – in burial, huts and clay figurines – continued through the introduction of iron, with occupation maintained at the site until recent centuries.

Metal-bladed tools gave agricultural communities in the West African forest south of the Western Sudan a real advantage. Patches of tropical rain forest could be cleared more effectively and quickly than with stone axes or fire: the ground could be hoed for the planting of root crops, and consequently expansion of settlement in the forest was made easier.

Iron Age societies in West Africa saw much development in the 1st millennium AD. Local and long-distance trade and the development of the agricultural potential of the forest area laid the basis for wealthy states or locally important chiefdoms and fine crafts, although the larger 'empires' were to develop in the savannas. At the burial site of Igbo-Ukwu* in eastern Nigeria a very rich deposit of grave goods includes remarkable objects in bronze displaying a sophisticated

Drawings of chariots, based on paintings and engravings from various sites in the Sahara

craftsmanship: ceremonial staffs, weapons, beads, pendants and decorated vessels. This site may date to the 8th–10th centuries.

A fine tradition in art is found in the later Iron Age from western Nigeria. At Ife★ (by Yoruba tradition, the place of the world's creation) naturalistic sculptures had links to pottery technology, and some pottery vessels had relief designs. The sculptures would have had a role in local cults. Broken potsherds were also used in the pavements of dwellings in what were now small towns. The sculpture period at Ife has been dated to the 11th–15th centuries. Rarer brass statuary (also naturalistic) comes from Ife, and some of the sculpture may represent kings of the town. Some continuity in art, and in the rest of the urban cultural tradition of western Nigeria can be traced through Old Oyo and other sites and exerted its influence on the Benin brasses. The walled town of Benin itself had a long history of settlement from the 13th century.

Elsewhere in coastal West Africa, village rather than town settlement was the pattern. There is good evidence of iron workings in what is now central Ghana, but no date is yet known for its introduction. Major social change came with the growth of the gold trade from the Akan goldfields of what is now Ghana. The site of Begho, probably the first of a series of 'international' market towns in the area north of the forest edge, was a centre for trade with the Muslim north, and it dates from at least the 14th century onwards. A large central market area separated artisans' and local merchants' quarters from Islamic traders. The finds from the excavations at Begho show the range of local products manufactured through the stimulus of trade, and the imports into medieval West Africa from the north. Archaeology is revealing Begho to modern scholars, but our knowledge of the medieval Western Sudanic kingdoms–Ghana,★ Mali,★ and Songhay★–comes largely from historical evidence and sources in the Islamic world which influenced these regions.

Eastern and southern Africa

Through archaeological excavation we have considerable information on settlement sites from the Iron Age of Bantu-speaking Africa. Today, Bantu-speaking, iron using agricultural societies are to be found in a zone extending from Cameroon to the area east of the Congo rain forest, and south to the Cape Province of South Africa. It is commonly assumed that the spread of iron also marked the expansion of populations of negroid physical type–the ancestors of present-day Bantu-speakers–into the southern savannas of Africa. The limited early physical remains discovered tend to support this, although an Iron Age expansion of Bantu-speakers would have absorbed earlier Khoisan★ populations, some of whom could conceivably have already learnt how to smelt iron.

Vessel from Igbo-Ukwu, Nigeria, cast in bronze by the lost-wax process in the form of a waterpot enclosed in rope-work

The initial expansion of Bantu-speakers may have been eastwards from the Cameroon area at the north-west of the equatorial forest in the 1st millennium BC. Either here or further east they obtained knowledge of iron technology and of the cultivation of some crops, including sorghum, the prehistoric Iron Age cereal staple of the savannas, and they also herded cattle and sheep. These cultural elements gave the Iron Age societies clear advantages over hunter-gatherer and herder groups.

In the lake area of East Africa the early Iron Age tradition, distinguished archaeologically by pottery style, was established by c.400 BC. Tall cylindrical clay furnaces for the smelting of iron from ore show the beginning of the smelter form used into modern times. Iron objects are rare on archaeological sites: perhaps because broken implements were re-forged and not discarded. Stone tools continued to be used alongside metal in much of the Early Iron Age.

The Early Iron Age spread southwards, probably in two distinct cultural 'streams' about AD 300–400. The rapidity of this movement and its extent is remarkable: its limits on the west were the rain forest and desert edge, but to the south the tradition penetrated to much of the Indian Ocean coast of South Africa, limited by the western edge of the summer rainfall belt needed for sorghum cultivation. This spread may reflect not so much large mobile populations as population expansion made possible by the advantages conferred by iron technology and mixed agriculture in rich areas previously occupied by hunting bands. Some groups of hunter-gatherers* continued to coexist with the Iron Age, while the Khoisan populations of most would have been absorbed by the predominantly negroid Iron Age groups.

Early Iron Age settlements in eastern and southern Africa shared common features, many of which continued through the Later Iron Age to recent times. Settlement was normally in villages of round huts with walls of poles and clay, and most probably grass roofs. Villages were scattered within fertile lands, and rarely needed to be in a defensive position. Pits in some villages may have been for burial, or more probably for food storage. A mixed agricultural base was supplemented by hunting and food gathering. Crafts undertaken by members of the household included pottery making. Iron Age pottery, handmade and fired in an open hearth, was very conservative in forms and in decorative techniques, as a result of which archaeologists can use change in pottery style to indicate social links and social developments. At Lydenburg* in the Transvaal, clay was used for moulded heads, perhaps used in ceremonies.

Iron smelting techniques used into the 20th century can offer insights into Iron Age technology. Top: a working smelter at Garu, Ghana specially constructed for Ghana National Museum researchers in 1973. Right: a smelting furnace photographed in Northern Rhodesia (now Zambia) in the 1920s

Iron smelting was undertaken in or near many villages where suitable ores could be found, and bladed tools and weapons were forged. Copper was rarer but is nonetheless found in many Early Iron Age sites. Copper ores or cast objects were traded widely from small sources or the major deposits of south-eastern Zaire and northern Zambia. Copper was used for objects of personal decoration, but also came to be valued as a currency. Conversely, cowrie shells from the Indian Ocean coast were introduced as currency, but were then used for ornamentation as well.

The richest Early Iron Age societies known seem to be those of what is now the Shaba Province of south-eastern Zaire. Grave goods in excavated burials are of fine iron and copper objects, seashells and some glass beads and pottery wares distinct from the Early Iron Age elsewhere. This wealth may reflect trade and the surplus from mining activity. It has been suggested that population growth and pressure in the Shaba region was one of the factors contributing to the major social and cultural changes that affected eastern and southern Africa from the 7th century, changes that are often classified as marking the beginning of the Later Iron Age. It may be, however, that the penetration of much of eastern Bantu Africa★ by pastoralists from the Eastern-Sudanic-speaking world to the north was an equally important factor.

This Later Iron Age complex is marked by changes in pottery style and settlement over a wide area, and probably represents population spread, with new language elements, absorbing earlier Iron Age and Khoisan groups remaining in the area now settled. In much of the savanna region these new societies were not dissimilar to those of the early Iron Age in the scope of their economy and material culture, and in settlement patterns, but some factors, particularly mining and trade, created new social developments. The Arab/Swahili★ coastal settlements were a source of rich trade items, which were exchanged for the goods of the interior by African traders. The influence of the copper mines of the interior is seen in the flanged crosses and long ingots of copper found at sites in Central Africa. At Ingombe Ilede on the Zambezi River burials of the 14th or 15th century show the wealth obtained in trading: in grave goods of shell, gold and glass beads; hoes and gongs of iron; and cotton cloth with copper-working tools.

Within what is now Zimbabwe (formerly Rhodesia) gold working has been identified at numerous ancient mines of the Later Iron Age. The economy based on agriculture, mining and trade supported new forms of society with rich chieftains and stone wall building. The most striking of many stone using sites of the Later Iron Age is Great Zimbabwe.★ Here was a natural citadel, and an obvious centre for both ritual and defence. The rulers of Iron Age Great Zimbabwe built an elliptical stone wall with a tall monument in the valley below the citadel, but the basic settlement within and beyond the wall followed the standard Iron Age model of clay huts of pottery using agriculturalists. Many trade objects of non-African manufacture

Copper ingot found in a grave at Ingombe Ilede, Zambia

found their way to Great Zimbabwe from the East African coast. The ritual role of Great Zimbabwe's rulers is emphasized by the finely crafted soapstone carvings, in particular the famous Great Zimbabwe birds. Though not in an area of gold mining, the site shows the wealth available from trading. Growing from initial settlement in the 11th century, Great Zimbabwe ceased its coastal links by the 15th century, perhaps as the result of political rivalry from neighbouring states.

The tradition of stone wall building continued later in other parts of what is now Zimbabwe and further to the south. Khani, Dhlo-Dhlo and other Zimbabwean sites have yielded trade goods of the 17th and 18th centuries which were imported as the coastal trade was transferred from Swahili to Portuguese settlements. To the south, in the Transvaal of South Africa, clustered settlements with stone enclosure walls were numerous into the early 19th century. Such settlements were, however, often disrupted and, in time, depopulated, following the rise of the Zulu kingdom★ and, then, European penetration and settlement in southern Africa.★   *R.M.D.*

Classical North Africa

Carthage

During the 8th century BC the Phoenician cities on the Lebanese coast established trading posts along the North African coast from Tripoli to the Atlantic. These formed a route to Spain, where the Phoenicians could obtain Spanish silver and British tin. From the middle of the 7th century BC Greeks founded agricultural settlements in Cyrenaica. Other Greek colonies in Sicily and southern Italy began to trade with Spain via the coast of France, where Marseilles was founded. In the 6th century BC commercial rivalry between Greeks and Phoenicians in the western Mediterranean led to battles for control of Sicily, Sardinia and Corsica. The leadership of the Phoenicians fell to Carthage, originally a colony of Tyre, which became a large independent city to which the other Phoenician settlements in North Africa were subject. Carthage was generally successful until defeated in Sicily by Syracuse, the largest Greek city on the island, at the battle of Himera in 480 BC. The Carthaginians retained western Sicily, but for the rest of the 5th century BC concentrated on expansion in North Africa.

Though Carthage began as a monarchy, from the 6th century BC it was a republic, governed by a council of elders and two annually-elected magistrates, the *sufets* or 'judges'. These were rivalled by the generals, one of whom, Mago, founded the Carthaginian empire in the 6th century. His descendants, the Magonids, dominated the government for a hundred years. One, Hanno, sailed perhaps as far as the Guinea coast of West Africa to extend Carthaginian settlement and commerce. This depended upon a powerful navy to monopolize the supply of Spanish silver, British tin, and North African and Sardinian grain to the rest of the Mediterranean. Inland, northern Tunisia was conquered and annexed to provide an agricultural base.

The peoples conquered here were known collectively as Libyans. They probably all spoke Berber languages, a series of dialects related to ancient Egyptian. Ways of life varied from the hill villages of the Atlas Mountains to nomadism in the desert. The Greeks of Cyrenaica took Libyan wives and admitted the children to citizenship. The Carthaginians had Libyan slaves and Libyan subjects. From these subjects they recruited heavily-armed infantrymen, the nucleus of the army; light infantry and charioteers were supplied by allied peoples with whom the Carthaginians traded. Townships on the Carthaginian model began to appear among the Libyan subjects on Carthaginian territory. Carthaginian influence on the clans of Numidia (modern Algeria) may account for the beginnings among them of kingdoms and capital cities. In the desert, the Libyan Garamantes★ of the Fezzan supplied the Carthaginians in the 'three

CLASSICAL NORTH AFRICA

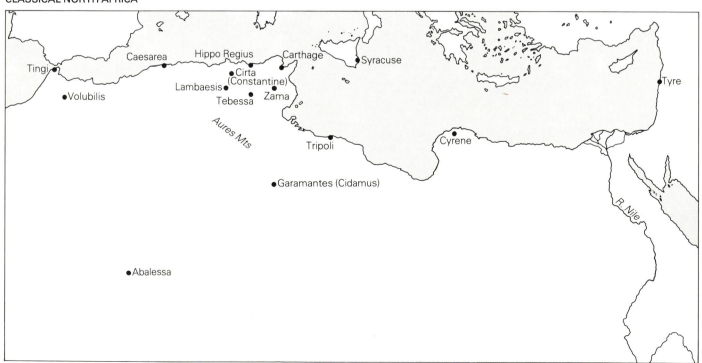

Punic mausoleum of the Numidian chief, Ateban at Dougga (ancient Thugga), Tunisia, c. 200 BC

cities' of Tripoli (Lepcis, Oea and Sabratha) with precious stones called carbuncles. The Garamantes, settled in the oases, copied Carthaginian funeral monuments. The Carthaginian cult of the dead, and to some extent their practice of child sacrifice, spread widely in North Africa. In exchange, the ram-headed Libyan sun-god Ammon, identified by the Greeks of Cyrenaica with Zeus, was identified by the Carthaginians with their own god Baal. His consort, the moon-goddess Tanit, may have been Libyan in origin.

The Punic wars

During the 4th century BC, while Cyrenaica was annexed to Egypt by Alexander the Great and his successor in the Nile Valley, his general Ptolemy, the wars between Carthage and the Greeks of Sicily resumed. Early in the 3rd century BC, however, the Greeks of Sicily were conquered by the Romans, and Carthage encountered a new enemy. The first of the Punic (Phoenician) wars lasted from 264 to 241 BC. Carthage lost its naval supremacy, was obliged to abandon

Sicily and eventually Sardinia, and was compelled to pay a large indemnity. The Libyan troops mutinied, but after their defeat, the general Hamilcar Barca began the conquest of Spain. His son Hannibal used this new empire as a base from which to invade Italy in the second Punic war (218–201 BC). Despite striking victories, Hannibal failed to capture Rome or to win support from Rome's Italian allies. When the Romans eventually landed in North Africa, Hannibal returned to be defeated finally at Zama (202 BC). Carthage was reduced to a tributary of Rome; though it survived and indeed prospered as the ruler of its North African hinterland, the jealousy of Rome culminated in 149–146 BC in its capture and destruction.

The Punic wars provided the kings of Numidia with a great opportunity. Syphax, king of the Masaesylii in western Algeria, supported the Romans in the second Punic war, while the kings of the Massylies, in eastern Algeria, allied with Carthage. It was Masinissa, however, the king of the Massylies, who turned to Rome in time to share in the Roman victory at Zama, and to be rewarded with hegemony over Numidia and lands as far east as the three cities of Tripoli. During his long reign, until his death in 148 BC, Masinissa's imitation of Carthage led to the widespread adoption of the Punic language and script, the Carthaginian religion, and Carthaginian municipal institutions at his capital Cirta (Constantine) and elsewhere. The practice of Carthaginian agriculture led to increased production of grain for export, and to the cultivation of olives.

These developments continued after the fall of Carthage in 146 BC, modified by the growing influence of Greek and Latin culture. The Romans colonized Carthaginian territory as their province of Africa. Meanwhile the Numidian kingdom was split up among the descendants of Masinissa, notably after an attempt by one of them – Jugurtha – to beat off the Romans and reunite the kingdom had failed in 105 BC. The kingdom of Mauretania in northern Morocco, whose king Bocchus helped in Jugurtha's overthrow, gained western Algeria, but, like the Numidian principalities, depended heavily on Rome. These client states were further weakened in the Roman civil wars of the 1st century BC. Siding eventually with Pompey, the Numidian kingdoms were finally annexed by Caesar and his heirs in 46–40 BC. Mauretania survived until AD 40, when the last king was murdered by the Emperor Caligula.

Roman Africa

The Roman Empire in North Africa, then, stretched along the Mediterranean coast to the west of Egypt in five provinces: Cyrenaica with its capital at Cyrene; Africa Proconsularis with its capital at a rebuilt Carthage; Numidia with its capital at Cirta (Constantine); Mauretania Caesariensis with its capital at Caesarea (Cherchel to the west of Algiers); and Mauretania Tingitana with its capital at Volubilis (Walila near Fes). The most important was Africa Proconsularis, which included Tripolitania, modern Tunisia and the

Before European Colonization

uplands of eastern Algeria around the head of the Medjerda valley. As successor to the state of Carthage and the fertile domains of Masinissa, it produced most of the grain and olive oil, which were the staple exports of North Africa. It contained most of the Roman cities, the largest being Carthage and the inland city of Theveste (Tebessa). Numidia was constituted for defence, with the headquarters of the 3rd Legion strategically placed at Lambaesis to command the approach from the desert to the south-west. The two Mauretanias were guarded only by mounted patrols of auxiliary troops.

The Roman Empire in North Africa closely followed the coastal belt of Mediterranean climate except in Africa Proconsularis and Numidia, where the line of frontier forts took in the oases of southern Tunisia and the desert south of the Aures Mountains. The Moroccan Atlas and the Atlantic plains were excluded. For 200 years there was little trouble with the nomads of the Sahara, although the tribes of the Moroccan Atlas may have presented a threat. The mountain peoples within the Roman frontier, in the ranges of the Aures and Kabylia, for example, were confined to the hills. Partly by administration, partly by the growth of the market economy, others were drawn into the settled agricultural population, which now extended well beyond the limits of Greek and Carthaginian rule. Numerous colonies of veteran Roman soldiers were established as far west as Mauretania in the 1st century BC and later, but the majority of peasants and landowners were of native origin. The demand for grain, olive oil and wine made production profitable, and the cultivated area expanded, dams being used to irrigate otherwise barren land. As a result North Africa yielded a regular surplus enabling it to supply two-thirds of Rome's annual grain requirement.

At the heart of the system the Roman towns were designed to incorporate the peoples of North Africa into the society and civilization of the empire. Laid out on the Roman plan of straight streets centred on the crossroads and chief public buildings in the middle, they frequently required the construction of aqueducts to supply water. Governed in Roman fashion by elected magistrates, their inhabitants enjoyed either Roman citizenship or associated status. Thus the provincial population became actively engaged in the Roman way of life. The wealthy and ambitious spent their time and money in the service of the emperor, their fellow-townsmen and themselves when they took charge of the city's affairs, and provided at their own expense the monuments, ceremonies and entertainments which established the Roman character of the town and its people. Latin replaced Punic as the urban language. Carthaginian religion was transformed into local Roman cults as Baal became Saturn, and Tanit the Heavenly Juno. Carthaginian art and architecture became increasingly Greek and Roman, and finally were largely swept away. North Africa became remarkable not only for its classical buildings, but for its splendid mosaics with their realistic portrayal of animals, birds, fish, mythological scenes and scenes from everyday life. The high point of Romanization was reached at the beginning of the 3rd century AD, when the Roman emperor was the North African, Septimius Severus. Not only did he patronize the cities of his native Tripolitania, but also extended Roman citizenship to all free men throughout the empire. The three cities of Tripoli backed on to the Sahara, where dealings with the Fezzan were more active than ever. The Garamantes imported wine, cloth, pottery and glass. In return they supplied the traditional carbuncles, with ivory from south of the desert. By the 4th century AD, Roman objects had reached the oasis of Abalessa in the Hoggar mountains, on the line of

The Medracen, a royal tomb of the Numidian kingdom in eastern Algeria, 2nd century BC

The Roman amphitheatre at El Djem (ancient Thysdrus), Tunisia, early 3rd century AD

rock paintings running from Libya to the Niger bend, where, for example, they were buried with a richly-ornamented female corpse in the so-called Tomb of Tin Hinan. Ivory had been produced in North Africa, but was now imported across the Sahara, as the North African elephant had been hunted to extinction. Its last home, Morocco, beyond the frontier of Mauretania, was also fast losing its other great beasts to the Roman circus games but continued to be a source of cedarwood. Although the Carthaginians may have acquired a little West African gold through their trading stations on the Atlantic coast, in Roman times Morocco did not serve as a second gateway to the desert.

Cyrenaica experienced a major revolt by its large Jewish community in AD 115. The Roman peace was more profoundly disturbed in AD 238, when a revolt in Africa Proconsularis led to the proclamation of the proconsul Gordianus, the governor of the province, as emperor. Though unsuccessful, the revolt began 50 years of troubles throughout the Empire. In North Africa cities were sacked by troops in AD 238 and again in AD 305. Forts along the Saharan frontier were abandoned, and Numidia and Mauretania Caesariensis were attacked by tribes from the south and west. At the end of the century the Emperor Diocletian withdrew from the

Mosaic at Utica, Tunisia, 2nd century AD. Utica was first capital of Roman Africa until Carthage was rebuilt in 40 BC

western part of Caesariensis, and from Mauretania Tingitana except for Tingi (Tangier). The remaining provinces were subdivided and grouped together in an African region ruled from Carthage; Cyrenaica was classed with Egypt and Syria. The reorganization was part of a general reform of the Empire under Diocletian and his successors in the 4th century AD, when order was restored, but government became more oppressive with armies of officials as well as soldiers. In the cities, reduced prosperity was apparent and populations declined under increasing taxation. In the countryside, production for the market began to give way to a subsistence economy.

Christianity

These changes were accompanied by a religious revolution. Christianity became widespread in North Africa in the 3rd century AD as the religion of small congregations led by priests and elected bishops. Intermittent persecution for refusal to acknowledge the divinity of the Roman emperor culminated under Diocletian. Under Diocletian's successor, Constantine, Christianity was abruptly transformed into the religion of both the Emperor and the state. The result in North Africa was disruptive. Strong opposition by those who had remained faithful during Diocletian's persecution to those who had apostatized or compromised with the authorities became opposition to the official Church when preference was given to these 'traitors' in the episcopate. Donatus, the opposition candidate for the bishopric of Carthage, became the leader of a rival Church, which throughout the 4th century AD was in the majority in the African provinces. The Donatists were not only hostile to official Christianity but to its chief supporters, the wealthier landowners, who may also

Ruins of the aqueduct which carried water from the spring at Zaghouan to the cisterns of Roman Carthage

Christian funerary mosaic, Tunisia, 4th century AD

have included the last of the pagans. These were terrorized by the so-called Circumcellions, Donatist peasants who seem to have courted persecution as a form of martyrdom. Matters came to a head at the end of the century when the Donatists were associated with the unsuccessful revolt of Gildo, a Berber prince from the mountains of Kabylia who commanded the Roman army in Africa, and in 397–8 put himself forward as a rebel candidate for the imperial throne. Augustine, the Catholic bishop of Hippo (Annaba, formerly Bone), was able to enlist the emperor's support for a persecution that virtually extinguished the Donatists. At the beginning of the 5th century AD the many splendid churches of North Africa attested the importance of Christianity as an essential feature of imperial rule.

The Vandal invasions and Byzantine Africa

Meanwhile the Empire was threatened from without. The widespread adoption of the camel by the peoples of the northern Sahara over the past two centuries had greatly extended the range of nomadism in the desert, and from the second half of the 4th century enabled nomadic tribesmen to raid Tripolitania and Cyrenaica. It was the barbarian invaders of the Empire in Europe, however, who put a sudden end to Roman Africa. In 429 the Germanic Vandals crossed the Straits of Gibraltar, capturing Carthage in 439. Settling as a military aristocracy of landowners in the old Carthaginian territory of northern Tunisia, they created a kingdom which lasted a hundred years. The Vandals were Christians who followed the Arian heresy, discriminating against the Catholic Church, and ending its period of greatness under St Augustine. The Roman cities were now largely abandoned, or transformed into villages. Rural life was less disturbed, with native landowners and their peasants surviving under Vandal overlordship on the high plains of eastern Algeria. The return towards a subsistence economy, however, brought a return towards tribal society, just as the contraction of the state to the area around Carthage led to the reappearance of tribal chieftains. Romano-Berber kingdoms formed in the mountainous regions of Roman Africa, and further to the west in the lost provinces of Mauretania. These were Christian, using Latin in their inscriptions, but it may be that Berber had already begun to encroach upon Latin as the vernacular language of areas where Latin had previously gained ground from both Berber and Punic. Much more alien were the camel-riding Lawata of the desert, worshipping the old god Baal, who defeated the Vandals and settled in the steppes of Tunisia.

The Roman Empire survived in the eastern Mediterranean with its capital at Constantinople (Byzantium). In 533, under the Emperor Justinian, the Byzantines overthrew the Vandals, and gradually reconquered Roman Africa, that is, eastern Algeria, Tunisia and Tripolitania. Cyrenaica had remained attached to Egypt. The government was military, and the country heavily fortified. Christianity and the Church were used diplomatically to bring about alliances with Berber chiefs and peoples. The new rulers were Greek, but Latin-speaking Catholics were encouraged to re-create something of the landowning society of the past. This restoration of authority in areas that had escaped control for a hundred years provoked opposition from Donatist communities which had survived in the more remote regions. Towns remained small, and new churches were built on sites away from the old city centres. The province no longer lay close to the heart of a vigorous economy, but on the far horizon of a shrunken empire. Nevertheless, olive oil continued to be exported; Carthage remained a great port through which Constantinople communicated with the western Mediterranean. At the beginning of the 7th century AD the regime was strong enough for the governor, the exarch, to mount an attack on Constantinople which installed his son Heraclius as emperor. When after his defeat of the Persians in the 620s, however, Heraclius lost both Syria and Egypt to the Arabs, Byzantine Africa was left exposed to Arab attack.   *M.B.*

North-East Africa before the rise of Islam

Indigenous elements

All but a very few of the peoples of North-East Africa speak languages belonging to three branches of the Afro-Asiatic family: Cushitic, Omotic and Semitic. The distribution of the several distinct languages of each of these branches has changed greatly over the centuries through major shifts in population and the assimilation of the cultural traits of intruders. The presence of isolated groups speaking languages of Africa's other language families in the Sudan borderlands indicates that earlier peoples gave way before speakers of Agew and Beja, the two Cushitic languages once common from the Jema River and the Blue Nile (called Abbay in Ethiopia) to northern Eritrea. Three waves, the earliest beginning before the Christian era, carried the cattle-breeding ancestors of the Afar, those of the Somali and finally, after AD 1400, those of the Oromo (Galla) north-eastwards out of the same nuclear area near Lake Abaya in the Ethiopian Rift. The Afar settled between Massawa and the lower Awash River before these lowlands became intensely desertified. The Somali reached the Ogaden in the interior of the Horn where they lived in uneasy symbiosis with a variety of neighbours. The Somali remained in close contact with each other for many centuries before dispersing early in the 2nd millennium AD. The Afar and Somali adopted the Arabian camel, whose grazing habits permitted them in time to drive out hunters, cattle-keepers and cultivators. The camel also permitted some Afar and Somali to become avid long-distance traders. There is no reason to think, however, that either the Afar or the Somali were in place along the coasts they now inhabit early enough to have been influenced by the intermittent voyages down the Red Sea of the ancient Egyptians in the later 2nd millennium BC or by those King Solomon sent c.1050 BC. Only greatly expanded archaeological work will, in any case, make clear whether or not the land of incense known to the Egyptians as Punt* and in the Old Testament as Ophir was on the African side of the seas the Egyptians and ancient Israelites sailed.

The history of south-western Ethiopia remains almost totally obscure before AD 1000. We know, however, that in addition to being expert cattle-breeders, the Cushitic- and Omotic-speaking peoples there included skilled hoe-cultivators who domesticated *ensete* (the 'false banana') and devised the irrigation and terraced farming which distinguished southern agriculture from the plough-cereal complex of the Cushitic Agew- and Semitic-speaking northerners. Traditions of highland farmers between the Omo Valley and the basin of the White Nile reveal that principles of social organization (such as age-grade sets) and religious beliefs (including belief in a benign creator-deity of the sky) which have been associated with the Cushitic Oromo migrants were being evolved by Omotic-speakers before AD 1000. The phallic stone monuments west of the Rift Valley lakes remain enigmatic but are ascribed in local traditions to still earlier times. No later than the first millennium AD, Omotic-speakers must have been creating the sacral kingship associated with soil fertility and cattle which gave rise in the first half of the 2nd millennium to the autocratic kingdoms of Enarya and Janjero west of the upper Omo.

The earliest documented kingdom in the southern highlands is that of Cushitic farmers, the Sidama, in the plains of Shewa surrounding what is now the site of Addis Ababa. By the later part of the first millennium AD, they had erected a powerful state, Damot, in response perhaps to incursions by the Semiticized Agew, who at Aksum in the first centuries AD founded the first great empire in North-East Africa. Because the Aksumites left written records and imposing ruins and were in touch with the literate societies of South Arabia and the eastern Mediterranean much of their history is known. How the amalgam of African and alien elements which they left as a legacy to all other Ethiopians was fused remains uncertain.

Royal burial monument, Aksum (c. AD 400): carved details on the monolithic stele echo architectural features of timber and dry-stone Aksumite buildings

South Arabian borrowings in northern Ethiopia

Building in dressed stone, writing (a South Arabian Semitic language–Sabean–in a South Arabian script) and iron technology were introduced from the middle of the first millennium along two chains of trading stations which extended into what is now Tigre province from the ancient port of Adulis and its inland emporia, Coloe and Matara, on the edge of the Eritrean escarpment. The ruins of the temples and other buildings of all of these sites are indistinguishable from those found at earlier sites in South Arabia. One chain continued down the eastern ridge of the Tigrean plateau as far south as the district of Azbi. Another veered south-westwards below the Mereb River through Yeha to Haoulti some 20km south of the plain where Geez-speakers (originally from south-eastern Eritrea) built the town of Aksum a couple of hundred years later. The dramatic achievements of c.500–300 BC, it is now argued, followed upon many centuries of infiltration by small groups of South Arabian hunters, traders and farmers.

Small incense burners dedicated to the Sabean moon-god are to be found–with identical decoration–both in southern Arabia and east and north-east of Aksum. This example is from Melazo, near Aksum

Ethiopia's modern Semitic languages–Tigrinya and Tigré (spoken respectively in Tigre and Eritrea), Amharic (native to the eastern highlands, and Ethiopia's official language for the last 700 years), and Harari and the Guraghé cluster in the south–do not descend from Geez (also known as Ethiopic, as is its script) as was once believed. For hundreds of years the literary language of all Christian Ethiopians, Geez is coming to be seen by scholars as merely a sister language with other Ethiopian Semitic languages rather than as one of their roots. Migration by Semiticized Agew out of a nuclear area in south-eastern Eritrea as much as 3000–4000 years ago is thought to have carried an earlier language than Geez throughout Tigre and down the eastern highlands into the Rift. From this 'proto-Ethiopic' all present-day Ethiopian Semitic languages, including Geez, were developing while the northern highlands passed through their Sabean and early Aksumite periods.

Botanists have shown that the favoured cereal crops of the northern highlands, a strain of sorghum, and a short grass called *teff* (*Eragrostos abyssinica*), were domesticated locally. Linguists add that the word for plough and other agricultural vocabulary in Ethiopian Semitic is of Agew origin. Apparently, then, the earliest immigrants from South Arabia did not create the food-producing revolution. Moreover, South Arabian influences do not seem to have been crucial for the development of centralized monarchy. In the *Kebre Neghest* (*Glory of the Kings*), Ethiopian monks composed a great national saga for the Christian Empire from the Ethiopian story of an early queen, Makeda, and biblical references to a queen from Sheba (or Saba: the south) but they also incorporated pre-Christian legends of the Agew and the Barya-Kunama groups whom the Agew and the Beja displaced in the Eritrean highlands. If anything, however, these pagan myths of the curtailment of blood sacrifices to a snake cult, and the consequent invention of a kingship to which women might succeed suggest that early political development arose independently out of the social transformations associated with the indigenous development of agriculture rather than as a result of ideas spread from South Asia. Not until c.500 BC is there abundant and unmistakable evidence in the triangle between Adulis, Azbi and the neighbourhood of Aksum of the imitation of South Arabian culture.

Probably it was in the development of long-distance trade in partnership with the Beja and Agew that the early immigrants from South Arabia made their greatest contribution to change in the northern highlands. Since the time of Solomon and earlier, the eastern Mediterranean had been supplied with items of luxury from Africa by overland caravans from entrepôts in South Arabia. Large markets grew up in North-East Africa only later. New opportunities in commerce opened with the establishment of regular seaborne trade to the straits by Alexander's successors in Egypt, the Ptolemies, from 285 BC. Roman occupation of Egypt increased the demand for African luxury goods as well as for silk, which was transhipped at

South Arabian ports. Competition for the transit trade across the highlands seems to have prompted the rise in the Christian era of leaders using the military title *negus* rather than the priestly or royal titles of South Arabia which had been in favour a few centuries earlier.

The Aksumite hegemony

A pilot's guide to the Red Sea, *The Periplus of the Erythrean Sea*, dated from the later 2nd to the early 3rd centuries AD relates that the small town of Adulis had the most important port on the African coast. Ivory, tortoise-shell, incense, rhinoceros horn (prized abroad as an aphrodisiac), and obsidian were exported from Adulis and the adjacent coast in return for Egyptian and Indian cloth, swords and other blades, beads and glassware, and Indian iron and sheet metals from the Mediterranean for making ornaments and weapons for the hunt and for war. The whole of the coast from considerably north of Adulis to the straits was subject to Aksum. Although ships at anchor at Adulis might be attacked by the peoples of the mainland, the king of Aksum had a firm hold over Coloe and other inland marts for ivory. Ivory hunted in the wide valley of the Tekeze, the major tributary of the Atbara, was accumulated in the capital itself. The king was reputed to know Greek and to be shrewd, even grasping, in business.

Archaeological evidence tends to show the sudden rise to empire of an upstart town. The Aksumite rulers assumed a new title, King of Kings (*Neguse Neghest*), perhaps a superlative of *negus*. Their inscriptions recount triumphant expeditions of far-ranging conquest beyond the Tekeze, to the coast as far as the straits and into northern Yemen, where inscriptions from the second quarter of the 3rd century AD confirm that there was a brief occupation from Africa. Aksum's pre-Christian inscriptions refer to the subjugation of the Habasha, perhaps meaning the ancestors of the Tigrinya-speakers of

KEY

| Bigo | Towns | | MALI | States and regions |

NORTH-EAST AFRICA BEFORE THE RISE OF ISLAM

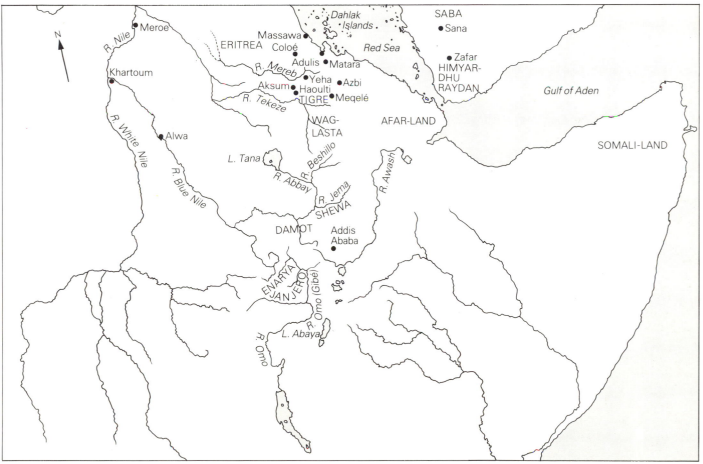

Azbi and the rest of eastern Tigre. Greek inscriptions at Aksum refer to the subjection of Ethiopia: probably referring to parts of the eastern Sudan, as the then current Greek usage described everything south of Egypt as 'Ethiopia'. Inscriptions also describe expeditions against recalcitrant tributaries–and to their being resettled–and against Beja marauders who interfered with the king's caravans.

Military prowess may not alone account for Aksum's pre-eminence. The Aksumites may have commanded the loyalty of the Agew to a degree that the leaders of the older centres did not. The name Aksum itself combines the Agew word for water with the Geez for official, *shum*, a reference to the vast rock cisterns above the town (in Tigrinya, *May-shum*, the chief's water). The buildings at Aksum are markedly different except in decorative motif from those modelled on South Arabian styles at surrounding sites. Rubble walling replaced dressed stone. Massive stelae deftly carved from single blocks of quarried granite, and harking back to the unworked slabs of basalt called *hawlti* found in many places in Tigre rather than to any South Arabian precursor, became the favourite Aksumite monument. These, and the Cyclopean walls of royal burial chambers beneath the stelae and on the necropolis which overlooks the town prove that the masonry skills learned from South Arabians were being redirected to locally inspired forms, not lost. Similarly the astral symbols of disc and crescent revered by the South Arabians are perpetuated in Aksumite royal art, but a dynastic god, Mahram, has been added to the Sabean pantheon. In Greek, the Aksumites equated Mahram with Ares, the god of the tumult and destructiveness of battle. Sabean continues to be used for inscriptions, but Geez and Greek parallel texts also appear, the former written either in Sabean script or in a variant in which the South Arabian characters have been modified to represent vowels as well as consonants. Thus readers of Ethiopic and its modern sister languages have the convenience of a full syllabary.

Mediterranean influences contributed to Aksum's amalgam of cultural elements. Aksumite coins adhere to the weights of Roman coins of the early 2nd century and bear inscriptions in Greek along with the crescent and disc of the Sabeans. The Greek practice of using letters of their alphabet with bars above and below to write numerals has been taken over whole into Geez inscriptions and continues to be used until this day. In Christianity, finally, the Aksumite rulers found a charter for proto-nationalism to bridge the linguistic and other differences which divided the peoples of their conglomerate empire before political and economic vicissitudes disrupted Aksum's military and mercantile power towards the end of the first millennium.

Christian Egypt and the conversion of Aksum

Christianity had been taken up early in the 2nd century by some of the learned Jews of Alexandria. Adherence among the Coptic-speaking peasantry and villagers of Egypt and among the numerous urban Greeks who had lived among them since the time of the Ptolemies grew during the violent persecutions of the 75 years before Constantine's edict of toleration in 313. Official religion and popular cults in the first centuries of Roman rule had lost their appeal as the trade of towns declined from AD 250. Poor harvests, brought on by a series of low Niles, made taxation more burdensome to the countryside, where monastic settlements offered leadership and protection.

Alexandria produced some of the early Church's foremost theologians. Often they were at loggerheads with the clerics who were influential at Constantinople either on doctrinal questions or because of the Egyptian's claim to precedence based on the pretence that the see of Alexandria had been founded by St Mark himself. One of its most troubled tenures began with the election in 328 of Athanatius. He proved to be as great a teacher to the whole Church as his fellow African bishop, St Augustine (d.430). Exile was forced upon Athanatius four times by sectarians who, through imperial favour, sought to tamper with the creed agreed to at the Council of Nicea in 325, when the teachings of the Egyptian Arius emphasizing the humanity of Jesus were condemned. Athanatius led the fight against this and other heresies.

In alliance with the Pope, Alexandrian interpretations prevailed at Church councils for over a century. At Chalcedon in 451, however, the extreme views on the unity of Christ's two natures taught by one of Athanatius's least tactful and less orthodox successors were rejected by bishops alarmed at the arrogance of the see of St Mark. Thereafter, the Church in Egypt began slowly to divide into a majority dominated by Coptic-speaking monks, whose well-endowed monasteries reached the peasantry and small townsmen, and Greek-speaking townsmen who declared for Chalcedon in order to demonstrate their loyalty to the foreign bishops whom the emperors had imposed upon the Egyptian clergy. Their detractors derided the Alexandrians and their sympathizers as 'Monophysites' and falsely accused them of denying the dual nature of Christ by their emphasis on his divinity. Egyptian reaction to the Emperor Justinian's attempts from 527 to reassert imperial authority further split the Church in Egypt. Aided by Persian and Arab occupation in the 7th century, the anti-Chalcedonians in Egypt separated the Coptic Church. It was to this vibrant and assertive community that the Aksumites attached themselves in the early 4th century, to follow the Copts gradually thereafter into isolation from the Greek and Latin branches of Christendom.

Before his first exile in 335, Athanatius (d.373) was visited by Frumentius, who was returning home to Tyre after some years at the Aksumite court to which he and his brother had been taken in their youth. The teacher they had been accompanying to India and the crew of their ship had been murdered by brigands at Adulis. The two boys' knowledge of Greek made them favourites of the king to whom they were released by their captors. On the king's death, Frumentius shared with the queen in the regency until Ezana, her son by the old king, came of age. Thus the two brothers had obtained permission for foreign Christians to meet for communal worship. Frumentius petitioned Athanatius to send someone to evangelize the country and was himself sent back as Aksum's first bishop. Thereafter, until the 1950s Ethiopia had as its primate a foreigner appointed from Egypt. In Ethiopia, Frumentius is remembered as *Abba Salama Kesate Berhan* (Father of Peace, the Bringer of Light). At mid-century, he was still at work and Ezana still reigned. It was reported in the Roman world that Frumentius had ordained a local clergy and converted great numbers of the Aksumites, including the king. Ethiopian Church historians place Frumentius at the time of two legendary twin rulers, Abreha and Atsbeha, and claim that the ancient Ethiopians progressed from Judaism to Christianity. In reality, until their conversion to Christianity the ancient Ethiopians worshipped the South Arabian, and their own indigenous gods.

Archaeological evidence shows a dramatic change from Ezana's reign. Elements of syncretism also appear. Ezana's coins are the only ones to bear crescent and disc for a time, and crosses for another period. One of his longest inscriptions boasts of a long expedition westwards to the Nile, where the Aksumites drove off Nuba intruders from Meroe★ and themselves sacked what is described as the half-ruined capital of the kingdom of Kush★ before retiring to the highlands. Uniquely in this one of his several surviving inscriptions, Ezana invokes the Trinity, avoids all references to Sabean deities and calls himself the servant of the Lord of Heaven and Earth, *Egziabeher* (still the Geez name for God), rather than son of Mahram, as in other instances. Yet the giant stelae with platforms to receive gifts for the dead continued to be erected for royal burials at Aksum.

The full translation of the Bible, the establishment of monasteries and, probably, the conversion of the countryside date to the end of the 5th and the early 6th centuries, when Aksum became a haven for anti-Chalcedonians and most notably for refugees from the Syriac-speaking Churches of the Levant. Ethiopians call this the second conversion. The initial effect of the introduction of Christianity was to align the Aksumites more closely with Greek-speaking traders and with outlets for African trade under Roman rule. In the three centuries before the Arab occupation of Egypt in 645, Aksum reached the apogee of its power as a mercantile state.

The best account of Aksum surviving in Graeco-Roman literature was written by the well-travelled Egyptian monk, Cosmas Indicopleustes. He visited Aksum and Adulis in 525, towards the end of the reign of Kaleb, and found the country full of churches. Indeed, archaeologists confirm traditional accounts that Kaleb put down apostacy and insurrection at the still flourishing market and temple site of Matara with such violence that much of the town had to be rebuilt. At Debre Damo, a flat-topped mountain between Aksum and Matara, one of the Syrian saints had suppressed a snake cult to found a monastery, which became the greatest fount of learning in the Christian empire until the 13th century. Here Kaleb built in timber and drystone-walling the magnificent chapel which stands to this day. Traditions of the Amharicized Agew of Wag and Lasta, along the upper Tekeze south of Tigre, most frequently recall Kaleb as the founder of the churches of what was then the borderlands of the Aksumite domain.

Cosmas repeats information given him by traders who had gone on the expeditions which the king sent annually many weeks beyond the frontier to barter iron bars, salt and meat for gold nuggets. The governor of Wag-Lasta was responsible for escorting these caravans to the west of Lake Tana. The spread of independent Agew into the highlands west of the upper Tekeze and within the bend of the Blue Nile was accelerated by this commercial penetration. The *Periplus* mentions gold only when listing exports from the East African coast. At some later date than the writing of this guide, therefore, and probably because of their closer contact with the Roman world, the Aksumite princes organized caravans to tap supplies of gold which formerly found their outlet through the Sudan.

Before the middle of the 4th century Constantine's successor sent missionaries to South Arabia. Many Christian communities sprang up. The elected rulers of Himyar and Dhu Raydan, the successor confederation to Saba, who made their capital at Zafar south of Sana

Timber and drystone-walled church at Debre Damo built in the 5th century AD by King Kaleb

wavered between Christianity and Judaism, the religion of merchants who were in league with the Romans' enemies, the Sassanian Persians. In 525 Kaleb sent a fleet with an army to intervene in a succession struggle. The Jewish faction at Zafar had bested the Christian candidate whom Kaleb and the Romans supported and had begun ruthlessly to extirpate all Christian strongholds in the Yemen. The invaders placed a Christian prince once more over Himyar. Thereafter Kaleb's son and successor, Gebre Mesqel (Servant of the Cross), appointed as viceroy the Aksumite commander, Abreha, who had usurped power.

Although Abreha showed scant respect for his nominal overlord at Aksum, he cooperated with the Romans by attacking Persian clients in South Arabia in 548. With much energy too, he built a fine cathedral at Sana to draw pilgrims and their caravans away from the shrines of pre-Islamic Mecca. In the year that the Prophet was born (570), it is said, Abreha (or a namesake) rashly marched into the Hejaz to destroy Mecca. The expedition aborted with terrible losses and South Arabia erupted in civil war. At the behest of an anti-Christian faction, the Persians, who were renewing their war with the Roman Empire, occupied South Arabia in 572. The Christian parties in Himyar and its sister states were crushed. The agricultural and commercial prosperity of South Arabia also suffered. Aksum's international trade was further dislocated while the Copts welcomed the Persians into Palestine and Egypt in 616–20 and, ten years later, the Byzantines then drove them out. The mercantile base of Aksum's wealth was disrupted until the victories of the Arab Muslims from mid-century once more reunited South Arabia, the northern Red Sea, Egypt and the Levant.

Christian Nubia

Something of Christian belief and ritual had long been seeping southwards from Upper Egypt when the first formal mission arrived at Faras, the capital of the northern-most Nubian kingdom of Nobatia in 543. It had been sent by Justinian's wife, the Empress Theodora, who favoured the anti-Chalcedonians. To judge by the evidence of their burials, commoners as well as their kings rapidly converted. Because Nobatia, its rival, had attached itself to the so-called Monophysites, the neighbouring kingdom of Makuria, with its capital at Old Dongola, welcomed missionaries sent from the opposing party and sympathetic to the Greek-speaking Church in Egypt in 569–70. At the invitation of the king of the most southerly kingdom, which had its capital on the right bank of the Blue Nile half way between Sennar and Khartoum, the anti-Chalcedonian bishop of

Wall painting of the Nativity (late 10th to early 11th century) from a cathedral excavated at Faras in Nubia

Nubia left Faras in 580 for Alwa. He reported finding Ethiopians there but dismissed them as heretics. No important link between the two African churches, even as they grew increasingly isolated, has yet been documented, although the decoration of later Aksumite churches bears some similarity to the wealth of religious painting in Nubia. Instead Christian Nubia, as had Kush, looked northwards.

Christians in all three of the Nubian kingdoms adopted Greek as their liturgical language and preserved Byzantine practices although acknowledging in the 8th century the right of the See of Alexandria to appoint the several Nubian bishops. Inscriptions in Coptic, and in Nubian written in Coptic script, also sometimes appear in the northern kingdoms which had amalgamated under the leadership of Old Dongola before the Arabs attacked them shortly after the occupation of Egypt. After the second Battle of Dongola in 651–2, the Arabs accepted a truce rather than face the expert Nubian archers once more. Referred to as the *Baqt*, the agreement between the Nubians and Egypt's Muslim rulers required an exchange of payments. The Nubians promised an annual quota of slaves in return for Egyptian produce. They also promised to protect foreign Muslim traders and to permit them public worship. For over six centuries no further attempt to conquer these Christian states was made in spite of Nubian raids into Upper Egypt. Instead, the *Baqt* reinforced Nubia's commercial orientation northwards down the Nile.

Aksum moves south

Aksum, like its neighbours in the Sudan, was shielded from the direct consequences of Arab Muslim expansion. Arab traditions claim that a King Asham of Aksum gave sanctuary to companions of the Prophet during the *hejira* to Medina, and that Asham's successor, his son, Arma, was so warmly sympathetic towards Islam when emissaries came from Muhammad at Mecca offering condolences on the death of the kindly Asham that the Prophet excluded the Ethiopians from the enemies of Islam. In fact, the thrust of Arab conquest simply bypassed North-East Africa for more attractive areas. Indirectly, the convulsions caused within the Byzantine Roman world did disturb Aksum, which turned its attention southwards away from the Red Sea for several generations.

Ethiopian Muslims retain the tradition that King Asham, whom they hold to have been a convert to Islam, is buried between Azbi and Tigre's present capital, Meqelé. Thus as early as the first quarter of the 7th century, perhaps, the Aksumite capital had begun the shift southwards which brought the empire's centre of gravity into the corridor between the upper Tekeze, the Beshillo (a tributary of the Blue Nile), and the tributaries of the middle Awash. Here animist Agew, Amhara and Sidama came belatedly under the influence of Christian Aksum during a great revival of its energies *c*.800–950 (at the very time when Christians were ceasing to be the majority of the population in Egypt). Parts of the north had been overrun by animist

Agew from west of the Tekeze and by Beja pastoralists pushing in from the eastern Sudan. It is these upheavals that account for the decline of the town of Aksum at the end of the 7th century. The prelude to and perhaps the underlying cause of Aksumite withdrawal from the north-east for a time was the loss of maritime trade to Arab Muslims during a long struggle that lasted into the 8th century. By then Muslim rulers of the Dahlak Islands had replaced the traders of Adulis. The African coast remained nominally under Aksumite rule although in the hands of pirates and independent pastoral peoples. Christianity retained its hold over the highland population despite the incursions of animists.

The later princes of the Aksumite dynasty established themselves in what had been Aksum's southern borderlands and there controlled the slave trade, which the *Periplus* had mentioned only at ports beyond the straits, as well as the gold trade, which Cosmas described. Thus they became the most important of the inland partners of Muslim traders in the Gulf of Aden and on the Dahlak Islands. The resilience of the Christian empire in the last quarter of the first millennium owes much to the sense of destiny created by a fusing of Old Testament stories with local legend.

As eventually compiled in the *Kebre Neghest*, the Christian kingdom's imperial saga explains how the Emperor Constantine divided the world with his fellow Christian emperor at Aksum. The Biblical scraps about a queen from Sheba (or Saba) have also been elaborated around a folk hero, Menelik I, who is remembered to have excluded women from royal succession. Menelik is presented as the son by Solomon of the mythical Makeda whom clerical writers saw as the queen from Sheba. Jewish companions sent back with Menelik after he too visited Jerusalem are said to have stolen the Ark of the Covenant. Thus Aksum shared the world with Rome and was endowed as a second Jerusalem and an earthly Zion (Zyon) under a putative branch of the House of David. No mention is made in the *Kebre Neghest* of Islam, although the Geez version appears to be a translation through Arabic from a Coptic original that was circulated in the 13th century as part of propaganda against the family of Agew origin from Lasta,★ which had usurped the throne from the last of the Aksumite dynasty *c*.1150. Apparently, as one might have expected, Ethiopian monks in Egypt and on pilgrimage to the Holy Land had early begun to search for Biblical references to their part of what the Greek version of the Bible called Ethiopia (*viz.* all the lands south of Egypt). It is likely that something of this Solomonic myth, in which Rome's first Christian ruler also appears, was part of the folk beliefs spread by the Ethiopian clergy during the brilliant reigns of Kaleb and his son, Gebre Mesqel. This composite legend of the origins of the Christian monarchy inspired all succeeding generations of Christian Ethiopians however removed they and their ancestors were in fact from the small triangle in the northern highlands where Aksumite civilization had arisen.

R.A.C.

The spread of Islam in North Africa

The Arab conquests

The Arabs who conquered Egypt and Cyrenaica between AD 639 and 644 belonged to a religious community whose members constituted an army. They were 'the Faithful' who had conquered Syria from the Byzantine Empire, and Iraq from the Persians, and were engaged upon the conquest of Iran. Driving the Byzantines* from Egypt with some assistance from the native Copts,* they replaced Alexandria as the capital by a garrison city called Fustat. Here they collected the tribute of the conquered country, maintaining for this purpose the Byzantine administration, strengthened by the departure of the great Greek landowners whose estates had escaped government control. About a hundred district governors from the Coptic upper class were appointed to take charge of agriculture and irrigation, to collect taxes in cash and kind, and to levy a new poll-tax on the adult male population. The Monophysite Coptic Church was recognized as the true Church of Egypt, and recovered all that it had lost during Byzantine persecution.

The Christian Copts, classed as subjects under Arab protection, were largely forbidden to adopt the faith and join the ranks of the conquerors. To maintain their numbers, the Arabs looked to the Berbers of Libya, whom they raided and enslaved, enlisting them in the army as clients and thereby admitting them to the religious community as *muslims*, people who had made their *islam*★ or submission. An early raid on Christian Nubia★ led to an agreement to continue the existing exchange of Egyptian grain for black slaves; an attack on Byzantine Africa in 647 defeated and killed the exarch (governor) Gregory. About 670 the Arabs established a new garrison city at Kairouan, south of Carthage.★ By 705 Carthage had been captured, the Romano-Berber princes defeated, and Byzantine Africa incorporated into the Arab Empire as the province of Ifriqiya. By 715 the governor of Ifriqiya, Musa ibn Nusayr, with contingents of Berber clients and allies, had advanced through northern Morocco to conquer Spain from the Visigoths.

The Arab Empire, ruled from Damascus by the Commander of the Faithful, stretched from the Atlantic to Central Asia. Powerful and wealthy Arab nobles commanded armies and governed provinces with retinues of slaves and personal clients. Coptic peasants, however, were on the verge of rebellion against high taxation. Discontent was rife among the faithful. The army, becoming a body

KEY

| VILI | Peoples | | Bigo | Towns | | MALI | States and regions |

THE SPREAD OF ISLAM IN NORTH AFRICA

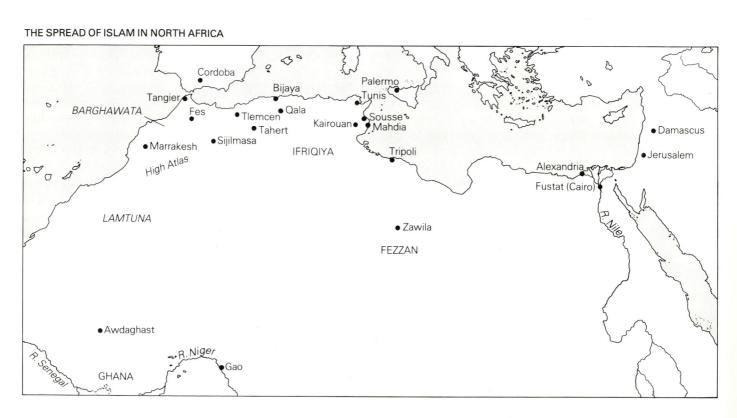

The Great Mosque of Kairouan, Tunisia, 9th century: the south wall showing the dome above the *mihrab*

of registered soldiers, was split into factions and divided between Arabs and non-Arabs. Those excluded from its ranks were similarly divided. More important, they were jealous of the privileges of the few. The Umayyad dynasty held the office of Commander of the Faithful in the name of God, but its right was challenged from various quarters. In 739 the Berbers of North Africa rebelled, choosing a new ruler whom they regarded as leader of the community. The Umayyads, however, were overthrown in 750 by revolutionaries from Central Asia, who installed a candidate from the house of the Prophet Muhammad.

The growth of Islam

The new rulers, the Abbasids, moved the capital of the empire from Damascus to Baghdad in Iraq. There they perfected an absolute monarchy housed in a palace city which contained the royal household, the ministries and the professional army. Egypt was ruled through a governor, a financial superintendent and a postmaster in charge of communications with the capital. Great estates were given to supporters of the regime, while tax-farmers began to take over the collection of revenue. Arabic replaced Greek as the language of written records, and was adopted by the educated Copts who mainly staffed the administration. Ifriqiya, reconquered with difficulty from Arab as well as Berber rebels, was granted virtual independence in

800. Its governor, Ibrahim ibn al-Aghlab, built himself a palace city in imitation of Baghdad outside the original capital, Kairouan. He recruited an army of slaves, probably from Europe, to dominate the Arab troops who garrisoned the outlying districts. Descendants of the Kharijites, the original rebels of 739, enjoyed independence in the northern Sahara and western Algeria. Spain was ruled by the last of the Umayyads. In northern Morocco Idris, in flight from Arabia where his family had challenged the Abbasids' right to the throne, founded the city of Fes and a local dynasty, the Idrisids.

As caliphs, or successors of Muhammad, at the head of the religious community, the Abbasids claimed religious authority. In the hundred years from 750 to 850, however, the faith was defined by scholars who handed down their teachings from master to pupil. They taught a heavenly Law which the ruler should enforce, but could not change. The majority of Muslims were Sunnites, whose versions of the Law were authorized by the Sunna, the Custom of the Prophet (essentially legal rulings drawn from the Quran and the *hadith*–sayings attributed to the Prophet, and subsequent judicial interpretations of these two sources). These Sunni scholars (*ulama*, sing. *alim*, 'the wise'), differed on non-fundamental points of law and were consequently divided into schools, of which one, the Shafiite, originated in Egypt. The most widespread in North Africa, however, was the Malikite school, of which Kairouan became a distinguished centre. Teaching was in the mosques, the places of worship built initially in the middle of the garrison cities, where the community assembled every Friday to hear the prayer recited in the monarch's name. By contrast with the Sunnites, who had accepted the succession of caliphs of the Umayyad and Abbasid dynasties, the Shiites emphasized the political and legal authority of Ali, the husband of Muhammad's daughter Fatima, and his offspring, who included Idris, the founder of Fes. The Kharijites in North Africa divided into a number of sects with their own traditions. Such differences created hostility, but were trivial compared with the general agreement on the form of the Law.

By the middle of the 9th century the community of the faithful, no longer an army, had become a cross-section of the population of Egypt and North Africa (in Arabic, the Maghrib, 'the West'). Believers were now generally known as Muslims, and their religion as Islam. In Egypt they were settling as peasants on the land, and beginning to assimilate the rural Copts, perhaps by intermarriage. Literate Copts, employed as clerks in the administration, became identified with this kind of occupation. This identification, together with the wealth and learning of the Egyptian Church, helped Christianity to survive as a minority religion. In Ifriqiya these same factors were insufficient, and native Latin-speaking Christianity had died out by the 12th century. Islam in the Maghrib was a dynamic civilization which during the 9th century not only conquered and colonized Byzantine Sicily, but the remoter regions of North Africa

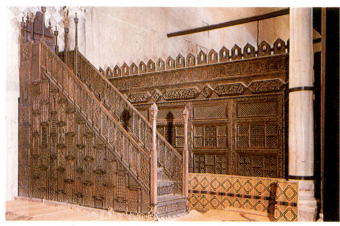

The Great Mosque of Kairouan, Tunisia: 9th century pulpit and 11th century screen for the sultan

itself. Soldiers, nomads, merchants and adventurers were joined by holy men who settled in the countryside as far away as southern Morocco. The term *murabit* (marabout), originally one dedicated to the holy war against the infidel, eventually became the common name for such a saintly and ascetic person. The holy man acquired all the characteristics formerly possessed by priests, monks and hermits, Christian and pagan.

In the 9th century a major political and economic role was played by the Ibadites, a Kharijite sect centred on southern Tunisia and Tripolitania, with a city at Tahert in western Algeria and adherents at Zawila in the Fezzan. Zawila supplied Ifriqiya and Egypt with slaves from the Central Sudan;* the Ibadites, travelling south-westwards to the Niger bend at Gao, obtained the gold of Ghana.* Thus they created a network of trade routes in the Sahara feeding the arterial route from Spain through North Africa to Egypt, where it branched up through Syria to Iraq and down the Red Sea to India. The route, created by the Arab conquests, survived the dissolution of the Arab empire. It restored commercial prosperity to North Africa, and stimulated the discovery of the new world to the south of the desert. It also ensured that the Maghrib developed alongside the Middle East within the growing civilization of Islam.

The Fatimids

In the century from 850 to 950, the Abbasid empire disintegrated, and the Abbasid caliphs became nominal rulers of the Islamic world under the protection of a Persian dynasty. Egypt, briefly independent under the Tulunid dynasty (868–905), became finally independent under the Ikhshidids in 943. Palace cities were built outside the old capital Fustat, and the new rulers used the country's wealth to maintain a substantial army, to govern much of Syria, and to pose as guardians of the Holy Places of Mecca and Medina. A still

more ambitious state was created in Ifriqiya, where the local dynasty of the Aghlabids was overthrown in 909 by an insurrection of mountain tribesmen inspired and led by a holy man, a prophet who preached the coming of the Mahdi, 'the Rightly-Guided One' destined to prepare the ground for the reign of the true representatives of God on Earth. These were the Fatimids, called after Fatima, daughter of Muhammad and wife of Ali, from whom they claimed spiritual descent. The Mahdi, the first of the line, set out to overthrow the Abbasids from the west as the Abbasids had overthrown the Umayyads from the east.

Mahdia, 'the city of the Mahdi', was built on the coast of Tunisia as a base for the invasion of the Middle East. First attacks on Egypt, however, failed. To the west the Fatimids came into conflict with the Umayyad rulers of Spain, turning northern Morocco and western Algeria into a battleground for tribal chieftains in the service of the rival dynasties. In 945 they were almost overthrown by the revolt of the Kharijite Abu Yazid.

The Great Mosque of Kairouan, Tunisia: the *mihrab* (niche indicating the direction of Mecca)

The Ribat of Monastir, Tunisia: a coastal castle serving as a retreat for Muslim holy men, built 8th–11th centuries

The final attack on Egypt did not take place until 969, after a long campaign of propaganda and diplomacy financed by Western Sudanese gold. This was procured in unsurpassed quantities by Ibadite merchants who opened up a more direct route across the desert from Sijilmasa in south-eastern Morocco to Awdaghast on the borders of Ghana. The army, led by the Slavonic general Jawhar, encountered little resistance from the demoralized Ikhshidid rulers of Egypt; a new palace city called al-Qahira (Cairo, 'the Victorious') was built to the north of Fustat, and in 973 the Fatimid monarch Muizz arrived from Ifriqiya.

The Fatimids were Shiites, who claimed the right to rule the Muslim world in place of the Abbasids, the representatives of Sunnite Islam. But the Abbasids had ceased in practice to govern even Iraq, and the Fatimids were not strong enough to recreate the old empire of the faithful. Instead they sought recognition, not from the mass of the people, but from the rulers of the many states into which the Islamic world was now divided. Their power was based upon the government of Egypt and Syria, whose taxes paid for a mixed army of Berbers, Turks and Sudanese, and a wealthy aristocracy of members of the royal family, their servants and viziers. Around this nucleus were regions such as the Yemen, Mecca and Medina, and Ifriqiya under the Zirids (Berber princes from the central Maghrib to whom the Fatimids had entrusted their North African dominions), whose rulers acknowledged Fatimid overlordship. Beyond these regions missionaries were sent to work for the establishment of similarly pro-Fatimid regimes. The Christian states of Nubia* and Ethiopia* were included through their connections with the Coptic Church, which acted as an intermediary between Cairo and the Christian kings. The trade route down the Red Sea to India enabled Fatimid merchants and missionaries to create colonies as far away as India itself.

Decline of the Fatimids

Since recognition of the Fatimid monarch as the Imam or leader of the entire Muslim community was so important to the dynasty, it was a blow when in 1048 the Zirid sultan of Ifriqiya, already independent, recognized the Abbasids. The Abbasids were now championed by the Seljuq Turks, a Central Asiatic horde which took over Iraq and moved on into Syria. The threat of invasion, coupled with prolonged famine, brought about a revolution in Egypt which ended in 1074 when the Armenian general Badr al-Jamali took power on behalf of the sovereign. With Syria and Palestine largely lost, the army was reformed, tax farms were given to soldiers, and new provinces replaced the small administrative districts of Egypt. In 1094 Badr al-Jamali was succeeded by his son al-Afdal. The claims of the dynasty were upheld mainly to provide the real ruler with a title to govern in the name of the Imam, and to maintain the connections established by the Fatimids along the important route to India. The rivalry with the Turks ended with the capture of Jerusalem by the 1st Crusade in 1099, and the creation of the Crusader states in Palestine and Syria. Instead of pursuing the holy war against the infidel, however, al-Afdal withdrew his larger but more lightly-armed forces after their defeat by the Frankish knights. Egypt retreated into isolation.

The break with Cairo in 1048 was part of an unsuccessful attempt by the Zirids to maintain control of Ifriqiya. With the departure of the Fatimids for Egypt, prosperity declined, and the government at Kairouan became unpopular. In the mid-11th century the former Roman and Byzantine province disintegrated into a series of city states, militarily dependent on the confederation of Arab tribes known as the Banu Hilal who had pushed into the country from the Libyan desert. The Zirids were confined to Mahdia, while Kairouan dwindled to a small town. Their cousins, the Hammadids, left Qala, their capital in the mountains of Algeria, and moved to Bijaya (Bougie). Here and elsewhere in the Muslim world the cities showed a trace of Roman town planning in the central mosque, which took the place of the forum, surrounded by market streets. But the streets had become winding, the houses were enclosed, and quarters were built around cul-de-sacs shut off at night. Government was by officials under the prince in the palace citadel. Village and tribal communities were largely self-governing. The nomadic Arab tribes were intermediate between the state and this rural society, lording over less military peoples within their territories.

The Almoravids and the Almohads

Morocco in the 11th century saw a new state created in a region which had lain largely outside the Roman Empire. Nomads, merchants, warriors and holy men had moved into the districts north and south of the High Atlas; on the Atlantic coast a Berber people, the Barghawata, made holy war on their neighbours. In the mid-11th century a holy man of the High Atlas, Ibn Yasin, preached militant Islam to the Berber-speaking Tuareg nomads of the western Sahara. The Lamtuna submitted, and under Ibn Yasin's direction became the Holy Men, the Murabitun or Almoravids, an army drilled by prayer and dedicated to fighting for the faith. Both Sijilmasa and Awdaghast were taken, and the gold trade of the Western Sudan was brought under control. Ibn Yasin was killed in 1057, but his chief commander, Abu Bakr, ruled the desert until his death in 1086, during which time, it is said, he conquered the black kingdom of Ghana. In 1070 he founded the city of Marrakesh north of the High Atlas, from which his cousin Yusuf ibn Tashfin conquered Morocco, western Algeria, and Muslim Spain.

The Almoravids in the Maghrib and in Spain remained a foreign army and a foreign aristocracy. Despite their piety, prowess and wealth in Western Sudanese gold, they were swept away by a similar, still more thoroughgoing movement among the Berbers of the High Atlas. The Muwahhidun or Almohads, 'the Unitarians', were created by the scholarly Ibn Tumart, who came as a new Mahdi, sent by God to lead the Muslim community. After his death about 1130, his caliph or deputy Abd al-Mumin had conquered Morocco by 1147, and by 1163 ruled North Africa as far as Tripoli. By 1172 Abd al-

The al-Azhar Mosque, Cairo: court, Fatimid period. Founded in the 10th century, al-Azhar became a university

Mumin's son and successor ruled Muslim Spain as well. The dynasty governed this vast empire in the name of the Mahdi. The Berbers of the High Atlas formed the aristocracy and the nucleus of the army. The students of Ibn Tumart's doctrine, that the faithful should eschew traditional judicial interpretations of the Law and go directly to the Quran and the sayings of Muhammad for guidance, formed a corps of administrators. Success depended upon an astonishing ability to muster and move a large and disciplined army to meet attacks by nomads in Ifriqiya and by Christians in Spain. At the height of their power the Almohad caliphs were great patrons of the arts and sciences; the empire was prosperous, with Morocco now the centre of affairs in the Maghrib. The breakdown came at the beginning of the 13th century, when Ifriqiya became autonomous under an Almohad sheikh of the Hafsid family, and the caliph was defeated by Castile in 1212. When the throne was seized in 1227 by a candidate who repudiated the Mahdi and massacred the Almohads, the Hafsids declared themselves independent in Ifriqiya, the Ziyanids in Tlemcen, while Muslim Spain, except for Granada, was reoccupied by Portugal, Castile and Aragon.

Crusaders and Turks in Egypt

After the murder of al-Afdal in 1121, the Fatimids survived until the 1150s, when Egypt attracted the attention of the Christian kings of Jerusalem and of the Turks in Damascus, the leaders of the Muslim opposition to the Crusaders. Both saw the country as good land to be distributed as fiefs for the maintenance of mounted knights, expensive soldiers essential to victory. Turkish knights, less heavily armoured than the Crusaders, but trained as horse archers as well as spear-and-swordsmen, were called *mamluks* ('slaves') since they were normally, after purchase, trained in the households of already qualified soldiers who constituted an oligarchy to form companies in the service of their lords. Repeated invasions of Egypt by Crusaders and Turks ended with the conquest of the country in 1169 by the forces of Damascus. The Turkish commander, Saladin–a Kurd–destroyed the Egyptian army, and divided the land among his *mamluks* who paid some of the revenue to the state, keeping the remainder. When the Fatimid caliph died in 1171, he was not replaced. Instead, Saladin was sufficiently powerful to take over the government of Damascus, and in the name of the Abbasids to conduct the war against the Crusaders which ended with the capture of Jerusalem in 1187. His empire survived the attack of the 3rd Crusade to be inherited by his family, the Ayyubids. Egypt did little more than provide the resources for the active Syrian policies of the dynasty, until in 1250 it was invaded by the army of the 7th Crusade. During the invasion the Ayyubid sultan died, his *mamluks* rebelled, and placed one of themselves, Aybeg, on the throne. Thus began the Mamluk★ 'dynasty' which was to control Egypt until overthrown by the Ottomans★ in 1517.

M.B.

Islam and Christianity in North-East and East Africa

The Indian Ocean trade until the arrival of the Portuguese

Ease of sea communications has bound coastal eastern Africa and Madagascar to the Indian Ocean world. From November to April prevailing winds bear sailing ships from western India, the Persian Gulf and southern Arabia towards Africa. The same steady winds brought Indonesians from Borneo to Madagascar by outrigger canoes in the first half of the 1st millennium AD. These first settlers of the island brought bananas, root crops and rice cultivation. They also introduced Indonesian architecture and their Malayo-Polynesian language. All these cultural traits, except language, spread to the Bantu-speakers of the African coast of the Mozambique Channel, peoples whom the Malagasy raided for slaves. By the 16th century independent colonies of Africans were well-established on the western coast of Madagascar. Cultural exchange was also two-way. Iron working,* which began *c.*1000, cattle keeping techniques, religious ideas and chiefly office came from, or at least by way of, the African coast. From the 12th century onwards Arabic-speaking Muslims also landed, some coming from the Kenya coast. By the 16th century Muslim Arab settlements exported cattle to Arabia and supplied the whole East African coast with rice. About 1550 Malagasy royal lineages emerged to dominate large sections of the island. The infusion of a variety of Asian peoples, including some Muslims, and the development of overseas commerce were, however, only two of many factors contributing to this profound change.

KEY

| Bigo | Towns | | MALI | States and regions |

ISLAM AND CHRISTIANITY IN NORTH-EAST AFRICA

The monsoon of June to October carried traders back from East Africa towards India. The rising demand for African goods transformed the network of local trade in East Africa. Early in the 2nd millennium AD seasonal coastal markets and fishing villages developed into small cosmopolitan city-states with substantial buildings and complex cultures and economies: a change associated with the permanent settlement of Muslim traders. Arabic and Persian enriched the Bantu languages spoken by the small groups of fishermen and local traders visiting the cost between the Juba and the Zambezi. A coastal Bantu – Swahili – developed. Loan words for commerce also appear in the Cushitic language of the Somali of the coast north of the Juba. Neither Swahili nor Somali was supplanted by Arabic although numerous immigrants from the Persian Gulf and Arabia settled among the Somali, and groups also ventured further south. Everywhere, hunters, cattle breeders and cultivators near the African coasts were drawn into the mercantile economy which world demand and Afro-Asian partnership at the coast had created. Coastal trading by African seamen is recorded by the *Periplus of the Erythraean Sea* (late 2nd or early 3rd century AD). Greater demand stimulated it, but Indian Ocean shipping was in Asian hands.

The type of goods available meant that overseas trade rather than exchanges among Africans predominated. From the time of the *Periplus* until the Portuguese* disrupted the trade at the end of the 15th century, the African market satisfied itself by importing India's cheap textiles and metal goods and by buying glazed pottery and porcelain from China and Persia, as well as glass beads from outside Africa. For such manufactures Africans bartered a range of raw materials: incense, ivory, tortoise shell, rhinoceros horn, coconut oil, timber, grain and pig-iron. Gold and slaves had been of scant importance according to the *Periplus*, but came onto the market in increasing quantities thereafter. Slaves came from the North-East African interior in response to Muslim demand. Gold continued to be supplied through Christian Ethiopia from the upper Nile. The opening of deposits on the highlands of Great Zimbabwe* from the 10th century dramatically affected the fortunes of East African trading centres. The rise of Mogadishu on the Benader coast as East Africa's principal mart at the beginning of the 2nd millennium AD rested on its control of the trade.

After 1150, Arabs and traders of Arabian origin who had been settled for several generations on the Benader coast, migrated southwards to the outposts of the seaborne trade along the Swahili coast which they called Zanj. Previously only a handful had been so adventurous. Soon after 1200, Kilwa, on one of the islands off the southern Tanzanian coast, emerged as Mogadishu's leading rival. From the mid-13th century Kilwa was pre-eminent under a Muslim dynasty which boasted of having come from Shiraz in Persia by way of Mogadishu. For generations before 1250 the Shirazi had married into merchant and chiefly families along the Benader coast and among the

Swahili. This so-called Shirazi dynasty was replaced at Kilwa at the end of the 13th century by another Arabo-African line. By then Kilwa appointed the governors of Sofala, the principal outlet for Zimbabwean gold on the Mozambique coast. For 150 years thereafter Kilwa prospered as an emporium and as a centre for light manufacturing. Pottery was made, despite the growing importance of imports, iron was smelted on a small scale, and copper was cast. Kilwans also themselves wove some of the cloth that – together with the glass beads which they imported – was the principal medium of exchange in the interior gold trade.

By 1331, when the Moroccan traveller Ibn Battuta visited, Kilwans were importing large quantities of silk and other fine textiles for their own use. From the end of the 12th century the rulers of Kilwa, like their northerly coastal neighbours, minted their own copper coinage, and imported pottery, including Chinese porcelain, began to be abundant, at least among the wealthy, who now built stone houses. The principal mosque was also much extended and a great palace-warehouse complex of dressed coral masonry was constructed before 1350. Vaults and domes may have been inspired by buildings at Aden, with which Kilwa traded directly, but the imbedding of Chinese ceramics in external walls is an exuberant contrivance peculiar to the Swahili. The geometric panels on the enclosures of pillar tombs along the Kenya coast are also locally inspired.

Pillar tomb at Gedi on the Kenya coast

The sultans of Kilwa ceased issuing coins *c*.1375. After two generations of economic decline, monumental buildings were once more undertaken after *c*.1425. From 1450, however, dynastic quarrels weakened the state to such an extent that in the decades before the arrival of the Portuguese, the centre of the East African trade had shifted northwards to the Kenya coast where Mombasa and the islands of Lamu and Pate prospered even after European shipping cut African middlemen out of much of the gold trade.

The spread of Islam

Within a century of the Prophet's death, individual Muslims were living at Mogadishu and on the Somali coast opposite Aden. Isolated Muslims—often refugee schismatics—had also established themselves down the whole East African coast by the end of the 1st millennium. With the arrival of numerous Arabic-speaking traders and a literate, learned community, orthodox Sunni Islam* established itself in all the coastal towns. In 1238 the Muslim community at Mogadishu was prosperous enough to raise a great Friday (main) mosque in stone. From mid-century a local Arabo-Somali dynasty supplanted the town's council of clans and foreign residents and established an Islamic state. Ibn Battuta reported the high degree of learning as well as of material comfort among urban Muslims during his trip from Zeila to Kilwa in 1331. Nevertheless, Islam remained a coastal religion in East Africa, without influence even on the

The 15th century extensions to the Great Mosque at Kilwa

mainland facing the island and peninsular settlements of traders. Because long-distance trade penetrated deep into North-East Africa and the Sudan, Islam was introduced there along with foreign manufactures as trade increased. It rivalled Ethiopian Christianity in the conversion of highlanders from traditional beliefs, and challenged Nubian Byzantine Christianity in the Sudan.

For some centuries Christian Nubia* retained its vitality despite the conversion to Islam of most Egyptians after 800, which isolated the Nubian Church. The migration into the eastern Sudan of Arab nomads and prospectors for gold further encircled the Nubian Christians, who clung to the arable land along the main Nile and on the Blue Nile as far south as the site of Sennar. Dynastic quarrels exposed the northern kingdom (with its capital at Old Dongola) to intervention from Egypt. From 1375 successful contenders relied upon Muslim allies and abandoned Christianity which, nonetheless, remained the popular religion for at least another generation. By the mid-15th century, however (unlike the situation in Muslim Egypt, where a Coptic minority remained significant) Christianity had virtually ceased to exist.

Soba, the capital of the southern Nubian kingdom of Alwa, was occupied at the end of the 15th century by a northern Sudanese Muslim leader who had established himself at the confluence of the White and Blue Niles. In 1504 almost all the riverain Sudan came under the rule of the Funj, a warrior aristocracy of Muslims. In alliance with peoples of the White Nile, the Funj established a sultanate at Sennar on the left bank of the Blue Nile. Upstream, on the right bank, Soba was in ruins. The king of Alwa and many of his subjects seem to have retreated up the Blue Nile to the gold-bearing area of Fazughli beyond Funj control, where they may have remained Christian into the 17th century. By their hold over the gold of the upper Blue Nile, these displaced rulers obtained horses. Their cavalry menaced the Funj until the latter occupied Fazughli about 1685, and may also have aided the northern Ethiopians during Muslim invasions of the Christian empire in 1529–43. Even after 1685, it took a generation for the last vestiges of the Nubian Church in Fazughli to disappear.

In North-East Africa, Christianity and Islam both expanded at the expense of local cults. Among the northern Somali the slow process of conversion to Islam is associated with the founding of the major clan divisions as late as the mid-12th century under the inspiration of learned holy men from southern Arabia who married into Somali chiefly families and displaced local magicians and diviners. Further south, the Hawiya Somali clans who had settled the lower Webi Shebele by 1100 also controlled Merca and Brava. Through these ports Muslim Arab traders penetrated the fertile valley of the Webi under Hawiya protection. Learned Muslims also came inland by this route, and in the 14th century an Arabo-Hawiya confederation, Ajuran, was founded.

Ajuran was the first large Somali state. Islam then made inroads among the pastoral Somali of the Ogaden from Ajuran centres of teaching and piety. The majority of the herdsmen living in the lowlands between the Gulf of Aden and the Harar plateau, however, were converted through the military activities of the highland Muslim states, which were dominated by merchant princes and warriors speaking Semitic languages related to today's Harari. This process was not completed until the 16th century when the Harari Ahmed ibn Ibrahim (d.1543) succeeded in incorporating large numbers of Somali irregulars into the armies he launched in a jihad (holy war) against the Christian empire of Ethiopia.

During the centuries from the Arab occupation of Egypt (645) until the Portuguese challenge to Muslim naval supremacy in the Gulf of Aden and the Red Sea, the Ethiopian Christian empire expanded its dominion over much of present-day Ethiopia while retaining its hold over part of the lands north of the Mereb River (modern Eritrea). Arab Muslim traders flocked to North-East Africa by way of the old route across the Mereb into Tigre, but made few converts away from the coast and its offshore islands. They did, however, become indispensable intermediaries in the long-distance trade which the later emperors of Aksum* and their successors tried to monopolize. Along a newer route inland from the Somali port of Zeila, Arab and Muslim coastal traders settled at staging posts up to the escarpment north of Addis Ababa and in the approaches to the Rift Valley. For generations they lived as clients of local chiefly families who were animists. The Shewan highlands of the district of Addis Ababa were most favoured by the development of transit trade

to Zeila. The later Aksumite rulers, having revived the power of the Christian empire at a new capital south of Aksum from 850, sought to expand their hold over the outlying settlements of Semitic-speakers down to the Shewan highlands. For some 30 years until the end of the 970s, however, a warrior queen of the Cushitic Sidama of Damot rallied animists to block this expansion. The Amhara, Argobba and other Semitic-speaking peoples south of Tigre (whose ancestors had settled the eastern highlands before the rise of Aksum) remained largely animist and independent for several more generations. Only from the beginning of the 13th century under the Zagwe (ze-Agew – 'of the Agew') dynasty, which had been established c.1150, did the Christian state resume its expansion. By then, it faced the competition of Islam and of an Islamic state in eastern Shewa.

The first important conversions to Islam in the Ethiopian highlands occurred early in the 12th century among the ancestors of the Argobba farmers and professional traders who today survive in scattered settlements along a crescent swinging from the escarpment in south-eastern Wello province through Shewa to the outskirts of Harar town. A Sultanate of Shewa emerged in the central portion of this crescent, in the lowlands between the eastern edge of the Shewan escarpment and the middle Awash, astride the Zeila-bound routes of the Rift Valley slave trade. The ruling family claimed Meccan descent and exercised paramountcy over the many small trading centres in which resident Muslims from the coast and Arabia had finally gained the upper hand. From 1125 the Sultanate of Shewa came into conflict with Amharic-speaking pioneers whose ancestors living on both sides of the Beshillo (an eastern tributary of the Blue Nile) had absorbed

'Sidama stones' are so called by the present inhabitants of the Rift Valley southwest of Addis Ababa since they believe that these monoliths were erected by their predecessors, the Sidama. Many are anthropomorphic, probably representing important deceased warriors or leaders, and are decorated with representations of ornaments which may have been attached to the burial wrappings of the deceased. These examples are now in Addis Ababa but were formerly about 100km to the south-west. They may date only from the 17th century but are representative of a style that goes back to earlier centuries of the history of the several Cushitic-speaking peoples whom Christianity, Islam and the Oromo migrations later influenced

Christian Tigrean migrants from c.800. Thus priestly Christian families were present among the still predominantly animist Amhara before they set off southwards in the mid-11th century in search of virgin lands. By the 13th century Shewa was a cultural boundary between Christianity and Islam.

Muslim and Christian empires in Ethiopia and the Horn

About 1150 the Aksumite dynasty was overthrown by the Agew commander of Lasta, an enclave of Cushitic speech at the headwaters of the Tekeze between the southern Tigreans and the Amhara and northernmost Argobba. The notables of Lasta had enriched themselves in the service of the Aksumite rulers since at least the early 6th century by their control of the Tekeze fords, and by administering state caravans to the gold-fields west of Lake Tana. The new dynasty had long intermarried with the Aksumite imperial family, as did other provincial magnates, and were devout Christians, despite Agew reverence for sacred groves and caves. For literary purposes and the liturgy, they, like all Ethiopian Christians, adopted Geez, the Semitic language of Aksum. However, the tenacity in this corner of the empire of northern Ethiopia's ancient Cushitic language, Agew, reinforced the reputation of the nine rulers of the Zagwe dynasty as upstarts.

The Ethiopian Church reveres the most famous of the Zagwe rulers, Lalibela (reigned c.1200–30), as a saint. At his capital, which was renamed after him, he reproduced the sacred places of Jerusalem by having 11 large churches sculpted from the living rock. Other Zagwe rulers were also great builders and lavished endowments, especially upon the monastery of Debre Libanos of Shimenzana in south-eastern Eritrea. Lalibela commanded some 60 000 professional soldiers and expanded the empire west to Lake Tana. He attempted the conquest of the animist Agew of Gojjam and the Sidama of the kingdom of Damot. These and other accomplishments of what Ethiopian Church historians continue to regard as the Christian empire's dark age were not sufficient to protect the Zagwe from seditious propaganda from their opponents which continued to refer to their usurpation of the Aksumite throne. The clergy of Aksum and of the great monastery of Debre Damo in Tigre, which the Aksumite rulers had favoured, kept this memory alive. The provincial notables of Enderta in south-eastern Tigre also championed the campaign of vilification, which culminated in their bringing from Egypt, in 1225,

Top: St George's Lalibela, the most flamboyant of the several churches hewn from the solid rock built in the 12th and 13th centuries at the Zagwe capital. St George's retains many of the architectural features of Aksumite timber construction. Right: by contrast, the Immanuel church, also at Lalibela, imitates in sculpting from solid rock almost all the features found in the timber and drystone 5th century church at Debre Damo (see page 109)

while Lalibela still ruled, an Arabic text of the compilation, *The Glory of the Kings (Kebre Neghest)*. This purports to prove that the legitimate kings of Ethiopia, to whom, it was claimed, Providence had entrusted the Ark of the Covenant, were those descended from Solomon, and Sheba, the legendary queen of Aksum.

A southern chieftain of the recently converted Amhara, Yekuno Amlak (born *c.*1230), allied himself with the clerical and noble opponents of the Zagwe in Tigre to found a new imperial dynasty. Like the first of the Zagwe rulers, Yekuno Amlak could claim descent through marriage from the later Aksumite emperors. He pretended, moreover, that through him this so-called Solomonic dynasty was being restored. In this he was aided by a new school founded in 1248 at the 9th century Aksumite island monastery of St Stephen on Lake Haiq by a celebrated Agew teacher, Iyesus Moa (d. 1292). Wherever the many distinguished students trained by Iyesus Moa travelled to complete their education, they spread the renown of Yekuno Amlak, who, as the local governor, had showered the new school with his munificence. Yekuno Amlak had been enriched by the market near Haiq where the Zeila route through Argobba-land reached the Christian empire. Profiting from succession disputes among the Zagwe princes, Yekuno Amlak detached the Amhara from the empire and then, from 1268, reunited its warring provinces. Within two years, he had defeated the fugitive Zagwe emperor in Tigre with the assistance of a faction there. For 30 years from his death in 1285, however, the quarrels of his sons and grandsons paralyzed the Christian state.

From 1285, Umar Walasma, the Muslim lord of Ifat in north-eastern Shewa, defeated the Sultan of Shewa, annexed his territories and founded a new Muslim dynasty combining Ifat and Shewa under its rule. The enlarged Ifat encroached upon Damot to the west just as the Christian Zagwe had tried to. The Walasma dynasty's principal concern was, however, to dominate the Zeila trade. Moreover commercial rivalries kept the Muslim and nominally Muslim principalities of the Rift from uniting in more than temporary alliances under the Walasma. Muslim expansiveness was further checked by developments within the Christian empire. With the accession of Yekuno Amlak's grandson, Amda Siyon, in 1314, succession struggles came to an end, allowing energies to be directed once again towards imperial expansion.

During the reign of Amda Siyon (1314–44), the *Kebre Neghest* was at last translated into Geez, and it is from this period that the earliest Christian royal chronicle survives (an Arabic account of the Sultanate of Shewa also exists). Amda Siyon instituted the practice of confining all of the male relatives of the emperor, except his sons, at the remote mountain monastery of Gishen. Thus most of his successors until the second half of the 16th century avoided dynastic wars. Amda Siyon reasserted the authority of the Solomonid dynasty of the Amhara over Tigre, Lasta and the other old Christian provinces and then annexed Gojjam and Damot as far as the headwaters of the Awash. He also made tributary Hadya, a nominally Muslim principality in the region of the Rift Valley lakes south-west of the Awash, and the foremost market for slaves. To complete his hold over the Zeila trade, the Emperor attacked Ifat. The pastoral Muslims of the lowlands east of Shewa rallied to Ifat, but the sultan, a grandson of Umar Walasma, was killed in 1320 and the highland parts of Ifat-Shewa became tributary to Amda Siyon under another of Umar's grandsons, Sabredin, whom Amda Siyon made governor. However in 1332 Sabredin organized a Muslim league among the trading states which revolted against Christian rule. The same year, Amda Siyon led a great campaign towards the east, reconquering Ifat-Shewa and its allies and killing Sabredin.

After this defeat most of the Walasma family split into factions vying for the favour of the Christian emperor but two of Sabredin's great-grandsons, Haqedin II and his younger brother, Seadedin, denounced their supine relatives who compliantly paid tribute and willingly sojourned at the Christian court in order to obtain appointments over the former sultanate of Ifat-Shewa. They fled the court and in 1375 set up their headquarters near the site of Harar town beyond the range of the emperor's garrisons. There they supplanted the sultans of Adal, who had suffered defeat with Sabredin in 1332. The two brothers then extended their sway over a confederation of small trading states and peoples from the middle Awash to the Gulf of Aden including lowland pastoralists who had remained aloof from previous Christian–Muslim struggles. The Gadabursi clans of the Dir Somali between Harar and the coast, for example, claim that their subgrouping arose out of the followers of one of the lieutenants of Seadedin in the last decade of the 14th century. The new Walasma empire of Adal was, however, limited, in the lowlands, to a corridor through the pastoral Somali to Zeila. Like Ifat-Shewa, the heartland of the new Walasma kingdom was a highland region of Semitic-speaking cultivators and professional, long-distance traders. Muslims had been settled for many generations already between the site of Harar town (founded 1520) and what is now Dire Dawa in the lowlands just to the north. By the 15th century a chain of small towns and caravanserai built in stone rose along the crest of the highlands west of the site of Harar town. Surrounded by terraced fields of the mildly narcotic *chat* (Arabic *qat*), coffee and other commercial crops, these centres overlooked the lowland routes between Zeila and eastern Shewa. Local notables provided a class of knights who were the backbone of Adal's army.

However, Christian pressure continued: in 1403 Seadedin Walasma was executed at Zeila by Dawit II during an extended raid by that emperor to the coast. Seadedin's ten sons fled to the Yemen, which for 200 years had flourished under a line of rulers who had laid claim to both Zeila and the island of Massawa (which had replaced the Dahlak Islands as the outlet for the northern route from the Ethiopian

St John composing his Gospel: a 15th century manuscript kept at one of the island monasteries of Lake Tana

highlands and which Dawit's son and short-lived heir Tewodros I raided in 1412–13).

Disputed successions convulsed the Christian empire after Dawit's second son, Yishaq, died in 1430 while campaigning against Adal. By the time that his younger brother, Zera Yaqob (1434–68), was released from Mt Gishen to bring order to the army and the kingdom, the youngest and most intrepid of Seadedin's sons, Ahmed Badly, had recovered the throne of Adal with Yemeni help. He is said to have drawn even the Muslims of northern Ethiopia into his alliances against the Christian empire. Not until he was killed in 1445 did the tide turn. Thereafter, in the interests of trade, the Walasma sultan of Adal resolved to avoid further military conflict with the Christian state.

As well as consolidating his power along the Muslim frontiers of the Christian empire and safeguarding trade routes, Zera Yaqob sought to reorganize and expand the Ethiopian Church. In particular, he sought to bring under central control the dynamic, but divided monastic movement which had expanded with the boundaries of the empire into remote areas. The majority of monasteries followed the teachings of St Tekle Haymanot (d.1313), himself the most celebrated Amhara student of Iyesus Moa. After a stay at his teacher's old monastery, Debre Damo in Tigre, the saint retired soon after 1300 to a retreat between the Blue Nile and Addis Ababa, later called Debre Libanos of Shewa. His successors there joined the bishops appointed from Cairo by the Copts – who accompanied the emperor's itinerant court – in denouncing the uncanonical marriages of Amda Siyon and his successors, who, in retaliation, hounded into exile the more militant of the Shewan monks. Among the many new monasteries founded by fugitive monks north of the Blue Nile, and by Tekle Haymanot's former associates in Tigre, a semi-independent ecclesiastical hierarchy determined by discipleship emerged, with the abbots of Debre Libanos at its apex. Meanwhile parish priests from the half-literate, married peasantry and the richly endowed court clerics continued to look towards the authority of the Coptic bishop.

A second, smaller, monastic movement was founded in the north by Abba Ewostatewos (d. c.1352). Like the House of Tekle Haymanot, that of Ewostatewos advocated poverty rather than depending upon secular munificence. But its founder also condemned the slave trade and other backsliding among Christian officials and challenged the leaders of the most venerable of Tigre's monasteries. The followers of Tekle Haymanot developed an ardent veneration for the Virgin; those of Ewostatewos revived Old Testament practices, despite bans by the Coptic hierarchy, which Debre Libanos and the court respected. Much persecuted, the House of Ewostatewos gained great popularity in parts of what is now Eritrea where its sectarianism reinforced centrifugal forces while the order worked prodigies of evangelization. Renegade Sabbatarian monks also were responsible for the growth of Judaism among Agew-speakers west of the Tekeze who had resisted Christian rule since later Aksumite times (hence Ethiopia's Bet Israel community, commonly called *Falasha*, 'Outsiders').

Zera Yaqob drew the divided monastic movement together at a council in 1450 at which observance of both Saturday and Sunday and the cult of Mary were accepted as orthodoxy. Revitalized, the church played a major part in his attempt to centralize political power. He endowed lavishly the new monasteries but subjected them to the supervision of abbots of Debre Libanos who were tied to the court and required all monks to instruct parishioners or to serve the state.

As long as the imperial army remained strong, the divisions between the diverse peoples gathered up into the Christian empire since the reign of Amda Siyon were suppressed. Powerful officials were imposed from the court. Permanent garrisons of horsemen in the old Christian provinces and in the tributary Muslim principalities of the south cowed the restless local notables and gentry who ran day-to-day affairs. Most of Amda Siyon's successors fathered heirs by Tigrean mothers in order to reinforce the dynasty's bond with the north. In obstinate defiance of their Egyptian bishops, however, the Shewan emperors had secondary wives as well as numerous concubines. The queens' male relatives supplied courtiers with roots in the several provinces.

While such 'court-country' links helped strengthen a successful emperor they also, however, expanded the number of factions which emerged when there was no clear succession to the throne. Zera Yaqob's son, Beide Maryam (r.1468–78) in any case relaxed the draconian policies by which his father had kept provincial and court factions in check. Beide Maryam was succeeded by his six-year-old son Eskender (r.1478–94), and factiousness intensified. When he himself died, one faction of the army declared Eskender's son, himself then only six years old, emperor as Amda Siyon II, while another faction brought Eskender's brother, Naod from Mt Gishen. Amda Siyon II died after six months and Naod replaced him as emperor (r.1494–1508). In 1508 a clique led by Eleni, one of Zera Yaqob's queens (a convert from Islam) and the Egyptian bishop rejected a mature son of Naod in favour of a juvenile, Lebne Dengel (r.1508–40) so that they might exercise the regency. As he came of age the new emperor proved an intrepid commander, but arrogant and wilful and lacking in political acumen.

The revival of Muslim imperialism

The last two decades of the 15th century was a period of mounting danger for the Christian empire. From the 1480s the Walasmas' authority in Adal was undermined by an ambitious general, Mahfuz. The success of the raids which he led against the Christian empire's borders overshadowed the Walasma Sultan and his urban merchant allies who became discredited in the eyes of the professional cavalrymen of the Harar highlands. Sheikhs from Arabia found ready employment with the war party and further enhanced Mahfuz's reputation. In 1516 Lebne Dengel killed Mahfuz in battle but his daughter, Del Wambera, encouraged her husband, Ahmed ibn Ibrahim al-Ghazi, to pursue her father's turbulent policy.

In the bitter struggle within Adal between the partisans of war and those of trade, Ahmed ibn Ibrahim became the leader of Mahfuz's veterans. In 1520 Abu Bakr Walasma, a son of the recently assasinated sultan of Adal, transferred his residence to Harar and transformed the agglomeration of villages into a major market town and centre of learning. By shrewd alliances with only nominally Muslim Somali, Abu Bakr forced the Semitic-speaking, highland knights and their companions to recognize his accession to the Sultanate of Adal. In attempting to deprive Ahmed ibn Ibrahim of his command in 1526, however, the new sultan was killed. Ahmed placed Abu Bakr's brother on the throne as a figurehead. By a combination of cajolery, punitive attacks and offers of a share in booty, Ahmed then drew the Somali and other pastoralists into an alliance with him against the Christian empire.

For at least a century contacts had grown up between Ethiopia and Europe which rested on European interest in the Prester John legend, which posited the existence of a Christian king in the 'East' who might prove useful to Europeans in their own struggles against Islam. In 1512, by which time Ethiopians had begun – in the face of Mahfuz's successes – to appreciate the potential benefits of an alliance with a European power, the Empress Dowager Eleni replied to messengers from Portugal* by proposing an alliance against Adal. An embassy (from Portuguese India) did not, however, arrive until 1520, by which time Lebne Dengel had been sufficiently successful against the Muslims to make him indifferent to Portuguese aid. When a Muslim army, which was larger and much better equipped and organized than any earlier expedition, invaded in 1529, the emperor confidently raised a greater one calling up troops from every province including Tigre and today's Eritrea. Dozens of his best commanders and thousands of their expert horsemen were killed in a great cavalry battle on 7 March 1529 at Shimbra-Kure at the foot of Mt Zuqwalla, which commands the Awash plain some 60km south of the site of Addis Ababa.

The balance of power in North-East Africa had shifted. Self-satisfied, the emperor's regiments had ignored changes in technology – such as the supplanting in Muslim armies of the toe stirrup by one which gave greater weight to the lance. The Christian empire lacked easy access to the chain mail, helmets and steel sabres which Ahmed ibn Ibrahim imported for his best soldiers. In the next few years the technological balance was to shift even further in favour of the Muslims: in 1531, for example, they began to make use of Turkish artillery brought from the Yemen.

As well as exposing the Christian court's technological inadequacies, military defeat also revealed its failure to bind the diverse peoples of the empire together; local loyalties remained strong even in the older, Christian provinces. For a generation, under a gifted commander, Muslims united with the partly-Islamicized peoples of the Horn in a war of religion and looting. As long as they were victorious, these allies attracted into their service auxiliaries from among the Christian notables of the highlands. For centuries the Solomonids alone in North-East Africa had enjoyed the advantage of combining military superiority with statesmanship and the ability to infuse their followers with a sense of divine mission. Ahmed ibn Ibrahim, whom Christian writers nicknamed *Gragn* (The Left-handed), brought this combination to the eastern Semitic- and Cushitic-speaking peoples of the region. A generation of internecine war followed.

R.A.C.

Bantu Africa

c.1000-1500

In most parts of Bantu-speaking Africa the early 2nd millennium AD seems to mark the beginning of a new period. Over much of the region, archaeologists have found pottery that they call 'Later Iron Age', as it contrasts quite sharply with earlier local Iron Age★ styles. To some extent, this change reflects the movement of peoples; it may also be linked to economic changes. On the inland plateaux there was a marked increase in cattle-keeping, due perhaps to the introduction of milking. There is also evidence to suggest that methods of iron working became more efficient, and that as a result the clearance of woodland became easier than before. The pottery record indicates a broad continuity from the cultures of the later Iron Age to those of the present century. The main language groups recognized today probably took shape between AD1000 and 1500, and it was in this period that kingdoms first emerged in Bantu Africa.

The ideology of kingship in this region may have owed something to contacts with the Nile Valley, and ultimately ancient Egypt,★ but its scale and success depended on a variety of local factors. Competition for control over cattle and other resources, such as fish, game or mineral deposits, might lead to the ascendancy of certain lineages, and these in turn might be associated with men already acknowledged as priests, rain-makers or arbitrators. Thus arose hereditary chiefs, whose right to rule was shared—and often disputed—by their kinsmen. The more important chiefs were regarded as 'divine kings' whose own physical health was thought to epitomize the condition of their country: to preserve the welfare of people, animals and crops they had to observe taboos and rituals. These were supervised by priests who might also be councillors and king-makers; like kings and chiefs they were dignified by hereditary titles, and in conquered territory some of them might represent the original inhabitants.

On the northern frontier of Bantu-speaking East Africa, kingdoms first took shape among the agricultural peoples living between the source of the Nile and Lake Kivu. The original stimulus may have been the arrival of non-Bantu cattle-keepers from the north, who built the great earthworks at Bigo in western Uganda, about the 14th or 15th century. This may indeed have become a capital for the kingdom of Bunyoro, which seems always to have regulated relations between herdsmen and farmers. The same economic function was served by new kingdoms further south, among the Haya, and also in what are now Rwanda and Burundi, where grassy plains abut on fertile hillsides and herdsmen gained power by lending cattle to farmer-clients.

Elsewhere in East Africa kingship was still unknown; indeed, settled populations were still few and far between. Along the coast,

however, groups of Swahili-speakers had clustered in small city-states which traded across the Indian Ocean and had begun to adopt Islam. Arabs settled in these states, especially from the 12th century onwards, and at Kilwa★ they gained control of the trade in gold from the Mozambique coast; the profits from this enabled them to build a magnificent palace, in coral ragstone, in the 14th century.

West of Lake Tanganyika, in what is now Zaire, there was evidently some social stratification by the 12th century in the upper Lualaba region: excavations around Lake Kisale have revealed the graves of people adorned with copper, iron and ivory jewellery. We cannot say what kind of leadership prevailed there, but it may be the existence of such an elite that accounts for local traditions about the founder of the first kingdom among the Luba peoples. Further west, in the open savanna of Shaba and northern Angola, oral traditions of early migration and kingship probably refer to the spread of prestigious symbols, such as bracelets and iron bells, among lineage groups that had acquired religious and economic prominence; by the 15th century, several such groups seem to have become nuclei for

Copper and iron objects from excavations at Sanga, near Lake Kisale, Zaire

0   5cm

BANTU AFRICA

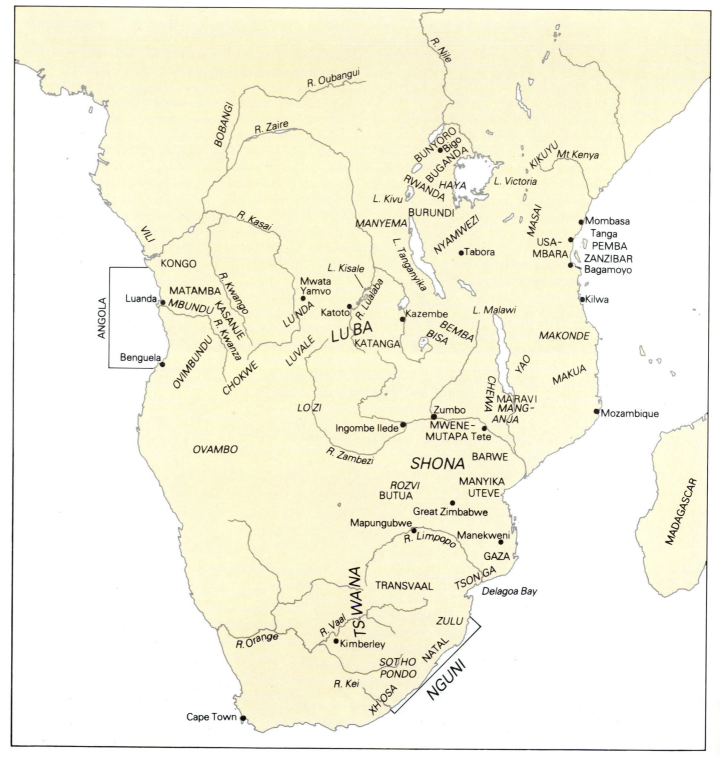

kingdoms among the Lunda and Mbundu peoples. Such centralization of authority would have owed little or nothing to the ownership of cattle, which in most of the Zaire basin was precluded by disease spread by tsetse fly; instead, it may well have derived from increasing trade in metals and forest products. This was especially likely around the mouth of the Zaire River, where we can be fairly sure that the Kongo kingdom had taken shape by 1400. When the Portuguese★ first visited the capital in 1485, they found that the king used as a form of currency shells from an offshore island nearly 250km away.

South of the Zambezi, as in East Africa, the control of cattle was clearly a key factor in the growth of hierarchical government. Our best evidence for this comes from stone-walled enclosures (*mazimbabwe*) on the Zimbabwean plateau and at Manekweni, near the coast of Mozambique. Several of them were probably built about the 14th century, and they seem to have been capitals for polities comprising both farmers and transhumant herdsmen. The most famous is Great Zimbabwe, not only because its drystone granite masonry is especially fine but also because excavations have shown that its inhabitants traded gold from nearby mines for coastal imports, including Chinese porcelain. Such luxuries, and the huge scale of building works, point to the existence of a ruling elite or central authority which may well have had indirect contacts with rulers further north: there is a marked resemblance between ceremonial

Great Zimbabwe: right: a general view of part of the site, with the 'elliptical building' in the foreground. Above: the completely solid, drystone 'conical tower' within the 'elliptical building'

KEY

VILI	Peoples
LUBA	Language groups
Bigo	Towns
MALI	States and regions

iron bells found at Great Zimbabwe, at Katoto in Shaba, and at Ingombe Ilede on the middle Zambezi, an outpost for trade in gold, copper and ivory in the 15th century. During the same period a kingdom was formed lower down the Zambezi by the Mwenemutapa dynasty; this was based on the management of both cattle and gold-mining, and it soon extended its influence over kingdoms further east, such as Manyika and Uteve.

Across the Limpopo, the period between 1000 and 1500 witnessed the continued migration of farmers into new land, as far south as the River Kei. Cattle-keeping increased, and in the southern Transvaal large villages were centred on cattle enclosures, with some use of stone-walling. Traditions indicate the emergence of dominant lineages among ancestors of both the Sotho-Tswana and Nguni-speaking peoples, but the only evidence of a particular political unit during this period comes from Mapungubwe hill, above the middle Limpopo River, where by the 15th century a prosperous elite traded copper and ivory for gold, exotic beads and pottery.

c.1500–1800

In the 16th century Europeans began to trade along the coastlines of Bantu Africa. By the end of the century parts of the western coast were firmly drawn into the Atlantic slave trade,* while there were Portuguese outposts along the Kwanza River in Angola and along the lower Zambezi. Portuguese intruders brought to Africa crops that they had found in the Americas, notably maize and cassava. The diffusion of new food crops along the trade routes of the interior may well have promoted population growth in some areas; it certainly gave a new impetus to agricultural colonization. It is also in the course of this period that the outlines of political history in Bantu Africa first come into focus around the names of historical, rather than merely legendary, characters. This is due partly to the written records of European visitors on or near the coast, and partly to oral traditions: many refer in some detail to the 18th century, while some relate distinct events that may be dated a good deal earlier.

Among the lake kingdoms of East Africa, Rwanda and Buganda first rose to prominence in the 17th and 18th centuries. The heartland of Rwanda may have been the scene of especially crowded intermingling between herdsmen and farmers; at any rate, by 1800, the kingdom had expanded eastwards to include Gisaka, and the king presided over a hierarchy of provinces and districts governed by fellow-members of the Tutsi minority. Meanwhile, Buganda expanded from the shores of Lake Victoria to take over parts of Bunyoro; like Rwanda, it evolved a territorial hierarchy of chiefs, though here the economic underpinning consisted not of herds of cattle but of landed estates on which the prolific banana could sustain a chief's followers. Elsewhere in the interior the only other kingdom of comparable size to emerge in this period was also in a banana-growing area – the hills of Usambara. In other parts of Tanzania there

were several clusters of small chiefdoms by 1800, while in western Kenya and eastern Uganda lineages or age-sets remained the basis of political organization. Along the coast the Portuguese had gained a precarious hegemony over a few city-states by 1600, but in the later 17th century they began to be displaced by Arabs from Oman. In the 18th century a new dynasty in Oman developed Zanzibar* as a rival to Mombasa for the trade of the western Indian Ocean. Trade with the mainland opposite expanded, and by 1800 this had prompted the growth of new towns such as Tanga and Bagamoyo.

On the west coast Europeans made a much greater impact. At first, Portugal treated the Kongo king as an ally, but by 1600 the search for slaves induced Portuguese traders and settlers in Angola to stir up civil war. Dutch intrusion made matters worse, and by 1700 the king and his senior chiefs were virtually impotent. Slaves from this region were now mostly shipped from the Vili kingdoms, further up the coast. Here the Portuguese had little influence, and they concentrated on Angola. In the 1620s they were fiercely resisted by the Mbundu queen, Nzinga, but she had to retreat inland to Matamba, where she eventually agreed to collaborate with them. However, the Portuguese could not prevent either Matamba or its neighbour, Kasanje, from exporting slaves to parts of the coast beyond their control. And further inland lay the Lunda empire of Mwata Yamvo. By the early 18th century Mwata Yamvo was selling slaves to the west, but he was also pushing eastwards, to the salt and copper of Shaba. A Lunda general, Kazembe, created a new kingdom on the Luapula River; his successors introduced cassava from the west and continued to send tribute to Mwata Yamvo, but by 1800 Kazembe had also opened up a trade route, via the Bisa people, to the Portuguese and Arabs on the east coast. Meanwhile, in southern Angola the Portuguese based on Benguela had secured new partners in the slave trade: the Ovimbundu kingdoms. Well before 1800 European goods were trickling through Ovimbundu country as far east as the Luvale people of western Zambia, and soon afterwards Ovimbundu traders visited the Lozi kingdom, on the flood-plain of the upper Zambezi.

In south-eastern Africa the Portuguese were for a long time interested in gold and ivory rather than slaves. It was to gain access to gold-mines that they expelled Muslim traders from the lower Zambezi, and by the mid-17th century they had acquired some influence over the kingdoms of Mwenemutapa, Manyika, Uteve and Barwe. Further west, on the Zimbabwean plateau, was a kingdom rich in cattle, which they called Butua. Here, in the 1680s, a new ruler, Dombo, drove a Portuguese army back to Tete, in the Zambezi valley; he also ousted them from the eastern kingdoms. This setback caused the Portuguese to develop trade in gold and ivory north of the Zambezi with the Chewa king Undi, and in copper from Zambia. By the 1720s Dombo's successors (whose people were now called Rozvi) had re-established the gold trade, but the Portuguese were allowed no nearer than Zumbo (on the Zambezi) and Manyika. North of the

Zambezi the ivory trade had contributed in the early 17th century to the growth of the senior Maravi kingdom, that of Kalonga, but this was undermined both by internal disputes and by the emergence of the Yao people as the principal ivory traders between the east coast and the middle Zambezi. In the later 18th century the Yao began to take their ivory to the Swahili at Kilwa rather than to the Portuguese, partly because the latter were now more eager for slaves to sell to the French sugar islands of Réunion and Ile de France (Mauritius). By 1800 agents of the Portuguese were raiding for slaves among the Makua and Makonde, and also among the Mang'anja and Chewa.

We still know few details of the history of the Bantu peoples south of the Limpopo before 1800, though some trends are clear enough. Small-scale chiefdoms were widespread by 1700, and while many continued to be split by succession disputes the 18th century also saw the growth of several substantial kingdoms. Among the Tsonga this was a response to increased trade in ivory and copper, for which traders from several European countries competed at Delagoa Bay. Coastal trade may also, by 1800, have contributed to political centralization among the Tswana of the western Transvaal. South of Delagoa Bay the early adoption of maize in fertile country by the northern Nguni may have caused a quite rapid rise in population; it

Kazembe, the Lunda general and state-builder

was probably rivalry for pasture as much as trade which by 1800 had prompted some of their rulers to make radical changes in military organization. By contrast, the southern Nguni ran a brisk trade in cattle and copper with the Dutch in the 18th century, but this eventually provoked conflict which undermined Xhosa chiefs.

c.1800–80

Until the 19th century the peoples of Bantu Africa had mostly managed to keep white intruders at bay, even if some areas had suffered from slave-raiding. Thereafter, the balance of advantage began to move steadily towards Europeans, whose industrial revolution hugely increased their capacity for trade and warfare. By 1850 the slave trade was in decline, but there was a fast-growing demand for African products: above all ivory, but also palm oil, beeswax and rubber. By extending contacts and markets, overseas trade could stimulate production for local use, especially of ironwork. Exotic crops were widely adopted. But 'legitimate' trade could be just as ruthless and destructive as the slave trade. The rivalries of alien traders and their African partners were aggravated by swelling imports of firearms, and the political map was transformed. Rulers emerged whose power was based on violence and terror rather than on traditional kinship loyalties or religious beliefs. Several kings sought to strengthen their position by appointing subordinate leaders on the basis of achievement rather than birth, but some also faced growing discontent among both priests and oppressed subjects. The political and commercial changes created new bases for communal identity, and many of the 'tribal' names known today were first used in the 19th century; the expansion of trade also spread the use of trade languages, such as Swahili. The course of these changes may be traced both in oral traditions and in the often voluminous records of white explorers, traders and missionaries, who by the 1880s had penetrated all but the remotest parts of Bantu Africa.

In East Africa the growth of trade with Europe was channelled through the Arab regimes on the coast. Ivory was the main export, but from the 1830s slaves were needed for clove plantations on Zanzibar and Pemba. These slaves were brought mostly from the hinterland of Kilwa, though further west slaves were bought for use in traders' settlements up-country, such as Tabora. By 1850 mainland Tanzania was criss-crossed by caravan routes used both by Arabs and Swahili from the coast and by traders from the interior, such as the Nyamwezi. One route ran north into Buganda, which laid more of its neighbours under tribute and dominated Lake Victoria with fleets of canoes. In the 1860s and 1870s new leaders established extensive if fragile hegemonies in western and southern Tanzania. The sultanate of Zanzibar set up customs posts in several coastal towns, but it exerted no real power in the interior and by 1870 it was much influenced by the British. Highland Kenya was as yet scarcely affected by the expansion of trade; here the main development was the continued move southwards of Kikuyu cultivators until they came up against Masai herdsmen around the site of Nairobi.

Along the west coast patterns of trade and political power shifted as slavers were outlawed and forced to operate outside the main ports, while the growth of legitimate trade favoured new areas: the Zaire estuary, for instance, became more important while the Vili kingdoms declined. Up-country, the Bubangi people monopolized the trade along the middle Zaire and Oubangui River. The decline of the slave trade weakened the Portuguese in Angola; their colony did not expand much, while they quite failed to destroy Kasanje. By the 1850s much ivory and beeswax were being supplied by the forest-dwelling Chokwe, whose hunters infiltrated the Lunda empire of Mwata Yamvo; they sold to both the Portuguese and the Ovimbundu, who also bought slaves beyond the upper Zambezi. By 1870 parts of the far interior had been subdued by invaders from the east. Arabs and Swahili from the east coast settled in Manyema, where they raided for ivory. Further south, the Luba had created an extensive empire by 1800, but this was eroded by traders from both east and west. One was Msiri, a Nyamwezi, who created the new state of Katanga and overran part of Kazembe's kingdom; this was in any case overshadowed by the rising power of the Bemba.

Much of Africa south of Lake Tanganyika was convulsed during the 19th century by black invaders from South Africa. In the 1820s the chiefdom of the Zulu, a group of Nguni-speakers, was mobilized by Shaka to form well-drilled regiments. Armed with short stabbing-spears, they subdued their neighbours; many people fled from the Zulu menace and some adopted similar methods. By 1830 Moshweshwe had formed the nucleus of a new kingdom among the Sotho, in the Drakensberg mountains. Over the next ten years there was a series of migrations northwards across the Limpopo. Sebitwane took his Sotho-speaking Kololo to the upper Zambezi, where they lorded it over the Lozi until they were overthrown in 1864. Mzilikazi's Ndebele, from the Transvaal, defeated the Rozvi and settled around Bulawayo. Soshangane left the borders of Zululand for southern Mozambique, where he created the Gaza kingdom. Zwangendaba crossed the middle Zambezi with an army which grew very rapidly through the recruitment of captives, though it soon split up: Ngoni kingdoms were formed in eastern Zambia, in south-eastern Tanzania and in Malawi, where they clashed with Yao traders who settled round the southern end of the lake. On the middle and lower Zambezi, Portuguese estates crumbled under attacks by Ngoni and Gaza; from the ruins emerged new leaders, mostly of African descent, who used slave armies to carve out still more new kingdoms and carry the slave trade far into what is now Zambia.

Meanwhile white settlement in South Africa* was increasing fast, and whites steadily encroached on Bantu territory. The Xhosa were gradually conquered by the British from the Cape, while other Nguni were absorbed into the British colony of Natal. The Dutch settlers known as the Boers moved on to the inland plateau and subdued groups of Tswana, and it was Boer threats that induced Moshweshwe to accept British protection in 1870. Three years earlier, diamonds had been discovered at Kimberley, and the white man's search for cheap labour soon made itself felt throughout southern Africa; by 1879 it had drawn the British into fighting, and eventually defeating, the Zulu kingdom.

A.D.R.

The Western and Central Sudan

West Africa may be divided into two major climatically-determined, latitudinal vegetation* zones: in the south tropical forest and, to the north of the forest, the savanna (grassland) or Sudanic zone–covering 75 per cent of the region–with woodland cover varying from relatively thick bush to scattered trees. The north of the Sudan, the Sahel, forms the 'shore' (Arabic, *sahil*) of a third zone, the Sahara.

The West African tropical forest has been inhabited for several millennia, and the spread of iron technology* made it possible for increasingly sophisticated societies to settle or develop in it; the classic early case being the culture (8th–10th centuries AD) associated with the site of Igbo-Ukwu* in eastern Nigeria. Nevertheless, many of the states that were later to become prominent in the forest (such as those of the Yoruba* in Nigeria or the Akan* in Ghana) had their origins in the southern savanna or on the savanna/forest fringes, and links with more northerly societies through trade or the spread of political ideas or personnel were important in their development.

The Sudan has a number of features that make it particularly suitable for human settlement and for the development of complex, large-scale polities. It is relatively open to human movement (important, for example, for communications within an empire or kingdom, or for the development of long-distance trade), has a number of extensively navigable rivers, above all the Niger, and provides conditions–notably the absence, or (compared with the forest) relatively low level, of tsetse fly infestation–which allow the keeping of cattle, horses, donkeys and oxen for food, transport and military use: even the camel may be used in parts of the Sahel where suitable dune-grazing is available.

Sudanic states and empires to the 17th century

Trans-Saharan trade between North Africa and the black peoples of the West African Sudan– who, before the dessication of the Sahara,* had in any case inhabited areas much further north–pre-dated Carthaginian* and Roman* settlement in North Africa. Trade, mediated by Berber-speaking desert peoples such as the Garamantes,* was probably then on a limited scale, and was horse- or perhaps oxen-borne. Expansion of trans-Saharan trade–now camel-borne–with the Arab conquest* of North Africa in the 7th and 8th centuries must be seen as a major stimulus to the creation of black polities. From the 8th century on North African Arabic writers make increasingly precise references to kingdoms in the Western Sudan (the area to the west of, and including, the Niger bend) straddling the Sahel-Saharan fringes: Takrur in the far west on the Senegal, Ghana further east in the open Sahel, and Gao (the nucleus of the later Songhay empire) on the Niger bend. Further south, on the upper Niger and its affluents, an incipient kingdom of the Malinke people– the likely forerunner of the empire of Mali–was mentioned in the 11th century. These polities, in various combinations and with varying political superstructures, were to form the matrix of the Western Sudanese politico-commercial empires until the 1590s.

In the Central Sudan (between the Niger bend and Lake Chad) Kanem to the north-east of Lake Chad (the precursor of Bornu) was a small kingdom known to Arabic writers by the 10th century. At about the same time, beyond direct contact with Saharan societies–and therefore unknown to North African writers–Chadic-speakers had begun to spread westwards from the Chad basin into the northern savannas of what is now Nigeria, creating *Kasar Hausa* (Hausaland), a distinctive culture of settled agriculture and increasingly important market and administrative centres.

Early European theories about the more precise forces that led to the establishment of centralized states in the Western and Central Sudan rested on essentially racist assumptions, but also on local traditions probably distorted by relatively late Islamic ideology, and envisaged 'white', dynamic, horse-riding pastoralists (the Berber-speaking nomads, or even 'Judaeo-Syrians') imposing states on earthbound, passive black agriculturalists, creating dynasties that later took on a blacker hue. Pastoralists do create states–as in the case of Kanem, created by *black* pastoralists (the Zaghawa and other groups)–but settled agriculture has often provided a firmer basis for complex political organization. For example, archaeological findings at 1st millennium BC sites in southern Mauritania (in the area where Ghana was to flourish in the 1st millennium AD) suggest that by 900– 600 BC a centralized state had been created by black neolithic agriculturalists, probably, like the people of metropolitan Ghana, Soninke, a Mande-speaking people. If anything, this early state, necessitated by the internal dynamics of agricultural expansion in a

KEY

▮ Desert	▮ Tropical forest	Bigo Towns
▮ Savanna	*VILI* Peoples	MALI States and regions

WEST AFRICAN PEOPLES AND STATES 12TH-17TH CENTURIES

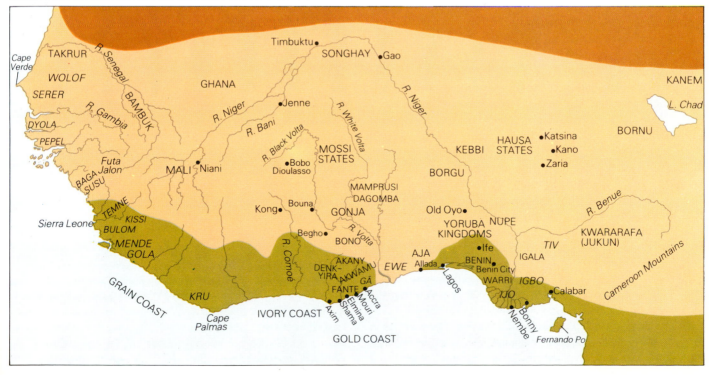

marginally cultivable area, was *destroyed* by nomadic incursions; Ghana may represent a later parallel form, made more viable by iron-working, perhaps stimulated by continued contact with nomads – especially trade – but not created by them.

Long-distance trade created the wealth which enabled sophisticated political superstructures to be erected over agricultural societies. Takrur, first mentioned in Arabic sources in the 11th century, Gao (especially in the late 11th and early 12th centuries), and, in particular, Ghana (from at least the 9th to the 13th century) were noted for their northward export of gold most of which, at this period, was mined in Bambuk, between the upper Senegal and Faleme rivers. Major imports into the Sudan included Saharan salt, an expensive essential broken into smaller packages and traded further south, luxury goods for court consumption such as Saharan copper, fine cloth and beads, and militarily important horses.

Takrur and Gao were kingdoms rather than true empires; the bulk of Ghana's population seems to have been Soninke, and its major imperial venture, the attempt to control important Saharan centres, led to a speedy response from the Sanhaja nomads, organized in the Almoravid* movement, who aspired to maintain control over the Saharan trade. In 1076/7 they imposed their domination over Ghana, perhaps by outright conquest, perhaps by imposing a Muslim dynasty in a form of indirect rule. Ghana was still a major power in the first half of the 12th century, but by the beginning of the 13th century was apparently ruled by the Susu, southern Soninke, formerly Ghana's subjects, who also ruled the Mande-speaking Malinke. Between about 1230 and 1255 a major victory over the Susu by Sundiata, a Malinke warrior, led to the foundation of a new dynasty and the beginnings of the Mali empire.

Mali (flourished *c*.1250-*c*.1460) and its successor, Songhay (*c*.1460–1591) were both at their respective heights substantial imperial systems with a more easterly commercial focus than Ghana. From their homeland on the upper Niger – out of range of desert intrusions – Mali's rulers made full use of river communications to extend and control their possessions and expand trade. Mali in the 14th century ruled the Gambia and lower Senegal valleys to the west, controlled Gao, and had developed Timbuktu as another major desert-side trading town. From the Niger downstream of Gao traders from Mali had, by the mid-14th century, struck east to penetrate Hausaland. From Jenne, upstream of Timbuktu on the Bani River, Mande-speaking traders (often called Dyula) began to establish in the 14th and 15th centuries a trading diaspora – a network of commercial settlements outside the formal bounds of the empire – towards the south-east, ultimately linking the empire with the Akan states,* whose traded gold substantially augmented the supplies from Bambuk and Bure (Mali's nearest goldfield). In addition the Akan forests (and those further west) supplied kola nuts, prized as a valuable non-alcoholic stimulant by Muslims, which were traded north-west to the Niger bend and also along a new, north-easterly route which linked the Akan with Hausaland via Borgu.

Mali's riverborne imperium was heavily dependent on the submission of the Sorko fishermen – the most powerful of the groups making up the Songhay people – who controlled river transport. With a long history of independent statehood, centred on Gao, the Songhay were uneasy with rule from Mali. By the early 15th century they had begun to raid metropolitan Malian territories and their ruler, Sonni Ali (1462–92) transformed Songhay into an empire stretching upstream above Jenne. Beyond this point Mali survived as a sizeable independent kingdom whose main interests now lay westwards towards the coast. The Mande element remained central to the new empire: Mande-speakers (perhaps in some cases Mandeized Songhay) continued to man and further develop much of the trade diaspora, and Sonni Ali's greatest successor, the Askia (ruler) Muhammad (1494–1528), who seized power from Sonni Ali's son, was probably of Soninke ancestry. Muhammad expanded the empire to its greatest extent, controlling parts of the southern Sahara and perhaps, briefly, making tributary the Hausa states of Katsina, Kano and Gobir to the east. His reign was followed by 60 years of disputed successions, culminating in the 1590–1 conquest of the empire by a Moroccan force sent by Ahmad al-Mansur.*

In the 17th century – partly as a result of disturbed conditions in the Niger bend – trans-Saharan routes shifted yet further east. Before this the Central Sudan was less profoundly transformed by commerce than areas further to the west, largely because it had little or no gold to trade. From its beginnings Kanem's major international trade was in slaves* (probably a relatively minor item in Western Sudanese exports), although when its monarchy was at its strongest, as for example in the early 13th century, it expanded along the trade routes towards the Fezzan, in the process controlling the valuable salt trade from the deposits at Bilma. Early consolidation east of Lake Chad was thwarted by revolts and intra-dynastic rivalries, and in the 1390s the Kanem court fled to the west of the lake, re-establishing itself in the province of Bornu. By the beginning of the 16th century Bornu was an important power, rivalling Songhay for influence in the southern Sahara and over the Hausa states, and establishing close diplomatic and commercial links with Ottoman* North Africa, notably during the reign of Mai Idris Aloma (1569/70–*c*.1619).

The history of Hausaland is obscure until the 15th and 16th centuries when Kano, Katsina and Zaria enter written records as its most significant states. Engaged in frequent defensive and offensive campaigns towards the south, particularly against the Benue valley confederation of Kwararafa,* the Hausa states also developed as major commercial centres. Dyula traders pioneered routes to Hausaland from the 14th to the 16th century (and as well as spreading Islam may also have played a role in political centralization). By the 17th century Hausa (or Hausaized Mande) traders had taken over many routes, especially, for example, the kola road from Gonja (north of the Akan states) to Hausaland, and traded their own craft goods (especially leather-work and dyed cotton cloth), slaves, kola, hides and skins, gold, ivory, perfume, wax, ostrich feathers, salt and tobacco across West Africa and into the trans-Saharan system.

The Lake Chad cradle, from which Hausa and Bornuan culture emerged, seems also to have been the source of forces that led, more or less directly, to the formation of a more southerly tier of states whose ruling dynasties, established over and partly assimilated with autochthonous groups, claim north-easterly origins. The cavalry states of the interrelated Mamprusi, Dagomba and Mossi (established in their modern location in northern Ghana and Upper Volta from the 15th century on) and the Borgawa (Borgu) may be direct offshoots of the Hausa/Bornu expansion. Alternatively, they may represent parallel developments, and longer-established states with these traditions, such as Nupe, the Yoruba states, Benin, the Aja states and, perhaps, the small polities of the Ewe and Gã are perhaps best seen as parts of a wider process that *includes* the developments in Hausaland and Kanem/Bornu.

Islam and political change

Islam inevitably accompanied trade along the routes from North Africa to the West African Sahel, but until the 18th and 19th centuries, when Islamic theocracies attempted to impose orthodoxy on relatively large areas, Islam was limited in rigour, social range and number of adherents. A common early pattern, as in the urban centres of Ghana and Gao, was one of accommodation between Islam and traditional religions. In Ghana, in the mid-11th century, the capital consisted of two towns 10km apart, one Muslim (with 12 mosques) and one, inhabited by the king, surrounded by the shrines of traditional religious cults, but with a mosque for visiting Muslims. Muslims, some perhaps Soninke, acted as intermediaries between the king and foreign traders, and some were senior royal officials. Formal adherence by a ruler to Islam was a development from this situation; it did not bring revolutionary change. In exceptional cases, as perhaps in Takrur in the 11th century, initial conversion of the ruler appears to have led to a rapid spread of the religion among his subjects; elsewhere, as in 14th century Mali, rulers who had become converts often felt obliged to countenance pagan practices at court in order to safeguard their own positions as traditional rulers. Increasingly, though, such rulers attempted to fulfil the major obligations of Islam, including pilgrimage to the Holy Places. Perhaps the most spectacular hajj was made by Mansa Musa of Mali (?1312–?37) in 1324, but other rulers, including other Malian kings, and Askia Muhammad, also made the journey. Such visits to the heart of the Muslim world impressed Sudanese rulers with the inadequacies of Islamic practice in their own domains; one significant effect of this was their request for advice from Muslim jurists on

proper forms of Muslim government. The most influential of such advisers–his advice formed an important part of the intellectual armoury of 18th and 19th century Islamic reform movements in West Africa–was Muhammad al-Maghili, a North African who, in the 1490s, advised the rulers of Katsina and Kano and Askia Muhammad of Songhay. Despite such encounters, however–and there is some evidence that Askia Muhammad for one tried to establish Islam as a state religion–Islam remained a minority faith confined largely to the royal courts, traders and major urban centres, some of which, such as Timbuktu, Jenne and Kano became important centres of Islamic scholarship. The dispersion from such centres of Dyula traders, themselves often learned men, or accompanied by learned kinsmen, was one of the major means whereby Islam was spread across the Sudan. Dyula traders were, however, characteristically quietist in their religion; where they were involved in the creation of new polities, as perhaps in Gonja, established in the 16th or 17th century in what is now northern Ghana, Islam remained an adjunct to the creation of state power–in this case by barely-Islamized Mande warrior groups–not its motivating force.

The migrations of the pastoral people known as Fulani were however ultimately to make Islam a major force–the state religion–in wide areas of the Sudan. The early history of the Fulani–speakers of a West Atlantic language (Fulfulde or Fula★)–is obscure. They include physically distinctive groups, which may indicate that they originated as an admixture of Berber and black peoples. By the 10th century most Fulani seem to have settled in the middle and lower Senegal valley–the Futa Toro–the area controlled by the state of Takrur. By the 15th century many had migrated to the well-watered Macina area of the Niger bend, and in the 17th century Fulani from Macina swelled an earlier smaller migrant group settled on the Futa Jalon plateau (modern Guinea). By the 15th and 16th centuries Fulani had settled across Hausaland, reaching Bornu, and, by the 18th century, northern Cameroon. Migrants were pastoralists and almost all pagan, but they were accompanied, or closely followed by the *torodbe* ('those who pray to Allah'), a Fulfulde-speaking group best characterized by its *métier*, an adherence to Islam and the pursuit of Islamic learning.

The first manifestations among the Fulani of a tradition of jihad– the process which sought to convert unbelievers (peacefully at first, by force if necessary), purify Islam and create social and political institutions that accorded with Islamic law–were centred in the Futa Toro where, since the 16th century, power had been held by a pagan Fulani dynasty. In the 1660s and 1670s an ultimately unsuccessful Berber-led jihad with considerable Fulani support was followed by a successful Fulani-led jihad in Bondu (between Futa Toro and Futa Jalon). Some of the followers of its leader, Malik Si, had been drawn from Futa Jalon, where Muslim and pagan Fulani lived alongside and under the nominal jurisdiction of earlier immigrants, the Susu-speaking Jalonke. Increasingly the Fulani were engaged in a trade to the coast in cattle, hides and slaves, and this has been put forward as an economic explanation of the Fulani attempt to shake off Jalonke rule there. Yet the situation was complex: for some time after the declaration of a jihad (c.1726), the Muslim Fulani allied with certain Jalonke groups and fought against pagan Fulani. The ultimate outcome was the creation of an imamate, consolidated as a federation by the 1760s, which survived until the French* invasion of 1896–7. The Futa Jalon jihad was followed by new risings in Futa Toro, led by Sheikh Sulaiman Bal, who had studied in Futa Jalon: by 1776 Sulaiman had overthrown pagan rule and established a Muslim state.

The Futa jihads created imamates that were relatively small and homogeneous; that led by Usuman dan Fodio (1754–1817) – the Shehu – and his successors in the Hausa areas of northern Nigeria, which began (in its military phase) in 1804 had, by the 1830s, resulted in the establishment of a federation of 15 emirates centred on capitals at Sokoto and Gwandu. The Sokoto Caliphate covered 470 000 sq km, including territory as far south as Ilorin (carved out of the Yoruba empire of Oyo) and Nupe, and survived intact until the British* conquest of 1900–6. The Shehu, a member of a particularly scholarly *torodbe* lineage began preaching in about 1774. By the late 1780s he was settled in the north-western Hausa state of Gobir, where he attracted a considerable body of followers. Like most Hausa states Gobir was Islamized, but had a government that mixed Islam with traditional practices. At first, then, the Shehu's community was tolerated, but when it appeared to be a political threat its members were attacked. The Shehu ordered a *hijra* (modelled on Muhammad's flight from Mecca), the prelude to jihad. Jihad in Gobir was emulated

Fulani cavalrymen photographed in northern Cameroon in 1932

by a series of autonomous local movements led mainly by Fulani, some former pupils of the Shehu, against their Hausa rulers. In the east jihadists faced resistance from a Muslim power, Bornu. The Mai (ruler) of Bornu called in a Kanembu Muslim cleric, Sheikh Muhammad al-Kanemi (d.1837/8), who organized military (and intellectual) resistance. Bornu retained most of its territory but al-Kanemi's intervention brought fundamental change. He organized what amounted to a parallel administration to that of the Sefawa dynasty (which had been in continuous power since the foundation of Kanem); in 1846 the creation of a new, al-Kanemi dynasty was formalized in a seizure of power by al-Kanemi's son, Umar.

The most geographically-distant adherent of the Shehu's jihad was Seku Ahmadu Lobbo (1775/6–1845), a *torodbe* who studied and taught near Jenne until his community was expelled because of its vehement criticisms of Muslim backsliding in the area. Ahmadu's community then settled in Macina, where Fulani were ruled by a weakly-Islamized sub-clan of military specialists (the Dikko) which was the subordinate partner in an alliance with the pagan Bambara state of Segou. Ahmadu's preaching appealed to many Fulani who felt oppressed by Dikko rule and disliked the alliance, and when his community was attacked he asked for (by 1815/16) a flag – the emir's symbol of authority – from the Shehu, a request abandoned when the Shehu died. By 1818 a successful jihad had led to the creation of a compact state (centred on a new capital, Hamdallahi) administered on rigorously Islamic lines.

Despite Macina's internal orthodoxy its rulers felt obliged to maintain good relations with neighbouring pagan powers – notably Segou; it was this accommodation that in 1862 laid Macina open to attack from the forces of Al-Hajj Umar (1794–1864) and its absorption into the empire ruled by Umar's successors until the completion of its conquest by the French in 1893. Born in Futa Toro, Umar went on hajj in about 1825; in Mecca he was appointed *kalifa* for West Africa of the Tijaniyya sufi order, and returned home between 1829 and 1840 via North Africa, Bornu, Sokoto and Macina. Umar's Tijani adherence and his claim that it was superior to all other sufi orders set him apart from other jihad leaders, who all adhered to the Qadiriyya; those in Futa Toro, Futa Jalon and Macina were hostile, and he settled in Dinguiray on the edge of the Futa Jalon plateau. From this base, from 1848 on, with the help of thousands of supporters from Futa Toro armed with modern weapons, Umar waged jihad against pagan polities. He conquered the Bambara state of Kaarta (1857), attempted to forestall the French advance on his recruiting grounds in the Senegal valley (1857–60) and conquered Segou (1860–2), a move that provoked opposition from Macina and, in turn, its conquest. The empire was highly decentralized after Umar's death, but put up a strong resistance to growing French pressure after 1880.

Resistance to the French was to become the major preoccupation of the other major state that arose in the 19th century Sudan, that led by Samori Turé (c.1830–1900), a Malinke war-leader. Although Samori was a Muslim, and in the early 1880s declared himself imam, and demanded that his subjects all become Muslim–a policy abandoned after it provoked revolts–he was not a jihadist. His empire can perhaps best be seen as an attempt, conscious or unconscious, to revive elements of the Malinke commercial and political unity that had been achieved by the rulers of Mali. Samori's state emerged (c.1874) with a capital at Bissandugu, out of a complex mix of pagan and Muslim polities, armies and commerce. It expanded more widely than other states in the area because of Samori's close links with the commercial networks of the Dyula–who were able to supply him with modern weapons–and his highly rational approach to military organization (itself the core of political organization in his state) and the supply and maintenance of ordnance. By 1880 Samori controlled the headwaters of the Niger, including the Bure goldfields; but from 1882 onwards his empire was penetrated by the French advance. In 1891 a French column, severely harassed by Samori's guerrillas en route, captured Bissandugu, sacrificed by Samori in a scorched earth retreat. Throughout 1892–3 Samori and his forces withdrew east into what is now Ivory Coast, establishing a second empire which held off the French until 1898 when Samori–once again moving west–was captured.

The French conquest–involving the dismemberment of major Sudanese polities–was virtually complete; meanwhile the northern Nigerian emirates of Nupe and Ilorin had been captured for Britain by forces of the Royal Niger Company,★ the prelude to a conquest of the rest of the Sokoto Caliphate, which, unlike the Islamic empires in French territory, was to survive the conquest as a major instrument– its archetype–of the British policy of indirect rule.★   *R.G.T.*

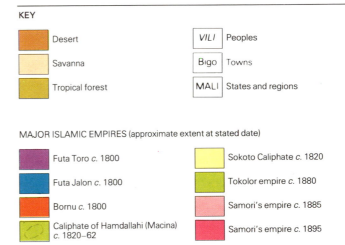

KEY

Desert	*VILI* Peoples
Savanna	Bigo Towns
Tropical forest	MALI States and regions

MAJOR ISLAMIC EMPIRES (approximate extent at stated date)

Futa Toro c. 1800	Sokoto Caliphate c. 1820
Futa Jalon c. 1800	Tokolor empire c. 1880
Bornu c. 1800	Samori's empire c. 1885
Caliphate of Hamdallahi (Macina) c. 1820–62	Samori's empire c. 1895

WEST AFRICAN PEOPLES AND STATES 18TH AND 19TH CENTURIES

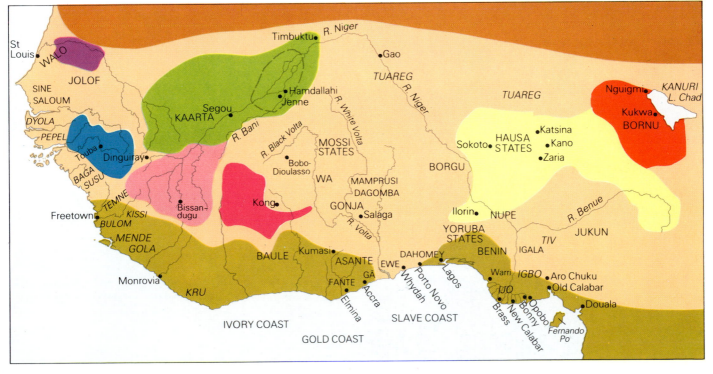

Europe, North Africa and the Sahara, 1250–1835

Mamluk Egypt

The Mamluk* sultans who came to power in Egypt in 1250 quickly took over the Ayyubid empire in Egypt and Syria. In 1260, at the battle of Ayn Jalut in Palestine, they defeated the pagan Mongols who had captured Baghdad in 1258, and threatened to overrun the entire Islamic Middle East. The victory established them as the leading Muslim power, and their army as the finest in the region. By 1291 first Baybars, then Qalawun and his son, al-Ashraf Khalil, had eliminated the Crusaders from Syria and Palestine. For a hundred years thereafter the supremacy of the Mamluks was scarcely challenged.

The succession to the throne was semi-hereditary, as sons tended to succeed fathers. The army from which the sultans came, however, maintained its professionalism by excluding the soldiers' offspring and recruiting from newly-acquired slaves. The *mamluks** continued to be well-armed horsemen, grouped in companies in the household and personal service of their amirs ('generals'), of whom the greatest was the sultan. They were recruited as youths by a slave trade from Central Asia and the Caucasus, and trained as warriors by their masters, the amirs.

On completion of this education, each received a grant of land (*iqta*, 'fief') to maintain himself as a knight throughout his active career. He was responsible for its cultivation, keeping certain revenues and remitting the rest to the state. If he became an amir with his own *mamluks*, his portion was enhanced. It could not be inherited by his children, and was reallocated at his retirement. In this way the government found the means to meet part of the cost of the army, while providing for the collection of its basic revenue.

Even before the Crusaders were obliged to withdraw to Cyprus and Rhodes, Alexandria attracted the Italian merchants whose business had flourished in the Holy Land. The economic growth of Western Europe since the 11th century had reversed the position which had prevailed in the Dark Ages, when Europe had supplied the Middle East and North Africa with commodities such as timber and slaves. Now European manufactures like cloth were exported at a profit to pay for goods imported from the Far East. Egypt's trade with India provided the Venetians with spices which were brought up the Red Sea to Aydhab, transported to the Nile at Qus, and sailed down the

KEY

Bigo Towns   MALI States and regions

EUROPE, NORTH AFRICA AND THE SAHARA

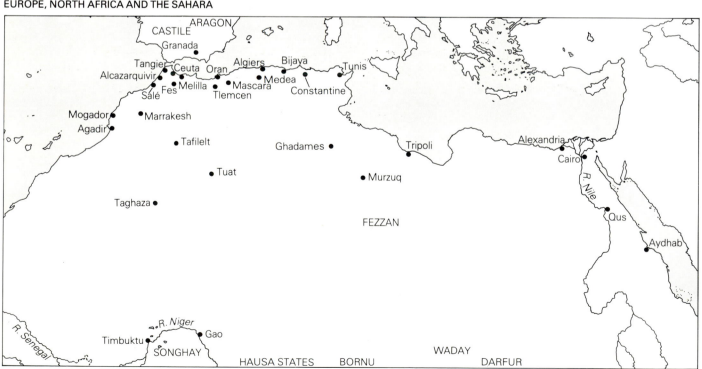

The 'Tombs of the Mamluks', Cairo, 14th–15th centuries: in the background, the Citadel of Saladin

river through Cairo to Alexandria. Egypt's own industries, notably clothmaking, may have suffered, but the Indies trade thrived in the hands of the Karimi merchants who controlled the Red Sea traffic. In the Mediterranean the Italians took charge under agreements with the Mamluk sultan which allowed them to reside at Alexandria, and to import and export at fixed rates of duty. Within Africa slaves continued to be imported from the region of Ethiopia* and Nubia* (whose Christian kingdom disappeared early in the 14th century as a result of Mamluk intrigue). But the chief development was towards the west, where the trans-Saharan routes from as far away as the River Senegal were drawn towards Cairo, partly because of the growing pilgrimage from the Western and Central Sudan,* which passed through Egypt on its way to the Holy Places of Islam.

The Maghrib, 13th–15th centuries

In the Maghrib the Hafsid sultan of Ifriqiya was widely recognized as the true heir to the Almohad caliphate, but his power was confined to eastern Algeria, Tunisia and Tripolitania. His capital was Tunis, now the biggest city and port of Ifriqiya. Western Algeria was ruled from Tlemcen by the local dynasty of the Ziyanids (or Abd al-Wadids). In Morocco the last descendants of Abd al-Mumin* were eliminated in 1269 by the Marinids. This dynasty, based upon Fes, maintained the imperial ambitions of the Almoravids* and the Almohads*, invaded Spain, attacked and took Tlemcen, and conquered Ifriqiya in the middle of the 14th century. With the break-up of the Almohad empire, however, the pattern of Muslim sultanates and Christian kingdoms in North Africa and Spain was firmly established, and the Marinids' military adventures ended with the death of their last great sultan in 1359. The states which outlasted individual rulers were loosely-organized collections of cities and tribes to whose governors and chiefs the sultan delegated his authority in return for taxes, tribute and military service. From his palace citadel he ruled over his capital and its environs, and maintained a standing force which might tour the country to receive hospitality and demonstrations of loyalty, collect taxes and presents, and deal with the recalcitrant.

This force, originally composed of slave troops, was now often supplemented or replaced by Christian mercenaries. For long periods these mercenaries were an aspect of the dependence of the Ziyanids of Tlemcen and the Hafsids of Tunis upon the kingdom of Aragon, to which they paid tribute. The Hafsids permitted priests and monks to attend the troops and the European merchant community, although the opportunity which some of these missionaries sought to evangelize the Muslim population never arose. More important concessions were made to the Aragonese merchants of Barcelona. At Tunis and Bijaya (Bougie) they lived in their *funduq* or hotel-warehouse under their own supervisor, as did the Genoese, Pisans, Venetians and so on. Tunis was a major entrepôt for seaborne trade, almost entirely in European hands, between the eastern and western Mediterranean. Tlemcen, on the other hand, where the Aragonese merchants predominated, was the chief centre for the Western Sudanese gold trade, which flourished at least until the second half of the 14th century, while the empire of Mali* was at its height. North Africa supplied the products of the pastoral economy, wool and leather. Bijaya, providing the essential commodity wax, gave its name to the French wax candle (*bougie*). Morocco gave the Spaniards the merino (Marinid) sheep.

Commercial relations were punctuated by wars, like the French attack on Tunis in 1270 and the Marinid invasion of Spain in 1340, inevitably religious in character. Always there was piracy, which North Africans regarded as a continual holy war against infidels who

Game of chess, Moorish style, from the *Chess Book* of Alfonso the Wise of Castile, 1252–84

had not concluded a treaty of peace. New factors were the Black Death in the middle of the 14th century, the subsequent reorganization of the European economy, and the political and economic changes of the 15th century in the Iberian peninsula. Commercially the eastern Maghrib benefited as the Venetians sought compensation for the closing of many of their outlets in the Middle East; black slaves were bought for domestic, agricultural and industrial work in Sicily and Italy. Some were required for a new purpose, the cultivation and manufacture of sugar on plantations in southern Europe. In the 15th century the Hafsids in Ifriqiya enjoyed a long period of peace and prosperity, extending their suzerainty over a much-weakened Tlemcen. Morocco, on the other hand, never recovered from the confusion following the death of the sultan Abu Inan in 1359. By the middle of the 15th century Marrakesh was virtually independent of Fes, and in 1465 the Marinids were overthrown. Their successors, the Wattasids, ruled only the northern half of the country.

Portugal, Spain and the Ottoman empire in North Africa, 1415–1587

In 1415 the Portuguese* captured Ceuta, and by the beginning of the 16th century a string of stations down the Atlantic coast of Morocco formed part of their trading network around the coast of Africa. In 1492 the Spaniards took Granada, followed by a series of ports along the Mediterranean coast of North Africa, including, in 1534, Tunis. This extension of the Spanish empire, however, was countered from the east, where the old order had also been overthrown by a new power. Perhaps because recurrent outbreaks of plague reduced the agricultural revenue of Egypt, the Mamluks in the 15th century were crippled by lack of cash, in spite of state monopolies upon trade in such commodities as spices. The temporary disappearance of the spice trade through Alexandria followed the Portuguese discovery of the sea route to India in 1498, and the havoc caused to Muslim shipping left the Mamluk sultan unable to campaign effectively against the Ottoman Turks. In 1517 Egypt was conquered and annexed by the Turks, whose empire now covered the Balkans, Anatolia, and the Arab lands of the Middle East. The Ottoman army consisted of the janissaries, an infantry of slave origin levied from the Christian population of the Balkans, armed with handguns; the spahis, light cavalry; and a large corps of field artillery. This armament made it the most modern force in the world; there was also a fleet of galleys crewed by the seamen of the Aegean, pirates whose activities linked them with the corsairs of the Maghrib in the holy war against the infidel.

The raids of the North African corsairs were the chief reason for the Spanish advance. The Hafsids and Ziyanids were incapable of resistance but the pirates fought on, joined by others from the east, led by the brothers Barbarossa. Helped by contingents of janissaries, the newcomers began the conquest of Algeria and Tunisia on behalf

Illuminated Quran (1568) written for the Sultan of Morocco in a typical Maghribi script

of the Ottoman Empire. The hitherto minor port of Algiers became the base from which, between 1516 and 1574, the Spaniards were expelled from North Africa with the exception of Oran, Mers el-Kebir and Melilla in Morocco. As Ottoman viceroys with the title of *beylerbey* (supreme commander), Khayr al-Din Barbarossa and his successors ruled from the borders of Morocco as far as Egypt. In 1587 this dominion was incorporated into the Ottoman Empire as the regencies of Algiers, Tunis and Tripoli. With the creation of these separate provinces, the modern divisions of Algeria, Tunisia and Libya were established.

The Saadians and the Alawites in Morocco, 1511–1727

The 16th century revolution in Morocco was made from within by a campaign which began in the south in 1511 and ended with the final capture of Fes from the Wattasids in 1554. The Saadian dynasty which then took power claimed descent from the Prophet, and vital to its success was the support of scholars and holy men.

Since the time of the Almohads the doctrines of Sufism (Islamic mysticism) had created schools of devotees who followed, in addition to the Law, the *tariqa*, or way, of a teacher. In rural areas at least, such teachers were the *murabits* or marabouts, the holy men, who combined scholarship and asceticism in their *zawiyas* or monastic settlements, where they studied and prayed with their disciples, and where they were buried in domed chapels. The disciples in turn established their own *zawiyas* according to their master's teaching, forming larger or smaller brotherhoods to which most men of religion were affiliated. The *zawiyas*, in town and country, made an important contribution to the social as well as the religious life of the Maghrib. In Morocco they were especially influential because of their hold over the tribes, whose warriors looked to the marabouts to keep the peace, but also to give a political lead in time of trouble.

The *zawiyas* helped to bring the Saadians to power. They were alienated but not destroyed when the new dynasty tried to bring them under control. Precariously poised between the Portuguese, and the Turks in Algiers, the Saadians defeated the Portuguese at the battle of Alcazarquivir (al-Qasr al-Kabir) in 1578. For 25 years under Ahmad al-Mansur al-Dhahabi (the Golden Conqueror) the regime was wealthy and strong. Marrakesh was once again the capital, where the sultan assembled a strong force of renegade Christian infantry in imitation of the Turkish janissaries, and used it to try to capture the source of Western Sudanese gold. The expedition of 1590–1 overthrew the Sudanese empire of Songhay*, and took Timbuktu, which became the headquarters of the Arma, the musketeers and their descendants who ruled in the region of the city for over a hundred years. The Saadians derived little benefit. On the death of Ahmad in 1603, a quarrel over the succession brought about the collapse of the dynasty. Great marabouts divided the country into regions of which they became the rulers, until in the 1660s Mawlay al-Rashid, the leader of another family of *sharifs* or descendants of the Prophet from south-eastern Morocco, captured Fes and restored the sultanate. The new Alawite dynasty was securely established during the long reign of his brother, Mawlay Ismail, 1672–1727.

Ottoman North Africa in the 17th and 18th centuries

In the Ottoman provinces the 17th century saw a movement towards independence from Istanbul, and a constitutional conflict for power within each provincial government. The pasha, the governor appointed by the Ottoman sultan, who conducted the administration through the *divan* (council), lost much or all of his authority. The quarrel was between the *aghas* (generals) with their military command, the *beys* (great office-holders) with their wide patronage, and the *deys* (junior officers) of the elite corps of janissaries. These were variously supported or opposed by the *taifas* of the *rais*, the companies of corsair captains in the North African regencies, and by the *kouloughlis*, the offspring of the janissaries who, like those of the *mamluks* were forbidden to join the troop, although they might enlist in other regiments. After many fluctuations, and wars between Morocco, Algiers, Tunis and Tripoli from about 1680 to 1710, the outcome in the 18th century was a series of monarchies independent of Istanbul in all but name. In Algiers the ruler was the Dey, chosen by the janissaries, who were now recruited in Anatolia from Turkish volunteers. The Dey ruled the district of Algiers, assigning the rest of the country to the three Beys who governed at Constantine in the east, Medea to the south, and Mascara in the west. Tunis was ruled by hereditary Beys of the Husaynid dynasty, and Tripoli by the Karamanlis, a dynasty of *kouloughli* origin with the title of pasha. Only in Egypt was the acquisition of power less formal, less complete. There the Mamluks had survived the Ottoman conquest of 1517 as an aristocracy endowed with tax-farms instead of military fiefs. These

Qarawiyyin Mosque, Fes, Morocco, 12th century: the entrance to the prayer-hall viewed from the entrance to the court

tax-farms became virtually private property in return for an inheritance tax which replaced payments to the treasury. The Mamluks, whose leaders had the title of Bey, were divided into feuding factions which inhibited the creation of a new monarchy. Nevertheless, the Shaykh al-Balad, 'Head of the City/Cairo', the chief of the dominant faction, was the effective ruler of the country.

Europe and North Africa, 16th–19th centuries

From the 16th century onwards, the expansion of world trade following the discovery of the sea routes to the Americas and the Indies greatly reduced the economic importance of North Africa. Although the spice trade returned to Alexandria, Egypt was no longer the main link between East and West. The Ottoman Empire, on the other hand, demanded not only black slaves* and gold, but Egyptian crops to feed its cities. With good administration, agricultural productivity rose only to fall back as the Mamluks escaped the control of Istanbul. Further west, the situation was complicated by piracy. Developed into a major enterprise by the 16th century wars, raiding by the corsairs continued into the 17th century as a highly profitable business in which captured goods were sold off at bargain prices, often for return to Europe, Christian captives were held for ransom, and European governments were induced to buy immunity with tribute. By the 18th century, however, piracy from Tripoli in the east

to Salé (Sallee) in Morocco had become little more than a threat with which North African rulers exacted payment from the states of Europe. More important was the export to Europe of North African commodities, particularly grain. During the reign of Sidi Muhammad (1757–90) even Morocco, which had largely severed commercial relations with Europe, briefly opened its relatively insignificant ports. European merchants in the Maghrib as well as in Egypt continued to reside as privileged foreigners under their national consuls, who, as the power of the European nations grew, became figures of considerable political importance.

North Africa's relations with the Sahara and the Sudanese belt south of the desert centred upon the central and eastern routes across the desert, as the Hausa states,* Bornu,* Waday* and Darfur* emerged as important centres of government and trade. Black slaves were still in demand, by the nomads and oasis-dwellers of the Sahara as well as by the city peoples of the north. The Fezzan, with its capital at Murzuq, came increasingly under control from Tripoli. At the beginning of the 19th century, Tripoli seemed the obvious starting-point for British expeditions into the interior, just one example of the way in which Europe had suddenly become dominant. The Napoleonic Wars had given a boost to North African exports of grain and cattle, and a final fillip to piracy. Their conclusion confronted the North Africans with the reality of European power. Piracy was brought to an abrupt end. In 1830 the French captured Algiers, and went on to annex the country. The French action was, however, exceptional. While the influence of the European consuls increased, Muslim rulers were generally free to seek their own advantage from the relationship. The archetype was the new ruler of Egypt, Muhammad Ali,* who after the invasion of Egypt by Napoleon in 1798 had arrived with the Ottoman forces sent to recover the country with the British. Appointed Ottoman viceroy in 1805, he finally broke the power of the Mamluks in 1811, and went on to capture Mecca and Medina, conquer the Nilotic Sudan in 1820–2, invade Greece, and finally, in 1831–3, conquer Palestine and Syria. To create this empire, and to establish himself as an absolute monarch, he relied on a European-style conscript army of Egyptians, a Western educated administration to supervise it, and a cash crop, cotton, to pay for it. His success was not repeated. Yusuf Pasha, the Karamanli ruler of Tripoli, lost his throne in 1835, when his debts and his high taxes provoked a revolt which ended with the return of Libya to the status of a province of the Ottoman Empire. At Tunis, on the other hand, the Bey found a new source of income from olive oil, which took the place of grain as Tunisia's major export, and in 1831 created his own conscript army. With the accession of the new sultan, Mawlay Abd al-Rahman, in 1822, the Alawite dynasty in Morocco recovered from the rebellions of the reign of his predecessor, Sulayman, and by readmitting European merchants, began to take its own first steps towards modernization.   *M.B.*

The Portuguese in Africa, c.1450–1650

The exploratory voyages of Portuguese seamen along the Atlantic coasts in the 15th century were part of what is commonly called in European history the 'Age of Discovery'. Exploiting and adding to the accumulated technological knowledge of the medieval world, and financed by the growing merchant class of southern Europe, Iberian shipping in less than a hundred years circumnavigated Africa, explored the Indian Ocean trade routes, reached China and Japan and crossed the Atlantic Ocean to 'discover' the Americas. The various civilizations of the world were brought together intellectually and commercially more than ever before, and the foundations of an international commercial system dominated by Western Europe were laid.

The main inspiration for Portuguese expansion sprang from a mixture of economic, religious and strategic factors. Initially, the need to expel Muslim forces from the key ports of North-West Africa was paramount. Although the Islamic powers had been defeated in Portugal in 1249, they still occupied Granada in Spain and dominated North Africa* and the Middle East, cutting off Europe from direct access to the trade of Africa south of the Sahara and of the Far East. If Portuguese ships could indeed sail out into the Atlantic and reach the coasts of West Africa, they might outflank the Muslim enemy and gain direct access to the sources of West African gold, short-circuiting overland routes and troublesome middlemen. Religious zeal added impetus to these economic imperatives. A continuing belief in an African Christian kingdom, that of the mythical Prester John,* motivated the search for a ruler who might be a potential ally against the Muslim enemy.

The initial push against the Islamic forces in North Africa resulted in the fall in 1415 of the important commercial and naval base of Ceuta, which was used by Muslim powers as a springboard for attacking the Iberian peninsula and Christian shipping. In the course of the 15th and early 16th centuries most of the Moroccan ports, such as Tangier (1471), Larashe (1473), Azzamur (1486) and Agadir (1505), came under either Portuguese or Spanish occupation. Although they could not organize a unified defence to save the coastal towns, Moroccan rulers were able to resist attempts by European forces to penetrate into the interior.

The Portuguese already had some quite accurate information on the trans-Saharan trade, as shown in a famous 14th century Majorcan map which gave the location of caravan routes and the Western Sudanese kingdom of Mali.* However, the occupation of Ceuta brought a closer awareness of the gold trade to the south and was a catalyst for further voyages down the North-West African coasts. Prince Henry the Navigator, the first Portuguese governor of Ceuta, was a prime patron and organizer of the expansion southwards. The school that he established at Sagres on the south-west tip of Portugal became a centre for maritime research where scholars collated and improved on sailing, navigation, mapping and shipbuilding techniques. An increasingly influential merchant class in Oporto and Lisbon was eager to invest in commercial ventures, especially after the first cargoes of gold and slaves had been brought back from the Guinea coast in 1441.

West and West Central Africa

Once the shallows, currents and winds of the dreaded Cape Bojador had been negotiated in 1434, and it was ascertained that caravels equipped with lateen sails could indeed travel northwards into the prevailing winds and return home safely, Portuguese exploration of the African coasts gained momentum. By the time Prince Henry died in 1460 the Senegal and Gambia rivers had been passed, the previously uninhabited Cape Verde Islands discovered, and Sierra Leone reached. In 1471 ships attained the Mina coast (also called the Gold Coast), the closest coastal point to sources of West African gold. In the next year the Bight of Benin was navigated and the uninhabited island of São Tomé, which was to become an important entrepôt in the Gulf of Guinea, located. Other landmarks in the epic of Portuguese expansion were the arrival of Portuguese ships at the Zaire estuary, where contact was made with the ruler of Kongo (1483), Bartholomew Dias's rounding of the Cape of Good Hope in 1487 and, 11 years later, Vasco da Gama's voyage along the East African coasts before crossing the Indian Ocean to Calicut in India.

Several general themes emerge in the history of African–Portuguese interaction on the coasts of West and West Central Africa in the 15th and 16th centuries. The foremost was trade. The stock African exports were gold, slaves, ivory and pepper; also such other valuable commodities as copper, silver, indigo, amber, wax, civet, hides and beads. In return African rulers and entrepreneurs demanded cloth, iron bars, horses, copper basins, brass manillas and guns, although the latter were seldom supplied. Commercial enterprises might be undertaken by individual ships, which would stop wherever there was a safe anchorage and a good market. More settled patterns of commerce were also established, depending on such factors as pre-existing African trade networks, the type of goods available, African politics and the high mortality rates among Europeans.

At the most crucial trading points along the west coast permanent factories and forts were built. The precedent was set in 1448 with the construction of a fort on the island of Arguin off the Mauritanian coast, intended as an entrepôt for the adjacent coastline and, in particular, designed to divert trade from trans-Saharan routes. But the Arguin base never attracted much gold from interior sources and networks, and slaves became the main export, even this trade declining by the end of the 15th century as other areas on the Senegambia coast to the south grew in significance. Santiago, the most fertile of the Cape Verde Islands, was also fortified. The archipelago became important commercially after the islanders were granted the privilege of trading with the area from Senegal to Sierra Leone by the Portuguese Crown in 1466.

The most important stretch of coast for the Portuguese was the 250km of Mina coast from where trade routes radiated inland from fishing and salt-making communities to reach the Akan goldfields in the interior. Here they began building the fort at Elmina in 1482. Land was rented for the site with the reluctant agreement of the two local rulers of Komenda and Fetu. Other minor fortifications were erected at Axim to the west, and at Shama and Accra further east. Such establishments were to protect the Portuguese monopoly against attacks from European competitors, rather than from African opponents. Even at the peak of Portuguese power, political authority seldom extended beyond the immediate environs of a fort.

Brass casting from Benin (Nigeria) of a Portuguese musketeer, 16th or 17th century

West African ivory carving – probably a salt-cellar – of uncertain precise origin, one of a large number produced in the 16th century by African artists for the Portuguese market

Portuguese policy in West Africa aimed at maintaining a maximum profit with a minimum commitment of manpower and resources, already over-extended in the far-flung overseas empire. Indeed, the weakness of Portugal's position and its need for African allies was shown in a dispute at Accra in 1576 that resulted in the fort being destroyed and trade there stopped for the next 50 years. The main factor that made a limited presence possible and profitable was the efficiency of African commercial networks in bringing trade goods from the interior to the coast. In the Gold Coast local merchants were not only in touch with the Akan area, but with Mande traders★ and regions of the Niger bend.

East of the Gold Coast the Portuguese were early impressed with the kingdom of Benin,★ in what is now Nigeria and here they anticipated some success with missionary work as well as commercial profit. From 1487 to 1507 a factory was maintained at the Benin river port of Ughoton, exporting good quality pepper to Europe, and cloth, beads and slaves to the Gold Coast. But early hopes quickly faded. High mortality rates, the prohibition by the Portuguese

Crown of the private pepper trade which competed with the royal monopoly in Indian pepper, and a prohibition by Benin after 1516 on the export of male slaves, which it needed to man its armies, were all factors in the failure to establish a lasting relationship. It was also significant that the *oba* (ruler) of Benin remained indifferent to the goods the Portuguese offered. His state was already oriented to a dynamic African trade system which reached through Yoruba and Igbo neighbours to the Western and Central Sudanese network in the north. Only the importation of firearms would have convinced the *oba* of the value of a European alliance, and these the Portuguese would not supply.

An important dimension of Portuguese commercial activities in West and West Central Africa in the 15th and 16th centuries was the success of the Portuguese in insinuating themselves into pre-existing African trade networks. As a poor and underpopulated region of Europe with little manufacturing industry, their success depended heavily on their ability to identify and respond to African tastes and demands for goods that were available on other parts of the coast, as well as those brought from Europe. For example, in order to buy gold on the Mina coast, they transported slaves, cloth and beads from Benin; Benin cloth and São Tomé palm-oil were taken to points south of the Equator such as Loango and Luanda where the Portuguese were active traders; slaves were taken from Kongo and Angola to work on plantations on São Tomé; African labour from the Upper Guinea mainland was transported to work on the cotton and indigo plantations of the Cape Verde Islands; while cloth, manufactured and dyed on the Cape Verde Islands, was traded along the Upper Guinea Coast and shipped to the Gold Coast.

Another early development was the growth of Portuguese settlements. These were first established on the Portuguese Atlantic islands–Madeira (c.1419), the Azores (c.1439), the Cape Verde Islands (1456–60), and São Tomé and Príncipe (c.1570). The settlers were of diverse origins. They might include administrators, soldiers, missionaries and traders, but also deportees from Portugal; the *degredados*, unwanted elements such as Jews, beggars and convicts. Another element in the population of the Cape Verde Islands and São Tomé was African slaves from the mainland. Mulatto offspring were common and a new class of Afro-Portuguese emerged. These people, in time, forgot their ties with Portugal and accommodated themselves to the local African communities in which they lived. Yet they also acted as brokers of Portuguese trade and culture. In Upper Guinea the *lançados*, as they were known, spread out in numerous coastal and riverain settlements between the Gambia and Sierra Leone, trading through Mande middlemen with sources as far as the Upper Niger. Further south in the colony of Angola, *pombeiros*, who were often Afro-Portuguese, organized caravans from coastal points such as Luanda and Benguela to interior markets. In most regions, however, such as the Gold Coast, Benin and Loango, African rulers resisted efforts to encroach on their position as coastal middlemen.

By the late 15th century, the slave trade was well-established. The main impetus came from the expansion of sugar cultivation from the Mediterranean to the Atlantic islands, where it was introduced with spectacular success. In particular, sugar worked by slaves from Benin, Kongo and Angola was the basis for the development of the island of São Tomé whose prosperity peaked in the years 1530–60. After the 1570s, when there were serious slave rebellions, many settlers left for Brazil to participate in the burgeoning sugar industry of the regions of Pernambuco, Bahia and Rio de Janeiro. This 'sugar revolution' in the New World in turn encouraged the growth of the trans-Atlantic slave trade.★

Portuguese relations with the Kongo★ and Mbundu★ peoples, living south of the Zaire River in the region of modern Angola, demonstrate the contradictions inherent in their interactions with African societies. After early expeditions went to the Kongo with instructions to promote trade and to evangelize the people, the *manikongo* (ruler) was baptized in 1491. Each side could see potential benefits in the new alliance. For Kongo rulers it meant access to European goods, technology and literacy; for the Portuguese, potential economic gain and their most persistent attempt at acculturation of an African society. Kongo youths were sent to Europe for education and, with the permission of the ruler, missionaries were active in the Kongo capital. The relationship did not work out as foreseen, however. Unlike the Gold Coast, the Kongo region had no lucrative mineral to export, and Portuguese and São Tomé traders quickly turned to the export of slaves. The able Kongo ruler, Afonso I (ruled 1506–43) complained of the disruption this caused in his state in a letter to the Lisbon Crown in the 1520s, but, unlike the *oba* of Benin, the *manikongo* could do little to reverse the trend. The Portuguese missionary effort made slow progress due to African resistance and to high mortality rates. Instead of becoming a religion of the masses, Christianity was adopted by a small ruling elite, who made it a royal cult underpinning their political authority.

Searching for other sources of slaves, São Tomé traders had also moved south in the early 16th century to the Kwanza River, an important trade artery to the interior. Following on these unofficial traders the Portuguese Crown sent embassies in the 1520s and 1560s, to the court of the *ngola a kiluanje*, the ruler of the western Mbundu state of Ndongo. In 1571 a charter to settle the area was given to Paulo Dias de Novais, whose expedition founded the Portuguese establishment at Luanda in 1575. During the next 30 years Portuguese military forces struggled unsuccessfully against disease, inadequate supplies and Mbundu resistance, to gain access along the Kwanza route to the salt mines at Kisama and to the rumoured but non-existent silver mines at Cambambe. By the early 17th century the slave trade had become the main *raison d'être* of the small colony of Angola, and it was to remain so for the next two centuries.

East Africa

The interaction of Portuguese and African societies on the coasts of East Africa was rather different from that on the Atlantic coasts. A chain of Swahili city-states★ from Sofala in the south to Mogadishu in the north represented a blending of African, Arabian and Persian cultures and commercial interests. For centuries these societies had been in touch with traders from the Red Sea, the Persian Gulf, India and the Far East, exchanging African commodities such as gold, ivory and slaves for beads, textiles, glassware, porcelain and other items. After the voyages of Vasco da Gama, the prime interest of the Portuguese was to secure the sea route across the Indian Ocean to the Spice Islands. They justified the ruthlessness of their attacks on the Muslim city-states of East Africa (beginning in 1502) on religious grounds, but economic and strategic considerations were obviously paramount.

Fort Jesus, Mombasa, Kenya

South of Cape Delgado the main goal was to secure naval supremacy in the Mozambique channel and to gain access to the gold trade of the plateau regions south of the Zambezi River which were part of the declining Mwenemutapa★ state. The trading entrepôt at Sofala, used by Swahili and Arab traders as the southern depot of the Kilwa-Mwenemutapa trade, was secured and fortified in 1505. Following this, in 1507, a fort was built on Mozambique Island, which became the Portuguese headquarters in the region. Efforts to control the gold trade were unsuccessful since, after the Portuguese capture of Sofala, Swahili traders diverted the trade to points on the coast further north. A further effort to make direct contact with the Mwenemutapa area was made in the 1530s when Portuguese forces moved inland along the Zambezi valley to establish and garrison two forts at Sena and Tete. From there, several sporadic attempts were made to advance south of the river into the Mwenemutapa area, to set up *feiras* (markets) which would be points of Portuguese influence, to open up missionary work, and to intervene in local politics. Such efforts, like those at Sofala, were counter-productive. The Portuguese were unable to gain permanent access to the minerals of the region, and their political initiatives only served to underline the weakness of the Mwenemutapa ruler in the eyes of his subjects and his neighbours. As Mwenemutapa further declined, the centre of political authority in the region passed to the Changamire state, which lay further south beyond the reach of Portuguese influence. By the second half of the 17th century, the official Portuguese presence in Zambezia was limited to a handful of soldiers in the fever-ridden garrisons of Sena and Tete, and to the small community on Mozambique Island. At the same time, a mixture of Portuguese settlers, adventurers and *degredados* of Portuguese, Indian and African origin remained in the Zambezi valley, intermarrying with local women, acquiring land, trading, and using their firearms to influence local politics. These *prazeros* (*prazo*: a plantation or estate) kept alive Portuguese influence at a time when the official presence was almost non-existent.

North of Cape Delgado Portuguese forces moved swiftly to secure strategic points such as Kilwa,★ Mombasa and Malindi. Their ships, armed with heavy cannon, bombarded the coastal towns into submission, while the traditional rivalries of coastal ruling families were exploited. In 1593, having overthrown the Mombasa ruler with the help of his Malindi neighbour, the Portuguese built Fort Jesus, which remained a bastion of their east coast influence for the next hundred years.

Ethiopia

In the late 15th and early 16th centuries the Portuguese finally encountered an African Christian kingdom in the state that dominated the western highlands of Ethiopia.★ The same mixture of strategic, commercial and religious considerations were present in this relationship as elsewhere. The Catholic Portuguese and the Coptic Christian state had a common cause in repulsing the expanding power of the Ottoman Turks in the Red Sea. After the capture of the Ethiopian port of Massawa in 1536, the Ethiopian ruler welcomed the intervention of Portuguese forces with firearms on his side. For more than a century, until about 1650, Portuguese missionaries, soldiers and diplomats remained in the country until a conflict between Jesuit priests and the monks of the established Coptic Church sparked off a civil war that ended with the expulsion of European influences from the North-East African highlands. Thus ended the abortive Portuguese efforts to gain control of the Red Sea trade routes. The Christian Ethiopian state retreated into an isolation that removed it from interaction with Europe until the 19th century.

European competition and Portuguese decline

By the mid- 17th century the hegemony that Portugal had enjoyed in European-African relations for almost two centuries was ended. In West and West Central Africa, French and English interlopers had intermittently challenged Portugal's monopoly since the 1530s. After Spain had taken control of the Lisbon monarchy in 1580, the possessions of the Iberian enemy became fair game for English, French and Dutch ships. It was the Dutch who succeeded in dislodging the Portuguese from their supremacy on the Atlantic coasts of Africa. They established a fort at Mouri on the Gold Coast in 1612 and captured Elmina in 1637. The Portuguese were also expelled from São Tomé and Luanda in 1641, but recovered these posessions seven years later to re-establish their influence, if not their dominance, in the southern Atlantic trading system. On the east coast more advanced Dutch and English shipping pioneered new routes across the Indian Ocean which bypassed the East African coast. It was the Omani* Arabs who wrested Mombasa from Portuguese control in 1698.

In the long run the Portuguese did not have the resources, manpower or shipping to control and consolidate their vastly dispersed empire, which stretched from Brazil to Africa and across the Indian Ocean to the Far East. Ironically, those who most kept alive Portuguese influence were often those who were largely independent of any control from Lisbon – the lançados, the pombeiros and the prazeros. For over 200 years Portugal had maintained footholds on the African continent, but with a few exceptions, such as Kongo, they scarcely affected the patterns of African life. Yet there were some lasting influences. Portuguese was widely used as the language of trade in West and West Central Africa; important foodcrops, such as maize and manioc, were introduced from the Americas and were adopted as African staples; and Portugal had drawn Africa into an international trading system wider than ever before, a trend further intensified by English, Dutch and French competitors in the 17th century and after. *P.M.M.*

The slave trade era

Dimensions and directions of the trade

More slaves were exported from Africa in the two hundred years from the mid-17th to the mid-19th century than at any other comparable period in the history of the trade. In 1969 a statistical assessment of the total trans-Atlantic slave trade was published by Professor Philip Curtin, and his findings, with some minor revisions, remain the most generally accepted assessment for the volume of that trade. As many as 11–12 million people left Africa for the Americas, 80 per cent of these in the period 1701–1850. This figure does not take into account those who were exported in the slave trade across the Sahara and the Indian Ocean, mainly, but not entirely, to the Muslim world.*

There were several reasons for the expansion of the slave trade in this period. The stimulus came mainly from an increase in the demand for sugar in Europe and a corresponding need for more

SLAVES EXPORTED FROM AFRICA TO THE AMERICAS

Period	Slaves exported
Before 1600	330 000
1601–1700	1 609 000
1701–1810	7 262 000
1811–1870	2 278 000
Total 1600–1870	11 479 000

Source: J.D. Fage, *A History of Africa* (New York, 1978), based on Philip D. Curtin, *The Atlantic Slave Trade: a Census* (Madison, 1969)

Cape Coast Castle, Ghana

labour in the plantations of the Americas. In the early 17th century the Dutch edged out the Portuguese* as the super-power in the African trade, to be superseded themselves at the end of the century by Britain and France. Having acquired expertise in the sugar industry during their occupation of Brazil,* 1630–54, the Dutch transferred this know-how to the islands of the Caribbean,* where sugar plantations prospered, especially on the French island of Saint Domingue and the British possessions of Jamaica and Barbados. The need for an adequate work-force became even more pressing in the 18th century, as other labour-intensive crops, such as cotton, tobacco, rice, indigo and coffee, were developed in South America, the West Indies, and the southern USA,* and gold-mining became an important industry in Brazil. Answers to the question of why the labour problems of the New World were 'solved' by forcibly transporting men, women and children some 6500km across the Atlantic have now moved beyond previously-accepted, yet patently erroneous, pseudo-scientific theories that suggested that black people could withstand tropical climates and thus work better than whites. Of the several explanations for the trans-Atlantic slave trade,

the most important concerns resistance to disease. The sparse local American Indian population was decimated by imported European diseases such as smallpox; European mortality rates were high due to a host of tropical ailments to which they had little immunity; Africans, accustomed to the tropical disease environment and also to the diseases of the Euro-African landmass, had the lowest mortality.

The organization of the trade

How was the slave trade organized, and how did it affect African societies? There was little that was haphazard, either in the way slaves were obtained or in the transactions between agents of European trading companies and African merchants at coastal markets.

Slaves were commonly acquired through wars, raids or tribute. They were most often victims of localized conflicts, taken in the course of the expansion or the break-up of political entities, rather than in wars induced to obtain captives who could be sold. They were frequently criminals and debtors, the modern practice of incarceration being little known in African societies. Another category was drifters or refugees, or those who could not claim the protection of a

powerful family and who became vulnerable in lineage-oriented societies. Occasions when Africans would willingly sell their relations into slavery were rare, such actions arising in times of great stress; for example during a prolonged drought when disease and starvation might be the alternatives.

Buying and selling operations became highly conventionalized at many points on the coast. African currencies, such as iron bars in Upper Guinea, ounces of gold-dust on the Gold Coast, cloth and cowries in the Bight of Benin, brass manillas in the Niger delta-Cameroon region, and lengths of cloth on the Loango coast, were adopted as standard units of value. European goods and African slaves were valued according to such units of account, leaving the selection of European goods to be included in the payment for a slave as the main subject for negotiation. Items most demanded by African businessmen were guns and powder, cloth, spirits and tobacco, and hardware. Local rulers often required the payment of fees and customs duties, which might be paid in more exotic prestige goods.

Local conditions determined the precise nature of the organization of the trade, and different parts of Africa – and in particular West and West-Central Africa – felt the full impact of the slave trade at different times between the 16th and 19th centuries.

Senegambia and the Upper Guinea coast

Of considerable importance in the early years of the slave trade (the Senegambia alone exported about one-third of the slaves that left Africa before 1600), the region between the Senegal River and Sierra Leone was not of much significance after the mid-17th century. By that time previously unsettled conditions on the coast and its immediate hinterland, caused by the break-up of the Jolof state in the Senegambia and the invasions of the Mane in Sierra Leone, had subsided. In the 18th century slaves tended to come from inland areas. Long distance caravans, which carried on a brisk intra-African regional trade in items such as salt, kola nuts and cloth, would arrive from the Upper Niger at markets on the Gambia and Senegal rivers.

The first day of the Yam Festival at Kumasi, Asante, 1817 (see page 148). Plate from T. Edward Bowdich, *Mission from Cape Coast Castle to Ashantee* (1819)

They might also bring captives derived from the expansionist wars of the new Bambara states, Kaarta and Segou.* Slaves for coastal markets were also generated in the mountainous Futa Jalon* region by the Fulani jihad (Islamic holy war), a forerunner of the Islamic reform movement that was to engulf the Western Sudan* in the 19th century. But slaves remained only one of several exports from this region; indeed, in the 18th century, the value of other goods that were bought by European merchants, such as ivory, camwood, gum and beeswax, was greater.

The Windward Coast and the Gold Coast

Along the Windward Coast, lying between Sierra Leone and the Gold Coast, the slave trade was never of great consequence. The absence of natural harbours, and treacherous offshore conditions deterred European shipping. In striking contrast was the region to the east, the Gold Coast, which experienced the greatest concentration of European interests in West Africa. Here, by the early 18th century, competing commercial companies from England, Holland, Denmark, Sweden and Brandenburg, had built some 30 forts to protect their trade from rivals.

The existence of gold mines in the hinterland of the Gold Coast meant that for centuries African trade networks had been developed to allow the passage of goods over long distances. From the 15th century or before, Mande-speaking trade specialists, the Dyula,* had extended routes from the Niger port of Jenne to the forest regions, where they bought gold and kola nuts to sell in the markets of the Western Sudan or to trans-Saharan merchants. Another route reached out from the coastal forests to the Hausa* area in the north-east. As in other parts of Africa, such pre-existing commercial systems facilitated the transport of slaves to the coast. However, it was not until the early 18th century that slaves superseded gold as the principal overseas export of the Gold Coast.

The wealth that commerce generated and an increase in the scale of organization were major factors in the development of centralized political systems in the Gold Coast region. By the 17th century three important states, Akwamu, Denkyira and Akyem, vied with each other for political and economic supremacy, only to be overtaken in the early 18th century by the power of Asante. This kingdom was a confederation of Akan-speaking peoples who recognized the paramouncy of the ruler of Kumasi as *Asantehene* (ruler of all the Asante). Within about 70 years Asante had defeated its three major rivals and absorbed much of their territory; seized control of the gold-bearing regions and the principal routes to the coast; expanded northwards to make tributary the states of Gonja and Dagbon (Dagomba) in the savanna; and threatened the position of the Fante as middlemen on the coast. By the early 19th century the stage was set for the confrontation of British and Asante power, a major theme of Gold Coast history in the immediate pre-colonial period.

The Slave Coast

In the second half of the 18th century, and in the 19th century, the number of slaves exported from areas east of the Gold Coast increased dramatically. This was partly due to changing political conditions, but also reflected the growing efficiency of African institutions in adapting to meet the demands of foreign trade. As in the case of Asante, expanding commercial contacts, at first northwards with the Western Sudan and then with Europeans on the coast, aided the growth of state systems. In the 17th and 18th centuries the dominant power was the northern, savanna-based Yoruba state of Oyo, the armies of which had carved out an empire that reached Yoruba forest communities in the south and the fringes of the Hausa region to its north. As its much feared cavalry raided neighbouring territories, taking prisoners and extorting tribute, Oyo dispatched slaves to the ships of French, English and Portuguese traders at the Slave Coast ports of Whydah, Porto Novo and Badagri.

By about 1730 Dahomey, one of several small Aja states in the hinterland of the Slave Coast, and itself a tributary state of Oyo, had asserted its supremacy over its neighbours and had become the main intermediary in the slave trade between Oyo and the coast. Dahomey proceeded to evolve a highly authoritarian and militarized state, the principal economic base of which was the slave trade. Its major continuing weakness through the 18th century was its dependent status in relation to Oyo, which remained the main source of the slaves exported at Slave Coast ports. In the early 19th century, however, Yoruba satellite states started to break away from the Oyo empire, and its northern provinces became subject to the expanding forces of the Muslim Sokoto* caliphate. This was the beginning of a period of civil war among the Yoruba, which provided large numbers of captives for the Atlantic trade, many of whom were exported through the ports of Dahomey.

The Niger delta-Cameroon region

Along the many rivers of the Niger delta and east as far as the Cross River, Ijo and Efik communities had traded with each other, and with the Igbo of the hinterland, for centuries in items such as fish, salt, building materials and agricultural produce. This commerce had initiated a move from small isolated communities based on kinship ties to more consolidated settlements, a process that was further accelerated by the demands of overseas trade. The organizational demands of the slave trade, which involved not only the buying of slaves in the interior but their transport in canoes to the coast, the provision of foodstuffs, security arrangements and the negotiation of prices with European merchants, aided the rise of trading oligarchies and the emergence of city-states.

The most important source of slaves was the densely-populated Igbo hinterland. One Igbo response was that of the Aro people whose main settlement was at the town of Arochuku, the site of the most prestigious of Igbo religous shrines. People came from miles around to consult the oracle which would adjudicate important disputes, condemning many to slavery. Not only did the shrine generate wealth for those who controlled it; other Aro carried its prestige with them. Since they had some amount of ritual immunity from attack, they were allowed to establish settlements through much of the Igbo area. Turning their many connections to commercial advantage, they consolidated the trade routes of the region into a network that dispatched slaves to coastal markets.

The Loango-Angola region
The Portuguese effort to bring large areas of Angola under their rule through military conquest had petered out by the mid-17th century, leaving the Portuguese with a coastal strip between Luanda and Benguela and a hinterland about 150km deep. Among African peoples a new political situation had emerged which affected the conduct of the slave trade. The western Mbundu state of Ndongo, ravaged by combined Portuguese and Imbangala attacks, virtually disappeared from the map, while two new states, Matamba, settled by Mbundu refugees and Kasanje, established by the Imbangala, controlled access to the interior through their dominance of the upper Kwango valley. By the last quarter of the century these two kingdoms had established themselves as intermediaries in the slave trade between caravans that arrived from the coast and those which came from the Central African savannas east of the Kwango. The latter region was dominated in the period c.1650–1850 by the Lunda empire. Combining an effective political structure, which integrated subject peoples into the state, with an efficient tribute system that supplied slaves for export, the Lunda became the main source of slaves for the Angolan coastal markets.

By the second half of the 18th century, however, the Portuguese trade was threatened by Dutch, British and French competitors, who frequented the ports on the Loango Coast north of the Zaire River and offered cheaper, better quality goods and firearms to African merchants. Responding to these better trading incentives, the Vili of Loango exploited their already-established commercial networks south of the Zaire River to tap the markets of Kasanje and Matamba, thus diverting large numbers of slaves who would otherwise have been channelled to Luanda and Benguela. At the same time, newer sources in Gabon and along the Zaire River added to the prosperous slave trade of the Loango Coast. The abolition of the trade north of the Equator in 1815 gave the West Central African slave trade a further boost and it continued as late as the 1860s by which time the principal markets in Brazil and Cuba had been closed. Politically, the slave trade helped to cause the decline of states such as Loango, Kakongo and Ngoyo, as their rulers were unable to maintain a monopoly of foreign trade, and a new class of entrepreneurs, who vied with each other for economic and political power, emerged. Thus, the experience of this region of Africa was contrary to parts of West Africa, such as Asante, Dahomey and Oyo, where overseas trade was a factor in the consolidation, not fragmentation, of political authority.

Southern and eastern Africa
In South Africa a major event during the period under consideration was the establishment of a supply station at the Cape by the Dutch East India Company in 1652. Joined by French Huguenot refugees in the late 17th century, the colony soon expanded beyond the scheme envisaged by the Company directors. As an economy based on the port at Cape Town, wine and wheat production in the Cape, and pastoralism in the more arid lands of the interior was developed, a plural society in which whites played a dominant role was established. Indigenous Khoi were employed as domestic servants and labourers, and slaves were imported from Guinea, Angola, Madagascar, south-eastern Africa and Malaysia. The use of African labour and the alienation of African land were firmly entrenched principles by the time the South African white frontier met that of expanding Bantu pastoralists in the late 18th century.

Before the 19th century the prosperity of the Swahili★ city states of East Africa seems to have been based primarily on their commercial dealings with each other, with the immediate hinterland of the coast, and with other settlements on the Indian Ocean seaboard. There is little evidence for long-distance caravan trade; goods which reached the coast seem to have done so through a relay trade and local networks. Although slaves had been dispatched in Arab dhows across the Indian Ocean for centuries, exports do not seem to have reached major proportions. South of Cape Delgado the gold trade that had lured the Portuguese along the Zambezi valley had been reduced to a trickle by the 18th century, and ivory was the main export sent to the markets at Kilwa and Mozambique by African traders such as the Yao. Remnants of Portuguese influence survived through small garrisons on the Zambezi and on the Mozambique coast, and through the owners of the Zambezi *prazos* (plantations or estates).

The 19th century saw change of revolutionary proportions in many areas of eastern Africa. One new element in the situation was an increasing demand for ivory, both in traditional markets in India and in the Western world, where ivory or ivory-inlaid objects were the height of fashion. Another factor was a spiralling demand for slaves, for the French sugar plantations on Mauritius and Réunion, for Brazil (after the abolition of the West African trade started to have effect), and for Omani clove plantations in East Africa.

The intervention of the Omani Arabs★ in East African affairs, especially during the reign of Sayyid Said ibn Sultan, was the main force for change. The Omani rulers had considered East Africa as part of their sphere of influence since their forces had ousted the Portuguese from Mombasa at the end of the 17th century, but it was

Sayyid Said who realized the economic potential of the region, especially in relation to his homeland. In 1837 Omani forces occupied Mombasa and in 1840 the sultan moved his capital to the island of Zanzibar. He then began to introduce a profitable export crop, cloves, into Zanzibar and the neighbouring island of Pemba; with such success that Zanzibar had become the major world producer by the 1860s. Slaves brought from the East African mainland supplied the labour for the clove plantations.

In pursuit of new sources of ivory and slaves, Swahili caravans began to open up a vast trading network through eastern Africa in alliance with various African societies. The Nyamwezi, east of Lake Tanganyika, who had already established their own trading relations with the Katanga region, were among the first to enlist as guides, porters, interpreters and purveyors of food. Their skills as elephant-hunters were both modified and sharpened through the use of guns supplied by the coastal traders. Others, such as the Kamba north of Mombasa, and the Yao between Lake Malawi and the coast, became prosperous participants in the expanding east coast trade. The activities of coastal traders had other effects in the interior. Swahili market towns such as Tabora and Ujiji became centres for the spread of Islam and Islamic cultural influences; Swahili became a widely-spoken language; the use of guns altered previous patterns of political power, and a more fluid situation paved the way for the rise of opportunists and innovators such as Mirambo of the Nyamwezi, the Yeke leader, Msiri, and the famous Swahili trader, Tippu Tib, who intervened in local politics and created new states that they themselves dominated. The short duration of the East African slave trade and the intensity with which it was pursued brought suffering and lawlessness to many parts of eastern Africa.

Tippu Tib, the Swahili trader

The impact of the trade

In conclusion, the use of the term the 'slave trade era' for the period, c.1650–1850 in African history needs to be reviewed. As this discussion has shown, the overseas slave trade was a major force for change in many societies. On the other hand, some areas of the continent, for example, the intra-lacustrine region of East Africa, Ethiopia and southern Africa, were little affected. Even in those regions that were involved, few were touched on a continuous basis since the focus of the trade shifted over time—for example, the Senegambia and Upper Guinea in the 15th and 16th centuries; the Bight of Benin (from the Gold Coast to Cameroon) in the late 18th and 19th centuries; and East Africa in the 19th century. Furthermore, generalizations about the effects of the slave trade must be treated with care. The long-accepted view that the demographic effect of the trade was universally a disaster are presently being reconsidered. Regions of eastern Nigeria and Malawi that were prime targets for the trade as recently as 100 or 150 years ago now support some of the densest populations in Africa. This suggests that for some regions population levels were sustained by natural increase in spite of the loss through the trade. Finally, it should be noted that even in those areas where the export of slaves was sizeable, it remained a branch of economic activity usually dominated by a small elite. Most Africans continued to be absorbed in local and regional systems of production and exchange.

P. M. M.

Slave market in Zanzibar, 1872

The prelude to European occupation, 1820–85

There was a profound transformation in the relations between Africa and Europe during the 19th century. Fundamental to this change was the Industrial Revolution, that combination of technological advances and organizational innovations that gradually altered the bases of the Western European economies from rural agrarianism to urban industrial capitalism. Europe became increasingly dependent on the wider world for raw materials for its factories, food for its workers, and markets for its cheap, mass-produced goods. The value of world trade increased roughly tenfold between 1820 and 1880, and accumulated European capital increasingly flowed overseas to finance mining, railway construction, shipping, and agricultural production. This period also saw a massive outpouring of European population to all corners of the world. Compared to the Americas and Australia, Africa was a minor recipient of this emigration: nevertheless, between 1790 and 1875 the European population of Africa increased from about 32 000 to nearly 750 000, and its share was responsible for a dramatic change in existing relationships between Africans and Europeans.

Britain was the unchallenged industrial and naval power during the first half of the 19th century. Thereafter its supremacy was increasingly challenged by France and Germany in Europe, as well as by the USA. Competition became sharper from the 1870s on – in response to a series of economic depressions – as each industrialized nation sought to protect its markets. Protective tariffs were introduced; consular services were extended to facilitate the negotiation of commercial treaties, and a judicious application of military force was increasingly obvious in dealings with overseas trading partners.

The abolition of the slave trade* by Denmark (1792), Britain (1807), Holland (1814), and France (1815) provided an additional rationale for European interference in Africa. The slave trade continued despite these prohibitions: more than 2 000 000 slaves were exported between 1810 and 1870. Most went to Brazil and Cuba: Portugal did not prohibit the slave trade until 1836, and even then did little to discourage it in its coastal African settlements. The necessity for anti-slavery naval squadrons increased the European (primarily British) military presence along the African coasts.

European penetration of the interior, however, was a very hazardous undertaking during the first half of the century. The activities of the Association for Promoting the Discovery of the Interior Parts of Africa – the African Association – illustrate this. This body, formed in Britain in 1788, embodied commercial, scientific and humanitarian interests, and was particularly intent on establishing the source and navigational capabilities of the Niger River. Nearly all of its agents – including the famous Mungo Park (1771–1806) – perished in the attempt. In spite of these early reversals, British explorers, and a considerable number of Germans in British employ, continued to push into the interior. The two most successful of these early explorers were David Livingstone (1813–73) (in southern Africa) and Heinrich Barth (1821–65) (in inland West Africa); both wrote accounts of their journeys which caught the public imagination. The academic and scientific community indicated their new interest in overseas areas by the formation of national geographical societies: France (1821), Prussia (1828), Britain (1830), Russia (1845) and Spain (1877).

Heinrich Barth (1821–65)

David Livingstone (1813–73)

Henry Morton Stanley (1841–1904)

In the 1870s Germany and Belgium joined Britain as major patrons of exploration. The focus of penetration moved to Central Africa, to the watersheds of the Nile and the Congo rivers. In 1876 King Leopold II* of Belgium convened an international conference of African specialists at Brussels to coordinate scientific exploration and anti-slavery activities in Central Africa. The International African Association, with affiliated national committees, was born. This association soon became the vehicle of Leopold II's personal ambitions, while the various national committees pursued their own nationalistic biases. The German committee (one of the most important) was similar in aims and membership to the already existing *Deutsche Gesellschaft zur Erforschung Äquatorialafrikas* (1873), and they merged in 1878 to form the *Afrikanische Gesellschaft in Deutschland*. The many German expeditions sent out between 1873 and 1889 had a distinctly scientific bias, whereas those operating under the sponsorship of Leopold II emphasized their anti-slavery role and were more militarily aggressive.

The increased (and more combative) European penetration from the 1870s on was made possible by new technological advances. Steam power, for example, transformed ocean transport and naval logistics. The African Steam Ship Company was formed in England in 1851 and began a regular service to West Africa the following year. It was joined by the British and African Steam Navigation Company in 1868, and by French and German steamship lines in the 1870s. The opening of the Suez Canal in 1869 drastically shortened the distance to East Africa. The development of the machine-gun, light artillery, and the repeating rifle now made it feasible for small European forces to operate against numerically superior African armies in difficult terrain. Finally, the availability of quinine as an anti-malarial drug made life in the African tropics considerably less hazardous.

The Christian missionary effort in Africa in the first half of the 19th century was predominantly British and Protestant, and was inspired by the Evangelical revival in Europe as well as by the anti-slavery campaign. The most important bases of early missionary activity were Sierra Leone in West Africa and the Cape Colony in the south. The Church Missionary Society (CMS) arrived in Sierra Leone in 1804, followed by the Wesleyan Methodists in 1811; the London Missionary Society arrived at the Cape in 1799. The major Roman Catholic initiative, based in France, came substantially later and was focused on East Africa. In 1863 the Holy Ghost Fathers (*La Congrégation du St Esprit*) began their work in Zanzibar and on the mainland opposite. A greater urgency was given to Catholic evangelization by Cardinal Lavigerie, who founded the White Fathers (*La Société de Notre-Dame d'Afrique*) in 1868, a missionary society that worked first in Algiers and then established itself in the interior of East Africa after 1878. The above-mentioned organizations were the more successful pioneers of both confessions, but their numbers did not substantially increase until after the colonial conquest at the end of the century. Their religious impact was also limited: converts to Christianity – with very few exceptions – were gained only among freed slaves and refugees.

North Africa: consuls and capital

Although the Ottoman sultans theoretically ruled Egypt until 1914, their control continued to be largely nominal following the Napoleonic occupation of Egypt (1798–1801). An Albanian officer in the Ottoman army, Muhammad Ali,* had seized effective control of the country by 1811 and established a family dynasty. During the next three decades he constructed the strongest army in the Ottoman Empire and transformed the government and economy of Egypt.

At the centre of this transformation was the army. An officer and technical corps was trained (often by French and Italian officers) in newly-established schools; more than 200 students were educated abroad between 1826 and 1847. An industrial base (armaments, textiles, tanneries, shipbuilding) was established to supply the army. Tax collection, land-ownership, and trading monopolies were more efficiently structured and controlled in order to finance the army. Muhammad Ali extensively used European expertise and models to further his aims, but he was never mastered by them.

The Egyptian army proved its military superiority in the Arabian peninsula and Syria. European diplomats, concerned that the fragile core of the Ottoman Empire was being threatened, forced Egypt to withdraw from its Middle Eastern conquests in 1841. Thereafter, Egyptian expansion was focused southwards on the sources of the Nile. By 1880 Egyptian administrators or traders were penetrating the Great Lakes region, the fringes of the Congo forests, and the borderlands of the Ethiopian highlands.

After Muhammad Ali's death in 1848 his successors drifted into

Muhammad Ali confers with British representatives in 1839

financial difficulties and laid the way open for foreign intervention. Khedive Ismail (ruled 1863–79) sought to accelerate the modernization of Egypt but borrowed recklessly to do so: the foreign debt increased thirtyfold during his reign. The recruitment of foreign advisers, as well as the relaxation of trading restrictions, increased the number of Europeans resident in Egypt from a few thousand in 1860 to over a hundred thousand in 1876. This in itself increased the possibilities of friction, since most European countries did not recognize Egyptian legal jurisdiction over foreign residents. In 1875 a desperate Ismail was forced to sell his shares in the Suez Canal to Britain. In the following year, in order to guarantee the repayment of foreign debts, he was forced to accept British and French joint-controllers of Egyptian revenue and expenditure. In 1879 he was finally deposed by the Ottoman sultan acting under pressure from the European powers. This set the scene for a nationalist reaction resulting in the British military intervention in 1881–2, one of a number of key incidents which lay behind the subsequent European 'Scramble'★ for Africa.

In the face of French expansion★ in North Africa – signalled by the invasion of Algeria in 1830 – the rulers of Morocco and the nominally Ottoman province of Tunisia also sought to modernize their respective administrations and armies. They were much less successful than their counterparts in Egypt, yet were faced with the same external pressures caused by foreign indebtedness, aggressive commercial penetration, and the legal immunity of foreign nationals. By the mid-1870s most of North Africa had relinquished much of its economic autonomy.

West Africa: slave trade to 'legitimate' commerce

Freetown was established on the Sierra Leone coast in 1792 to accommodate free black Americans from Nova Scotia and Jamaica. These settlers, long removed from their African roots, were devout Christians and firm believers in the superiority of European civilizations. They were soon to be outnumbered by 'recaptives' – some 60000 men and women liberated from slave-ships by the British anti-slavery squadrons. These new settlers (who came to be called Creoles) accepted the Christian, European ethos of the pioneering community while retaining a very distinct African identity. Many of them – particularly those from the Yoruba area of Nigeria – re-established links with their homeland.

Education was eagerly sought by the Creoles and their descendants. Even university-level education became available locally: Fourah Bay College, founded by the CMS in 1827, was affiliated in 1876 to Durham University in England. From the 1840s literate Creoles spread through West Africa as merchants, missionaries, civil servants, and employees of European commercial companies. Two of the more prominent examples of this diaspora were James Africanus Horton (1835–82) and Samuel Ajayi Crowther (1808–91) – respect-

ively of Igbo and Yoruba ancestry. Horton graduated in 1859 as a medical doctor from King's College, London; he eventually became head of the army medical services in the Gold Coast and was the author of many books on African topics including political treatises as well as technical works on medicine, climate and geography. Crowther became the first Bishop of the CMS Niger Mission in 1864. During the 19th century it was the Creoles who were the most effective proselytizers of Christianity and European ideas in West Africa.

Liberia★ was founded in 1822 for free black Americans who wished to escape discrimination in the USA by returning to Africa. It was also seen as a dumping ground for slaves freed by the US Navy. However, very few recaptives were actually set free in Liberia, and the influence of the original black American immigrants – the Americo-Liberians – remained dominant. This lack of an indigenous base was one of the reasons why Liberians never had such a wide impact on West Africa as the Creoles. In 1847 Liberia proclaimed itself an independent nation but the USA delayed recognition until 1862, and it was many years before it received substantial international recognition.

Britain was the most important trading power in West Africa during the first half of the 19th century; France was a distant second. The Danes and the Dutch withdrew from their West African trading posts in 1850 and 1872 respectively. As the exports of slaves declined, a new trade in vegetable oils arose. Palm-oil and groundnut (peanut) oil were increasingly used in Europe for the production of soaps, candles and lubricants. Soap was required for cleansing the populations of the growing urban centres, candles were in demand for lighting, and lubricants were needed to oil industrial machinery. In addition, French housewives increasingly used groundnut oil for cooking in preference to the more expensive olive oil. Palm-oil was

European palm-oil traders with their 'boys' at Opobo, Nigeria

extracted from the fruit of the oil palm that grew in the tropical forest zone 50 to 100km from the coast. The main centres of production were in what is now Nigeria. The major customer was Britain, whose imports rose from about 100 tonnes in 1807 to over 31 000 tonnes in 1854. Groundnuts grew in the drier savanna zone. Export production of groundnuts began along the Gambia River in the early 1830s, spread to southern Guinea and northern Sierra Leone in the late 1830s, and to Senegal and Portuguese Guinea in the early 1840s. France became the major customer for groundnut oil.

From mid-century Britain and France began to be more aggressive in their dealings with African societies. This was particularly true from the 1870s, when the declining profitability of the vegetable oil trade (caused by Asian competition as well as the rising production of mineral oils) led to an increase in disputes between African and European merchant groups. Britain sent its first resident consul to West Africa in 1849; gunboat diplomacy became increasingly common. In 1851 Lagos was bombarded and—ten years later—was declared a British Crown Colony. In 1874 a successful British expedition was launched against the Asante,* and the southern Gold Coast was declared a Crown Colony in the following year. Between 1854 and 1865 the French in Senegal, led by an energetically expansive governor, Louis Faidherbe, were increasingly in conflict with surrounding Muslim states. There was a lull in the late 1860s and early 1870s but by 1879, stimulated by the onset of trade depression, the French government had begun to plan for a major extension inland including the development of a river-rail transport system linking Dakar with the upper Niger via St Louis and the Senegal River. The Dakar-St Louis railway, begun in 1882, was completed in 1885. A line begun inland at Kayes on the upper Senegal in 1881 had only progressed 53km towards the Niger by 1884.

Increased conflict between Africans and Europeans was accompanied by increased tension between European powers. The French, alarmed by the acquisition of Lagos, began extending their commercial activities to the palm-oil areas that had formerly been a British preserve. Further complications were added by the increasing number of German merchants active in West Africa.

East and Central Africa: ivory and the Zanzibari sultanate

Although the Arab state of Oman had expelled the Portuguese* from the East African coast, it was unable, because of domestic difficulties, to assert its own authority over this area during the 18th century. Zanzibar and Kilwa were the only major coastal towns to maintain a nominal allegiance to Oman. Mombasa fell under the rule of a renegade Omani clan, the Mazrui, and became the most powerful city-state along the coast.

Although Arab merchants continued to visit the East African littoral, trade was stagnant by comparison with the situation in previous centuries. During the 19th century, however, East and

Ivory for export being weighed in Zanzibar, c. 1890

Central Africa became the major producers of ivory in the world. More than 55 000 elephants were being slaughtered annually in the latter part of the century to meet the incessant demand. Ivory was destined for Indian bangles or for the cutlery handles, combs, piano keys and billiard-balls of the emergent European (and American) *nouveaux riches*.

As the profitability of the ivory trade became apparent, the rulers of Oman in Arabia moved to reassert their control over the East African coast. Sayyid Said ibn Sultan reconquered the secessionist strong-hold of Mombasa in 1837 and transferred his residence to Zanzibar in 1840. After his death in 1856, a succession crisis prompted Britain to impose a settlement in 1861 that separated Oman from its East African possessions. The Sultanate of Zanzibar now became an African entity, exerting a variable control from the Somali coast in the north to the Rovuma River in the south.

Zanzibar became the principal commercial entrepôt on the East African coast. Commercial treaties were signed with the USA (1833), Britain (1839), France (1844) and the North German Hanseatic states (1859). Strong trade links existed with India, and Indians (who were British subjects) dominated the financial structure and customs administration of Zanzibar. Arab-Swahili traders pursued the retreating ivory frontier and by the 1880s were active deep in the Congo forests. Swahili, the language of Zanzibar and the coast, became a commercial *lingua franca* of the interior. Islam also made a limited impact along the trade routes.

During the Napoleonic Wars Britain had promoted Omani interests in the Persian Gulf and had subsequently extended this support to East Africa. This policy was part of a wider Indian Ocean strategy designed to limit French influence and protect communication links with the empire in India. After the opening of the Suez

Canal in 1869 British trade with East Africa expanded considerably. The implementation of a series of anti-slave trade treaties (1822, 1845, and 1873) made the sultans increasingly vulnerable to British consular pressure and control.

Across the continent the slave trade from the Portuguese ports of Luanda and Benguela continued unchecked until mid-century. Brazilian, Portuguese and Cuban slave dealers replaced French and British merchants. West Central Africa became the last major source for the Atlantic slave trade. After 1850 slaves were replaced by ivory and—from the 1870s—wild rubber. (Rubber was crucial to the expansion of the new electrical and transport industries; the leading world producers of rubber by 1900 were the Congo Free State, Angola, the Gold Coast, French Guinea and Brazil.) Portuguese influence in the area was weak, but sufficient to delay the emergence of any strong European rivals, although France had a foothold in Gabon. By the 1880s West Central Africa was the area in which European interests were least clearly defined.

Halt of a Boer Family on Trek by Samuel Daniell

Ethiopia

The period from 1769 to 1855 is known in Ethiopian history as the *Zamana Mesafent*, 'the era of princes', a time when the Ethiopian monarchy led a nominal existence, a powerless pawn in the hands of successive regional warlords. The most powerful of these leaders seized the throne himself in 1855 and was crowned Tewodros I. His drastic attempts to enforce internal unity lost him domestic support; his impatience with diplomatic representatives cost him external support. When a British expedition invaded Ethiopia in 1867 to release hostages, they met little resistance. Tewodros committed suicide in defeat.

Faced with the growing threat of Egyptian imperialism, Tewodros's successor, Yohannes IV, made concessions to powerful local rulers to attain a semblance of internal unity. Egyptian invasions from the Red Sea in 1875 and 1876 were soundly defeated, and large quantities of modern weapons fell into Ethiopian hands. Ethiopian-Egyptian relations were only regularized in 1884 when the Mahdist revolt★ in the Sudan made mutual friendship desirable. Conflict with the powerful southern state of Shoa was averted in 1882 when Yohannes agreed that Menelik of Shoa would succeed him as ruler of Ethiopia.

Ethiopia therefore entered the 1880s relatively united and free of external control. The Egyptian defeats had demonstrated that Ethiopia had the potential to mount a massive military effort against foreign aggression.

Southern Africa: the growth of white settlerdom

Britain seized the Cape Colony from the Dutch in 1806. There were about 20 000 descendants of Dutch settlers, the Boers, resident at that time, most of them within a restricted radius of Cape Town. On the interior frontier, however, there were settlements of Trekboer pastoralists and hunters engaging in intermittent trade and warfare with their African neighbours.

British-introduced land policies and judicial reforms, as well as the abolition of slavery in 1834, led to the major Boer exodus known as the Great Trek. Between 1836 and 1846 more than 10 000 Boers left the Cape Colony to settle in the far interior beyond British control, penetrating into areas temporarily depopulated by the impact of the disruptive expansion of the Zulu★ state. Britain blocked the Boers' westward access to the sea by annexing Natal in 1842 and providing it with British settlers. The Trekboers then proceeded to form two small republics in the northern interior—the Transvaal★ and the Orange Free State.★ These were officially recognized by Britain in 1852 and 1854 respectively. The new Trekboer states led a precarious existence, rent by internal disunities and periodically threatened by surrounding African states.

The key centre of European activity in southern Africa was the Cape Colony. Britain's raw wool imports had increased 800 per cent between 1830 and 1870, and the Cape Colony was second only to Australia as a source. By 1870 it provided 12 per cent of Britain's raw wool imports, exceeding the value of Britain's palm-oil imports from West and West Central Africa. The 1867 discovery of diamonds in Griqualand (quickly annexed by the Cape Colony) led to an accelerated inflow of capital and immigrants and greatly enhanced state revenues. In 1872 the Cape Colony was granted self-government. By the 1870s there were approximately 180 000 whites in the Cape Colony, 16 000 in Natal, and 70 000 in the two Boer republics. Even before the discovery of gold in 1886 southern Africa was well on its way to rivalling Algeria as the main area of white settlement in Africa.

L.E.L.

The Scramble for Africa

Divergent explanations of the European partition of Africa sometimes reflect distinctions between the long-term forces of imperialist penetration and the dramatic 'scramble' for political control in the 1880s and 1890s. Since the 16th century groups of Europeans and Africans had been drawn into a nexus of unequal relationships, and many African peoples had become in some degree dependent— economically, culturally, more rarely politically—upon external power. But it was only in the 1880s that European governments began to claim exclusive political rights over African territory, first on the coasts, then inland. By 1900 diplomatic agreements among Europeans had partitioned the greater part of the continent into formal colonial empires. These spectacular changes can best be explained in relation to discontinuities in the longer span of Afro-European relations.

The 'Great Depression' of the international capitalist economy during the last three decades of the 19th century made prices and profits unstable; merchants trading in Africa warned their governments that their future prosperity might depend on developing new African outlets for exports and investment. But African societies already penetrated by foreign capitalists also suffered from economic instability. Egypt* in 1882 provided the most striking example of internal discontent directed against a regime which had become heavily dependent on foreigners. West Africa was another area where—because of the decreasing profitability of the palm-oil trade— relations between Africans and Europeans were deteriorating.

As conditions within Africa became less stable, other European governments became less willing to let their interests depend on the maritime dominance of the British navy. The Anglo-French entente, maintained with greater or less cordiality since the Napoleonic Wars, began to wear thin under increasing friction, and finally collapsed after 1882, along with the joint control which the two governments had tried to maintain in Egypt. With the unexpected notification of German political claims in Africa, the delicate balance that enabled Europeans to reconcile their interests with respect for Africans' political independence was destroyed; British, French and German

Alexandria 1882: the British responded to anti-European nationalism with a naval bombardment and occupation

governments, pressed by 'merchants, missionaries and other martial classes', rushed to protect their present and prospective interests before the open door was shut by rivals. Frenchmen moved to prevent the British from consolidating their control of the River Niger; Gladstone's government in Britain sought methods to prevent France dominating the Congo. The German Chancellor, Bismarck sent agents to protect endangered commercial interests in Namibia, Eweland (present-day Togo), Cameroon, and Zanzibar; and Leopold II of Belgium (in his personal capacity) seized the opportunity to promote his territorial ambitions in Africa wherever possible.

No European government wished, however, to mortgage its foreign policy for the sake of African interests of marginal importance. The international conference summoned at Berlin in November 1884 was intended to control, not to extend, the scramble for political titles that was already under way. It originated in Bismarck's desire to concert a common policy with France in tropical Africa. Partly moved by reasons of European diplomacy, he also aimed to frustrate Britain's attempts to secure maximum commercial advan-

'How do we stand now in the world?' Cartoon of Bismarck, 1884

tages in Africa with a minimum of political responsibility. Britain had attemped this by making Portugal the guardian of free trade in the Congo, by claiming exclusive commercial privileges on the Niger, and by upholding a South African exclusive claim on the Namibian coast. But the Berlin Conference agenda was limited to securing free trade in the Congo basin and free navigation on the Congo and Niger rivers, and to defining procedures to ensure that European powers claiming African coastline in future should make their occupation effective. Territorial questions were explicitly excluded, although many bilateral negotiations proceeded simultaneously.

In many ways the direct results of the Conference were more limited still. Restrictions were placed on the rights of European powers to levy duties on trade in the wide area defined as the 'Conventional Basin of the Congo'; but the Congo Free State,* for which Leopold's skilful diplomacy secured international recognition while the Conference was sitting, was subsequently able to follow highly restrictive and oppressive economic policies. A British trading company, the Royal Niger Company,* also retained the means of effectively excluding foreign competitors from the Niger and Benue rivers. The approved procedures for securing international recognition of European claims to African coastline left room for the elastic device of 'protectorates', which, it later transpired, could be made to mean more or less whatever the protecting Europeans chose to make them mean. In any case, only relatively small stretches of coastline still remained unclaimed by 1885. This was no revolutionary plan for partition, but a delaying tactic, an attempt by European statesmen with little knowledge and no deep interest in Africa to find means 'of ensuring the continuation of the traditional free-trading system on its coasts and great rivers'.

Although the Berlin Conference was not the dramatic event often portrayed in textbooks, it does provide a convenient historical watershed. During the next 15 years rivalries between Europeans moved rapidly inland from the coasts, as soldiers, merchants, missionaries, mining prospectors, and ambitious proconsuls glimpsed new worlds to conquer; and gradually public and politicians in France and Italy, Germany and Britain came to attach higher value to the opportunities that formal empire over Africans seemed capable of bringing. Armed missions confronted each other in remote African villages, brandishing mutually incompatible treaties purporting to confer sovereignty over the same African ruler (who had rarely intended to surrender his independence to either). If such disputes were to be regulated without inter-European war, some ground rules were necessary; the civil servants who poured incomprehendingly over inaccurate maps worked these out gradually, extending the general approach of Berlin from the coasts to the interior. Although the Conference had not partitioned Africa, it provided a framework that allowed Europeans to partition the continent without major conflicts among themselves.

Conflicts between Europeans and Africans were, of course, another matter. Article VI of the Berlin Act did provide for the 'preservation and improvement of the native tribes'. But the weak voice of international conscience could not prevent the new colonial governments interpreting this obligation as they thought fit: at least until this theme was taken up in the League of Nations Mandate system of 1919 under which the conquered German colonies were divided among the Allies, who were, theoretically, supposed to rule them according to strict guidelines laid down by the League. *J.D.H.*

African resistance

The greater part of the African continent was occupied by the European colonial powers in the quarter century between 1878 and 1903 – when the Sokoto* caliphate in what is now northern Nigeria finally fell to the British. The only substantial parts of the continent that had been occupied before 1878 were the coastal zones of Angola* and Mozambique,* colonized by the Portuguese in the 16th and 17th centuries, Algeria*, taken by the French after fierce resistance in the 1830s, and the Senegal* River valley, occupied by the French in the 1850s. It is a slow-dying myth that Africans by and large offered little resistance to colonial conquest and in many cases welcomed it. In fact, the majority of states and peoples did resist, however in-effectively, and many peoples once occupied took up arms against their colonial masters as soon as they perceived them to be at a disadvantage, in an attempt to regain their lost independence.

It is arguable that the Scramble* for Africa, as the late 19th century European occupation of the continent came to be called, would not have been possible, or would at least have been infinitely more difficult at the time, but for two factors. The first was the discovery of quinine as a prophylactic against malaria, which enabled European officers to lead troops – mainly African – into the interior. The second was the invention of the machine-gun culminating in the rapid-firing, easily transportable Maxim, which enabled small forces to deal with numerically overwhelming armies that were fighting on familiar terrain. Europeans suffered notable defeats at the hands of African armies when they had no apparent technological advantage or when this did not outweigh the numbers opposing them, or, most important, the skill with which those numbers were deployed. Examples are the Asante (Ashanti) defeats of the British in 1823 and 1863, and the Zulu victory over them at Isandhlwana in 1879.

The history of the European occupation of Africa raises four major questions. Was the European conquest inevitable? Why did some peoples resist while others did not? Why were some peoples more successful in their resistance than others? How far, once conquered, did they accept the fact of colonial rule? By the end of the 19th century African society was still essentially agricultural with limited resources to finance long-term wars. African warfare was usually limited to the dry season. Invading European armies were geared to year-round warfare and were supported by the comparatively much richer resources of industrial society. Furthermore the conquest was achieved at a time of rapid advances in gun technology, and though Africans did have some access to this, the guns they received in trade were usually models which were obsolescent in Europe. Finally, the European powers, so often at war with each other, conducted their colonial adventures at a time of domestic peace. There were only two major confrontations between European forces in the course of the conquest, the guidelines of which had been laid down (and were generally followed) at the Berlin Conference:* between French and British forces on the Niger in Borgu in 1896 and on the upper White Nile at Fashoda in 1898. In the event, clashes were avoided by negotiations in the chanceries of Europe.

The reasons for the failure of African armies to resist the Europeans were complex. In certain cases African peoples saw a distinct advantage in the European presence since it secured external trade. Others collaborated with Europeans against African enemies, seeing

Sayyid Muhammad Abdille Hassan led military resistance to British and Italian expansion in Somaliland, 1900–20

African forces were widely used to crush African resistance: French colonial troops rest during a pacification mission in the Ivory Coast, *c.* 1900

the latter as the most immediate danger, then found that they were unable to extricate themselves. Some signed treaties with Europeans, discovering too late that the complications were otherwise than they had supposed. Many failed to resist because they had seen the futility of such a course demonstrated by their neighbours.

The general failure of African armies to deal effectively with the invaders was principally due to the fact that their organization and tactics were designed to deal with African military situations: internal rebellions or threats from neighbours, who had similar military technologies. Rarely were these suited to dealing with the European invaders, especially as threats from neighbouring states continued; for there were few instances of African states settling their differences to present a common front against the new enemy. Furthermore, few states had all-season standing armies for few could afford to take able-bodied men permanently off the land. European armies, by contrast, had standing armies, albeit primarily composed of African troops, trained all year round in the drill and tactics associated with their superior weapons. Africa produced few generals who could adapt their armies to the new contingencies, Samori,★ in West Africa, being a notable exception. He appreciated that the head-on confrontation appropriate for armies deploying similar technologies was suicidal in the face of an enemy of superior fire-power. Instead he resorted to guerrilla tactics, which enabled him to engage the French for over seven years. Indeed guerrilla tactics were the only answer to the

situation confronting African states and peoples. Thus politically decentralized societies organized around kinship ties like the Igbo and Tiv (Nigeria), Tallensi (Ghana) and Nandi (Kenya) gave the invading forces much greater problems than many centralized states since their village by village, hamlet by hamlet resistance was akin to guerrilla warfare.

The European armies were rarely welcomed despite propaganda to this effect. Thus the British portrayed their conquest of the Sokoto caliphate as one in which they were hailed by the 'oppressed peasantry'. The truth was that it led to a mass emigration – a *hijra* – of rulers and ruled eastwards to the Sudan. The massive risings by the Shona and Ndebele against the British in Southern Rhodesia, the Maji Maji rebellion against the Germans in East Africa, and the Herero and, later, Nama risings in German South West Africa, and Abd al-Karim's revolt in Morocco against the French and Spanish were notable indications of resentment against the new colonial situation. The lack of acceptance of defeat is best brought out by the massive risings in French Black Africa and significant disturbances elsewhere during the First World War,★ when it was perceived that the colonial masters were at a disadvantage, as the exodus of administrators and traders to the European front seemed to suggest. This was the last chapter in the history of the sort of resistance which aimed at recreating the pre-colonial polities. Once more the colonial powers, though now at war with each other, demonstrated that they had the technology and resources to regain control. Further resistance was to be within the framework of the new colonial states and would be geared to taking control of these. It was led not by the pre-colonial elites but by those created by the colonialists. *M.C.*

French expansion: North Africa

By the beginning of the 19th century the maritime power of the corsairs of Algiers* had virtually disappeared, and they had not established an effective administration over their hinterland. However, the area did provide the grain that fed the armies of Napoleon, and in 1808 the Emperor sent a spy to draw up plans for a possible invasion. The attack was delayed for more than 20 years until the restored Bourbon monarchy, tottering towards its fall, sought an overseas adventure to rally disaffected elements round the Crown. In 1827 the Dey of Algiers struck the French Consul with a fly-whisk and refused to apologize. In June 1830, seizing upon this as a pretext, a French army invaded. What government there was collapsed, the Dey went into exile, and the French, with no experience of ruling Muslims and, indeed, only one officer who spoke the Arabic language, found themselves compelled to organize a new administration. There was no certainty that Paris would not abandon its conquest, so considerable power was put in the hands of friendly local rulers and, in particular, much of the west was left to the Amir Abd al-Kader, who created an efficient state around Mascara.

Soon after the conquest, however, unofficial groups of Europeans arrived to establish small farms and market gardens around the towns and eventually their presence and their political influence, despite their small numbers, made withdrawal impossible. Marshal Bugeaud, appointed governor in 1840, adopted a policy of recruiting French peasants to settle on the land in armed groups, and largely through his efforts the European population had grown to 150 000 by the 1850s. Naturally, the local population, led by Abd al-Kader fought for its lands and liberties, and there was constant warfare. Particular attention was paid by the colonial authorities to increasing the number of French citizens. Naturalization was offered to any Algerian who applied for it, and in 1870 local Jews and all Europeans who had been born in the country were decreed to be French.

The permanent acquisition of a new province had not been the original aim of the attack on Algiers, but the absorption of Tunisia was an act of deliberate policy. As early as 1836 the French had warned the Ottoman sultan, nominally suzerain of Tunisia, not to interfere there, and in 1846 they had feted the Bey of Tunisia in Paris as an independent sovereign. By the end of the 1870s the extravagance of the Bey, encouraged by European governments and bankers, had plunged the country deeply into debt, thus affording its creditors ample excuse for interfering in the administration. There was fierce competition between the British, French and Italians for influence until the British, involved elsewhere, lost interest. Italy was forestalled by a French invasion of Tunisia in April 1881. There was little opposition and the Bey, by the Treaty of Bardo, agreed to accept French 'protection' and 'advice upon necessary reforms'.

The Dey of Algiers strikes the French Consul: the pretext for the French invasion of Algeria in 1830

By 1880 the French were still no more than 500km south of Algiers, but the following two decades saw their rapid expansion from Senegal* into the West African interior and a consequent drive southwards from Algiers to link the two possessions. In 20 years the territory of Algeria was at least quintupled in size.

There had been an early clash between the French in Algeria and the Moroccans, for in 1844, when Abd al-Kader had revolted, the sultan sent troops to his aid. French and Moroccan forces clashed on the Oued Isly, after which a treaty demarcated the northern part of the frontier but left the southern portion vague. A strong sultan, Hassan I (ruled 1873–94) endeavoured to modernize his country but was systematically obstructed by the French, who saw a potential threat to their position in Algeria if a successful Muslim state existed on their border. There was constant interference and by 1900 the Moroccan government was near collapse. The French encroached across the undefined boundary and, when resisted, exacted reparations from the sultan, who had lost control of the tribes. It was clear that the main obstacle to French ambitions was the rivalry of other European powers, which were eventually bought off. Even before completing agreements with the other European powers the French had occupied Oudjda in the east, after the murder of one of their agents in Marrakesh, and the western province of Chaouia, after the killing of eight Europeans in Casablanca in 1907. In order to protect the occupied territory it always appeared necessary to 'pacify' the next tribe and so, half unwillingly, the French were drawn further inland until, by the end of 1911, they had reached Fes and the foothills of the Atlas Mountains. In March 1912 Sultan Mulai Hafid called for French protection, accepting the Treaty of Fes in March 1912, and protectorate status similar to that of Tunisia.

Unlike Tunisia, however, there was fierce resistance, for the Berber tribesmen of the mountains had rarely been dominated even by the strongest of sultans. General Lyautey, the first Resident General, started to subdue them in the name of the sultan but it was not until 1934 that the last resistance was extinguished.   *R.L.B.*

French expansion: tropical Africa

The French empire in tropical Africa originated in diverse initiatives by private individuals and state servants; it acquired an appearance of coherence only later, when governments of France's Third Republic found it politically expedient to assume responsibility. The first main thrust originated in the long-established colony of Senegal, and was led by military officers. In the 1880s the colony proper consisted of four municipalities – Saint-Louis, Gorée, Dakar and Rufisque; but sporadic offensives by 19th century governors had established French hegemony, more or less effectively, over much of the territory of the modern Republic of Senegal. In 1879 the French government embraced ambitious schemes for railway development backed by political authority; these involved penetration of the Tokolor empire (founded by Al-Hajj Umar,* d.1864), under the direction of an autonomous military headquarters. Officers of the Colonial Army now perceived opportunities to win martial glory for themselves in the Western Sudan,* while offering French nationalists vicarious compensation for the German defeat of France in 1870. During the 1880s political indecisiveness in Paris and military resistance in Africa constrained the military to advance cautiously, alternating aggression with diplomacy in their dealings with the Muslim empires of Ahmadu* (Al-Hajj Umar's son and successor) and Samori.* But in 1889 and 1891, the local military command seized the initiative by launching full-scale attacks on both states.

French business interests in Senegal tended to oppose the methods of the military, but elsewhere French traders sponsored supplementary expansive thrusts. In 1865 they had instigated treaties with African rulers in the 'southern rivers', which grew into the colony of Guinea; in the 1880s government agents began to penetrate the Futa Jalon uplands, and the colony assumed strategic and commercial importance as an alternative route to the upper Niger River. On the Ivory Coast, where French interests after 1871 were represented solely by the firm of Verdier from La Rochelle, a French exploration of 1887–9 revealed trading routes through the forest to the savanna

zone. In the 1890s the government assumed responsibility, thrusting rapidly northwards to complete the campaign against Samori; the final subjection of the Baule and other forest peoples was deferred until 1908. In both colonies substantial French commercial penetration followed the conquest.

In the region of Dahomey, French commerce was longer established; colonization originated in the tactical alliance between Marseilles merchants fearing domination by Lagos and a royal lineage with dynastic ambitions. In 1883 this led to a French protectorate over the coastal enclave of Porto Novo, where commercial and missionary influence was already strong. This commitment drew French officials into growing conflict with the proudly independent and militarily formidable Fon kingdom of Abomey. After much vacillation Paris authorized a military expedition in 1892, which eventually deposed King Behanzin and broke up his state. The new colony now provided a base for penetrating the middle Niger and upper Volta valleys, and eventually linked up with the military advancing through the Western Sudan.

Seku Ahmadu, ruler of the Tokolor empire, 1864–93

French colonial troops in Dahomey (now Benin), *c.* 1900

French activity in Central Africa was less dynamic. Although their freed slave settlement at Libreville amounted to little, the French retained the commercial station in Gabon which they had occupied in 1843. When Savorgnan de Brazza discovered a route from the Ogoué valley to the Congo's inland waterways, this became the base for vast French claims in Equatorial Africa. This area was little developed by African commerce, and colonial administrators became dependent to an exceptional degree on forced labour and harsh methods. In the 1890s the colonial government, starved of revenue, granted exclusive rights to exploit the natural resources of ivory, rubber and timber to a number of concessionary companies, many of which dealt brutally with Africans and were unscrupulous in their business methods.

After 1863 the Merina monarchy in Madagascar had adopted a course of self-modernization, embracing Protestant Christianity and seeking foreign support for administrative reforms. Foreign traders, missionaries, fortune-hunters and proconsuls all had ambitions, but French and British influence balanced each other out until the relations of the two governments deteriorated in 1882. Thereupon the French government, pressed by settlers in the Indian Ocean islands of Réunion and Mayotte, asserted rights over the Sakalava of the north-west, invaded the littoral, occupied Diégo Suarez, and forced the appointment of a French Resident at Tananarive. Having secured British acquiescence in 1890, the French used Malagasy reactions against European encroachments as a pretext for occupying Tananarive in 1895, then finally annexed the whole island the following year.

During the 1880s only a minority of French politicians, though a growing one, regarded expansion in Africa as desirable, and public interest was generally low. Sometimes the parliament could be induced to vote funds, as for the railway programme of 1879; and after 1882 anti-British moves were in accord with popular feeling. But politicians tended to retract as soon as there was danger of additional expense or military commitments.

After 1890 those interested in Africa united in various organizations, collectively known as the colonial party, which cut across political alignments. Under the leadership of the Algerian-born Eugène Etienne this pressure group secured official support for private expeditions and exercised a strong influence on French external policy. Though business interests were well represented, tropical Africa was of marginal interest to French capitalism, compared to Tsarist Russia or the Ottoman Empire; the colonial movement flourished by temporarily diverting the attention of chauvinistic politicians, intellectuals, and journalists towards African objectives. Fantastic projects achieved wide publicity, like that of a consolidated empire linked by transcontinental railways and turning on the hinge of Lake Chad; wild notions of displacing Britain from Egypt★ prompted the abortive Fashoda expedition of 1898. Meanwhile a weak civilian administration struggled to recover control of the new empire from the military – a process not complete in intractable territories like Mauritania and Niger until the 1920s. The mainland colonies were combined into the quasi-federations of West Africa★ (1895) and Equatorial Africa★ (1910). Frenchmen now faced the problems of creating administrative systems that would reconcile the aspirations of French nationalism and French commerce with the claims of the French Republic to represent universal principles of human rights.

J.D.H.

British expansion

By 1885 earlier trading or anti-slave trade activities had shaped the embryos of four British colonies in West Africa: on the River Gambia, along the shores of Sierra Leone and the Gold Coast, and in southern Nigeria, where in 1885 an Oil Rivers Protectorate was proclaimed eastwards of the Crown Colony of Lagos. But no inland boundaries had been established, and effective control rarely reached as much as 150km from the sea. In East Africa the British presence was less positive. Britain's campaign against the Arab slave trade had secured its paramountcy at Zanzibar,* but in 1885 the southern half of the ostensibly Zanzibar-controlled coast was declared a German protectorate. British missionaries had penetrated far inland to Buganda, and both missionaries and traders were active by Lake Nyasa (Malawi) in the hinterland of Portuguese Mozambique. The British interest at Aden led in 1885 to the proclamation of a protectorate over the Somali coastlands on the opposite side of the Gulf of Aden. But neither here, nor elsewhere in East Africa, was there any official British presence on the mainland, save in Nyasaland, to which a consul had been sent in 1883.

Prior to 1895 Britain had little positive colonial policy for these tropical African interests. The countering of rival European claims or activities was thought to be primarily a matter for diplomacy. Thus the colonies that emerged in East Africa (as also the Oil Rivers Protectorate) were for much of the period 1885–1914 the responsibility of the Foreign Office, not the Colonial Office. But since diplomacy alone could not prevail against actual French or German advances in Africa, British commercial capital was sought to develop positive British interests on the ground. There were sufficient trading profits in the Oil Rivers of the Niger delta to enable the Royal Niger Company (RNC), chartered in 1886, to begin the conquest of what became the Protectorate of Northern Nigeria. But, since the British occupation of Egypt in 1882 was thought to require control of the source of the White Nile, the Foreign Office was more concerned with East Africa. The Imperial British East Africa Company, chartered in 1888, was encouraged to occupy Uganda, but it lacked an adequate commercial base to maintain this enterprise so far in the interior. In 1893, therefore, Britain took direct action, and soon after built the Uganda Railway,–at a cost of £8 million–from the Indian Ocean to Victoria Nyanza through the East African Protectorate (the later Kenya Colony). Such an investment was totally exceptional at this time. It may be compared with the acceptance of an annual subsidy of £10 000 from Cecil Rhodes's British South Africa Company* to help transform the consular jurisdiction in Nyasaland into a primitive colonial administration; Nyasaland's subsequent development was related to that of the two Rhodesian colonies.

Joseph Chamberlain (Colonial Secretary, 1895–1903) brought a

Macupa Bridge, linking Mombasa Island with the Kenya mainland at the coastal end of the Uganda Railway

more forward British colonial policy. A professional colonial service began to replace earlier haphazard recruitment to colonial administrations. In West Africa the French military advance from Senegal* had already cut off British traders' access to the interior from the Gambia, and was threatening the access of those operating from Sierra Leone, the Gold Coast and southern Nigeria. Following the French model of recruiting African soldiers to serve under European officers, an inland protectorate was created for Sierra Leone, and the militant kingdom of Asante and its hinterland north of the Gold Coast were occupied. The RNC was divested of its political role, and the conquest of the Sokoto* caliphate was completed in 1900–06.

The prime responsibility of government in the new colonies was to establish a general framework of law and order that would encourage African farmers to produce exportable surpluses, and European entrepreneurs to enter and acquire these in exchange for European exports or to develop new mining and other large-scale economic activities. Colonial administrations were intended to support themselves from taxes levied on the expected increases in wealth and trade. In practice the cost of establishing effective control over sizeable territories tended to exceed the revenue that could be raised from direct or indirect taxation. Africans were unused and often hostile to European demands which provoked resistance.* In 1898 in Sierra Leone, and in 1900 in Asante, the imposition of British control provoked major revolts, while eastern Nigeria was not finally 'pacified' before 1918 nor British Somaliland until much later.

In the coastal regions of the Gold Coast and Nigeria, long acquaintance with European trade and education did help Africans to generate new wealth by offering for export such agricultural produce as cocoa and palm-oil and palm kernels, and it was feasible to build

Frederick Lugard (1858–1945): agent of British expansion, colonial official, and theorist of colonial rule

Belgian expansion

European information about the hinterland of West Central Africa was sketchy in the 1870s. Europeans bought products such as wax, ivory, coffee, palm-oil and, increasingly, rubber on the Angolan coast and in the Zaire estuary, but knew little about the complex commercial network upon which this trade rested. The general recession in the African trade of the 1870s was a background factor in the European Scramble★ for Africa but, in this area, the timing of partition was largely determined by the decision of King Leopold II of Belgium to seize a piece of what he regarded as 'this magnificent African cake'. His move (1877–8) was ill-prepared, but he found inspiration in the accounts of the explorers V.L. Cameron and H.M. Stanley, in Gordon's exploits in the Sudan, and through his acquaintance with the Dutch owners of a trading house on the lower Zaire River

Leopold was a visionary who had hitherto dabbled in various far-fetched schemes in Asia. His oft-repeated conviction was that Europeans should be 'on the watch' for spoils in the outlying areas of the world economy. He was, as an individual, concerned single-mindedly with profit and it has often been suggested that his expansionist enterprises were unsupported by any general imperialist feelings in Belgium. Certainly there was opposition in Belgium to state-sponsored enterprises overseas, but this did not preclude the involvement of Belgian capital in Africa. Belgian industrial, commercial and financial interests were tightly enmeshed with other Western European interests and Leopold found much support–particularly from the international merchant bankers of Antwerp, as well as from private bankers of various nationalities either based in, or having connections with, Belgium.

From 1876 to the early 1880s Leopold presented himself and his Congo Association as altruistic and scientifically oriented. Nevertheless at the 1884–5 Berlin Conference★ his *Etat Independent du Congo* (Congo Free State) (EIC) was recognized as a sovereign state. The term 'state', however, soon became a misnomer as Leopold turned the EIC into what amounted to a privately-owned chartered company. Centring its operations on the network of navigable rivers crossing the equatorial forest, the EIC had, by 1891–2, succeeded in creating a monopoly aimed exclusively at generating profit by the enforced production of rubber and ivory. At Leopold's prompting, bankers floated firms in Belgium which colluded with the EIC in monopolizing the Congolese rubber trade. The same individuals sometimes held stock in similar enterprises operating elsewhere, notably in the French Congo, but capital was concentrated in the EIC, where the 'rubber system' was most violently implemented.

From the 1890s the system was operated by small armed garrisons of African mercenaries, under the overall supervision of European agents. It only gradually came to an end between 1906 and 1910. By

railways to extend both effective control and the export economy into the interior. In East Africa, however, the construction of the costly Uganda Railway had preceded effective European penetration. In an attempt to accelerate the growth of traffic and revenue, European settlers were encouraged to farm the southern Kenyan highlands, where Kikuyu farmers had withdrawn in face of the pastoral expansion of the Masai. But this did not immediately produce income comparable to that coming by 1914 from the cotton exports of African farmers in southern Uganda, and it created serious problems for the future.

The British occupation of southern Uganda had been facilitated by treaties with its principal African kings, which allowed them considerable powers of local government and which recognized African rights in land. Political agitation from European-educated Africans had secured comparable recognition for African land rights in West Africa, while the conqueror of northern Nigeria, Frederick Lugard (who had earlier served in Uganda), had also chosen to govern there through the traditional rulers. By 1914, when Lugard effected the amalgamation of the northern and southern Nigerian colonies, this 'indirect rule' was beginning to be seen as the preferred British method of governing tropical African colonies where limited revenues restricted the expensive employment of European officials in direct administration. *J.D.F.*

'In the rubber coils. Scene – The Congo "Free" State.' Cartoon from *Punch*

that time military opposition from Swahili competitors had long been crushed, and Luso-African armed caravans or upheavals by harrassed villagers never posed a significant threat. Leaks by missionaries or independent observers proved more of an embarrassment, as they brought to light the human and ecological waste generated by the system. These witnesses fed an international campaign against the EIC (led by E.D. Morel, who founded the Congo Reform Association in 1904). Up to the end, however, Leopold believed that some cosmetic treatment would suffice to guarantee the continuing operation of this immensely profitable enterprise. Fundamental social and economic changes lay behind the success of humanitarian campaigns against the EIC. On the one hand, rubber production rapidly declined after years of over-exploitation of wild vines, while, on the other, British, American, and (cautiously at first) Belgian firms were taking a stake in mineral prospecting and exploitation. Belgium annexed the EIC in 1908, and this political change further encouraged the major Belgian banks to continue expanding their colonial portfolios. By the outbreak of the First World War, important mining enterprises were taking shape in the savanna regions of Katanga, Kasai, and Ituri. Following the annexation, big business, Church, and state coalesced into an openly Belgian rather than Leopoldian enterprise. *J.-L.V.*

Portuguese expansion

In the 1880s Portugal, a minor peasant and fishing kingdom sometimes described by contemporaries as the sick man of Western Europe, laid claim to five African colonies, three small and two large. The claim was based on 400 years of commercial contact primarily connected with various branches of the international slave trade.

West Africa

The Cape Verde Islands were not much affected by the Scramble★ for Africa and continued their pattern of salt mining, ocean-fishing, goat-rearing, telegraph-operating and the replenishment of liner coal-bunkers disturbed more by vagaries of climate than by colonial conquest. Guinea-Bissau also had a small Creole population, which gave colonial administrators an entrée from which a small mainland colony was created. São Tomé, off the Nigerian coast, was much wealthier, with tropical plantations of coffee and cocoa. As a Portuguese colony it was able to import slaves until 1908 without attracting international condemnation. After that date most mainland labour, from both Angola and Mozambique, had to be repatriated after fixed periods of plantation service.

Angola

In 1884 Angola consisted of five Portuguese enclaves on the coast of Central Africa and an ill-defined hinterland through which trade paths reached deep into what is now Zaire and Zambia extracting beeswax, red rubber and, above all, chained gangs of slave-workers in exchange for wine, rum and gunpowder. Portugal established an internationally recognized claim to about 1.3 million sq km of this hinterland and then spent 50 years of intermittent military investment in conquering it. Resistance was fierce and recurrent. The great central Bailundu rebellion shook the colony in 1902. The old Kongo kingdom revolted in 1913, and the Ndembu chiefdom, not far from the capital city of Luanda, had to be resubjugated in 1907. The Kwanyama, on the Namibian border, were among the hardest to conquer, and the 1915 war against them came to dominate the military legends of the Portuguese empire. The last wars occurred in the 1920s in Lunda territory, where diamonds had been discovered.

Mozambique

The Portuguese penetration of Mozambique was less direct, though no less violent, than the colonial conquest of Angola. Abortive attempts were made to find colonial allies among the *prazo*★ principalities, founded on the basis of an early phase of Portuguese activity on the Zambezi. When the resistance proved too costly for Portugal, it sought international aid. Mozambique was parcelled out

Quilimane, Mozambique, c. 1900: Africans carrying a European in a palanquin

to multinational private-enterprise colonizers with varying charters of franchise. The northern Niassa Company precariously recovered the costs of conquest by forcible extraction of peasant surplus. The central Mozambique Company used military force to recruit labour for sugar plantations whose profits were well disguised in complex share dealings. In the south Witwatersrand labour recruiters paid fees, which, together with Transvaal railway and harbour dues, enabled direct rule by Portugal to be financed. The international financing of the conquest of Mozambique did not prevent rebellions from occurring. The largest was the Barwe rebellion of 1917, which coincided with the short-lived German invasion of northern Mozambique. *D.B.B.*

German expansion

The unification of Imperial Germany was completed in 1871. Neither this new state nor its constituent sections had previous experience with overseas colonial possessions. This situation was altered with the declaration of protectorates over the ill-defined coastal areas of South-West Africa (1884), Togo (1884), Cameroon (1884), and East Africa (1885). Metropolitan responsibility for these territories lay initially with the Political Section of the Foreign Office; a Colonial Section was eventually created in 1890 within the same ministry. Only in 1907 was a Colonial Office created with specific ministerial responsibility for the colonies.

The German Chancellor, Otto von Bismarck, was determined that merchant groups should bear the responsibility and expense of administering these new territories. In Togo and Cameroon prominent traders were given consular responsibility. The German East Africa Company (*Deutsch-Ostafrikanische Gesellschaft*) and the German Colonial Company for South-West Africa (*Deutsche Kolonialgesellschaft für Südwestafrika*) took control of their respective areas. It soon became apparent, however, that merchants did not have the financial or diplomatic resources to dominate African polities and to mediate between conflicting European claims. By 1890 the German government was being reluctantly dragged into the affairs of the African interior.

It was the use – or threat – of military force that enabled German control to be extended in the 1890s and maintained thereafter. The army (*Schutztruppe*) of each colony – with one exception – consisted of African troops led by German officers. The exception was German South-West Africa, where strong racial attitudes permitted only a white military force: Togo possessed a police force rather than an army but there was no real difference in training and function. By 1914 the German colonies could deploy a total armed force of nearly 7000 men. Although well trained and equipped, it was smaller than the African colonial armies of Britain, France, Belgium or Portugal.

Once military control had been established and taxation introduced, German officials sought means to stimulate an export economy in order to make their respective colonies economically self-sufficient. In South-West Africa the promotion of white settlement became the key economic policy from the 1890s. This meant that the Herero and Nama peoples in the south were increasingly subject to seizure of land and cattle: they had already been seriously weakened by the 1897 rinderpest epidemic, which had destroyed many herds. Armed revolt broke out in 1904 and 15 000 troops had to be sent from Germany. By 1907 over 80 per cent of the Herero and 50 per cent of the Nama had been annihilated.

In East Africa, the largest of the German colonies, official policy was more variable. However, white settlement and compulsion in African agriculture were increasingly favoured after 1902. The Maji Maji rebellion spread rapidly across the south of the colony in 1905, precipitated by grievances connected with tax, labour, agricultural compulsion and the loss of traditional privileges. The conflict lasted for two years; an estimated 200 000 people died in the conflict and subsequent famine.

In Cameroon large parts of the colony were turned over to concessionary companies – on the model of the Congo Free State* – which ruthlessly extracted produce (mainly wild rubber) and labour from the African population. This provoked a series of uprisings in the south, which began in 1904 and were not effectively suppressed until 1910.

In Togo there was minimal interference with a strong pre-colonial pattern of export production. Consequently, Togo was the one German colony to escape widespread violence in this period.

military character by 1914. Only two out of 21 districts in German East Africa still remained under military rule, and seven out of 24 districts in Cameroon. Togo and South-West Africa had complete civil administrations. In German East Africa (in the interlacustrine area) and in Cameroon (in the northern Islamic states) administrative units called 'residencies' were created where German officials operated as advisers rather than direct administrators. This practice (based on British experience) occurred only in areas that had highly developed state structures and were remote from the territorial administration.   *L.E.L.*

Italian expansion

Italy found itself a latecomer to the European partition of Africa. Viewed from Rome, the French occupation of North Africa,★ followed by Britain's occupation of Egypt★ in 1882, not only enhanced the power of Italy's European rivals but also threatened to end Italian dreams of occupying the Mediterranean coast of Africa.

The first opportunity to join the Scramble★ for Africa came in 1885, when Italian forces successfully occupied the Red Sea port of Massawa despite fierce resistance from Emperor Yohannes IV of Ethiopia. One year later Britain, which had occupied the northern half of Somaliland in an effort to protect trade links with its colony in Aden, invited the Italians to do likewise in the southern half, a move the British hoped would contain French expansion in and around Djibouti. In 1890 an advance into the interior led to the capture of Asmara. Further Italian advances were abruptly halted when the Ethiopians decisively defeated the Italians at the battle of Adowa★ in 1896. By the peace treaty signed in Addis Ababa in that year the Italians recognized the independence of Ethiopia in return for the right to continue their occupation of the ports of Massawa and Assab, which they later organized into a colony and named Eritrea.

By the early 1900s Ethiopia's loss of its outlets to the sea, the illness of Menelik★ and the revolt of the Somalis was threatening to revive factional interests within the region. Britain, Italy and France, in an effort to avert the break-up of Ethiopia and a consequent intensification of their own rivalries, signed a tripartite convention in 1906 under which each agreed to maintain the *status quo* in Ethiopia. However, they also agreed on a division of their interests, should the *status quo* be broken: Italy's interest in Eritrea and Somaliland was recognized, as was its sphere of influence in the adjacent areas of the Blue Nile. While this recognition carried little significance as long as Ethiopia remained united, it was a key factor in Italy's African policy after the First World War.★

To the north, Italian penetration of Tripolitania and Cyrenaica (now Libya) dated from the last decade of the 19th century, when the

German East Africa: top: German soldiers hanging Africans during the Maji Maji rebellion. Above: Germans and Africans in a sisal-processing factory near Dar es Salaam

Between 1907 and 1914 there was little military opposition, and Germany's consolidation of its colonies proceeded at a rapid rate. The economy of each colony was restructured to concentrate on export production. White settlers were given increased control over economic and political structures, while Africans were seen increasingly as a source of labour for the plantations and mines: the white population trebled in this period, and the number of Africans engaged in wage labour doubled. Railways were now considered to be the moving force of economic expansion and integration. By 1914 there were 4500km of rail operation in the colonies, most of which was constructed after 1907.

The administration of the German colonies had lost much of its

Banca di Roma began acquiring financial interests in these territories, which were still nominally part of the Ottoman Empire.* By 1908 its investments had doubled, a reflection of growing Italian involvement in commercial establishments, small workshops and farms, as well as the territories' educational and cultural life. In 1911, for trivial reasons, Italy declared war on Ottoman Turkey and later landed troops in Tripoli. Local resistance to the invasion, and to Italy's subsequent declaration of annexation, was fierce, particularly in Cyrenaica where the Sanusiyya, an Islamic sufi brotherhood, fought a protracted war against the Italians until 1917, when they were eventually defeated by the British after Italy had joined the Allied Powers.

Under the terms of a truce negotiated first with the British and then with the Italians, the leader of the Sanusiyya, Muhammad Idris, obtained Allied recognition of his position as Amir in Cyrenaica in return for his promise to stop Sanusi attacks on coastal towns in the Libyan territories and in Egypt. But the future of the country was not to be decided until after the war, when the Allies in the Treaty of Lausanne (1923) agreed to recognize Italian claims to both Tripolitania and Cyrenaica.   *P.A.S.*

Spanish expansion

Spain's expansion in the 19th century stemmed from its government's desire to maintain past glories in a world almost monopolized by more powerful competitors. After the loss of Caribbean and Pacific colonies in the late 1890s, the only field for expansion was south of Gibraltar, but even there Spain came late to the feast and had to be content with crumbs. Political will and resources were wanting. Two geopolitical domains have to be considered: north-western Africa and the Gulf of Guinea.

On the Moroccan coast Spain possessed two penal settlements: Ceuta (Portuguese since 1415, under the Spanish Crown from 1580) and Melilla (Spanish from 1497) and minor coastal islets. In 1859 a war with Morocco heralded a short-lived spate of interest in African affairs. It can be conveniently held as the starting point of a less desultory policy, but at that time, in Spanish eyes, Morocco was more an unruly neighbour than a potential colony. Above all, Madrid was anxious to keep England and France off the southern shores of the Straits of Gibraltar. The creation of the *Real Sociedad Geográfica Española* (1877) and the *Sociedad de Africanistas y Colonistas* (1883) spurred the launching of various politico-commercial missions beyond the Saharan façade fronting the Canary Islands. In November 1884 Captain Emílio Bonelli took possession of Villa Cisneros and La Giiera. The following month Spain proclaimed its annexation of the coast between Cabo Bojador and Cabo Blanco. The

territory was to be governed from Las Palmas. Except for explorations, and the signing of a protectorate treaty in 1886 in what is now Mauritania, the interior was left to the nomads, while protracted negotiations (1886–91) with France took place.

In 1893 new hostilities with Morocco ended inconclusively in the hinterland of Melilla. The partition of Morocco was in the offing, but Spain was in no strong position to bargain successfully with France. The subsequent Franco-Spanish treaties and conventions (1900, 1902, 1904, 1912) all tended to restrict Spanish claims in Morocco and the Sahara. In 1909 a bloody campaign behind Melilla started the Spanish occupation of the Rif, one of the most difficult parts of Africa to subdue. Northern Morocco, which was constituted into a Spanish protectorate (1912), was to become the nightmare of the Spanish government until the late 1920s. South of the French protectorate over Morocco, the site of the small enclave of Ifni remained a political

The Rif War, 1909: Moroccan prisoners being taken into the Spanish fort at Melilla

no-man's-land, while Cabo Juby (now Tarfaya) was occupied in 1916. For all purposes, Spanish Sahara remained a myth.

South of the Equator, the Spanish presence was somewhat less tenuous but amounted to little anyway. In 1778 Portugal had ceded Fernando Po and Annobón to Spain, but the first Spanish expedition had ended in disaster. Under British vigilance Fernando Po became a haven for liberated slaves and Spain was politically absent until 1858. The islands were at first ruled from Cuba, which hampered effective administration. A few Spanish traders settled in the Islets of Corisco and the Elobeys, off the mainland (Rio Muni), and in Cabo San Juan on the mainland. In spite of Spanish explorations in the 1870s and 1880s the hinterland was virtually closed to Spanish endeavours, and the mainland coastal settlement of Bata remained a French possession until ceded to Spain in 1900. Fernando Po was much more developed thanks to the entrepreneurial skills of a handful of cocoa-planters (some of them English-speaking Creoles), an energetic governor, Angel Barrera, and labour recruited (sometimes forcibly) on the West African mainland (notably in Liberia).   R.P.

Southern Africa

In the late 19th century southern Africa was transformed from an area of little more than strategic interest to the European powers to one of vital importance to the world economy. This rapid change in the status of the region was brought about initially by the opening of the diamond diggings in Griqualand West in 1867, and subsequently by the discovery of immense gold deposits on the Witwatersrand in 1886. By the end of the century the Transvaal had already become the world's largest single source of gold, accounting for almost a third of the world's output.

Rapid industrialization in the Transvaal transformed the economic and political complexion of the entire subcontinent. The economic centre of southern Africa moved suddenly northward from the Cape Colony to the previously bankrupt Afrikaner state, the South African Republic. Overseas capital poured into the republic (£60 million by 1897), and between 1886 and 1899 almost 100 000 new immigrants arrived in South Africa, most of them bound for the industrial region around the mining capital of Johannesburg. Railway development gathered pace and harbour facilities in the British-ruled Cape Colony and Natal were expanded and improved. Because of rural poverty and the need for cash to pay taxes and rents, Africans were prepared to travel long distances to find employment in South Africa's new industrial heartland, where wages were more attractive than elsewhere in the subcontinent. By 1899 the gold mines employed an African migrant labour force of almost 100 000.

British interests in southern Africa, which before the mineral discoveries had pivoted on maintaining the security of the strategically important naval base on the Cape peninsula, suddenly changed with the development of gold mining. Much of the capital invested in the industry was British, and most of the new immigrants who settled in the Transvaal (the Uitlanders) came from Britain. Yet Britain's pre-eminent influence in the region was immediately threatened by the new wealth of the Transvaal and by the policies pursued there by President Kruger's government. In order to retain political control of the republic, Kruger's government introduced legislation to deny equal franchise rights to the Uitlander community. Efforts were also made to achieve greater commercial autonomy from Britain, to extend the frontiers of the republic, and to forge closer relations with a number of overseas governments. Moreover, the gold mining industry was hampered by restrictive economic policies introduced by Kruger's government to ensure that the Afrikaner oligarchy maintained close control over, and prospered from, industrial development. In these circumstances the security of Britain's naval base, and the financial interests of British investors in the Transvaal, seemed decidedly threatened. Furthermore, the possibility of federating the settler polities of the region under British auspices, the cornerstone of imperial policy in the 1870s, appeared more remote than ever before.

The first efforts to reassert British supremacy in southern Africa were made, by Cecil Rhodes, a vigorous imperialist, the most successful Kimberley diamond magnate, and, from 1890, Prime Minister of the Cape Colony. Inspired by a desire to pave the way for further British colonial expansion in the interior, to discover a 'second Rand' to counterbalance the wealth of the Transvaal, and to block the northward expansion of the republic, Rhodes persuaded the British government in 1888 to grant a royal charter to his British South Africa Company in order that it might conquer and administer the region north of the Limpopo River on Britain's behalf. Two years later the first white settlers entered the area that in previous centuries had formed the heartland of the Great Zimbabwe* and Mwenemutapa* (Monomotapa) empires, but which during the colonial period was destined to bear its conqueror's name – Rhodesia. The Shona and Ndebele, who resisted the pioneers' encroachment, were ruthlessly suppressed, much of their most fertile land was seized for white settlement, and a large proportion of their livestock was

Right: the discovery of diamonds initiated the economic transformation of South Africa: workers searching gravel at Kimberley, *c.* 1890. Below: Ndebele prisoners at Fort Mangwe during the 1896 revolt against European rule in Southern Rhodesia

confiscated or slaughtered. A rudimentary company administration was established, and company agents were dispatched by Rhodes to lay claim to the region beyond the Zambezi River.

It soon became evident that the enormous mineral wealth Rhodes had hoped to discover in the north was a pipe-dream, and that his strategy to compel the Transvaal to enter the British fold had failed. Recklessly, he sought to engineer an Uitlander coup to overthrow Kruger's government. With the connivance of a number of British colonial officials the plot was hatched in December 1895, but the planned insurrection in Johannesburg collapsed, and the invading force from the Bechuanaland Protectorate led by L. S. Jameson, which was intended to link up with the insurgents, was easily defeated. The Jameson Raid destroyed Rhodes's political career and further embittered Anglo-Boer relations. Following the raid, the British Colonial Secretary, Joseph Chamberlain, and the High Commissioner to South Africa, Sir Alfred Milner, mounted progressively more intense diplomatic pressure on Kruger's government to enfranchise the Uitlanders without delay. Kruger sternly resisted, since to have acceded to the British demands would have undermined Afrikaner domination of the republic's affairs and ultimately jeopardized its independence. The two sides entered into war on 11 October 1899.

After suffering serious initial reverses the British army occupied the Transvaal and its sister republic, the Orange Free State, during 1900, but it was not until May 1902 that the Afrikaner governments agreed to peace terms and accepted the British annexation of their countries. In the aftermath of the South African War Britain sought to consolidate its military victory by encouraging large-scale British immigration into the Transvaal and by destroying Afrikaner nationalism through an all-embracing policy of anglicization and the promotion of rapid economic development. However, relatively few British immigrants were attracted to the Transvaal, and by 1905 it was evident that Afrikaner nationalism could be destroyed neither by force of arms and political domination nor by social engineering. In 1906 self-government was restored to the Transvaal by the new Liberal government in Britain (self-government was granted to the Orange River Colony, as the Free State was known under British rule, in the following year). From the British point of view, however, the war had not been fought completely in vain, for in 1910 the unification of the four settler colonies under British auspices was finally achieved. Although dominated politically by the Afrikaner population of the Union, South Africa remained part of the British Empire and subsequent Commonwealth for the next half-century. Against the wishes of South Africa's white political leaders, the three British High Commission Territories in southern Africa, Basutoland, the Bechuanaland Protectorate and Swaziland, were not incorporated in the Union. The question of Southern Rhodesia's* association with the Union was left to be resolved at a later date. *P. W.*

Ethiopia

As a result of the Mahdist rebellion* in the Sudan a number of towns with Egyptian garrisons and European inhabitants were besieged. The British government, anxious to obtain the help of Emperor Yohannes IV* of Ethiopia in their evacuation, signed a treaty with him, in June 1884, specifying that Ethiopia should have free transit through the port of Massawa 'under British protection' for all goods, including arms and ammunition.

The Ethiopian commander, Ras Alula, duly relieved six garrisons in the Sudan, but the 1884 agreement was short-lived, for in February 1885 Italy* occupied Massawa. This was done with the consent of the British government, which favoured Italian expansion in the hope that it would curb that of France. The Italians, though at first promising free movement of goods through the port, soon seized the neighbouring coast, advanced inland, and instituted an arms blockade. They were, however, defeated by Ras Alula at the battle of

King Menelik of Shoa, Emperor of Ethiopia, 1889–1913

Dogali in January 1887. The Italians responded by preparing for a war of revenge. Yohannes, faced with this threat, transferred a garrison from Galabat on the Sudan frontier, whereupon the Mahdists attacked at that point. The Emperor hastened to repel them, but at the close of a victorious battle was killed by a sniper's bullet. News of his death led to confusion in northern Ethiopia, which was intensified by a serious outbreak of cattle disease and subsequent famine. In the ensuing period of difficulty the Italians advanced inland, occupying Asmara, and established their Red Sea colony of Eritrea in 1890.

Further south, meanwhile, King Menelik* of Shoa had been strengthening his position. In May 1889 – less than two months after the death of Yohannes – he signed a treaty of perpetual peace and friendship with Italy at the village of Wuchale. By this agreement the Italians recognized him as Emperor and conceded his right to import arms through Italian territory; he in return recognized Italian sovereignty over the Eritrean plateau, including Asmara. The most important clause of the treaty was, however, Article XVII, which was soon the basis of dispute. In its Amharic version the text states that Menelik should have the power to avail himself of the services of Italy in communications with other powers; but in the Italian version this was made obligatory. On the basis of this, the Italians claimed, in October, to have established a protectorate over Ethiopia in accordance with the General Act of Berlin.

Menelik devoted the ensuing years to importing arms, mainly from France and Russia, and at length denounced the Wuchale treaty in February 1893, declaring 'Ethiopia has need of no one; she stretches out her hands to God.' The Italians subsequently overran most of Tigre, but Menelik, advancing into the province at the close of 1895, defeated them decisively at the battle of Adowa on 1 March 1896. The invaders were obliged to sign the peace treaty of Addis Ababa in October, whereby the Wuchale agreement was annulled, and the absolute independence of Ethiopia affirmed. *R.K.P.P.*

Liberia

Liberia was founded in 1822 by a philanthropic association, the American Colonization Society, as a settlement for free people of colour from the USA. About 13000 black Americans emigrated to Monrovia and other smaller settlements during the following 50 years, and nearly 6000 slaves recaptured at sea were liberated there. On 26 July 1847 the settlers declared themselves an independent sovereign black republic, the first in Africa, and adopted a constitution based on that of the USA; Joseph Jenkins Roberts became the first president. For over 20 years the government was controlled by mulattoes; the first full-blooded African president, Edward James

Roye, was elected in 1870, and the True Whig Party that he founded became the dominant party in the republic. The republic had difficult relations both with indigenous African peoples and with encroaching colonial powers. Initially forced to defend their foothold on the coast against indigenous African attack, the settlers were by the late 1830s able to start extending their control into the hinterland, in keeping with their doctrine of 'manifest destiny' to civilize the interior. The pace of annexation increased as rival colonialists appeared in the late 19th century, and an interior administration similar to that established by colonial regimes was set up. Some indigenous people were assimilated into the settler group, and Liberians such as Benjamin Anderson made epic explorations of the interior, but not until 1904 were indigenous Africans regarded as eligible for citizenship. By then, Liberia had been hemmed in by French and British expansion,* and large tracts of territory had been shorn from the republic by the colonial powers. The republic's economy was based on trade with the interior and was initially prosperous, but in the last three decades of the 19th century economic recessions in Europe and inability to compete with overseas steamship companies severely weakened this trade, and forced successive Liberian governments to seek foreign loans which compromised their independence. In 1909 the USA helped prevent Britain and France from taking over Liberia as a protectorate because of non-repayment of loans. It was, however, more by its own vigour than by foreign help that the Americo-Liberian republic was able to survive the European Scramble* for Africa. *C.S.C.*

Egypt

Throughout the colonial period Egypt retained a nominal independence. Although an autonomous province of the Ottoman Empire, the country was arguably the main prize in the Scramble* for Africa, which, in part, its occupation precipitated. Concern over the nationalist threat to European financial interests and British strategic considerations, posed by Arabi Pasha, who became Egypt's minister of war in 1882, led to the despatch of a British expeditionary force. Following the battle of Tal al-Kabir in September, the British occupied Egypt. The importance of controlling the Suez Canal, the lifeline of its imperial communications, especially as German influence in the Near East increased, precluded Britain's early withdrawal, and a permanent occupation ensued. The form of the Ottoman khedivial regime was retained in order to placate European, especially French, opinion. Real power, however, lay with British 'advisers', under the British Agent and Consul-General. This post was occupied by Sir Evelyn Baring (Lord Cromer) from 1882 until 1907, during whose tenure the pattern of British control was established.

The period up to the outbreak of the First World War witnessed important social and economic advances but a relative stagnation in political affairs. Sound fiscal management corrected the disastrous state of Egyptian finances. Special attention was paid to irrigation works, which were modernized and extended. The fellahin (peasants) were relieved of some of the worst aspects of oppression. Cotton became the country's main cash crop, and contributed to an increased, if narrowly based, prosperity. British education policy, which was criticized as illiberal, created, ironically, a disaffected class with severely limited employment prospects. This combined with rising resentment of foreign domination to fuel the establishment and growth of various nationalist groupings, none of which, however, succeeded in organizing a mass following. Notable were the Nationalist Party led by Mustafa Kamil (1874–1908) and the Constitutional Reform Party of Shaykh Ali Yusuf. A further irritant to Egyptian nationalist aspirations was the British handling of affairs in the Sudan. Egypt was obliged to withdraw from its territories south of Wadi Halfa in the face of the Mahdist revolution (1881–5). Following the Anglo-Egyptian conquest of the Sudan (1896–8), the Condominium Agreement (1899) established a joint British and Egyptian rule there, but Egyptian participation was from the outset circumscribed.

Under Cromer's successors, Sir Eldon Gorst (1907–11) and Lord Kitchener (1911–14), political reforms aimed at expanding the power of Egyptian political institutions were undertaken. The Organic Law of 1913 established a Legislative Assembly with considerable authority, but at the outbreak of the First World War it was prorogued. When Britain declared war on the Ottoman Empire in November 1914, Egypt's anomalous status (which remained that of an Ottoman possession) was altered by the unilateral British declaration of a protectorate. The reigning khedive, Abbas II Hilmi, was deposed and replaced by his uncle, Hussayn Kamil, as sultan. The British Agent and Consul-General was thereafter styled High Commissioner. Further political developments were postponed by the war, in which Egypt played an indirect but significant role. The demands made on Egypt during the war alienated large and important sections of the population, and were partly responsible for a nationalist upsurge in 1919.

M.W.D.

Left: President J.J. Roberts of Liberia arriving at Monrovia, January 1849, after a visit to England. Right: cartoon of Khedive Abbas II Hilmi

AFRICA IN 1914

The First World War

The importance of the First World War as a turning point in African history has until very recently been underestimated. It marked the end of the European Scramble* for Africa begun some 30 years before. Despite dramatic challenges made to the authority of the colonial powers during the war, by its end they were firmly in control of the peoples they administered and were to remain so until the close of the Second World War.* The social and economic consequences of the war were widely felt: directly by well over a million Africans recruited as soldiers, carriers and labourers; indirectly by the many millions involved in production of foodstuffs and raw materials required by the European belligerents. Although the African campaigns were marginal to the course of the war, they had profound effects on the peoples in whose lands they were fought, notably in German Cameroon* and German East Africa.* Finally, the war saw an end to serious attempts by Africans to regain the lost independence of their pre-colonial polities. Henceforth, political agitation would be focused on unpalatable aspects of the colonial system and attempts to gain access to the power-structure of the colony-states established by the Europeans over the preceding 40–50 years. With the exception of Ethiopia and the small Spanish territories, which remained neutral, the whole of Africa became involved directly or indirectly on one or other side during the war. Liberia began as a neutral but sided with the Allies when America entered the war in 1917. Massive recruitment of Africans as soldiers followed the outbreak of the war. These troops were used in Europe, in the Middle East and in the campaigns in the four German colonies. It is estimated that over a million African soldiers were recruited during the war, while countless more men, women and children were impressed as carriers and labourers for the Togo, Cameroon, East African and Middle Eastern campaigns. Very few of these were genuine volunteers and in French Black Africa, where recruitment was compulsory, thousands emigrated to neighbouring British territories, where military exactions were less onerous, fled to the bush, or mutilated themselves to avoid conscription. The exigencies of war brought home to millions of Africans the realities of the new colonial regimes, which hitherto had only marginally affected their daily lives.

The most immediate impact of the war was the invasion by Allied forces of the four German colonies to deny the Germans use of their ports and to neutralize their African radio communications system. Togo was occupied after a brief campaign launched shortly after the declaration of war and was divided for administrative purposes between France and Britain. The campaign in Cameroon took much longer partly because of the larger size of the territory and its difficult terrain, partly because of the skill of the German commanders, who, as in the case of the British, French and Belgians, did battle with African troops. Cameroon, like Togo, was divided between France and Britain, the larger part being administered by France. Only in German South-West Africa was the war exclusively between whites: neither the Germans, who had just completed the suppression of the Herero and Nama revolts, nor the white South Africans, wished to arm their African populations. The South Africans, with greater resources in men and materials, overran the German colony and effectively incorporated it as a fifth province of the Union. The German East African campaign lasted for the duration of the war, as a result of a brilliant guerrilla campaign led by General von Lettow Vorbeck who, at the head of a force of 14 000 askaris (African troops), pinned down over 150 000 Allied troops. The bulk of German East Africa came under British administration, under the terms of the League of Nations Mandate, though the small but populous kingdoms of Ruanda and Burundi wer awarded to the Belgians. German South-West Africa (now Namibia*) was put under South Africa. In Egypt, as a result of Turkey's entry into the war, Britain's forces there were strengthened and a Turkish expeditionary force was repulsed at the Suez Canal. Thereafter the main cause for concern was the activities of the Sanusi* in revolt against the Italian administration in Libya.

British and French troops were not engaged in invading the German territories, but in suppressing revolts that were widespread in French West Africa and Nigeria. Some of these revolts were inspired by the desire to recapture a lost independence, the prospect of which seemed possible as Africans witnessed an exodus of European administrators and traders to fight on the Western Front. Others were in protest against obnoxious aspects of colonial rule, such as forced labour, compulsory recruitment, excessive taxation and the imposition of unpopular chiefs. The revolts in French West Africa led to large areas of the federation being out of administrative control, and tied down substantial forces that otherwise would have been sent to Europe. The most serious revolt was the Sanusi-inspired revolt by the Tuareg in Niger, which was suppressed by a joint Anglo-French expedition. Despite the initial successes of these risings, they

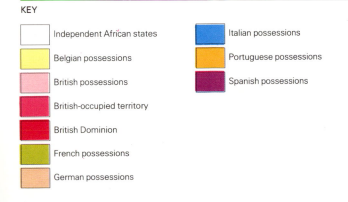

KEY

- ☐ Independent African states
- ☐ Belgian possessions
- ☐ British possessions
- ☐ British-occupied territory
- ☐ British Dominion
- ☐ French possessions
- ☐ German possessions
- ☐ Italian possessions
- ☐ Portuguese possessions
- ☐ Spanish possessions

were all suppressed and the Europeans once again demonstrated the superiority of their military technology. This was not seriously to be challenged again by Africans until the 1950s.

Protest against the colonial authorities after the war was by and large peaceful and aimed at securing greater participation in the political processes of the imposed colony states and reform of their

---

Below: German askaris on the march during the East African campaign. Bottom: French West African troops waiting to go into action during the Gallipoli campaign in Turkey, Spring 1915

abuses. The educated elite and those few Africans prospering from the colonial economic system spearheaded protest. The war had encouraged hopes among the elite for at least greater participation in the political and economic institutions of their countries. In the first place many Africans had been hastily recruited and trained to fill positions hitherto reserved for whites. In the case of North Africa many Tunisians and Algerians had gone to work in the factories of wartime France and returned inspired with egalitarian political ideas acquired at the work-bench. The boom in prices for some products coupled with the exodus of white traders brought African merchants, hitherto progressively pushed aside by European and Lebanese competition, renewed prosperity. Above all, war opened up new horizons for Africans. Previously largely enclosed within a bilateral relationship with their European rulers, Africans were now irrevocably exposed to–and felt themselves part of–the whole African continent and the rest of the world. In particular President Woodrow Wilson's Fourteen Points inspired demands for self-determination in Tunisia, and encouraged West African nationalists to hope that they would gain greater involvement in the determination of their own affairs from the Versailles Peace Conference. In South Africa, the Native National Congress sent a delegate to London in 1919 to remind the king of the contribution made by the South African Native Labour Corps to victory and to express the hope that their loyalty would be rewarded. *M.C.*

Colonial doctrines and practices

Underlying the conquest and subsequent rule of Africa by European powers was a belief that these actions were justified by the superiority of Western civilization. This belief had been reinforced by the rapidly-growing technological capacity of the West, by the development of pseudo-scientific theories of racial superiority, and by the emergence of such new philosophies as Social Darwinism with its insistence that 'fit' social groups eliminating or subordinating 'unfit' ones represented the natural order. European guardianship or trusteeship could therefore be seen as an end in itself, a necessary and inevitable exercise of authority over peoples incapable of managing their own affairs. It was more usually presented, however, as a means to effect the modernization of African societies, a mechanism by which the supposed superior knowledge, structures and values of the West could be diffused to backward regions. The proponents of these views denied any internal capacity for social transformation in African societies. Less frequently stressed by theorists of colonial empire, although emerging from time to time in defence against metropolitan criticism of colonial expenditure, were the gains to Europe. These were seen as being predominantly economic in character – access to markets for manufactures and to supplies of raw materials needed for Europe's continuing industrialization. Recognition of the twin goals of colonial rule was most explicit in Lord Lugard's concept of the 'dual mandate' (1922), in which Britain's responsibility in Africa was defined as the promotion of the moral and material well-being of the local inhabitants and the exploitation of African resources for the benefit of the world as a whole.

The broad idea that colonial administrations could, and should, advance the complementarity or interdependence of Europe and Africa found a narrower expression in the body of neo-mercantilist thought which had arisen to challenge the free trade reasoning of 19th century liberalism. Neo-mercantilism – the doctrine holding that metropolitan and colonial economies should be enclosed within a watertight imperial system – was never a wholly dominant intellectual tradition in Europe, but overlapped with, and reinforced, ideas about the desirability of administrative and cultural assimilation of colony to metropolis that surfaced most strongly in the policies of France and Portugal. The concept of association, a looser relationship which permitted a high degree of local autonomy in fiscal and budgetary matters, was more attractive to the British and Belgians, in part because it was more in tune with free trade ideals to which they remained committed for longer, but also because it accorded with previous domestic and imperial experience.

In translating general precepts about rights, responsibilities and relationships into specific policies, officials were guided by the administrative experience acquired in African territories already under their authority – Cape Colony and Natal in the case of the British, or Algeria for the French. Other imperial 'laboratories' such as India were also important influences. While the Belgians came to Africa lacking in lore, they tended to look to the example of their close neighbours, the Dutch, in South-East Asia. Almost invariably, however, abstract theory and earlier experience had to be adapted to local conditions and circumstances. This was particularly true of the primary political task of the colonial regime, namely the seeking out of mediating groups (chiefs, councils, civil servants, soldiers) who would act as agents of control over indigenous societies as well as communicators between the people and the European rulers. British theorists of 'native administration' espoused the ideals of Indirect Rule, according to which traditional authorities would be permitted to continue to exercise many customary powers.

French traditions emphasized Direct Rule, in which the colonial administration would either ignore indigenously-legitimized leaders or reduce them to a subordinate position with derivative powers. While the contrasting approach resulted in a certain difference in national styles – British officials, for example, being more ready than French to create artificial 'chiefs' in small-scale societies – in practice local political realities, coupled with lack of finance for a developed system of bureaucratic control, meant that the French often employed traditional elites in ways little different from those of Indirect Rule.

Large areas of agreement about economic policy existed within European colonial circles. Prevailing theories of international trade, which stressed the gains to be made from production of commodities for which there was some natural comparative advantage, predisposed colonial governments to the promotion of export-led growth. So did the fiscal benefits of the indirect taxation of trade. The role of the state, as perceived by influential politicians in France and Britain, was to provide investment in infrastructure, especially communications and public health, so as to attract private capital from Europe into Africa. Where debate commonly arose was over the kind of private capital to be attracted, and its likely impact on African societies. Investment in mineral exploitation was welcomed, because the best available technology seemed to require large-scale capitalist organization, but in tropical and sub-tropical agriculture advantages of scale, and of any particular configuration of technology and organization, were much less clear-cut. The local (African) smallholder, the immigrant (European) settler-farmer or proprietary planter, and the large, metropolitan-based corporate plantation all had their advocates among policy-makers; but the extent to which they became the dominant producers for overseas markets in any particular colonial territory rested upon local environmental factors as well as on official preconceptions. Climatic and disease conditions, for example, rendered West Africa and large parts of West Central Africa less attractive to European colonists than East or North-West Africa.

177

Incoming settlers and plantation managers, demanding administrative assistance in securing land and labour, drew deeply from the wellsprings of racism in European thought to justify their privileged position within the colonial economic structure. The primary goal of the European powers was to incorporate Africa into the international economy. They achieved this in a variety of ways with a diversity of consequences, establishing a relationship between Africa and the outside world that survived the demise of colonialism.   *J.F.M.*

French North Africa

After initial French uncertainty about Algeria's post-conquest status, the territory was proclaimed part of France in the 1848 constitution of the Second Republic and was organized into three *départements*, each administered by a *préfet*, while overall control was retained by the Ministry of War. As the number of settlers (*colons*) increased, the country was divided into *territoires civiles*, where there was a large European population organized in *communes* as in France, *territoires mixtes* where the *colons* were in a tiny minority and *territoires Arabes* where there were no *colons*. Outside the *territoires civiles* rule was by army officers who were often deeply resented by the *colons*, whom they endeavoured to hold in check. Constant civilian opposition led in 1880 to the ending of military control everywhere except in the southern territories. The French Constitution of 1870 declared Algeria an integral part of France, with representation in the Senate and Chamber of Deputies and overall responsibility transferred to the Ministry of the Interior. This assimilation was carried to its extreme in 1881 when specific aspects of Algerian administration were put under the appropriate ministry in Paris. For example, the Ministry of Health decided whether to raise the salary of a doctor in Ouargla while bureaucrats at the Ministry of Education decreed that Algerian children should use the same textbooks as used

North African service in the First World War was rewarded with a limited post-war extension of French citizenship: North African troops prepare couscous somewhere in France

in Burgundy, however unsuitable they might be. This ridiculous situation lasted 15 years after which more local power was given to the Governor-General of Algeria. There was no relaxation, however, in the control of the Muslim population, for the legal code known as the *indigénat* decreed that Muslims could be imprisoned for up to six months without appeal for actions that were not crimes under French law. The *indigénat* was administered by magistrates, only seven out of 300 of whom, in 1903, understood Arabic. In 1898 nominal indigenous representation was granted by the election of a minority of docile notables to the purely consultative *délégations financières*. In 1912 conscription was introduced for the Muslims, 173 000 of whom served in the First World War.* As a reward French citizenship was extended to certain categories in 1919. Settler opposition blocked an attempt to extend this even further in 1935.

Tunisia was controlled differently, coming, as a nominal protectorate, under the French Foreign Office. It retained the appearance of a sovereign state with its own flag, national anthem and monarch (the Bey) in whose name all laws, although initiated by the French Resident-General, were issued. The Bey had his own cabinet with the Resident-General as Foreign Minister and the French Commander-in-Chief as Minister of War. Other ministers, and local administrators, were Tunisian, but each had attached to his office a French official, who was in fact the controller and overseer of his actions in the smallest detail. The sensitive area near the Libyan frontier was always under direct French military rule.

In Morocco the system was similar although army control was stronger (much of the mountainous area was under martial law throughout the period of the protectorate) although the Sultan and some of the chiefs achieved greater independence. Spasmodic attempts to create a Ministry of North African Affairs in Paris always failed because of the constitutional differences between Algeria and its neighbours.

The Maghrib changed drastically during the century ending in 1939. There was an exchange of population, with 1 million Europeans being settled in Algeria, 200 000 in Tunisia and over 250 000 in Morocco while large numbers of North Africans found work in France. In Algeria grants and confiscations meant that the *colons* held all the best land, where they introduced modern farming methods – including new crops such as wine-grapes – and transformed the countryside. In Morocco and Tunisia protectorate status meant that expropriation was more difficult, but even so settlers acquired great estates.

Before 1939 there was little export of manufactured goods although numerous small industries grew up to serve local needs. Oil had not yet been found in Algeria, so its exports were mainly agricultural. The French, however, gave a great impetus to mining in Tunisia and Morocco. The two protectorates ranked among the top four world exporters of phosphates, and in Morocco – where 40 per cent of all capital invested before 1939 was directed towards mining – coal, cobalt and nickel were also exploited.

The French paid particular attention to the development of communications: on their arrival in Fes, the Sultan's carriage was the sole wheeled vehicle in the city, but it was soon possible to go by train to Tunis. Excellent roads were constructed and air travel began. Large centres grew up and Casablanca developed from a town of 10 000 in 1908 to be the third largest city in Africa. This resulted in great social changes as people left the countryside to find work in the new industrial areas and the often squalid *bidonvilles* (shanty towns) became a feature of the landscape.

The *colons* had believed that 'any native who could read was a danger to France', so little was done in Algeria for the education of Muslims although facilities for Europeans were excellent. In Tunisia there had been a more developed system before the Protectorate was declared, and more children attended school there than in its much larger neighbour. As the government needed indigenous officials, an attempt was made to form an intellectual elite which received training as Frenchmen. In Morocco, the first French Resident, General Lyautey (1912–25) saw the extension of education as a means of winning support for French rule and took a personal interest in intelligent students, urging them to go to universities in France. His successors built many schools among the Berbers to discourage them from seeking an Arab education and fitting them for service in the army or the administration. Lyautey also pioneered the use of medical doctors to penetrate and win over unsubmitted areas, so public health for Muslims received more attention than it did in the rest of the Maghrib, where it was largely neglected. *R.L.B.*

French Black Africa

The federations

French-ruled Black Africa (*Afrique noire française*) was divided into two huge federations: French West Africa, with its capital at Dakar, and French Equatorial Africa, with its capital at Brazzaville. French West Africa consisted of the constituent colonies of Mauritania, Senegal, French Soudan (now Mali), Niger, Dahomey (now Benin), Ivory Coast, Guinea and Upper Volta. Upper Volta was created in 1920, dismembered in 1932, when it was divided among its neighbours Ivory Coast, Niger and French Soudan, but was reconstituted in 1947. French Equatorial Africa consisted of the constituent colonies of Chad, Oubangui-Chari (now the Central African Republic), Moyen-Congo (now the Democratic Republic of the Congo) and Gabon. After the First World War* the greater part of German Cameroon, and just over half of German Togo were placed under French administration by League of Nations Mandate. Theoretically both these colonies were administered separately from their two neighbouring federations; in practice their administrations differed only in their being subject to restrictions on military recruitment, and in being required to submit annual reports on their administration to the Permanent Mandates Commission in Geneva. Between 1934 and 1936 Togo was administered as part of Dahomey and then, until 1945, it was placed directly under the Governor-General of French West Africa, who served as its High Commissioner.

Each federation was headed by a governor-general, who was directly responsible to the Minister of Colonies in Paris. Unlike his British counterpart, the governor-general had no legislative authority but could only propose laws to the Minister of Colonies, who enacted them by decree after consultation with the Cabinet. The Chamber of Deputies only rarely initiated colonial legislation. The governor-general was responsible for the overall political direction of his group of colonies and their economic development. He controlled the budget for the group while the departments responsible for agriculture, health and sanitation, posts and telegraphs and public works were all organized on a federal basis. He was advised by a Council of Government, which consisted of the secretary-general to the federal government, the army and navy commanders, the heads of the four federal services, the lieutenant-governors of the constituent colonies, one African representative for each colony nominated by the respective lieutenant-governor, and the president of the *Conseil-Général* of Senegal in the case of French West Africa. The Council of Government only had a deliberative role and could not enact legislation, as did the councils in the British colonies.

The colonies

The constituent colonies were headed by lieutenant-governors, who were principally concerned with the political situation in their colonies and with implementing the economic policies laid down by their governor-general. Their independence of action was severely limited: not only did the governor-general control their budgets and most important services, but he was also the intermediary in communications with the Minister of Colonies.

Road repair by forced labour, Dahomey (now Benin), 1933

Blaise Diagne, Deputy for Senegal, 1914–34

On the credit side of an otherwise harsh administrative regime that denied Africans all political and legal rights was an excellent health service and the elements of an educational service that produced in many colonies the first generation of Western-educated elites who, in the 1950s, were to claim independence from the French.

The only exception to this regime was the colony of Senegal where the inhabitants of the four communes of Dakar, Saint Louis (the colonial capital), Gorée and Rufisque had the status of French citizens, even though the majority were Muslims and did not accept French personal law. As *citoyens* they sent an elected deputy to the French Chamber of Deputies, and elected their own municipal councils and mayors, as well as half the members of the *Conseil-Général*, which passed the budget for the whole colony. In all other respects the areas outside the four communes in Senegal were administered on the same basis as the rest of French Black Africa.

Up until 1945 very little was done by the French to develop their Black African territories, the majority of which were among the poorest on the continent. They were looked on principally as suppliers of raw materials – foodstuffs in particular – for the metropolis, and administrative taxation and labour policies were directed to ensuring their maximum productivity.   *M.C.*

The constituent colonies of the two federations were uniformly administered. Each was divided into *cercles* headed by a French *commandant*; the *cercles* were in turn divided into subdivisions headed by a French *chef*. The latter directly controlled the activities of the African *chefs de canton*, some of whom were chosen on the basis of traditional claims to office, others on the basis of proven loyalty to France or their literacy in French. The village chiefs were responsible for the day to day administration of the African population, who were classified as French *sujets* (subjects) as distinct from *citoyens* (citizens). This latter status could in theory be attained by Africans who had sufficient French education and were monogamous Christians; by 1940 less than 2000 Africans had been formally assimilated in this way. As *sujets*, all adult Africans were subject to the *corvée* (forced labour on public projects), to the *indigénat* (a summary code of administrative justice under which alleged offenders could be imprisoned without trial by the French administrative officer), to obligatory military service in the case of males, and to compulsory crop cultivation. The village chief was responsible for keeping order in his village, producing labour and military recruits and ensuring cultivation of crops when required by the administration. He was also responsible for collecting taxes, which were fixed at a rate that forced men in areas that did not produce cash crops, such as Niger and Upper Volta, to seek work in richer colonies like Ivory Coast and Senegal. In certain instances – particularly in the Congo, Ivory Coast and Cameroon – labour was compulsorily recruited for private enterprise particularly on plantations.

British West Africa

In British West Africa the period between the two world wars was comparatively tranquil. There were few risings against the colonial regime, while nationalist protest until the late 1930s was largely conducted in a gentlemanly, 'constitutionalist' fashion, and was confined to the coastal capitals of Lagos, Accra and Freetown. Only in the 1930s – with the return of Nnamdi Azikiwe* from America (first to the Gold Coast to edit the *African Morning Post* and then to Lagos where he set up *The West African Pilot* in 1937) and the foundation of the Sierra Leone Youth Movement by I.T.A. Wallace-Johnson in 1938 – were the British authorities given a foretaste of the style of politics that was to predominate after the Second World War.* Whereas until then nationalists had been content to demand reforms in the colonial system largely directed at giving them greater participation in it, Azikiwe, Wallace-Johnson and, to a lesser extent, J.B. Danquah in the Gold Coast began to challenge the right of the British to administer them at all.

The inter-war years saw little economic development, for the depression that followed the First World War and the world economic crisis of the 1930s meant that there were few funds available for either public or private investment. With the notable exception of Sir Gordon Guggisberg, the development-conscious Governor of the Gold Coast (1919–27), the predominant attitude of colonial rulers as far as the economies of the West African territories was concerned was a *laissez-faire* one. The expatriate import-export companies, such as the United Africa Company and John Holt, had practically a free hand, and fixed the prices paid to producers so that there would be no competition among the companies. The most notorious example of this was the price-ring formed by the expatriate cocoa buyers in the Gold Coast and western Nigeria which provoked a prolonged hold-up of sales by cocoa-farmers that ultimately brought about government intervention. This was a presage of the increasing role of government in the economy during the war and after.

The war was to increase dramatically the level of economic activity in West Africa. On the eve of the outbreak, however, it was not even as high as it had been in the early 1920s, as the trade figures for Nigeria show:

NIGERIA'S OVERSEAS TRADE, 1921 AND 1938

Date	Imports	Exports	Total trade
1921	£10 237 000	£8 258 000	£18 495 000
1938	£ 8 632 000	£9 702 000	£18 334 000

Source: Michael Crowder, *West Africa under Colonial Rule* (London, 1968)

I.T.A. Wallace-Johnson (1894–1965): the most radical of the West African nationalists of the inter-war period

If there was no economic revolution in the lives of the people administered by the British during the inter-war years, a profound if largely unobserved social revolution was taking place. In this 20-year period, large numbers of children attended European-type schools opened by government or missionaries, or founded by parents who saw Western education as the only way to advancement in the colonial order. Some, like Azikiwe and Kwame Nkrumah,* sought abroad the university education that was not available at home. It was the increasing number of colonial subjects with secondary or university education who became sensitized to the paradox of a democratic government in Britain – about which they were taught in school – governing autocratically in the colonies. They began to demand that Britain should practice what it preached. The British, however, made only minimal concessions to the democratic ideal in the West African colonies. In 1923, for example, Governor Sir Hugh Clifford restored the Nigerian Legislative Council, which that most autocratic of colonial governors, Lord Lugard, had abolished. However, only four of the unofficial seats were elected ones. The rest were held by Nigerians nominated by the colonial government, which, as in the legislative councils of the other West African colonies, had an official majority. The executive councils presided over by the governors had no African members and also had official majorities. Thus the governors could always ensure the enactment of legislation which they initiated.

As far as participation by Africans in their own administration was

concerned, the colonial regime concentrated on the Native Authorities which were organs of local self-government with limited executive and legislative powers. But this in no way appeased the educated elite, for the Native Authorities were based on those who would have ruled in pre-colonial times – emirs and chiefs – in whom sole executive, judicial and legislative authority was often vested. Such a system worked relatively well in an area like northern Nigeria where emirs had been accustomed to such powers, and where social change was minimal. The presence of traditionally strong chiefs was, however, no guarantee of the effectiveness of the Native Authority system – particularly where education and economic development had spurred social change, as in the Akan areas of the Gold Coast. The system could provoke overt opposition in areas where the authority of chiefs had been severely circumscribed in pre-colonial times or where, as in south-eastern Nigeria, there had been no executive chiefs at all. When these chiefs – created by the colonial authorities in the case of south-eastern Nigeria – attempted to collect taxes, they provoked great resentment on the part of the people they were supposed to govern. In south-eastern Nigeria there were riots in 1929 against the colonially created chiefs which led the colonial administration to restructure the Native Authorities to conform to the pre-colonial pattern of authority, which had usually been that of the elders.

Whatever changes the colonial rulers made the educated elite did not feel that they had a place in these Native Authorities, even though

Tanganyika

Tanganyika was formed from the reduced area of the former German East Africa.★ (The former residencies of Ruanda and Urundi were excised and placed under Belgian rule.) The new colony was administered by Britain under a League of Nations Mandate. An *ad hoc* administration based on the German system was continued until 1925. Thereafter a system of Indirect Rule based on the West African (and particularly Nigerian) model was introduced. Native Authorities – based on what were thought to be pre-colonial political tribal units – were established with salaried chiefs, courts and treasuries. Legislation made this system uniform throughout the territory.

The fall of world prices in the early 1930s occasioned by the world economic crisis led to a rapid decline in agricultural production which threatened the financial solvency of the colonial administration. The official response was legislation and unofficial coercion which increasingly regulated the kind and quantity of crops produced by African cultivators, and then closely determined how those crops were marketed. The economic and political position of Indian merchants and European sisal plantation owners was enhanced, but these immigrant groups never sought to control administrative policy to the extent that occurred in neighbouring Kenya.

Kenya

Kenya (the name substituted for the East African Protectorate in 1920) had the largest concentration of European and Indian settlers in East Africa. Although the white settlers were not able to achieve their goal of self-government (as in Southern Rhodesia★) they exerted a disproportionate political influence on the colonial administration. Africans were encouraged to participate in decision-making only at a parochial level, particularly in the Local Native Councils established in 1924–5.

The inter-war economic crisis affected each racial community in different ways. European settlers, who controlled, but under-utilized, 20 per cent of the arable land, were given government loans and preferential access to agricultural extension services and transport facilities. They were also protected against African competition in the production of livestock and certain crops such as coffee. The role of Indian merchants was generally strengthened. The African population – as in Tanganyika – was coerced into increased agricultural production and lower wages. These policies, combined with rapid population growth and an unequal racial division of land, led to severe land shortage and soil deterioration in the African areas. The Kikuyu peoples were particularly badly affected. African political organizations, which became prominent in the 1930s (the Kikuyu Central Association, North Kavirondo Central Association, Taita Hills Association, and the Ukamba Members Association), were primarily concerned with land grievances.

A cocoa plantation (1922) in the part of former German Cameroon administered by Nigeria after the First World War

it was hoped that they would use their education and talents to help modernize local government institutions rather than concern themselves with those at the centre. But the educated elite increasingly saw the Native Authorities as representing divisive elements in the state, reflecting as they did differences between peoples inhabiting the colony-states, and vesting powers in chiefs who were concerned with preserving the past, and did not look beyond the frontiers of their Native Authorities. The elite identified increasingly with their respective colony-states, which they wished to transform into nations independent of alien rule.   *M.C.*

British East Africa

The history of East Africa in the inter-war period was characterized by measures to standardize 'native administration' in the 1920s, by drastic attempts to counter the disruption caused by the economic crisis in the 1930s, and by an underlying struggle between white settlers and Indian merchants to influence political decisions at the territorial level. Nascent African associations were beginning to emerge which questioned some of the assumptions of colonial rule. British-administered East Africa was estimated in 1939 to have a population consisting of 15.7 million Africans, 133 000 Indians, and 33 000 Europeans.

Uganda

Uganda had an insignificant European agricultural community, which ceased to be of any economic importance from the early 1920s on. The economic initiative lay rather with African peasants cultivating cotton. Cotton cultivation spread rapidly throughout Uganda in the inter-war period and became the main export item. The main grievance of African producers in this period centred on the virtual monopoly – encouraged by government regulation – of cotton buying and ginning enjoyed by Indian and European merchants.

Efforts were made – as in the other East African colonies – to standardize the methods of African administration. This involved both the restriction of the unique wide autonomy given to the

Below: an Indian trader and African labourers with a consignment of seed cotton *en route* to the ginnery, Lake Kyoga, Uganda. Bottom: Sayyid Ali ibn Hamoud, Sultan of Zanzibar, with the British Consul-General and his staff

kingdom of Buganda under an agreement made with the British in 1900, and the extension of a chieftainship system (based on the Bugandan model) to other societies in Uganda, which had previously lacked hierarchical, centralized forms of government.

Zanzibar

Zanzibar was theoretically under the control of the Governor of Kenya until 1925. Thereafter, the Sultan of Zanzibar was the nominal head of government with a British Resident and his officials exerting effective control. It became official British policy to support the political dominance of an Arab land-owning aristocracy. This policy was threatened by the Depression, which placed many Arab (and African) clove planters deeply in debt to Indian financiers. In 1934 the administration responded by applying a moratorium on debts owed by Arabs and Africans, and by restricting the transfer of land to Indians. In 1937 Indian merchants were excluded from the export clove trade. They (and their associates in India) responded with a crippling boycott. In the following year a compromise restored Indian commercial rights and established a reduced level of debt to be repaid by planters. War-time prosperity soon led to the elimination of many of these debts.

L.E.L.

British Central Africa

Southern Rhodesia

By 1920 most whites in Southern Rhodesia wanted 'responsible government' – rule by a government elected by themselves – in place of administration by the British South Africa Company★ (BSAC). The BSAC wished the country to become a fifth province of South Africa, but this option was rejected by a white referendum in 1922. Instead, in 1923, Britain gave the settlers internal self-government, while retaining control over foreign policy and a power to veto laws affecting the constitution and African rights. This did not, however, prevent the Southern Rhodesian government from passing laws to protect whites against economic competition from Africans. The Land Apportionment Act of 1930 gave the 50 000 whites exclusive access to half the country, including the best farming land. The land rights of Africans, who then numbered about 1 million, were largely confined to reserves, many of which were infertile or overcrowded. A few 'native purchase areas' were created for African commercial farmers, but they were handicapped by discriminatory marketing arrangements and inadequate facilities. Most African men became ever more dependent on selling their labour, yet in the last resort they remained dependent on the reserves, for pass-laws prevented them from settling permanently in towns. Besides, the prospects of African wage-earners were severely restricted by the Industrial Conciliation

Hanging up tobacco leaves to dry, Southern Rhodesia, c. 1930

Act of 1934, which legalized an industrial colour bar and denied African workers effective bargaining powers. Thus African incomes were systematically minimized to ensure the survival of white-owned enterprise. As a result, between 1920 and 1940 the country reduced its dependence on immigrant labour from Mozambique, Nyasaland and Northern Rhodesia, even though the number of African wage-earners almost doubled. The output of gold, the chief export, had stagnated during the 1920s, but it rose steadily after 1931, while exports of asbestos, chrome and tobacco also increased.

Northern Rhodesia

The administration of Northern Rhodesia was transferred in 1924 from the BSAC to the Colonial Office. The white population – less than 4000 in 1921 – was given representation in a Legislative Council. Elected members were outnumbered by civil servants, but the government sought to encourage white immigration by reserving for European use the best farmland, along the railway and in the far north and east. As in Southern Rhodesia, many Africans were moved into reserves which soon became overcrowded; yet the expected influx of whites did not take place and land kept empty for them reverted to bush. Throughout the 1920s the country remained very poor. Its chief export in 1926 was tobacco, and in 1928–30 zinc and vanadium from the mine at Broken Hill.

Meanwhile, however, the basis had been laid for future prosperity: modern techniques of prospecting had located vast deposits of copper near the headwaters of the Kafue River. Two mines were developed by Rhodesia Selection Trust, and two by the Anglo-American Corporation. By 1932 their joint output had overtaken that of the Katanga mines and thereafter Northern Rhodesia was established as the fourth largest copper producer in the world. By 1940 24 000 Africans worked on the copper mines, and nearly 2500 whites. Many

Africans had gone on strike in 1935; this prompted the white mineworkers to form a trade union and to reinforce an informal colour bar in the industry. This was one reason why African miners struck again in 1940. The government made a few belated reforms, but like the mine companies it continued to regard African workers as only temporary visitors from the countryside. Besides, those employed within Northern Rhodesia were still outnumbered by those working beyond its borders, mainly in Southern Rhodesia and Tanganyika but also in South Africa. The growing prosperity of the copper industry, stimulated by rearmament in Europe, was little help to the government, for Britain took half the income tax levied on the mine companies, and in any case much of their pre-tax profits was drained away in royalties exacted (on a dubious legal title) by the BSAC.

Nyasaland

Policy in Nyasaland was shaped partly by local white pressure but still more by larger imperial interests. Planters in the Shire Highlands, growing tea and tobacco, retained access to very cheap labour, and though by the 1930s many Africans grew cotton and tobacco, their needs were firmly subordinated to those of white employers. Yet the latter's exports were worth much less than those of Europeans in Southern Rhodesia or Kenya; in 1939 the white population was still barely 2000; and their representatives in the Legislative Council were all nominated by the Governor. The expansion of cash-crop production, whether white or black, was inhibited by the high freight rates charged by the railway that from 1924 linked Nyasaland to the sea at Beira. This had been underwritten by Britain in order to maintain influence in Mozambique, and thus elsewhere in southern Africa. The railway's debt charges, however, had to be paid by the Nyasaland government. This was a crippling financial burden, which virtually precluded any spending on social services or other public investment in local production. In 1936 the government committed itself to the systematic export of African labour, chiefly to Southern Rhodesia and South Africa, areas that had in any case long been the chief source of cash for people in the northern districts.

Plans for amalgamation

During the 1930s moves were made towards uniting the British territories in Central Africa. The growth of the Copperbelt had shown whites in the south that Northern Rhodesia was no longer a poor relation, and Godfrey Huggins, who became Prime Minister of Southern Rhodesia in 1933, argued strongly in favour of amalgamation. He was supported by many whites in the north, who feared that the Colonial Office would never let them obtain self-government on their own. In 1938 a Royal Commission from Britain encountered solid opposition to amalgamation from African witnesses in Northern Rhodesia and Nyasaland, and further debate was interrupted by the Second World War.★   *A.D.R.*

Egypt and the Sudan

The inter-war period was a time of troubles in Egypt and the Sudan, dominated by the demands of emerging nationalisms on the one hand, and by British determination, on the other, to secure imperial interests. These two forces were fundamentally incompatible: in the mid-1930s, however, the gap between them was narrowed – if only temporarily – through concessions made by the British aimed at gaining nationalist support against the growing threat from the Axis powers.

Immediately after the conclusion of the First World War,* the dormant force of Egyptian opposition to British occupation burst to the surface. The protectorate which had been declared by Britain in 1914 had been seen in Egypt as a war-time measure that should now be abolished in preparation for Egyptian independence. The British intention of retaining the protectorate, combined with the justified grievances of the peasantry who had suffered from the demands of the British war effort, gave popular force to the demands of the nationalists led by Saad Zaghlul. When the British government refused to negotiate, widespread disorder resulted. The High

Commissioner, Sir Reginald Wingate, was recalled and superseded by Lord Allenby, and order was restored. British efforts at conciliation were vitiated by an unwillingness to give up the protectorate and by Zaghlul's hold on Egyptian popular opinion. To break this impasse the British government unilaterally declared Egyptian independence in February 1922, but reserved for future negotiations arrangements for the defence of Egypt, the safeguarding of imperial communications, the protection of minorities, and the question of the Sudan. Although the nationalists rejected these limitations, Egypt became a constitutional monarchy with a bicameral parliament in 1923. In January 1924, after a stunning election victory, Zaghlul's party, the *Wafd*, came to power with Zaghlul as the first democratically chosen prime minister of a nominally independent Egypt.

In the Sudan the effects of the war were more positive, in that the economy benefited from the demands for food and animals made by the Egyptian Expeditionary Force in the campaign against the Turks. But the Egyptian nationalist rising in 1919 and a new political consciousness among educated Sudanese produced an anti-British movement. This culminated in a series of demonstrations and other incidents in 1924, fomented by the White Flag League and other organizations. In November of that year the Governor-General, Sir Lee Stack, who was also *sirdar* (commander-in-chief) of the Egyptian

Saad Zaghlul (centre) with his ministers, 1924

army, was assassinated in Cairo by Egyptian extremists. Blaming the recent disturbances in the Sudan on Egyptian agitation, and anxious to take advantage of the shock occasioned by Stack's murder, Allenby issued an ultimatum to the *Wafd* government, demanding the evacuation of Egyptian army units from the Sudan and announcing that irrigation from the Nile in the Sudan's Gezira Scheme would be increased to an 'unlimited' extent. Zaghlul resigned. As the evacuation of the Egyptian units progressed, members of a Sudanese battalion refused the orders of British superiors and were killed, resisting to the last man from the military hospital buildings in Khartoum.

The cathartic effect in the Sudan of the events of 1924 ushered in a period of relative quiet and political reaction. Egypt's part in the Condominium* by which it ruled the Sudan jointly with Britain was abolished in all but name. The British-manned Sudan government blamed the educated elite for the disturbances, and in an attempt to neutralize them and to diminish the influence of the country's powerful religious leaders, it adopted the Nigerian model of Indirect Rule as its administrative policy. During the governor-generalship of Sir John Maffey (1926–33) the role of the educated class was consequently reduced, while traditional authority was enhanced. By the mid-1930s, however, the British had begun to realize that the Sudan's traditional political system was far too decayed to be usefully revived, and a more balanced administrative policy was resumed. At the same time, a more sophisticated secular nationalist movement, less radical than the anti-British groups of 1924, began to emerge. This led, in 1938, to the establishment of the Graduates' General Congress, which was hampered, however, by a lack of mass support.

In Egypt the period following the British ultimatum and the resignation of Zaghlul in 1924 was characterized by a series of unsuccessful negotiations between Britain and Egypt over the 'reserved points' in the 1922 declaration. The Sudan, claimed by Egyptian nationalists as Egyptian territory, but governed still under the terms of the 1899 Condominium Agreement, was an insoluble issue. Zaghlul, although kept from power, continued to dominate politics until his death in 1927. The Nile Waters Agreement in 1929 eased the tension caused by the Gezira clause in Allenby's ultimatum by allotting a greater share of water which could be used for irrigation to Egypt. In 1936, as a consequence of the growing threat posed by Italy* in North-East Africa and increasingly disturbing developments in Europe, an Anglo-Egyptian treaty was signed. Largely avoiding the question of the Sudan's constitutional status, the treaty provided for an Anglo-Egyptian military alliance and the maintenance of a British garrison in the Suez Canal Zone. In the aftermath of this agreement, the Montreux Convention of 1937 called for the abolition of the Capitulations (treaties by which the European powers and the USA enjoyed special rights in Egypt), and Egypt became a member of the League of Nations.   *M. W. D.*

Italy and the Horn

Italian colonial policy after the First World War* was greatly influenced by Mussolini's seizure of power in 1922. The fascist regime embarked on fierce military operations in 1922–9 to gain control of the Libyan province of Cyrenaica, then only nominally under Italian rule, and likewise occupied the Nogal area of Italian Somaliland in 1925–6. In the early 1930s Mussolini turned his attention to Ethiopia. In 1932 he sent his Minister of the Colonies, General De Bono, to inspect Eritrea. On his return the fascists agreed that Italy's 'colonial future must be sought in East Africa.' Investment in Eritrea and Somaliland was increased, roads were improved, and harbours were expanded at Massawa and Mogadishu.

The pretext for Italy's invasion of Ethiopia came in 1934 when an

Below: Ras Tafari (later Emperor Haile Selassie) after becoming Regent of Ethiopia in 1916. Bottom: Italians in Mogadishu, Italian Somaliland celebrate an Italian victory in Ethiopia, 1936

Anglo-Ethiopian boundary commission was confronted by Italian troops at Wal Wal, 100km on the Ethiopian side of the frontier with Italian Somaliland, where Ethiopian and Italian soldiers clashed on 5 December. Italy demanded an apology and recognition of Italian sovereignty there. Emperor Haile Selassie refused, proposing international arbitration. Mussolini rejected this, whereupon the Emperor appealed to the League of Nations, which procrastinated for 11 months while the Italians prepared for war. Britain and France meanwhile agreed in the event of a conflict to rule out military sanctions against Italy or the closure of the Suez Canal.

Mussolini attacked on 3 October 1935. The League condemned Italy, but imposed only limited economic sanctions. The British Foreign Secretary, Sir Samuel Hoare, and the French Premier, Pierre Laval, devised a compromise, which was unacceptable to either party and led to much indignation in Britain. Hoare resigned.

Despite vast military superiority the Italians at first made slow progress. Mussolini, fearing the imposition of further sanctions, ordered the use of poison gas. Ethiopian resistance began to crumble early in 1936 and Italian troops entered Addis Ababa on 5 May, the Emperor having left for Europe. Mussolini proclaimed the creation of the Italian East African empire on 9 May. Haile Selassie addressed the League of Nations in June, but it shortly afterwards abandoned sanctions.

The Italians, mainly for strategic reasons, devoted most of their efforts in Ethiopia to road-building. Other economic activity took second place. Trade stagnated, partly because of the demonetization of the Maria Theresa dollar (Ethiopia's traditional currency) and the explusion of foreign traders. Attempts at large-scale Italian settlement were limited for lack of funds. Laws were enacted prohibiting inter-racial cohabitation, and Addis Ababa and other towns were divided into European and 'native' quarters. Education for the subject population was restricted to prevent the emergence of a 'native intelligentsia'.

Armed resistance meanwhile continued, particularly in Gojam, Amhara and Shoa. An attempted assassination of the Italian Viceroy, General Graziani, in February 1937, was followed by the massacre of several thousand Ethiopians. Many survivors fled to join resistance forces. Graziani, unable to crush the rebellion, was replaced by the Duke of Aosta, who adopted a more liberal, though still avowedly racist policy.

Mussolini's entry into the European war in June 1940 isolated his empire. The Italians overran British Somaliland, but in January 1941 Allied forces attacked from the Sudan and Kenya, while Emperor Haile Selassie entered Gojjam to lead a patriot army. The fascist empire crumbled rapidly. Addis Ababa was occupied by South African forces on 6 April, the Emperor returned to the capital on 5 May, and the last Italian forces surrendered at Gondar in November.   *R.K.P.P.*

Belgian Africa

The limits of growth under constraint, 1919–24

The First World War seriously damaged Belgium's economy and, in the immediate post-war years, its capitalists sought to re-establish its position as a supplier of bulk or semi-processed commodities by greatly expanding the Congo's tropical produce and minerals production. A related objective was to reduce foreign control over mineral extraction and processing. Major Belgian investments were made in communications, and in developing mining enterprises in Upper-Katanga, Kasai and Kilo Moto, each of which employed more than 20 000 African labourers by the mid-1920s.

Mining was almost entirely controlled by the *Société Générale de Belgique* and other great financial interests (such as *Empain* and the *Banque de Bruxelles*). A pioneering multi-national, Lever, with its *Huileries du Congo Belge*, had also entered the Belgian Congo. In the early 1920s, however, such large enterprises still did not dominate the economy. Rather, the weakness of the Belgian currency encouraged numerous small firms and petty traders to engage in the trade in such commodities as palm-oil and copal. Paid for in devalued francs these were then sold on the world market for sterling.

By 1924, however, the export boom faced breakdown. Railways and ports were unable to handle the load and, more fundamentally, African societies were disrupted to the point of collapse by the export drive. In particular they faced massive dislocations of manpower, enforced savings through the manipulation of import duties, compulsory labour on a vast scale (notably on road construction) and the demand both for export produce and food for local consumption.

Extracting oil from palm nuts with a hand-press in a village in the Belgian Congo, 1920

Disruption was such that large companies came to fear that their labour reserves would not be able to reproduce themselves – a fear echoed by missionaries and colonial administrators.

Disruption bred social unrest – notably the Kimbanguist movement in the Lower Congo in 1921 – but, by the mid-1920s, natural forces (such as the continuing long-term effects of major epidemics: the last being the influenza pandemic of 1918–19), and repressive government policies had cowed African opposition. Opposition was, in any case, deeply divided, not least because of the localist policies of the highly decentralized administration, Christian missionaries and labour recruiters, who sowed the seeds of later more potent ethnic divisions. The demands of economic efficiency, then – the need to maintain the export drive – rather than the need to respond to active social unrest, was the main impetus for the reform of the colonial system which began in the second half of the 1920s.

Towards a new colonial order, 1924–33

Homogeneous in both their social background and their interlocking economic interests, the managers of state, Church, and large-scale capitalist enterprise were readily able to plan a reoriented colonial policy. Most urgent in their view was the need to encourage the development of a productive, efficient African population, ensuring that its familiar, 'customary' surroundings would be outwardly respected, while this rural society was linked organically to the capitalist sectors of the economy. Through the late 1920s and early 1930s, in a remarkable exercise of social engineering, mixed state-big business *ad hoc* committees developed blueprints for a new colonial order. To save manpower, communications were decisively improved, the large industries brought more capital-intensive tech-

A model industrial village established by *Union Minière* at Elisabethville, Belgian Congo, 1928

niques, and the practice spread of stabilizing African families in model industrial camps. In 1925–6, as a part of this colonial overhaul, the state began subsidizing large-scale elementary education by Roman Catholic missions, nearly all of which were Belgian. It was felt that mission schools would exercise both a moral and a 'Belgianizing' influence in rural areas.

The world economic depression of the 1930s brought investment to a halt, and this slowed down industrial production as well as the rise in productivity which had taken place after 1926. Thousands of jobs were lost in mining and in processing activities, but in several branches of colonial industry the period won a reprieve for the old style labour-intensive organization of production. On the whole, however, the recession offered the opportunity to implement some essential aspects of the new colonial policy. In particular, it squeezed out many small firms, ushering in a period of dominance by large-scale capital. It led to the unprecedented mobilization of African villagers for market-oriented agriculture and it dealt a deadly blow to the 'wasteful' collecting economy. Through the introduction of a production-oriented form of indirect rule, state officials hoped to be in a position to manage the orderly reproduction of a stable, healthy, rural society, a prerequisite of further accumulation of capital. By 1936 there were an estimated 950 000 cotton growers at work in the Congo.

'Total civilization', 1934–9

The expression 'total civilization' is borrowed from Governor P. Ryckmans. It captures the essence of an 'ethical policy' carried out through technocratic, authoritarian rule. During this period, mining remained a corner-stone of the colonial economy, and it is in the mining camps that the blueprint for a 'total civilization' came nearest to reality. At the same time, it was more clearly recognized that African agriculture was after all the main component of Congo's national product. Processing of agricultural produce by European settlers or industrialists was regarded as a preliminary step to the development of an industrial production economy geared to the local market. In fact, this programme called for long-term accumulation in the Congo, at the price of eventual transfers of activity from metropolitan to colonial branches of Belgian industry. Also basic to the operation of the system was the steady transfer of remittances from the Congo to Belgium. The export of colonial capital to Belgium gathered momentum in the 1930s.

This period is marked by the powerlessness of African resistance, as had been made clear by the Kwilu revolt of 1931 (which had cost one European and 400 African lives). Beyond the occasional flare-up of millenarian movements, or the silent obstruction of the rural masses, new great divides opened in African society. They separated the literate from the illiterate (*basendji*), and they posed fresh challenges to colonial rule.   *J.-L.V.*

Portuguese Africa

The period between the world wars was not one of great colonial initiatives in Portugal. From 1910 to 1926 an increasingly unstable democratic republic found little time, funds or manpower to devote to African affairs. After 1926 a corporative state, loosely modelled on Benito Mussolini's Italy, was created by army officers, who were increasingly guided by a former university teacher called António Salazar. In the 1930s Salazar restricted colonial development by insisting on balanced books without metropolitan assistance. Throughout this period Portuguese emigrants steadfastly refused to choose the colonies in preference to Brazil, and Portuguese investors equally declined to risk capital in Africa. Angola remained a convict colony in the popular mind, and much of Mozambique was effectively an extension of British imperial interests. The three small Portuguese colonies of West Africa attracted even less attention.

Angola

The inter-war years saw some revival of the Angolan coffee industry as shopkeepers branched out into small plantation production. When, in 1929, the Benguela railway reached the copper mines in the Belgian Congo,* new markets for maize and dried fish developed. Diamonds were located in the remote north-east province and significant quantities of gem stones were marketed through the South African company De Beers. All these activities required labour. So did the annual maintenance of seasonal tracks. The major function of local government became the recruitment of unwilling labourers who were compulsorily allocated to state and private enterprise and often dispatched on contract to distant parts. Some Angolans were also recruited for work in the neighbouring industrial colonies ruled by Belgium and Britain.

Mozambique

Labour was more comprehensively and systematically recruited in Mozambique than in Angola. Sugar plantations operated on a far larger scale than the Angolan coffee farms of the period and so controlled local, regional and long-distance supplies of male labour. Female labour was in some areas compelled to grow government crops of rice. The buying and trucking of cashews was frequently in the hands of Indian shopkeepers. In coastal areas peasant coconut producers were gradually squeezed out by large firms to become wage-earners. The largest single labour migration was the southern migration to the gold mines of South Africa. Workers who failed to sign up with the Witwatersrand recruiters were liable to serve six months *chibalo* (forced labour) on the road gangs. In exchange for the right to recruit Mozambique labour, South Africa used the port of Lourenço Marques for part of the Transvaal's international trade.

This transit traffic through Beira gave Mozambique a reliable national income independent of any local productive enterprise. This income was fortified by fees on migrant labour, which were partially paid in gold.

D.B.B.

Spanish Africa

From 1912 to 1920 Spanish administrations in northern Morocco had to contend with the opposition of various chieftains. This persistent struggle was intensified in 1921 when Spain suffered the worst European defeat in African history. The Abd el Krim brothers, and especially Mohammed, led a rebellion which inflicted upon the Spaniards the resounding defeat of Anual (21 July 1921), killing the commander-in-chief, General Silvestre, and between 13 000 and 19 000 Spanish soldiers. They swept away all the garrisons from the eastern Rif, only stopping short of Melilla. From then on, the fight against the Rifians was to fully occupy the Spanish army for six years. The army's frustrations were instrumental in the coming into power of the dictator Primo de Rivera, who pulled out of the interior at a tremendous cost: the evacuation of Chaouen (Nov-Dec 1924) cost the lives of 800 officers and 17 000–20 000 casualties among the ranks. However, notwithstanding his unusual abilities as a warrior and a statesman, Abd el Krim was no match for the combined forces of Spain and (from 1925) France. In September 1925 the Spanish counter-offensive began to roll the Rifians back. Abd el Krim surrendered to the French in 1926. Mopping up operations lasted until the spring of 1927 within 'Spanish Morocco'. Spain's difficulties and humiliations in its protectorate were partly responsible for the demise of the monarchy (1931) and the outbreak of the Spanish Civil War. Whatever economic development was planned for the Spanish zone (mostly mining) was, in turn, halted by the war, to which Morocco contributed large contingents on Franco's side.

Further south, Ifni was peacefully occupied in 1934 after the French had eventually subdued Berber resistance in southern Morocco. The occupation of the Sahara took place in the same year, but scientific exploration there only started in 1945. In Spanish Guinea, Rio Muni was totally pacified in 1925-6. Catholic missions and lumbering companies penetrated the country occupied by the Fang ethnic group. The Civil War left very minor scars in the colony but lack of funds delayed development until well after the end of the war, when a heavy-handed paternalism combined with Catalan capitalism began to tap Spanish Guinea's timber resources and to develop cocoa and coffee plantations.

R.P.

Southern Africa

In 1919 whites in South Africa possessed more power than any other settler group on the continent. During the 19th century superior force had enabled them to occupy much of the better agricultural land, and the spoils of an expanding industrial economy based on immense mineral wealth were theirs. Africans were assigned to the least favourable and most remote areas, where, finding increasing difficulty in supporting a rapidly growing population, they served as a reservoir of cheap unskilled labour for the white economy. Whites possessed a monopoly of political power, and in 1910 they had succeeded in eliminating any control of their affairs from Europe, the only settler group in Africa to do so.

Although throughout the inter-war period industry and commerce were controlled by English-speaking settlers, Afrikaners maintained firm control over the country's political system. Afrikaners were able to dominate political life partly because they outnumbered English-speakers in the ratio of about 3:2, and partly because when the Union constitution was formulated the rural districts, predominantly Afrikaner, were deliberately over-represented in parliament to offset English-speakers' electoral power in urban and industrial centres.

South Africa's wealth was unevenly distributed not only between the white and black populations, but also between different members of the white community. In the gold-bearing areas of the Rand near Johannesburg there existed a large white working class made up of skilled and semi-skilled workers and thousands of 'poor white' Afrikaners driven off the land by rural poverty. White workers were represented by powerful trade unions and were concerned to defend their status as an aristocracy of labour against the growing number of Africans employed in industry. When in 1922 the mine-owners threatened to employ Africans as skilled workers at lower wages than the whites enjoyed, a well-organized strike took place in defence of the industrial colour bar, the means by which white workers maintained exclusive control of skilled occupations. Violence erupted, and J.C. Smuts, the Prime Minister, used troops to put down the rebellion. In the 1924 general election Smuts's South African Party, which stood for Anglo-Afrikaner cooperation and a paternal policy towards Africans, was defeated, and a coalition of the Labour Party, which represented the views of the rebellious white

One of the demonstrations of white trade unionists that led up to the 1922 strike. The banner reads, 'Workers of the World Fight and Unite for a White South Africa'

miners, and the Afrikaner National Party, formed by General J.B.M. Hertzog in 1914, took office. Both the Labour Party and the National Party stood for the consolidation of white privilege, and in particular for the maintenance of the rights of the white working class.

Hertzog remained Prime Minister until 1939, after 1933 as the leader of a new political party, the United Party, formed when the Nationalists combined with Smuts's South African Party to combat jointly the effects on South Africa of the world economic depression. The vigorously nationalist right wing of Hertzog's party, led by D.F. Malan, refused to support the new arrangement and instead went into political opposition as the Purified National Party. In this way the National Party that has governed South Africa since 1948 came into being. However, much of the groundwork for its post-war apartheid* programme was undertaken in the two decades before it assumed office, for between 1924 and 1939 white privilege was progressively extended in almost every sphere of South African life. The industrial colour bar was consolidated: the rights of white workers were further protected by a series of legislative measures; government control over the labour market was extended; the unequal distribution of land in South Africa, whereby the majority African population was legally confined to only 13 per cent of the country's land area, was further entrenched; and in 1936 the parliamentary representation of Africans in Cape Province, a legacy of the days before Union, came to an end when African voters were removed from the common electoral roll and given the right to elect three whites to sit in parliament on their behalf.

The progressive erosion of African liberties and opportunities for social advancement did not pass by unchallenged. The main African political organization, the African National Congress (ANC), founded in 1912, consistently spoke out against white policies and pressed forward claims for more land, better wages and improved educational and employment opportunities. Largely controlled by lawyers, clergymen and journalists, the ANC sought to redress African grievances by constitutional means in close collaboration with liberal whites. Its influence upon government policy was negligible. The only mass protest organization to emerge during the inter-war years was a trade union, the Industrial and Commercial Workers' Union of Africa (ICU), founded in 1919 by a Nyasa clerk, Clements Kadalie, which, at the height of its activities, claimed a membership of over 100 000. The ICU was able to achieve some limited success in improving conditions for Africans both in the industrial areas and in the countryside, but it lacked good organization and a coherent programme. It failed to organize the urban African working class effectively, and by the late 1920s the movement had disintegrated because of internal weaknesses and official suppression.

During the inter-war years white South African politicians were anxious to extend the union. After the First World War* South Africa was granted a Mandate to administer the former German colony of

Clements Kadalie: founder of the Industrial and Commercial Workers' Union of Africa

South-West Africa on behalf of the League of Nations. In practice, South Africa governed the territory as if it were a province of the Union, brutally suppressing local resistance to its rule. South African politicians were less successful in persuading Britain to hand over to their control the neighbouring High Commission Territories of Basutoland, Bechuanaland and Swaziland. Although remaining British colonies, these territories nonetheless were completely dependent economically upon the Union, where most of their menfolk worked as migrant labourers. The possibility of Southern Rhodesia* joining the union evaporated in 1922 when, immediately before the ending of British South Africa Company administration, settlers there chose colonial self-government rather than incorporation in the Union and Afrikaner domination.

P.W.

Pan-Africanism and African nationalism to 1939

By 1939 African political groups existed in nearly every territory of the continent. Most were very small and only in North Africa did they attempt to secure a mass following and demand national independence. Although African political activity was widespread in the inter-war years, its purpose was to criticize and gain concessions from colonial rulers, not to take over power from them. Indeed, the ingredients for effective nationalist policies rarely existed. The process of territorial integration had then only recently been completed, often by continuing conquest. Modern economic development was just beginning, large areas of Africa were governed by traditional rulers under a system of indirect rule, and the number of formally educated Africans was extremely small.

Nationalism and pan-African sentiment in sub-Saharan Africa has its roots among the small educated elite in the coastal settlements of West Africa in the 19th century. The elite, composed largely of 'returned' Americans of African descent and freed slaves, or their descendants, was the product of Christian mission education and strongly influenced by 19th century ideas of progress and modernization. Members of the elite held leading positions in Church, state and commerce in the European colonial settlements, particularly Freetown, Sierra Leone, and controlled the government of the independent republic of Liberia,* which had been founded by black Americans. The elite not only expected to increase their role in colonial administration but also attempted, in the 1860s and 1870s, to establish modern 'national' governments for certain West African peoples. The outstanding intellectual figure of 19th century West African nationalism was Edward Wilmot Blyden (1832–1912), a West Indian, who believed that blacks could only achieve their full potential in Africa. He therefore advocated a 'back to Africa' movement for Afro-Americans and the creation of a unified pan-West African state, wrote widely on these topics, and was active politically in Sierra Leone, Liberia and Nigeria.

The European 'Scramble'* for Africa and the prevalent ideas of white racial superiority resulted in Africans being excluded from many social and political positions. This led many African Christians to challenge foreign mission control and to break away to form their own independent 'Ethiopian'* or 'Zionist' churches. Such churches were numerous and their beliefs and practices diverse. They became a means whereby Africans asserted their identity and they also often acted as vehicles for political and economic grievances against colonial rule. For example, independent churches were involved in anti-colonial rebellions in Natal (1906) and Nyasaland (1915) while sects in Central Africa in the 1920s and 1930s preached a form of millenarianism that predicted the imminent end of white rule. A

Edward Wilmot Blyden: pioneer pan-Africanist thinker and West African nationalist

cultural nationalism also developed among the elite of West Africa which promoted African customs, languages and the writing of history.

The first African political organizations were formed in the late 19th and early 20th centuries. In West and South Africa they were led by the educated elite who sought to protect their own economic and political interests and, more broadly, to protest against the loss of African rights in general. Groups such as the Aborigines Rights Protection Society in the Gold Coast (1897), the African National Congress in South Africa (1912) and the National Congress of British West Africa (1920) were constitutional-minded bodies that expressed their grievances through meetings, the local press, and the occasional delegation. In East Africa the various political associations that emerged out of the crisis of the First World War, like the Young Kavirondo Association (1921) and the Kikuyu Central Association (1924), were dominated initially by traditional rulers and tended to express the discontent of single ethnic groups. None of these political groups advocated separation from the European powers but rather reform of the colonial government, a solution to African economic grievances and, in Central and East Africa, an end to land alienation and limits to white settler control. Most groups were small and their support mainly urban and local. In certain cases they could command influential support, as in Dakar, where in 1914 Blaise Diagne was elected as the first African to represent Senegal in the French National Assembly. As is indicated by the names of organizations such as the Rhodesian Bantu Voters Association and the Tanganyika African Association, most political groups functioned within the territorial boundaries of a single colony. A few had wider, pan-African visions. The leaders of the National Congress of British West Africa, for example, envisaged a union of British West Africa. Diagne looked towards a unified French-speaking West African state.

As these various political groups did not aim to take over territorial governments are we justified in calling them 'nationalist'? Opinions

The deputation sent to London by the National Congress of British West Africa in 1920

Jomo Kenyatta – later first president of Kenya – speaking at a political meeting in Trafalgar Square, London, c. 1936

vary, as do definitions. Certainly these political organizations represented African interests against the incursions of foreign control and can therefore be regarded as the forerunners of the later mass nationalist parties that emerged after the Second World War.* In Central and East Africa modern nationalist parties claim a continuing link, both human and symbolic, with the political groups of the inter-war years and back to the movements of primary and secondary resistance to colonial rule. African political activity in the first four decades of the 20th century took various forms – revolts, strikes, voluntary associations, independent churches and schools – many of which had little to do with direct nationalist policies. Yet interwoven within some of these activities lie the strands of future nationalist expression. For example, the Kitawala (Watchtower Movement) and Kimbanguist independent churches, persecuted by the Belgian authorities in the Congo from the 1920s onwards, provided some of the strongest support for the nationalist cause in the late 1950s.

In the 1920s and 1930s a number of new influences bore upon African politics. Socialist ideas were promoted particularly by French-speaking black intellectuals and workers in Paris. However, the most effective adoption of socialist ideas was in the Industrial and Commercial Workers Union* (ICU) founded by Clements Kadalie in South Africa in 1919. Within a few years the ICU claimed 100000 members throughout the country, had branches in Central Africa, and was involved in overtly political activities. Africans studying abroad during the inter-war years formed political unions which promoted a more radical anti-colonial line. Students who had belonged to the West African Student Union in London on their return to Africa helped form local youth groups such as the Nigerian Youth Movement (1936). Through a more militant press they helped whip up African grievances and at local elections successfully challenged

the old and cautious elite politicians. It is, however, important not to exaggerate the political influence of those Africans who had studied abroad. Ordinary men – clerks, farmers, and traders – constituted a substantial and often decisive backbone to the various African associations and political groups.

Pan-African ideas had a significant influence in African politics in the inter-war years. The first pan-African congress was held in London in 1900; others were to follow after 1919. Overwhelmingly the membership was black American and was to remain so until the fifth congress at Manchester in 1945. Pan-African sentiment was encouraged in Africa in the early 1920s by the short-lived United Negro Improvement Association formed by Marcus Garvey* (1887–1940) in New York. Garvey's populist racial politics and his message of a united 'Africa for the Africans' received little sympathy from the more intellectual pan-Africanists represented by the dominant figure of W.E.B. Du Bois (1868–1963). Nevertheless Garvey's influence throughout the continent was considerable, encouraging African political aspirations and also a sense of racial pride. During the 1930s Léopold Senghor,* Aimé Césaire and other French-speaking intellectuals from West Africa and the Caribbean formulated the concept of *négritude*. This proclaimed a pride in the African heritage and renounced the French colonial idea of assimilation. *Négritude*, which can be seen as an expression of cultural isolation, had only slight influence on ordinary Africans. A more effective cement for pan-African feeling and protest in both Africa and the Americas was the Italian invasion of Ethiopia* in 1935. By and large, pan-Africanism was a sentiment that rarely overcame the ethnic divisions existing within each African territory let alone those that marked off different parts of the continent. Its contribution to African nationalism has been more rhetoric than reality.   *D.K.*

The Second World War

The Second World War marked a turning point in the colonial history of Africa. Not only did it bring an end to the world economic depression; it also led to a restructuring of the world political order that was to have long-term consequences for the future of Africa. The economies of the principal colonial powers in Africa, France and Britain, were shattered by the war. France was overrun by the Germans, while Britain lost its Far Eastern colonies to the Japanese, a 'coloured' race, thus destroying the myth of white invincibility. France and Belgium, vanquished by the Germans, existed as free entities only in their equatorial African colonies. The colonial relationship came under increasing criticism from the Americans and Russians, albeit from radically different political perspectives. The Americans entrenched their anti-colonialism in the Atlantic Charter, signed by Franklin Roosevelt and Winston Churchill, which confirmed the 'right of all people to choose the form of government in which they live', and stated that the aim of the Allies was 'to see the sovereign rights and self-government restored to those who have been forcibly deprived of them.' Churchill subsequently denied that these sections of the Charter applied to Britain's African colonies. But they proved an inspiration to many shades of African nationalists. Russian criticism of imperialism also inspired African nationalists, even if on a lesser scale than the Charter. The *Groupes d'Etudes Communistes*, set up by French Communists in French West Africa after it had rallied to General de Gaulle, had an important influence on the ideological and organizational orientation of what was to become its largest political party, the *Rassemblement Démocratique Africaine*, founded in Bamako in 1946.

The war likewise modified the political and economic views of those colonial powers that participated in it–France, Britain and Belgium. By contrast, Spain and Portugal, which remained neutral throughout, were little affected by it. In the face of German propaganda, both the French and the British had to appeal to their subjects to remain loyal and encourage them so to do with promises of political and social reform. Thus at the famous Brazzaville Conference of 1944, which considered the future of their empire, the French introduced a programme of massive economic and social reform–FIDES: *Fonds d'Investissement et de Développement Economique et Sociale*–as well as the outline of a new constitution whereby Africa would be closely integrated in a French Union. At the same time, Africans would have a much larger say in their own affairs, and the abuses of the colonial regime–forced labour, the status of *sujet* and the *indigénat*,* or summary administrative justice–would be abolished. The British introduced their Colonial Development and Welfare programme during the war and in the non-settler colonies initiated constititional changes that gave Africans increased–if only marginally so–participation in the political process. The Belgians did not contemplate political concessions, but did introduce a development programme for their vast Congo estate.

Africa was directly involved in the war militarily, economically and socially. The entry of Italy into the war on the side of the Germans threatened the access of the Allies to the Far East by the Suez route. Not only did Italian East Africa guard the entry to the Red Sea, but Libya could serve as a base for a combined Italian-German invasion of Egypt. Italian East Africa was quickly overrun by Allied troops and Haile Selassie* was restored to the Ethiopian throne. The Libyan campaign lasted until 1943 and the Axis forces were only driven out after a combined American-British invasion of French North Africa, which, under the terms of the French armistice with the Germans, was 'neutral'. Many African troops were involved in these campaigns, as in those of the First World War.*

The British in West Africa felt threatened by the neighbouring French colonies, which, though neutral under the Vichy regime of Marshal Pétain, they feared would be used as a German base. An abortive invasion by British and Free French forces of Dakar, the capital of Vichy French West Africa failed. But assistance to Free French forces in Equatorial Africa helped rally all the constitutent colonies around the black Guyanese Governor of Chad, Félix Eboué who had declared support for De Gaulle from the outset. After the Allied invasion of French North Africa the government of French West Africa also rallied to the Allied cause.

Large numbers of Africans were used as troops in these campaigns, and in the Burma campaign against the Japanese. Even greater numbers were involved in the production of raw materials essential for the Allied war effort. After the fall of the British and Dutch colonies in the Far East to the Japanese, Africa became vital as a

French West African troops, *c.* 1940

British East African troops examine a shrine in a bombed Buddhist temple at Kalewa, Burma, 1944

The Maghrib

Morocco

The conquest of Morocco had necessitated much heavy fighting on the part of the French, but Moroccan resistance had been inspired not by nationalist ideals but by communal particularism: generally as soon as a group had submitted, its members had joined with the French against its neighbours. Even Mohammed Abd el-Krim,* who had united much of the Rif against the French and the Spanish between 1921 and 1926, had fought for his own community rather than for Morocco as a whole. In 1930, however, effective nationalist protest emerged in the urban centres when, as a part of their policy of dividing the Arabs and Berbers, the French reorganized the administration of traditional justice in a way that could provoke the cry that 'Islam is in danger'. A group of traditionally educated young Moroccans in Fes, led by Allal el-Fassi, started demonstrations which led to violence and arrests. Shortly afterwards other Moroccans who had received a Western education and were centred

The monarch as religious leader: King Mohammed V of Morocco (on horseback) on his way to the mosque at Rabat

source of supply of palm products, tin and rubber, as well as foodstuffs. Much of this was secured by forced labour, compulsory crop cultivation and requisition. At the same time the boom resulting from the war led to considerable development in Africa. Ports such as Dakar and Dar es Salaam were enlarged, and towns like Kano, Fort Lamy and Khartoum expanded rapidly as staging posts on the route to the North African front. But prices for African produce did not increase in line with the world market price, as price controls were imposed by colonial governments. There was a general shortage of imports, leading to inflation. The large number of peasants who came to towns like Lagos, Brazzaville and Casablanca could not find adequate accommodation and lived in appalling conditions in hastily erected shanty towns. In North Africa conditions were made worse by bad harvests in 1943 and 1944. The rapidly expanded urban proletariat, suffering from steep inflation and fixed wages, living in inadequate accommodation, proved a fertile breeding ground for the aspirations of nationalists anxious to take over from the colonial governments.   *M.C.*

on Rabat, proposed reforms of the protectorate administration which the French rejected with contempt. In 1944 the two nationalist streams converged to form the *Istiqlal* (Independence) Party, which, for the first time, called for an end to the French protectorate.

In 1947 Sultan Mohammed V, who had increasingly come to support the demands of *Istiqlal*, made a speech in Tangier stressing his country's Arab heritage and pointedly omitting to express gratitude to France. He had emerged as the real leader of the Moroccan independence movement, and embarked on a policy of competing with the French for influence among the traditionally organized rural population, obstructing French administration in every way possible. The French demanded that he should formally condemn *Istiqlal*: when he refused, they instigated a rural-based rebellion against him. When this failed to move him, he was arrested in August 1953, declared deposed and exiled to Madagascar. The Moroccan people refused to recognize his successor and armed opposition started in the mountains and the city slums. By 1955 the revolt had reached a high pitch, and the French government decided to concentrate its resources against the nationalist rebellion in Algeria. Mohammed V was brought back from exile, and in March 1956 Moroccan independence was recognized.

Tunisia

Nationalism in Tunisia had emerged tenuously before the First World War★ in the shape of a group of reforming intellectuals who had called themselves the Young Tunisians but had sought to be recognized as Europeans rather than aspiring to national independence. Later, in 1920, there had arisen the *Destour* (Constitution) Party which, although nationalist, had been very Islamic-oriented, reactionary and totally unorganized. In the early 1930s, however, a more radical group, led by a lawyer, Habib Bourguiba,★ emerged within the somnolent *Destour*, which for the first time involved women, artisans and peasants in politics. In 1934 Bourguiba created his own highly organized and deeply motivated *Néo-Destour* Party, formed a close alliance with the nascent trade unions, and forced the old *Destour* out of existence. Whereas in Morocco the Islamic and secular nationalist movements had merged, in Tunisia the leadership was entirely in the hands of Westernized intellectuals. Bourguiba spent long periods in jail (1934–6, 1938–43) or in exile (1945–9), while the French repression encouraged increasingly radical leaders to emerge. During the Second World War,★ while held in German-occupied France, Bourguiba had repeatedly refused to collaborate with the Axis powers, and the French also ignored him. After his release he went to Cairo in 1945 to work for North African independence and to enlist the support of the Arab League. On his return to Tunisia in 1949 – still working closely with the trade unions – he started a campaign of urban terrorism and guerrilla activity aimed at attracting the attention of the UN and world public opinion.

Habib Bourguiba's triumphant return to Tunisia in 1955

In 1952 he was again arrested and spent three years in confinement while the struggle continued. As with Morocco, the French decided that Tunisia should be sacrificed to enable efforts to be concentrated on saving Algeria. In 1954 Tunisia was granted autonomy and then – at the insistence of Bourguiba and the *Néo-Destour* – complete independence in March 1956.

Algeria

In Algeria before 1939 political movements led by Western-educated intellectuals had called for equality with the French settlers (*colons*) rather than national independence. One of their leaders, Ferhat Abbas, spoke of 'one France from Dunkirk to Tamanrasset', declaring that there had never been an Algerian nation. A more radical, Marxist-oriented approach, more strongly nationalist, had emerged in France in the 1920s among Algerian migrant workers. Its leader, Messali al-Hajj, returned to Algeria in 1936, and in 1937 founded the *Parti du Peuple Algérien* (PPA). Messali was in prison or under house arrest during the Second World War and was only released in 1946; meanwhile Abbas, Algeria's nationalist leader by default, continued to press for equality with the *colons* and respect for Islamic institutions rather than pressing for independence. The strength of the popular support for a more radical approach was already clear by May 1945 when a demonstration in Setif led by PPA activists was bloodily repressed. The French then conceded some of the demands of the moderates, including indigenous representation in an Algerian assembly. In 1948 and 1951 elections were held but the results were so evidently rigged by the French that faith in the

King Mohammed V

Born in 1910, Mohammed ben Youssef (Muhammad ibn Yusuf), Alawite Sultan of Morocco, became King Mohammed V of Morocco after independence in 1956. Succeeding his father, Mawlay Youssef, as sultan in 1927 at the age of 16, he inherited a throne that was central to the protectorate system through which the French ruled Morocco, but that had little executive power, since most royal decrees (*dahirs*) were prepared by the French authorities and merely presented to the sultan for signature. Despite signs of sympathy for the Moroccan nationalist movement in the 1930s and 1940s, it was not until after the Second World War,* that Mohammed – inspired, it is said by a meeting with Franklin Roosevelt in 1943 – exercised his right to withhold his signature from decrees in protest against the protectorate. In 1953 this intransigence led to his being deposed and exiled to Madagascar, ostensibly at the request of a number of notables from the rural areas. However, other sections of the population refused to accept his successor, an Alawite prince, as sultan, and in November 1955, Mohammed was recognized again as the legitimate ruler. His prestige enabled him, as the supreme representative of the traditional leaders of Morocco, to dominate the newly-independent state down to his death in 1961. *M. B.*

Habib Bourguiba

Born at Monastir, Tunisia in 1903, Bourguiba began his career as a French-trained lawyer and a member of the Tunisian nationalist *Destour* Party, which he joined in 1921. In 1934 he broke away from the party to form the *Néo-Destour*, which gradually took over the campaign for Tunisian independence, employing more radical political methods than had its predecessor. After riots and a general strike in 1938 Bourguiba was arrested with other nationalist leaders and was imprisoned until 1943. In 1945 he went to Cairo, returning to Tunisia in 1949. Rearrested for political activities in 1952, he remained in prison in France until 1954, but continued to dominate the movement for national independence, obliging the French to recognize him in 1955 as the sole leader acceptable to the country. In 1955 he engineered the expulsion from the *Néo-Destour* of his chief rival, Salah ben Youssef, and became prime minister at independence, and then president in 1957 when the Bey was deposed. He was declared life-president in 1975. His hold on power has been virtually unchallenged, despite long periods of illness in the 1970s. *M. B.*

democratic process was lost. A guerilla group, among whose leaders was Ahmed Ben Bella,* had already emerged in 1948, but the French felt that the movement had rapidly died out and were therefore taken by surprise when on 1 November 1954 coordinated armed attacks were launched against them throughout Algeria by the newly formed (July 1954) *Front de Libération Nationale* (FLN). By mid-1955 the French realized that they had a major uprising to suppress in a territory in which oil had recently been discovered, and began the process of abandoning Tunisia and Morocco. The war was to continue until nearly 10 per cent of the Algerian population had been killed, and although the French nearly succeeded in stamping out internal revolt they could do little against raids from external bases in Morocco and Tunisia, and assistance from the Arab League and other allies of the FLN. The *colons* would not agree to concessions to the FLN, for any settlement would have harmed their privileged position. When Paris tried to negotiate, the *colons* revolted too. The Fourth French Republic was toppled and General de Gaulle, brought back to power, realized that a military solution or the wooing of conservative elements against the FLN would prove impracticable. In May 1961 he made a final effort by offering Algeria independence provided that France could retain the Sahara, where the oilfields were situated. The FLN refused to compromise, and with France deeply divided and financially embarrassed by the war, de Gaulle forced his supporters, who had relied on him to save Algeria for France, to accept defeat. An armistice was signed at Evian in March 1962, and in July France formally recognized Algerian independence. *R. L. B.*

Libya, Egypt and the Sudan

Libya, Egypt and the Sudan were all spared direct involvement in the First World War.* The strategic importance of this region, however, ensured that, to varying degrees, they would become a battleground in the Second World War.* In the Sudan, British-led forces contended with the Italians invading from Eritrea, until the battle of Keren in March 1941 removed the Axis menace on that front. The security of Egypt, focal point of British imperialism in the Near East, was in great danger until the decisive battle of El-Alamein in November 1942. Libya was traversed by Italian, German and Allied forces in ferocious campaigns until finally wrested from the Axis in 1943. The war intensified the nationalist pressures against foreign domination which had already been building up in the region.

Libya

Libya achieved its independence in 1951, the first of the European possessions in Africa (after Egypt, which had never been annexed by the British and had always been technically independent) to do so, when the three component territories of Cyrenaica, Tripolitania and Fezzan emerged as a united kingdom. These territories had been administered sketchily by French and British military administrations after 1942–3, but in 1950 the UN insisted that Libya be declared independent. The pre-eminent position of the Sanusiyya,* a cohesive *sufi* order that had assisted the British war effort, was reflected in the fact that its leader, Sayyid Idris al-Mahdi al-Sanusi, was chosen by a national assembly as king of the new state. King Idris, a moderate, pro-Western ruler, remained in power until overthrown by a military coup in 1969.

Sudan

In the Sudan the road to independence was more complex. The Graduates' Congress, the country's first credible political grouping, clashed with the British during the war, and was gradually rent by the same sectarian rivalries that had hampered previous secular movements. A long-standing and fundamental polarization re-emerged: on the one hand, supporters of Sayyid Abd al-Rahman al-Mahdi, son of the Mahdi* who had driven out the Egyptians in the 1880s, and head of the Ansar (the Mahdist community: originally the Mahdi's army) favoured complete independence, but cooperation with the British; the followers of Sayyid Ali al-Mirghani, head of the Khatmiyya *sufi* order, on the other hand, together with most of the secular nationalists, favoured union with Egypt as the best way to secure the Sudan's future and frustrate Abd al-Rahman's personal ambitions. In 1944, in an attempt to moderate and influence the nationalist movement, the Sudan government established the Advisory Council of the Northern Sudan, which, however, was

boycotted by those who advocated union with Egypt. A Legislative Assembly for the entire country was elected in 1948. Meanwhile the Egyptian government continued to press its claims to the Sudan in negotiations with Britain and, in 1947, at the UN. In 1952 Egypt's new revolutionary regime dropped the claims, and in January 1953 reached an agreement with the Sudanese political parties. In February an Anglo-Egyptian agreement provided a timetable for the Sudan's self-determination. The country's first prime minister, Ismail al-Azhari, was an avowed supporter of union with Egypt, but political realities dictated the abandonment of that stance, and the Sudan finally achieved independence on 1 January 1956.

Egypt

Political evolution in the Sudan had, as from 1899, been closely linked to developments in Anglo-Egyptian relations. Those relations had been soured beyond redemption during the Second World War, when the British military occupation of Egypt had made clear the narrow limits of Egypt's nominal independence. After the war successive Egyptian governments attempted to renegotiate the 1936 Anglo-Egyptian treaty,* but without success. Control of the Suez Canal and the future status of the Sudan remained apparently insurmountable obstacles to agreement.

The changed international and national circumstances of the immediate post-war years produced a radical reaction in Egypt, as extremists, especially of the right, gained control of political momentum through a wave of violent demonstrations and assassinations. The political parties proved incapable of mobilizing support or of influencing events. On them, and on the monarchy, was blamed Egypt's failure in the 1948–9 war against Israel. A Free Officers

Members of the Egyptian Military Revolutionary Council after the proclamation of a republic in 1953

Gamal Abdel Nasser

Gamal Abdel Nasser, the son of a post office clerk, was born on 15 January 1918 in Alexandria, Egypt. Educated in secondary schools in Alexandria and Cairo, by 1935 he was already active in politics as a student leader. He briefly studied law at Cairo University and then in 1937 entered the Cairo Military Academy, from which he graduated in July 1938. He served in Egypt and the Sudan (1939–43) and then became an instructor at the Military Academy. After graduating from the Staff College he saw service in the Egyptian army in the war in Palestine against the Israelis (1948–9) and then returned to the Staff College as an instructor. Along with other radical officers Nasser had begun to establish a secret revolutionary group as early as 1942; by 1949 the Society of Free Officers had taken

final shape as a well-organized movement. The Free Officers seized power in a coup in July 1952, and in 1954 Nasser ousted General Neguib and became President. He negotiated the withdrawal of British forces (1954), sought assistance from the Communist bloc (1955), and nationalized the Suez Canal (1956), a move that led to an Anglo-French-Israeli invasion. After the war Nasser sought to unify the Arab world and consolidate socialism in Egypt. His military involvement in the Yemen (1962–7), austere policies, and autocracy increasingly alienated him from Egyptians, but even after the disastrous war with Israel (June 1967) he retained considerable popularity. When he died suddenly on 29 September 1970 millions of Egyptians came to Cairo to demonstrate publicly their deep grief.   *H.-H.K.*

Movement in the army, established shortly after that defeat and led by Colonel Gamal Abdel Nasser,★ determined to restore the dignity and integrity of Egypt, and thus to remove foreign control. In July 1952 it succeeded in overthrowing the government, forcing the abdication of King Farouk, and installing itself in power. In 1953 the monarchy was abolished and Egypt became a republic. The problem of foreign domination, symbolized by Britain's retention of control over the Suez Canal, was not finally solved until the Suez War★ of 1956, after which Egypt took over the canal and all foreign troops were evacuated from Egyptian soil.   *M.W.D.*

French West Africa

Modern political organization among the African peoples of France's West African colonies can be dated from constitutional reforms in 1945, which provided deputyships for each colony in the French National Assembly. African political demands were initially articulated by a small French-educated elite, which pressed for greater African political rights (*assimilation*) within a French institutional structure, rather than for an independent African nationalism. The very word 'independence' was not publicly put forward as a desirable goal by any French West African politician until 1957, and the issue of territorial independence only became truly salient when General de Gaulle organized a referendum on the subject in 1958.

While all African political parties or movements were thus very belatedly drawn to the theme of independent territorial nationality, there were wide variations in activity between territories. The earliest politically-organized mass involvement was in the Ivory Coast in 1948–50, where the *Parti Démocratique de la Côte d'Ivoire* led by Félix Houphouët-Boigny★ was repressed by the local colonial administration because of its affiliation to the French Communist Party. This repression took the lives of more than a hundred African subjects, and was ended only by Houphouët-Boigny's disaffiliation from the Communist Party in 1950, and his subsequent firm allegiance to the French metropolitan government of the day.

Senegal was the next territory to be the scene of mass African political activity, in the years 1951–2, with electoral contests between the urban-centred socialists led by Lamine Guèye, and the *Bloc Démocratique Sénégalais* led by Léopold Senghor★ which appealed to the newly-enfranchised rural majority. This competition was on the whole peaceful, and it resulted in Senghor's enduring personal ascendancy in Senegalese politics, but 'anti-colonial struggle' was a notion quite strange to both the major contestants, equally committed as they were to metropolitan French culture and institutions.

The *Loi Cadre* reform, passed by the French parliament in 1956, indicated the metropolitan desire to anticipate African demands by the creation of elective government structures (under French tutelage) in each of the overseas territories. This focus on the individual territories, rather than on the federation centred at Dakar

Félix Houphouët-Boigny

Born at Yamoussoukro in the Ivory Coast on 18 October 1905, Houphouët-Boigny was educated at medical school in Dakar, Senegal and returned home to become a successful medical practitioner, a wealthy coffee planter and a chief. He attained political prominence in 1944 by organizing a strong union of African coffee planters, which in 1945 was transformed into the *Parti Démocratique de la Côte d'Ivoire*, one of the earliest mass political parties in colonial Africa. The same year he was sent to Paris as a delegate to the constituent assembly that shaped the new Fourth French Republic. He was subsequently elected as a deputy to the French National Assembly in 1946, 1951 and 1956. He served in the French Cabinet from 1956 to 1959. Houphouët-Boigny – unlike other post-war nationalist leaders in French West Africa – consistently opposed the creation of a strong Francophone federation in West Africa. His idea of autonomous territorial development was to prevail. He became President of the Ivory Coast at independence in 1960. *D.C.O'B.*

Léopold Senghor

Born on 9 October 1906 in Senegal, Senghor was educated at secondary schools in Dakar and Paris and then at the University of Paris. He was a secondary school teacher in France from 1935 to 1948 and had established a reputation as a leading poet of the *négritude* movement before beginning his political career in 1945, when he was elected a Socialist Party deputy to the French National Assembly. In 1948 he formed his own political party, the *Bloc Démocratique Sénégalais*. His party, under a series of names, has dominated Senegalese political life since its decisive victories in the elections of 1951 and 1952. Senghor, who became President of Senegal at independence in 1960, has consistently and successfully sought to absorb the various parties and movements that have attempted to contest his personal hegemony, his crucial asset being a close and even cordial relationship with French political leaders. He has favoured close ties between Senegal and France, and is recognized as the elder statesman of Francophone Africa. *D.C.O'B.*

Sékou Touré

Born at Faranah, French Guinea on 9 January 1922, Touré was the son of a peasant farmer. He attended Quranic and missionary schools, and then technical school in Conakry, but was expelled for leading a strike. He became a post office employee in 1937 and in the early 1940s became active in trade union organization. He was elected general-secretary of the post and telegraph workers' union in 1945. In 1946 he was a founder member of the inter-territorial political party, the *Rassemblement Démocratique Africain*. Touré's national party, the *Partie Démocratique de Guinée* (PDG), founded in 1947, was originally an outgrowth of the trade union movement, but Touré's own boundless energy and personal magnetism established his own and the PDG's claims to be leaders of nationalist politics, particularly after a series of strikes in 1953 which Touré helped organize. In 1957 he became Vice-President of the Government Council of Guinea – effectively prime minister – and in 1958, when Guinea declared independence and withdrew from the French Community, President of the Republic of Guinea. *D.C.O'B.*

201

which had formerly supervised all France's West African territories, provoked Senegalese charges that France was now intent on 'balkanizing' West Africa. Paris deputies for each West African territory meanwhile hastened home to secure their newly-provided domestic power base. Guinea, under the leadership of Sékou Touré* and the *Parti Démocratique de Guinée* was, from 1956 to 1958, politically the most active territory of the, by 1957 defunct, French West African Federation.

General de Gaulle's assumption of power in France in the summer of 1958 was followed by a constitutional referendum in November. Each of the overseas territories was offered a choice between immediate independence or membership in the French community; only Guinea voted for independence, and it was duly punished by the immediate withdrawal of all forms of French aid. African political leaders in all the other territories (with the marginal exception of Niger) successfully encouraged the electorate to vote for membership in the community. This prudence was rewarded two years later (1960) when the French government gave independence to all the West African territories. Constitutions were drafted on the French Fifth Republic model, and seven sovereign states thus followed Guinea in attaining an independent status. De Gaulle's government, beset by all the problems surrounding the war in Algeria,* seems indeed to have been eager to grant independence to West Africa before it was demanded. All the independent states that emerged from the West African federation, except Sékou Touré's Guinea, remained firmly within France's sphere of influence.   *D. C. O'B.*

French Equatorial Africa and Cameroon

French Equatorial Africa (FEA) comprised four federated territories – Gabon, the Middle Congo, Oubangui-Chari (now the Central African Republic) and Chad – at the onset of the Second World War.* Ex-German Cameroon was not part of FEA, but administered by France and Britain under League of Nations mandates. The governors of the French FEA colonies sided with General de Gaulle's Free French and the Allies against Pétain's Vichy government. Brazzaville became the headquarters of Free French Africa, and in 1944 De Gaulle chaired the Brazzaville conference to determine the common future of France and its African colonies in peacetime. The conference marked a turning-point in French colonial history as it sowed the seeds of decolonization, which matured 14 years later.

Cameroon's status was very different. After the end of the war, the defunct League of Nations mandates were converted into UN trusteeship agreements. The Northern and Southern Cameroons continued to be run by Britain as parts of Nigeria, while the larger French Cameroun was treated like a French Equatorial territory. But the UN provisions for self-determination and the consequent freer climate of political debate meant that Cameroonians were always conscious of the reality of eventual independence.

Under the Fourth French Republic, France created, in addition to an area council in Brazzaville, territorial assemblies where for the first time African politicians could deliberate on domestic policy, though they had no real executive powers. These led to the development of national consciousness and sounded the death knell of the federal ideal. The French attempted to solve the problems of postwar economic depression in FEA with a development fund (FIDES – *Fonds d'Investissement et de Développement Économique et Social* designed chiefly to improve the poor transport infrastructure. Its investment activities over the next ten years probably helped to keep the territories more closely linked to France. It was later replaced by new French and European Economic Community development funds which continued even after independence.

The 1956 *Loi Cadre** (framework law) offered the prospect of limited autonomy for French African territories. Two years later De Gaulle returned to power and abandoned the principle of a French Union amalgamating France and its overseas possessions in Africa and elsewhere. Instead he proposed an international 'French Community' under which France would control defence, economic and foreign policy, while the member states would have internal self-government. All the territories of FEA accepted this proposal by referendum. Even French Cameroun, never officially part of the Community, adopted a comparable government structure. Britain meanwhile decided that the Northern and Southern Cameroons were not economically viable as independent states whether separately or together.

Several prominent political leaders emerged. Two were former Catholic priests: Barthélémy Boganda founded a pan-African party (*Mouvement pour l'Évolution Sociale de l'Afrique Noire*) in Ubangui-Shari, and Fulbert Youlou led the Congolese. Only in Cameroun was there violent political activity. The pro-reunification *Union des Populations du Cameroun* under Ruben Um Nyobe launched a guerrilla campaign against French rule: over 10 000 people were killed in the subsequent repression, and a pro-French party, the *Union Camerounaise* under André-Marie Mbida, and later led by Ahmadou Ahidjo, eventually took power.

French Cameroun and the FEA states were all given independence under separate presidents in 1960, becoming the Republics of Cameroun, Gabon, the Congo, Chad, and Central Africa. The British Cameroons were offered a choice only between becoming part of Nigeria or joining the new Cameroun Republic in UN-organized plebiscites. In 1961 the Northern Cameroons elected to become part of Nigeria, and the Southern Cameroons joined former French Cameroun in a federation   *A. P. H.*

Madagascar

Madagascar's wartime French governor was pro-Vichy, but the ultimate cause of Allied wartime intervention was the desire to protect Cape sea routes and to pre-empt Japanese plans to establish military bases on the island. In May 1942 Allied forces led by the British navy invaded, forcing the pro-Vichy administration to surrender in November. The administration of the colony was then handed over to the Free French.

In 1946 France converted its colonies into 'overseas territories' and abolished forced labour. All Malagasy became French citizens, but only those highly educated became electors for three of the five seats in the French National Assembly. Liberalization permitted the establishment of political parties: the pro-independence *Mouvement Démocratique de la Rénovation Malgache* (MDRM), led by Raseta and Jacques Rabemananjara, represented mainly the educated classes of the Merina ethnic group; as a counterweight, though ostensibly to protect the coastal people, the French promoted a second party, the *Parti des Déshérités Malgache*, which included among its leaders Philibert Tsiranana. The MDRM won all three Malagasy seats in the 1946 elections.

A nationalist insurrection followed on 29 March 1947; armed rebels attacked French settlers, administrative buildings and military posts mainly on the eastern coast. Although the rebellion was clearly orchestrated, probably by nationalist secret societies, the MDRM leadership not only did not sponsor it but publicly called for calm. Fifteen months of repression followed – with deaths varyingly estimated at between 11 000 and 80 000. Armed repression and the judicial process were used to suffocate nationalist demands. The rebellion's 20 military leaders were executed, six MDRM leaders condemned to death, but reprieved (and later granted amnesties in 1954), and the MDRM dissolved.

After the passing of the 1956 *Loi Cadre*★ (framework law) proposing universal adult suffrage and a share in executive power, the nationalists espoused more moderate arguments for independence. Tsiranana's new predominantly coastal party, the *Parti Social Démocrate*, was created in 1957, again with French backing. He won increasing electoral support until by 1960, when he became president of the independent republic, his party had captured almost all the seats in the legislature: only the sustained opposition of Richard Andrianamjato's urban and ethnically Merina *Parti du Congrès de l'Indépendance de Madagascar* preventing the *de facto* creation of a one-party state. Tsiranana signed cooperation agreements with France that preserved French bases and overall financial and economic control in exchange for the transfer of sovereignty and French aid. He saw his role as maintaining Madagascar's traditional lifeline with France rather than seeking new allies among the uncharted political landscapes of nearby East Africa or the Indian Ocean islands – or looking further afield.   *A.P.H.*

Parti Social Démocrate election posters showing Philibert Tsiranana and the party symbol – a wild cat

The Horn of Africa

During the 1940s and 1950s the Horn largely stood outside the mainstream of African nationalism. In Ethiopia, which regained its independence from Italian occupation in 1941, the Emperor Haile Selassie★ re-established his control and created a centralized regime which allowed little scope for political participation. One chamber of parliament–the Chamber of Deputies–became popularly elected under a revised constitution introduced in 1955; the Senate remained appointive. The Chamber of Deputies, however, lacked control over an executive still directly appointed by the Emperor, and exercised little influence, and no political parties were formed. The principal pressures came in the 1940s and early 1950s from dissatisfied members of the traditional ruling class, graduates returning from education abroad and officers in the armed forces. A combination of these pressures erupted in a brief abortive coup in December 1960.

Aden Abdullah Osman   Abdar-Rashid Ali Shermarke

The former Italian colonies of Eritrea and Somalia, administered by Britain after 1941, were disposed of by the UN; Eritrea was federated with Ethiopia in 1952 while Somalia became an Italian-administered UN Trust Territory in 1950. In Eritrea, where about half of the population initially favoured union with Ethiopia, initial goodwill was dissipated by Ethiopian actions designed to reduce any regional autonomy, and the political parties formed in the 1940s were suppressed. In Somalia, the Italian trusteeship was initially opposed by the principal party, the Somali Youth League (SYL), which had been founded in 1943 and represented most Somalis other than the sedentary groups of the Juba basin. However, the SYL came to cooperate with the trusteeship administration, and comfortably won the elections held in 1956 and 1959. Unlike most nationalist parties, it had no single dominant leader, its principal personalities being Aden Abdullah Osman and Abdar-Rashid Ali Shermarke.

In British Somaliland nationalist activity scarcely started until 1954, when political consciousness was aroused by the transfer to Ethiopian administration of grazing lands used by Somali nomads, and the first elections did not take place until February 1960. All parties, including the dominant Somaliland National League led by Mohamed Haji Ibrahim Egal, favoured union with Somalia, which was achieved when the two territories united as the independent Somali Republic in July 1960. No significant nationalist movement developed in the French Somali Coast (known after independence as Djibouti★), which voted heavily to remain associated with France in the 1958 French colonial referendum.   *C.S.C.*

Haile Selassie

Emperor of Ethiopia from 1930 to 1974 Haile Selassie (*né* Tafari Makonnen) was born in 1892, the son of Emperor Menelik's★ cousin Ras Makonnen. Tafari succeeded his father as governor of Harar province, a position that gave him considerable wealth. After the deposition of Menelik's grandson Iyasu in 1916, he became Regent for Menelik's daughter Zawditu, and heir to the imperial throne. On Zawditu's death in 1930 he was crowned Emperor, adopting the name Haile Selassie ('Power of the Trinity'). Continuing Menelik's modernizing work, he established ministries, schools and hospitals, issued anti-slavery decrees, and set up a government bank. Confronted by Italian invasion in 1935 he appealed to the League of Nations, which imposed ineffective sanctions against Italy. His own forces engaged the Italian army in March 1936, but were defeated, and Haile Selassie escaped to lay Ethiopia's case before the League in Geneva, after which he went into exile in Britain. Italy's entry into the European war in 1940 made Haile Selassie an ally of the British, who helped him liberate Ethiopia in 1941. After his restoration he was much concerned with post-war reconstruction, and development, and later with pan-African politics. He was deposed in 1974 and died a prisoner in 1975.   *R.K.P.P.*

Belgian Africa

Developments after independence in the former Belgian Congo (known as Zaire* after 1971) demonstrated that the broad concept of anti-colonial struggle encompassed a number of different, often contradictory social forces. Much more had been at stake in the last years of Belgian rule than merely opposition to the foreign colonial oligarchy. The social forces which were to collide when the Belgians withdrew were already becoming apparent during the Second World War.*

In 1941, when first white, then African employees struck at *Union Minière* (the leading mining enterprise of Katanga), industrial trade unions were still prohibited and the strike caught both management and colonial administration unprepared. An African demonstration was brutally suppressed in Elisabethville and, for a few years, the African workers of the Katanga copperbelt were cowed. In 1945, however, there were further strikes in Katanga and in the Leopoldville and Lower Congo areas and a town riot at Matadi. Essentially immediate reactions to a steep rise in the cost of living, these urban protests were paralleled by movements in the rural areas more indicative of long-standing frustrations and resentments and of a latent opposition to various aspects of colonial supremacy. The white God was challenged – for example by a Watchtower-inspired prophetic movement at Masisi (1945); the white civilizer was maligned – in Kasai there were lingering rumours of white cannibals, *mitumbula*, feeding upon black children; white power was doubted – on various occasions rumours spread that *Germani*, or black Americans, would come as liberators and dispensers of wealth.

The armed forces (the *Force Publique*) were the guarantee of Belgian rule under such circumstances but the fear of armed mutiny always loomed large in the colonial mind, especially during the war when troops served abroad and caught sight of the outside world. A mutiny did take place at Luluabourg (1944); others, in Katanga, were forestalled. The Luluabourg incidents petered out with some looting by small groups of disbanded soldiers but from them sprang an opportunity for the *évolués* – office clerks, teachers, male nurses, etc. – to assert their class consciousness. The *évolués* were indecisive and divided. In the wake of military unrest some had thought in terms of a military coup against the government, others pressed the authorities to grant them a special status and a share in the government of the illiterate masses.

Such war-time developments indicated the main conflict areas within Congolese society. After 1945 the country entered a period of rapid industrial and urban growth. Imbued with the complacency of technocrats, Belgian colonial circles were convinced that the key to political immutability lay in sustained economic expansion and increased welfare, together with careful social engineering. Indeed,

Top: home of an *évolué* in the 1950s at Leopoldville. Above: a maize mill in Kasai province in the 1950s

at first, this policy seemed successful but, from 1956, mechanization and a steadily growing European labour force began to slow down the creation of job openings for Africans. By the late 1950s, in a development that boded ill for the future, African urban unemployment was growing. Some observers perceived, however, that the low productivity of African agriculture represented the main long-term

Patrice Lumumba

A Tetela born in the Kasai province of the Belgian Congo on 2 July 1925, Lumumba was educated to post-primary level, and then served for several years as a post office official in Stanleyville (now Kisangani) where he helped organize *évolués*.* In 1957 he moved to Leopoldville (now Kinshasa), where he soon played an active political role, forming, in 1958, the *Mouvement National Congolais* (MNC) a political party that advocated a strong unitary state, drawing its main support from minority ethnic groups. The MNC secured 40 per cent of the vote in the 1960 elections; it was the only one able to claim national (rather than regional) support. Shortly before independence Lumumba was appointed prime minister of the first Congolese government. Within days of the proclamation of independence on 30 June 1960, army mutinies and regional secessions threw the country into chaos. At the prompting of the army chief of staff Colonel Joseph-Desiré Mobutu,* Lumumba was forced from office, imprisoned and finally sent to Elisabethville (now Lubumbashi). He was summarily executed on 17 January 1961 at the instigation of the secessionist Katangan government, a fate that established him for many Africans throughout the continent as a martyr to the cause of African political independence.   *J.-L. V.*

threat to colonial development. Throughout the period the gap between urban and rural incomes widened and, in several parts of the country, there were the ingredients of an agrarian crisis in the making. The tightening web of regulations, obligations, etc., only proved self-defeating as it bred resentment and encouraged the exodus towards the towns.

A distinguishing feature of Belgian rule in the post-war Congo was the absence of any firm political will to associate the aspiring African bourgeoisie with government. Traditionally the Congo was the preserve of capital and Church, and, in the absence of political life, up to 1957, legalistic debates on the responsibility of local councils or on a status for 'civilized Africans' were coupled with intimidation, these contradictory tendencies serving as substitutes for political enfranchisement. From 1955 there had been cosmetic operations of public relations between white and black while, gradually, new regulations dismantled the colour-bar system piecemeal. Nevertheless the rapidly growing class of *évolués* began to realize that their offers of collaboration with the white colonial bourgeoisie – however servile – would never be wholly accepted, and that in any case such collaboration would eventually threaten their sense of identity. The Church played on this latent fear and, in 1956, gave its blessing to a programme of gradual emancipation which a few African intellectuals from the Upper Congo published in *Conscience Africaine*, their Leopoldville periodical. Soon after the *Alliance des Bakongo* (ABAKO), a Lower Congo cultural association from Leopoldville came out with more vigorous demands for emancipation 'now'. Both the Minister of Colonies and the Governor-General dismissed these as 'nonsense'.

In the following years external factors accelerated change in the Congo. Patrice Lumumba's* encounter with Kwame Nkrumah* (Accra, December 1958) for example, gave fresh resolve to his leadership of the *Mouvement National Congolais*, the only mass movement with a 'Jacobin' platform, clearly committed to the fostering of national unity. Deeper trends were, however, local and, in particular, the urban/rural relationships proved crucial. Urban leaders tried to build up their factions by developing constituencies in their home areas. There, in turn, rural discontent found its expression in populist, ethnically based movements which often submerged all authority, including that of the political leaders. In the Lower Congo area, the proximity of Leopoldville only made the situation more explosive. On 4 January 1959 urban riots took everyone by surprise in Leopoldville and, in the following months, the colonial administration faced total collapse in Lower Congo. This was the only total checkmate to colonial power in Congolese history, but it also showed the limits of ABAKO's control of the situation.

In this atmosphere of emergency select committees were hastily convened in Brussels to improvise the transition from colony to independent republic. Significantly, this unprecedented intervention of Belgian politicians into Congolese affairs had as its corollary the exclusion of the colonial administration and of the white middle class (settlers, traders, industrialists, etc.) from all negotiations leading to independence.

On 30 June 1960 the Congolese *évolués* were left to solve their factional struggles, to resist the mounting wave of rural radicalism and to try to arbitrate between rival ethnic claims. Their future relationship with the main sectors of the colonial economy remained to be decided. Their most immediate problem was to confront the mutiny of the *Force Publique*: with the military riots of Thysville (4 July), an old colonial nightmare had finally come true.   *J.-L. V.*

British West Africa

By 1945 the political climate in West Africa had changed radically. A new generation of political leaders had emerged determined to gain self-government and eventual independence. For their part, the British colonial authorities accepted this aspiration but visualized self-government and independence as a distant prospect. By contrast, the nationalists increasingly demanded a rapid transfer of power, if not 'self-government now'. The British perspective on the proper pace for transfer of power is clear from the constitutions promulgated for Nigeria and the Gold Coast in 1946, both of which made very modest advances in devolution of power to Africans, and both of which were bitterly attacked by local nationalists.

Though the four British colonies in West Africa shared certain services in common and had had their economies coordinated by a British Resident Minister during the war, the response of the colonial governments to demands made by the nationalists was primarily based on considerations of the situations as they perceived them in each of the four territories rather than as part of an overall strategy as was the case in French West Africa★ and French Equatorial Africa.★ Similarly, there was little contact and certainly no coordination between nationalists in British West Africa such as existed between political leaders in the constituent colonies of French West Africa. The prime source of strength of the nationalists in all four territories was the growing anti-colonial feeling among the people and a growing desire to participate in their own government. This was bolstered by the rapid expansion of education as well as economic improvement in all but The Gambia. Nationalists in all four territories faced a similar problem, the lack of a common culture, language and history among the peoples they sought to lead to independence.

Gold Coast to Ghana

The new constitution introduced in 1946 provided for an elected African majority for the first time in a British colony in Africa. But it was violently criticized by nationalists, for the majority was in the great part indirectly elected from among the chiefs. At the same time the British retained firm control of the Executive Council.

Nationalists under the leadership of Dr J.B. Danquah formed the United Gold Coast Convention party (UGCC) to oppose the new constitution. They brought back as their Secretary, Kwame Nkrumah,★ who had made a reputation for himself as an anti-colonialist in the USA and Britain, where he had helped organize the Manchester Pan-African Congress of 1945.

Kwame Nkrumah

Born in Nkroful in the Western Province of the Gold Coast Colony in 1909, Nkrumah was the son of a goldsmith. After elementary education and a year as a pupil teacher, he trained as a teacher at Achimota College, taught from 1930 to 1935 and then left for the USA. He graduated from Lincoln University (BA, 1939; B. Theol, 1942) and the University of Pennsylvania (MSc, 1942; MA 1943), financing his studies through unskilled labour. He lived in London from 1945 to 1947 and was joint-secretary of the 1945 (Manchester) Pan-African Congress. His nationalist activities caught the attention of the leaders of the United Gold Coast Convention (UGCC),★ who invited him to return to the Gold Coast to become the Convention's Secretary in 1947. In 1948, after violent demonstrations against the colonial government, he was imprisoned for a short while, together with other UGCC leaders. In 1949, however, he broke with the UGCC to form the more radical Convention People's Party (CPP),★ which organized 'Positive Action' campaigns in 1949–50 to demand immediate independence. Nkrumah was arrested again but was released after a CPP election victory in 1951 and appointed Leader of Government Business in the Legislative Assembly. Further election victories followed in 1954 and 1956, and in 1957 Nkrumah became first Prime Minister of Ghana. In 1960 a republic was declared and Nkrumah was elected President. He pursued policies of African socialism,★ pan-Africanism★–which he attempted to effect through the short-lived Ghana-Guinea-Mali Union (1958–60) and his active role in the creation of the Organization of African Unity★–and fostered a self-projected 'personality cult' which came to be known as Nkrumaism. He was overthrown in a military coup in 1966 while in Peking, died in exile in 1972, but was buried with full honours at his birthplace.   D.G.

The UGCC capitalized on urban discontent and the anger of cocoa farmers, whose trees had been compulsorily destroyed to contain disease. After violent demonstrations and riots against expatriate business following a price-fixing agreement, Danquah, Nkrumah and other UGCC leaders were jailed. However, a subsequent government commission recommended a new constitution with a directly selected African majority in the legislature and an African majority of 8 out of 11 places in the Executive Council. While Danquah accepted the new proposals, Nkrumah did not. He formed his own Convention People's Party (CPP) and demanded full 'self-government now'. In 1950, as a result of his Positive Action Campaign, which gained more support and resulted in strikes and riots, he was jailed together with other CPP leaders. His party won the election and he emerged from jail to form the first African government in colonial Africa.

Thereafter the Gold Coast made steady progress towards independence. This was facilitated by the warm relationship that developed between Nkrumah and the British governor, Sir Charles Arden-Clarke. In 1954 Ghana attained full internal self-government and the only obstacle to early independence was the growing opposition to Nkrumah from regionally-based parties. Such was the extent of this opposition, especially in Ashanti, that Britain insisted that Nkrumah test his popularity at a general election before conceding independence. The CPP won 72 of the 104 seats and on 6 March 1957 the Gold Coast, taking the ancient name of Ghana,* became the first black African country to gain its independence from colonial rule.

Nigeria

Nigeria's road to independence was longer because Nigeria was less homogeneous than Ghana. The chief problem was the integration of the north and south, which until the introduction of the 1946 constitution had been effectively administered as separate entities.

The first session of the Nigerian Legislative Council under the 1946 Constitution: a northern member takes the oath

Nnamdi Azikiwe

The son of an Igbo army clerk, Azikiwe was born on 16 November 1904 in Zungeru, Northern Nigeria. He attended mission schools and worked as a government clerk before leaving for the USA in 1925 where he worked at a variety of jobs to finance his university education. After graduating from Howard, Lincoln, Pennsylvania and Columbia universities he returned to West Africa in 1934. In January 1935 he became editor of the radical nationalist *African Morning Post* in Accra (Gold Coast), returning to Nigeria in 1937 to launch a new daily paper, the *West African Pilot*. This, and the nationalist political organization, the National Council of Nigeria and the Cameroons, which he founded in 1944, were major vehicles for the spread of nationalist ideas beyond the capital, Lagos. Azikiwe became Eastern Region Premier during the period of internal self-government that preceded independence. After independence, he became Governor-General and in 1963, when Nigeria became a republic, President, a 'ceremonial' office, but his term was curtailed in 1966 by military rule. He played a minor role in the Biafra★ secession movement, but sought reconciliation with Federal leaders before the end of the civil war. In 1979 Azikiwe returned to active political life when he stood—unsuccessfully—as a candidate in the presidential elections.   *D.W.*

There were serious imbalances in development and education, and while the north was predominantly Muslim, much of the south was Christian. The 1946 constitution brought the north within the competence of the Legislative Council for the first time, and provided for an elected African majority—as with Ghana, largely indirectly elected. The Executive Council remained firmly under British control. Nationalists, led by Dr Nnamdi Azikiwe★ and his National Council of Nigeria and the Cameroons (NCNC), protested violently against the constitution, which they complained had been foisted on them without consultation.

These protests led to a constitutional review in which all sections of the country were consulted. The constitution that emerged entrenched the three regions that had been established in 1946. The largely consultative regional assemblies were now given legislative powers and their own executive councils. The federal pattern of Nigeria's constitutional development was established and the subsequent elections were fought by largely regional based parties; the NCNC, drawing its strength from the east, the Action Group (AG) from the west, and Northern Peoples Congress (NPC) from the north.

Subsequent constitutional negotiations focused on two main problems: the allocation of power between the regions and the centre, and the date for independence. The north, anxious not to be submerged by the more advanced south, wanted time to prepare itself. The south was anxious to take independence as soon as possible.

Constitutional negotiations (1954–9) produced a federal constitution, and in the 1959 general election immediately prior to independence no one party emerged with an overall majority. From the point of view of their political philosophies the natural alliance would have been between Azikiwe's NCNC and Obafemi Awolowo's AG, but personal and ethnic rivalry led to a coalition government between the NCNC and the NPC.

Sierra Leone and The Gambia

The smaller territories of Sierra Leone and The Gambia attained independence in 1961 and 1965 respectively. In the case of The Gambia independence was delayed because of its tiny size and population. It was thought to be unviable as a separate state, but attempts to link it with neighbouring Senegal,★ of which it forms a natural geographical part, were strongly resisted.

In both colonies devolution of power by the British and the extension of the franchise to all adults saw the transfer of political power from the educated coastal elites to the economically and educationally backward peoples of the Protectorates. Thus in The Gambia independence was gained without violence under the leadership of a veterinary surgeon, Dauda Jawara, who was a Mandinka from up-river. In Sierra Leone a doctor from the inland Mende ethnic group, Milton Margai, steered the colony to independence. Margai managed to contain the bitterness of the Creoles of Freetown, who felt themselves disinherited, and incipient rivalry between the two principal ethnic groups of the interior, the Mende and the Temne, but immediately before independence a trade union leader, Siaka Stevens, demanded that a general election be held to test Margai's strength. This was refused, and there were violent protests by Stevens' followers, many of whom were Temne. Although Margai himself kept the country firmly under his control, this violence was an augury of the future pattern of events after his death.   *M.C.*

British East Africa

Kenya

In the Second World War* Kenya supplied food to British forces in Ethiopia, Somalia and the Middle East. For the first time white farming became really profitable, and white settlers gained a larger share in government. Yet in 1948 the total white population was less than 30000, whereas there were 5 million Africans. Land shortage was acute, especially among the Kikuyu bordering the 'white highlands' – fertile areas which had been reserved for white occupation. In 1946 Jomo Kenyatta* returned from England and in 1947 became president of the Kenya African Union (formed in 1944 to back the first African nominated to the Legislative Council). Within the next few years groups of landless Kikuyu began to plan violent action against whites and chiefs, and in 1952 the government declared a state of emergency. In 1953, in a controversial trial, Kenyatta was convicted of managing the rebel organization known as Mau Mau, which waged a guerrilla war from camps in the Aberdare Mountains.

By 1955 Mau Mau had been largely suppressed; 32 white civilians and 13000 Africans had been killed, while 80000 Kikuyu were in detention camps. By 1957 putting down the rebellion had cost £50 million: half came from the British government, which thus took a belated lead in shaping policy for Kenya. Settler aspirations were sharply checked, while an African peasantry was created through a massive programme of land reform and subsidies for African agriculture. In 1959 Africans finally gained the right to buy land in the 'white highlands'. Meanwhile, in 1957 Africans had been directly elected to the Legislative Council on a restricted franchise. The emergency was ended in 1960, Kenyatta was released in 1961, and a general election produced the country's first African government: a coalition between Kenyatta's Kenya African National Union (KANU) and the Kenya African Democratic Union (KADU), which was an alliance between pastoral peoples and those of the coast. In May 1963 an election based on universal adult suffrage enabled KANU to form a government, and independence followed in December. A year later Kenya became a republic and KADU merged with KANU.

Uganda

In Uganda, European settlers were of no importance; decolonization there was complicated instead by the special position of the kingdom of Buganda. Its people, the Ganda, numbered only 836 000 in 1948 – one-sixth of the total population – but were the most prosperous and best-educated group in the territory and enjoyed a large measure of internal autonomy. Ganda peasants resented the exactions of landlord-chiefs but looked for reform to their king, the Kabaka, Frederick Mutesa II, rather than to the British. Other peoples in Uganda sought to challenge Ganda predominance by increasing their own local autonomy. In 1952 a new governor, Sir Andrew Cohen, set about preparing the country for self-government. From 1954, for the first time, the Legislative Council included elected members; half were Africans. But in 1953 the Colonial Secretary, Oliver Lyttelton, carelessly caused the Ganda to fear that East Africa, like British Central Africa,* would be yoked in a federation. The Kabaka withdrew his support for Cohen, who deported him to Britain. He returned in 1955, but the Buganda government continued to aim at secesssion. From 1960 this was resisted by two territory-wide parties: the Democratic Party (mainly Roman Catholic) and the Uganda People's Congress (UPC) (mainly Protestant). Late in 1961 Buganda agreed to accept a federal status within Uganda and the general election in 1962 enabled the UPC leader, Milton Obote (from Lango district), to form a government for the country as a whole. Uganda achieved independence in October; in 1963 it became a republic, with the Kabaka as president.

Tanganyika

Tanganyika had been ruled by Britain under mandate from the League of Nations; in 1946 it became a UN 'trust territory' a status that required Britain to prepare it for independence. But in Tanganyika, as elsewhere, the war had strengthened the settler economy; it now received further encouragement from the government. Meanwhile diamonds soon became a major export. The British government wasted £36 million on an ill-planned scheme for the mechanized plantation production of groundnuts. Little was done to encourage African agriculture. African farmers and herdsmen, however, were harassed by a large-scale programme of land conservation. In the early 1950s the Tanganyika African Association, which had been founded in 1929, was reinvigorated both by members who had received higher education and by support from farmers and urban workers. In 1954 it was renamed the Tanganyika African National Union (TANU) and under its new president, Julius Nyerere,* pressed for an end to British rule. The British aim, as in Central Africa, was a 'multi-racial' society in which no one racial group would predominate politically, even though in 1956 there were about 8.5 million Africans, 77000 Asians and only 20000 Europeans. The widespread use of Swahili simplified political communication and in the general elections of 1958–9 TANU won seats for European and Asian as well as African candidates. Elections in 1960 enabled it to form a government, led by Nyerere; independence followed in December 1961. Nyerere resigned to concentrate on party organization but when Tanganyika became a republic in 1962 he was elected president.

Zanzibar

When, in the mid-1950s, the prospect of decolonization began to open up in the islands of Zanzibar and Pemba, the Arab minority sought to pre-empt or co-opt African competition. The Zanzibar

Jomo Kenyatta

Born at Ngenda in Kenya in the 1890s, the son of Kikuyu agriculturalists, Kenyatta (*né* Kamau) attended a mission school between 1909 and 1914 and was baptized Johnstone Kamau in 1914; he changed his name to Kenyatta in the 1920s. He worked for the Nairobi Municipality between 1922 and 1928, meanwhile becoming involved with Kikuyu political organizations. In 1928 he became secretary of the Kikuyu Central Association, and in 1929 went to London as its representative, returning to Kenya in 1930. In 1931 Kenyatta returned to England, where he studied anthropology at the London School of Economics; wrote *Facing Mount Kenya* (1938), a landmark of cultural nationalism; and helped organize the 1945 Manchester Pan-African Congress. In 1946 he returned to Kenya and immediately assumed the nationalist leadership, becoming president of the newly-formed Kenya

African Union in 1947. In 1953 Kenyatta was convicted on sketchy evidence of 'managing' the Mau Mau* guerrilla movement and was sentenced to seven years hard labour. By 1959 the Mau Mau emergency was over, and in 1960, while Kenyatta remained in prison, a new political party, the Kenya African National Union (KANU) was formed and Kenyatta was named its president. He was released in August 1961, but despite KANU victories in the 1962 elections, was banned from forming a government. KANU won further elections in 1963 and Kenyatta became Prime Minister of independent Kenya. On 1 June 1963, when Kenya became a republic, Kenyatta became president, a position he retained until his death on 22 August 1978. Kenyatta was conservative, tolerant and pragmatic, and the Kenya over which he presided came to be regarded as moderate, stable and pro-Western. *G.A.*

Julius Nyerere

Nyerere was born in March 1922, the son of a chief, at Butiama in north-western Tanganyika. He attended government primary and secondary schools, and gained a Diploma in Education at Makerere College, Uganda in 1945, and an MA at Edinburgh University in 1952. He taught in Tanganyika 1946–9 and 1953–5. He was a founder member of the Tanganyika African National Union (TANU) established in 1954, and became its first president, abandoning teaching in 1955 to devote himself full-time to political organization and campaigning. In 1957 he became a nominated member of the Legislative Council but after two meetings resigned in protest at British policies. In 1958, however, at the first general elections held in Tanganyika, he won a seat as the Member for the Eastern Province and after a second election in 1960 he was appointed Chief Minister, and at independence in

December 1961 became Prime Minister. Six weeks later Nyerere resigned to devote himself to TANU organization but in October 1962, when Tanganyika became a republic, he was elected President, and became President of Tanzania* (a union of Tanganyika and Zanzibar) in 1964.

Nyerere's government has followed egalitarian policies at home, with a stress on rural development, and he himself lives simply, avoids pomp and elaborate security, and receives a salary equivalent to only US$500 a month. He has become a leading world figure, advocating a new world economic order under which poor countries, like Tanzania, would have greater chances for betterment. In Africa he has been an active supporter of liberation movements against white minority rule in southern Africa, but has also been one of the few African presidents to speak out against repressive black African regimes. *T.A.*

John Okello, leader of the 1964 revolution in Zanzibar

Nationalist Party (ZNP)–mainly but not exclusively Arab–was opposed by the Afro-Shirazi Party (ASP), led by Abeid Karume, which was weakened by divisions between immigrant and indigenous Africans but received help from TANU. In 1961 the ZNP formed a coalition with a splinter-group from the ASP; the ZNP secretary, the socialist radical A.R. Mohamed ('Babu'), broke away to form a new party. In July 1963 an election based on adult suffrage returned the coalition, but the ASP gained more than half the votes. This precarious situation broke down soon after independence in December. In January 1964 a Kenyan, John Okello, overthrew the Zanzibar government; some 5000 Arabs were killed, as many fled into exile, and the rest were dispossessed. Okello himself was soon displaced by an alliance between Babu's men and Karume's ASP. The new regime promptly forged links with East Germany and China. In April 1964 Tanganyika and Zanzibar became a united republic which took the name Tanzania in 1965.

The East Africa High Commission

Between the wars Kenya, Uganda and Tanganyika had a common currency and postal systems and a common market. In 1948 the East Africa High Commission was set up to run communications; collect income tax, customs and excise duties; and promote research. It was responsible to the Central Legislative Assembly, composed of civil servants, elected immigrants and nominated Africans. Uganda and Tanganyika complained that the system unduly favoured Kenya, which was both East Africa's workshop and the chief outlet for its exports. The East African Common Services organization, which replaced the Commission in 1961, made allowance for the advent of independent governors, and the financial relations of the three countries were made more equitable, but Kenya continued to gain most from membership.

A.D.R.

British Central Africa

The Second World War* and post-war reconstruction gave a boost to Southern Rhodesia's economy. The country increased exports of chrome and asbestos, though not gold, and tobacco production expanded fast after the war. The government fostered iron and steel and textile industries; manufacturing rapidly became important. By 1958 the white population numbered 205 000. More and more Africans lived in towns, and white beliefs in segregation came under strain. Godfrey Huggins, who had been Prime Minister since 1933, provided government support for African secondary education and agriculture, hoping to give a black elite a vested interest in the existing society. Black workers staged a general strike in 1948, but most were short-stay migrants and prolonged united action was beyond their power.

In Northern Rhodesia the mine companies could not keep pace with British demands for copper during the war, but afterwards they invested heavily in expanding output. This responded impressively to rising prices, boosted by sterling devaluation in 1949 and by war in Korea from 1950. The mine companies were finally able to pay regular dividends, while the government also benefited considerably, especially since in 1949 it gained a share in the British South Africa Company's mining royalties. Government spending on 'development' favoured white business: the white population grew rapidly through immigration and by 1953 reached almost 50 000. The African countryside was largely neglected, but the condition of Africans in towns was somewhat improved. The Colonial Office promoted the emergence, in 1947–8, of African trade unions, and

these enjoyed the same rights as white unions. Thus some African workers were able to secure a modest share in the new prosperity; moreover after 1953 the mine companies slightly modified the industrial colour bar, enabling Africans to do some of the jobs previously reserved for whites.

Nyasaland's exports also increased very rapidly after the war, though they were worth only a small fraction of those from either of the Rhodesias. Many white planters now concentrated on tea; much of the rising demand for tobacco was now met by Africans. There was little immigration of Europeans; they numbered only 5000 in the early 1950s. Yet African production was now constrained by growing pressure on the land: the territory was much smaller than either of the Rhodesias but its population – over 2 million – was considerably larger. Officials applied unpopular conservation measures in overcrowded rural districts, and the economy continued to depend heavily on migrant labour.

After the war, white settlers renewed demands for the amalgamation of the Rhodesias and Nyasaland. They were partly prompted by fears of African advancement, especially in Northern Rhodesia; indeed, both there and in Nyasaland Africans were nominated in 1948 to the Legislative Councils. Moreover, many whites of British origin in Southern Rhodesia sought amalgamation in order to avoid being swallowed up by South Africa,* where in 1948 Afrikaner nationalists gained power. The Labour government in Britain ruled out amalgamation, but it was keen to see a federation in which Britain could retain control over African affairs in the northern territories. However, Africans there remained firmly opposed to any close association with the settler regime in the south, of which many had first-hand experience as labour migrants. Local welfare associations,

Kenneth Kaunda

Born on 28 April 1924 at Lubwa, Northern Rhodesia, the son of a missionary, Kaunda was educated at a local mission school and at the secondary school in Muwali. From 1943 to 1949 – apart from a period as an assistant mines welfare officer – he was a teacher, and then returned to Lubwa to farm. His political talents were directed into a farmers' association and then into the newly-formed African National Congress (ANC) led by Harry Nkumbula. In 1953 Kaunda became ANC secretary-general but grew disillusioned with the ANC because of its failure to block the establishment of the Central African Federation.* In 1958 Kaunda and other radical ANC leaders declared their goal

to be an independent nation, and rejected Nkumbula's decision to participate in elections based on a new constitution that allowed only a very limited franchise to Africans. In 1958 the radicals split from the ANC to form the Zambia African National Congress (ZANC): in 1959 the colonial government declared a state of emergency, banned the ZANC and jailed Kaunda and others. In 1960 Kaunda was released and was elected president of the United National Independence Party, which had been founded while he was in prison. He became prime minister after internal self-government was granted in 1962, and at independence in October 1964 became President of the Republic of Zambia.   *G.A.*

The Struggle for Independence

led by mission-educated clerks and teachers, combined to form embryo political parties, the Nyasaland Congress (1944) and the Northern Rhodesian Congress (1948). In Southern Rhodesia a Bantu National Congress had been founded in 1934, but there was no mass support for its campaign against amalgamation, since this seemed no great threat to Africans already under settler rule. In 1951 the Labour government in Britain was replaced by a Conservative one, which ignored African protests and imposed federation on Central Africa in 1953.

The Central African Federation was dominated from the first by Southern Rhodesia. Huggins (who became Lord Malvern in 1956), became the Federal Prime Minister. Southern Rhodesia supplied more than half the elected members of its parliament and gained the lion's share of federal expenditure; the south became in effect the Federation's workshop, while uneven redistribution of federal tax revenue meant that Northern Rhodesia suffered a net loss each year of £10 million to the other territories. Social services for whites expanded much faster than those for blacks, and few Africans from any territory qualified for entrance to the multi-racial university college founded at Salisbury in 1957. Since the Federation was so dependent on revenue from the Copperbelt, it was much affected when the copper boom ended in 1956. Many Africans were thrown out of work, while many in the south were also thrown off the land as the government replaced communal by individual tenures in an attempt to improve farming methods.

Far from entrenching the power of white settlers, federation boosted the growth of African nationalism. By the late 1950s popular discontent in all three territories was being mobilized by a new generation of literate young Africans who sought to emulate Ghana's achievement of independence in 1957 and pressed for 'one man, one vote'. In 1958 Dr Hastings Banda returned to Nyasaland after many years overseas and took over the Congress party there; in 1959 Kenneth Kaunda★ and other radical nationalists broke away from the Northern Rhodesia Congress to form the United National Independence Party. In 1961–2 the British government acknowledged that it was not prepared to keep the northern territories in the Federation by force and allowed Africans to take a majority of seats in their respective legislative councils. These concessions were bitterly resented by Malvern's successor as Federal Prime Minister, Sir Roy Welensky (a former trade union leader in Northern Rhodesia). In 1961–2 the Southern Rhodesian government banned successive parties led by Joshua Nkomo, a former railway workers' leader from Bulawayo, in the heart of Ndebele country. In 1963 the Reverend Ndabaningi Sithole broke away from Nkomo's Zimbabwe African People's Union★ to form the Zimbabwe African National Union,★ which drew support from Shona-speaking areas. By this time, however, federation had been challenged by white nationalists in Southern Rhodesia who had no patience with the pretensions to racial

Lord Malvern (left) and Sir Roy Welensky

'partnership' of the ruling United Federal Party. In the 1962 elections it was defeated by the Rhodesian Front, which aimed to make the country an independent state under white rule.

At the end of 1963 Welensky bowed to the inevitable and the Federation was dissolved. In a vain attempt to prevent the Rhodesian Front from seizing independence illegally, Britain gave Southern Rhodesia the greater part of the Federation's military assets. In July 1964 Nyasaland became the independent state of Malawi; in October, Northern Rhodesia became the Republic of Zambia. The British government was only prepared to grant independence to Southern Rhodesia on terms quite unacceptable to the Rhodesian Front. African resistance was ruthlessly suppressed by the Southern Rhodesian government, and on 11 November 1965 the Prime Minister, Ian Smith, made a unilateral declaration of independence (UDI). *A.D.R.*

South Africa

South Africa emerged from the Second World War* with a larger and more varied industrial base and a more diversified labour force. Large numbers of Afrikaners had entered skilled, high paid jobs, while even greater numbers of Africans had become full time wage labourers; many, however, continued to migrate between their homes in the 'reserves' and the industrial urban areas. Social and economic tensions were accentuated. In 1946 African miners on the goldfields struck, and were severely repressed by the United Party government led by Jan Smuts. This vacillated between liberal and autocratic actions. Its liberal face frightened the almost wholly white electorate, and in 1948 the Afrikaner National Party (NP), in coalition with a smaller party, came into power and has won every subsequent election.

The ideology of the NP was apartheid, a policy that looked forward to the complete separation – geographic, political and social, if not economic – of the whites on the one hand, and the 'non-whites' – Africans, Coloureds and Indians – on the other. The most imposing features of apartheid, notably the creation of Bantustans* or

Africans, Coloureds and Indians protest, c. 1952 against the apartheid policies of the South African government

D.F. Malan, Prime Minister of South Africa, 1948–54, one of the architects of the National Party's apartheid policy

Homelands* were implemented after 1961. Between 1945 and 1961 NP governments enacted a great mass of discriminatory legislation aimed against the non-whites. This sought to control every aspect of their daily lives, and to ensure the privileges and prosperity of the whites, who numbered less than one quarter of the population. Examples of this legislation include the Group Areas Act (1950), which designated residential areas as being exclusively for particular racial groups; the Immorality Act (1950), which outlawed sexual relations and marriage between whites and non-whites; and the Bantu Education Act (1953) which separated the African and European education systems.

The response of Africans and other non-white groups to the economic and social unheavals they were undergoing, and to the government's actions, which augmented these stresses and strains, was one of prolonged resistance. African political and industrial unrest reached a climax in the 1950s. In 1952 (the tercentenary of the first white settlement at the Cape) the African National Congress (ANC) organized a widespread passive resistance campaign against discrimination in general and, in particular, against the legislation which obliged Africans in urban areas to carry identification passes. In 1953 the Congress Alliance of the ANC and Coloured, Indian and sympathetic white parties drew up a Freedom Charter for South Africa which demanded full rights for all citizens, white and non-white. The government's reply was large-scale arrests and bannings – by which individuals were prevented from carrying on their occupations and were rendered politically impotent, and yet more laws aimed at the suppression of non-white opposition.

Faced with government repression, in 1959 African opposition split: one branch, the ANC, continued to support the aims of the

Albert Luthuli

Luthuli was born in Southern Rhodesia (now Zimbabwe) c. 1898 of Zulu parents. His father died shortly after his birth, and his mother returned with Luthuli to her native Natal in South Africa. Luthuli was educated in mission schools and then taught at a mission college for 15 years. In 1936 he was elected to a minor Zulu chieftainship, a position which increased his awareness of the inequalities and injustices suffered by black South Africans. He joined the black nationalist African National Congress (ANC) in 1946, and was elected president of the Natal branch in 1951. In 1952 he became national president of the ANC, and his refusal to resign led to his being deposed as a chief by the government. In 1953 his political activities led to his being banned from entering the larger centres of South Africa, and in 1954 a further banning order confined him to the Lower Tugela magisterial district and debarred him from attending public gatherings. Although ill-health and continual banning orders made it difficult for him to give vigorous administrative leadership to the ANC, he exerted a powerful moral influence in a period when apartheid* measures were becoming harsher – and were meeting increased African resistance. His moderate policies, however, did lose him support among ANC radicals, who formed the rival Pan-Africanist Congress (PAC) in 1958. Both the ANC and the PAC were banned in 1960 amid increasing and more violent African resistance to pass law restrictions. Luthuli's advocacy of non-violence led to his being awarded the Nobel Peace Prize in 1961. In 1962 he published an autobiography, *Let my people go*. In July 1967 he was killed by a train while crossing the tracks near his home.   *L.E.L.*

Hendrik Verwoerd

Verwoerd was born in September 1901 in the Netherlands, but came to South Africa in 1903 when his parents emigrated as missionaries. He was educated at the staunchly Afrikaner university at Stellenbosch (BA 1921, MA 1922, PhD 1925) and then pursued further studies abroad. In 1928 he was appointed to the chair of psychology at Stellenbosch University. While at Stellenbosch Verwoerd joined the National Party (NP) and became a member of the *Broederbond*, the highly influential, semi-secret inner circle of leaders of Afrikaner cultural and political nationalism. In 1935 he was appointed editor of a new Afrikaans-language newspaper, *Die Transvaler*, which began publication in 1937. During the Second World War Verwoerd propagated Afrikaner nationalist views in his newspaper, for example opposing South African military participation on the Allied side. In 1948 the general elections were won by the NP and Verwoerd was elected to the Senate. In October 1950 he became Minister of Native Affairs and introduced – among other pieces of discriminatory legislation – measures to separate black education from the white system (Bantu Education Act 1953) and regulations that began the process of resettling blacks outside white-occupied urban areas. In August 1958 he became Prime Minister, and soon initiated a policy of establishing separate black states – the Bantustans – within South Africa. In 1960 he fulfilled a longstanding ambition by masterminding moves to transform South Africa into a republic, but was unable to maintain its membership of the British Commonwealth in the face of the hostility of other members to South Africa's apartheid* policies; hostility which had been intensified by the 1960 Sharpeville* massacres. Verwoerd was assassinated in parliament in September 1966 by a deranged parliamentary messenger.   *A.A.*

Sharpeville, 21 March 1960

Freedom Charter; the other, the Pan-Africanist Congress (PAC), followed a more nationalist African line. The PAC organized further demonstrations against passes, and it was during one of these, at Sharpeville in the southern Transvaal, that the police fired on an unarmed crowd on 21 March 1960 and killed 67 people. A state of emergency was declared, and both ANC and PAC turned to more violent actions. Both parties were banned, and, after massive repression–culminating, by 1964, in the imprisonment of Nelson Mandela and other leaders of the ANC, and Robert Sobukwe of the PAC–open resistance was largely broken. Meanwhile, in 1961, South Africa had shown its defiance of world opinion by leaving the British Commonwealth, and declaring a republic. *A.A.*

Portuguese Africa

The history of the decolonization of the Portuguese empire in Africa is quite different from that of the other European empires for three main reasons. First, Portugal in the 1960s was not a democracy. Its authoritarian government was able, if it chose, to declare war without the regard for public opinion which influenced British and French governments. Between 1961 and 1974 it censored news, played down reports of casualties, arrested dissidents, and put about half of its budget into fighting African wars. In the end the European-manned Portuguese army rebelled and put an end to the wars, thereby recognizing colonial freedom.

Second, Portugal was a poor country. Industrialized nations, by contrast, found that they could maintain close ties of economic partnership with former colonies, or even economic domination over them. If, however, in 1961, Portugal had granted flag independence to its colonies, they might have become neo-colonial satellites of, for example, West Germany or the USA, since Portugal itself could not have satisfied their need for capital, technology or skills. Antonio Salazar, the Portuguese prime minister, therefore determined to retain the formal, old-colonial links. He astutely pressed the Kennedy administration into reversing US policy on self-determination for Africa; instead the USA began supporting Portuguese resistance to national emancipation. The lever on Washington was Portugal's strategic refuelling base on the Azores Islands, which the US Air Force wished to use.

Third, Portugal's two largest colonies bordered South Africa. The maintenance of white supremacy in the industrial south looked profitable to Western investors, and Portugal's colonies were therefore a potential buffer between Black Africa and white-ruled Africa. Members of the North Atlantic Treaty Organization therefore decided to stretch their geographic limitations and to allow military aid to Portugal to be used in the indirect defence of South Africa. This was made more effective by an influx of white settlers. By 1970 Mozambique and Angola had about 500 000 whites between them, a proportion comparable to that in Rhodesia (now Zimbabwe*), which was the third link in the chain of colonies isolating South Africa from independent Black Africa.

The colonial wars in Portuguese Africa lasted 13 years, longer than, and at times as brutal as, the only comparable African war, that in the settler colony of Algeria.* War began in Angola in 1961, followed by Guinea-Bissau in 1963 and Mozambique in 1964.

The 1961 Angolan war of independence had begun in the cotton fields. Since the 1940s Kimbundu-speaking peasants in the Luanda hinterland had suffered poverty, and sometimes famine from a government policy of compulsory crop growing. In January 1971, in a reluctant display of final despair, they turned to violence, and burnt down the cotton warehouses. A month later, urban blacks also launched a violent uprising and tried to free their leaders from prison. The immigration of semi-educated whites had been steadily eroding city jobs at even quite menial levels and had caused acute black discontent. The newly-arrived white workers felt threatened by the unemployed blacks, and invaded the slums with firearms soon after: in March, an even larger and more destructive conflagration occurred in Angola's northern coffee estates. Africans who had been dispossessed of their land, and unpaid plantation workers killed 200 white settlers and many black immigrant coffee harvesters. In retaliation, white militias liquidated Westernized Africans from schools, churches and other centres capable of providing anti-colonial leadership.

Eduardo Mondlane

Born in 1920 in southern Mozambique, Mondlane was the founder of modern Mozambican nationalism. The son of a chief, he had a peasant childhood but won a scholarship to attend secondary school in South Africa. He subsequently studied at the Jan Hofmeyr School of Social Studies and Witswatersrand University but was deported from South Africa because of his part in founding an organization of Mozambican students. He completed his higher education by going to Portugal in 1950– where he forged close friendships with other young nationalists from the Portuguese African colonies, including Agosthino Neto and Amilcar Cabral–and then to the USA, where he studied sociology and anthropology at Oberlin College and Northwestern University, completing a PhD at the latter before becoming an officer of the UN Trusteeship Commission.

Returning briefly to Mozambique in 1961, Mondlane saw that peaceful decolonization was ruled out and decided to commit himself to the independence struggle. He kept in touch with small nationalist groups that had formed following a massacre of peasants at Mueda in 1960–1, but did not join any of them, arguing instead that they should unite. He successfully brought the three main groups together at a conference in Dar es Salaam, where the *Frente de Libertação de Moçambique (Frelimo)* was founded on 25 June 1962. Mondlane was elected *Frelimo* president and shortly afterwards he resigned his post as a professor at Syracuse University in the USA and devoted himself full-time to the new movement, which launched a guerrilla war against Portugal in September 1964. Mondlane was assassinated in Dar es Salaam on 3 February 1969, blown up by a parcel bomb allegedly sent by Portuguese agents.   *T.H.*

Amilcar Cabral

Born at Bafata on the mainland of Portuguese Guinea on 24 September 1924, Cabral was the son of a Cape Verdian official and landowner from the island of São Tiago. After attending school in Cape Verde, Cabral studied agronomy and hydraulics engineering in Lisbon for five years, returning to Portuguese Guinea in 1953, where he took up an appointment as an agricultural engineer. He carried out an extensive agricultural census during which he travelled throughout Portuguese Guinea, obtaining an intimate knowledge of the condition of the peasantry which made him increasingly opposed to Portuguese colonial rule. In 1955, under pressure from the colonial administration, he returned to Lisbon, but later worked in Angola, where he associated with Angolan revolutionary leaders, and established a clandestine political party, the *Partido Africano da Indepên-*

dencia da Guiné e Cabo Verde (PAIGC). Although the PAIGC initially worked peacefully in urban areas, increasing Portuguese repression forced it into the rural areas, and in 1959 Cabral returned from Angola to set up PAIGC headquarters in Conakry, Guinea. There he began a large-scale guerrilla training programme, and by 1963 guerrilla warfare against the Portuguese had been initiated. Cabral's grasp of peasant needs enabled him to formulate a revolutionary strategy of compelling utility and relevance to the situation in Portuguese Guinea, stressing mass participation and improvements in health, education and women's rights. Cabral was also a talented military leader, able to bridge ethnic divisions, and by the early 1970s PAIGC controlled more than half of Portuguese Guinea. He was assassinated on 20 June 1973 by a PAIGC dissident widely believed to have been in the service of the Portuguese.   *J.E.C.*

Portugal succeeded in suppressing the great Angolan rebellions of 1961 and in containing the continuing guerrilla war. But the cost was so great that Salazar's policy of restricted economic nationalism had to be modified. Foreign investment was allowed to build an industrial base with which to finance the war. As a corollary, educational opportunities had to be liberalized to enable more blacks to gain the necessary education to work in the modern sector of the economy. Even this was not adequate and a policy of Africanizing the colonial army was embarked upon. As a last resort, new economic opportunities were offered to black coffee growers to minimize their disaffection. Their Baptist religion became unofficially tolerated, they were given technical advice and credit comparable to that given to white settlers, and they were permitted to establish cooperatives independent of the entrenched white marketing firms. Meanwhile the war continued in eastern Angola, where two political movements each fielded guerrilla armies, though neither was able to break the colonial deadlock that had been reached in the early 1970s.

In 1973–4 *Frente de Libertação de Moçambique (Frelimo)* guerrillas broke through into the centre of Mozambique and caused the Portuguese army to sue for peace after the latter had overthrown the governing dictatorship in Lisbon. In Angola, where the nationalist movement was split between Agosthino Neto's *Movimento Popular de Libertação de Angola* (MPLA), Holden Roberto's *Frente Nacional de Libertação de Angola* (FNLA), and Jonas Savimbi's *União Nacional de Independência Total de Angola* (UNITA), the Lisbon coup encouraged the internationalization of the war. Zaire moved first, anxious to avoid the establishment of a left-wing government which might inflame the aspirations of its own rural populations, and supported Roberto's forces. When this initiative faltered, South Africa moved in to support Savimbi, a strategy which so offended African sensibilities that Cuba was able to enter the war with some 10 000 troops and to rescue the regime of Neto to which the retiring Portuguese had informally given possession. The internationally orchestrated civil war tore the country apart and destroyed the central economy which had been relatively immune to the long, but remote, military stalemate of the war against Portugal. The American oil wells of Cabinda, were the only large industry to survive almost unscathed. By 1976 the worst of the war was over, though South African intervention remained a threat, and urban-rural tensions and bleak poverty remained.

The Mozambique war of liberation began more slowly, faltered as the lines of communication from the northern border became over-extended, and suffered a severe setback in 1969 when Eduardo Mondlane,* *Frelimo's* pre-eminent leader, was assassinated. Portugal, meanwhile, rallied international support by involving South Africa and European states in the building of a 2 million kwh hydro-electric dam on the Zambezi. The bait to foreign involvement proved inadequate, however, and Portugal fought the last years of rearguard colonial defence bitterly and without ground allies. Portuguese commandos and special security police were demoralized by the international response to brutal repressive policies. The small, white settler communities south of the Zambezi panicked when their highland settlements were penetrated by guerrilla irregulars, who, in 1973, began to sabotage the railway to Rhodesia. The war ended in April 1974. Independence was achieved in June 1975; the intervening period being taken up with last-ditch attempts by the Portuguese to negotiate a continued political association with Mozambique.

In Guinea-Bissau, at the time of the Lisbon coup, the *Partido Africano da Independência da Guiné e Cabo Verde* (PAIGC) already controlled large rural swathes in the north and south and had set up an alternative black government which had begun to attract international recognition. Power was therefore handed over smoothly to the PAIGC. The smallest colonies, the two island groups of Cape Verde, and São Tomé and Príncipe, gained their freedom as a by-product of the mainland wars. Their politics were dominated by drought, famine and overpopulation.   *D.B.B.*

The colonial legacy

Although the relatively short period of European colonial rule may be seen in hindsight as a mere episode in the long sweep of history, inducing fewer fundamental changes in African societies than was once supposed, the problems and difficulties of post-colonial Africa rest as much, if not more, on the innovations of the colonial era as on the continuities from the pre-colonial past. This is most obviously true of the character of the post-colonial state–with its birthright of artificial boundaries, politics strongly affected by ethnicity,* and uncertain relationships between military and civilian powers–but it is also the case in respect of the post-colonial economy. Indeed, reflecting the view that political predicaments often stem from underlying economic circumstances, interest in, and debate over, the colonial legacy has increasingly focused upon Africa's modern economic history.

Did colonialism promote 'development' or 'under-development'? At issue is rather less what actually happened than how to evaluate these events. European rule completed the integration of Africa into the world system of production and exchange, and facilitated the penetration of European, and latterly American, capital into the continent. The colonial economies evolved as peripheries of the core industrialized economies. Structural change took the form of a rapid expansion of the export sector, supplying agricultural and mineral products to overseas markets and normally specializing in one or two commodities. In cocoa-growing Gold Coast (now Ghana), peanut-producing Senegal, and cotton- and coffee-trading Uganda indigenous agriculture was the basis of the export sector, whereas the wine of Algeria, coffee of Kenya and tobacco of Southern Rhodesia (now Zimbabwe) came from the estates of immigrant European farmers. Several economies had mineral as well as agricultural exports, but Northern Rhodesia (now Zambia) was unusual in its reliance upon a single mineral, copper, for its foreign exchange earnings. Such was the importance of externally-oriented production that growth and fluctuations in the typical African economy largely reflected outside conditions, particularly international prices for the staple export commodities and movements in the terms of trade between manufactures and primary produce. Foreign capital, companies and personnel were pre-eminent in trade, banking, mining, manufacturing (mainly a post-1945 phenomenon) and, in certain cases, commercial agriculture. Sectors producing for the internal market – for foodstuffs, construction materials or consumer goods – grew more slowly, and partly as a derivative of external trade. Large parts of the countryside tended to have little significant exchange production, being bypassed by the modern transport and communications networks necessary to commercial activity, and remained locations of low productivity, subsistence-orientated agriculture which released labour to the more favoured areas.

To one school of thought, principally within the Western liberal tradition, these changes represented processes of 'development'. Despite the fact that, on the eve of independence, total per capita incomes were low relative to the industrialized economies, and even allowing for such features as the use of coercion to secure labour during the early decades of the colonial presence, the results of European rule were generally held to be 'progressive'. The productive capacities of African societies, it is argued, had been enlarged through the introduction of modern technology, and total per capita output had increased over time. The national product may not have been distributed equally, and it was less than certain that the real incomes and levels of welfare of the broad mass of the population had risen. Nevertheless, one could point to the wider provision of education, roads, health facilities and other services by the state, more especially during the post-1945 phase of colonial 'development and welfare', as an indication of spreading social benefits. Colonialism, it could be argued, had launched Africa on a developmental path, providing a foundation from which further extensions of the forces of production were possible.

The alternative interpretation, which emerged strongly during the post-independence decades, brings together elements of nationalist and Marxist perspectives. It suggests that integration into the international economy produced not 'development', the first steps on a path to cumulative economic transformation, but rather 'underdevelopment', a diversion into an evolutionary dead end. The structuring of the African economies by the colonial powers, it is argued, created a condition of dependence on the West that continues to stifle and stunt post-colonial economies. The manifestations of dependence include over-reliance on overseas markets, susceptibility to fluctuations in commodity prices, the growth of foreign debt, the dominant position of foreign companies within the economy, and the alleged willingness of the post-independence political and administrative elites to cooperate with foreign capital. Dependence results in 'underdevelopment' because it permits the exploitation of Africa by the West, even after the end of formal colonial authority, principally through the repatriation of profits by Western firms operating in the continent, and by means of 'unequal exchange' which ensures that the gains from trade accrue mainly to the West. The full potential of Africa's resources, therefore, was not realized under either the colonial authorities or the great majority of independent governments.

Adjudication between these two positions is rendered difficult by the ambiguity of the terms 'development' and 'underdevelopment', both of which can mean a condition as well as a process. The proponents of 'underdevelopment' in particular cloud the distinction by their tendency to argue that because African economies are not in a 'developed' condition, in the sense of being high-income, industrialized economies, then they must have undergone a process of 'underdevelopment'. It would be possible, however, depending upon choice of meaning, to state that African economies 'developed' into 'underdevelopment'. The 'underdevelopment' school's charges of exploitation are also difficult to substantiate. To be sure, monopoly and coercion existed in some places at some times, but they were by no means universal features of the colonial situation. 'Unequal exchange' does not appear a particularly useful concept, in that equity in trade is largely a matter for subjective evaluation, and it is not at all clear that leakages of national income through repatriated profits is the major or even an important barrier to the bringing of Africa's unused resources into production. On balance, it seems more realistic to perceive the economic transformation carried out by the European rulers as involving processes of 'dependent development', in which there were both stimuli to, and constraints upon, the growth of productive capacities. A highly ambivalent relationship with the world's core industrial economies (capitalist and socialist) was the colonial legacy to Africa.

J.F.M.

The National Theatre in Lagos, Nigeria: one of the projects commissioned for the Second All Black and African Festival of the Arts (*Festac*), 1977

CONTEMPORARY AFRICA

THE STATES OF AFRICA

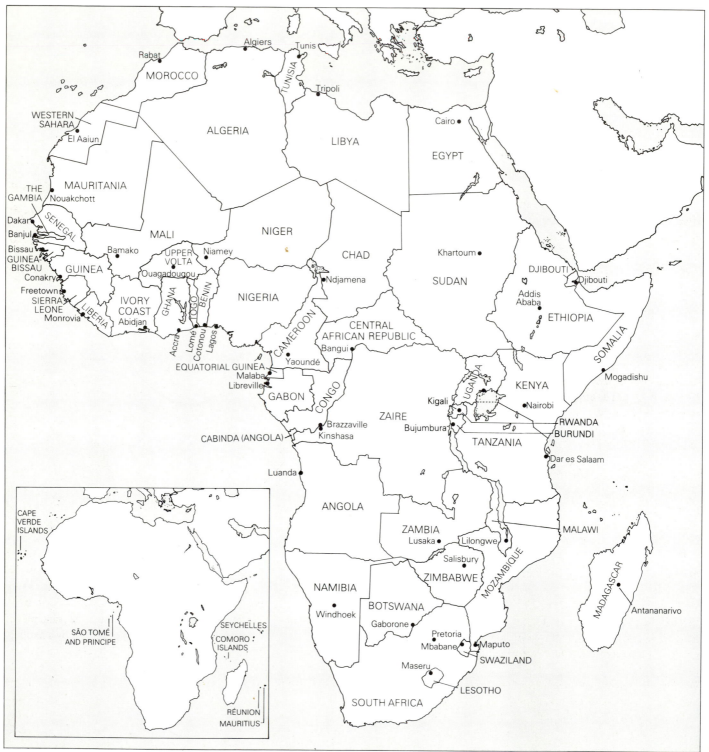

MOROCCO

Rabat

Algiers

TUNISIA

Tunis

Tripoli

WESTERN SAHARA

El Aaiun

ALGERIA

LIBYA

EGYPT

Cairo

MAURITANIA

THE GAMBIA

Nouakchott

Dakar

SENEGAL

Banjul

Bissau

GUINEA-BISSAU

GUINEA

Conakry

Freetown

SIERRA LEONE

LIBERIA

Monrovia

Bamako

MALI

UPPER VOLTA

Ouagadougou

IVORY COAST

Abidjan

GHANA

Accra

TOGO

Lomé

Cotonou

BENIN

Lagos

Niamey

NIGER

NIGERIA

CHAD

Ndjamena

CAMEROON

Yaoundé

EQUATORIAL GUINEA

Malabo

Libreville

GABON

CONGO

Brazzaville

Kinshasa

CABINDA (ANGOLA)

Khartoum

SUDAN

CENTRAL AFRICAN REPUBLIC

Bangui

ZAIRE

DJIBOUTI

Djibouti

Addis Ababa

ETHIOPIA

SOMALIA

Mogadishu

UGANDA

Kigali

KENYA

Nairobi

RWANDA

Bujumbura

BURUNDI

TANZANIA

Dar es Salaam

Luanda

ANGOLA

ZAMBIA

Lusaka

Lilongwe

MALAWI

Salisbury

ZIMBABWE

MOZAMBIQUE

MADAGASCAR

Antananarivo

NAMIBIA

Windhoek

BOTSWANA

Gaborone

Pretoria

Mbabane

Maputo

SWAZILAND

Maseru

LESOTHO

SOUTH AFRICA

CAPE VERDE ISLANDS

SÃO TOMÉ AND PRINCIPE

SEYCHELLES

COMORO ISLANDS

RÉUNION

MAURITIUS

Algeria

Area (km²)	2 381 741
Population 1980 (UN projection)	19 828 000
GNP per capita 1977 (US$)	1110
Capital	Algiers
Currency	Dinar

Since independence in 1962 the government of Algeria has been dominated by the army, and, until his death in 1978, specifically by the controller of the army, Houari Boumedienne.

Boumedienne's combination of state socialism with Arabism and Islam came to characterize the regime. As Chief of Staff of the *Armée de la Libération Nationale*, (ALN), Boumedienne ensured that Ahmed Ben Bella, one of the original leaders of the insurrection in 1954, was able to take over the nationalist movement on his release from imprisonment in France in 1961, and then the government of the newly-independent country. While Boumedienne overcame the military opposition of the guerrilla leaders who had continued to operate inside Algeria, Ben Bella defeated politically Ben Yousef Ben Khedda, the head of the provisional government, who had negotiated the Evian Agreement* on Algerian independence; Ferhat Abbas, who demanded the supremacy of an elected assembly; and Mohamed Khider, who tried to take power by virtue of his position as general secretary of the *Front de la Libération Nationale* (FLN), the party of government. Ben Bella's chief use of power was to initiate, in 1963, worker self-management (*autogestion*) for agricultural estates and industrial enterprises that had been vacated by the almost total departure of the French, and now belonged to the state. His attempts to remove Boumedienne's supporters from the government, however, resulted in the coup of June 1965, when Ben Bella was placed under house arrest, and Boumedienne became President of the Council of the Revolution and prime minister.

Following the coup, Ben Bella's supporters united with opponents of Ben Bella and Boumedienne, like Mohamed Khider and Belkacem Krim, in opposition in Europe, where Khider was assassinated in 1967, and Krim in 1970. While Ben Bella had pursued popularity through frequent public appearances and tours, Boumedienne was little seen. The government was in the hands of the so-called Oujda group of his supporters, who had formed around him in Morocco during the war. The economy came increasingly under state control, while worker self-management was still embryonic; the official policy was to use the oil and gas revenues of the country to create heavy industry as the basis for economic growth. In 1971, after the national company, *Sonatrach*, had progressively acquired a larger and larger share in its operation, the mainly French-owned oil and gas industry

Workers on a worker self-managed agricultural estate in Algeria receive their wages

was finally nationalized. The administration and local government were modelled on the French system with its *communes* and *départements*, and was, like it, strongly bureaucratic, with the addition of the army as an agent of control. Assemblies elected for the *communes* in 1967 and the *wilayas* or *départements* in 1969 were heavily directed by the government. There was no national assembly, and the national party, the FLN, was strictly subordinate to rather than in control of the government.

In 1971 Boumedienne turned to the question of land reform. The aim was to solve the problem of land hunger and rural unemployment outside the area under self-management, which now showed signs of success. Land in excess of what the owner and his family could cultivate alone was redistributed to peasants organized in cooperatives, a major act affecting the property of the Algerian middle classes on which the regime relies for its personnel. The reform, however, was largely unopposed. In 1976 the question of popular participation in national affairs was revived in a debate organized throughout the country on the National Charter, which laid down the principles of Algerian socialism and was overwhelmingly approved by a national referendum in June. This was followed in 1977 by elections to a new national assembly, the candidates coming, as in the local elections, solely from the FLN. Power neverthelesss remained with the President and his largely military adherents, who between them resolved the problem of succession created by Boumedienne's death at the age of 46 in December 1978, with the choice of Chadli Bendjedid – the acting defence minister – as the new president.

In foreign affairs Algeria has been cautious, looking to France and the West, to the USSR and to China for assistance. It has been close to Syria in support of the Palestine Liberation Organization and, as a member of the Organization of Petroleum Exporting Countries, has advocated a high price for oil. A long-standing border dispute with Morocco, which led to a clash in 1963, has since 1975 taken the form of support for *Polisario*★ military forces fighting Moroccan troops in Western (formerly Spanish) Sahara.★   *M. B.*

Angola

Area (km²)	1 246 700
Population 1980 (UN projection)	7 181 000
GNP per capita 1977 (US$)	330
Capital	Luanda
Currency	Kwanza

The official end to Portugal's presence in Angola on 11 November 1975 saw the country in open civil war, with three claimants to governmental legitimacy. In Luanda the *Movimento Popular de Libertação de Angola* (MPLA) established a 'People's Republic of Angola', while both the *Frente Nacional de Libertação de Angola* (FNLA) and the *União Nacional de Independência Total de Angola* (UNITA) set up rival regimes respectively at Ambriz and Huambo. A few days later, UNITA and FNLA reluctantly combined at the instigation of their foreign backers to form a coalition 'Popular Democratic Republic of Angola'. At independence, however, MPLA's control of the district capitals and seaboard towns had collapsed in the face of a combined South African and UNITA-FNLA advance. With the arrival of Cuban regulars and greatly increased levels of Soviet military assistance, the MPLA was able to halt the South African-supported advance about 400km south of Luanda on 20 November. To the north, the FNLA was similarly repulsed and on 16 February 1976 the last major area of resistance at São Salvador was taken. This change in the military balance prompted a South African withdrawal from forward positions in January, leaving the poorly organized and still mutually hostile UNITA-FNLA to garrison the southern provinces. MPLA then launched a major offensive and by 12 February had captured all the major towns previously in UNITA-FNLA hands. On 27 March the last South African troops were pulled out with only small, isolated bands of UNITA guerrillas being left to operate in Huambo and Bie provinces and from across the Namibian border. By this time, the MPLA's Peoples' Republic had been recognized by both the Organization of African Unity★ (11 February) and Portugal (12 February).

Immense tasks of reconstruction faced the new government. These were made especially difficult because of shortages in all types of technical and managerial personnel following the departure of over 600 000 whites before independence and critical losses in basic infrastructure such as bridges, trucks and rail-links. Great damage to the food-growing regions of the central plateau and to the coffee plantations in the north was compounded by the loss of over 90 per cent of the Ovimbundu migrant workers to UNITA strongholds in the south. Thus production of coffee, the main export crop, as well as sisal and cotton has slumped to under 30 per cent of pre-war levels.

Despite these formidable problems, Angola's trade balance remained in surplus in the late 1970s, chiefly because of tax and royalties collected from the American subsidiary, Cabinda Gulf Oil. Indeed, some two-thirds of government revenue was derived from this single source. National policy is to seek a controlling interest in foreign companies rather than outright nationalization. Peasants and workers cooperatives are envisaged as the basis of the new Angolan economy but their extension beyond formerly abandoned enterprises is inevitably gradual. In this phase of reconstruction and economic recovery a policy of pragmatism has therefore been pursued, with official encouragement for a private sector in small-scale artisan and service activities.

In the political field, MPLA underwent a major restructuring in 1978 in response to the factional activity surrounding an attempted coup by MPLA dissidents on 27 May 1977. Renamed 'MPLA Party of Labour' at its first Congress in December 1977, it has assumed a vanguard role in the building of a new society. Nevertheless, a considerable distance has yet to be travelled before Angola can be said to possess a fully integrated set of political institutions.   *J.E.C.*

Benin

Area (km²)	112 622
Population 1980 (UN projection)	3 534 000
GNP per capita 1977 (US$)	200
Capital	Cotonou
Currency	CFA franc

After becoming independent from France as the Republic of Dahomey in 1960, the country went through a decade of acute political instability, with six bloodless coups between 1963 and 1973. Economic difficulties (with a chronic budgetary deficit) provide some of the relevant background to this political turmoil. Dahomey also had a problem with the enforced repatriation of its relatively well-educated nationals who had occupied administrative posts throughout the former French West African Federation. This led to the growth of a civil service far beyond the country's resources.

A series of military political interventions (in 1963, 1965, 1967, 1969 and 1970) revolved around competition between the country's three principal civilian politicians – Hubert Maga, Sourou Migan Apithy and Justin Ahomadegbe. In 1972 Major (now Colonel) Mathieu Kerekou led a *coup d'état* and took over the government. Since then the Kerekou regime has consolidated its power and tightened internal security. In 1974 Marxism-Leninism was adopted as the official ideology, and at the end of 1975 the country was renamed the People's Republic of Benin. Leftward moves led to a steady deterioration of relations with France, and in 1976 all French financial aid was cut off. There have reportedly been unsuccessful attempts at military coups, as well as a chronic political disaffection centred on exiled civilian politicians, and in 1977 an invasion force of foreign mercenaries briefly controlled Cotonou airport. The Kerekou regime (already the longest surviving since independence) still relies on a national army of 2000 men, reinforced by the national gendarmerie: its popular base is chiefly in the relatively backward, underpopulated north. Without significant mineral resources, Benin stresses the need for self-sufficiency through improved agricultural production, and has achieved some success – notably in a tripling of rice production between 1972 and 1978. *D.C.O'B.*

Botswana

Area (km²)	600 372
Population 1980 (UN projection)	795 000
GNP per capita 1977 (US$)	440
Capital	Gaborone
Currency	Pula

Since independence in 1966 Botswana has seen its economic prospects transformed and its political system remain tranquil and democratic. Independence came during a particularly severe drought that left one person in six dependent on food aid handouts. Since then, diamond, copper, nickel, and coal mines have been developed (although only the first is notably lucrative) and in 1969 the customs union agreement linking Botswana, Lesotho and Swaziland to South Africa was revised in favour of the three Black states. In 1976 Botswana broke away from the southern African monetary union and created its own currency, the pula. Nonetheless, the country remains very poor and the predominantly rural population remains vulnerable to droughts. It is large, sparsely populated, and surrounded almost entirely by South Africa, Namibia and Zimbabwe.* During

the conflict in Rhodesia (now Zimbabwe) it had to cope with refugees and cross-border raids by Rhodesian forces, and in 1977 was forced to form a small army. Its previously very limited scope for manoeuvre in relations with the white minority states will presumably be eased by the 1980 election of a black government in Zimbabwe.

Bostwana is one of the few remaining parliamentary democracies in Africa. The ruling Botswana Democratic Party of President Seretse Khama won the 1965 (pre-independence), 1969 and 1974 elections, but three opposition parties (the Botswana Independence Party, the Botswana National Front, and the Botswana People's Party) have seats in the National Assembly. Politics have tended to be relaxed and low-key but tensions are increasing as a result of rapid economic growth and, particularly, the situation in neighbouring countries. *C.S.*

Sir Seretse Khama, President of Botswana, 1966–80

Burundi

Area (km²)	27 834
Population 1980 (UN projection)	4 288 000
GNP per capita 1977 (US$)	130
Capital	Bujumbura
Currency	Burundi franc

Belgium ceded its authority in Burundi in 1962 to a nation-state based on the traditional Tutsi★ monarchy, headed by the ageing Mwami (king) Mwambutsa IV and led by a political party, *Unité pour le Progrès National* (*Uprona*). The kingship provided a superficial unity, with a balance struck, in the first three years of independence, between the minority Tutsi and majority Hutu★ ethnic groups in government. This unity began to crack in July 1966 when Mwambutsa was deposed by his son, Prince Charles Ndiseye–who became Mwami Ntare V–with the backing of Captain Michel Micombero. Within four months Micombero, who had become prime minister, had abolished the monarchy, inaugurated a republic and had set the country on the path of overt Tutsi domination. Hutus were progressively purged from positions of authority: by 1972 only two of the 26 member *Uprona* executive, the *Conseil Suprême de la Republique*, were Hutu, 23 being Tutsi-Hima from Bururi province. A Hutu coup failed on 29 April 1972, and was followed by the systematic massacre of over 100 000 Hutu by the army and the *Jeunesse Révolutionnaire Rwagasore* (a 'youth' movement closely

Voters wait to cast their ballots in the 1960 Burundi elections

associated with *Uprona*). About 120 000 other Hutu had fled to Tanzania by July 1973. On 1 November 1976 Lieutenant Colonel Jean-Baptiste Bagaza, representing a different group of Bururi Tutsi families, seized power in a bloodless coup, and has since made some attempts to eliminate the corruption attendant on minority rule by the Tutsi.

I.L.

Cameroon

Area (km²)	475 442
Population 1980 (UN projection)	8 088 000
GNP per capita 1977 (US$)	340
Capital	Yaoundé
Currency	CFA franc

Cameroon has been led by Ahmadou Ahidjo for over 20 years, first as prime minister and, after the independence of French Cameroun in 1960, as president. The British-administered UN trust territory of the Southern Cameroons voted to enter into a federation with the new republic in 1961. The federation lasted until the two countries decided to merge and declared the United Republic of Cameroon in 1972. The country therefore has English- and French-speaking areas; both are official languages of the united republic, though many African languages are used as the mother tongue in different areas.

Ahidjo's government continued to face opposition from the left-wing *Union des Populations du Cameroun*★ (UPC) which had been banned by the French in 1955 but which had become a clandestine guerrilla movement. By 1960 this opposition had flared into an insurrection among the Bamileke★ (who constitute Cameroon's largest ethnic group) which was only put down with the assistance of French troops. The last remnants of UPC resistance inside Cameroon were only eradicated in the early 1970s, but by then Ahidjo had established an authoritarian state ruled by a single party, the *Union Nationale Camerounaise*.

The economy is based on the export of cash crops. Cocoa (Cameroon is the world's fifth largest producer) and coffee account for well over half of the country's exports. Cotton is grown in the dry north, and is increasingly used in local cloth production, while the equatorial forests of the south provide sizeable exports of timber. Cameroon had one important industry on independence, an aluminium plant at Edea, but as all the alumina used in the plant is imported and almost all the aluminium production exported, the industry serves chiefly to export hydro-electric energy embodied in aluminium. Offshore oil production has begun near the Nigerian border; nearly a million tonnes of crude oil were produced in 1978, the first full year of operation. An oil refinery is now being built near Victoria.

Most industry is concentrated around Douala, the largest town (population: 458 000), main port and also the rail terminus. Yaoundé, the capital, lies 250km inland and serves mainly as an administrative centre. The old German-built railway between the two towns was extended recently to reach Ngaoundéré.

Cameroon maintains particularly warm relations with France, is associated with the European Economic Community through the Lomé Convention, and is a founder member of the *Union Douanière et Economique de l'Afrique Centrale*★ customs union of which the other members are Gabon, Congo and the Central African Republic. *A.P.H.*

Cape Verde Islands

Area (km²)	4033
Population 1980 (UN projection)	323 000
GNP per capita 1977 (US$)	140
Capital	Praia
Currency	Cape Verde escudo

Cape Verde suffered cruelly under 515 years of Portuguese rule. During the 20th century alone some 100 000 people died in the islands during successive famines. So when in 1956 Amílcar Cabral,★ himself of Cape Verdean origin, founded the *Partido Africano da Independência da Guiné e Cabo Verde* (PAIGC) in Guinea-Bissau★ to fight the Portuguese, many Cape Verdeans joined him. After the Portuguese government collapsed in 1974, Cape Verde, like the other colonies, proclaimed itself an independent republic, on 5 July 1975.

PAIGC became the ruling party of both Guinea-Bissau and Cape Verde; although its decisions were binding on both countries, each has its own government and assembly. The Cape Verdean government, under the leadership of President and Prime Minister Aristides Pereira Pedro Pires, has adopted policies of austerity and self-help, suited to an impoverished country, preached by Cabral. Labour intensive development schemes, chiefly road construction and water conservation have been undertaken. Education has been a priority: illiteracy at independence was about 70 per cent. Dependent on imported food – chiefly from the USA, which has a large immigrant Cape Verdean population – the country has nevertheless managed to preserve friendly relations with the other power blocs, an effective policy of non-alignment. Large-scale emigration to Europe has relieved unemployment and the remittances of emigrants have provided much needed foreign exchange. *C.F.*

Central African Republic

Area (km²)	622 984
Population 1980 (UN projection)	2 004 000
GNP per capita 1977 (US$)	250
Capital	Bangui
Currency	CFA franc

Oubangui-Chari★ gained internal self-government from France as the Central African Republic in 1958 with Barthélémy Boganda★ as prime minister. His death in 1959 effectively ended the proposed federation with Chad, Gabon and the Congo, and the Central African Republic gained independence from France alone in 1960 under Boganda's successor, David Dacko. President Dacko ruled over a deteriorating economy until his overthrow in a military coup led by Colonel Jean-Bedel Bokassa on 1 January 1966. The export economy – based mainly on cotton, coffee, timber and diamonds –

Jean-Bedel Bokassa, President of the Central African Republic, 1966–79, after his coronation as emperor in 1977

temporarily improved, but by 1968 relations with France were strained, and the republic briefly left the pro-Western *Union Douanière et Economique de l'Afrique Centrale** to form, with Zaire and Chad, the short-lived *Union des Etats de l'Afrique Centrale.** In the 1970s relations with France became more cordial: several Frenchmen were appointed to authoritative government posts, France began constructing a military base and concluded agreements on the as yet unexploited uranium deposits.

Despite substantial subsidies from France, financial difficulties abounded, exacerbated by the prevalence of administrative corruption. By 1979 agricultural production had not fully recovered since the serious 1973 drought, and transport blockages since 1977 had adversely affected exports and caused petrol rationing. Only the ivory trade—largely illicit—was booming; diamond production remained well below former levels.

Bokassa's military self-promotion from colonel to field-marshal paralleled his elevation from president to life-president (in 1972) and—shortly after declaring the republic an empire—to emperor (in 1977). The Napoleonic-style coronation (paid for largely by France) reputedly cost $20 million, whereas annual income per capita was $250. Despite an imperial court, a prime minister, and Dacko back in favour as personal adviser, Bokassa became increasingly autocratic. Several assassination attempts were reported and in early 1979 urban riots were suppressed by Zairean troops. Revelations about the Emperor's personal involvement in the massacre of more than a hundred schoolchildren who had demonstrated against his rule forced France to cool its relations with Bokassa. Later, in September 1979, the French government helped organize the coup that overthrew Bokassa (who went into exile in the Ivory Coast) and replaced him as head of state by Dacko.   *A.P.H.*

Chad

Area (km²)	1 284 000
Population 1980 (UN projection)	4 473 000
GNP per capita 1977 (US$)	130
Capital	Ndjamena
Currency	CFA franc

Independence from France was proclaimed on 11 August 1960. The new prime minister, François Tombalbaye, immediately set about consolidating his personal power. Gabriel Lisette, the founder of the ruling party, the *Parti Progressiste Tchadien* (PPT) was purged; a presidential regime was established in 1962, and in 1963 all parties except the PPT were banned.

Tombalbaye's single party policy was opposed by Muslim politicians and his 'national loans' policy—the imposition of a development levy—led to outbreaks of peasant revolt. In 1966 these rebellions were given some form by the establishment, with Sudan's assistance, of *Frolinat* (the Chad National Liberation Front). In 1969 French forces intervened to help Tombalbaye against the rebels and in 1971 Tombalbaye sought national reconciliation by inviting Muslim politicians to join his government.

In 1973, against a background of continuing *Frolinat* military activity, Tombalbaye dissolved the PPT and, following the example of his ally General Mobutu of Zaire,* adopted a policy of 'authenticity' and national revival under the aegis of a new political movement, the *Mouvement national pour la révolution culturelle et sociale.* Authenticity in part involved the revival of intimidating ritual initiations, designed to cow Tombalbaye's opponents: those who refused to undergo initiation were executed. In April 1975 a *coup d'état* overthrew Tombalbaye, who was killed, and set up a Supreme Military Council led by General Félix Malloum. *Frolinat* continued its opposition and, by early 1978, with Libyan help, had conquered the whole of northern Chad. Renewed intervention by French troops saved Malloum but in August 1978 he was replaced by Hissène Habré, a former *Frolinat* leader. By February 1979 Malloum and Habré were in open conflict, religious and ethnic conflicts had been exacerbated and Chad had become even more divided, anarchic and threatened by the ambitions of its neighbours, notably Libya.   *B.L.*

Comoro Islands

Area (km²)	2236
Population 1980 (UN projection)	347 000
GNP per capita 1977 (US$)	180
Capital	Moroni
Currency	CFA franc

The four Comoro Islands were administered as a French overseas territory until 1975. One, Mayotte, remains a French possession today. The other three, Ngazidja, Nzawani and Mwali (formerly, respectively, Grande Comore, Anjouan, and Moheli) voted massively in favour of independence in a French-organized referendum in 1974 (whereas two-thirds of Mayotte's electors voted to remain French) and seized independence—which France had agreed to grant five years after a favourable vote—in July 1975 under Ahmed Abdallah. He was ousted within a month and the State of Comoro was led for over two years by Ali Soilih, who attempted to implement radical economic, social, administrative and religious reforms.

Ahmed Abdallah returned from his Paris exile after a European mercenary invasion eliminated Ali Soilih in May 1978, and became the sole president of the Federal Islamic Republic of the Comoros. He established links with conservative Arab oil-producing states and restored French aid to an economy entirely agriculture-based but producing barely half the food requirements of its 300 000 inhabitants, plus some export crops–copra, vanilla, cloves and perfume oils. France also now provides military assistance although the problem of Mayotte remain unsolved. *A.P.H.*

Congo

Area (km²)	342 000
Population 1980 (UN projection)	1 532 000
GNP per capita 1977 (US$)	500
Capital	Brazzaville
Currency	CFA franc

The Congo gained full independence from France on 15 August 1960. The first President, Abbé Fulbert Youlou, leader of the *Union Démocratique pour la Défense des Intérêts Africans* followed policies of cooperation with France and support for the Western bloc. In August 1963, however, urban unemployment, anti-trade union government proposals, ethnic favouritism, and plans for the establishment of a single political party stimulated an uprising which led Youlou to resign.

Youlou was succeeded by a government which advocated Marxist-Leninist socialism under the direction of a new political party, the *Mouvement National Révolutionnaire* (MNR). The MNR, however, faced ethnic and political conflict, and opposition to its position as the sole political party. After disturbances and anti-government conspiracies, the army, led by its commander-in-chief, Marien Ngouabi, intervened in 1968 and took over power, maintaining avowedly socialist policies under the direction of the *Parti Congolais du Travail* (PCT). The 1970s saw a continuing struggle for power among the military leaders. In March 1977 Ngouabi was assassinated and was succeeded by Colonel Joachim Yhombi-Opango; in February 1979 Opango was eased out of power by pressure from the left–whose continued accusations against him of corruption and high-living led to his imprisonment in August–and was replaced by Colonel Denis Sassou Nguesso.

The Congo's heavy dependence on primary product exports has meant that all the military/PCT regimes have, to a lesser or greater extent, tempered socialist policies with 'pragmatism'. Until the discovery of offshore oilfields the Congo depended on the export of timber and agricultural products, mainly to France. Oil exports boomed in 1974, but by 1975 production had fallen off because of technical problems and the oil companies' reactions to Ngouabi's nationalization proposals, and other exports declined in the face of the general world recession. By 1976–77 the Congo, overcommitted to development projects, faced a balance of payments deficit of US $160 million. The oilfields are small and will be exhausted by the early 1980s; nevertheless, the rest of the economy has stagnated and in 1978 (after an upturn in production) crude oil constituted 69 per cent of exports. Nguesso's intervention may imply a shift back to the relatively leftist policies of Ngouabi which had been diluted by Opango: this was certainly the tenor of the new regime's public pronouncements. By late 1979, however, Nguesso had shown no signs of taking a rigorously socialist path in practice. The mix of 'socialist' and 'pro-Western' policies continued. In June 1979, for example, the Congo opened negotiations with Western-oriented Zaire aimed at increasing cooperation between the two countries; in November a visit by Nguesso to Paris to seek French aid coincided with the announcement that 600 Congolese children had been sent to Cuba for education. *M.S.*

Djibouti

Area (km²)	21 783
Population 1980 (UN projection)	119 000
GNP per capita 1977 (US$)	Not available
Capital	Djibouti
Currency	Djibouti franc

Before and since independence, Djibouti has been dominated by its neighbours and their links with its two main ethnic groups: Ethiopia with the Afars, and Somalia with the Issas. Independence was delayed until June 1977 because of these tensions and was immediately followed by the Ethiopia-Somalia war in the Ogaden.★ For Djibouti the war was a catastrophe. The Afar/Issa balance was upset and Afar members of President Hassan Gouled's government resigned in 1978, claiming that their community was being persecuted. Thousands of refugees flooded across the border into Djibouti and the economy, based almost entirely on port trade, slumped following a breakdown of the rail link to Addis Ababa, which is vital to both countries. However, a large French military presence provides political stability, and Ethiopian successes in the Ogaden led to both the beginning of a restoration of the old ethnic balance and a reopening of the railway line, which gave promise of an economic revival. *C.S.*

Egypt

Area (km^2)	997 667
Population 1980 (UN projection)	42 144 000
GNP per capita 1977 (US$)	310
Capital	Cairo
Currency	Egyptian pound

After 70 years of British rule the first native Egyptian regime since 525 BC came to power through a coup on 23 July 1952. It was led by General Muhammad Neguib and a number of other soldiers, including Colonel Gamal Abdel Nasser* and Colonel Anwar Sadat, who constituted the Free Officers Movement. Within four years Egypt had become the leader of the Arab world, the alien monarchy had been abolished and a republic had been proclaimed (1953), much-needed land reforms and other economic reorganization had been instituted, and the hated British military presence had been removed (1956). The revolutionary officers were, however, divided over political and economic policies. By November 1954 the relatively conservative Neguib had been replaced by Nasser as president and leader of the revolution – positions which Nasser retained until his death in 1970 – and all political parties had been banned (including, most importantly, the religiously conservative Muslim Brotherhood, and the Communist Party).

In January 1953 the governing Revolutionary Command Council formed the Liberation Rally as an 'embryo' political organization for the prospective single party state. This failed to mobilize mass support, however, and in January 1956 (the same month that Sudan* became independent of Egypt) the government proclaimed a new constitution and established the National Union as the sole political organization. After the elections of June 1957, in which women were allowed to vote for the first time, a one party state was finally established. Nationalization, and the Egyptianization of posts of responsibility became subsequent official policy, partly as a reaction to continuing foreign influences. By 1962 these policies had developed into the concept of Arab Socialism, the principles of which were embodied in the Charter of National Action (May 1962). Subsequently, all Egyptian industries and agricultural enterprises were nationalized, and were placed under the direction of the Arab Socialist Union (successor to the National Union). Although these policies caused internal disillusionment and economic hardship, Nasser's charisma as a national leader prevailed, and neutralized much potential opposition.

From 1953 on Egypt became increasingly renowned in the Arab and African world as a revolutionary state. Its apparently radical economic and political reforms, strong anti-imperialist stance and support for the non-aligned movement* (for example at the Bandung Conference* in 1955) gave Egypt the leadership of the Arab world and even, with Kwame Nkrumah's Ghana,* joint leadership of the Afro-Asian bloc. Also in 1955, Nasser invited the Communist bloc to provide Egypt with military and economic assistance, and in July 1956 Nasser nationalized the Suez Canal Company. In retaliation Britain, France and Israel invaded Egypt in October. Both the USA and the USSR pressed for a ceasefire and this was enforced early in November by the UN, Egypt subsequently agreeing to compensate the shareholders of the Suez Canal Company. The border between Israel and the Gaza Strip was patrolled by UN troops, who were stationed on the Egyptian side.

Nasser's attempts to unify the Arab world after the Suez crisis – notably the establishment in 1958 of the United Arab Republic with Syria, from which Syria withdrew in 1961 – were largely unsuccessful. Nevertheless, Egypt's standing as the most active revolutionary Arab power remained undiminished. For example, it was deeply involved in the Yemen in supporting republican forces against the Saudi Arabian-backed royalist regime (1962–7), and championed anti-Zionism, a course that led to the 1967 Six Day War against Israel in which Egypt was defeated, losing territory in the Sinai peninsula – including oilfields – and revenue from the Suez Canal, which was to be blocked by sunken ships until cleared and reopened in 1975.

Egypt faced major problems of reconstruction as a consequence of the 1967 defeat. The armed forces were reorganized, and Nasser relied increasingly on the USSR to re-equip, advise and instruct them. At the same time relations with the West were improved in order to alleviate foreign exchange shortages, and Egypt also became heavily dependent on financial aid from Saudi Arabia, Kuwait and Libya.

Nasser died in September 1970 and was succeeded by his vice-president, Anwar Sadat. Over the next decade Sadat began to dismantle much of the socialist planning and economic organization inherited from Nasser; turned Egypt away from the USSR and increasingly towards the West; and, from a position of strength, sought accommodation with Israel, a policy which, in turn, led to changes in Egypt's relations with its Arab neighbours.

Sadat began to implement major 'liberalizing' political and economic changes only after the boost given to his popularity by Egypt's military successes against Israel in 1973. In 1974 most political prisoners were amnestied, press censorship was relaxed, and police powers were restricted. In 1976 and 1977 measures were introduced to allow the formation of political parties for the first time since 1953, although there were restrictions aimed at proscribing parties that were regarded as extremist. Sadat's reforms to the economy centred on measures introduced in 1973 which allowed the creation of a private enterprise sector alongside the public sector and encouraged the inflow of foreign investment. His moves towards creating a free market economy have not gone unchallenged: critics

President Anwar Sadat (left) with President Jaafar al-Nimeiri of Sudan (centre) and President Muammar Qaddafi of Libya

Jerusalem to negotiate with the Israeli government, an initiative that led to the signing of a peace treaty with Israel in March 1979 providing for a phased Israeli withdrawal from Sinai. Egypt's relations with other Arab powers were profoundly affected by the treaty with Israel, which was widely seen as a betrayal of the Palestinian cause. In 1972 Libya and Egypt had agreed on a programme of gradual union of the two states, but Sadat became less and less enthusiastic as Libya's President Qaddafi sought to accelerate the merger. Sadat's Israel policy contributed to a worsening of relations that culminated in a break in diplomatic relations in 1977 followed by recurrent border clashes. After the 1979 Egyptian treaty with Israel, member states of the Arab League decided to withdraw ambassadors from Cairo, and a withdrawal of Arab aid meant at least a temporary increase in the already heavy Egyptian reliance on the USA for arms and financial assistance.   *H.-H.K.*

point in particular to the failure of the new policies to take account of the needs of the poor, who continue to face a high rate of inflation (accelerated by the relaxation of controls on, for example, rents) and cannot afford the luxury goods that have swamped the market since the easing of trade restrictions. Popular anger was most decisively expressed in January 1977 when serious urban rioting with considerable loss of life followed the announcement that food subsidies would be withdrawn, a response which led to the implementation of stiff measures against opposition outside the approved party structures but also forced a partial reinstatement of subsidies.

Sadat's dismissal of a number of pro-Soviet ministers in May 1971 was an early sign of his coolness towards the USSR. Soviet assurances about arms deliveries seemed increasingly suspect, and in July 1972 Soviet military advisers were expelled from Egypt and Sadat began to seek arms supplies from the West. Like Nasser he was under recurrent pressure to reopen full-scale hostilities with Israel, and he repeatedly assured the Egyptian people that preparations were underway. A joint Syrian-Egyptian attack came suddenly on 6 October 1973. Egyptian forces swept across Sinai and, although later rolled back by the Israelis, shattered the myth of Israel's invincibility. Major gains to Egypt sprang from the diplomatic intervention of the oil-producing Arab states, who threatened an oil boycott of Western powers supporting Israel. This encouraged the USA to put in motion negotiations between Egypt and Israel which, by 1975, had led to Israeli withdrawal from a strip of the territory seized in 1967 – including the Egyptian Sinai oilfields. Egypt's relations with the USA continued to blossom, and in March 1976 Sadat abrogated the Soviet-Egyptian Treaty of Friendship. In November 1977 he travelled to

Equatorial Guinea

Area (km²)	28 051
Population 1980 (UN projection)	339 000
GNP per capita 1977 (US$)	340
Capital	Malaba
Currency	Ekuele

Granted independence by Spain on 12 October 1968, Equatorial Guinea was ruled until August 1979 by one of the most ruthless dictators of recent times, Life President Francisco Macias Nguema. After quashing an abortive coup in March 1969, Nguema rapidly set about eliminating all his opponents, real or imaginary, including his successive Cabinet members. The almost total departure of Spanish administrators and settlers in 1969 disrupted the economy and social services of an otherwise moderately prosperous colonial preserve. Firmly in control of the single political party, the army and a youth militia of thugs, the President succeeded in making Equatorial Guinea a hermit country. By the late 1970s one-third of the population lived in exile (probably 100 000 persons). Tension with Gabon in 1972 over the supposedly oil-rich islets of Corisco eased off, and repatriation to Nigeria of about 15 000 labourers from Fernando Po (renamed Macias Nguema Byogo) was partially offset by forced labour conscription from Rio Muni, but the general decline of economic life, the constant deterioration of living conditions, a pervasive atmosphere of terror (mostly against literate citizens), the disappearance of all liberties and the banning of the Catholic Church (1978) contributed to discredit the regime. Nevertheless, it was able to survive thanks to Soviet, Cuban and Chinese help plus some investments from France, and assistance from the European Economic Community. In August 1979, however, Nguema was overthrown in a coup and was executed the following month by a military regime headed by Lieutenant-Colonel Teodoro Obiang Nguema Mbasogo. *R.P.*

Ethiopia

Area (km²)	1 221 900
Population 1980 (UN projection)	31 522 000
GNP per capita 1977 (US$)	110
Capital	Addis Ababa
Currency	Birr

For the first 14 years after most African states became independent Ethiopia presented an enviable picture of stable continuity. The Emperor Haile Selassie★ continued his already long reign and, as the much respected doyen of African leaders, hosted the 1963 conference which founded the Organization of African Unity.★ Internally, both an attempted coup led by the commander of the imperial bodyguard in December 1960 and the evident differences between Ethiopia and other African states led the imperial government to more determined efforts at modernization and reform. Administrative detail, hitherto concentrated in the Emperor's hands, was progressively delegated, especially to Aklilu Habte-Weld, Prime Minister from 1961 to 1974. New ministries, including those for planning and land reform, were established and manned by educated civil servants. New judicial codes were enacted and local development projects encouraged. The elected Chamber of Deputies, though lacking political parties, played an increasingly vocal role in legislation.

These essentially administrative efforts at modernization suffered from a failure to expand the political base of the regime, which was heavily concentrated on the palace. Any new initiatives required the Emperor's consent and, even when this was given, often could make little headway against established interests; land reform was one of these. While Haile Selassie remained extremely skilled at managing court factions, he thus progressively lost authority among new social groups whose aspirations had no outlet. The university students were the most vocal of these, and were involved in regular clashes with government authorities from the mid-1960s onwards, but many of their views were shared by junior civil servants and army officers. Equally, no effective channels existed for representing the views of people outside the educated group, with the result that the provinces especially became increasingly separated from the regime. In Eritrea in the north a guerrilla movement, the Eritrean Liberation Front

(which later split into three main sections), became active in the mid-1960s and by the end of the decade posed a serious military threat to government forces. A number of minor but significant opposition movements and revolts took place in the Galla- and Somali-inhabited southern provinces. The government proved equally weak in the northern heartland of traditional Ethiopia, where a revolt took place in Gojjam province over a new tax in 1968, and totally inadequate efforts were made to deal with a very serious famine in Wollo province in 1973.

When these pressures erupted in a series of strikes, riots and army mutinies early in 1974, the government offered pay increases and constitutional reforms, which could not contain the situation. Effective power passed progressively to the Derg, a committee drawn from the junior officers and other ranks of the armed forces. In September 1974 the Derg deposed the Emperor, and in November executed over 50 leading members of the old regime. The new government took equally forcible action over the nationalization of urban and rural land and of many businesses, and attempted a military solution to the guerrilla insurgency in Eritrea. Local government responsibilities were given to peasants' associations in the countryside and urban dwellers' associations in towns. Conflicts took place within the Derg, two successive chairmen of which were executed, and by 1976 Major Mengistu Haile-Maryam emerged as its unquestioned leader. In 1977 he renounced Ethiopia's longstanding relationship with the USA, declared a Marxist-Leninist regime, and

Major Mengistu Haile-Maryam (front row left) with other members of the 120-strong Ethiopian Derg (ruling committee) which seized power in September 1974

sought Soviet and Cuban military aid in order to combat secessionist movements in Eritrea and the Somali-inhabited south-east and to overcome other internal opposition movements. By March 1978 combined Ethiopian and Cuban forces had driven Somalian government troops out of the Ogaden, but they continued to face resistance from irregular Somali guerrilla forces. Eritrean liberation movements were equally recalcitrant, and the Ethiopian government seemed bent on a military solution rather than seeking to negotiate over any form of autonomy for Eritrea.   *C.S.C.*

Gabon

Area (km²)	267 000
Population 1980 (UN projection)	546 000
GNP per capita 1977 (US$)	3730
Capital	Libreville
Currency	CFA franc

Gabon became independent of France on 17 August 1960 under the *Bloc Démocratique Gabonais* (BDG) led by Léon M'Ba, a veteran nationalist who received 99.6 per cent of the votes cast in the 1961 presidential election. M'Ba was deposed by a military coup in February 1964, but was reinstated after French military intervention. In November 1967 M'Ba died, and power passed peacefully to his young vice-president, Albert-Bernard Bongo. Bongo has maintained close relations with France, and has pursued a generally pro-Western foreign policy – to the extent of maintaining relations and trade with white-ruled South Africa and Rhodesia. Although his government faced increasing economic difficulties in the late 1970s, Gabon remained stable politically, Bongo successfully concentrating political power in his own hands.

Until the late 1960s Gabon's main foreign exchange earner was timber. In the 1970s, however, its vast mineral wealth attracted considerable foreign aid and investment, notably from France: among Francophone African countries, Gabon receives the highest per capita aid from France. Exploitation of offshore oilfields began in 1957, but was not important until the late 1960s. Between 1966 and 1976 oil production expanded from 1.4 million to 11.3 million tonnes per year. By 1976 Gabon's small population enjoyed a per capita Gross National Product ($2540 per year) second only in Africa to Libya. Oil reserves, however, are limited and production began to fall off unexpectedly rapidly in 1977. Gabon's reserves of other minerals, especially manganese, iron and uranium are much more substantial, but their full exploitation has been hampered by transport difficulties. Nevertheless, by 1976 Gabon supplied 25 per cent of the manganese consumed by the Western economies, and substantial amounts of uranium. Transport difficulties will be overcome by the completion in the 1980s of the Trans-Gabon railway – the first stage of which was opened in January 1979 – which will link the coast with the north-eastern iron deposits and the south-eastern manganese and uranium mines.

Meanwhile, however, Gabon has encountered increasing budgetary and external debt problems: heavy investments in development projects were made during the oil boom, and other mineral revenues have not yet reached a level sufficient fully to sustain current expenditure and debt repayments. The onset of these problems was accelerated by the high cost of the Organization of African Unity* summit held in Libreville in July 1977 – estimated at two-thirds of export earnings for the year. In August 1977 Bongo announced an austerity programme, one effect of which was severe unemployment. In the past Gabon had suffered from severe labour shortages, which had been alleviated by immigration from other African states. Now, in an astute political move, Bongo laid the blame for such manifestations of the economic crisis as inflation on these foreigners: in 1978, for example, 10000 immigrants from Benin were expelled. While continuing to welcome foreign investment, Bongo also pursued, from 1974 on, a policy of 'Gabonization' in employment, and also placed restrictions on the repatriation of the profits of foreign companies. Gabon's 1976–80 development plan sought to lessen the imbalance in the economy between the mineral export sector and agricultural production (both for export and local consumption). Local self-sufficiency is particulary important if Gabon is to improve its balance of payments position, since in the late 1970s 85 per cent of its food requirements were imported. Substantial industrialization remains a much more distant prospect – in the late 1970s Gabon's industries employed only 10 per cent of the work force – but is perhaps the only way in which Gabon can utilize its vast mineral wealth for its own long-term benefit.   *R.C.*

The Gambia

Area (km²)	11 295
Population 1980 (UN projection)	563 000
GNP per capita 1977 (US$)	200
Capital	Banjul
Currency	Dalasi

The Gambia gained independence in February 1965 with a government led by Dauda Jawara's Protectorate People's Party – now the People's Progressive Party (PPP), at first in coalition with the opposition United Party (UP). At subsequent elections the UP–which has been in opposition since 1965–has steadily declined in strength. In 1970 The Gambia became a republic with Jawara as the first president. Jawara has remained in firm control despite opposition from various quarters; for example, protests from members of the Mandinka ethnic group, who argued that he was neglecting his own people after he had sought to broaden support for the originally Mandinka-based PPP, and accusations that he had leaned too far towards the West.

The Gambian economy remains almost entirely dependent on the export of groundnuts and groundnut products which provide over 90 per cent of foreign exchange earnings; a precarious dependence in view of recurrent drought and fluctuations in world prices. Nevertheless Jawara's government has fostered increased production and improved quality. Rice production–for local consumption–is being developed, and cotton production is expanding rapidly. A modest tourist industry has also been developed since the mid-1970s. So far serious inflation and shortages of food have been avoided, although unemployment has begun to become a problem in Banjul.

The Gambia's future was once thought to lie in union with Senegal,* whose territory surrounds all but its narrow coastline. There is little Gambian enthusiasm for this, but the two countries cooperate, and as a member of the Economic Community of West African States* and other African groupings, and as a recipient of aid from the West, the East and the Organization of Petroleum Exporting Countries, The Gambia is not isolated. *D.W.*

Ghana

Area (km²)	238 537
Population 1980 (UN projection)	11 446 000
GNP per capita 1977 (US$)	380
Capital	Accra
Currency	Cedi

When Ghana became independent on 6 March 1957 the national treasury was full, the Convention People's Party (CPP) was strongly established throughout the country, Kwame Nkrumah* was an African hero, and pan-Africanism* seemed about to be reborn in Accra. Development was in full swing, encompassing an accelerated plan for education and large industrial schemes, represented preeminently by the Volta Lake and River Project and its aluminium smelter. By 1979 the economy was crippled, with an inflation rate of over 100 per cent per year. An under-capitalized, declining cocoa

industry could no longer pay for imports. The CPP was no more than a memory, and the claims of the People's National Party (PNP)–victorious in the 1979 general elections–to be its successor remained as yet untested.

Nkrumah was ousted by the army in February 1966 and died in exile in 1972. From 1966 until 1979 (except for the period between October 1969 and January 1972) the military remained in power, but experienced internal political upheavals. Brigadier Emmanuel Kotoka, the principal author of the coup against Nkrumah, was assassinated in an attempted coup led by junior officers; his successor Lieutenant General Joseph Ankrah was removed from office shortly afterwards. Brigadier Akwasi Afrifa presided over the country's return to civilian rule in October 1969, but the Second Republic, led by Dr Kofi Busia's Progress Party government, only survived until January 1972 when Colonel Ignatius Acheampong seized power. Acheampong was himself deposed in July 1978 by Lieutenant General Fred Akuffo, who was able to do little to repair the by then tattered economic and political fabric. In June 1979 non-commissioned officers and privates led by an air force lieutenant, Jerry Rawlings, deposed Akuffo. They secretly tried him (for economic crimes) and executed him, Acheampong, Afrifa and other leading military figures. A 'house-cleaning' regime, the Armed Forces Revolutionary Council (AFRC), was established, but handed over power to an elected PNP government led by President Hilla Limann in October 1979.

The political changes which followed independence appear less dramatic if the record of party conflict before 1957 is considered. It is the terrible downturn in the economy which is puzzling. It is as if the relative prosperity of the 1950s, following the Korean War boom, persuaded Ghanaians that they could always live well today on tomorrow's income. Ambition outran performance. Imports of luxury goods (including food) and of semi-finished materials for what was hoped would be a rapid 'industrialization' produced a mounting deficit of huge proportions. Cocoa farms were neglected and disease spread among the trees, few young people entered farming, high prices across the frontiers led to smuggling, and the rise in the price of imported oil after 1973 finally brought the country to what amounted to bankruptcy. Desperate remedies were tried during these years: import controls, a floating exchange rate, loans from the International Monetary Fund, a massive devaluation in 1971 and 1978. Early in 1979 Akuffo replaced the entire currency in an effort to reduce liquidity: bank deposits were exchanged at par, but cash at a discount. Rawlings' AFRC concentrated on combating the corruption and profiteering that accompanied economic decline but although its policies improved the morale of the poorer sections of the community for a while, it did little to improve the desperate economic situation which Limann's civilian government inherited almost unchanged.

Who should rule in Ghana has always been open to dispute in two ways. Since independence the shift in the social basis of power which took place in the 1950s–following the first general election in 1951– has been consolidated. A growing educated class of businessmen, civil servants, teachers and members of the professions control most of the positions of power when elections are held and when the military keep out of office. Chiefs are important, but usually only locally. The senior members of the professions are afforded respect, but are too few to exert much influence. Farmers, urban artisans and labourers are to a great extent excluded from any direct say in national politics because of their lack of education in the national language, English. In theory, therefore, the state should be kept steady by the broad number of 'middle-educated' leaders. Unfortunately, however, these leaders are divided by civilian and military interests, and by regional and/or ethnic loyalties.

The army numbers some 15 000 and has its own corporate interests that bestow a large degree of autonomy on its actions. When offended by politicians, it can attack, and no one can prevent its entry into politics. In the first coup in 1966 the army intervened because it disliked Nkrumah's autocratic rule, and was afraid of being displaced by rival forces built up by the president. In 1972 it was opposed to Busia on similar grounds (though less plausibly) and was spurred on by Acheampong's own ambition for office. Once in power, however, the armed forces have been divided, and are no more able to govern effectively than the civilian politicians. Hence the alternation between civilian and military rule.

Communal problems ought not to be great in view of Ghana's relatively long history of ethnic interaction and high level of education, yet they have figured prominently in the years since independence. The ethnic centre of the country lies among the Akan–that is, the Asante, Brong, Fante and Akuapem–in the central and southern regions. But the Akan are often divided among themselves because of a long history of rivalry between local chiefdoms. North of the Akan lie heterogeneous communities which can join together politically because they are northern and poor. To the east are the Ewe-speaking peoples of the Volta Region, who are divided territorially between Ghana and Togo.* As a minority they are suspected, rightly or wrongly, of being 'over-clannish': hence there were pro- and anti-Ewe factions in the critical 1969 election; a less prominent feature of that of 1979. There is also a Gā-speaking minority in and around the capital, Accra, and it, too, has usually acted politically like a 'third force'. When the government acts internationally, Ghana has a strong sense of national identity, but when political disputes take popular or, indeed, civil-military form, the fractures are more likely to be along lines of communal division or between the followings of powerful political patrons than based on ideology or class solidarity.

It is true that there has been a vague pro- and anti-Nkrumah sentiment since the mid-1960s in the sense of would-be radical versus

conservative policies, but that apparent division has more rhetoric to it than substance. Nor is it easy to see a reformist way forward from the present. No changes in the constitution or in ideology, nor the move from military to civilian rulers, nor the economic formulae pressed on successive governments by external advisers, seem likely to alter the basic dilemma.   *D. G. A.*

Guinea

Area (km²)	245 857
Population 1980 (UN projection)	5 014 000
GNP per capita 1977 (US$)	210
Capital	Conakry
Currency	Syli

Guinea was the first territory of the former French West African Federation to become an independent republic (in 1958), after registering a massive electoral majority in favour of immediate independence in General de Gaulle's constitutional referendum of that year. De Gaulle took Guinea's option as a personal affront, and instructed the outgoing French administration to take reprisals. Files and equipment were destroyed, while French personnel, technical assistance and financial aid were abruptly withdrawn. The new government of President Sékou Touré* was thus compelled to build a wholly new administrative machine. This was done on the basis of the ruling party, the *Parti Démocratique de Guinée* (PDG), which was indeed remarkably successful in building a party state.

The PDG regime has been effective enough in domestic political control but it has owed its survival to foreign assistance from various quarters–the USSR especially from 1958 to 1961, and the USA since that time. Overseas economic interest in Guinea has focused on that country's bauxite reserves (two-thirds of the world's total, and accounting for up to 97 per cent of Guinea's export revenue). The economy has stagnated or regressed in all other sectors, and Guinea remains an extremely poor country. Domestic economic problems and a sense of diplomatic isolation partly explain periodic political crises in Guinea. There have been six major internal convulsions over alleged plots against the regime since independence: foreign 'enemies' have ranged from the USSR (1961) to the USA (1966) and Portugal (1970), with France chronically hostile for 18 years from independence. After the brief invasion of a mercenary force in 1970, distrust and fear of domestic or foreign enemies of the regime became dominant in local politics. President Sékou Touré regularly spoke of a 'permanent plot' against himself and his government, and a formidable apparatus of internal coercion was established to meet real or imagined challenges. Guinea's climate of suspicion and fear seems to have been at its worst during the 'Fulani plot' of 1976: here a whole ethnic group (one-third of Guinea's population at independence) was accused of plotting against the regime. Touré's own firmest support has come from his own ethnic group, the Malinke, and his government has included an increasing number of his relatives (especially by marriage).

Guinean foreign policy was dramatically reorientated at the end of 1978 and during 1979; changes which may mark Guinea's emergence from the era of the 'permanent plot'. In December 1978 Guinea was reconciled with France: President Giscard d'Estaing visited Conakry, and after three days of talks it was agreed that commercial, cultural and financial agreements would be entered into. In July 1979 framework agreements were signed in Paris; meanwhile Sékou Touré had resumed friendly relations with Guinea's Francophone neighbours, Senegal and Ivory Coast. Guinea's reconciliation with France and its African allies was part of a broader initiative that sought, in particular, to attract new foreign investment and technical assistance. Since 1979, for example, Sékou Touré has visited the USA, resumed relations with West Germany and has improved terms for foreign investors in Guinea.　　　　　　　　　　　*D.C.O'B.*

Guinea-Bissau

Area (km²)	36 125
Population 1980 (UN projection)	573 000
GNP per capita 1977 (US$)	160
Capital	Bissau
Currency	Peso

Guinea-Bissau's independence was recognized by Portugal under the terms of the Algiers Accord on 26 March 1974. In November 1975 the *Partido Africano da Independência da Guiné e Cabo Verde* (PAIGC) officially entered the capital. Although the transitional period was relatively free of conflict owing to PAIGC's authority as the only effective liberation movement, party and administrative structures in the urban areas were weak and many groups previously dependent on the colonial economy and army were antipathetic. Consolidation of PAIGC legitimacy was, therefore, first priority. 'Dynamizing groups' in workplaces and neighbourhoods, together with the formation of mass organizations for youth, women and workers, have been instrumental in mobilizing support for the regime. The first nation-wide elections for regional councils were held in December 1976 as a preliminary to the formation of a new, enlarged Peoples' National Assembly. At the same time, the new social structures of

Luiz Cabral (right), President of Guinea-Bissau, 1974–80, in conversation with members of the liberation army in June 1974

peoples' stores, courts and village committees have been extended beyond the old liberated areas.

Guinea-Bissau entered independence in a state of chronic poverty with an exclusively agricultural economy debilitated by war. In the late 1970s efforts were devoted to achieving self-sufficiency in food production and cutting rice imports. Long term plans involve diversification to include sugar cane and tropical fruits in addition to the old colonial monoculture in groundnuts, and several small-scale processing plants have been established. The organization of cooperatives is proceeding gradually using demobilized soldiers.

Foreign policy maintains links with the East and Nordic states, but also welcomes aid and assistance from Western Europe and international agencies. The daunting economic and social problems of both Guinea-Bissau and Cape Verde* underline the low priority now given to formal unification, a measure even less likely after the November 1980 coup that overthrew the government of Luiz Cabral, a Cape Verdian.　　　　　　　　　　　*J.E.C.*

Ivory Coast

Area (km²)	322 462
Population 1980 (UN projection)	7 820 000
GNP per capita 1977 (US$)	710
Capital	Abidjan
Currency	CFA franc

Since independence in 1960 the Ivory Coast has been ruled without interruption by a single party, the *Parti Démocratique de la Côte d'Ivoire* (PDCI), and by a single president, Félix Houphouët-Boigny.* No formal opposition has been tolerated, and the regime has relied on a massive programme of French technical assistance and investment, and a French military garrison. The regime has thus been secured in place by France's trust in the moderate policies of Houphouët-Boigny and the PDCI. Some political unrest was manifest in the early years after independence, especially among leftist students and trade unionists: two plots against the regime were revealed in 1963, and were followed by purges within the governing party and a reduction in size of the national army.

There has been continuing resentment among educated Ivorians about the slow pace of Africanization since independence, with French nationals still occupying many positions at all levels, particularly in industry and commerce. These and many other grievances were openly expressed in a series of 'public dialogues' with the president and leading government figures in 1969. In general, the internal political situation in the Ivory Coast has been remarkably calm, perhaps as a result of a steadily sustained economic growth – agricultural production almost exclusively (cocoa, coffee, etc.), to which, in the late 1970s, was added the promise of substantial reserves of offshore oil. There have been minor regionalist disturbances, notably in 1969 and 1970, but on the whole the government's policy of reconciliation has been effectively applied. A military plot was uncovered in 1973, and seven officers were subsequently sentenced to death. In a dramatic move in 1977 three senior ministers were dismissed following rumours of widespread high-level corruption: later Houphouët-Boigny gave his own extensive plantations to the nation and criticized the high-living of some of his colleagues.

Despite his age and periodic ill-health Houphouët-Boigny's political power is unchallenged, although there has been speculation about the succession. In 1976 the President of the National Assembly, Phillipe Yacé was named in a constitutional amendment as successor in the event of Houphouët-Boigny's death, resignation or incapacity through ill-health.

In foreign policy Houphouët-Boigny has defended what he terms 'neutrality in Africa' which, in effect, means support for moderation, pro-Western policies, and a bitter opposition to the expansion of communist power. His most controversial initiative has been his proposal for a dialogue between Black African states and South Africa, launched in 1971, which led to secret talks in 1974 between Houphouët-Boigny and the Prime Minister of South Africa, Balthazar Vorster. Houphouët-Boigny has also repeatedly called for Western aid to enable Africa to resist the expansion of Soviet power, and in this context he warmly welcomed the public reconciliation of France and Guinea* in 1978.   *D.C.O'B.*

Kenya

Area (km²)	582 646
Population 1980 (UN projection)	15 688 000
GNP per capita 1977 (US$)	270
Capital	Nairobi
Currency	Kenya shilling

Kenya became independent on 12 December 1963 with Jomo Kenyatta* as Prime Minister and leader of the Kenya African National Union (KANU). It became a republic in December 1964, with Kenyatta as the first president. In the years just before independence KANU, whose support came mainly from the Kikuyu and Luo ethnic groups, had been opposed by the Kenya African Democratic Union (KADU), which drew its support from pastoralist and coastal peoples. In 1964, however, KADU merged with the ruling party and Kenya became a *de facto* one party state. In 1966 there was a split in KANU when Oginga Odinga – who had for some time led a radical group that expressed unease at growing class differentiation in Kenya and had called for mass nationalization – formed an opposition party, the Kenya People's Union (KPU). In July 1969 the assassination of the Minister of Finance, Tom Mboya, precipitated a political crisis, and riots at Kisumu were followed by the banning of the KPU and the imprisonment of its principal members. KANU had no rivals, yet the expression of discontent was still catered for in general elections: for example at the December 1969 elections all party members were declared eligible to stand and 77 of the 158 sitting MPs lost their seats. Similarly, in the October elections that followed Kenyatta's unopposed re-election as president in September 1974, 88 MPs were rejected by the electorate, including 17 ministers. By the mid-1970s parliament had far less life than its electors, having become increasingly powerless and subject to Kenyatta's autocratic whims: on a number of occasions it was, for example, prorogued for no reason. Opposition inside parliament now centred on a small group within KANU led by J. M. Kariuku which continued to attack corruption, social inequality and foreign dominance of the economy. Kariuku's assassination in March 1975 sparked off a new political crisis, during which most of Kenyatta's critics were detained, parliament was once again prorogued and party elections due in April 1977 were postponed.

Kenyatta died in August 1978 and was succeeded by his vice-president Daniel arap Moi. Moi immediately took note of some of the criticisms that had been made by Kenyatta's opponents. In particular, corruption in the civil service, public corporations and the police was investigated, and in December 1978 all political detainees were released. Limits on opposition were, however, retained: in

November 1979 Moi was the sole candidate in the presidential elections, five other candidates, including Odinga, having been barred.

The Kenyan economy rests primarily on agriculture, the major export crops being tea, sisal and pyrethrum. Kenya lacks major sources of raw materials, and industrial production consists chiefly of food processing and the assembly of consumer goods from imported parts. Oil refined in Kenya is exported widely in East Africa, and tourism* is a major foreign exchange earner. Although the Kenyan economy has continued to grow fast, and stability and a government ideology committed to capitalism have attracted much foreign investment, the country faces a number of related problems that are likely to become increasingly intractable. Much of the best agricultural land that became available by purchase from white settlers is in the hands of a wealthy minority, and the emphasis on export cash crop production has led to a neglect of food production for local consumption. A growing proportion of the population thus faces high food prices and is unable to acquire land to grow its own – or may even be forced to sell out to wealthier land-owners – and the problem is exacerbated by Kenya's particularly high rate of population growth. Urban unemployment, fuelled by large-scale migration from the rural areas is a major problem exacerbated by the capital-intensive nature of most existing industries. The Kenya government has for some time been formally committed to land settlement schemes and the development of labour-intensive industrial projects but these have had little impact so far.   *G.A.*

Lesotho

Daniel arap Moi during the ceremony at which he took over as President of Kenya after the death of Jomo Kenyatta in 1978

Area (km²)	30 355
Population 1980 (UN projection)	1 284 000
GNP per capita 1977 (US$)	230
Capital	Maseru
Currency	South African rand

Lesotho gained its independence from Britain in 1966. It is one of the poorest countries in the world, partly because most of its best land – which it still claims – was ceded to South Africa as the price of the kingdom's annexation by the British as a protectorate. Despite being entirely surrounded by South Africa, Lesotho preserved its integrity as a political unit through its protectorate status, but has been increasingly dependent on its neighbour economically. In the 1970s, for example, over half Lesotho's male population provided a quarter of the temporary contract labour in South African mines.

Apart from some diamonds and much water, natural resources are few. Its mountain goats yield the finest mohair, and its mountains are also a tourist attraction which is being developed, although largely by South African-owned enterprises. So far, other economic development has concentrated on halting erosion, improving agriculture, starting a few industries and developing infrastructure in the difficult terrain. Economic interdependence with South Africa is reinforced by Lesotho's participation in customs and monetary union agreements, its budget is heavily dependent on revenues from the union supplemented by international aid.

The bitterly divisive pre-independence election of 1965 was won by Chief Leabua Jonathan leading the relatively conservative, Catholic-based, South African supported Basotho National Party which narrowly defeated the royalist, but radical Basotho Congress Party (BCP). Both sides were optimistic in the next election in 1970. However with the BCP apparently in the lead, Chief Jonathan stopped the announcement of results and then, in what amounted to a coup, suspended the constitution. A counter-coup was crushed and, after a short period of exile, the monarch Moshoeshoe II was reinstated as head of state, but with narrowly limited powers. Despite another small, violent uprising by opposition forces in 1974, a national government including representatives of all parties has been proposed. Meanwhile, having curbed the opposition, Chief Jonathan's government has itself become increasingly critical of South African policies, refusing, for example, to recognize the neighbouring Transkei* despite the economic benefits which such a move would probably bring.   *P.M.*

Liberia

Area (km²)	111 369
Population 1980 (UN projection)	1 937 000
GNP per capita 1977 (US$)	430
Capital	Monrovia
Currency	US dollar

Until April 1980, when a military coup overthrew the True Whig Party (TWP) government, Liberia's history had exhibited remarkable continuity. The Americo-Liberians*–descendants of freed slaves from the USA, and less than 3 per cent of Liberia's population–were politically dominant, and their party, the TWP, had held power continuously since 1878, since 1955 as the sole political party. This oligarchy had survived partly because of the paucity and political fragmentation of the indigenous population, but also because–since 1944 when William Tubman became president–the indigenes had been granted representation in the legislature and had been incorporated into the TWP patronage network. Indigenous participation was, however, carefully controlled–only, significantly, in the army did the indigenes' presence grow overweighty–and under Tubman, and William Tolbert (President 1971–80), the TWP 'machine' controlled the flow of wealth and power to the lowest levels. The economic structure increasingly reinforced the TWP's predominance. The pattern of foreign financed and managed production for export of primary raw materials had been set by the establishment of the Firestone rubber plantations in 1926, but by the 1960s iron ore had become a more important export earner, with the government taking a half share of profits; funds that fuelled the TWP machine.

Until the late 1970s opposition was muted, centring mainly on student groups in the USA. In 1978 one such group, the Progressive Alliance of Liberia (PAL), established an office in Monrovia and began campaigning against the TWP's monopolization of power. In April

1979 when it was hinted that the producer price of rice would be increased to encourage local production, PAL organized anti-government demonstrations during which at least 50 people were killed. Leaders of PAL were arrested and charged with treason but later amnestied. In December PAL became a political party–the Progressive People's Party (PPP). In March 1980 PPP leaders called for a general strike, a move followed by their mass arrest on charges of sedition and treason. On 12 April, however, trials were forestalled by a coup led by Master Sergeant Samuel Doe during which Tolbert was killed. Doe established a People's Redemption Council (PRC) composed of army non-commissioned officers, which oversaw a cabinet that included many of the leaders of anti-TWP movements. The PRC began a purge–at first bloody, with 13 public executions–of Americo-Liberians whom it considered guilty of corruption and maladministration. Subsequently, during 1980, Doe patched up relations with other African leaders, who were initially horrified by the executions, and negotiated the continuance of the traditional special relationship with the USA. However, no major policy initiatives had emerged and the future prospects for civilian rule remained uncertain.   *D.W.*

Libya

Area (km²)	1 759 540
Population 1980 (UN projection)	2 638 000
GNP per capita 1977 (US$)	6680
Capital	Tripoli
Currency	Dinar

Libya became independent in January 1952 under King Idris, the head of the Sanusiyya* order and amir of Cyrenaica. The recruitment without elections of a constituent assembly by the UN Commissioner appointed to prepare the country for independence within the shortest possible time had given prominence to the leaders of traditional society in the three provinces of Tripolitania, Cyrenaica and the Fezzan at the expense of the modernists of the Tripolitanian National Congress Party. The elections for a national assembly in March 1952 confirmed the conservative character of the new government. The king ruled through ministers, the most important of whom were Cyrenaicans connected with the Sanusiyya order. Benghazi, in Cyrenaica, formed a second capital. The country was extremely poor, with a very small population, and the government depended for revenues upon the rents and aid provided by Britain and the USA in return for military bases. These alliances confirmed the pro-Western character of the regime.

The position changed in the 1960s with the discovery of oil. Oil revenues permitted the expansion of irrigated agriculture on the lines laid down by the Italians in the 1930s. They led, also, however, to a great increase in private wealth and corruption, and to major social changes with migration from the rural areas into the cities. Dissatisfaction culminated in 1969 in the coup by young army officers led by Muammar Qaddafi.

The new regime closed the Western military bases, and became strongly Arab nationalist, especially in relation to Israel. As the most influential figure in the Revolutionary Command Council of army officers governing the country, however, Colonel Qaddafi has developed an idiosyncratic political philosophy compounded of Islamic religion, Arabism, and popular socialism. Abroad this has led to proposals and declarations of union with Egypt and Tunisia in 1973, to support for the Muslim opposition in Chad, and – until his overthrow in 1978–9 – for President Idi Amin in Uganda. Internally, a greater degree of administrative unification has been accompanied by measures to involve the people in government. In 1971 a national party, the Arab Socialist Union, was created, incorporating the trade unions. In 1973 Qaddafi called for a spontaneous political, social and cultural revolution, and established a number of popular committees to carry this out. His aim contrasted with the professional direction of the country and the economy, which was left to bureaucrats and technocrats, under the general supervision of his colleague, Major Abd al-Salam Jallud. Conflicts generated by the contrasting approaches seem to have underlain the attempted coup of 1975, when Major al-Mahayshi, minister for planning, fled abroad.

In 1976 Qaddafi began the publication of his *Green Book*, setting out his ideas. At the same time an elected General People's Congress was convened to continue the work of the Arab Socialist Union –

which it replaced – and the popular committees set up in 1973. Qaddafi himself has led a life in accordance with his ideas; simple and open to the people. It remains to be seen if oil revenues can generate the productive employment, notably in agriculture, to give his vision substance.   *M.B.*

Madagascar

Area (km²)	587 041
Population 1980 (UN projection)	9 329 000
GNP per capita 1977 (US$)	210
Capital	Antananarivo
Currency	Malagasy franc

The period 1960–72 did not witness any sudden change in Franco-Malagasy relations. After independence in 1960 the French stayed on in large numbers and held the key positions in trade, commerce, communications, defence and security. In the private sector the first president, Philibert Tsiranana, permitted French firms to monopolize the import-export trade and to control agriculture and mineral exploitation. French aid and technical assistance was prominent, but accompanied by slow progress in development projects. Profits from trade and commerce continued to flow out of the island to France and virtually nothing was reinvested in Madagascar. Industrialization was minimal and some 85 per cent of the population continued to live in the rural areas and to make their living from agriculture. Throughout the 1960s Tsiranana's opponents, some of whom sprang up from within the ranks of the ruling *Parti Social Démocrate*, attacked this colonial type relationship. Opposition to France and Tsiranana bubbled over in May 1972 when his security forces fired on a group of protesters in the capital, killing 34. The rioting which followed toppled Tsiranana and led to the appointment of a military government headed by General Gabriel Ramanatsoa, who quickly negotiated the withdrawal of French forces, began the indigenization of education, and established relations with Arab and Communist countries. He was not, however, radical enough for the left-wing and was replaced by a naval officer, Lieutenant Commander Didier Ratsirika.

Ratsirika has taken the island far left by nationalizing almost all foreign holdings, though in so doing he has worsened Madagascar's already gloomy economic situation. The population is increasing at about 2.2 per cent a year; urban centres are expanding; unemployment is high; basic foodstuffs are often in short supply; and the education system produces more graduates than the economy can absorb.   *S.G.*

Muammar Qaddafi, Head of State of Libya since 1969

Malawi

Area (km²)	118 484
Population 1980 (UN projection)	5 577 000
GNP per capita 1977 (US$)	140
Capital	Lilongwe
Currency	Malawi kwacha

After 18 months of responsible internal self-government, Malawi (formerly Nyasaland) became independent on 6 July 1964. Dr Hastings Kamuzu Banda, representing the strongly conservative nationalism of the Malawi Congress Party (MCP), crushed opposition from the youthful and progressive, mission-educated elite within two months of independence. In September he forced six Cabinet members to resign after they had demanded rapid Africanization of the civil service and a non-aligned foreign policy. Under repression from a white-led police force and army, dissidents went into detention or into exile. An abortive raid led by one of Banda's radical opponents, H. B. M. Chipembere, operating from the Mangoche hills with strong support from the Yao ethnic group in February 1965, and a hopelessly miscalculated incursion led by the former Minister of Home Affairs, Yatuta Chisiza, in October 1967, left Banda free to assume a personal dictatorship.

After grandiose claims to Tanzanian territory and the establishment of full diplomatic relations with South Africa after a visit from the South African prime minister, Mr Balthazar Vorster, in 1970, Malawi became the pariah of Black Africa. This idiosyncratic diplomacy was rewarded by foreign investment and large South

African loans to build a new capital in Lilongwe and a rail link from the Indian Ocean port of Nacala. Made Life President in July 1971, Banda set the style for his ministers and top party faithful with his ownership of a major group of companies, several farms and palaces and the accumulation of wealth through capitalist enterprise. Manufacturing industry has expanded greatly but is capital-intensive, supplying only 15 per cent of the country's jobs. Agricultural labourers, the backbone of the profitable tea and flue-cured tobacco industry, are some of the poorest paid in southern Africa.

By the mid-1970s Malawi was a police-state with strong regional discrimination against Tumbuka-speakers from the north. In 1977 the arrest of Albert Muwalo, secretary-general of the MCP—who was subsequently executed, and the imprisonment of his ally, Focus Gwede, the head of the Special Branch, resulted in the release of hundreds of detainees, many of whom have resumed their former jobs. Relations with Zambia and Tanzania have improved, and dependence on South Africa will lessen with new rail links from Lilongwe to Chipata in Zambia in the 1980s.   I. L.

Dr Hastings Kamuzu Banda (left) visiting a farm

Mali

Area (km²)	1 240 000
Population 1980 (UN projection)	6 470 000
GNP per capita 1977 (US$)	110
Capital	Bamako
Currency	Mali franc

Previously the French colony of Soudan, Mali attained its separate independence in 1960 after an abortive federation with neighbouring Senegal in 1959. The ruling party at the time of independence was the *Union Soudanaise*, controlling all 80 seats in the National Assembly, and within four years stifling all party opposition. The first president, Modibo Keita, launched a policy of socialist modernization accompanied by much austerity: 'economic independence' dictated that Mali leave the franc zone in 1962, a move followed by rapid inflation and hardship. In 1967 the government felt compelled to swallow its pride and effectively rejoin the franc zone, but economic difficulties persisted and formed the background to a successful, bloodless (and initially popular) military *coup d'état* in November 1968.

Military government in Mali has been accompanied by the personal ascendancy of the current president, Colonel Moussa Traoré, who has frequently declared but not yet implemented his programme of return to civilian rule. In 1976 the military government did announce the creation of a 'mass political party', the *Union Démocratique du Peuple Malien*, while members of the Modibo Keita government remain constitutionally banned from political activity. Keita himself died in prison in 1977.

Economic hardship in Mali, highlighted by the severe drought of 1972–4, led to many reports of serious state mismanagement of the economy. Government officials were alleged to have been involved in misappropriation of drought relief funds, and the extension of state commercial control has clearly led to smuggling on a very large scale. France's continued willingness to provide budgetary aid and technical assistance to this impoverished country appears to be motivated by fears that isolation could only push Mali into Soviet and Cuban arms. *D. C. O'B.*

Mauritania

Area (km²)	1 030 700
Population 1980 (UN projection)	1 427 000
GNP per capita 1977 (US$)	270
Capital	Nouakchott
Currency	Ouguiya

Previously governed as a colony within the Federation of French West Africa,★ Mauritania became independent in 1960. The government was directed by President Moktar Ould Daddah, and controlled by his political party, the *Parti du Peuple Mauritanien* (PPM). Organized opposition was virtually impossible under the PPM, which controlled all seats in the National Assembly. There have, however, been recurrent tensions between the agriculturalist black population of the south and the semi-nomadic pastoralist Arabo-Berber population of the desert north. These tensions became acute in 1968 following a government decision to make Arabic an official language (together with French) and in the early 1970s with the reorientation of foreign policy away from Black Africa and towards the Arab world.

From 1974 until 1979 Mauritania's history was dominated by the affairs of the Western Sahara,★ the Spanish colonial territory that was divided between Mauritania and Morocco by the Madrid agreement of 1975. The Western Saharan liberation movement, the *Frente Popular para la Liberacíon de Sakiet el Hamra y Rio de Oro* (*Polisario*) has bitterly fought this agreement, and called instead for a separate Sahraoui republic. With Algerian support, *Polisario* was capable of a sustained guerrilla offensive, directed more successfully against Mauritania than against Morocco. Mauritania's economy, already severely weakened by the severe drought of 1969–74, and dependent for export revenue on the MIFERMA iron mines, was unable to meet the challenge of increased military expenditure, which in any case failed to prevent *Polisario* sabotage.

The civilian PPM regime was displaced in July 1978 by a military *coup d'état* which brought Lieutenant Colonel Mustapha Ould Salek to power. *Polisario* then announced a cease-fire. In August 1979 a formal peace agreement was signed, and Mauritania relinquished its claim to the southern part of Western Sahara. *D. C. O'B.*

Mauritius

Area (km²)	2040
Population 1980 (UN projection)	969 000
GNP per capita 1977 (US$)	760
Capital	Port Louis
Currency	Mauritius rupee

After obtaining independence from Britain in March 1968, Mauritius remained in the British Commonwealth and became an associate state of the European Economic Community (EEC). The prime minister since independence has been Sir Seewoosagur Ramgoolam (Labour Party) who leads an increasingly fragile coalition which includes Gaetan Duval, the former opposition leader. New opposition arose from the left in 1970 in the shape of the *Movement Militant Mauricienne* (MMM). After a dock strike in August 1971 the MMM leader, Paul Bérenger was briefly detained and the MMM fragmented. The Mauritian population is mixed; approximately 70 per cent Indo-Mauritian, 27 per cent Creole and Franco-Mauritian, with a small minority of Chinese. Population density is high at over 500 per sq km and there are severe unemployment problems, particularly among the young who are reluctant to stay in the agricultural sector. The land is extremely fertile and the climate ideal for tropical crops. The economy is dominated by cane sugar, which provides 40 per cent of national income and over 80 per cent of exports. In 1978 665 000 tonnes was produced, most of which was exported to Britain. Tea used to follow sugar products as the second most important export, but tourism has now overtaken it as a foreign exchange earner. Since 1971 the government has promoted Export Processing Zones, which now include textile factories, electronics assembly plants and diamond-cutting shops. Favourable investment terms, readily available labour and the access to EEC markets offered by the Lomé Convention have resulted in a manufacturing boom. In 1978, however, the EEC began to restrict textile exports to Europe, while changes in EEC agricultural policy may threaten future exports of sugar. *A. P. H.*

Morocco

Area (km²)	458 730
Population 1980 (UN projection)	20 384 000
GNP per capita 1977 (US$)	570
Capital	Rabat
Currency	Moroccan dirham

Morocco has been ruled since independence in 1956 by a monarchy. The authority of Mohammed V* was clearly established in 1955, when his restoration as the head of an independent state was the only way out of the impasse created by his deposition in 1953. His prestige was reinforced by his wealth, his following among the rural notables, and the campaign on his behalf by the guerrillas in the countryside. The *Istiqlal*, the chief nationalist party, under the leadership of Allal el-Fassi, was urban-based with a considerable membership, but its mass appeal was subordinated to the cause of Mohammed as the legitimate sovereign. The *Istiqlal* could not therefore come to power as the undisputed party of government, nor were its leaders necessarily chosen by the King for the premiership. It was weakened in 1959 when its left wing split off to form the *Union Nationale des Forces Populaires* (UNFP). When Mohammed V died in 1961, his son and successor Hassan II drafted a constitution, which was approved by a national referendum in 1962, giving the monarch presidential powers over a cabinet of ministers. In the elections that followed in 1963 for the first Moroccan national assembly, a royalist coalition, the *Front pour la Défense des Institutions Constitutionelles* (FDIC), won as many seats as the *Istiqlal* and UNFP combined, though with a smaller proportion of votes. The architect of the constitution and the coalition was Ahmed Reda Guedira, the King's chief minister; the core of the FDIC was a new party, the *Mouvement Populaire*, representing the King's support in the countryside. This support increased as widespread patronage created vested interests in the regime.

Riots in the main cities in 1965, sparked off by unemployment and rising prices, brought about the suspension of parliamentary government. During the next five years the *Istiqlal* was not only excluded from office but driven into opposition by the King's policies. The regime acquired a bad name with the disappearance (and presumed murder) in Paris in 1965 of Mehdi Ben Barka, the leading-figure of the UNFP. In 1970 a second constitution was approved by referendum, and in 1972 a third, both intended to translate the national appeal of the monarchy into the reliable support of local assemblies and a Moroccan parliament composed of 'neutrals' and royalists. Opposition from within the armed forces, however, resulting in the abortive coups of 1971 and 1972, put an end to both

King Hassan II of Morocco

these attempts to create an institutional framework for Moroccan politics. Governing through cabinets appointed by, and responsible to himself, the King turned instead to the reform of the military, and to silencing the UNFP. Trials of scores of its members for terrorism and subversion in 1973–4 split the party between the more revolutionary followers of Mohammed al-Basri and those of Abderrahim Bouabid, who in 1975 formed the new *Union Socialiste des Forces Populaires*.

The strongly nationalist *Istiqlal*, on the other hand, led by Mohammed Boucetta since the death of Allal el-Fassi in 1973, was attracted by the King's campaign to annex the Spanish Sahara, with its large deposits of phosphates to add to those of Morocco. This was accomplished, in concert with Mauritania—at least nominally—after the death of Franco in 1975, but Morocco has met fierce resistance from the Algerian-supported Saharan nationalist movement, *Polisario*.* In 1978, in another major foreign policy move—in line with its inclination towards France and the USA and its interest in African affairs—Morocco sent troops to pro-Western Zaire* to support the government in its conflict with Angolan-based rebels.   *M.B.*

243

Mozambique

Area (km²)	783 030
Population 1980 (UN projection)	10 375 000
GNP per capita 1977 (US$)	150
Capital	Maputo
Currency	Mozambique escudo

Mozambique won its independence on 25 June 1975, nearly 11 years after the *Frente de Libertação de Moçambique* (*Frelimo* – Mozambique Liberation Front) led by Dr Eduardo Mondlane* had launched a guerrilla war to end Portuguese rule. By 1974 *Frelimo* was tying down more than 60 000 Portuguese troops and its success was instrumental in prompting the army coup that overthrew the Portuguese dictatorship in April 1974, opening the way to Mozambique's independence. *Frelimo* and the new Portuguese regime signed accords in September 1974 formally ending the war and setting up a pre-independence 'transitional government'. Brief resistance from some of the country's 280 000 white settlers was quickly neutralized and most then started leaving.

Since independence, led by Samora Machel, *Frelimo* has instituted major social reforms, and at its 1977 third congress formally declared its adherence to Marxism-Leninism. Many small businesses and plantation farms abandoned by their Portuguese owners had already been nationalized, and now insurance companies and banks were taken over too, along with the country's largest mining company, the largest agricultural company and the oil refinery. However, not all private business was nationalized, and *Frelimo* remained keen to attract Western technology and investment.

Frelimo describes its political system as resting on 'people's democratic power'. However, democratic rights have been restricted by the establishment of a one-party system under the 1975 constitution. *Frelimo* is flanked by several 'mass organizations' and a network of neighbourhood *grupos dinamizadores* (dynamizing groups). There is a secret police force, and some oppositionists have been detained in 're-education centres'. However, political opposition has been minimal since *Frelimo* retains the prestige of having led the independence war.

In its foreign policy *Frelimo* is committed to non-alignment and has not allowed foreign powers to set up military bases on its territory. Its primary aim has been to attract aid from all possible sources. It has also cemented close ties with its African neighbours, especially Zambia and Tanzania, with which it was closely allied in supporting the nationalists fighting for majority rule in Zimbabwe.* From 1976 to 1980 the Zimbabwe African National Union maintained base camps in Mozambique and, in retaliation, Rhodesian forces

Samora Machel (centre) President of *Frelimo* since 1970 and President of Mozambique since 1975

repeatedly raided deep into Mozambiquan territory. Mozambique's relations with South Africa have, however, been more cordial – for pragmatic economic reasons. Mozambique earns essential foreign exchange by selling South Africa electricity from the Cabora Bassa dam, sending migrant labour and granting port facilities. South Africa is also Mozambique's cheapest source of manufactured imports.

Mozambique's economy is too weak to allow the *Frelimo* government to end its economic ties with South Africa. There is very little manufacturing industry, and few of the country's rich mineral resources have yet been exploited. Agricultural commodities have traditionally accounted for about 60 per cent of exports. Under colonial rule exports normally covered only about half of the import bill, the deficit being made up by invisible earnings, mainly from South Africa. In the first five years of independence this situation worsened, as the economy suffered from the exodus of the whites, the world recession, a decline in earnings from South Africa, and, until 1980, the closure of the border with Zimbabwe.   *T.H.*

Namibia

Area (km²)	824 292
Population 1980 (UN projection)	1 024 000
GNP per capita 1977 (US$)	1000
Capital	Windhoek
Currency	South African rand

In 1966 the General Assembly of the UN revoked South Africa's mandate over the territory of South West Africa–renamed Namibia by the UN in 1968. Undeterred, the South African government went ahead with its scheme of apartheid, or separate development for Namibia under which 60 per cent of the land was to have been allocated to the whites–10 per cent of the population. The main African nationalist party, the South West Africa People's Organization (SWAPO), which had its initial support from the Ovambo people (the largest group, who lived in the north straddling the border with Angola), began an armed struggle against South African rule in the late 1960s. In 1971 there was a prolonged African general strike and this increased the scale of violence. Ovambo and another 'homeland' were granted limited self-government in 1973, but the Africans who tried to work this system incurred the wrath of those who opposed it.

The turning point in the military and political struggle over Namibia came when Portugal granted independence to Angola in 1974. Civil war then broke out, with the intervention of South African forces (operating from bases in Namibia) on one side and Cuban and Russian on the other. The withdrawal of the South African forces and the victory of the *Movimento Popular de Libertação de Angola* in Angola,* not only greatly increased tensions within Namibia, and the scale of SWAPO military actions, but also caused the South African government to attempt a new political solution. White political groups and representatives of non-whites who did not support SWAPO formed the Democratic Turnhalle Alliance (DTA), and South Africa agreed in September 1977 to grant independence to Namibia in December 1978 under an arrangement with the DTA, which excluded SWAPO and which was to be based on the earlier scheme of group separation. This was followed by an intensification of SWAPO guerrilla activity. Meanwhile, Western members of the UN Security Council tried to mediate between the South African government and SWAPO, and in April 1978 South Africa agreed to the holding of UN-supervised elections that would elect an assembly to draft a constitution that would provide for independence by the end of 1978. However, in September 1978 the South African government decided to go ahead without UN supervision, and in December 1978 elections–which were regarded as invalid by the Western powers and were boycotted by SWAPO–were held for a constituent assembly, the DTA winning 41 out of 50 seats. The assembly subsequently agreed that a further round of elections–supervised by the UN–would be held in 1979. However, by mid-1980 no agreement had been reached between the UN Commissioner for Namibia and the South African government on the way in which these elections would be conducted, and it remained uncertain whether Namibia was to continue as a satellite of South Africa–its likely fate under a DTA government–or would become an independent state with a government possibly hostile to South Africa. *A.A.*

Niger

Area (km²)	1 267 000
Population 1980 (UN projection)	5 272 000
GNP per capita 1977 (US$)	160
Capital	Niamey
Currency	CFA franc

Previously a French colony, Niger gained independence in 1960 and was then governed for 14 years by President Hamani Diori and a single party, the *Parti Progressiste Nigerien*. Opposition, notably from Djibo Bakary's illegal *Sawaba* party, was ruthlessly suppressed. Discontent against the regime persisted nonetheless, and grew more acute with the drought of 1970–4. The government was accused of corruption and inefficiency in its handling of the economy and distribution of food relief aid. In April 1974, a military *coup d'état* led by Lieutenant Colonel Seyni Kountche overthrew the Diori regime, abolished civilian political institutions, and set up a supreme military council.

Since 1974, with the world oil price rises, Niger's uranium reserves (the largest in Africa, and fifth largest in the world) have assumed a new value. As the world price for uranium quintupled in five years, Niger's production more than tripled. Two principal uranium mines, financed respectively by French and Japanese capital, accounted for almost half of Niger's export revenue by 1978. The country has a continuing problem in its lack of trained personnel, and also has difficulties in the provision of a transport outlet, but it has discovered very substantial mineral reserves (coal, phosphates, and oil as well as uranium).

President Kountche's government has been firm in its handling of domestic opposition, but has also included many civilians in top official posts. Economic management has improved overall since the military takeover, and the regime has succeeded in maintaining good relations with France while diversifying its sources of overseas aid and investment. The government has declared its support for international projects in transport, water and mineral prospecting. President Kountche feels secure enough to turn his attention to foreign affairs, acting, for example, as mediator in an attempt to settle the Chad-*Frolinat*-Libya dispute in 1978. *D.C.O'B.*

Nigeria

Area (km²)	923 768
Population 1980 (UN projection)	72 596 000
GNP per capita 1977 (US$)	420
Capital	Lagos
Currency	Naira

Within four years of independence on 1 October 1960 Nigeria was on the verge of civil war. The patiently negotiated federal constitution could not contain the intense rivalries between the three major ethnic groups as represented by the three major political parties: the Hausa-dominated Northern Peoples Congress (NPC), the Igbo-dominated National Council of Nigerian Citizens–formerly the National Council of Nigeria and the Cameroons–(NCNC), and the Yoruba-dominated Action Group (AG).

The fragile coalition of the NPC and NCNC which formed the federal government was united on one thing: the destruction of the AG. Within two years the AG's leader, Chief Obafemi Awolowo, and his leading supporters had been jailed for treason, a state of emergency had been declared in the Western Region, the AG's principal base, and the AG government there neutralized and replaced by a pro-NPC government. Furthermore the Western Region had been split in two, with the non-Yoruba areas given separate statehood. On the other hand the minority ethnic groups in the Northern and Eastern Regions were denied the states they continued to agitate for.

The coalition partners soon fell out among themselves over the provisional results of the 1962 census, which indicated that the Northern Region had a substantially larger population than the three southern regions combined. Since parliamentary seats were allocated on a population basis, it seemed that Nigeria would be perpetually dominated by the north. The Federal Prime Minister, Sir Abubakar Tafawa Balewa, tried conciliation by ordering a fresh census, but its preliminary results, which appeared in February 1964, again gave the north a majority of 29.7 million as against a combined total for the south of 25.8 million–and fuelled a fresh crisis.

The NCNC and AG now allied against the NPC and its dependent ally in the Western Region, S.L. Akintola, who formed his own party, the Nigerian National Democratic Party, to fight the federal elections scheduled for December 1964. These were held against a background of labour unrest, rising prices and political violence. The results were inconclusive because in many areas the AG and NCNC boycotted the elections, claiming that they were rigged. Crisis was again averted by Balewa agreeing to form a government of national unity and to hold fresh elections in the affected constituencies. The situation continued to deteriorate and the Western Region elections of November 1965 were held in a state of near anarchy, which continued after Akintola claimed victory on the basis of polls that had been clearly rigged.

The deteriorating situation was brought to an end by a *coup d'état* in which the federal prime minister and the premiers of the Northern and Western Regions were assassinated with many top army officers, mainly of northern origin. The organizers of the coup eventually submitted to the head of the army, Major-General J.T. Aguyi-Ironsi, who took over as head of state.

The coup was at first widely welcomed. But Ironsi's military government soon appeared to be pursuing policies favourable to his own ethnic group, the Igbo. By proposing a military constitution for the country, he instilled fear into northerners, who saw themselves being swamped by the better educated southerners, who hitherto had not been able to get places in the northern civil service. Their fears were heightened by the fact that the major who had engineered the coup had killed the federal prime minister, who was a northerner, the Northern Region premier and many northern officers, while sparing Igbo regional premiers. There were anti-Igbo riots in northern cities; Ironsi was assassinated by northern officers and once more the country was plunged into anarchy.

Lieutenant Colonel Yakubu Gowon, the senior northern officer, proved to be the only person who could control the largely northern rank and file, and so became head of state. He was not recognized as such by the Eastern Region military governor, Colonel Chukwuemeka Odumegwu Ojukwu. Further anti-Igbo riots, and failure to agree on an acceptable compromise constitution for the future of Nigeria, led to Ojukwu's decision to secede from Nigeria in May 1967 and create the state of Biafra. On the eve of secession Gowon decreed that Nigeria was now a 12-state federation, thus breaking the monolithic north into six states, and the east into three. Two of the eastern states comprised minorities, which had long been agitating for separate states. But Ojukwu continued with his secession. Biafra gained considerable support overseas during the three-year civil war, but the rest of Nigeria, after initial doubts as to whether it would hold together, rallied behind Gowon and the federal government forces finally put an end to secession in January 1970.

The following years were involved in reconstruction of a shattered economy, made easier by oil revenues. Despite widespread accusations during the war of genocide by the Federal Government, no Biafrans were executed for their part in secession, few were detained while many regained their former posts in government.

Gowon's post-war regime came to be marked increasingly by inefficiency and corruption, and popular discontent was increased by massive inflation that followed the huge pay increases made to civil servants in December 1974 and generalized throughout the private sector. His decision to delay the promised return to civilian rule in 1976 eroded the once widespread popular support he had enjoyed. In July 1975 when Gowon was away at the Organization of African Unity* Conference in Kampala his government was overthrown and a longstanding rival and critic, Brigadier Murtala Mohammed, took over as head of state. He gained great popularity, as he initiated a programme of reforms, including a house-cleaning of inefficient and corrupt public servants, and promised to create new states and return to civilian rule by 1979. Although he was assassinated in February 1978 before he could realize his programme, it was faithfully followed

General Olusegun Obasanjo, retiring President of the Supreme Military Council, and the new civilian President of Nigeria, Shehu Shagari after the ceremony at which power was handed over in October 1979

by his successors and after a Constituent Assembly had adopted a US-style constitution Nigerians went to the polls in August 1979. The new civilian government, led by President Shehu Shagari assumed power in October, inheriting massive problems: a poor financial situation, resulting from international inflation as well as the profligate spending of the military regimes, exacerbated by civilian commitments to an oversize army and a universal free education scheme; increases in corruption—despite official campaigns against it; and considerable labour unrest.   *M.C.*

Réunion

Area (km²)	2510
Population 1980 (UN projection)	548 000
GNP per capita 1977 (US$)	Not available
Capital	Saint-Denis
Currency	French franc

A volcanic island with fertile soils and abundant rainfall, Réunion has an ethnically mixed population (the island was uninhabited when first settled by the French) rapidly increasing at 3 per cent a year. This has caused overcrowding, high unemployment and a 'poor-white' poverty trap, problems only partially solved by official encouragement to emigrate to France.

The island has the status of a French overseas department, and has three representatives in the French National Assembly and two in the Senate. In 1973 it was made the headquarters of French military forces in the Indian Ocean after their forced withdrawal from Madagascar. A minority campaigns for independence though a larger proportion favours complete integration with France.

The economy is heavily dependent on sugar cane for export to France. Rum, vanilla and perfume oils are also sold overseas, but export receipts cover only one-third of the import bill, the rest being covered by French subsidies and private remittances.   *A.P.H.*

Rwanda

Area (km²)	26 338
Population 1980 (UN projection)	4 865 000
GNP per capita 1977 (US$)	130
Capital	Kigali
Currency	Rwanda franc

The *Parti de l'Emancipation du Peuple Hutu (Parmehutu)* – the political organ of the Hutu* ethnic group, the subservient majority in the Tutsi*-ruled kingdom of Rwanda, a Belgian colony since the First World War – seized power with Belgian connivance, and under the leadership of Grégoire Kayibanda in January 1961. Kayibanda formed the first independent government but the defeated Tutsi-dominated *Union Nationale Rwandaise* in exile undertook a number of raids led by *inyenzi* ('cockroaches') guerrillas during the first two years of independence. Popular reaction to the Tutsi minority, which had flared into a widespread uprising in November 1959, resulted in large-scale killing of Tutsi, with an estimated death toll of 10 000 in response to *inyenzi* raids. Government response to ethnic killing was tardy and emphasized the fear of continuing Tutsi hegemony.

After a decade of *Parmehutu* rule Tutsi still held prominent positions in education establishments and the still important Catholic Church. Moreover *Parmehutu* became increasingly dominated by the ethnically conscious Gitarama sub-group of the Hutu from the central region which had created a dangerous regionalism from which the agriculturally rich north felt excluded. Growing disorder in schools, seminaries and in the university, with the expulsion of Tutsi in racist attacks, preceded a military coup on 5 July 1973. The new military government of General Juvenal Habyarimana, himself a northerner, with strong representation from the northern provinces of Gisenyi and Ruhengeri, set itself the task of healing ethnic and regional conflicts.

In July 1975 the *Mouvement Révolutionnaire National pour le Développement* superseded *Parmehutu* and in subsequent years an increasing number of civilians were given ministerial posts. Military rule has seen an improvement in relations with both Burundi and Uganda although disruption during Idi Amin's tyranny in Uganda* greatly damaged Rwanda, whose trade and oil largely passed south. Belgian control over the Rwandan economy, especially in the mining sector, was not lessened under Habyarimana's government.   *I.L.*

São Tomé and Príncipe

Area (km²)	964
Population 1980 (UN projection)	85 000
GNP per capita 1977 (US$)	420
Capital	São Tomé
Currency	Dobra

São Tomé and Príncipe gained independence from Portugal on 12 July 1975 after elections confirming the *Movimento de Libertaçao de São Tomé e Príncipe* (MLSTP) – led by Manuel Pinto da Costa and Miguel Trouvoada – as the single ruling party. The new government inherited an economy marked by chaos and under-production, particularly on the *roças* or cocoa plantations, which provide the basis of the island's livelihood. An end to contract labour from other colonies and political mobilization of native workers cut production by half. Nationalization of the plantations in November 1975 has been accompanied by only a limited recovery. In tackling these problems, the government is hampered by severe shortages in technical and managerial expertise. Cuba currently provides some 75 per cent of all skilled personnel. Long term plans call for expansion in maize, tropical fruits and fishing in an effort to reverse the present policy of importing nearly all the republic's food. São Tomé adheres to a policy of non-alignment, perhaps inevitably, given its present dependence on international markets and aid programmes. There is, however, increasing cooperation with Gabon, MLSTP's base during the years of exile, and the Francophone zone. *J.E.C.*

Senegal

Area (km²)	196 192
Population 1980 (UN projection)	4 989 000
GNP per capita 1977 (US$)	420
Capital	Dakar
Currency	CFA franc

Senegal, whose capital, Dakar, was also the capital of the French West African Federation,* became separately independent in 1960. Léopold Senghor, the man elected first president, has dominated the country's political life ever since. There were indeed many challenges to Senghor's hegemony in the early years after independence, but by 1966 all the opposition parties had joined the governing *Union Progressiste Sénégalaise*. A student strike at the University of Dakar in June 1968 (modelled on the Paris demonstrations of the previous month) provoked a national general strike, and presidential control was reasserted by a discreet show of military force and a constitutional amendment giving formal recognition to the trade unions.

After 1968 the country's life was dominated less by political events than by the harsh climatic realities of the Sahelian drought (1968–73, and again in 1977). The national economy has long been dependent on the peanut as a virtual export monocrop, and in the drought years peasants across the country reverted to subsistence farming to survive. The government, which relied economically on peanut production, turned overseas for financial and other assistance – while also benefiting from some success in its industrialization programme around Dakar.

Partisan political activity was allowed to re-emerge from 1974, and in 1976 a constitutional amendment provided for the creation of three competing parties – Senghor's governing *Parti Socialiste* (PS), Abdoulaye Wade's *Parti Démocratique Sénégalais*, and Mahjmout Diop's *Parti Africain de l'Independance* (PAI). The PAI, which had been banned since 1961, now filled a constitutionally allocated slot for a 'Marxist-Leninist or Communist' legal opposition. Presidential, legislative and municipal elections were duly held in February 1978, and produced the expected triumph of Senghor and his PS (83 per cent of the popular vote). Both of the recognized opposition parties, as well as others that remained legally unrecognized, protested against the count.

Senghor's relations with France remained cordial, and French budgetary and technical assistance underpinned the government. The maintenance of a French military base in Dakar partly explains the regime's remarkable durability. *D.C.O'B.*

Seychelles

Area (km²)	119
Population 1980 (UN projection)	66 000
GNP per capita 1977 (US$)	Not available
Capital	Victoria
Currency	Seychelles rupee

Spread over 850 000 sq km of ocean 92 picturesque islands form the Seychelles Republic, which gained independence from Britain in 1976. Most of the inhabitants live on Mahé Island.

The first president, James Mancham, was deposed in June 1977 by his then prime minister, Albert René. President René proceeded to convert the republic into a one-party socialist state while maintaining the tax privileges and property rights of foreign investors.

Tourism began only after the 1971 inauguration of the international airport, and rapidly dominated the economy; the 1978 total of 62 000 tourist visits represents one tourist per inhabitant. As a result, agriculture and fishing have been neglected. Food imports rose sixfold between 1970 and 1976 and traditional agricultural exports – copra and cinnamon bark – are in decline. Tourism earnings offset most of the trade deficit, but the hotel construction boom is now over: the government plans to modernize fisheries and to turn the Seychelles into a tax-haven. Suggestions that the USSR will be given naval base facilities have always been denied. *A.P.H.*

Sierra Leone

Area (km²)	71 740
Population 1980 (UN projection)	3 392 000
GNP per capita 1977 (US$)	200
Capital	Freetown
Currency	Leone

Sierra Leone became independent in April 1961 with a government formed by Sir Milton Margai's Sierra Leone People's Party (SLPP). The SLPP victory marked the triumph of the majority up-country Protectorate people over the Creole* politicians of Freetown and the western coastal areas around it—the Colony—who had claimed the right to maintain the political supremacy that they had enjoyed during colonial rule because of the Colony's higher standard of education and its population's British citizenship.

The unity established by the SLPP in what became known as the Provinces was, however, precarious. Siaka Stevens, a powerful lieutenant of Sir Milton, had formed the All People's Congress (APC) in 1960, a party with a more radical stance than the SLPP, and with leaders from the Northern rather than the Southern and Eastern provinces, and after independence it became an effective opposition. In the 1967 general elections the APC gained a narrow majority over the SLPP—now led by Sir Milton's brother, Sir Albert Margai—but the army intervened to prevent Stevens from assuming office and military rule was established. In 1968, however, a privates' coup overthrew the regime, and Stevens was invited to become prime minister. By 1980 Steven's government faced widespread opposition—exacerbated by the heavy expense of an Organization of African Unity* summit conference in Freetown—after a decade of political upheavals including attempted coups followed by execu-

tions, attempts on Stevens's life, widespread civil disturbances, elections that returned the APC to power but were widely regarded as having been rigged, and the declaration in 1978 of a one-party state.

Sierra Leone's political problems have been exacerbated by its poor economic performance. Foreign exchange has come mainly from diamond and iron-mining, but Sierra Leone's official exports of diamonds have constantly fallen in volume—a decline masked by rising world prices—partly because of a high level of smuggling, and the single iron ore mine was closed in 1975. Expansion of other mineral production, notably rutile and bauxite, offers some hope, but agriculture has remained largely stagnant despite considerable investment in large-scale projects. *D.W.*

Somalia

Area (km²)	637 657
Population 1980 (UN projection)	3 652 000
GNP per capita 1977 (US$)	110
Capital	Mogadishu
Currency	Somali shilling

For Somalis, the creation of an independent Somali republic in 1960 was only a beginning of their struggle for national unity. It linked those Somalis formerly ruled by Britain and Italy; it excluded those living in Kenya, Ethiopia and Djibouti. The idea of 'reunification of all Somalis' has dominated post-independence politics and, indirectly, the economy too. Parliamentary government survived until 1969, aided by the common commitment to reunification. But personal and clan disputes grew, coming to a climax with the 1969 elections and the assassination of the president, Dr Abdar-Rashid Ali Shermarke, soon afterwards. The army took power in a bloodless coup and its commander, Major-General Mohammed Siad Barre, became president. The new government, always austere, became increasingly radical in its philosophy. Socialism at home and irredentism abroad both favoured close ties with the USSR, since the West (linked to Kenya and Ethiopia) was unwilling to accommodate Somali requests for military aid. This friendship came to an abrupt end in November 1977 when Somalia severed diplomatic relations following an escalation in the Ogaden war against Ethiopia* and increasing Soviet intimacy with the new rulers of Ethiopia. In March 1978 when the West refused to fill the vacuum created by this move, Somalia was left without foreign military assistance (although economic aid was offered in its place) and was forced to withdraw from the Ogaden. By

President Siaka Stevens of Sierra Leone (left, signing) with William Tolbert, President of Liberia, 1971–80

Women militia march-past in Somalia

1980 the USA was showing a tentative interest in military links. Meanwhile, however, Somalia continued to face the effects of guerrilla warfare by Somali irregulars against Ethiopian forces in the Ogaden: Ethiopian attacks on Somalian border settlements, and an enormous inflow of Somali refugees.

A high military profile since the 1960s has taken its toll on the economy, which is badly served by both climate and geography. But, because of its strategic position, Somalia has never been short of offers of aid. In the 1960s substantial amounts of foreign aid were received but much was wasted. The Siad Barre government has emphasized self-reliance. It launched a major literacy drive following the adoption of a Somali script in 1972. This coincided with one of the worst droughts in recorded history. An energetic campaign combined drought relief, the teaching of literacy and the settlement of nomads. *C.S.*

South Africa since 1961

Area (km²)	1 221 037
Population 1980 (UN projection)	28 533 000
GNP per capita 1977 (US$)	1340
Capital	Pretoria
Currency	Rand

The crisis that the white regime in South Africa faced after Sharpeville* in 1960–1 led not only to widespread repressive measures, but also to the determination to apply what were termed the 'positive' aspects of apartheid.* It was hoped that African nationalist demands and aspirations could be diverted by the creation

of ten African states or 'homelands'* (Bantustans), based on the existing 'reserves' within South Africa. Apartheid–or separate development, as it came to be called–accepted that large numbers of Africans would continue to live and work in the urban industrial areas, but that they would be citizens, not of South Africa, but of a particular homeland. It was acknowledged that the homelands could not then, and increasingly would not be able to, accommodate all the people belonging to a 'national' group. Nevertheless, the regime went ahead with this device to maintain white supremacy.

The cornerstone of the Bantustan policy was the Promotion of Bantu Self-Government Act of 1959, which maintained that the 'Bantu peoples' formed separate 'national units' rather than 'a homogeneous people,' thereby ignoring over two centuries of interaction which had produced an African urban working class. In terms of demographic arithmetic–let alone of any other rational or moral argument–the restriction of Africans–who formed over 70 per cent of the population–to 13 per cent of the land of South Africa is a policy of questionable validity. Much of this 13 per cent is poor land, and few of the country's rich mineral resources are situated in it. Yet National Party governments have been determined to press ahead with separate development.

Black South Africans seek places on an overcrowded workers' train

Of the homelands–Transkei, Ciskei, Kwazulu, Qwaqwa, Bophuthatswana, South Ndebele, Lebowa, Gazankulu, Venda, and Swazi–the first to start along the road to self-rule was Transkei. Granted self-government in 1963, under the firm control of the traditionalist Chief Kaiser Matanzima, Transkei was formally granted independence in 1976, to be followed the next year by Bophuthatswana, which consists of six separated blocks of territory, surrounded by 'white' land. Neither Transkei nor Bophuthatswana have received any recognition outside South Africa. The leaders of the eight other homelands have refused to accept this kind of independence. Indeed, Gatsha Buthelezi has used his position as leader of Kwazulu to launch outspoken criticisms of separate development.

By the time of the independence of Transkei, the South African economy, which had enjoyed almost unbroken growth in the 1950s and 1960s, had run into trouble. Although many industries still required more skilled labour–a requirement that white workers could not meet–many less-skilled Africans became unemployed. In many instances the government's only response was to 'remove' the individual unemployed to his homeland (which he had probably never seen), and thus to make him the responsibility of the hard-pressed homelands authorities. This 'dumping' of Africans caused increasing resentment and insecurity among people living in the urban areas. After a decade of apparent quiescence since Sharpeville, African resistance became more pronounced. In 1973 there was a large and partly successful strike in Durban, and then much unrest among African gold miners–all of which culminated in the uprisings of 1976–7.

The immediate cause of these disturbances was the discontent of black schoolchildren and students in the so-called townships, in particular Soweto, the huge city to the south-west of Johannesburg. Attempts by the white authorities to introduce Afrikaans as the language of instruction in schools led to spontaneous demonstrations by young people. The violent response of the security forces led to active support of the demonstrations by many older Africans, and the uprising spread to most of the other towns and cities of the Transvaal and into the Cape, where Africans were joined by Coloured (mixed-race) people. African militancy was much encouraged by the success of the African struggle against Portuguese rule in Mozambique* and by the withdrawal of South African forces from Angola.*

The white regime responded to the 1976–7 uprisings in much the same way as it had after the Sharpeville incident of 1960. The new African organizations–the South African Students' Organization and the Black People's Convention–were banned and many individuals were arrested. By the end of 1977 at least 24 of those arrested since the beginning of the demonstrations had died in custody–including Steve Biko, the most forceful and charismatic of the student leaders–and numerous others had been sentenced to long

of the great Muslim sectarian leaders for mass support, resulting in an unhealthy polarization. A more fundamental problem has been the tense and often explosive character of north-south relations. Under the Anglo-Egyptian Condominium,* the already serious differences between the predominantly Muslim, Arabized and relatively sophisticated north, and the non-Muslim, black peoples of the south were exacerbated. At independence political dominance came into the hands of the northern religio-political groupings. Violent disturbances in the south, beginning in 1955, assumed the proportions of a civil war in the early 1960s.

The parliamentary system inherited by the independent Sudan seemed unable to cope with these problems. In 1958 the army assumed power in a bloodless coup, and ruled until 1964, when massive popular opposition brought about a return to parliamentary government. This second parliamentary period (1964–9) witnessed an unprecedented degree of inter-party wrangling and manoeuvering, a complete breakdown of order in the south, and an apparent

Jaafar al-Nimeiri, President of Sudan (left) with Julius Nyerere, President of Tanzania

Scene from the Soweto riots, June 1976

periods of imprisonment. No major concessions were made by the government – although attempts were made to win over the Coloured and Indian communities by promises of limited political representation in the future. Above all, the homeland policy was maintained unchanged, and the South African government remained arrogantly impervious to international criticism of the appalling conditions prevailing in the homelands. Non-white opposition to white minority rule remains very close to the surface, and whites rely essentially on military force and efficient security to maintain their position of dominance.   *A.A.*

Sudan

Area (km²)	2 505 813
Population 1980 (UN projection)	21 420 000
GNP per capita 1977 (US$)	300
Capital	Khartoum
Currency	Sudan pound

Although the Sudan was one of the first states in Africa to achieve independence (in 1956), its history since then has been characterized by political instability. The generally elitist nature of political parties since their inception in the 1940s forced them to look to the followings

inability on the part of politicians to deal with the country's pressing economic and political problems. In 1969 the military again took power under the leadership of Major-General Jaafar al-Nimeiri. His regime managed, at least temporarily, to suppress opposition both from the right (the *Ansar*, or followers of the Mahdi, whose political arm was the *Umma* party), and the left (the Communists and other leftists who had helped Nimeiri to power). In 1972 the debilitating civil war was finally brought to an end after a peace conference in Addis Ababa, and the south was granted limited autonomy.

The Sudan today is a presidential republic with a unicameral legislature. It is a one-party state, the official Sudan Socialist Union being endowed with a special status by the constitution of 1973. Under this constitution (the Sudan's first), the president (who, since a plebiscite in 1971, has been Nimeiri) is vested with great power. Opposition to the regime has come largely from the supporters of the former *Umma* party and its leader, Sayyid Sadiq al-Mahdi. A number of coups have been attempted since 1969, the most serious having occurred in 1971 and 1976. In 1977 Sayyid Sadiq returned to the Sudan from exile and agreed to work in concert with Nimeiri.

The Sudan's foreign policy has been moderate and generally pro-Western. As a member of both the Arab League and the Organization of African Unity,★ the Sudan has played an active mediating role. In recent years the troubling developments in the Horn of Africa and the activities of the Libyan regime have brought the Sudan closer to the West, whence technical and military assistance is sought. The Sudan's economic and political relations with Egypt remain close, although attempts at political union have faltered. The economy is mixed, with heavy reliance on the agricultural sector, especially cotton. Oil exploration has been encouraging but inconclusive. Major development schemes are under way, financed largely by Arab and Western funds. These aim at developing the Sudan's enormous capacity for food production, in the hope of transforming the country into the 'bread-basket' of the Arab Near East.   *M.W.D.*

Swaziland

Area (km²)	17 363
Population 1980 (UN projection)	543 000
GNP per capita 1977 (US$)	580
Capital	Mbabane
Currency	Lilangeni

Swaziland boasts the longest reigning monarch in Africa and one of the most traditional systems of government on the continent. Having initially opposed modern partisan politics, the 80 year old king (or

Ngwenyama), Sobhuza II, shrewdly formed his own political party and won all seats in the 1967 pre-independence elections. At the next general election in 1972, however, the main opposition party won three of the 24 seats. The King reacted strongly to this minor opposition success by a series of moves culminating with the abrogation of the constitution and the dissolution of political parties, which, he claimed, were 'alien' to Swazi traditions. Any hopes that the short-lived experiments with political parties would be revived were quashed in March 1977 when the King proclaimed the abolition of the parliamentary system and the substitution of traditional tribal communities, or *tinkhundla*. Since the royal family is at the centre of both political power and land tenure, the system is truly feudal. But it is not oppressive: numerous traditional safeguards exist against the arbitrary use of power. Moreover, a shrewd foreign policy has saved the country from censure in Africa either for its domestic politics or for its ambivalent relations with South Africa.   *C.S.*

King Sobhuza II of Swaziland

Tanzania

Area (km²)	945 087
Population 1980 (UN projection)	18 052 000
GNP per capita 1977 (US$)	200
Capital	Dar es Salaam
Currency	Tanzania shilling

Three main themes have dominated Tanzanian government policy since independence was achieved in 1961. They are the struggle to create an egalitarian society and avoid the rise of a privileged elite; support for African liberation movements, and a fight to be truly non-aligned. In all affairs, the thoughts and guidance of President Julius Nyerere* have dominated.

Tanzania's internal policy was vague until 1967 when Nyerere authored, and had the ruling party, the Tanzania African National Union, adopt the Arusha Declaration. The Declaration stated that all major institutions of finance and production should be in the hands of the state, and that the nation should develop through the efforts of Tanzanians rather than relying on foreigners and foreign businesses.

The most controversial part of the Arusha Declaration was the leadership code, which prohibited leaders, meaning party or government officials, from having more than one income or from owning properties for rent. Many officials had to choose between government or party service and their private business interests, and some chose the latter. Nyerere's number two man, Oscar Kambona, fled the country and has been trying to organize an opposition from exile ever since.

Tanzania's socialist policies have resulted in slower development than in neighbouring capitalist states, but distribution of wealth has

March-past of women of the Tanzanian People's Militia

been more even in Tanzania. Nyerere argues, and most observers agree, that it will be at least another 20–30 years before his socialist experiment can be judged a success or failure.

Soon after the island of Zanzibar's revolution in 1964, a loose union was formed with mainland Tanzania. The union was strengthened in 1975 when the ruling parties of the two parts of the union were merged to form the Chama Cha Mapinduzi Revolutionary Party and a new constitution was adopted that allowed Zanzibar and the mainland to each have separate government institutions, but which made the new single party supreme.

Tanzania's staunchly non-aligned stand has brought it into conflict with several big powers; for example Tanzania won its fight with West Germany over the right to recognize both Germanies. But the policy has won Tanzania international respect and allowed the country to receive aid from both East and West.

Ever since it achieved its own independence Tanzania has devoted a large portion of its diplomatic and material resources to aiding independence struggles in other African countries. Tanzania encouraged and played host to the formation of the *Frente de Libertação de Moçambique*★ (*Frelimo*), trained the *Frelimo* army and served as a rear base for *Frelimo* during a ten year long war for independence. Soldiers have also been trained in Tanzania for Zimbabwe, Angolan and South African nationalist movements.

In 1979 Tanzania became the first African country to have ever defeated another African country in a war by occupying its territory. In a war set off by an invasion of Tanzanian territory by the army of Uganda's Idi Amin, Tanzanian forces fought for eight months and overthrew the Amin regime. *T.A.*

Togo

Area (km²)	56 000
Population 1980 (UN projection)	2 596 000
GNP per capita 1977 (US$)	300
Capital	Lomé
Currency	CFA franc

Togo's path to independence was marked by conflict over the question of the reunification of the Ewe people, who had ultimately been split between British and French colonial administrations. In 1956 the French government–which opposed reunification of any kind–organized a plebiscite in the UN Trust Territory of Togo which indicated that the population wished to form an autonomous republic within the French Community. Nicolas Grunitsky, leader of the *Parti de l'Unité Togolaise*, became Prime Minister. The plebiscite

had, however, been rigged, and in 1958 a UN-supervised general election was won by the rival *Comité de l'Unité Togolaise* led by Sylvanus Olympio–an advocate of ultimate Ewe unification–who became president when Togo achieved full independence on 27 April 1960. The struggle between Grunitsky and Olympio, both southern Ewes and members of interlocking elite families with some non-African ancestry, continued until January 1963, when Olympio was murdered in an uprising of army NCOs (among whom was Sgt Etienne Gnassingbe Eyadema, a northerner). The unresolved problems of ex-servicemen discharged from the French army lay behind the uprising, but its main result was the return of Grunitsky, who became President. Grunitsky's government, however, faced continued opposition from pro-Olympio elements, and in January 1967 Eyadema–by then a Lt Colonel–seized power, ostensibly to prevent civil war.

Eyadema, who became Togo's first general in December 1967, has repeatedly spoken of a return to civilian rule but, despite several plots against him, remained in power at the end of 1979. In part as a counter to opposition groups he has laid heavy stress on national unity and his own part in creating it. All existing political parties were banned in 1967 and a sole political movement, the *Rassemblement du Peuple Togolais* (RPT), was formed in 1969. In the same vein, like his ally and friend, President Mobutu of Zaire★–to whom he sent military aid during the Shaba rebellion (1978)–Eyadema has fostered an ideology of 'authenticity', stressing indigenous values 'while remaining open to modernity'. 'Authenticity' has been used as a weapon against political enemies: in November 1977 a major plot against Eyadema

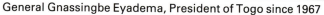

General Gnassingbe Eyadema, President of Togo since 1967

was forestalled, and at a trial in August 1979 members of the Olympio, da Souza and Lawson families were implicated and convicted, and were castigated as 'anti-national' aliens because of their partially foreign antecedents. In December 1979 Eyadema announced forthcoming parliamentary and presidential elections but this did not, apparently, presage any relaxation in his grip–the RPT was to be the sole participating party, and an RPT rally unanimously selected Eyadema as the only presidential candidate.

Taking production for home consumption and export (chiefly coffee and cocoa) together, agriculture is the most important sector of the Togolese economy. Since the early 1970s, however, phosphates have become an increasingly important export. In 1973 phosphates constituted 46 per cent of exports by value; in 1974 this increased to 76 per cent. Despite a slump in prices in 1975–6, production has continued to expand rapidly. Nevertheless, Togo's balance of payments was only kept in credit in the late 1970s by transfers in the form of aid–largely because of the country's high propensity to import. Eyadema's ideology of 'authenticity' has perhaps been more positively realized in foreign affairs and economic policy than in domestic politics. Despite continuing heavy dependence on French aid, Eyadema has been more critical of French policy than many other Francophone African leaders. For example, he has attacked French manipulation of the Franc Zone and also successfully worked with Nigeria to create the Economic Community of West African States* (ECOWAS), refusing to join the purely Francophone *Communauté Economique de l'Afrique de l'Ouest* (CEAO). His most striking move came in 1974 when he nationalized the largely French owned phosphate mining company.   *R.C.*

Tunisia

Area (km²)	163 610
Population 1980 (UN projection)	6 561 000
GNP per capita 1977 (US$)	860
Capital	Tunis
Currency	Tunisian dinar

At independence in 1956, the government of Tunisia was taken over by the *Néo-Destour* party under its leader Habib Bourguiba.* As prime minister, Bourguiba supervised the newly-elected constituent assembly in the preparation of a constitution. In 1957 he deposed the traditional ruler–the Bey–to become president of the new republic, an office which he now holds for life. Despite differences with France during the Algerian war (French aircraft attacked the Tunisian village of Sakiet Sidi Youssef in 1958) and over Bizerta (where French forces fought to retain a naval base in 1961), his regime has been notable for its pro-Western policies. Within Tunisia it has been authoritarian, with the president in control of the party, and the party in control of the government. Under the constitution of 1959 the national assembly became a body serving mainly to ratify legislation; the party congress, normally held every five years, has been more creative. From 1958 the party organization was made to coincide with the administrative districts of the country, helping to make it an institution of government. The strong trade union movement, the *Union Générale Tunisienne du Travail* (UGTT), has acted as an extension of the party.

The main issues have been economic policy and planning, and the question of Bourguiba's successor. Ahmed Ben Salah, dismissed as leader of the UGTT in 1956, was given control of planning in 1961. In accordance with the party's change of title in 1964 from *Néo-Destour* to *Socialiste Destourien*, Ben Salah's plans were for state investments financed by foreign loans, notably from the USA. The programme, however, was not a success, largely because of the failure of the agricultural cooperatives. In 1970 Ben Salah was dismissed, tried on several charges and imprisoned. Since then the emphasis has been upon free enterprise, which has been largely responsible for the growth in the important tourist industry established in the previous decade.

Ben Salah's failure questioned the policies and the leadership of the party. In 1971 the party congress was the occasion of much discussion. Critics like Ahmed Mestiri, however, were quickly disowned. Despite a long illness, Bourguiba asserted his authority, which was clearly re-established at the party congress of 1974. Since 1970 his chief supporter and presumed successor has been the prime minister, his old colleague, Hedi Nouira. Nouira has governed firmly, calling out the troops in 1978 to deal with riots in the course of a strike, for which Habib Achour, the leader of the UGTT, was held responsible.   *M.B.*

Uganda

Area (km²)	241 139
Population 1980 (UN projection)	13 222 000
GNP per capita 1977 (US$)	260
Capital	Kampala
Currency	Uganda shilling

At independence in 1962 long-standing conflict between the major nationalist party, the Uganda People's Congress (UPC), led by Milton Obote, and the Kabaka (king) of Buganda,* Frederick Mutesa II, was superficially healed by the formation of a coalition between the UPC and the Bugandan *Kabaka Yekka* party. Obote became prime minister and Mutesa was appointed president; a federal constitution perpetuated the wide autonomy Buganda had enjoyed before independence. Conflict between Mutesa and Obote continued until May 1966 when Obote launched a pre-emptive attack on Mutesa's palace, after which the Kabaka fled into exile. Obote then sought to bolster his position by introducing increasingly radical policies and by promoting his supporters in the army, notably Idi Amin, who became army commander in 1966. In 1969 Obote proposed a Common Man's Charter, and in 1970 announced a 60 per cent nationalization of large-scale commerce, banking and plantations.

Elections were scheduled for April 1971, but in January Amin seized power while Obote was abroad. Shrewdly, Amin secured the support of the Baganda at home, and Britain and Israel abroad, while conceding nothing of substance in return. Meanwhile, he set about liquidating members of the pro-Obote Lango and Acholi ethnic groups in the army. In a succession of purges over the next seven years, potential sources of opposition were removed but, at the same time, Amin's power-base shrank. The honeymoon with the West ended in 1972 when 40 000 Ugandan Asians were expelled within six weeks. This act brought Amin a popularity in Africa that was not completely expunged by the massacres of thousands of indigenous citizens; in 1975 he became Organization of African Unity★ Chairman for the year. Exiles invaded Uganda in 1972 but were easily repulsed. By 1978, however, Amin had begun to turn against his closest supporters. The army, which split into rival factions, was unable to withstand a Tanzanian invasion in 1979; Amin escaped

abroad, and his regime collapsed. Two caretaker civilian governments experienced increasing administrative difficulties in the face of continuing political and economic anarchy. In May 1980 a military government seized power, but promised to hold elections: the same month Obote returned from exile.

C.S.

Upper Volta

Area (km²)	274 200
Population 1980 (UN projection)	6 774 000
GNP per capita 1977 (US$)	110
Capital	Ouagadougou
Currency	CFA franc

Previously a colony within the French West African Federation, Upper Volta became independent in 1960. The first president was Maurice Yameogo, with his party, the *Union Démocratique Voltaique* (UDV), quickly banning organized opposition. In 1966 the military intervened to overthrow the Yameogo regime, and a new government was formed under the presidency of Lieutenant-Colonel Sangoule Lamizana. The country was then ravaged by the Sahelian drought from 1969 to 1974, and much of the rural populace was brought to the brink of starvation: their hardship would have been much worse without a large-scale international relief operation, although there were disturbing reports of corruption and inefficiency in the local distribution of overseas food aid.

Political parties were allowed to re-emerge after 1970, in which year were held the first elections since the military seizure of power. Three main parties, and numerous minor ones, have competed for seats in the national assembly, but President Lamizana and the military exercised the real power. Since 1976 Lamizana has responded to popular demand for a return to civilian rule, and the old civilian factions and personalities have re-emerged. Legislative and presidential elections were duly held in April and May 1978. Lamizana was confirmed president by an electoral majority, while the UDV won a narrow and bitterly disputed majority in the legislature. A new cabinet was formed by Prime Minister Joseph Conombo, with 19 civilians and two military officers.

Upper Volta remains an extremely poor country, one of the world's 25 poorest according to UN income statistics, and its (limited) economic viability is assured by remittances from more than half a million agricultural workers employed on plantations in countries to the south (especially Ivory Coast). Most of its own territory is desert or semi-desert, and the relatively dense population is thus much at the mercy of climatic variations.

D. C. O'B.

Ugandan students celebrate the establishment of the first civilian government after Idi Amin's overthrow in 1979

Western Sahara

Area of former Spanish Sahara (km^2)	265 990
Population 1980 (UN projection)	79 000
GNP per capita 1977 (US$)	Not available
Capital of former Spanish Sahara	el Aaiún
Currency	Spanish peseta

Resistance to Spanish rule in the Western Sahara erupted into open revolt in 1957 but was suppressed by a joint Franco-Spanish military expedition. Spain's original interest in Western Sahara stemmed from the fish resources off its coast and the colony itself remained an economic backwater until the exploitation of phosphate deposits in the 1970s. By 1975 2.6 million tonnes of dry phosphate were being exported annually. Francoist Spain initially resisted demands for a

Algeria has given considerable support to the Western Saharan liberation movement: Sahraoui refugees in a camp near Tindouf, Algeria greeting leaders of *Polisario*

self-determination referendum which had been put forward from 1966 by the UN.

Morocco, which claimed Western Sahara on grounds of traditional allegiance to Morocco's Alawite sultans, supported referendum proposals, confident that a majority would seek integration with Morocco. Contrary to expectation, however, an indigenous Sahraoui nationalism had emerged by the late 1960s and early 1970s. The desert tribes had always enjoyed *de facto* independence of Morocco and had had their own cultural traditions but the rise of Sahraoui nationalism was also encouraged by modern developments: the continuation of Spanish colonial oppression long after France had abandoned its Maghribian colonies and the sedentarization, urbanization and education that followed the development of phosphate exploitation.

In 1967 Mohammed Bassiri founded a Sahraoui liberation movement, the *Harakat Tahrir Saguiet El-Hamra wa Oued Ed-Dahab*, but this was crushed by the colonial authorities in 1970. In 1973 a group of young Sahraoui students founded the *Frente Popular para la Liberacíon de Sakiet el Hamra y Rio de Oro (Polisario)*. Guerrilla warfare against Spain, under the leadership of Mustapha El-Ouali Sayed, began immediately.

In 1974, shaken by the sudden collapse of Portugal's African empire, the Franco regime announced its intention of withdrawing rapidly from Western Sahara. Spain planned to hand over to a pro-Spanish regime, under the Saharan National Union Party (PUNS)–a Spanish inspired faction–and a Spanish organized assembly of conservative tribal notables, the *Djemaa*. These traditionalist forces were, however, decisively outflanked by *Polisario*, whose wide popular support was confirmed by a May 1975 UN mission.

King Hassan, however, acted to ensure that *Polisario* did not take over and that there was no referendum. He massed troops on the border and, in September 1974, reached agreement with Mauritania (a rival claimant) to partition the Western Sahara when the Spaniards left. In December Morocco and Mauritania persuaded the UN to submit their claims to the International Court of Justice.

The Court's advisory opinion (October 1975) rejected both claims. King Hassan, taking advantage of Spain's political weakness as Franco neared death, responded by marching a civilian army of 350 000 'Green Marchers' as well as military units across the Saharan border on 6 November. Spain rapidly capitulated and on 14 November signed an agreement with Morocco and Mauritania effectively ceding the colony. On 14 April 1976 Morocco and Mauritania formally partitioned the territory–Morocco receiving the northern two-thirds, including the phosphate mines, and Mauritania receiving Tiris El-Gharbia in the south.

Polisario had declared the foundation of the Saharan Arab Democratic Republic on 27 February and about half the Sahraoui population fled to refugee settlements in Algeria. Armed by Algeria, *Polisario* spread guerrilla war into Mauritania and southern Morocco. By 1978 it had brought Mauritania to its knees, prompting its army to stage a coup in July and promise to end the war. In August 1979 Mauritania signed a peace agreement with *Polisario*, relinquishing its claim to Tiris El-Gharbia, which was then immediately annexed by Morocco. Ceasefire in Mauritania allowed *Polisario* to concentrate on Morocco and by late 1979 the guerrillas were in effective control of the desert terrain of Western Sahara and southern Morocco.   *T.H.*

Zaire

Area (km²)	2 344 885
Population 1980 (UN projection)	27 952 000
GNP per capita 1977 (US$)	130
Capital	Kinshasa
Currency	Zaire

The Republic of Zaire (until 1971 called the Democratic Republic of the Congo, or more simply Congo-Kinshasa) is Africa's third biggest country in terms both of population and surface area. It is almost completely landlocked: over 9000km of land frontiers are supplemented by a mere 37km of coastline. Its resources could make it the most powerful nation in Africa, but recurrent political and managerial difficulties and widespread corruption have sapped its potential, and in the late 1970s the country was saddled with an unserviceable foreign debt of $3.6 billion.

Although the Belgian Congo had experienced phenomenal export-led growth (based on both agricultural and mineral raw materials) during the 1950s, the country was extremely ill-prepared for independence. A development plan produced by a Belgian academic, Professor von Bilsen, in 1956, which suggested that the colony should be groomed for independence in 30 years, was received with disbelief in Belgian government and business circles. But the 'wind of change' in Africa, notably in the neighbouring French territories, forced the Belgians to accord independence in June 1960, with Patrice Lumumba* as Prime Minister and Joseph Kasavubu as President of the new republic.

Within five days the army had mutinied and attacks on Europeans became widespread. A month later, the copper-rich, south-eastern province of Katanga seceded under its premier, Moise Tshombe. Secession was maintained for nearly three years, backed by Western business interests, notably the *Union Minière du Haut-Katanga*, which produced all the copper and cobalt. Kasai province also attempted to secede. Direct intervention by the big powers was avoided by the dispatch of UN forces. UN troops remained until 1964 but were not used against the Katangese secession until after Lumumba had been unseated by Colonel Joseph-Désiré Mobutu, and then assassinated in January 1961. In 1964 Mobutu, who had emerged as the strong man, invited Tshombe back from exile to form a government.

By this time, although secessionist movements had been crushed, the economy was in complete disarray and living standards for most of the African population had reverted to subsistence level. The national army was sustained by Belgian and other European mercenaries, whom President Kasavubu and Prime Minister Tshombe refused to dismiss. In 1965 the reign of politicians ended when General Mobutu took power in a bloodless coup.

Mobutu's initial economic and monetary reforms (the nationalization of the *Union Minière* in 1966, a massive devaluation in 1967) succeeded in stabilizing the economy and produced a growth rate of 6 per cent per year between 1969 and 1973. But Mobutu also aimed to centralize and personalize his power. His political party, the *Mouvement Populaire de la Révolution*, became the sole party in 1971. He then embarked on a campaign for 'authenticity', abolishing Christian names–he himself became Mobutu Sese Seko, attacking the powerful Catholic clergy, renaming the country, its major river, and its currency 'Zaire' and ordering that Zaireans address each other as 'citizen' (*citoyen, citoyenne*). His 1973 policy of 'Zaireanization' imposed local control on foreign-owned businesses. Although this was reversed in 1976, and further foreign investment encouraged, the damage had already been done. Managerial chaos, declining production, the increased cost of oil and food imports, and a fall in copper prices resulted in GDP declining by 5 per cent a year during 1976–8. The traditionally healthy trade balance went into deficit, foreign exchange reserves vanished, and Zaire became the first African country to default on its international debt.

Prospects for economic recovery were helped by the signing in August 1979 of a $150 million IMF standby agreement coupled with strict conditions. The currency was progressively devalued by 100 per cent in early 1979 and some debts were rescheduled. Oil production began with 8.3 million barrels in 1977, and one of the world's largest hydroelectric schemes at Inga, has been established with all three phases expected to be in operation by 1980. The Mobutu government still retains the backing of the West because of substantial fixed investments (Belgian investments alone are valued at $ billion), the country's strategic position, and its role as a supplier of key minerals.

President Mobutu Sese Seko (left) talks to one of his officers during operations against the Shaba rebellion in 1978 which was finally crushed with Belgian, French and Moroccan help

But production of copper and cobalt, which now provide 70 per cent of export earnings (1978 output was 391 000 tons and 13 000 tons respectively), was hit by two further rebellions in Shaba (formerly Katanga) province in 1977 and 1978, both of which could only be quelled by the 34 000-strong army with the assistance of foreign forces. Many technical and managerial posts vacated by Europeans after the 1978 uprising remain unfilled, although an estimated 30 000 whites (mainly Belgians) still live in the country. Mineral exports are further depressed by transport difficulties contingent on the political situation in southern Africa. The three traditional rail routes (Beira, Benguela and Tazara) remain blocked, increasing Zaire's dependence on the southern rail route through Zambia, Zimbabwe and South Africa. It is from these last two countries that many essential imports – maize, wheat, coal and coke – are supplied. Dependence on the white-ruled south, neglect of agriculture – food imports cost over $300 million per year – inflation running at 100 per cent per annum and unbridled corruption at all levels of government and administration are major problems facing Mobutu's government and threatening its survival.

A. P. H.

Zambia

Area (km²)	752 614
Population 1980 (UN projection)	5 875 000
GNP per capita 1977 (US$)	450
Capital	Lusaka
Currency	Zambia kwacha

Zambia (formerly Northern Rhodesia★) achieved independence from Britain on 24 October 1964 as a republic with Kenneth Kaunda★ as president and leader of the United National Independence Party (UNIP). Three interrelated problems have dominated Zambian history since independence: the state of the copper-mining industry; the fact that Zambia is land-locked; and the confrontation with the white-controlled south.

On 14 December 1964 the British South Africa Company★ – which had continued after independence to exact royalties from the mining companies – surrendered its country-wide mineral rights to the Zambian government for £4 million. In 1968 the government initiated a programme of state participation in commerce and industry, taking a 51 per cent stake in 26 companies, including, in 1969, the two mining houses – the Anglo-American Corporation and the Roan Selection Trust. Copper provides approximately 90 per cent of Zambia's export earnings, and up to 50 per cent of government revenues. The 1975–8 slump in copper prices, together with transport difficulties, was a disaster for the economy – in 1977, for example, copper's contribution to government revenues fell to nil, and in 1977–8 mine operating costs were barely covered by foreign exchange earnings. Zambia had inherited an unbalanced economy from the colonial period, and although it has great agricultural potential, rural development has received low priority since independence; maize often has to be imported and agriculture is disproportionately dependent on about 350 white farmers. In 1975, however, Kaunda called for a major change of economic strategy, stressing the need for rural reconstruction and increased self-sufficiency in food production, but at the beginning of the 1980s Zambians still faced considerable shortages and serious inflation, hardships that were exacerbated, at least in the short-term, by government retrenchment.

Zambia's economic difficulties have been intensified because the country is land-locked – and therefore dependent on neighbouring countries for the transport of its imports and exports to and from seaports – and because it has given unstinting help to black liberation movements in Mozambique,* Angola,* Rhodesia (now Zimbabwe*) and Namibia.* By 1978, for example, there were an estimated 8000 Zimbabwean guerrillas based in Zambia and a further 15 000 Zimbabwean schoolchildren. Rhodesian forces raided into Zambia in 1978 and 1979, and in 1978 South African planes had attacked South West African Peoples' Organization* camps in western Zambia. Until the opening in 1975 of the TanZam* (Tazara) railway linking Zambia with Dar es Salaam in Tanzania, Zambia was dependent on rail routes through Rhodesia to the Mozambican port of Beira, and via Zaire to the Angolan port of Lobito – the Benguela railway. In January 1973 the white Rhodesian government retaliated against Zambian support for Zimbabwean guerrillas by closing the border between the two countries, thus cutting the southern rail route. Zambia rerouted its copper exports via the Benguela railway thus – at crippling cost to itself – taking an active part in applying UN sanctions against Rhodesia. In August 1975 the Benguela railway was closed because of guerrilla action in Angola, and Zambia's bulk export-import routes would have been completely cut had it not been for the completion of the Tazara railway. However limited port facilities at Dar es Salaam meant a serious hold-up of traffic, and in October 1978 Zambia was forced to negotiate for the reopening of a southern route – to South Africa – although Kaunda continued to oppose the March 1978 'internal settlement' in Rhodesia and the border remained closed apart from railway traffic. Majority rule in Zimbabwe, achieved in 1980, will undoubtedly ease Zambia's economic problems, but much will remain to be done in building a more balanced economy.

Political developments in Zambia have reflected the state of siege that the country has faced on all fronts. Kaunda's policies have been characterized by an emphasis on national unity – in the face of

considerable actual political conflict – both to foster economic development and to counter subversion from outside. In 1971, the Vice-President, Simon Kapwepwe, a long-standing political associate of Kaunda resigned from UNIP to found the United Progressive Party (UPP). This was banned in February 1972, and Kapwepwe and other members were arrested. In December 1972 Zambia was proclaimed a one-party state with UNIP as the sole party; only after this, in January 1973, were Kapwepwe and most of the UPP's former members released. Kaunda was re-elected president in 1973 – although 20 per cent of those who voted registered a 'no' vote and nine government ministers were unseated. In September 1977 Kapwepwe rejoined UNIP but considerable division – revolving above all around economic policy and relations with white southern Africa – continued to exist within the party. In 1978 Kapwepwe put himself before the UNIP conference as a candidate to be selected for the presidential elections to be held at the end of the year. He was disqualified from standing by amendments to the party constitution, and in December 1978 Kaunda was re-elected president of Zambia for a further five year term.

G.A.

Zimbabwe

Area (km²)	390 245
Population 1980 (UN projection)	7 495 000
GNP per capita 1977 (US$)	500
Capital	Salisbury
Currency	Zimbabwe dollar

The Rhodesian Front (RF) representing the whites – less than 5 per cent of the population of Southern Rhodesia* – declared independence from Britain illegally and unilaterally on 11 November 1965 after the British Prime Minister, Harold Wilson, had removed the threat of military intervention. Ian Smith, with a strong popular appeal among the whites, had been chosen by the RF to stop moves towards ultimate African majority rule that had been outlined in the 1961 Constitution. Britain's subsequent repeated attempts to restore Rhodesia to legality, particularly negotiations on HMS *Tiger* (1966) and HMS *Fearless* (1968), took place against a background of alleged British government collusion with major oil companies in the breaking of sanctions against the illegal regime.

The declaration of independence had modified the 1961 Constitution only to the extent of curtailing judicial appeal to the British Privy Council and replacing the British governor with an 'Officer Administering the Government'. Continued white political and economic power was not adequately guaranteed by these new amendments, so a new constitution and a Land Tenure Act were passed by the Rhodesian parliament in 1969. The new constitution gave the whites 50 seats in parliament while African representation was henceforth to consist of eight 'tribal' seats elected through electoral colleges of chiefs, and eight directly elected seats–a reduction in directly elected seats on the 1961 Constitution. African representation was only to be increased when the African proportion of income tax assessment exceeded 16/66 (the original proportion of African to total parliamentary seats) of total assessment. This guaranteed white political supremacy, as Africans only paid 1 per cent of national income tax in 1969, and there was an immediate shift in tax structure to give greater predominance to indirect taxation. The 1969 Land Tenure Act consolidated the system of segregation in land tenure established in 1931, and divided the country into a patchwork of racially defined land ownership. The 6 million Africans were allocated 100–110 million hectares of Tribal Trust Lands consisting mainly of overcrowded areas with much soil erosion; 12 million hectares were African Purchase Areas–a safety valve for the small African middle class that had emerged in the late 1950s. The white population of 250 000 was allocated 110 million hectares of the best land, mainly in the highveld.

Although there were significant guerilla incursions by African nationalist (Zimbabwean) forces in the 1960s, it was the opening up of a new front in the north-east by guerrillas based in Mozambique during the 1972–3 rainy season that marked the beginning of a war that would ultimately force concessions from the RF. The guerrilla war began in earnest after the most glaring of the British attempts to be rid of the Rhodesian issue, the agreement of 24 November 1971 between Ian Smith and the British Foreign Secretary, Lord Home, which would have kept African rule at bay for at least 70 years. On 16 December 1971, a bishop of the United Methodist Church, Abel Muzorewa, with a council of ten, formed the African National Council (ANC) to combat the Smith-Home agreement. Muzorewa emerged as a nationalist leader from the ANC's successful opposition to the proposals.

Mozambiquan independence in 1974 dramatically changed the political configuration of southern Africa and forced on Ian Smith the South African policy of 'detente'. In November 1974 Joshua Nkomo, the veteran African nationalist leader of the 1950s (leader of the Zimbabwe African People's Union–ZAPU), Ndabaningi Sithole (leader of the Zimbabwe African National Union–ZANU), Robert Mugabe (ZANU), and other leading nationalists were released from detention to attend talks in Lusaka, Zambia. These were unsuccessful, as were a second set of negotiations held in August 1975 under the umbrella of Muzorewa's ANC. By the end of 1976 Sithole had become unacceptable to the guerrilla forces of ZANU and, with Mozambique now seeking a political solution to the Rhodesian conflict, Mugabe took over the leadership of the ZANU executive with the support of its

Chief of Defence, Josiah Tongogara. Meanwhile, in September 1976, Smith had been pressed by US Secretary of State, Henry Kissinger, and the Prime Minister of South Africa, Balthazar Vorster, into announcing a move to majority rule within two years, and a conference in Geneva was planned to discuss details. In preparation for the conference ZANU concluded a working arrangement with ZAPU to form the Patriotic Front (PF). The Geneva Conference (December 1976) was a failure–Smith had no intention of handing over power, and PF leaders had no confidence in his promises of an interim administration.

After the conference there was an intensification of guerrilla activity, with both ZANU and ZAPU guerrillas active in increasing numbers. Under pressure from the war and sanctions, the Smith regime finally concluded an 'Internal Settlement' with Muzorewa's new party, the United African National Congress (UANC) on 3 March 1978, possibly in the belief that the other major co-signatory, Sithole could call in large numbers of his former followers in the ZANU guerrilla army. Elections took place in April 1979–without PF participation–with 85 per cent of the country under martial law and at least 10 per cent of the population restricted to 'protected villages'. 'Peace' was the only theme of the elections; not mentioned was the January 1979 Constitution which gave the white population 28 per cent of parliamentary seats.

Muzorewa's UANC took a majority of the African seats, and in June Muzorewa became Prime Minister of Zimbabwe-Rhodesia. Nevertheless, the war continued to escalate, and in August 1979 an initiative by the independent African states involved in the war was taken up by the British government, which organized the Lancaster House Conference in London to negotiate an independence agreement involving the PF. In December 1979, after 14 weeks discussion, unilateral independence was ended by the appointment of a British Governor, Lord Soames, to Southern Rhodesia. After a ceasefire had been concluded between the PF and the Rhodesian Security Forces, and complicated arrangements had been put into effect to call in the guerrilla forces, Commonwealth-supervised elections were held in February 1980. The white population was granted 20 seats on a separate electoral roll, all of which were won by the RF. Mugabe's ZANU(PF) won 57 of the 80 'common roll' seats; Nkomo's PF (formerly ZAPU) won 20 seats, and Muzorewa's UANC only three. On 18 April Zimbabwe became independent with Mugabe as Prime Minister leading a ZANU(PF) government with PF and white representation. Mugabe's government, which took up an avowedly conciliatory stance, faced immense problems in reconstructing a war-torn economy, absorbing the rival guerrilla armies of ZANU and ZAPU, and satisfying the expectations of the African population–particularly their desire for a reallocation of land, an expansion of educational opportunities and the Africanization of private and public employment.   *I. L.*

Ideologies

The European impact upon African societies resulted in more than economic, political and social change. It also introduced a new set of political and social theories and theologies. In the realm of politics the most significant was undoubtedly the most powerful ideology of 19th century Europe, nationalism.* Although there are as many varieties of nationalism in Africa as there have been nationalist movements, the attraction of the core of the ideology initially to Westernized African intellectuals and later to a wider constituency is clear enough.

Unlike other ideas in the Western political gun-locker, such as socialism or liberalism, nationalism furnished modern African leaders with a clear mandate for self-rule. The history of much of Europe in the 19th century had involved the assertion of the right to self-rule by populations previously either submerged or divided by an earlier state system. The criteria for such claims were weakly defined but usually invoked common history, language and customs. Thus for European and African alike a claim to constitute a nation actively challenged alien over-rule. Again in 19th century Europe it had been the clarion call of emergent classes eager to press for what we would today call 'modernization'. This aspect of nationalism accorded with the desire of African nationalists to restructure African society so that the technological and material achievements that had been so instrumental in permitting Africa to be overrun by Europe could also be attained by Africans. This involved an acceptance of the bureaucratic, modern state rather than the traditional polity, and of a society that rewarded merit rather than one which accorded people privilege by dint of inheritance. It is an anti-aristocratic ideology and its proponents in Africa have only rarely been 'traditional' leaders; it was always the ideology of those who sought to curb the pre-colonial powers of chieftaincy and those who had most to gain from the demise of traditional notions of redistribution and ascribed status. Although there is dispute about this, it can be argued that nationalism in Africa always remained the ideology of a relatively limited section of African colonial society which was able to convince larger numbers of people that their misfortunes were explained by colonialism and that the best way of eliminating alien rule was to follow a nationalist party.

To a large extent the ideology was determined by the nature of pre-colonial society and that society's relationships to colonial structure. For example pre-colonial West Africa produced far earlier political responses of a nationalist sort than East or Central Africa. In West Africa a growing number of coastal and largely urban people had become involved in trade with Europe, with Christianity, and with Western education from the 18th century. This Westernized elite first wished to assert its essential similarity to Europeans and its social distance from the inhabitants of the interior. But the close of the 19th century saw such expectations dashed by European exclusivity, and predatory and racialist commercial expansion: consequently an essentially Europhile ideology rapidly became both more resistant and more African. Nonetheless the social origins and history of those elites ensured that they remained to a large extent dissociated from the 'grass roots' by the weakness of their ethnic affiliation, their distinctive and syncretic life styles and, of course, their relatively privileged class position in the colonial economy.

In East Africa the modern elite was a far more consciously created colonial elite with virtually no pre-colonial history. No less concerned with betterment than its West African counterparts, it was, however, much more clearly composed of 'men of the people'. Colonial insistence on administrative divisions based upon ethnicity underlined a tendency for East and Central African nationalists to be more particularist and less universalist than their West African equivalents. Similarly, the presence or absence of settlers is an important element of explanations of distinctions between brands of African nationalism. In colonies where wealth was created primarily by peasant production untrammelled by a settler community the relative freedom of aspiration is clear in the essentially opportunistic nature of nationalist ideology. Essentially, the early demands for participation and freedom from prejudice when frustrated gave way eventually to a realization that capture of the state alone could open a closed colonial economy. But the history of settler colonies is more marked by the gradual, steady erosion of a variety of individual freedoms. Nationalist politicians in such colonies proffered, for much of the colonial period, far more defensive ideologies less concerned with creating more opportunity than with combating the diminution of previously open chances.

Colonial structure was an important determinant of the content of nationalist ideas in other ways. For example, the much earlier appearance of the demand for independence in Anglophone than in Francophone Africa is in part explained by the tight rein the French exercised on the vast bulk of Africans designated as 'subjects' rather than 'citizens'. More importantly, the federal structure of French West and Equatorial Africa, which persisted into the 1950s, made it especially difficult for nationalists to define the 'nations' they wished to liberate. In British West Africa, by contrast, the constitutional reforms of the last half of the 1920s forced nationalists, who had until then been essentially pan-West African nationalists, to become territorialists. Those reforms made it imperative to create local, territorial political associations to contest territorial elections. By the 1930s in Anglophone West Africa quite distinctive Nigerian, Gold Coast and Sierra Leonean nationalisms, with distinctive styles and personalities and fewer inter-territorial links, were discernible. By the 1950s Francophone nationalists were still locked in combat about the territorial nature of what was clearly to become formally independent in the near future. Similarly, the peculiar lack of national ideology, as opposed to ethnic and particular organization, in the Belgian Congo is to a very large extent to be explained by colonial structure. Here a highly decentralized, regionalized administration had created a largely regionalized, poorly educated and politically repressed modern elite. Only Patrice Lumumba's *Mouvement Nationale Congolais* proffered a Congo-wide ideology, his enemies being content with particularist ideas.

The radical political analyst Frantz Fanon characterized all nationalist movements as essentially bourgeois and tools of neo-colonialism* but such a judgement glosses over the variety of ideologies which have emerged in Africa. Fanon died before he could witness the triumph of the liberation movements in Portuguese Africa* in 1974. The leaders of all three of these movements, locked as they were by the 1960s in wars of national liberation, produced ideology and practice which have been noticeably more radical than those of the rest of Africa, with the exception of South Africa. Forced to mobilize on a scale far removed from the relatively more docile occupation of rallying support in colonial elections, the ideology of the Portuguese-speaking leaders is notably anti-bourgeois and cannot simply be regarded as nationalism. Other African leaders have claimed that their ideology and style of rule have been 'African socialist'. Using such an ideology, both Kwame Nkrumah* of Ghana and Sékou Touré* of Guinea made some attempts to socialize their states, but the claims of President Kenyatta* to African socialism in a Kenya committed to unconstrained capitalism and ruled in a markedly authoritarian fashion were highly questionable.

Moreover, the utility of nationalism declined once formal independence was achieved. The ideological gap cannot be said to have been filled in many African states. Some leaders have been active in seeking ideas and techniques to transform their societies. Julius Nyerere* of Tanzania, for example, had adopted an openly rural based, 'populist', non-capitalist road to socialism as a state ethic. Persistent non-socialist phenomena, like private property in Tanzania, indicate the difficulties leaders of countries with essentially weak state apparatuses experience in squaring sincere intentions with achievements. At the other extreme, Félix Houphouët-Boigny* of the Ivory Coast practises and preaches a brand of *laissez-faire* pragmatism which has undoubtedly attracted considerable foreign investment but which has also stifled dissent. But for many African states ideology is an area of intellectual activity temporarily in cold storage while military rulers hold power. Few of the military rulers, and their civilianized versions like Mobutu Sese Seko of Zaire, have produced ideological justifications of their over-rule that have much moral or intellectual weight.

Few modern Africans would fail to identify with the old and exciting idea of pan-Africanism.* Despite the enormous diversity of the continent most people have a profound sense of being African. Some visionaries, like Nkrumah, believed that that wish could be transformed into a United States of Africa and it was for this purpose,

initially at least, that the Organization of African Unity* was devised. The theoretical underpinnings of it are unquestionable–rational resource development, manpower planning, market coordination and enlargement of scale to hold outside predators at bay. The formidable obstacles in the way of consummating this ideal are not unconnected with nationalism. The idea of the nation, and its reification in the nation state is now part of African history. Breaking down barriers is a threatening process in which national pork-barrels shrink, carefully won and even more carefully enshrined areas of privilege are diluted, and the strong must support the weak. The very particularism of the ideology of nationalism, its celebration of vernacular values and enmity towards universalism, makes the pan-Africanists' task today more and more difficult.   *R.R.*

Forms of government

Single party government

The great majority of African states were provided at independence with constitutional frameworks modelled on those of the outgoing European colonial powers. Only two states passed through the period of colonial rule in Africa without coming under European hegemony–Liberia,* where, from 1870 until 1980, the True Whig Party maintained the world's longest lasting single-party regime; and Ethiopia,* where Haile Selassie's* monarchy was revived after the shortlived Italian occupation of the 1930s. Many other new African states could at least claim to derive their form of government from the paramilitary institutions of anti-colonial revolt rather than from a servile imitation of their former colonial masters, notably Algeria, Angola, Mozambique and Guinea-Bissau.

Those African states that inherited a European-style democratic constitution had in principle the machinery for multi-party electoral competition–the 'Westminster model' in former British territories; constitutions closely modelled on that of the Fifth Republic in France's ex-colonies. Party competition did not, however, survive in most states for more than a few years after independence. In some states a single party already had a virtual monopoly of support from its identification with the nationalist movement. In other cases the party with an electoral majority–however slim–at independence quickly set about eliminating opposition parties by all the means available to government–usually charging opponents with subversion–and in due course banning any form of political opposition.

While the single-party regime emerged very rapidly in most African states, it proved durable in only a few important instances. The last surviving single-party governments characteristically have owed their survival and consolidation as 'party states' to the personal ascendancy of a single leader. Sékou Touré* (Guinea), Habib

Bourguiba* (Tunisia), Julius Nyerere* (Tanzania), and a few other party leaders are still in a position where the state has become virtually identified with their own personalities.

Military governments

In the absence of a leader with political credentials from the nationalist movement, the ruling single party has often been displaced without difficulty by military coup. The military have the advantage of a relatively disciplined organization, their own means of transport and communications, and a virtual monopoly of modern armaments. The soldiers are also prepared, at least in their training, to act swiftly in crisis situations. It has seldom proved difficult for the African military to justify their political intervention, and even to win initial widespread popular support, by castigating civilian politicians for their corrupt and arbitrary rule. The African military characteristically presents itself in a puritanical light, as the guardian of national honour and identity, in contrast with the decadence, nepotism and corruption of civilian rulers. This soldierly puritanism has perhaps taken its most extreme form in Muammar Qaddafi's Libya,* but it is an important element in military politics throughout Africa.

The austere virtues affected by Africa's military rulers, who now govern in a majority of states, have proved to be accompanied by significant political disabilities. Military rule in Nigeria,* for example, was at first (1966) welcomed by most Nigerians, but within a short period divisions within the army plunged the country into bloody and protracted civil war. A measure of the complicated responsibility for this bloodletting must go to the political inexperience of the new military rulers, but the events of 1966 in Nigeria highlight a general characteristic of African military rule: the state's political divisions are reproduced within the military itself. As long as the army remains outside political life, isolated by the barracks and the officer's mess, it can preserve a sense of corporate unity contrasting with society at large, but once the soldiers take direct political control, they find society's divisions (ethnic, regional, religious) penetrating their own ranks. Moreover, once political power is based explicitly on armed force, those who wield power must always beware of counter-claimants from within their own ranks. Thus the Nigerian officers (predominantly Igbos) who seized power in January 1966, and took drastic measures for the displacement of that country's federal civilian institutions, were overthrown by a second coup in July of the same year by officers and men who feared and resented what they saw as an Igbo tribal conspiracy.

Military rulers since that time, in Nigeria and elsewhere in Africa, have gradually accumulated political experience, and they have sought to protect the army from the divisive effects of direct political involvement. They have, in particular, built up the strength of paramilitary gendarmeries, which are entrusted with the suppression of civil disturbances, allowing the regular army to remain within its own institutional boundaries. Military rulers have also found it useful, even necessary, to co-opt civilian advisers to assist them in governing. The civil service in African states has in general worked readily enough with military rulers, but the military have also periodically sought the advice of civilian politicians and have even in certain states prepared the way for a full return to civilian rule. For example military governments have organized elections in Upper Volta (1978), Ghana (1979) and Nigeria (1979), and in Algeria, since the National Charter of 1976, the ruling military hierarchy has sought to revive the moribund *Front de Libération Nationale* as a governing political party. However, although the late 1970s saw a drift towards civilian rule, it seems reasonable on the basis of past experience to assume that the military will in some manner (direct or indirect) remain very much at the centre of political life in most African states. The difficulties faced in these states in meeting popular economic expectations, while at the same time containing the potentially divisive forces of communalism* within their frontiers, have set a pattern of lasting political instability in African states. Regimes faced with such instability have been drawn to authoritarian courses of action, with scant regard for constitutional or legal constraints. Where the regime has become involved in external war, as in Ethiopia/Somalia, Morocco/Mauritania/*Polisario*,* or in southern Africa, the reinforcement of domestic military authoritarianism has been a logical political outcome.

Presidentialism

Whether the sovereign authority be military or civilian, there is at least one political feature common to virtually all African states – the concentration of power in the hands of a single figure at the top of the governmental hierarchy. This personalization of power – presidentialism – reached perhaps its most notorious extremes in the persons of Emperor Bokassa in the Central African Empire* and Idi Amin in Uganda,* but the tendency to identify the state with a single personality is present in most African states. The presidential palace is the focal point of political authority in such states, and the president (or king in Morocco, or, until 1979, emperor in Central Africa) has power that effectively overrides or disregards that of parliaments, courts or cabinet ministers. Louis XIV's celebrated maxim *l'état c'est moi* could truly be adopted by the rulers of a majority of African states today. Some features of the personalization of power in Africa may be taken as an exercise in public relations, reflecting the aspirations of individual rulers rather than the underlying political realities, but others (powers of arbitrary arrest, detention and execution at the ruler's whim) are real enough. There is nonetheless a wide variation within the category of Africa's presidentialist regimes, from the violent caprices of Uganda's Amin to the pedantic, tranquilly paternal authority of Léopold Senghor's* Senegal or Félix Houphouët-Boigny's* Ivory Coast.

The personalization of African political power, the drift towards *de facto* monarchy in most states, has of course been accompanied by new political problems. There is at least the danger of the atrophy of institutions, as parliamentary and judicial powers tend to wither under the absolute authority of presidential monarchs. Some African presidents, however, have shown themselves concerned to preserve legal political competition in elected parliaments, either by allowing controlled multi-party electoral politics or by allowing relatively free elections within a single governing party. Complete freedom of the judiciary may be out of the question, but again some presidents display a measure of respect for the due process of law. The critical problem for Africa's presidentialist regimes lies in the provision for an orderly political succession: given the existing military political involvement in most African states, and the atrophy of civilian political institutions, the spectre of the military coup haunts these states as the most likely form of political succession.   *D.C.O'B.*

Legal systems

The legal systems of African states, largely based on European laws transplanted during colonial rule, include significant remnants of lively indigenous legal traditions which were distinctive features of social life in pre-colonial Africa. Islamic law is of fundamental importance in North Africa and in Muslim communities elsewhere. African governments today face difficult problems of adapting legal systems to contemporary social and economic needs.

African customary laws
The indigenous legal systems of pre-colonial African societies varied greatly. Some communities developed centralized types of government with chiefs or kings who could make laws by decree, appoint judges, hear appeals, enforce judgments and punish offenders. Other communities were 'chiefless', conducting their affairs by mutual collaboration, respect for established traditions and the observance of intricate personal or family rituals, and resolving disputes through mediation by priests, divination by oracles or arbitration by elders. Some features of these legal systems were general: they were unwritten, being developed, operated and preserved through oral traditions; the source of rules of behaviour lay in the customs of the community, so that these are essentially systems of 'customary laws'. A common feature was the importance of litigation—skills in the presentation, arguing and judgment of a case being developed almost as an art form. Skill in judging cases was a talent much prized in chiefs and elders and the public conduct of litigation, with the cross-examination of witnesses, participation in argument by members of the public and the recollection of previous cases as 'precedents',

served to restate and reinforce community standards and to teach children proper modes of conduct.

Intricate patterns of behaviour, based on customary law, developed, especially concerning family structure—for example, marriage and inheritance—but also concerning economic life, regulating markets, employment and the tenure and use of land. In the absence of prisons, penalties for offenders were either severe for serious crimes—for example, death for dangerous witchcraft—or took the form of compensation for victims—such as the deceased's relatives in most kinds of homicide—often with ritual observances. Customary laws were essentially flexible and adaptable, integrated with the moral and religious life of the community and well known in the community concerned.

Different colonial rulers adopted different policies towards customary laws. France generally sought to replace such laws ultimately by French law, whereas British policies of Indirect Rule through African chiefs involved the recognition and preservation of customary laws except insofar as they were thought to deny basic British principles of justice or morality. A significant consequence of British policy was the establishment of systems of 'African (Customary, Local) Courts' in which chiefs (or, later, full-time judges) applied customary laws (and some written laws) to Africans only. In the Republic of South Africa a formalized system of 'native law', partly codified and elaborated by judgments of government officials in 'Native Courts', has largely replaced various systems of traditional customary laws.

Islamic law
The Sharia, the body of Islamic law based on the Holy Quran and the opinions of jurists of the various schools, was long ago applied as the basic legal system across North Africa, in the inland Muslim communities of West Africa and from Zanzibar along the East African coast. It continues to apply, subject to certain reforms introduced by legislation mainly in Algeria, Egypt, Morocco, Tanzania and Tunisia, and inescapably mixed with local customs in other states (e.g. Sudan, Nigeria). In North Africa the Maliki and Hanafi versions are mainly followed; in East Africa mainly the Shafii, and in Nigeria the Maliki schools apply.

Imported legal systems
The transplantation of European laws by the various colonial powers was a formative event in the evolution of legal systems in Africa. Britain introduced English law, with its characteristic techniques of 'common law', in which rules are found in judges' decisions in previous cases as judicial precedents as well as in statutes (legislation, usually Acts of Parliament, and subsidiary legislation, e.g. ministerial regulations). A system of general courts modelled on those of England was established in each territory, with jurisdiction over all

Left: elders of the Somba people (Benin) hearing a case according to customary law. Below: the Alkali (*qadi*, Muslim judge) of Kano (Nigeria) in the late colonial period. In many states of Africa customary and Muslim legal systems are incorporated into, or complement, imported legal systems such as the British-style system illustrated opposite

the inhabitants. There were some changes from English practice: trial by jury, an essential feature of serious criminal charges in England, was not generally introduced in Africa; the legal professions that grew up were united, usually as advocates (not divided into barristers and solicitors, as in England); some laws were codified in comprehensive statutes–for example, unlike England, most British dependencies had codes of criminal law and procedure (which have remained in force to the present).

French territories received the contrasting 'civil law' system, with the Napoleonic codes (the basis of law in France, much of Europe and elsewhere). Other European models of the civil law were received in the Belgian Congo and Ruanda-Urundi, in the Spanish and Portuguese territories and in Italian Somaliland. South Africa, from the time of Dutch settlement in the 17th century, adopted Roman-Dutch law, to which many principles of English law have been added. This type of legal system spread also to other southern African territories, so that it now applies in Botswana, Lesotho, Swaziland and Zimbabwe. In the Republic of South Africa the legal system has been fundamentally affected since 1950 by legislation implementing the policy of separate development (apartheid),* imposing racial segregation and greatly extending discretionary governmental and police powers.

In other colonies of European settlement differences between imported and indigenous legal concepts–especially, for example, concerning land rights–were key factors in stimulating the growth of nationalism and even rebellion (e.g. Algeria, Angola, Kenya, Mozambique and Rhodesia–now Zimbabwe). Of the older independent states, Liberia adopted the common law as applied in the USA

(1820) while the written laws of Ethiopia (which, exceptionally, include ancient records of legal practice many centuries ago) include basic modern codes, mainly of civil law type, together with elements of common law. Traditional customary laws retain vitality and significance for most citizens in Liberia and Ethiopia.

Modern legal systems

African states face a variety of problems in seeking to modernize their legal systems. The constitution of a state is the foundation of its legal system, and the search for effective and appropriate constitutions has led to constitutional changes and experiments in most states since independence. For example, strong presidential government, often in a single-party system, is common (e.g. Guinea, Tanzania, Malawi, Zambia, Sudan, Mali, Sierra Leone, Zaire). In many states constitutional government has been replaced at some point by military rule following coups; yet traditions of legalism and the desire for legitimacy prompt even usurping rulers to adopt formal measures purporting to bestow legality and normally to preserve the bulk of existing legal systems. However, in revolutionary Ethiopia old laws have been changed and new laws made to destroy the old socio-political structure, seen as irremediably exploitative, and to implement socialism.

Inheriting from colonial rule the mixed legal systems, with laws of indigenous and foreign origin, and often Islamic law, coexisting, with resulting unresolved conflicts and uncertainties of law, most African states have made some attempts to harmonize, some even to unify, their laws. This has been seen as a necessary element of nation-building, the move towards a national legal system applying to all, in place of diverse laws applying according to ethnic, religious or local factors. In most states court systems have been unified, with the former African (customary) courts, where they existed, being abolished or integrated with the general courts. Notable exceptions are Nigeria, where Customary (Area) and Sharia Courts continue, and Malawi, where Traditional Courts are designed to administer justice in accordance with fundamental African concepts.

For most inhabitants of tropical African states customary laws, whether or not officially recognized, continue to be of primary importance, governing basic personal and property matters like marriage and family life, inheritance and land rights. Few states have sought to integrate the different laws of marriage and divorce, as Tanzania did in 1971. Cameroon and Somalia, each formed by the combination of adjacent territories formerly under different colonial rulers, have yet more complex problems: their legal systems contain substantial elements from both common law and civil law models, with numerous occasions when unresolved divergences of principle and practice arise.

Most African states face pressing problems of economic and social development, for which law can be an important instrument; but

The prosecution counsel at a subversion trial in Accra, Ghana

existing legal systems require extensive adaptation to serve development needs, having themselves been, especially in the colonial phase, the instruments of under-development. African socialism, widely current in various formulations, has not yet produced a distinctive type of legal system. Special laws to protect, but also to control, foreign investment are common. Nigeria has an elaborate new legal code to enforce indigenization* (i.e. Nigerian participation) in principal commercial and industrial undertakings.

Land is basic to African economies and most states have reformed the laws controlling its use and occupation in recent years. Some states (e.g. Kenya) have replaced the limited family rights recognized at customary law by absolute individual titles under statute law; rather more states (e.g. Tanzania, Zambia and Nigeria) have abolished unlimited individual titles in favour of rights of occupancy for limited periods (e.g. 99 years) on condition that the land is developed.

Although, for practical as well as ideological reasons, many states have expanded their public economic sectors, establishing new 'parastatals'–public corporations* to control or operate key economic and industrial activities–no states–even those which have adopted a more rigorous version of socialism (e.g. Guinea, Tanzania, Somalia, Ethiopia, Mozambique, Angola)–have yet adopted social-ist legal systems of the Soviet/East European models. Some Muslim states (e.g. Libya, Somalia) seek to evolve legal systems based on Islamic socialism; south of the Sahara indigenous traditions generally combine with the lasting effects of colonialism to inhibit juristic innovation at this yet early stage of independent Africa.

The legal systems of African states in the future will no doubt embody characteristic features from their existing legal systems, including indigenous concepts, although these are perceptibly weakening under current economic and social pressures. *J.S.R.*

Energy

The ultimate energy resource in Africa, as elsewhere, is the sun. At present, however, its energy is tapped directly only to a limited extent, for instance for drying crops or fish, or for producing salt by evaporation. Increasing interest is now being shown in using solar energy more extensively, through the medium of electricity, but that still lies in the future.

One way in which the sun's energy is tapped indirectly is through vegetation,* both natural and cultivated. Thus 'energy resources' include the forests* and woodlands that are so extensive in tropical Africa. Most firewood is cut and consumed within the subsistence sector of the economy but local scarcity is now causing more and more to be marketed. 'Energy resources' also include all the food crops by which the people of Africa maintain their own energy and that of their livestock, since many activities which consume energy from oil or electricity elsewhere in the world, such as farming operations or transport,* here depend largely on human or animal effort.

In addition to the continuing dependence of so many people on these sources of energy the inanimate and commercialized sources of energy upon which all countries increasingly depend are important in Africa, particularly local coal and gas, local and imported oil, and local hydro-electric power.

As the table above indicates, Africa's share of world consumption of energy in these forms is only 2 per cent, and its per capita consumption is only 20 per cent of the world average. Even these figures fail to reflect the lowly position of most African countries in the world's energy economy, for South Africa alone consumes over half the continental total, and per capita consumption in most individual countries is between 3 and 10 per cent of the world average.

The common practice of placing South Africa among the 'developed' countries is open to question both in terms of most national averages, which are often comparable to those of Latin American countries, and the well-being of the majority of the population; but energy consumption is one respect in which the country's position is not only totally different from most in Africa, but is comparable to that of such European countries as Italy and Romania. Among the more populous African countries, Egypt, Algeria, Tunisia, Zambia and Zimbabwe also have a relatively high level of consumption, reflecting their partially industrialized economies. On the other hand, recorded commercial energy consumption per capita in impoverished Mali, Upper Volta, Niger, Chad and Ethiopia is less than 10 per cent of the already low African average. While this shows how little such countries now contribute to pressures on the world's energy resources, it also shows how much scope there is in theory for their demand to increase if and when they take a real share in world development.

COMMERCIAL ENERGY CONSUMPTION, 1976: WORLD, AFRICA AND SELECTED AFRICAN COUNTRIES

Country	Coal	Oil/gas	Hydro-electricity	Total	kg-coal-equivalent per capita Total
	millions of tonnes coal-equivalent				
WORLD	2 696	5 395	227	8 318	2 069
AFRICA	77	83	5	165	397
South Africa	70	17	0.4	87.4	2 985
Egypt	1	16	0.9	17.9	473
Algeria	–	12	–	12	729
Nigeria	0.3	5	0.3	5.6	94
Morocco	0.7	4	–	4.7	273
Libya	–	4	–	4	1 589
Zimbabwe	3	0.9	0.6	4.5	634
Zambia	0.8	1	0.8	2.6	548

Source: *World Energy Supplies 1972–6* (UN, New York, 1978)

The table above also shows how the relative contributions of different energy sources vary greatly from one country to another. In South Africa coal contributes much the largest share and imported oil most of the remainder. In Zimbabwe, too, coal is dominant, but imported oil and hydro-electricity are both important. By contrast, both Algeria and Nigeria use little coal and have no need to import oil: their energy comes mainly from local oil and gas. Although the contribution of hydro-electricity to total commercial energy consumption is only 3 per cent for Africa as a whole, it rises to 6 per cent if South Africa is excluded; and it accounts for virtually all the electricity generated in Cameroon, Ghana and Uganda.

Coal

Since we have noted South Africa's dominance in continental energy consumption, and the unusually high share of coal there, it follows that its coal consumption totally dwarfs that elsewhere. This is equally true of production, South Africa's 60 million tonnes accounting for over 90 per cent of the annual continental total. This reflects in part the level of industrial development and the lack of other energy resources there; and also the fact that while Africa's known coal reserves are substantial, 85 per cent are concentrated in this one country, remote physically and at present politically from potential consumers elsewhere.

The remaining reserves are also mainly in southern Africa: 8 per cent are in Zimbabwe and 6 per cent are in Swaziland. Annual production in Zimbabwe exceeds 3 million tonnes and is of great

Firewood is a major energy source in Africa: Xhosa girls (South Africa) load firewood for head-carriage home

economic importance, but that in Swaziland is little over 150 000 tonnes. Other minor producers are Zambia, Mozambique, Nigeria and Morocco, but annual output from the small and poor deposits is under 1 million tonnes in each case.

Oil and natural gas

The present known oil reserves in Africa – some 7000 million tonnes – represent about 10 per cent of the world total, but they are heavily concentrated in just three countries, Libya, Algeria and Nigeria.

Virtually no oil was produced in Africa until the 1950s, and it was the closure of the Suez Canal in 1956 that led the multinational oil companies to seek supplies in countries bordering the Mediterranean and Atlantic. Nigeria and Libya are now the most important producers, followed by Algeria. Production in Angola was cut in the 1970s by political conflict there, and it is now larger in Gabon, which is far more affluent than most small African countries as a result. In all these countries most of the oil is exported overseas, although some is sold elsewhere in Africa. The main remaining producer is Egypt, which satisfies its own relatively large requirements with some to spare for export.

In each of these countries natural gas is found associated with the oil, and reserves are again highly concentrated in Algeria, Libya and Nigeria, which have 4.5 per cent, 2 per cent and 1.25 per cent of the known world reserves respectively. Algeria is thus better endowed

Drilling rig in the Zelten oilfield, Libya

OIL RESERVES, PRODUCTION AND TRADE, 1976: AFRICA AND SELECTED AFRICAN COUNTRIES

Country	Reserves	Production	Exports	Imports
		millions of tonnes		
AFRICA	7 000	287	261	31
Libya	3 240	93	89	—
Nigeria	1 660	103	100	—
Algeria	1 230	50	44	—
Tunisia	300	4	3	1
Egypt	220	17	7	1
Angola	180	5	4	—
Gabon	80	11	10	—
South Africa	—	—	—	15

Sources: *World Energy Supplies 1972–6* (UN, New York, 1978); *Statistical Yearbook 1977* (UN, New York, 1978)

with gas than with oil, and accounts for 60 per cent of African production, half being used locally and half being exported in liquefied form. In Libya most is exported in this way. Plans to earn revenue from natural gas in the same way in Nigeria have been delayed, and while a little is used industrially there (some within the oil industry itself), disturbingly large quantities go to waste at present. Tunisian reserves are smaller, but still sufficient to provide a valuable future energy source there if the problems of transporting the gas from remote southern source areas to northern consuming areas can be overcome.

Although oil consumption in Africa falls far short of production, so that the continent has a surplus of this vital energy source over effective requirements, large quantities are imported from elsewhere, as a result of the way in which the international oil companies are organized, the need for diverse refined products – some of which can only be produced from certain grades of crude oil, or by technologies that are not available locally – and the political barriers that divide Africa. The largest importer is South Africa, which obtains its oil mainly from the Middle East. The majority of other countries also depend heavily on imported oil, but in some cases the imports are from within Africa. Thus Nigerian oil is supplied to Ghana, Sierra Leone and Senegal, and oil from Gabon is sent to Cameroon, Congo and Ivory Coast.

Hydro-electricity

One of the main uses for imported oil in African countries is generating thermal electricity, and so the pattern of electricity production indicated in the table opposite does not entirely reflect local energy resources. However, for some years water power has made a larger contribution to total electricity generation in tropical Africa than in most parts of the world, and its share is increasing.

Since 1973 higher oil prices have greatly increased the competitive position of hydro-electricity wherever there is a physical potential.

While it is extremely hard to say whether Africa is well or badly placed relative to other continents with regard to natural resources as a whole, the position with regard to hydro-electricity is quite clear. Although estimates vary considerably, all observers agree that its potential capacity is higher than that of any other continent – largely because of the flow characteristics of many of its rivers – and represents between 25 per cent and 40 per cent of the world total.

As yet water power remains largely an unexploited resource. Less than 1 per cent of the potential has been tapped, and Africa has only 2 per cent of the world's installed generating capacity. This clearly reflects the lack of effective demand for electricity at the present level of economic development. The people of Africa have huge unsatisfied needs for energy, which electricity could often appropriately provide, but the costs involved are too great. Hydro-electric schemes require substantial capital investment, often beyond the means of African countries, especially when the rivers' seasonal flow necessitates huge storage dams; most large projects have depended on overseas loans. Energy-consuming industries are present to only a very limited extent; and most people could not consider using electricity in the home, especially as charges would be raised by the

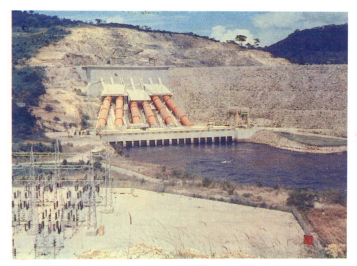

View of the Volta Dam, Akosombo, Ghana showing transmission equipment and the tubes leading to the underground generators

ELECTRICITY GENERATION: AFRICAN COUNTRIES, 1976

Country	Total	Hydro-generated
	millions of kwh	
South Africa	79 100	2 000
Egypt	11 000	7 000
Zambia	7 000	6 800
Zimbabwe	5 700	4 900
Algeria	4 600	500
Ghana	4 200	4 200
Zaire	3 500	3 400
Nigeria	3 400	2 500
Morocco	3 300	1 000
Mozambique	1 900	1 500
Tunisia	1 500	100
Libya	1 500	
Cameroon	1 300	1 300
Angola	1 300	1 000
Kenya	1 100	700
Ivory Coast	1 000	400
OTHERS	7 200	3 100
Total	138 600	40 400

Source: *World Energy Supplies 1972–6* (UN, New York, 1978)

costs of distribution to the scattered rural majority. Some of the most favourable sites are, of course, very remote from such concentrations of demand as do exist.

Nonetheless hydro-electricity is contributing substantially to total commercial energy consumption in several countries, and major schemes such as those at Kariba on the Zambezi, Akosombo on the Volta, and Aswan on the Nile have drawn worldwide attention. Numerous smaller hydro-power stations also exist, but their aggregate contribution to total energy supplies does not match that of the dozen largest schemes, and costs per unit tend to be higher for small schemes than large. The distribution of large power stations is clearly related to both physical potential and the pattern of demand. The former Northern and Southern Rhodesia (now Zambia and Zimbabwe) together offered a demand sufficient to justify the Kariba project, while Egypt's needs justified the massive investment at Aswan. The Volta scheme depended not only on Ghana's relative prosperity, but also on the establishment of aluminium smelting to provide a major consumer.

While South Africa offers the greatest demand for power, hydro-electricity potential there is very limited, partly because of the highly seasonal flow of most rivers. It was, in fact, an assured South African demand that encouraged the Portuguese to proceed with one of Africa's largest projects, that in Mozambique at the Cabora Bassa gorge on the Zambezi. Today this is one of several respects in which independent Mozambique is tied to South Africa, for it will be many years before effective local demand matches the generating capacity at Cabora Bassa.

Much the greatest potential within Africa is offered by the lower reaches of the Zaire River because of its huge and seasonally steady water flow. The potential at Inga Falls alone may be 28 000 megawatts (MW), or more than the present hydro and thermal total for the whole continent, and it can be approached in easy stages. The first generators were installed in 1972–4, and by 1978 the capacity had reached 920 MW. However, even this relatively modest output depended on building power lines 1700km inland to the copper mines. Further investment at Inga will clearly depend on an improvement in the state of the Zaire economy and on the growth of effective demand, or on agreements to supply other countries from this potentially low-cost site.

Other energy sources

Africa may have 30 per cent of the world's reserves of the main nuclear fuel, uranium. Small quantities are already mined in Gabon and Niger, but entirely for export to Europe; the prospects for nuclear power stations in tropical Africa seem remote in view of the huge capital costs. The largest reserves of uranium are in South Africa, which could perhaps afford these costs, but coal still provides a cheaper basis for electricity generation there.

Possibly of more interest in Africa in the foreseeable future is geothermal energy, for which there is a considerable potential throughout the eastern African Rift Valley zone, most notably in Ethiopia. However, before a contribution can come from this source, much fuller research will be required in relation to both the resources available and the technology required.

The best prospects for new sources of energy are provided by solar energy, especially since it does not seem to be much influenced by economies of scale. Capital costs should be relatively low, and power can be efficiently provided for the widely-scattered small-scale demands of rural areas, for example to pump water for irrigation.

The atomic research plant at Pelindaba, South Africa

There is an urgent need for cooperative effort among African countries and through international research and development, involving governments and universities, to discover how this source of energy can best be harnessed.

Contemporary change

The energy situation, and thus the whole development situation, in Africa was drastically altered by the activities of the Organization of Petroleum Exporting Countries in the 1970s. The oil resources of major producers increased in value, and countries with some domestic oil, or with other major energy resources, such as Egypt, Zaire, Zambia and South Africa, were shielded from part of the impact. But those largely dependent on oil imports, such as Senegal, Sierra Leone and Tanzania, suffered a severe setback. Worst hit of all were the poorest African countries, the Sahel states of Mali, Upper Volta, Niger and Chad, which were already suffering from disastrous droughts (creating extra needs for transport, etc.); for although their commercial energy consumption is tiny, this means that there was little scope for cutting back, while as landlocked states they also bore the increased costs of hauling oil from the ports. One consequence was the increased demand for firewood among people who had begun to use kerosene for cooking.

Thus throughout much of Africa there is now increased incentive both to make fuller use of resources such as water power, and to investigate the use of solar energy. Over the next ten years, countries like Zaire and Guinea can perhaps make fuller use of their opportunities for large-scale hydro-electricity generation. Others, such as Ethiopia, might be able to bring more benefit to their people through a larger number of small schemes on their many fast-flowing rivers, especially if technological research were directed to this scale of operation. In Niger, Chad, Mauritania and Somalia solar energy now seems to offer the best prospect. The remaining technical problems could probably be overcome within the 1980s: whether they will be largely depends on whether those who command the world's technological research are willing to redirect a small part of their attention to the critical problems of the poorest countries, and are capable of genuine cooperation with the people of those countries in working out how new techniques can actually be put into practice where they are most needed.   *A. O'C.*

Water resources

To review in brief the water resources of a continent the size of Africa some generalizations are necessary. At one extreme, the continent encompasses in the Sahara and along its margins one of the most extensive land areas of gross water deficiency. By contrast in the lower

Zaire basin lies one of the world's largest undeveloped hydro-power potentials in a zone of equatorial forest, sustained heavy rainfall and excessive surface runoff.

In a continent so fundamentally dependent on agriculture★ to sustain its population and population growth (through the production of subsistence crops) and to support its development and foreign earnings (through the production of export crops), a continent hoping for significant industrial growth yet to a large degree deficient in fossil fuels (except for Algeria, Libya, Nigeria and to a lesser degree southern Africa) water resources assume a paramount importance. Most fundamental in any consideration of African water resources is rainfall★–its amount, reliability and variability. Alongside the soil★ (and, locally, mineral deposits★) rainfall is the major natural resource of most intertropical African nations, a resource frequently counterbalanced to a large degree by the fact of high to very high evapotranspirational water losses. Water availability is a vital factor in land use in Africa; it explains to a large degree not only the nature of agricultural and pastoral production but also the gross patterns of population distribution and concentration. It is in most areas of Africa the limiting factor on development. This holds true particularly for eastern and interior West Africa.

In discussing water resources in the context of Africa three broad topics call for special emphasis; water for crop production, water for the needs of people and stock and water for hydro-power generation.

Water for crop production

It may have been in the Nile valley in Egypt that irrigation of crops was first developed, a technology developed as the result of understanding the effects of the natural flood regime of the lower Nile. This technology did not spread to Black Africa, possibly

Traditional well near the ruins of ancient Thebes, Egypt

because it was unnecessary and irrigation of crops is little practised in intertropical Africa except locally on plantations. The natural flood regimes of the rivers do, however, often provide water for seasonal exploitation of flood plains. 'Flood retreat agriculture' is locally important in parts of Africa but large-scale control or effective manipulation of flooding is rare. Controlled irrigation on a large scale is restricted to Egypt and North Africa and to southern Africa, and in these zones ground water resources are also exploited on a considerable scale.

In the wetter parts of intertropical Africa rain-grown crops can be produced throughout the year, often in abundance. In the drier areas or areas with markedly seasonal water surpluses where rainfall is erratic, and variable in amount and arrival, the peasant cultivators have learned to adapt their cropping and land management practices to these largely unpredictable patterns, e.g. by cultivating a range of crops with different water requirements and duration of growth, by planting the same crop over extended periods in small amounts and, on the margins of relatively stable cultivation, by combining cultivation with pastoralism★ or resorting during periods of drought to hunting and gathering.★

Major improvements in agricultural productivity have been achieved through research on rainfall variability, cropping techniques, land management, plant breeding and crop water needs, but there are large areas of Africa where there is a massive dearth of data on local water resources – either rainfall, streamflow or ground water. Thus many improvement schemes founder through lack of background data – whether these be aimed at improved agricultural output, as was the colonial ground nut scheme in Tanganyika, or at improved water supply or at power development.

Water supply for people and stock

In large areas of Africa water for drinking and other uses (e.g. washing) is inadequate either in amount, availability or quality. It tends to be most easily and cheaply available in the urban centres where adequate finance and modern technology have been applied and least satisfactory in rural areas where effective demand is low and per capita consumption least. Reliable and good quality supplies of water are generally widely available in urban centres, but in rural areas most people must depend for washing, and for drinking water for themselves and their livestock on traditional, frequently far-off, often polluted and seasonally erratic supplies. For long, too, it was believed that the major development constraint in the enormous rangelands of Africa was the deficiency in water points (wells, boreholes, reservoirs and dams).

Improved rural water supply has been identified as a key to progress in many area, e.g. the Sahel zone, the Sudan, Kenya and Tanzania, calling as it does for relatively unsophisticated technology though large overall investment. It was argued that an improved

water supply would improve the health of the people and the resistance of stock to disease, that it would thus speed up economic development in rural areas by increasing output from both cultivators and pastoralists and that it would relieve the major part of the agricultural work force (i.e. the women) from the time-consuming and relatively unproductive task of fetching water, thereby redirecting their efforts to crop production and care of stock. A very high proportion of Africa's rural population suffers from debilitating disease leading to an often crippling reduction in their energy and effectiveness at work. These and the high infant mortality might be reduced by the provision of improved water supplies. It was

Left: Lack of basic data on water resources is a major problem in Africa: a plot for measuring rainfall, surface runoff and soil loss in Tanzania. Below: Deficiencies in rural water supplies can lead to long journeys and long queues: a small borehole in northern Uganda with containers waiting to be filled

argued that reduced infant mortality would reduce the birth rate and thus break a critical development block when per capita production could overtake population growth. But experience tends to show that improved water supplies in rural areas do not achieve these ends. If the system is not properly maintained, a greater population is put at risk. Abundant cheap water encourages irrigation which in the absence of improved sanitation encourages the spread of water-borne diseases such as bilharzia. Provision of uncovered water tanks encourages the spread of malaria. As water collection is regarded as a social function, female labour is not necessarily released for alternative employment and, if it were, it might not be possible for surplus production to be either consumed or marketed.

Where improved water provision has been installed in pastoral areas its effect has often been to concentrate the animal stock in that locality and to keep numbers artificially high in drought years. Overconcentration of stock depletes the local feed of the area around the water point and erodes the soil. Within a few years stock die of hunger, not of thirst, and the investment is wasted. In the pastoral land of Africa the approach to a water point is almost invariably marked by vegetation and soil deterioration. In the absence of ecological investigation and proper control this appears in fact to be normal.

Water for power generation

The use of water for the generation of electric power is generally regarded as a later stage of resource use after more basic needs for drinking water and crop production have been satisfied. Yet because of a desire to industrialize rapidly and external offers of aid and technical expertise in the field of water power development, many African countries have favoured this alternative, and enormous investments have been made in the development of hydro-electricity* schemes in, for example, Egypt, Nigeria, Ghana, Zambia, Zimbabwe and Angola. In part this is a reflection of the natural potential of the continent (Africa possesses a hydro-electric potential in excess of the whole of North America) where only 5 per cent of the developable capacity is as yet exploited. Africa has the lowest percentage of its hydro-power resources developed or properly evaluated of any continent.

But serious problems stand in the way of developing this vast energy potential. Probably no African country has the resources, be they technical or financial, to develop its water resources unaided or to use to advantage the power that would be generated. The Owen Falls scheme in Uganda provides an early example of the problem, the Aswan High Dam in upper Egypt a more recent and spectacular one. Such schemes are therefore frequently prestige projects, superficially indicators of material progress, readily justified internally and attracting foreign aid of various kinds. But the leaders of the developing countries of Africa often fail to realize their inability

Many hydro-electric dams in Africa have more capacity than can be utilized locally: the Owen Falls Dam at Jinja, Uganda

to control and operate these projects and the extent to which they may constrain future development options in both financial and political terms. Many of these large schemes have had severe and unforeseen adverse ecological consequences, e.g. in the spread of water-borne diseases and pests which may in the long-term and in some instances counterbalance the economic advantages foreseen. A full evaluation of the repercussions of large scale water resource manipulations is needed before, not after, they are implemented.   *P.H.T.*

Forestry and timber

The forests of Africa vary in nature from semi-desert scrub to the tropical evergreen forests of the equator and from high altitude forest to coastal mangrove swamps. A few general statistics are given in the first table on page 278.

Forest of some kind, then, covers about a quarter of the 3000 million hectares of Africa and, of this forest area, some 300 million hectares can be used to produce industrial forest products.

The second table on page 278 shows volumes of wood consumed and percentages for different uses. It is noteworthy that the overriding needs from conventional forest products are for wood fuel and building material.

The estimate shows that there are 35 000 million cubic m. of wood available from the commercial forest to supply the industrial wood needs so that, at present rates of exploitation, it would, in theory, take 150 years to cut over the whole forest and this would allow time for a new crop to grow. Planted forest, as opposed to natural forest, covers

FOREST AREAS AND GROWING STOCK VOLUME IN AFRICA

| | Region of Africa | | | | |
	West	East	North	South	Total
Total forest area *millions of hectares*	495.7	241.7	9.2	15.9	762.5
Forest as percentage of total land area	39.5	26.3	1.6	6.0	25.4
Commercial forest area for industrial products *millions of hectares*	*	*	*	*	295
Estimated growing stock volume *millions of cubic metres*	*	*	*	*	35 000

* Not available

Sources: 'Wood World Trends and Prospects' (*FAO Basic Study* no. 16, 1967); 'The Outlook for Timber in the United States' (*United States Department of Agriculture Forest Service Research Report* no. 20, 1973)

FORESTS PRODUCTS PRODUCTION IN AFRICA, 1977

| | Roundwood production | |
	millions of cubic metres	*percentage of total production*
Fuel	297	86.6
INDUSTRIAL ROUNDWOOD		
Saw and veneer logs	21	6.1
Pulpwood	6	1.7
Other roundwood	19	5.6
Total roundwood	343	100

Source: *Yearbook of Forest Products Statistics 1966–77* (FAO 1979)

only some 3.1 million hectares or 1 per cent of the commercial forest area. It would appear, therefore, from these statistics that there is plenty of wood to go around, but the unequal distribution of the forest causes severe shortages of forest products in some parts of the continent. For this reason it is necessary to consider the people's needs and the forest zones together.

The desert

Here there are no trees and very little, if any, vegetation. Populations are very dependent on isolated oases and wells where date and other palms provide food, building materials and fuel, and other trees, shrubs and herbs provide animal feed.

The sub-desert, arid grassland and wooded steppe

This type of vegetation covers much of the Sahelian zone and the Kalahari area. Most of these areas contain nomadic tribes whose livelihood depends on livestock. They are nomadic because of seasonal variations in climate, rainfall and growth of vegetation for animal feed. In many areas the animal population is too large for the tree vegetation to be able to survive the repeated browsing, trampling and soil compaction which causes the limited rain which does fall to run off the soil surface rather than sink into it. There is little doubt that overgrazing has contributed to the southward creep of the desert. This is most noticeable during dry climatic periods such as the early 1970s. The supply of wood fuel for cooking in these areas is often critical with people having to walk up to 30km to collect it.

The problems of establishing fuel plantations are numerous, notably the inhospitality of the climate to tree growth, the grazing and the lack of administrative control due to the nomadic way of life. Certain countries have started to attempt to tackle some of these problems and Nigeria has recently been planting large areas of shelter belts. Considerable interest is now being shown in growing multi-purpose trees, some of which provide fuel, food for animals and food for human beings as well as protection from erosion.

The savanna forests

These range from the less arid grasslands with a few trees to almost closed forest with scattered patches of grassland. They provide their inhabitants with wood fuel and building poles in greater quantities than the previous zone but the vegetation has often suffered badly from fire and shifting cultivation. Many of the savanna areas would be high forest but for these factors and they are often ideal for the establishment of plantations of trees for industrial use such as pines, eucalypts, gmelina and other native or exotic trees. Some of the natural trees give high value timber but only in relatively small quantities per acre.

Okoume logs being sorted for export in Gabon

Montane forests

These range from grassland with a few trees to closed high forest often containing very large trees, often conifers. The forests are notable for the well marked strata of different plant communities which change with altitude. They often protect very steep slopes and provide sources of water for the surrounding flatter land; removal of the forest can result in serious erosion and impoverishment of land not only on the mountains but also in surrounding plains as has occurred in parts of Ethiopia, Algeria and Tunisia. Often the climate and soils on the mountains are better for tree growth than on the plain, and tree plantations for industrial use can be grown on them more successfully than elsewhere, thus combining protection of soil and production.

The communities that live in or near these forests normally obtain fuel and building poles from them and often also a considerable quantity of food in the form of meat, fruit and roots. In the drier areas they provide much needed browsing and grazing for domestic animals, and overgrazing is one of the major dangers. Strict reservation and grazing control is, therefore, particularly important, but has not always been applied.

Moist forest at low and medium altitudes

These forests include the equatorial tropical evergreen forest and moist deciduous and semi-deciduous forests. They contain very large numbers of tree species and they contribute a major part of all industrially used wood produced in Africa. They cover about 9 per cent of the continent and there is little doubt that large areas of them have been cleared by man and that they would be much larger without his influence.

Over the whole of the tropics some 16 million hectares of this forest type are being cleared every year. In Africa the clearing is taking place mainly after commercial felling of the forest for industrial wood products. About 10 per cent of the total growing stock goes for saw and veneer logs, since only large trees and a limited number of species are taken. The rest is normally burnt on site and then the land is cultivated.

Nigeria, once a large exporter of logs and manufactured wood products, is now a net importer of sawn timber, and the Ivory Coast, currently one of the larger exporters, is expected at the present rate of progress to run out of natural forest in the next one or two decades.

These forests in spite of their reduction in extent still provide large quantities of food, fuel and building materials for the people living in or around them. The pygmies live entirely within them and obtain all their food and shelter from them.

Temperate forests

These are found in the extreme north and south of the continent in Algeria, Tunisia and Morocco where pine, cedar and oak forests, some badly degraded, are found on the mountains, or in the Cape region of South Africa. They are mainly of local importance, but Tunisian cork oak forests are managed for cork production for export.

Plantations

Research into plantation forestry has been carried out in many African countries but, until recently, extensive commercial plantations were confined to relatively few. Kenya and South Africa have plantations dating from well before the Second World War and are now largely dependent on plantation forestry for industrial forest products. Plantations have also been established in North African countries for a long time and Libya has plantations of eucalyptus and acacia established to stabilize desert sand.

More recently Nigeria, Malawi, Zambia and Swaziland have established large industrial plantations and other countries are now doing so, but the areas established so far are small compared with the areas of natural forest. Ethiopia is at present engaged in a scheme to establish, through the participation of the local population, large areas of fuel and pole plantations to supply local needs.

Administration of forest services and forestry

Forest is owned largely by central government, local government or village communities and very little is in private hands; research is normally done by central governments. The percentage owned by central and local governments varies according to the degree of federalism in the general organization of government. Forest services in many countries are coming under increasing pressure to de-reserve many of the natural forest reserves for agricultural use and central governments with a firm commitment and will to maintain and manage sufficient forests for the needs of the people are better able to resist these pressures than local governments. The local governments may, however, be better placed to manage small plantations for local use.

African countries, with a few exceptions such as Zaire, are likely to be able to supply large export markets for tropical woods for only the next 10–20 years and few if any are planning to supply more than their own future needs for tropical hardwoods once the exploitation of existing untouched natural forest is complete.

Forest products

Wood fuel is by far the largest wood use, and supply of it is critical in the sub-desert areas and in savanna areas which are mainly grassland and have few trees. Poles are extensively used for building both for walls in mud and wattle construction and for roofing. They are also used for transmission lines and to a lesser extent for pit props. Sawn timber is used extensively in building construction, joinery and furniture. Pit-sawing is still practised in many places particularly in the more remote areas while sawmills of varying degrees of sophistication are widespread.

Plywood and veneers are manufactured in many countries and particle board in a few. Pulp and paper is being manufactured in an increasing number of countries as import bills for paper rise. The industry is still, however, quite small and finds it difficult to compete with pulp from temperate regions both in terms of quality and price on the world market. The table below shows export and import figures for 1977, but it should be noted that these include intra-African trade and do not therefore represent total inflow or outflow from Africa. It can be seen, however, that the value of imports was almost double that of exports although the volumes exported were larger. Unprocessed logs still accounted for 79 per cent of all exports in terms of volume.

AFRICAN WOOD EXPORTS AND IMPORTS, 1977

	Exports	Imports	Exports	Imports
	millions of cubic metres		millions of US$	
Logs in round	6.7	0.62	526	63
Sawn timber	1.1	4.7	136	744
Panels	0.3	0.37	64	91
	millions of tonnes		millions of US$	
Pulp	0.73	0.19	116	73
Paper	0.116	1.03	27	548

Source: *Yearbook of Forest Products Statistics 1966–77* (FAO 1979)

Pulp mill in Swaziland

The forests of Africa, therefore, have both a protective and a productive role vital to the welfare of its people. These roles are often poorly understood or ignored and in some areas the human population is suffering accordingly. The mixing of agriculture and tree growing for fuel, forage, fruits and even industrial products needs to receive, in future, much more attention than in the past, as should a more thrifty and less wasteful use of the natural forest resources which remain.

R.A.P.

Minerals

Approximately 30 per cent of the world's mineral resources are in Africa. In 1960 mining and quarrying contributed 4.1 per cent of Africa's total Gross Domestic Product; in 1975 the figure had reached 19.3 per cent. Minerals account for half of Africa's total exports; at the end of the 1970s Africa was producing about 5 per cent of total world mineral output.

Over half the world's newly-mined gold comes from Ghana, South Africa, Zaire and Zimbabwe although the area of the Witwatersrand in South Africa is by far the most important gold-producing area in the world. Cameroon, Congo, Ethiopia, Gabon, Ghana, Kenya, Liberia, Madagascar, Nigeria, South Africa, Sudan, Tanzania, Zaire, Zambia and Zimbabwe all produce gold, though in most cases in small quantities. Total African output in 1975 was 751 010kg, of which South Africa accounted for 713 400kg, Zimbabwe 17 000kg, Ghana 16 295kg and Zaire 3210kg. World production in 1975 was 1 262 931kg.

Africa produces the greater part of the world's diamonds, the first discovery in South Africa being made in 1866. The diamond-

AFRICA'S SHARE OF WORLD MINERAL PRODUCTION, 1977

Mineral	Percentage of world production
Gold	74.5
Diamonds	70.9
Cobalt	56.2 (1976)
Chrome ore	43.8
Manganese ore	36.5
Uranium ore	30.2
Crude phosphates	25.8
Copper ore	19.6
Bauxite	14.9
Crude petroleum	10.2
Iron ore	8.0

Source: calculated from data in *Africa South of the Sahara 1980–81* (London, 1980)

producing countries in Africa include Angola, Botswana, Central African Republic, Congo, Ghana, Ivory Coast, Liberia, Namibia, Sierra Leone, South Africa, Tanzania and Zaire.

Zaire is the world's leading diamond producer, though almost all its output consists of industrial diamonds; South Africa and then Namibia lead in gemstones. Tiny Lesotho opened a diamond mine at Letseng-la-Terai in 1977. In 1975 Africa produced 21 676 000 metric carats of industrial diamonds and 8 954 000 metric carats of gemstones. By 1977 the continent produced an estimated total (industrial diamonds and gemstones) of 34 350 metric carats out of a world total of 47 750 metric carats.

Africa's share of world copper production is 20 per cent and in 1977 the continent produced 1 502 700 tonnes of copper ore out of a world total of 8 113 700 tonnes. The main producers were: Zambia, 658 100 tonnes; Zaire, 498 000 tonnes; and South Africa, 216 100 tonnes. Other African producers are Algeria, Botswana, Congo, Kenya, Mauritania, Morocco, Mozambique, Namibia, Uganda and Zimbabwe. Together Zambia and Zaire produce more than 1 million tonnes a year while the Zambian copperbelt and the copper region of Shaba Province in neighbouring Zaire between them contain the largest concentration of copper and cobalt in the world.

World copper smelter production in 1977 came to 8 174 400 tonnes; Africa's share of this was 1 357 200 tonnes. Nickel, sometimes found associated with copper, is produced in Botswana, Morocco, South Africa and Zimbabwe. Total production in 1977 came to 49 400 tonnes out of a world total of 690 600 tonnes.

Two-thirds of the world's cobalt—one of the most precious minerals—comes from Africa. Of a total world production of 35 400 tonnes (1976), 23 100 tonnes came from Africa: 18 100 tonnes from Zaire, 3000 from Zambia and 2000 from Morocco. Zaire possesses 70 per cent of the world's known cobalt reserves.

Africa has an estimated 90 per cent of chromium ore (chromite) and currently supplies about 30 per cent of exports. Although Madagascar and Sudan produce some chrome the major reserves on the continent lie in South Africa and Zimbabwe. In 1975 Africa produced 1 289 700 tonnes of chrome ore out of a world total of 3 707 000. Of that amount South Africa accounted for 906 300 tonnes and Zimbabwe 295 000 tonnes; the following year South Africa had enormously increased its production to 2 409 000 tonnes.

Growing world energy demands are putting a premium upon uranium resources as the industrialized countries turn to large-scale nuclear power programmes. At present one-third of proven reserves of uranium outside the USSR and Eastern Europe lie in Africa, which meets 20 per cent of world demand. In 1977 Africa produced a total of 8260 tonnes of uranium out of a world total of 28 578 tonnes.

World reserves of uranium were estimated in 1975 to stand at 1 080 500 tonnes; Africa had 283 800 tonnes of this. The breakdown in Africa was: South Africa, 186 000 tonnes of reserves; Niger, 40 000;

Algeria, 28 000; Gabon, 20 000; Central African Republic, 8000; and Zaire, 1800. Since then the world balance has been altered dramatically in Africa's favour by huge discoveries in Namibia. Uranium deposits at the Rossing mine area are estimated to be in excess of 300 000 tonnes (almost 50 per cent as much again as South Africa's reserves) and other finds also have been made. Namibia should emerge as the world's leading uranium producer in the 1980s. Elsewhere in Africa there are uranium traces, and large deposits are believed to exist in the north of Chad. The African continent ranks third after North America and Australia as a source of uranium.

Although Africa only produces about 6 per cent of the world's bauxite, it possesses huge untapped resources of it. Guinea is estimated to have one-fifth of the world's reserves of high grade bauxite. In 1977 five African countries (Ghana, Guinea, Mozambique, Sierra Leone and Zimbabwe) produced 12 246 000 tonnes (world production came to 83 754 000 tonnes). Guinea supplied 11 320 000 tonnes of the African total.

World primary aluminium production was 14 411 700 tonnes in 1977. Of this Africa produced 356 700 tonnes, made up of Ghana, 152 300; South Africa, 77 800; Cameroon, 63 300; and Egypt, 63 300. It should be noted, however, that relatively cheap African hydropower* is sometimes used to smelt imported bauxite or alumina. Ghana, for example, is well endowed with high quality bauxite, and exports bauxite for smelting in Scotland, but the whole of its production of aluminium—the largest in Africa—is smelted from alumina imported from elsewhere—particularly from Jamaica.

Opencast copper mine at Kolwezi, Zaire

Natron (sodium carbonate) being collected from the soda-pans at Lake Magadi, Kenya

Africa produces one-third of the world's manganese. Gabon, Ghana, Morocco, South Africa and Zaire produced a total of 3 587 100 tonnes of manganese in 1975: of this South Africa accounted for 2 006 400 tonnes and Gabon for 1 115 500 tonnes. The world total for the year came to 9 263 200 tonnes. Especially high quality manganese is found in Ghana and in the 'Kalahari' field in South Africa.

Algeria, Congo, Morocco, Namibia, Tunisia and Zambia are lead producers though their combined output in 1977 came to only 139 000 tonnes of a world total of 2 511 000 tonnes.

Africa also accounts for a quarter of the world's phosphate supplies. In 1977 Morocco, Senegal, South Africa, Togo and Tunisia produced between them 27 770 000 tonnes of phosphate rock out of a world total of 115 883 000 tonnes. Morocco is by far the largest source of phosphates in Africa, producing 17 027 000 tonnes of the 1977 total.

Africa accounts for only a small proportion of the world's zinc – 270 000 tonnes out of 4 866 000 world output (excluding the USSR and Eastern Europe) in 1977. Its main producers are Algeria, Congo, Morocco, Namibia, South Africa, Tunisia, Zaire and Zambia.

One-sixth of the world's antimony comes from Africa, which produced 13 612 000 tonnes in 1976 out of a world total of 76 231 000 tonnes. By far the largest amount came from South Africa (11 766 000 tonnes); other producers were Algeria and Morocco, with small amounts from several other countries.

In Africa only Nigeria and Zaire possess tin and only Nigeria has produced it on any scale, although its output has been declining since 1968. In 1974 Nigeria's production of tin concentrates was 5455 tonnes and Zaire's was 4436 tonnes.

There are abundant resources of iron ore in Africa. Liberia is the largest producer of the metal, achieving an annual export figure in the range of 23 million tonnes. In 1977 African iron ore output came to 56 200 000 tonnes; the world total was a mammoth 852 000 000 tonnes. Algeria, Ghana, Zimbabwe, South Africa, and Egypt have their own smelters and Nigeria is due to start producing its own steel in the 1980s. Although Africa only produces about 15 per cent of the world total of iron ore the continent has established reserves of about 3000 million tonnes. Total African crude steel production in 1976 came to a mere 8 460 000 tonnes. World production was 681 000 000 tonnes.

There are huge reserves of coal in Africa. The following countries now mine coal, although often on a very limited scale: Algeria, Botswana, Morocco, Mozambique, Nigeria, South Africa, Swaziland, Tanzania, Zaire, Zambia, and Zimbabwe. The scale of coal production during the 1970s may be gauged by the figures for 1976. South Africa mined 75 229 000 tonnes that year; although figures for Zimbabwe were not available it mined about 3.5–4 million tonnes. Zambia produced a mere 720 000 tonnes, followed by Morocco with 708 000 tonnes. Other production is on an even smaller scale, in no way reflecting the available reserves.

At the end of the 1970s Swaziland had one mine in operation producing 150 000 tonnes a year to cover all its internal requirements and was then considering opening another mine to produce 2 million tonnes a year once export markets had been established. Swaziland's reserves were estimated at 1000 million tonnes of reasonable quality

African miners drilling in a South African gold-mine

Oil-well near Warri, eastern Nigeria

coal. South Africa is the world's sixth largest producer of bituminous coal and has coal reserves of 68 000 million tonnes. Neighbouring Botswana has established a huge belt of coal seams running diagonally from north-east to south-west across the country for some 500km.

Apart from the major minerals Africa also has most of the rarer ones such as beryllium, germanium, hafnium, lithium, niobium and platinum. South Africa has half the world's resource of platinum and is the largest producer. The continent is the principal producer of radium, scandium, caesium and corundum. South Africa and Namibia supply slightly over half the world's vanadium with South Africa contributing the greater part of this metal: in 1975 South Africa produced 10 971 tonnes and Namibia 562 tonnes of a world total of 21 882 tonnes. In the case of cadmium Africa only produces 251 000 tonnes, a small proportion of total world output and of that Zaire and Namibia between them contribute 247 000 tonnes. Africa indeed dominates the world market in strategic minerals such as cobalt, chromium, lithium, beryllium, tantalum and germanium.

African crude oil production increased enormously in the 1970s: Nigerian production, for example, increased from 13.3 million tonnes in 1965 to 111.6 million tonnes in 1974. Africa has approximately 10 per cent of known world oil reserves and production in the 1970s reflected this. In 1976 world production was approximately 2900 million tonnes, of which Africa provided about 285 million tonnes. The leading producers were Nigeria, with 103 million tonnes; Libya, 93 million tonnes; Algeria, 50 million tonnes; Egypt, 16 million tonnes; and Gabon, 11 million tonnes. Lesser producers include Congo, Zaire, Angola and, with very small offshore fields, Ivory Coast and Ghana. Natural gas is found with oil in many African fields. Between them Algeria, Libya and Nigeria

have about 8 per cent of known world reserves. Algeria leads production with 5947 million cubic m in 1975, of which approximately half was exported.

High oil prices in the 1970s have meant that exploration for new fields in Africa has been one area of mineral prospecting which has been particularly active, and new fields which in the past might have proved uneconomical are regularly opened up. Many of the *known* reserves of other minerals, for example coal, remain unexploited. Moreover, the estimate that 30 per cent of total world mineral reserves lies within Africa must remain tentative, for large areas of the continent have still to be surveyed in detail. How, and when Africa's remaining mineral reserves will be used, or, indeed discovered will depend on the wider political and economic ramifications of mineral exploitation★ and energy★ use. *G. A.*

People as a resource

Population characteristics

Resources in the physical environment are latent and potential until taken up and used by people. Land must be used or power generated by human exploitation. Resources have no meaning without people and, in the complex of economic activity and social organization, people themselves are resources. Not only do people exploit, they may be exploited.

In Africa, where levels of technology are low and mechanized systems of production are limited, manpower is inevitably a major factor in development. Numbers of people matter particularly in agriculture but also in many other productive processes. Not only is quantity important, quality is of major concern. In much of Africa where levels of formal education★ are low, as reflected in rates of literacy and numeracy, qualities of persistence and adaptability are high. Hard-won intuitive experience has made it possible for people to survive, if not to flourish, in physical conditions which are rarely favourable, frequently marginal, and often difficult. But such adaptability and varied response are only some aspects of the diversity of human quality in Africa. There is great variety in racial and ethnic characteristics, in languages and cultures, in traditional social organization and in contemporary political institutions. All these combine in the human resources of the continent. The majority of the population are indigenous Africans, but there are important minorities settled in Africa that have originated elsewhere.

The total population of Africa is in the region of 430 million though deficient censuses make accurate assessment difficult. This figure represents approximately 10 per cent of the world population. Growth to this present size has been most rapid in this century and has doubled within the last three decades. Such rapid growth has been determined by falling levels of mortality (to a present 18–20 per 1000) with maintained high fertility rates (at present 45–48 per 1000). These combine to give an annual rate of natural increase of between 2.5 and 2.9 per cent, the highest of the continental rates. Mortality has fallen largely as a result of preventive measures and general improvements in factors affecting public health. However the burden of disease★ still weighs heavily on the peoples of Africa, both the well-known 'tropical' diseases and those which are common to other parts of the world. Malaria remains a major scourge, contributing to high levels of infant and child mortality and debilitating those in the older age groups. This and other diseases considerably reduce the efficiency of people as a resource. Difficulty in adjusting to significant reductions in mortality contributes to reluctance to change attitudes and practices which would lead to lower fertility. Attempts to reduce fertility through the introduction of family planning programmes have met as yet with only limited success, even in countries disposed to such measures. The present youthful age structure in all countries with large numbers in the reproductive groups, sets the likely pattern for continuing population increase to the end of the present century.

Compared with other continental areas the overall average population density (10 per sq km) is low. But like all such generalized figures this is misleading in respect of the variety of densities which occur within, and between, different parts of the continent. There are major desert areas, particularly in northern Africa, which are virtually uninhabited. Egypt is a striking example of high population concentration in the Nile valley and delta (nearly 1000 per sq km) which contrasts with the rest of the country which is very sparsely populated. Throughout Africa there are major though not comparable variations in population densities with a tendency for concentrations in 'islands' of high density which occupy relatively limited areas. These concentrations are related in many instances to relatively favourable physical conditions (e.g. soil fertility, water supply) but they have also been much influenced by historical circumstances in the more distant past and by political, economic and social factors in the present century. These are concentrations of people mainly in rural areas for compared with other continents the proportion of Africa's population living in urban places is low – less than 20 per cent. In the towns and cities of course the highest absolute densities of population occur.

Land and people

Relationships of people with land, the interactions of human with environmental resources, are highly complex. Numbers involved exclusively in subsistence production are now small. Indigenous hunting/gathering★ economies are practised by very few. People with predominantly pastoral★ ways of life have been less changed than those involved in agriculture,★ who in varying degrees have been drawn increasingly into wider systems of exchange at local, regional, national and international levels. However, all forms of rural economic activity have experienced pressure from increasing population and some have been modified substantially as a result. The pressures are in some instances Malthusian – population growth outstrips food production – manifesting themselves in various forms of rural poverty and deprivation – declining fertility and soil erosion, poor crop yields, malnutrition and under-nutrition, and forced movement. These circumstances may be exacerbated by a capricious physical environment to produce widespread suffering, as with the drought★ in the Sahel regions of Africa in the first half of the 1970s. Even where adjustments have been made in agricultural economies to meet the needs of increasing population and the demands for the production of crops for export, where population growth has served as a stimulus to change, these adjustments have been accomplished with only relative success. Needs and demands are met by the increasingly intensive use of land with increasing labour inputs but only with continuing small-scale organization, little change in the basic technology of production and low per capita production levels. In limited areas involving limited numbers of people various forms of settlement schemes which introduce new organization, new cultivation methods, new crops or improved strains, and more modern technology have met with limited success. The use of land for farming by Europeans, in the Maghrib and East Africa in the past and continuingly in parts of southern Africa, has demonstrated possibilities for large-scale production involving modern technology, but these successes have been dependent on the alienation of the best quality land and the availability of cheap African labour. With political independence land formerly farmed by Europeans has been returned to use by Africans either under socialist policies involving cooperatives, as in Algeria, or under a mixed economy, as in Kenya.

Migration

In the equation relating people and land the latter represents a relatively fixed capital resource: people are much more mobile, and the transference and redistribution of human resources take place in a variety of ways. The most major single transference was the forced movement of people taken as slaves★ out of Africa to meet the economic demands of Europeans in the Americas and Arabs in the Middle East. Within Africa traditional economies have involved population mobility in response to environmental factors. Pastoralists move in search of pasture and water, and shifting cultivators move to clear new land as soil exhaustion follows short periods of cultivation with no input to restore fertility. Environmental hazards★ may increase the need for such movements and recent drought has forced pastoralists to abandon their traditional economy, if only temporarily, for other means of economic support. Large-scale involuntary mobility has resulted from political instability, particularly within the last two decades, with the international movements of large numbers of refugees as from the south of Sudan into East Africa and from Angola into Zaire, and internal refugee movements such as were caused by the civil war in Nigeria. Political ideology may influence population mobility and redistribution as with the socialist *ujamaa* and 'villagization' policies of Tanzania which are directed to concentrate dispersed population, to promote economic development and to facilitate the provision of social infrastructure.

The construction of dams★ (on the Nile at Aswan, Niger at Kainji, Volta at Akosombo, and Zambezi at Kariba) and the flooding of vast areas of river valleys to provide water for hydro-electric power generation and for irrigation have forced the resettlement of population and often major changes in economic practice.

Involuntary movements often result in permanent changes of residence and in many instances there is no alternative, but the permanence of refugee movements whether from environmental or political disasters is difficult to determine. There is a marked tendency for people to return to areas from which they have fled if an improvement in circumstances makes this possible. However, relatively spontaneous movements also result in the permanent relocation of population as cultivators occupy sparsely habited or uninhabited lands, in some instances lands which are made habitable by the eradication of disease or by the development of improved water supplies for domestic use and for irrigation.

Africa has also been and continues to be characterized by movements which are temporary and which involve periods of absence from but not permanent changes in places of residence. Such movements over both short and long distances involve varying lengths of absence, and are essentially circulatory in nature. They are motivated by a complex of factors some of which are social in character (e.g. visits for kinship or ethnic festivals), but the majority are rooted in economic circumstances and often in economic necessity. In areas of more precocious agricultural, mining and industrial development there are demands for wage labour★ and these draw in population from areas which are less well-developed, particularly where there is land hunger and where there are restricted opportunities for earning a cash income. Some circulatory movements involve what are essentially forms of daily or weekly commuting, others last for several months and may be seasonal in their periodicity. In the latter case those who seek work elsewhere do so during months when there is reduced economic activity in their home areas, absenting themselves during the dry season and returning to farm at the commencement of the next wet season. The temporary absences may involve whole family groups but more often they involve only active adult males. Migrations by unaccompanied males were particularly common in the past and especially when movements over long distances were physically demanding. Changes have occurred as a result of improvements in communications.

However, in some parts of Africa there have been, and still are, restrictions which permit the movements of men only and prevent them being joined by their dependents. These restrictions were imposed formerly on labourers migrating to the Copperbelt in Zambia and are imposed now in South Africa. The South African mines have been dependent on cheap sources of labour from a wide range of countries in southern parts of the continent, recruited for specified periods of time by an organization which arranges return transport between home places and places of work and the transmission of remittances back to the families of those employed. This system for the deployment of human resources is one of the most organized in the world, though the economic, moral and political ethics of the migratory labour system in southern Africa and indeed of migrant labour in other parts of Africa are open to question. Migrant labour tends to lead to a limited acquisition of skills, due among other things to frequent turnover; migrants generally are exporting their strength rather than their skill. Preventing migrants from being accompanied by their dependents lead to disruptions in family life and in wider social relations. Source areas of migrant labourers are denied important elements of manpower to the detriment of their economic development and become increasingly dependent on remittances from those away. In southern Africa the developed capitalist and, in this case, white core area of economic development drains away human resources from the poor and under-developed periphery, as do similar less advanced economic 'islands' in other parts of the continent. While there has been undoubted exploitation in the South African migrant labour system, it may be argued alternatively that in some source areas of labour the marginal opportunities offered by their environments are so limited that there is not the scope for the fullest deployment of their human resources. Thus, notwithstanding disadvantages, these resources might be better utilized by being employed for periods elsewhere. And it has been shown that some societies have been capable of adapting to the absence of a considerable proportion of the active adult male labour force without severe detriment to their economies.

While temporary absences and circulatory movements have been or continue to be important in the transference of human resources in Africa there are also the developments of movements of people away from the rural areas to the towns. This rural-urban migration, implying the permanent transfer of population, has received the lion's share of attention in studies of population movements in recent years. The manifestations of these movements are to be seen in urban growth rates several times greater than rates of increase in the population overall. Annual urban growth rates are in excess of 6 per cent and may rise as high as 10–12 per cent. The population of Lagos, the largest urban centre in Nigeria, increased from 300 000 to 1 000 000 in less than three decades and there are an increasing number of similar 'millionaire' cities in Africa. Such expansion is due in part to the maintenance of high natural rates of increase among urban dwellers but it is contributed to most markedly by incoming migrants from rural areas. Despite the outflows occurring from them, rural areas continue to experience population growth because of the high rates of natural increase. As yet no major large-scale rural depopulation has occurred but the balance in the proportions of rural and urban population is now changing markedly in some countries, particularly in North Africa.

Urban populations

Rates of urban growth in Africa are now considerably greater than they were in the industrializing world in the 19th century but the reallocation of human resources which these indicate is not underpinned by comparable economic growth. People are leaving rural areas because of pressure upon resources not because of an agricultural revolution which is resulting in increased productivity due to scientific and technological changes. Furthermore, they are not being absorbed economically in the cities through an industrial revolution which is creating large-scale demands for labour. Industrialization is limited throughout the continent apart from South Africa, and labour demands in the primary and secondary sectors of employment are very restricted. Demands are limited also in the tertiary sector, which in any case is contributing little to the generation of wealth. Many who move from rural to urban areas have been described as 'migrating to unemployment' and are supported, particularly in the very early phases of their urban lives, by relations and friends and by employment in what are called 'informal activities', both legal and illegal.

The numbers of urban migrants produce not only economic pressures but also considerable stresses upon the social infrastructure of towns – on housing, water supply, waste disposal and transportation systems, and on medical and educational facilities. Considerable proportions of the populations of larger cities are housed in the temporary structures of shanty towns or *bidonvilles*. Not only is there mobility to towns but also considerable mobility after arrival in towns – movements in search of employment and accommodation and, when these are found, movements between one and the other.

Faced with these urban problems in all their many forms various attempts have been made to exercise some control over urban growth both by attempting to limit movements into towns and to make rural areas more attractive so that people will be less disposed to leaving them. Most success in the former has been achieved in the authoritarian circumstances of South Africa, through influx control which limits the numbers of blacks in towns and requires them to be registered in employment, and at the same time classes them as temporary urban sojourners who are legally citizens of the Bantustans* which are now being established in the Republic. In Tanzania programmes to redistribute the population and improve

economic and social infrastructure in the rural areas are intended thus to reduce the urge to move into towns. Only partial success is being achieved and as in other instances, even where there is a degree of authoritarianism involved, there is a major gulf between the establishment of policies and the ability to implement them effectively. For many people the towns, with all their social and economic disadvantages, seem to offer more than rural areas. Whether, as time passes and disadvantages become greater, frustrated expectations may explode in urban social and political instability is a question which must occupy the concerns of the majority of governments in Africa.

Future prospects

The reallocation of African human resources, largely through spontanous action though sometimes with official sanction and control, is largely concerned with the limited acquisition of modern skills, particularly those acquired through formal education. In the majority of African countries rates of illiteracy are high, school enrolment rates are low and the resources for education are severely limited. Improvements are being made through internal effort often coupled with international unilateral and bilateral aid. Nigeria, with major revenues from oil, is now embarked on a programme of universal primary education as well as strengthening its secondary and higher levels. The economies of many other countries do not permit comparable ambitious developments. Where such developments are possible the evidence to date suggests that the improvements being effected may bring further problems in their train. People in both rural and urban areas who acquire even minimal educational skills may then consider themselves fitted for better economic opportunities than they would otherwise expect to achieve. In this way the nature of human resources is changed. The problem becomes particularly serious in rural areas when agricultural activities acquire low social and economic status. If as a result increased numbers leave these activities, production for internal consumption and for export may be reduced seriously. Already there are instances of countries in Africa which need to import food while the potential for internal food production goes unrealized. Given the present and foreseeable limitations for urban employment, any further increase in numbers moving into towns would only exacerbate the possibilities for frustrated expectations.

Africa's human resources display a variety of qualities, particularly the ability to adapt to, and to cope with, difficult circumstances. Given present and foreseeable formidably high rates of population increase and the redistributions and transferences of population which are already occurring, it remains to be seen whether human resources can be utilized to their best potential to produce for African peoples life which is economically more abundant, socially satisfying and politically stable.

R. M. P.

Hunting and gathering

In Africa south of the Sahara most of the rural population live by agriculture* or by pastoralism.* But, in a number of areas, there are small populations who now, or until recently, obtained their subsistence only by exploiting wild foods: by hunting, trapping or scavenging game animals, birds and reptiles; by fishing; and by gathering insects, birds' eggs and nestlings, rodents, wild roots, fruits, mushrooms, and the honey produced by several different species of wild bee.

The best known of such groups are the Bushmen, or San, living in the dry savanna of Botswana, Namibia and Angola and the Pygmy or Pygmoid groups of the tropical forests of Burundi, Rwanda, Uganda, Zaire, the Congo, the Central African Republic, Cameroon and Gabon. Less well-known and often very small groups live in southern Ethiopia, southern Somalia, Kenya, Tanzania, Zambia and Madagascar. Although found in many countries, hunter-gatherers form well under 1 per cent of the populations of sub-Saharan Africa. A few groups are quite substantial: the Mbuti Pygmies of the Ituri forest of eastern Zaire number several thousand. The total population of Bushmen in 1963/1964 was approximately 44 100. Of these, some 9300, concentrated in Namibia and Botswana, were then living largely by hunting and gathering while the remainder were incorporated into the agricultural economy.

Almost all African hunter-gatherers live in small nomadic units, numbering only a dozen or two and moving frequently, often as much as every week or two. They live at population densities which rarely exceed one person per 2 sq km and are usually very much less than this. Their subsistence techniques are quite varied, though almost all groups depend in part on the use of bows and poisoned arrows and on spears for hunting, on axes for cutting out bees' nests in hollow trees to extract honey, and on digging sticks for gathering wild roots. Most of the tools, weapons and other equipment used in hunting and gathering are made with considerable skill but without much investment of time or labour. The Dorobo or Okiek of the high mountain forests of Kenya are unusual in the substantial amount of labour they invest in constructing and maintaining individually-owned wooden beehives suspended high in the forest trees. In most of these societies hunting methods usually involve only very limited cooperation or coordination. An exception is the system of net-hunting used by the Mbuti Pygmies for hunting small forest animals. Here women and children act as beaters to drive animals into a net set up by a group of men. More usually African hunter-gatherers rely on individual tracking and stalking of the animal being hunted. These various traditional methods of hunting and gathering are, in general, no threat to the future availability of game and other food supplies. Some African governments give their hunter-gatherer populations special exemption from the rigours of the game laws in recognition of their special dependence on hunting.

In the past scientific writings on hunter-gatherers often gave a rather distorted view of this way of life. Because hunting and gathering preceded agriculture historically, it was widely assumed that this mode of subsistence must have been harsher, must have involved greater struggle, than agricultural forms of subsistence which developed later.

Only recently has sufficient research been carried out to allow the effective testing of these notions. From research conducted among the Mbuti of Zaire, the !Kung Bushmen of Namibia and Botswana and the Hadza of Tanzania, we now know that certainly in these instances, and probably far more generally, this way of life is much less harsh than had been thought. Life is not a relentless struggle with nature. Members of these societies are usually able to obtain the food they need to meet their nutritional requirements in a straightforward and matter of fact way without undue difficulty; in general, they probably obtain a greater yield for a given amount of labour than they would in most systems of simple peasant agriculture. The diet usually consists mainly of a variety of wild plant foods that can be obtained predictably and regularly. Meat is a valued supplement obtained less often. Although there are marked seasonal variations in the availability of food, severe shortage or famine is almost unknown. People are protected from famine by two factors: firstly, the wild foods they eat are indigenous and less susceptible to drought or pests than are cultivated crops, many of which, maize for example, are not indigenous to Africa; secondly, they are protected by the fact that they depend on a number of different foods and if one type of food fails, then alternatives are available. Medical studies have now confirmed the absence of malnutrition among the !Kung Bushmen and the Hadza.

Frequent nomadic movements are not, as was once thought, a simple product of local shortage of food and an indication that hunter-gatherers are under constant pressure to obtain enough to eat. Rather, they take advantage of the fact that they have highly portable equipment to move for a wide variety of reasons, although they always seek, if possible, to improve their access to food. Movement is not, in general, seen as difficult but is positively valued. An outbreak of illness, a death or a quarrel are all usually followed by movement to a new site. People often move camp to trade or simply to visit. When they kill a large animal, they often find it more convenient to move their camp to the carcase than to move the carcase to the camp.

The traditional view of the social organization of these societies was that they were divided into relatively autonomous land-owning patrilineal bands of perhaps a few dozen or even as many as one or two hundred people. Recent research suggests that groupings are far more flexible and less elaborately structured. In some of these societies groups of people do assert rights over land and its ungarnered produce. Among the !Kung Bushmen, for example, rights are claimed over water and plant foods, but outsiders who seek permission are apparently invariably given access. The rights appear to serve simply as a classificatory device, an expression of individual and group identity. In other societies, such as the Hadza, people are explicit about the absence of constraints. People associate themselves with particular localities but live, hunt and gather anywhere they choose without seeking permission. The evidence from African hunter-gatherers contradicts the popular contention that man is fundamentally territorial, universally asserting exclusive rights over territory.

Below: !Kung Bushman with hunting bow and poisoned arrow. Top right: *Panjube* (*Adenium* sp.), the plant from which the Hadza make their arrow poison. Bottom right: Hadza hunter carrying zebra meat

These societies, in general, lack unilineal descent groups of the sort that are so familiar in African agricultural and pastoral societies. Relationships between kin are informal and involve few obligations to provide goods or onerous services. There are obligations to be generous and, in particular, to share the meat of large game animals, but people accept few commitments to others, even very close kin. In contrast to agricultural and pastoral societies, the stress is not on claims, obligations, credits and debts, but on generalized generosity and mutuality. The few formal obligations that are accepted are usually to spouses and relatives by marriage.

These basic social characteristics—loose and flexible social groupings, relatively uncommitted and informal social relationships—are consistent with, though not an inevitable product of, an economy focused mainly on the present and relatively unconcerned with the past or the future. People work for short periods and then use the products more or less immediately. There are no accumulated

material assets to be managed and then transmitted from one generation to the next. In contrast, in agricultural and pastoral societies people work in partnership with others and only receive a yield for their labour much later. Delay imposes a requirement for systematic, ordered and patterned relationships between kin and others who associate in production that will eventually provide a reasonably predictable yield for those who have worked. Assets are accumulated and are transmitted according to specific rules to heirs, who depend on receiving them.

Not all African hunter-gatherers are present-oriented and relatively free of commitments and dependencies. For example, the Okiek of the mountain forests of Kenya, with their heavy investment in stocks of wooden beehives, depend on each other for the protection and management of their assets and for control over inheritance. As one would expect, the social organization of the Okiek is more similar to the organization of their agricultural and pastoral neighbours than it is to that of most other African hunter-gatherers.

Government policies towards African hunter-gatherers have, in general, sought to sedentarize them and to persuade them to live by agriculture. Even the most cautious observer would have to admit that most such schemes have failed to achieve their declared intentions. Sedentarized hunter-gatherers are far more likely to become apathetic refugees, demanding regular hand-outs of food from government, than they are to become self-dependent farmers. Surprisingly little attempt has been made so far to involve hunter-gatherers in the wider economies of the countries in which they live by developing equitable marketing arrangements that would permit them to hunt and to gather products for sale as well as for their own needs. Game-cropping of large animals may be difficult to carry out and to administer without producing too high a kill-ratio, but it would surely be possible to improve marketing arrangements for honey, nuts and the skins of small fur-bearing animals such as hyrax. Care would have to be taken to avoid the situation of some South Indian hunter-gatherers, who collect a wide range of forest products for sale, but who are obliged by the government to sell the products to the agents of a single contractor who has bought the concession from the government and who accordingly expects to buy products from the hunter-gatherers at far below the market price.

Wild foods – plant and animal – still provide an important reserve for agricultural and pastoral peoples in time of serious famine thoughout much of the dry-belt of East and Central Africa. In this context the specialized knowledge and skills of hunter-gatherers can serve as an asset not just for themselves but also for their pastoral and agricultural neighbours. *J.W.*

Top: Hadza woman digging up edible roots with her digging-stick. Bottom: !Kung Bushman processing *mongongo* nuts, a major source of food

Pastoralism

Approximately 40 per cent of the world's pastoralist population is to be found in Africa. Even so, the 17.3 million people directly, or predominantly, depending on their animals for their livelihood constitute only about 5 per cent of Africa's total population as seen in the table below. Pastoralism is most significant in the semi-arid zones and countries between, roughly, isohyets marking annual rainfall of 200 and 600mm. In areas wetter than this it makes little sense to raise animals extensively when much greater productivity per hectare may be achieved from crops. The bulk of the continent's pastoral economies are to be found in a great arc surrounding the tropical rain forest and savanna regions. Some countries lie almost entirely within this rainfall zone and it is in these that pastoral populations outnumber settled cultivators and urban dwellers. In Mauritania and Somalia, for instance, 70 per cent of the total population is estimated to be in the pastoral sector. In other countries which have very extensive arid and semi-arid regions the proportion of pastoralists is surprisingly small, as in Algeria (3 per cent) and Morocco (1 per cent), largely as a result of concentrations of settled people along coastal belts and the rapid decline of nomadism and stock raising before alternative opportunities such as oil-generated growth. Quite frequently countries are sharply divided into agricultural and pastoral regions, such as in the Sudan and Niger, where there is a fairly clear north–south divide.

KEY

■ Main cattle producing areas   ▨ Distribution of tsetse fly

DISTRIBUTION OF CATTLE AND TSETSE FLY

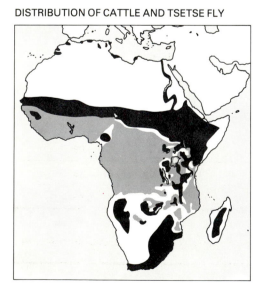

A further factor influencing the distribution of livestock in Africa is the incidence of animal disease, particularly trypanosomiasis carried by the tsetse fly as shown on the map below. There is a close correlation between the incidence of tsetse and the absence of, particularly, cattle: smaller stock are often resistant to the disease. One numerically minor exception to this rule is the small *N'gana* breed of cattle found along parts of the forest region of the West African coast which has developed a high degree of resistance. The wetter areas also breed ticks and also bacterial and viral conditions

SIZE AND IMPORTANCE OF PASTORAL POPULATIONS IN AFRICA

Region	Country	Human pastoral population[1]	Pastoral population as percentage of total population
AFRICA	Algeria	500 000	3
NORTH	Egypt	100 000	<1
OF THE	Libya	300 000	14
SAHARA	Morocco	200 000	1
	Tunisia	60 000	1
Region sub-total		1 160 000	
WEST	Chad	1 800 000	50
AFRICA	Upper Volta	800 000	15
SOUTH	Mali	1 500 000	30
OF THE	Mauritania	1 500 000	70
SAHARA[2]	Niger	800 000	20
	Senegal	350 000	10
Region sub-total		6 750 000	
EAST AND	Angola	500 000	8
SOUTHERN	Botswana	14 000	2
AFRICA	Ethiopia	1 600 000	4
	Kenya	1 500 000	12
	Somalia	1 700 000	70
	Sudan	3 900 000	22
	Tanzania (Masai only)	100 000	<1
Region sub-total		9 314 000	
AFRICA Total		17 224 000	4.9

< = less than

[1] The 'pastoral population' in some countries is recorded by the authorities as being the same as the *nomadic* population. In some parts of Africa this would underscore the pastoral population significantly

[2] There are major pastoral populations in Nigeria but census data is not adequate enough to allow their enumeration here

Source: S. Sandford, 'Pastoralism under Pressure', ODI *Review* (2, 1976)

that are inimical to cattle keeping.

The distribution of different types of livestock is illustrated in the table below. The type of animal kept relates broadly to the prevailing environmental conditions. In the driest areas camels predominate among the large stock and gradually cattle assume a greater importance as average rainfall totals increase. The main form of stock organization again relates to the climatic conditions. Most animals in Africa, in fact virtually all, are raised on natural grazing and browse resources, and these vary both spatially and temporally. In consequence the pastoralists have to maintain a very mobile form of economy and life style to exploit seasonal changes and different niches in the environment. Exactly how this is done varies greatly from region to region, but in the main it involves either a horizontal movement, such as the southward summer movement of the Fulani from the Sahara fringes into the savanna zone after the harvest, or a vertical movement, such as that effected by the Nuer (Sudan) as they move up from the flooded plains on to higher ground during the rainy season.

LIVESTOCK POPULATIONS IN SELECTED AFRICAN COUNTRIES,[1] 1977

Region	Country	Cattle	Camels	Sheep/goats	Total[2]	Livestock units per capita human population[3]
AFRICA NORTH OF THE SAHARA	Algeria	1 300 000	135 000	11 760 000	2 351 000	0.26
	Egypt	2 148 000	101 000	3 331 000	2 153 000	0.11
	Libya	152 000	60 000	4 250 000	607 000	1.21
	Morocco	3 650 000	210 000	19 240 000	5 054 000	0.51
	Tunisia	890 000	190 000	4 550 000	1 357 000	0.52
Region sub-total		8 140 000	696 000	43 131 000	11 521 000	0.28
WEST AFRICA SOUTH OF THE SAHARA	Chad	3 716 000	316 000	4 896 000	3 778 000	1.08
	Upper Volta	1 900 000	5 000	3 677 000	1 893 000	0.39
	Mali	4 076 000	188 000	8 494 000	4 298 000	0.81
	Mauritania	1 400 000	700 000	7 800 000	2 600 000	2.06
	Niger	2 900 000	265 000	8 760 000	3 461 000	0.79
	Nigeria	11 500 000	17 000	31 700 000	12 387 000	0.33
	Senegal	2 440 000	6 000	2 655 000	2 223 000	0.56
Region sub-total		27 932 000	1 497 000	67 982 000	3 065 000	0.51
EAST AND SOUTHERN AFRICA	Angola	3 050 000	—	1 130 000	2 553 000	0.64
	Botswana	2 400 000	—	1 550 000	2 075 000	3.45
	Ethiopia	26 119 000	966 000	40 213 000	25 882 000	1.08
	Kenya	7 350 000	540 000	8 200 000	7 240 000	0.65
	Somalia	2 654 000	2 000 000	15 424 000	5 666 000	2.07
	Sudan	15 892 000	2 813 000	26 840 000	18 211 000	1.43
	Tanzania	14 817 000	—	7 700 000	12 624 000	0.93
Region sub-total		72 282 000	6 319 000	101 057 000	74 250 000	1.08
ALL REGIONS		108 354 000	8 512 000	212 170 000	116 412 000	0.68
OTHER AFRICA		53 255 000	107 000	79 511 000	50 662 000	0.49

[1] Principally those countries in which pastoralism is a significant form of economic activity
[2] Using FAO 'livestock units': cattle = 0.8; camels = 1.0; sheep/goats = 0.1
[3] It is possible only to relate the livestock totals to the agricultural population as a whole (i.e. cultivating and herding). It is not possible to link directly the pastoral populations and the number of animals attributable to these populations alone

Source: adapted from FAO Production Yearbook (1977)

It is already becoming clear that the apparent 'sameness' of pastoralism is a myth; indeed, African pastoralism is extraordinarily diverse and complex. For instance, many communities such as the Karimojong (Uganda) maintain a 'mixed' economy in which the women, children and elders remain, for much of the time, in one main area and subsist from a risky agriculture and a milch herd/flock while the young men take off in the dry season to set up camps on the wetter, western plain where it is possible to find grazing and, more particularly, water. Further complexity may be added by stressing the many other roles that pastoralists play and the use they make of their animals. In West Africa pastoralists maintained a rather unequal symbiosis with cultivators by moving onto their land after harvest, the animals grazing the stubble, the herds depositing manure on the fields and both people and animals gaining access to the watercourses. Others acted also as carriers, for example during the period of trans-Saharan caravan trade which linked North Africa with sub-Saharan Africa through great emporia such as Timbuktu. Remnants of this still survive in the salt traffic of the Tuareg from the Sahara to the markets such as that at Segou (Mali). Further diversity may be illustrated by the hunting and gathering activities of some tribes supplementing their animal products and the use of animals to establish semi-feudal dominance over settled people such as the *buhake* system of the Tutsi in Rwanda/Burundi in which cattle were loaned to agriculturalists who looked after them and received a share of any increase in the herd.

At the centre of pastoral life, however, is the powerful element of risk. It is a rough rule of thumb that there is an inverse correlation between rainfall totals and variability, i.e., the drier it is, the greater the risk of a failure of the rains. Hence drought is a fact of life in the pastoral areas and it should be remembered that where the rainfall totals are low anyway, a shortfall is likely to be far more critical in terms of production.

To counter this risk pastoralists have, over the ages, adopted many risk-minimizing strategies. These include splitting the herd among relatives and friends over a wide area to reduce concentrated pressures; raiding; keeping different types of animals which exploit different niches in the environment (goats browse, cattle graze) and hunting and gathering in times of stress. In many cases, though by no means all, animals provide the basis of the community's subsistence security: they give food directly and they may be traded in times of stress. One particularly unusual feature of pastoral life in Africa, distinguishing it particularly from livestock economies in the developed countries, is the fact that animals are kept overwhelmingly for their recurrent rather than terminal products. Thus it is a form of 'dairying' under extremely extensive conditions. The animals provide milk and sometimes, as among the Masai, blood, which is tapped from the living animal, and are used as suppliers of meat only under unusual circumstances such as ritual ceremonies or times of hardship. This is less true of the small stock but, even there, the animals are kept mostly for their milk. It has been estimated that approximately 1000kg per person of biomass is required to maintain survival in a pastoral economy based on direct subsistence and about 500kg where the animals feature in an exchange for grain. This translates into a relatively large number of animals as the productivity of the herds and flocks is low by western standards. FAO estimates that the average Malian animal (cow) per lactation produces 197kg compared with the average US cow which provides 4413kg. In terms of meat, the average figures per animal for Africa as a whole, Mali, the Sudan and the USA are, respectively, 137kg, 90kg, 165kg, and 246kg. It should be remembered, however, that the animals to be found in most of Africa's pastoral areas have been bred over the years for survival rather than productivity. It is important that they can survive ticks, virus diseases and poor pasture and this is one reason why older animals are so rarely culled while they are productive: they have proven their worth as survivors. Furthermore the herd structure of many pastoral systems reveals very sharply the reasons why animals are kept within the subsistence framework. Whereas such rough pasture would almost automatically be put under male stock in the developed world as part of a beef-producing system, in the pastoral areas the females predominate very solidly.

In addition to the subsistence role of livestock it is necessary to consider also the other functions which stock fulfil within many pastoral societies. They may confirm a marriage arrangement by exchange of bridewealth; give status to their owner; build up a network of obligations and patronage; focus power and develop interpersonal relations. Much has been written in this context to explain the 'numbers' mentality of many pastoralists. More correctly the basis of quantity rather than quality (though survival is a quality much valued) is to be found in a combination of the above 'social' factors and the concept of insurance. Although pastoralists may be able to supplement their diet with some agriculture, fishing, hunting, etc., often their main line of protection lies in the animals themselves. The more one has, the more are likely to survive.

It is not possible, with the data available, to reconstruct the workings of pastoral economies in the past. It would seem likely that their growth rates were held down by periodic catastrophes such as drought and disease, but some writers have suggested that more purely pastoral societies were self-regulating in size and growth. The simple truth is that we do not know. There were periodic major outmigrations of pastoral peoples, or people who adopted pastoralism, such as the spread of the Fulani east from Senegal and the Futa Jalon commencing before the 10th century, the expansion from Ethiopia in the 11th century and the dramatic southward spread of the Nilotics from the southern Sudan probably from the 15th century. Whether this was a response to overpopulation, overgrazing or some other cause is almost impossible to say.

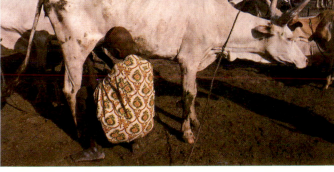

The coming of colonialism caused many changes. Previously pastoralists had often held the upper hand (e.g., the Tutsi, Fulani) over their more settled and vulnerable neighbours. This hegemony was broken and in the rapid growth of the cash crop colonial economy the pastoralists became the poor relations. Migrations and movements were severely curtailed, some environmental checks on cattle and human numbers were modified (wells, virus diseases), and large areas of previously grazed land abandoned when some pastoral tribes were struck by the twin scourges of rinderpest and smallpox at the end of the 19th century. Much has been written on the surge in the growth of animal numbers, especially since the Second World War, as a result of improved water facilities and veterinary medicine as well as the need to find more animals to support a growing human population. It is extremely difficult to find reliable evidence to back up this hypothesis, though this does not invalidate it.

Whether or not the herds were subject to extraordinary growth, there was a marked trend during the colonial era to favour the expansion of agriculture into areas which had previously served as dry-season grazing land. This happened in Masailand in Kenya, along the savanna-Sahelian fringe in West Africa, and in the Sudan. As a result pastoral communities found themselves confined to a diminishing area which was inadequate, particularly in the dry season. At the same time the impact of commercialization on the pastoral economies was fairly light. Pastoralists have chosen to retain the major part of the productive capacity of their herds and flocks. If they have sold animals, as in the case of many Sahelian countries, they have received only 11 per cent of the final selling price of the meat. Up to 14 different taxes are levied in some countries on animals sold into the cash market. In many cases it has simply not been sensible for pastoralists to transfer risk onto the commercial economy as the terms of trade measured in calories for grain purchased have been heavily weighted against the pastoralists. Also the distribution network for food in these areas is often unreliable and more risky than the drought. There were few opportunities, except in countries like Algeria, for the pastoralists to migrate or invest elsewhere, though this has happened in the Sudan. The consequence of this was that the rangelands came under extraordinary pressure, especially around the newly constructed watering points. In many cases it remained the most rational thing for the herder to maximize the number of his animals, especially as the money economy did not replace the many other functions which the animals fulfil. In aggregate the sum of these individually rational actions became corporate irrationality leading to the process now popularly known as desertification. Other aspects of the pastoral economy were also undermined, such as the carrying

Top: Somali herdsmen with cattle, camels and sheep at a waterhole in northern Kenya. Centre: Dinka boy milking a cow, Sudan. Bottom: Fulani drovers with cattle, Cameroon

DESERTIFICATION RISK

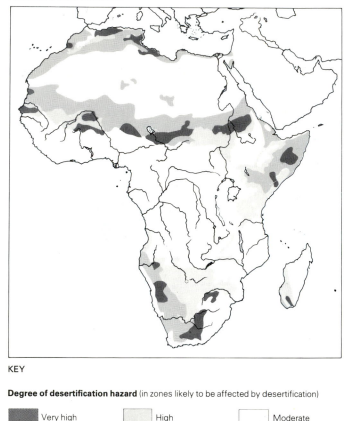

KEY

Degree of desertification hazard (in zones likely to be affected by desertification)

Very high   High   Moderate

trade, which was taken over by motor transport. The net result has been that the areas now suffer greatly during the periodic droughts as the environment and the economy have both been undermined. During the 1968–73 drought in the Sahel it was estimated that as many as 40 per cent of the animals died; this at least giving the grazing some respite. As droughts in these areas tend to bunch over several years, the suffering is cumulative and many pastoralists migrated to areas as distant as central and southern Nigeria. However there is nothing for them to do in these areas and once the drought is over they return to continue their traditional practices. They cannot easily move out of pastoralism, for in most cases there simply is not the land available for them to settle (except in areas such as the Sudan).

This process threatens some countries with the loss of not only productive resources but also a major element of their export economy. Livestock and livestock-related products form 24 per cent (by value) of Mali's exports, 30 per cent of Chad's and 83 per cent of Somalia's. Yet this is at a time when Africa is spending $265m. per annum on imported meat and meat products. The coastal areas of West Africa have a growing demand for meat and protein, especially in Nigeria, and this is being met increasingly by imports from the developed world. Nigeria in 1977 imported meat and meat products worth $32 million, Egypt $58 million, and Zaire $19 million. An astonishing $518 million was spent in Africa in 1977 on imported milk. Nigeria spent $10 million on imported canned beef.

A major research effort is under way to investigate the workings of the pastoral systems in Africa even though this is late in the day. A new International Livestock Centre for Africa has been set up with bases in Nigeria, Ethiopia, Kenya and Mali. The Desertification Conference in Nairobi stressed the idea of integrating pastoral areas of sources of immature stock with feedlots for fattening in wetter areas. There are many who are sceptical about this concept as, in the main, the problem remains that the animals kept by the pastoralists are overwhelmingly for subsistence, which does *not* mean *meat*. Thus any changes to be made in pastoralism must take account not only of a major restructuring of diet and subsistence security by also the numerous functions of livestock in these societies. A further complication lies in the fact that there is a conflict between the individual ownership of animals and the communal ownership of grazing land. This makes many forms of improvement extraordinarily difficult to implement. Not least of the problems is the fact that decision makers are almost entirely urban based and derived from the agricultural areas.

There is no simple solution to this problem of overpopulation and environmental destruction. It is clear that a whole range of changes needs to be made at a high level of integration and there are few, if any, successful models to follow. Ideally, the fine adjustment of nomadism and transhumance should continue, as there seems to be no better way of exploiting this type of physical environment. Again, ideally, numbers would be regulated so that stocking rate does not exceed the carrying capacity of the land. This could mean high rates in good periods and a means of rapid destocking in times of drought. The potential for increased productivity under controlled management is considerable. At the moment the priority is still to stop the destruction.

P.R.B.

Agriculture and fishing

Agricultural regions

There are three major zones of African agriculture whose characteristics are related to regional variations in climate.* In the North African winter-rainfall zone crops include wheat, vines, and olives. Cotton, sugar cane and rice are grown under irrigation. In the tropical summer-rainfall zone yam, cassava, cocoa and oil palm are important in the wetter, forested areas while grains and grain legumes, e.g.

maize, sorghum, millet, groundnuts and cowpeas, predominate in the drier, savanna areas.

A third, central and southern African region from Zambia to the Cape of Good Hope is partly tropical and partly sub-tropical. The region is distinctive because of the activities of white settlers, and the system of labour migration* which has built up around the southern African mining/industrial complex.

Stock rearing, important mainly around the margins of the Sahara in North and West Africa, interpenetrates eastern and southern Africa more comprehensively. Freshwater fishing rises to prominence where there are major rivers and lakes. Ocean fishing is of some importance, especially off the continent's western coastline.

Food crops

Major domestic foodstuffs include cassava, sorghum, millet, maize, yams, bananas and plantains, rice and wheat. Africa has about 10 per cent of the world's population, but 40 per cent of world cassava output. Cassava is a hardy tropical root crop which grows well in the high rainfall zone but is sufficiently drought resistant to be grown also in the savanna zone of the tropical region. Cassava alone provides up to 10 per cent of Africa's food energy requirements. The root of bitter varieties needs careful processing to rid it of poisonous hydrocyanic acid. The resulting meal (*gari*) or flour is readily stored and transported, convenient to prepare, and in much demand in urban areas. Cassava leaves, when properly prepared, constitute a valuable, protein-rich vegetable and are an important item of diet in Sierra Leone, Liberia, Zaire and elsewhere in central and eastern Africa.

Sorghum and millet are major grain crops in the drier parts of the tropical zone. Some quick-maturing varieties of millet can be grown where rainfall is less than 400mm a year. Output of each grain is about 10 million tonnes a year, equivalent to 20 per cent of world production and 10 per cent of Africa's food energy requirements. The tropical grasslands north of the Equator are the main zone of concentration but both crops are grown from Egypt to the Cape.

Africa accounts for about 16 per cent of the world's output of yams and sweet potatoes. The white yam is the traditional staple of the forest zone and forest margins in the eastern part of West Africa.

STAPLE CROPS: CASSAVA AND WHEAT

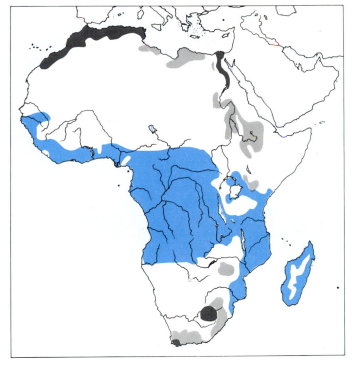

STAPLE CROPS: MILLETS, SORGHUM AND YAMS

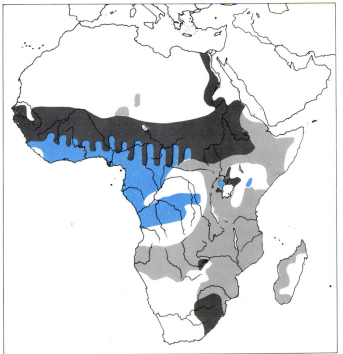

KEY

Cassava and wheat

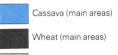

Cassava (main areas)

Wheat (main areas)

Wheat (secondary areas)

Millet, sorghum and yams

Millets and sorghum (main areas)

Millet and sorghum (secondary areas)

Yams (main areas)

Mixed millets, sorghum and yams

Winnowing millet in northern Kenya

STAPLE AND CASH CROPS: MAIZE

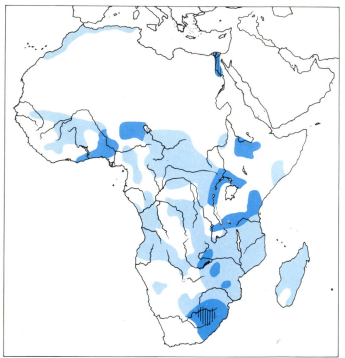

Cultivation is labour-intensive and requires skilled attention. Price rises in recent years have meant that many urban consumers can no longer afford yam and now manage with cassava instead. The sweet potato and cassava have both gained ground at the expense of yam cultivation, especially in areas of high population pressure and consequent soil impoverishment. Like cassava the sweet potato also produces valuable edible leaves.

Maize is cultivated in all parts of the continent. It is of greatest significance, both for subsistence and as a commercial crop, in central and southern Africa. In West Africa maize is dominant in a region focused on southern Benin, but otherwise is mainly a secondary food crop, especially valued in drier areas as a hunger breaker before the

STAPLE AND CASH CROPS: OIL PALM AND DATES

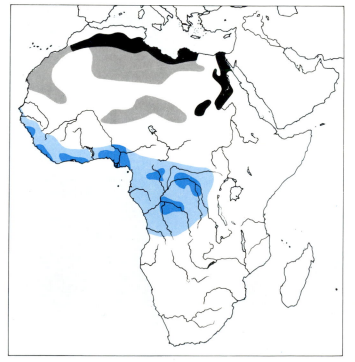

KEY

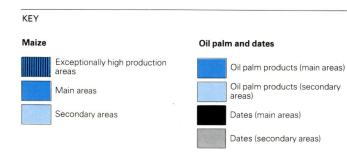

Maize

⬛ Exceptionally high production areas

🟦 Main areas

🟦 Secondary areas

Oil palm and dates

🟦 Oil palm products (main areas)

🟦 Oil palm products (secondary areas)

⬛ Dates (main areas)

⬜ Dates (secondary areas)

STAPLE AND CASH CROPS: GROUNDNUTS AND CITRUS

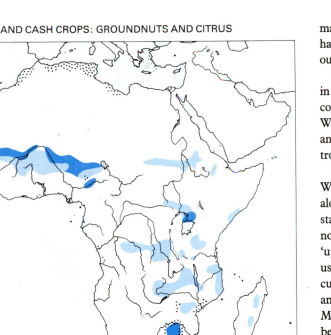

STAPLE AND CASH CROPS: BANANAS AND ENSETE

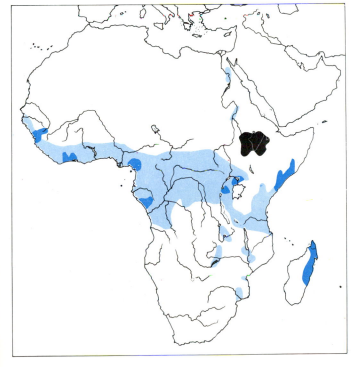

main harvest and in high rainfall areas because two crops can be harvested per year. Africa produces 8 per cent of the world's maize output.

Rice and wheat flour (for bread) are important convenience foods in urban areas throughout Africa. Africa is not self-sufficient in either commodity, accounting for only 2–3 per cent of world output. Within Africa 92 per cent of wheat output comes from South Africa and the zone from Morocco to Ethiopia. A little wheat is grown in the tropics under irrigation in the dry season.

Rice is a major crop in Egypt, Madagascar and the western half of West Africa. In Ivory Coast, Liberia, Sierra Leone, Guinea, and along major rivers in The Gambia, Senegal and Mali rice is the major staple, occupying the place of yam further east. African red rice has now been almost entirely supplanted by Asian varieties. Traditional 'upland' cultivation is still important but swamp rice cultivation, using irrigation, has been encouraged in recent years. Rice cultivation has been introduced with considerable success in central and southern Nigeria, northern Ghana and parts of Tanzania and Malawi. Despite an increase in rice output of more than 45 per cent between 1961 and 1976, compared to a world increase of 35 per cent in the same period, most African states continue to import heavily. (African imports amount to 11 per cent of world trade in rice.) Egypt is a major rice exporter, however (88 per cent of African exports and about 2 per cent of world trade in rice in 1976).

'Cash' crops for export

'Cash' crops—major foreign-exchange earners—include cocoa, palm produce, rubber, coffee, cotton, groundnuts, tea, tobacco, sugar, and from the sub-tropical regions within Africa wine, olives, rice and citrus fruit. As a result of specialization because of optimum environmental conditions in particular areas, production of each crop tends to be concentrated in two or three countries. Rubber output is principally from Liberia, and tobacco from Zimbabwe. Ivory Coast, Ethiopia and Uganda between them account for 48 per cent of the African coffee crop, and Ghana, Nigeria and Ivory Coast, 82 per cent of the cocoa crop. Egypt and Sudan produce more than half the cotton grown in Africa. Palm-oil and palm-kernel production is restricted to the forest zone of western Africa from Sierra Leone to

KEY

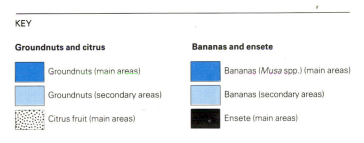

Groundnuts and citrus

Groundnuts (main areas)

Groundnuts (secondary areas)

Citrus fruit (main areas)

Bananas and ensete

Bananas (*Musa* spp.) (main areas)

Bananas (secondary areas)

Ensete (main areas)

Tobacco harvesting in Zimbabwe

CASH CROPS: RUBBER AND TOBACCO

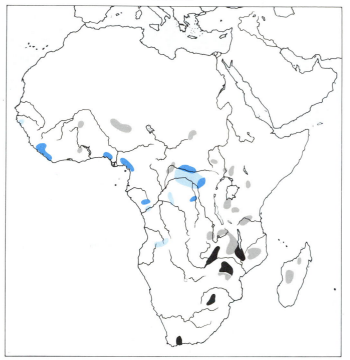

CASH CROPS: COFFEE, SUGAR AND GRAPES

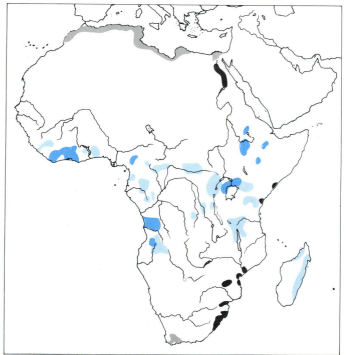

northern Angola. Nigeria, despite the effects of the civil war (1967–70), remains the most important producer, but internal demand for palm-oil has become so great that exports have ceased. Groundnut cultivation is perhaps the most widespread cash-crop activity in Africa, in part because local markets provide an alternative if world demand slackens. Nigeria, the largest producer of groundnuts in the 1960s, was by 1975 in third place behind Senegal and Sudan and narrowly ahead of Zaire. Groundnut production was badly affected by the West African drought (1969–73). Although absolute output continued to rise during the period 1967–75, Africa's share of total world output of major cash crops fell. In the case of cocoa, for example, the African share dropped from 71 per cent to 63 per cent.

KEY

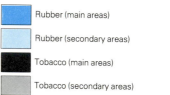

Rubber and tobacco

- Rubber (main areas)
- Rubber (secondary areas)
- Tobacco (main areas)
- Tobacco (secondary areas)

Coffee, sugar and grapes

- Coffee (main areas)
- Coffee (secondary areas)
- Sugar (main areas)
- Grapes (main areas)

CASH CROPS: COCOA AND TEA

CASH CROPS: COTTON AND CLOVES

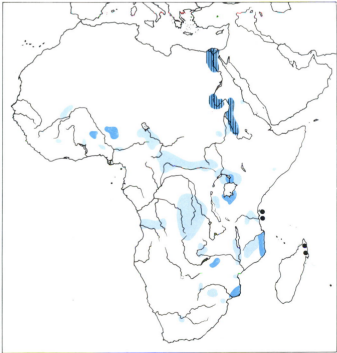

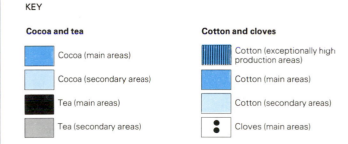

Top: tea-picking in Kenya. Bottom: splitting cocoa pods in Ghana

KEY

Cocoa and tea

Cocoa (main areas)

Cocoa (secondary areas)

Tea (main areas)

Tea (secondary areas)

Cotton and cloves

Cotton (exceptionally high production areas)

Cotton (main areas)

Cotton (secondary areas)

Cloves (main areas)

INDICES OF LOCATIONAL CONCENTRATION FOR MAIZE, CASSAVA AND TRACTORS; FAO INDEX OF PER CAPITA AGRICULTURAL PRODUCTION: SELECED AFRICAN COUNTRIES

Country	Indices of locational concentration[1]			FAO Index of per capita agricultural production 1975[2]
	maize 1976	cassava 1976	tractors 1975	
Algeria	<0.1	—	3.0	65
Angola	1.2	2.3	1.4	73
Benin	1.2	1.2	<0.1	109
Burundi	0.7	2.3	*	192
Cameroon	1.0	1.2	*	123
Central African Republic	0.4	4.6	*	91
Chad	<0.1	0.1	<0.1	69
Congo	0.2	5.4	0.5	78
Egypt	1.2	—	0.6	98
Ethiopia	0.7	—	0.1	80
Ghana	0.7	1.7	0.3	92
Guinea	1.2	1.1	<0.1	91
Ivory Coast	0.3	1.0	0.3	124
Kenya	1.7	0.5	0.4	92
Lesotho	2.2	—	1.0	92
Liberia	*	1.8	*	109
Libya	<0.1	—	*	141
Madagascar	*	1.6	0.3	93
Malawi	4.1	0.2	0.2	117
Mali	0.2	0.1	0.1	67
Mauritania	<0.1	—	*	65
Morocco	0.4	—	1.1	94
Mozambique	0.8	2.5	0.6	87
Niger	<0.1	0.6	<0.1	73
Nigeria	0.3	1.6	0.1	83
Rwanda	0.3	0.9	*	109
Senegal	0.2	0.2	0.1	99
Sierra Leone	0.1	0.3	0.1	101
Somalia	0.6	0.1	0.4	102
South Africa	4.8	—	6.9	104
Sudan	<0.1	0.1	0.6	125
Tanzania	1.8	3.1	*	91
Togo	1.0	1.9	0.1	84
Uganda	0.9	0.8	0.1	88
Upper Volta	0.1	<0.1	<0.1	86
Zaire	0.3	3.9	0.1	88
Zambia	2.5	0.3	0.8	95
Zimbabwe	3.7	—	*	85

Sources: FAO Statistical Publications

Farming systems

Of Africa's limited share of the world's tractors (2 per cent of about 17 million), 30 per cent are to be found in North Africa and about 45 per cent in the Republic of South Africa, thus serving to emphasize the distinction between sub-tropical Africa, where temperate latitude crops and technologies are appropriate and tropical Africa where different farming systems prevail. Tropical Africa is still the province of the small-scale farmer utilizing principally family labour, only occasionally supplemented by draught animals or mechanization. In some cases, where governments and capitalist business interests have established large estates and plantations, for crops such as tea, sisal, palm-oil and rubber, field work may still be largely by hand (e.g. rubber tapping and tea picking). Technical justification for a plantation is more often to be found at the processing stage. Large palm-oil mills recently established in Nigeria and Sierra Leone are efficient only if there is a guaranteed input. Plantations (now often incorporating peasant out-grower schemes) are the best way of ensuring that the processing plant works to capacity. These circumstances apart, large-scale mechanized farming schemes in the tropics have often proved to be more problematical than profitable, while the peasant farmer, although using 'traditional' methods and hand cultivation, has registered notable successes, for example in cocoa cultivation in Ghana and groundnut cultivation in Senegal.

Thus the various 'traditional' farming systems within tropical Africa, are not simply 'survivals' from a bygone age. Shifting cultivation and its cognate farming systems have a surprising degree of efficiency, not easily bettered by proposed replacements. In addition, the farming systems concerned have continued to develop with time. Population pressure is held to be one factor stimulating such development. As population pressure on land increases, agricultural production is intensified. A typical sequence involves shifting cultivation without fixed farm boundaries, giving way to rotational bush fallowing (where farmers return to recognizable farm plots after a period of a few years) and then to very short 'planted fallows', after which an infield-outfield system may emerge in which the main emphasis is placed on intensively manured and permanently cultivated plots close to the farmstead. Shifting cultivation only survives where population pressures are less than 8–12 persons per sq

NOTES TO TABLE

*Not available   < = less than

[1]Values for maize, cassava and tractors are indices of locational concentration. An index of 1.0 indicates that the country in question has the same percentage of Africa's total for the feature in question as the country's percentage of Africa's total population. A value of less than 1.0 indicates less concentration than would be expected in population terms. A value greater than 1.0 indicates a greater concentration than would be expected in population terms

[2]Base year (100) = 1960. Figures in the table indicate 1975 per capita agricultural production as a percentage of the figure for 1960. World average = 106; Africa average = 95

km, but rotational bush fallowing continues until rural population densities exceed 150–200 persons per sq km. It has also been suggested that as agriculture is intensified to cope with land shortage, returns per man day decline, even though overall output rises, i.e. low intensity-low output farming systems survive up to the point change becomes a necessity due to land shortage. For this reason it is dangerous to conclude too much from evidence to the effect that African yields of maize, rice, etc., are sometimes less than half the world average yield per hectare, for it may be that this has been achieved with less than half the average labour input and expense. Certainly yield figures by themselves do not proclaim, as some have supposed, that African soils are inherently 'infertile' or necessarily inferior to soils in temperate regions. The distribution of African peasant farming systems correlates quite closely with population density figures. The area around the major northern Nigerian city of Kano and the central zone of eastern Nigeria are two areas where permanent-field cultivation has developed. Both regions contain localities where rural population densities exceed 500 per sq km. Conversely, the main belt of shifting cultivation, namely from the Zaire River estuary to Tanzania, corresponds to an area of markedly low population density.

In shifting cultivation farm holdings tend to vary with family size because labour shortage rather than land shortage is the major constraint on production. Most systems of land tenure often loosely described as communal are in fact sets of land rights vested in the extended family rather than the individual. Some families control more land than others. Outright purchase or sale of land is still often difficult or impossible, but pledging, leasing and renting for cash are increasingly common. Opinion is sharply divided as to whether lack of a 'normal' capitalist land market inhibits agricultural change. Forest-zone farms are typically about 0.5 to 1 hectare, sometimes subdivided into separate plots. Savanna farms tend to be larger, i.e. up to 5 or more hectares, due to the fact that land is easier to clear, but in general is less fertile when cleared.

Irrigation

Irrigation is of long-established importance in some parts of Africa, e.g. the Nile valley. Most of Africa could, in theory, benefit from irrigation. Even high-rainfall areas experience a water deficit in the dry season. Initial development costs, however, are high, and, where large dams are involved, ecological and social dislocations often prove to be serious. For the Sahel* region it is estimated that irrigation is feasible on about 10 per cent of the presently cultivated area. Only about 10 per cent of this potential has been realized so far. The

Top: oil-palm farm in Rwanda. Centre: Bush-clearing for farming in progress in western Nigeria. Bottom: a forest farm in western Nigeria

Digging irrigation canals in Sudan

emphasis will remain on dry-land farming, despite recurrent drought problems, because many of the crops which benefit most from irrigation are not in great demand locally. Irrigation often only makes sense where there is an assured overseas market for crops such as cotton or sugar cane, or where a low-cost scheme is able to supplement the main farming activities, making use of seasonally under-employed labour during the dry season.

Livestock

It is estimated that Africa has 11 per cent, 13 per cent and 25 per cent respectively of the world's sheep, cattle and goats. Domestic birds, i.e. chickens, guinea fowl, ducks, etc., are of widespread importance, but pigs are insignificant in most areas.

In the drier grasslands ringing the Sahara (rainfall 100–800mm) nomadic pastoralism* continues to be important. Other methods of livestock management include ranching, which is of considerable significance in southern Africa, and of growing interest to governments elsewhere, and 'supplementary' livestock rearing as practised by settled agriculturalists throughout Africa. the latter practice, it should be stressed, is rarely 'mixed farming' in the sense of livestock management fully integrated into the farming system, but a low-intensity activity in which off-farm surpluses of labour, land and food are converted to livestock primarily as a means of investment and saving. A recent study in eastern Nigeria shows that small livestock (mainly goats) and chickens can constitute up to 10 per cent of family income. They forage for themselves, scavenging compound refuse, and only require attention during the dry season when farm work is at a low ebb. The great advantage of small domestic livestock is that they can be converted to food or cash at any time that a social, nutritional or financial crisis demands. The trypanosomiasis-resistant dwarf cattle

of the West African forests, the *muturu*, were once important elements in local farming systems, but have yielded to the goat in most areas, partly because as more land is brought into cultivation it becomes essential to change to a type of livestock that can eat a wider range of vegetation than cattle, and can therefore be fenced in, in order to prevent damage to growing crops.

In parts of East Africa, e.g. Uganda and Tanzania, livestock management by settled cultivators is an especially important phenomenon. Interest focuses on cattle as a means of utilizing rough grazing and 'investing' food and labour surpluses. In some areas this has reached such proportions that cattle grazing represents a major activity within the farming system. In the drier parts of East Africa, however, e.g. in much of Kenya, nomadic pastoralism prevails.

Cattle rearing in the wetter savannas of tropical Africa is severely hampered by trypanosomiasis, a disease transmitted by tsetse flies. The area affected by trypanosomiasis appears to have increased during the late 19th and early 20th centuries, most probably as a result of population dislocations resulting from slave raiding and European expansion. (A reduction in population density encourages regrowth of the orchard bush constituting the tsetse flies' favoured habitat.) Rinderpest, introduced as an accidental by-product of European colonial involvement in north-eastern Africa, was a major scourge between 1890 and the 1920s, with herd mortalities up to 90 per cent in some areas. Much development effort in the last 60 years has gone into controlling these two major diseases. The fight against rinderpest has been a success. There is still considerable argument as to how to control trypanosomiasis, some authorities arguing that the low-cost ecological methods of disease control developed by African cattle peoples prior to the turmoils of the 19th century are still best.

Livestock in Africa are principally important for meat and hides. Cattle transport themselves over long distances, and the savanna to forest meat supply has long been a feature of inter-regional agricultural trade within West Africa. Burgeoning cities provide an increased market for meat, much of which has now to be imported. Hides figure quite importantly as exports. Kano goat-skins have long been known in Europe as 'Morocco leather'. Wool has been quite an important export from North Africa, but tropical African sheep are meat rather than wool producers. Modern poultry farms and piggeries are prominent around many major urban centres.

Lack of draught animal power and the plough have often been cited as reasons for 'underdevelopment' of agriculture in tropical Africa. Despite problems of soil management and animal health, schemes to introduce ox-ploughing and 'mixed farming' have been enthusiastically pursued, with some success in, for example, The Gambia, Ghana, and northern Nigeria. Nevertheless, recent research suggests that animal power is not always an efficient use of available resources, and that tillage is not the only constraint on farm size and productivity. Weeding or harvesting may be more significant bottlenecks, and these are activities in which animal power is of less use. If an ox consumes more than it produces, bearing in mind the need for dry-season feed, the 'green manure' value of rough grazing, and labour diverted from other productive activities to care for the animal and maintain the plough, then African farmers may be right to reject ox-ploughing. Animal power is of great viability in sub-tropical Africa, and the plough is a long-established feature of indigenous agriculture in, for example, North Africa, Ethiopia and Lesotho.

Fishing

Annual fish landings in Africa are in the order of 5 per cent of world output, and are equivalent to an annual consumption of 9kg per person. Most communities with access to lakes and all-season rivers engage in part-time fishing for family consumption. Fishermen along major rivers, e.g. the Niger, or by large lakes such as Lake Chad are full-time specialists, much of whose catch will be smoked and transported to far-distant markets. Fishing has been encouraged by the creation of major artificial lakes, for example, Volta in Ghana and Kainji in Nigeria. Nevertheless, the main prospect for increasing fish supplies rests with ocean fishing. Up to two-thirds of Africa's fish supply comes from marine sources. The western seaboard states dominate output, accounting for 90 per cent of ocean landings. South Africa and Namibia are together the largest contributors (40–45 per cent) but Senegal, Ghana, Angola and Nigeria account for a further 35 per cent. Nigeria is unusual in having a sizeable sea-fishing industry and an equivalent or even greater output from inland fisheries (including fish from the Niger, the coastal lagoon system, and lakes Kainji and Chad). North Africa, with 20 per cent of Africa's population, accounts for 10 per cent of the total fish catch, Morocco being the largest single contributor.

Inshore sea fishing in Sierra Leone

Fishing offers great scope for development through the application of modern technology. At present much of the benefit is reaped by fleets from rich countries fishing in African waters. Japanese, Russian and Italian trawler fleets are prominent in the well-stocked fishing grounds off the western African coast between Liberia and Mauritania. The potential for African fisheries is underlined by the success of the Holy Apostles of Aiyetoro commune on the sea coast of the western flank of the Niger delta, where an Ilaje fishing group have, largely through their own efforts, built a modern ocean-going trawler fleet and industrialized their fish processing activities, thereby transforming standards of living in the period since their settlement was founded in 1947.

Agriculture in the economy

Agriculture is still what most people in Africa do for a living. The percentage of the work-force engaged in agriculture (here taken to include livestock rearing, forestry and fishing) in 1978 varied from about 90 per cent for the Sahel states to about 30 per cent for South Africa and oil-rich Libya. The figure in most tropical African countries is between 60 per cent and 80 per cent. Agricultural commodities are major foreign exchange earners for countries lacking mineral resources, e.g. groundnuts in Senegal, tea in Kenya, and cotton and coffee in Uganda. Only in South Africa, Zimbabwe, Egypt and Algeria does the manufacturing industrial sector begin to rival agriculture and mineral exploitation and even then production for export is not a major emphasis. However, agriculture invariably contributes less overall to Gross Domestic Product (GDP) than might be supposed from the agricultural sector's importance as a generator of employment. The average figure for the agricultural contribution to GDP for Africa as a whole is 25 per cent (whereas the average for

River fishing in Cameroon

work-force employed in agriculture is 75 per cent and for export earnings from agriculture, 60 per cent). Guinea with an estimated 50 per cent of GDP contributed by agriculture and Zimbabwe with 17 per cent, are near the top and bottom of the scale respectively. Figures such as these are sometimes read as evidence of a fundamental crisis of low productivity. Caution needs to be exercised on two counts, however. The first is that agriculture is still firmly household or 'subsistence' oriented in many countries. GDP calculations tend to underestimate the true importance of goods and services circulating at the household level (even in the USA it has been suggested that non-quantifiable domestic transactions – e.g. housework – might constitute as much as 30 per cent of the 'true' GDP). The second point is that if agriculture is less productive than it should or might be, this is as a result of development policies which over the years have deliberately 'milked' agriculture to stimulate growth elsewhere. Colonial governments helped pay for themselves out of farmers' taxes (either as export or income taxes) and cash cropping was stimulated to provide a tax base. More recently government produce marketing boards (for crops such as cocoa and palm produce in West Africa and some food crops, such as maize, in East Africa), set up originally to protect producers from the uncertainties of market price fluctuations, have had the effect of transferring rural earnings to urban areas, because the differences between world market prices and prices paid to the farmers have been absorbed as administrative overheads and invested in industrial and commercial ventures of little direct relevance to farm producers. Corresponding direct investment in agriculture has been low. For example at a time when agriculture accounted for about 50 per cent of Nigerian GDP, the government allocation for agriculture during the 1962–8 Development Plan period was only 13 per cent of planned public expenditure, of which more than a third was never actually spent.

The situation in southern Africa calls for further comment. Here in the first phase of colonization, a productive peasant agricultural sector provided both food and capital (through taxation) for development. For example in the fiscal year 1904–05 African taxes provided 41 per cent of Rhodesian government revenue, whereas non-African residents contributed only 27 per cent. Subsequently, African agricultural productivity and competitiveness declined in the face of white settler agriculture depriving African farmers of better quality land, and government discrimination against African farm produce through tariff and produce-grading controls. With research, extension, transport and marketing facilities firmly directed to serve the interests of the white farming community, African agriculture has been unable to transcend its 20th century state of depression. Rural populations now subsist on inadequate amounts of marginal land using survival strategies rescued from pre-colonial agriculture. The fact that subsistence is possible at all in these circumstances is tribute to the efficacy of the ecological knowledge and skill of the African farmer. This part-employed, self-sustaining, 'rural proletariat' is of great significance to the southern Africa urban-industrial complex as a source of ready labour whose bills for social overheads and the maintenance of normal family life have already been paid by subsistence agriculture. In southern Africa much emphasis has been placed, in agricultural 'development' terms, on preserving these vital rural subsistence capacities through 'conservation' measures, especially soil erosion protection.

Long-distance migratory labour, back-stopped by 'subsistence' agriculture, has not been so strikingly all-dominant elsewhere in Africa. Nevertheless, it was a by no means unknown feature of colonial economies as far apart as Algeria and Malawi. Sahel migrant workers in France and northern Ghanaian workers in the forest-zone cocoa belt are two among many possible examples which show that post-colonial governments outside southern Africa have not been able to discard the system.

African agriculture in the colonial and post-colonial worlds has also been badly affected by extended periods of adverse terms of trade. For example, London prices for Kenya, Uganda and Malawi teas were actually lower in 1969 than in 1960. Furthermore the tea producers' share of the final price declined from 67 per cent in 1955 to 44 per cent in 1974. It remains to be seen whether more favourable price trends established in the late 1970s for many tropical commodities can be maintained.

As agriculture modernizes, fertilizer and machinery import prices begin to be of great significance. Africa is still very dependent on overseas fertilizer supply. Most prices went up by 400 per cent or more between 1971 and 1975 and supplies were inadequate even at 'energy crisis' prices. Developed-world mechanized agriculture is as a whole very dependent on fossil fuel energy inputs, and countries without oil resources are beginning to question the wisdom of encouraging similar dependence in Africa. On the other hand multi-national agricultural business interests have a vested interest in promoting existing technology. Alternative technologies, some of which build upon the energy efficiency characteristic of tropical shifting cultivation, are possible. Research on the familiar traditional practice of intercropping, for example, has revealed that because mixed crops planted in the same field maximize utilization of sunlight, water and plant nutrients and minimize pest and disease attack, yields are both higher and less variable than under mono-culture and returns per man hour are maximized. Intercropping has been discouraged in the past partly because it was inimical to the spread of mechanization, but partly because its merits were simply not understood.

One of the long-standing problems of African agriculture is the inappropriateness of much agricultural research effort. There is evidence that sorghum, millet and white yams were first domesticated in Africa. Over 18 per cent of the world's cultivated crop hectarage is planted to crops of African origin. And yet the amount of research directed towards these crops is insignificant by comparison with the research effort devoted to temperate-zone food crops or tropical 'cash' crops, such as cocoa and rubber, which are of primary interest to the developed world. There has been the beginnings of a change in this balance through the establishment of institutions such as the International Institute of Tropical Agriculture in Ibadan, Nigeria, devoted to fundamental research into tropical food crops. Small domestic livestock are also beginning to attract attention, and effort is being devoted to improving technologies for storing, marketing and transporting crops.

It is claimed that indigenous marketing systems work with considerable 'efficiency'. Food-crop producers in Nigeria, for example, typically receive 50–60 per cent of the final purchase price for their commodities. Even so, exploitation by middle-men (and moneylenders) is an ever-present possibility and the extension of cooperative activities is thought to be a way forward.

Dilemmas of agricultural development

Agricultural work-forces continue to diminish (and their average ages to rise) throughout Africa, and progress towards greater per capita productivity is by no means universal. Rural annual population growth of 2–3 per cent is outstripped by urban growth rates of 5–10 per cent. Africa's 10 per cent population in urban centres over 50 000 will have increased to 20–30 per cent by the end of the present century, creating a disproportionate growth in demand for foodstuffs. Urban wage levels are higher and the quality of urban life is more attractive than rural areas. This is especially true of oil-producing states, where agricultural output has begun to slump alarmingly. Algeria uses up to one-third of revenues from oil to meet the food import bill. Whereas diminished foodstuff self-sufficiency is in itself not necessarily a bad thing–if accompanied by greater specialization in activities for which the economy has a comparative advantage–the growing dependency of many African countries on North American food supplies without corresponding development elsewhere in the economy is a cause for concern. By the mid-1970s overt attention was being paid to this problem, for example 'back to the land' schemes such as Nigeria's Operation Feed the Nation, but overall government investment levels in agriculture are still disappointingly low. It may be argued that a major contribution comes in the form of indirect investment in rural roads and education, but as often as not those improvements serve to steepen the rate of decline in the agricultural sector by encouraging the flow of young people to cities. Even where resources have been committed directly–and in this respect the World Bank and other international agencies have been especially active in Africa since the 1960s– problems still abound. Integrated rural development and Green Revolution technology continue in the main to bypass the mass of the

An officer of the Gambian Ministry of Agriculture giving advice to farmers on the storage of groundnuts

rural poor in favour of wealthier 'middle peasants' and capitalistic farmers. Some would argue that the overriding problem is that African agriculture is far too 'open' to swings in the world economy and to the profit-making propensities of multi-national agricultural business interests, an openness which the World Bank and Green Revolution may exacerbate rather than cure. By 1980 the key problems were being faced with new determination and this was perhaps a hopeful sign. *D.O.A., J.A.K.&P.R.*

Environmental hazards

Major natural disasters in Africa are nearly all associated with one factor: rainfall, and in particular rainfall failure. Other forces are much less important. The Atlas Mountains of Morocco and Algeria and the Rift Valley stretching from north-eastern to east-central Africa are both areas of seismic instability, but major destructive earthquakes are extremely rare, and nothing in recent African experience matches the seismic hazards of South and Central America or western Asia. Coastal Africa is not particularly noted for major destructive winds, although cyclones, for instance, frequently wreak damage on parts of the Indian Ocean coast.

Floods

Among natural hazards associated with rainfall, drought is most significant in Africa but floods should not be ignored. Worldwide, floods predominate among natural disasters, particularly in tropical regions where most annual rainfall is concentrated in one, or at most two seasons. In Africa flood destruction is rarely spectacular, since it is usually the result of limited flash-floods from one unusually heavy fall of rain, often in areas of relatively low overall precipitation. These may be short-lived and too localized to produce disaster on a provincial, let alone national, scale and yet such hazards can entirely destroy crops and homes, and can carry away human beings and livestock. On the other hand, some farmers actually depend on rivers annually flooding. This is particularly true in semi-arid areas such as the middle reaches of the Senegal River in West Africa or the Omo River in south-western Ethiopia, where 'flood-retreat cultivation' of grain crops is undertaken on the river banks as the flood subsides, making rich alluvial soils productive where resources would be unavailable for large-scale irrigation or where local precipitation is insufficient for rain-fed cultivation. However, such cultivation may be destroyed if a late bout of torrential rain, possibly far upstream, causes the river to flood again.

Most riverain societies of Africa have not developed such cultivation systems and when, occasionally, a great river inundates the surrounding countryside, the human and national economic toll can be great. Mozambique has often been the major African victim of this kind of disaster; for example yearly floods between 1976 and 1979 caused an estimated annual average of $40 million worth of destruction in an already hard-pressed economy. Numerous major and minor rivers flow through Mozambique to the Indian Ocean: the country reaps the benefits of alluvial soils at the cost of a high flood risk. In addition there are, on average, six cyclones of varying intensity on the coast each year. In 1977 Cyclone Emily contributed to the country's worst floods in 60 years, which killed 300 people and affected some 400 000, half of whom stayed in relief camps for many months. The other major factor, coinciding with the cyclone, was the discharge of large volumes of water from the new Masingir Dam on a tributary of the Limpopo as well as from other dams on southern international rivers running from South Africa and Swaziland. In

POTENTIAL LOSSES TO AGRICULTURAL PRODUCTION IN MOZAMBIQUE FROM FLOOD DAMAGE

Crop	1975 value of production millions of US$	Percentage of GDP	Percentage of crop at risk	Value of potential loss millions of US$
Maize	25.8	15.9	50	12.9
Sugar cane	8.6	5.3	100	8.6
Rice	8.1	5.0	100	8.1
Cotton	6.1	3.8	30	1.8
Irish potatoes	0.9	0.5	50	0.5
Sunflower	0.7	0.4	50	0.4

Source: B. Wisner, 'Flood Prevention and Mitigation in the People's Republic of Mozambique', *Disasters* (3, 1979)

LOSSES DUE TO THE 1978 ZAMBEZI FLOOD IN MOZAMBIQUE

Type of loss	Province Tete	Manica	Zambezia	Sofala	Total
Lives lost	31	3	2	9	45
Homeless persons *thousands*	89.6	22	30	77.4	219
Croplands lost *thousands of hectares*	25.1	9.5	9	17.9	61.5
Schools lost	53	14	20	68	115

Source: B. Wisner, 'Flood Prevention and Mitigation in the People's Republic of Mozambique', *Disasters* (3, 1979)

1978 discharges from the Kariba and Cabora Bassa dams exacerbated the catastrophic flooding of the Zambezi valley in Mozambique. Nevertheless although man has a hand in intensifying floods in the country, the chief risk is from localized torrential rainfall which overwhelms the banks of rivers and their tributaries.

Irrigation canals can also exacerbate flooding. In Sudan, for instance, much of the food production in the vast arid regions depends on irrigation schemes running off the White and Blue Nile rivers and their tributaries. In July 1978 part of the Gezira and White Nile region received torrential rains which, within a period of two weeks, exceeded the average annual total of rainfall. On this flat terrain, damaged canals overflowed into fields already flooded by the rains. About half a million people were directly affected, and 32 villages were cut off by the floods, while more than half of the 900 000 hectares under crops were in jeopardy.

In the typical African context, flood prevention is a difficult matter. Cooperation between governments may help in some measure to alleviate the dangers of combined discharge from major dams, while the building of floodways and drainage works can protect the low-lying districts of towns and cities. The problem in rural areas, however, is more intractable. Most African countries have neither the financial nor technical resources to build permanent flood barriers in more than a very few places. Given conducive social conditions, communal efforts can be directed at the creation of dykes, floodwalls, river diversions and terraces; the resettlement of villages away from flood-plains is a possibility in countries such as Tanzania where this kind of social engineering has been part of the country's recent political experience. In general, however, African farmers have good reasons for establishing themselves where they do. Alluvial soils are at a premium, although sometimes flood-prone, and land hunger increasingly limits the mobility of subsistence farmers. In the foreseeable future it is likely that local people will continue to regard flood damage as a risk which they cannot avoid or which, viewed over a span of years, is insufficient to warrant the investment of critically scarce resources and labour.

Drought and famine

At least it is possible for African governments and farmers to do something to prevent flooding. There is almost nothing they can do to prevent drought. The 'seeding' of rainclouds is experimental, expensive and dependent on techniques only available to rich nations, while the long-term, large-scale conservation of water on the ground is far beyond the resources of any Black African state and big dams are usually investments for hydro-electric power, whatever the secondary gains for irrigated agriculture.

The 1970s witnessed a particularly severe drought period in the semi-arid Sahel zone just south of the Sahara as well as in much of the Horn of Africa. This and subsequent international discussion of the problem of desertification may have fostered the impression that drought in Africa usually comes in massive doses and hits at already dry zones. Like floods, however, small-scale droughts of limited duration, causing serious but localized losses, are far more common than the large events which are better publicized and better studied. A rough rule-of-thumb for Kenya, for example, is that in each ten-year period there will be at least one small, localized drought in some district annually, two to three regional droughts affecting less than 10 per cent of the country's population over a two-year period, and one major drought affecting 10 to 15 per cent of the population and requiring full-scale mobilization for the redistribution of national grain surpluses and stores–a 'national emergency'.

Again like floods, drought is not confined to one type of ecological zone. Just as floods can strike normally arid areas, relatively humid areas can experience serious rainfall deficits. In Sierra Leone, for instance, annual rainfall is generally in excess of 2000mm and seldom varies by more than 5 to 10 per cent from one year to another. But in 1973 rainfall was from 10 to 30 per cent below the mean annual total over much of the country, and up to 40 per cent below in extreme eastern and western areas. As a result, rice planters experienced food shortages on a scale unknown for 30 years and cash-crops (cocoa, coffee, palm produce) were reduced over a period of two years or more. Similarly, drought in the Lower Zaire Province of Zaire in 1978 was severe enough to cause some starvation and calls for international relief.

Nevertheless it is true that the most disastrous droughts tend to strike in the more arid regions, those where mean annual rainfall is below 1000mm. What makes for disaster–human mortality and severe economic and social disruption–is that the countries involved are among the continent's poorest, with few means to respond to catastrophic food shortages, while the local subsistence economy is particularly vulnerable in that quite small rainfall margins in the relatively short rainy season are of critical importance. The list of the countries worst affected by the long drought which finally produced a starvation crisis in 1973 is indicative: Mauritania, Mali, Upper Volta, Niger, Chad, western and northern parts of Sudan, Ethiopia and Somalia. Parts of other countries were affected by the drought, notably Senegal, The Gambia, northern Nigeria and northern Kenya, but here human starvation was largely averted because of larger national food stocks or better possibilities for importing food early, a better infrastructure of roads and transport for relief distribution, a larger number of accessible urban centres, and, not least, large southward, highland or coastal areas outside the main drought area which could absorb, if only temporarily, some refugees from the drought.

Any such generalization is subject to exceptions, and here the case of Ethiopia presents the greatest challenge. It is likely that 100 000 or more drought victims perished from starvation and related disease between 1972 and 1975; probably considerably more than famine deaths across the Sahel. Ethiopia is one of Africa's poorest and most densely populated countries, with few roads penetrating the rugged terrain, and a high proportion of the mortality occurred in north-eastern farming areas although the far less densely populated rangelands inhabited by pastoralists were also severely affected. On the other hand, much of the most productive area of the country in the centre and west had good harvests in the critical 1972–3 period (see table on page 308), and the government held appreciable foreign assets which could have been converted to food imports. Much of the human loss could probably have been avoided if the Ethiopian government of Haile Selassie had responded less tardily to early warning from its own agricultural survey department (international agencies have also been criticized for their failure to apply sufficient pressure) and if the system of land tenure had not been so heavily weighted against the rights of farmers, many of whom were tenants of absentee landlords, to retain the product of their labours.

As with other natural catastrophes, there has been a tendency for observers to look upon the human disasters ensuing from drought in Africa as 'acts of man' rather than 'acts of God'. Just as earthquake victims in Central America may be those whom the social and economic system has consigned to precarious shanty towns on the margins of cities, so drought victims in Africa are those who have been consigned to the margins of productive land where they are increasingly vulnerable to the vagaries of climate. This notion gained considerable strength as a result of the Sahel drought. The very word 'sahel' derives from the Arabic term for 'edge' or 'border', in this case the southern margin of the Sahara Desert. A band of low scrub and grasses some 200 to 300km wide and stretching from Mauritania to the western part of the Sudan, the zone has a normal upper rainfall limit in the south of some 500mm per year and a lower limit in the north of about 200mm, although pastoral populations exploit the grass cover further north where rainfall may be below 100mm per year. In areas where rainfall is more than about 250mm farmers are usually able to cultivate grain (mostly sorghum and millet). Thus the Sahel is the meeting place of cultivators and pastoralists who depend

OVERALL CROP PERFORMANCE IN THE 1972–3 DROUGHT IN ETHIOPIA

Region	Number of districts reporting	Crop performance: percentage of districts reporting in each category			
		above normal	normal	below normal	substantially below normal
Arussi	20	5	70	15	10
Bale	11	82	9	9	0
Begemder and Simien	29	21	72	7	0
Eritrea	23	4	78	9	9
Gemu Goffa	17	6	82	12	0
Gojjam	22	14	82	4	0
Hararghe	22	23	39	30	9
Illubabor	14	22	64	14	0
Kefa	9	33	45	22	0
Shewa	72	17	54	21	0
Sidamo	23	22	78	0	0
Tigrai	42	6	84	2	8
Wellega	35	0	86	14	0
Wello	21	0	10	38	52
Total	370	14	65	14	7

Source: A. M. Hussein (ed.), *Rehab; Drought and Famine in Ethiopia* (London, 1976)

Top right: Galla pastoralists searching for forage and water during the 1973 drought in Ethiopia. Bottom right: Animal victims of the Sahelian drought, Niger, 1973

to varying degrees on an economic exchange of grain and livestock, but who also increasingly compete for the same land for cultivation and grazing. The drought which began in 1969–70 and reached a climax in 1972–3 hit both groups of people. There is some evidence that pastoralists, who are in a minority, suffered more deaths than farmers, and pastoralists who lost all or most of their herds faced greater long-term hardship than farmers who could at least hold on to their land, unlike some of their counterparts in Ethiopia.

Among the largely Muslim rural populations of the Sahel the drought was widely ascribed to the will of Allah and was considered by many of the older generation as a punishment for growing laxity in religious observances and moral conduct. This explanation may be considered to embrace a pressing social and economic problem, for town life and paid labour, often far from home regions, attracts young men and also some women away from the rigours of rural life, and pastoral families feel especially keenly the loss of young herdsmen who are needed to take livestock for far-grazing during the dry season.

International discussion of the Sahel disaster has focused on the special vulnerability of Sahel populations. Increasing populations depend on decreasingly productive land, which is overgrazed and overcultivated, and there is less and less room for manoeuvre when drought strikes. One school argues that since colonial times Sahel farmers have been encouraged to pursue an unbalanced economy, producing cotton and groundnuts for the international market and

paying insufficient attention to domestic food production and the preservation of soil quality. On the other hand it may not be unduly optimistic to note that local people must still have retained an impressive level of adaptation to environmental hazard since there was a mortality of well under 1 per cent of the population affected by the worst period of consecutive drought experienced in the Sahel since 1913.

Famine on whatever scale is, however, an unacceptable tragedy, particularly if a more secure future does not beckon. In the short term there has been a partially successful international effort to set up regional food stocks and contingency plans to respond to such disasters in Africa. This system, though inspired by drought, could insure countries against the worst human effects of other ravages, such as plagues of desert locusts (which threatened the Horn of Africa in 1978) or less dramatic epidemics of crop pests (grasshoppers, army-worm or cassava mite, which is spreading in East and Central Africa). In the long term there is considerable argument about how to safeguard populations in hazard-prone areas through development programmes. But here the subject rapidly moves away from the specific problem of natural hazard to the general problem of the eradication of poverty.

Disease

Although natural catastrophes periodically take a heavy toll in Africa they are, by any standard, outweighed by the ever-present natural

INFANT GROUPS AS A PERCENTAGE OF TOTAL POPULATION AND INFANT MORTALITY AS A PERCENTAGE OF TOTAL MORTALITY: THREE AFRICAN COUNTRIES AND DENMARK

Country	Group as percentage of total population		Deaths as percentage of total mortality	
	age 0–1 year	age 0–4 years	age 0–1 year	age 0–4 years
Liberia (1970/71)	3.1	17	43	57
Chad (1963/64/72)	—	15	—	37
Central African Republic (1959/60/65/66)	—	16	—	49
Denmark (1969)	1.5	8	2.2	2.9

Source: Based on data from *Action for Children* (Dag Hammarskjold Foundation, Uppsala, 1975)

hazard of acute and chronic disease. Over much of Africa life expectancy at birth is still barely 50 years, some 20 years less than the norm in developed countries. Most of this deficit is the result of accident and disease.

The visitor to Africa is sometimes struck by an apparent paradox. Having heard that life expectancy in Africa is short and disease is rife, he may be surprised to find an apparently strong, well-nourished and seemingly fit population by the standards of the industrialized world. The paradox is real: Africans suffer under an appalling load of infectious disease but much less from obesity, heart disease, stroke, diabetes, malignant disease and the other major causes of morbidity and mortality in the materially more affluent world. Moreover, disease does not strike at random but discriminates between adults and the young, between the sexes, the rich and the poor, and between different ecological settings. Approximately 25 per cent of the African population is below five years of age and it is in this group that most mortality from infectious disease occurs. Mortality in the first year of life is often found to be as high as 100 per 1000 in different regions, and between one and four years of age 30 per 1000 per annum. The table above shows the contrasting pattern of mortality in Africa and Europe.

Africa's major diseases are those which are found anywhere under conditions of material poverty; they are diseases which still occur in the developed nations but with a much reduced incidence. Worm infestations, intestinal infections, respiratory infections, tetanus and the common infectious diseases of childhood have in total a far greater impact on health than the more 'exotic' tropical diseases with which Africa is often associated. Indeed, with some exceptions, the term 'tropical disease' is something of a misnomer since it includes many infections which were common in Europe and North America until a century ago. Leprosy, cholera and some types of malaria, for example, were all found much farther north than their present distributions. Many others, including typhoid, plague, rabies and a range of intestinal infections and parasites are still found in parts of the industrialized world.

Although to speak of the 'average' in a continent as large and varied as Africa is inappropriate, the problems and diseases which affect the under-five age group are, nonetheless, remarkably similar from place to place. The newborn African child is on average much lighter than his Western counterpart. In part this may reflect the relatively small size of the mother but in areas where falciparum malaria is common, infection of the placenta may reduce the birth weight still further. Most infants are born healthy but are at risk from a number of infections. Neonatal tetanus causes many deaths in the week after birth. This results from contamination of the umbilical cord from the use of dirty instruments or medicaments: in parts of West Africa for example, cow dung is used as an umbilical dressing.

The overwhelming majority of African babies are breast-fed. During the first four to six months of life, when this is often the child's only source of food, the child may enjoy a period of comparatively good growth and freedom from disease, in part from the continuing immunity transferred from the mother before birth and from breast milk, and in part from the freedom from direct infection from food. With the introduction of solid food the diet becomes a major hazard. 'Weanling diarrhoea' affects many children at this time as the weaning foods used are often bacterially contaminated. This often causes a reduced rate of growth and chronic illness. Epidemics of diarrhoea from a range of different infectious agents leads to dehydration and death for many more.

Measles, often coming in seasonal epidemics at intervals of two or three years, takes a huge toll from the first years of life. Although this disease is now widely regarded as a trival and, with vaccination, increasingly rare disease in the developed countries, its effect on the younger, lighter African child already suffering from a range of other infections is devastating. In Africa the case mortality may average 3–5 per cent, although this may be conservative. A mortality of 38 per cent was recorded during an outbreak in Mali. Whooping cough in the African child may also be very serious and cause death or residual lung damage and disability. Polio is comparatively rare, although it exacts a constant toll of life and, perhaps worse, leaves many survivors crippled and an economic and social burden to their families. Surveys in southern Africa show up to 6 per cent of children suffering from some degree of residual paralysis. Malaria in some

parts of sub-Saharan Africa may cause as many as half of all deaths below five years of age. First infection often occurs in the first year of life. Recurrent bouts of fever and a high risk of death from cerebral malaria and anaemia give way by the age of three to four years to a relative immunity for survivors. Tuberculosis is common in young African children.

Malnutrition may in some degree affect as many as half of all children in the rural areas and slums of Africa. At the extreme it presents itself in two main forms. Marasmus, when the child is wasted, is the most common and can be found in every area of the continent. Kwashiorkor is associated with swelling (oedema) of the feet and may occur in children who have more body fat and who are seemingly 'better nourished'. Isolated cases of kwashiorkor are seen in many areas; but it is most common in those places where the diet is based on cassava, as in an expanding area of West Africa, and in the areas where the staple diet is plantain. Both of these foods are low in protein. But the direct causes of malnutrition are still to a large extent a matter of debate. Outright food shortage in the family, at least outside of famine conditions and of the cash economy of towns (as opposed to 'self-sufficient' rural areas) is probably the least common cause. Infection, by increasing the requirement of food, reducing absorption and causing a loss of appetite accounts for much malnutrition. Late weaning, the use of starchy weaning foods and bad mothercraft have probably been blamed too much and too widely as the primary cause. The African household is more often than not kept swept and clean. But bacteriological cleanliness is impossible to achieve when there are few utensils, an earth floor, a pit privy or no regular means of sanitation. The demands on a mother's time may also be many. In The Gambia, for example, a baby born early in the year when the demands for agricultural labour are least may be kept at the breast for several months. Later in the year when the mother must travel to distant rice fields, the baby must be left behind, and of necessity solid food will be introduced at an early age.

At older ages mortality from infectious disease falls, although the adult African may still be regularly affected by ill-health. In much of monsoon Africa, each adult can regularly expect a bout of malaria in the mid-rains as immunity is re-established. Many may expect to suffer regularly from diarrhoea and dysentery; many develop tuberculosis. Much misery, loss of labour and sometimes death are still caused by illness and conditions which are no more than an irritation elsewhere. Hernias, hydroceles, infections of the hand and foot, accidents, cataract, conjunctivitis, blindness from the late effects of trachoma and a host of other minor and not so minor diseases may occur. Gonorrhoea and other venereal diseases are of epidemic proportions even in rural areas over much of Africa and are a leading cause of female infertility. Women may expect to have regular pregnancies beginning at an early age and to suffer the risk of chronic ill-health from anaemia and death in pregnancy and childbirth.

THE PATTERN OF INFECTION OBSERVED IN A GAMBIAN CHILD FROM BIRTH (8 JANUARY 1962) TO TWO YEARS

Age in months	Infections noted
0+	—
3	P; DV; RTI
6	P; D; RTI ⎫
9	⎬ M
12	C; WC ⎭
15	RTI; DV; SS
18	RTI; C; D; A; SS ⎫
21	P; M; RTI ⎬ M
24	⎭

Key: P = pyrexia (fever); D = diarrhoea; V = vomiting; RTI = respiratory tract infection; C = conjunctivitis; WC = whooping cough; SS = skin sepsis; A = ascariasis (roundworm); M = malaria

Source: adapted from *Technologies for Rural Health* (Royal Society, London, 1977)

Of the 'tropical' diseases many are important, but to a very variable extent in different areas of the continent. Schistosomiasis is outranked only by malaria and tuberculosis as a public health problem and affects some tens of millions of people. Two main forms are found: *Schistosoma mansori* and *S. lenatobium*, the former causing recurrent bloody diarrhoea, and the latter the loss of blood in the urine. Prevalence rates vary widely, but in some areas where the infection is common it may be considered to be abnormal not to pass blood in the urine by adolescence. The disease is spread by contact with water containing specific types of snail, and is becoming more widely distributed with the extension of irrigation in agriculture. Leprosy is endemic in much of Africa and at any one time may affect about 0.5 per cent of many populations. Onchocerciasis ('river blindness') caused by a filarial worm and spread by the black fly is responsible for much blindness in the river valleys of West and Central Africa. Trypanosomiasis ('sleeping sickness'), transmitted by the tsetse fly may be becoming more common after a period of decline. Cholera, reintroduced to sub-Saharan Africa in the early 1970s, is now found continent-wide. Epidemics have caused great loss of life in many areas, and mortality from untreated cholera may rise to as high as 60 per cent of sufferers. Huge epidemics of meningococcal meningitis occur in the dry season in a broad sweep from Ghana and Upper Volta across the Sahel to Ethiopia.

Natural catastrophes in Africa receive more international media coverage and public concern than the daily toll of disease. In 1973 the popular image of Ethiopia as a land of exotic imperial splendour was suddenly replaced by the image of 100 000 people starving to death. But a rough calculation suggests that the normal difference in death rates between Ethiopia and Europe means that some 500 000 'extra deaths' occur yearly in Ethiopia, and the vast majority of these are due to disease and chronic malnutrition.   *J.H.&J.S.*

Conservation

National parks and game reserves are the backbone of nature conservation in Africa. While there are many reserves of lesser status, and some statutes to control hunting and other threats to wildlife in most countries, there is seldom the cash, the staff, or the wide public support to ensure their effectiveness. Indeed, the visitor to Africa who is enthusiastic about nature conservation, his picture derived perhaps from the cinema or television, will find that the majority of Africans believe on the contrary that there are national tasks that are far more important. To a few nature conservation may even be seen as no more than an elitist foreign notion.

It is true that much of the structure of nature conservation dates from before independence. The first national parks (in 1929) were created by one of the most centralized administrations, namely the Belgian Congo (now Zaire). The French colonial territories in West Africa followed this lead and were followed in turn by the British territories in East Africa, southern Africa and finally British West Africa.

The areas chosen as parks were usually zones that were thought to be uninhabited and unsuitable for agriculture. In many places they served as a 'no-man's-land' along a national frontier. The prime function of the parks or reserves was the protection, usually for viewing, but at first sometimes for the hunt, of large and spectacular species, notably the elephant, lion, and the various antelopes. One early concern was to protect smallholdings from depredation by marauding animals. Hence fences or deep ditches were built up against inhabited land, not to keep people out, but to keep marauding animals in. Some parks, especially in East Africa, were also conserved for their natural topographic beauty (as in Kenya and Uganda).

Even before the age of cheap energy in the west, some parks, mainly those in East and South Africa, were attracting large numbers of visitors. They employed a range of expatriate and local staff in various wardening capacities, and usually boasted a comfortable rest-house and a number of guides.

After independence, despite some radical reappraisal of the role of such blatantly un-African institutions, most parks were retained. They served the two purposes of prestige (as elsewhere in the world) and as a source of much-needed foreign currency. Kenya, in particular, earns more from tourism★ – itself overwhelmingly dependent on the wildlife parks – than from any other source. The number of visitors to the Kenya parks rose from about 11 000 in 1965 to 1 534 000 in 1975. Many other countries would like to believe that their parks have some of this potential. Most governments can afford the luxury of a park since few are in areas of serious land-use conflict, although none is completely free of these. In Kenya Kikuyu smallholdings have now spread right to the boundary of the Aberdare National Park and there are reputedly many losses of cattle to wild marauding carnivores. In the south of Kenya and in Tanzania the livestock of the Masai still graze part of the Masai Maru Reserve and the Serengeti Park. The attractiveness of the idea of parks lingers on despite these conflicts and new ones are still being created.

The map on page 313 shows the parks in sub-Saharan Africa that meet the rather stringent criteria of the International Union for the Conservation of Nature (IUCN). This means that most of them are, among other things, owned by the state and free of other land users. Several other reserves of lesser status appear on the IUCN list, many indeed meeting its requirements as national parks, but not named as such in the country concerned. Several more areas are termed parks in various countries but are not acknowledged by the IUCN. Many of these less closely controlled parks have facilities quite equal to many of those on the IUCN list.

Elephants and tourist buses in a game park in Kenya

The savannas of eastern and southern Africa undoubtedly have the greatest potential for viewing the large and spectacular species. In West Africa hunting has eliminated many of these animals or reduced them to very small numbers. While elephants still survive, few can be seen west of Nigeria and few enough in Nigeria itself. The giraffe has disappeared from most of the Sahel. Lions are very rare, and only the smaller antelope survive and then in small numbers. The water-loving hippopotamuses and crocodiles are to be seen in some rivers, but the rare dugongs are so shy that few can hope to see them. There has been a similar depredation of the larger animals in the Sudan. Where visitors 50 years ago reported giraffes and kudus in central Kordofan, their visits are now very rare, if not unknown. Only in the south of the Sudan do these species survive.

The rich grasslands of East Africa not only allow easy viewing, but may also have a higher inherent carrying capacity for the popular species. The Serengeti National Park in Tanzania boasts 24 species of antelopes, as well as elephants, black rhinoceroses, giraffes, hunting dogs, buffaloes, lions, civets, genets, cheetahs, caracals, servals, hyenas and zebras, to name only a few species. The grazing ungulates occur in staggeringly large numbers. In South Africa the Kruger Park boasts equivalent numbers of species. Most of the larger parks support a residential visitor centre aimed almost wholly at the tourist market. Their accommodation is often luxurious and they allow painless and excellent viewing, often at close quarters. Most too are well served with a network of all-weather roads, and a subsidiary network of dry-season tracks that can even take domestic cars. Most will supply guides, and some even offer viewing from the air.

The original philosophy behind the creation of the parks, following largely the notion pioneered in the USA (which, unlike Europe, also had large wilderness areas), was to set aside an area from which interference would be excluded and in which the animals were free and unmolested. This was seen as sufficient to ensure the survival of the protected species. There was no thought of management beyond that needed to ensure that visitors should get the best opportunity to see the animals and rest in comfort and safety and that marauding should be kept to acceptable limits. Some artificial waterholes enabled the animals to be seen even more easily.

Had the land use inside and outside the parks remained unaltered, this policy might have succeeded, but changes have occurred in both. It was not then understood just how widely the management of grazing by herdsmen had modified the vegetation: deliberate burning and domestic grazing had often been the factor that had kept the scrub at bay and had therefore allowed the expansion of grassland and its ungulates. In some wetter places clearance for agriculture had kept the thick forest back: in the high and wet Aberdare Mountains few spots of primary forest remained uncleared, and protection has meant, in many places, the invasion of dense woodland which discourages some species and makes viewing difficult.

The more important agent of change was outside the park boundary. An explosion in the human population, and the creation of peace, allowed the settlement of land on a scale never seen before in Africa. This expansion of cultivation inevitably funnelled the large mammals into the parks, and drastically affected their patterns of seasonal migration between others. Few of these changes have been properly documented, so that it is usually impossible to assign with certainty the blame for what appears to be an overpopulation of animals or unusually high levels of disease among them to climatic or cultural changes or to 'natural' fluctuations. The case of the elephants in Tsavo National Park in Kenya is an example: is their wholesale destruction of trees due to natural migration, to overpopulation due to changes in the land use of the surrounding area, to climatic changes, or even to some biological cycle? Whatever their cause, these changes mean that more and different kinds of management are needed. Animal populations now often need to be kept in check by culling, and grasslands may have to be cleared by fire if the large herds of grazing animals for which the parks are well known are to be maintained. It is clear that much more needs to be known about the animals and their history before a sound policy can be evolved.

KEY

▪	Under 250 000 sq km
◾	250 000 – 500 000 sq km
◼	500 000 – 1 million sq km
⬛	Over 1 million sq km

NATIONAL PARKS APPROVED BY THE IUCN (1978)

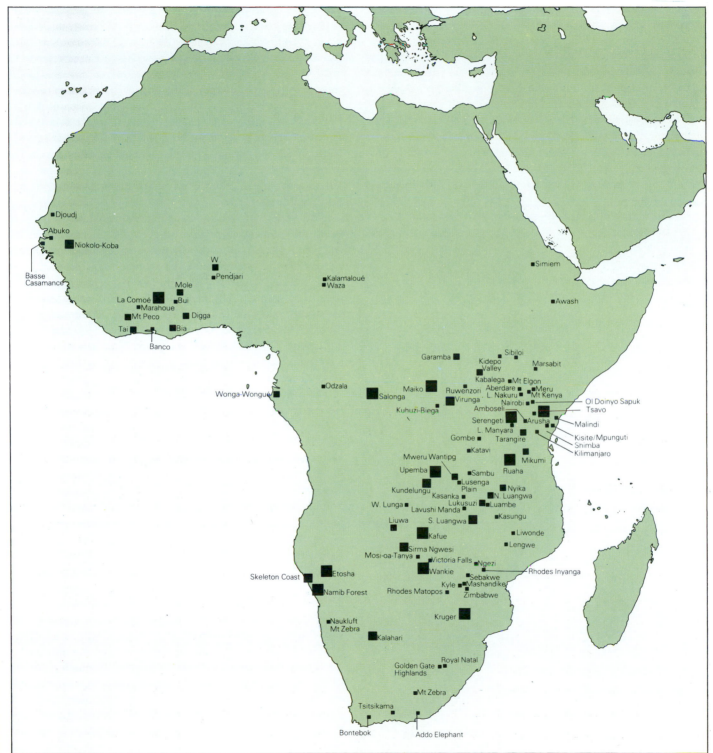

A serious concern among nature conservationists is that a policy that depends only on isolated reserves inevitably leads to these becoming 'islands' in a sea of cultivation. Theory predicts that such isolation will inevitably lead to a slow loss of species (as on real islands). The Mkomazi Game Reserve in Tanzania, for example, has already lost four large mammal species out of its complement of 43 in the 25 years since its establishment. Theory predicts that only 22 will survive in 300 years time even if there is some immigration.

The most serious threat to the large game, however, is neither the pressure of land use, nor slow decline, but the devastating depredation by hunters. Hunting under licence was permitted on a small scale in many parks at first, but this privilege has been progressively curtailed. The real threat now is the organized poacher, hunting often at night when game can be dazzled by car headlights, and killing in large numbers to sell horns, skins or ivory very profitably to the tourist or abroad to markets such as South-East Asia where there is a huge demand for ivory and rhinoceros-horn. The whole enterprise from the kill to the export is illegal in most countries, and yet vast. In East Africa the most serious threat is to the rhinoceros, but the elephant, dik-dik, cheetah and some other species are also endangered. There are those who seriously believe the rhinoceros will soon become extinct in some East African countries. Even the elephant may follow. Many believe that this trade can only be stopped by ensuring that tourists deny themselves any animal souvenirs. Nevertheless, political and moral pressure on some governments to ensure that their anti-poaching laws are enforced may also have some effect.

Not surprisingly, the largest of Africa's plants were also those which most dramatically suffered the burden of exploitation: the continent's forests* have everywhere been exploited for their timber. Regrettably, the foresters, unlike the animal hunters, have been slow to revise their wasteful and thoughtless exploitation. Many forests have been repeatedly plundered for their largest and most ecologically and economically important trees. Huge hectarages, especially in the uplands, have been totally cleared and planted with alien species. While these provide a greater renewable resource than the original forest, few elements of the native flora or fauna can survive in them.

The concentration on the conservation of large organisms has fortunately meant that large reserves have been created. The Serengeti National Park in Tanzania is 14500sq km in extent, and Ansongo-Menaka National Park in Mali is 17500sq km. The real beauty of large reserves lies in the fact that in order to be big enough to hold the largest organisms they are also likely to hold numerous small creatures, who can live there in comparative safety from interference. Because management is unlikely to be applied to them and little interest focused on them adverse situations are unlikely to be created. Moreover, when so much remains to be discovered about the fuctioning of ecosystems, especially in areas where few of the extant organisms are well known, the conservation of habitats is, for the present, the only feasible approach. Even for such a well-known group of organisms as the birds, new species are discovered in Africa almost annually, so that any manager of a reserve may expect to have under his control numerous creatures as yet unknown to science. The African parks and reserves are therefore a very precious resource for the scientific community at large, the responsibility for which must be shared with richer countries. However, despite the many reserves that now exist, the conservationist in Africa, as elsewhere in the world, cannot afford to be complacent if he is to retain the wealth of the African vegetation* and fauna,* especially as effective conservation outside the reserves has been neglected. *A.W. & B.W.*

Ivory poachers dismembering an elephant in East Africa

Development

By any reasonable criteria the vast majority of the nations which comprise the African continent rank among the world's poor. Per capita income is low, agriculture is plagued by low productivity and industrial activity though growing, is still a relatively small part of the economy as a whole. Moreover, Africa's poverty is not limited to strictly economic difficulties; health care is uniformly inadequate, nutrition is poor and education remains deficient in quantity and largely inappropriate in quality.

Measuring development

Although a number of statistical criteria have been advanced to measure development the most widely used and accepted are based on estimates of a nation's Gross National Product (GNP) or Gross Domestic Product (GDP). A number of criticisms have, however, been levelled against the reliability and accuracy of these figures. First, it has been argued that these statistics tend to underestimate the value of goods and services produced in the subsistence sector of the economy. This criticism is especially important in the African context, in which subsistence production tends to be dominant. Second, when these national product statistics are divided by a nation's population to create per capita product figures they tend to disguise the wide differences in income within nations. In Africa, as in most of the rest of the 'developing world', income differences within nations are much greater than in the industrialized world so that per capita national product statistics cannot be taken as an accurate representation of the condition of the average inhabitant. Third, since the value of the currencies of many African nations are controlled by their national treasuries, the conversion of the local value of goods and services into international equivalents, usually the US dollar, is fraught with difficulties. Thus, a clear understanding of the value and stability of a given nation's currency becomes essential to a realistic evaluation of national product statistics. Finally, and perhaps most importantly in the African context, the collection of valid economic and social statistics for many nations on the continent is nearly impossible. Not only national product statistics but virtually all other statistical materials must be treated with extreme care in the African context as a consequence of the lack of reliability of the primary data on which such statistics are based.

Population and development

The problem of economic development is often associated with 'overpopulation' in an erroneous manner. This is especially true in the case of Africa. In general the continent is lightly peopled, having an average population density of only 14 per sq km, which compares with a world average of about 30 per sq km. The average, however,

POPULATION, AREA, GROSS NATIONAL PRODUCT (GNP) PER CAPITA AND GROWTH OF GNP: SELECTED AFRICAN COUNTRIES

Country	Population mid-1976 millions	Area thousands sq km	GNP per capita 1976 US$	Percentage average annual growth of GNP 1960–76
Algeria	16.2	2 382	990	1.7
Angola	5.5	1 247	330	3.0
Benin	3.2	113	130	0.1
Burundi	3.8	28	120	2.3
Cameroon	7.6	475	290	2.8
Central African Republic	1.8	623	230	0.3
Chad	4.1	1 284	120	−1.1
Congo	1.4	342	520	2.8
Egypt	38.1	1 001	280	1.9
Ethiopia	28.7	1 222	100	1.9
Ghana	10.1	239	580	−0.1
Guinea	5.7	246	150	0.4
Ivory Coast	7.0	322	610	3.4
Kenya	13.8	583	240	2.6
Lesotho	1.2	30	170	4.6
Liberia	1.6	111	450	2.0
Libya	2.5	1 760	6310	10.2
Madagascar	9.1	587	200	−0.1
Malawi	5.2	118	140	4.1
Mali	5.8	1 240	100	0.9
Mauritania	1.4	1 031	340	3.7
Morocco	17.2	459	540	2.1
Mozambique	9.5	783	170	1.4
Niger	4.7	1 267	160	−1.1
Nigeria	77.1	924	380	3.5
Rwanda	4.2	26	110	0.8
Senegal	5.1	196	390	−0.7
Sierra Leone	3.1	72	200	1.1
Somalia	3.3	638	110	−0.3
Sudan	15.9	2 506	290	0.4
Tanzania	15.1	945	180	2.6
Togo	2.3	56	260	4.1
Tunisia	5.7	164	840	4.1
Uganda	11.9	241	240	1.0
Upper Volta	6.2	274	110	0.8
Zaire	25.4	2 345	140	1.4
Zambia	5.1	753	440	1.7
Zimbabwe	6.5	390	550	2.2

Source: *World Bank Statistical Yearbook 1978* (Washington DC, 1978)

STRUCTURE OF POPULATION: SELECTED AFRICAN COUNTRIES

Country	Percentage of population					
	in urban areas		below age 15		of working age (15–64 years)	
	1960	1975	1960	1975	1960	1975
Algeria	31	50	44	48	52	49
Angola	10	18	43	42	55	55
Benin	10	18	44	45	53	52
Burundi	2	4	43	43	55	54
Cameroon	13	24	39	40	59	57
Central African Republic	19	36	42	42	54	55
Chad	7	14	45	40	53	57
Congo	27	40	42	42	55	54
Egypt	38	48	42	41	55	56
Ethiopia	7	11	43	44	54	54
Ghana	23	32	47	48	52	50
Guinea	10	20	42	43	55	54
Ivory Coast	11	20	42	43	55	54
Kenya	7	11	47	47	51	51
Lesotho	1	3	38	38	57	56
Liberia	9	28	41	41	56	55
Libya	23	31	43	44	53	53
Madagascar	12	18	45	45	53	52
Malawi	4	6	40	45	56	51
Mali	10	14	44	44	54	53
Mauritania	7	11	42	42	55	55
Morocco	30	38	45	47	53	49
Mozambique	4	6	42	43	56	54
Niger	6	9	46	46	52	52
Nigeria	18	29	45	45	54	53
Rwanda	2	4	45	44	52	53
Senegal	22	28	43	43	56	54
Sierra Leone	12	15	42	43	54	54
Somalia	18	28	44	45	54	53
Sudan	9	13	44	45	53	52
Tanzania	5	7	46	47	51	51
Togo	10	14	45	46	53	52
Tunisia	32	47	43	44	53	52
Uganda	5	8	44	44	53	53
Upper Volta	5	8	42	43	55	54
Zaire	20	26	44	44	53	53
Zambia	18	37	47	48	51	50
Zimbabwe	16	20	48	48	49	51

Source: *World Bank Statistical Yearbook 1978* (Washington DC, 1978)

conceals a great diversity. In some areas, notably the Nile Valley and parts of Nigeria, population densities approach Asian levels while in the Sahelian states, Central and southern Africa densities fall below 10 per sq km. While overpopulation is not a pressing problem for the continent as a whole in an absolute sense, even lightly peopled areas can be said to have a 'population problem' in relation to the utilization of the resource base which is available to them. In numerous areas farming techniques are extensive and require large amounts of fallow land to refertilize the soil; in others, on the fringe of deserts, nomadic and semi-nomadic pastoralists★ require great tracts of land to prevent overgrazing, which will in turn have tragic ecological effects.

Similar difficulties arise in relation to the increasingly urban nature of the continent's population. Pushed off the land by the growing difficulties of subsistence farming in an increasingly commoditized society and drawn to urban areas by the prospect of wage employment, no matter how illusory, an ever larger proportion of the population finds itself swelling the ranks of the unemployed and under-employed in cities such as Lagos, Cairo and Nairobi. These migrants stretch the social services of these urban centres well beyond breaking point and constitute a major development problem.

The structure of the population, with its extreme bias to the very young, constitutes yet another development difficulty. Throughout the continent child mortality remains high, thus large families remain the best insurance against poverty in old age, and although children play an important role in subsistence farming and craft activity, they do constitute a disproportionate burden on the adult working population.

There is little prospect of resolving the difficulties posed by the location and structure of Africa's population without a major attack on both the rural conditions which lead to large family size and migration, and the low level of industrial development which condemns large segments of the urban population to a marginal existence. Only through such essential modifications of the economy will the development problems generated by the nature of Africa's population be ameliorated.

Agriculture and development

Throughout the continent agriculture★ remains both the basis of the economy and the major occupation of the vast majority of the population. With the exception of a small plantation sector, agriculture remains overwhelmingly the preserve of small peasant cultivators. In general, agricultural techniques have remained unchanged over a long period of time. However, important innovations have been made by peasant farmers especially in the adoption of new crops over the past century. The most important of these have focused on export production, with coffee, cocoa and, in the plantation sector, tea being among the most important.

The most serious problem confronting the agricultural sector

CONTRIBUTION OF AGRICULTURE TO GROSS DOMESTIC PRODUCT (GDP) AND AVERAGE GROWTH PER YEAR: SELECTED AFRICAN COUNTRIES

Country	Percentage contribution of agriculture to GDP		Average annual growth of agricultural sector of GDP	
	1960	1976	1960–70	1970–6
Algeria	21	7	4.4	6.2
Angola	50	29	4.0	−0.7
Benin	*	39	*	−0.3
Burundi	*	64	*	1.0
Cameroon	48	33	6.5	3.4
Central African Republic	45	37	0.8	1.9
Chad	55	52	1.8	−1.3
Congo	16	15	4.6	−7.2
Egypt	30	29	2.9	3.0
Ethiopia	65	50	2.2	0.9
Ghana	41	49	3.7	1.3
Guinea	*	43	2.1	10.2
Ivory Coast	43	25	4.2	3.5
Kenya	38	30	5.9	1.6
Lesotho	73	38	*	*
Liberia	40	29	6.3	4.9
Libya	14	3	23.3	3.8
Madagascar	37	29	*	1.2
Malawi	58	45	2.9	5.5
Mali	55	38	1.3	−0.8
Mauritania	57	35	2.4	−2.1
Morocco	29	21	4.2	0.6
Mozambique	55	45	2.1	2.1
Niger	66	47	3.3	−4.0
Nigeria	63	23	−0.5	−0.2
Rwanda	81	52	*	3.3
Senegal	30	28	1.9	3.4
Sierra Leone	*	32	1.4	2.0
Somalia	45	31	−1.5	−1.2
Sudan	58	41	3.3	8.8
Tanzania	57	45	3.7	2.5
Togo	55	25	4.3	3.0
Tunisia	24	21	4.6	9.4
Uganda	52	55	2.8	1.3
Upper Volta	55	34	0.0	3.2
Zaire	30	16	3.9	1.9
Zambia	11	14	2.0	3.2
Zimbabwe	18	16	*	*

* Not available

Source: *World Bank Statistical Yearbook 1978* (Washington DC, 1978)

today is the increased pressure of having to feed a rapidly growing urban population. Attemps to increase food production have focused in large measure on the introduction of technological innovation. Over the last few decades mechanization, irrigation, improved seed strains and the increased use of fertilizers have figured importantly in the attempt to increase output. In general, however, these technological solutions have met with limited success.

Although attempts to resolve the problem of agricultural development through the introduction of various technological solutions continue, it has now been generally recognized that the low productivity of the agricultural sector is at least as much a problem of social organization as of technological deficiency. Thus land reform (particularly in North Africa), cooperatives, credit schemes, farming collectives–notably *ujamaa* schemes in Tanzania–and state-run farms (particularly in Guinea) have all made an appearance on the African scene. No single strategy has, however, proved to be outstandingly successful.

A closely related problem is the manner in which the agricultural sector is related to other areas of the economy. It is generally conceded that any significant, long-term gains in agricultural productivity will have to be linked to advance in agro-allied industries such as fertilizer, insecticide, and farm equipment production. Unfortunately, the African economy is characterized by the dearth of such linkages and the creation of mutually reinforcing ties between agriculture and industry remains a major challenge.

Development and trade

The role of Africa in the international market is that of a primary goods exporter and an importer of manufactured goods. Thus, the degree to which international trade* benefits the nations of Africa in economic terms is directly dependent upon the terms of trade between primary and manufactured goods products. Throughout the period 1954–6 to 1968–70 the continent experienced a 10 per cent deterioration in the terms of trade, a deterioration which was largely due to the increase in manufactured goods prices. From 1973 onward Africa has benefited from a major commodity boom, accompanied by about a 40 per cent improvement in the terms of trade over the period 1970–6.

Because the terms of trade are calculated on the basis of the ratio of the unit value of imports to the unit value of exports without regard to changes in quantity they are apt to be misleading. While it is true that over the last six or seven years Africa has been able to obtain higher prices for its exports, it has only been able to increase the volume of its exports by some 2 per cent. On the import side, however, the growth in volume has been some 50 per cent. The orthodox view of this state of affairs stresses that it demonstrates Africa's growing ability to import manufactured goods from the developed world. However, the current situation also highlights several important problems in

TERMS OF TRADE[1]

Region	1960	1965	1967	1968	1969	1971	1972	1973	1974	1975	1976
Developed market economies	96	98	99	99	99	99	100	99	87	90	89
Developing market economies	103	99	99	100	101	104	102	112	156	140	146
AFRICA	104	96	100	102	106	101	101	113	154	130	141

[1]Unit value index of exports divided by the unit value index of imports. 1970 = 100

Source: *Statistical Yearbook 1978* (UN, New York, 1979)

the structure of Africa's commerce with the rest of the world. First, because Africa has only been able to marginally increase the volume of its exports, it has only minimally benefited from the current commodity boom. Second, the major consequence of the boom, the increase in imported manufactured goods, has had negative effects on African manufacturing, with the annual rate of growth in this sector dropping from over 9 per cent during the period 1961–5 to less than 3 per cent in 1976.

In order to understand why the improvement in the terms of trade has not been translated into a stimulus to development in the manufacturing sector it is necessary to enumerate some of the major obstacles to industrial development on the continent.

Industry and development

Although the level of industrial activity in Africa remains low in comparison to that in the developed nations, the rate of industrial growth on the continent has been comparatively high. An examination of the period 1930–60 reveals that while industrial activity in Africa grew at an average rate of about 6 per cent per year, the rate of growth for industrialized nations was about 4.5 per cent and for the world as a whole 4.6 per cent. This high rate of growth reflects in large measure the negligible base of industrial activity at the origin of this statistical series. In the 1970s African industrial growth slowed as a consequence of the worldwide recession.

A major problem of economic development lies in the structure of the continent's industrial sector. At present, primary industries such as mining and minerals processing industries dominate the non-agricultural areas of the economy. These are, for the most part, of long standing and their expansion has had little impact on the remainder of the economy. Their lack of linkages to secondary industry has prevented them from becoming an important force for economic growth and some observers have even maintained that their continued expansion has created a distortion in the continent's economy.

The manufacturing sector is of more recent origin than primary goods production and it is to this sector that the continent's hopes for

rapid economic development are tied. With the exception of North Africa, which has taken advantage of both its geographical position and cheap labour supply to compete in the European market, African manufacturing* has tended to concentrate on light manufacturing directly linked to a strategy of import substitution. Among such locally produced import substitutes, cigarettes, beverages and textiles have figured prominently. More recently, the assembly of imported components into finished vehicles and electronics equipment has gained importance.

A major problem in the development of the manufacturing sector has been the limited size of most national markets, although here Nigeria and Egypt constitute important exceptions. Attempts to resolve this difficulty through the creation of regional customs unions, such as the now defunct East African Community* and the Economic Community of West African States (ECOWAS),* have proved only marginally successful and have lacked necessary political stability. A second difficulty with the development of manufacturing and industry in general has been that of foreign ownership. Put bluntly, the calculations of foreign investors are rarely in total agreement with the economic development strategies of African states. Moreover, some African economists have argued that foreign ownership has militated against the development of managerial skills among African nationals and that foreign control of production processes has worked against a diffusion of technical skills.

In general, then, the major difficulties of African industrial development centre on its lack of integration with the economy as a whole and its primary resource based focus. Thus it can be seen that any real evaluation of a nation's industrial growth must take into account not only growth rates but the structural nature of that industrial growth.

Social welfare

Nutritionists regard an average daily intake of at least 2500 calories as an important prerequisite of a healthy life. Nearly every African nation has a sizeable proportion of its inhabitants subsisting below this prescribed level. Moreover, Africans—especially the young—are

PERCENTAGE CONTRIBUTION OF INDUSTRY TO GROSS DOMESTIC PRODUCT (GDP) AND AVERAGE ANNUAL GROWTH OF INDUSTRIAL SECTOR: SELECTED AFRICAN COUNTRIES

Country	GDP percentage contribution of industry		Industrial sector of GDP average annual growth	
	1960	1976	1960–70	1970–6
Algeria	24	57	10.5	16.4
Angola	8	27	9.8	11.6
Benin	*	20	*	9.8
Burundi	*	15	*	4.3
Cameroon	10	20	7.7	3.3
Central African Republic	12	23	2.8	2.8
Chad	12	14	3.9	8.1
Congo	18	43	7.6	22.6
Egypt	24	30	5.4	4.3
Ethiopia	12	15	7.4	16
Ghana	19	25	6.7	4.2
Guinea	*	33	6.2	3.8
Ivory Coast	14	20	11.6	7.9
Kenya	18	23	7.5	9.8
Lesotho	*	8	*	*
Liberia	37	37	7.8	0.3
Libya	89	65	31.3	−7.4
Madagascar	10	20	*	2.0
Malawi	11	22	13.9	12.4
Mali	10	17	4.0	8.9
Mauritania	21	37	15.8	7.1
Morocco	24	31	4.2	7.8
Mozambique	9	15	10.8	−3.8
Niger	10	24	11.1	10.0
Nigeria	11	50	13.8	12.6
Rwanda	7	22	*	8.4
Senegal	20	24	3.7	3.9
Sierra Leone	*	23	5.5	4.7
Somalia	17	8	3.3	10.3
Sudan	15	16	1.7	2.8
Tanzania	11	16	8.0	2.9
Togo	16	21	7.3	7.0
Tunisia	18	30	8.7	10.1
Uganda	13	8	7.8	−6.7
Upper Volta	13	19	3.8	7.0
Zaire	27	30	35.9	5.0
Zambia	63	41	−0.1	3.4
Zimbabwe	35	40	*	*

*Not available

Source: *World Bank Statistical Yearbook 1978* (Washington DC, 1978)

in general deficient in protein intake as well. The major reason for these deficiencies is the low productivity in the agricultural sector. An important secondary reason in some areas is that the shift of production into cash crops for export has changed dietary patterns. This is especially important in areas which have shifted from grain or yam production into the cultivation of cassava, which while requiring lower labour inputs is quite low in protein content. Dietary deficiencies are in no small way related to another major development problem, the high incidence of disease.

Nutritional deficiency is directly responsible for clinical malnutrition* and related problems such as the deficiency disease, kwashiorkor. In addition, it lowers resistance to other endemic diseases on the African continent, such as malaria, cholera and pneumonia. Sanitation remains largely non-existent in the overcrowded slum quarters of major cities while most rural areas are unlikely to have supplies of pure water. This situation inevitably gives rise to the high incidence of parasitic diseases, such as hookworm and schistosomiasis. For most of the continent the provision of medical care* such as hospitals and doctors remains woefully inadequate.

The expansion of education* on the African continent constitutes a major paradox of development. At independence the first generation of political leaders stressed the expansion of the educational system as a major feature of the development effort. The aim was twofold. On the one hand education was seen as a way of breaking the intellectual bondage of colonialism, on the other it was seen as the chief means of creating the appropriate skills necessary to advance economic growth. Consequently, enrolments expanded dramatically and education came to absorb a large share of the national financial resources. The result of this massive social investment has in many ways been disappointing.

Education, particularly the humanities-oriented education which was inherited from the former colonial powers, has done little to transform the African economy. Technological education has, in general, been thoroughly neglected. Thus the skills necessary for the creation of a well trained agricultural and industrial workforce have not been created despite the large financial commitment. In addition the problem has been compounded by the creation of a large class of school leavers, who, having been trained in the humanities, find that their lack of technical skill dooms them to a life of unemployment or severe under-employment. The task of retooling the educational systems of the continent remains a major one with only minimal progress having been made in this area.

The evolution of development strategies

The attainment of political independence in Africa was accompanied by optimistic predictions of rapid economic growth and development. By 1980, after two decades of independence, both politicians and economists had had to adjust to the reality of limited growth and the real possibility of economic stagnation. The limitations of development models and theories have become glaringly obvious and much of what has been written on the subject has been called into question by the experience of the 1960s and 1970s. At present it is fair to say that there is little consensus regarding either the origins of the development problem or its solution.

Development economics as a branch of economic science had its origins in Africa's colonial period. Colonies were almost universally seen by the colonizers as 'estates to be developed' and nearly all colonial powers paid at least lip-service to what was seen as the obligation to exploit the resources of colonial areas for the benefit of 'civilization'. Needless to say, however, during the colonial period development focused on those sectors of the economy which were seen as potentially profitable investments by the colonizers. Thus, emphasis was on the development of extractive industry and export crop agriculture and the necessary infrastructural improvements to make such endeavours viable. Comparatively little attention was paid to food production or social welfare measures and almost no effort at all was made to create an indigenous manufacturing sector. In addition, such development schemes as did exist were hampered by colonial fiscal restraint, the insufficient understanding of local ecological conditions and the often heavy-handed and oppressive implementation of social policies.

From 1945 on, the role of the colonial state in economic development was greatly expanded. The Keynesian reaction to the chaos of depression and war opened the door to the possibility of greater governmental interference in the workings of the economy and was instrumental in the creation of state-owned and run cooperatives and marketing boards in colonial areas such as Africa. Moreover, this shift in economic policy dovetailed with the needs of the colonizers themselves. The Second World War left the colonial powers both indebted and in danger of losing a large amount of their share of world trade. State management of the colonial economy permitted the profits accruing to the colonial governments to be used to repay war debts while produce marketing boards assured the continuation of imperial dominance in African commerce.

It was the post-war period which saw the budding discipline of development economics attain academic respectability. Development economics was concerned to reconcile the emerging nationalist demand for political independence with the Western need to maintain the supply of vital mineral and agricultural produce from colonial areas. The particular school of thought which reconciled these potentially conflicting interests was what has come to be known as 'growth economics'. As set forth by writers such as W.W. Rostow, W.A. Lewis and others, growth theory maintained that regions such as Africa could only develop by following the historic path of Western economic growth, a major aspect of which was a continued and expanded participation in the international market. Such a policy

assumed continuing dependence on primary goods exports and was in reality the continuation of earlier colonial policy with only slight modifications. The increase in state control did, however, provide indigenous nationalists with a role to play in the 'growth' economy through the administration of marketing boards, cooperatives and supply companies. In doing so nationalism was made compatible with the maintenance of a Western-dominated international economic order.

Thus the transition to independence did not signal a major break with the colonial experience of economic development. The newly independent nations of the African continent inherited dependent export-oriented national economies and had neither the capital, skills or leadership to embark on radically different economic policies. Attempts were made to lessen the dependence on the former colonial masters through overtures to the UN, the World Bank and the development agencies of the USA, yet here too thinking was largely dominated by the growth school.

The central proposition of the growth school, that African economies could follow the historical path of Western development by increasing their participation in international trade, has given rise to a number of criticisms in the years since independence. Much of this criticism centres around the proposition that the economic development of the West in itself precludes African emulation. Those who hold this view maintain that Western development took place at a generally lower level of technical expertise and in a period in which far smaller amounts of capital investment were needed for the establishment of a viable manufacturing sector. They further argue that the colonial experience itself has so distorted the African economy by emphasizing primary-goods production and export that the continued or expanded participation of Africa in the world economy as a primary-goods exporter can only lead to a worsening of the situation or what has been termed by critics 'growth without development'. A more recent criticism holds that successful imitation of the Western experience is impossible because the Western nations themselves were able to attain their present economic levels through access to the relatively cheap energy sources of the colonized world whereas at present such resources command extremely high prices relative to the past.

A second major tenet of the dominant growth school is that all savings in the economy should be reinvested in order to assure rapid economic growth. This proposition gives rise to a number of problems in the African context. Throughout the continent present levels of consumption are extremely low and there is tremendous pressure on governments to divert savings from investment to consumption. This is especially important in the realms of social services and education, which, although sometimes classed as social investments, do not directly lead to an increase in economic output as defined by the growth theorists. Moreover, the focus on economic growth does not address the important problem of economic inequality. In Africa, as in most developing regions, income distribution is highly uneven and a number of governments have concerned themselves with the closing of such income differentials. Such a course of action runs in diametric opposition to growth theory, which maintains that income differentials are necessary to promote needed savings and thus investment, the rich having (at least in theory) a much greater propensity to save – and invest – than the poor.

The emergence of such criticisms of the growth school of development has dovetailed in fundamental terms with the growing frustration of a number of African leaders who have witnessed their nations' failure to make significant economic gains in the post-independence period. Ghana under Kwame Nkrumah,* Algeria under Houari Boumedienne, Guinea under Sékou Touré,* and Tanzania under Julius Nyerere* have all invoked policies which challenge the growth school. More recent innovators in the field of economic development include the former Portuguese colonies of Angola, Mozambique and Guinea-Bissau as well as the Republic of the Congo. Though diverging with reference to particular policies, all have stressed a variant of socialism based on self-reliance and a commitment to higher living standards for the mass of the population as a precondition for economic development.

Socialist innovators have faced many of the same problems as those who have chosen or adhered to the policies of the growth school. The economic heritage of colonialism – chronically low levels of investment and productivity and inadequate management and planning – have all blocked progress on the development front. Only in mineral-rich Algeria have socialist policies made important gains in the manufacturing sector. Moreover, the deteriorating terms of trade for primary producers in the 1970s have forced states such as Tanzania to place even greater stress on the production and export of raw materials.

Given continuing world economic recession and Africa's chronic economic problems there is little reason to be optimistic with regard to economic development policies of whatever persuasion. Only in the case of petroleum production have mineral-rich African nations' export earnings kept pace with the dramatic inflation of the 1970s. Further, the deteriorating world economic situation has led the traditional aid donors in the West to curtail the flow of concessional capital resources. In such a climate African development promises to be a slow and painful process.

Changing aid strategies

Both the economic goals of development assistance and the strategies to meet them changed in the 1970s. For much of the 1960s the main focus of development assistance was the creation of what was seen as the necessary infrastructure of development. Roads, power-generating stations and the development of deep-water ports ranked high on the list of assistance priorities. The development of natural resources, especially mineral deposits and light manufacturing were also considered of prime importance.

The relative failure of such assistance to produce any dramatic gains in economic development and the emergence of a severe crisis in food production in Africa led to a major re-evaluation of the

INFLOW AND REPAYMENT OF MEDIUM- AND LONG-TERM PUBLIC LOANS: SELECTED AFRICAN COUNTRIES

Country	Gross inflow		Repayment of principal millions of US$		Net inflow	
	1970	1976	1970	1976	1970	1976
Algeria	292	1 938	33	433	259	1 505
Benin	2	31	1	6	1	25
Burundi	1	4	—	2	1	2
Cameroon	28	193	4	22	24	171
Central African Republic	10	23	2	5	8	18
Chad	6	26	2	5	4	21
Congo	30	53	6	10	24	43
Egypt	302	1 418	247	552	55	866
Ethiopia	27	73	15	14	12	59
Ghana	40	47	12	23	28	24
Guinea	110	661	10	37	102	642
Ivory Coast	76	355	27	109	49	246
Kenya	30	204	7	20	23	184
Lesotho	—	2	—	—	—	2
Liberia	7	34	11	14	−4	20
Madagascar	11	20	5	9	6	11
Malawi	38	36	3	7	35	29
Mali	21	39	1	3	20	36
Mauritania	4	158	3	65	1	93
Morocco	163	707	36	128	127	579
Niger	16	12	2	4	14	8
Nigeria	61	65	36	211	25	−146
Senegal	19	70	5	24	14	46
Sierra Leone	8	24	10	17	−2	7
Somalia	4	56	1	2	3	54
Sudan	39	389	21	63	18	326
Tanzania	50	117	10	15	40	102
Togo	5	62	2	9	3	53
Tunisia	82	365	44	69	38	296
Uganda	26	31	4	3	22	28
Upper Volta	2	25	2	3	—	22
Zaire	32	329	30	14	2	315
Zambia	335	270	31	45	304	225

Source: *World Development Report 1978* (World Bank, Washington DC, 1978)

development assistance strategy in the early 1970s, focusing on a reappraisal of the role of agriculture in the continent's economic development.

Rural development now forms a fundamental part of what has come to be known as the 'basic needs' strategy of development assistance. The basic needs strategy is an attempt to provide those who are considered Africa's poorest, the rural subsistence agriculturalists, with such necessities as safe water and primary education along with improved seed strains, fertilizers and technical assistance. The strategy is designed to improve agricultural productivity and at the same time halt the flow of migrants to the already overcrowded urban centres of the continent. Moreover, by doing so it is hoped that the output of food products will be sufficiently increased so as to permit the diversion of limited foreign exchange from food importation to more productive uses. The success or failure of the basic needs strategy will ultimately rest on whether there has been a correct appraisal of both the needs and desires of the long-neglected rural population and whether local government and elites will lend their cooperation to such an improvement in rural conditions.

The development assistance controversy

In order to understand the controversy surrounding development assistance it is necessary to understand that such assistance was first conceived in the period following the Second World War as a supplement to the commercial flow of capital and expertise from the developed to the underdeveloped nations of the world. Until the mid-1960s the view that such resources would 'flow naturally' from the one area to the other formed the basis of a consensus among development economists. Development assistance was to undertake those investments which private capital would not–such as the creation of basic infrastructural improvements. Thus from its origins, development assistance was closely associated with an economic viewpoint which rested on a faith in *laissez-faire*, private foreign investment as the major engine of growth.

Needless to say, development assistance has taken a considerably different outlook in the years since these views were current. It is today generally understood, if not always viewed with approval, that development assistance goes far beyond the role of merely supplementary investment. Indeed, for some of Africa's poorer nations development assistance funds have become the major form of capital importation.

The close historical relationship between development assistance and direct foreign investment has generated a number of problems. First, many African nations, though in desperate need of capital and technical expertise, are wary of the motives which lie behind the donor's generosity. President Nyerere of Tanzania is only one of many leaders to argue that the dependence on assistance funds places limitations on the choice of development strategies, particularly in those cases in which a state-planned or socialist path of development is chosen. The fact that assistance has at times since independence been used as an economic weapon in the ideological war between East and West, in which Africa has been a major arena, has compounded such difficulties. Other critics maintain that assistance funds are merely another device to tie the economies of Africa to the states of the industrial West. They point to the fact that much assistance is 'tied', meaning that it may only be used to purchase goods from the donor nation. As much assistance is in the form of loans which eventually must be repaid, there is a tendency for the line between assistance and such stimuli to overseas exports as state guaranteed credits to be blurred.

Although there is no lack of criticism of the nature of development assistance, few African leaders, if any, have called for its abolition. Africa is desperately in need of capital transfers to finance its own autonomous development. Thus many nations are faced with the apparent paradox of decrying development assistance and at the same time demanding that the industrialized states set aside a larger portion of their GNPs to assist the international poor. The increased use of multi-lateral institutions such as the UN and the World Bank, as well as assistance from what are seen as politically neutral areas such as Scandinavia, has been one way in which the political problems of aid have been lessened, though even here charges have been made that certain international agencies, especially the World Bank, have suffered from American domination.

Another major paradox of the development assistance picture is that after nearly three decades of sustained capital transfers, both private and public, the nations of the African continent are more heavily indebted than at any time in the past. Critics of development assistance maintain that this is primarily due to the structure of the world economy and Africa's role in it as a primary producer, a role, they argue, which development assistance has served to perpetuate.

Although the future role of development assistance in Africa is open to many questions arising from the controversy surrounding it, it is certain that the need for such assistance will be necessary for many years to come. If assistance is to be effective it will have to be responsive to the needs and desires of the continent's inhabitants and will have to be allied with a determined effort to change Africa's position in the world economy. Such changes will depend not only on the willingness of the donor nations to permit assistance to be used for such purposes, but will also depend on the ability of the continent's leaders to forge viable development plans for the future which embrace such goals.

Foreign investment

The effects of foreign investment constitute a major area of controversy among economists and politicians who are concerned with the growth and development of the African economy. One of the major difficulties in understanding the various points of view presented in the literature on foreign investment and its effects is the lack of agreed definition and the lack of a clear dividing line between direct foreign investment and other forms of capital flows, such as export guarantees, suppliers' credits and foreign aid. Thus it is necessary at the outset to delineate the major forms which direct foreign investment commonly takes.

The most obvious form of direct foreign investment is that in which

BALANCE OF PAYMENTS AND DEBT SERVICE RATIOS: SELECTED AFRICAN COUNTRIES

Country	Gross current account balance[1] millions of US$		Interest payments on external public debt millions of US$		Debt service as percentage of			
					GNP		Exports	
	1970	1976	1970	1976	1970	1976	1970	1976
Algeria	−116	−542	10	341	0.9	5.7	3.2	14.1
Benin	1	−21	—	1	0.7	1.7	2.2	4.9
Burundi	*	*	—	1	0.2	0.6	*	*
Cameroon	−26	−83	4	19	0.9	1.8	3.1	6.0
Central African Republic	*	9	—	2	0.9	1.8	3.2	7.2
Chad	2	−3	—	2	1.0	1.4	3.5	4.8
Congo	*	−218	3	6	3.2	2.3	*	5.3
Egypt	−116	−730	38	77	4.1	6.0	28.7	17.6
Ethiopia	−25	−22	6	11	1.2	0.9	11.3	6.3
Ghana	−56	−72	12	17	1.1	0.5	4.9	4.6
Guinea	*	*	4	17	3.8	6.1	*	*
Ivory Coast	−26	−139	12	66	2.7	4.0	6.7	9.1
Kenya	−38	−61	11	23	1.2	1.4	3.7	3.6
Liberia	*	*	6	6	5.5	2.7	*	*
Madagascar	*	*	2	5	0.8	0.7	3.5	*
Malawi	−32	−71	3	6	1.8	1.9	7.0	7.2
Mali	−2	−32	—	9	0.4	0.5	1.8	3.2
Mauritania	−12	−52	—	3	1.5	14.7	3.2	33.2
Morocco	−101	−1308	23	89	1.8	2.5	7.7	12.6
Niger	1	−8	1	2	0.9	0.9	3.8	7.3
Nigeria	−348	−311	20	39	0.7	0.9	4.1	2.3
Rwanda	*	16	—	—	—	—	1.3	0.6
Senegal	−15	−37	1	18	0.7	2.1	2.4	5.7
Sierra Leone	−13	−59	3	4	3.0	3.7	10.0	8.3
Somalia	*	−69	*	*	*	*	2.0	3.0
Sudan	−30	−110	12	55	1.2	2.6	10.3	16.7
Tanzania	−29	10	6	13	1.3	1.1	5.0	4.3
Togo	4	−61	1	4	0.9	2.0	2.9	9.9
Tunisia	−36	−147	17	41	4.4	2.4	17.1	6.8
Uganda	24	−45	4	2	0.6	0.2	2.5	1.6
Upper Volta	9	−40	—	1	0.6	0.7	3.9	4.8
Zaire	−54	−544	9	35	2.2	1.6	4.6	12.9
Zambia	131	−571	23	52	3.2	2.4	5.4	8.9
Zimbabwe	*	*	4	2	0.6	0.2	*	*

* Not available
[1] Current account balance before interest payments on external public debt

Source: *World Bank Statistical Yearbook 1978* (Washington DC, 1978)

STOCK OF FOREIGN (PRIVATE) DIRECT INVESTMENTS AND GROWTH TRENDS: SELECTED AFRICAN COUNTRIES

Country	Stock at end of year millions of US$ 1967	1972	Percentage of table total 1967	1972	Percentage growth 1967–72
Algeria	703	250	11.2	2.8	−64
Angola	193	290	3.1	3.2	50
Benin	18	25	0.3	0.3	40
Burundi	14	18	0.2	0.2	27
Cameroon	150	210	2.4	2.3	40
Central African Republic	37	50	0.6	0.6	37
Chad	18	20	0.3	0.2	12
Congo	90	100	1.4	1.1	11
Egypt	58	100	0.9	1.1	72
Ethiopia	50	70	0.8	0.8	39
Ghana	260	360	4.1	4.0	38
Guinea	93	175	1.5	2.0	88
Ivory Coast	202	340	3.2	3.8	69
Kenya	172	235	2.7	2.7	37
Lesotho	0.5	2	—	—	300
Liberia	300	360	4.8	4.0	20
Libya	578	1560	9.2	17.4	170
Madagascar	72	95	1.1	1.1	31
Malawi	30	55	0.5	0.6	83
Mali	7	8	0.1	0.1	23
Mauritania	101	150	1.6	1.7	48
Morocco	179	250	2.8	2.8	39
Mozambique	102	125	1.6	1.4	22
Niger	23	35	0.4	0.4	50
Nigeria	1109	2100	17.6	23.5	89
Rwanda	15	17	0.2	0.2	12
Senegal	154	210	2.4	2.3	37
Sierra Leone	68	75	1.1	0.8	10
Somalia	13	15	0.2	0.2	19
Sudan	37	35	0.6	0.4	−5
Tanzania	60	65	1.0	0.7	8
Togo	42	65	0.7	0.7	53
Tunisia	135	200	2.1	2.2	48
Uganda	48	30	0.8	0.3	−38
Upper Volta	16	18	0.2	0.2	11
Zaire	481	620	7.7	6.9	20
Zimbabwe	237	315	3.8	3.5	33

Source: Carl Widstrand (ed.), *Multinational Firms in Africa* (Dakar and Uppsala, 1975)

a private investor maintains some degree of control over the uses to which his investment funds are put. This is usually the case in various types of industrial and commercial investments even where the host government participates in the enterprise and also exercises some investment control. Also included in direct foreign investment are re-invested earnings of foreign investors, even though these are generated within the host country. Re-invested earnings are included in foreign investment because they represent the undistributed profits of foreign investors and could potentially be repatriated were it decided not to continue to re-invest. A second major area of foreign investment are 'portfolio investments'. A portfolio investment usually takes the form of a commercial loan by a private bank to the host government, although a number of development agencies, notably the International Bank for Reconstruction and Development (World Bank), are major sources of portfolio investments. In a portfolio investment the investor usually maintains some control over the uses to which funds are put but generally much less control than in direct commercial and industrial investments. Finally, export credits and export credit guarantees, which are extended to importing countries by private firms, banks, or governments of exporting nations, are usually included as foreign investments though they may also be considered by some economists as a form of aid if they are provided at terms which are 'softer' than those available in the open financial market.

In sectoral terms the major field for direct foreign investment on the African continent has been in the petroleum industry, which is responsible for over 40 per cent of all direct investment on the continent. Mining and smelting follow in importance at a distant second with somewhat over 20 per cent while other major areas such as agriculture and trade constitute approximately 7.5 per cent and 6 per cent of total direct foreign investments respectively. Moreover, in nearly every country on the continent foreign investment is concentrated in one, most important sector, which is usually also the major export of the host nation.

One important effect of the high concentration of direct foreign investment in petroleum production and other extractive industries is the uneven distribution of investment from external sources around the continent. The major oil producers, Algeria, Nigeria and Libya, alone account for some 30–40 per cent of the continent's total foreign investment while other important mineral producers such as Gabon, Zaire, Zambia and Liberia account for an additional 15–20 per cent.

With very few exceptions the flow of foreign investment has followed from the well-established economic linkages with the former colonial power. Thus, investment funds of British origin account for some 72 per cent of the direct foreign investment in former British colonies while investments of French origin make up a similar proportion of the total foreign investment of former French ruled areas. This pattern of historical dominance of the foreign investment field has been altered only in those nations where a concerted effort has been made to alter the source of investment funds, such as Guinea; in those cases where the economic weakness of the former colonial power has made investment dominance impossible, such as former Portuguese colonies; or in those situations in which the economy of the former colony has grown quite rapidly, such as Libya and Nigeria.

The foreign investment controversy

Until quite recently it was generally agreed that direct foreign investment in the African context constituted a beneficial force and contributed greatly to the growth of the African economy. This view had its origins in the experience of the industrialized nations for whom foreign investment historically acted in precisely such a manner as well as the recognition of undeveloped investment opportunities. In addition, advocates of direct foreign investment have maintained that it leads to increased employment, an improvement in the productivity of labour and a stimulus to the host countries' economies by providing access to advanced technology, up- to-date managerial skills and often an improved infrastructure.

Critics of this view have generally been those for whom economic development is seen more in terms of a qualitative change in the structure of the economy rather than as a simple evaluation of the statistical evidence presented by the indices of growth. Such critics maintain that direct foreign investment cannot play a similar role in the development of the economies of areas such as Africa as it did in the now industrialized nations for a number of reasons. First, much of the direct foreign investment in the 19th century was associated with the creation of railways and other infrastructural elements while at present, in Africa, the focus is on extractive industries with few linkages to the rest of the economy. Second, they argue that much of the 19th century flow of investments went to areas of European settlement in which European emigrants, often highly skilled, created the managerial and technological framework for their utilization, while today managerial and technologically skilled positions often remain the preserve of temporarily resident, non-African personnel, who do not train African replacements. Third, they often argue that the rapid advances in technology itself and the fact that modern technology is often highly capital-intensive means that the increases in employment opportunities are likely to be quite small by contrast with the opportunities provided by the relatively labour-intensive techniques of the previous century. Finally, critics of direct foreign investment as an engine of economic development maintain that in the long run it leads to an overall net outflow of capital from the host country when profits are repatriated to the home country of the investor, and that this repatriation inevitably creates balance of payments difficulties.

Foreign investment and the multi-national corporation

The rise to prominence of the multi-national corporation has added a new dimension to the issue of foreign investment in Africa and elsewhere. The multi-national corporation is not simply a firm which has investments or commercial interests in more than one country – its sheer size gives it unprecedented economic power. Of the 99 largest 'economies' in the world multi-nationals account for 40, being larger than all but a handful of African nations. Moreover, multi-nationals tend either to dominate those industries which they enter or to work in close cooperation with other multi-nationals with similar interests, as in the petroleum industry. They also tend to be the most important centres of research and development for their given areas of focus while concentrating decision-making and technological skill in their home bases of operations. In addition, the individual operations of a multi-national often produce only either partially finished or component products which are then finished or assembled in another part of the multi-national's global 'factory'.

All of these characteristics of the multi-national firms are of great importance to the growth and development of the African economy. Aside from those issues concerning technological transfer and the development of managerial skill common to all foreign investment, multi-national corporations also raise important issues of economic sovereignty. While defenders of the growth of multi-national enterprises see them as generating the efficient use of capital, labour and natural resources, critics maintain that the global integration of such enterprises perpetuates a division of labour which intensifies the extractive and resource-based nature of the African economy. Further, critics argue that multi-nationals create 'branch-plant' economies in areas like Africa in which only a portion of any given line of production takes place. The creation of such fragmented branch-plant operations, they contend, constitutes in and of itself a formidable barrier to the transfer of technology. An examination of patents issued in African countries provides a useful illustration of this point, as in nearly every country on the continent foreign-held patents exceed 90 per cent of the total granted.

Yet another important issue raised by the activities of multi-national corporations and foreign investment in general is that of national economic sovereignty. While multi-nationals may indeed be efficient in the allocation of capital and manpower resources on a global scale, such efficiency may come into serious conflict with the economic development strategy of the host nation. The issue of national economic sovereignty is especially important in Africa where a number of nations have chosen socialist or other state-directed development strategies based on long term planning.

The issue of economic sovereignty also arises in connection with taxation and labour relations. Since the component firms of a multi-national company are often in the position of buying or selling to other components of the parent firm, it is relatively easy for them to over-invoice or under-invoice imports and exports in order to minimize declared profits for taxation reasons or in order to evade value-added or trade duties. Moreover, such accounting manipulations may also be useful in dealing with strident union demands or critical political pressure. In such a situation the lack of indigenous market and managerial expertise is likely to make the monitoring of the activities of such large foreign investors difficult in the extreme.

Given that most African nations are in dire need of investment capital and are loath to impose restrictions which might dissuade potential investors the problems of direct foreign investment on the continent are likely to remain. One possible way in which some of the less acceptable practices and policies of foreign investors might be curtailed would be through regional cooperation in the establishment of a code of norms for investors. Little progress has, however, been made in this direction. Thus the role of direct foreign investment in the growth and development of the African economy is likely to remain the subject of sustained comment and controversy. *R.W.S.*

Agriculture and peasantry

Most people in Africa are peasants or members of peasant families. Over 80 per cent of Africans live in rural areas and derive their living from agriculture, while three-quarters of the economically active population works directly in agriculture. The great majority of these people are peasants. They are members of households which work relatively small areas of land mainly by their own labour, and produce for their own consumption and, in varying degrees, for sale or exchange. Poverty in Africa is overwhelming, and the possibilities for development of the continent depend on the labour and conditions of production of this vast army of small agricultural producers.

Rural change
The first 20 years of political independence in Africa was a period of almost unprecedented change for many African agriculturalists. Others experienced an acceleration of changes that had begun during the colonial period. During the colonial period in many parts of Africa the possibility of substantial agricultural expansion was closed to the mass of rural producers, or was subordinated to the interests of the colonial state or of foreign settlers. In Kenya, for example, peasants were legally or administratively prevented from cultivating lucrative cash crops, such as coffee, which were reserved for the European settlers. In the Portuguese colonies, conversely, peasants were forced to grow cash crops (for example, cotton) for sale at low prices to the authorities even if their own food production fell below consumption requirements. The characteristic experience, however, was of agricultural stagnation for peasant producers: where

there was substantial cash crop expansion through unforced indigenous enterprise (for example palm-oil in Nigeria, or cocoa in Ghana), African peasants were often deprived of substantial amounts of the proceeds by the activities of commercial buyers, who agreed among themselves on prices and buying quotas and, later, through the colonial marketing organizations which controlled producer prices, ostensibly with the object of buffering producers from the impact of fluctuations in world commodity prices. In some cases, moreover, opportunities for cash crop expansion were limited to restricted groups, such as traditional rulers and other colonial favourites.

The termination of colonial rule removed the most blatant of such restrictions; others remained, and were perhaps intensified. It is arguable, for example, that West African export crop producers at the beginning of the 1980s gained even less from what amounts to the taxation of their earnings by marketing boards–through, for example, government investment in rural areas–than they had done in the years immediately before independence. More generally, though, it can be said that independence has opened up the peasant sector to the forces of the world market where agriculturalists had been isolated from it before, and has intensified their impact where an indigenous export agriculture sector had already been created. Pre-capitalist agricultural communities have become major export crop producers, and the traditional structures of land tenure and political authority have rapidly crumbled in many parts of Africa–either under the power of new money-based relationships, or because of deliberate intervention by the political authorities. The demise of self-sufficient agricultural communities and the rise of peasants producing for and buying from the national and world markets has had widespread social effects. These include rapidly increasing migration of rural people to Africa's cities, changes in work patterns on the farm (in sexual division of agricultural work and income, and in the hiring of agricultural labourers) and, with these developments, growing class differentiation among the peasantry.

In these circumstances of rapid, often turbulent, change the agricultural sector must nevertheless provide the food for Africa's growing population, an increasing proportion of which produces no food for itself. Farmers must also provide the bulk of the economic surplus to fuel the long-term diversification and industrialization of African economies.

Agricultural production
The record at the beginning of the 1980s was not encouraging. In the 1970s Africa as a whole had suffered the biggest drop in per capita food production of any region in the world. By the late 1970s African per capita food production was roughly 10 per cent below the level of the early 1960s. Nor was this the result of catastrophic falls in production in a small number of countries (although the Sahelian

PERCENTAGE OF POPULATION ENGAGED IN AGRICULTURE: CONTRIBUTION OF AGRICULTURE TO GDP, 1976;[1] AND PERCENTAGE CONTRIBUTION OF MAJOR AGRICULTURAL PRODUCTS TO EXPORT EARNINGS, 1976:[1] WORLD, AFRICA AND SELECTED AFRICAN COUNTRIES

Country	Percentage of population in agriculture	Percentage contribution of agriculture to GDP	Major agricultural exports and percentage share of these in export earnings
WORLD	47	*	*
AFRICA	65	*	*
Algeria	53	7	*
Angola	60	29	*
Burundi	84	64	Coffee 89
Cameroon	82	33	Coffee 32, Cocoa 20
Central African Republic	89	37	Cotton 23 (1975), Coffee 23 (1975)
Chad	86	52	Cotton 64 (1974)
Egypt	52	29	*
Ethiopia	81	50	Coffee 56, Pulses 10
The Gambia	79	*	Groundnuts 91
Ghana	54	49	Cocoa 56, Timber 15
Guinea	82	43	*
Ivory Coast	81	25	Coffee 34, Cocoa 18
Kenya	79	30	Coffee 28, Tea 10
Lesotho	86	38	*
Liberia	72	29	*
Libya	20	3	*
Madagascar	85	29	Coffee 27 (1975), Vanilla 7 (1975)
Malawi	85	45	Tobacco 45, Tea 18
Mali	88	38	Cotton 44, Groundnuts 11
Mauritania	84	35	*
Morocco	53	21	*
Mozambique	67	45	*
Niger	90	47	*
Nigeria	56	23	Cocoa 3
Rwanda	91	52	Coffee 77, Tea 7
Senegal	76	28	Groundnuts and groundnut oil 20
Sierra Leone	67	32	Cocoa 9, Coffee 8
Somalia	81	31	Livestock 61, Bananas 16
South Africa	29	9	*
Sudan	78	41	Cotton 51, Groundnuts 20
Tanzania	83	45	Coffee 31, Cotton 15
Togo	70	25	Cocoa 18, Coffee 12
Tunisia	43	21	*
Uganda	83	55	Coffee 82, Cotton 6
Zaire	76	16	Coffee 14
Zambia	69	14	*

*Not available   [1] Unless otherwise stated

Sources: FAO estimates *World Development Report* (World Bank 1978); *International Financial Statistics* (IMF January 1978)

drought★ exacerbated the problem). Roughly two-thirds of all African countries have suffered declines in per capita food production – and those countries contain 90 per cent of the continent's population. Evidence compiled by the Economic Commission for Africa★ underlines the intractability of the problem. Per capita food production declined, even though the use of fertilizer has increased enormously, as has the use of tractors. By as early as 1974 fertilizer use was 145 per cent higher than a decade before and tractor use 60 per cent higher. The problem is that the business of growing Africa's food is for the most part untouched by these advances in agricultural technology. Even where the technology is available, other factors – poor communications, unfavourable prices, inadequate marketing and processing, corruption – more often than not counteract technology's full potential.

The effect on nutrition standards is serious. Even with an understanding of nutritional needs improving with the expansion of formal education,★ and with countries spending scarce foreign exchange on imports of cereals and animal protein, the estimated per capita calorie availability still falls substantially short of requirements, and there are regional, class and other variations much worse than the average.

The production of cereal crops fared particularly badly in the 1970s. Maize, sorghum, millet, wheat and rice are the major African cereals: production rose only slowly and, except in the case of maize, almost certainly slower than population growth. Production of root crop staples such as cassava and yams – particularly important in West African countries – apparently fared better, though not much. Production of other important foods – beans, palm-oil, meat – stagnated or fell back.

The production of major export crops was somewhat more healthy, although in most cases the rapid expansion of the 1960s and early 1970s had tailed off by the opening of the 1980s. African countries produce a substantial share of world coffee: the share has grown from about 20 per cent of world production in the early 1960s, to fluctuate in 1980 between one-quarter and one-third. The major producers are Ivory Coast, Kenya, Uganda, Angola and Tanzania. East African countries (especially Kenya, Malawi and Tanzania) are also the major tea producers. While tea production roughly trebled in the 1960s and 1970s to a 1980 level of about 170 000 tonnes, African production was then still less than 10 per cent of world output. West African countries, Ghana and Ivory Coast in particular, account for about two-thirds of world cocoa production, and over one-third of the total production of palm products (concentrated overwhelmingly in West Africa, and Nigeria in particular). The continent also has a significant share in world production of groundnuts (30 per cent, concentrated in Senegal and The Gambia), cashew nuts (roughly 50 per cent of world output, with Mozambique a major producer) and sisal (50 per cent, Tanzania being the biggest producer). African countries have a small but economically significant share in world production of tobacco (especially Zimbabwe), cotton (Egypt is the largest producer), cane sugar (predominantly eastern and southern countries) and fruit and vegetables (North African countries, with other producers such as Kenya and Ivory Coast moving up).

The health of export agriculture is of course affected by world economic conditions, and the inflation and recession of the 1970s was partly responsible for the faltering of African agricultural exports. When deflated on the basis of the UN index of prices of exported manufactured goods, the real value of African agricultural export commodities was by 1980 lower, despite the price rises of the early 1970s, than it was in 1970. The terms of trade for African agricultural producers have deteriorated.

The peasantry's future

The major difficulties for African peasants are thus economic and political: problems of markets, terms of trade, and government policies on rural development. There are also ecological issues: desertification, particularly affecting pastoralists★ in East Africa and the West African Sahel zone; population densities and pressure on land in fertile areas, even though overall *average* density is low; fragile soils★ and climatic patterns. These factors have an important political dimension, since they are immediately affected by changes in land tenure, pricing and other policy decisions, and the types of technology in use.

The difficulty of maintaining or increasing living standards is severe enough for the minority of peasants producing for the export market: for the subsistence and food-crop producing majority, life has been much harder. The subsistence sector has suffered from gross neglect, in part because of real difficulties in devising agricultural services to deal with its particular problems, but also because subsistence producers have often been seen merely as regrettable evidence of economic backwardness. Peasants producing food for the domestic market have received a little more attention, but in most African countries, as elsewhere, producer prices have been kept disadvantageously low, to the benefit of the urban middleman and – sometimes – the urban consumer.

The social and economic impact of agriculture's disabilities varies according to the proportion of population involved in agriculture and the sector's contribution to the economy. There are clearly different orders of problem in sub-Saharan Africa, with over 80 per cent of the population living in rural areas and agriculture typically accounting for over one-third of Gross Domestic Product (GDP), and in North Africa, where agriculture contributes only 20 per cent to regional GDP, and where non-agricultural employment is much more important. For almost all African countries, however, the threatened or actual decline of peasant agriculture presents severe policy problems: rural-urban migration and the consequent growth of

PRODUCTION OF SELECTED CROPS: WORLD, AFRICA AND LEADING AFRICAN EXPORTERS (1976 AND 1977)

Country	Production *thousands of tonnes* 1976	1977	Country	Production *thousands of tonnes* 1976	1977
cocoa			*rubber*		
WORLD	1362	1408	WORLD	3596	3613
AFRICA	850	906	AFRICA	223	237
Ghana	320	310	Nigeria	85	90
Ivory Coast	230	240	Liberia	73	80
Nigeria	165	210	Zaire	27	27
Cameroon	82	90			
coffee			*sisal*		
WORLD	3659	4340	WORLD	423	471
AFRICA	1260	1274	AFRICA	229	213
Ivory Coast	308	291	Tanzania	119	110
Ethiopia	193	175	Kenya	34	34
Uganda	192	202	Angola	25	20
Madagascar	93	95	Madagascar	22	21
cotton lint			*staple foods (a) cereals*		
WORLD	12264	14250	WORLD	1465877	1459012
AFRICA	1086	1242	AFRICA	68472	65731
Egypt	396	435	South Africa	10004	12087
Sudan	124	208	Nigeria	8489	8426
Tanzania	69	59	Egypt	8188	7997
Nigeria	61	73	Morocco	5656	2888
groundnuts			*staple foods (b) roots and tubers*		
WORLD	17871	17455	WORLD	563261	570211
AFRICA	5123	4473	AFRICA	78157	78814
Senegal and The Gambia	1347	845	Nigeria	28230	27730
Sudan	827	850	Zaire	12722	12905
Nigeria	500	330	Ghana	4430	4430
Zaire	319	330	Tanzania	4322	4431
palm products (a) kernels			*sugar cane*		
WORLD	1491	1514	WORLD	694225	737483
AFRICA	702	723	AFRICA	57237	60027
Nigeria	321	340	South Africa	19221	19770
Benin	70	70	Egypt	8446	8000
Zaire	64	65	Mauritius	6600	6900
Sierra Leone	51	50	Mozambique	2600	2700
palm products (b) oil			*tea*		
WORLD	3426	3751	WORLD	1633	1758
AFRICA	1293	1321	AFRICA	156	190
Nigeria	655	660	Kenya	62	86
Ivory Coast	158	185	Malawi	28	32
Zaire	155	145	Uganda	15	15
Cameroon	80	82	Tanzania	14	17

Source: FAO estimates

uncontrolled urban settlement, unemployment and mass poverty, balance of payments difficulties because of a relative decline in export values and an increase in food imports, and the long-term deterioration of the major productive base of most African economies.

Part of the solution to these problems may be found in international and domestic prices more favourable to the peasant producers of export and food crops, though the political difficulties are evident. But crucial changes are also likely to be necessary in national agricultural institutions: in patterns of credit and extension services, in the direction of agricultural research, and in the organization of production itself. In Africa agrarian reform is at a very early stage. A few countries with substantial land inequalities have undertaken tenure reforms, but these have not necessarily affected the majority of peasants (e.g. Algeria) or have in some respects accentuated inequalities (Kenya). Where ambitious settlement schemes have been undertaken (Ghana, Somalia, Sudan, Egypt and elsewhere) the record is mixed and the effect confined. In cooperative organizations there have been significant African success stories, but it is commonly accepted that the best recipe for cooperative success is to organize relatively well-off peasants producing a high-value crop – hardly the major problem area. The more ambitious schemes of cooperative or collective production, such as those in Algeria, Tunisia, and Mozambique, have experienced considerable difficulties of low production, peasant reluctance and inexperience with new organization. It is difficult to envisage their widespread introduction in most African countries in the short or medium term. Nevertheless, even with more favourable prices the maintenance of the peasantry is likely to depend in the end on institutions for mass diffusion of improved agricultural technologies and the provision of a degree of social insurance and of social services in the African countryside. The pressures of modernization have reduced the capacity of peasant communities to provide these things for themselves: there is little sign that a continuation of export-oriented individual production backed up by services inaccessible to most peasant producers will succeed where it has failed up to now. *G.B.L.*

Craft production

Before imported goods reached them – at various times in different parts of the continent – African communities obtained locally their essential tools, weapons, cooking utensils, containers, clothing, and housing. Not all communities made all these items for themselves; local trade distributed the products of specialized craftsmen. Most communities also produced items of personal adornment, musical instruments, ritual and ceremonial objects and other articles which added to the richness of individual and communal life.

The technology which produced these things, though it differed widely, rarely demanded equipment not made by the craftsmen themselves or their neighbours; and originally most of the raw materials could be produced locally. When external trade made available imported raw materials, they were generally processed on traditional equipment. The same is true today when much of the raw material is scrap – imported iron bars or pieces of spring from large motor vehicles made into hoes in traditional forges, or imported yarn woven on traditional looms.

African technology was, in purely technical terms, less advanced than that of pre-industrial Europe or South-East Asia; just as the plough and the transport wheel were unknown to Africa south of the Sahara, so also were the potter's wheel and kiln-fired pottery, the lever-action bellows, saw, lathe, and spinning wheel. The pedal loom was known only in West Africa and the northern savanna belt, and (apart from Ethiopia) only in a narrow form much less efficient (in terms of man-hours) than the hand-looms of Europe and Asia. Only in leather-dressing in a few areas could African craftsmen, though still using the simplest means, compete with the technologically more advanced world of Europe.

It was confidently assumed, particularly by those seeking to sell the products of industrialized Europe to Africa, that local goods would rapidly give way before the competing factory-made articles. The extent to which this actually occurred varied, not only in different parts of the continent, but also in different industries; pottery, iron, leather and textiles can be taken as examples.

Pottery

Pottery is still widely made in Africa, usually by women, by techniques including coiling, hollowing, moulding, and combinations of these methods. Except for recent deliberate introductions by non-Africans, of rather limited success, the potter's wheel is not found south of the Sahara, though various slow turntables are known. No settling tanks are used – the admixture of coarser particles in the clay makes a more fire-resistant pot – but the clay is kneaded and beaten after digging, and grog of various kinds added if necessary. Firing is usually in a bonfire with the heat retained by grass, ash or earth. Glazes are unknown, but fine finishes are given by burnishing (in parts of Central Africa plumbago is used to give a metallic sheen); plunging the hot fired pot into green leaves gives a black finish which also makes the pot less porous, and other vegetable substances are used to give different finishes.

Production costs virtually nothing; equipment consists of a piece of stick or a bamboo ring, palm fruits or maize cobs, smooth stones from the brook, an old pot or plate to serve as base or turntable, and perhaps a small wooden comb or carved roulette, a string of beads or a

Potters in the Republic of Benin

piece of cord for decoration. If the woman digs her own clay and grinds her own grog, anything she gets from selling her pots is pure gain; she is usually part of a household which provides her basic necessities of food and housing, and to which she contributes domestic labour.

Pots can therefore be sold cheaply enough to compete with imported iron 'missionary' pots and the ubiquitous coloured enamelled ironware. While enamelled ironware is cleaner and more attractive for eating, and the iron cooking pot is less liable to break, food is less liable to burn and keeps hot longer in a clay pot, and water keeps cooler in a porous vessel. For some special vessels, such as the narrow-mouthed pots for collecting palm wine, there are no real alternatives. In most households local pottery is found alongside imports from the industrial world. Pot-making is hard, dirty work. If local pottery industries disappear, the cause is not so much competition from imports as new and more attractive employment opportunities for women.

Iron-working

Centuries before the first Europeans sailed into the Gulf of Guinea, most parts of Africa had learned to smelt iron. Smelting, the burning of charcoal mixed with iron ore in an enclosed space so that the oxygen from the ore combines with the charcoal to leave metallic iron, is carried out in two types of furnaces: a tall, relatively permanent one, which, if well sited, does not require the use of bellows, and a much smaller furnace used for a single season, with which bellows must be used. Both types were normally constructed by the smelters, who were also usually the iron-ore miners and often made their own charcoal.

Good iron could be made by this method, but there was never enough of it. From early days, iron bars from Europe were much in demand, as today are hoe blanks and scrap-iron from motor vehicles. Smelting disappeared, first from areas near the coast, and, as imported iron reached the interior, it became confined to more and more remote areas. In some areas, such as eastern Africa, the final disappearance was preceded by a boom caused by an increase in internal trade.

The smelting process produced a bloom which could be wrought into hoes, spears and arrowheads by the blacksmith. Only the local smith could, and can, give the hoe blade the exact angle demanded by local farmers. The smith still makes tools for other craftsmen, though no longer weapons; he is still an essential part of the community, though he no longer commands the awe which surrounded the smelter.

There has been some modernization of the smith's equipment. The traditional bowl or 'drum' bellows has widely given place to the European type; sometimes the smith works at a European-type anvil. Most of his tools are still of his own making, but a few may be imported. There is less tendency than in Europe for the smith to move into the modern sector of vehicle-repairing, which is largely recruited by more or less formal apprenticeship; some smiths, and other craftsmen including the Kamba in Kenya, have moved in.

Leather-working

Most pastoral or semi-pastoral peoples have used leather in various forms for clothing, footwear, containers and sometimes tents. Their skill varied enormously; some were content with stiff, half-cured skins, others were able to produce soft, supple and graceful garments, elaborately decorated bags and sandals, and saddles which were often ornamental as well as functional. In the cavalry states the leather-worker was as much a military necessity as the smith. Much of the decorative leather-work of the pastoral Tuareg was done by the women of the all-inclusive artisan group known as smiths.

Leather-workers in Jos, Nigeria

The leather-workers of the Hausa areas of what is now northern Nigeria and southern Niger were perhaps the most accomplished. Tanned and dyed goatskins, produced by simple but well-understood techniques of scraping, tanning with acacia bark, and dyeing with vegetable dyes, were exported across the Sahara, to become some of the 'Morocco' leather used for binding Europe's books—one of the very few instances of an African handicraft building up an export market outside Africa. The Saharan caravans themselves used leather sacks and bags from Hausaland, the most important being the water-bags made in what is now Niger. The export of dyed goatskins greatly increased in the late 19th century, but collapsed with changes in European and American demand for leather and the decline of the caravan trade. Under colonial rule saddles and harness became luxuries rather than military necessities, and the new export crop, groundnuts, was packed in imported sacks, not leather bags. Even the Tuareg of the desert, always needing more leather goods than they produced, no longer had the resources they formerly commanded.

The demise of the Hausa leather industry appeared imminent when the railways brought cheap imported goods into northern Nigeria. Instead, the leather-workers began to produce decorative leather-work, no longer for the local elite alone but for merchants, non-Africans and other strangers. It was sold all over the Hausa trading network, so that there are few markets, airports, or curio shops where Hausa leather-work cannot be bought.

In addition, the leather-workers turned to new materials. Sandals, now often have soles made from old vehicle tyres; and many forms of plastic are used, both for decoration and as parts of leather goods. Imported dyes are now also used, replacing the old rust-reds with a bright crimson. There must have been a decline in the industry from its 19th-century heyday, but it shows no signs of dying out.

Textiles

Not all African peoples have made woven textiles; pastoral peoples often used tanned skins instead, while beaten and felted bark-cloth was widely distributed, and reached a high standard of craftsmanship in Uganda. The finest woven textiles were made from un-spun palm fibres in the Congo—the well-known 'plushes' and 'velvets', together with more workaday cloth which became a currency. Expensive to produce on a technically inefficient upright loom with a pull-heddle, these cloths, though they survived centuries of Portuguese contact, disappeared under the violent disruption of early French and Belgian colonialism, and gave way to the cheaper and more washable products of European industry.

Top: cloth being dyed in indigo dye-pits in Fes, Morocco. Bottom: a village weaver in northern Nigeria weaving narrow strip cloth on a pedal loom

The fixed-heddle horizontal loom of eastern Africa (found also occasionally in West Africa) is also much less efficient than the European or Indian pedal loom; yet its products survived for centuries while the eastern African coast was in touch with India and Europe. The older trade networks carried little Indian or European cloth inland before the 19th century; by mid-century it was beginning to replace the local weave.

Local cloth, to judge from surviving specimens, was often coarse and unattractive, and must have been expensive, in man-hours, to produce. Prestige was all on the side of the imported cloth – to become civilized was to 'become an Arab', *ustuarabu*; to become a Muslim or a Christian was to wear cotton cloth in quantities the local looms could not have produced. Nationalism came too late to eastern Africa for local cloth to be used as a symbol; by the turn of the century local weaving had largely died out, except in such places as Ufipa (in what is now western Tanzania), which wove a cloth of sufficiently high quality to compete with imports.

In West Africa, however, a very considerable hand loom industry survives. The main loom is the pedal loom. In its narrow form as used in West Africa (where cloth is commonly woven approximately 10cm wide, then sewn together), it is still much more efficient than other African looms. Except on the coast, local cloth remained competitive in price until modern transport penetrated the interior of West Africa. The looms themselves, though they have the same working parts as an Indian or European hand loom, are constructed by the weavers from 'sticks and pieces of string'. The weaver's womenfolk could grow, card and spin the cotton, and he himself was generally a farmer for part of the year. In the absence of any alternative economic opportunities during the dry season, this was virtually a costless industry. There were, indeed, some full-time weavers (often provided with food by members of the household); these were generally under patronage of a king or chief. Many of the finest weaving traditions in West Africa for example, that of Asante,★ seem to derive from such a court industry, and these have often found a market among the new elites. Cloth which suffered most from the competition of machine-made imports (and now of cloth locally machine-made) is the coarse, poor cloth which had nothing to recommend it but its cheapness.

Weaving has undoubtedly declined in West Africa, though the more decorative cloth from Akwete, Igala, Nupe, and various Yoruba areas still finds a market. It is easy to exaggerate the decline of West African weaving; some index to its persistence is given by the imports of imported cotton yarn. In the 1890s some 90 000kg of cotton yarn for weaving were imported into West Africa from England, and a similar quantity into Senegal from France. By 1910–14, Nigeria alone was importing some 300 000kg a year; by the 1950s Nigerian imports had risen to some 1.1 million kg, and by 1961 to over 1.8 million kg.

The impact of imports

The replacement of an intermediate product – cotton yarn, smelted iron – by an imported substitute is characteristic of the impact of imports on African crafts; in many cases the imported substitute is now replaced, in part at least, by scrap. For example, in the Bida glass industry locally-made glass has given way to the use of broken bottles.

Characteristic, also, is the survival of the local industry alongside rising imports. With a fast-expanding population, there is often room for both, and the local product is often more efficient for local use; cloth from West African looms stands up better than the imported product to local methods of laundering; local sandals are often more appropriate than cheap manufactured shoes.

Apart from the early adoption of the pedal loom, there has been little adoption of imported technology; most craftsmen have preferred to remain not only the owners, but actually the producers of their means of production. The use of imported intermediate materials, however, has meant a departure from costless production; the craftsman now needs plenty of money rather than a large family. This problem has sometimes been met by working on the material owned by the customer (and, formerly, by the patron). It represents a basic structural change in the craft industries, whose long-term effects cannot at present be foreseen. *M.J.*

Mineral exploitation

Many of the major mining industries of today were initially developed with great skill by Africans for local and regional use. However, the modern mining industry is on a much vaster scale and has a completely different character, being oriented to supplying the hungry needs of the West. 'Developing market economies' produce 33 per cent but consume only 6 per cent of nine key base metals. For Africa, excluding the Republic of South Africa, the figures are even more extreme.

Excluding South Africa, the most commercially valuable mineral resources presently being exploited on the African continent are the petroleum deposits of Nigeria, Libya, Algeria and, to a lesser extent, Gabon, Tunisia, Egypt, Angola and the Congo. The pressing energy needs of the West have made oil big business wherever it is found. A second major mining complex is centred around the copper resources of Shaba (formerly Katanga) province, Zaire and Zambia in south-central Africa. There are also a host of scarce precious and industrial metals found only in limited locations on the globe: gold, mined in Ghana; tin, mined in Nigeria and Zaire; cobalt, of which Zaire is the world's major producer, and diamonds, found largely in Africa. Large-scale African diamond-exporting countries include Namibia, Angola, Sierra Leone, Zaire and Botswana. Finally, Africa produces

THE MOST SIGNIFICANT MINERAL EXPORTS OF AFRICA BY VALUE

Country	Product	Value millions of US$
Nigeria	Petroleum	10 114.1 (1976)
Libya	Petroleum	6 504.4 (1975)
Algeria	Petroleum	3 655.7 (1975)
Gabon	Petroleum	894.6 (1976)
Zaire	Copper	770.4 (1974)
Zambia	Copper	734.9 (1975)
Morocco	Phosphates	495.5 (1976)
Tunisia	Petroleum	323.0 (1976)
Liberia	Iron ore	293.6 (1975)
Egypt	Petroleum	281.1 (1976)
Algeria	Petrol products	230.9 (1975)
Angola	Petroleum	194.6 (1973)
Mauritania	Iron ore	149.6 (1976)
Namibia	Diamonds	119.7 (1972)
Congo	Petroleum	117.2 (1975)

Sources: National trade statistics

a variety of commoner metals, generally located with relative convenience to European industrial consumers and of high mineral quality. Important examples are Gabonese manganese, Guinean bauxite, Mauritanian and Liberian iron ore, and phosphates from Morocco, Senegal, Togo and Tunisia.

Major mining operations in Africa remain thoroughly under the domination of big American and European corporations. The character of mineral production and use has led to control by a few firms in each field, mining operations often being substantially integrated with processing, manufacturing and marketing. The 'Seven Sisters' of the oil business—Shell, British Petroleum (BP), Gulf, Exxon, Mobil, Chevron, Texaco—hold the commanding heights of the petroleum market. Flanking them are 'small' independents, whose capital value exceeds the Gross National Product of most African states. Until recently, one giant—*Union Minière du Haut Katanga*—controlled Congolese copper production and two – Anglo-American and Roan Selection Trust—controlled Zambian production. Swaziland iron ore is fed directly into the mills of Nippon Steel. Niger uranium mining was developed in the 1970s with the specific aim of serving the needs of the French atomic energy programme. Much African mineral production has been under the grip of consortia. The role of the consortium has been of increasing importance; several companies often prefer to unite to organize a single mining corporation to minimize risks and distribute the product for the purpose of their operations in a single African country.

Most African mineral production serves the needs of the countries of the European Economic Community. The USA is an important consumer, however, notably of Nigerian petroleum. Japan, the industrialized country most dependent on imported raw materials, is playing a role of growing significance in the African minerals trade, generally in the form of consortium participation.

A particular feature of gem and base metal production in Africa is the pivotal role of South African mining houses. The Anglo-American interest is particularly important in Zambian copper production and in diamond mining in Botswana, Namibia and Tanzania. The DeBeers subsidiary of Anglo-American has a virtual corner on all world diamond purchase. Charter Consolidated provides technical and other services for Mauritanian copper mines, the American firm Amax is involved in Liberian iron ore, while Lonrho controls the major Ghanaian gold producer, Ashanti Goldfields; all have their profits and assets base in Zimbabwe and South Africa.

Mining capital displays few signs of integration into the national economies of African countries. A recent study commissioned by the World Bank concludes that 'the record of the world mining industry in responding to the needs of the developing countries is dismal.' Mining operations are generally extreme examples of what are usually termed 'enclave' economies. In colonial times, mining enterprise often relied on migrant wage labour★ working to meet tax payments while the administration directed them more or less voluntarily towards the mines. Wages were extremely low and living requirements were mainly supplied by subsistence agriculture. The tendency has been away from migrant labour towards a smaller, more permanent labour force, sometimes relatively well-paid, with increased application of machinery. In 1968 almost 50 000 Zambian copper miners earned on average twice the general wage in the country and almost nine times the cash income of peasant farmers. Many African miners, however, earn far less than this. Where at least a portion of mining activity remains alluvial, there remain possibilities for small-scale operations and African entrepreneurship. A large work-force can supplement earnings with other economic activities. Examples are tin mining in Nigeria and diamond mining in Sierra Leone and most other producer countries. In other branches of mining, production is highly capital-intensive and wages represent only a small portion of total costs of production. The immense Libyan petroleum export industry only employed a total of 10 000 workers in 1970. Both small-scale mining, in which diggers sell their produce to a company, and big capital-intensive operations, which have a proportionately small wage bill as compared to costs, are situations which discourage sustained labour militancy. However, in certain mining industries, notably Ghanaian gold and Zambian copper, miners have played a crucial political role through union organization and strike action.

Wages are the main direct input of mining companies into African hands. Only to a limited extent do companies purchase supplies from the country in which they operate. Indeed they require massive purchases of imports to the detriment of national balances of payments. In general, mineral products have been shipped out of Africa with a minimum of value-adding processing, except where transport costs have been crucial, as with southern-central African copper.

Mining generally requires a substantial new transport* infrastructure. In Sierra Leone, Mauritania, Liberia, among other countries, railways and port facilities have been installed to service mineral exports. This has powerfully affected the geography of economic development and services which follow the 'line of rail', often with no relevance to the overall needs of the population and consuming a huge proportion of available resources.

The major contribution mining makes to the national economies of Africa comes in the form of state taxation of mines and state investment in mining. Since the Second World War, but particularly following decolonization, African governments have taxed mining concerns more and more heavily, and, in an increasing number of African states, government revenues depend heavily on minerals taxation. Most governments have also insisted that senior staffing in mining operations be indigenized. Pressure to introduce value-adding processing within Africa has led to increased refining and smelting activity.

Up to a point mining companies have accepted the conditions imposed upon them by indigenization and taxation measures. However, particularly when mineral resources are available elsewhere, companies are prepared to disinvest and ultimately move out of a particular country entirely. DELCO, which had been mining iron ore in Sierra Leone for 40 years, simply shut in 1975 after running down operations for some years. Without actually disinvesting, companies have ceased to put capital into exploration, expansion, new equipment or infrastructure unless they have been able to obtain a more favourable business climate. In Nigeria, exploration for new petroleum deposits virtually ceased until negotiations with oil companies took a favourable turn for BP and Shell in 1977. Under strained circumstances, the capital outflow from Africa is high.

During the 1970s African governments apparently moved further down the road of assuming control of their own resources. One major development has been the formation of producer associations, of which the most successful has been the Organization of Petroleum Exporting Countries (OPEC), of which Libya, Algeria and Nigeria are all crucial members. Similar organizations have been founded to improve prices in copper and bauxite, while tin producers have sponsored an organization since the economic crisis of the 1930s.

In addition, African governments have increasingly insisted on a direct minority or majority share in mineral companies. In Nigeria a state oil development company was formed in 1971 to provide a direct national stake in petroleum. In the same year Algeria nationalized

oil production, with Zaire and Zambia nationalizing copper, Mauritania, iron ore, and Togo, phosphates, in following years.

Such measures must be understood as attempts by African states to obtain a better deal *within* existing trade relationships. In any case under the cover of nationalization, mining companies are often able to retain effective managerial control of decision-making and very favourable compensation terms. Indigenization* is most likely to be effective in areas such as personnel departments, not overall planning. In Zambia the most important impact of nationalization has been government pressure to extend exploration and increase exports, thus intensifying the already extreme dependence of the Zambian economy on copper mining. Copper nationalization has induced little real change in mining strategy. To the extent that state investment enables them to avoid political criticism, control labour more effectively and share expenditures and risk, companies often welcome and even solicit state participation.

Producers' associations such as OPEC appeared at first sight to hold the world to ransom, but in the mid-1970s, when new fields out of OPEC range were brought into production and the Western economies remained depressed, OPEC proved unable to stem falling prices. With their control of processing, integration with production of consumer goods and technological know-how, the corporations remain in a very strong position. A nationalized company must still often sell its product to a subsidiary of the old organization. Libya nationalized BP in anger at British policy in the Persian Gulf but found itself forced to pay economic compensation in 1975 in order to continue doing business with the West. Precisely as African and other Third World countries create more demanding and uncertain conditions for Western oligopolies, the corporations have become busier seeking alternative mineral resources (such as the seabed) and technologies (such as solar and thermal energy) to free themselves from operating under such conditions. Minerals exploration today is overwhelmingly concentrated in the developed countries. The lion's share since 1945 has gone to the USA, Canada, Australia and South Africa.

Petroleum and base metal resources in the abundance in which they are found in Africa would appear to provide a potential basis for industrialization.* Even were Africa to apply creatively a new appropriate technology suited to the needs of its people, these resources would be bound to play a major part. Some minerals, notably coal, which have been of limited interest to Western capital, remain almost entirely undeveloped.

So far only Algeria has applied mineral resources to industrial development on a significant scale. Algeria now produces steel, chemical fertilizers and is constructing plants for aluminium electrolysis and petro-chemicals. Vehicle assembly in Algeria is designed to use a proportion of local raw materials. Apart from Algeria, Zimbabwe and Egypt are the only steel-making countries in Africa north of the Limpopo, although Nigeria will be bringing its

AFRICAN MINERAL DEPENDENCY: MINERAL EXPORTS AS A PERCENTAGE OF TOTAL EXPORTS BY VALUE (COUNTRIES WITH THE HIGHEST PERCENTAGE)

Zambia	(1977)	97.4
Libya	(1975)	95.1
Algeria	(1975)	94.3
Guinea	(1975/6)	94.2
Nigeria	(1977)	92.2
Mauritania	(1976)	91.3
Gabon	(1976)	90.9
Zaire	(1974)	87.2
Liberia	(1975)	79.1
Sierra Leone	(1976)	70.3
Congo	(1977)	70.2
Togo	(1975)	64.6
Niger	(1975)	60.8
Tunisia	(1976)	53.5
Namibia	(1971)	53.0

Sources: calculated from data in *New Africa Yearbook* (London, 1979); *The Middle East and North Africa 1978–9* (London, 1978); *Africa South of the Sahara 1978–79* (London, 1978)

first steel mill into operation in the early 1980s and the Ivory Coast and Libya also have plans for steel production. In most African countries, cement factories and petrol refineries are the only heavy industries using local minerals. Only a very small part of African mineral production goes into inter-African trade. At the same time, the very character of the technology which Africa imports from the West has brought about increasing imports of manufactured goods and machinery that frequently contain African raw materials. The rise in oil prices in 1973 had a severe negative effect on the balance of payments of most African countries.

Minerals production is only one side of the dependent character of African economies which presents the long-term threat of, at best, stagnation and, at worst, a progressive breakdown of the productive system as a whole. As a result, we can expect conflict over mineral resources to play an increasingly significant part in Africa's economic and political relations with the world. *W.M.F.*

Industrialization

Strategies of industrialization

The traditional craft* industries of Africa continued throughout the colonial era, and many of them are still flourishing in the present period of regained independence. Nevertheless, they can by now meet only a small proportion of the popular demand for farm tools, textiles, furniture and cooking utensils.

The development of larger-scale manufacturing in Africa began as an attempt to supply new needs that had been created by the establishment of colonial administrations and the arrival of foreign officials and settlers. Thus during the first half of the 20th century it could be confidently predicted that almost every African territory would contain one or more of the following: a brewery, an ice factory, a soft drinks bottling plant, a bakery, a cement factory and a printing works. At this period shoes, cloth and clothing, cutlery, paper products, enamel-ware, hardware, bicycles, radios, commercial motor vehicles, cars and omnibuses and all similar articles were imported, initially from Europe or the USA, and later also from Japan, India and other countries that had begun to progress towards industrialization.

The first modern factories set up in Africa were not the result of any official policies of encouraging industrial development. They concentrated on articles that were highly perishable (e.g. bread or ice), or that cost very much more to transport after assembly (e.g. furniture) or after the addition of a cheap local commodity (e.g. water in soft drinks). At the same time a limited range of factories was established to process commodities intended for export, either in order to reduce bulk and weight, or else to preserve a perishable substance. Thus, every cotton-growing area that had been developed by the encouragement, or even insistence, of colonial agricultural officials needed one or more ginneries. Similarly, tanneries were set up in animal-rearing regions, and oil mills in areas where oil-palms were prevalent.

This pattern of manufacturing dependency, mirroring as it did the political dependence of almost all the African continent, was gradually eroded from two directions. On the one hand ambitious African craftsmen, who saw their traditional skills declining in value, began to seek ways of infiltrating the modern sector of the economy. Blacksmiths started to make spoons, knives and scissors and even ploughshares alongside their traditional hoes and axes; carpenters collaborated with commercial vehicle owners to build the vehicle frames and even crude coach bodies to mount behind imported cabs on bare chassis. Tailors hired apprentices in larger numbers and bought sewing machines, and then began to make shirts, shorts and dresses in anticipation of demand, rather than merely to order as before. Such enterprises very often live and die with their initial proprietors, and have contributed very little to the establishment of larger-scale and longer-lasting industrial undertakings. On the other hand foreign businessmen, particularly the representatives of companies operating in several territories, saw opportunities of making near-monopoly profits by basing manufacturing primarily on raw materials obtainable locally. In Egypt great sugar estates were developed in the south, and both local crushing mills and a large refinery just south of Giza have been producing sugar on a massive scale for the last 70 years. In the West African forest zone sawmills have been using local logs to produce sawn timber and—more recently—plywood for both export and local markets; groundnuts grown in the savanna areas, especially in Nigeria and Senegal, are now crushed locally to produce valuable cattle-cake for local farmers as well as groundnut oil to meet the rising demand in urban areas.

Such restricted industrial self-sufficiency was hardly satisfactory to the aspirations of African nationalists. In the struggle for independence, the fact that freedom from foreign domination would not automatically give Africans control of the factories, which they saw as the 'commanding heights' of their own economies, was noted and resented. A number of interrelated sets of attitudes towards African industrialization in the period after the Second World War up to and after independence can be delineated. Colonial governments, accepting the view that the developing world 'attached a mythical value to the factory chimney', set about identifying types of industry that could prudently be installed in a state shortly to become independent. First, they asked what could be made locally instead of being imported—the import-substitution policy—and then, using tariff rebates, tax holidays and similar fiscal concessions, they tried to persuade foreign companies to set up factories to manufacture such daily necessities as shoes, bicycles, cardboard boxes, cans, writing instruments, electric light bulbs, etc., in the colonial territory. The manufacturing companies were often happy to do this, since they could thereby hope to secure the profits from serving a growing market, and might also exclude competitors. These policies have been continued in almost all African countries after independence.

At the same time, however, African intellectuals were noting that foreign companies which set up factories employing imported machinery, imported raw materials and imported experts could constitute a drain on a country's resources for a substantial period. New plants, they complained, were either using old machinery no longer efficient enough to produce in competition with the most modern plant abroad—in which case it seemed that the African states were being fobbed off with the second best—or else they used the most modern and sophisticated machines and provided disturbingly little employment. Such factories were occasionally also taking advantage of the rather generous interpretations of the term 'manufacturing' that were used locally, and were carrying out such minimal processes on imported semi-manufactured raw materials that they became known as 'finishing touch' industries. For example, the foreign companies would import potable spirits in bulk at very high proof, merely diluting and bottling them in Africa, or they might import lengthy rolls of toilet paper, merely slicing and wrapping these before offering them for sale. In either case they would still claim the tax reliefs appropriate to manufacturers.

To this paradoxical course of events—a desire for the implantation of manufacturing industry, yet dissatisfaction with its results—the African states have reacted in a number of ways. One group, scorned

by its fellows for its lack of independent spirit, has taken the view that the best policy is that which leads to the most rapid expansion of the economy. If this involves being very accommodating to foreign investors and giving them almost complete freedom to invest, to export their profits and to employ their own nationals at will, the price is considered to be worth paying. This attitude, now increasingly modified under the pressure of public opinion, has been that of Kenya, Senegal and Ivory Coast, and it has certainly enabled otherwise small and weak states to achieve a remarkable rate of growth of the Gross National Product (GNP), even if the advancement of Africans of managerial ability to positions of authority has been slow.

A second group has preferred independence at all costs, or nearly so, and has readily expropriated foreign enterprises, setting up state-owned corporations* in their place. Such states have hitherto failed to run the nationalized factories as efficiently as their previous owners, a problem created by the 'civil service' mentality of local employees and by its non-applicability to commercial life; confiscated factories have ceased to make profits, and these nations' consequent rates of economic growth have been very slow. Anxious to advance on every front simultaneously, and to retain complete independence, such states as Guinea, Ghana and Tanzania have demonstrated repeatedly that demagogy and patriotism cannot replace careful book-keeping and attention to detail as methods of ensuring profit from investment in manufacturing. Many observers have commented that while African factory hands can be trained to be just as productive as workers in other countries, skilled craftsmen are so ambitious to move upwards to managerial positions that they cannot be persuaded to carry out for long the functions which are so vital to efficient and profitable production. (Mineral exploitation* in these states has often been left to foreign firms, and governments have reaped useful incomes from the profits these have made.)

A third approach to industrialization is that now coming to be associated with the school of regional planners and the concept of the growth-pole strategy. According to the latter, the most valuable industries in a developing state either provide the raw material for subsequent local processing, or else draw on other industries for their raw materials, since in this way industries support one another, and the surplus production or extra demand of one manufacturing plant becomes the reason for the establishment and profitability of another, either within the same politico-economic unit (in economic space) or within the same region or manufacturing centre (in geographic space). Such a philosophy has been followed almost instinctively in the longer-established manufacturing states of Africa, both around the Rand in the Republic of South Africa and in the neighbourhood of Cairo in Egypt. In Nigeria, as indeed in West Africa as a whole since the founding of the Economic Organization of West African States (ECOWAS),* and also in the former French Equatorial Africa, where the system of the *Union Douanière et Economique de l'Afrique Centrale* (UDEAC)* was devised, there is appreciation of the advantages of an unified strategy of industrial location* and expansion, but there are also many separate governments each needing popular support; the result is that agreements concerning the allocation of particular types of industry prove very hard to honour, particularly in the face of eager foreign firms offering developer-financing (with the foreign firm supplying capital and building the plant) and turn-key deals (with the foreign firm selling a complete 'package' – a ready to operate factory), for setting up new plants. Pending the creation of precise agreements between national and regional authorities on the allocation of industries, such states tend to see 50–100 per cent of their industrial expansion taking place at their principal ports, which are generally also their capital cities.

A major problem of all industrial developments in Africa is that economic advisers inevitably look at strategies followed in the past by currently successful industrialized countries: even if the experience of the United Kingdom no longer seems relevant, that of Japan or more recently still of South Korea or Taiwan appears to afford a useful guide. On the one hand the possibilities of export-led industrialization must by now seem extremely meagre, since there are no longer any populous countries left in the world that are able or willing to constitute an outlet for exports coming from African states. On the other hand the actual volume of consumer goods emerging from African factories is so small that these plants alone could never constitute an adequate market for the capital goods produced by a full-scale iron and steel complex, say, or a petro-chemical complex that might be established in Africa to serve the needs of all the members of the Organization of African Unity;* nor could their unsophisticated farming systems make effective use of the fertilizers that might be produced by such industrial giants. In consequence, while, for example, Nigeria's former regions and present states have disputed for the right to contain that country's long-awaited iron and steel plant, it can be argued that if West Africa is to have a single such complex, Nigeria is not necessarily the right state to have it anyway, and that even if it were that its prospects of profitability would be better if other tropical African countries agreed not to compete.

Types of industry

The situation is evidently complex. While it may be stated with some confidence that every African state is in favour of industrialization, convinced of the value to society at large of the increased output per man-hour that factory working can bring, and scornful of the disadvantages that the process is said by some to involve, the stage by now attained varies substantially between countries, whether we look at manufacturing in absolute terms as in the table opposite, or as affecting different proportions of the population of each state as in the map overleaf.

MANUFACTURING IN AFRICA: ABSOLUTE NUMBERS OF INDUSTRIAL WORKERS IN SELECTED COUNTRIES

Region[1]	Country	Number of industrial workers
NORTH	Algeria	125 800
	Egypt	653 600
	Libya	8 100
	Morocco	140 500
	Sudan	17 900
	Tunisia	53 700
WEST	Benin	1 400
	The Gambia	1 000
	Ghana	55 600
	Guinea	3 000
	Ivory Coast	36 800
	Liberia	2 200
	Mali	8 400
	Mauritania	2 000
	Niger	5 200
	Nigeria	148 600
	Senegal	14 700
	Sierra Leone	47 400
	Togo	2 400
	Upper Volta	2 200
NORTH CENTRAL	Burundi	1 200
	Cameroon	17 200
	Central African Republic	6 000
	Chad	4 600
	Congo	10 100
	Equatorial Guinea	1 800
	Gabon	4 800
	Rwanda	5 300
	Zaire	85 900
SOUTH CENTRAL	Angola	84 500
	Botswana	1 200
	Lesotho	700
	Malawi	20 100
	Mozambique	88 700
	Swaziland	5 900
	Zambia	48 900
EAST	Ethiopia	51 200
	Kenya	75 100
	Madagascar	25 500
	Mauritius	22 900
	Somalia	5 800
	Tanzania	48 700
	Uganda	40 700
SOUTH	South Africa	1 125 000
	Zimbabwe	122 300

[1]See inset map on page 340

Source: UN and ECA statistics

MANUFACTURING IN AFRICA: FACTORY WORKERS AS A PROPORTION OF TOTAL POPULATION

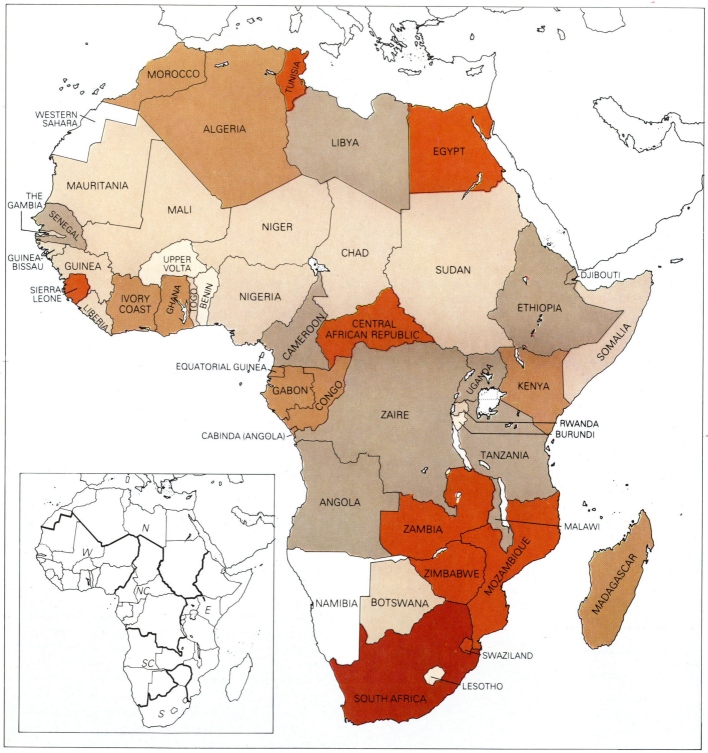

MANUFACTURING IN AFRICA: THE PATTERN OF INDUSTRY BY REGIONS

	North	West	North Central	South Central	East	South	**Africa**	**World**
				Region[1]				
Total number of factory workers *thousands*	999.5	330.9	136.5	250.0	279.9	1 247.3	3 244.1	*
Factory workers per thousand inhabitants	11.7	3.0	3.3	10.1	4.9	44.7	9.4	*
PERCENTAGE OF FACTORY WORKERS ENGAGED IN EACH OF THE FOLLOWING ISIC CATEGORIES								
31 (food, beverages and tobacco)	22.3	22.1	29.1	44.0	33.4	15.1	22.5	13.6
32 (textiles and clothing)	37.1	29.1	23.6	16.9	27.1	20.4	26.8	22.2
33 (wood and furniture)	2.1	15.6	19.7	6.5	8.0	6.5	6.8	6.7
34 (paper, printing and publishing)	4.8	4.7	1.8	7.9	4.1	5.6	5.2	5.0
35 (chemicals, petroleum and plastics)	10.6	9.0	8.1	6.4	4.7	6.1	7.8	7.9
36 (non-metallic mineral products)	6.5	3.3	3.1	7.8	4.7	9.8	7.3	5.7
37 (basic metal industries)	2.1	0.4	1.2	1.0	0.6	7.6	4.1	4.9
38 (fabricated metal products – machinery and equipment	12.5	10.4	9.5	8.7	15.5	27.0	17.7	31.6
39 (other manufactures)	1.1	5.2	4.0	0.7	1.7	1.8	1.9	2.4
$\Sigma\|W-R\|$ (the sum of divergencies between World and African regional percentages in each ISIC category)	55.1	56.6	63.5	70.9	52.2	17.9	30.7	—

*Not available

[1]See inset map on page 340. North = Algeria, Egypt, Libya, Morocco, Sudan, Tunisia. West = Benin, The Gambia, Ghana, Guinea, Ivory Coast, Liberia, Mali, Mauritania, Niger, Nigeria, Senegal, Sierra Leone, Togo, Upper Volta. North Central = Burundi, Cameroon, Central African Republic, Chad, Congo, Gabon. Rwanda, Zaire. South Central = Angola, Botswana, Lesotho, Malawi, Mozambique, Swaziland, Zambia. East = Ethiopia, Kenya, Madagascar, Somalia, Tanzania, Uganda. South = South Africa, Zimbabwe. Excluded for lack of information: Equatorial Guinea, Guinea-Bissau, Mauritius, Namibia, Western Sahara

Source: ECA data and author's research

Such figures give a general picture of the contrasts between the stages of industrialization attained in various parts of Africa, but they disregard the highly contrasted pattern of industry to be found within each state or region, using this term in the structural sense of the proportion of the labour force employed in the main types of industry. From the tables published by the UN Economic Commission for Africa (ECA),* the table above has been constructed to show the percentage of industrial workers in the various International Standard Industrial Classification (ISIC) categories. The figures collected and published by the ECA cover virtually the whole of the continent, being much more comprehensive than those published by the UN Statistical Division in New York, and to the ECA data we have added figures for South Africa and Zimbabwe. The national figures have then been grouped into six regions (see inset map opposite) for presentation in the table above.

The significance of this table is best appreciated by comparing the proportion of the industrial workers in each region, category by category, with the African and global values. Starting with the South region, we see that that region's similarity to the world pattern is quite striking, the sum of the divergencies amounting to 17.9 only, while for all other regions it is more than 50, and for the particularly underdeveloped South Central region it rises to 70.9. To turn to particular industrial categories, the fact that the South and North regions come lowest in terms of the percentage of industrial workers engaged in ISIC 31 (food, beverages and tobacco) may be taken as evidence of their relative industrial advancement and wealth, and hence as an oblique illustration of Engel's Law, which states that as a family grows wealthier it spends a declining proportion of its income on food. Yet the fact that the West region comes much lower than the South Central in this respect is more probably to be explained in cultural rather than economic terms, because yam, cassava and

KEY

Factory workers per 1000 total population

Data not available

Less than 1 per 1000

1–2.5 per 1000

2.5–5 per 1000

5–10 per 1000

10–25 per 1000

More than 25 per 1000

sorghum eaters from the former are less likely to have their staple food processed by factory workers than are those who eat wheat, as bread, or maize ground into mealie flour. The exceptionally high values for 31 for the East and South Central regions reflect also the importance of food-processing industries, e.g. tea and coffee, in Kenya, Uganda, Ethiopia and Malawi. Similarly the high values for 32 (textile-based industries) in the North region are due to the presence of locally-produced raw materials, especially cotton; conversely the mining and associated metalworking plants of the South region explain its high value for 38, metal products and machinery. Indeed apart from the freak high values of 33 (wood-based industries) in the West and North Central regions (based on local forest resources), it may be said that there is a central group of industrial categories, from 33 to 37, which vary relatively little from region to region, totalling from 22.1 per cent in the East region to 33.9 per cent in the North Central and 35.6 per cent in the South, while on either side of these, categories 31 and 32 vary from 35.5 per cent (South region) to 60.9 per cent (South Central region), and 38 (fabricated metals and machinery) ranges from 27.0 per cent in the South region to as little as 8.7 per cent in the South Central.

So far we have been arguing that the manufacturing industries present in any African state are at least as much an expression of its stage of economic development as they are a reflection of the raw materials locally available, with the implication that any state wishing to proceed with a programme of rapid and far-reaching industrialization should pay as much attention to inducing the right attitudes towards investment, productivity and sound accounting among its citizens as to the search for suitable industrial raw materials. Nevertheless, the presence within a state of a supply of good coking coal, high quality iron ore, petroleum, bauxite or other minerals, or the possibility of producing meat, sugar, hides, timber or natural fibres, indubitably constitutes a valuable resource, suggesting which products it would be most prudent to develop at the beginning of the industrialization process, and what lines to pursue without fear of interruption from future shortages of materials or from political interference.

Of these two groups of raw materials the renewable, i.e. the animal and vegetable, present greater statistical difficulties than the mineral: it is virtually impossible to make an inventory of their availability, or to map their occurrence. This is because the supply of timber,* say, is partly a question of what is now growing in the forests, and partly a question of what land can be spared for permanent timber production, and how much it can be made to yield. Similar arguments apply to the cultivation of cotton, jute or other fibres, which can replace, or more probably supplement, food crops wherever they can yield an adequate cash return. The rearing of animals for meat, wool and hides for processing in a factory will eventually be controlled by similar considerations, but hitherto it is only in Egypt or in the Saharan oases that competition between animals and man for land for food is keenly felt.

While, therefore, it has proved possible, as for example in the *Oxford Regional Economic Atlas of Africa*, to draw a series of maps of the present distribution of those crops which form the raw material of manufacturing, it would be absurd to attempt to plot the potential extension of each. This is an economic issue at least as much as an agronomic one. In central Sudan, for example, there is already a major irrigated sugar-growing and sugar-refining scheme nearing completion, which might have been very profitable if original estimates of the cost of construction had proved realistic and if sugar prices had stayed at their freak levels of the early 1970s, but which now seems certain to be run at a loss for years to come. Moreover, the same area in Sudan is also a potential cotton and groundnut-growing area, depending on prices and on the willingness of Sudanese share-cropping tenants to grow these crops, and it could no doubt be used to grow wheat, rice, timber, castor oil or sesame.

The workability of a mineral resource* is also a function of its degree of concentration, its accessibility and the current level of prices obtainable. Thus in south-western Sudan there is a long-known deposit of copper, Hofrat en Nahas, which has been investigated many times, but whose remoteness and relatively low quality have never made it seem worth exploiting; least of all with copper prices exceptionally depressed. Essentially the same is true of bauxite and iron ore, it generally being cheaper to extract high quality ores and to transport them over long distances than to work poorer deposits because they are nearer.

Many of the industrial raw materials of Africa were initially exploited with the object of immediate export, as for instance when cotton-growing was inaugurated in the Sudan Gezira from 1926, or when the arrival of the Nigerian railway in Kano in 1912 led to a very substantial increase in the cultivation of groundnuts; similarly Nigerian petroleum was exported in a raw state after its discovery in 1956, and began to be refined locally from 1965, while Algerian iron ore, which has been exploited for export for many years, began to be smelted in Algeria in 1972. These reflections on the availability of industrial resources suggest an alternative way of appraising the present state of manufacturing in Africa, by classifying industries into five categories.

Agro-based industries, using locally grown natural products as raw materials and processing them locally as far as possible. This group of commodities may ultimately be intended for export, or for the local market.

Import-substitution industries, which take the list of currently imported articles as a target, and aim to replace them as far as possible, whether the raw materials used are local or imported.

Heavy industries, representing major investments in plant for processing iron ore and similar raw materials, which are intended to produce the materials for further treatment, and thus to trigger off broader-based industrial expansion in the country where they are set up, and possibly in neighbouring states as well.

Of these the first two are not, of course, mutually exclusive. In sub-tropical countries brewing and distilling will be agro-based, and principally use local raw materials, but near the Equator grape juice, malt and hops (though not molasses) are more likely to be imported; shoe factories generally use the hides from local beasts for local leather, but when they turn to using plastics for soles or uppers, these, or at least the chemicals from which they have been derived, are often imported still; corned beef from local cattle is sold in cans made from imported tin-plate, even in tin-producing Nigeria; most African countries now make Virginia-type cigarettes, but the percentage of local tobacco used varies enormously, from 100 per cent in Zambia or Zimbabwe, to nil in Egypt, where the collection of duty is still regarded as more important than the saving of foreign exchange involved. It is for such reasons that two categories only are provided in the diagram below to distinguish between light and heavy industries, following the classification employed by the ECA which puts ISIC groups 31, 32, 33, 34, and 39 in the former category, and groups 35, 36, 37 and 38 in the latter. It is recognized that several of the light industries are not yet based on local raw materials, for reasons already considered, and that some may never be, e.g. metal

furniture in the smaller states or specialized forms of printing, and similarly that the heavy industries, as here defined, are very far from being the major chemical and metallurgical works to which the term would be applied in industrially more advanced regions of the world.

Hitherto we have been regarding industry as a source of paid employment. If we wish to consider the actual commodities or substances that industry exists to provide, the tables of commodity production data from the UN Statistical Yearbooks give an overall view. The tables overleaf, although supplemented by separate enquiries, are by no means always as complete as one would wish.

Of the various agro-based industries (see table on page 344) it is probably best in this context to consider a few examples which, at least in Africa, are virtually never based on imported raw materials: sugar, tobacco products (save in Egypt, as noted above), cotton yarn, and margarine.

The crops and forest trees in question grow well in a tropical climate, and the chief problem posed by this table is to decide whether the absence of a particular item is due to faulty reporting, or to the fact that Sudan, for example, though a major producer of cotton, had at

KEY

Light industry   Heavy industry   For key to regions see inset map on page 340

MANUFACTURING IN AFRICA: EMPLOYMENT IN LIGHT AND HEAVY INDUSTRY, BY REGIONS

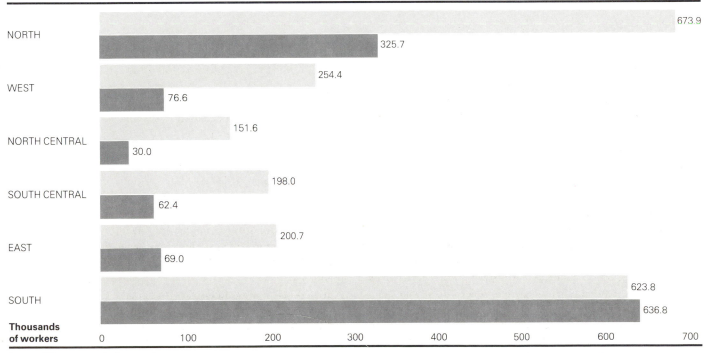

Source: ECA data and author's research

the time in question (1977) not yet begun to spin its own cotton yarn. Where a basic crop like sugar is not reported, this presumably means that commercial cultivation has not been undertaken. The importance of cigarette manufacture is interesting: in even the poorest countries money is to be made by avoiding import duties and making cigarettes on the spot, and while tobacco is dietetically valueless its manufacture provides jobs.

Import substitution is probably best illustrated by listing the

PRODUCTION OF CERTAIN AGRO-BASED INDUSTRIES IN AFRICA, AND WORLD TOTALS, 1977[1]

Country	Sugar thousands of tonnes	Cotton yarn thousands of tonnes	Margarine thousands of tonnes	Wheat flour thousands of tonnes	Cigarettes millions
Algeria	25	9.3 (1975)	8.5 (1976)	659 (1974)	10 217 (1976)
Angola	65	3.1 (1973)	3.1 (1974)	82 (1973)	2 500
Chad	15	—	—	*	*
Cameroon	35	—	—	31 (1976)	1 755
Congo	16	—	—	5	1 380 (1976)
Egypt	657	210.4	133	2 896	24 980
Ethiopia	137	9.8 (1976)	—	80 (1976)	1 572 (1976)
Gabon	*	—	—	18 (1975)	332 (1975)
Ghana	25	—	—	52 (1975)	2 339 (1975)
Guinea	13	—	—	—	*
Ivory Coast	37	6.0 (1975)	—	119	3 240
Kenya	185	219.0 (1975)	—	155	3 944
Liberia	*	—	—	—	100
Libya	*	—	—	88 (1975)	263
Madagascar	110	6.2 (1971)	—	—	1 804
Malawi	95	—	—	—	487
Mali	152	—	—	—	*
Mauritius	705	—	—	—	888 (1976)
Morocco	260	14.3 (1974)	2.5	781 (1973)	9 043 (1976)
Mozambique	320	3.4 (1976)	1.5 (1974)	65 (1976)	3 100
Nigeria	40	5.0 (1975)	5.1 (1975)	280 (1975)	13 000
Senegal	40	0.2 (1975)	—	82 (1975)	2 265
Sierra Leone	*	—	—	21 (1975)	1 503
Somalia	35	—	—	—	*
South Africa	2 369	37.9	77.8	917	22 620
Sudan	151	*	—	223 (1975)	730
Swaziland	238	—	—	—	*
Tanzania	108	—	—	72 (1976)	3 659 (1976)
Tunisia	10	7.4 (1976)	0.5	300	5 399
Uganda	20	—	—	9	1 867
Upper Volta	10	0.5 (1976)	—	—	460 (1976)
Zaire	65	*	2.0 (1976)	—	2 860 (1976)
Zambia	71	—	3.5 (1972)	90	1 350
Zimbabwe	200	*	*	*	4 600
WORLD	91 826[2]	*	6 180[2]	130 100[2]	3 321 560[2]

*Not available   [1]Unless otherwise stated   [2]Estimate

Source: *Statistical Yearbook 1978* (UN, New York, 1979)

countries which have their own factories producing certain widely used commodities: gasoline, pneumatic tyres, cement and radio receivers.

The table below indicates that cement production is one of the basic industries to be found in any country trying to reduce its dependence on imports from abroad, while petroleum-refining occupies an essentially similar role, with the additional feature that those countries which are substantial producers of petroleum are likely also to establish additional refining capacity for export (except Nigeria, whose refinery capacity is incapable of meeting the vast internal demand). The manufacture of tyres and the assembly of radios are by contrast useful but far less essential elements in the process of eliminating the demand for imports from abroad.

Lastly we come to heavy industry, particularly the processing of iron and steel. These industries are much desired by ambitious and patriotic Africans, but at a time when every major steel-making country in the world is suffering from excess capacity and under-employment the validity of the arguments for investing in this field

PRODUCTION OF CERTAIN IMPORT-SUBSTITUTES IN AFRICA, AND WORLD TOTALS, 1977[1]

Country	Gasoline thousands of tonnes	Cement thousands of tonnes	Tyres thousands	Radio receivers thousands
Algeria	787	1 777	378 (1974)	21 (1976)
Angola	61	650	195 (1974)	38 (1974)
Benin	—	164 (1976)	—	—
Congo	—	45	—	—
Egypt	1 530	3 169	479	265
Ethiopia	75	100 (1976)	—	—
Gabon	122	93 (1975)	—	—
Ghana	225	700 (1976)	178 (1972)	90 (1975)
Ivory Coast	254	918	—	80 (1975)
Kenya	366	1 144	—	—
Liberia	67	100	—	—
Libya	589	659	—	—
Madagascar	97	52	—	—
Malawi	—	94	—	32 (1972)
Mali	—	50	—	—
Morocco	380	2 614	379 (1976)	157 (1975)
Mozambique	65	220	—	24 (1974)
Niger	—	40	—	—
Nigeria	726	1 260	754 (1976)	112 (1976)
Senegal	135	329	—	—
Sierra Leone	42	—	—	—
South Africa	3 539	6 573	4 017	385
Sudan	130	178	—	—
Tanzania	105	247	—	177 (1975)
Togo	—	228	—	—
Tunisia	141	629	135	71
Uganda	—	80	—	—
Zaire	32	489	*	*
Zambia	190	332	8	28
Zimbabwe	—	486	*	—
WORLD	562 436	*	759 000	126 566

* Not available   [1] Unless otherwise stated.

Source: *Statistical Yearbook 1978* (UN, New York, 1979)

PRODUCTION OF HEAVY INDUSTRY IN AFRICA, AND WORLD TOTALS, 1977[1]

Country	Sulphuric acid	Pig-iron and ferro-alloy	Crude steel	Unwrought aluminium	Copper smelter production
			production thousands of tonnes		
Algeria	*	389	213	—	—
Egypt	30	569 (1976)	263	—	—
Ghana	—	—	—	153	—
Morocco	358 (1976)	12	—	—	—
Mozambique	23 (1974)	—	*	—	—
South Africa	31 210	6 894	7 178	78	218
Tunisia	1 208	136	156	—	—
Zaire	173	—	—	—	452
Zambia	275	—	—	—	660
Zimbabwe	*	300	300	—	28
WORLD	110 890	498 300	667 000	13 500	8 150[2]

* Not available   [1] Unless otherwise stated   [2] Estimate

Sources: *Statistical Yearbook 1978* (UN, New York, 1979)

must be questioned: certainly no African state can look forward with confidence to the export of steel products as a source of profit. In the table above, which shows the beginnings of heavy industry in Africa, the only really substantial figures, 6.6 million tonnes of pig iron and 6.9 million tonnes of crude steel for casting in South Africa, represent in each case little more than 1 per cent of world production in 1976, which is an indication that the continent still has a long way to go in this sector.

Future growth of African industrialization, though eagerly desired throughout the continent, is difficult to predict with confidence. The post-1973 global increase in energy prices severely hit all oil-importing states, while even in those with unexpected increases in foreign earnings from petroleum exports the enlarged money supply produced severe inflation and the disruption of previous economic activities. Almost everywhere in the continent the profitability of industry is increasingly doubtful, and that modernization of agriculture* which could truly support African industrialization, by providing the demand for capital goods, the source of raw materials and the wealth that would make import-substitution irrelevant, still seems impossibly far away.   *K.M.B.*

Industrial location

Industry here refers specifically to manufacturing, that is factory production: the processing of raw materials or the fabrication of produced or processed parts into new products. Repair work such as vehicle and clock repairs, though sometimes loosely referred to as

manufacturing, falls outside this definition. Strictly speaking, repair operations are service functions which belong to the tertiary or service sector.

The term 'industrial location' is used to describe the occurrence and distribution of industry in Africa in two related senses. In its narrower sense the term refers to the site or spot, for instance, roadside or city centre location; in its wider sense location refers to the locality or the region, say, urban or rural area, or forest zone location.

In countries where initial benefits, such as good transport facilities, cheap power and good water supply, are scarce and highly localized, the pattern of industrial location is generally one of great concentration in a few favoured centres. Vast areas of the territory, where such facilities are not adequately provided, become neglected and devoid of industrial activity. Efforts to put industries in such places would therefore be very expensive since such basic infrastructure must be part of the industrial development package of the entrepreneur.

Factors and patterns of industrial location in Black Africa

Industrial activity of the medium- or large-scale type is relatively recent in most African countries, hardly predating their political independence. Throughout the colonial period Black African countries were used by their colonial masters both as sources of cheap raw materials for the metropolitan industries and as markets for the latter's products. For the effective maintenance of such a relationship some form of modern transport* system was necessary. Mainly rail and road, the routes were everywhere of a coast-interior alignment for speedy evacuation of natural resources (agricultural and mineral products) and for the importation of manufactures. Few attempts were made to link up major internal routes for the effective articulation of local and regional economies.

The effect of the colonial origins of modern route systems in Black Africa has been mainly to give very few and relatively well-served urban centres considerable advantages of accessibility. With such a headstart in the economic development race, within the urban system of each country, such towns quickly developed into big centres for the generally inefficient articulation of local and regional trade. It is in such rapidly growing centres that most characteristically urban activities develop and more infrastructural facilities are set up, to the neglect of numerous other towns. Such growing services and facilities constitute the attractive elements of an industrial environment. It is not surprising that what little large- and medium-scale manufacturing has developed in Black Africa is concentrated in the few centres of this type. In fact, in many countries it is the port-cum-capital (often the first contact point of the country with the outside world) that develops into a primate city and captures the bulk of the industrial establishments. For example, the table below shows that as many as ten of the 19 capital cities shown claimed at least 50 per cent of the entire industrial establishments in their respective countries by 1971. Indeed, three capitals, Libreville (Gabon), Banjul (The Gambia),

PERCENTAGE OF MANUFACTURING INDUSTRY LOCATED IN CAPITAL CITIES: SELECTED AFRICAN COUNTRIES, 1977

Country	Capital	Percentage share of industry
Gabon	Libreville	100
The Gambia	Banjul	100
Liberia	Monrovia	100
Senegal	Dakar	81
Burundi	Bujumbura	80
Sierra Leone	Freetown	75
Tanzania	Dar es Salaam	62
Sudan	Khartoum	60
Guinea	Conakry	50
Cameroon	Douala	50
Egypt	Cairo	47
Ethiopia	Addis Ababa	47
Kenya	Nairobi	47
Zambia	Lusaka	35
Nigeria	Lagos	35
Congo	Brazzaville	33
Zaire	Kinshasa	30
Ghana	Accra	30
Uganda	Kampala	28

Sources: K. M. Barbour, *The Growth, Location and Structure of Industry in Egypt* (New York, 1972); A. L. Mabogunje, 'Manufacturing and the Geography of Development in Tropical Africa', *Economic Geography* (49, 1973)

and Monrovia (Liberia), had a 100 per cent claim. In most other countries the greater part of the industrial establishments not located in the capital city are in one or two other cities. For example, Jinja and Tororo claimed over 80 per cent of the remaining industrial establishments in Uganda. The Accra/Tema-Kumasi-Sekondi-Takoradi triangle in southern Ghana accounted for over 80 per cent of Ghana's non-capital based industrial establishments. The picture is much the same for Mombasa and Kisumu in Kenya, for Kankan and Dabola in Guinea, and for Alexandria and Mehalla el Kubra in Egypt.

This characteristic structure of industrial location in Black Africa reinforces the enclave structure which is an enduring feature of the colonial heritage throughout Africa. Since the most important industrial elements of these African countries comprise public utilities and state corporations, it can be argued that the most dominant factor influencing industrial location decision-making even by private entrepreneurs is the policy of the governments of the respective African countries.

Large-scale industries in Black Africa are mostly not only city-based but also market-oriented in their location. There are, however, many examples of industrial location which are influenced by raw materials supply. In some cases industries are located at the source of materials, in others—where there is dependence on imported materials—they are established in port-towns (in other words they are urban-based).

Mainly because of their high material index (excessive weight of input compared with weight of resulting output), industrial establishments such as integrated cement plants, sugar mills, glass, ceramic and brick factories are normally material-rooted or supply-based in order to minimize transport cost on weight or bulk-losing materials. This is not true, however, of a good many sawmills, paper mills, vegetable oil and livestock feed mills, because, although their major raw materials are weight- or bulk-losing, their other input requirements—power, chemicals and skilled labour—are city based; that is, away from the source of their raw materials. And the more transport facilities improve, the more the industries are liberated, as it were, from their sources of raw materials to the outskirts of big cities, where they compete with weight- or bulk-adding as well as perishable goods industries.

Because most African countries are still technologically very weak and consequently dependent on imported material inputs (both primary products and intermediate goods), their main ports are invariably their major industrial centres. This is evident from the table. As their first contact points with the sources of imported inputs, the ports in effect become the material sources and logical location of most supply-based industrial activities—in keeping with the cost-minimization principle. This implies that as technology improves and greater self-reliance becomes possible in African countries, more of the currently coast-based industries now constrained by import needs will probably locate inland near the domestic resource base.

Industrial activity in small towns and rural areas has been at a low level mainly because of poor infrastructural facilities. These require a large population with considerable purchasing power as the minimum threshold for their effective provision and maintenance. The small amount of industrial activity so far developed in such locations is generally on a small enough scale to be adaptable to some forms of improvisation: bore holes for piped water, and portable generating plants for power.

Many of such industrial establishments have been set up through the initiative and drive of small rural communities performing as cooperatives. Others represent the single-handed effort of certain individuals striving to bring some form of economic development to their otherwise agricultural communities. Not only does manufacturing in such an environment help to diversify the rural economy, it also improves local income through employment and dependence on local resources. Above all, it gives the rural community a sense of belonging to the modernization drive which industrialization has so far brought to a very limited geographical area. It is interesting to note that the decision to locate manufacturing industries in such ill-equipped and unattractive rural areas has not been motivated by profit maximization. The industrial entrepreneur is seeking satisfaction more in social welfare terms than in private benefit-cost terms. The many examples of this in Nigeria are typical of a widespread phenomenon in many African countries today. *J.O.C.O.*

Wage labour

Before the second half of the 19th century only limited coastal trading areas of Africa with extensive overseas contact had reached a level of economic development which required the use of hired labour. In the interior wage labour was virtually non-existent, and slave and communal labour was used to perform public works and to create the agricultural surplus needed to support rulers, armies, and other non-productive elements within pre-colonial societies. After they had established political supremacy over these societies and emancipated the slaves, European administrators, settlers, and entrepreneurs began to recruit a voluntary wage labour force for the purpose of governing and exploiting the resources of the newly acquired territories. This proved to be difficult, for although local populations rapidly developed a desire for cash and new goods, they were reluctant to accept the low wages, hard work, and harsh discipline offered by expatriate employers. So, in order to force young men into wage employment and to reduce the level of wages that was required to attract new labourers, colonial governments, particularly those of sub-Saharan Africa resorted to measures such as rural taxation, land alienation, and forced labour.

These policies introduced the idea of wage labour to African societies and stimulated a flow of young men out of subsistence farming regions and into the expanding cash-crop and urban areas where employment, wages and new social experiences were to be found. Most migrants preferred to work for African cash-crop farmers, but where such opportunities were absent (as in the Sahel regions of West Africa) or restricted by government policy (as in Kenya) they had no option but to accept employment in road and railway construction, commercial and plantation farming, mining and other jobs created by the growth of the cash economy. These migrant labourers—invariably illiterate and unskilled—shifted frequently between jobs in countries where they were free to do so. Most worked for wages on a seasonal basis, earning enough to pay taxes and to buy some goods, then returning to their home areas for the few months of the year when their labour was needed on subsistence farms.

The distance which migrant labourers had to travel to find work varied from under 150km in relatively prosperous areas such as Ghana and the Ivory Coast to over 1500km in the parts of eastern and southern Africa supplying labour to the mines of South Africa and the Rhodesian Copperbelt. The flows of migratory labour crossed territorial borders and created regional, rather than national, labour markets. The mobility of the early African wage labour force compensated for the scarcity of labour in the areas of greatest demand and in doing so removed what had been one of the most important obstacles to the exploitation of the continent's resources in the pre-colonial period.

Until the 1930s the demand for workers in Africa's labour markets was equal to or greater than the supply. Since that time the supply of labour has expanded rapidly as a result of improved transport* and communications, improved working conditions, family and ethnic connections in urban areas and unrealistic expectations of life and work in town among rural communities. Simultaneously, the number of new jobs available has expanded slowly or even diminished. Slow rates of growth in most African economies, the improved productivity of workers and the introduction of capital- rather than labour-intensive industrial techniques have all contributed to the stagnation of demand.

This pattern of supply and demand in the labour market has had a number of effects on the structure of the African wage labour force. Firstly, the wage labour force in all African countries is a small, and in many cases a declining proportion of the total population and total labour force. Excluding the Republic of South Africa, North Africa has the highest proportion of wage labourers in the total labour force at approximately 35 per cent. East and Central Africa follow at 15 per cent each, while in West Africa only 6 per cent of the labour force is in wage employment. These regional figures disguise wide national variations within each region. In North African countries the proportion of wage labourers in the labour force is uniformly high, ranging from 30 per cent to 50 per cent of the total. In West Africa the figure varies from 2 per cent in the landlocked Sahel state of Upper Volta to 20 per cent in Liberia, where large rubber and mining enterprises dominate the economy. Similarly, in East Africa Ethiopia's wage labourers represent only 7 per cent of the total labour force, whereas the figure for Zambia with its large copper mining industry is 27 per cent. Finally, in Central Africa the proportion ranges from 5 per cent in Cameroon to 25 per cent in Angola. Only in the plantation dominated economy of Mauritius, where 85 per cent of the labour force works for wages, is there a sharp deviation from this general pattern.

A second effect of the excess of supply over demand in Africa's labour markets is large-scale unemployment. In most major urban areas of Africa this is a major social problem and seems likely to remain so for many years to come. Unemployment rates as high as 27 per cent in Algeria, 17 per cent in Kenya and between 15 per cent and 35 per cent in Nigeria have been recorded. Even these high levels of unemployment and the associated evils of urban poverty, housing shortages and inadequate sanitation have failed to stem the flow of aspirant wage labourers to the towns.

The unemployment problem has been alleviated to some extent by the third result of excess labour supply. During the last three decades Africa's main urban areas have developed a large 'informal' economy consisting of petty trading, small-scale manufacturing, the provision of personal services and a wide range of illegal activities. While most

Labourers from Lesotho seeking work at the South African mines recruiting office in Maseru, Lesotho

towns have a core of committed skilled and semi-skilled wage labourers, the far larger number of unskilled workers alternate between urban and rural areas, and within the urban areas they alternate between, or even combine, wage labour and employment or self-employment in the informal urban economy.

The distribution of Africa's non-agricultural wage labour force among different occupations reveals the extent to which most African countries have failed to develop a significant industrial or manufacturing sector in the national economy. Outside of South Africa all African countries have more wage labourers employed in the service sector (finance, commerce, transport, communications and other services) than in the industrial sector (mining, manufacturing, construction and public utilities). In countries with mining and manufacturing industries such as Ghana, Zaire, Mauritania, Zambia, Malawi and Liberia, between 40 and 45 per cent of non-agricultural wage labourers are engaged in industrial activities. Elsewhere in the continent the proportion is smaller. For example, in Mali the proportion is only 10 per cent, in Chad it is 26 per cent, and in Algeria, 30 per cent. More specifically, in the majority of African countries public and private services employ most wage labourers (30–40 per cent), followed by construction (15–20 per cent), manufacturing (10–20 per cent), mining (5–15 per cent), and transport (5–15 per cent).

The limited growth of manufacturing industry in Africa is reflected in the sexual composition of the wage labour force. Throughout Africa women form at least half of the total labour force, particularly in trading and small-scale agriculture.* However, unlike the industrialized countries of Europe and America, where large numbers of women are employed in manufacturing, in Africa only a small number of women have been absorbed into the wage labour force. In most countries the proportion of female wage earners is under 10 per cent. Again Mauritius, with almost 20 per cent of females in the wage labour force, provides the main exception to the general continental pattern.

A final significant feature of the modern African wage labour force is the large number of workers employed in public services and institutions and in state-owned enterprises. Throughout North, West, Central and East Africa between 35 per cent and 45 per cent of all wage earners are employed in the public sector. This pattern of employment is the result of three trends in post-war African economies. Firstly, since that time most governments, colonial and independent, have been committed to a policy of active intervention in the economy to create new enterprises and to plan economic growth and development. Secondly, since the period of decolonization large numbers of foreign-owned agricultural and industrial enterprises have passed into the hands of national governments. Finally, African governments have been keen to alleviate the pressing problem of urban unemployment, particularly among the growing number of young school-leavers. Consequently, high levels of overmanning and 'underemployment' have been tolerated in the public sector.

The dominant role of the state in most African economies has had a decisive impact on the political status and activities of the wage labour force. Wages in Africa have always been low. In the colonial period this was justified in terms of the low productivity of African labour, the limited economic needs of workers and their lack of commitment to wage employment. Wages were therefore set at a low level by a monopolistic combination of government and expatriate employers, and only raised in times of severe economic hardship or when political stability was threatened by discontent amongst urban workers. In the 1940s trade unions emerged throughout Africa to organize and express this discontent. The principal features of the wage labour force – unskilled, illiterate and uncommitted – presented con-

siderable obstacles to successful unionization, but colonial governments were very sensitive to the growth of mass protest movements and in most cases attempted to steer the unions into 'responsible' policies. However, these attempts generally failed, and trade unions played a leading role in the nationalist movements of the late colonial period. Taking West Africa as an example, it is clear that the relationship between trade unions and nationalist parties was in some cases, for example Guinea and the Ivory Coast, a close one. In other countries, for example Ghana and Nigeria, the relationship was less formal and less intimate.

Since the period of decolonization the organized wage labour force has remained on close terms with government only in a few radical states, such as Algeria, Mozambique and, to a lesser extent, Tanzania. Elsewhere the relationship has been characterized by varying degrees of hostility. Like their colonial predecessors, independent African governments have fixed wages at low levels, justifying such policies in terms of the need to conserve funds for capital investment, the need to create an attractive investment

Members of the Railway and Port Workers' Union of Ghana at a union meeting in Sekondi, Ghana

climate for foreign capital, and the need to equalize rural and urban standards of living. Underlying these justifications has been the concern of governments, particularly military regimes, to redirect scarce resources away from the wage labour force and towards the ruling elite.

In addition to these economic considerations, African governments have been perturbed by the potential political power of wage labourers who play a key role in the national economy and who are concentrated in the principal centres of administration, industry and commerce. Consequently post-colonial African governments, even those led by former active unionists, have used a variety of tactics to diminish the political and economic power of the wage labour force. For example, in Ghana trade unions have been incorporated into a central Trades Union Congress which is under constant pressure to pursue moderate demands. In Kenya and Zambia governments have attempted to merge the trade union movement into the structures of the ruling party. In almost every country controlled by a military regime severe legislative restrictions on the activities of trade unions have been introduced.

These policies of control have met with only limited success. Many unions have proved reluctant to see their independence disappear, and when they have complied with the wishes of government, rank and file union members have frequently engaged in political or industrial action against the instructions of their officials. Thus it appears that in contrast to the wishes of most African governments, the wage labour force will continue to play an important role in determining the political future of the continent.   *J.F.C.*

State-ownership and indigenous entrepreneurship

Economic decolonization and the possibilities of creating a productive pattern of national or indigenous capitalist development are two major challenges to independent Africa. Central to the achievement of these tasks is the state: as a direct investor itself, or as the regulator of patterns of foreign investment and through the protection and promotion of indigenous enterprise and technology.

Historically, the state in Africa has generally supported foreign capital. Under colonial rule state-ownership was mainly limited to public utilities and functions related to the infrastructural and service requirements of colonial agricultural, trading and mining interests. In the agriculturally richer colonies, the state sector also included the marketing boards, whose revenues partly helped finance provision of public utilities and infrastructure. With the approach of independence, larger or relatively well-endowed countries such as Nigeria, Kenya and Ivory Coast saw the expansion of foreign capital from commerce (importation and distribution) into local assembly or production. This was often encouraged by state provided finance, protection and tax incentives, in an effort to maintain inflows of investment as well as to promote import substitution in some cases.

With the exception of Ghana, where direct, productive state investment took place under Kwame Nkrumah,* state enterprise *per se* remained weak in most countries. Similarly, indigenous private entrepreneurship, where it existed on any significant scale, was underdeveloped and restricted to commercial and service activities and small-scale capitalism. Since the mid-1960s state initiatives have dramatically increased, though patterns of intervention have taken divergent forms and have resulted in mixed achievements.

Thus, even in Nigeria, where – with political pressures for greater autonomy from foreign capital, oil based resources and market size – conditions would appear more favourable than elsewhere, state intervention has resulted in minimal new entrepreneurial opportunities being opened up for indigenous businessmen. At the same time compulsory partial localization of share ownership has enlarged the capital base of foreign controlled companies in higher technology sectors. Alternatively, in Ghana, direct state investments in new industry under Nkrumah, themselves heavily dependent on external finance and technology, have been undermined by subsequent regimes, while in Tanzania nationalized state enterprises have entered into a range of technical partnership arrangements with multi-national corporations. In contrast, in the Francophone countries, even the relatively expansive Ivory Coast, state intervention in favour of national or indigenous enterprise has been virtually non-existent.

One sector into which state-ownership has been extended in almost every country where it exists is petroleum and mineral extraction.* Large industries have been wholly or partially nationalized in Nigeria (petroleum), Zaire and Zambia (copper), and Mauritania (iron). Lesser industries have been taken over in Ghana (diamonds, bauxite, gold and manganese), Senegal and Togo (phosphates), Sierra Leone (diamonds), and Guinea (bauxite). Among the latter, with the exception of Ghana and Guinea, little else has been touched. In nearly all cases the operation of these industries remains in foreign hands, under appropriate management, engineering, marketing and other service contracts, although the Nigerian National Petroleum Corporation has become involved in drilling and exploration activity. Politically, state intervention in the petroleum and mineral sector appears to have been limited hitherto to the maximization of planning control and resources for national development. In this profitable sector, multi-national corporations have usually been undertaxed and recalcitrant in indigenizing their management, while at the same time being relatively free in determining levels of production and hence major government revenue. Also Africans' convictions that they are being exploited by foreigners tend to be particularly strong in

NATIONALIZATION AND INDUSTRIALIZATION: SELECTED AFRICAN COUNTRIES, 1960–76

Country	Foreign direct investments millions of US$ 1967	1973	Nationalization and indigenization
Benin	18	30	NATIONALIZATION Selective. Most manufacturing, banking, insurance, petroleum distribution, telecommunications, and port facilities. But not large trading houses (e.g. *Société Commerciale de l'Ouest Africaine*, John Holt)
Cameroon	150	240	NATIONALIZATION Electric power
Central African Rep.	37	55	NATIONALIZATION Petroleum distribution, shoe manufacturing (Bata)
Congo	90	110	NATIONALIZATION Selective. Timber operations, sugar mill, insurance, petroleum exploration, and distribution
Ethiopia	50	80	NATIONALIZATION Comprehensive. Essential industry (e.g. food, beverages, textiles, leather, chemicals, iron and printing), petroleum distribution, banking, insurance and plantations
Gabon	265	425	NATIONALIZATION Projected iron mine (Bethlehem Steel), cement plant, and some petroleum distribution
Ghana	260	410	NATIONALIZATION Selective. Large mineral enterprises: gold (*Lonrho*), diamonds (Consolidated African Selection Trust), bauxite (British Aluminium) and manganese (Union Carbide) – 55 per cent. Large timber operations – 55 per cent. Large enterprises producing basic necessities (e.g. sugar, fertilizers, and rubber products) – 55 per cent. Petroleum refining – 100 per cent. Authorized but not implemented: aluminium industry (*Valco*) – 30 per cent; petroleum production – 20 per cent. INDIGENIZATION Comprehensive. Wholly reserved to Ghanaians: small retail and wholesale enterprises; all enterprises in 19 categories of simple industry (e.g. surface transport, bakeries, and real estate). Required Ghanaian participation: large retail and wholesale; 46 categories of industry – 40/50 per cent. Banking – 40 per cent. Small timber and mineral enterprises – 40 per cent. Small enterprises producing basic necessities – 50 per cent
Guinea	93	180	NATIONALIZATION Selective. Large bauxite operations (*Friguia*) – 49 per cent. Most manufacturing and commerce. Petroleum distribution. Small disputed bauxite operation (*Alcan*) taken over in 1961. INDIGENIZATION Foreign businessmen banned in 1968
Kenya	172	280	NATIONALIZATION Minor. Banking – 60 per cent. Petroleum refining – 50 per cent. Electric power – 51 per cent. Some farms for redistribution to Kenyans. INDIGENIZATION Comprehensive. All enterprises outside of six cities; dealing in commodities mainly consumed by Africans (e.g. sugar and rough textiles); wholesale and retail; export-import, brokerage, manufacturer's representatives, and real estate. Implemented gradually but forcefully since 1967
Madagascar	72	140	NATIONALIZATION Selective. Banking, insurance, cinemas, large trading house (CMM) and electric power
Malawi	30	70	INDIGENIZATION Asian traders forced to leave rural areas
Mali	7	9	NATIONALIZATION Comprehensive. Accomplished in the early 1960s
Mauritania	101	170	NATIONALIZATION Iron mining (*Miferma*) – 100 per cent; copper mining (*Somima*) – 100 per cent
Nigeria	1109	2400	NATIONALIZATION Massive but selective. Petroleum production (Shell-BP, Phillips-*Agip*, *Safrap*, Mobil, Gulf) – 55 per cent. Banking – 40 per cent. Some petroleum distribution (Shell) – 60 per cent. INDIGENIZATION Comprehensive. Wholly reserved to Nigerians: all enterprises in 22 categories; all small enterprises in 33 categories of more complex industries. Nigerians must hold 40 per cent share in large enterprises in the 33 categories
Senegal	154	230	NATIONALIZATION Phosphates (*Compagnie Sénégalaise des Phosphates de Taiba*) – 50 per cent
Sierra Leone	68	80	NATIONALIZATION Diamonds (Sierra Leone Selection Trust) – 51 per cent
Somalia	13	17	NATIONALIZATION Banking, insurance, electric power, sugar mill, petroleum distribution, and shell fishing plant
Tanzania	60	80	NATIONALIZATION Comprehensive. Plantations, manufacturing, large buildings, hotels, banking, insurance, petroleum distribution, export-import, and wholesaling
Uganda	48	19	NATIONALIZATION Comprehensive. Small copper mine, plantations, banking, insurance, export-import, petroleum distribution, wholesale and retail trade, and virtually all manufacturing. INDIGENIZATION Comprehensive and abrupt with the expulsion of Asians by Idi Amin's government
Zaire	481	640	NATIONALIZATION Massive but selective. Copper (*Union Minière*) – 100 per cent. Diamonds (MIBA). Petroleum production – 15 per cent. Plantations, petroleum distribution, transport, many large manufacturing and commercial enterprises – 100 per cent. INDIGENIZATION Comprehensive. Retail, wholesale and some other enterprises indigenized in 1973; large enterprises including those indigenized in 1973 taken by government in 1974 in preparation for later sale to the public; in 1975 some former owners were offered 40 per cent equity in their former enterprises. Net result is widespread, uneven takeover
Zambia	421	300	NATIONALIZATION Massive and comprehensive. Copper mining (Anglo-American, Roan Selection Trust) – 51 per cent. Most manufacturing, transport, freehold land, banks, newspapers and hotels. INDIGENIZATION Decree covers most wholesale and retail trade, and other categories of small business. Largely thwarted by loopholes

Source: adapted from Leslie L. Rood, 'Nationalization and Indigenization in Africa'. *Journal of Modern African Studies* (14, 1976)

this sector where wasting assets – irreplaceable natural resources – are visibly being taken away.

Beyond the strategic petroleum and mineral sector further state intervention or investment has been affected by a number of factors, including the ideological orientation of the national leadership; the relative strength of domestic and foreign private capitalist groups; and the circumstances and structure of the national economy.

Ideologically inspired comprehensive nationalizations have taken place in Tanzania (Arusha Declaration, 1967), Zambia (Mulungushi Declaration, 1968), Uganda (Common Man's Charter and 'Move to the Left' 1969–70), Ethiopia, Somalia, Congo, Benin, Guinea and Mali. They have included banking and insurance, petroleum refining and/or distribution, transport, freehold land, large buildings, hotels, plantations, import-export and wholesale trades, and large industries or those manufacturing essential goods. Ideologically motivated state intervention has been carried out in the belief that only public ownership of the means of production and distribution can ensure a pattern of development whose benefits will be widely spread. Within this category, especially in the more underdeveloped economies, there has also been no immediate alternative to public sector growth, in the absence of any significant private indigenous capitalist class.

At the same time other countries, without necessarily any strong ideological orientation, have also extended areas of public ownership, not only over the so-called 'commanding heights' (e.g. banking and insurance) but also into other spheres, although this has been more selective and most have only been on an equity participation basis. They include some of the richer and/or larger states: Nigeria (banking and insurance), Zaire (plantations, petroleum production and distribution, transportation and many large manufacturing and commercial companies), Ghana (timber, large enterprises producing basic necessities, petroleum production and distribution) and Kenya (banking, petroleum refining and electric power). Many of these initiatives have been accompanied by diplomatic assurances to both foreign and domestic private capital about the limited intentions underlying changing investment laws. In Zaire enterprises taken over in 1973/4 were intended for later sale to private citizens, while in 1975 some foreign businessmen whose enterprises were earlier expropriated were offered back a proportion of their former equity.

Although new state investment of a directly productive nature has hitherto been limited, public investment in the social sector has been greater. Apart from utilities and services under public ownership since the colonial period, or more recently added to it as a result of nationalization, the state since independence has invested for example in public housing (through the Ghana State Housing Corporation or in northern Nigeria the Kaduna State Housing Authority), in road transport (through the Ghana State Transport Corporation or through the State bus lines of the Nigerian Federation) and in employment-creating projects (public works,

state manufacturing). The state has also created organizations aimed at reducing the cost of living through the supply of essential goods and commodities at controlled prices from state industries (the Ghana Industrial Holding Corporation, the National Development Corporation of Tanzania or the Ugandan Development Corporation) or through state trading corporations (The Ghana National Trading Corporation, the State Trading Corporation of Tanzania or the National Supply Company of Nigeria).

In the non-socialist and to some extent the socialist oriented countries it is in the financial sector that state participation is most likely to divert resources towards a more productive pattern of investment – including both state and indigenous private enterprise. The state in nearly every country has taken equity in foreign owned banks* – a move in Nigeria explicitly linked to assisting the indigenization programme, while in Tanzania the National Bank of Commerce now allocates a majority of its credit to state enterprise. In addition to the Industrial Development Corporations set up in most Anglophone countries a number of years ago (and in Nigeria the Regional Development Corporations), the 1970s saw the proliferation of new government financial institutions such as the Nigerian Industrial Development Bank and the Nigerian Bank for Commerce and Industry, and in Ghana the National Investment Bank, Capital Investments Boards and Regional Development Corporations.

In parallel with the beginnings of state participation and investment in industrialization are the recent efforts of some governments to accommodate in various ways the growing indigenous entrepreneurial class, where it exists as a political force, as in Nigeria, Kenya, and, increasingly, Ghana, or where its creation is desired ideologically, as it has been in Zambia and Zaire.

One of three major approaches has been adopted where African governments have attempted to encourage and promote indigenous entrepreneurship. The first two essentially involve various forms of state protection and patronage: restrictive foreign investment laws, the discriminatory allocation of manufacturing and trading licences, preferential loan capital concessions and contracts from government agencies and institutions. The first approach, as it has been applied in Kenya and Zambia, has been more *ad hoc*: carried out through the denial of licences – mainly to Asians. In Kenya the programme has been carried out gradually but successfully since 1967, but in Zambia it was partly thwarted by loopholes. The second approach, as exemplified by the 1970 Ghana Business Promotion Act and 1975 Investment Policy Decree and the 1972 and 1977 Nigerian Enterprises Promotion Decrees, has been more systematic, taking place within a defined legislative framework and with a specific government regulatory authority to oversee implementation. In each case, legislation has required the transfer of a range of enterprises in largely small-scale trading and services from foreign (often Levantine and Asian) to indigenous ownership and the sale of a proportion of equity (40–60 per cent) in larger-scale enterprises, including manufacturing. In Ghana certain sectors referred to earlier are reserved for minimum state equity participation, reflecting the legacy of state sector primacy under Nkrumah.

The third 'approach' to indigenization is characterized by its relatively disorganized styles of implementation. These have amounted to expropriation and expulsion of alien businessmen, as with the Asians in Idi Amin's Uganda, or their expulsion from the rural areas, as in Malawi and Zaire, or their banning, as in Guinea in 1958. In Zaire, although the 1973 exercise was initiated by clearly defined legislation, no machinery was established to oversee transfer, with fairly disastrous consequences.

Apart from the immediate problems related to the effectiveness of even systematic state organization for supervising foreign disinvestment (alien evasiveness, corruption of officials, competing demands of indigenous businessmen), one of the long-term effects of more successful programmes carried out in Ghana and Nigeria will be of a socio-political nature. Sale of shares has inevitably benefited managerial, bureaucratic and professional strata, and this, together with their recent acquisition of land and urban property since independence, will set up an inequitable pattern of income distribution in the future.

Equally important, the same indigenization programmes have not contributed significantly to the enhancement of indigenous control (managerial or shareholding) or to technology transfer. First, minimal new entrepreneurial opportunities have been opened by the sale of entire businesses to indigenous elements. In Ghana in 1975 85 per cent of the entrepreneurs operating in reserved areas were Ghanaian and only 106 enterprises were thus affected by the 1970 Ghana Business Promotion Act and a mere 34 by the Investment Policy Decree of 1975. In Nigeria, even as early as 1967, 56 per cent of those areas subsequently exclusively reserved in 1972 were already under indigenous ownership and the Nigerian Enterprises Promotion Decree of that year thus affected only 357 enterprises in the whole federation. Within the limited scope of those actually affected, other obstacles have occurred, including the extreme smallness of scale of some enterprises and their consequent unmarketability, difficulties in evaluating certain enterprises for disinvestment, such as verifying minimum capital/turnover, identifying precisely the range of goods and services carried on and distinguishing wholesale from retail activity.

In other spheres indigenous participation has been largely of a passive financial nature. Although in Nigeria shareholding has been extended to 60 per cent in some spheres, these are mainly in the commercial sector, while indigenous shareholding continues on a minority (40 per cent) basis in the higher technology, foreign controlled industries. Accommodation of upper income groups into the financial structure of multi-national corporations, as share-holders, only serves further to reinforce the position of those corporations in which individuals from whom the local ruling group is drawn now have a stake.

Against this background, greater possibilities for economic decolonization and the creation of national or indigenous patterns of productive development appear to lie in the emerging sector of new 'joint ventures' between the state and foreign private capital and technology. Marked expansion of this sector has taken place in Kenya, Nigeria and Ghana, and includes industries such as vehicle assembly, cement, electronics, matches, textiles, beer, soaps and detergents and glue. As against their declared benefits to the national economy, in terms of providing access to foreign controlled technology, some analysts consider that not only are the net costs of joint ventures greater than might appear, but that technology transfer is either illusory or inappropriate and the resultant production is oriented towards domestically consumed luxuries.

The dominant motivation of government for entering into joint ventures appears to be much the same as in the mineral sector: to take a share in the surplus value – in this case as a return on providing the foreign partner with state controlled advantages such as tariff and market protection, tax and import duty concessions, political security and guarantees against expropriation, priorities in government contracts as well as privileged access to a range of facilities including, for example, state financial institutions and foreign remittance guarantees.

The future development of state or indigenous enterprise in Africa faces a number of constraints, some of them widely recognized. They include availability of investment funds, inadequate infrastructure, shortage of managerial and technical manpower and attitudes towards business and towards the state sector. Attitudes towards the state sector tend to be soured by the earlier poor performances of corporate public management. At the same time, the attitudes of indigenous businessmen have often been characterized as dominated by commercial rather than productive perspectives, preferring softer options for middleman roles – either as clients of state patronage or in profitable distributorships of foreign manufactured goods. *P.D.C.*

Appropriate technology

During the early years of technology transfer from industrialized nations to the developing world much frustration was suffered in Africa because whole industries were imported completely unmodified and without consideration of local economic and technical resources. In the 1960s Dr E.F. Schumacher, a British economist, introduced his concept of 'Intermediate Technology' (IT) and formed the Intermediate Technology Development Group (ITDG).

Schumacher's ideas sought to provide an explanation of the relative failure of much of the development work then being undertaken, which was based on relatively advanced techniques, such as semi-automated industry in the towns and more mechanized farming in the rural areas. By contrast, Schumacher and his followers sought to develop technological advances that were 'intermediate' between traditional and highly sophisticated technologies, and most important, that could be developed using simple, easily available materials and local skills.

The ox-plough, introduced in several African countries by agricultural extension services and rural development specialists, is a good example of Schumacher's concept. It stands, so to speak, half-way between the traditional hand-operated hoe and the modern diesel tractor. Intermediateness, of course, is relative: in the societies of the Middle East and Asia which have known and used ox-drawn ploughs for thousands of years such a technology can be called traditional, and the intermediate level of technology would be more adequately represented by a small mechanical cultivator. In tropical African societies the ox-plough is usually a major innovation and represents a big technical step forward.

Schumacher was very concerned that development work was not improving rural or urban employment prospects, and he advocated the setting up of more rural-based industries. His ITDG set up a number of projects in Africa in an effort to get IT off the ground. In Botswana a project was started to make rainwater catchment tanks for rural primary schools. In northern Nigeria support was given to an engineer at Ahmadu Bello University, Zaria to help manufacture low cost medical equipment for hospitals. A technical group in Kumasi, Ghana was given support in setting up facilities, which grew into the well-known Technology Consultancy Centre (TCC). In Zambia small machines for manufacturing egg boxes were designed to try to solve Zambia's egg distribution problems.

As interest developed in IT, and as more and more people became involved, it was realized that if a new piece of equipment or technique was being introduced, it not only had to be appropriate to the people's needs but also had to take into consideration social and cultural conditions. Eventually this wider viewpoint became more popularly known as Appropriate Technology (AT).

AT has been called the social and cultural dimension of innovation. Its philosophy holds that the value of a new technology lies not only in its economic viability and technical soundness, but also in its adaptation to the local social and cultural environment. One of the main shortcomings of IT, for example, had been its failure to recognize the important role women play in agricultural work: in many societies women grow and process the food for the family and market, and also control and operate the water supply. So any new equipment for crop processing or for use in the field has to be checked

Left: ox-ploughing at an agricultural training centre in Nigeria. Right: a locally constructed wind-pump in Tanzania

to see that it is socially acceptable to women. For example, in the southern Sudan a need was recognized to ease the hard work of the women in grinding dura (sorghum) grain into flour. A well-known international group designed a pedal-operated grinder that would do the job reasonably well and could be made locally. After a short trial period one of the machines was left in a village for long-term trials and acceptance but was little used. Women in this area, it turned out, did not ride bicycles; and the machine was classified locally as a bicycle. Men did ride bicycles, but felt that dura-grinding, however it was done, was women's work.

There are many other examples of newly introduced technologies that clash with the cultural patterns of a particular society or modify roles of men and women in the village. In other places, for example, strains have been caused by ostensibly quite beneficial innovations, such as a new water supply to a village, which have changed the life-style of village women overnight. If several hours a day were taken up by collecting water, then when water is readily available all the newly available hours have to be taken up by doing something else. This can and, in some places does, cause social strains.

The ITDG was not the only group that observed the problems being caused by certain types of development: all over Africa innovative people were trying out their own solutions. The Church, too, has always tried to play an active part in local development. In Kenya, in 1966, the National Christian Council of Kenya set up two experimental rural training centres that they called 'village polytechnics'. The objective of these centres was to train school leavers in a practical manner for rural employment. They were not set up purely as vocational training because it was recognized that their job was of much wider educational value. They took in boys and girls to give them the basic skills of carpentry, building, agriculture, etc., as well as teaching self-reliance. Now over 20 centres are in operation, all situated in rural areas and therefore able to concentrate on training for appropriate local conditions.

A similar centre was started in Botswana – Swaneg Hill School – for similar reasons: growing unemployment and the problem of young people leaving school with no practical training or skills. A small school was started first to cope with some of the young people who could not get school places. This was closely followed up by the establishment of what were called 'brigades' to train young men in particular skills to enable them to get a job or start working on their own. The first one was the builder's brigade. This took on boys to do a sort of apprenticeship. Later other brigades were set up covering carpentry, mechanics and farming, and a textile workshop was established for girls.

Without doubt the biggest interest in AT has been shown by non-government groups. AT centres or village centres are springing up in every country. The main universities in Africa are becoming very interested and are setting up AT units to deal with local problems. The most well-known of these is the TCC in Kumasi, Ghana, run as an autonomous unit within the University of Science and Technology. The work of such units is wide-ranging, and includes technical and commercial advice to businesses and governments and the establishment of local production units to manufacture such things as steel bolts, saw-benches, water tanks, weaving machines, animal feeds and soap.

In the past many African governments regarded AT as greatly inferior to the conventional technologies of the industrialized countries. One of the few exceptions was Tanzania, where the 'villagization' programme seemed to offer an opportunity to incorporate AT into the national plan. President Julius Nyerere* himself has said that he thought AT would play an important part in his country's development. More recently, however, other governments have been expressing an interest in AT, especially as many of the UN agencies have adopted the concept and have been encouraging it.

Government interest was attracted in East Africa in the 1970s when UNICEF organized an East African Regional Seminar on village technology which was held in Kenya. In conjunction with the Kenyan social services ministry, a village technology demonstration and development unit was established and a permanent exhibition built. The exhibition featured a wide range of full-scale exhibits of AT covering the production, storage and processing of food, home improvements, building techniques, use of solar, wind and water energy,* and the conservation and protection of water resources.* The exhibition created as much if not more interest than the seminar itself.

Soon after, in Tanzania, the Commonwealth Secretariat put together a 'rural technology meet'. This was a practically-oriented conference on developments in agricultural technology that were being researched in all the British Commonwealth countries of East and southern Africa. The government officials who attended this meeting were encouraged to set up national appropriate technology committees to coordinate the work in their own countries and for mutual cooperation.

Initially, AT was associated almost exclusively with the development of rural areas and the establishment in them of small industries. As a result it was given a low priority by national governments in Africa. The international call to improve conditions, communications and facilities in rural areas met only with a lukewarm response. By the 1980s, however, AT was being looked at on a much wider front, and had moved on to embrace more advanced technology. African leaders are becoming increasingly aware of, and uncomfortable with, their technological dependence on industrialized countries. Most now realize that importing 'advanced' technology may only increase their dependence on rich powerful countries and does nothing to build up their own technological capacities.   *P. S.*

Regional groupings

African states have found it expedient, like most states of the world, to combine for a multiplicity of purposes and in a variety of ways, but perhaps nowhere else is the tendency quite so pronounced and the pattern of inter-state cooperation quite so complex. In Africa there is considerable duplication, overlapping and instability. Some of the regional organizations have been short-lived, and others have scarcely had much life breathed into them.

The complexities of African regional groupings are due to several factors operating simultaneously and sometimes at cross-purposes. The ideology of pan-Africanism* is one such factor. It rejects the colonial division of Africa, advocates planning on a supra-national scale, and expresses the belief that all African states share a common cause requiring combined action. This ideology has had to contend however with the vastness and the diversity of the African continent. Most regional organizations are not in fact a reflection of pan-African aspirations but a direct response to two quite different factors. The first is the insistence of African governments on the right to exercise their own discretion in deciding how far and for what purpose they should combine with one another. The second is the imprint of colonial rule which both partially unifies and partially divides the African states, for example, into a group of Francophone and a group of Anglophone states. It is the joint operation of these two factors, cutting across that of pan-Africanism, which has led to the multiplicity and complexity of regional groups. Although such groupings are sometimes hailed as stepping-stones to pan-African unity, at other times denounced as a hindrance, the relationship between pan-Africanism and regionalism is a tenuous one. Both are reactions to the accumulated divisions and handicaps imposed by colonialism, pan-Africanism being the more emotionally charged and vaguer dream, regionalism being the more pragmatically measured response. They are best understood, however, as distinct phenomena, occasionally interacting, sometimes appearing to conflict, at other times seeming to be complementary.

From this standpoint, the various regional groupings may be arranged into three broad categories. A first category consists of the pre-1963 alliances, notably those which had their origins and took their names from conferences held at Brazzaville in December 1960, at Casablanca in January 1961 and at Monrovia in May 1961. These were rival caucuses of more or less radical and more or less moderate states, divided mainly by differing reactions to conflicts in Algeria and the Congo (later Zaire), and also by difficulties in drafting a common charter which would unite them all. Once the Algerian and Congolese conflicts were resolved, agreement on a charter was also forthcoming and, by May 1963, the two main rivals, the Casablanca and the Monrovia groups, had clearly become redundant. So also had

the Union of African States, formed by Ghana, Guinea and Mali in July 1961. The Brazzaville group, formally constituted as the *Union Africaine et Malgache* (UAM) in September 1961 was, however, reluctant to concede that it no longer had a purpose. As a group of Francophone states, all maintaining a close working relationship with France and the European Economic Community (EEC), it stood out as a suspected agent of neo-colonialism. It itself had little confidence that the Organization of African Unity* (OAU)–despite the reassuring wording of its charter–could act as a shield against subversive activities which some African leaders, notably Kwame Nkrumah,* seemed more or less openly to encourage. After lengthy discussions throughout 1963–4, during which relations with Ghana failed to improve, the decision was taken in February 1965 to maintain the organization, with a slight change of name to *Organisation Commune Africaine et Malgache* (OCAM), and at the cost of Mauritania's withdrawal. More than any other grouping, the UAM/OCAM was a test case for determining the legitimate limits of regional organizations. Its lack of geographical contiguity, its close association with France, and the comprehensive scope of its activities–economic, technical, cultural as well as political–stood in the way of acceptance. But its own persistence, despite the hesitancy of some of its members, and the renewal of factionalism within the OAU, made for acquiescence in a *fait accompli*. It was even able, on occasions, to attract new members from former Belgian colonies, Rwanda, Zaire, and former British colonies, Mauritius and Seychelles. But in recent years it has been weakened by several withdrawals and overshadowed by the institution of Franco-African summit meetings, which have been held on a regular annual basis since 1975.

In a different, second, category of regional groupings are the various customs unions and economic communities. Despite the importance attached by pan-Africanism to such institutions, it is arguable that very few, if any, would have come to be established had they not already been in operation prior to independence. Indeed, as colonies became self-governing many of them chose to dismantle whatever regional authorities there were rather than reinforce and expand them. This 'balkanization' has often been laid at the door of neo-colonialism,* which, it is argued, seeks to divide and weaken the pan-African movement. The ex-colonial powers were certainly not disinterested bystanders but their efforts were in fact directed more often to the upholding of regional arrangements than to their dismantlement. More decisive factors were the timing of each colony's independence and the African leaders' own calculations of costs and benefits. If self-government came about simultaneously there was some hope of maintaining existing joint authorities, provided they were seen to be advantageous. In 1961, Julius Nyerere* suggested the postponement of Tanganyika's own independence, in the hope of hastening Kenya's independence and of forming a federation with Kenya and Uganda, so that the existing customs union, common currency, joint research institutions, and integrated communication services could be maintained. In the end, the member-states preferred to re-establish these as inter-governmental rather than as federal institutions.

The widespread decolonization undertaken by France in 1960, and the fact that some of its territories were ill-prepared for self-government, made for a similar measure of continuity. Gabon, Congo, Chad and Oubangui-Chari (renamed Central African Republic) simply reconstituted the existing federal arrangement to take account of their desire for separate sovereignty and shortly afterwards, in 1961, even managed to extend the area of economic integration to include Cameroon, founding thereby the *Union Douanière et Economique de l'Afrique Centrale* (UDEAC). There was less harmony and continuity in French West Africa, where Guinea had already taken its independence in 1958 and Ivory Coast preferred a direct and close association with the wealth of France rather than a federation with its impecunious neighbours. Despite this, the retention of the franc-zone *Communauté Financière Africaine* (CFA) currency, the formation of a joint airline, *Air Afrique*, and two overlapping and restricted customs unions, the *Communauté Economique de l'Afrique de l'Ouest* (CEAO) and the *Conseil de l'Entente*, are reminders of the former federation. Where decolonization was not simultaneous and economic self-sufficiency was more feasible, as in North Africa, British West Africa, and British Central Africa, each colony or protectorate tended to go its own way. It is only since 1975, with the formation in 1975 of the Economic Community of West African States (ECOWAS), that the process of economic disintegration has been set in reverse.

Economic groupings of this kind are difficult to operate in any circumstances, and particularly so when, as in Africa, all the member-states tend to be exporters of a narrow range of primary products and to be poorly developed in other respects. The more comprehensive the aim, the more probable the stress and strain. Initial technical difficulties in production, consumer habits, long distances and poor communications can make the promotion of local manufactures a costly business. Cheaper imports have to be kept out by a tariff wall or by quantitative restrictions. This reduces import duties, an important source of revenue for most states. The location of new industries★ is a particularly contentious issue. Their equitable distribution among member-states is relatively uneconomic but a concentration in areas already more developed, so as to reap the benefits of external economies, can be explosive. Compensatory devices, such as a transfer of funds from the more to the less developed states, are often only additional bones of contention. For example, the frictions that developed between Kenya and its two partner-states, Tanzania and Uganda, finally killed off the East African Community in 1977–8. Difference in attitudes to state and private enterprise, difficulties in organizing meetings of the three

presidents after Idi Amin's seizure of power in Uganda, and disputed management of common services, especially the railways and the airlines, proved too heavy a handicap. UDEAC has, however, managed to survive, except for Chad's departure in 1968, but only by agreeing to considerable administrative decentralization and some break-up of common services. The fact that these four governments of different political outlook have managed to maintain a certain degree of economic integration is a hopeful sign.

It is sometimes argued that economic integration cannot be effectively maintained unless backed up by political unification, but UDEAC is a witness to the contrary. On the other hand, the theory that economic integration has a reinforcing dynamic of its own, brought about by the need to resolve periodic crises, has little support in African experience. Hopes for ECOWAS lie in it being able to profit from earlier African experience and also from that of the EEC. As in the Treaty of Rome, economic integration is to be achieved step by step over a period of 15 years, with much of the detailed arrangement left to further negotiation. Likewise, definitions of the origin of traded products – a knotty problem – are borrowed from the Lomé Treaty of Association with the EEC. The successful operation of ECOWAS will depend on the willingness of each member-state to renounce the right to make unilateral decisions over a whole range of economic and financial matters, and also on avoiding an inequitable distribution of benefits in favour of Nigeria, which has half the community's population and over a third of its Gross National Product.

The final category of regional organizations is a varied collection of *ad hoc* authorities, established for some quite specific and limited purpose. Typical of such purposes are:

(a) the development or preservation of some natural asset which can only be exploited effectively in common, e.g. a major river, an important source of water and food such as Lake Chad, mineral deposits which straddle frontiers and require new transportation facilities;

(b) services which would be uneconomic for a single state, such as an airline, a shipping company, training and research institutes, or which require wider collaboration for their effective operation, such as a meteorological service, the control of drought, pests and endemic diseases;

(c) mutual consultation on scientific and technical matters, such as public finance, statistics, broadcasting or the introduction of new crops, e.g. rice.

Such activities are usually uncontroversial being clearly of mutual benefit and amenable to bureaucratic management. They are also less costly to finance and are generally supported by international agencies. They are therefore relatively successful, although some of the joint economic enterprises, such as *Air Afrique*, and the joint exploitation of mineral resources, as in the Liptako-Gourma region of Mali, Niger and Upper Volta, can suffer from quite serious disputes.

Membership is a function of the particular activity and can range from a few neighbouring states to a broad spread across Africa.

The three sets of regional groupings, superimposed one upon the other, produce a bewildering picture of overlapping areas, functions and membership. It makes for difficulty in attempting to rank the various organizations in any order of importance, efficiency or viability. Some of the more ephemeral, such as the Casablanca and Monrovia groups of the early 1960s, are of considerable historical interest. The more problematical, such as the economic communities of Equatorial and West Africa, hold out perhaps the greatest promise, if only they can survive. The more technical *ad hoc* authorities attract less attention but provide a close network of inter-state cooperation. A vital element in the picture is the pattern of external linkages, be these bilateral, e.g. with the former colonial power, or multilateral, e.g. with a consortium or with an international organization, such as the Economic Commission for Africa,* the UN Development Programme, the World Bank, and the EEC. Which regional organizations thrive best is to some extent a consequence of the external support they receive. Just as vital, however, is the personal support of the respective heads of state, who have the authority to strike the necessary bargains at critical moments. Most regional organizations do in fact operate through periodic meetings of heads of state, assisted by ministers or by a separate council of ministers, and a small secretariat or management committee. Without such support, from outside and from above, a regional organization is unlikely to show much sign of life. *S.K.P.-B.*

AFRICAN REGIONAL ORGANIZATIONS

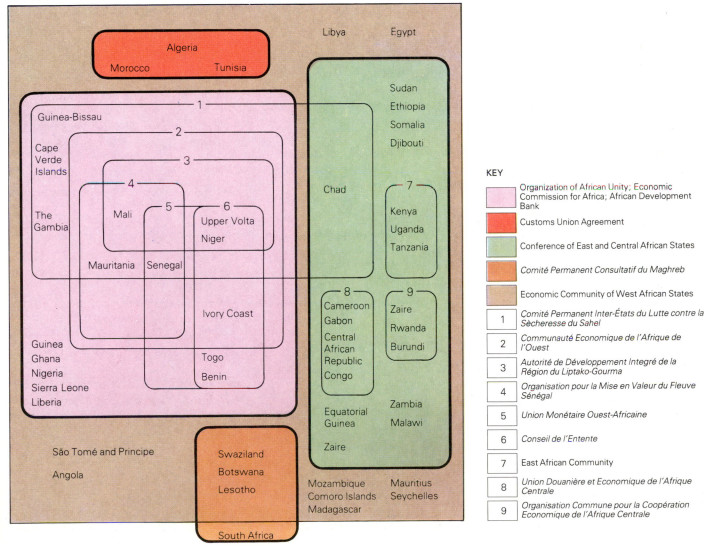

KEY

Organization of African Unity; Economic Commission for Africa; African Development Bank

Customs Union Agreement

Conference of East and Central African States

Comité Permanent Consultatif du Maghreb

Economic Community of West African States

1   *Comité Permanent Inter-États du Lutte contre la Sècheresse du Sahel*

2   *Communauté Economique de l'Afrique de l'Ouest*

3   *Autorité de Développement Integré de la Région du Liptako-Gourma*

4   *Organisation pour la Mise en Valeur du Fleuve Sénégal*

5   *Union Monétaire Ouest-Africaine*

6   *Conseil de l'Entente*

7   East African Community

8   *Union Douanière et Economique de l'Afrique Centrale*

9   *Organisation Commune pour la Coopération Economique de l'Afrique Centrale*

Transport

Simple forms of transport

The vast majority of Africans are dependent on agriculture* or 'fringe' urban activities in which simple forms of transport have to be used because, at least superficially, they are cheap. Human porterage is almost universal. Agriculture produce, including export items such as cocoa, groundnuts and palm-products are carried from farm to home or market. Trade goods are carried in small quantities in towns by human porterage, and many imported goods are finally distributed by head-carriage. Human porterage, unquantified as it is, is undoubtedly still one of Africa's principal means of moving goods at the local level.

Over longer distances, or for large quantities, animals may be used to carry directly or, more rarely, to haul carts, but widespread aridity and the high incidence of tsetse-borne animal disease reduces the contribution animals can make. In dry scrub and true desert areas only the camel may be used. In semi-arid regions the donkey is useful because of its relatively high tolerance of such conditions. There is still considerable scope in Africa for the development of an 'intermediate' transport technology, either by the application of animal power to improved designs of cart or by greater use of bicycles, small motorcycles or vehicles modelled on these. In general, there is greater use of such forms of transport in the Francophone than in the Anglophone territories.

The transport provided by these simple means is of limited capacity and cheap only over short distances and for small amounts. The basis for economic development must be the provision of high capacity and lower cost transport for a larger volume and wider range of goods and for larger numbers of people over increasing distances.

Water transport

Africa's rivers are not for the most part ideally suited to navigation. Had they been so, development might well have started earlier and proceeded faster. Most of the rivers, because of the continent's plateau nature, feature alternate sections of low gradient and rapids (e.g. Nile, Zaire) while seasonal rainfall results in marked variations in flow. Shifting sand-bars at river mouths often make access difficult or impossible except for the smallest vessels or local craft such as canoes. Interruptions to navigation are, therefore, both geographical and seasonal. However, on these rivers and also on lakes and coastal lagoons a great variety of local craft, powered by paddle, sail and, now, motors serves local needs. The sailing 'cutters' of the Gambia River and the 'bullom' boats of Sierra Leone are typical, while on the Niger large motorized canoes are used extensively for passengers and freight.

The Gambia River is exceptional in that small ocean-going vessels can penetrate 275km inland, and the traditional small sailing cutters are giving way to push-tow units and self-propelled barges for the movement of groundnuts. Navigation on the Senegal River is restricted by seasonality of flow and shallow depths at the bar. The

Head-carriage in Lagos, Nigeria

Riverboat on the Niger at Mopti, Mali

Niger is navigable only in sections and for parts of the year while on the Benue the river port of Makurdi can be reached during six months of the year but Garoua for only two. There are plans for improvement of the Niger and the construction and operation of the integrated iron and steel plant at Ajaokuta could provide considerable river traffic. Sections of the Nile are significant but navigation is not easy especially on the upper stretches. Although navigable to Matadi by ocean-going ships the use of the 14 500km of navigable waterway provided by the Zaire-Oubangui is limited by falls which have to be bypassed by rail links (e.g. Matadi-Kinshasa, Kisangani-Ubundu) and by sections with seasonally restricted depths. Despite its inadequacies river transport provides the basis of Zaire's national transport system, and is also significant for the Central African Republic and the Congo. The East African Lakes provide useful waterway links often in conjunction with railway services as on Lake Victoria. In Ghana the artificial Lake Volta is already used for passenger and roll-on/roll-off freight services.

Rail transport

Because the rivers did not provide obvious routes to the interior the European powers started to construct railways to establish 'effective control'. By the First World War a series of well defined colonies had emerged, each served in isolation by a rudimentary transport system often based on a railway line. Although many of these railways had a political purpose they did in some cases stimulate economic development and have had a continuing profound influence on the

Diesel-hauled train on the Sierra Leone Railway

geographical pattern of economic activity and on later elaboration of the transport infrastructure. Ghana's so-called 'Golden Triangle' of concentrated economic activity closely parallels the Accra/Tema-Kumasi-Takoradi rail links, the Mombasa-Kampala axis has been called 'main street–East Africa' while in southern Africa much economic activity is located adjacent to the 'line of rail' between Bulawayo and Salisbury (Zimbabwe) and Livingstone and Ndola (Zambia).

The railways were able to provide cheap bulk transport and were a main factor in creating or sustaining colonial economies based overwhelmingly on a limited range of primary products deriving from agriculture, forestry★ and mining★ activity. Export traffic still accounts for well over 75 per cent of the traffic of most African railways and in the case of specially constructed mineral lines (e.g. Mauritania, Liberia) the exports may be virtually the entire traffic.

Of nearly 75 000km of railway in Africa 30 per cent is to be found within South Africa, which country accounts for well over half of the total African rail freight. A true railway 'network' exists only in South Africa: elsewhere in the continent the lines are mainly of the type once described as 'weak lines of strong faith'. They consist of the penetration routes of the colonial era, piecemeal developments within each territory, each to different gauge and often of very low design standards so that costs of construction were minimized.

In general Africa is a continent in which railways have been extended in recent years. Some new lines have served to elaborate or provide missing links in the existing, usually government owned, networks. Examples of this type would include the Kotoku-Achiasi line in Ghana, the Ruvu-Mnyusi link in East Africa, the Mpimbe-Vila Cabral link between Malawi and Mozambique, the Cameroon railway extension to Ngaououndéré and the Bauchi line to Maiduguri in Nigeria. Others have been built, sometimes by private companies, to serve specific economic enterprises, usually mines. Examples are the Kasese extension in Uganda to tap the Kilembe copper deposits; the Kadake-Ngwenya line to export iron ore from Swaziland; the Cuima and Mocamedes lines in Angola for iron ore; the Mauritanian and Liberian lines for iron ore; and the line begun in 1974 in Gabon, which should be completed in the early 1980s, will reroute manganese exports through a Gabonese port, and will eventually make possible the exploitation of iron ore deposits in the north-east.

Without large quantities of bulk traffic many of Africa's general purpose lines are unprofitable but may possibly be justified on political or strategic grounds. The Tazara (TanZam) Railway linking Zambia and the Tanzanian port of Dar es Salaam and the Zimbabwean Beitbridge link to South Africa are the best examples. Proposals to extend the Cameroon railway into Chad or the Central African Republic and the Benin railway into Niger might be justified as necessary routes to land-locked countries, although it is doubtful if existing or potential traffic would make them economic.

Road transport

Road transport is particularly important in Africa because of the lack of navigable waterways and the low capacity relative to demand of the railways. Even where the main haul is by another mode, road transport invariably serves as the initial collector and final distributor of goods and has a flexibility of route, vehicle type and capacity which allows it to adapt more readily than water transport or railways to local geographical conditions and demand.

The small number of cars in most African countries reflects income levels: most are to be found in countries such as South Africa, Zimbabwe and Kenya, where Europeans make up a larger proportion of the population, or those countries where there is a relatively higher national income (e.g. some Maghrib countries, Egypt, Nigeria). A number of African countries now have relatively well-developed road transport industries, the growth of which is related to general economic progress.

Rapid urbanization* is a further stimulus to road transport, and cities such as Cairo and Lagos have an urban transport problem as serious as, if not more serious than, that found in any large city. For the stimulation of rural economic development there is really no alternative to road transport.

Most of Africa's roads are of earth, being very dusty in the dry season and possibly impassable during the rains when there is usually severe disruption to the movement of essential goods. Unlike railways, roads have the advantage that they can be upgraded as demand requires using mainly local materials and expertise. In many

countries (Gabon, Chad, Niger, Central African Republic) there is virtually no surfacing of roads outside a few main towns while in most others surfacing to all-weather standards is restricted to main inter-urban links. The Trans-African Highway will provide an all-weather route from Mombasa to Lagos and with its feeder routes will eventually link a number of important 'growth poles' in East, Central and West Africa. The gradual extension of the surfaced road across the Sahara will give a valuable back-door route into West Africa.

Road transport is a fruitful area for smaller-scale local investment. The bulk of transport in the rural areas and the towns is still satisfied by informal services provided by taxis and mixed freight/passenger trucks, such as the 'mammy lorries' of West Africa, which are ideal where the demand is dispersed and where separation between passenger and freight transport is by no means complete.

Air transport

Although still insignificant overall, air transport in Africa is favoured by the great distances, difficult surface terrain and the large areas generating little traffic. For the landlocked states air transport is crucial for over-flying neighbours. For the initial exploration, establishment and sometimes continued servicing of isolated mining enterprises (Zouerate iron ore mine in Mauritania, oil wells in the Sahara or Niger Delta) air transport either by helicopters or short take-off aircraft is invaluable. In large countries such as Ethiopia or Zaire air transport provides the main links between capitals and main regional centres. National airlines often begin with domestic routes but in many cases (e.g. Ghana, Nigeria) become international, long-haul carriers which 'fly the flag'.

For the most part Africa's bulky raw material exports are not suited for air transport, although political necessity (e.g. Zambia after Rhodesia's UDI,* Uganda under Idi Amin) may lead to its use. Some higher value, lower bulk exports (fresh fruit from Ivory Coast, frozen meat from Chad, flowers and spices from Kenya) can support the cost of air freight. Consumer and capital good imports are more suitable air freight particularly where port congestion (e.g. Lagos, Dar es Salaam) increases the cost of surface transport. The Peugeot car assembly plant at Kaduna, Nigeria, is entirely dependent on air freighted components.

Mixed passenger/freight trucks loading in Nigeria

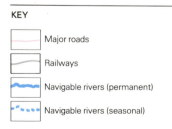

KEY

	Major roads
	Railways
	Navigable rivers (permanent)
	Navigable rivers (seasonal)

TRANSPORT

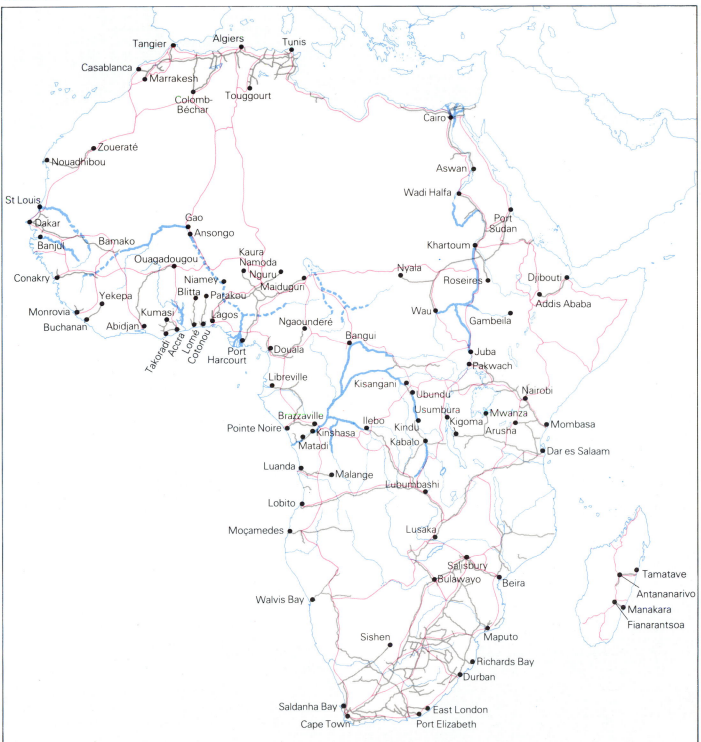

CIVIL AVIATION: SCHEDULED SERVICES,[1] 1976

Country	Passengers carried (thousands)		Freight[2] carried (millions tonnes/km)	
	Total	International	Total	International
Algeria	1 682	863	9.1	8.1
Benin	40	40	13.1	13.1
Cameroon	248	68	8.6	6.5
Central African Republic	98	40	13.2	13.1
Chad	72	40	14.0	13.1
Congo	77	40	13.5	13.1
Egypt	1 113	812	20.7	20.4
Ethiopia	288	145	17.7	15.8
Gabon	190	90	13.7	13.5
Ghana	215	101	3.5	3.4
Guinea	65	20	0.2	0.1
Ivory Coast	114	40	13.3	13.1
Kenya	450	399	17.9	17.8
Libya	670	334	6.3	6.3
Madagascar	262	63	6.7	4.6
Malawi	94	65	4.5	4.4
Mali	55	40	1.3	1.3
Mauritania	94	47	13.7	13.3
Morocco	809	695	17.6	17.5
Niger	75	40	13.2	13.1
Nigeria	485	105	7.3	6.8
Senegal	120	77	13.2	13.2
Somalia	38	19	0.2	0.1
South Africa	2 999	603	146.3	118.4
Sudan	265	165	7.3	6.7
Tanzania	310	207	3.2	2.8
Togo	44	44	13.1	13.1
Tunisia	809	725	6.7	6.7
Uganda	74	69	7.4	7.4
Upper Volta	42	40	13.1	13.1
Zaire	463	87	53.5	29.5
Zambia	260	87	19.3	18.8
AFRICA Total	13 249	6 575	519	449

[1]Figures for total services cover both domestic and international scheduled services operated by airlines registered in each country. Scheduled services include supplementary services occasioned by overflow traffic on regularly scheduled trips and preparatory flights for new scheduled services
[2]Freight means all goods, except mail and excess baggage carried for remuneration

Source: *Statistical Yearbook 1977* (UN, New York, 1978)

INTERNATIONAL SEABORNE TRADE (EXPORTS AND IMPORTS) PASSING THROUGH AFRICAN PORTS, 1975

Country	Crude oil and petroleum products (cargo in thousands of tonnes)		Dry cargo	
	Exports	Imports	Exports	Imports
Algeria	37 673	287	5 000	7 500
Angola	7 103	40	8 887	2 810
Benin	—	172	108	475
Cape Verde	—	57	20	89
Cameroon	—	367	820	948
Comoro Islands	—	10	12	55
Congo	1 780	284	935	353
Djibouti	—	509	160	250
Egypt	1 123	2 220	1 400	9 000
Equatorial Guinea	—	20	45	125
Ethiopia	113	624	440	224
Gabon	10 793	6	800	462
The Gambia	5	27	101	100
Ghana	305	1 300	2 190	2 276
Guinea	—	263	1 500	337
Guinea Bissau	—	31	45	135
Ivory Coast	137	1 504	3 398	1 934
Kenya	632	2 876	1 157	1 283
Liberia	—	572	26 100	600
Libya	72 310	1 012	2	8 607
Madagascar	230	760	587	429
Mauritania	—	97	9 500	310
Mauritius	—	293	614	530
Morocco	17	2 929	15 431	4 354
Mozambique	51	518	9 164	3 025
Nigeria	85 217	799	2 250	3 801
Réunion	1	129	249	691
São Tomé	—	5	25	35
Senegal	56	1 403	2 600	675
Seychelles	—	25	11	78
Sierra Leone	1	327	3 249	490
Somalia	—	90	525	390
South Africa	227	16 185	20 458	10 571
Sudan	—	1 760	1 050	800
Tanzania	211	837	874	2 765
Togo	—	126	2 575	404
Tunisia	12 484	1 410	2 878	2 495
Western Sahara	—	80	2 100	250
Zaire	46	1 000	487	303
AFRICA Total	230 695	40 954	127 748	69 967

Source: *Statistical Yearbook 1977* (UN, New York, 1978)

Ocean shipping and seaports

Over 90 per cent of Africa's trade* is with overseas areas and the ports play a critical role in the progress of development. The rapid expansion of trade in recent years has been possible only because port capacity has been greatly increased. Many long established ports (Casablanca, Algiers, Alexandria, Mombasa, Durban, Cape Town, Lagos, Takoradi) have been extended either for conventional cargo handling or in some cases (Cape Town, Lagos) for containers. A large number of specialized terminals have been built to handle bulk exports of oil (Algeria, Nigeria, Libya, Gabon), phosphates (Togo, Western Sahara, Senegal, Morocco) and iron ore (Mauritania, Liberia, South Africa). Completely new general cargo ports, such as San Pedro in Ivory Coast and Tema in Ghana, have become main focal points of regional development and much of Africa's industrial capacity is located at the ports. Port development has not always kept pace with demand so there has been an increase in port congestion at places such as Lagos, Lobito, Dar es Salaam and Alexandria. In some ports dramatic expansion has taken place (e.g. Lagos's Tin Can Island development).

African states are now attempting to carry more of their own trade and are establishing shipping lines to do this, either state-owned (Ghana – Black Star Line, the Nigerian National Shipping Line) or private (Denco of Liberia, Nigerian Green Lines). Liberia as the world's largest flag of convenience is exceptional in that virtually none of this is used for its own trade.   *D. H.*

Kipevu deep water berths, Mombasa, Kenya

Markets

A common feature of most parts of Africa is the market place, through which a great deal of marketing, especially at the local level, takes place. African markets are colourful, lively, noisy and exciting places to visit. Their economic importance is obvious: in these market places – which are to be distinguished from small places of *ad hoc* trading and the wider economic concept of the 'market' – sellers and buyers exchange goods and services. They are also significant social and political institutions that must be included in any economic or socio-political analysis that seeks to take full account of the most immediate and vital concerns of the bulk of the population.

The market place is very widely distributed in Africa, being found in some form or another almost everywhere. Most market places, wherever they occur and whatever type they belong to, are open, with temporary stalls, with poor, crowded and often insanitary conditions, and with few lock-up or storage facilities. Only in some of the larger towns do market places contain permanent, concrete stalls; and completely covered market places are rare. Yet in spite of their generally untidy, congested and chaotic appearance, African market places are in fact usually well organized. Similar products are often sold in the same area of the market place, sellers are subject to some form of market authority, including market fee collection and supervision, and division of labour and patterns of specialization by ethnic group, age and sex are also common. This remains true whether markets are small rural centres, containing only a handful of sellers and buyers, or large, as in some of the great urban markets, which may contain many thousand people at any one time.

The almost bewildering variety of types of African markets reflects not only the great range of ecological conditions in the continent but also the widely differing economic and social circumstances. Certainly it is difficult to generalize usefully about African markets and it is sensible to make some kind of classification, based on one or more of several possible criteria – location, size, size of trade area, physical form and internal arrangement, function in the chains of distribution, or the kinds of goods and services provided. Perhaps the two most useful classifications of African market places depend upon two other criteria: distribution and timing.

The ubiquitous distribution of markets masks the important distinction to be drawn between those markets that are truly indigenous, traditional or pre-colonial in origin, and those that are of more recent origin – colonial or post-colonial. Indigenous market places in Africa seem to be very largely confined to northern and western Africa, with smaller pockets in parts of eastern and north-eastern Africa. One possible explanation for this restricted distribution is that while some indigenous markets may have arisen out of the needs of local or neighbourhood exchange, traditional markets seem

to be associated with long-distance (or at least external) trading contacts in areas of relatively high population density and where political control could guarantee the market peace. Therefore the market place as a feature of pre-colonial Africa was absent where these conditions did not exist. In northern and western Africa these conditions existed: elsewhere markets are mostly of colonial origin.

A second distinction can be drawn between market places – both traditional and modern – that are daily and those that are periodic: that is, occurring less frequently than daily. Periodicity, which is characteristic of over 75 per cent of all African markets, is a logical response to conditions of limited demand. The most common periodicity in Africa as a whole is probably the seven-day (weekly) market. However, the length of a market 'week' varies from area to area so there is a great range of possibilities, as can be illustrated from West Africa, where markets occur generally at two-day to eight-day intervals and, more exceptionally, at 12-, 16- and 24-day intervals.

Periodic markets are often related in a 'ring' or 'cycle', as shown in the map opposite of markets in the Akinyele area of western Nigeria. In this specific ring, eight periodic markets are noted, seven taking place at eight-day intervals, and one at a four-day interval. The markets operate on successive days in such a way that each of the seven eight-day markets takes place on a day on which it is the only one of the seven operating within the ring. After all the markets have had their turn, there is one marketless day, after which the process is repeated in the same order. The eighth market occurs every four days and so operates simultaneously with one market on the first day and with another market on the fifth day of each eight-day period. This integrated timing and pattern of marketing is logical and convenient: it expresses a need to contact a wider and more varied section of people and goods than is possible when only one market is involved.

From the economic point of view there seems generally in Africa to be a broad distinction in function between periodic and daily markets. Periodic markets are mostly rural in location. Their primary function – at least in those areas, such as West Africa, where markets are indigenous – seems to be mainly the injection of local foodstuffs and craft products into the exchange economy by wholesale buying and selling. In those areas, such as much of East Africa, where markets are of much more recent origin, they seem to act primarily as centres for the distribution into the countryside of imported, especially consumer, goods from the urban centres.

Daily markets are usually associated with urban life and their dominant interest is the retail buying and selling of local and imported goods. There is therefore much less variation in the types of goods sold in such daily markets. Indeed, they may be looked upon as open shops in many ways and the growth of permanent, covered lock-ups, shop-houses and, eventually, shops and shopping streets

seems to be a logical and certainly very common development around such daily markets. Moreover, the relationship between the urban daily markets and the rural periodic markets is usually clearly evident. A two-way movement of trading takes place. From the rural periodic 'bulking-up' market comes produce (agricultural and craft industrial products originating in the countryside) for sale in the urban daily retail markets. From the daily markets and shops traders take out into the rural periodic markets consumer goods, including goods imported from abroad, for sale to rural farm populations.

MARKETS IN THE AKINYELE AREA OF NIGERIA

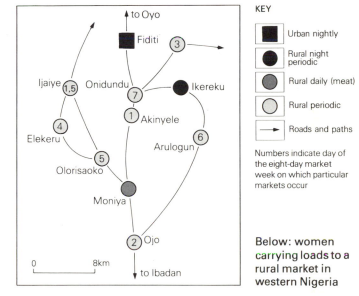

Below: women carrying loads to a rural market in western Nigeria

Treichville market, Abidjan, Ivory Coast

MARKET PERIODICITY IN WEST AFRICA

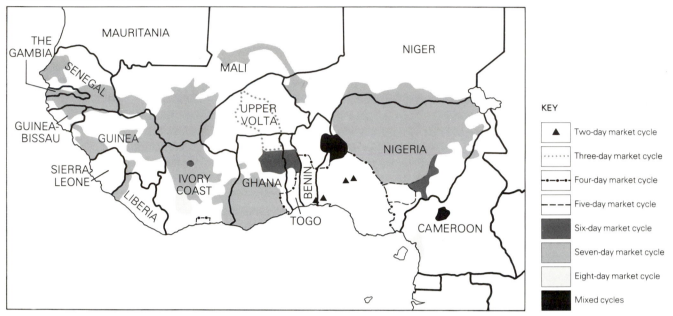

KEY

▲ Two-day market cycle

Three-day market cycle

Four-day market cycle

Five-day market cycle

Six-day market cycle

Seven-day market cycle

Eight-day market cycle

Mixed cycles

The social and political functions of the market place in Africa are declining in many areas, but they are still very important. To some writers, indeed, the 'non-economic' aspects of markets, especially rural markets, are at least as significant as the economic aspects. Certainly they provide places for social intercourse and human interaction in circumstances where alternative foci are few or lacking. They also provide places where social contacts and obligations can be perpetuated. Moreover, markets provide services such as cooked foods, locally-made beer, tailoring, barbers, and the repair of bicycles, watches and shoes. Frequently, too, the market place forms an integral part of the social and political focus of a settlement, lying beside the chief's house, mosque or court. Finally, many writers have commented on the importance of the market place as a centre for the dissemination of information of all kinds – political, health and educational especially.

What of the future of market places and their associated local marketing in Africa? It is easy to point to their apparent weaknesses. The large-scale movement of men and women to and from rural periodic markets carrying local foodstuffs and cottage industrial products is at first sight wasteful in time and energy. In the area covered in the map of Akinyele area – something under 800 sq km – on seven out of eight days up to 5000 women from farms and settlements in the area converge on the market operating on that day. The large numbers selling and the small profits made suggest underemployment of labour, a liking for trade as an activity, and few other activities offering larger returns for the capital and labour commanded. Admittedly, the turnover is often small and slow. But the loads that can be carried by a woman headloading along bush paths for several kilometres are limited: a woman in Yorubaland (southwestern Nigeria) is generally thought to be capable of headloading 35kg compared with 55kg for a man. Consequently, the daily repetition of such movements is likely to be necessary if local produce is to be distributed effectively. The result is a very considerable movement of people to and from markets. In the Akinyele ring a woman living between market 1 and market 6 attends five of the markets shown: she walks up to 14km to market, covers 80km or more a week in travelling on foot to and from market, usually with a basket or calabash of goods on her head and a baby on her back, and is occupied in travelling and trading or buying in the markets five out of every eight days.

There is some evidence that certain of the economic roles of the market place are being taken over by other trading mechanisms and the market place bypassed. Increased urbanization* and, especially, improved transport* are already making their effects felt on traditional marketing structures. Certain crops, such as cocoa, coffee and many other export cash-crops are already marketed largely outside the market place.

Whatever happens in the countryside, there is little doubt that the market place will for long continue to dominate the retail structure of most African towns. It is perhaps too easy to assume that markets are out of place in a modern city – that they are inefficient if rather attractive anachronisms – and it is by no means certain that open markets are not ideally suited to the prevailing physical, social and economic conditions in Africa. *B.W.H.*

Finance and banking

Although North Africa, with its long-standing commercial and financial ties with Europe, and the Cape, with its settler population, had developed local banks earlier, it was not until the late 19th century that modern banking expanded significantly in Africa. The indigenous societies of Africa had evolved their own systems of credit, currency and exchange, but as more of Africa was incorporated into the world capitalist economy these systems came under increasing stress. However adequate they may have been for Africans, European merchants felt constrained by them and sought to introduce currencies with which they were more familiar, and also needed the banks' credit and discounting services.

In 1853 the *Banque du Sénégal* began operations under a French charter which gave it the sole right to issue currency in the colony of Senegal. It was the first modern credit institution in the French African territory and in 1901 was renamed the *Banque de l'Afrique Occidentale*. The first British banking venture in Africa came in 1862 in the Cape Colony with the establishment of the Standard Bank of British South Africa. This was the first bank to bring international capital to South Africa on a large scale. In North Africa British bankers chartered the Anglo-Egyptian Bank in Alexandria in 1864.

There followed a pause until the end of the century when two more British banks began operations. Alfred Jones, the head of Elder Dempster Lines, founded the Bank of British West Africa in 1894 and the bank opened its first two branches in Accra and Lagos in 1896. In the same year the National Bank of India opened offices in Mombasa and Nairobi, beginning operations in East Africa which have continued to the present under the name of National and Grindlays Bank. The last major European entrant into the field of African banking appeared in 1917 when the Colonial Bank, a British bank from the West Indies, opened its first West African branch. The Colonial Bank expanded in West Africa with the backing of Barclays Bank. In addition to these banks there were some German, Italian, Dutch and Belgian banks, but they never developed on a large scale.

These European banks were designed to serve colonial trade in Africa and it is this influence that has marked their development until the present period. The banks provided currency for European firms, handled transfers of funds to European markets, discounted bank notes and provided credit on the security of the export crops or minerals that were the basis of trade. Banks were established in the centres of European commerce. In areas where there was a large settler population, such as southern Africa and later East Africa, or in areas that were more completely integrated with the world capitalist economy, such as Egypt or Algeria, banks developed more extensive services for the settlers and merchants. In other areas bank services remained minimal and bank policy was dictated by the European head office. Bankers had few dealings with Africans.

Banks laboured assiduously to get the accounts of the colonial governments, a steady source of income that offset seasonal trade fluctuations. Government accounts were often linked to the privilege of issuing currency, another lucrative source of income. Thus the Bank of British West Africa, the *Banque de l'Afrique Occidentale*, the National Bank of India and the Standard Bank of British South Africa all handled at one time government accounts and currency issue.

In the British territories currency boards were eventually set up to manage currency affairs. The first of these was the West African Currency Board (1912), followed by the East African Currency Board (1919) and the Central African Currency Board (1939). The currency boards, responsible to the Secretary of State for the Colonies issued local currencies based on sterling. They guaranteed the free exchange of the local currency for sterling at a fixed rate and in unlimited amounts. In the French territories the *Banque de l'Afrique Occidentale* continued to function as a bank of issue until 1955.

During the colonial era two periods – the interwar economic crisis and the boom of the 1950s – were important for the further development of banking in Africa. During the interwar crisis a number of smaller banks were forced under and the survivors underwent a process of consolidation. The Bank of British West Africa, in order to increase its capital, established working agreements with Lloyds Bank, Standard Bank of South Africa and the banks that eventually formed the National Westminster Bank. More importantly, 1925 saw the creation of Barclays Bank (Dominion, Colonial and Overseas), an amalgamation of the Colonial Bank, the National Bank of South Africa and the Anglo-Egyptian Bank. This bank, popularly known as the 'Empire Bank', was the first transcontinental bank in Africa.

During the 1950s these banks, as well as many new ones, expanded rapidly. Standard Bank had 600 offices in 1953, in 1963 it had almost 900; the Bank of British West Africa had 39 in 1951 and 110 in 1960. This expansion was a consequence of the boom in the export economy and also of the new interest in economic development in Africa. The banks began to support development* in the late 1940s with several loans to colonial governments.

In the long run a more important factor supporting expansion was the strong demand by African businessmen for a banking system that met their needs as well as those of the European trading firms. Thus for the first time the banks turned their attention to African customers, partly because the trading firms that had formerly provided credit to African middlemen no longer did so. In addition new banks, owned and run by Africans, were beginning to appear. Although there had been attempts to start such banks in the 1930s only one bank, the National Bank of Nigeria (1933), survived. Not until the late 1940s did any new successful African banks appear. Nigeria experienced the strongest indigenous banking movement, but European banks throughout Africa realized the seriousness of the challenge.

The independence of most African countries in the 1960s brought some change to the banking and financial structure in Africa. Most independent Anglophone states established central banks to issue currency, hold government accounts and regulate commercial banks and credit policy. The Francophone states followed a more dependent policy. Most remain members of the franc zone. Their currencies are tied to the French franc and freely convertible, and 65 per cent of their foreign reserves must be held in francs. These countries do not have central banks but are members either of the *Banque Centrale des États de l'Afrique de l'Ouest* or the *Banque des États de l'Afrique Centrale*. Until 1973 the headquarters of both were located in Paris.

Independence focused attention on the banks' role in national economic development and raised questions concerning staffing, ownership, credit and foreign exchange policy. Banks were prime candidates for indigenization* programmes. At first indigenization took the form of employing more Africans and at higher levels, but eventually foreign banks were required to sell part of their shares to African investors, so that most foreign banks now have some African participation in both staff and ownership. African participation has involved governments in banking because many countries do not yet have a sufficiently large bourgeoisie to invest in banks. The state has taken the shares in their place.

A number of African states have gone beyond indigenization and have nationalized all banks. This programme of expropriation, affecting both foreign and domestic banks, has been part of government attempts to build socialism and has allowed greater control of financial and monetary policy.

Despite the greater involvement of Africans in banking since independence there has been only a slow change in the orientation of banks in the past 20 years. Banks still act primarily as the agents of capitalist incorporation, a reflection of the continued dependence of the African economy. Thus most banks continue to serve the needs of the trading companies first; the fact that these firms may now be African-managed means little. The local sector is still starved of credit. Even a country as wealthy as Nigeria has had to institute credit guide-lines to encourage lending to agriculture* and industry.

Although agriculture is the mainstay of African economies, it suffers from a lack of finance. Commercial banks claim that they are not well suited to lend for the small and short-term needs of the African farmer and have been slow to develop agricultural credit because of its low profit margin. In response to this, governments have supported agricultural credit banks and cooperative banks to meet rural requirements, but these have been plagued by organizational and managerial problems and often have not received sufficient funds.

Local industry has been slightly more fortunate since most independent states quickly created development banks. These banks have also been supported by multilateral aid institutions such as the World Bank. Furthermore, commercial banks have been more willing to lend to support industrialization* because they are more accustomed to such lending and because most projects involve foreign participation, capital and technology. They fit better the mould of the traditional import-export orientation of the commercial banks. In recent years a plethora of specialized credit bodies have emerged to serve the needs of the small bourgeoisie. Mortgage banks are probably the most important of these, although the most interesting are the automobile finance companies that have been set up in some Francophone countries by automobile importers specifically to help the African bourgeoisie finance the purchase of imported cars.

With the exception of the ten countries that have nationalized their banks, European banks continue to play the dominant role. Some countries have no indigenous banks but are served only by international banks. Nigeria, which possesses the most developed banking structure in sub-Saharan Africa, has 18 banks of which seven, the largest, are national subsidiaries of international banks. For the foreign banks the post-independence period has been one of adjustment and consolidation, but also one of continued expansion. The old, French, *Banque de l'Afrique Occidentale* was reorganized in 1965 with the aid of the First National City Bank of New York and became the *Banque Internationale pour l'Afrique Occidentale*. In 1965 Standard Bank took over the old Bank of British West Africa and with the backing of the Midland Bank, the National Westminster Bank and the Chase Manhattan Bank formed the Standard Chartered Group, a transcontinental rival to Barclays. The post-independence period has also been marked by the entrance of new capital, particularly American, into African banking. Libya, which itself nationalized its banks, has become an international banker with banks in the Central African Republic, Chad, Mauritania, Mali, Togo, Uganda and Algeria.

International finance has been strengthened by the activities of multilateral financial aid institutions in the post-war period. The number of these institutions has swelled so that now there are special ones for Africa: the African Development Bank, the African Development Fund, the Arab Bank for Economic Development in Africa and the African Agricultural Credit Commission. The most important of these multilateral bodies is undoubtedly the World Bank and its affiliates, the International Development Association and the International Finance Corporation. The World Bank group is the chief source of development finance in Africa, as commercial banks have found themselves overextended in some areas and face the limiting effects of inflation on their supply of capital. The World Bank has also stepped in to provide finance for development in fields, such as agriculture and education, where the commercial banks have felt the risks were too great and the returns too small.

Another international organization, the International Monetary Fund (IMF), has begun to play a greater part in African finance. Using its ability to provide credit to stabilize currencies and cover foreign exchange deficits, it can force governments to follow credit and monetary policies that are favourable to continued international banking activity, as has been demonstrated by the case of Zaire. Faced with default on massive public debts held by international bankers, the Zairean government agreed to allow the IMF to manage its financial affairs and to carry out economic reforms in return for a rescheduling of the Zairean debt and the continued flow of foreign capital. The dependence on foreign banks, although in a new form, continues.

After two decades of independence the nature of banking in Africa remains little changed, dominated by a few large international banks and oriented to the needs of the international, rather than the national, economy. There have been some recent developments, such as the formation of the West African Clearing House in 1975 to handle bank transfers among the West African states and thus eliminate the process of clearing funds through London and Paris, but it is not yet clear whether these are superficial changes or whether they will be able to serve as the basis for an independent African banking system.   *J.P.O.*

Trade patterns

Africa's trading patterns reflect its level of economic development. It remains by far the least developed region in the world, with manufacturing* and processing at a comparatively simple stage and primarily directed towards home markets.

Export industry has scarcely started in sub-Saharan Africa and is confined to a handful of North African countries. As a result Africa remains almost as dependent as it was at the time of independence on imports of most capital goods, particularly machinery and transport equipment and the more sophisticated manufactures, chemicals and products of heavy industry. Though it has developed local light industry, manufacturing everyday essentials, the demand for branded consumer goods and better quality manufactures from industrial countries remains as high as ever.

Africa's lack of industrialization and export industry also dictates its export pattern. Between 1970 and 1975 manufactures accounted for only 7.6 per cent of total exports from the continent. As in colonial times it remains basically the supplier of primary commodities needed by the industrial world. Because of the rise in the value of crude oil,* Africa is now exporting a greater proportion of primary

products than it was at independence. By 1976 primary products accounted for nearly 90 per cent of Africa's exports with crude oil accounting for over 60 per cent of the total, or two-thirds of Africa's total exports.

The countries of developing Africa (excluding South Africa) accounted for 4.1 per cent of total world exports in 1977 and 4.6 per cent of world imports. In the 15 years after independence Africa exported more than it imported and used the surplus to pay for invisibles and services provided by the industrial powers, but since the oil crises in 1975 this surplus has become a deficit, because of sustained inflation.

Developing African countries exported $45.9 billion in 1977 compared with total world exports of $1130 billion. Significantly, despite the oil crisis and inflation which followed, Africa's share of world trade has changed very little since the later 1960s because Africa's oil-producing states have boosted the overall export total, though the volume of some agricultural commodities has been static and prices have done little more than keep up with world inflation. But the need to maintain habitual volumes of imports, and world inflation, have meant that Africa has been spending proportionately more on imports since 1975.

AFRICA'S TRADE BALANCE

	1960	1965	1970	1975
		billions of US$		
Exports	4.8	7.4	12.2	33.9
Imports	5.3	6.7	10.5	39.3
Trade balance	−0.5	+0.7	+1.7	−5.4

Sources: *World Bank Tables*, 1976; *ECA Survey*, 1976

Africa's exports grew at 12 per cent in money terms during the 1960s and at 24.8 per cent during the 1970s. This spurt was largely caused by inflation particularly in crude oil prices. The fact that Africa kept its share of world trade was largely because the four significant oil exporters–Nigeria, Libya, Algeria and Gabon–have increased their oil prices in line with OPEC policy. Africa's exports of crude oil increased in value from $269 million in 1960 to $19300 million in 1975 and have practically doubled since.

Other African countries, without oil, enjoyed a brief commodity boom for minerals and tropical crops immediately after 1975, but since then the prices of these commodities have declined and with them the value of these countries' exports.

Thus the consequences of the escalation in oil prices have been very different for the oil and non-oil producers in Africa. In 1974, for the first time, the value of exports from the four leading oil producers exceeded the value of exports from all the other African countries together. Since then the situation has been exaggerated by further oil price increases. Exports of the oil exporters quadrupled in 1970–5, and are still increasing, while those of other countries, on average, only doubled.

Among the non-oil producers there are also sharp differences in relative trade performance. The terms of trade, which show the ratio of import to export prices, had been moving steadily against all developing countries in the 1960s. The position improved sharply with the mini-commodity boom of 1973–4 and the larger boom of 1976–7. In Africa the producers of tropical beverages – particularly coffee, cocoa and tea – saw their terms of trade improve sharply compared with the average price of manufactured imports. Though prices of these crops declined in 1978, the terms of trade were still favourable for the producers compared with the prices prevailing in 1970. However, Africa's exporters of minerals, particularly copper, exported mainly by Zambia and Zaire, found themselves considerably worse off in 1979 than they were in 1970.

Structure of exports

At independence agricultural products formed about two-thirds of Africa's exports with minerals forming much of the remainder, but the rise in production and price of crude oil has totally reversed this situation. Crude oil alone now accounts for two-thirds of Africa's exports and the rising price of oil ensures that this situation will be still further exaggerated in future.

Meanwhile agricultural production has been growing slower than in most other regions in the world and has scarcely been sufficient, at an average growth rate of 2.5 per cent since independence, to keep up with population increase. Farmers have concentrated increasingly on providing foodstuffs for the local market and less on export crops, with a result that agricultural exports show little growth.

Although the pattern of exports has altered between primary commodities, Africa remains as heavily dependent as ever upon them. Most countries are dependent on export earnings of one or two main primary commodities and are highly susceptible to price fluctuations in these commodities. The following countries are dependent for more than 70 per cent of their export revenue on one product: Burundi and Rwanda (coffee), The Gambia (groundnuts), Libya and Nigeria (crude oil), Mauritius (sugar), Mauritania (iron ore), Zambia (copper), Chad (cotton), Réunion (sugar), Dahomey (palm-oil). A number of other countries are dependent for 70 per cent of earnings on two main products only: Liberia (iron ore and rubber), Sierra Leone (diamonds and iron ore), Botswana (meat and diamonds), Uganda (cotton and coffee), Ghana (cocoa and timber), Congo (diamonds and timber), Algeria (crude oil and citrus fruit), Gabon (crude oil and timber), Somalia (live animals and bananas).

Africa produces almost all the world's diamonds, over 80 per cent of its gold, 30 per cent of its phosphates, 25 per cent of its manganese, and 20 per cent of its copper. It produces 10 per cent of its iron ore

from reserves which amount to more than 3000 million tonnes, and over 9 per cent of its crude oil. Bauxite, of which Africa produces 6 per cent of world supplies, is even more abundant than iron ore and is scarcely exploited yet. In chromite, Africa has about 90 per cent of world reserves and supplies about 30 per cent of world exports. Africa also dominates world markets in strategic minerals such as cobalt, chromium, lithium, beryllium, tantalum and germanium. It is the principal producer of other strategic minerals such as radium, scandium, caesium and corundum. About one-third of the world's proven reserves of uranium outside the USSR and Eastern Europe are located in Africa, and Africa already exports 20 per cent of the world supply of this increasingly important mineral.

Africa's exports in value order are ranked in the table opposite. It shows clearly the soaring rise in the value of petroleum. Copper exports which were worth 38 per cent of the value of petroleum exports in 1970 have remained steady in volume terms, but in value they have been outstripped by oil. By 1975 copper, the main African producers of which are Zambia, Zaire, South Africa, Zimbabwe and Namibia, was worth only 7 per cent of oil exports.

Africa's second most valuable export after oil is gold. This comes mainly from South Africa, and as a result does not appear in the Economic Commission for Africa's table, which refers to developing countries only. South Africa's gold exports were worth $2430 million in 1977 and though production is declining, have risen since with rising world prices. Other smaller African gold producers are Zimbabwe, Ghana and Zaire.

Coffee, cocoa, cotton and phosphates come next in the ranking of African exports. Each accounts for approximately 3 per cent of the total; the precise position in the ranking varies according to sharply fluctuating commodity prices rather than to any substantial change in the volumes produced.

The tropical beverages are the main export earners for the countries bordering the Equator. Africa produces and exports about one-third of the world's coffee. The high coffee prices of 1976–7 were good for exports of the main producers (in rank order) Ivory Coast, Uganda, Ethiopia and Angola.

Africa produces two-thirds of the world's cocoa, with about a quarter of African exports coming from Ghana. Since 1977 the Ivory Coast has overtaken Ghana to become the world's largest cocoa exporter, followed by Ghana, Nigeria and Cameroon.

Cotton is one commodity where production is declining in the face of competition from man-made synthetics and the increasing difficulty in finding labour willing to harvest the crop. It is the main export of Egypt, Sudan, Chad, Mali and Upper Volta.

Tea is grown in the tropics at higher altitudes. Africa produces only 10 per cent of world production, but its share is expanding. The leading African exporter is Kenya, followed by Malawi, Mozambique, Tanzania and Uganda.

EXPORTS OF SELECTED COMMODITIES (TOP TWENTY BY 1975 VALUES) FROM AFRICA, 1970–5

Commodity	Total value *millions of US$*						Volume of exports *as a percentage of 1970 volume (1970=100)*				
	1970	1971	1972	1973	1974	1975	1971	1972	1973	1974	1975
Crude petroleum	3 925	4 828	6 006	8 788	22 600	19 300	94.6	98.0	96.0	90.2	82.0
Copper	1 473	1 069	1 155	1 680	2 290	1 250	96.8	105.9	103.7	111.1	100.0
Coffee	828	793	895	1 193	1 334	1 200	101.4	106.8	118.0	118.5	109.0
Cocoa	696	592	563	740	1 100	1 150	109.0	91.0	83.0	81.0	79.0
Crude phosphates	162	170	206	262	1 270	1 150	102.8	121.1	130.4	148.0	115.0
Cotton	780	848	851	1 039	1 240	1 000	102.5	95.0	90.0	67.0	63.5
Wood	256	265	340	647	654	560	103.5	124.2	144.4	138.1	128.7
Iron ore	299	316	331	408	491	500	100.7	100.7	113.7	109.5	100.0
Sugar	153	174	214	288	532	480	100.4	109.2	124.0	110.0	98.0
Groundnuts and oil	230	175	228	248	250	270	69.3	84.0	73.0	45.0	57.0
Diamonds	270	236	252	295	321	260	87.4	93.3	81.0	84.9	73.3
Tobacco	82	102	119	154	168	230	124.4	143.0	170.0	180.0	210.0
Palm-oil and kernels	124	131	89	115	280	190	100.0	91.0	70.0	93.0	106.0
Citrus fruits	125	129	132	180	156	180	90.0	90.0	115.0	93.0	84.8
Wine	196	70	89	198	148	150	42.0	50.0	62.0	55.0	45.0
Tea	84	86	108	109	120	136	102.4	128.6	129.8	124.0	126.0
Rubber	85	73	63	108	158	100	103.0	95.0	100.0	105.0	90.0
Sisal	44	36	44	78	168	95	78.0	76.9	59.1	71.2	51.4
Olive oil	23	51	124	85	206	90	209.0	477.0	208.0	352.0	145.0
Rice	92	68	61	75	112	80	77.0	66.4	41.0	37.0	37.0

Source: *Economic Conditions of Africa* (ECA, 1976)

The table shows that Africa was 84 per cent dependent on its top 20 commodity exports (including petroleum) in 1975. The next 20 commodities in importance account for only 5 per cent of total exports.

Africa is beginning to process some of its agricultural and mineral products by refining metals such as copper and iron ore and processing vegetable oils such as groundnut and palm-oil. There has also been considerable progress in branding and marketing commodities such as Botswana beef, Ivory Coast pineapples, Kenya coffee and other fresh produce which is air-freighted to Europe. But manufacturing is in its infancy and is confined to a few countries such as Egypt (clothes, shoes), Ivory Coast and Mauritius (textiles and ready-made garments), and Morocco and Tunisia (processed foods and textiles).

Structure of imports

The composition of Africa's imports varies hugely between countries according to their wealth and level of industrialization. Since independence local, secondary, import substitution industries have been set up in most countries and these produce most basic consumer goods in the clothing, drink, food and textile sectors. In 1960, at the time of independence, 42 per cent of developing Africa's imports were consumer goods and 30 per cent were capital goods. Gradually this situation changed as Africa has become more self-sufficient in consumer goods, and by 1975 the position was reversed, with 42 per cent of imports being taken by machinery and transport equipment alone and consumer goods forming a smaller percentage.

Considerable increases in imports have also been registered in such categories as crude raw materials, chemicals, iron and steel, non-ferrous metals and other manufactures. The most dramatic increase of all came in crude oil imports, which now account for up to a quarter of the import bills of many middle income countries. In 1960 11 per cent of Kenya's import bill was for fuel, by 1976 it was 27 per cent.

Average import values grew at a rate of 6 per cent a year for the first four years of the 1970s and then jumped by 25 per cent in 1975, due to world inflation and increased expenditure by Africa's oil producers. Imports of non-oil producing countries grew by an average of less than 2 per cent a year up to 1974 and then by 14.5 per cent in 1975.

The structure of imports varies vastly between African countries according to their wealth and the advancement of their own industrial sector. In 1970, for example, Rwanda spent 64 per cent of its import bill on consumer goods and 24 per cent on capital goods, while Kenya spent 38 per cent on capital goods and only 10 per cent on consumer goods. Oil exporters, following Nigeria's example, have been spending an increasing proportion of their earnings on capital goods to build up their industrial base.

AFRICA'S IMPORTS, 1971 AND 1975

Category of import	Value millions of US$ 1971	1975
Food, beverages, tobacco	1 765	5 502
Cereals	476	1 740
Crude materials	628	1 500
Textile fibres	104	226
Fertilizers and minerals	45	99
Metal ore and scrap	29	44
Oils and fats	220	537
Mineral fuels	694	3 347
Chemicals	1 108	2 833
Machinery and transport	5 546	17 061
Cars and parts	354	968
Other manufactures	3 601	9 904
Textile yarn and fabric	818	1 590
Iron and steel	654	2 453
Non-ferrous metal	140	308
Other metal manufactures	467	1 490
Clothing	196	463
Total imports	13 497	40 766

Source: *UN Bulletin of Statistics*, May 1977

SOURCES OF AFRICA'S IMPORTS

Source area	Value billions of US$ 1971	1975	Percentage of total imports 1971	1975
NON-COMMUNIST INDUSTRIAL COUNTRIES				
European Economic Community	*	16.47	*	40.4
France	*	0.617	*	1.5
Japan	*	0.383	*	0.9
Others	*	15.587	*	39.0
Total industrial countries	10.61	32.44	78.7	79.6
DEVELOPING COUNTRIES				
Africa	0.70	1.49	5.2	3.6
Middle East	0.35	1.71	2.6	4.2
Asia	0.47	1.38	3.5	3.4
Total developing countries	1.67	5.85	12.4	14.3
COMMUNIST COUNTRIES	1.21	2.47	9.0	6.1
Total imports	13.49	40.76	100	100

Source: *UN Bulletin of Statistics*, May 1977

Direction of trade

Historically, Africa has always sold more than four-fifths of its exports to the industrial world. The average for the period 1972–7 was 82.8 per cent. It exported 11.5 per cent to the developing world and 5.2 per cent to the centrally planned economies.

Over 50 per cent of Africa's exports go to Europe, where the old colonial commercial links are still strong and enhanced by the privileged trading relationship with the European Economic Community (EEC) under the Lomé Conventions. Next important customers are the USA, Japan and the Communist countries.

Africa's imports also come mainly from Europe (55 per cent) and from other major trading powers, with Japan having displaced the USA from second position in the late 1970s. Britain supplied Africa with about a third of its requirements in 1973, but by 1979 it ranked at about the same level as West Germany and France, which has emerged in recent years as Africa's major supplier.

Under the Lomé Conventions Africa can sell almost all its products to the EEC duty free, except those goods which compete directly with agricultural products covered by the Common Agricultural Policy. In practice this means that over 90 per cent of Africa's exports are admitted to Europe duty free, yet Africa's share of EEC imports has been slowly declining over the last 15 years, as more countries have aimed at European markets.

European exports, however, are doing well in Africa. Since 1975 they have expanded faster than sales to any other world market and by 1976 accounted for 7.6 per cent of total EEC exports. Nonetheless, Africa still runs a favourable trade balance with the EEC.

Intra-African trade

Despite the political motivation to develop intra-African trade, it accounts for only a tiny proportion of the continent's global trade. The figure has declined slightly from 5 per cent in the 1960s to 4.2 per cent in the 1970s. This compares unfavourably with trade within the regions of other groups of developing countries. For example, Asian and Latin American trade is about 20 per cent internally directed.

Intra-African trade is low because manufacturing industry is aimed at internal markets and because exporting is a difficult business due to poor communications, complicated customs regulations, and tariff structures which give little advantage to neighbouring states.

There are comparatively few examples of African countries importing raw materials from each other because of the general industrial underdevelopment; exceptions are the use by many West African countries of Nigerian crude oil for refining locally, and Cameroonian imports of Guinean alumina for manufacture of aluminium tools and equipment. Nigeria has plans to use Guinean iron ore in the steel industry which it is now developing.

Intra-African trade takes place mainly within the various continental regions—north, west, east and southern Africa. The

AFRICAN AND WORLD EXPORTS: ORIGIN AND DESTINATION, 1966–77

	DESTINATION OF EXPORTS BY MARKET TYPE			Developing market economies				
	World		Developed market economies	Latin America & Caribbean	Africa	Middle East	other Asia	Communist economies
Sources of exports	Value billions of US$	Percentage annual growth	Percentage of total exports	Percentage of total exports				Percentage of total exports
WORLD								
1966–71 annual average	265.4	12.1	69.8	6.0	3.8	2.4	6.3	10.5
1972	415.6	18.7	71.8	5.7	3.5	2.5	5.8	10.2
1973	577.0	38.8	71.0	5.4	3.5	2.6	6.2	9.9
1974	835.6	44.8	70.1	6.6	3.8	3.4	6.4	8.6
1975	873.8	4.6	65.7	6.7	4.7	5.0	6.3	10.6
1976	990.5	13.4	67.4	6.2	4.3	5.1	6.1	9.7
1977	1 130.2	14.1	67.1	6.1	4.6	5.3	6.2	9.3
1972–77 annual average	803.8	21.0	68.3	6.2	4.2	4.3	6.2	9.6
AFRICA								
1966–71 annual average	10.2	12.0	82.0	1.7	5.0	1.2	2.1	7.0
1972	14.5	13.2	80.7	3.5	3.9	1.0	2.4	7.6
1973	20.6	42.1	81.5	3.8	5.0	0.9	1.8	6.5
1974	38.4	85.9	84.2	4.7	3.9	0.9	1.3	4.7
1975	33.9	−11.6	78.3	6.6	5.5	1.3	0.9	6.6
1976	41.8	23.3	82.5	5.2	4.3	1.5	0.8	4.7
1977	46.0	9.9	86.3	4.9	3.2	1.2	0.8	3.6
1972–77 annual average	32.6	24.8	82.8	5.0	4.2	1.1	1.1	5.2

Source: *World Bank Annual Report, 1978* (World Bank, Washington DC, 1979)

problem here is that the regions produce very similar agricultural products – citrus, corn and wine in North Africa, tropical cash crops and foodstuffs in East and West Africa. This precludes much trade within regions while bad communications hinder trade further afield.

Intra-African economic groupings have also been of limited value in stimulating regional trade. West Africa has never had a customs union on a regional basis though this is the long term objective of the Economic Community of West African States (ECOWAS).*

The East African Community* between Kenya, Uganda and Tanzania, which was the most successful free trade area in Africa, collapsed in 1976–7 for a number of political and economic reasons. One of the most important was that Kenya's superior manufacturing capacity gave it an export advantage over its neighbours. When Tanzania closed its frontier in 1977 local industry flourished, but Kenyan industry found its most important African market closed.

In French-speaking Africa the *Conseil de l'Entente** – grouping the

Ivory Coast, Benin, Niger, Togo and Upper Volta – and the overlapping *Communauté Economique de l'Afrique de l'Ouest** (CEAO), grouping the Ivory Coast, Mali, Mauritania, Niger, Senegal and Upper Volta, do allow preferential trade between these states. It consists largely of trade between the more advanced coastal countries which send manufactures inland in exchange for foodstuffs and meat, particularly animals on the hoof.

Smuggling accounts for a large, but unquantifiable, volume of trade, particularly in West Africa, where countries with higher customs duty levels and weaker currencies are exposed to the smuggling of imported goods from countries with lower tariff systems and comparatively open frontiers. In this way branded manufactures are exchanged for export commodities. For example, there is considerable smuggling of cocoa out of Ghana in exchange for a whole range of foreign consumer goods through the neighbouring states of Togo and Ivory Coast.   *A.R.*

White settlerdom in South Africa

Figures compiled by international agencies place South Africa in a group of 'other developed areas', between industrial countries and less developed areas, on a par with Portugal and below Greece and Spain. In 1973, for instance, per capita Gross Domestic Product (GDP) for South Africa was US $1100; for Portugal, US $1000 and for Spain, US $1730. But most figures relating to the South African economy are distorted, because the economy is skewed, if not in a unique, then in a peculiar fashion. The estimated population of South Africa in 1978 was just under 27 million. This total was broken down, for political and economic purposes, into the following 'racial' categories: White, 4 378 000; Coloured (mixed race), 2 433 000; Asian, 765 000; African, 19 370 000. The validity of these categories in any absolute sense is open to question (and will be noted below), but, to use them in their widely accepted sense, it would appear that, on the most favourable estimate, between the late-1960s and the mid-1970s, 16.7 per cent of the population received two-thirds of the disposable income, while 71.2 per cent received some 25 per cent. GDP can be divided roughly between that accruing to capital and that to labour: in South Africa some 40 per cent of GDP accrues to capital, and this is *almost entirely* white owned; of the GDP accruing to labour, a large proportion goes into white salaries and wages, on a ratio of 5 to 1 (or even higher). Although the trend has been for non-white wages to increase proportionately higher than white wages, the per capita income ratio is something in the order of 10 (white) to 1 (non-white).

The reasons for this remarkably skewed economy are to be found deeply embedded in the political structure of South Africa and in the historical development of the political economy. The political structure is dominated by white settlerdom (16.7 per cent of the total population). In the late 19th century most of the region was divided between four settler polities: the Cape Colony, with a 'colour-blind' franchise based on education and property qualifications; the British colony of Natal, with a franchise limited to all intents to whites; and the Boer (Afrikaner) republics in the Transvaal and the Orange Free State, which uncompromisingly limited the vote to whites. After the war of 1899–1902, which was fought to determine both the control and the nature of the area's economic development, the four settler colonies formed the Union of South Africa in 1910, under the constitution of which only the Cape retained a franchise open to some non-whites. In the Cape, African and Coloured voting rights were abolished in the 1930s and 1950s respectively. In the national elections of the 1960s and 1970s only whites voted.

The minority white population is heterogeneous, the main division being between Afrikaans-speakers and English-speakers. The Afrikaners are descended from the Dutch, French and German settlers of the 17th and 18th centuries; the English migrated to South Africa mainly in the 19th century. Since the beginning of the 20th century Afrikaners have been in a majority of about two-thirds. It took several decades of nationalist contest before the Afrikaners became fully articulated politically, but since the victory of the National Party (NP) in the 1948 election Afrikaners have been in the political ascendancy. The NP has increased its parliamentary majority and its share of the white vote in all subsequent elections. The control of the state by whites has assured the maintenance of the wage and job colour bars in industry.

Historically, the non-whites have always occupied subordinate positions within the white-dominated polities. As slaves and servants, as tribesmen who had been conquered and whose lands were expropriated, non-whites in South Africa became, by the end of the 19th century, a proletariat. Legislation by whites, dating back to the earliest days of their settlement, discriminated against the ancestors of the Cape Coloured people, Africans (who spoke a number of related Bantu languages), and Indians. Discrimination and segregation were designed to keep these people politically powerless, socially separated and economically subordinate. The coming to power of the NP in 1948 did not inaugurate anything new, although NP governments have tackled the task of maintaining white supremacy with unparalleled vigour and ruthlessness, introducing a mass of further discriminatory and segregation legislation, and a new word–apartheid–into South African politics and onto the international stage.

Apartheid is an Afrikaans word meaning 'separateness'. It was first used as a political concept by academics, and was adopted as a slogan by the NP. At one level of application it has signified the mass of conventions and laws which have guaranteed the whites' social and economic privileges. At another level, and increasingly from the early 1960s, apartheid has been concerned with what appears to be a political restructuring of South Africa. This has been the implementation of the Bantustan or Homeland policy. As a result of the colonial wars of the 19th century, Africans were dispossessed of all but 13 per cent of the land of South Africa. This land had become the Reserves, which were rigidly defined by the 1913 and 1936 Native Lands Acts. NP policy has been to promote self-government, leading to quasi-independence, of these scattered territories. All ten Homelands have advanced some way along this road which leads logically to the break-up of South Africa; in 1976 Transkei and in 1977 Bophuthatswana were granted independence by South Africa (a status which was recognized nowhere else). The citizens of these independent homelands have no rights in 'white' South Africa, in which country they are foreigners. Yet nearly one half of the total African population lives in urban areas that are situated in white South Africa; and another large group of Africans lives on white owned farms as labourers. Most Coloured and Asian people live in or near urban areas. There is no large South African town whose non-white population does not outnumber whites. Separate development (as apartheid is now called) is aimed at defusing the aspirations and demands of non-whites, by providing them with their areas for supposedly autonomous political development; it is not meant to alter radically the economic structure of the country. The non-whites remain in such large numbers in the urban areas because the requirements of the economy demand that they do so. The frustrations of Africans and Coloureds with the bleak working and living conditions in the urban areas, which their role in the political economy determined, have culminated in two major outbreaks of violence – the shootings at Sharpeville* in 1960 and the Soweto/Cape Town riots* in 1976.

The economic structure of South Africa is a singular example of the uneven development of capitalism. Industrialization started in the 1870s with the exploitation of diamonds and gold. Gold mining in particular created long-surviving industrial patterns, especially labour migration.* In many respects South Africa remains a peripheral region of international capitalism. In the early days all the large amounts of capital required for the expensive mining operations came from metropolitan sources, predominantly Britain. By the end of the 1970s something approaching $20 billion (US) had been invested in real terms, South Africa being one of the largest single areas of investment for the Western bloc. Britain still leads the field, with £5000 million followed by the USA and West Germany: this capital flow is enticed by a rate of interest which is twice as high as the world average. Although the South African economy generates much local capital, increasingly from Afrikaner sources, it could not continue to operate at present levels without this huge influx. Furthermore, a very high proportion of South African trade is with the five main Western countries. Of this trade, gold is still the largest export. South African gold underpins the monetary system of the West and its price greatly increased in the 1970s.

Within South Africa the pattern of capitalist development exhibits other features of unevenness. The skewed nature of income distribution has been noted. Industrialization occurs in a number of fairly small areas – the southern Transvaal/northern Orange Free State triangle, the main ports, Durban and Cape Town, and one or two other zones. All industrial growth has taken place in the 'white' area. In addition, much of white agriculture has been capitalized and mechanized. Most of 'white' South Africa is economically rich, by any standards; all of 'black' South Africa is poor and undeveloped. It has been argued that the South African political economy is a classic example of the development of underdevelopment; the Homelands can be seen as mere reservoirs of labour (note the old term, 'reserve') and dumping grounds for the growing unemployed – some 25 per cent or more of the productive African labour force. Increasing unemployment is an effect of the marked change in the nature of the South African economy, from labour- to capital-intensive forms

of industrial and agricultural production.

Two of the major flaws in separate development, the incapacity of the Homelands to provide homes and livelihoods for even half the African population, the majority of which will continue to live and work in 'white' areas, and the 'problem' of the Coloureds and Asians, who have no 'homelands', resulted in a change of emphasis in official policy in the late 1970s. As well as continuing to divide South Africa into small political units (except for the white or 'common' area, which remains very large), the South African government has attempted to create a non-white elite urban proletariat. Policy is more overtly class- and less racially-based. The non-white elite, so it is argued, will see in its acceptance of white control the guarantee of its relative stability and prosperity. In part this tendency is dictated by changing factors (the need for a smaller, highly skilled labour force); in part by the political requirements of the white group.

The political economy of South Africa has been explained in a number of ways by academics and by people active in its maintenance or supersession. One rather crude approach sees South Africa in the racial terms of the white protagonists, in particular of Afrikaner nationalism. The conflict is between European Christian National values and 'communistic' barbarism. Afrikaner nationalist interpretations have been anti-internationalist and anti-capitalist. The obverse of this in certain respects has been the attitude of some of the African spokesmen of Black Consciousness. Another, more academic, explanation analyses South Africa as a plural society, using sociological models and sophisticated concepts of race and racism. Some pluralists adopt a seemingly neutral attitude to the role played by capitalism in the historical development of South Africa. Liberal interpretations are more positive in this respect, even if unconsciously so. In spite of irregularities, capitalism is seen as being beneficial to all the peoples of South Africa, at least in the long run (capitalism is 'colour-blind'). And capitalism is basically antagonistic to apartheid, which is an anachronism. This is the argument of the capitalists themselves, who see increased foreign investment and economic intervention as the cure of the racial ills brought about by apartheid. Radicals and Marxists reject the liberal/capitalist interpretation. The political economy of South Africa is, they argue, a highly complex totality, with apartheid one of its main political elements and capitalism the basis of the economy. If there are conflicts between the two, these are resolved mutually. The major conflict in the South African situation is the result of the inherent contradictions in a specific manifestation of capitalism. The analysis of South Africa is fundamentally on a class basis, racial categories and racism being part of the ideological apparatus of the dominant class; this interpretation applies not only to the actual South African situation, but also to liberal and pluralist explanations. But few observers of the South African political economy see its future as anything but a long period of severe conflict. *A.A.*

Tourism

Tourism in Africa today has its roots in the development of tourist attractions in colonial days and the pattern of modern tourist penetration in Africa follows the colonial path. Colonial rule saw the expansion of road communications *within* African states but the poor development of communications *between* them. It also did very little to overcome the enormous difficulties of contact between the separate regions of the continent, in particular between the north, west and east.

Communications have not improved much since independence. Africa's capital cities often maintain stronger links, through air travel and telecommunications, with their respective former colonial capitals than with each other. Francophone Ivory Coast and Senegal, for example, attract a very high proportion of their tourists from France, while Kenya and the Seychelles have tourist industries run largely by British businessmen that attract a high proportion of English-speaking tourists. Where substantial expansion of the industry has taken place since independence (as in these four countries) the new influx of tourists has been from the other Western economic giants, for example West Germany and the USA, rather than from other African countries. The tourist industry is, in fact, one of the most striking reminders of the very recent passing of colonialism in Africa and of its replacement by new links with European and other Western societies.

There are significant differences in tourist 'penetration' between different regions of Africa. 'Mass' tourism is only to be found in North Africa and southern Africa. North Africa's historical links with the Mediterranean and southern Europe, its sunny climate, and its relative geographical closeness to major tourist markets make it an important and well-established destination for European seekers of sun, seaside and cultural exoticism at a comparatively low cost. Egypt, Tunisia and Morocco are each hosts to well over a million tourists every year. The southern African tourist industry is smaller and more idiosyncratic but also rests on a mass market. Distance from mass markets in Europe and North America means that foreign visitors to South Africa must be relatively affluent; nevertheless in 1978 it attracted about 230 000 visitors from Europe and 100 000 from other non-African countries.

Within southern Africa a major tourist industry is developing which draws on the mass of the white South African population. While foreign visitors to South Africa are lured with inexpensive pseudo-exotic confections – as one tourist advertisement put it, 'Only in South Africa can you visit a Hindu temple in a Chinese rickshaw pulled by a Zulu warrior' – Lesotho, Botswana and Swaziland are developing tourist industries oriented towards escapist white South Africans that provide them with luxurious hotel facilities as well as allowing the possibility of a brief respite from the racial and social prohibitions imposed by apartheid.* Swaziland, for example, is near enough to the major urban centres of South Africa to allow weekend visits by whites; one of its major attractions being its casino, since organized gambling is prohibited in South Africa. Similarly, in Lesotho the Maseru Holiday Inn and Casino, a Hilton Hotel and a second casino have been built in the capital. Such developments bring little economic benefit to the countries involved; most of the supplies needed for the hotels are imported, and most of the profits are repatriated by the foreign majority shareholders. Expansion has been impressive; between 1968 and 1978, for example, tourist visitors to Lesotho increased from 4000 to 132 000 a year. The market

Gateway to the Mt Kenya Safari Club, Kenya

Lagos beach, Nigeria

is apparently still expanding since a hotel-casino complex – 'Sun City' – has also been projected for the nominally independent black 'homeland' of Bophuthatswana,* 160km from prosperous white Johannesburg.

Distance from major white markets (and the lack of development of a significant black African tourism) has meant that outside of North Africa and southern Africa tourism has been limited, resting essentially on an affluent minority market of tourists in, for example, the UK, France, the USA, West Germany and Japan, who can afford to travel long distances to enjoy such legendary attractions as game parks, forests, mountains, lakes, and ocean shores, and to observe the mythical 'uncorrupted tribal society' that tourist publicity tends to conjure up. Most successful in tapping this market has been Kenya (where tourists spent an estimated £K60 million – approximately £71 million sterling – in 1978), but the 'tourist frontier' has also begun to spread from established North African resorts, down the west coast to Senegal, The Gambia and Sierra Leone. In the 1976–7 season, for example, over 20 000 air charter tourists visited The Gambia and spent approximately £1.6 million there.

Conditions for tourism

Each African country caters for some sort of travel, even if only for businessmen, traders and officials, and most have tried in some way to exploit their many tourist attractions, both for immediate economic gain and to encourage wider development of the country's resources. Africa's potential for tourism depends not only on the number and quality of tourist attractions but also on each country's ease of access from the tourist markets and its ability to accommodate, cater for, entertain and transport foreign visitors. Africa's tourist facilities have generally been expanded in the post-independence era, particularly in Egypt, The Gambia, Ivory Coast, Kenya, Malawi, Mauritius, Senegal, Seychelles, Swaziland and Tunisia. In other countries the general standards of accommodation have improved but are often without adequate back-up services – for example, private beaches, efficient catering, transport facilities – for the type of tourism that attracts a mass market. Moreover, the general economic and organizational difficulties that beset the continent have often taken their toll of grandiose tourism 'master-plans'. Although tourist centres are sometimes 'enclaves' isolated from the everyday life of the countries in which they are situated, it often proves difficult to insulate them from civil disorder, rampant inflation, widespread petty theft, electricity blackouts, water shortages, lack of spare parts for plumbing or air-conditioners, and food, alcoholic beverage and fuel shortages, all or some of which may be prevalent, particularly in the poorer countries. Where such problems are overcome it is often at great cost in foreign exchange, which might be spent more profitably in other sectors of the economy.

Apart from such questions of infrastructure, the development of a significant tourist industry depends also on political factors, notably the attitudes of African governments to the likely social and political effects of an influx of relatively affluent and probably culturally distinctive foreigners. At one extreme a few countries, such as Guinea, have placed very tight long-term restrictions on the entry of foreigners of any sort. Idi Amin's Uganda* placed a ban on tourist entry from September 1972 to September 1973, and what had once been a relatively flourishing industry only began to recover after his overthrow. Other governments have been hesitant about encouraging an unrestricted inflow of tourists, particularly when there is no clearly discernible economic benefit. Tanzania, for example, until the break-up of the East African Community* and the closure of the border with Kenya in 1977, received a high proportion of its tourist arrivals in the form of visitors to *Kenya* on one-day excursions which were paid for in Kenya and therefore largely benefited the Kenyan economy. Moreover, such small benefits were often seen as not counterbalancing the adverse effects of tourism on a country whose government was seeking to build socialism and self-reliance, and the more rapid development of tourism since the late 1970s (with tourists mainly entering directly into Tanzania) has been under the close control of the Tanzania Tourist Corporation.

A Mombasa beach hotel, Kenya

Types of tourism

African countries have potential for several basic types of tourism and travel: wildlife tourism, 'tropical' tourism based on coastal attractions, climate and water sports, adventure tourism, cultural travel and exchanges and business travel. For any one trip to Africa an individual would be likely to combine some of these types. Business travel is frequently associated with 'tropical' tourism in Africa, and many purely business travel destinations have begun to develop facilities for luxury or package tourism. Thus Gabon, Liberia and Sierra Leone have built new beach hotels as a by-product of their commercial attractions.

The sites that currently attract the greatest numbers of foreign visitors are: in North Africa, the Mediterranean coasts, the ancient cities and early ruins of Egypt, Sudan and North-West Africa; and in East Africa the game parks and Indian Ocean coasts. In 1978, indeed, Egypt (with 1.1 million tourist arrivals – 20 per cent of the African total), Tunisia, Morocco and Kenya accounted for 75 per cent of Africa's visitors from Europe and North America. Apart from southern Africa with its coasts, mountains, game parks and concocted exoticism, the other significant countries for tourist arrivals in 1978 were Ivory Coast, Senegal, Togo, The Gambia, Cameroon, Sudan, Madagascar, Gabon and Tanzania.

In West Africa much of the tourism is still a coastal phenomenon. Although there are, for example, important historical sites inland – such as the ruins associated with the ancient empires of the western Sahel* zone and northern Nigeria – this is a very underdeveloped tourist area, partly because these sites are less spectacular than those in, for example, Egypt and are therefore of specialist interest, and partly because of formidable transport difficulties in reaching them. Tourism in such areas is very much the preserve of the 'adventure' tourist. Many of such sites are perhaps most easily reached from the north, and the trans-Saharan crossing from North to West Africa has proved to be a persistent, if minor, aspect of 'adventure' tourism; in addition many travellers make limited forays into the desert from

North Africa rather than complete crossings.

Africa's wildlife tourism is its most unusual feature: other continents have game preserves, but none on such a scale. There are, however, conflicts of interest between those who are managing wildlife conservation* policies and tour operators, whose activities, if uncontrolled, would lead to the destruction of the very assets that provide their profits. In fact, a similar kind of long-term responsibility is required in a less dramatic degree for nearly all kinds of tourism in Africa, particularly when local residents fear, or do not know how, to protest against their loss of rights. In North Africa, for example, stretches of beach that once provided an independent livelihood to whole fishing villages have been turned over to sunbathers. Employment in menial occupations in tourist hotels can be a poor substitute for the traditional way of life.

Cultural tourism does not seem to carry with it any comparable social or economic risks. Travel may be designed around a programme of appreciation of local music, arts and crafts, theatre, dance and language. While most countries have established important cultural centres, and museums and traditional festivals flourish, there has been very little construction of tourist 'packages' that can sensitively provide enjoyment of these local resources. On the contrary, the tendency (as for example in South Africa, but also in Kenya) has been to concoct watered-down versions of 'traditional' cultural forms that bear little or no relationship to the real local heritage. The most successful manifestations of 'cultural' tourism have, in fact, been 'one-off' ventures, notably the massive Second All Black and African Festival of the Arts (*Festac*) sponsored by the Nigerian government and held in Lagos (and other Nigerian centres) in January 1977, which brought African and foreign black artists and intellectuals together from all over the continent and from outside for the first time – the first festival held in Dakar in 1966 was confined to Africans. However, *Festac* was an event that completely contradicted the general rule that tourism in Africa is an industry dominated by foreign interests.

The wider development of such tourism – which implies considerable development of intra-African flows – is desirable but probably unlikely. Poverty (both from the point of view of the development of transport and communications, and from the point of view of individual African's ability to afford tourist travel) is the major stumbling block: whereas only 12 per cent of Africa's tourists come from elsewhere in Africa, in Europe 80 per cent of tourists are from European markets. If then African countries are to benefit from what appears to be likely to continue to be the prevalent type of tourism – visitors from rich countries overseas – the main problems would appear to be ensuring that real economic benefits are forthcoming and, less tangibly, ensuring that economic benefits are not counterbalanced by damage to the culture and morale of their peoples. *R.M.S.*

TOURISM: COUNTRIES WITH MOST VISITORS, 1974

Country	Number of foreign visitors
Morocco	1 340 000
Tunisia	716 000
Egypt	679 476
South Africa	608 425
Kenya	379 600
Algeria	249 000
Zimbabwe	238 821
Tanzania	177 500

Source: *Tourism International Yearbook 1976* (London, 1976)

The changing family

In indigenous African societies the kinship unit, which may be understood in general terms as the extended family, has traditionally been the core unit of social organization. As is typical in agrarian societies the world over, the extended family has tended to be the basic unit of production, distribution, consumption, usual source of immediate authority and general agency of social control. Kin solidarity is a dominant ethical theme in matrilineal, patrilineal, and bilateral descent and inheritance systems alike. Kin constitute an important reference group for family members, who typically relate to wider communities as a segment or representative of their particular family. At the same time, this unit claims a special right to the perpetual loyalty of its individual members. Even if adult members have been working for several years away from home they may still be called to account for their behaviour or career progress by the extended family; the Igbo people of eastern Nigeria offer a particularly striking example.

Today the typically communalistic extended family is undergoing some alteration. At the same time, however, forces of change are encountering some countervailing factors that support the continuity of extended kin solidarity. Members of contemporary families find themselves attempting to work out contradictions between old and new (perhaps 'Western' is the most appropriate term) values and definitions of relationship. These old and new norms can be found operating in varying combinations in each family situation.

At least three contexts involving different rates and types of family change may be identified. Certainly change comes more slowly to rural areas. Yet there are no major populations so isolated from centres of change that they remain untouched, and norms may be challenged abruptly as one or more family members migrate in search of employment. A second context, which includes a large proportion of the rapidly growing urban population, is that of the first generation urbanites whose social world spans both places of work and origin, as they typically maintain an active social role in the home community to which most will eventually return. Finally, there are those who are the product of more than one generation of urban-based family life. Our discussion of change focuses on these last two categories, where the most widespread and rapid change occurs.

The fundamental agent of change in Africa may be identified in general terms as urbanization*–more particularly, the diffusion of cultural styles (urbanism) and institutional arrangements associated with the growth and spread of the city. In cities, for example, 'modern' institutional arrangements encourage what may be called 'individualized contract'–the tendency for individuals to be regarded as social atoms of society who incur debts and enjoy rewards as *individual* employees or as individual subjects of the state. This opposes the perception of oneself as a component of a family group, as a part of a *whole*. Non-customary legal systems* reinforce this trend, tending to interpret 'family' in the Western sense, and, increasingly, to articulate rights and obligations in terms of husband, wife, and offspring (the nuclear family). The 'ideology of the couple'–the perception of the couple as a special, exclusive relationship–is growing in strength. This orientation is supported by the growth in popularity of the idea of romantic love as a goal and primary motive in marriage. Research indicates that the idea of the conjugal family along the lines of the Euro-American model is most prevalent among younger persons, those with higher education and incomes, and urbanites. Within such a relationship the tendency would be to come to view members of a wider (extended) family group as 'outsiders'; to insulate socially the married couple. This nucleation of the family unit is reinforced, as elsewhere in the world, by urban housing designed and constructed to fit the needs of a streamlined family unit, thus lending a structure of privacy to the world of the urban couple.

There are, however, a number of factors that reinforce the more traditional extended family structure in the process of urbanization. There is widespread evidence from sub-Saharan Africa that kinship plays a vital role in propelling migrants to employment careers in rapidly growing cities. After obtaining an education in rural areas, migrants are assisted to urban centres characterized by overcrowding and high rates of unemployment where they are sustained, chiefly by family sponsors, while they seek a livelihood. They thus incur 'debts' both to individual family members and, more importantly, to the kinship unit as a whole. This sense of obligation–the need to repay the debt–is reinforced by customary law* which may threaten the individual with sanctions of censureship in the rural area. Reciprocation of duty, however, is also likely to be supported by an individual's strong feelings of loyalty to his place of origin and to his particular family. Reciprocation most typically takes the form of remittances, usually of some portion of the monthly salary, or intermittent but significant gifts of cash and goods. Most of this finds its way back into the rural areas; some may go to help kin living in towns or cities. Although distance from kin may physically isolate migrants and suggest that extended family ties would be undermined over time, regular communication between migrants and rural kin, and family members in other cities, remains the norm. Improved transport and communications have eased this process and reduced the effective distance between family members. Research from Ghana and Tanzania, for example, has shown that remittances to home tend to increase as migrants become more established and better able to contribute to (especially ageing) rural kin. The tendency for the demand or request for support, by a seemingly ever-widening pool of kin, to increase at a pace equal to the fortunes of urban entrepreneurs or employed persons has, at times, been labelled 'parasitic' by Western observers. Very often, however, the foundations of the present good fortune of individuals can be attributed to earlier family sponsorship. Moreover, in the absence of alternative agencies of social welfare, rural kin can maintain the migrant's claim to agricultural land, which symbolizes security in the uncertainty of rapid change. Urban-based kin can also be an important source of support in various crises. In a real sense, then, the extended family remains an economic unit—though a more complex one than previously. The Ijebu Yoruba of Nigeria reportedly conceive of this system as 'farming the city'. This supports, once again, the point raised earlier; the importance of recognizing that continuity is a part of family change in Africa.

What will happen to the African family in the increasingly urban future is a perplexing question. There has been general speculation that it will conform to the more simplified Western model. Research (for example from Lagos and Douala) indicates, on the other hand, that urban based families undergo a considerable extension and elaboration over generations of urban living, as the extended kin network remains an important context of reference, interaction, and support. At the same time, however, young single or married urbanites will continue to attempt to assert a certain amount of independence, economic autonomy, and to perceive the emotional content of their relationship as exclusive of outside kin. This orientation, at its extreme, will be more tenable and sustained among the small minority of couples who can be certain they will not need to rely on family support in the future. Testimony is abundant, however, that younger adults typically seek a limited *insulation*—not *isolation*—from the wider family and its affairs. In fact, where both husband and wife have urban incomes there is some tendency to maintain separate accounts, at least in part to prevent easy access by a spouse's relatives to one's own reserves.

The practice of plural marriage (polygyny) has come to be viewed critically among certain groups, as has the practice of maintaining an 'outside' (informal or casual) wife. Where women have access to status and economic independence outside the family structure, e.g. through education, employment or trade, their attitude towards husbands taking a 'junior' wife (i.e., a 'subordinate' to an existing wife) has become more negative. Again, among younger adults, men and women with more education and with urban experience, plural marriage declines in popularity, probably in line with the rise of the 'ideology of the couple'. It is necessary to recognize, at the same time, that plural marriage has not become an altogether unpopular idea, for example among well established (usually older) men with higher incomes in regions that have customarily prescribed more wives for the economically successful.

Whether the family will continue to move towards conformity with the Euro-American type in the future will likely depend in large part upon the economic growth of the country or region concerned and how that growth is distributed between rural and urban populations;

what alternative agencies of social welfare arise to replace the family's social security function; and the extent to which current (indigenous or modified) cultural patterns remain adaptable to changing demographic and economic conditions. *W.G.F.*

Social stratification

The emerging patterns of social stratification in Africa reflect both the evolution of traditional forms and the creation of new forms as Western social and economic forces penetrate the continent to an increasing depth. In some measure these new forms resemble those familiar in the West, and have been described in such Western terms as middle and working class. However, the development of Africa has not been autonomous but dependent upon the West, and its stratification exemplifies this status.

Traditional patterns of stratification are far from uniform. At one end of the spectrum are many societies, such as the Tiv of Nigeria, that are substantially egalitarian. Territorial groups are based upon descent. The principal social divisions are between men and women, old men and young men. The latter work to support, in part, the former; the elders maintain their authority with ritual sanctions. But though the youths may resent specific incidents of their subordination they do not rebel against it, for they will in turn become elders. By contrast, in many kingdoms, such as those of the Yoruba of Nigeria, or the Akan of Ghana, the king and his titled chiefs display great affluence, as do wealthy traders. However, although the kingship is hereditary, other positions of power and wealth are open to most citizens, and many who have reached high positions have come from humble families. Furthermore, the estate of a wealthy man tends to be distributed widely among his children by his many wives; none receives enough to enable him to replicate his father's status without further effort. Thus these societies stress not only the unequal endowment of individuals at birth but also the virtues of personal achievement thereafter and therefore contain substantial elements of equality of opportunity, if not egalitarianism. Further along the spectrum are other kingdoms, exemplified by most of the kingdoms of the West African savanna, in which political office is restricted to a dominant ethnic minority; thus Fulani families govern the Hausa emirates of Nigeria. Elsewhere a dominant clan may rule, as among the Swazi or Zulu in southern Africa. Origin myths serve to validate and perpetuate this social ranking though these may, in modern situations serve little effect; they did not, for instance, prevent the massacre of the dominant Tutsi by the Hutu of Rwanda.* In the western Maghrib the Berbers continued to practice their traditional way of life, combining agriculture and pastoralism, while the coastal cities were dominated by an Arab or Arabized population.

The trans-Atlantic slave trade* and that of the Arabs on the eastern coasts of Africa facilitated the growth of many African kingdoms. But the rulers ultimately consumed the wealth generated in ostentatious display; little was invested to increase production. Thus an affluent court or capital with a complex hierarchy of officials coexisted with villages still largely egalitarian and descent-based.

The early decades of colonial rule established an extractive economy, agricultural products and minerals providing the raw materials for Western industry. Many of the crops were, however, grown by farmers within the indigenous forms of land tenure; the mines were worked by labourers who migrated for short periods in their youth and then returned to a traditional model of rural living. In the newly created colonial states a very small expatriate minority of officials, traders and missionaries was dominant.

In some areas these expatriates settled–in Algeria, the Ivory Coast, and Kenya, for example–and established agricultural estates. In southern Africa the early Boer settlers and their successors not only seized most of the land from the Africans but also established a prosperous industrial economy. Aliens also occupied the middle strata of many societies–the Asians as traders and clerks in East Africa, the Lebanese as traders in West Africa, the French petit-blancs (white small-shopkeepers and minor functionaries) in Senegal and the North African colonies; these groups effectively limited the advance of the indigenous population into positions in the modern economy and society.

In the post-colonial state the superstructure erected over the traditional societies has been taken over by Africans. They have filled the administrative offices and, with the increase in social services, they have expanded enormously the state bureaucracy. Independence led to the rapid development of a nascent manufacturing industry,* but mainly as the result of Western enterprise. African politicians and civil servants have exercised a limited control over its development. Many have grown wealthy from perquisites obtained through their decision-making roles. Few Africans have either capital or skills to develop businesses on the scale of the expatriate firms, though many are becoming small-scale entrepreneurs in property-owning or farming, especially where the estates of erstwhile settlers have been seized or sold.

The prime qualification for entry into this new dominant group is education. As a result its members are often of diverse social origin. In some cases, as among the Ganda of Uganda, a dominant indigenous group sought adherence to the mission churches and their schools as a means of buttressing its position; in other cases the underprivileged in traditional society sought through education an alternative route to high status. One consequence of the rapid growth of the African dominant elite is that most of its members are of humble rural origin. Yet, once at the top, they can, through their wealth and influence, and through the advantaged upbringing of their children, ensure that their own offspring retain a place in the upper strata.

Though colonial officials and many settlers have departed, the number of non-Africans in other roles–for example as technicians or businessmen–has increased in most societies. They are transient, and so marginal to the stratification system; yet their affluent life style serves as a visible model for the African dominant groups and this in turn contrasts markedly with the poverty of both rural and urban masses.

Agriculture* has tended to remain stagnant, receiving little direct investment. Yet the farmers through the sale and export of their crops have in large measure financed the recent development of the state. Patterns of rural social structure are being only slowly modified and traditional attitudes persist in this politically fragmented stratum. The lack of opportunities has led millions of youths to migrate to the bigger cities in search of a better future.

Here few jobs await them. Industry tends to be capital-intensive. Crippling foreign debt repayments are reducing public expenditure–in bureaucratic expansion for instance. A few men and women obtain stable wage employment in industry or the public sector, being paid relatively well by local standards (though low wages by international standards are an inducement for foreign firms); many more receive a minimum wage as daily paid labourers–a wage often much lower then locally recognized subsistence levels. The remainder create employment for themselves as artisans, petty traders or professionals (such as lawyers and doctors) serving rich or poor. The poverty of the self-employed (apart from the professionals) is reflected in their residence in the peripheral shanty towns of the cities.

Attempts to analyse the stratification of these African societies in classic Western class terms is fraught with difficulties. The dominant African elite is an upper class in terms of its consumption patterns; but it owns neither the land, which is still largely held by the peasants, nor industry, which is mostly foreign-owned. It exerts some control over production within constraints of dependence upon the Western economy. Though collectively its members are seen by the masses as enjoying a highly privileged position, tension is mitigated by the belief that individuals have succeeded by their own efforts and by the continued ethnic identification of persons with their communities of origin. The masses realize that they are being exploited, but peasants do not fully realize the extent of their indirect taxation, factory workers are ignorant of their firms' profits, and the self-employed see only the constraints to their advancement. Opposition tends to be focused diffusely upon 'the government' and not upon a particular economic system. The corruption of one regime is resolved by the initial purges of its successor. Lacking education and experience, the poor have no vision of an alternative form of society; trade unions, highly organized in the manufacturing sectors of most states, are often coopted by government and limit their demands to wages rather than to issues of ultimate control.

In their poverty the urban poor must retain their relationship both with their communities of origin and with their neighbours of like origin. These provide them with social security and with the patronage which they see as essential to their personal advancement. Such ties inevitably tend to weaken any consciousness of common class interests among the poor as a whole.

The dominant elite itself promotes an ideology of self-help and individual social mobility. Nationalistic slogans serve to unite the citizenry against an often ill-defined foreign domination. Ethnic rivalries within the state, consequent upon the continuance of traditional social structures mask, as in the Nigerian civil war, more deep-seated political and economic divisions. Only, as in southern Africa, where the ethnic divisions are hierarchically ranked, do the criteria of ethnicity★ and class become almost congruent to create a powerful movement among the poor for their liberation.   *P.C.L.*

Urbanization

In 1975 one African in four lived in an urban area. This reality stands in sharp contrast to the conventional, rather bucolic image of the 'dark continent'. Although Africa remains the least urbanized continent, urban growth, explosive since the Second World War, appears set to continue at a rapid pace. It has been estimated that the urban population in the year 2000 will be 42 per cent of the total population, or 350 million, a figure equal to the continent's total population in 1970.

Urbanization is frequently assumed to be closely linked to industrialization. However, major cities flourished in various parts of Africa well before the age of the Industrial Revolution, and while it is true that many more urban centres came into being after the establishment of colonial rule, they were primarily geared to the requirements of commerce and administration. Even after independence, Africa continued to be primarily a producer of raw materials and to this day few African cities are based on industry★ or mining.★

Various parts of Africa have a long urban history. Indeed, the capitals of the kings of ancient Egypt★ were established in their imposing splendor two millennia before the founding of Rome. Alexandria became the most important centre of Hellenistic and Jewish culture and by 30 BC was the largest of the Roman provincial capitals. Carthage★ rivalled Rome in the 3rd century BC. A millennium later, the spread of Islam through North Africa brought a dramatic expansion of Mediterranean trade, and intellectual pursuits and the arts flourished. Existing settlements, like Tunis, expanded and new towns, like Marrakesh, gained prominence.

Across the Sahara, the gold trade provided the basis for the emergence of empires and their capital cities. In the 11th century

Timbuktu: René Caillié's impressionistic view of 1828

Koumbi-Saleh, the Muslim section of the capital of Ghana,★ was said to have a dozen mosques. Gao, the capital of the vast Songhay★ empire, had an estimated 75 000 inhabitants in the 16th century. Timbuktu, a smaller city of perhaps 25 000, was famous throughout the Muslim world as a centre of religion and learning.

On the east coast of the continent, it was the Indian Ocean trade that brought into being major ports such as Sofala, Kilwa, Mombasa, and Malindi.★ They exchanged ivory, gold, and copper for merchandise that came from countries as distant as China. The stone ruins of Great Zimbabwe,★ 400km inland, bear witness to the stature of one of the kingdoms that supplied the maritime trade.

Today, the level of urbanization in Africa is low compared with the rest of the world, but its urban population is growing faster than that of any other major region. A comparison by country reveals two significant patterns. Level of urbanization closely correlates with level of economic output: the poorest countries tend to be the least urbanized. This pattern holds worldwide. To conclude that urbanization is a prerequisite of economic growth, however, would be premature, as we shall see. The second pattern, and partly related, is a distinct regional division. North Africa, the region most urban prior to colonial rule, continues to lead the continent in level of urbanization. Even the poorest country in the region, Egypt, is more highly urbanized than the several countries of tropical Africa that have higher incomes. West Africa is characterized by a wide range in levels of both income and urbanization, from the barren lands of the Sahel to the lush cash-cropping regions in the south. East Africa is the poorest and least urbanized region, and Madagascar fits the same pattern, but it is here that urban growth is proceeding most dramatically. Middle Africa appears as a better-endowed region with higher levels of urbanization. The peculiar pattern of Zaire can be

GROSS NATIONAL PRODUCT (GNP) PER CAPITA, PROPORTION OF POPULATION LIVING IN URBAN AREAS,[1] AND ANNUAL GROWTH IN URBAN POPULATION, 1950–80: AFRICAN COUNTRIES WITH A POPULATION OF OVER 5 MILLION IN 1980

Region	Country	GNP per capita US$ 1977	Percentage of total population in urban areas		Urban population thousands			Percentage annual growth in urban population		
			1980[2]	1950	1960	1970	1980[2]	1950–60	1960–70	1970–80[2]
AFRICA		490	29	31 818	49 506	80 373	132 951	4.5	5.0	5.2
NORTH AFRICA										
	Algeria	1 140	61	1 948	3 287	6 529	12 065	5.4	7.1	6.3
	Egypt	340	45	6 532	9 818	14 080	19 119	4.2	3.7	3.1
	Morocco	610	41	2 345	3 412	5 236	8 265	3.8	4.4	4.7
	Tunisia	840	52	1 103	1 521	2 234	3 394	3.3	3.9	4.3
WEST AFRICA										
	Ghana	370	36	727	1 575	2 511	4 104	8.0	4.8	5.0
	Guinea	200	19	148	315	543	956	7.8	5.6	5.8
	Ivory Coast	770	38	367	662	1 192	2 099	6.1	6.1	5.8
	Mali	120	20	277	452	751	1 284	5.0	5.2	5.5
	Niger	190	13	111	169	337	660	4.3	7.1	7.0
	Nigeria	510	20	3 595	5 642	9 009	14 811	4.6	4.8	5.1
	Senegal	380	25	563	704	930	1 265	2.3	2.8	3.1
	Upper Volta	140	8	122	207	366	575	5.4	5.9	4.6
EASTERN AFRICA										
	Ethiopia	110	14	761	1 284	2 315	4 562	5.4	6.1	7.0
	Kenya	290	14	336	597	1 145	2 223	5.9	6.7	6.9
	Malawi	150	34	107	152	407	1 874	3.5	10.4	16.5
	Mozambique	140	9	136	242	468	901	5.9	6.8	6.8
	Sudan	330	25	572	1 212	2 571	5 305	7.8	7.8	7.5
	Tanzania	210[3]	12	285	485	920	2 131	5.5	6.6	8.8
	Uganda	250 (1976)	12	204	396	783	1 577	6.9	7.1	7.3
MIDDLE AFRICA										
	Angola	280	21	301	493	848	1 508	5.1	5.6	5.9
	Cameroon	420	35	400	675	1 185	2 450	5.4	5.8	7.5
	Zaire	210	40	2 493	3 602	6 556	11 049	3.7	6.2	5.4
	Zambia	460	38	428	742	1 290	2 235	5.7	5.7	5.6
	Zimbabwe	460	23	242	446	898	1 721	6.3	7.2	6.7
	South Africa	1 400	50	5 261	7 424	10 281	14 154	3.5	3.3	3.2
	Madagascar	230	18	338	569	977	1 718	5.3	5.6	5.8

[1] As far as data permits, the varied concepts of 'urban' population as nationally defined in each instance have been used. Growth rates are compounded annually
[2] Estimate   [3] Mainland Tanzania only

Sources: *World Bank Atlas 1979* (World Bank, Washington DC, 1979); 'Patterns of Urban and Rural Population Growth' (UN Population Division, draft manuscript, 1979)

related to its political difficulties over the last two decades. The Republic of South Africa is set apart from the rest of the continent by both its vigorous industrial sector and its repressive policy towards Africans. If industrialization has raised incomes, the lion's share has gone to the white minority, and severe restrictions on the urban residence of Africans have established a pattern of rather slow urban growth.

Urban growth is fed by two demographic processes: natural population growth and rural-urban migration. The population of Africa grows at about 2.6 per cent a year. If we assume that the natural growth of the urban population proceeds at a similar pace, then it appears that about half of urban growth is the result of rural-urban migration. Attention focuses on rural-urban migration because of the substantial contribution it makes to urban growth, because it may be presumed to respond more rapidly than fertility to policy initiatives, and because any changes in migration behaviour affect urban labour markets immediately, whereas a half-generation lies between modifications in fertility and their impact on the labour force.

The body of research on rural-urban migration in Africa is substantial, and the evidence overwhelming: the great majority of people move for economic reasons. When people are asked why they move, the better prospects in the urban economy usually stand out in their replies. Migration streams between regions can be shown to correspond to income differentials. Over time, as economic conditions at alternative destinations change, migration streams switch accordingly. And when a migration stream ceases, this can be traced to new opportunities in the rural area which previously sent migrants.

Short-term employment in urban areas, say a few months to two or three years, followed by a return to a rural home area was a common pattern in colonial days. It is tempting to speculate that such circular migration is the initial response of a 'traditional' society to new opportunities to earn wages and acquire manufactured goods, that is, to visualize 'tribesmen' making short forays into an alien environment. The facts indicate otherwise. Circular migration was a function of the recruitment of men at low wages. Where employees had access only to bachelor accommodation, both aspects, the cheap-labour policy and the limitation of recruitment to men, were brought into sharp relief. Most strikingly, in environments characterized by circular migration, major employers were able to establish a more stable labour force by providing remuneration sufficient to enable workers to bring wives and children. Thus the *Union Minière du Haut Katanga* changed its labour policy in the copper mines in what is now Shaba Province, Zaire, as early as 1927. A measure of compulsion was involved in that workers had to bring their wives, but the region soon boasted a stable labour force. By 1957 the average length of service of African employees in the Katanga mines was 11 years.

In parts of British colonial Africa circular migration was not just the outcome of policies adopted by employers; impermanent settlement of indigenous workers in urban areas was politically intended and policies were adopted to that purpose. In South Africa the gold mines are prohibited by law from providing family accommodation for more than 3 per cent of their African work force. Many men are recruited on short-term contracts not only in the mines but in various other sectors of the economy. The number of African migrants in the country has been estimated at about half of those in registered employment. Furthermore, over the last two decades, major efforts have been directed towards uprooting the many Africans who have long been settled in urban areas. Racial oppression has thus created a paradox: the most industrialized country on the continent, where a large proportion of the African population has worked in mines, factories and services for several generations, has the highest proportion of short-term recruits in its labour force.

In colonial days, the demand for labour frequently exceeded the supply, and various forms of forced labour were resorted to. Sometimes this was the only means of meeting labour requirements

in areas where the money economy had not yet made much of an impact and people did not aspire to the goods that money could buy. Generally, however, forced labour was the tool of a cheap-labour policy. Money was attractive enough, but the wages offered were too low and working conditions too harsh to draw sufficient numbers of workers.

With the approach of independence the labour market changed dramatically in many African countries. Employers who had complained about shortages of unskilled labour, about high labour turnover, and about widespread absenteeism, were now besieged by crowds of unemployed, and reported rates of labour turnover and levels of absenteeism lower than those in industrialized countries. Urban wage increases, intended to buy political support from crucial sectors of the labour force, had stimulated rural-urban migration well in excess of urban employment opportunities. Substantial urban

Prosperity and poverty are often sharply contrasted in African cities. Left: central Nairobi, Kenya. Below: a Nairobi shanty town

unemployment and under-employment raised the spectre of a threat to the established order and posed a question as to the economic implications of continued rapid urban growth, an issue to which we shall turn shortly. Also drastically affected were the considerations underlying individual, or more typically family, decisions on rural-urban migration.

The emergence of urban unemployment forced migrants into long-term migration. With the job search taking months, circular migration was no longer a viable proposition. The migrant had either to re-establish himself permanently in the rural economy or to commit himself to remain in town for an extended period. Many who stayed at their urban jobs continued to leave wives and children in their rural area of origin. Throughout much of Africa the subsistence and/or cash incomes to be gained from agriculture are substantial in comparison to very limited urban earning opportunities for women; their contribution to family income is significant in relation to the urban incomes of many men. For a wife to come to town means abandoning agricultural production without compensation, and facing severely limited earning opportunities in the new urban setting. The higher cost of urban living usually falls squarely on the husband's meagre wages. Family separation is therefore widespread not only among short-term but also among long-term migrants. Extended family support typically facilitates such simultaneous involvement in the urban and the rural economy.

Rural-urban migration has become long term, usually spanning a working life, but it is not permanent in the eyes of many urban dwellers. The majority are first-generation migrants and most of these maintain close ties with what they consider their rural 'home'. They visit and in turn are visited by their country cousins, they exchange gifts, and messages flow to and fro. This relationship is cemented by an emotional commitment to kin and to the community in which the migrant grew up; it is based on an economic imperative: the rural home community provides social security for the migrant. In the urban setting unemployment and under-employment are widespread, and unemployment compensation remains virtually unknown. Social security systems covering disablement and old age are still in their infancy. For the majority of urban dwellers, the only social security, meagre but reliable, is that found in the solidarity of the village. Links with people back home assure the migrant of a refuge in hard times; being recognized as 'our son abroad' translates in many parts of Africa into an effective claim to partake of the communally held land on return.

Continued substantial rural-urban migration, in the face of pervasive urban unemployment and under-employment, presents a paradox: why should men leave their farms to join the urban unemployed? Why do so many unemployed stay on in town instead of returning to rural areas where they have claims to land or opportunities for employment? The assumption is easily made that there is a rural-urban gap in communication, that those who set out on their journey to the city fail to appreciate how difficult it has become to secure employment there. Certainly, the city holds bitter disappointment for many, but by and large migrants are quite well informed, thanks largely to their connections with earlier migrants. Most migrants have a pretty accurate idea of what to expect – and their decision to migrate is rational in economic terms: they are participating in a lottery, trying their luck in the urban economy game. It is a lottery because so much of the hiring is haphazard. And it is a very serious gamble. Rural income is foregone, costs are incurred in migration, and severe hardships are experienced because of unemployment. But new migrants keep setting out for the African equivalent of the American frontier, new opportunities in the city.

Migrants have to survive until they find employment. The extent to which not only relatives but also friends provide assistance is impressive, but as time goes by an increasing proportion of migrants have to fend for themselves. If they have not been able to secure employment, they are forced to look for casual work, to accept employment well below the legal minimum wage, or to engage in petty self-employment. Job seekers who survive in these ways appear to be most prevalent among street vendors, porters and domestic servants. For obvious reasons, there is little information about those unemployed who get involved in illegal activities with their attendant risks.

Rural-urban migration is a rational response to the rural-urban gap in life chances. Such information as is available for income comparisons is less conclusive than is commonly assumed, but it is quite obvious that the more important urban centres in particular offer better opportunities for education and training. Furthermore, a whole range of amenities not available in rural areas is found in the towns, especially in the capital cities, and such amenities as public housing, piped water, electricity, and medical care are typically heavily subsidized. The rural-urban gap translates quite literally into a difference in life chances: infant and early child mortality is fairly generally recognized to be lower in towns than in rural areas, in spite of poor living conditions and a high incidence of tuberculosis.

The visitor to Africa who ventures beyond the tourist facilities soon becomes aware of severe urban poverty, but it takes a close look at rural reality to fully appreciate the extent to which the rural masses have been neglected. This neglect was tragically revealed when hundreds of thousands died during the Sahelian drought. If the drought appeared to be the immediate cause of their ordeal, the facts are that little had been done to protect them against such a not altogether unexpected eventuality, and that the calamity was compounded by the reluctance of political leaders, e.g., Haile Selassie in Ethiopia, to acknowledge the famine and to request international relief.

The political leverage of the rural masses is severely circum-

scribed. Elections that would allow them to give effective expression to their demands have become rare events. Rural rebellions usually cannot threaten the national centre of power and are contained by *ad hoc* concessions. So peasants, frustrated in their aspirations, take up the remaining option: they vote with their feet and move to the city.

This massive rural-urban migration imposes heavy economic costs on African nations. In nearly every country additional land could be brought under cultivation, and thus the emigration of able-bodied adults means a loss of potential output. The migrants come to cities that are unable to fully employ to productive ends the labour force already in place. Finally, these additions to the urban population require more resources for survival than their rural counterparts. The rural-urban gap in life chances continues to spawn substantial rural-urban migration that constitutes a major element in rapid urban growth that must be characterized, in the light of conditions outlined here, as *over-urbanization*.

Such a perspective throws doubt on the conventional assumption that urban growth is the necessary correlate of economic growth. Much of the wealth of Africa is produced in rural areas. These areas not only feed the urban population but also produce the coffee, cocoa, tea, cotton, groundnuts, palm-oil, rubber, tobacco, meat, and timber that earn precious foreign exchange. The products of the labour of peasants and plantation workers pay for investment and consumer goods that go largely to urban areas. Certainly, cities have grown around mining centres, industrial activity has contributed to urban growth, and labourers are needed to tranship goods, clerks to organize trade, and civil servants to run the public administration. It appears, however, that one reason that the more affluent countries of Africa are more urbanized than their poorer neighbours is to be found in their tendency to channel their greater resources disproportionately into the urban sector – thus attracting rural-urban migrants – not for productive purposes but to support an ever-expanding bureaucracy and showy public works.

J.G.

Ethnicity and communalism

The structural foundation for communalist politics in modern African states lies in the creation of these states by the European colonial powers at the end of the 19th century. The colonial boundaries established were not intended to correspond to any pre-existent African entities, and the colonies each characteristically included within their frontiers a rich diversity of already established, social, cultural and political solidarities. Some pre-colonial political systems such as Asante, Buganda and Morocco, had been relatively centralized and territorially unified; many other societies had been decentralized and virtually without political structure. The colonial state was to introduce something quite new to these entities by its insistence on its own novel and fixed territorial boundaries. The new colonial state included within its frontiers peoples speaking numerous different languages,* adhering to a wide range of religions with kaleidoscopic patterns of social loyalty. This internal variety is the background for the emergence of a sense of ethnicity and communalism in the modern African state.

Colonial rule established a new and relatively stable political structure within which different African societies competed with one another for the available economic goods and resources. In making available new resources colonial modernization also tended to exacerbate rather than calm feelings of communal competitiveness. The development of the cash economy (trade, commercial agriculture, light industry) created new economic opportunities and thus a situation in which some communities by skill or good fortune secured

new advantages. A tribe or an Islamic brotherhood which controlled land which was now to be commercially developed, for example, got ahead in economic terms, and thus took on a shared sense of communal superiority over its less fortunate or skilful neighbours. The growth of colonial towns, similarly, greatly benefited communities which had historically owned or controlled the land on which the new towns arose. The development of modern communications, the establishment of road and rail links between previously isolated communities, made it possible for people to compare their own situation with that of others of whose very existence they may previously have been unaware.

Two linked communalist political developments have thus been set in motion with the creation of the modern African state (whether colonial or post-colonial). First, it becomes possible for communities with a shared language, religion or regional origin to acquire a heightened sense of their own corporate existence. In the extreme cases, the dimensions of a shared language and culture are only grasped when the new communications facilities make it possible for

State meets community: President Léopold Senghor and leaders of the Mouride Muslim brotherhood at Touba, Senegal

previously isolated communities to see their situation as part of a whole. For example, the Igbo of eastern Nigeria traditionally lived in relatively isolated villages or groups of villages. Only with colonial rule did the full geographical extent of the Igbo cultural and linguistic area become apparent to individual Igbo. Second the new pride of one community tends to excite jealousies and hostilities among others. Competition in trade, or for the recognition of land rights, or for urban jobs, tends to exacerbate communalist hostilities.

The town is the focus of communalist politics, and in the towns it is the beneficiaries of a modern education who can provide a communal political leadership. Communal competition, especially for jobs in government service or in industry, is centred on the towns. Urban voluntary associations provide assistance on a communal basis, help in finding housing, and eventually, jobs for migrants to urban areas. Those who direct such associations are almost necessarily those with modern educational skills, at the least with basic literacy enabling them to write letters on behalf of illiterate members. When mass electoral politics is possible, the educated urban elite can provide a democratically elected communal leadership. In the terminal colonial period, or sometimes in the early years after independence, electoral competition served further to extend communal hostilities as the educated minorities appealed for support to the rural communal homelands – where many voters may not previously have seen themselves as engaged in political competition on a communal basis. The basic point here is to understand that modern African communalism is characteristically brought from the town to the countryside, is created by urban job competition, and is directed by those with the best modern education. In its modern form communalism is not a reversal of history, nor a re-creation of traditional loyalties (except in the rhetoric of urban communal politicians); it is something politically new – in its own way, almost as new to Africa as territorial nationalism.★

Communalist politics is, of course, at least potentially a threat to the unity of African states, and that potential threat is certainly used to justify the reluctance of today's state leaders to allow free electoral competition or unrestricted freedom of the press.★ A very wide range of political options is open to the states' political leaders, depending on a variety of local circumstances. The states of North Africa, whose citizenry share a religious identity in Islam,★ are relatively fortunate, although communal tensions persist on a regional basis, and are perhaps most acute (particularly in Algeria) between Berber and Arab linguistic communities. South of the Sahara communal situations are very widely varied. Although Islam in states of the Sahel zone commands the doctrinal allegiance of the great majority of citizens, Islam in Black Africa subdivides into numerous *sufi* brotherhoods – and brotherhood loyalties can be the basis of communal strife. The Arabic language is known only to a religiously-learned few in the Sahelian states (Mali, Niger, Senegal, etc.) and does not provide a bond of unity as in North Africa. South of the semi-desert Sahel, in states of the tropical forest, religious identities vary across a wide range. Christianity★ has made progress, especially in the towns of the West African coast, in East Africa (Uganda above all), in Zaire and southern Africa, but it competes not only often with Islam but with very numerous pre-existent 'traditional' religions.★ A religious element is indeed often present in Black Africa's communal politics, but the core social identity is less frequently religious than ethnic. The 'tribal' form of communalism, ethnicity based on shared language and culture, is prevalent in most Black African states. Ethnic identity commonly overlaps with loyalty to a geographical region (most troublesome when that region overlaps the boundaries of the modern state, but always potentially disruptive when numerous ethnic groups are contained within a single modern state boundary) and it very often overlaps with feelings of religious distinctiveness.

The mere existence of communal differences, such as are found in some form in all modern African states, does not, of course, in itself necessarily dictate a pattern of political competition between the communities which make up these states. But the differential effect of modernization, through the institutional mechanisms of the market economy and of the state itself, does provide ample opportunity for the spreading spirit of communalist competition. As some communities secure advantage in economic or political terms (because, for example, of the favourable natural resources of their area, or their location near efficient transport or the capital city) and with that material advantage a feeling of socially shared superiority, so also they tend to provoke resentment on the part of other communities which have fallen behind. Such communalist resentments are most keenly felt by peoples in close daily contact with one another, and in the place where such contact is concentrated – the towns.

All the leaders of modern Africa states are, of course, aware of the potential dangers to them which are in some measure inherent in communalist politics – at the worst, dangers of secession, irridentism or internal war. The reaction of modern African political regimes has been in the very broadest terms a common one: the concentration of political power around a single man. This concentration of power at the political centre does not in itself do away with the problem of communalism, particularly when the ruler is seen to exercise his power to the advantage of some communities at the expense of others. Most African rulers, however, have shown themselves to be conscious of a need, in the interests of their own political survival, to practise some form of 'ethnic arithmetic'. The ruler may surround himself with an inner core of political associates drawn from his own community, but he sees his interest in associating representatives of the state's other principal communities within his government. Where the ruler fails to provide adequate political representation for various communities within the state boundaries, then indeed he runs the danger of state disintegration. Biafra* remains the outstanding example of the perils along that path, but the Biafran disaster may have given warning to politicians across the entire African continent: a warning in the first place to communalist politicians of the political dangers in pushing their case to military extremes; a warning also to the established rulers of African states of the dangers of provoking too keen a sense of isolation and powerlessness in a particular community. African states it would seem now must learn to live with their poly-communal realities, and in the great majority of cases (although with enduring political tensions) that learning process is fully under way.   *D.C.O'B.*

Traditional medicine

Every African people has its own distinctive medical practices whose origins often lie in the distant past and which are closely related to its own particular culture. For many years these practices were regarded with suspicion by Europeans, who condemned them as 'primitive' or superstitious. To this day, however, the traditional healer provides the main means of combating disease for most ordinary people, who often see the hospital and modern doctor as somewhat alien and forbidding. Indeed, for many ailments traditional medicine may be regarded as satisfactory. Not for nothing was West Africa in the 19th century called 'the white man's grave'. Yet while Europeans, who usually spurned the local healers, died by the hundred, Africans were often able to find adequate relief by using indigenous remedies.

While brief generalizations can be misleading, it is possible to draw a broad distinction between two kinds of traditional theories of disease to be found in Africa. There are theories of natural causation and theories which suppose that a human or supernatural agency has inflicted the disease. Because the latter often has important social and religious consequences in local cultures, most literature dealing with traditional medicine concentrates upon these malevolent people and beings. But it would seem that many African peoples do regard illness in its everyday manifestations as having natural causes.

Among the Yoruba of Nigeria, for example, healers think that most illnesses are caused by the activities of worms (such as tapeworm) and germs or 'insects' in the body. The 'insects' are said to be 'so small that you cannot see them' and in fact they correspond closely to the concept of bacteria. For the Yoruba, germs and worms have an inherently beneficial role to play in the body. They digest the food, bring strength, fertility and so on. By eating too much of the wrong food, drinking to excess, working in the sun or otherwise mistreating his body, however, a person will encourage the germs and worms to become overactive and they will then cause an ailment.

It would seem that this germ and worm theory of disease is not peculiar to the Yoruba: there are indications that it exists elsewhere, for example among the Thonga of South Africa. However, little research has been done to investigate it and other similar theories.

From all over Africa, but especially in the forests of West Africa, there have been reports of elaborate and sophisticated knowledge of medicinal plants, which enable healers to construct medicines in the form of infusions, tinctures, powders, etc. Although specialists often have a very extensive knowledge – perhaps of thousands of plants – ordinary people may also be found to have a good working knowledge which allows them to cure simple ailments.

Among pastoral peoples, who have the opportunity to examine the carcases of animals, surgical techniques are sometimes highly developed. The Masai of East Africa and the Fulani of West Africa have a high reputation in this field. Often, where pastoral and

Mr Adebawo, a herbalist of Ibadan, Nigeria with some of his medicines

agricultural peoples meet, the pastoralists will provide surgical services – setting bones and extracting teeth – to the agriculturalists, who, in turn, provide pharmaceutical treatment for the herdsmen.

In nearly every part of Africa, though in varying degrees, illness is attributed to human or supernatural malice. Human beings who cause disease are usually called in the literature 'sorcerers' or 'witches'. There are communities where this distinction does not apply, but, broadly, a sorcerer is someone who uses medicine for evil purposes. The term sorcerer is used because, to foreigners, some African medicines appear 'magical' and require the use of incantations or rituals. A witch is someone who has inherited the power to harm people, though in general he will not use medicinal techniques, and can cause harm inadvertently, merely through thinking

Isoma, one of the rituals of the Ndembu people (Zambia) is performed to alleviate the ill-will of ancestors – manifested in female infertility – whose veneration had been neglected. In this part of the ritual cold water is poured over the couple being treated

malicious thoughts. Witches and sorcerers are not universally regarded as wholly evil. The possession of such powers is sometimes regarded as necessary for rulers who may use them for socially useful purposes.

Supernatural beings too, spirits, ancestors, gods, and the High God, may bring misfortunes or even death upon an individual, and an illness caused in this way may be regarded as a punishment for evil-doing. The ancestors are commonly regarded as the guardians of moral authority – for example among the Lugbara of East Africa or the Mende of Sierra Leone – and they will support social authority by bringing disease upon deviants. When a Mende has discovered that his ancestor has made him ill, his family will gather around the graveside of the ancestor, confess the fault and beg forgiveness so that the patient will recover. Often the fault may not be strictly moral, but rather a failure to perform the correct rites for a god or an ancestor. And there are occasional gods and spirits who are vindictive enough to bring illness without the victim having committed any but the most trivial misdemeanour.

Where it is felt that an illness is not entirely due to natural causes, it is common for divination procedures to be used to discover the source of the affliction. Sometimes it is necessary to know only in general terms that sorcery or witchcraft or the wrath of a god has caused the ailment, but sometimes the name of a human culprit may be revealed. In such cases there may be far-reaching social consequences, for the miscreant may be punished or be made to make amends. Occasionally, witch-finding becomes a major preoccupation and accusations of sorcery can become a central feature of social structure.

Traditional medicine is still of major significance in all parts of Africa, though it is assailed on all sides. It is still derided by some of those trained in Western techniques; and there are several Christian churches – the Aladura of West Africa, for example, – who condemn it for its pagan associations and urge a reliance on faith-healing. The proliferation of 'quack' doctors has tended also to cast doubt upon the majority who are seriously concerned for their patients' welfare. Nevertheless, without the traditional healers, modern medicine* would be overwhelmed by a deluge of patients, and there is reason to believe that the traditional techniques are often successful. *A.D.B.*

Modern medicine

Modern health services today exist in every African state, some of them reaching a high degree of sophistication, but for centuries the bulk of health care was provided by a variety of practitioners of traditional medicine,* who are still important, particularly in rural areas. After a period of being generally despised by the medical profession, there is now a movement to cooperate with, and to improve, the better elements of traditional practice; for example, improvement in technique for normal deliveries, supportive therapy in psychiatric disorders, and the isolation and testing of active ingredients in herbal preparations. In 1979 Dr T. A. Lambo, deputy director-general of the World Health Organization (WHO), a Nigerian psychiatrist who had earlier demonstrated the great value of involving the local community in rehabilitating and treating the mentally ill, announced that the *Instituto Italo-Africano* in Rome had been designated as the first WHO collaborating centre for traditional medicine.

By comparison with China and India, however, traditional medical care is less organized in Africa, and is often viewed with great suspicion by professionals. Most Africans still turn first to traditional healers, and only accept scientific care as a second line of defence. In some countries there is a clearly recognized line of demarcation as to which diseases are best treated by which system of care. How effective the involvement of healers in a modern health service will be remains uncertain.

Apart from traditional practitioners (who base their treatment solidly on the accumulated, generally approved experience of particular ethnic groups) and members of the modern medical profession, there are a number of 'illegal' practitioners who often portray themselves as a combination of 'witchdoctor', qualified physician and learned man familiar with all human experience, derived from traditional beliefs, Islam, Hinduism, Christianity, and even space-age technology. Though clearly responsible for the neglect of serious conditions and, indeed, often the death of their 'patients', legal action is seldom taken to stop them. Less eclectic in their claims are faith-healing groups, Christian* for the most part, which have rapidly increased in number since the end of colonial rule. These are similar to such groups anywhere in the world, but are more numerous in Africa where there is often little other provision for health care.

Medical missions

Often the first to bring modern medical services to Africa were medical missionaries. Until recently most regarded traditional healers as enemies although Dr David Livingstone, who travelled widely in Africa as a missionary and explorer from the 1840s until his death in 1871, was an exception, exchanging remedies and ideas with African healers as freely as with the Portuguese or Arabs whom he met. Livingstone left behind no medical institutions, but his work as a medical missionary inspired many who later founded dispensaries, clinics and simple hospitals all over Africa.

Other early pioneers of modern medical care included Anne Marie Javouhey, a nun of a closed order on the island of Gorée, off Dakar, Senegal, who left her convent to start nursing patients in their homes there and, in the 1820s, was called in to reform nursing practice in the hospitals in Freetown, Sierra Leone and Bathurst, The Gambia. European missionaries also founded multi-purpose institutions in various parts of Africa which combined colleges, schools, technical training, simple medical care and limited medical training. Among the most significant of these were the Lovedale Missionary Institution established by Dr James Stewart in Cape Province, South Africa in 1841; the Livingstonia Hospital founded by Dr Robert Laws on the shore of Lake Malawi in 1875; and the Hope Waddell Institute founded in 1895 in Calabar, Nigeria. Nigeria's first general hospital was founded in 1895 by Jean Coquard, a French priest unqualified in medicine. Virtually self-taught, he became a competent surgeon and worked in Abeokuta until his death in 1933. The most famous of such institutions was founded by Dr Albert Schweitzer in 1913 at Lambaréné in Gabon and was run by him until his death in 1965.

All over Africa simple medical help was given in response to great need at mission stations, and lay missionaries were often trained to provide this before they sailed from Europe. Thus even before fully trained personnel became available mission stations were the nucleus of primary health care. In the 1960s some 1800 mission hospitals were in operation in Africa – about half of the total hospitals. The emphasis in training was to provide staff for the hospital where the training was given, and then for outlying dispensaries. Initially training was at a simple auxiliary level, unrecognized by government; later many courses were approved for the training of fully qualified nurses and midwives, and were often grant-aided.

Medical students were always given their training by universities – at first outside Africa – or by governments, not by missions, but Makerere University Medical School, at Mulago, Kampala in Uganda is a direct descendant of the Mengo school for the training of medical assistants established during the First World War. Mengo hospital was founded by Dr Albert Cook of the Church Missionary Society as Uganda's first hospital in 1898. By the 1920s he and his wife had built 21 health centres in Buganda and staffed them with midwives they had trained. Many of these women were also employed by the government as nursing staff. The Christian Medical College at Kilimanjaro, Moshi in Tanzania, built in the 1970s, also assists in medical undergraduate training by association with the University of Dar es Salaam.

Most medical missionaries were, and remain, non-African, but a West African, Dr Adrien Atiman, worked with the White Fathers in Tanzania for 40 years, and other eminent men, such as the Nigerian Dr Akanu Ibiam, also chose missionary careers. Other Africans were given assistance by missions in gaining medical qualifications overseas: notable among these were the Sierra Leoneans James Africanus Horton* and William Broughton Davies, qualified in Britain in the 1850s, and the Liberian S. F. Magill, who graduated in the USA. The greatest educational contribution of missions was, however, in the provision of auxiliary and nurse-midwifery courses in which a very high standard was achieved in many parts of Africa.

Antenatal and child-care services were exceedingly poor in most of Africa until the 1950s. A great forward movement resulted from the organization of 'under-fives' clinics, and improved obstetrics services at that time, particularly in Nigeria, at Ilesha and Ibadan. The children's clinics provided immunization against smallpox, tetanus, whooping cough, tuberculosis and, later, measles and poliomyelitis, with simple curative care and screening for serious illnesses, and health education for parents–particularly regarding nutrition. Infant and child mortality rates fell dramatically where such clinics operated, and the concept spread rapidly across the continent, until there were many hundreds. Severe protein malnutrition–kwashiorkor–was first clinically described in Ghana, and in the 1960s nutrition rehabilitation centres were set up, where mothers were encouraged to teach other mothers how to improve diet and cooking practices with locally obtained supplements. Aid agencies began to favour the support of such centres and, even more, development schemes which brought together improvements in agriculture and health practice. Naturally, in periods of famine, war

A mobile clinic administering to Masai in East Africa

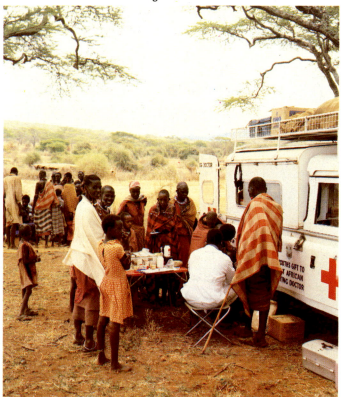

or natural disaster food supplies need to be brought in from outside Africa, but schemes such as Christian Rural Service in Rwanda and Uganda, or Faith and Farm in Nigeria taught self-reliance, and although small in scale had in them the seeds of future success.

Missions have also greatly contributed to the physical rehabilitation of the disabled, particularly those suffering from leprosy, polio and cerebral palsy, and the blind, deaf and dumb. Social rehabilitation is also organized by several missions, in the care of orphans, unmarried or deserted mothers, alcoholics and drug addicts, and those made destitute by unemployment, war or famine.

In a few countries during recent years mission or church hospitals have been absorbed into state health services. Most of Nigeria's 100 hospitals are now state district hospitals, but staffing, and the character of the institution is frequently continuous with the past. Cooperation between different missions and government has been much improved by the setting up of Christian associations, such as the Private Hospitals Association of Malawi and the Church Health Association of Ghana, with the encouragement of the Christian Medical Commission of the World Council of Churches, which has also endeavoured to redirect the energies of churches into primary health care.

Government health services

Almost all government services in Africa began as colonial medical services, primarily set up to treat, in early years, civil servants, troops, prisoners and the police, and–to a lesser extent–the indigenous populations of administrative towns, but gradually expanded to cover smaller towns and rural districts. The character of the service was moulded by the policies of the metropolitan country. British colonies centred their service upon the District Medical Officer (DMO), trained either at the London School of Hygiene and Tropical Medicine, or the Liverpool School of Tropical Medicine. The DMO was often given the overwhelming task of combining responsibility for the district with medical superintendence of the hospital, and found touring the dispensaries often burdensome. This burden was partly relieved when the British copied the French and Belgian mobile health team concept.

France trained naval and army doctors beyond the needs of the armed forces in order to be able to second them to serve in its tropical dependencies, and a great many of these remained after independence to serve national governments. Like the British doctors, they were also trained in tropical disease by military and university schools, and research centres such as the Pasteur Institute in Paris. There are now 11 Pasteur Institutes in Africa (though they have often been renamed)–in Algiers, Kumba, Brazzaville, Addis Ababa, Conakry, Abidjan, Casablanca, Tunis, Dakar and Antananarivo. The heart of French colonial health services was not a static hospital, but a mobile team dedicated to the control and eradication of a limited number of important diseases. The *Organisation pour la Collaboration et Coopération contre les Grandes Endemies* set up centres at Ouagadougou, Cotonou, Bamako and Dakar, and the *Office de la Recherche Scientifique et Technique Outre-Mer* in Paris gave rise to centres at Abidjan, Bouaké, Cotonou, Dakar, Kumba, Ndjamena, Brazzaville, Libreville, Niamey, Yaoundé and Antananarivo.

The Belgians in the Congo (now Zaire) specialized in a district laboratory service, as well as endemic disease control. The German approach was not dissimilar but it concentrated upon the health of plantation workers, and miners, and produced effective health legislation and better medical supervision for them. The Italians had over 1000 doctors in Ethiopia during their occupation between 1935 and 1941, but all left with the defeat of the regime. The Portuguese—in common with all colonial powers—did good work in the control of sleeping sickness, but little else of note.

Medical education

Apart from the medical schools of South Africa and Egypt, Britain and France did more in medical education than other colonial powers. Particularly famous are the medical schools at Dakar (Senegal), Makerere (Uganda), Khartoum (Sudan), Ibadan (Nigeria) and Accra (Ghana). Today there are 47 degree-awarding schools in Africa, although 14 countries have none, and most students in these lands do not find places elsewhere, either within or outside Africa. There is a considerable brain-drain of doctors, nurses, physiotherapists and others from those who have trained abroad, most being attracted to the USA or Europe. Only Mauritius and Madagascar are staffed entirely by indigenous doctors. In Benin, The Gambia, Mali, Nigeria, Senegal, Togo and Sierra Leone some 50–70 per cent are nationals, whereas only 10 per cent are in Botswana, the Central African Republic, Chad, Malawi and Zambia. Big cities—capitals in particular—are always best served, as the table shows. Thus the UN objective of 1 doctor to 10000 people is remote for most African countries, and much the same applies to suggested ratios for nurses (1:5000), midwives (1:1000), health inspectors (1:15000), and health auxiliaries.

INHABITANTS PER DOCTOR: SELECTED AFRICAN COUNTRIES, 1975

Country	Capital	Rest of country
Gabon	1000–2000	10–20 000
Zambia	1000–2000	10–20 000
Kenya	1000–2000	20–30 000
Uganda	1000	30–40 000
Sierra Leone	1000–2000	30–40 000
Guinea	5000–6000	90–100 000

Source: *WHO African Technical Papers* (9, 1975)

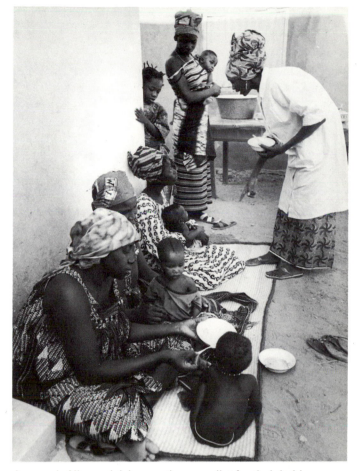

A nurse in Niger advising mothers on diet for their babies

Although schools for training medical auxiliaries have blossomed since about 1960, they are often still given little priority and poor facilities. The concept of 'barefoot' doctor or village health worker is still in the experimental stage, in no way comparable to developments in China. Tanzania has made the greatest effort here, but even there remote agricultural families, hunter-gatherers and nomadic herdsmen remain unreached, apart from occasional visits by a flying doctor service. Even urban populations may be ill-served. Unemployed poor living in gross overcrowding, unable to afford immunization or simple medical care, often also suffer from the effects of unbalanced diets and scarce, polluted water supplies.

Control of communicable diseases

By the 1950s mass WHO control schemes, using penicillin, had freed Africa from yaws, a painful disabling chronic infection. By 1978 smallpox was eradicated, persisting last in Ethiopia and Somalia. Cholera and tuberculosis, meningitis and typhoid are far from conquered, but six major diseases—malaria, schistosomiasis (bilharzia), leprosy, leishmaniasis, sleeping sickness (trypanosomiasis) and the filariases, including onchocerciasis (river blindness)—are now the target of a special programme of WHO.

Malaria has been eradicated from many countries both in the New and Old Worlds, but nowhere in Africa. Until primary health services are stronger, and problems of mosquito resistance to insecticides, and parasite resistance to antimalarials are overcome, there seems little hope of more than limited control until the perfection of vaccines now under development. Snails carrying the parasite that causes schistosomiasis have spread into every lake, river, stream and irrigation canal causing ill-health, especially in children, anaemia, and, in some countries, such as Egypt and Zambia, bladder cancer, yet control measures (consisting of the clearing of aquatic vegetation, the use of molluscicides, and the treatment of patients) are rarely seen and often ineffective. Each major river dammed, as at Kainji on the Niger, Akosombo on the Volta, Aswan and Owen Falls on the Nile, and Kariba on the Zambezi, leads to a further spread.

Of the 12–15 million people with leprosy worldwide, some 5 million live in Africa, and only a third of these are in reach of

Treatment of leprosy by sulphone injection in Cameroon

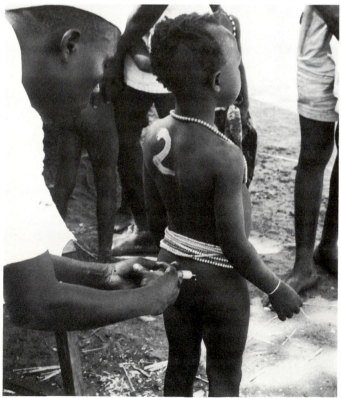

treatment. Dapsone, a cheap and effective drug made available in 1949, replaced the unsatisfactory chaulmoogra oil, and made outpatient treatment possible after—or even without—a brief spell in hospital. Leprosy settlements declined, and their hospitals are now needed only for the care of drug reactions and for neglected patients who need reconstructive surgery. Indeed these hospitals ought now to be wards in general hospitals but such are still few and far between. A trial of BCG vaccine in Teso, Uganda, gave encouraging results, unfortunately not confirmed by work in Papua and Burma. Newer drugs and their resistance problems are being studied and, using armadillos as host animals, production of a vaccine may be feasible in the 1990s. Centres for training in leprosy control and rehabilitation exist in Ethiopia, and are designed to help the whole continent.

Sleeping sickness, an immense scourge in history, has been much reduced by 60 years work, though recent resurgence in war-affected zones is causing concern. It is controlled by the elimination of breeding grounds for the tsetse fly, uprooting trees, destroying bush, and spraying insecticides on both riverine and savanna bush; and by the use of drugs, themselves somewhat toxic, to clear infection in people. There is some evidence now of spread from cattle to man, a new and frightening prospect. Research into the use of sterile male tsetse flies, released into the wild, and into the release of worms that parasitize tsetses has so far been disappointing, but WHO are concentrating on new drugs.

Onchocerciasis, or river blindness, caused by a worm spread by black flies which breed in rapidly flowing rivers, affects over 20 million people, and can lead to adult blindness rates of 20 per cent. It has led to the abandonment of many fertile valleys, and, together with malnutrition and sleeping sickness, has held up the development of poor savanna areas. The vectors have been destroyed on the Nile in Uganda, and in the rivers of Mt Kenya by adding DDT, but the endemic areas of West Africa stretch from the Gambia to Ethiopia. In the Volta River basin a 20 year programme using helicopters will, it is hoped, clear the disease from Benin, Chad, Ghana, Ivory Coast, Mali, Togo, Niger and Upper Volta. In general, blindness, caused by onchocerciasis, and by cataract, trachoma, measles, leprosy and smallpox, is a major problem in Africa about which far too little is being done.

Several university links within and outside Africa from many parts of the world, in diverse political situations, have greatly benefited research and training, and some of these have continued for 10–20 years. A good example is the cooperation of the Royal Dutch Tropical Institute of Amsterdam and the university and laboratories of Nairobi, and of Dar es Salaam. International agencies of many kinds have played and will play important roles in African medical care, disease control, and in emergency and long term relief in war, disaster and famine, but those schemes which encourage national self-reliance are the most important.   R.S.

Education

The 1970s clearly marked Africa's return to itself, to a search for an educational expression that reflects the unique nature of African cultures and responds to local needs for economic and social development. African states have begun intensifying their efforts to move away from the education systems that they inherited from the colonial era: to make the transition from elitist to mass education, to link school with production and community development, and to strengthen patriotic and cultural identity. These are the goals and although a start has been made on all these fronts, the road to realizing them is very long and difficult, for Africa as a whole remains the continent with the least 'formal', school-based education.

Enrolment

Universal enrolment at the primary level is a main objective of all African countries. Quantitative progress has been impressive, for example, a 24 per cent increase in enrolment ratios at the primary level between 1960 and 1975. The gains continue to be substantial as more and more countries launch universal primary education schemes. At the post-primary level the enrolment ratios showed an increase of 9 per cent in the period between 1960 and 1975. By 1980, however, growth rates at this level had begun to accelerate because of

the expansion of middle school education. Although few figures are available for pre-school education, mainly because it remains almost solely within the private sector, it too is on the rise, particularly in urban areas. By 1980 the relative number of pupils in formal vocational and technical schools had not risen much above the early 1970s figure of about 10 per cent of the total secondary population.

The greatest progress has been made in enrolments in higher education, with an annual average increase of 9.8 per cent between 1965 and 1974. Before 1950 there were only four higher education establishments in sub-Saharan Africa (excluding South Africa); by 1980 there were 63 universities. Another related sign of improvement has been the decrease in the proportion of African students studying outside the continent. Despite these relative advances, however, it can be seen from the graph below that the number of African students in higher education as a proportion of total population is still well below that of other regions.

Impressive as the overall growth figures are, they have not, except in the case of university enrolments, reached the 1980 target goals adopted in 1961 by the Addis Ababa Conference of African States on the Development of Education: that is, universal primary enrolment, and secondary education for 30 per cent of those completing primary education. A comparison of enrolment ratios reveals the great divergencies in access to education between African countries. Within countries as well there are considerable disparities in

HIGHER EDUCATION IN AFRICA COMPARED WITH OTHER AREAS, 1960–75

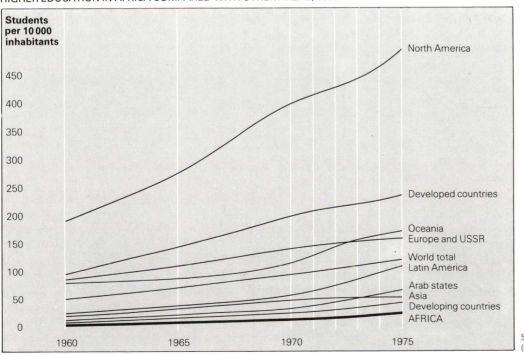

Source: *Statistical Yearbook 1976*
(UNESCO, Paris, 1977)

ENROLMENT RATIOS FOR PRIMARY, SECONDARY, AND HIGHER EDUCATION: SELECTED AFRICAN COUNTRIES, 1960 AND 1975

	Primary school enrolment percentage of age group[1]		Secondary school enrolment percentage of age group[1]		Higher education enrolment percentage of age group 20–24 years[1]	
	1960	1975	1960	1975	1960	1975
LOW INCOME COUNTRIES						
Benin	26	44	2	11	*	1
Central African Republic	32	79	1	8	*	<1
Chad	16	37	<1	2	*	<1
Ethiopia	5	23	1	6	<1	<1
Guinea	30	28	2	14	*	1
Kenya	47	109[2]	2	13	<1	1
Lesotho	83	102[2]	3	12	<1	1
Madagascar	52	80	4	11	*	1
Malawi	63	61	1	3	*	<1
Mali	7	22	2	3	*	1
Mozambique	48	52	2	6	*	<1
Niger	5	17	<1	2	*	<1
Rwanda	49	58	2	2	*	<1
Sierra Leone	23	35	3	11	<1	1
Somalia	9	58	1	4		1
Tanzania	24	57	2	3	*	<1
Uganda	49	53	3	6	<1	1
Upper Volta	8	14	1	2	*	<1
Zaire	60	90	3	11	<1	1
MIDDLE INCOME COUNTRIES						
Algeria	46	89	8	19	<1	3
Angola	21	79	2	11	<1	1
Cameroon	65	111[2]	2	12	*	1
Congo	78	153[2]	4	46	1	3
Egypt	66	72	16	40	5	13
Ghana	59	60	3	35	<1	1
Ivory Coast	46	86	2	17	<1	2
Liberia	31	62	2	16	<1	2
Mauritania	8	17		3	*	*
Morocco	47	61	5	16	1	3
Nigeria	36	49	3	10	<1	1
Senegal	27	53	3	11	1	2
Tunisia	66	95	12	20	1	4
Zambia	48	96	1	14	<1	1
Zimbabwe	98	99	6	9	<1	*
INDUSTRIALIZED COUNTRIES						
South Africa	89	107[2]	15	96	3	5

*Not available   < = less than
[1]Data reported for a number of countries are for years other than those specified
[2]In many African countries primary schools enrol pupils who are older than the usually defined age range of 6 to 11: hence figures larger than 100 per cent

Source: *World Development Report* 1978 (The World Bank, August 1978)

education opportunity, both in access and quality, between urban and rural children and between boys and girls. Female ratios, although improving, are still relatively low. There are also substantial ethnic and socio-economic variations in access to education. Finally, it must be pointed out that the population in the age group 5 to 14 is expanding rapidly and is expected almost to double between 1975 and 1985. With universal primary enrolment as an objective, this presents great difficulties as ever-increasing numbers of children enter the first year of school. It also means that primary education takes an increasingly high proportion of the education budget.

Costs

The amount of money that African governments spend on education, 20–30 per cent of national budgets, expresses their belief and hope that education can be translated into economic and social development. For the whole of Africa the average annual increase of public expenditure on education as a percentage of Gross National Product (GNP) was 12.7 per cent for the period 1965–74 (13.6 per cent for non-

Arab African states). The public expenditure per pupil increased in the same period from US$5 to US$15 (US$4 to US$12 in non-Arab African states). By comparison, the figures for the world as a whole in the same period were 11 per cent and US$41 to $98 respectively. Africa simply has less to spend on education than any other region.

The secondary and higher sectors in the 1960s absorbed an increasing share of the education budget as compared to the primary sector, reaching an average of 52 per cent in 1970. This proportion is expected to continue to increase, particularly in the wealthier countries as the distribution of the total school population between different levels continues to change in favour of secondary and higher education (projected figures for 1985 of 79 per cent primary, 18.2 per cent secondary and 2 per cent higher education). Regardless of the relative allocation of public expenditure on education it will continue to rise on all fronts. It now seems likely that educational expenditure in terms of GNP will rise beyond the level of 5.78 per cent envisaged by the Addis Ababa Conference.

One of the reasons why education costs are so high is that the system is inefficient; almost a quarter of the school population is made up of students who are repeating courses they have failed, and a

Pupils in a rural school in Kenya

PUBLIC EXPENDITURE ON EDUCATION AS A PERCENTAGE OF GROSS NATIONAL PRODUCT AND TOTAL PUBLIC EXPENDITURE: SELECTED AFRICAN COUNTRIES, 1965 AND 1975

	Education expenditure			
	as percentage of GNP[1]		as percentage of public expenditure	
Country	1965	1975	1965	1975
LOW INCOME COUNTRIES				
Benin	3.9	7.2	22.8	39.0
Burundi	2.0	2.4	20.0	22.0
Central African Republic	2.7	3.0	16.5	17.0
Chad	2.8	2.2	17.1	11.9
Ethiopia	1.2	2.5	4.5	15.6
Guinea	4.9	5.9	13.9	15.9
Kenya	4.6	5.9	18.3	20.5
Lesotho	3.8	4.4	13.6	13.4
Madagascar	*	4.0	27.0	17.8
Malawi	3.6	2.4	15.4	13.4
Mali	4.5	4.4	28.7	*
Mozambique	*	*	3.9	6.6
Niger	1.2	2.0	10.7	16.6
Rwanda	2.6	3.2	23.4	26.6
Sierra Leone	2.7	3.3	17.2	18.9
Somalia	1.4	2.7	6.5	9.2
Tanzania	3.3	3.8	23.7	15.0
Uganda	2.1	3.4	12.3	15.7
Upper Volta	2.1	2.9	17.0	16.1
Zaire	3.4	4.2	16.0	19.3
MIDDLE INCOME COUNTRIES				
Algeria	4.0	6.5	14.8	14.3
Angola	*	2.2	4.9	11.9
Cameroon	3.6	3.8	18.0	19.6
Congo	4.4	5.4	18.2	18.2
Egypt	4.8	5.4	12.9	18.4
Ghana	4.5	4.3	17.7	19.7
Ivory Coast	5.4	5.9	20.6	29.6
Liberia	*	1.9	8.7	11.4
Mauritania	1.9	4.1	14.1	19.5
Morocco	3.9	5.3	*	20.5
Nigeria	2.4	4.1	20.7	24.2
Senegal	3.1	2.5	*	20.5
Togo	2.0	5.3	14.4	15.0
Tunisia	4.0	6.1	23.6	20.6
Zambia	6.0	5.3	12.9	17.9
Zimbabwe	3.4	3.6	17.3	15.8

*Not available
[1]Data for a number of countries are for years other than those specified

Source: *Statistical Yearbook 1976* (UNESCO, Paris, 1977)

majority of primary pupils drop out before they acquire lasting literacy skills. Recently there has been an attempt to reduce the numbers of repeaters by automatic class promotion, but this still does not solve the wastage problem. Another related serious constraint is the lack of teachers. In order merely to maintain the 1972 pupil-teacher ratio of 40:1 the number of primary school teachers would have to grow by 88.9 per cent between 1972 and 1985. Not only are most classrooms severely overcrowded, many are manned by untrained, inexperienced teachers. For example in 1975, 40 per cent of primary school teachers in Kenya, and 33 per cent in Nigeria were completely untrained. Only 35 per cent and 1 per cent respectively had completed secondary school plus teacher training. The majority of primary school teachers in Africa who are trained at all enter training college after completing primary school, or only part of the secondary school course. The problems of quantity and quality in African education exist together. The basically political decision to democratize the education system has resulted in a lack of all resources necessary to operate efficiently schooling at all levels.

Educational reforms

In colonial days, and immediately after independence a person with even a primary school education was almost assured a white-collar job in an urban area. Now, employment opportunities of any kind are simply not keeping pace with the numbers of school leavers, with or without diplomas. The problem of unemployed youth is big and growing. A number of countries have responded to the immediate problem by introducing special programmes of national or community service and non-formal education schemes that allow continuance of educational opportunities.

But, more fundamentally, Africans are intensively involved in redefining ultimate goals and trying to tie educational objectives to them. This is not an easy task and contradictions are not uncommon. Nevertheless, it is from this process that the major reforms in African education up to 1980 have come. A key idea underlying reform movements is that the results of education should not be measured solely in terms of the growth in GNP, for the rise in GNP has not meant for the masses a comparable rise in their standard of living. Rather, education should be looked at as part of a coordinated effort to raise the masses out of ignorance, disease and poverty. To this end there has been a great proliferation of innovative attempts to link school education to production and community development. Small- and large-scale projects are under way where schools are growing crops and raising animals for market and to a lesser degree are manufacturing articles to sell. In extending services to communities, school children are, for example, digging latrines, planting trees, and teaching adults to read. An ever-increasing number of universities are attempting to reach the non-academic public through extramural activities, and by opening programmes to new categories of students.

They are being asked to direct their research efforts towards practical applications in response to local socio-economic development problems and towards enriching the life of the rural areas.

A closely related aspect of African reforms is that they are seeking to link school with the cultural roots and current life of the community. There is a growing interest in rediscovering and preserving traditional culture. Often this interest is approached critically. Some African educators, mindful of the dangers of being carried away by a nostalgia for the past, are searching their indigenous heritage – local history and folklore, traditional arts, crafts, professions and technologies, social customs and religious beliefs – for features which are relevant to the solution of current problems.

In the attempt to reach the two related goals of production and cultural identity, Africa today is a hive of innovative activity. National institutes of education, usually associated with universities, and curriculum units within ministries of education have sprung up for the purpose of curriculum research and development, producing learning aids and training education staff. New educational technologies related to the use of television★ and radio,★ the setting up of vernacular and rural presses and the expansion of correspondence learning systems are being devised. There are more professional teacher associations than ever before, and many of them are involved in curriculum work and the development of learning materials. There are attempts being made to modify the operation of teacher training institutions and to educate teachers for a new role that goes beyond classroom teaching to include community involvement and adult education, local curriculum development, and a reconsideration of the relationship between teacher and student.

Of crucial importance in relation to the strengthening of cultural identity and the integration of the individual into the community is the rise of linguistic institutes to promote the mother tongue or

Pupils in a northern Nigerian school being taught the Hausa language simultaneously in Roman and Arabic script

LANGUAGE OF PRIMARY INSTRUCTION: TEN AFRICAN COUNTRIES

Country	Medium of instruction Primary school class (1 2 3 4 5 6 7)	Medium used in subject texts (other than language subjects)
Lesotho		English used (apart from some Sesotho religious texts) but a commission has recommended the extension of the Sesotho medium
Swaziland		English used; some schools which follow the 'English through activity' scheme use English as a medium throughout
Botswana		English used, but a 1977 commission recommended that Setswana be used as the medium up to primary class 4
Zambia		English used, but official policy advocates the wider use of the indigenous languages
Tanzania		Swahili is the medium in all schools
Kenya		Texts in Swahili have been prepared for use up to primary class 4. All others are in English. Some schools are following the New Primary approach which uses English medium
Uganda		Maths and social studies texts in six local languages have been prepared for use up to primary class 3. Otherwise English is used
Nigeria		Texts for use up to primary class 3 have been produced in the three main local languages. All others are in English. States with multiple languages still use English medium
Ghana		English is used. The diagram is applicable to state-run schools. Many private primary schools use English throughout
Sierra Leone		English is used. Policy statements suggest a future switch to the use of indigenous languages in the lower classes

Note: African languages = dark grey. English = light grey
Source: H. Hawes, *Curriculum and Reality in African Primary Schools* (London, 1979)

tongues as the medium of instruction in schools. Many African educators, seeing school education given solely in a foreign language as a factor hindering children's educational progress and making for cultural alienation, are trying to work through the knotty problems of the language or languages to be used, costs of materials, staffing problems, absence of technical terms, and so on. The mother tongue question, particularly in multi-lingual African countries, remains a highly volatile curricular issue.

Educational change

Although these reform efforts indicate directions of change, they are relatively uncommon in the total African education context. For the most part what goes on in most schools at all levels in Africa today remains remote from the day-to-day experience and immediate environment of the students and teachers. On the whole, school is still an alien institution in many communities, more bookish, more academic and more biased towards a model urban environment than most African educational reformers would like. Not only is school, through its rigid selection process, regarded by children, teachers and parents as the main vehicle for escaping poverty, but the major behavioural role of education systems in Africa, as in many other parts of the world, is to select those who would most benefit their nation by further academic training. Towards this purpose African school systems tend to be highly centralized, deploying common syllabuses, examinations and certificates. The ultimate spoils of academic success are paid employment, prestige and privilege. Although, as noted earlier, there has been a dramatic move for the democratization of education which is allowing more and more children to attend school, the competitive struggle for further academic training still dictates what teachers and children do in schools and what parents expect them to do.

Agricultural and trade schools are wrapped up in this academic selection bias as well. Often they exist as parallel institutions offering practical courses and are frequently looked upon as second best by the students streamed into them who have failed to gain admission to the higher levels. The proliferation of private pre-schools in recent years, although oriented to some degree to the objectives of basic education, is viewed by most as the first, headstart step on the ladder to academic success. There is also a thriving business in private out-of-school preparation of students as external candidates for various certificates and diplomas.

It must be pointed out, however, that some African countries, notably Tanzania, are trying to devise new systems of assessment of student ability and performance whereby the level of participation in development and community advancement can be measured and rewarded. And there is growing evidence recently that parents are becoming more concerned about the results of the highly selective process and its consequences for those who are dropped at various stages along the way. They see their children drifting back to the village having been unable to find jobs in the urban areas and are beginning to ask why schools cannot provide locally applicable skills.

Basic, life-long education

Although it is clear that African governments are still committed to universal primary and secondary schooling, it is felt that the formal school system must be backed up by new types of out-of-school educational activities. Basic education for all for the purposes of development is the new and perhaps revolutionary idea coming out of Africa today. Its modern philosophical basis was outlined in *Education for Self-Reliance* a published statement made by Tanzania's President Julius Nyerere in 1967. Nyerere's theme was taken up by the UNESCO-sponsored International Commission on Education which elaborated it in a publication entitled *Learning to be*, and was also endorsed by the Conference of Ministers of Education of African Member States held in Lagos in February 1976.

Basic education, easier to define than to put into practice, is applied education, immediately relevant to 'minimum survival needs', as opposed to most school education, which teaches the concepts and learning skills of academic disciplines, all of which may eventually be useful, if modified by real life experience, sometime in the quite distant future. Thus, the emphasis is on health, improved production and self-employment skills, all grounded in the local physical and social environment. There has been a substantial increase in non-formal education programmes for out-of-school youth, from the brigades in Botswana to the *Comités Culturels et de Plein Air* in Mali. Also, it is being realized that the African adult population constitutes a potentially great 'teacher reserve'. The life skills of mothers and fathers must be upgraded, not only so that they can improve their immediate conditions but because they can only teach their children what they themselves know. In this regard there is renewed interest in indigenous non-formal apprenticeship systems where youth and artisans make their own arrangements for education and training by the communities' skilled craftsmen. The apprenticeship system is long-established in Africa, but could benefit from support provided by the 'formal' sector of education.

Although these ideas are particularly attractive to politicians, as they seem to offer direct ways out of the impasse of attempting to do more with less, in practical terms implementing basic education in Africa has inherent problems. There are dangers that in its various forms basic education may be looked upon as inferior education, as a way to keep people in the village and on the farm, and as an admission that African countries cannot in the near future reach the standards of the industrialized. Yet any realistic educator in Africa today, and there are very many, sees no other way to apply education in all its forms and at all levels in order to raise the living standards of the poor people and achieve an identity uniquely African. *G. W. K.*

Communications media

The press: past

The colonial press was the first to appear in Africa with the publication of the *Cape Town Gazette* in 1800, although Marc Aurel, a French printer, produced 30 issues of Bonaparte's military order *Courier de l'Egypt*, in Cairo on 15 August 1798 during the Napoleonic occupation of Egypt. These were essentially broadsheets, and were subsequently printed at irregular intervals.

The Royal Gazette and Sierra Leone Advertiser, first published in 1801, was the earliest newspaper to appear in West Africa and was followed by other publications representing the interests of the various colonial administrations, missionary societies, and settler communities throughout the continent over the next 150 years. This gave impetus to the growth of an African-produced press, particularly in those regions, as in parts of West and North Africa, where indigenous societies vigorously resisted the European attempts to impose their authority. The first paper of this kind was the *Liberia Herald* founded in 1826 by a freed black American slave, Charles L. Force. English-speaking liberated slaves from North America and the West Indies brought to this region, notably the Gold Coast, Liberia and Sierra Leone, technical knowledge, capital and, above all, a political awareness which readily found a vehicle in newspaper publication, of which notable examples were the *Gold Coast Times* (1879), the *Gold Coast Independent* (1895) and the *African Interpreter* (1867). Equally lively were the Egyptian nationalist newspapers of the late 19th century, especially *Al Ahram*, *Al Misr* and *Al Watan*, which were all influential in shaping political events.

Newspapers in various African vernaculars were first published by missionaries in West Africa, but later, under indigenous direction, played an important role in mobilizing anti-colonial movements. In Nairobi, for example, Bugandan exiles published several radical papers for circulation in Uganda, and the Kenya Central Association was, by 1925, producing a party newspaper edited by Johnstone Kamau (later known as Jomo Kenyatta*). During the 1950s and 1960s African political leaders such as Kwame Nkrumah,* Julius Nyerere,* Léopold Senghor* and Nnamdi Azikiwe* made devastating use of their own newspapers, either in the final stages of the independence struggle, or to mobilize post-independence parties.

The press: present

The nature of the press in contemporary Africa reflects both the legacy of colonial control over the flow of information and the diversity of political, social and cultural institutions. A commonly held belief that most African governments exercise a strict and repressive control over their newspapers fails to take into account the wider function of the press in the African context and the degree of 'freedom' which effectively exists.

While the dominant pattern is one of government ownership, the emphasis is more on how the national leaders perceive the role and function of the press, and whether this role can effectively be imposed on a particular press that has developed its own strong tradition. Nigeria and Kenya are two examples of countries where investigative journalism often criticizes government policy.

In most of Africa, however, the press is totally harnessed to government aspirations. National leaders have effectively adapted the press to function along the same lines as the former colonial government information services, and in many cases their daily newspapers are little more than ministry broadsheets.

A major characteristic of the press in Africa, is the paucity of national daily newspapers. By 1977 there were approximately 170 dailies serving 55 nations with a total population of just under 420 million. High costs of newsprint and printing machinery, distribution problems, illiteracy and a low population density ratio all militate against the expansion of newspaper publication in Africa.

NUMBER AND CIRCULATION OF NEWSPAPERS, 1976/77

Area	Number of daily newspapers	Circulation millions of copies	Circulation per 1000 inhabitants
World	7 900	408	130
AFRICA	170	6	12
Europe (excluding USSR)	1 660	115	243
Latin America	1 075	23	76

Sources: calculated from data in *The Middle East and North Africa 1978–79* (London, 1979); *Africa South of the Sahara 1978–79* (London, 1978); *Statistical Yearbook 1977* (UNESCO, Paris, 1978)

The adopted colonial practice of teaching through the medium of European languages in schools has reinforced the tradition of printing mainly in English and French and, as some would argue, has strengthened the press's role as a medium through which the ruling urban elites and intelligentsia voice their needs. The reality may be that printing daily newspapers in the vernacular would not be economical, considering the scale of polylingualism on the continent. Discounting the Arabic publications of North Africa, there are now less than 25 African-language dailies throughout Africa.

Radio: past

The earliest radio broadcasts were made from South Africa (1924), followed by a small service in Kenya (1927) and another in Salisbury (1932), all providing musical entertainment and relays from London for their European communities. Wired services (broadcasts sent to subscribers by land-line from a central receiver) were started in Sierra

Leone in 1934, the Gold Coast in 1935 and Nigeria in 1936.

During the war radio was developed as a vital means of communications especially in North and East Africa, and by 1945, the British Broadcasting Corporation was recommending that national networks in English-speaking Africa should be developed along lines similar to the Corporation's in the United Kingdom. This did in fact become the pattern: the French model, however, was quite different, reflecting the more direct and centralized policy of governing from Paris.

Broadcasting in the vernacular started during the war in the Gold Coast, Kenya and Northern Rhodesia, and British policy by the early 1950s was, for mainly political reasons, directed towards the development of African language services. A similar pattern did not appear in Francophone territories until the late 1950s and early 1960s.

The format for most of Africa was of colonial transmission networks sufficiently powerful for domestic purposes, but inadequate for external broadcasting. The two major exceptions were Cairo Radio and the South African Broadcasting Service. African political leaders had no access to radio – as they had to the press – until the Nasser* revolution in 1953, when Cairo Radio increased its broadcasting capacity to cover the continent. Initially it served to unite the Arabic-speaking peoples of North Africa in their struggles against colonialism, for example through the programmes beamed to Algeria during the late 1950s and early 1960s. Later, exiled political leaders from tropical Africa made use of the facilities, and were transmitting programmes in the vernacular to their people, much to the concern of the colonial authorities. In part to counteract this influence, the South African Broadcasting Service started an external African Service in 1958 and expanded its domestic African-language network 'Radio Bantu'.

Despite the pretensions to impartiality on the part of the numerous statutory broadcasting corporations in much of colonial Africa, the role of radio in the propaganda war was firmly entrenched by the decade of formal independence.

Radio: present

Radio is the most widespread and influential medium now used in Africa. There are more than three times as many transmitters as there are daily newspapers and for the rural masses radio is the main link with the rest of the country in which they live and the outside world. As the colonial authorities found, it is adaptable to polylingualism, and easily propagated. Consequently, it has become an instrument of information dissemination, entertainment and control and a vital means of governing in many African nations.

In over 90 per cent of African countries radio broadcasting comes under the direct control of the ministry of information or a similar government agency. This control may be justified economically and

politically. Independent commercial radio could not exist in most nations since advertising revenue potential is limited, and licence-fee collection would be impracticable. More important, however, governments feel that such a ubiquitous medium should be fully exploited to serve the needs of the nation, and not be given over to private interests. Many state-owned stations do, however, carry commercial advertising. Apart from ubiquitous music programmes, light entertainment generally ranks low in African radio, although indigenous history and culture, together with educational programmes are often presented in lively and imaginative ways. For example, government budget proposals on agriculture, or methods of family planning, might be simplified and conveyed by means of catchy songs and proverbs.

Although radio is ostensibly used to mobilize and integrate the nation, the prevailing patterns of government ownership and control make for highly centralized systems which reinforce the economic and socio-cultural gap between urban and rural communities. The latter are precluded from having effective input to the system and, consequently, radio may become little more than a public relations mouthpiece for political leaders and urban elites. A notable exception is the Nigerian federal system of broadcasting which provides for autonomous state-owned services representing the particular needs of the various regions. While the regional stations are free to choose their own content, they must transmit certain national programmes, such as major political statements and national news items. More than 30 languages are used for domestic broadcasting in Nigeria; a feat unsurpassed in Africa.

Technical problems still persist in many countries, particularly for transmission facilities in the medium waveband because of a limitation on frequency-spectrum space. Furthermore, vast distances coupled with low-powered transmitters result in uneven and poor quality coverage in many large countries. At the other extreme, some nations have developed powerful external services, often for specific reasons, such as Libya's 'Palestine Service' beamed to Israeli-occupied territories, and the South West African People's Organization's twice daily transmissions to Namibia from Lusaka and Dar es Salaam. However, while Egypt, Nigeria and South Africa have world-wide external services broadcasting in over 80 languages, the pattern for Africa as a whole remains one of interspersed networks of varying capacities, with very few interconnection facilities for international or domestic broadcasting.

Television

Discounting a brief appearance in Morocco in 1956, the earliest television broadcasting service in Africa was in western Nigeria (WNTV) in 1959, followed by Egypt in 1960. By 1963 national systems had been set up in Kenya, Nigeria, Rhodesia (now Zimbabwe) and Sudan. In 1977 34 nations had television, some little more than a single urban service; all government controlled and mostly installed by British and North American media interests. Extensive national networks exist where governments have utilized television for educational purposes. For example, the Ivory Coast's national education system was completely restructured to allow for audio-visual television teaching, and other states that have developed similar systems include Algeria, Egypt, Ghana and Zambia.

While most governments justify expenditure on television by extolling its educational value, many systems do not possess the transmission capacities for universal coverage, and often lack the resources for producing local programmes. Consequently, television has tended to become an urban-oriented service providing much imported Western entertainment for the wealthy. Furthermore most systems are dependent on foreign technical assistance and imported spare parts. An exception is the Egyptian television service, which not only makes its own productions and syndicates them to other Arabic-speaking North African countries, but manufactures television receiver sets and other components.

The controversy over television and its imported 'Western culture orientation' continues amongst African media spokesmen, although, paradoxically, those who have fully utilized its potential are the more radical socialist states. It may well be that the future of television broadcasting in Africa will depend on the function it is expected to fulfil by the national governments.

Africa and the international media

Most of what Africa hears or reads about itself emanates from the international mass media, which are fundamentally Western-oriented. In the world communications network Africa has very little control over the flow of information, both to and from the continent. Although a skeletal system of 14 satellite ground stations ties Africa into the world network *Intelsat*, high operating costs prohibit utilization for broadcasting and restrict usage to telephonic and telegraphic traffic.

International news agencies often form the major communications links between Africa and the rest of the world. The largest are *Agence France Presse* (AFP), Associated Press (AP), Reuters, *Tass*, and United Press International (UPI). In the colonial era AFP and Reuters dominated and it was not until the late 1960s that others seriously entered the continent. The two American agencies, AP and UPI, monopolize the photographic wire services and are steadily expanding their news-service 'clientele'. *Tass*, with over 20 offices, is, however, the second largest agency on the continent after AFP.

In the immediate post-colonial period AFP and Reuters helped a number of countries in setting up their own national agencies. These included Algeria, Congo, Ghana, Kenya and Senegal. By 1978 there were at least 37 national news agencies on the continent. These individual agencies, however, have neither the finances nor capacity

to enter the world market, but it is hoped that the future emergence of a pan-African news agency as envisaged by the Organization of African Unity* may be more effective in redressing the two-way flow of information. The recent improvements made by the International Telecommunication Union in the telecommunications infrastructure for Africa should encourage the creation of such an agency.

Publishers

Book publishers, unlike their newspaper counterparts, have grown considerably in number over the past 20 years. Outside of Egypt and South Africa, there were only a handful of African-based publishing houses by the 1950s. The most notable were Mbari Publications of Nigeria (publishers of the journal *Black Orpheus*, and the first house to publish Wole Soyinka's* *Three Plays*), East African Publishing House, and the African University Press in Lagos, the latter two started by the English publishing house, André Deutsch.

By 1976 there were over 340 houses, including international subsidiaries, institutional and state-owned publishers, and indigenous privately-owned enterprises. At least 25 per cent publish in the

BOOK PRODUCTION, 1960 AND 1976

Area	Titles produced 1960	Titles produced 1976	Titles per million inhabitants 1960	Titles per million inhabitants 1976	Percentage share of books produced 1960	Percentage share of books produced 1976
World	332 000	591 000	144	186	100	100
AFRICA	5 000	11 000	19	27	1.5	1.9
Europe	163 000	269 000	383	565	49.1	45.6
USA and Canada	18 000	91 000	91	382	5.4	15.4

Source: *Statistical Yearbook 1976* (UNESCO, Paris, 1977)

vernacular, and a further 25 per cent produce some material in an African language.

The greatest expansion has been in educational publications, and governments are the major customers throughout the continent, with the African subsidiaries of the large international houses, such as Longman, Macmillan and Oxford University Press, being the main suppliers in this field. Despite their increasing importance, especially in the promotion of African fiction, indigenous publishing houses have encountered numerous obstacles, such as poor financial backing, production problems, lack of marketing knowledge and overwhelming competition from the established international houses.

Consequently, in some countries the state has entered publishing in order to promote African interests, as in Algeria, Libya, Ghana and Zambia, although in most instances the international companies have continued to supply the greater proportion of material. *S.J.M.*

Traditional religions

In Africa today each society, or ethnic group, has its own system of religious belief and action, some 'traditional' or 'tribal', others Christian or Islamic. Sometimes some members of a particular society retain their traditional beliefs, while others are adherents of Christianity* or Islam,* a situation which may lead to conflict or competition.

African traditional religions predate the intrusive religions– Christianity and Islam. 'Traditional' here refers to the local religions that lack written sacred books and that have not achieved the generally accepted status of a 'world religion'. The old-fashioned term for traditional religions was 'animist', but is now considered misleading. Each traditional religion is a central element of a particular people's culture, together with its language, sense of history, and traditional political system. These religions are those of relatively small-scale societies and are crucial for each society's sense of identity.

Much has been written on the supposed unique qualities of African religions, but their thought and practice are essentially similar to those of all religions, although obviously there are also many distinct features, just as there are in the nature and form of African societies. Like all religions, those of Africa comprise both belief and rites. Beliefs include notions about various mystical and spiritual forces that are held to exercise power and influence over living people. They also include theories about the origins of these forces and the people upon whom they impinge. Rites are performed by living people in order to come into communication with these forces and thereby ensure 'proper' relationships both between themselves and those forces, and also between one another.

All African religions include a belief in a creator-deity, or High God, omnipotent, everlasting and possessed of many attributes, each of which is reflected in a particular name which arises on appropriate occasions. Deities are usually regarded as male, although some are thought of as female. Most are believed to dwell in the sky above and beyond the human world; many also have immanent or terrestrial aspects, which may be harmful in contrast to the generally benign nature of the deity in the sky. There are, typically, myths of the divine creation of the world, and of a later withdrawal away from the human world to become a remote and otoise deity, often regarded as beyond human contact or knowledge.

Contact with the High God is, in most African societies, with various spirits or refractions of it, which can take many forms and be given many roles and functions. These manifestations may be associated with diseases, epidemics and natural disasters, with events and powers external to a given society (such as the appearance of foreigners or events associated with them), or be free-ranging and

A shrine of the Asante people (Ghana) featuring a carved wooden stool, a symbol of authority in Asante society

thought to seize and possess individuals as the whim take them. In the older literature terms such as 'fetish' are often used to refer to these spirits. Spirits may be considered as representations of the many powers, external to ordinary human beings, that affect them during the course of their lives and that are regarded as in general beyond control and even understanding as to their motives. Since they are invisible, they may be physically represented by means of carved figures, masks, and the like; and because they are typically considered to range freely through space and, indeed, time, they may temporarily be localized by being given shrines where human beings can contact them. Spirits are usually morally neutral: they may bring both good and evil, according to their believed motives and caprices and to the moral behaviour of the living.

Apart from beliefs about spirits, there are, in many African religions, beliefs in the mystical powers of ancestral spirits, ghosts, or shades. Unlike spirits, these forces are in a sense human: their motives, at least, are the same as those of their living descendants, and in general belief they are extensions of the living, even though incorporeal and 'inhabiting' some space uninhabited by the living. Since in most African societies the dead are buried in graves, it is to be expected that most religions hold that the dead continue to exist in a land of the dead under the surface of the Earth; many religions hold that they live in the forest or the wilderness, areas distinct and separated from the everyday world of living communities. The dead are thought generally to watch over the stewardship that the living carry out in their names, and to send sickness as a sign of displeasure at offences that affect the wellbeing or continuity of the clan or lineage of which both dead and living are members.

As in all religions, it is accepted that the creator-deity, spirits, ancestors, and the living (and often the unborn) are all members of a single community. The living cannot fully conceptualize, comprehend, and thereby control and predict, the actions of the other forces. They may observe and experience the consequences of these actions and from them adduce the nature and motivations of these forces. And they may, it is thought, in perhaps all African religions, also come into direct or indirect contact with them, at specific times and in particular situations. By so doing they activate, or reactivate, the proper or ideal relations between these diverse members of a single moral order, relations which are usually dormant even though recognized to exist.

Means of communication include prayer, sacrifice, offerings and divination, on the part of the living; and the sending of sickness, possession, visions, dreams, and omens, on the part of spirits and ancestors. Which means are used depends on many factors: the particular forces believed to be involved; the particular situation of sickness or other circumstances; the status of the living person. Prayer is typically made to a deity considered to be omnipotent and remote from living men so that there can be no place set aside for close contact. Sacrifices are made to deities, spirits and ancestors, the offerings including domestic animals, non-animal objects, beer and other drinks, all substances that in one way or another symbolize the nature of the person for whom the sacrifice is made and the force to

Libation to the gods and the ancestors being poured by a priest of the Gã people in Jamestown, Accra, Ghana

which it is offered. The central act of sacrifice contains many meanings, any one of which may be uppermost in any particular society: to recognize the power of a deity, to express kinship with ancestors by sharing food with them, to remove sin by consecration of a sacrificial victim and thereby purify both the sinner and his community, to remove a dangerous spiritual force and to drive it back to its proper position outside the realm of the living.

The living members of a particular community typically contact the various spiritual forces through ritual specialists. These include functionaries such as rainmakers and priests of many kinds (who are especially important in centralized states where the royal and chiefly courts may include large numbers of ritual officials), who usually represent local communities on a ritual level; the elders of families and lineages, who may sacrifice to the dead on behalf of their living members; diviners, who can contact spiritual forces to discover the identity of those affecting the living by sickness or misfortune, using many methods of oracular consultation, possession, trance, and dreams; and prophets, who have appeared throughout African history, regarded as emissaries of deities and seeking to lead people to a new form of society in times of widespread troubles.

Beliefs in the activities of witches and sorcerers are traditionally widespread. They are believed to be living people with the power to harm those whom they dislike, typically because of envy or jealousy of others' success. Witches are thought to have an innate power to harm or even kill mystically, whereas sorcerers are said to use magical object and 'medicines' to achieve their ends. This distinction is a common one, but is not always found. Their activities are generally discovered by diviners and 'witchdoctors', who can also neutralize their powers. Witches and sorcerers may include both men and women, traders and other outsiders often being considered powerful practitioners.   *J. M.*

Christianity

Christianity was first established in Africa in the 1st century, when Christians dispersed from the Holy Land throughout the Mediterranean world, including Egypt and especially the city of Alexandria with its large Jewish and Greek-speaking population. The Coptic churches which were founded have remained in Egypt to this day. Christianity spread from Egypt along the North African coast as far as Mauritania during the first three centuries AD, and southwards into Nubia★ and the Sudan, where it flourished from the 6th until the 16th century, when the Nubian Christian kingdoms were finally defeated by Muslim Arabs. Coptic Christianity reached Ethiopia★ in the 4th century: the *Abuna*, or head of the Ethiopian Church, was, until 1959, under the authority of the Coptic Patriarch of Alexandria.

Outside North Africa and Ethiopia Christianity has spread throughout the continent as a consequence of mission evangelization. We may perceive four main phases of mission enterprise, although the divisions between them are of course not everywhere very precise.

The first phase of evangelization was associated mainly with the Portuguese,★ who wished to establish links with the supposed Christian Ethiopian king Prester John. During the 15th and 16th centuries the Portuguese established Christian churches in Elmina,★ Benin,★ Angola★ and Kongo,★ among other places. The king of Kongo was converted to the faith, setting up a Christian kingdom at San Salvador. In the same period the Portuguese established churches at Mombasa★ and elsewhere along the East African coast as well as in a few places in southern Africa. The weakening of Portuguese rule and Portuguese participation in the slave trade brought their Christian effort to a virtual halt by the end of the 16th century, leaving few traces behind it.

The second phase began in the 18th century, after a century or so of virtually no missionary activity from Europe. This phase was largely a Protestant one, marked by the founding of Protestant missions in Europe, followed by the setting up of missions mainly in western and southern Africa and the establishment of Freetown (Sierra Leone), Monrovia (Liberia) and other settlements of freed slaves. Besides evangelization there was some educational and medical activity. The missions were weak, however, and much of their work was concerned mainly with the small populations of the coastal trading towns who were already strongly influenced by Europeans.

The third phase began towards the end of the 19th century, and was associated with the formal advent of colonial government in almost all parts of Africa. Missions spread, often competing against each other, from the coastal areas throughout the hinterland. The late 19th and early 20th centuries were the times of high missionary enterprise, missions providing in many areas both evangelical, educational and health services and in some areas becoming virtual extensions of colonial governments, although usually retaining both a degree of independence of–and often opposition to–these governments and their policies.

The final phase, which in some parts (especially the West African coast) overlapped with the previous one, has been marked by the growth of independent African Churches, both in the sense of their becoming Churches as distinct from mission enterprises and also in that of being distinct movements often strongly opposed to European-controlled mission Churches.

The consequences of this period of often intense missionary activity have in general been twofold: the growth of indigenous Christian sects and Churches that are in various kinds of relationship to the traditional faiths; and various changes in the social and political aspects of African cultures, not all of them due only to Christian impact but all to varying degrees affected by it.

The process of Christian conversion has varied from one part of Africa to another over the past hundred years. In some areas, such as Buganda (Uganda), entire populations accepted the new faith quickly; in others, such as most of the traditionally pastoralist areas, there were only a handful of converts. In some areas, such as most of southern Africa, the chiefs were the first to be converted, in others, such as the Akan kingdoms of Ghana, they were the last; in some areas mainly women have become Christians, in others both sexes–the main factor here being probably the indigenous status of women, who, if lowly regarded, may accept a new faith largely in order to become independent of their men.

In almost all of Africa the missionaries came as part of the colonial experience, and despite their frequent attempts to mitigate its more severe effects (especially in southern and eastern Africa) they were on the whole regarded as being closely associated with colonial rule. In many areas missions were given responsibility for education* and health services.* This development often helped them to make converts, but they were regarded as participating in the new power of colonial governments, so that they were often in an anomalous position. On the one hand, people were wary of them; on the other, those Africans who wished to share in the new power, wealth and way of life associated with it not unnaturally tended to join the missions, particularly since to do so was often the only way to acquire a Western-type education. The mission phase was followed–or, more accurately, came in many areas to be associated with–the growth of new Christian movements.

There seem to be three main factors relevant to the development of these new Churches. The first has been the problem of accommodating Christian beliefs to the realities of African social and cultural life, especially in those cases where the missions have shown themselves intolerant and ignorant of traditional religious beliefs and social practices. Examples are the beliefs in the powers of the dead and witches, and the incidence of polygyny, which have usually been forbidden by missionaries. They have failed to understand that these beliefs may form an integral part of an internally consistent system of thought and enable people to make sense of their everyday experience; and the practice of polygyny has social and economic implications for the orderly maintenance of social norms, so that its prohibition may often profoundly affect everyday family and domestic life. Africans have, not unnaturally, often found it possible to accept many traditional beliefs and practices as being consistent with Christian life, and have established their own separate sects and Churches which they consider to be as sincerely Christian as the established missions. The second factor is closely related: this is the relationship of Christianity with notions of African identity and history. Africans do not wish to regard Christianity as an essentially European faith; they often point to Ethiopia as an example of Christianity that is fully African and long-established. Many separatist Churches have been known as 'Ethiopian' Churches, as a sign of the emphasis placed on their African identity and tradition as distinct from those of the European-controlled missions. The third main factor has been an organizational one, especially in those areas (e.g., much of southern Africa) where the missions have been seen as parts of white-controlled Churches which have exercised a colour bar, so that African members have been given a subordinate role in mission affairs. Seeing this as a negation of the Christian message, many African Christians have set up their own Churches, which they can control and in which they can acquire higher status than they could in the white-controlled Churches. This has been particularly evident in the case of Protestant missions, where the teaching that an individual may directly and personally contact God–who might tell him to set up a new Church–has sanctioned this very separatism.

Josiah Olunowo Oshitelu, founder and first primate of the Church of the Lord (Aladura), an independent African Church established in Nigeria (1930) and now widespread in West Africa

Another central aspect of the reaction against mission Churches is represented in the acceptance of forms of spirit possession and Pentecostalism. The belief in direct communication between God and the living is clearly relevant in wishes to ignore or to remove intermediaries in the form of clergy and the authority that they exercise over their congregations. There are also less overt reasons to do with the increased importance and autonomy of the individual in the modern (and often urban) world as against those of traditional groupings that are under the control of traditional holders of authority. In this context also changes in political and familial systems have been significant. Many of the new Churches developed political aspects in the anti-colonial movements associated with nationalist aspirations, and were led by Christian prophets whose messages were as much political as religious. Examples are many: in the growth of independent Churches in Kenya that became associated with the Mau Mau* movement; the independent Churches in South Africa; Alice Lenshina's Lumpa Church in

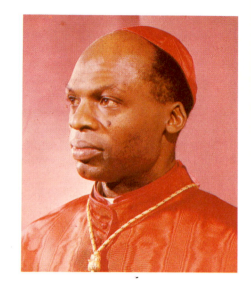

Right: Cardinal Laurian Rugambwa, Bishop of Bukoba, Tanzania, who was created Africa's first cardinal in 1960. Below: members of an indigenous Christian sect in Zimbabwe using the power of Christ to cast out devils

Zambia; the many Churches in the Congo region. Indeed, some of these movements developed into actual political parties.

Nevertheless, of the approximately 100 million people – about 25 per cent of the whole population of Africa – who would have claimed to be Christians in the late 1970s, perhaps 75 million belonged to the Roman Catholic Church. A further 15–20 million belonged to one or other of the world-wide Protestant denominations, while only 5–10 million belonged to indigenous African Churches. If reliable, these figures would seem to indicate that a major religious revolution has taken place in Africa during the past hundred years, and much of it since the end of the colonial period.   J.M.

Islam

Apart from Christianity* the other world religion that has entered Africa and has profoundly affected both traditional African religion and African societies is Islam. Like Christianity, Islam in Africa has at times been closely associated with forms of colonialism – although not directly with the European colonialism of the late 19th century which so encouraged the spread of Christianity. But culturally at least there have been marked differences between the two faiths in the history of their spread through Africa, especially in their geographical distribution and in the historical fact that Islam has frequently spread by direct force of the sword rather than by means of peaceful persuasion.

Islam entered North Africa* from Arabia in the 7th century and spread along the Mediterranean as far as Spain. It was essentially an urban religion in North Africa, with little impact among the Saharan peoples to the south. By the 11th century it had begun to move southwards, the Berbers having accepted the faith; and this movement was intensified with the southerly invasions of the Almoravids,* into the southern Saharan borderland. States there traded with the Muslim world of the Mediterranean and were also visited by North African traders, so that Islam has been known for a long period in the region but had not spread among the local populations, although the rulers of the states seem to have become Muslims themselves. Islam enabled trading partners to establish links over great distances, and the use of Arabic writing was also an important factor in trading enterprises, assisting in the rise of a class of educated clerks and officials who were important in the government of these West African states until the colonial period.

The medieval states of the Sahel region of West Africa, and their successors, were at the bounds of the Islamic world, but, largely because of their importance as suppliers of gold and slaves, an important part of it. This importance declined after the coming of the Portuguese* along the West African coast, and the states grew weaker and Islam stagnated in the region until the 19th century.

There had been great changes in Islam in North Africa, largely related to the appearance there of reformist Muslim *sufi* brotherhoods, and this spread to West Africa where local Muslims began to advocate a purification on Islam. The most important consequence was the series of jihads (holy wars) across the savanna zone from Senegal to the Sudan, culminating in the conquest of many non-Muslim states and the establishment of Muslim kingdoms such as the emirates of northern Nigeria and the Sudanese state of the Mahdi.* The pattern of rulers and aristocrats being Muslim – and so literate members of an international 'class' – and the mass of the population retaining all or much of their traditional faiths has been a widespread one in West Africa. Often, of course, Islam has spread throughout an entire population, usually with elements of the pre-Islamic religion also being kept, as is permissible in Islamic law.

In East Africa the impact of Islam was rather different. The routes for traders and others from Egypt southward up the Nile valley were for long blocked by the Christian kingdoms of the Upper Nile. Islam entered East Africa proper directly from Arabia to the Somali and Swahili coasts from the 9th century onwards, and the coast has remained Muslim until the present day. However, unlike the situation in West Africa, Islam has never spread inland to any extent except for small settlements of former slave traders in Tanzania and Zaire. In recent centuries there has been settlement of Muslims from the Indian sub-continent, essentially urban traders and dwellers. Central and southern Africa have never accepted Islam, except for a few small communities such as the 'Malays' among the Cape Coloured people.

Islam in Africa has always been associated with trade, and until recently with the trade in slaves to the Arab world. There has therefore often been a division in many areas where Arab slave trading was prominent between Muslims and non-Muslims, the latter associating the former with slavers. Elsewhere, such as in the coastal areas of West Africa, the slaves used by the local populations were acquired from Muslim traders from the hinterland, so that Islam was here associated with the slaves and so given low prestige, Muslims usually being made to occupy *zongo* (strangers' quarters) outside the walls of the towns and cities. Since the abolition of slavery this situation has changed, of course, but the association of Islam with trade (and especially long-distance trade) has persisted. It has often been useful, if not necessary, for would-be traders to accept Islam. Particular trade monopolies (for example, the trade in livestock) are often associated with Muslim groups, as with the Hausa in West Africa and the Somali in East Africa, who maintain their distinctiveness from non-traders in both economic and religious terms. Similarly in political terms, a convert to Islam has often been able to opt out of onerous traditional political and familial obligations by placing himself under Islamic law.

There are variations in the schools of Islamic law. In eastern Africa most Muslims accept the tenets of the Shafii school, whereas in western, northern and central Africa the majority accepts the teachings of the Maliki school. This school in particular allows the partial recognition of traditional customary law, which has led to a great deal of local adaptation to indigenous rules of inheritance and family law and traditional social customs to do with the position of women.

Like Christianity, Islam has probably seen its greatest expansion in the last hundred years, and particularly since European colonization. Many colonial administrations gave special assistance to Christian missions: while they often 'protected' predominantly Muslim areas, they did not actively encourage Islamic expansion. However, other

Festival celebrating the end of Ramadan in Cameroon

factors, notably peaceful conditions, improved communications, migration and urbanization have aided the acceleration of conversion to Islam. Estimates from the early years of political independence suggest that the Muslim population of Africa stood then at *c.*100 million. Half of these lived in the states of North Africa, where they were in an overwhelming majority. In sub-Saharan Africa perhaps half of the Muslim population (*c.*25 million) lived in West Africa – with more than 15 million in Nigeria alone. Outside West Africa Muslims were in a majority in the Sudan and Somalia. No later estimates exist but it is likely that the Muslim population of sub-Saharan Africa has increased disproportionately. Whereas adherence to Islam in North Africa is almost complete and therefore increases only as the population increases, in sub-Saharan Africa, Islam steadily continues to gain new adherents above and beyond the

natural increase of existing Muslim communities.

It is clear that one trend in the ever-changing religious situation in Africa is the fuller participation of Africans themselves in Christianity and Islam – this is more marked in the case of Christianity, Islam rarely making distinctions between peoples of different races and cultures. Another trend is the increasing degree of acceptance, adaptation and tolerance between the 'new' and the 'traditional' faiths; if the former are to become part of everyday social life they have to adjust to the qualities, needs and tensions of everyday life to which the 'traditional' faiths are so successfully adapted. As an example, beliefs in the powers of witches do not necessarily fade away in the new cities, but may continue to enable people to control something of the pressures and antagonisms to which they are subject in an urban scene. The former intolerance and ignorance of one faith by another continue to fade, a process which is part of the development and widening of scale of African societies.   *J. M.*

African pilgrims in Mecca during the 1978 hajj

Traditional arts and crafts

Our knowledge of the development of visual art in Africa is fragmentary in the extreme. It begins with the paintings and engravings on rock surfaces at numerous sites in North Africa and the Sahara. This rock art has been grouped into a sequence of periods on stylistic grounds, which presumably reflects the changing populations of the areas although there is little archaeological evidence to substantiate this classification, and the art appears to have developed through some 5000 years to the present century: some of the engravings executed in the Tibesti region, for example, depict aeroplanes and motor vehicles. Rock art is also found at sites in West and East Africa, and especially in southern Africa, where it is presumed to be Bushman★ work, although as in the Sahara there is little in the way of evidence either to support authorship or to indicate significance. Painting is not, of course, restricted to the surfaces of rocks: throughout the continent the walls of houses and shrines are painted; and body painting, as well as other kinds of adornment, is equally widespread, often indicating lineage, age-grade or cult affiliation or the temporary status of a person during a *rite de passage* such as initiation or marriage.

The earliest known sculptures are the pottery heads, figures and fragments of the Nok culture★ of the central area of Nigeria, dated to between 500 BC and AD 200. Other and later examples of pottery sculpture are found in the Segou region of Mali (possibly 16th century), at Ife in the Yoruba-speaking area of Nigeria (11th-15th centuries), in the Sao culture of northern Cameroon (10th–16th centuries), at Luzira in Uganda (as yet undated), and at Lydenburg in South Africa, where a number of heads, dated to *c*.AD 500 have been found. Pottery sculpture is still widespread, as, for example, among most of the peoples of southern Nigeria; and the unfired mud statuary of the Edo and Igbo peoples may be a related tradition.

The Nok culture also provides the earliest evidence of iron-working★ in sub-Saharan Africa, where iron follows directly upon stone without an intervening Bronze Age. Once they do appear, alloys of copper (more often than not some variety of leaded brass; though tin-bronzes do also occur) are found almost exclusively in a ceremonial context. The earliest evidence of this comes from the Igbo village of Igbo-Ukwu★ in Nigeria, where sites of 9th century date have revealed a quantity of cast bronze regalia, some associated with the burial of a king. These castings bear no relationship in style to the famous brasses of Ife (11th–15th centuries) or of Benin,★ Nigeria (15th–19th centuries). Benin is of particular interest, as it is possible to correlate stylistic developments in the art with oral traditions and the writings of European visitors over some 400 years, and to interpret art objects of, say, the 16th century in the light of present day ritual and political institutions.

Stone sculptures probably datable to no later than the 16th century have been discovered in Sierra Leone, and also among the Kongo★ of the area around the mouth of the Zaire River. Stone statuary also occurs at Ife, at the Yoruba village of Esie (where the figures depicted are regarded by the local people as the original inhabitants turned to stone), in the middle Cross River area of south-eastern Nigeria, in Ethiopia and at Great Zimbabwe.★

Ivory was already being carved with extraordinary skill in the 16th century at Benin and by the Sherbro of the coastal regions of Sierra Leone. The earliest surviving wood sculptures are probably the portrait figures of kings of the Kuba (Zaire), some of which, if those known today are indeed the originals, are thought to date from the 17th century. Other early wood sculptures include a Yoruba divination tray collected in the 17th century (and now at Ulm in Germany), the figures carved to commemorate deceased elders by the Ibibio-speaking Oron group near the mouth of the Cross River in south-eastern Nigeria, the oldest of which might be late 18th century, and some of the wooden figures of culture-heroes carved by the Chokwe of Angola, which are mid-19th century or earlier. Wood does not survive for any great length of time in Africa due to the ravages of insects, weather and fire. Nevertheless it is reasonable to assume that wood sculptures of the past 100 years or so represent developments of much older traditions. However, some of the finest works of art in wood known to us date only from the 1920s; for example, the sculptures of famous Yoruba masters such as Olowe of Ise (d.1939) and Areogun of Osi-Ilorin (*c*.1880–1954).

African sculpture is, of course, the work of individuals. Among some peoples woodcarving is essentially a self-taught spare-time activity at which anyone can try his hand, and it brings a man no special status in his community. Elsewhere, a woodcarver may have learned his art by apprenticeship to a master for some years. He will belong to a professional guild and he will be a more or less full-time specialist. In such circumstances a skilled carver is likely to be recognized as such in his community and his work known over a relatively wide area. Metal working is almost always a full-time profession. Sculptors using wood or metal are invariably male whereas mural painting and pottery,★ whether domestic ware or sculpture, are usually the work of women. There are exceptions; such as Hausa men potters in some areas of northern Nigeria and the brass casters of Benin, who also manufacture pottery sculpture.

The earliest textiles★ in sub-Saharan Africa are the bast fibre fragments excavated at Igbo-Ukwu (9th century AD) and the cotton and woollen cloths discovered in the Tellem caves of the Bandiagara escarpment of Mali, which were associated with archaeological remains dated to the 11th century and earlier. It is evident from the latter that a well-developed textile industry was already flourishing at that date in that area. West Africa has, without doubt, been one of the major world centres of cotton cultivation. Other fibres employed in weaving including wool, particularly in North Africa, silk, and raphia, which appears to have been woven throughout the sub-Saharan area, although for the recent past it is best known from Zaire. The Kuba, in particular, excel in the embellishment of raphia cloth with cut-pile embroidery. West Africa is also famous for its indigo-dyeing, and various methods of resisting the dye are employed to create pattern, especially in Senegal, Ivory Coast and by the Yoruba of Nigeria.

In addition to wood, metal, pottery and so forth, there are many less enduring forms created with beads, basketry, feathers, leaves, wax and so on, often *ad hoc* creations of an ephemeral nature. Even wood sculptures may be decorated and redecorated by their owners with seeds, beads, mirrors and paint, and the costumes accompanying masks may be renewed. An object can hardly be said to be finished when it leaves the sculptor, as it may subsequently pass through a variety of subtle changes (reflecting, perhaps, a greater concern with process rather than form in Africa).

Just as a work of art can only be fully understood in the light of the physical processes in which it is involved, so it also needs to be placed in the particular African intellectual context. A sculptured human figure may be intended as a portrait of a deceased chief or important ancestor, or it may in some sense represent a god or one of its devotees, or some essentially impersonal force manipulated to human advantage through curative rites; but it may equally well be an ornament for a rich man's house. Masks serve to disguise their wearers, perhaps while impersonating an ancestor or some other spirit, and yet within a masking society it is often the case that while certain masked figures have great ritual significance, others are simply entertainers. The symbolic loads carried by these objects will, inevitably, depend upon the context in which they are used; and the most that can be said in a general sense is that visual forms in whatever medium participate in some kind of conceptual system. For example, among the Lega of Zaire or the Asante of Ghana this participation is by means of the associations of particular objects with proverbs, whereas at Benin the content of art provides visual metaphors which can be said to define the qualities of kingship, and other key concepts, themes or preoccupations of that culture. It often happens, again as among the Lega, that the value and significance of particular forms, colours and shapes of human manufacture have their place within visual systems of communication that also include such things as bones, claws, and electric light bulbs: in such a case, of course, the term 'art' is perhaps better applied to the entire assemblage in virtue of the imaginative associations of its various component parts.   *J. P.*

The following illustrations of arts and crafts provide a few examples of the variety of styles, materials and techniques to be found in Africa

Pottery head from Luzira, Uganda

Pottery is almost universal throughout Africa. Vessels, lamps, drums, thatch fineals and animal or human figures are moulded by hand (without the use of a wheel) and fired in bonfires. This produces a biscuit-fired ware which, in spite of a greater fragility than, say, European ceramics does have certain practical advantages for domestic pottery. The Luzira head, one of numerous examples of pottery sculpture in Africa, was discovered near the northern shore of Lake Victoria. Nothing is known of its age, significance, or of the culture which produced it

Pottery head of the Nok culture, Nigeria (*right*)

The Nok culture flourished about 2000 years ago in the central area of Nigeria. It provides the earliest evidence of iron-working in sub-Saharan Africa and also of sculpture. This example was discovered during tin mining near Jemaa on the southern escarpment of the Jos plateau. Nok sculptures portray people and animals. Some of the heads are near life-size and clearly broken from substantial figures. The ability to fire large and complex pottery statuary successfully under primitive technological conditions indicates a high level of accomplishment, shared, indeed, in Africa, only with ancient Ife

Saharan rock painting from Tassili, Algeria (*below*)

Rock art in the Sahara can be divided into four main periods. In the earliest wild animals are depicted, perhaps indicating a hunting economy, while subsequent periods show cattle, as in this example, horses and camels respectively. Rock art found elsewhere, as for example in southern Africa (where it is probably Bushman work), exhibits other sequences of stylistic development. Nothing is certain of the significance of Saharan rock art. In southern Africa, however, the frequent appearance of the eland, a species important in Bushman cosmology rather than in hunting, suggests something of the ideological basis of these visual forms

Cast bronze altar stand from Igbo-Ukwu, Nigeria (*top*)

Although the dating of the sites excavated at the Igbo village of Igbo-Ukwu in eastern Nigeria has excited some controversy, the probability remains in favour of the 9th century AD, in which case Igbo-Ukwu provides the earliest evidence for the casting of copper and its alloys in sub-Saharan Africa. This altar stand (if that is what it is) comes from a hoard of ceremonial objects. Another site revealed the burial chamber of a king. The apparently sudden appearance of these objects in a developed style and of technical excellence, with no known antecedents – and the same is equally true of Nok – is but one of the mysteries of African art history

Cast brass figure from Ife, Nigeria (*centre*)

The origins of Ife sculpture are uncertain, for yet again there are no obvious immediate antecedents to suggest the development of its naturalistic style. The Nigerian kingdom of Benin, however, claims to derive its kingship as well as its brass casting from Ife, but the precise nature of this presumed relationship remains unclear. The figure shown here is thought to represent a king and was discovered, by accident, together with other brass and pottery sculptures at a site which has subsequently been dated by carbon 14 and by thermoluminescence to between the 12th and 15th centuries. In Yoruba mythology Ife is the place where the gods came down from the heavens to create the world, and the various Yoruba kingdoms trace their origins to it

Ivory mask from Benin, Nigeria (*bottom*)

This mask, carved in the early 16th century in the shape of a king's head, was worn by the king of Benin. It hung from his waist when he wore ceremonial dress. In Benin only the king was permitted to wear ivory, because it is white, a colour appropriate to Olokun, the King of the Water and – together with the leopard, though for very different reasons – a source of royal imagery. Around the top of the head are carved several Portuguese heads. The king's monopoly of trade with Europeans is perhaps symbolized by this feature

Brass plaque from Benin, Nigeria (*below*)

Rectangular brass plaques depicting court ceremonial, battles, etc., were cast, probably in the 16th and 17th centuries, and mounted on the pillars supporting the roof of the royal palace in Benin. Here, a king holds a pair of leopards, a reference perhaps to the leopard as 'King of the Bush' and a metaphor of royal power and authority. The killing of the animal by anyone except the king–who sacrificed a leopard annually to his own head–was forbidden. The significance of the mudfish in place of legs on the figure of the king is uncertain

Wrought iron staff from Benin, Nigeria

This is the staff of a diviner-healer. The chameleons and long-beaked bird represented on it belong to a class of species which represents the dissolution of the boundary between man and animal. Both doctors and their morally-inverted counterparts, the witches, transform themselves into such creatures (which are thus not *real* animals at all) in order to conduct their activities

Maravi elephant masquerader from Malawi (*below*)

Many African 'works of art' – like this assemblage of sticks, cloths and leaves – are purely ephemeral constructions put together as occasion demands, and therefore never reach the salerooms or museums of Europe or the USA. Many African masks are not sculpted wood, and even those which are will only ever be part of some larger assemblage. Masquerades frequently employ visual metaphors of power, and images of animals may be significant in this regard as representing powers otherwise beyond human control but which, nevertheless, can be brought under control in masquerade form

Igbo wood tableau from Nigeria (*left*)

This extravagant sculpture incorporates leopards, Europeans on horseback, mothers with children, rams, birds and snakes. Some of these figures are carved separately and nailed on. The purpose for which it was made is uncertain. Perhaps it was intended as an *ikenga*, the spirit of a man's right arm (i.e. of his personal abilities to achieve success), though the usual form of this Igbo artefact – a stool surmounted by a pair of horns – is absent. Alternatively it could be a 'trophy' carried by some age-grade or other association at public festivities as an advertisement of its qualities and achievements, as is suggested, indeed, by the various figures carved on it

Nuba body-painting from Sudan (*right*)

The visual enhancement of the human body by means of paint, hair-styling, scarification, clothing and jewellery may be carried out for reasons that are primarily aesthetic. Nevertheless such decoration is also likely to indicate something of the wearer's status. Among the south-eastern Nuba body decoration will indicate age-grade status, clan affiliation, ritual conditions, etc. Each clan section, for example, has its own characteristic colour. These are either red or yellow but as each clan section has its own source of ochre; there are slight differences of shade which are discernible by the Nuba themselves

Bambara altar from Mali (*right*)

This object in the shape of a quadruped is made of an indeterminate composition (said to include clay, beeswax and saliva) on a framework of sticks, and is caked in dried blood. The Bambara people have a sequence of male initiatory cults, each of which makes use of altars (or 'fetishes') such as this, though not always or necessarily in some recognizable shape. They are made up of materials of symbolic value in which the power of the cult is located and on which blood sacrifices are made to generate and direct that power

Konso grave figures from Ethiopia

Several peoples in North-East Africa, including the Konso of southern Ethiopia, set up sculptures over the graves of brave or otherwise outstanding deceased men. The figures serve to mark the grave but whether they also in any way 'represent' the deceased or his attributes is uncertain. Figure sculpture has no consistent significance throughout the continent and it is impossible to guess the context of any particular example. A wooden figure could represent a deceased elder (Oron-Ibibio, Nigeria); a culture hero (Chokwe, Angola; Kuba, Zaire); a spirit-spouse (Baule, Ivory Coast); a cult devotee (Yoruba, Nigeria); or it could act as the repository of magical power for the community (Kongo, Zaire)

Kuba wood figure from Zaire (*right*)

Since the reign of Shamba Bolongongo (whose image is illustrated here) in the mid-17th century, each Kuba king is supposed to have had his image carved in wood during his installation rites; the carving is believed to house his spirit double. These figures are regarded as portraits, although all the known figures of this type are clearly idealized (which does not, of course, rule out portraiture in some sense). The identity of the king is established by the emblem, in this case a *mancala* board, carved at the base of the sculpture

Chokwe wood figure from Angola (*far right*)

The sculpture of the Chokwe people of northern Angola can be divided into two distinct periods related to the two phases in its history over the last 200 years. Works of the first period, which include the figures of a chief playing the *mbira* (a musical instrument) illustrated here, were carved at a time when the Chokwe were ruled by the Lunda. After *c.*1860 the Chokwe rose up against the Lunda and, indeed, proceeded to dominate them; but the sculptures of this latter period are not regarded as so ambitious as works of the earlier period

Lega ivory and wood figures from Zaire

The Lega regard membership of their all-pervasive, though voluntary, *Bwami* association as the essence and ultimate goal of life. Bwami also represents the effective system of power and authority. There are several grades, and membership is open to both men and women under appropriate conditions. Each grade possesses a secret assemblage of significant objects, including sculptures as well as natural and other manufactured objects. Each of these possesses straightforwardly verbal and proverbial meanings; and in the course of initiation into the association objects and meanings are revealed to the entrant who thereby acquires knowledge and wisdom

Yoruba dyed textile from Nigeria (*right*)

Indigo-dyeing is almost as widespread in Africa as weaving. Patterns are made by tying or stitching the cloth or painting it with some starchy substance before immersing it in the dye. Later, when the stitching or starch is removed, a pattern will remain, whitish on an indigo ground. The Yoruba cloth shown here is called *Ibadandun* – 'Ibadan is a happy place' – so-named because the design, which was painted with starch, includes a representation of the pillars of Ibadan town hall. These cloths are made for use by women as wrap-around skirts

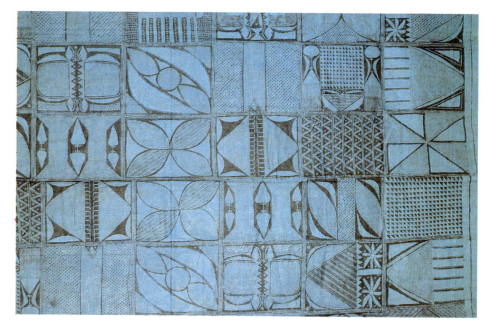

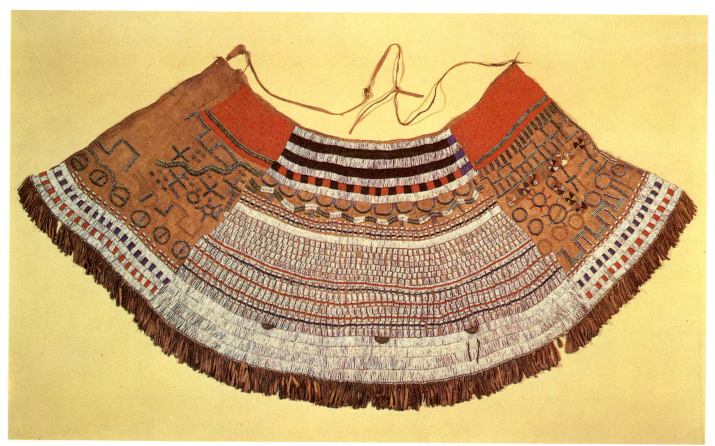

Asante silk textile from Ghana (*right*)

Weaving reaches its greatest technical complexity in Africa among the Asante and Ewe peoples of Ghana. Using two pairs of heddles a weaver can combine warp and weft striping and extra weft float patterns to create textiles such as this example, which the Asante call *adweneasa* ('my skill is exhausted'). These cloths are always woven, whether of cotton or silk, in 10cm-wide strips, which are then sewn together selvedge to selvedge. The silk cloths were first woven in the 17th century when Asante weavers first unravelled European silk cloths to weave the yarn into their own prestige fabrics

Iraqw hide skirt from Tanzania (*left*)

Two-dimensional African arts include painting, weaving and dyeing, and appliqué (in cloth, leather, etc.) and embroidery using cotton, or silk or, as in this example from the Iraqw people of Tanzania, glass beads. Glass bead embroidery is also found among the Yoruba of Nigeria, in the grasslands of Cameroon, among the Kuba of Zaire–where it is employed principally in regalia–and among nomadic or pastoral people such as the Fulani, the Masai and the Bushmen. Particular patterns can indicate the age and marital status of both men and women. The beads employed are mostly of European origin

Yoruba wood doors from Nigeria

These doors were carved c.1915 for the palace of the King of Ikere-Ekiti, one of the kingdoms of eastern Yorubaland, by a sculptor famous in that area, Olowe (d.1939) who came from the village of Ise. His personal style is distinctive and immediately recognizable in an area noted for fine sculptors. The figures on the doors, which are characteristically carved in unusually high relief, depict the king receiving his first British administrator: the hammock was the normal mode of travel for British officials in southern Nigeria before the development of motorable roads, and such travellers were accompanied by carriers with head-loads as depicted here

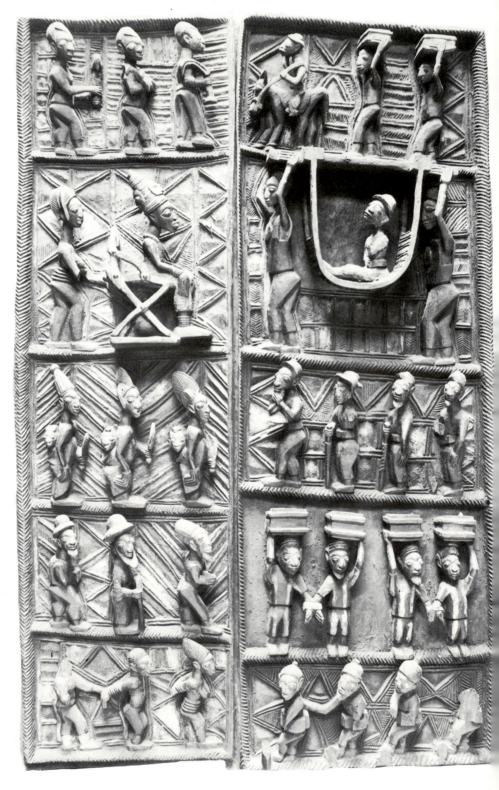

Traditional architecture

In most parts of Africa there was traditionally little physical distinction, except that of size, between the houses of the rich and those of the poor. The provision of housing was accorded a high priority in most societies, and building materials that were readily available locally–usually vegetable matter, mud, or stone–were shared in such a way that every family possessed a house appropriate to its needs. Specialist, full-time builders hardly existed, except in some urban areas, and in a few hierarchical societies where specialists were employed full-time in the building or repair of palaces. More usually, and to this day in many rural areas, every man put up and periodically renovated his own house (although sometimes, as in some Masai villages in East Africa, building was purely woman's work), often with the help of his family or neighbours. How long this took varied from society to society. Sometimes a house would be put up in a day after perhaps weeks of preparatory work, as among the Kikuyu of Kenya, where custom was emphatic that the house must be finished in a day, for leaving work unfinished overnight was thought to be an invitation to evil spirits. In other societies a complete homestead took several years, or seasons to complete, for building was often dry weather work.

The houses that were built were personal adaptations of a community solution. Each new house reflected society's pattern, but was adapted to satisfy the particular needs of the individual family and builders. The styles had been worked out communally over several generations and so were closely tailored to the needs of the people who lived in them. It can almost be said that in many societies the driving force was conformity rather than innovation. What was

valued was the idea of perpetuating a life-style through the generations, and social sanctions were used to enforce this ideal. So in many societies everyone aspired to live in a similar house; aspirations to wealth in the form of cattle or crops, which, if achieved, might manifest themselves in larger or grander houses, were discouraged.

Houses rarely outlived a single generation; in most societies every family experienced house building or fundamental repair one or more times during a lifetime. This was one of the factors binding a community together through involving every member in the need to provide shelter. Moreover, houses that needed constant renewal and rebuilding enabled families not only to participate in the process of creating the physical environment but also to have accommodation exactly tailored to their needs. There could always be a quick response to changed family circumstances. As buildings could be put up exactly where they were needed, there was no question of people adapting themselves to buildings that may have been unsuitable or inadequate. Consequently, in many societies buildings were almost physical manifestations of kinship and marriage arrangements. For example, in societies where married sons continued to live in the family house, houses might be extended to provide semi-autonomous facilities for the sons' wives and children; similarly, in a polygynous society, a man's marriage to a new wife or wives might entail the construction not only of new rooms, but also of new, separate cooking areas.

The technology used in building was limited less by the total level of skills available within a particular society than by the skills that were widely available. Houses had to be erected quickly and a large number of people, all of whom had to master the necessary skills, were involved in construction. The need for readily accessible raw materials was also a constraint on the use that might be made of

The casbah at Ait Benhaddan, Morocco

Nupe house, Nigeria

A village of the sedentary Danakil (Afar) people on a salt caravan route in Ethiopia

Top: a Tambernu house in the Republic of Benin. Bottom: the mosque at Larabanga, northern Ghana

available technology. Transport was generally difficult–pack-animals were often not available because of disease, rivers were often unsuitable for navigation–and therefore costly, and so little or no trade in building materials took place. Materials were usually obtained locally, within portering distance of the building site. Each society, then, had to regulate the exploitation of its local building materials to ensure that the community's building enterprises were in harmony with supply.

Houses were not only one of the links between people and their immediate environment; they were also one of the means through which community identity was expressed. There are more than 1500 different peoples living in Africa and, in general, each can be said to have a unique material culture, not in every detail but certainly in aggregate. Although certain styles of building can be recognized over large areas, all the different peoples within a particular area build

houses that differ only in detail. House styles can, then, almost be thought of as the badge of the particular peoples who build them, asserting differences between them and their neighbours.

The space between individual buildings in African villages is almost as important as the buildings themselves. As the weather is warm and dry for most of the year, craftwork, cooking and eating can be performed outside, and a demarcated space is sufficient for many activities. A low shelter from the wind is all that is needed for a dry season kitchen, or a shady tree for a meeting place. Most African houses that are still built in the traditional style are not collections of rooms within a single building, as is the case in many parts of Europe and North America, but a collection of similar one-roomed buildings united by the space between them and perhaps surrounded by a fence or wall, which in some cases also links the 'rooms' and demarcates them into functional areas. What distinguishes one house from

Mousgoum house, Cameroon, showing the characteristic dome-shaped construction and raised decoration

Top: courtyard of a house at Oulata, Mauritania. Bottom: communal fortified storehouses at Kabao, Libya

another is the number and arrangement of the buildings, which depend on who is living in the house, and the relationship of individuals with each other.

Perhaps the most visually unusual examples of African houses are built by the Mousgoum people, who live on the flood-plain between the Logone and Chari rivers just south of Lake Chad. In the dry season the area is virtually a desert, but it becomes swampy in the very short wet season. Out of this flat plain Mousgoum villages appear like huge clusters of upturned pots. Each house contains between 4 and 20 pointed clay domes decorated all over with a striking relief pattern of raised lozenges. The buildings are arranged in circles with the doors opening onto a central yard. There is a sleeping room for each wife (which sometimes also includes a pen for sheep or goats), a kitchen and a granary, a room for the head of the household and a room shared by the unmarried boys. The homestead is completed by a stable, and

perhaps a store and an entrance room. Most of the doorways are framed inside by remarkable cusped shelves supported on mud pillars and flanked by incised patterns on the walls. These exquisite examples of geometrical perfection, achieved by eye alone, are found only among the Mousgoum people.

By contrast the Chagga of northern Tanzania live in dispersed settlements on the lush fertile slopes of Mt Kilimanjaro, and they build their houses in a style that is to be found with variations all over East Africa from Ethiopia to Tanzania; round thatch buildings with the thatch extending to the ground, all roof and no walls. Again, as in Mousgoum houses, each wife in a polygynous household has a building of her own. Inside, it is divided into bays by a central passageway, on one side of which there is sleeping accommodation, and on the other a stall for animals. Above the bays a platform spans the building. It is reached by a notched ladder and is used for storing fodder and as a place for children to sleep. Each family homestead is surrounded by its own banana grove and a dry stonewall or a small hedge of *masala*, the Chagga plant of peace and pardon. Each clan area, which consists of many dispersed settlements linked by paths, is demarcated by a larger hedge or earth bank. One fascinating feature of Chagga settlement is the large network of passageways and caverns whose entrances are usually hidden. In the recent past they seem to have been used as bolt-holes or places to hide from attackers, but whether this was their original function is unclear. Today it is very difficult to find examples of traditional Chagga houses: cement blocks and corrugated metal roofs are much preferred.

Before the Second World War many clusters of thatched houses were spread across the western grassland of Cameroon. Today it is difficult to find good examples of these mushroom-shaped palm and bamboo buildings. Instead bricks and corrugated sheeting have become the norm, and we can only appreciate the wealth and beauty of the architecture of the Bamileke and Bamoun people from old photographs. Once the lush grassland vegetation of the valleys supported small kingdoms with dozens of densely populated villages–clusters of extravagantly tall structures with high conical roofs covered with thick grass thatch. Each house consisted of four to eight square-plan buildings. The walls were made of two or three layers of tightly-laced palms (one layer laid vertically, one horizontally, one diagonally), sometimes mud-plastered, and surmounted by a steep conical thatched roof supported on a circular platform on top of the walls. The room for the head of the household was distinguished by a circle of pillars forming a kind of verandah. The whole homestead and the surrounding fields were enclosed by neat

Below: Chagga houses (in what is now Tanzania) *c*. 1900. Top right: traditional Zulu houses (South Africa), and, in the foreground, an example of the style that has largely replaced them. Bottom right: Mangbetu houses (in what is now Zaire) *c*. 1950

fences. The Bamileke also built elaborate chiefs' houses and shrines, similar in construction to ordinary houses but having a wealth of carving on the verandah posts and on the heavy wooden door-frames.

Buildings of palm and bamboo, rectangular or square in plan, are found all over Central Africa from Cameroon to western Tanzania. Most are not as tall as the Bamoun and Bamileke houses. Along the lower reaches of the River Zaire, very long buildings joined together end to end to form 'streets' are found, while in Tanzania Nyakyusa houses have the ridge-pole raised at each end to give a scooped profile to the roof. Mud is hardly used in this area, while in West Africa it is the most common building material. There it is used as puddled-mud and erected in courses or layers, as a plaster over a lattice framework, as mud bricks laid in mud mortar, or as a mortar and plaster for small stones. The houses of the Dogon people of Mali are a good example of this last method of construction.

The Dogon live on the 300m high Bandiagara escarpment in Mali, and have attracted much attention from anthropologists. Perched precariously on the slopes of the barren escarpment, their villages of densely clustered houses have largely remained untouched by the Muslim horsemen of the plains. At first glance Dogon villages appear to be disorganized, but in fact both houses and settlements as a whole are laid out according to a precise symbolism. Each village is said to represent the world egg out of which all life vibrates. It also represents a person lying in a north-south direction with the village smithy placed at the head, various shrines at the feet, and the family homesteads at the chest. Similarly, the buildings within a house represent parts of a prone body: the kitchen represents the head, various shrines the feet and so on. Because of the terrain the precise layout – in terms of dimensions – varies, but the essential spatial relationship between buildings remains the same in all houses. The houses are tiny mud and stone buildings with low flat roofs, while the granaries are taller, square or round-plan buildings with conical thatched roofs.

The Hausa live in densely populated villages and towns in northern Nigeria. In the towns their houses are built of pear-shaped mud bricks laid in rows with points uppermost, embedded in mortar and plastered on both sides. The houses are encircled by tall mud walls, which ensure privacy for the women inside, essential in this mainly Muslim society. The houses usually contain between five and ten rectangular or round-plan buildings, sometimes built into the surrounding wall. A distinctive feature of Hausa architecture is the mud vault used to roof some of the buildings. Vaults are constructed of mud arches reinforced with palm fronds and spanned by split palms arranged in a herringbone fashion and plastered over with more mud, which is decorated with paint or incised designs.

Top: Pastoral Fulani houses, Niger. Centre: Nuba house, Sudan. Bottom: Dinka houses, Sudan

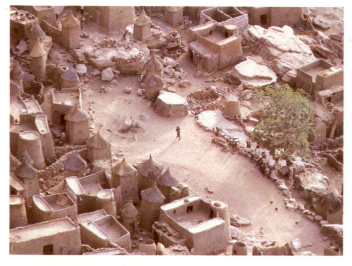

Left: villages of the Dogon people (Mali) which are located on the lower slopes of the Bandiagara escarpment. Above: a decorated mud-walled house in Zaria, Nigeria

Plastered mud walls are particularly receptive to mural painting, and incised and sculpted decoration. Almost all the mud buildings of West Africa are decorated in some way, usually at points of structural or social significance–doorways, thresholds, finials and so on. In Hausaland sculpted mud decoration in spirals, loops and interlaced patterns is found around the main entrance doorways of houses, and in the 1960s builders began decorating the whole of the facade of some houses.

Such changes in decorative fashion are superficial when set against the stylistic continuities of Hausa architecture, and such continuities may well stretch back for centuries in many parts of Africa. In Ethiopia a pottery model of a house has been excavated which bears a remarkable similarity to houses still built today by Tigre farmers, and it is probably not just an isolated example. It is conceivable that some present day African villages are continuations of early Iron Age villages. Although African houses are often rebuilt at least once every generation, they are usually modelled on a 'standard' pattern, and this continual renewal seems to ensure the survival of house types in much the same way as oral tradition preserves histories.   *S.D.*

Contemporary painting and sculpture

Africa's artistic heritage is usually thought of in terms of sculptures created in pre-colonial times, of which the magnificent Benin★ ivory pectoral mask chosen as the symbol of the Second All Black and African Festival of the Arts, held in Lagos in 1977, is a supreme example. For insomuch as African art has gained world attention it is because of the influence of traditional masks on such European artists as Pablo Picasso and Constantin Brancusi or the high prices fetched nowadays by Benin bronzes and Senufo, Yoruba and Fang wood-sculptures in the salerooms of Europe and America.

The contemporary art of Black Africa, created during and since the colonial period, has received fairly scant attention outside the continent. Certainly few modern African artists have gained international reputations such as those enjoyed by writers like Léopold Senghor,★ Wole Soyinka,★ Mongo Beti,★ Chinua Achebe★ or Ngugi wa Thiong'o.★ And yet, as the exhibition of modern art at the first Festival of Negro Arts held in Dakar in 1966 showed a largely unsuspecting international audience, there are a number of African visual artists with similar potential.

Makonde wood sculpture by Rashid Rukombe (Tanzania)

Untitled beadwork picture by Jimoh Buraimoh (Nigeria)

Right: *Crane and fish* by E.S. Tingatinga (Tanzania). Below: *Folly*, oil-painting by Demas Nwoko (Nigeria)

The exhibits then were dominated by the work of artists who had formal, largely Western-style training and by 1980 the majority of artists whose works was exhibited in Africa or abroad still came from this background. Yet the average visitor to the capitals of African states will see little, if anything, of this art unless he chances on it in a public building or in the foyer of his hotel. Rather his lasting impression of modern African art is likely to be of the displays of polished ebony heads, gracefully carved antelopes, romantic paintings of palm trees and canoes mixed with recently carved 'antiquities' or Benin bronzes hot from the furnace that are to be found for sale in every big airport or hotel.

Artistic activity in Africa today ranges far beyond the work of the school-trained artist. Indeed, it is a major fallacy that the so-called traditional artist is a man of the past. True, the spectacular spread of Christianity* and Islam,* together with Western technology and values, since the imposition of colonial rule entailed a rapid decline in both the number of artists and their output; but not their extinction.

Many Africans still practise their traditional religions* and cult objects are eaten by termites, broken, or stolen for the international antiquities market, and have to be replaced. Furthermore, the tourist

Popular art: a truck in Lagos, Nigeria decorated with a kung fu motif and a slogan in Yoruba

Popular art: a potter in the Republic of Benin at work on a pot decorated with a snake and human figures

trade provides an outlet for copies of traditional sculptures whether sold as such, as at the Abidjan Museum in the Ivory Coast, or masquerading as the real thing. However, by and large the work of traditional artists has declined both in quantity and quality as a result of the European conquest at the end of the 19th century.

Many of those who would have worked for the traditional market are now exclusively preoccupied with production for the new tourist trade. Nowhere is this changeover more dramatically illustrated than in Benin City, Nigeria, where the brass-workers who once produced almost solely for the Oba's palace now do so almost solely for the growing tourist market. Most tourists return home with an 'authentic' African souvenir whether it be a Benin bronze or a Bambara antelope mask copied from the originals, or a piece representative of the new genres of tourist art.

Behind this tourist art lies a vigorous popular art, often created by the same men. Bars have to be painted with murals, arresting shop-signs designed, and commercial motor vehicles decorated with the currently fashionable motif. This popular art, often of high originality, is the principal contact most Africans have with art created exclusively for decorative and aesthetic effect as distinct from ritual purposes. As in the Western world, the gallery-going population is restricted to a small elite.

The work of the African artist who produces individual paintings and sculptures for sale in art galleries or by private treaty can be divided into two main categories: that of the school-trained and that of the so-called untutored artist. By and large the former look down on the latter group, even though their work has obtained a wider international audience.

The phenomenon of the untutored contemporary artist is widespread in Black Africa. It results from the establishment of a series of art workshops by Europeans anxious to harness the artistic talent manifested in the traditional arts of Africa to new modes and forms of expression, permitting it to express its innate African qualities, without, as Frank McEwen, director of the Salisbury Workshop, put it, imposing on pupils the 'corrupting' influences of Western art schools.

The earliest to establish this type of teaching was Kenneth Murray at Government College, Umuahia, Nigeria in the 1930s. Here students were not initiated into perspective and proportion but were encouraged to draw their inspiration from indigenous crafts and traditions, an approach which he believed was the only way whereby a truly contemporary Nigerian art would evolve.

Workshops at which standard Western art-teaching methods were eschewed and where the supervisors just provided the materials and instructed pupils in the techniques of mixing paint or making prints were established in Lubumbashi (Belgian Congo) in 1944 by Pierre Romain-Defossés, in Cyrene (Southern Rhodesia) by the Reverend Edward Paterson in 1939, at Poto-Poto in Brazzaville (French Congo) by Pierre Lods in 1951, by McEwen in Salisbury (Southern Rhodesia) and by Ulli Beier, not himself an artist, in Oshogbo (Nigeria) in the 1960s. Some of the products of these workshops have enjoyed considerable international success.

Even more remarkable have been the stylistic similarities between the artists supervised by Beier's wife, Georgina, in Oshogbo and those she subsequently grouped around her in Papua New Guinea. It is clear that many of these untutored artists have indeed been influenced by the work of their supervisors and most of them have had access to Western art books. Sadly, once their supervisors have left, little development has been noticeable in the majority of their work.

Few artists produced by these workshops have subsequently undergone formal art training. Ben Enwonwu, who first practised art under Murray and then won a scholarship to the Slade School of Fine Art in London, is a notable exception. His paintings and sculptures show all the skill one would expect of a graduate of that school and he is one of few modern African artists with an international reputation.

The great majority of practising artists, however, were trained at one of the university-level art schools which were founded or upgraded during the 1950s and 1960s. The most notable are to be found in Zaria (Northern Nigeria), Khartoum (Sudan), Addis Ababa (Ethiopia), Makerere (Uganda), Kumasi (Ghana), and Dakar (Senegal). All these schools have given their students courses in the basic principles of Western art, but either through the vision of their directors or as a result of protest by their students they have

Detail from repoussé aluminium panel by Asiru (Nigeria)

increasingly tried to respond to African cultural circumstances.

While many of the products of their schools emerge as competent draughtsmen or designers with little to distinguish them from their Western counterparts, the more talented have come out with styles and themes that are recognizably African without being eclectic with regard to traditional art.

None of these schools has a pervading style, as do the workshops. One can, however, detect in some of them periods when a particular teacher was influential. But with a range of different teachers at any one time, and frequent changes of staff, uniformity of approach has not generally been any more of a problem than in the average Western art school. One only has to compare the work of Khartoum's most famous products, Ahmed Mohamed Shibraim and Ibrahim es Salahi, who is perhaps the finest African contemporary artist, to see how different their approach is.

This diversity within one school is even more strikingly illustrated by the work of that cluster of talent that graduated from the Zaria school in the early 1960s: Uche Okeke, Yusuf Grillo, Demas Nwoka, Simon Okeke, Bruce Onobrakpeya and Jimoh Akolo, each of whom has his own very individual style, and each his own themes. Nor can one easily perceive any overall theme in the work of contemporary African artists. The style and preoccupations of the sculptures of Vincent Kofi from Ghana are very different from those of his Ivory Coast neighbour Christian Lattier.

What does characterize the best of contemporary African art is its vigour and freshness, its mood of exploration, its refusal to be tied down by contemporary Western fashion. Only when it is consciously eclectic, seeking to declare itself African by using ill-digested traditional motifs, does it become trite and fall into the category of superior tourist art.

M.C.

Dance

Dance in Africa may be divided into three categories: traditional, neo-traditional, and theatrical. Traditional dance has evolved over generations as an essential part of ritual and social life in African societies, serving a social purpose as well as providing a source of delight and entertainment. Dance is central to ritual, for example, when the Yoruba priests of the god Sango (Nigeria) depict the thunder and lightning of their tempestuous deity through the dramatic intensity of their dance gestures, they restate the nature of his power to the worshippers, who in turn pay homage with formal songs and dances. Dance can play a socio-political role when rulers state their authority through their performance. An Asante king in Ghana wins the respect of his subjects as he expresses kingship in a dance of skilful assurance. His gestures are answered by his chiefs, each expressing the nature of his office through the rhythmic patterns of his dance. Thus dance portrays individual and group roles.

Sango priests (Nigeria) worship their deity through the gestures of their dance

Gwandara women elders (Nigeria) perform a ceremonial dance

The working movements of farmers and fishermen are formally stylized in dances expressing their strength and virility as men, while in some societies their wives and daughters use more restrained movements to express the qualities expected of women. This contrast is clearly expressed in the vigorous dances of young Zulu men of South Africa and the subtle foot patterns of Zulu women. Men and women have distinctive dances and rarely perform together with the exception of popular recreational dances. In many cultures a hunter gains courage through a ritual dance that ensures the protection of his guardian spirits. After a successful kill he may re-enact the hunt for his community in a mimetic dance that serves to placate the spirit of the animal. Thus dance defines the skill of a man and acts as a form of communication and cohesion within a community.

Many cultures in Africa are horizontally divided into age-sets, each with its characteristic dance. Children and adolescents have distinctive dances and dance-games, and occasions on which they learn the arts of their elders and thus absorb the beliefs, customs and mores of their society. Young men and women have courtship dances, which lead into the more authoritative rhythms of the married state and finally into the measured dances of the elders, for age presents no barrier to dance in Africa. In a Yoruba village the elders on reaching the age of 65 are initiated into the delicately refined movements of the appropriate dance.

A Masai (Kenya) and a Baraba (Nigeria) warrior dance for the same purpose but use a totally different form. At a conscious level the form is an expression of their role, but it is unconsciously grounded in movement habits dictated by the physical circumstances in which the dancers live and the material culture, traditions and temperament of their people. In Nigeria the Ijo of the Niger Delta, who travel by canoe and live in villages which are regularly flooded, dance as though balancing on an uneven surface, whereas the Tiv, who farm the firm earth of the savanna, place their feet solidly on its surface as they form a circle to dance as a team.

A dance leader followed by his team

In the majority of cultures the traditional calendar focuses on regular ritual festivals which combine ceremony with entertainment to reach climactic heights at the appearance of lavishly costumed masquerade figures whose dance, incantation and song serve to relate the sacred and the secular. In other cultures the arts are interrelated in ritual dramas portraying the mythological history of the people, as in the eight day Ozidi Saga of the Ijo; or storytelling is elaborated to include mime, dance and song in a form of 'whole theatre', as seen in the spectacular performances of the Tiv Kwagh-hir. Thus dance is an essential element in an interrelated complex of the arts.

On all occasions dance is inseparable from music, and the dancers usually follow the rhythmic lead of the musician or singer. A dancer's skill is assessed on his ability to follow the rhythms of the leading instrument of the musical ensemble and to catch changes and nuances within the rhythmic pattern. Thus precision is recognized in terms of rhythmic discipline rather than the creation of exact geometric patterns in space – the criteria of excellence for Western dance.

Traditional dance is an integral part of daily life within a homogenous community. When such dance is transplanted from its familiar setting onto an urban stage to entertain a cross-cultural audience, then its function is radically changed. This affects the form, as dancers are required to perform within the set limits of a stage and before an audience whose members are probably unfamiliar with the original intention of the performance. The organizers of such events are often civil servants rather than choreographers. They demand that the dancers present variety, accenting the spectacular elements of their dances within a strictly limited time, and may

Team dances are a common feature of African tradition and are based on an age-grade or an extended family unit. The team is organized by a leader chosen for his dance skill and his creativity in initiating new styles within the traditional form. He is responsible for training and rehearsing the dancers, who perform in unison after him as he follows the dictates of the music. In some societies, such as the Yoruba, which stress hierarchical authority, dancers move freely as individuals within the group, each relating directly to the leading musician. In this free-flow pattern the creation of new movements results from the improvisation of the individual, often in competition with his fellow dancers. A third type of formation combines team with individual dance when soloists emerge to add a personal style to the performance of the group, as seen in the dances of the Gwari people of Nigeria.

Village dancers are surrounded by their audience, whose presence delineates the shape and extent of the performing area. In this close-knit relationship members of the audience are familiar with the art forms which are presented as a restatement of their beliefs and customs. The audience participates by voicing praise and criticism to ensure that the performers respect their tradition and make innovations that are in accord with it. Skilled dancers are selected by elders to perform at marriages, funerals and other important public ceremonies. There are times for informal recreation when anyone may dance in a style of his own choosing, as seen in popular 'highlife' and 'soul' clubs, which have flourished since the radio became part of village life and introduced generalized forms of popular music.★

Dancers of the Ghana National Dance Ensemble re-enact an Akan ceremonial dance

redesign the costume to meet urban tastes or reflect national sentiments. Thus movements are radically changed to meet new needs without the required consideration for artistic standards. Civic and traditional arts festivals and in some instances national dance companies produce what may be termed neo-traditional dance in which the externals of the form echo past traditions with little reference to their original intention. Dances that are deeply embedded in ritual seldom survive this treatment, though team dances, which have been performed on a variety of social occasions within their original culture, are often successfully redesigned by their dance leaders to meet the needs of an urban audience; thus the competitive nature of an arts festival can, in some instances, lead to the development of dances of a high standard of excellence.

Theatrical dance is emerging as an important aspect of contemporary African theatre. Choreographers design dance-dramas or combine with directors to produce works in which the arts are related rather than isolated into a distinct specialization as in Western theatre. Choreographed works usually combine movements abstracted from a wide range of cultures, or present a dramatized setting in which village dances may retain their vitality of form and purpose.

Dance in Africa has never been static, as it is a vital expression of a way of life. Therefore theatrical artists with creative insight remain within the essence of their traditions by creating works based on African rhythms which express life in contemporary society. *P. H.*

The 'Spirit of the Moon' (danced by Labayo Ogundele): a scene from a dance-drama choreographed by Peggy Harper for the University of Ife Theatre (Nigeria)

Drama and cinema

Drama

Drama in Africa derives from two sources that often conflict. The traditional performing arts enable the African dramatist to rediscover, after colonialism, an essential African identity; but Western drama, the other source, shows how performance can be made into an enduring play text. The development of African drama in the 1960s and 1970s has manifested the contradictions resulting from this dichotomy. Play texts can be the means whereby African playwrights achieve recognition and intellectual status; but they indicate a derivative form and even, at times, a derived content. Furthermore, intellectual recognition often means losing the mass audience that the traditional performing arts enjoyed, and continue to enjoy. However, as an expression of the African mind, traditional performances can also reflect a narrow ethnic or religious chauvinism, and to revive them is to alienate further a younger generation dazzled by urban technology and eager to escape the label 'bush'. Most Africans want a genuinely African and popular drama; but it is difficult to know precisely what such a drama is.

The work of J.P. Clark, one of the first published Nigerian playwrights, reveals these conflicting sources. *Song of a Goat* and *The Masquerade* derive from Aristotelian concepts of tragedy; a later play, *Ozidi*, recreates on the stage a traditional Ijo saga. The Ghanaian playwright Efua Sutherland has written *Edufa* based on Euripides' *Alcestis*, and *The Marriage of Anansewa*, a play developing the story-telling art of the Akan-speaking people. The Nigerian Ola Rotimi turned from Greek sources to writing plays based on 19th century Yoruba and Benin history (*Kurunmi* and *Ovonramwen Nogbaisi*). And history, particularly colonial history, has obsessed Francophone West African playwrights like Jean Pliya from the Republic of Benin (*Kondo le Requin*), the Cameroonian Jean-Baptiste Obama (*Assimilados*), and Bernard Dadié from the Ivory Coast (*Beatrice du Congo*). In other plays, Dadié and others reflect the French comic tradition; and spectacular ballets re-form traditional dances for the modern theatre.

The plays of Wole Soyinka, Africa's outstanding playwright, reflect perhaps more than any other author's work the profound complexities of form and content in African drama. His early plays (*The Lion and the Jewel* and *The Trials of Brother Jero*) still most popular in performance, are satirical comedies with Nigerian content treated naturalistically. His political plays (*A Dance of the Forests; Kongi's Harvest* and *Madmen and Specialists*) are concerned with the tensions of modernization in a still deeply traditional society. In his later plays, like *The Bacchae of Euripides* and *Death and the King's Horseman*, as well as in his critical study *Myth, Literature and the African World*, he confronts the Western mind with universal themes

The urban black theatre in South Africa is similar in its cultural synthesis, as in Credo Mutwa's *uNosimela*. Playwrights must find ways of showing both the evils of apartheid★ and their own surviving humanity, while still being allowed by the authorities to perform. Plays like *Sizwe Banzi is Dead* by Athol Fugard, John Kani and Winston Ntshona, and *Survival* by Workshop '71, have also been performed abroad.

The differences between drama in West Africa and drama in southern and East Africa may be partly explained by the latter's experience of settler colonialism; but, paradoxically, drama in Botswana, Zambia and the countries of East Africa is less concerned with asserting African personality in the face of European racism than with criticism of contemporary society. Playwrights try to present their plays to the masses, attempting a social analysis from the masses' point of view. From the University of Dar es Salaam playwrights like Ebrahim Hussein, and the choreographer Godwin Kaduma, present plays in factories, dance-dramas in villages, and at the same time involve their student-actors in village work before and after a performance. In Mozambique the governing party, *Frelimo*, uses drama to orient the villages to their communal social tasks. In Zambia, Kabwe Kasoma and Stephen Chifunyise, among others, take their plays to remote areas and offer their audiences criticism of contemporary social behaviour. In Botswana theatre campaigns like *Laedza Batanani* ('The sun is up; let us come together and work') have stimulated social analysis and self-help among depressed communities, from role-play among the Basarwa (formerly called the Bushmen) in the Kalahari Desert to village community plays in many parts of the country. The work is established and has government

The Nigerian playwright, Wole Soyinka during the shooting of the film version of his play, *Kongi's Harvest*

Community theatre in a village in Botswana: this particular play deals with – among other things – drunkenness in the community and the embezzlement of village development funds

worked out in a Yoruba dimension. *Opera Wonyosi*, based on Brecht's *The Threepenny Opera*, satirizes Nigerian materialism. Soyinka is prepared to adopt a critical stance that is unpopular – not only towards the authorities but also towards his fellow intellectuals. So is the Ghanaian playwright Ama Ata Aidoo, for example in her play *Anowa*, which equates African complicity in the slave trade with the subservient role of African women.

These plays exist as texts. A rich popular theatre also exists, without texts, through professional touring companies who tour the towns of West Africa in converted buses and trucks. In Ghana and Togo such companies are known as concert parties; in Nigeria, mainly among the Yoruba, there are more elaborate touring companies (for example those of Hubert Ogunde and Duro Lapido), combining brass bands and local drums; mythical heroes with modern accoutrements; transvestism and female dancers; stories of chance and luck with party politics: a response to pre- and post-independence materialism.

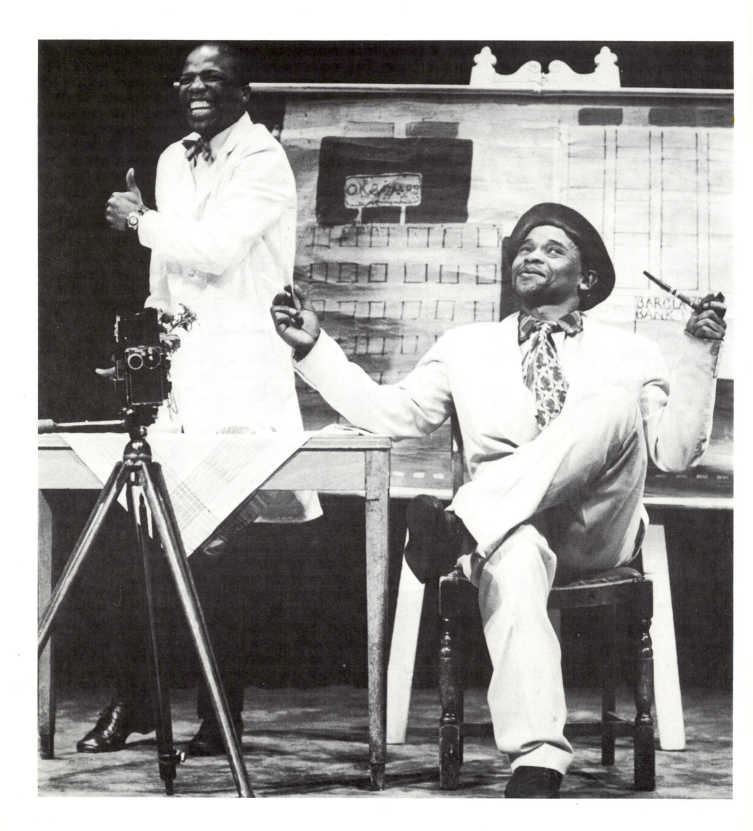

approval. In Kenya, however, the playwright and novelist Ngugi wa Thiong'o★ spent a year in jail for developing a play, *Ngahiika Ndenda*, with workers and farmers, in their own language, which was critical of the government's development policies.

Throughout Africa the language for drama is as important as its critical content. Egyptian playwrights, like Tewfik Al Hakim, write in modern Arabic; and Algerian playwrights like Kateb Yacine write in French and Arabic. Many African playwrights who previously wrote in English for an international readership, now write in the language of their own communities. Hussein's *Kinjeketile* was first written in Swahili. Kasoma's *Black Mamba Plays*, about the Zambians' struggle for independence, are in a mixture of the languages spoken in Zambia. Yulisa Maddy was imprisoned for his Sierra Leonean Creole play *Big Berrin*; and in Nigeria young Nigerian dramatists are expressing stringent satire in plays in pidgin.

Left: John Kani and Winston Ntshona in the London production of *Sizwe Banzi is Dead* by Kani, Ntshona and Athol Fugard. Below: Hubert Ogunde, the foremost impresario of modern Nigerian popular theatre and, since 1979, a film producer

Scene from the film, *Xala* directed by Sembène Ousmane

Cinema

The language issue is not so important in the emergent African cinema, because the film image itself is so powerful. Cinema in Africa is a new creative medium and not, like theatre, an extension of an existing one. It is much more popular than live theatre. Sensationalized feature films, like the Hong Kong-made kung-fu and Indian romance movies, are widely and repeatedly shown throughout Africa. Film-making since 1945 has largely centred on documentaries and anthropological records, and African governments have continued this sponsorship priority, and have not been concerned to set up feature film industries.

Foreign techniques have influenced African cinema. Nigeria's Ola Balogun was affected by Indian melodramas in making *Ajani-Ogun*; though his subsequent films, like *Amadi*, the first feature film made in a Nigerian language, Igbo, are much more individualistic. The Senegalese author, Sembène Ousmane,★ who is probably the best-known African film-maker, was influenced in his first film, *Borom Saret*, and even in his later socially critical films, *Le Mandat* and *Xala*, by the classic Russian directors. Film-makers in Niger have been guided by the Frenchman Jean Rouch, who has developed the style known as *cinéma vérité* or 'direct cinema', and who has trained film-makers from Niger to make excellent films on modest budgets (e.g. *Babatou et les Trois Conseils*). Rouch's first feature film, *Moi Un Noir*, used an actor, Oumarou Gande, who has now become a leading film-maker in Niger. He makes historical films, as does the Nigerian Adamu Hallilu (*Shehu Umar*, *Kantekebbi of Argungu*). Hallilu's films are in Hausa and are made with very large budgets. All African directors find that distribution of their films within Africa is difficult.

Reaching the theatre or cinema audience is difficult; but it must be faced, because for many Africans the creative media of theatre and cinema are very important for developing social awareness throughout the continent.

M. E.

Literature

Surrealism in the 1930s provided a philosophical basis for an intellectual rebellion by Francophone Africans against the colonization of their minds. The French colonial policy of trying to make intelligent Africans into black Frenchmen made a rebellion inevitable; and the impetus to the poetry movement known as *négritude* was given by the Surrealist attack in Europe on the tyranny of language and on bourgeois art. Caribbean and African writers like Aimé Césaire (from Martinique), Léopold Sédar Senghor★ (now President of Senegal), Jean-Joseph Rabéarivelo (Malagasy Republic), and Tchicaya U Tam'si (Republic of Congo) found in sensual rhythms and a collage of images the means to articulate their sense of dislocation and to rediscover the dignity of their discarded cultures. *Négritude* was then sharpened into political criticism by writers, like Yambo Ouologuem from Mali, who were published by the Parisian publishers *Présence Africaine*.

In Anglophone countries in the early 1960s poets began to express their dissatisfaction with the social and cultural objectives of *négritude*. Nigerian poets like Christopher Okigbo and Wole Soyinka,★ and the Ghanaian Kofi Awoonor wanted to be more concrete and to analyse the images for their inherent meaning for contemporary Africa. A further rebellion against all cerebral poetry came from the Ugandan Okot p'Bitek, whose *Song of Lawino* was seminal in its attack on all literary education. He, like his fellow Ugandan poet, Taban lo Liyong, turned to the oral poetry of his ethnic group for inspiration.

As political independence was established, the interest of intellectual West Africans shifted to the conflicting claims made upon them by the traditional world and by progress, and these dilemmas were explored in the novel. The best known African prose writer in English is probably the Nigerian, Chinua Achebe (*Things Fall Apart* and *Arrow of God*) and, in French, Camara Laye from Senegal (*The African Child* and *Dream of Africa*). Social criticism is expressed in the writing of Ayi Kwei Armah from Ghana (*The Beautiful Ones Are Not Yet Born* and *Fragments*), Sembène Ousmane,★ the Senegalese film-maker (*God's Bits of Wood*) and the Cameroonian Mongo Beti (*The Poor Christ of Bomba* and *Perpetua and the Habit of Unhappiness*).

This serious prose fiction is matched by locally best-selling novels which weave stories around contemporary popular themes, like the books of the Nigerian Cyprian Ekwensi (*Jagua Nana*) and T.M. Aluko (*One Man, One Matchet*), and the East African *Spear*

(1)   (2)

(3)

(4)   (5)

Contemporary African writers: (1) Yambo Ouologuem; (2) Okot p'Bitek; (3) Chinua Achebe; (4) Ayi Kwei Armah; (5) Mongo Beti; (6) Dennis Brutus; (7) Ngugi wa Thiong'o; (8) José Luandino Vieira

(6)

(7)   (8)

publications, which have large sales throughout Africa. Ekwensi himself emerged from an even less formal popular tradition of romantic novelettes known as Onitsha Market literature, which has been chronicled by the Nigerian critic Emmanuel Obiechina (*An African Popular Literature*).

Journalism in popular magazines, like *Drum*, was the first opportunity many black South Africans had to write. Bloke Modisane and Ezekiel Mphahlele moved on to autobiographies and autobiographical novels. Others, like Peter Abrahams (*Mine Boy*) and, later, Alex La Guma (*The Stone Country*) and Bessie Head (*Maru* and *A Question of Power*) have objectified their experience of discrimination into tightly-constructed novels. South African poets, too, like Dennis Brutus, Arthur Nortje and Masisi Kunene, have struggled to distil the experience of suffering and exile into accessible literary forms. Southern Africa also has an indigenous white literature, which at its best is also engaged in social criticism, like the novels of Alan Paton (*Cry, The Beloved Country*), Doris Lessing (*The Children of Violence* series), Nadine Gordimer (*The Late Bourgeois World*) and André Brink (*Looking on Darkness*).

Zimbabwe, Angola and Mozambique have also produced a politicized literature. Agostinho Neto, the President of Angola until his death in 1979, had a substantial reputation as a revolutionary poet; and José Luandino Vieira (*The Real Life of Domingos Xavier*) is a political novelist. In Kenya, Ngugi wa Thiong'o★ (*A Grain of Wheat*) has produced a major novel (*Petals of Blood*) which, like his plays, attacks present-day Kenyan society. Like his fellow-Kenyan writer, Meji Mwangi (*Going Down River Road*), he writes from the point of view of the urban and rural poor.

The language in which the literature is written remains an issue throughout the continent. There is a literature in Arabic (e.g. that of the Egyptian Naguib Mahfouz, whose *Miramar* and *Midag Alley* are in English translation); more and more drama, prose fiction and poetry appear in Swahili; and indigenous languages are increasingly used by popular writers. There is also a growing indigenous academic literary criticism, which is beginning to replace the earlier criticism by non-African critics, whose journals, like *Black Orpheus* and *Research in African Literatures*, did so much to stimulate writing. Pioneering African critics like Mphahlele and the Sierra Leonean Eldred Jones have been followed by Nigerians like Obiechina and Kolawole Ogungbesan, whose criticism is itself scrutinized by younger writers. They want to stimulate creative writing through indigenous-based literary journals, indigenous publishing organizations, and pan-African distribution networks. However, this literary activity will for the time being concern only the intellectual few. The majority of African populations are still illiterate; and those authors who wish to write creatively for this wider audience will choose to write for a performance medium: for the theatre★ or the cinema★, for television or for radio.   *M.E.*

Traditional music

Vitality and gentleness, full-bodied texture and tonal clarity, participation and display, are marvellously combined in the indigenous musics of sub-Saharan Africa. The secret of this alchemy is in their use of the human body as the prime instrument for making music. Individual, physical effort must be relaxed and economical, and the interaction of bodies must express their individuality in community. In sub-Saharan Africa music and bodily motion form an inseparable unity, and in music three features stand out above all others: antiphony (the alternate singing of solo and chorus), part-singing, and highly developed rhythm.

The Zulu of South Africa have a saying that is echoed in many other African societies: *umuntu ungumuntu ngabantu* – man becomes human through [association with] other human beings. This is both a statement of the fact that human qualities are learned, and a prescription for musical, as well as social, behaviour. The body is conceived as a social body, and music provides a framework through which people can create and experience a product that is greater than the sum of their individual contributions, and achieve, with collective discipline, personal freedom through transcendence.

These principles are embodied in a basic process of African musical performance which is found throughout western, central, eastern, and southern Africa. Should two people, brought up in an indigenous musical tradition, be asked to play together a succession of beats or an iambic figure (short-long beat), they will not play in unison, but rather at different tempi or in canon. Thus one person plays two to the partner's three beats, and the short beat of one person's iambic figure coincides with the other's long beat, producing a stream of short beats.

To do this is an exercise of individuality in community. Each player must hold fast to his own part, and the collective effort produces both new cultural forms for the ear and a richer experience for the participants: the right sound of the music cannot be detached from the experience of 'clicking', or 'falling into phase', that the players share.

The organizing principle is metre: music begins as a rhythmical stirring of the whole body. A drumbeat, for example, is part of a body movement in which the hand or a stick strikes the drum skin, so that for the player there are no rests between the sounds of the two beats. African musicians teach and discuss critically the correct performance of drum rhythms, and of other instrumental music, in terms of right and wrong body movements. Mnemonics such as *tibwi* and *gwitang* for an iambic figure tell a drummer whether to play in the

Zilli funeral drums of the Imia (Cameroon). Two types of drum are shown: the skin-covered membranophone and the wooden idiophone

Women of the AmaNazaretha Christian sect dancing on the mountain Nhlangakazi in KwaZulu, South Africa

centre or at the edge of the skin, with the tips of the fingers or the flat palm of the hand, and so on, in order to produce the right tones.

In African music drums are regarded as melodic instruments, and people say that they 'sing'. There are also the famous 'talking drums' of West Africa and the Congo regions, which are used to send verbal messages in a way similar to Morse code; but drum signalling is a linguistic phenomenon, which lacks the repetitive characteristic of musical metre. Similarly, the art of declamation is not generally classified in Africa as music. For example, Zulu praises are musically stylized speech rather than song, although they are recited on four fixed levels of pitch.

African song melodies are not merely intensified speech, although sub-Saharan African languages have a pronounced melodic quality and in some cases patterns of speech-tone cannot be altered without changing the meanings of words, as in Chinese. The rules for song melodies are frequently different from those for spoken language in their treatment of rhythm and tonality.

Because regular metre is the basic feature of musical expression among, for example, the Venda of southern Africa words that are recited like poetry are classed as *luimbo* (song); and because they depart completely from the rhythmic and tonal patterns of ordinary speech, they are really more 'musical' than melodies that follow speech-tone patterns more closely. This principle allows for greater freedom of contrapuntal invention in the chorus parts of songs, where melodies are not tied to speech-tone, and it also accounts for the fact that Venda did not find offensive the conflict between speech-tone and melody in European hymns, which they classified as choruses.

In some African musical systems patterns of speech-tone are maintained even in choruses, so that part-singing is not contrapuntal but in parallel motion. Even in these cases, however, song melodies are not exact replicas of spoken language: the pitches of speech-tone are relative, and musical invention makes for considerable variation within the required outlines of their patterns.

Musical systems are social products, and communal music and dance* pervade African social life. But they are not treated as ordinary, everyday social events: people expect some kind of transcendental experience in performing the music of spirit possession, of circumcision and other rites of passage, of ceremonial, and even of general entertainment. Music educates the emotions and cultivates people's sensitivity towards the feelings of others. These aims may or may not be stated specifically as the purposes of music or of the social event that it accompanies, but often they are inherent in the very conditions of performance. The social context provides only part of the meaning, and unless the music *and* the social context are right, the event is incomplete. For example, among the Venda of South Africa, members of possession cults could not be 'taken' by the spirits of deceased ancestors unless they were dancing with the group and in the area from which the ancestors came. But even when all these social conditions were right, they could not achieve the trance state associated with the cult ceremony unless the music was played correctly.

The special case of possession music is an extreme example of one of two ideal types of African music, which are often classified by contrasting terms that mean, roughly, 'ritual', or 'serious music', and 'play music'. Both contain elements of discipline and freedom in performance, but ritual music is more often meant to be repeated accurately on each occasion, while play music should reflect accurately the social occasion and hence contain topical improvisa-

A minstrel plays on the Luo lyre in Kenya

A *kora* player from The Gambia

tions. What is important is the transcendental nature of the *musical event*, whether the emphasis be on the transformation of people through the repeated music for trance, or the transformation of music through skilful invention and improvisation on basic structures in response to the immediate challenge of a social event.

The constant re-creation of music by performers and audience is as important a part of music experience as the special kinds of skill that music-making demands. The production of musical patterns in themselves is not as important as the meanings that these patterns are given, in specific contexts, in terms of attitudes and communication between people. And yet people are not able to use music creatively until they have mastered the conventions of their musical language which, in most of Africa, is combined with dance, ritual, drama, costume, sculpture and painting.

The ground rules of each musical system are generative and learnt through experiences that are shared by all members of the community. Principles of tonality and harmonic fluctuation, rules for the conversion of the speech-tone patterns of new words into appropriate melodies, when the musical framework of a song has been stated in the opening bars, and rules for the development of parts by different sections of a chorus, are as much present in the elementary songs of children as in the more complex music of adults, where the possibilities of the musical principles are more fully developed.

What happened traditionally in Venda was typical of many other societies, and may still apply even in areas that have been affected by massive social change. Children had the opportunity to hear the results of the operation of musical rules from the earliest age, they were keen to perform their songs correctly and to participate in the

Venda children (South Africa) try their skill at drumming during a possession dance while cult members sit in a group and rest

dances of older children, and they assimilated more of their musical system by sitting about with their mothers at adult events. The continuity of the tradition was further ensured by informal instruction in initiation schools. By the time they married, men and women had learnt, chiefly by osmosis, all the rules necessary to discriminate good from bad performances, new from old melodies, and the subtlety and significance of variation, and to pick up a new song quickly, to improvise new melodies to new words and new counterpoint to a given chorus. Some took the lead more than others, and acquired the reputation of being good singers, but it was generally accepted that any person who was sufficiently interested and enthusiastic could learn to perform music well.

Coordination of body movements and social participation are essential features of African music-making, but public solo performance is also valued. The kind of experience that musical events offer ranges from the fullest social participation to the maximum of spectacle, in which audiences thrill to the display of a master-drummer, a virtuoso harpist, or a player of *mbira*, the so-called 'thumb-piano' with tuned metal or wooden slats that are set on a resonator, and plucked with the thumbs.

The value of full participation is related to delight in the fullness of sound. If more than one person is present, why should only one tone be sung? Harmony is expected, whether through singing the same melody in parallel or through elaborating additional parts in counterpoint. The characteristically African responsorial form with solo call and chorus response enables the maximum of both display by soloists and participation by members of the chorus. Musical techniques stress the problem of coordination that ensemble playing poses, with its consequent experience for participants, rather than the technical difficulty of individual parts. Thus, almost as common as the use of interlocking parts in drum ensembles is the general principle of hocketing, in which individual singers or players produce small parts of melodies in consort. Good examples of this are found among the !Kung San people of the Kalahari and in the *domba* and *tshikona* forms of the Venda people.

Patterns of body movement and social participation also influence the music of the contemplative songs and instrumental soli that are played on zithers, lyres, bow-harps, xylophones, and the most widespread instrument that was invented in Africa, the *mbira*. Melodies are often generated by the flow of finger and hand movements in relation to the physical layout of instruments, or the fingers and/or thumbs of the left and right hands produce the rhythms that two or more people would play together on drums, in much the same way that a keyboard canon or fugue represents a number of separate voices.

Even when audiences are not actually joining in a performance, they can be deeply involved not only in the words and sentiments that are overtly expressed, but also in the music itself. People listen carefully to the social and political comment of minstrels in West Africa, especially those who accompany themselves on the *kora* harp-lute, and in southern Africa, where the most common solo instruments are various types of musical bow; and to housewives who share their gossip and criticism musically with other villagers, as they pound maize in the cool of the night. They are also able to listen carefully and critically to the music, because musical experience is common property and everyone participates in performance at some stages of his or her life. Above all, audiences are rarely recruited on a contractual basis, as are the audiences who pay to hear symphony orchestras or pop groups. If they are not there to perform, they share in musical events because they are kinsfolk, clansmen and women, neighbours, cult-members, fellow-novices, or associates of the performers, and therefore intimately involved in the social context of the music.

There is an overall contrast between the musics of the north of Africa and of those parts of sub-Saharan Africa where Islam is dominant, and the musics of the rest of southern, central and East Africa, and the coastal regions of West Africa. For example, in the former, classes of semi-professional and professional musicians have emerged so that music-making is less of a collective activity, and voice quality is noticeably thin and reedy, rather than open and resonant.

There are some correlations between ideology, social and political structure, and musical practice in Islamic parts of Africa, but there are too many exceptions elsewhere to postulate any generally valid correlations between song and musical styles and social formations. For example, although large orchestras and specialist musicians were associated with the courts of the powerful kings of Luba (Zaire) and Buganda (Uganda), one of the most complex of all African music styles, the choral and orchestral dance suites of xylophone ensembles

Chopi xylophonists, rattle players and dancers (Mozambique)

of the Chopi people in Mozambique, occurs in a much less stratified society. The music of the Babinga of the Congo forest and the !Kung of the Kalahari desert, who are hunter-gatherers, is richly polyphonic, although they are among the most homogeneous societies in Africa.

The distribution of musical styles in sub-Saharan Africa corresponds roughly with cultural and language zones, but almost universal are duple metre, with beats of equal length grouped in twos and threes, and time-keeping patterns with groups of unequal beats (e.g. short-short-long-short-long); call-and-response forms, in which a song is identified by its chorus line and the two parts often overlap and produce polyphony; syllabic treatment of words so that one syllable corresponds to one tone and off-beat phrasing of melodic accents and a strong metronome sense; and a regular alternation of tonality and 'harmonic' tension in the two parts of a vocal or instrumental cycle.

Universal laws of sound determine the overtones of a plucked string or overblown pipe and produce a hierarchy of tonal relations, but they do not determine the modes, scales, and tonal and harmonic principles that different communities have chosen in building their musical systems. The evidence from Africa shows very clearly that musical history cannot be seen as a progress from simple to complex in terms of the mathematical ratios involved in the laws of sound. Modes or scales that divide the octave into five intervals (pentatonic) are used in the music of the advanced traditional states of West Africa and Uganda, as well as by the !Kung hunter-gatherers of the Kalahari, while hexatonic and heptatonic modes are used in other African societies that are technologically and administratively neither as complex nor as simple as these two extremes. In some societies all three scales are used concurrently, reflecting the variety of musical systems that had been incorporated as a result of immigration and conquest, and to these are often added the scales and tone systems of Islamic or European musics.

The importance of many principles of traditional African music has been illustrated by responses to European music. Hymns, for example, have been re-harmonized and their melodies presented by church leaders in responsorial form, so that new members of a congregation could quickly participate in a new hymn. Tonic/sub-dominant/dominant chord sequences were added to the tonic/supertonic and tonic/mediant sequences of traditional music, and many hymns and urban secular songs were treated as choruses, so that speech-tone patterns of words could be ignored and greater contrapuntal freedom could be attained within the new tonal discipline.

There is as yet no evidence that traditional principles of music-making are in danger of extinction. In sub-Saharan Africa, musical practice continues to be collectively disciplined, cooperative and gentle, ritualistic but innovative and responsive to different and changing social situations. *J. B.*

Popular music

Popular music in sub-Saharan Africa is a product of the region's increasing urbanization and integration into the world economic and political order over the past century. Though some indigenous traditions have disappeared, modern styles have often retained African principles and processes of music-making while incorporating new materials. This is less a matter of passive acceptance than of positive selection consistent with the changing meanings, functions, and values of expressive culture in African society. Patterns of selection and transformation in popular culture provide insight into the social experience and creative response of the African masses, who profoundly influence the course of institutional change, but seldom write about it.

As distinct from its functional predecessor, recreational music, which appears to exist in nearly all African communities, popular music has its origins in the colonial experience and in the growth of large commercial centres. Unlike sacred and ceremonial music, recreational music is not customarily bound to formal institutional settings or purposes, and has therefore proved more amenable to innovation in response to social change. Traditional recreational styles have contributed materially to popular forms insofar as they are of value for African cultural reorientation to modern urban social conditions.

Certainly the role of popular music in structuring cultural transformation has made it a force for continuity as well as change. In pre-colonial urban communities, such as the Hausa states, now part of Niger and northern Nigeria, Arabian Islamic influence and institutionalized socio-political stratification created a class of specialized professional musicians whose status and functions have continued to reinforce the stability of the local political structure. The system of patronage remains, and modern political leaders and occupational groups as well as traditional aristocrats make use of praise singing and other musical services according to the old pattern. Although many performances are now available on disc or are played on the radio, and are therefore directed towards the entertainment of an undifferentiated public, Hausa urban music retains its 'traditional' (pre-colonial) Afro-Arabian character. Influential Western, Latin American, and other imported musics have had little discernible effect upon Hausa performance practice.

In non-Islamic areas, by contrast, the colonial experience and the influence of Christian missions on religion and education have created a number of coexistent but divergent patterns of popular musical development which reflect cultural change. Enforcing new modes of cultural behaviour, the missions introduced European sacred and secular musical expression in place of 'heathen' traditional styles to followers who had necessarily detached themselves to a

Military music was a major early influence on modern African popular music: the band of the King's African Rifles

greater or lesser extent from traditional communities. Forming a new colonial elite, African graduates of mission schools reinforced the prestige of church-sponsored musical performance in the growing towns, where the market for their services made them the demographic and cultural vanguard of urban communities.

In British and – before the First World War – German ruled Africa in particular, Christian African choirs, school concerts, and brass bands attained widespread popularity. In the closing decades of the 19th century, such performances had a great influence upon those Africans, of whatever degree of education or experience of European culture, who sought a livelihood in the new towns. Military garrisons in most colonies and episodes such as the South African War (1899–1902) aided the missions in promoting interest in brass and fife-and-drum bands among urban Africans, a trend much accelerated by African participation in the First World War.* Apart from the introduction of European instruments, the mission schools in particular were responsible for the entrenchment of the simplified 'tonic-solfa' notational system, based upon the unmodulated, movable *doh* and tonic-dominant-subdominant harmonies. This 'three-chord' system has become the basis of musical instruction, composition, and transmission in popular African music.

European folk and popular styles were also influential throughout the latter part of the 19th century, introducing instruments for solo accompaniment, such as the guitar and concertina. Adapted easily to indigenous traditions of itinerant solo musicianship, these instruments caught the interest of African musicians less by their prestige than because of their greater technical capacity for the expression of African as well as European folk musical ideas. Some of Africa's first genuinely popular music was non-traditional only in the choice of instrument and related performance techniques.

The late 19th and early 20th centuries also saw the beginnings of black American influence on emerging African Christian and popular musical culture. In addition to the black American settlement of Monrovia, Liberia, missionaries of various black Churches established themselves throughout British Africa. There they taught the singing of black American 'spirituals' and stimulated the creation of Christian folk religious song styles such as the 'Creole Shout' of Sierra Leone. Independent local Churches 're-Africanized' black American and European sacred songs into an indigenous popular hymnody which has provided the melodic basis of many of the continent's most famous and moving 'freedom' songs. Internationally famous popular styles such as West African highlife continue to owe a melodic and harmonic debt to the pervasive influence of such hymnody.

Equally important were black American and West Indian sailors, who taught their songs and solo instrumental styles to Africans in port towns from Freetown to Durban. Black companies such as McAdoo's American Jubilee Singers, who toured South Africa in the 1890s, or the vaudeville duo, Glass and Grant, who performed in Ghana in the early 1920s, had much influence on the development of modern African entertainment and stage traditions. Gramophone recordings, which appeared in Africa about the turn of the century, popularized American and European folk and popular styles, including ragtime, early jazz, 'cowboy' ballads, vaudeville tunes, and subsequently West Indian and Latin American music.

During the present century this range of imported and indigenous musical resources available to Africans has been exploited in the creation of new syncretic forms suited to new expressive cultural requirements. Until the Second World War* the administrative philosophy of Indirect Rule* made conditions for the emergence of local syncretic popular styles more favourable in the British territories than in those of the French, Belgians, or Portuguese.

Like the other powers, Britain trained Africans as artisans and soldiers, employing them when needed in areas far from their homes. This practice brought Africans from different ethnic groups and colonies together under European supervision and increased the potential for cultural exchange. So, for example, Gã carpenters and blacksmiths from coastal Ghana returned home from working in other West African colonies after the First World War with an occupational song form called *gombe*, which became an inter-ethnic working class folk music. Variants of the same form became popular in the coastal areas of Sierra Leone, Nigeria, and British Cameroon, and recently the style has been observed among young men's dance associations in Bamako, Mali.

Labour migration to mines and cities brought about intense African inter-ethnic cultural contact in the urban, European dominated environment. Throughout industrializing areas of the subcontinent a tradition of street music developed in which migrants combined traditional and foreign musical influences as they played

for drinks or coins in West African palm wine bars and South and Central African 'shebeens'. Many of these players returned home, bringing traditional recreational music under the influence of popular styles from the towns. Others remained permanently and joined an emerging class of semi-professional musical entertainers. In British Africa these tended to be of two kinds, differentiated by social class and educational status.

The first group belonged to the small middle class, which was demanding music for social occasions suited to its European influenced–and therefore prestigious–dance styles. Partly trained African vocal, keyboard, and brass performers attempted to duplicate European and American sacred and popular music at concerts and 'grand balls' for European expatriates or their white-collar African subordinates.

This is the origin of the dance-band tradition of West African highlife, which began in the coastal towns of Ghana in the 1920s. Ghanaian performers playing European dance music for the elite eventually began to add African melodies arranged 'by ear' in Western harmony to their repertoires. These particular pieces were named 'highlifes' by the poorly paid musicians, to some extent in ironic criticism of the free-spending life style of the new African administrative class. In industrialized South Africa elite bands played American jazz arrangements for sophisticated Johannesburg Africans, while the more versatile ensembles also played African melodies in a three-chord style called *marabi*.

Most active in the process of musical syncretism were the urban musicians who earned an irregular livelihood in the bars, dance halls, and parties of the African 'shanty towns'. A brief stay at a mission station or a period of employment in the European-managed sectors of the economy gave these performers sufficient interest in and access to the variety of musical influences in the urban environment. Seeking to please only themselves and their neighbours, they readily mixed African and Euro-American materials into new styles specifically suited to the expressive recreational needs of the expanding urban African working class. Good examples are the guitar band or 'palm wine' tradition of highlife, and the solo guitar or keyboard *marabi* players of South Africa, who injected a great deal more in the way of indigenous musical content into these forms than did the more Westernized dance bands.

The blending of African and Western musical materials proceeded according to the varying historical conditions of culture contact in Africa. Any overall unity in the process is in the direct involvement of the new popular styles in the dynamics of urban African social and cultural adaptation. Hence music and dance associations, performance activities of other voluntary organizations, and community entertainment events have all been closely linked with changing principles of social organization and identity. The general shift from ethnic-regional to local residential to social class bases of group affiliation in African cities has been achieved partly in recreational settings where musical expression has played a fundamental role.

The content of musical performances associated with these occasions for social interaction expresses the socio-cultural distinctions and aspirations upon which emergent patterns of identity and alliance are based. Culturally, such performance communication provides images that embody values, goals and concepts of ideal personality vital to the formulation of new adaptive strategies.

Important in this process of transformation is the distributive role of the mass media in their relation to the African audience and in particular, the urban musician. Since the 1920s recording and broadcasting media have been primarily responsible for making available the raw material of modern musical syncretism. Musicians themselves, often operating on the margins of organized society, have performed the role of 'cultural brokers' in this process, linking stratified or opposed social sectors and innovating new musical combinations which shape, as well as reflect, aspects of social and political change.

Consistent with the general trend of African modernization, musicians have emerged from their traditional role as semi-specialized communal artisans into nationally and internationally recognized cultural 'personalities'. Since the Second World War the rise of African nationalist movements and the search for new, thoroughly contemporary but strongly indigenous national cultural identities has greatly intensified this process.

In West Africa highlife has continued to absorb West Indian, Latin American, and black North American influences and changing styles while retaining its fundamentally indigenous character. The elite

One of the classic West African highlife bands of the 1950s and 1960s, E. T. Mensah and his Tempos from Ghana

dance band tradition has declined to a great extent, along with the colonial society which gave it life. Adult middle class West Africans, always preferring to distance themselves from the guitar band tradition, now often follow imported American styles. Young people of all classes, however, are attracted by the strongly indigenous basis of guitar highlife. This tradition has also benefited from the increasing dominance of the guitar in world popular music, and from its origins in the increasingly articulate culture of the urban African working class.

Throughout Black Africa, in countries as distant as Ghana, Kenya, and South Africa, musicians and the media have combined to produce broadly popular forms of dance music played on guitar, saxophone, keyboard, and percussion. The lyrics of these songs, continuing the traditions of recreational music, involve sharp and subtle commentary on social and political issues and personalities of vital concern to a modernizing, but not necessarily Westernizing, urban working class. While governments can be sensitive to criticism from such a widely distributed source, they have also made effective use of this attractive and communicative aspect of popular culture. Ghana's president, Kwame Nkrumah* sponsored government dance bands, and took the famous highlife ensemble, E.K.'s Band, on state visits to neighbouring countries. Zaire's President Mobutu Sese Seko has formally employed his country's popular *animation* (Congo) guitar bands to popularize his ruling party, the *Mouvement Populaire de la Révolution*.

African musicians in the French and Belgian territories began to participate more actively in the processes of musical syncretism in the nationalistic atmosphere which followed the Second World War. In Zaire, in particular, musical innovators such as Rochereau and groups such as *L'Orchestra O.K. Jazz* absorbed Latin American rhythms, including the bolero and rumba, along with European and Caribbean guitar styles, and mixed them with local playing traditions to create 'Congo' music. So appealing was this blend that it has spread throughout West, Central, and East Africa. Retaining its fundamental stylistic identity while absorbing progressive waves of Latin and black American influence, 'Congo' is today a vigorous international musical idiom.

No longer so popular internationally, highlife has likewise survived the challenge of the imports. In many cases the most famous contemporary bands have achieved their position in the forefront of national culture by introducing music with more rather than less traditional African content. A successor to Nigerian highlife, *juju* music, based on traditional Yoruba sources, has attained greater general popularity as exponents such as Sunny Ade increasingly 'retraditionalize' the more Caribbean-oriented *juju* of pioneer Ebenezer Obey. Bandleaders from other parts of Nigeria, with different styles, such as Victor Uwaifo, have followed a similar progression.

Right: African styles have increasingly influenced non-African musicians: Fela Anikulapo-Kuti with the English drummer, Ginger Baker. Below: the Cameroonian bandleader, Manu Dibango

The invigoration of new national cultures from traditional wellsprings has been to some degree inspired by developments in trans-Atlantic black music, including 'soul' music and African-influenced Jamaican *reggae*. Popular music has, in fact, made several return trips between Africa and the New World, and imported black styles remain among the most popular in African cities today. Of these, *reggae*'s explicitly black nationalistic cultural politics has proved as attractive as its infectious Afro-West Indian beat. Soul music, benefiting from the cultural dynamism and prestige of Black America and the productive and distributive dominance of American media, has become ubiquitous as urban African dance music. Predictably, creative African musicians such as Sonny Okosun (Nigeria) and Kori Moraba (South Africa) have produced competitive local versions of *reggae*, and the Nigerian Fela Anikulapo-Kuti's 'Afro-beat' represents only one major adaptation of soul music.

Popular African musicians seem likely in the future to retain and perhaps even strengthen their position as key cultural innovators and social commentators closely attuned to the overall direction of African modernization in the 20th century. Examining their achievements, one may dispute stereotypical notions of the imminent demise of 'authentic' African musical culture in the face of Westernization. Popular music can, on the contrary, provide a means of observing contemporary African culture as it is created by and presented to its participants.   *D.B.C.*

Nigerian popular music is particularly dynamic and innovative, with many bands that have developed new forms from traditional themes. Top, and bottom left: Sonny Okosun. Bottom right: Sunny Ade's band

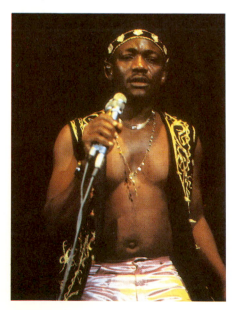

Sport

A barefooted Ethiopian called Abebe Bikila won the Olympic marathon in 1960: four years later he won again. Bikila's victories – which came during the key period of political decolonization – focused attention on Africa's arrival on the world athletics scene. Athletes from Africa had, however, made isolated apearances at earlier international competitions. As far back as 1912 teams from Egypt and white South Africa had participated in the Olympic Games: Egypt's Mohammed Hassanien taking part in the sabre and foil fencing competitions.

It was not until 1928, however, that Africans won Olympic medals. Mohammed el Quafi, an Algerian, competing for France, won a gold in the marathon and Egyptians won golds in wrestling (Ibrahim Mustafa) and weight-lifting (Said Nasser) and a silver and bronze in diving (Sinaika Zarid). In 1936 Egypt won two weight-lifting golds, a silver and two bronzes. For the next three Olympiads – London

The Ethiopian marathon runner, Abebe Bikila

(1948), Helsinki (1952) and Melbourne (1956) – the African medals table was dominated by one man, Alain Mimoun, an Algerian running for France. In 1948 he took the silver in the 5000m and in 1952 won silver medals in the 5000m and the 10000m. Mimoun ended his Olympic career with the gold in the marathon in 1956. In 1952 Ghana and Nigeria became the first Black African countries to participate at the Olympics. Melbourne welcomed Kenya, Ethiopia, Uganda and Liberia and in Rome (1964) 13 more African countries put in their first Olympic appearances.

Senegal's Louis Faal ('Battling Siki') became the first African to hold a world boxing title when he won the world light-heavyweight championship in 1922. In the 1950s Nigerians Dick Tiger and Hogan 'Kid' Bassey held, respectively, the world middleweight and world featherweight titles.

Within Africa itself organized sport began about a quarter of a century ago. International competition in the early days was mainly organized only between the colonies of a particular European power. The French, for instance, staged the *Jeux Inter-Africains* in 1959 in Bangui, Central African Republic for French-speaking countries only. The first step in holding pan-African games came during the third Friendship Games in Dakar, Senegal in 1963 when sportsmen from English and French-speaking countries competed against each other on the continent for the first time. It was there, also, that sports ministers began to discuss the organization of the first All-Africa Games. In 1965 some 3000 sportsmen from 30 countries competed against each other in the Congolese capital, Brazzaville in the first All-African Games. The Permanent Committee for the first Games, wanting to maintain the continuity of the competition, paved the way for the establishment of the Supreme Council for Sports in Africa (SCSA) in 1965, and in 1967 the Organization of African Unity* officially recognized the body.

By far the oldest international organized sporting body in the continent is the African Football Confederation, which was formed in 1957, the year it organized its first African football championships in Khartoum. This competition is now held every two years. Other international sporting bodies are being formed to develop the various sports in Africa. The African Boxing Union (ABU) was formed in 1973 during the third All-Africa Games to take care of professional boxing. The African Amateur Boxing Association looks after amateur boxing and holds regular championships, the seventh being held in Benghazi, Libya in 1979. Inspired by the Council of West Africa University Games, which has been organizing inter-varsity games in the region since 1965, African universities set up the Federation of African University Sports (FASU) in Lagos in 1971. The first FASU games were in Accra (1974) and the second in Nairobi (1978).

On the political front the SCSA has been fighting constantly to get the South Africans excluded from international sporting competitions or bodies. When South Africa participated in the Olympics between 1912 and 1936 with an all-white team, it was because that country's non-white population had not been given the chance to participate in regular South African sport. When the National Party came to power in 1948, however, this situation was formalized: the new policy of apartheid* was applicable in sport as in everything else. The South African National Olympic Committee had to stick to the apartheid laws and exclude Africans–however able they might be– from Olympic teams.

As African members of the International Olympic Committee (IOC) increased, moves began to expel South Africa from the IOC, and in 1964 the South Africans were barred from participation in the Tokyo Games. In 1968, however, some members of the IOC wanted South Africa to take part in the Mexico City Olympics, but African members, spearheaded by the SCSA, threatened to boycott the games if South Africa participated. After much argument the IOC eventually gave in and banned the South Africans from the Games. Two years later South Africa was expelled from the IOC and its racially-segregated sports organizations have been gradually thrown out of several international federations. Nevertheless the 1976 Montreal Olympics were boycotted by 22 African states because certain countries, particularly New Zealand, maintained sporting ties with South Africa.

The boycott was a bitter blow for the Games and the subsequent petty changes in South Africa's apartheid policy regarding sport have been mainly cosmetic. A few of the South African teams that have managed to compete abroad have included a handful of black or coloured sportsmen, but the fact remains that sport is still racially segregated inside South Africa. The Secretary General of the SCSA, Congo's Jean Claude Ganga, made this clear when he said that 'the presence of Black or Coloured players in a team in no way changes the fact of the apartheid policy practised in South Africa.'

African performances in the 1968 Olympic Games demonstrated conclusively that without African participation, future Olympics would be incomplete. Running at an altitude similar to their own (2250m), Kenyan and Ethiopian athletes dominated the middle and long distance events. They completely swept the medals table in the 5000m and 10000m and maintained Ethiopia's hold over the marathon: Mamo Wolde's gold marking his country's third consecutive victory. The deepest reservoir of running talent in the continent is in East Africa, which has turned out phenomenal middle and long distance runners by the dozen. Kenya leads the continent with the greatest number of talented runners emulating the exploits of stars like Kip Keino and Ben Jipcho. Tanzania can boast of Filbert Bayi who from 1974 until 1979 held the world record for the 1500m.

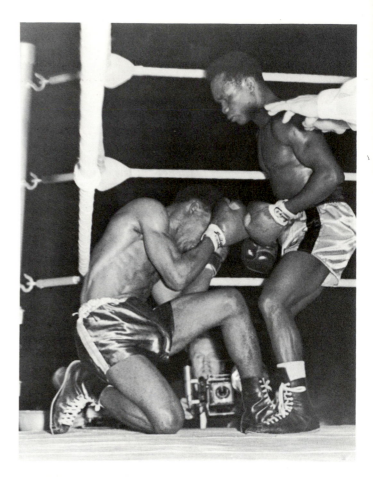

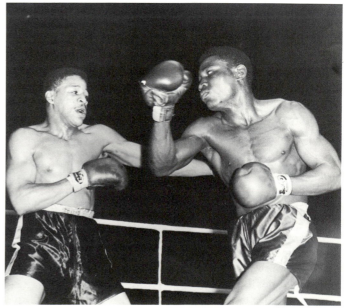

Top: Hogan 'Kid' Bassey (right) while world featherweight champion in a 1958 bout with Jules Touan of the Ivory Coast. Bottom: Dick Tiger (right) in a 1958 bout with Ellsworth Webb of the USA

Left: Kip Keino (Kenya) in the steeple-chase final at the 1966 Olympic Games. Above: the Mozambican-born Portu-guese international footballer, Eusebio. Below: Filbert Bayi (Tanzania), flanked by Malinowski and Coe

Football is by far the most popular sport in the continent. By world standards African football has not reached the heights that athletics has achieved although there are many skilful individual players, most of whom are playing in Europe and the USA. The most famous African footballer was Eusebio, who was born in Mozambique, then under Portuguese rule. He was chosen to play for Portugal and was the highest scorer, with nine goals, during the 1966 World Cup Finals in England.

African boxers, who are mainly amateur, are very successful. At the last two world boxing championships, two Africans emerged as champions, and at the Commonwealth Games, between 1970 and 1978, African boxers won 17 out of a total of 33 gold as well as numerous silver and bronze medals. Now African fighters are outgrowing amateurism and more are becoming professional. The last African to hold a professional world title was Ghana's David 'Poison' Kotey who was WBC world featherweight champion from 1975 to 1977. By 1979 a number of Nigerians and a Zambian held Commonwealth titles but were unable, despite pressing for them, to arrange world title fights, a situation which prompted the ABU to complain to the world boxing authorities.

Sporting activity in Africa continues to expand and the increase in pan-African competitions is a particular stimulus to young sportsmen. Each year larger segments of the African public are involved in African sports, new events are added to national programmes and new training facilities are established. Finance remains a stumbling block to rapid progress – as in so many other areas of African life – but African successes in sport at every level can be expected to increase steadily in number for the foreseeable future.   *D.D.*

Entertainment and leisure

Industrial societies treat productive labour as a category of activity which can be readily isolated. Where 'work' is a distinct category of input to the factory industrial process, so 'leisure' emerges as a category of output: a commodity to be consumed. Pre-industrial societies tend not to make such a clear-cut distinction between 'work' and 'leisure'. In hunting, for example, the line between sporting competition and group activity of productive significance may be finely drawn. Similarly, music, dance and dramatic arts may be so totally integrated within a ritual setting that they are not viewed as separate categories of activity.

The trend away from regarding culture, recreation and social activity as inseparable elements in community life was accelerated by the Industrial Revolution in Europe. The arts were for the first time sustained by the paying public rather than by aristocratic patronage. Most team sports achieved their current form in the mid-19th century and soccer had become a major spectator sport by 1900. Modern popular music, vaudeville, mass-circulation magazines, and 'package' tourism also have their roots in the massive social changes brought about by industrialization. Technological revolution in mass communications continues the process today.

Where similar changes have occurred in Africa they have often been deprecated by outsiders as representing a lowering of 'traditional' standards and an undesirable opening up of the continent to alien influence. This misunderstanding confuses form and content. Africa and Europe have responded in similar ways to similar processes of social and economic change. Growth of demand for spectator sport and consumer-oriented entertainment is in both cases a direct response to new patterns of leisure time availability and new opportunities for its use created by technological 'modernization'. When 50–100 years ago the Creole communities of Freetown (Sierra Leone) and Lagos (Nigeria) formed choral and dramatic societies to sing Handel and act Shakespeare they were responding to just as 'authentic' a social need as were the founders of the North of England 'oratorio societies' or Welsh valley choirs. Their choice of material showed a shrewd awareness of changed social relations rather than unthinking willingness to 'Europeanize'. In West Africa the present-day vigour of Krio drama★ (including Shakespeare, but now in translation), Yoruba folk opera, the Nigerian church choir repertoire (now influenced by popular music styles) and above all of popular music★ itself testify to the fact that new social and

Top: the Dunia Cinema at Makeni, Sierra Leone with posters for Indian- and Hong Kong-made films on display. Centre: Yoruba men at a party in Nigeria. Bottom: customers in a bar-restaurant in a Kinshasa hotel, Zaire

performance contexts for music and drama called forth by urban living are no longer dependent on 'imported' content but have led to authentic cultural development.

Some of the best material in African art and entertainment today represents a reworking of ideas from 'traditional' sources. 'Traditional' artists themselves are often able to make the transition, e.g. singers like Alhaji Muhamman Shata and Sarkin Taushi in northern Nigeria, by combining roles as praise singers, court musicians and recording studio stars. In other cases both form and content are new to Africa, having arisen in unprecedented settings. Three contexts stand out in this respect: the colonial army, the mission boarding school, and factory or mine employment.

During the colonial period army recruits, secondary school pupils and the labour force in mines and plantations were all young, worked in 'single-sex' institutions, were 'migrants' and found themselves alongside people from different ethnic backgrounds and speaking different languages. Above all they belonged to organizations in which 'leisure' had to fit the requirements of a tightly programmed working week. Team sports and various new forms of 'staged' musical and dramatic entertainments became popular in this context, and were frequently explicitly encouraged by the authorities. Mine managements might elevate talented musicians and entertainers among the workers to a semi-professional status. Bands or soccer teams provided an outlet for the skills of participants, entertainment for the rest of the labour force and prestige for the organization, just as happened, for example, with brass band movement in industrial northern England. Even today many of African's top soccer clubs are associated with business and industrial organizations or government departments, while the influence and significance of army military bands goes far beyond the playing of regimental marches and national anthems on official occasions deep into the world of popular entertainment, with military and police bandsmen regularly playing and recording first-rate dance music.

National, government-funded teams are perhaps the logical outgrowth of this process of sponsorship. Soccer, athletics, and cultural activities have been the most notable beneficiaries in post-colonial Africa. Since the late 1960s a generation of world-class athletes has emerged. Soccer players are beginning to follow suit. The process is much encouraged by investment in improved stadium and theatre facilities and by the organization of events such as the All Africa Games, and African arts festival such as *Festac* (Second World Festival of Black and African Arts and Culture, Nigeria, 1977).

Changes first introduced in the context of army, school, and

Top: a form of the board-game *mancala* (known locally as *ayo*) being played in Nigeria. Centre: the Argungu fishing festival, Nigeria: the floating calabashes are used to store the catch. Bottom: a young Namibian playing a home-made instrument

industrial activity have been sustained and rendered more general by the process of urbanization.* Africa is both the least urbanized and most rapidly urbanizing continent. In areas where towns date back into the pre-colonial period there are well-established differences within 'traditional' art forms corresponding to the urban-rural distinction. Elsewhere rural areas are the respositories of traditional entertainments and the towns focal points for the new. Availability of electricity frequently makes a crucial difference, as does the seasonal pattern of rainfall, which exercises an all-pervading influence on rural life but has little effect on urban activities. The dry season, a period of little work on the farm, is the time when most village entertainments and festivities take place. Leisure in the urban setting is contained within a regular pattern of weekends and public holidays.

Traditional sports and pastimes still survive. Some, for example yam hoeing competitions, are specific to the local environment. Others, such as wrestling, are widespread. Some traditional festivals and competitions, e.g. the Argungu fishing festival in northern Nigeria, have established themselves as tourist attractions.

Board games are common throughout urban and rural Africa. Several versions of draughts (checkers) are played, emphasis generally being placed on speed and quick wittedness. Without doubt, however, Africa's most significant board game is *mancala*, widespread under various names, and with variant rules throughout the continent and the black diaspora in the New World. The basic game is for two players, the board consisting of ranks of cups containing seeds or stones, and each player seeking to capture seeds on his opponent's side of the board. Play consists in picking up the contents of one cup under the player's control and distributing these around the board according to the rules of the game, generally anti-clockwise and one by one. In one version of the rules a player who ends by making a two or three on his opponent's side of the board captures those pieces. Play proceeds until no more pieces can be captured. Board layouts, numbers of pieces and rules vary from area to area. Some elaborately carved boards are works of art. In other cases the game will simply be played with stones and holes scooped in the ground. A good player knows the consequences of any given move over four or five circuits of the board. In this respect the game 'models' the kinds of coordinating decisions needed over the cycle of the agricultural year. The game, a great stimulus to mental arithmetic, ranks with chess and *go* in its intellectual demands.

Of modern sports, football is the most important. There can be few parts of Africa without a village soccer pitch. Table tennis runs soccer a close second in some areas. Cricket and rugby are popular in southern Africa and have small but lively followings in Anglophone East and West Africa. Tennis and swimming are major sporting interests of wealthier urban residents, and squash and golf show signs of following suit. These are all activities readily promoted within the framework of recreation clubs, which are frequently organizations of some social and political importance. In the colonial period sporting clubs were generally considered legitimate associations by even the most repressive regimes. Hence they have sometimes had a role to play in focusing radical political sentiment.

The growing market for leisure reading depends on international purveyors of paperback romance and adventure to a surprising extent. Except in areas with a strong literary tradition in the vernacular, few African authors have aimed at and captured a mass audience, with the possible exceptions of the Nigerian novelist Cyprian Ekwensi* and the novelettes of the Onitsha* Market tradition. Indigenous theatre, however, is a much more firmly established medium of popular entertainment. Touring concert parties combine music, dance, circus displays and magic with sharp social and political satire. Sketches and playlets are integral elements. In some cases the emphasis is on full-length musical plays (e.g. the operas of Hubert Ogunde, Duro Ladipo, Kola Ogunmola). At the other end of the spectrum is the popular music concert, known in Sierra Leone as a 'band-show', differing from a dance only in that the audience begins seated. All these entertainments can take place in any hall or wherever it is possible to rig up a portable generator.

Cinema*, on the other hand is more firmly tied to the urban setting because of the need for electricity. Indian romances, Hong Kong-made 'kung fu' films and Westerns are staple fare. Arabic-speaking and Francophone Africa has produced some quality feature films, notably the work of the Senegalese director, Sembène Ousmane.*

Other 'new' media* include radio, television and tape recording. Radio (rather than newspaper or television) is probably the most influential mass medium in Africa. Few villagers are now out of earshot of a transistor radio. As an entertainment medium the cassette tape recorder runs radio a close second. The machine is cheap, portable and independent of mains electricity. As a result instant music is now available in passenger trucks and taxis, and in the remotest village. (The gramophone is much more urban in its orientation, because of its dependency on mains electricity.) Bootleg cassette copying of hit records is a major 'informal sector' activity. Increased exposure to urban-recorded popular music increases demand. Major recording artists now sell to an international market. The music recording business in major centres, e.g. Lagos, Nairobi, and Kinshasa, continues to grow in importance. As yet television has had restricted impact in most parts of Africa. Improved coverage and some commitment to reaching mass audiences, e.g. government-funded community television halls, suggests that television may yet have the most impact of all on the use of leisure time.   *P.R.*

Zimbabwe's delegation to the UN, led by Prime Minister Robert Mugabe, takes its General Assembly seats for the first time at the 11th Special Session of the General Assembly on 25 August 1980

AFRICA AND THE WORLD

Pan-Africanism since 1958

In response to the widespread process of decolonization of the 1950s and 1960s the pan-African movement has been involved in a number of consequential adjustments, which have helped partly to clarify and partly to complicate still further some of its ambiguities. First, doubts as to whether pan-Africanism comprised only Black Africa, or the continent as a whole, were clarified when in 1958 Kwame Nkrumah* convened two conferences. To the first were invited all the independent African states. Of the eight taking part, only two, Ghana and Liberia, were quite clearly Black African. The others were Morocco, Tunisia, Libya, Egypt, Sudan and Ethiopia. At this conference the leading spokesmen of Black and Arab Africa Nkrumah and Gamel Abdel Nasser,* pledged themselves to joint diplomacy, coordinated economic planning and cultural interchange. A few months later took place an All-African Peoples Conference, which brought together party leaders from virtually the whole continent (including South Africa). These two conferences left no doubt about the continental dimension of the pan-African movement, a fact that was confirmed in 1963 when all the continent's independent states, now numbering 32 (South Africa excluded), established the Organization of African Unity (OAU).*

The use of this strictly geographical criterion for membership, to the exclusion of any extra-African representation, tended, however, to leave in a somewhat peripheral position the American and West Indian blacks, with whom the pan-African movement had origi-

The steering committee of the All African People's Conference at a reception in Accra (Ghana) in 1960

nated. Their continued participation depended henceforth upon alternative pan-African organizations, such as the 1966 and 1977 Festivals of Arts and the 6th Pan-African Congress, held in Dar es Salaam in 1974.

The pan-African movement thus came to be expressed, even at the political level, through differently constituted organizations— different not only in their geographical representation but also in what they represent. Pan-Africanism, as expressed through the OAU is restricted to the African continent and to its governments. The 6th Pan-African Congress, for its part, was conceived as a forum in which the official standpoints of African and Caribbean governments could be matched by the unofficial views of spokesmen from non-governmental bodies such as opposition political parties, trade unions, professional associations and universities. The OAU and the Pan-African Congress are alternative arenas, complementary yet also rivals for the political direction of the pan-African movement.

At the same time as the movement demonstrated its commitment to all-African and not just black solidarity, it continued to debate the relationship with other anti-colonial forces, notably communism and pan-Arabism. Marxist theories of economic exploitation, and the doctrine that Western imperialism is an out-growth of capitalism made for a close ideological bond between pan-Africanism and communism. This affinity, although weakened by the spectacle of Stalinist oppression and the readiness of the European powers to concede to their colonies political independence, has been resuscitated by more recent theories of neo-colonialism.* The governments of the newly independent African states, together with those of Asia, the Caribbean and South America, have proclaimed as an alternative the solidarity of the Third World,* directed against both Western

Left: a session of the 13th Assembly of Heads of State of the Organization of African Unity (Mauritius, 1976). Below: some of the participants at the 5th (Manchester) Pan-African Congress (1945), the founding conference of post-war pan-Africanism

and Soviet domination. This strategy of non-alignment allows each government to establish its own pattern of external relations. Most African states still look to European and North American countries for markets, capital investment, technical and military assistance. A few have preferred to establish a close working relationship with Soviet or other communist countries. It is much disputed, both within and without the pan-African movement, whether lopsided dependencies of this kind are primarily a reflection of great power rivalries or more a concomitant of instability within Africa itself. What is certain is the existence of a functional relationship between the two spheres of conflict. It is difficult for pan-Africanism to attain any internal cohesion in the absence of detente between the great powers, and vice-versa. The possibility, and even the desirability, of disassociating the pan-African movement from class struggles has always been problematical and perhaps never more so than today. It is a periodic source of disagreement within the OAU and was a subject of intense debate in 1974 at the 6th Pan-African Congress. There most of the African and Caribbean governments had to face denunciations from Marxist critics for allegedly perpetuating a neo-colonialist relationship with capitalist interests.

A special relationship between pan-Africanism and pan-Arabism has been founded on the contention that Zionism can be equated with apartheid. Most of the Black African states had initially established close diplomatic relations with Israel and welcomed its highly effective technical assistance, taking the view that Palestine was not an African problem. Attitudes changed in the early 1970s when it was seen that the Arab states had at their disposal a powerful means of influencing the Western powers in their policy towards not only Israel but also South Africa, namely control over the supply and price of oil. By the end of 1973, all the African states had broken off relations with Israel, and the Palestine Liberation Organization had been given observer status at the OAU. In return the Arab states had promised assistance in the liberation of southern Africa. It has proved however a somewhat contentious relationship. The inflated prices not only of oil but also of imported manufactures has caused many African states grave financial difficulties, only partially alleviated by loans and grants from the Arab states. The struggle against Israel also seems to have priority over the struggle against apartheid.

Thus, since 1958, pan-Africanism has become less focused on Black Africa, more ambivalent in relation to communism, and partially absorbed into wider Third World movements. *S.K.P.-B.*

The Organization of African Unity

The decision in May 1963 to establish the Organization of African Unity (OAU) has usually been portrayed as a compromise. The more radical African leaders, notably Kwame Nkrumah,* had persistently advocated a form of union wherein a central government was given all the necessary authority–diplomatic, military, economic and cultural–to complete the decolonization of Africa and to protect Africa from any kind of neo-colonialism.* The more cautious leaders clearly preferred a form of union that left to each member state the final responsibility for acting in unison.

The two conceptions of unity are quite different; insofar as the former entails at least a partial surrender of sovereignty, it was never a practical proposition. This applied even to Nkrumah's own early attempts at inter-state union, the Ghana-Guinea Union of October 1958, and the Ghana-Guinea-Mali Union first announced in December 1960. Although in both cases circumstances favoured close integration–both Guinea and Mali had become isolated from France and the rest of the Francophone countries–neither union, stripped of its rhetoric, was much more than an inter-governmental agreement to consult and to act in unison. Thus when the OAU was eventually established, there was virtually no disagreement about the institutions to be established under the charter. These were the Assembly of Heads of State and Government, the Council of Ministers, the Secretariat, the Council of Mediation, Conciliation and Arbitration, several specialized Ministerial Commissions, and a coordinating Committee for the Liberation of Africa. The Assembly meets for a few days each year, the Council normally twice a year and not quite so briefly. Both these bodies pass formal resolutions, each member-state having an equal vote. In the Assembly the support of a two-thirds majority of member-states is required. In the Council a simple majority of member-states is sufficient. There is, however, no recognized means of enforcing an Assembly or Council resolution. For instance, the December 1965 resolution to sever diplomatic relations with Britain because of its failure to take action over Rhodesia's Unilateral Declaration of Independence* was put into effect by only ten of the member-states. Unity and solidarity, one of the declared purposes of the OAU is therefore conditional on *ad hoc* agreements, freely entered into as and when issues arise. The inability of member-states always to agree certainly falls short of the ideal of unity of the OAU but it is not contrary to the text of the organization's charter. For this reason it is an exaggeration to contend, as some do, that the OAU has failed simply because of a lack of agreement on certain highly contentious issues or because member-states insist on retaining a right of independent action. Nor need any such demonstration of limited authority endanger its continuance as an organization. Indeed it is arguable that this very limitation is the condition of its survival.

This is not to say that there is no presumption in favour of a common line of action. The OAU not only symbolizes that elusive ideal: it can also sometimes inhibit member-states from deviating too far from certain norms enshrined in its charter. For example, all disputes between member-states should be settled peacefully, and certainly without recourse to any outside military assistance, since this leads inevitably to counter-intervention by other outside powers and a renewed division of Africa. Emergency outside assistance has none the less been sometimes invoked, notably by Ethiopia in its dispute with Somalia over the Ogaden,* and by Zaire in dealing with insurrections in its Shaba Province in 1978 sustained from within Angola. The OAU has been obliged to acknowledge that such invitations come within the right of self-defence. It would prefer, however, to find ways of preventing their occurrence and to this end has under consideration proposals to set up some kind of security council and joint defence force capable of keeping intra-African disputes within acceptable limits.

Similarly, there is a strong underlying consensus in favour of limiting contacts with South Africa. These are tolerated, with resignation when they are unavoidable, as in the case of Lesotho, whose territory is entirely surrounded by South Africa, with some indignation when they are voluntary, as in the case of Malawi–or as a temporary exception as with the 1974 negotiations over Rhodesia. There was, on the other hand, strong resistance to attempts by the Ivory Coast in 1971 to secure OAU approval for its policy of dialogue with South Africa. The OAU also imposed in 1976 a ban on recognition of the Transkei* or any other Bantustans that South Africa might establish. To this extent the OAU has proved an effective forum for the reassertion of principles which lie at the very heart of its existence.

The establishment of the Liberation Committee was of considerable potential importance because of the political recognition and military assistance that it could bestow on various nationalist movements. It has, however, been hampered by internal divisions, by the irregularity and inadequacy of members' contributions to its special fund, and by being frequently bypassed. All too often, as in the cases of Angola, Rhodesia and South Africa, rival nationalist movements have resisted the Committee's attempts to amalgamate them into a single force, each relying instead on the unilateral support of particular member-states. In the case of Angola,* the Assembly itself became openly involved but was still unable to make an effective choice, until the intervention of South African troops tipped the balance of OAU support overwhelmingly in favour of the *Movimento Popular de Libertação de Angola*. In an attempt to make the Committee more representative, its permanent membership has been increased from nine to 20, membership of the OAU itself having increased in the meantime from 32 to 49. This is a very large number of states to bring under the umbrella of a single organization. The pan-African ideology provides some cohesion but also some dissension in interpretation. The OAU has however demonstrated its capacity to be a forum of both consensus and disagreement, and therein lies hope for survival despite repeated prophecies of collapse.   *S.K.P.-B.*

The Economic Commission for Africa

The Economic Commission for Africa (ECA), an integral part of the UN Organization, was established in 1958 at a time when much of Africa was still in colonial hands, but it now acts in close partnership with the Organization of African Unity (OAU).* Its staff, appointed and financed by the UN, work under the direction of a Conference of Ministers, on which all the independent African States are represented (except South Africa, which was expelled in 1962). The ECA shares the pan-African ideals of the OAU in that it has championed continental unity in the struggle for economic and political independence. It has put forward far-reaching plans for rapid economic development, especially industrialization, aimed at achieving economies of scale in production and correspondingly large internal markets. Since most of the African states are far too small for the purpose, its planning has been on a supra-national scale. The ECA has, however, been faced with a number of difficulties. First, the huge size of Africa has obliged it to divide the continent into somewhat artificial sub-regions. Moreover, these do not correspond to the areas covered by the various inter-state organizations established by the African states themselves. Secondly, the ECA's plans, for example for integrated transport systems and for the location of basic industries, have often been unrealistic, in that the immediate benefits would have been very unequally distributed among the states concerned. Finally, the ECA is little more than a planning and advisory body. It can neither administer nor finance UN projects. These are the responsibility of other UN agencies, such as the UN Development Programme (UNDP), with which African governments deal directly, without necessarily paying attention to ECA recommendations. In any case, the African states can and do look to alternative sources of financial and technical assistance in drawing up their own national development plans. The ECA, therefore, has to rely upon the quality of its expertise, its powers of persuasion and on training African nationals in the skills of multi-national economic planning, project budgeting, etc. Periodically, in an attempt to establish a more effective rapport with African governments, it has redrawn the boundaries of its sub-regions and adjusted its methods of operation. It now tries to work more closely with existing inter-state organizations, and has based some of its own expert advisors in Multi-national Programming and Operational Centres, located in Niamey (Niger), Yaoundé (Cameroon), Kisenyi (Rwanda) and Lusaka (Zambia). It has also sought to establish closer working relationships with other international organizations in the field, notably by creating within its own Secretariat an ECA/UN Food and Agriculture Organization Division and an ECA/UN Industrial Development Organization Division, and by concluding an agreement with the

Arab Bank for Economic Development in Africa. Its achievements have so far been quite modest and quite out of proportion to the volume of studies it has prepared and the number of conferences it has convened.   *S. K. P.-B.*

Regional groupings: a listing

The following list of inter-governmental regional organizations excludes numerous *ad hoc* authorities of a technical nature, purely bilateral arrangements, organizations designed to attract a continent-wide membership, and organizations with some non-African membership, but includes some groupings that, although defunct, are of historical interest.

Autorité de Développement Integré de la Région du Liptako-Gourma
Founded: 1971. Members: Mali, Niger, Upper Volta. Functions: aims at joint development of the region, especially of its mineral resources. Overlaps functionally with River Niger Basin Commission.

Comité permanent inter-Etats du Lutte contre la Sècheresse du Sahel
Founded: 1973. Members: Chad, Mali, Mauritania, Niger, Senegal, Upper Volta. Cape Verde and Gambia joined 1976. Function: works in cooperation with the UN Sahelian Office (UNSO) to coordinate anti-drought measures in the West African Sahel belt.

Comité permanent Consultatif du Maghreb
Founded: 1964. Members: Algeria, Morocco, Tunisia (Libya withdrew 1970). Observer status: Mauritania. Functions: economic cooperation, limited and frequently suspended. Some functional organizations, e.g. *Centre Maghrebien d'Etudes Industrielles* (1967).

Conference of East and Central African States
Founded: 1967. Members: Burundi, Central African Republic, Chad, Congo, Equatorial Guinea, Ethiopia, Gabon, Kenya, Malawi, Rwanda, Somalia, Sudan, Tanzania, Uganda, Zaire, Zambia. Observer status: Algeria, Egypt, Guinea. Functions: early plans for an economic community were never institutionalized but meetings of heads of state normally take place every other year.

Communauté Economique de l'Afrique de l'Ouest
Founded: 1972–4. Members: Ivory Coast, Mali, Mauritania, Niger, Senegal, Upper Volta. Observer status: Benin, Togo and, since 1978, Guinea. Largely supersedes *Union Douanière et Economique de l'Afrique de l'Ouest* (UDEAO) (1959). Functions: operates a Development Fund and a regional corporation tax. Overlaps functionally with *Conseil de l'Entente* and the Economic Community of West African States.

Conseil de l'Entente
Founded: 1959. Members: Benin, Ivory Coast, Niger, Upper Volta. Togo joined 1966. Functions: facilitates mutual free trade and investment, by internal and external funding. A parallel Livestock and Meat Economic Community started 1970.

Customs Union Agreement
Founded: 1970 (revision of a 1910 agreement). Members: Botswana, Lesotho, South Africa, Swaziland. Function: customs union.

Economic Community of the Great Lakes Countries
Founded: 1976. Members: Burundi, Rwanda, Zaire. Function: convenes conferences of heads of state and councils of ministers to discuss economic matters.

East African Community
Founded: 1976. Superseded the East African High Commission and Central Legislative Assembly (1948–61) and the East African Common Services Organization (1961–7). Terminated by a series of unilateral actions 1977–8. Members: Kenya, Tanzania and Uganda. Functions: consisted of an Authority (the three presidents), a Legislative Assembly, 3 East African Ministers, several specialized Councils, three Tribunals and a Development Bank. Operated a common market, a common currency, and several common services (e.g. posts and telecommunications, railways and harbours, airways, research). Financed by a proportion of customs and excise duties and of income tax. Surviving institutions: East Africa Development Bank and East Africa Shipping Line.

Economic Community of West African States
Founded: 1975. To come into operation by stages over 15 years. Formal institutions established 1976–8. Superseded two preparatory groups, the West African Economic Community (1967) and the West Africa Regional Group (1968). Members: Benin, Cape Verde, Gambia, Ghana, Guinea, Guinea-Bissau, Ivory Coast, Liberia, Mali, Mauritania, Niger, Nigeria, Senegal, Sierra Leone, Togo, Upper Volta. Functions: negotiation of customs and free trade agreements between members; coordination of economic policies.

Lake Chad Basin Commission
Founded: 1964. Members: Cameroon, Chad, Niger and Nigeria. Functions: coordinates development of the Lake Chad waters and thereby agriculture, animal husbandry and fisheries.

Lakes Tanganyika and Kivu Basin Commission
Founded: 1975. Members: Burundi, Rwanda, Tanzania, Zaire, Zambia. Functions: coordinates hydro-meteorological research.

Organisation pour la Mise en Valeur du Fleuve Sénégal
Founded: 1972. Formerly *Organisation des Etats Riverains du Fleuve*

Sénégal (OERS) (1968), which superseded the *Comité inter-Etats des Riverains du Fleuve Sénégal* (1962). Members: Mali, Mauritania, Senegal, (Guinea withdrew). Functions: economic cooperation.

Organisation Commune Africaine et Mauricienne

Founded; Fluctuating membership of Francophone states, originally known as the Brazzaville group (1960). Formerly *Union Africaine et Malgache* (UAM) (1961), became OCAM (1965) after a brief existence as *Union Africaine et Malgache de Coopération Économique* (UAMCE). Redesignated *Organisation Commune Africaine, Malgache et Mauricienne* (OCAMM) when Mauritius joined in 1970 but reverted to OCAM when Madagascar withdrew in 1974. Functions: a variety of functional bodies, each with a variable membership not necessarily coinciding with that of OCAM itself, dealing with e.g. posts and telecommunications, tourism, industrial patents, and development banks. Other organizations, more indirectly associated with OCAM, operate in other fields, e.g. airways (*Air Afrique*) higher education, and culture.

Organisation Commune pour la Coopération Economique de l'Afrique Centrale

Founded: 1969. Members: Burundi, Rwanda, Zaire. Functions: economic cooperation.

River Niger Basin Commission

Founded: 1963. Members: Benin, Cameroon, Guinea, Ivory Coast, Mali, Niger, Nigeria, Upper Volta (Chad withdrew 1979). Functions: control of navigation and flooding.

Trans-African Highway Coordinating Committee

Founded: 1971. Members: Cameroon, Central African Republic, Kenya, Nigeria, Uganda, Zaire. Functions: coordination of planning and construction of a trans-African highway.

Trans-Saharan Highway Committee

Founded: 1977. Formerly *Comité de la Liaison Trans-Saharienne*, 1964. Members: Algeria, Mali, Niger, Nigeria, Tunisia. Functions: coordination of planning and construction of a trans-Saharan highway.

Union Douanière et Economique de l'Afrique Centrale

Founded: 1964. Formely *Union Douanière Equatoriale*, 1959. Members: Cameroon, Central African Republic, Congo, Gabon. Chad withdrew in 1968, but has had observer status since 1975. Functions: common market, coordination of larger-scale investment, central bank, some common services now largely decentralized, compensatory fund.

Union Monétaire Ouest-Africaine

Founded: 1962. Members: Benin, Ivory Coast, Niger, Senegal, Upper Volta (Mali withdrew 1962). Togo joined 1963. Functions: a central bank issues a common currency. A development bank was established in 1973.   *S.K.P.-B.*

Neo-colonialism

The theory of neo-colonialism was developed to explain the peaceful transfer of power to African colonies. One of its earliest and most influential exponents was Kwame Nkrumah,[*] the first president of Ghana. Nkrumah argued that although Britain, France and Belgium had surrendered political authority, they had retained effective power through their continued control of the economies of their former possessions. Indeed, he maintained that neo-colonialism was not only the final, but the most exploitative form of imperialism: 'For those who practise it, it means power without responsibility, and for those who suffer from it, it means exploitation without redress.' Other political economists and historians developed and refined the theory to explain African underdevelopment and the continued dependence of African states on the capitalist West.

While the theory of neo-colonialism remains controversial, and the concept is as often employed in political controversy as in serious political analysis, it is the case that the former colonial powers have remained a dominant external influence wherever there was a peaceful transfer of power. At independence most African states attempted to diversify their economic relationships, but colonial trade and investment patterns – the exchange of one or a very few raw materials for metropolitan manufactured goods – have been slow to change. Even where independence followed a violent struggle, as in

A French shopkeeper in Senegal

Algeria, many of the trade* and other economic relations established during the colonial period have survived decolonization. It is not clear whether, despite the guerrilla insurgency that preceded independence and the close relations with the USSR that developed subsequently, the same pattern will reassert itself in Portuguese relations with Angola, Mozambique, and Guinea-Bissau, but it seems probable, if only because the use of the Portuguese language in all three countries will tend to give Portugal a competitive advantage over other outside powers.

The contrasting styles of British and French colonial administration also had a divisive effect on relations between their former colonies after independence. The ex-British colonies all joined the British Commonwealth in the belief that membership was consistent with pan-African solidarity, policies of economic diversification, non-alignment and their own sovereignty. Nigeria, which originally had a defence treaty with Britain, abrogated it in 1962. By contrast, the ex-French colonies with the exception of Guinea, continued to be closely linked with France by a series of treaties covering cultural, financial and military affairs. The association of these states with the European Economic Community (EEC) under terms negotiated before independence, and the defence treaties that allowed African leaders to call on French military support against their domestic opponents, were widely denounced by Commonwealth African 'radicals' as evidence of neo-colonialism. When the Organization of African Unity (OAU) was established in 1963 this division was so deep that, although the charter bound all members to oppose neo-colonialism, agreement was only reached by avoiding all discussion of the EEC. Reconciliation was eventually achieved after Britain had joined the EEC in 1972. The Lomé Convention (1975), negotiated

under the auspices of the OAU, linked both ex-British and French colonies with the EEC regardless of their economic or political ideologies.

The involvement of external powers in African conflicts (Angola in 1975, Zaire in 1977 and 1978, Ethiopia/Somalia in 1978) reopened the question of Western neo-colonialism in intra-African diplomacy. The French, Belgian and Moroccan intervention in the two Shaba (Zaire) crises of 1977 and 1978, and the creation in 1978 of a Francophone pan-African military force (without reference to the OAU) was justified by France and its African allies by the communist threat to African regimes, and denounced by 'progressive' African regimes as evidence of continued Western imperialism. *J.B.L.M.*

Africa and the USA

The USA has been less deeply involved in Africa than in any other part of the Third World. Indeed, until the majority of African countries became independent in the 1960s, the only significant American involvement was in Liberia, which had been established in 1821 by the American Colonization Society as a home for freed slaves and became an independent republic in 1857 under strong American influence. Lacking deep historical roots or extensive material interests, US policy has tended to waver between romantic enthusiasm and simple neglect. The major positive influences have been the identification of American liberals and Afro-Americans with African anti-colonialism, and a more general public perception of the Soviet challenge to Western interests on the continent.

French troops in action in Chad in 1970 in support of the government of President François Tombalbaye

An American Peace Corps volunteer discusses dressmaking techniques with African girls in Zaire

During the Cold War the preoccupation with Western security led American administrations to temper the encouragement which President Roosevelt had earlier given to North African nationalist leaders to press for independence. The USA needed French cooperation within the North Atlantic Treaty Organization. It was not until 1960, when advances in military technology had rendered the American bases in North Africa dispensable, that this policy changed and President Kennedy lent his support to the African nationalist forces that were pressing for immediate transfer of power from Britain, France and Belgium.

In the early 1960s American anti-colonialism and anti-communism combined in a broad policy of support for the new states of Africa. President Kennedy came out strongly in favour of African non-alignment. Then, by seeking to resolve the Congo crisis (1960–4) through the UN, the USA contained Soviet influence and limited radical African criticisms of American imperialism. Simultaneously, the civil rights movement in the southern USA produced a strong romantic identification with the African campaign against colonialism and apartheid in southern Africa. In 1963 the US administration introduced a unilateral arms embargo against South Africa in response to African pressure in the UN Security Council. But it refused to take similar action against Portugal on the grounds that the USA could not afford to forfeit the Azores military base which was leased from Portugal.

The Congo operation, however, led to a reassessment of US interests in Africa. Against a background of domestic opposition to foreign aid and the gradual relaxation of tensions with the USSR, US involvement in Africa was scaled down. Moreover, while US private investment increased throughout the 1960s in both white-ruled southern Africa and in Black Africa – Nigeria in particular emerging as a major supplier of oil to North America after 1970 – the dominating obsession of the Vietnam war contributed to the policy of official neglect which characterized US Africa policy during most of the Johnson and Nixon presidencies.

The collapse of Portugal's African empire after the 1974 coup in Lisbon found the USA unprepared. The administration had previously concluded that the Portuguese, South Africans, and Rhodesians would continue to rule in southern Africa for the foreseeable future. Without any formal change of policy, the USA had acquiesced in the *status quo*. Indeed, imports of chrome from Rhodesia had been resumed in defiance of UN sanctions in 1971 by an amendment to US sanctions legislation by the US Congress. During the crisis in Angola,* Secretary of State Henry Kissinger attempted to counter Soviet and Cuban support for the *Movimento Popular de Libertação de Angola* by mounting a covert operation in support of the *Frente Nacional de Libertação de Angola* and the *União Nacional de Independência Total de Angola*, and by tacitly encouraging South Africa's direct military intervention. Domestic opposition to foreign

A South African worker in the Coca-Cola factory in Johannesburg

entanglements frustrated these aims; Congress vetoed the funds for the covert operation and the South African force was subsequently withdrawn. Under President Carter the USA attempted, with some success, to repair the damage done to its wider African relations by its perceived alliance with South Africa, for example by supporting a UN mandatory arms embargo. It failed, however, to persuade the USSR to curtail its own African involvements, which the Americans regarded as a threat to detente. The efforts of the USA, in collaboration with its Western allies, to secure a peaceful transfer of power in Namibia* and in Rhodesia had only partially succeeded – with the independence of Zimbabwe* – by 1980.   *J.B.L.M.*

Africa and the USSR

The USSR has no deep historical ties with Africa. The international communist movement was unimportant in the development of African nationalism, and – with a few exceptions – trade and economic relations between the USSR and Africa remain insignificant. African governments have been cautious of entanglements with Soviet power. Between 1975 and 1978, however, there were dramatic changes in Soviet relations with several African states. The Portuguese withdrawal from Angola precipitated a civil war, which was won by the *Movimento Popular de Libertação de Angola* (MPLA) with substantial Soviet and Cuban assistance. Treaties of friendship and cooperation were signed with Angola (1976) and Mozambique (1977). A similar treaty had been signed with Somalia in 1974, which also granted the USSR naval and air reconnaissance facilities in connection with Soviet naval activity in the Indian Ocean. But the Russians were expelled from Somalia and the treaty was abrogated after they had supported the Ethiopian government in resistance to the West Somali Liberation Front. The Somali revolt in the Ogaden province of Ethiopia was eventually crushed in February 1978, after military supplies and a Cuban expeditionary force had been introduced in a major Soviet air support operation. A treaty was signed with Ethiopia in 1978. Whether the decision to provide military support, as distinct from diplomatic backing, to its African allies followed a reassessment of Soviet ideological, economic and strategic interests in Africa remains unclear. Despite a change of emphasis, however, the new policy continues to reflect three traditional Soviet preoccupations.

The first is support for the Organization of African Unity* (OAU) policy of confrontation with white minority governments in southern Africa and for particular liberation movements. Historically, this policy can be traced to 1920, when the Comintern agreed to attack Western capitalism through its colonial rear. Africa was relatively unimportant in this strategy during the colonial period, but support for African liberation has been the cornerstone of Soviet African policy since 1960.

The USSR is also concerned to combat Western influence wherever this can be achieved without alienating African opinion or risking a major confrontation with the USA. Initially, this was done by concentrating Soviet aid and diplomatic effort in a few countries – Guinea, Ghana, Mali, Algeria and Egypt – that were held to have opted for the 'non-capitalist' road. But relations with these countries proved unstable, and the policy was quietly abandoned in the mid-1960s in favour of a pragmatic policy of correct relations with all African regimes. The most spectacular demonstration of the new pragmatism was provided by the civil war in Nigeria* (1967–70). The decision to provide substantial arms assistance to the federal

Angolan-manned Soviet armoured cars parade during celebrations of the MPLA victory against the Portuguese

government was taken only after the USA had declared its neutrality. The more direct intervention in Angola and the Horn similarly involved few risks. In the former case, the USA was constrained from active intervention by domestic opinion; in the latter, the USSR was acting in accordance with the OAU policy on territorial integrity.

The USSR has been concerned finally to contain Chinese influence. From the beginning the Sino-Soviet conflict was projected on to Africa. The two communist powers offered conflicting advice to the *Front de Libération Nationale* during the revolt in Algeria* and to the *Union des Populations du Cameroun* insurgents in Cameroon. They then engaged in diplomatic and ideological competition for African support within various front organizations, particularly the Afro-Asian People's Solidarity Organization. Finally, they supported rival liberation movements in southern Africa. One reason for the decision to ensure the MPLA's victory in Angola was almost certainly to prevent victory passing to the *Frente Nacional de Libertação de Angola* and the *União Nacional de Libertação Total de Angola*: movements supported by China. By 1980 it appeared that the Soviet Union had eclipsed Chinese influence in Africa, at least for the time being. *J.B.L.M.*

Africa and China

Two objectives have dominated the African policy of the People's Republic of China: national security, and the fostering of international socialist revolution. Since the late 1960s the search for security has tended to predominate as Chinese governments have increasingly come to fear what they regard as the imperialist ambitions of the USSR. African leaders have, in general, accepted what

Deputy Prime Minister Mikoyan of the USSR and President Nkrumah of Ghana during Mikoyan's visit to Ghana in 1962

is of advantage to them in relations with China (often while maintaining similar relations with the USSR) without committing themselves in any concrete way to China's fundamental objectives.

China was drawn towards Africa in the mid-1950s indirectly, through its search for security in Asia. A trade and non-aggression pact with India (1954) brought China into the 1955 Bandung★ Conference of non-aligned Afro-Asian states, which was attended by six African delegations. China's conciliatory stance won it friends and links were established, of which the most important, initially, were with Egypt. In 1956 an embassy was established in Cairo, substantial trade was initiated, and Egypt was given financial help during the Suez war. The first substantive rifts with the USSR over revolutionary strategy were apparent from 1957 on, when the Soviet government first expressed a desire for peaceful coexistence with the West. By contrast China urged militancy: for example it gave the *Front de Libération Nationale* in Algeria★ substantial credit for arms when the USSR was urging negotiations with France; and argued that Soviet resources should be used to consolidate the Communist bloc rather than being given as aid to 'bourgeois' regimes. In particular, China opposed Soviet aid (1958) to the Aswan High Dam project, which coincided with Nasser's clampdown on Egyptian communists.

China's attitude to aid in the 1950s was partly a reflection of its own poverty and internal development priorities; *trade* with Africa was expanded wherever possible and, once established, was not interrupted by periods of bad relations. The independence of 17 African states in 1960 (and the impending independence of many others) made it clear to China that it must enter the aid race if it were to assert its position as the leader of the Third World in the face of US and Soviet competition–which was increasingly seen as pernicious. China's large-scale aid ventures were directed at 'radical' states–

Guinea (1960), Ghana (1961), Algeria (1962), Mali (1962)–but there was a wide spread of smaller projects. Its major aid venture, in Tanzania, began as a direct counter to Soviet attempts to block the union of Zanzibar and Tanganyika in 1964, and its major project in Tanzania, the construction (1968–75) of the TanZam (Tazara) railway linking Tanzania with Zambia, was undertaken after both the USSR and Western powers had refused to help.

From the early 1970s onwards, while maintaining extensive trade and aid with 'radical' states, China has increasingly established links that appear incongruous unless seen in the light of anti-Soviet policies. For example, as well as 'balancing' Soviet aid (as in Mauritius in 1972), and replacing it (as in Egypt from 1976), China has established links with unmistakably conservative states such as Zaire (1973), Cameroon (1973), Gabon (1974) and found itself on the same side as South Africa in 1975 in supporting Zaire, the *Frente Nacional de Libertação de Angola*, and the *União Nacional de Independência Total de Angola* against the *Movimento Popular de Libertação de Angola* in Angola.★

R.G.T.

Africa and the Third World

Historically, the links between Africa and the 'Third World' countries in Asia, the Caribbean and Latin America were almost entirely the result of European colonialism. These links were of various kinds. In some cases, where the involvement during the colonial period had been close, the legacy from the past proved more problematic than the rhetoric of Afro-Asian solidarity might suggest. The emergence under colonialism of expatriate trading classes, such as the Lebanese in West Africa and Indians in East Africa, led to friction in the post-independence period–indeed, in Uganda to a mass exodus of Asians–as African governments attempted to advance the economic interests of their own nationals at the expense of more recent immigrants. Pan-Africanism★ also affected African relations with the Third World. Pan-Africanism had originally been conceived as a movement of worldwide solidarity among black people of African descent; with the formation of the Organization of African Unity★ (OAU) in 1963 it became the official ideology of the independent African states, whose leaders were grateful for the support of non-Africans but unwilling to grant them a formal status within the organization.

At the level of inter-governmental relations, however, where African leaders perceived an identity of interest and common problems, solidarity and the pursuit of common objectives has been from the start a central concern of African foreign policies. Since 1955 two such objectives have dominated Third World diplomacy. The first is the common commitment to anti-colonialism and racism; the

Chinese and Tanzanians at work on the construction of the TanZam railway linking Tanzania and Zambia

second to the reform of the international economy as a means of combating Third World poverty and economic underdevelopment. Africa was the last continent to be colonized by the European powers and the last from which they withdrew. Consequently, during the 1950s Africans were the beneficiaries of Asian pressure for decolonization and non-discrimination. Only three sub-Saharan African countries (Ethiopia, Liberia and the Gold Coast–now Ghana) were represented at the Bandung Conference in 1955, which established the Afro-Asian movement as a force in international politics. From the start, however, Egypt played a prominent part in both Afro-Asian and non-aligned diplomacy. Even the question of South African apartheid,* the issue which has dominated African diplomacy at the UN, was first brought before the Organization not by an African state but by India.

The position changed dramatically after 1960, when 17 African states joined the UN and the African group emerged as the largest single voting block. The African group took the lead in pressing for the final elimination of colonialism. Although the Africans continue to have the almost automatic support at the UN of Asian and Arab states on southern African questions (the latter group secured after 1973 by Africa's wholesale diplomatic defection from Israel), with the formation of the OAU and the collapse of the second 'Bandung' Conference in Algiers in 1964, the Afro-Asian movement declined rapidly in importance.

As members of the OAU all African states are also members of the non-aligned movement. At the 1961 Conference in Belgrade, Kwame Nkrumah* attempted unsuccessfully to commit the movement to a militant anti-imperialist policy. By 1963, however, when the OAU Charter was drafted the original conception of the non-aligned movement as a mediatory Third World force between the nuclear superpowers (Article III, 7 of the Charter) was in eclipse. By the early 1970s, when African governments, e.g. Zambia and Tanzania, were actively involved in the revival of the movement, its focus had changed. Non-aligned conferences provided them with an opportunity for rallying Third World support for the liberation struggle in southern Africa and for anti-Western pressure on economic issues. African countries have also been prominent in the UN Commission for Trade and Development (UNCTAD), where, as members of the Group of 77, they have demanded additional aid, preferences for Third World manufactured and semi-manufactured exports, and commodity stabilization and price enhancement schemes.

Until 1975 a dispute between the former French colonies, which favoured special arrangements between themselves and the European Economic Community (EEC) to the exclusion of other developing countries, and the Commonwealth African countries, which had traditionally favoured global arrangements, weakened the effectiveness of the Group of 77's strategy. In part this dispute reflected the fact that Africa contained many of the world's poorest

Poster of President Agosthino Neto and President Fidel Castro of Cuba, and welcoming crowd, during a visit by Castro to Angola

economies, whose vulnerability was increased by the quadrupling of oil prices by the Organization of Petroleum Exporting Countries in 1974. When the African countries finally resolved their differences and joined with others in the Caribbean and Pacific to sign the Lomé Convention with the EEC they included specific measures to assist the poorest countries, an approach which was carried over into the UNCTAD negotiations for a new international economic order. Meanwhile, there was also growing evidence of economic cooperation among Third World states themselves. Since 1974 the Arab states have emerged as major (although selective) aid donors to African countries, while countries such as India and Brazil are increasingly involved with African states in joint ventures and as alternative sources of manufactured imports.   *J.B.L.M.*

The Muslim world

Although the vast majority of black Africans who became resident in the Muslim lands from the Atlantic to the Ganges were hapless victims of slavery, there were others – pilgrims and scholars – who took up residence in Cairo or in the holy cities of Mecca and Medina and, in more than one case, were honoured as teachers or venerated as saints. Moreover, while the brutalities of capture in the African interior were no less for slaves destined for the north and east than they were for those headed for the Americas, and although the 'middle passage' of the Sahara was no less perilous than that of the Atlantic, the lot of the black African slave in Muslim societies and his chances of freedom and equality were significantly better than those of his trans-Atlantic counterpart. Plantation slavery was comparatively rare in the Muslim lands, though the use of slaves as soldiers was commonplace. Concubinage with slave girls was an accepted institution and the offspring of such unions were fully recognized. The mother could not be sold and she was free on her master's death. Only in the implicit condonation of castration of young males does Muslim society stand indicted more severely in matters of slavery than the Christian societies of the Americas, and even this barbarism allowed its victims considerable compensations through, for example, their ability to hold high political office.

The institution of slavery already existed in Arabia at the time of the rise of Islam in the early 7th century. Some of the slaves were black Africans, as was Bilal, the Prophet Muhammad's freedman and the first person to chant the Islamic call to prayer. The Quran took cognizance of the institution, but its injunctions and those contained in the reported sayings of Muhammad were such as to mitigate its effects. The law of Islam (Sharia), which was codified in the early centuries, devotes a good deal of space to the legal rights and disabilities of the slave, and to manumission. The law applied to all slaves irrespective of skin colour or origin, for following the creation of a vast Islamic empire stretching from the Pyrenees to the Indus, slaves were obtained from Europe and Asia as well as Africa.

Islamic law proclaims the basic freedom of man, but it permits the enslavement of a non-Muslim who has refused the summons to Islam and who has been taken captive in a resulting religious war (jihad). Most slaves, except Jews and Christians, became Muslims early on, but this did not affect their status. Those who came from Black Africa, being adherents of various African religions invariably adopted Islam. They were sold to Arab or other Muslim traders by local African rulers along the Sudanic belt of West Africa, along the banks of the Blue and White Nile and along the East African coast from the mouth of the Red Sea to Mozambique. Most of these rulers were themselves Muslims from the 11th century onwards.

The routes along which slaves passed out of Black Africa were

A slave caravan crossing the Sahara: plate from G. F. Lyon, *Travels in North Africa* (1821)

many and various, and differed somewhat according to period. From West Africa they generally passed first into North Africa, though some went straight to Egypt. From Morocco some passed into Europe* during the period of Muslim hegemony in Spain. From Cyrenaica in Libya others passed into Asia Minor and south-eastern Europe during the days of the Ottoman Empire (15th-19th centuries). The Saharan routes were difficult ones and only in the winter months could large caravans set out; even so, many slaves perished, mostly of thirst. The Nile valley was an easier route and it was supplied from the equatorial regions of the Sudan, western areas such as Darfur, Dar Fertit and Dar Runga, and from Ethiopia. Ethiopia and the Horn of Africa also supplied the Red Sea trade, which passed into Egypt, or to Mecca and Medina, whence some slaves would be sent on to Iraq and the Fertile Crescent. Slaves from the East African coast (Zanj) passed either into Persian Gulf ports, or went across the ocean to western India, especially Gujerat. India also imported slaves from Ethiopia, as the name by which they were known – Habshi – indicates.

Once in the country of sale, the slaves were handed over to a broker who sold them either at the public slave market or privately from his own house. New owners were generally given three days to discover and report any defects they had not observed at the time of purchase. Although it is difficult to generalize about an institution that existed over such a wide and varied area and for such a long period it seems probable that most slaves, both male and female, were purchased for domestic use. The men served the master, accompanied him on his outings and assisted him in his business. The women attended the

Slaves and merchants in the slave market in Cairo, Egypt, c. 1850

ladies, cooked and looked after children. Favoured ones become the master's concubines; a position as secure as that of a wife, for if a concubine produced offspring, she could not then be sold (whereas a wife could be unilaterally divorced), her children were free and she herself became free on her master's death. As a result, the majority of urban families, at least in North Africa, Egypt and Arabia, probably have some black African blood. Many rulers had black concubines in their harems and sons of African women did accede to power. Best known among these are the Fatimid ruler of Egypt, al-Mustansir (1036–94) and Mulay Ismail of Morocco (1672–1727). Ibrahim, son of the Abbasid caliph, al-Mahdi, often known as Ibn Shikla, was popularly declared caliph in Baghdad during the reign of his nephew al-Mamun and was acknowledged in this highest office of Islam for two years (817–19) by an important faction. Previously he had been governor first of Damascus, then of Basra, though his enduring fame rests on his reputation as a musician.

Black African males were also widely used as soldiers. Often they distinguished themselves as royal bodyguards, known for their courage and loyalty. They were first used in North Africa by the Aghlabid dynasty in Tunisia from 800 onwards; then by their successors the Fatimids both there and, after 969, in their new power base in Egypt. Farther west in Morocco black slave troops are first known to have been used under the Almoravids* (1056–1147) and their successors, the Almohads* (1130–1269) kept up the practice. In the 12th century black African Muslim volunteers from Ancient Ghana* are reported to have taken part in wars against the Christian kingdoms in Spain. Later, black slaves were used in much larger numbers in Morocco: first during the Sadian dynasty and much more extensively in the Alawid period under Mulay Ismail. Himself the son

of a black mother, Ismail energetically recruited black males and females, regardless of whether they were free or slave. The males underwent several years of technical and military training, at the end of which they were given brides from among the black girls who had been trained in the domestic arts. Their offspring were similarly trained and thus a self-perpetuating military aristocracy was created which continued to hold effective power for 30 years after Ismail's death.

In the east, too, black slaves were used as soldiers. There were some in the caliphal guard in 9th century Baghdad, and rulers in Arabia right down to the 20th century have often maintained black bodyguards. In India Black African soldiers have played the most significant role of all, often rising to important administrative positions and even becoming rulers themselves. In the late 14th century a eunuch called Malik Sarwar was appointed first vizier to the Sultan of Delhi, and then governor of the eastern provinces. On his death his adopted son, another black slave, succeeded him with the title Mubarak Shah and ruled in virtual independence of Delhi. On Mubarak's death in 1402 his brother Ibrahim succeeded and ruled for 38 illustrious years.

In 15th century Deccan and Bengal black Africans played important roles in government and administration. Black Africans were also important in the maritime province of Gujerat. Sultan Bahadur (1526–37) had some 5000 in his service. They were predominant in the Gujerat navy in the 16th-17th centuries both commanding and serving, and they ruled the island principality of Janjira. The most celebrated is probably Malik Anbar, who reached India via the Yemen in 1575 and served in the Deccan, championing resistance to Moghul imperialism. From about 1600 until his death in 1626 he was the real power in the sultanate. He reformed its financial administration and built up an efficient army. His court attracted poets and scholars, and he was famed for his public works and the fine buildings he put up during his years in power.

Several of these black Africans were eunuchs and eunuchs were often entrusted with considerable power. Their masters were assured of their absolute loyalty and were safe from the intrigues other men might foment on behalf of their sons. Not all eunuchs were Africans but from the 17th century black eunuchs became traditional holders of certain offices, and certain African Muslim courts, such as Songhay,* Kano* and Darfur, also began to employ eunuchs. The operation was usually performed on pre-adolescent boys, but was even then frequently fatal. Eunuchs were probably already mutilated before reaching their final destinations, but little is known about the centres where this was done. Ethiopia exported eunuchs and a Christian monastery in Nubia acted as an emasculation centre. The central African state of Baghirmi was also a major exporter of eunuchs in the 18th and 19th centuries. Some of these eunuchs were employed as guardians in the harems of persons of high rank while others were given military commands. The most famous of such eunuchs was the great Kafur. After being tutor to the sons of the first Ikhshidid* ruler of Egypt, he served as regent for first one son, then the other, after their father's death. On the death of the second son in 966 he assumed full power in his own right. At his death in 968 he had been the effective ruler of Egypt for 22 years.

The vast harem of the Ottoman sultan in Istanbul was watched over from the beginning of the 17th century by black eunuchs. The chief of these, the Kizlar Agha, had enormous power, since he had the easiest access of any man to the sultan. He was, as one modern writer has put it, the 'most feared, and consequently the most bribed, official in the whole of the Ottoman Empire'. In Mecca the custodianship of the Mosque of the Kaba, and in Medina that of the Prophet's mosque were traditionally entrusted to black eunuchs. When the Swiss traveller Burckhardt visited Medina in 1829 he found them to be among the most wealthy and respected citizens of that town, living in the best quarters, being addressed as 'Your Excellency' and having their hands kissed when they passed through the bazaar.

Although most black slaves performed domestic or military service they were sometimes used in agriculture or other productive sectors. Black slaves often tended date groves, from Bahrein in the east to the Dra valley in southern Morocco, and worked on sugar plantations in 9th century Persia. In the second half of the 9th century a huge number, mainly from East Africa, was engaged in clearing the saline marshes at the Tigris-Euphrates mouth and preparing the land for agriculture. It was among these that the great 'Zanj' revolt took place in 868–80, for a while threatening the Abbasid caliphate itself. Black slaves were also used in 19th century Egypt to boost cotton production (and also to serve in Khedive Ismail's army). In the Persian Gulf they have traditionally been pearl divers. In Nubia in the medieval period they worked the gold mines, and for centuries they dug salt in the Saharan mines of Teghaza. They have commonly been used as labourers on building sites.

Apart from the labour force the men provided and the progenitive role of the women, black Africans and their descendants have made numerous contributions to Islamic society. Some, such as Kafur, Mulay Ismail or Malik Anbar, played important roles as rulers and were enthusiastic builders of fine monuments and patrons of literature and learning. Kafur, for example, retained al-Mutanabbi, one of the greatest of all Arab poets, at his court. Other black Africans were themselves artists. Antara, a great pre-Islamic poet, al-Jahiz, a gifted essayist, Suhaym, Nusayb and al-Hayqutan, poets of the early period of Islam and Ibn Misjah and Ibn Shikla, great musicians of the 8th century–these, along with lesser figures and, no doubt, many who remain unsung, moulded their own African heritage into the Arab heritage which also became theirs.

Today the black African element in the Muslim populations of North Africa, Egypt, Arabia and the Persian Gulf can still clearly be

The Kizlar Agha (chief eunuch) of the Ottoman harem

seen. In some places black communities remain intact and tightly knit, especially in Morocco, Algeria and in such cities as Mecca and Medina. One isolated community still survives at Ulcinj in southern Yugoslavia, and the blacks in Jerusalem form a distinct group. Some of these groups, especially in North Africa, preserve their African customs, such as the *bori* possession cult of Hausa origin, or in Arabia (and to some extent Egypt) the *zar* possession cult of Ethiopian origin. More generally, however, Islam has proved an integrating social force and descendants of black Africans have found little difficulty in becoming acculturated to their host environment and identifying themselves with their lands of adoption.   *J.O.H.*

Europe

Until the 15th century most of Black Africa's contact with Europe was mediated by North African traders and armies. Some intercourse between cultures south of the Sahara and Europe was always possible by way of North Africa, which was linked through the Mediterranean with Europe. Evidence from both art and literature suggests that black Africans were present in the early Greek and Roman worlds. Significant numbers of black Africans were introduced into Europe by the spread of Muslim armies westward across North Africa and into the Iberian peninsula between the 8th and 15th centuries. By the end of the Middle Ages slavery had extended throughout the western Mediterranean; legal records from Portugal, Spain, France and Italy point to the increasing numbers of black slaves on the European markets in the 14th and 15th centuries–many the products of the Christian-Muslim wars and the longstanding Mediterranean slave trade.

During the decline of the Mediterranean slave trade and before the rise of the trans-Atlantic trade, Europe began receiving slaves directly by sea from the west coast of Africa. Portuguese expeditions down the West African coast in the mid-15th century launched this phase of the slave trade; over the next 150 years some 40–50 000 black African slaves were transported to Europe from western Africa. These migrations had varied effects on European society. No other cities could rival the 10 per cent population of Lisbon or the 3–4000 black slaves in Seville in the 16th century. Slavery of this volume was not a threat to the peasant economies of early modern Europe, although black slaves cultivated vineyards and sugar cane in Cyprus, Crete and Sicily in the late medieval era and, later, in the 15th and 16th centuries, in Mediterranean Spain and southern Portugal. A considerable number also worked the silver mines of Guadalcanal, Spain. Most frequently, however black slaves were urban based in southern Europe. In Renaissance Italy, for example, they were servants in wealthy urban households or novelties at courts, where they might be attired in oriental garb, a fashion that invaded France and England in the 17th and 18th centuries. Generally, they served in a variety of household and urban capacities, as attendants, porters, construction workers, tradesmen and the like. Some were even used as business agents and traders by their owners, or hired out to other employers. Exclusion from guilds did not prevent them from often learning and practising crafts.

Many free blacks coexisted with their enslaved brethren in early modern Europe and usually owed their manumission to faithful service or their own purchase of freedom. They tended to remain in the employ of their former masters or otherwise were limited to the most menial and unskilled jobs and to residence in lower class quarters of town. While baptism and participation in religious functions was not uncommon, this group faced discriminatory legislation and practices which, in Spain and Portugal in particular, associated blacks with Jews and Moors. That some group solidarity existed among the blacks is shown by their fraternal associations, which were located in such cities as Lisbon, Barcelona, Valencia and Seville in the 15th and 16th centuries. These orders welcomed slaves having their master's permission to join, and with minimal dues were able to assure their membership of Christian burials and provide the indigent with food and medicine. Some other blacks outside the orbit of slavery had a more provisional stay in Europe, venturing there with embassies from Ethiopia and West Africa, as travellers or students sponsored by European courts, religious groups or commercial agents, and as sailors and traders in the coastal cities.

From the later 16th century onwards the increasing demand for slaves in the Americas meant higher prices and a consequent reduction in the number of slaves sold to southern Europe. Slavery in Iberia declined as many blacks and their descendants were assimilated into the larger population, often through miscegenation. Superseding Portugal, the Netherlands, and Spain in overseas predominance, England and France took part in the Atlantic slave trade and developed slave labour systems in their lucrative American and West Indian colonies. This led to an influx of blacks into West European ports in the 17th and 18th centuries. A few of these immigrants were seamen and visitors arriving from Africa on missions similar to those in Iberia, and others were slaves imported directly from Africa mainly as domestic servants. However, most of the blacks who entered Europe during this period were servants from the colonies attending their masters. Planters took along their retinues of slaves for the social distinction this display afforded and for the benefit of a cheap labour supply. Many of the slaves remained in Europe, eventually gaining their freedom, and became a noticeable minority in European capitals and seaports. Dutch planters and commercial agents in the West Indies, apparently more frequently than their English and French counterparts, sent their mulatto offspring and some black slaves to the metropolis for vocational training or general education.

There were never more than 1–2000 black people in France at any one time during the 17th and 18th centuries, yet blacks and people of colour were perceived by the authorities as a growing menace to France. A royal declaration of 1777 complained that miscegenation was contributing to mixed colours and altered blood, and the following year inter-racial marriages were banned. In England Queen Elizabeth I had also been disturbed by the increase of blacks and in 1601 had issued orders to have 'Negroes and blackamoors' deported. But the real growth in the black population of England followed Elizabeth's reign, and by 1772 their numbers were estimated at 14–15 000, a figure that included slaves, runaways and free blacks. In the mid-1780s they were joined by black Loyalists who had sided with England in the American War of Independence as soldiers, sailors or labourers. Many blacks, unable to find work as domestic servants or wage-earners, became derelicts or else sought a marginal livelihood as crossing sweeps, entertainers, beggars and the like. A scheme to repatriate blacks to Sierra Leone★ in 1787 enjoyed little success, and the problem of England's 'black poor' continued into the next century.

During the 18th century various religious groups and Enlightenment theorists were finding slavery inconsistent with a commitment to natural rights and human equality. Knowledge of conditions on slave ships and on the plantations stirred people's consciences – along with the easily-observed hardships of blacks in Europe. With the decision by a court in 1772 that slaves could no long be compelled to depart England, the continuence of slavery in England fell into question and numerous slaves were in fact freed before full abolition in 1834. In France adherence to the revolutionary principles of 1789 and the example of a black uprising in the French colony of Saint-Domingue★ set the stage for emancipation decrees between 1794 and 1836. Even before the 18th century, all black slaves reaching the Netherlands were legally free; black slavery was abolished in Portugal in 1761–73; and Spain forbade the importation of slaves from its colonies in 1836.

Having attained freedom, blacks in Europe – some 20 000 strong in the early 1800s – became less of a separate group, and in time merged with the Europeans. By mid-century they were no longer the beneficiaries of anti-slavery sympathies, nor could they count on the assistance of traditional patrons. With the reduction in slave importations preceding abolition, little immigration occurred beyond the perennial trickle of black sailors in European navies and merchant marines, students from Africa and the West Indies, and visitors from these areas and the USA. Several hundred West Africans from European colonial and trading enclaves journeyed to the metropolises to study, favouring disciplines related to government, administration, law, medicine and missionary activity. This effort to create a Westernized African elite capable of identifying with European interests became less popular after the 1880s, when Europeans directly colonized the African continent; nevertheless, such movements of Africans to Europe continued into the 20th century.

Direct involvement in Africa through the establishment of imperial control facilitated black migrations to Europe even larger than those resulting from the enterprise of slavery in previous centuries. French colonies in Black Africa furnished nearly 200 000 soldiers for action on European battlefields in the First World War,★ and thousands came from French and English West Indian colonies. Other blacks from the colonies were incorporated into the civilian

The Servant (1618) by Diego Silva Velazquez

A Caribbean carnival procession in Notting Hill, London

African street-sweepers in Paris

labour force to alleviate manpower deficiencies in war industries. Following the war, black contingents participated in the occupation of Germany, an episode that ignited German and international charges of a 'black horror on the Rhine' until they were withdrawn in 1920. Smaller levies of black troops were enlisted in the Second World War,* but they saw limited action in Europe due to the early capitulation of Western Europe.

In both post-war periods Europe was receptive to West Indian and African labour because of enormous war losses. Numerous black veterans and demobilized labourers who remained in Europe after the wars, or their compatriots who later migrated there, found openings in public and maritime services, industry and clerical work. African and West Indian students continued to flock to the metropolises. Many of them were now politically oriented by the colonial experience and eager to lobby for black interests through the pan-African movements active in Europe.

As part of the gradual process of decolonization England, France and the Netherlands offered their present and former colonies the benefits of liberal immigration policies. With the promise of mutual economic advantage, unprecedented numbers of West Indians and Africans gravitated to Europe after the Second World War. Only rough net estimates of this phenomenon are possible, for many of these people later returned to their homelands and others have been clandestine immigrants. Also, domestic economic problems and social tensions have since caused Britain (1962 & 1971) and France (1974) to control the rate of black immigration to Europe. There are perhaps 70 000 black Africans currently in Britain, and blacks predominate among the approximately 600 000 West Indian residents. France has around 80 000 black Africans and an undetermined number from its racially-mixed overseas departments in the Caribbean, while the Netherlands hosts some 175 000 migrants from Surinam and the Dutch Antilles, most of whom are black. Many of these post-war immigrants have suffered from the encounter with urban, industrial society, and they have had difficulty getting skilled jobs, adequate housing, education and health services; yet others have benefited from the continuity of migration and assimilation, accelerated since the First World War, and have established themselves in European society.

W. H. A.

The Caribbean and Guyanas

The Caribbean islands were claimed for Spain by Columbus between 1494 and 1502, and the Spanish imported some African slaves to work gold from 1518 onwards. However, it was the 17th century conquest of the islands by England, France and the Netherlands, and their introduction of large-scale sugar growing that transformed territories like Barbados (English) and Saint-Domingue (French) from colonies of settlement to plantation colonies where a European minority supervised an African slave majority in the production of tropical agricultural commodities for the European market. Totally dependent on external sources for management, capital, labour, consumer goods and some staple foods, Caribbean and Guyanese plantation colonies were fragile, artificial creations at the mercy of external economic forces. Thus from the beginning they contained the seeds of their present social, economic and political schizophrenia.

The West Indies and the Guyanas received at least half of all Africans transported to the New World, and Africans rapidly and

Toussaint L'Ouverture, leader of the Saint-Domingue slave revolt

overwhelmingly outnumbered Europeans in most colonies. The tide of slaves flowing from Africa to the Caribbean was stemmed somewhat by the successful war of liberation waged against the French by an uneasy coalition of slaves and free people of colour in Saint-Domingue between 1791 and 1804. Similar efforts in France's other island colonies of Guadeloupe and Martinique met with only temporary success, and under Napoleon slavery was reinstituted there. The gradual nature of British-instituted abolition of the international slave trade, beginning in 1808, meant that Africans continued to enter many territories in the Caribbean and the Americas during much of the 19th century. The Cuban and Puerto Rican sugar economies, for example, expanded in the 19th century, and their slave trades were officially sanctioned by Spain until the 1860s. Meanwhile, although officially forswearing slavery in 1833 and 1848 respectively, Britain and France continued to exploit African labour by 'liberating' Africans from the Brazilian and Cuban slave trade and forcing them to migrate to the West Indies and Guyanas as indentured labourers.

Planters in all sectors of the Caribbean and Guyanas sought to expand or salvage the plantation system by substituting foreign labourers for slave labour, procuring them from Europe's empires in India, China and Indonesia, and, for Cuba, from Mexico. Attempts to attract new European settlers resulted in Europeans outnumbering Africans in Cuba (60 per cent European) and Puerto Rico (51 per cent European). So complex did migration within the New World become that the British West Indies actively recruited black North American workers, while other North American blacks made efforts to establish autonomous settlements in Haiti. Although in some territories, like Guyana, Trinidad and Surinam, numerous Asians remained as permanent residents, sometimes outnumbering the African population, in a 300-year period the African diaspora had already established an African social, cultural, economic and ultimately a political presence with which all Caribbean and Guyanese societies had to reckon.

Two major themes of the African diaspora emerged during slavery – the African majority's maintenance of internal autonomy informed by African values; and a minority's entry into the European orbit, usually through sexual alliances, adoption of European culture, and assumption of many intermediate positions in the European system, thus becoming, wittingly or unwittingly, agents of European control.

In coming to grips with their enslavement Africans tended at first to organize according to the norms of the broad culture areas from which they originated. Slave traders contributed to this development by concentrating their trade on specific parts of Africa, and slave owners reinforced this trend by showing preferences for slaves of specific ethnic groups. National and cultural associations provided displaced Africans with familiar models of internal social control, and where different nationalities were numerous enough they tended to associate in order to confront enslavement. In the process new units and even new languages were created, which, although based on familiar cultural principles, were not carbon copies of those in the homelands. The divisiveness of ethnic diversity thus gave way to the development of pan-ethnic links. It is not surprising that the modern ideology of pan-Africanism★ is in large part a product of the African diaspora in the New World, for it was through dispersal across the Atlantic and encounter in the Caribbean and the Americas that Africans became aware of a common continental origin, common values and a common oppression that demanded solidarity for survival and liberation.

Community-building and internal social control under the aegis of religious institutions of African origin, such as Vodun, Santeria and Myalism, were the most important aspects of the slaves' attack on slavery. Recent research suggests that Africans in the Caribbean and the Guyanas strove to reinstitute descent groups, and some succeeded in establishing nuclear families despite slaveowners' disregard for the ties of kinship. The inability of most planters to provide sufficient food for their slaves led to their encouragement of food crop cultivation and stock raising by slaves, and through distribution and sale of surpluses slaves developed internal marketing systems. All of these activities preserved African principles of cooperation. Slaves formed working combines at planting and harvest time and duplicated the communal financial savings institutions characteristic of a variety of African societies. Without these experiences slaves would not have developed the solidarity and social control necessary to confront the slave system.

Slaves challenged the system both indirectly and directly: indirectly through destruction of tools, work animals, cane-fields and other kinds of property, and through working slowly, malingering and work strikes; directly, through frequent armed revolts. Marronage–permanent withdrawal from the slave society–was often linked to armed revolt, but for a variety of geographical, demographic and strategic reasons was not always feasible. It took sizeable, unevenly or sparsely-populated territories with defensible jungle or mountain strongholds–like Jamaica, Saint-Domingue and the Guyanas–to harbour successful Maroon communities capable of forcing Europeans to recognize their independence. These forms of resistance are clear indices of the unacceptability of bondage, the will to confront slaveowners' military controls, the ability to organize large numbers of men and women for the struggle, and a clear vision of an alternative society.

Caribbean and Guyanese societies cannot be understood without reference to colour distinctions, because the superficial distinction of skin colour became a useful device for maintaining Europe's economic, social and political control. The dominant European group would undoubtedly have preferred a simple, two-tier caste system in which a closed, non-slave European group dominated a permanently enslaved African group. Sexual exploitation of African women accompanied economic exploitation, however, and a third, intermediate caste developed, composed of people of mixed ancestry. This group found manumission easier to achieve and lived primarily in urban areas. Denied most of the rights of Europeans, free people of colour remained dependent on Europeans for better material conditions and access to trades and service occupations. As the numbers of free coloureds grew, European colonial authorities sought alliances with them as a means of controlling slaves, freed people and even dissident European planter legislatures.

The illusion developed among coloured peoples that real power

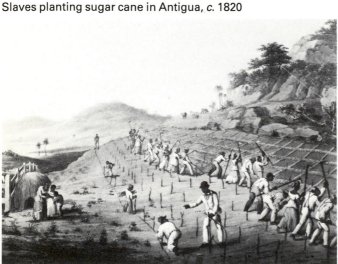

Slaves planting sugar cane in Antigua, c. 1820

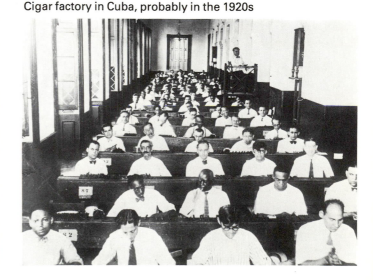

Cigar factory in Cuba, probably in the 1920s

could be achieved through partnership with some segments of the European population at the price of denying the culture and values of the black majority. As a result a wide void developed between brown and black peoples, a void that extended into the 20th century and that only those willing and able to assimilate European culture could cross. Brown- and light-skinned people did not hesitate to manipulate the darker lower classes for their own ends, as the Haitian and Jamaican cases demonstrate. At the time of the Saint-Domingue revolution, coloureds alternately allied with and fought against slave revolts as their own interests dictated, and in 19th-century Jamaica demagogic coloured politicians appealed to disenfranchised black peasants and workers to further their own economic and political interests.

In most of the Caribbean emancipation was followed by the failure of an already-declining sugar industry. Although the freed slaves developed a more diverse economy through new cash crops and, in Guyana, gold mining and lumbering, relatively few of them benefited from these developments in the long run. The white sector's continued concentration on plantation production limited the access of non-whites to land and marketing facilities for cash crops, and a regional diaspora occurred as some West Indians migrated to relatively higher wage markets in Cuba and Central America. Even in Cuba, however, cyclical sugar prosperity benefited only a few elite families and foreign capitalists, for while Cuba's per capita income was among the highest in the Caribbean, living conditions were among the worst, and black people tended to suffer the most.

In the 19th century, also, a variety of motives led some people back to Africa. Africa-born ex-slaves, soldiers and liberated Africans (Africans freed from slave ships) gravitated to a remembered homeland. Many others found opportunities in Africa in connection with European penetration of the continent – railroad building in Central Africa, Christian missions in West Africa, and European colonial administrations. In addition, West Indians played important roles in the settlement of Liberia.

West Indians continued to migrate overseas in the 20th century, mostly to North America and Europe, because of limited educational and employment opportunities at home. This development proved significant, because Caribbean and Guyanese students, professionals and workers overseas had an opportunity to mix and exchange ideas with each other, with African students and black North Americans. One result of the cross-fertilization of ideas was the pan-African movement, whose leaders before the Second World War were primarily West Indian and North American – men like H. Sylvester Williams and George Padmore of the West Indies, and W.E.B. Du Bois of the USA. While such men concentrated on calling conferences, passing resolutions and lobbying imperial governments in the name of anti-imperialism, Marcus Garvey*, a Jamaican, organized the Universal Negro Improvement Association. A grass-

Marcus Garvey (1887–1940), pan-Africanist leader, founder of the Universal Negro Improvement Association

roots international organization that stressed the African heritage, rejected European values and called for a return of blacks to Africa, Garvey's movement captured the imagination and support of people in the Caribbean, Guyanas, Central and North America as well as Africa, a considerable achievement in view of the opposition of the imperial powers.

Out of such movements and the labour unrest caused by the interwar economic crisis came unionization of workers, development of political movements, demands for adult suffrage and in some places, independence. As the 20th century histories of Cuba, Puerto Rico, Haiti and the Dominican Republic show, however, independence from Europe proves meaningless when the USA pursues a policy of economic penetration and military intervention. Although many of them have been formally independent since the 1960s, the Caribbean islands and the Guyanas remain dependent on the outside world. Only one, Trinidad, has a commodity, petroleum, that the industrial world desperately needs. Cuba, having removed itself from the orbit of the USA to that of the USSR, has nevertheless shown

The Cuban poet
Nicolás Guillén

that with determination and a cooperative patron state a Caribbean country can improve living conditions for most of its people; for that reason it has become a model of change for some of its neighbours.

The development of national consciousness and the desire for independence heightened the awareness of African origins and links and, for many, to emphasize these has been to declare cultural, and sometimes political, independence from the USA and Europe. C.L.R. James and Eric Williams analysed the slave trade and slavery to better understand and attack European imperialism. Aimé Césaire of Martinique and Léon Damas of French Guyana professed a pride in African civilization and sensibility which contributed to the concept of *négritude*★ – an assertion of a special African cultural mission to the world. Artists in all media in the 20th century have found African and Afro-West Indian themes a rich source of expression. National ballet repertoires incorporate their societies' heritage of African musical, oral and religious traditions. Haitian and Jamaican painters command a sizeable local and international following. The poetry of Cuba's Nicolás Guillén, Haiti's Jacques Roumain, Puerto Rico's Luis Palés Matos, St Lucia's Derek Walcott, Barbados' Edward K. Brathwaite, and novels of Jamaica's John Hearne, Haiti's Jacques Stéphen Alexis, Barbados' George Lamming, and Guyana's Edgar Mittleholzer display high literary standards. Coexisting with this more self-conscious cultural flowering is its wellspring – the energetic, still functioning popular culture of the working classes with its flamboyant and satirical masquerades, religious poetry and music. These, the vigorous growth of over 300 years of the African presence in the Caribbean and the Guyanas, are the key to understanding the African diaspora in the Caribbean. *M. E. S.*

Latin America

Within a century of the European arrival in the Americas at the end of the 15th century, Amerindian populations had been drastically reduced: in some areas, such as the Caribbean islands and coastal Brazil, Colombia and Venezuela, they were almost completely eliminated. As the Indian population dwindled, the colonists looked towards Africa as a source of impressed labour for their plantations, mines and workshops. For centuries the slave trade★ from Africa had provided Spain★ and Portugal★ with small but regular supplies of slaves, marketed originally by Arab★ traders and later by the Portuguese. Free and slave black people participated in the earliest Spanish expeditions to the Americas, including Columbus's voyages of discovery. Cortés's conquest of Mexico and Pizarro's conquest of Peru. Black people had also been profitably used as slave labour in the plantations of Madeira, the Cape Verde Islands and the Azores, and this particular use set a precedent for their importation to the New World.

The precise number of Africans shipped to the Spanish and Portuguese colonies between 1500 and 1850 will never be known. Realistic estimates range from 4 to 9 million, the majority of whom went to Brazil. Slaves from almost every part of sub-Saharan Africa were included in the trade. West Africans predominated in Mexico, northern South America, and the north-eastern region of Brazil. The Bantu-speaking peoples of the Congo and Angola were more numerous to the south and formed the largest ethnic group among Africans resident in Uruguay, Argentina and Chile. Slaves from Mozambique were less numerous and were concentrated primarily in

An 18th century artist's vision of Latin American race relations – black man and white woman beget mulatto offspring

southern South America. This distribution was due to the demands of the trade, which required that Africans spend as short a time as possible on the slave ships so as to increase the chances of their arriving at their destinations in an acceptable state of health. Trade routes therefore followed the prevailing winds, so that ships from Angola and the Congo headed directly west towards Rio de Janeiro, Montevideo and Buenos Aires, while slavers departing from west African ports sailed towards the Caribbean or towards Salvador (Bahia), the port of north-eastern Brazil.

Once arrived, the Africans were rapidly absorbed into an economy and society that desperately required their labour. That labour could take any one of a wide variety of forms. The majority of slaves brought to the Americas worked on plantations producing sugar and other tropical products for export. In Latin America, however, such labour was confined to the Caribbean basin and the coastal regions of Brazil, Ecuador and Peru. Elsewhere on the continent slaves worked at a multitude of jobs, performing the work that white people were either too few, too proud, or too lazy to do. Domestic servants cleaned, cooked, mended and kept house throughout the continent. Slaves mined for gold in Brazil and Colombia, and for silver in Mexico. They rode as cowboys in Argentina and Venezuela and worked as street vendors in cities from Mexico to Chile. Afro-Latin Americans – used here to refer to all those of African descent, whether 'pure' Africans or those of mixed racial ancestry – particularly excelled as skilled workers. Had it not been for the slave and free Afro-Latin American artisans, many, if not most, colonial Latin Americans would have gone unshod, unclothed and unhoused.

In the course of performing this labour many slaves were able to win their freedom and pass that precious inheritance on to their children. The majority purchased freedom with income earned by doing extra work for their masters or others needing their services; a minority were granted liberty outright by grateful or conscience-stricken owners. Large numbers sought the illegal freedom that could be obtained, even if only temporarily, by fleeing from their masters. It has been estimated, for instance, that by 1810 one-third of Venezuela's nominally slave population was in fact at liberty in the forests and savannas of the colony, having eluded pursuit by the authorities. Slaves who fled to remote and inaccessible regions were occasionally successful in establishing independent 'republics', the most persistent of which were located in Brazil, Colombia, Ecuador, Honduras and Venezuela. These settlements frequently included Indian peoples as well. As a symbol of African-Indian alliance against and resistance to European rule, the fugitive communities were a constant source of concern to the colonial administrators.

The number of slaves who acquired freedom varied greatly over time and from region to region, but it is clear that slaves in Spanish America and Brazil stood a significantly better chance of winning freedom than did slaves in the USA★ and the non-Spanish Caribbean★

colonies. In the early 19th century free people formed 11 per cent or less of the Afro-American population in the southern USA; they accounted for 50 per cent of the Afro-Latin American population of Peru, 75 per cent in the Caracas province of Venezuela, and 30 per cent in the Argentinian province of Buenos Aires. By 1850 approximately half of the Afro-Brazilian population was free.

But even those who acquired the status of free men and women could never expect to enjoy the same sort of freedom that was the birthright of any white person. Spanish and Portuguese law organized the New World societies into a clearly defined racial hierarchy, known in the Spanish colonies as the *Régimen de castas* (caste regime), in which free Afro-Latin American people were systematically deprived of rights automatically granted to their white compatriots. They were – to list only a few of a multitude of restrictions – barred from entering the clergy, becoming military officers or administrative officials, matriculating in the continent's universities, marrying white people, bearing weapons, and wearing certain types of clothing. Though some of this legislation was honoured more in the breach than in the observance, it was a recurring source of irritation and humiliation to those Afro-Latin American people who were supposedly 'free'.

The independence struggles of 1810–25 aroused considerable hope among Afro-Latin Americans for improvement in their legal, economic and social condition. The Spanish American revolutionaries actively sought Afro-Latin American support for their cause by promising an end to slavery and racial discrimination; royalists countered with similar promises. Consequently, thousands of Afro-Latin Americans, free and slave, fought valiantly on both sides of the conflict. Many of the revolutionary governments did in fact pass legislation and/or constitutional articles explicitly guaran-

A carnival in Rio de Janeiro, Brazil

teeing the equality of all citizens, but racially discriminatory laws and informal usages nevertheless continued until late in the century. Only in Central America, Chile, and Mexico was slavery abolished outright at the conclusion of the revolution; most Spanish American countries enacted programmes of gradual emancipation and waited until the 1850s and 1860s before eliminating slavery completely. The dependence of Brazil's plantation economy on slave labour was so deeply rooted that slavery was not abolished there until 1888.

Post-emancipation conditions did not prove kind to Afro-Latin Americans. Legal freedom made little difference to the lives of those who remained tied to the same forms of labour they had performed as slaves. The economically stagnant plantation areas offered little opportunity for economic and social advancement, and in the more rapidly developing areas, such as Argentina, southern Brazil and Uruguay, the former slaves found it difficult to compete on equal terms with the European immigrants who poured into those countries during the second half of the 19th century. The barriers between elites and non-elites, always difficult to cross in Latin American societies, proved virtually impermeable to Afro-Latin Americans. While a few were able to capitalize on boom conditions in parts of southern South America to acquire middle-class status, the great majority remained sunk in a poverty that was the direct inheritance of the colonial slave and caste regimes.

Further militating against the improvement of their conditions were the pseudo-scientific theories of race developed by European and North American thinkers during the late 19th century, and enthusiastically adopted by Latin American intellectuals. These ideologues urged their governments to promote European immigration in order to neutralize the supposedly retrograde genetic and cultural influence of the Afro-Latin American and Indian populations on the Latin American societies. Several nations adopted laws prohibiting black immigration; these were subsequently repealed in Mexico, Panama, Paraguay and Venezuela but still remain in effect in Chile and most of the Central American countries.

Such thinkers conveniently ignored the indispensable economic roles played by people of African ancestry in the development of the continent. They also deliberately overlooked the extent to which Latin American culture had been irrevocably shaped by the African presence. The music and dances of many Latin American countries, including the Brazilian samba, the Central American *cumbia* and the Argentine tango, are either directly derived from or strongly influenced by rhythms and steps imported from Africa. African religious practices not only altered the Christianity brought to the New World by the Europeans, but also went on to spawn completely new syncretic religions such as the Brazilian *candomblé* and *macumba*. In the area of literature, Afro-Latin American writers such as Machado de Assis, Abdias do Nascimento and Nicomedes Santa Cruz are counted among the region's finest.

Over the course of time recognizably Afro-Latin American populations have become concentrated in Brazil, coastal Colombia, Ecuador and Venezuela, and on the Caribbean coast of Central America. In southern South America – because of the early termination of the slave trade (relative, for instance, to that to Brazil or Cuba), the migration of millions of Europeans to the region between 1870 and 1914, and long-term mixing among the races – black African characteristics have largely been absorbed into the general genetic mix. Race mixture has gone on in Latin America ever since the first encounters between Africans, Europeans and Indians, and the process is now well advanced. Lines between the races are not easy to draw, nor do Latin Americans profess much interest in drawing them. Race is conceived of in these countries as a continuous spectrum rather than as a series of racial divisions, and the result is a system of racial classification and implied ranking considerably more complex than the North American dichotomy of 'black' and 'white'. While Latin Americans recognize the existence of blacks, browns, whites, and any and all combinations thereof, they tend to assign a racial label to a person as much on the basis of his economic and social status as on that of his physical appearance. Nevertheless, throughout Latin America dark skin colour tends to be strongly correlated with low social status.

Despite the fairly obvious racial inequities present in Latin American societies, the absence of the overt forms of racial discrimination historically practised in the USA has persuaded many observers that the Latin American countries do not suffer from the racism that has so long afflicted the USA. Afro-Latin Americans tend to concur, at least outwardly, and have displayed little or no interest

Market booths in Bahia, Brazil with inscriptions – one in Portuguese and the other (left) in Yoruba, a Nigerian language still widely used in Brazil in the context of religious cults

in applying the examples of the North American civil rights and black power movements to their own situation. Such racially-defined movements as the Brazilian Negro Front and the Autochthonous Negro Party (Uruguay), which arose during the 1930s, failed to generate mass support among the Afro-Latin American population, even though during the same period Marcus Garvey★ was attracting a wide following among English-speaking West Indians resident in Central America. It appears that young Afro-Brazilians are becoming increasingly sensitive to the subtle forms of racial exclusion prevalent in their country, but so far no concerted action along the lines suggested by the North American experience has been taken to combat that social ill. *G.R.A.*

North America

The USA

The first Africans arrived in the English colonies in North America during the 17th century. By that time African labour had already become established in Latin America★ and the Caribbean.★ At the end of the century, with the French and the English firmly established along the Atlantic seaboard, the slave trade to North America began in earnest. Nevertheless, North America received a small proportion of the Africans brought to the New World. During the 18th century, when slavery was a dominant form of labour, North America imported about 500 000 Africans – less than 5 per cent of the entire trans-Atlantic trade. Yet by 1865, when slavery was abolished, this population base had grown to approximately 4.5 million. This represented only 7 per cent of the US population, but was more than 40 per cent of all black Americans throughout the Americas. One of the most striking features of the black American demographic experience in the USA, then, was that the slave population – uniquely in the Americas – expanded by natural increase. The reasons for this enormous expansion are complex. Some of the causes may be found in the conditions of agriculture as well as the diet, disease environment and family organization of the slaves.

Until abolition, the black American population was concentrated in the states along the Atlantic and Gulf seaboards from Delaware to Texas. Tobacco, rice, cotton and sugar demanded the concentration of labour that the free population believed could only be supplied by African slaves. In the critical years before the Civil War both the population and the economy of the slave states were undergoing a severe crisis. In the North, humanitarian feeling had coincided with the growing unprofitability of slave-manned agriculture and enslaved blacks were in a small minority: in the border states of Delaware and Maryland free black Americans outnumbered the enslaved in 1860. In the lower South and Southwest, however, the

labour demands of cotton farming had attracted a large number of slaves – most bought from the tobacco-growing states – who far outnumbered the free black American population. In Mississippi, indeed, freedom was denied to anyone of black American descent. Elsewhere in the USA the number of slaves had diminished, although slavery was still an important issue in Missouri, and of growing concern to those northern states that had legally abolished slavery themselves and wished for universal abolition.

By 1860 black Americans could encounter three socio-legal conditions in the USA. The 15 northern states permitted free black Americans. The 16 southern states supported slavery, but those of the more southern, staple-producing states had a far greater interest in upholding slavery than the so-called 'border states', where wage labour challenged slavery and sharpened the concern over its future. This situation contributed to the political crises of the 1840s and 1850s over the admission of new states and whether they were to be 'slave' or 'free', which eventually led to the Civil War of 1861–5.

Slavery was the basis of white economic and political power in the South, and the white population there found it necessary to construct a series of rules and regulations, the Black Codes, which, while varying slightly from state to state, were designed to protect the superiority of the whites, coerce and control the slave population, and restrict the economic freedom of choice and opportunities of all non-whites.

The Black Codes were designed to minimize the distinction between the free black American and the enslaved black American in the South, and were the most extreme forms of racially-based exclusion and definition in the Americas. They denied elementary rights, such as freedom of movement, the right to own property, or the right to defend oneself against the personal abuses of the whites. Nor was the wilful killing of a slave by a white person regarded legally

A slave auction in Virginia, 1861

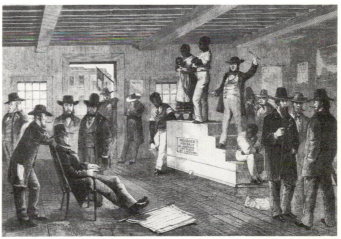

as murder. The malicious circumscription of the life of all black Americans by the whites created a vicious circle of increasing opposition and revolt by the slaves followed by increasing repression by the slaveowners and their allies. Until the Civil War two things helped maintain white supremacy: the numerical superiority of the whites, and the fact that, unlike any other American slaveholding society, the overwhelming majority of black Americans in North America were born into the slave-based society. They were not free people suddenly confined to the repressive regime of slaveowners. The repression and violence of the white Americans was possible because the minority of slaveowners persuaded the large majority of white non-slaveowners that slavery somehow protected whites from non-whites.

Nevertheless, despite severe handicaps and the lack of a continuous inflow from Africa, the black Americans forged a viable, dynamic society and culture, which retained many elements of the African heritage and operated in symbiotic relationship with the European and Indian cultures of North America. Slavery challenged, but did not shatter, the integrity of the black American family. Slavery oppressed and discomfited, but failed to eliminate consistent patterns of social behaviour that have parallels in African societies and social values. African patterns of kinship, the extended family and naming-practices among black Americans all reflect a social coherence and strong African legacy.

One of the prevailing myths about the black American community in North America is that slavery destroyed family life and left a permanent legacy of family instability. The fact that slavery disrupted families and, especially in the expanding cotton states, accelerated the forced separation of family members, should not obscure the general popularity and prevalence of the nuclear family among black Americans. Family life was certainly made difficult by the exigencies of slavery and the inordinate power of the slaveowners. But, where they could, slaves and non-slaves adjusted their concept of the family to approximate to the norms of the stable nuclear family. And the pattern continued in the post-slavery era until social mores and economic circumstances coincided to affect it – not just for black Americans but for all North Americans.

In slavery as well as freedom black Americans lived and worked as other Americans did. Most black Americans lived on farms or in rural areas until 1865, with about 10 per cent in the cities. Where they could, black Americans moved beyond the occupations of domestic servants, porters and unskilled labour to engage in skilled trades and industrial tasks. Throughout North America black Americans worked in textile and steel mills, railroads, docks and factories.

After the American War of Independence (1775–83), in which black Americans fought on both sides, a growing number of articulate black Americans began to urge the abolition of slavery. Some printed pamphlets, broadsides and newspapers, some trav-

elled throughout the free states urging support for total slave emancipation, and others used the strong religious organizations as a platform to attack slavery. In the early 19th century these black anti-slavery proponents had become a significant group, including David Walker, a printer in Massachusetts, Samuel Ringgold Ward, a Presbyterian pastor in New York, Lunsford Lane, an orator from North Carolina, and such ubiquitous speakers and organizers as Robert Purvis, who organized the first annual convention of free coloured people, Charles Remond, a delegate to the London Anti-Slavery Conference, and Charles Ray, a prominent member of the American and Foreign Anti-Slavery Society.

The most eminent of the advocates of the abolition of slavery was Frederick Douglass. Born a slave in Easton, Maryland in 1817, Douglass ran away from his master to Massachusetts, then a haven for escapees. There he polished his rudimentary education, and quickly became a distinguished orator and publisher of an anti-slavery newspaper. Douglass travelled to England and France, and used his speeches and his writings to attack slavery. During the Civil War Douglass recruited two regiments of black soldiers to fight for the North, and was appointed later as US Marshal for the District of Columbia. In 1889 Douglass, the pre-eminent black American of the 19th century, became his country's representative to Haiti.

Other black Americans also distinguished themselves in many fields. In 1835 and 1836 Henry Blair of Maryland patented two corn harvesters. Benjamin Montgomery, a slave owned by Jefferson Davis (president of the ill-fated Southern Confederacy), invented a propeller for boats in the late 1850s. Jan Matzeliger, a black immigrant from Dutch Guiana, patented a lasting machine in 1883 that virtually revolutionized the shoe industry in New England. In 1846 Norbert Rillieux of Louisiana patented the vacuum pan method of sugar refining, creating the greatest revolution in that industry since the invention of the rotary mill in 1449. In Detroit in 1852 Elijah McCoy's cup enabled engineers to lubricate machines while they were in operation. Granville Woods of Cincinnati, Ohio was a versatile inventor, whose designs were adopted by several major American companies at the turn of the century. Daniel Hale Williams, an anatomist trained at Northwestern University, was a pioneer in heart surgery. Charles Drew, the authority on blood plasma, was the first director of the American Red Cross Blood Bank. William A. Hinton, a clinical professor at Harvard University, originated the Hinton test for syphilis. George Washington Carver, an agricultural chemist at Tuskegee Institute, invented some 300 products from the peanut, and thereby re-invigorated the agricultural economy of marginally fertile southern lands.

The period from the Civil War to the late 1950s was a most difficult one for black Americans. In 1865, after the war, the Thirteenth Amendment to the Constitution abolished slavery. The post-war period required different sorts of adjustments to the new political order, to economic changes, and drastically new relations between those who had always been free and those who had only just become so. The South may have lost the war, but its ideas continued to prevail during the violent years that followed. Peace endured between the states, but not between white and black Americans. Virtually all the southern states passed laws restricting the electoral franchise, attacking the economic opoportunities, and defining the social conduct of black Americans. The subservient condition of black Americans under slavery was perpetuated not only legally, but also illegally through the violent activities of such white terrorist organizations as the Ku Klux Klan. Malicious destruction of private property, physical intimidation and even lynching helped maintain the gulf between white and black America. The suppression of black Americans can be seen in many fields–notably in politics. Between 1870 and 1980 only three persons of black American descent were elected to the US Senate: Hiram R. Revels and Blanche K. Bruce from Mississippi, and Edward Brooke from Massachusetts. The proportion in the House of Representatives over the same period has been only slightly better. Until the civil rights revolution of the 1960s black Americans endured second-class citizenship in the USA, defined and treated as an unwanted but necessary minority.

The concerted pattern of racial hostility did not entirely disillusion black Americans about their stake in the nation. During the 19th century a number of repatriation schemes began, but black Americans by and large decided to stay. They built schools, colleges and churches. Eventually black scholars graduated from the finest colleges in the land, and some, such as William Monroe Trotter, William E. B. Du Bois, Carter G. Woodson, and Eugene K. Jones, achieved international fame. In the first two decades of the 20th century associations such as the National Negro Business League, the National Association for the Advancement of Coloured People and the National Urban League began actively to oppose discrimination. Even as black Americans fought 'to make the world safe for democracy' in Europe, their own democratic rights were being denied at home. The USA took segregation to the battle lines abroad, for example, through the creation of all-black units. Although black Americans constituted 10 per cent of the population, they represented 13 per cent of conscripts, a pattern of over-representation repeated in all succeeding wars.

During the first half of the 20th century a massive migration from the southern states to the industrialized cities of the North took place. Black Americans began, against considerable odds, to join the mainstream of American life. For a short time in the mid-1920s Harlem became the most important centre of black American life and letters. The Harlem 'Renaissance' witnessed a flowering of music and literature dealing with the black American experience. Among its writers were Claude McKay, Alain Locke, Langston Hughes, Arna Bontemps, Countee Cullen, Wallace Thurman, Jessie Fauset, Jean

North and South: top: a Harlem restaurant in the 1920s. Below: selling herbal remedies in Winston-Salem, North Carolina

Toomer, and Nella Larsen. In music and theatre such artists as Eubie Blake, Florence Mills, Fletcher Henderson, Louis Armstrong, Ethel Waters, Paul Robeson, Marian Anderson and Duke Ellington emerged to delight audiences in America and abroad for decades to come. And jazz, born in New Orleans, captured Chicago, New York and then the rest of the world.

The Harlem Renaissance came in the wake of one of the most flamboyant figures of the age. Marcus Manasseh Garvey★ (1887–1940) was a Jamaican immigrant, who founded the Universal Negro Improvement Association as a pan-African movement designed to decolonize Africa and unite all Africans everywhere. An outstanding orator, indefatigable traveller, and constant dreamer, Garvey took his organization to Harlem in 1917, and spread his message through his newspaper, the *Negro World*. With branches in Africa, the Caribbean and Latin America, Harvey created an African Orthodox Church, and a shipping line – the Black Star Line – to transport his followers back to Africa and communicate between Africa and Africans of the diaspora. Garvey's scheme collapsed when he was convicted of fraud and, in 1927, deported. Nonetheless, his movement contributed greatly to restoring black pride and dignity.

In 1950 Ralph Bunche received the Nobel Peace Prize for his mediation of the Palestine dispute in the service of the UN. Four years later the US Supreme Court declared segregated schools unconstitutional, and, in effect, reversed the support it had given to that system since 1896. Throughout the South whites resisted, and the level of interracial violence increased. The symbol of the new passive revolution – which quickly became active – was the refusal of Mrs Rosa Parks of Montgomery, Alabama to surrender her bus seat to a white person. Her arrest resulted in a massive bus boycott. The ensuing struggle brought to the fore the Reverend Martin Luther King Jr (who won the Nobel Peace Prize in 1964) and his Southern Christian Leadership Conference. Other associations, such as the Congress of Racial Equality, and the Student Non-Violent Coordinating Committee joined the struggle for civil rights. In 1964 Congress passed a Civil Rights Law that declared segregation and discrimination illegal. By the beginning of the 1980s although conditions had improved considerably – and the list of martyrs had grown much longer – black Americans still had a long way to go to attain full equality in the country they had helped build and defend.

Canada

Except for the years immediately before and during the Civil War, Canada has never played host to a large number of black people. From a peak of about 50–60 000 in 1861, the black population in Canada declined to less than 20 000 in 1901 and, insofar as the black element in the Canadian population can be readily identified, stood at about 40 000 in 1980. Probably the first slaves to be brought direct from Africa to Canada were imported into French Canada in the late 1620s. Thereafter Canada became a significant, if relatively minor, part of the slave-owning territories of the British Empire, a situation complicated by an influx of blacks from other parts of North America. During the American War of Independence black slaves in what was to become the USA were encouraged to escape from their masters and assist the British, and were then granted their freedom. Most went to the West Indies but a considerable number, the 'Black Loyalists', were settled in Nova Scotia: meanwhile white 'loyalists' fled to Canada bringing their slaves with them. The Nova Scotian freed blacks were not treated as well in Canada as they had been promised – particularly as far as allocation of land was concerned – and 1200 of them formed the bulk of the participants who made a second attempt, in 1792, to form a settlement of freed slaves in Sierra Leone.* In the early 19th century US blacks continued to escape from slavery into Canada, a movement that was accelerated by the abolition of slavery in the British Empire in 1834, and culminated in the movements associated with the Civil War. Canada was only marginally affected – particularly in areas near the border with the USA – by the massive migration from the rural southern USA to the northern cities between the 1870s and the 1930s. Nevertheless, the first 40 years of the 20th century saw an upsurge of racism in Canada which has only begun to be fundamentally reversed since the early 1960s. While the Canadians did not construct an elaborate legal apparatus to restrict the lives of black Canadians, the Department of Immigration and Colonization carefully screened immigration of non-whites. No overt segregation existed, but subtle forms of discrimination achieved a socio-economic situation not very different from that in the USA. *F.W.K.*

Dr Martin Luther King Jr leads 10 000 civil rights marchers from Selma to Montgomery, Alabama, 25 March 1965

Further reading

GENERAL BOOKS

J. M. Abun Nasr, *A History of the Maghrib*, (2nd edn) Cambridge, 1975
J. F. A. Ajayi and M. Crowder (eds), *History of West Africa*, 2 vols, London 1971, 1974
M. Crowder, *West Africa under Colonial Rule*, London, 1968
P. Duignan and L. H. Gann (gen. eds), *Colonialism in Africa, 1870–1960*, 5 vols, Cambridge, 1969–75
J. D. Fage and R. Oliver (gen. eds), *The Cambridge History of Africa*, 8 vols, Cambridge, 1975–
V. Harlow and E. M. Chilver (eds), *History of East Africa*, vol. ii, Oxford, 1965
W. Knapp, *A Survey of North-West Africa*, (3rd edn), Oxford, 1977
D. A. Low and A. Smith (eds), *History of East Africa*, vol. iii, Oxford, 1976
R. Oliver and G. Mathew (eds), *History of East Africa*, vol. i, Oxford, 1963
The UNESCO General History of Africa, 8 vols, London, 1981–
M. Wilson and L. Thompson (eds), *Oxford History of South Africa*, 2 vols, Oxford, 1969, 1971

MAGAZINES AND JOURNALS

Africa, International African Institute, London
African Affairs, Royal African Society, London
African Arts, African Studies Center, University of California, Los Angeles
African Languages, International African Institute, London
International African Bibliography, Mansell, London
International Journal of African Historical Studies, Africana Publishing Corporation, New York
Journal of African History, Cambridge University Press
Journal of Commonwealth and Comparative Politics, Frank Cass, London
Journal of Modern African Studies, Cambridge University Press
Journal of Southern African Studies, Oxford University Press
Review of African Political Economy, Sheffield
Tarikh, Longman, London

THE PHYSICAL ENVIRONMENT

K. Boucher, *Global Climate*, London, 1975
C. Buckle, *Landforms of Africa*, London, 1977
R. J. Chorley (ed), *Water, Earth and Man*, London, 1974
J. I. Clark (ed), *An Advanced Geography of Africa*, London, 1975
T. N. Clifford and I. G. Gass (eds), *African Magmatism and Tectonics*, London, 1970
J. L. Cloudsley-Thompson, *Animal Twilight. Man and Game in Eastern Africa*, London, 1967
J. L. Cloudsley-Thompson, *The Zoology of Tropical Africa*, London, 1969
D. H. S. Davis, B. de Meillon, J. S. Harington and M. Kalk, *Ecological Studies in Southern Africa*, The Hague, 1964
A. de Vos, *Africa, the Devastated Continent*, The Hague, 1975
J. L. D'Hoore, *Soil Map of Africa at Scale 1:5 000 000: Explanatory Monograph*, Commission for Technical Cooperation in Africa, Lagos, 1964
FAO/UNESCO, *Soil Map of the World at Scale 1:5 000 000*, vol. vi, *Africa*, UNESCO, Paris, 1977
R. Furon, *The Geology of Africa*, London, 1963
J. F. Griffiths, *World Survey of Climatology*, vol. x, *Climates of Africa*, Oxford, 1972
A. T. Grove, *Africa*, (3rd edn), London, 1963
F. K. Hare, *The Restless Atmosphere*, London, 1960
G. M. Higgins *et al.*, *Report on Agro-Ecological Zones Project*, vol. i, *Methodology and Results for Africa*, FAO, Rome, 1978
B. Hopkins, *Forest and Savanna*, London, 1965
L. C. King, *South African Scenery*, (3rd edn), London, 1963
G. W. Lawson, *Plant Life in West Africa*, London, 1966
E. M. Lind and M. E. S. Morrison, *East African Vegetation*, London, 1974
K. A. Longman and J. Jenik, *Tropical Forest and Its Environment*, London, 1974
D. F. Owen, *Animal Ecology in Tropical Africa*, (2nd edn), London, 1976
H. H. Read and J. Watson, *Introduction to Geology*, vol. ii, *Earth History*, London, 1975
P. W. Richards, *The Tropical Rain Forest*, Cambridge, 1952
M. F. Thomas, *Tropical Geomorphology*, London, 1974
H. Walter, *Ecology of Tropical and Subtropical Vegetation*, London, 1971
R. O. Whyte, *Grasslands of the Monsoon*, London, 1968
J. T. Wilson (ed), *Continents Adrift and Continents Aground*, London, 1976

THE PEOPLES

P. J. Bohannan and P. Curtin, *Africa and Africans*, New York, 1971
J. D. Clark, *The Prehistory of Africa*, London, 1970
D. Dalby, *The Language Map of Africa*, London, 1978
O. Davies, *West Africa before the Europeans*, London, 1967
J. R. Gibbs (ed), *The Peoples of Africa*, New York, 1965
J. H. Greenberg, *The Languages of Africa*, Paris and The Hague, 1963
International African Institute (various authors), *Ethnographic Survey of Africa*, London, 1950–
R. Leakey and R. Lewin, *Origins*, London, 1977
J. Middleton (ed), *Black Africa: its Peoples and their Cultures Today*, New York, 1970
G. P. Murdock, *Africa: its Peoples and their Culture History*, New York, 1959
S. and P. Ottenberg (eds), *Cultures and Societies of Africa*, New York, 1960
D. W. Phillipson, *The Later Prehistory of Eastern and Southern Africa*, London, 1977
T. A. Sebeok (ed), *Current Trends in Linguistics*, vol. vi, *Linguistics in SW Asia and North Africa*, Paris and The Hague, 1970
T. A. Sebeok (ed), *Current Trends in Linguisics*, vol. vii, *Linguistics in Sub-Saharan Africa*, Paris and The Hague, 1971
W. E. Welmers, *African Language Structures*, Berkeley and Los Angeles, 1973

BEFORE EUROPEAN COLONIZATION

M. Abir, *Ethiopia and the Red Sea. The Rise and Decline of the Solomonic Dynasty and Muslim-European Rivalry in the Region*, London, 1980
W. Y. Adams, *Nubia: Corridor to Africa*, Princeton, 1970
I. A. Akinjogbin, *Dahomey and its Neighbours, 1708–1818*, Cambridge, 1967
C. Aldred, *Akhnaten and Nefertiti*, London, 1973
E. A. Alpers, *Ivory and Slaves in East Central Africa*, Berkeley and Los Angeles, 1975
E. V. Axelson, *Portuguese in South-East Africa, 1600–1700*, Johannesburg, 1960
E. V. Axelson, *Portuguese in South-East Africa, 1488–1600*, Johannesburg, 1973
M. L. Bender (ed), *The Non-Semitic Languages of Ethiopia*, East Lansing, 1976
D. Birmingham, *The Portuguese Conquest of Angola*, London, 1965
J. W. Blake, *West Africa: Quest for God and Gold, 1454–1578*, London, 1977
C. R. Boxer, *The Portuguese Seaborne Empire, 1415–1825*, London, 1969
D. Buxton, *The Abyssinians*, London, 1970
R. H. Chilcote (ed), *Protest and Resistance in Angola and Brazil*, Los Angeles, 1972
N. Chittick, *Kilwa. An Islamic Trading City on the East African Coast*, vol. i, *History and Archaeology*, Nairobi, 1974
F. Cooper, *Plantation Slavery on the East Coast of Africa*, New Haven, 1977
P. D. Curtin, *The Atlantic Slave Trade: a Census*, Madison, 1967
P. D. Curtin, *Economic Change in Pre-colonial Africa: Senegambia in the Era of the Slave Trade*, Madison, 1975
K. Y. Daaku, *Trade and Politics on the Gold Coast, 1600–1720*, Oxford, 1970
C. W. De Kiewiet, *A History of South Africa: Social and Economic*, Oxford, 1941
B. Doe, *Southern Arabia*, New York, 1971
I. E. S. Edwards, *The Pyramids of Egypt*, London, 1947
R. Elphick, *Kraal and Castle: Khoikhoi and the Founding of White South Africa*, New Haven, 1977
P. S. Garlake, *Great Zimbabwe*, London, 1973
P. S. Garlake, *The Kingdoms of Africa*, Oxford, 1979
R. Gray and D. Birmingham (eds), *Pre-colonial African Trade*, London, 1970
J. R. Harris (ed), *The Legacy of Egypt*, Oxford, 1971
A. C. Hess, *The Forgotten Frontier*, Chicago, 1978
P. M. Holt, *Egypt and the Fertile Crescent, 1516–1922*, London, 1966
A. F. Isaacman, *Mozambique: the Africanization of a European Institution: the Zambezi Prazos, 1750–1902*, Madison, 1972

C.-A. Julien, *History of North Africa*, London, 1970

R. K. Kent, *Early Kingdoms in Madagascar 1500–1700*, New York and London, 1970

M. L. Kilson and R. I. Rotberg (eds), *The African Diaspora: Interpretative Essays*, Cambridge, Mass., 1976

H. S. Klein, *The Middle Passage: Comparative Studies in the Atlantic Slave Trade*, Princeton, 1978

Y. M. Kobishchanov, *Axum*, London, 1979

S. Lane-Poole, *History of Egypt in the Middle Ages*, (2nd edn), London, 1914

M. Last, *The Sokoto Caliphate*, London, 1967

A. J. H. Latham, *Old Calabar, 1600–1891*, Oxford, 1973

P. M. Martin, *The External Trade of the Loango Coast, 1576–1870: the Effects of Changing Commercial Relations on the Vili Kingdom of Loango*, Oxford, 1972

B. Michael, S. Chojnacki and Richard Pankhurst (eds), *The Dictionary of Ethiopian Biography*, vol. i, *From Early Times to the End of the Zagwe Dynasty, c. 1270*, Addis Ababa, 1975

M. D. D. Newitt, *Portuguese Settlement on the Zambezi*, London, 1973

R. Oliver and B. M. Fagan, *Africa in the Iron Age*, Cambridge, 1975

D. W. Phillipson, *The Later Prehistory of Eastern and Southern Africa*, London, 1977

S. Raven, *Rome in Africa*, London, 1969

A. Roberts, *A History of Zambia*, London, 1976

W. Rodney, *A History of the Upper Guinea Coast, 1545–1800*, Oxford, 1970

A. F. C. Ryder, *Benin and the Europeans, 1485–1897*, London, 1969

S. H. Sellassie, *Ancient and Medieval History to 1270*, Addis Ababa, 1972

T. Shaw, *Nigeria. Its Archaeology and Early History*, London, 1978

P. L. Shinnie (ed), *The African Iron Age*, London, 1971

P. L. Shinnie, *Meroe: a Civilisation of the Sudan*, London, 1967

J. Strandes, *The Portuguese Period in East Africa*, Nairobi, 1961

T. Tamrat, *Church and State in Ethiopia, 1270–1527*, Oxford, 1972

J. S. Trimingham, *Islam in Ethiopia*, London, 1952

E. Ullendorff, *Ethiopia and the Bible*, London, 1968

J. Vansina, *Kingdom of the Savanna*, Madison, 1966

E. H. Warmington, *Carthage*, (2nd edn), London, 1969

THE EUROPEAN OCCUPATION

M. Abd al-Rahim, *Imperialism and Nationalism in the Sudan, a study in Constitutional and Political Development, 1899–1956*, Oxford, 1969

J. M. Ahmed, *The Intellectual Origins of Egyptian Nationalism*, London, 1960

S. Amin, *Neo-Colonialism in West Africa*, Harmondsworth, 1973

R. Anstey, *King Leopold's Legacy. The Congo under Belgian Rule 1908–1960*, London, 1966

R. Austen, *Northwest Tanzania under German and British Rule*, New Haven, 1968

D. Austin, *Politics in Ghana 1946–1960*, London, 1964

E. V. Axelson, *Portugal and the Scramble for Africa 1875–1891*, Johannesburg, 1967

P. T. Bauer, *Dissent on Development*, London, 1971

G. J. Bender, *Angola under the Portuguese. The Myth and the Reality*, London, 1978

G. F. H. Berkeley, *The Campaign of Adowa and the Rise of Menelik*, London, 1935

J. Berque, *French North Africa*, London, 1967

R. Bidwell, *Morocco under Colonial Rule*, London, 1973

H. Bley, *South-West Africa under German Rule*, London, 1971

E. A. Brett, *Colonialism and Underdevelopment in East Africa*, London, 1973

M. Brown, *Madagascar Rediscovered*, London, 1978

H. Brunschwig, *French Colonialism: Myths and Realities*, London, 1966

R. L. Buell, *Liberia, a Century of Survival*, Philadelphia, 1947

C. Bundy, *The Rise and Fall of the South African Peasantry*, London, 1979

G. M. Carter, *The Politics of Inequality: South Africa since 1945*, London, 1958

C. Clapham, *Haile Selassie's Government*, London, 1969

C. Clapham, *Liberia and Sierra Leone*, Cambridge, 1976

A. Clayton and D. C. Savage, *Government and Labour in Kenya, 1895–1963*, London, 1974

J. S. Coleman, *Nigeria: Background to Nationalism*, Berkeley and Los Angeles, 1958

M. Crowder (ed), *West African Resistance*, London, 1971

S. E. Crowe, *The Berlin West Africa Conference, 1884–1885*, London, 1945

P. D. Curtin (ed), *Imperialism*, New York, 1971

T. R. H. Davenport, *South Africa: a Modern History*, London, 1977

B. Davidson, *Africa in Modern History*, London, 1979

B. Davidson, *In the Eye of the Storm*, London, 1972

B. Davidson, *The Liberation of Guiné*, Harmondsworth, 1969

A. Del Boca, *The Ethiopian War 1935–1941*, Chicago and London, 1969

D. Denoon, *A Grand Illusion*, London, 1973

J. Duffy, *Portuguese Africa*, Cambridge, Mass., 1959

J. Dugan and L. Lafore, *Days of Emperor and Clown. The Italo-Ethiopian War 1935–1936*, New York, 1973

E. E. Evans-Pritchard, *The Sanusi of Cyrenaica*, Oxford, 1949

L. A. Fallers (ed), *The King's Men: Leadership and Status in Buganda on the Eve of Independence*, London, 1964

B. Fetter, *The Creation of Elisabethville, 1910–1940*, Stanford, 1976

R. First, *Libya: the Elusive Revolution*, Harmondsworth, 1974

Z. Gabre-Selassie, *Yohannes IV of Ethiopia*, Oxford, 1975

L. H. Gann, *A History of Southern Rhodesia: early days to 1934*, London, 1965

L. H. Gann, *A History of Northern Rhodesia: early days to 1953*, London, 1964

L. H. Gann and P. Duignan, *The Rulers of German Africa 1884–1914*, Stanford, 1977

I. Geiss, *The Pan-African Movement*, London, 1974

P. Gifford and W. R. Louis, *France and Britain in Africa: Imperial Rivalry and Colonial Rule*, New Haven, 1971

R. Gray, *The Two Nations*, London, 1960

R. J. Hammond, *Portugal and Africa, 1815–1910: a Study in Uneconomic Imperialism*, Stanford, 1966

W. K. Hancock, *Smuts*, (2 vols), Cambridge, 1962 and 1968

J. D. Hargreaves, *Prelude to the Partition of West Africa*, London, 1963

J. D. Hargreaves, *West Africa Partitioned*, vol. i, *The Loaded Pause, 1885–89*, London, 1974

T. H. Henriksen, *Mozambique: a History*, London, 1978

N. Heseltine, *Madagascar*, London, 1971

R. L. Hess, *Italian Colonialism in Somalia*, Chicago and London, 1966

T. Hodgkin, *Nationalism in Colonial Africa*, London, 1956

P. M. Holt, *Egypt and the Fertile Crescent, 1516–1922*, London, 1966

P. M. Holt and M. W. Daly, *A Modern History of the Sudan*, (3rd edn), London, 1979

A. G. Hopkins, *An Economic History of West Africa*, London, 1973

A. Horne, *A Savage War of Peace*, London, 1977

C. H. Huberich, *The Political and Legislative History of Liberia*, (2 vols), New York, 1947

J. Iliffe, *A Modern History of Tanganyika*, Cambridge, 1979

J. Iliffe, *Tanganyika under German Rule 1905–1912*, Cambridge, 1969

H. Johnston, *Liberia*, (2 vols), London, 1906

F. A. Johnstone, *Class, Race and Gold*, London, 1976

R. A. Joseph, *Radical Nationalism in Cameroun*, Oxford, 1977

R. W. July, *The Origins of Modern African Thought*, London, 1968

C. Kadalie, *My Life and the ICU* (ed S. Trapido), London, 1970

A. S. Kanya-Forstner, *The Conquest of the Western Sudan*, Cambridge, 1969

M. Khadduri, *Modern Libya, a Study in Political Development*, Baltimore, 1963

D. Kimble, *A Political History of Ghana, 1850–1928*, Oxford, 1963

A. J. Knoll, *Togo and Imperial Germany 1884–1914*, Stanford, 1978

R. Landau, *Moroccan Drama 1900–55*, London, 1956

R. Lemarchand, *Political Awakening in the Belgian Congo*, Berkeley, 1964

V. T. Le Vine, *The Cameroons from Mandate to Independence*, Berkeley, 1964

I. M. Lewis, *The Modern History of Somaliland*, London, 1965

C. Leys, *Underdevelopment in Kenya*, London, 1975

C. Leys and C. Pratt (eds), *A New Deal in Central Africa*, London, 1960

J. G. Liebenow, *Liberia, the Evolution of Privilege*, Cornell, 1969

G. A. Lipsky, *Ethiopia: its People, its Society, its Culture*, New Haven, 1962

W. R. Louis (ed), *Imperialism: the Robinson and Gallagher Controversy*, New York, 1976

W. R. Louis and J. Stengers, *E. D. Morel's History of the Congo Reform Movement*, Oxford, 1968

M. H. H. Macartney and P. Cremona, *Italy's Foreign and Colonial Policy*, London, 1938

J. S. Mangat, *A History of the Asians in East Africa*, Oxford, 1969

J. A. Marcum, *The Angolan Revolution*, Cambridge, Mass., 1969 and 1978

H. G. Marcus, *The Life and Times of Menelik II*, Oxford, 1975

M. D. Markowitz, *Cross and Sword. The Political Role of Christian Missions in the Belgian Congo, 1908–1960*, Stanford, 1973

J. Marlowe, *Anglo-Egyptian Relations 1800–1956*, London, 1965

P. Mason, *Year of Decision: Rhodesia and Nyasaland in 1960*, London, 1960

E. Mortimer, *France and the Africans 1944–60*, London, 1969

J. F. Munro, *Africa and the International Economy, 1800–1960*, London, 1976

J. F. Munro, *Colonial Rule and the Kamba*, Oxford, 1975

J. Murray-Brown, *Kenyatta*, London, 1972

P. M. Mutibwa, *The Malagasy and the Europeans*, London, 1974

A. Osuntokun, *Nigeria in the First World War*, London, 1979

R. Owen and B. Sutcliffe (eds), *Studies in the Theory of Imperialism*, London, 1972

R. Palmer, *Land and Racial Domination in Rhodesia*, London, 1977

R. K. P. Pankhurst, *Economic History of Ethiopia 1800–1935*, Addis Ababa, 1968

E. F. Penrose (ed), *European Imperialism and the Partition of Africa*, London, 1975

M. Perham, *The Government of Ethiopia*, London, 1969

C. Perrings, *Black Mineworkers in Central Africa; Industrial Strategies and the Evolution of an African Proletariat in the Copperbelt 1911–1941*, London, 1979

K. Post, *The New States of West Africa*, (2nd edn), Harmondsworth, 1968

C. Pratt, *The Critical Phase in Tanzania, 1945–1968*, Cambridge, 1976

T. O. Ranger, *The African Voice in Southern Rhodesia, 1898–1930*, London, 1970

T. O. Ranger, *Revolt in Southern Rhodesia*, London, 1967; new edn, 1979

A. Roberts, *A History of Zambia*, London, 1976

R. Robinson and J. Gallagher, *Africa and the Victorians*, London, 1961

C. Rosberg and J. Nottingham, *The Myth of Mau Mau*, New York, 1966

R. I. Rotberg and A. A. Mazrui (eds), *Protest and Power in Black Africa*, New York, 1970

R. I. Rotberg, *The Rise of Nationalism in Central Africa: the Making of Malawi and Zambia 1873–1964*, Cambridge, Mass., 1966

E. Roux, *Time Longer than Rope*, London, 1948

S. Rubenson, *The Survival of Ethiopian Independence*, London, 1976

R. Schachter Morgenthau, *Political Parties in French-speaking West Africa*, Oxford, 1964

H. J. and R. E. Simons, *Class and Colour in South Africa*, Harmondsworth, 1969

J. Suret-Canale, *French Colonialism in Tropical Africa, 1900–45*, London, 1971

V. Thompson and R. Adloff, *Djibouti and the Horn of Africa*, Stanford, 1968

V. Thompson and R. Adloff, *The Emerging States of French Equatorial Africa*, Stanford, 1960

V. Thompson and R. Adloff, *The Malagasy Republic*, Stanford, 1965

R. L. Tignor, *Modernization and British Colonial Rule in Egypt, 1882–1914*, Princeton, 1966

G. K. N. Trevaskis, *Eritrea, a Colony in Transition*, London, 1960

C. van Onselen, *Chibaro: African Mine Labour in Southern Rhodesia, 1900–1933*, London, 1976

P. J. Vatikiotis, *The Modern History of Egypt*, London, 1969

I. Wallerstein, *Africa: the Politics of Independence*, New York, 1961

P. Walshe, *The Rise of Nationalism in South Africa: the ANC, 1912–52*, London, 1970

P. Warwick (ed), *The South African War*, London, 1980

E. Webster (ed), *Essays in Southern African Labour History*, London, 1978

R. West, *Brazza of the Congo*, London, 1972

D. L. Wheeler and R. Pélissier, *Angola*, London, 1971

P. Wickins, *The ICU of Africa*, Cape Town, 1978

H. S. Wilson, *The Imperial Experience in Sub-Saharan Africa since 1870*, Minneapolis, 1977

H. S. Wilson (ed), *Origins of West African Nationalism*, London, 1969

J. Wright, *Libya*, London, 1969

C. Young, *Politics in the Congo. Decolonization and Independence*, Princeton, 1965

AFRICA SINCE INDEPENDENCE

H. Adam, *Modernizing Racial Domination. South Africa's Political Dynamics*, Berkeley, 1971

L. Adamolekun, *Sekou Touré's Guinea*, London, 1976

D. E. Apter, *The Political Kingdom in Uganda*, London, 1961

G. Arnold, *Kenyatta and the Politics of Kenya*, London, 1974

G. Arrighi, *The Political Economy of Rhodesia*, The Hague, 1967

D. Austin, *Ghana Observed*, Manchester, 1978

D. Austin and R. Luckham (eds), *Politicians and Soldiers in Ghana*, London, 1977

R. W. Baker, *Egypt's Uncertain Revolution under Nasser and Sadat*, Cambridge, Mass., 1978

P. Bechtold, *Politics in the Sudan: Parliamentary and Military Rule in an Emerging African Nation*, New York, 1976

M. Benson, *Tshekedi Khama*, London, 1960

H. Bienen, *Tanzania: Party Transformation and Economic Development*, (expanded edn), Princeton, 1970

L. W. Bowman, *Politics in Rhodesia: White Power in an African State*, Cambridge, Mass., 1973

M. Brown, *Madagascar Rediscovered*, London, 1978

B. Burton (ed), *Problems of Smaller Territories*, London, 1967

A. Callinicos and J. Rogers, *Southern Africa after Soweto*, London, 1977

G. Carter and P. O'Meara (eds), *Southern Africa in Crisis*, Bloomington, 1977

G. M. Carter, T. Karis and N. M. Stultz, *South Africa's Transkei: the Politics of Domestic Colonialism*, Evanston, 1967

J. Cartwright, *Politics in Sierra Leone 1947–67*, Toronto, 1970

C. Clapham, *Haile-Selassie's Government*, London, 1969

C. Clapham, *Liberia and Sierra Leone*, Cambridge, 1976

M. A. Cohen, *Urban Policy and Political Conflict in Africa: a Study of the Ivory Coast*, Chicago, 1974

R. Cohen, *Labour and Politics in Nigeria, 1945–71*, London, 1974

R. O. Collins, *The Southern Sudan in Historical Perspective*, Tel Aviv, 1975

S. Cronjé, *Equatorial Guinea: the Forgotten Dictatorship*, London, 1976

D. B. Cruise O'Brien, *Saints and Politicians. Essays in the Organisation of a Senegalese Peasant Society*, Cambridge, 1975

B. Davidson, J. Slovo and A. R. Wilkinson, *Southern Africa: the New Politics of Revolution*, Harmondsworth, 1976

A. Debel, *Cameroon Today*, Paris, 1977

S. Decalo, *Historical Dictionary of Dahomey*, Metuchen, 1976

S. Decalo, *Historical Dictionary of Chad*, Metuchen, 1977

S. Decalo, *Historical Dictionary of Togo*, Metuchen, 1976

S. Diallo, *Zaire Today*, Paris, 1977

J. Dunn (ed), *West African States: Failure and Promise*, Cambridge, 1978

W. J. Foltz, *From French West Africa to Mali Federation*, Berkeley, 1965

P. Fraenkel, *The Namibians of South-West Africa*, London, 1974

A. Gerteiny, *Mauritania*, London, 1967

P. Gilkes, *The Dying Lion*, London, 1975

R. Hall, *Zambia*, London, 1965

R. Hall, *The High Price of Principles: Kaunda and the White South*, London, 1969

T. H. Henriksen, *Mozambique: a History*, London, 1978

N. Heseltine, *Madagascar*, London, 1971

P. M. Holt and M. W. Daly, *A Modern History of the Sudan*, London, 1979

P. J. Imperato, *Historical Dictionary of Mali*, London, 1978

R. W. Johnson, *How Long Will South Africa Survive?* London, 1977

D. Jones, *Aid and Development in Southern Africa*, London, 1977

T. Jones, *Ghana. The First Republic*, London, 1976

R. A. Joseph, *Radical Nationalism in Cameroun*, Oxford, 1977

P. Kalck, *Central African Republic*, London, 1971

T. Kanza, *Conflict in the Congo. The Rise and Fall of Lumumba*, Harmondsworth, 1972

K. D. Kaunda, *Zambia Shall Be Free*, London, 1962

R. K. Kent, *From Madagascar to the Malagasy Republic*, New York, 1962

B. M. Khaketla, *Lesotho 1970: An African Coup under the Microscope*, London, 1973

A. Killick, *The Economy of Ghana*, New York, 1978

H. Kuper, *The Swazi*, New York, 1963

C. Lee, *Seychelles: Political Castaways*, London, 1976

C. Legum and T. Hodges, *After Angola. The War over Southern Africa*, London, 1976

C. Legum, *Ethiopia: the Fall of Haile Selassie's Empire*, London, 1976

C. Legum and B. Lee, *Conflict in the Horn of Africa*, London, 1977

G. M. E. Leistner and P. Smit, *Swaziland: Resources and Development*, Pretoria, 1969

R. Lemarchand, *Rwanda and Burundi*, London, 1970

V. T. Le Vine, *The Cameroon Federal Republic*, Ithaca, 1971
I. M. Lewis, *The Modern History of Somaliland*, London, 1965
C. Leys, *Underdevelopment in Kenya*, London, 1975
J. G. Liebenow, *Liberia: the Evolution of Privilege*, Cornell, 1969
I. Linden, *Church and Revolution in Rwanda*, Manchester, 1977
I. Linden, *'In Responsible Hands'*, Mainz, 1979
G. Lionnet, *The Seychelles*, Newton Abbot, 1972
J. Listowel, *Amin*, Dublin, 1973
R. Lobban, *Historical Dictionary of the Republic of Guinea-Bissau and Cape Verde*, Metuchen, 1979
M. Lowenkopf, *Politics in Liberia: the Conservative Road to Development*, Stanford, 1976
R. Luckham, *The Nigerian Military*, Cambridge, 1971
A. M. MacPhee, *Kenya*, London, 1969
J. Markakis, *Ethiopia: Anatomy of a Traditional Polity*, Oxford, 1974
D. Martin, *General Amin*, London, 1974
A. Mazrui, *Soldiers and Kinsmen in Uganda*, London, 1975
D. N. McFarland, *Historical Dictionary of Upper Volta*, Metuchen, 1978
C. McMaster, *Malawi. Foreign Policy and Development*, London, 1974
J. H. Mittleman, *Ideology and Politics in Uganda*, Cornell, 1975
E. Mondlane, *The Struggle for Mozambique*, Harmondsworth, 1969
D. C. Mulford, *Zambia: the Politics of Independence 1957–1964*, London, 1967
J. Murray-Brown, *Kenyatta*, London, 1972
B. U. Mwansasu and C. Pratt (eds), *Towards Socialism in Tanzania*, Toronto, 1979
J. Ostheimer (ed), *The Politics of the Western Indian Ocean Islands*, New York, 1975
S. K. Panter-Brick (ed), *Nigerian Politics and Military Rule*, London, 1970
J. Pettman, *Zambia: Security and Conflict*, London, 1974
K. Post and M. Vickers, *Structure and Conflict in Nigeria 1960–66*, London, 1973
C. P. Potholm, *Swaziland: the Dynamics of Political Modernisation*, Berkeley, 1972
C. Pratt, *The Critical Phase in Tanzania, 1945–1968*, Cambridge, 1976
P. Robson, *Economic Integration in Africa*, London, 1968
C. G. Rosberg and J. Nottingham, *The Myth of Mau Mau*, New York, 1966
N. Rubin, *Cameroun, an African Federation*, London, 1971
L. Rudebeck, *Guinea-Bissau*, Uppsala, 1974
P. Sanders, *Moshoeshoe, Chief of the Sotho*, London, 1976
R. Segal and R. First (eds), *South-West Africa: Travesty of Trust*, London, 1967
P. Selwyn, *Industries in the Southern African Periphery*, London, 1976
P. Short, *Banda*, London, 1974
A. Sillery, *Botswana: a Short Political History*, London, 1974
R. Stephens, *Nasser*, London, 1971
C. Stevens, *Food Aid and the Developing World*, London, 1979
C. Stevens, *The Soviet Union and Black Africa*, Macmillan, 1976
C. Stewart, *Islam and Social Order in Mauritania*, Oxford, 1973
G. W. Ström, *Development and Dependence in Lesotho, the Enclave of South Africa*, Uppsala, 1978
V. Thompson and R. Adloff, *Historical Dictionary of the People's Republic of the Congo*, Metuchen, 1974
V. Thompson and R. Adloff, *Djibouti and the Horn of Africa*, Stanford, 1968
V. Thompson and R. Adloff, *The Malagasy Republic*, Stanford, 1965
R. Titmuss and B. Abel-Smith, *Social Policies and Population Growth in Mauritius*, London, 1961
A. Toussaint, *History of Mauritius*, London, 1978
S. Touval, *Somali Nationalism*, Cambridge, Mass., 1963
M. Twaddle (ed), *Expulsion of a Minority: Essays on Ugandan Asians*, London, 1975
United Nations, *A Trust Betrayed: Namibia*, New York, 1974
A. van der Wiel, *Migratory Wage Labour: its Role in the Economy of Lesotho*, Mazenod, Lesotho, 1977
P. van Rensburg, *Report from Swaneng Hill*, Uppsala, 1974
P. J. Vatikiotis, *The Modern History of Egypt*, London, 1969
G. Williams (ed), *Nigeria: Economy and Society*, London, 1976
A. R. Zolberg, *One-party Government in the Ivory Coast*, Princeton, 1969

GOVERNMENT

A. Ajala, *Pan-Africanism*, London, 1973
A. Allott, *New Essays in African Law*, London, 1970
B. O. Bryde, *The Politics and Sociology of African Legal Development*, Frankfurt, 1976
T. O. Elias, *The Nature of African Customary Law*, Manchester, 1956
M. Gluckman (ed), *Ideas and Procedures in African Customary Law*, London, 1969
L. C. B. Gower, *Independent Africa. The Challenge to the Legal Profession*, London, 1967
R. W. July, *The Origins of Modern African Thought*, London, 1968
H. and L. Kuper (eds), *African Law: Adaptation and Development*, Berkeley and Los Angeles, 1965
H. F. Morris and J. S. Read, *Indirect Rule and the Search for Justice*, Oxford, 1972
K. Post, *The New States of West Africa*, (2nd edn), Harmondsworth, 1968
N. Rubin and E. Cotran (eds), *Readings in African Law*, (2 vols), London, 1970
N. Rubin and E. Cotran (eds), *Annual Survey of African Law*. London, 1967–
A. R. Zolberg, *Creating Political Order: the Party-States of West Africa*, Chicago, 1966

UTILIZATION OF NATURAL RESOURCES

BRALUP, *Rural Water Supply in East Africa*, BRALUP, Dar es Salaam, 1970
J. Caldwell and C. Okonjo (eds), *The Population of Tropical Africa*, London, 1968
R. Cruikshank, K. C. Standard and H. B. L. Russell, *Epidemiology and Community Health in Warm Climate Countries*, London, 1976
G. Dahl and A. Hjort, *Having Herds*, Stockholm, 1976
D. Dalby, R. J. Harrison Church and F. Bezzaz, *Drought in Africa, 2*, London, 1977
FAO, *Land and Water Survey*, FAO, Rome, 1967
J. Ford, *The Role of the Trypanosomiases in African Ecology: a Study of the Tsetse Fly Problem*, London, 1971
S. George, *How the Other Half Dies: the Real Reason for World Hunger*, London, 1976
D. B. Grigg, *The Agricultural Systems of the World: an Evolutionary Approach*, Cambridge, 1974
W. A. Hance, *The Geography of Modern Africa*, New York, 1975
W. A. Hance, *Black Africa Develops*, Waltham, 1977
W. A. Hance, *Population, Migration and Urbanization in Africa*, New York, 1970
R. B. Lee and I. Devore (eds), *Man the Hunter*, Chicago, 1968
R. B. Lee and I. Devore (eds), *Kalahari Hunter-Gatherers: Studies of the !Kung San and their Neighbours*, Cambridge, Mass., 1976
L. Marshall, *The !Kung of Nyae Nyae*, Cambridge, Mass., 1976
I. Masser and W. T. S. Gould, *Inter-regional Migration in Tropical Africa*, Institute of British Geographers, Special publication, 8, London, 1975
T. Monod (ed), *Pastoral Societies in Tropical Africa*, London, 1975
D. Morley, *Paediatric Priorities in the Developing World*, London, 1977
A. M. O'Connor, *The Geography of Tropical African Development*, (2nd edn), Oxford, 1978
P. O'Keefe and B. Wisner (eds), *Land Use and Development in Africa*, London, 1978
S. H. Ominde and C. N. Ejiogu (eds), *Population Growth and Economic Development in Africa*, London, 1972
R. M. Prothero (ed), *People and Land in Africa South of the Sahara*, New York, 1972
U. Riise and E. Skofteland, *Hydrology in Developing Countries*, Oslo, 1979
H. Ruthenberg, *Farming Systems in the Tropics*, (2nd edn), London, 1976
T. Scudder, *Gathering among African Woodland Savannah Cultivators: a case study: the Gwembe Tonga*, Zambian Papers no. 5, Institute of African Studies, University of Zambia, 1971
H. Sheets and R. Morris, *Disaster in the Desert. Failures of International Relief in the West African Drought*, Washington DC, 1974
A. J. Smith (ed), *Beef Cattle Production in Developing Countries*, Edinburgh, 1976
M. F. Thomas and G. W. Whittington (eds), *Environment and Land Use in Africa*, London, 1969
C. M. Turnbull, *Wayward Servants: the Two Worlds of the African Pygmies*, London, 1965

UNESCO, *The Sahel: Ecological Approaches to Land Use*, Paris, 1975
G.F. White, D.J. Bradley and A.U. White, *Drawers of Water: Domestic Water Use in East Africa*, Chicago, 1972
J. Woodburn, *Hunters and Gatherers. The Material Culture of the Nomadic Hadza*, London, 1970

POLITICAL ECONOMY

L. Adamolekun, *Sekou Touré's Guinea*, London, 1976
E.O. Akeredolu-Ale, *The Underdevelopment of Indigenous Entrepreneurship in Nigeria*, Ibadan, 1975
S.A. Akintan, *The Law of International Economic Institutions in Africa*, Leyden, 1977
S. Amin, *Unequal Development*, London, 1976
K.M. Barbour, *The Growth, Location and Structure of Industry in Egypt*, New York, 1972
N. Bastor (ed), *Measuring Development*, London, 1974
P. Bohannan and G. Dalton (eds), *Markets in Africa*, Evanston, 1962
R. Bosson and B. Varon, *The Mining Industries and the Developing Countries*, London, 1977
C. Bundy, *The Rise and Fall of the South African Peasantry*, London, 1975
C. Chime, *Integration and Politics among African States*, Uppsala, 1977
J.I. Clarke, *An Advanced Geography of Africa*, Amersham, 1975
I. Clegg, *Workers' Self-Management in Algeria*, London, 1971
W.F. Crick, (ed), *Commonwealth Banking Systems*, Oxford, 1965
J. Crossley and J. Blandford, *The DCO Story: a History of Banking in Many Countries*, London, 1975
R. Cruise O'Brien (ed), *The Political Economy of Underdevelopment. Dependence in Senegal*, London, 1979
J.R. Day, *Railways of Southern Africa*, London, 1963
J.R. Day, *Railways of Northern Africa*, London, 1964
P.D. Dunn, *Appropriate Technology*, London, 1979
Economic Commission for Africa, *African Statistical Yearbooks*, Addis Ababa
Economic Commission for Africa, *Survey of Economic and Social Conditions in Africa*, Addis Ababa, 1976
J.B. Eicher, *Nigerian Handicrafted Textiles*, Ife, 1976
A.F. Ewing, *Industry in Africa*, Oxford, 1968
W. Fagg and J. Picton, *The Potter's Art in Africa*, London, 1970
R. First, J. Steele and C. Gurney, *The South African Connection*, London, 1973
Frances Stewart, *Technology and Underdevelopment*, London, 1977
R. Fry, *Bankers in West Africa: the Story of the Bank of British West Africa*, London, 1976
E.L. Furness, *Money and Credit in Developing Africa*, New York, 1975
R. Gardi, *African Crafts and Craftsmen*, New York, 1969
N. Girvan, *Corporate Imperialism: Conflict and Expropriation*, New York, 1976
P.C.W. Gutkind, Robin Cohen and Jean Copans (eds), *African Labour History*, London, 1978
F.E.I. Hamilton (ed), *Spatial Perspectives on Industrial Organization and Decision-Making*, London, 1974
W.R. Hance, *African Economic Development*, New York, 1962
R. Harris (ed), *The Political Economy of Africa*, New York, 1975
A. Hazlewood, *Economic Integration: the East African Experience*, London, 1975
D. Heathcote, *The Arts of the Hausa*, London, 1976
J.A. Henry, *The First Hundred Years of the Standard Bank*, London, 1963
B.W. Hodder and U.I. Ukwu, *West African Markets*, Ibadan, 1969
B.S. Hoyle and D. Hilling (eds), *Seaports and Development in Tropical Africa*, London, 1970
International Monetary Fund, *Surveys of African Economies* (5 vols), Washington DC, 1968–73
W. Isard, *Location and Space Economy*, Cambridge, Mass., 1956
A. Jalloh, *Political Integration in French-speaking Africa*, Berkeley, 1973
R. Jeffries, *Class, Power and Ideology in Ghana: the Railwaymen of Sekondi*, Cambridge, 1978
N. Jequier, *Appropriate Technology: Problems and Promises*, London, 1976
P. Kilby, *Industrialization in an Open Economy – Nigeria 1945–1965*, Cambridge, 1969
T. Killick, *Development Economics in Action*, London, 1978
M. Klein (ed), *Peasants in Africa: Historical and Contemporary Perspectives*, London, 1980

A. Leftwich (ed), *Economic Growth and Political Change in South Africa*, London, 1973
C. Leys, *Underdevelopment in Kenya*, London, 1975
A. Losch, *The Economics of Location*, New Haven, 1954
Makmood Mamdani, *Politics and Class Formation in Uganda*, London, 1976
C. Meillassoux (ed), *The Development of Indigenous Trade and Markets in West Africa*, London, 1971
K. Morton and P. Tulloch, *Trade and Developing Countries*, London, 1978
B.W.T. Mutharika, *Towards Multinational Economic Cooperation in Africa*, New York, 1972
W.T. Newlyn and D.C. Rowan, *Money and Banking in British Colonial Africa*, Oxford, 1954
T. Newman, *Contemporary African Arts and Crafts*, London, 1974
S.A. Ochola, *Minerals in African Underdevelopment*, London, 1975
A.M. O'Connor, *The Geography of Tropical African Development* (2nd edn), Oxford, 1978
Oxford Regional Economic Atlas of Africa, Oxford, 1965
R. Palmer and Neil Parsons (eds), *The Roots of Rural Poverty in Central and Southern Africa*, London, 1977
J. Picton and J. Mack, *African Textiles*, London, 1979
Richard Sklar, *Corporate Power in an African State*, Berkeley, 1975
H. Robinson and C.G. Bamford, *Geography of Transport*, London, 1978
P. Robson, *Economic Integration in Africa*, London, 1968
W.W. Rostow, *The Stages of Economic Growth*, Cambridge, 1960
I. Roxborough, *Theories of Underdevelopment*, London, 1979
R. Sandbrook and R. Cohen (eds), *The Development of an African Working Class*, London, 1975
L. Schatzl, *Industry in Nigeria*, Munich, 1973
E.F. Schumacher, *Small is Beautiful*, London, 1973
I. Shivji, *Class Struggles in Tanzania*, London, 1976
I.G. Shivji (ed), *Tourism and Socialist Development*, Dar es Salaam, 1973
R. and J. Simons, *Colour and Class in South Africa, 1850–1950*, Harmondsworth, 1959
R. Sklar, *Corporate Power in an African State*, Berkeley, 1975
R. Synge (ed), *Travellers' Guide to Africa*, London, 1974, 1978, 1980
C. van Onselen, *Chibaro: African Mine Labour in Southern Rhodesia, 1900–1933*, London, 1976
P. Walshe, *The Rise of African Nationalism in South Africa*, London, 1970
A. Weber, *Theory of the Location of Industries*, Chicago, 1909
H.P. White and M.B. Gleave, *An Economic Geography of West Africa*, London, 1971
World Bank, *World Bank Annual Reports*, New York, 1970–9
J. Woronoff, *Organizing African Unity*, New York, 1970
G. Young, *Tourism, Blessing or Blight?* Harmondsworth, 1973

SOCIETY

R. Ainslie, *The Press in Africa*, London, 1966
D.R. Aronson, *The City is Our Farm: Seven Migrant Ijebu Yoruba Families*, Cambridge, Mass., 1979
F. Barton, *The Press of Africa – Persecution and Perseverance*, London, 1979
D.A. Clarke (ed), *Acquisitions from the Third World*, London, 1975
M.A. Cohen, *Urban Policy and Political Conflict in Africa: a Study of the Ivory Coast*, Chicago, 1974
A. Damiba, *Education in Africa in the Light of the Lagos Conference 1976*, Paris, 1977
B. Davidson, *The Lost Cities of Africa*, (revised edn), Boston, 1970
E.E. Evans-Pritchard, *Witchcraft, Oracles and Magic among the Azande*, Oxford, 1937
E. Faure, *Learning to Be*, Paris, 1972
M. Gelfand, *Livingstone the Doctor. His Life and Travels*, Oxford, 1957
G. Gerbner (ed), *Mass Media Policies in Changing Cultures*, New York, 1977
J.L. Gibbs (ed), *Peoples of Africa*, New York, 1965
N.M. Goodman, *International Health Organizations and Their Work*, London, 1971
J. Gugler and W.G. Flanagan, *Urbanization and Social Change in West Africa*, Cambridge, 1978
P.C.W. Gutkind and P. Waterman (eds), *African Social Studies: a Radical Reader*, London, 1977
W.A. Hance, *Population, Migration, and Urbanization in Africa*, New York, 1970

H. Hawes, *Curriculum and Reality in African Primary Schools*, London, 1979
M. H. King, *Medical Care in Developing Countries*, London, 1966
H. Koebing and H. Walser (eds), *Selected Essays of Erwin H. Ackerknecht*, Baltimore, 1971
L. Kuper and M. G. Smith, *Pluralism in Africa*, Berkeley, 1969
P. C. Lloyd, *Africa in Social Change*, Harmondsworth, 1967
P. C. Lloyd (ed), *The New Elites of Tropical Africa*, London, 1967
J. B. Loudon (ed), *Social Anthropology and Medicine*, London, 1976
I. L. Markovitz, *Power and Class in Africa*, New York, 1977
P. Marris, *Family and Social Change in an African City: a Study of Rehousing in Lagos*, London, 1961
M. Marwick (ed), *Witchcraft and Sorcery*, Harmondsworth, 1970
A. A. Mazrui, *Cultural Engineering and Nation Building in East Africa*, Evanston, 1972
S. W. Mead, *Broadcasting in Africa: a Continental Survey of Radio and Television*, 1974
T. A. M. Nash, *Africa's Bane. The Tsetse Fly*, London, 1969
J. K. Nyerere, *Education for Self-Reliance*, Dar es Salaam, 1967
E. Oluwasanmi (ed), *Publishing in Africa in the Seventies*, Ife, 1975
C. Oppong, *Marriage Among a Matrilineal Elite: a Family Study of Ghanaian Senior Civil Servants*, Cambridge, 1974
A. R. Radcliffe-Brown and D. Forde (eds), *African Systems of Kinship and Marriage*, London, 1950
R. Sandbrook and R. Cohen (eds), *The Development of an African Working Class*, London, 1975
R. Schram, *A History of the Nigerian Health Services*, Ibadan, 1971
D. R. Smock and K. Bentsi-Enchill (eds), *The Search for National Integration in Africa*, New York, 1976
O. Stokke (ed), *Reporting Africa*, Uppsala, 1971
A. Tuden and L. Plotnicov (eds), *Social Stratification in Africa*, New York, 1970
H. W. Turner, *History of an African Independent Church*, (2 vols), Oxford, 1967
V. W. Turner, *The Drums of Affliction*, London, 1968
G. M. Van Etten, *Rural Health Development in Tanzania*, Amsterdam, 1976
W. Weekes-Vagliani, M. Bekombo and L. Wallisch, *Family Life and Structure in Southern Cameroon*, Paris, 1976
C. Wilcocks, *Aspects of Medical Investigation in Africa*, London, 1962
D. Wilcox, *Mass Media in Black Africa*, New York, 1977
H. M. Zell, *The African Book World and Press: a Directory*, London, 1977

RELIGION

J. Beattie and J. Middleton, *Spirit Mediumship and Society in Africa*, London, 1969
E. Evans-Pritchard, *Witchcraft, Oracles and Magic among the Azande*, Oxford, 1937
E. Evans-Pritchard, *Nuer Religion*, Oxford, 1956
D. Forde (ed), *African Worlds*, London, 1954
M. Fortes and G. Dieterlen (eds), *African Systems of Thought*, London, 1965
M. Gluckman, *Law, Politics and Ritual in Tribal Society*, Oxford, 1965
M. Griaule, *Conversations with Ogotommeli*, London, 1965
I. Lewis (ed.), *Islam in Tropical Africa*, London, 1966
R. G. Lienhardt, *Divinity and Experience: the Religion of the Dinka*, Oxford, 1961
J. Middleton, *Lugbara Religion*, London, 1960
J. Middleton and E. H. Winter, *Witchcraft and Sorcery in East Africa*, London, 1963
R. Oliver, *The Missionary Factor in East Africa*, London, 1952
G. Parrinder, *African Traditional Religion*, London, 1954
G. Parrinder, *Religion in Africa*, London, 1969
G. Parrinder, *Religion in an African City*, London, 1953
J. D. Y. Peel, *Aladura, a Religious Movement among the Yoruba*, London, 1968
B. C. Ray, *African Religions: Symbol, Ritual and Community*, London, 1976
B. Sundkler, *Bantu Prophets in South Africa*, London, 1948
J. V. Taylor, *The Primal Vision*, London, 1963
P. Tempels, *Bantu Philosophy*, Paris, 1959
J. S. Trimingham, *Islam in the Sudan*, London, 1949
J. S. Trimingham, *Islam in West Africa*, Oxford, 1959
J. S. Trimingham, *Islam in East Africa*, Oxford, 1964
V. W. Turner, *The Forest of Symbols*, Ithaca, 1967

V. W. Turner, *The Drums of Affliction*, London, 1968
F. B. Welbourn, *East African Rebels*, London, 1961
M. Wilson, *Communal Rituals of the Nyakyusa*, London, 1959

ARTS AND RECREATION

K. B. Anderson, *African Traditional Architecture*, Oxford, 1978
K. Awoonor, *The Breast of the Earth*, New York, 1975
F. Bebey, *African Music: a People's Art*, London, 1975
U. Beier, *Contemporary Art in Africa*, New York, 1968
D. Biebuyck (ed), *Tradition and Creativity in Tribal Art*, Los Angeles, 1969
D. Biebuyck, *Lega Culture*, Berkeley, 1973
J. Blacking, *Venda Children's Songs: a Study in Ethnomusicological Analysis*, Johannesburg, 1967
D. S. Blair, *African Literature in French*, Cambridge, 1976
R. Brain and A. Pollock, *Bangwa Funerary Sculpture*, London, 1971
J. F. Carrington, *Talking Drums of Africa*, London, 1949
W. Cartey, *Whispers from a Continent: the Literature of Contemporary Black Africa*, London, 1971
H. Cole and D. Ross, *The Arts of Ghana*, Los Angeles, 1971
T. Cope, *Izibongo: Zulu Praise-Poems*, Oxford, 1968
P. Dark, *An Introduction to Benin Art and Technology*, London, 1973
O. R. Dathorne, *African Literature in the Twentieth Century*, London, 1976
W. D'Azevedo (ed), *The Traditional Artist in African Society*, Bloomington, 1973
S. Denyer, *African Traditional Architecture*, London, 1978
E. Elisofon and W. B. Fagg, *The Sculpture of Africa*, London, 1957
J. Faris, *Nuba Personal Art*, London, 1972
A. Forge (ed), *Primitive Art and Society*, London, 1973
D. Fraser and H. Cole (eds), *African Art and Leadership*, Madison, 1972
C. Heywood (ed.), *Aspects of South African Literature*, London, 1976
L. Holy and D. Darbois, *Masks and Figures from East and South Africa*, London, 1967
R. Horton, *Kalabari Sculpture*, Lagos, 1965
A. M. Jones, *Studies in African Music*, (2 vols), London, 1959
E. D. Jones (ed), *African Literature Today*, (periodical), London, 1972–
B. King and K. Ogungbesan (eds), *A Celebration of Black and African Writing*, London, 1977
P. R. Kirby, *The Musical Instruments of the Native Races of South Africa*, London, 1934
J. Knappert, *Four Centuries of Swahili Verse*, London, 1978
R. Layton, *Anthropology and Art*, London, 1979
M. Leiris and J. Delange, *African Art*, London, 1960
J. C. Mitchell, *The Kalela Dance*, Manchester, 1956
M. W. Mount, *African Art: the Years since 1920*, Newton Abbot, 1973
B. Nettl (ed), *Eight Urban Musical Cultures*, Urbana, 1978
Ngugi wa Thiong'o, *Homecoming*, London, 1972
J. H. K. Nketia, *African Music in Ghana*, Evanston, 1962
J. H. K. Nketia, *Drumming in Akan Communities of Ghana*, Edinburgh, 1963
J. H. K. Nketia, *Folk Songs of Ghana*, Legon, 1963
J. H. K. Nketia, *The Music of Africa*, London, 1975
E. Obiechina, *An African Popular Literature: a Study of Onitsha Market*, Cambridge, 1973
P. Oliver, *Shelter in Africa*, London, 1971
S. Ottenberg, *Masked Rituals of Afikpo*, Seattle, 1975
J. Picton and J. Mack, *African Textiles*, London, 1979
L. Prussin, *Architecture in Northern Ghana*, Berkeley & Los Angeles, 1969
T. O. Ranger, *Dance and Society in East Africa*, London, 1975
J. S. Roberts, *Black Music of Two Worlds*, New York, 1972
A. Roscoe, *Uhuru's Fire: African Literature East to South*, Cambridge, 1977
T. Shaw, *Nigeria. Its Archaeology and Early History*, London, 1978
W. Soyinka, *Myth, Literature and the African World*, Cambridge, 1976
R. F. Thompson, *Black Gods and Kings*, Los Angeles, 1971
R. F. Thompson, *African Art in Motion*, Los Angeles, 1973
H. Tracey, *Chopi Musicians: their Music, Poetry and Instruments*, London, 1948
M. Trowell, *African Design*, London, 1960
V. Turner, *The Forest of Symbols*, Ithaca, 1967
J. Vansina, *Children of Woot*, Wisconsin, 1978
P. Vinnicombe, *People of the Eland*, Pietmarisburg, 1976
K. P. Wachsmann (ed), *Essays on Music and History in Africa*, Evanston, 1971

C. Wauthier, *The Literature and Thought of Modern Africa*, London, 1976
H. Weman, *African Music and Church in Africa*, Uppsala, 1960
M. Wenzel, *House Decoration in Nubia*, London, 1972
F. Willett, *Ife in the History of West African Sculpture*, London, 1967
F. Willett, *African Art*, London, 1971

INTER-AFRICAN RELATIONS

A. Ajala, *Panafricanism*, London, 1973
Z. Cervenka, *The Unfinished Quest for Unity: Africa and the OAU*, London, 1977
E. C. Chibwe, *Afro-Arab Relations in the New World Order*, London, 1977
I. Geiss, *The Panafrican Movement*, London, 1974
C. Legum, *Panafricanism*, (2nd edn), London, 1965
B. W. T. Mutharika, *Towards Multinational Economic Cooperation in Africa*, New York, 1972
J. S. Uppal and L. R. Salkever (eds), *Africa: Problems in Economic Development*, New York, 1972
I. Wallerstein, *The Politics of Unity*, New York, 1967
M. Wolfers, *Politics in the OAU*, London, 1976
J. Woronoff, *Organizing African Unity*, New York, 1970

INTERNATIONAL RELATIONS

S. Amin, *Neo-Colonialism in West Africa*, Harmondsworth, 1973
Z. Brzezinski (ed), *Africa and the Communist World*, Stanford, 1963
B. Gosovic, *UNCTAD: Conflict and Compromise*, London, 1972
A. Hutchison, *China's African Revolution*, London, 1975
R. W. Johnson, *How Long Can South Africa Survive?* London, 1977
R. Kanet (ed), *The Soviet Union and the Developing Nations*, Baltimore, 1974
D. Kimche, *The Afro-Asian Movement*, Jerusalem, 1973
C. Legum (ed), *Africa Contemporary Record*, 1–9, London, 1969–1977
R. Legvold, *Soviet Policy in West Africa*, Cambridge, Mass., 1970
C. Leys, *Underdevelopment in Kenya*, London, 1975
R. Lowenthal, *Model or Ally? The Communist Powers and the Developing Countries*, London, 1977
J. Mayall, *Africa: the Cold War and After*, London, 1971
A. Mazrui, *Towards a Pax Africana*, London, 1967
J. D. B. Miller, *Politics of the Third World*, London, 1965
W. A. Nielson, *The Great Powers and Africa*, London, 1969
K. Nkrumah, *Neo-Colonialism: the Last Stage of Imperialism*, London, 1965
K. Nkrumah, *Challenge of the Congo*, London, 1967
A. Ogunsanwo, *China's Policy in Africa 1958–71*, Cambridge, 1974
C. Stevens, *The Soviet Union and Black Africa*, London, 1976
C. C. Twitchett, *Europe and Africa: From Association to Partnership*, London, 1978
I. Wallerstein, *The Modern World System*, New York, 1974
S. R. Weissman, *American Foreign Policy in the Congo*, Cornell, 1974

THE AFRICAN DIASPORA

A. H. Adamson, *Sugar Without Slaves: the Political Economy of British Guiana, 1838–1904*, New Haven, 1972
C. Bagley, *The Dutch Plural Society*, London, 1973
L. E. Barrett, *The Rastafarians: a Study in Messianic Cultism in Jamaica*, Rio Pedras, Puerto Rico, 1968
L. Bennett, Jr. *Before the Mayflower. A History of the Negro in America, 1619–1964*. Baltimore, 1964
E. K. Brathwaite, *The Development of Creole Society in Jamaica, 1770–1820*, Oxford, 1971
R. Brunschvig, *Abd*, in *The Encyclopaedia of Islam*, (vol. i), Leiden, 1960
M. Campbell, *The Dynamics of Change in a Slave Society, A Socio-Political History of the Free Coloreds of Jamaica, 1800–1865*, Rutherford, New Jersey, 1976
A. Césaire, *Return to My Native Land*, Paris, 1968
A. Césaire, *Discourse on Colonialism*, New York, 1972
T. Clark, *Puerto Rico and the United States, 1917–1933*, Pittsburgh, 1975
D. W. Cohen and J. P. Greene (eds), *Neither Slave Nor Free: the Freedman of African Descent in the Slave Societies of the New World*, Baltimore, 1972
A. F. Corwin, *Spain and the Abolition of Slavery in Cuba, 1817–1886*, Austin, 1967
G. Coulthard, *Caribbean Literature: An Anthology*, London, 1966

G. Coulthard, *Race and Colour in Caribbean Literature*, London, 1962
M. Crahan and F. W. Knight, (eds), *Africa and the Caribbean: the Legacy of a Link*, Baltimore, 1979
P. Curtin, (ed), *Africa and the West: Intellectual Responses to European Culture*, Madison, 1972
P. D. Curtin, *The Atlantic Slave Trade. A Census*, Madison, 1969
C. N. Degler, *Neither Black Nor White: Slavery and Race Relations in Brazil and the United States*, New York, 1971
F. Fernandes, *The Negro in Brazilian Society*, New York, 1969
J. H. Franklin, *From Slavery to Freedom, a History of Negro Americans*, New York, 1967
C. Goslinga, *The Dutch in the Caribbean and on the Wild Coast*, Gainesville, 1971
H. G. Gutman, *The Black Family in Slavery and Freedom 1750–1925*, New York, 1976
D. Hall, *Free Jamaica, 1838–1865: An Economic History*, London, 1969
J. S. Handler, *Plantation Society in Barbados*, Cambridge, Mass., 1978
J. S. Handler, *The Unappropriated People: Freedom in the Slave Society of Barbados*, Baltimore, 1974
M. M. Horowitz, (ed), *Peoples and Cultures of the Caribbean*, Garden City, 1971
L. Hughes and M. Meltzer, *A Pictorial History of the Negro in America*, (3rd edn), New York, 1969
C. L. R. James, *The Black Jacobins: Toussaint L'Ouverture and the San Domingo Revolution*, New York, 1963
L. Johnson, *The Devil, the Gargoyle, and the Buffon: the Negro as Metaphor in Western Literature*, Port Washington, 1971
R. July, *The Origins of Modern African Thought*, New York, 1967
M. L. Kilson and R. I. Rotberg (eds), *The African Diaspora*, Harvard, 1976
F. Knight, *The African Dimension in Latin American Societies*, New York, 1974
F. W. Knight, *Slave Society in Cuba during the Nineteenth Century*, Madison, 1970
F. W. Knight, *The Caribbean: The Genesis of a Fragmented Nationalism*, New York, 1978
H. E. Lamur, *The Demographic Evolution of Surinam, 1920–1970: a Socio-demographic Analysis*, The Hague, 1973
K. O. Laurence, *Immigration into the West Indies in the 19th Century*, Barbados, 1971
B. Lewis, *Race and Colour in Islam*, New York, 1971
G. K. Lewis, *The Growth of the Modern West Indies*, New York, 1968
G. K. Lewis, *The Virgin Islands: A Caribbean Lilliput*, Evanston, 1972
J. Leyburn, *The Haitian People*, New Haven, 1966
K. Little, *Negroes in Britain*, London, 1947
D. Lorimer, *Colour, Class and the Victorians: English Attitudes to the Negro in the Mid-Nineteenth Century*, Leicester, 1978
T. Martin, *Race First: the Ideological and Organizational Struggle of Marcus Garvey and the Universal Negro Improvement Association*, Westport, Conn., 1976
S. McCloy, *The Negro in France*, Lexington, 1961
S. T. McCloy, *The Negro in the French West Indies*, Lexington, 1966
R. Mellafe, *Negro Slavery in Latin America*, Berkeley, 1975
C. Mesa-Lago, *Revolutionary Change in Cuba*, Pittsburgh, 1971
S. Mintz and R. Price, *An Anthropological Approach to the Afro-American Past: a Caribbean Perspective*, Philadelphia, 1976
M. Morner, (ed), *Race and Class in Latin America*, New York, 1970
M. Morner, *Race Mixture in the History of Latin America*, Boston, 1967
G. Myrdal, *An American Dilemma*, (2 vols), New York, 1944
P. Newman, *British Guiana: Problems of Cohesion in an Immigrant Society*, London, 1964
R. Price (ed), *Maroon Societies: Rebel Slave Communities in the Americas*, Garden City, 1973
K. Ramchand, *The West Indian Novel and Its Background*, New York, 1970
L. B. Rout, *The African Experience in Spanish America*, Cambridge, 1976
S. Ryan, *Race and Nationalism in Trinidad and Tobago*, Toronto, 1972
F. Snowden, *Blacks in Antiquity: Ethiopians in the Graeco-Roman Experience*, Cambridge, Mass., 1970
R. B. Toplin, (ed), *Slavery and Race Relations in Latin America*, Westport, 1974
E. Williams, *Capitalism and Slavery*, New York, 1961
R. W. Winks, *The Blacks in Canada. A History*, Montreal, 1971
D. Wood, *Trinidad in Transition: the Years after Slavery*, London, 1968

Acknowledgements

The publishers gratefully acknowledge permission to reproduce the following illustrations:

Action (Peace Corps Volunteer Group) 464l; Africana Museum, Johannesburg 192; All-Sport Photographic Limited 451, 453b; Ardea London 31, 54, 55, 56; Collection of the Art Institute of Chicago 473; Ashmolean Museum 94t; Aspect Picture Library 127br; Barnaby's Picture Library 52, 83b, 92, 113, 118, 121t, 140, 271, 275, 333b, 401, 425l, 442r, 455b; Professor John Blacking 444; Dr Michael Brett 102, 103, 104, 114, 115; BBC Hulton Picture Library 150t, 151c, r, 164, 186, 215b, 384, 416br, 459b, 470, 481; British Institute of Recorded Sound 443r; Reproduced by Permission of the British Library 476l; Courtesy of the Trustees of the British Museum 139, 414, 417, 418r, 419b, 421tl, 422r, 424; A. D. Buckley 391; Camera Press Limited 39br, 194r, 198b, 200, 201c, b, 203, 204, 207, 211, 212, 213, 216t, 218b, 223, 225, 231, 238, 240, 241, 243, 244, 250, 251, 252, 253b, 254, 255, 256, 259, 269, 280, 281, 282t, 299t, 302, 331, 365, 410t, 432, 465, 466l, 467, 468, 478t; Dr Richard Caulk 109, 120, 121t, 123; Courtesy of Christies 421tr; Clarendon Press 194l; Bruce Coleman Limited 83t; Colorific Photo Library Limited 80c, 85, 216b, 442l, 443l, 479; Colorsport 453tl; Commonwealth Institute 367, 378l, 379, 394, 422l, 431tr, cr; Contemporary Films Limited 439t; Creole Records 449t; Michael Crowder 333t, 431bl, br, 433; Professor Philip D. Curtin 268b; The Decca Record Company Limited/P. René-Worms 449b; Susan Denyer 428l, br; E. C. P. Armées–France 176t; Sara Ellis 129, 157, 469, 471; Foreign and Commonwealth Office Library 182; Werner Forman Archive 88, 90, 94b, 106, 119, 142, 144, 145, 406, 421b; Roger Delpit/Fotogram 474r; The Fotomas Index 184b; Susan Griggs Agency Limited 268t, 303t, 426l; Librairie Hachette 161; George Hallet 441t; Peggy Harper 434, 435, 436; Heinemann Educational Books Limited 440tl, tr, br, 441bl, br; Georg Gerster/John Hillelson Agency Limited 110; Hoa-Qui 427l, 463; Michael Holford Photographs 91, 138; J. C. N. Humphreys (Africana Museum) 170b; Robert Hunt Library 176t; Alan Hutchison Library 39bl, 48, 50, 78, 80r, 82, 86, 93t, 167t, 201t, 221, 232, 274, 283, 293, 296, 301t, 303bl, 309, 312, 314, 332, 355l, 360l, 362, 378r, 386, 387, 399, 410b, 411, 412, 426tr, 427tr, 429t, c, 430tl, bl, 446, 454c, b, 466r; Anthony Hutt 427br; Imperial War Museum 196l; Intermediate Technology Development Group/Centre for World Development Education/Dick Stanley 355r; International Defence and Aid Fund 79; International Library of African Music 445; Instituto Nacional de Antropologia e Historia, Mexico 478b; Bhupendra Kania 440bl; Keystone Press Agency 187t, 199, 218t, 227, 236, 253t, 258, 440c; Adrian Kohler/University College of Botswana 437b; Alisdair and Venice Lamb 423; Henri Lhote 415t; Livingstone Museum, Zambia 99; The London Library 146/7; The Longman Group Limited 409; The Mansell Collection 93b, 150b, 152, 156, 158, 165, 171, 172, 173, 185, 475, 476, 480, 483; E. Bradley Martin 154; Amplicaciones Reproducciones MAS 168/9; The Middle East Picture Library 272; Ministry of Information, Senegal 389; Ministry of Information, Nigeria 425r; Murphy Hershman 350, 407, 450; National Archives of Nigeria 193; National Archives of Zimbabwe 214; National Geographic Magazine 60t (© Peter Jones), 46 (© Albert Moldray), 53 (© Baron Hugo van Lawick); Courtesy of the National Library of Jamaica 477; National Museum of Nigeria 87; New African/Ingelore Frank 349; Peter Obe Photo Agency, Lagos 247; Oxfam/Pierre Ségoud 309b; Klaus Paysan 80l; Dr D.W. Phillipson 60–70; Photoreportage Belin 196r; John Picton 415b, 416bl; Picturepoint London 155, 360r, 366; Pitt Rivers Museum, Oxford 98b; Leonard M. Pole 98t; Popperfoto 101, 105, 116, 137, 153, 163, 166, 167b, 170t, 184t, 187b, 206, 208, 215t, 226, 261, 298, 420, 429b, 430r, 455c, 459t, 464l, 484; Courtesy of the Powell Cotton Museum 134; Paul Richards 301c, b, 454t, 455t; Leni Riefenstahl 419t; Royal Court Theatre 438; Royal Geographical Society 151l; Professor Matthew Schoffeleers/African Arts Volume V, No. 4, 418l; Dr Thurston Shaw 97, 416t; S & G Press Agency Ltd 452; Stage Photo Service, Lagos 437t; The Star Private Collection © The Argus Company 191; Syndication International Ltd Library 453tr; Richard Taylor/'World About Us' 439b; Professor P. H. Temple 35, 46, 276, 277; Roger Thomas 273, 426br; M. B. Thorp 39t, c; John Topham Picture Library 127t, 217, 282b, 361, 428tr; Annie Treasure 474l; © Crown Copyright/Tropical Products Institute 305; Professor Victor Turner 392; United Nations 278, 457 (Saw Lwin); Dr J.-L. Vellut 188, 189, 205; Roger Viollet 159, 162, 178, 180, 181, 195, 198t; Ian Watts/Africa 458; West Africa 209, 299b, 448; Dr J. C. Woodburn 288, 289; World Health Organization 395, 396

Jacket photographs: front: ZEFA; back: Frank Willett left; Alan Hutchison Library top and centre right; Colorific Photo Library bottom right

A condensed version of the article, 'Contemporary painting and sculpture' by Michael Crowder first appeared in The Times, 18 January 1977

The publishers are grateful to the following for reference material used in the compilation of maps:

K. Boucher, Global Climate, English Universities Press, London, 1975: 40r, 41, 42l

D. Dalby, Africa South of the Sahara, 1978–9, Europa Publications, London, 1979 and J. Greenberg, The Languages of Africa, Mouton, The Hague, 1963: 76

J. F. Griffiths, World Survey of Climatology, vol. x, Climates of Africa, Elsevier, Amsterdam, 1972: 40l, 43l, 44

J. R. Harlan, 'Agricultural Origins: Centers and Noncenters', Science 1971: 71

B. W. Hodder and U. I. Ukwu, Markets in West Africa, Ibadan University Press, Ibadan, 1969: 367

Claude Meillasoux (ed), The Development of Indigenous Trade and Markets in West Africa, International African Institute/Oxford University Press, London, 1971: 368